THE UNITED STATES AND MEXICO AT WAR

Editorial Board

THE UNITED STATES AND MEXICO AT WAR

Nineteenth-Century Expansionism and Conflict

Edited by
DONALD S. FRAZIER

MACMILLAN REFERENCE USA
Simon & Schuster Macmillan
NEW YORK

Simon & Schuster and Prentice Hall International
LONDON   MEXICO CITY   NEW DELHI   SINGAPORE   SYDNEY   TORONTO

Copyright © 1998 by Simon & Schuster Macmillan

All rights reserved. No part of this book may be reproduced or transmitted in any form or by any means, electronic or mechanical, including photocopying, recording, or by any information storage and retrieval system, without permission in writing from the Publisher.

Simon & Schuster Macmillan
1633 Broadway
New York, NY 10019

Printed in the United States of America

Printing Number

10 9 8 7 6 5 4 3 2 1

LIBRARY OF CONGRESS CATALOGING-IN-PUBLICATION DATA

The United States and Mexico at war : nineteenth-century expansionism
 and conflict / edited by Donald S. Frazier.
       p.   cm.
   Includes bibliographical references and index.
   ISBN 0-02-864606-1 (alk. paper)
   1. Mexican War, 1846–1848. 2. United States—Foreign relations—
Mexico. 3. Mexico—Foreign relations—United States. 4. United
States—Foreign relations—1815–1861. 5. Mexican War, 1846–1848—
Influence. 6. United States—Territorial expansion. I. Frazier,
Donald S. (Donald Shaw), 1965–   .
   E404.U66   1997
   973.6'2—dc21   97-42964
                                                                CIP

This paper meets the requirements of ANSI-NISO Z39.48-1992 (Permanence of Paper).

Editorial and Production Staff

Project Editor
Dorothy Bauhoff

Manuscript Editors
Sarah Gardner Cunningham
John W. Hopper
Nancy G. Wright

Development Editor
Stephen Wagley

Editorial Assistants
Anthony Coloneri
Christina Grillo

Proofreaders
Carol Holmes
Helen Wallace

Production Director
Dabney Smith

Cartographer
Donald S. Frazier

Translator
The Horse's Mouth Language Services

Indexer
AEIOU, Inc.

MACMILLAN REFERENCE
Elly Dickason, *Publisher*
Paul Bernabeo, *Editor in Chief*

Contents

PREFACE

The year of publication of this work—1998—marks the 150th anniversary of the signing of the Treaty of Guadalupe Hidalgo. Regrettably, few recognize the treaty's name, let alone realize that it was one of the most important events in the history of North America, and certainly the history of Mexico and the United States. This accord, signed by representatives of two nations who had been for several decades either on the brink of combat or, from 1846 to 1848, actually at war, radically altered the course of U.S. and Mexican history. The Rio Grande became the demarcation between the industrializing, expansive nation to the north and the struggling, strife-torn republic to the south. The territory that changed hands—the Mexican Cession—would deliver to the United States additional land and resources to fuel its growing economy and provide opportunity for its swelling population. For Mexico, the loss of the territory was, in many ways, an abandonment of its future and national patrimony. It is indeed ironic that the gold discovered in California in 1848 would be stamped into coins bearing the eagle of the United States, not the eagle and snake of Mexico.

Two momentous events occurred in 1821 that would forever change history. Mexico gained its independence from Spain, bursting on the political scene as a young, proud republic. That same year, U.S. settlers came to Texas, then a remote territory on Mexico's northern periphery. They were welcomed as the vanguard of a new strain of citizen that would bring all that was good about the American character—industry, thrift, and innovation. As events would show, however, these men and women would actually turn out to be the unwitting advance agents of a spirit—later identified as Manifest Destiny—that was already gnawing at the soul of the United States. When English Puritans came to the United States in 1630, they had carried with them an unshakable belief in their role as agents of God and in their unmistakable mission to carry their civilization to the wilderness of North America. As generations passed, this vision became part of the national mythos. By the nineteenth century, Americans came to believe that their destiny, as revealed and supported by the meteoric rise of the United States, was to control the North American continent. This belief, fueled by the popular press and politicians alike, dwelt within most citizens of the United States, in weaker or stronger concentrations, and informed their worldview. By allowing U.S. citizens to settle in Texas, Mexico had un-knowingly invited into their nation the contagion that would eventually lead to its dismemberment.

A stronger nation might have resisted such an insidious invasion. Mexico, however, was weak. Gutted by its war for independence from Spain; torn apart by political factions and recurring civil war, revolution, and foreign intervention; raided by Indians; straddled with debt; housing a stratified and mutually antagonistic society, and with no real sense of nationalism, Mexico could do little more than protest.

Within years of colonization, the Texans rebelled, or seceded, depending on the viewer's perspective. Quickly, suspicion between the United States and Mexico turned to crisis, crisis turned to conflict, and by 1846, conflict led to war.

But what would this war be called? In the United Sates, it was simply the Mexican War, or the War with Mexico. South of the Rio Bravo del Norte—the Rio Grande—the citizens of that republic knew it as the War between the United States and Mexico, the War of U.S. Aggression, or simply the Invasion of Forty-Seven. This last name is the most curious, since the war began in 1846 and raged throughout Mexico's northern states. It reveals, however, the state of disunity in Mexico at the time: the invasion was not taken seriously until the capital was in peril.

This war, this episode in both nations' development, is often overlooked because of its chronological proximity to other events in both U.S. and Mexican history such as the U.S. Civil War, the Mexican War of the Reform, or the French Intervention. But the U.S.–Mexican War and the issues that spawned it dominated the course of the early nineteenth century in North America. In many ways, the struggle between the two nations caused their later internal catastrophes. Without Stephen F. Austin's arrival in Texas in 1821, there would have been no Alamo in 1836, there may never have been annexation of Texas in 1845, and perhaps no war in 1846, no Mexican Cession, and no territories to exacerbate the question of slavery. Similarly, the failure to defend itself from U.S. aggression led Mexico to examine its internal affairs and resulted in a new sense of nationalism and a period of internal reform.

Because of the importance of these events, Bruce Winders and I urged our publishers to create a reference work on the subject—including events from 1821 to 1854—as a concise, first source for generations of future scholars investigating this era. The late Charles E. Smith endorsed our vision and used his vast understanding of his craft and industry to be an advocate and early adviser for the project. Soon, associate editors Paul Lack, Pedro Santoni, and Sam Haynes joined the team and helped in a thousand different ways. Outside agencies and individuals, too, contributed to this project. Dr. William Schultz gave access to his treasure trove of unpublished daguerreotypes; W. Michael Mathes provided the cover art from his own collection. Josefina Vázquez of El Colegio de México maintained a critical eye on this project's progress, and the Sam Taylor Foundation of the United Methodist Board of Higher Education provided some financial support for research. The editorial staff at Macmillan—especially Dorothy Bauhoff, Sarah Cunningham, and Paul Bernabeo—proved invaluable in coordinating a project that soon had nearly two hundred contributors, all of whom, by design, were to represent differing perspectives on our topic in over six hundred articles. These contributors, from Mexico, the United Sates, the United Kingdom, the Czech Republic, Canada, and Germany, have made this book, and their scholarship and insights are pathbreaking and profound. In fact, many articles they penned are the first real inquiries into their subjects. I wish I could thank them all personally for their hard work, diligence, and patience.

Undertaking such an ambitious project, with issues sensitive to readers on both sides of the U.S.–Mexican border, required certain editorial decisions that, we hope, will reflect our desire for an inclusive and balanced perspective. No attempt has been made to require all our contributors to agree on topics that invite controversy. Indeed, one of the strengths of this work is its sense of the different voices that have recorded this multifaceted history and, today, attempt to interpret it. We have on occasion pointed out particular areas of disagreement; not surprisingly, these often occur in descriptions of legendary heroes such as los Niños Héroes or the defenders of the Alamo.

We have to an extent attempted to keep our terminology true to the period. We have used the Spanish-language form of the name for places that were, previous to 1848, in Mexican territory, even if those names were later anglicized. We have used the nineteenth-century spelling for the Mexican city of Vera Cruz (though we have preserved the modern spelling of Monterrey to differentiate it from the California city of Monterey). And we have honored the request of several of our contributors to use the term "Texian," not "Texan," to describe the residents of Texas in the years before annexation. Our illustrations provide a bit of the visual flavor of the times, as they all (with the exception of the tactical maps) date from the period. They include daguerreotypes taken during the 1840s and engravings made for early publications on the war.

It is our hope that this book, the work of a dedicated and resourceful group of international historians, will advance scholarship on a long neglected period of North American history. Errors or weaknesses in concept, fact, or interpretation are mine, as general editor.

Donald S. Frazier
Abilene, Texas

DIRECTORY OF CONTRIBUTORS

STEVE ABOLT
Fort Worth, Texas
  Flags: U.S. Flags
  Flags: Militia Flags
  Uniforms: U.S. Uniforms

CAROL JACKSON ADAMS
Salt Lake Community College
Salt Lake City, Utah
  Bancroft, George
  Elections, U.S.: Election of 1824
  Gilmer, Thomas W.
  Gregg, Josiah

H. ALLEN ANDERSON
Texas Tech University
Lubbock, Texas
  Indian Policy: Texan Policy
  McLeod, Hugh

FAUSTINO AMADO AQUINO SÁNCHEZ
Museo Nacional de las Intervenciones
Mexico City
  Corona, Antonio
  Tolsá, Eugenio
  Vander Linden, Pedro

KAREN L. ARCHAMBAULT
Old Dominion University
Norfolk, Virginia
  Elections, U.S.: Election of 1848
  Gold Rush

SHANNON L. BAKER
Texas Christian University
Fort Worth, Texas
  Chase, Ann

DURWOOD BALL
University of New Mexico
Albuquerque, New Mexico
  Cañoncito, Battle of
  New Mexico: Overview
  New Mexico: Revolt of 1837

S. KIRK BANE
Arkansas Tech University
Russellville, Arkansas
  Ide, William B.

ALWYN BARR
Texas Tech University
Lubbock, Texas
  Béxar, Siege of

JOHN M. BELOHLAVEK
University of South Florida
Tampa, Florida
  Benton, Thomas H.
  Benton-Brown Compromise
  Cushing, Caleb

JAMES D. BILOTTA
North Tonawanda, New York
  Fillmore, Millard

SUSAN EASTON BLACK
Brigham Young University
Provo, Utah
  Mormon Battalion
  Mormonism
  Utah

JOHN PORTER BLOOM
Las Cruces, New Mexico
  Immigration: Immigration to New Mexico
  Mesilla Valley
  Pueblo Indians
  Río Grande Campaign
  Santa Fe–Chihuahua Trail

CASSANDRA BRITT
Newport News, Virginia
  Jackson, Andrew
  Webster, Daniel

JIMMY L. BRYAN, JR.
University of Texas at Arlington
Arlington, Texas
  Ford, John Salmon
  Harney, William S.
  Navarro, José Antonio
  Parrott, William S.
  Smith, Persifor F.
  Walker, Samuel
  Yell, Archibald

JURGEN BUCHENAU
University of Southern Mississippi
Hattiesburg, Mississippi
  Diplomacy: Mexican Diplomacy

JASON BULLOCK
Abilene Christian University
Abilene, Texas
Wickliffe, Charles A.

LEE BURKE
Dallas, Texas
Carson, Christopher ("Kit")

STEVEN R. BUTLER
Descendants of Mexican War Veterans
Richardson, Texas
Monuments and Memorials
Pensions, U.S.
Thornton Affair
Veterans Organizations

RANDOLPH B. CAMPBELL
University of North Texas
Denton, Texas
Houston, Sam

GREGG CANTRELL
Sam Houston State University
Huntsville, Texas
Austin, Stephen F.

JEFFREY CARLISLE
Denton, Texas
Apaches: Lipan Apaches
Flacco the Elder

THOMAS B. CARROLL
Palo Alto Battlefield National Historic Site
Brownsville, Texas
Matamoros

TY CASHION
Texas A&M University, Commerce
Commerce, Texas
Coahuila y Texas

JOSEPH E. CHANCE
Edinburg, Texas
Brazos Santiago
Camargo
Cerralvo
China
Davis, Jefferson
Marshall, Thomas
Prisoners of War: Mexican Prisoners
Rancho Davis
Ridgely, Randolph
Supplies: U.S. Supplies
Victoria and Tampico, Occupation of
Walnut Springs

PAUL COE CLARK, JR.
Armed Forces Staff College
Norfolk, Virginia
Espionage

DON M. COERVER
Texas Christian University
Fort Worth, Texas
Almonte, Juan Nepomuceno
Sonora Revolt of 1837
Sonora y Sinaloa

DAVID COFFEY
Texas Christian University
Fort Worth, Texas
Mackenzie, Alexander Slidell
Patterson, Robert
Perote Castle
Tampico: City of Tampico

M. BRUCE COLCLEUGH
New Orleans, Louisiana
Anaya, Pedro María
Andrade, Manuel
Baz, Juan José
Blanco, Santiago
Guerrillas
Juvera, Julian
Mexico, 1821–1854
Otero, Mariano
Recriminations, Mexican

DAVID J. COLES
Florida State Archives
Tallahassee, Florida
Butler, William O.
Gaines, Edmund P.
Huejutla Expedition
Perry, Matthew C.
Price, Sterling
San José, Siege of
Stockton, Robert F.
Wool's March

CLAY COTHRUM
The University of Tampa
Tampa, Florida
Pakenham, Richard

DALLAS COTHRUM
University of Texas at Tyler
Tyler, Texas
Calhoun, John C.
Clay, Henry

A. CAROLINA CASTILLO CRIMM
Sam Houston State University
Huntsville, Texas
Garza, Carlos de la

JAMES E. CRISP
North Carolina State University
Raleigh, North Carolina
Huston, Felix

THOMAS W. CUTRER
  Arizona State University West
  Phoenix, Arizona
    Hays, John C.
    McCulloch, Ben
    Scott, Winfield
    Scott's Armistice

CARLYN E. DAVIS
  McMurry University
  Abilene, Texas
    Bear Flag Revolt
    Ritchie, Thomas

JOHN L. DAVIS
  The University of Texas at San Antonio
  San Antonio, Texas
    Texas Rangers

PAUL K. DAVIS
  University of Texas at San Antonio
  San Antonio, Texas
    Rusk, Thomas J.

JOSEPH G. DAWSON III
  Texas A&M University
  College Station, Texas
    Doniphan, Alexander W.
    Doniphan's March
    Sacramento, Battle of

JESÚS F. DE LA TEJA
  Southwest Texas State University
  San Marcos, Texas
    Seguín, Erasmo
    Seguín, Juan Nepomuceno

ARNOLDO DE LEÓN
  Angelo State University
  San Angelo, Texas
    Border Cultures
    Racism
    Texas Revolution: Causes of the Revolution

JAMES M. DENHAM
  Florida Southern College
  Lakeland, Florida
    Hawkins, Charles E.
    Jesup, Thomas S.
    Mexía, José Antonio
    Moore, Edwin Ward
    Navy, Texan
    Tyler, John

WILLIAM A. DePALO, JR.
  University of New Mexico
  Albuquerque, New Mexico
    Alcorta, Lino José
    Army, Mexican: Organization of the Mexican Army
    Army, Mexican: Postwar Reforms
    Canalizo, Valentín

    Freaner, James L.
    Frontera, José
    Gaona, Antonio
    Jarero, José María
    León, Antonio
    Military Academy, Mexican
    Recruitment: Mexican Recruitment
    Rincón, Manuel
    Sierra Gorda Revolt
    Urrea, José
    Vázquez, Ciriaco

MERTON L. DILLON
  Ohio State University
  Columbus, Ohio
    Abolitionism
    Free-Soil Party
    Liberty Party

VIRGINIA DOGGETT
  McMurry University
  Abilene, Texas
    Constitution, Mexican: Constitution of 1824

FRED DOMINGUEZ
  Abilene Christian University
  Abilene, Texas
    Mier y Terán, Manuel de

JODELLA KITE DYRESON
  Ogden, Utah
    Bell, Peter H.
    Borden, Gail
    Conventions of 1832 and 1833
    Immigration: Immigration to Texas
    Maverick, Samuel
    Robertson, Sterling C.

ANTONIO ESCOBAR OHMSTEDE
  Centro de Investigaciones y Estudios Superiores en
    Antropología Social
  Mexico City
    Huasteca Revolts
    Indians: Indian Raids

CHARLES L. ETHERIDGE
  McMurry University
  Abilene, Texas
    Thoreau, Henry David

DIANA EVERETT
  Edmond, Oklahoma
    Cherokees

PAUL FINKELMAN
  Cleveland State University
  Cleveland-Marshall College of Law
  Cleveland, Ohio
    Slavery
    Wilmot, David
    Wilmot Proviso

RICHARD V. FRANCAVIGLIA
University of Texas at Arlington
Arlington, Texas
Geography and Climate
Railroads

DONALD S. FRAZIER
McMurry University
Abilene, Texas
Andrade, Juan José
Army Life: Life in the Mexican Army
Borginnis, Sarah
Boundary Disputes
Bowie, James
Chihuahua, State of
Communications
Cos, Martín Perfecto de
Cuba
Cuevas, Luis Gonzaga
Finances: Mexican Finances
Jordan, Samuel W.
Lancers
Landero, Juan José
Lombardini, Manuel María
Mejía, Francisco
Mora, José María Luis
Mora y Villamil, Ignacio
Morales, Juan
Navy, Mexican
Ortega, José María
Patria Chica
Privateers
Soldaderas
Spain
Supplies: Mexican Supplies
Tactics: Mexican Tactics
Torrejón, Anastasio
United States, 1821–1854: Sectionalism
Valencia, Gabriel

KEVAN D. FRAZIER
West Virginia University
Morgantown, West Virginia
Finances: U.S. Finances
Museums and Archives

LARRY GARA
Wilmington College
Wilmington, Ohio
Pierce, Franklin

MARK L. GARDNER
Cascade, Colorado
Army, U.S.: Army of the West
Bent, William
Brazito, Battle of
Magoffin, James
Martínez, Antonio José
Mountain Men
New Mexico: U.S. Occupation
Nuevo Mexicanos
Santa Cruz de Rosales, Battle of

Santa Fe: City of Santa Fe
Taos Revolt
Traders Battalion

MIGUEL ANGEL GONZÁLEZ QUIROGA
Universidad Autónoma de Nuevo León
Monterrey, Nuevo León
Nuevo León

CARLOS GONZÁLEZ SALAS
Tampico, Tamaulipas
Ramos Arizpe, Miguel

NORMAN A. GRAEBNER
Charlottesville, Virginia
Causes of the War: U.S. Perspective

DAVID ALAN GREER
Texas Christian University
Fort Worth, Texas
Oregon Territory
Territories: U.S. Territories

RICHARD GRISWOLD DEL CASTILLO
San Diego State University
San Diego, California
Claims and Damages: U.S. Claims
Gorostiza, Manuel de
Legacy of the War: Legacy of the War in the United
States
Los Niños Héroes
Treaty of Guadalupe Hidalgo

L. MARSHALL HALL
Longwood College
Farmville, Virginia
Bennett, James Gordon
Buchanan, James
Cadwalader, George
Dallas, George M.
Trist, Nicholas P.

STEPHEN L. HARDIN
The Victoria College
Victoria, Texas
Fannin, James
San Jacinto, Battle of
Texas Revolution: Course of the Revolution

DANIEL S. HAWORTH
University of Texas at Austin
Austin, Texas
Álvarez, Juan
Army, Mexican: Overview
Bustamante, Anastasio

SAM W. HAYNES
University of Texas at Arlington
Arlington, Texas
Black Bean Episode
Cabinet, U.S.
Cameron, Ewen

Democratic Party
Elections, U.S.: Election of 1844
Fisher, William S.
Green, Thomas Jefferson
Henrie, Daniel Drake
Mier Expedition
Polk, James K.
Prisoners of War: Texan Prisoners
Santa Fe: Santa Fe Expedition
Shannon, Wilson
Somervell Expedition
Thompson, Waddy
Vasquez Expedition
War Aims: U.S. War Aims
War Message, Polk's
Woll's Expedition

DAVID S. HEIDLER
Colorado Springs, Colorado
Marcy, William L.
Twiggs, David E.
Worth, William J.

JEANNE T. HEIDLER
Colorado Springs, Colorado
Marcy, William L.
Twiggs, David E.
Worth, William J.

CORY HENDRICKS
McMurry University
Abilene, Texas
Snively Expedition

MARGARET SWETT HENSON
University of Houston—Clear Lake (retired)
Houston, Texas
Burnet, David G.
Decree of 1830
Texas Revolts of 1832
Texas Tories
Zavala, Lorenzo de

OCTAVIO HERRERA
Universidad Autónoma de Tamaulipas
Ciudad Victoria, Tamaulipas
Canales Rosillo, Antonio
Occupation of Mexico
Río Grande, Republic of the
Tamaulipas

LAURA HERRERA SERNA
Museo Nacional de las Intervenciones
Mexico City
Mexico City

HARRY P. HEWITT
Midwestern State University
Wichita Falls, Texas
Boundary Commissions
Díaz de la Vega, Rómulo
Emory, William H.

THOMAS HIETALA
Grinnell College
Grinnell, Iowa
Ashmun Amendment
Congress: U.S. Congress
Corwin, Thomas
Expansionism and Imperialism
Green, Duff
Hannegan, Edward A.
Walker, Robert J.

RON HINRICHS
San Pasqual Battlefield Volunteer Association
Escondido, California
La Mesa, Battle of
San Pasqual

HARWOOD P. HINTON
Austin, Texas
Wool, John E.

DANIEL WALKER HOWE
University of California, Los Angeles
Los Angeles, California
Whig Party

LINDA SYBERT HUDSON
Kilgore, Texas
Cazneau, Jane McManus Storm

CRAFT HUGHES
McMurry University
Abilene, Texas
Weapons: Weapons Technology

J. PATRICK HUGHES
Leavenworth, Kansas
Kearny, Stephen W.
May, Charles

NATHANIEL CHEAIRS HUGHES, JR.
Chattanooga, Tennessee
O'Hara, Theodore
Pillow, Gideon

DAVID D. JACKSON
Summerlee Foundation
Dallas, Texas
Mississippi Rifle

PERRY D. JAMIESON
Air Force History Support Office
Bolling Air Force Base
Washington, D.C.
Tactics: U.S. Tactics

ROBERT W. JOHANNSEN
University of Illinois at Urbana-Champaign
Urbana, Illinois
Douglas, Stephen A.
Literature

All of Mexico Movement
Army Life: Life in the U.S. Army
Hamer, Thomas L.
Lane, Joseph

ISAAC MCDANIEL, O.S.B.
Saint Meinrad College
Saint Meinrad, Indiana
Religion

ARCHIE P. MCDONALD
Stephen F. Austin University
Nacogdoches, Texas
Fredonia Rebellion
Travis, William B.

ROBERT RYAL MILLER
Berkeley, California
San Patricio Battalion

ALLAN R. MILLETT
The Ohio State University
Columbus, Ohio
Marines, U.S.

STEVEN H. MINTZ
University of Houston
Houston, Texas
Elections, U.S.: Election of 1840

NASSER MOMAYEZI
Texas A&M International University
Laredo, Texas
Sierra Madre, Republic of the

ANGELA D. MOORE
Old Dominion University
Norfolk, Virginia
Monroe Doctrine
Van Buren, Martin

CHRISTOPHER MORRIS
University of Texas at Arlington
Arlington, Texas
Missouri Compromise

EDWARD H. MOSELEY
University of Alabama
Tuscaloosa, Alabama
San Juan de Ulúa
Vera Cruz Campaign
Vidaurri, Francisco

JAMES R. MUNSON
Longwood College
Farmville, Virginia
Alleye de Cyprey, Baron
France
Guizot, François

MARK E. NACKMAN
Tarrytown, New York
Texas: Nationalism in Texas

JAMES E. OFFICER (DECEASED)
University of Arizona
Tucson, Arizona
Arizona

JOSEF OPATRNÝ
Charles University
Prague, Czech Republic
Ostend Manifesto

ROBERT F. PACE
Longwood College
Farmville, Virginia
Agriculture
Elections, U.S.: Election of 1828
Elections, U.S.: Election of 1836
Elections, U.S.: Election of 1852
Louisiana Purchase

JOSÉ DE LA CRUZ PACHECO ROJAS
Durango, Durango
Durango, State of

T. MICHAEL PARRISH
Lyndon Baines Johnson Library
University of Texas at Austin
Austin, Texas
Bliss, William W. S.
Taylor, Zachary
Taylor's Armistice

JEFFREY L. PATRICK
National Park Service, U.S. Department of the
Interior
Republic, Missouri
Buena Vista, Battle of
Conner, David

MARÍA TERESA PAVÍA MILLER
Universidad Nacional Autónoma de México
Mexico City
Bravo, Nicolás

JEFFREY M. PILCHER
The Citadel
Charleston, South Carolina
Castes
García Conde, Pedro
Jalapa
Pastry War of 1838
Peña y Barragán, Matías de la
Rea, Joaquín
Tampico: Battle of 1829
Trías Álvarez, Ángel

MATTHEW PINSKER
Millersville University of Pennsylvania
Millersville, Pennsylvania
Spot Resolutions

MARK PITCAVAGE
Institute for Intergovernmental Research
Tallahassee, Florida
Militia, U.S.

RANDALL C. PRESLEY
Abilene Christian University
Abilene, Texas
Lafragua, José María

RONALD J. QUINN
San Diego Coast District
San Diego, California
California: Overview

W. DIRK RAAT
State University of New York
Fredonia, New York
Adams-Onís Treaty
Gadsden Purchase
Mexican Cession
Treaty of 1832

CARLOS RECIO DAVILA
Saltillo, Coahuila
Saltillo

ANDREAS REICHSTEIN
University of Hamburg
Hamburg, Germany
Empresarios
Land Grants
Land Speculation

TOM REILLY
California State University, Northridge
Northridge, California
Newspapers: U.S. Press

DENNIS REINHARTZ
University of Texas at Arlington
Arlington, Texas
Cartography

DOUGLAS W. RICHMOND
University of Texas at Arlington
Arlington, Texas
Class Structure in Mexico
Collaboration in Mexico
Territories: Mexican Territories
Tucson
Victoria, Guadalupe

ROBIN ROBINSON
Arizona State University
Tempe, Arizona

Armijo, Manuel
Salas, José Mariano

LELIA M. ROECKELL
Bronx Community College of the City University of
New York
Bronx, New York
Clayton-Bulwer Treaty
Great Britain
Hamilton-Gordon, George

ANDREW ROLLE
Henry E. Huntington Library
San Marino, California
Frémont, John C.

YOLANDA GARCIA ROMERO
North Lake College
Irving, Texas
Women: Women in Mexico
Zozaya, María Josefa

ALAN ROSENUS
Saratoga, California
Vallejo, Mariano Guadalupe

MITCHEL ROTH
Sam Houston State University
Huntsville, Texas
Kendall, George Wilkins
War Correspondents

MARK SAAD SAKA
Sul Ross State University
Alpine, Texas
San Luis Potosí: State of San Luis Potosí
San Luis Potosí: City of San Luis Potosí
Bocanegra, José María

ELIZABETH SALAS
University of Washington
Seattle, Washington
Camp Followers: Mexican Camp Followers

LINDA K. SALVUCCI
Trinity University
San Antonio, Texas
Trade

ROBERT D. SAMPSON
Decatur, Illinois
O'Sullivan, John L.

JOSEPH P. SÁNCHEZ
National Park Service
Albuquerque, New Mexico
Ampudia, Pedro
Arista, Mariano
Herrera, José Joaquín de
Palo Alto, Battle of

PEDRO SANTONI
California State University, San Bernardino
San Bernardino, California
Carbajal, Francisco
Cortina, José Gómez de la
Couto, José Bernardo
de la Rosa, Luis
Garay, Francisco de
Gómez, Gregorio
Gómez Farías, Valentín
Gómez Pedraza, Manuel
González Cosío, Manuel
Historiography
Jarauta, Celestino Domeco de
Juárez, Benito
Lerdo de Tejada, Miguel
Micheltorena, Manuel
Militia, Mexican Civic
Ocampo, Melchor
Parrodi, Anastasio
Peña y Peña, Manuel de la
Pérez, Francisco
Polkos Revolt
Rangel, Joaquín
Téllez, Rafael
Terrés, Andrés
Zerecero, Anastasio

THOMAS F. SCHILZ
San Diego Miramar College
San Diego, California
Indian Policy: U.S. Policy
Indians: Overview

JOHN H. SCHROEDER
University of Wisconsin—Milwaukee
Milwaukee, Wisconsin
Adams, John Quincy
American Peace Society
Giddings, Joshua
Immortal Fourteen
Public Opinion: Popular Sentiment in the United
States
Texas: Annexation of Texas

WILLIAM J. SCHULTZ, M.D.
Olmsted Family Practice Group, Inc.
Sugar Creek, Ohio
Health and Medicine
Photography

TRACY M. SHILCUTT
McMurry University
Abilene, Texas
Immigration: Immigration to California
Johnston, Albert Sydney
Temple, Henry John

JENNIFER A. SHIMP
McMurry University
Abilene, Texas
Ugartechea, Domingo de

STANLEY E. SIEGEL
University of Houston
Houston, Texas
Diplomacy: Texan Diplomacy
Diplomacy: U.S. Diplomacy
Donelson, Andrew Jackson
Elliot, Charles
Henderson, James P.
Jones, Anson
Lamar, Mirabeau B.
Politics: Texan Politics
Treaties of Velasco

HAROLD DANA SIMS
University of Pittsburgh
Pittsburgh, Pennsylvania
Freemasonry
Guerrero, Vicente

WILLIAM B. SKELTON
University of Wisconsin—Stevens Point
Stevens Point, Wisconsin
Polk-Scott Feud

ROBERT W. SLEDGE
McMurry University
Abilene, Texas
Protestantism

GENE A. SMITH
Texas Christian University
Fort Worth, Texas
Jones, Thomas ap Catesby
Larkin, Thomas O.
Monterey, California: Monterey Incident of 1842

THOMAS TYREE SMITH
United States Army
Fort Bliss
El Paso, Texas
Army, U.S.: Army of Observation and Occupation
Forts
Mexico City Campaign: The March to Mexico City
Military Academy, United States

REYNALDO SORDO CEDEÑO
Instituto Tecnológico Autónomo de México
Mexico City
Bustamante, Carlos María de
Congress: Mexican Congress
Constitution, Mexican: Constitution of 1836
Constitution, Mexican: Constitution of 1842
Constitution, Mexican: Constitution of 1843
Tornel, José María

MIGUEL SOTO
Universidad Nacional Autónoma de México
Mexico City
Alamán y Escalada, Lucas
Bermúdez de Castro, Salvador
Paredes y Arrillaga, Mariano

RONALD L. SPILLER
Edinboro University of Pennsylvania
Edinboro, Pennsylvania
Cerro Gordo, Battle of

RAYMOND STARR
San Diego State University
San Diego, California
Monterey, California: City of Monterey
Treaty of Cahuenga

DONALD F. STEVENS
Drexel University
Philadelphia, Pennsylvania
Conservatives, Mexican
Léperos
Moderados
Puros

JOSEPH A. STOUT, JR.
Oklahoma State University
Stillwater, Oklahoma
Crabb, Henry
Filibustering
Oury, William Sanders
Walker, William

ANA ROSA SUÁREZ ARGÜELLO
Instituto José María Luis Mora
Mexico City
Politics: Mexican Politics
War Aims: Mexican War Aims

EDWIN R. SWEENEY
St. Charles, Missouri
Apaches: Chiricahua Apaches
Apaches: Gileño and Mimbreño Apaches

CRAIG L. SYMONDS
United States Naval Academy
Annapolis, Maryland
Navy, U.S.

LAWRENCE D. TAYLOR
El Colegio de la Frontera Norte
Tijuana, Baja California, Mexico
Alvarado, Juan Bautista
Ayutla Revolution
Californios
Claims and Damages: Mexican Claims
Indian Policy: Mexican Policy
Ortiz de Ayala, S. Tadeo
Peonage

PAUL E. TEED
Saginaw Valley State University
University Center, Michigan
Parker, Theodore

JERRY THOMPSON
Texas A&M International University
Laredo, Texas
Cortina, Juan

GUY P. C. THOMSON
University of Warwick
Coventry, England
Music: Mexican Music
Puebla: State of Puebla

ANDRÉS TIJERINA
Texas A&M University, Kingsville
Kingsville, Texas
Tejanos
Trans-Nueces

ADRIAN G. TRAAS
Alexandria, Virginia
Chapultepec, Battle of
Contreras and Churubusco
Topographical Engineers

SPENCER C. TUCKER
Virginia Military Institute
Lexington, Virginia
Alvarado Expedition
Bomb Brigs
Lower California Campaign
Naval Blockade
Steamships
Tabasco River Expedition
Tuxpan, Battle of
Weapons: Coastal and Naval Weapons

RON TYLER
Texas State Historical Association
Austin, Texas
Art

LINDA D. VANCE
Descendants of Mexican War Veterans
Austin, Texas
Camp Followers: U.S. Camp Followers
Magoffin, Susan
Women: Women in the United States

PAUL J. VANDERWOOD
San Diego State University
San Diego, California
Banditry

JESÚS VELASCO MÁRQUEZ
Instituto Tecnológico Autónomo de México
Mexico City
Legacy of the War: Legacy of the War in Mexico
Newspapers: Mexican Press
Public Opinion: Prewar Sentiment in Mexico
Public Opinion: Mexican Perceptions during the War

RICHARD WARREN
St. Joseph's University
Philadelphia, Pennsylvania
Elections and Coups, Mexican

ROBERT S. WEDDLE
Bonham, Texas
Presidios

ROBERT P. WETTEMANN, JR.
Texas A&M University
College Station, Texas
Brown, Jacob
Corpus Christi
Fort Texas
Fort Texas, Siege of
New Orleans
Recruitment: U.S. Army Recruitment
Shields, James
Smith, Justin

AMY M. WILSON
McMurry University
Abilene, Texas
Beach, Moses Y.
Fueros
Pico, Andrés
Pico, Pío de Jesús

RICHARD BRUCE WINDERS
The Alamo
San Antonio, Texas
Army, U.S.: Organization
Atrocities
Aztec Club
Civil War Generals
Deserters
Encarnación, Hacienda de
Foraging
Historiography
Huamantla, Battle of
Mexican Spy Company
Mexico City Campaign: Defending the Road to
  Mexico
Missions
Monterrey, Mexico, Battle of
Mounted Rifles, U.S.
National Road, Mexico
Numbers and Losses
Patronage in the U.S. Military
Politics: U.S. Politics
Prisoners of War: U.S. Prisoners
Puebla: Siege of Puebla
Republicanism, U.S.
Slang
Ten Regiment Bill
Thorns, Horns, and Stingers
Tornel Decree
United States, 1821–1854: Sectionalism

Voltigeurs and Foot Riflemen, U.S.
Volunteers: U.S. Volunteers
Volunteers: Remustered Volunteers

JOSH LEE WINEGARNER
McMurry University
Abilene, Texas
Apaches: Mescalero Apaches
California: U.S. Occupation
Laredo and Nuevo Laredo
Tampico Expedition

BETSY WINGERT
McMurry University
Abilene, Texas
Catholic Church

LEE ANN WOODALL
McMurry University
Abilene, Texas
Flags: Texan Flags
Zacatecas

ROBERT WOOSTER
Texas A&M University, Corpus Christi
Corpus Christi, Texas
Texas: Conflicts with Mexico, 1836–1845

DONALD E. WORCESTER
Texas Christian University (emeritus)
Fort Worth, Texas
Borderlands

A. J. WRIGHT
University of Alabama at Birmingham
Department of Anesthesiology Library
Birmingham, Alabama
Anesthesiology

KEVIN R. YOUNG
Forest View Historical Services
San Antonio, Texas
Alamo
Bradburn, Juan Davis
Coleto Creek, Battle of
Crockett, David
de la Peña, José Enrique
Flags: Mexican Flags
Goliad Massacre
Knights of the Golden Circle
Uniforms: Mexican Uniforms

DAVID T. ZABECKI
American Military Academy
Freiburg, Germany
Flying Artillery
Ringgold, Samuel
Weapons: Field Artillery

LIST OF ARTICLES

BUCHANAN, JAMES
L. Marshall Hall

BUENA VISTA, BATTLE OF
Jeffrey L. Patrick

BURLESON, EDWARD
Kenneth Kesselus

BURNET, DAVID G.
Margaret Swett Henson

BUSTAMANTE, ANASTASIO
Daniel S. Haworth

BUSTAMANTE, CARLOS MARÍA DE
Reynaldo Sordo Cedeño

BUTLER, ANTHONY W.
Curt Lamar

BUTLER, WILLIAM O.
David J. Coles

C

CABINET, U.S.
Sam W. Haynes

CADDO INDIANS
David La Vere

CADWALADER, GEORGE
L. Marshall Hall

CALHOUN, JOHN C.
Dallas Cothrum

CALIFORNIA: OVERVIEW
Ronald J. Quinn

CALIFORNIA: U.S. OCCUPATION
Josh Lee Winegarner

CALIFORNIOS
Lawrence D. Taylor

CAMARGO
Joseph E. Chance

CAMERON, EWEN
Sam W. Haynes

CAMP FOLLOWERS: MEXICAN CAMP FOLLOWERS
Elizabeth Salas

CAMP FOLLOWERS: U.S. CAMP FOLLOWERS
Linda D. Vance

CANALES ROSILLO, ANTONIO
Octavio Herrera

CANALIZO, VALENTÍN
William A. DePalo, Jr.

CAÑONCITO, BATTLE OF
Durwood Ball

CARBAJAL, FRANCISCO
Pedro Santoni

CARSON, CHRISTOPHER ("KIT")
Lee Burke

CARTOGRAPHY
Dennis Reinhartz

CASTES
Jeffrey M. Pilcher

CASTRO, JOSÉ
Ward M. McAfee

CATHOLIC CHURCH
Betsy Wingert

CAUDILLOS
John Lynch

CAUSES OF THE WAR: MEXICAN PERSPECTIVE
John Lynch

CAUSES OF THE WAR: U.S. PERSPECTIVE
Norman A. Graebner

CAZNEAU, JANE MCMANUS STORM
Linda Sybert Hudson

CERRALVO
Joseph E. Chance

CERRO GORDO, BATTLE OF
Ronald L. Spiller

CHAPULTEPEC, BATTLE OF
Adrian G. Traas

CHASE, ANN
Shannon L. Baker

CHEROKEES
Diana Everett

CHIHUAHUA, STATE OF
Donald S. Frazier

CHINA
Joseph E. Chance

CIVIL WAR GENERALS
Richard Bruce Winders

CLAIMS AND DAMAGES: MEXICAN CLAIMS
Lawrence D. Taylor

POINSETT, JOEL
Curt Lamar

POLITICS: MEXICAN POLITICS
Ana Rosa Suárez Argüello

POLITICS: TEXAN POLITICS
Stanley E. Siegel

POLITICS: U.S. POLITICS
Richard Bruce Winders

POLK, JAMES K.
Sam W. Haynes

POLKOS REVOLT
Pedro Santoni

POLK-SCOTT FEUD
William B. Skelton

PRESCOTT, WILLIAM HICKLING
Robert W. Johannsen

PRESIDIOS
Robert S. Weddle

PRICE, STERLING
David J. Coles

PRISONERS OF WAR: MEXICAN PRISONERS
Joseph E. Chance

PRISONERS OF WAR: TEXAN PRISONERS
Sam W. Haynes

PRISONERS OF WAR: U.S. PRISONERS
Richard Bruce Winders

PRIVATEERS
Donald S. Frazier

PROTESTANTISM
Robert W. Sledge

PUBLIC OPINION: PREWAR SENTIMENT IN MEXICO
Jesús Velasco Márquez

PUBLIC OPINION: MEXICAN PERCEPTIONS DURING
THE WAR
Jesús Velasco Márquez

PUBLIC OPINION: POPULAR SENTIMENT IN THE UNITED
STATES
John H. Schroeder

PUBLIC OPINION: POLITICAL SENTIMENT IN THE UNITED
STATES
Ward M. McAfee

PUEBLA: STATE OF PUEBLA
Guy P. C. Thomson

PUEBLA: SIEGE OF PUEBLA
Richard Bruce Winders

PUEBLO INDIANS
John Porter Bloom

PUROS
Donald F. Stevens

Q

QUITMAN, JOHN A.
Robert E. May

R

RACISM
Arnoldo De León

RAILROADS
Richard V. Francaviglia

RAMOS ARIZPE, MIGUEL
Carlos González Salas

RANCHO DAVIS
Joseph E. Chance

RANGEL, JOAQUÍN
Pedro Santoni

REA, JOAQUÍN
Jeffrey M. Pilcher

RECRIMINATIONS, MEXICAN
M. Bruce Colcleugh

RECRUITMENT: MEXICAN RECRUITMENT
William A. DePalo, Jr.

RECRUITMENT: U.S. ARMY RECRUITMENT
Robert P. Wettemann, Jr.

REJÓN, MANUEL CRESCENCIO
Aaron P. Mahr Yáñez

RELIGION
Isaac McDaniel, O.S.B.

REPUBLICANISM, U.S.
Richard Bruce Winders

RESACA DE LA PALMA, BATTLE OF
Aaron P. Mahr Yáñez

RIDGELY, RANDOLPH
Joseph E. Chance

RINCÓN, MANUEL
William A. DePalo, Jr.

THE U.S. AND MEXICO AT WAR

Map Key and Military Glossary

Geography

Trees or chapparal

Marsh

Cultivated fields

Pedregal (lava field)

Strategic elevations

Rivers

Tactical elevations

Fords

Orchards

State boundaries

Human Construction

Bridges

Railroads

Tactical towns

Strategic towns

Buildings

Churches

Roads

Forts

Entrenchments

Obstructions

Military

Mexican Infantry

U. S. Infantry

Dragoons

Cavalry

Artillery

Headquarters

Engagements

Steam warships

Sail warships

Sinking vessels

Supply wagons

Troop movements

Attacks

Retreats

Encampments

Art.	U.S. artillery serving as infantry
NG	Mexican Guardia Nacional militia
AM	Mexican Activo militia
Guardacostas	Mexican coastal garrison troops
Line	Mexican lina units
Light	Mexican ligero units
US	U.S. regulars
MS, AR, KY, OH, TN, LA NY, PA, IL, IN, TX, SC	U.S. volunteers
Voltigeurs	U.S. light infantry
USMR	United States Mounted Rifles

LIST OF MAPS

A

Aberdeen, Earl of

See **Hamilton-Gordon, George**

Abolitionism

Opposition to the spread of slavery into the territories and to the admission of new slave states was a long-standing abolitionist policy designed to hasten the end of slavery. Admission of Missouri, annexation of Texas, and war with Mexico all demonstrated, abolitionists believed, that their anti-extension policy had been defeated by Southern power and corrupt majority will.

When Congress decided in 1790 that the Constitution prevented it from interfering with slavery within the states, abolitionists lost the possibility of significant aid from that source. For a long time most abolitionists reluctantly accepted this states' rights position as constitutionally correct. At the same time, however, they argued that Congress legally could—and must—restrict slavery by keeping the territories free and by admitting no new slave states.

In 1819, when Missouri proposed entering the Union as a slave state, antislavery forces marshaled in opposition. Although their efforts failed, the Missouri Compromise established a generation-long North–South equilibrium that abolitionists defended. Its disruption by the expansionist policies of the 1840s and 1850s produced a hailstorm of abolitionist protest, intensified Northern resentment of Southern influence in national affairs, and brought about a political realignment that would lead to secession and civil war.

The Quaker abolitionist editor Benjamin Lundy lived in Texas in the early 1830s and witnessed its developing revolution. The movement for Texas independence, he concluded, was part of a conspiracy developed in the South to

acquire new slave territory for the United States. Lundy's *War in Texas* (1836) conveyed this interpretation to a Northern audience already suspicious that an aggressive "slave power" aimed to control the country. Aided by the flood of anti-Texas petitions that abolitionists sent to Washington, D.C., Representative John Quincy Adams used Lundy's argument in congressional debate to help frustrate annexation.

His success was brief. James K. Polk's election to the presidency in 1844 on a platform calling for expansion on several fronts meant that the Republic of Texas would at last be annexed. Abolitionists regarded this event as the gravest of defeats and as conclusive evidence that slaveholders ruled the nation. Their only recourse, so the most extreme of them asserted, was to separate from the slaveholding Union. Just as "immediate abolition" was the radical cry of the 1830s, so "no union with slaveholders" became the abolitionists' slogan in the 1840s.

Abolitionist reaction to President Polk's request for a war declaration in 1846 was predictable. War against Mexico, in their view, was waged solely to acquire slave territory and consolidate Southern political power. Perhaps Quaker abolitionist John Greenleaf Whittier best captured the hypocrisy abolitionists discerned in the Mexican adventure: "Christian America, thanking God that she is not like other nations . . . goes out, Bible in hand, to enslave the world."

Polk charged such critics with prolonging the war and giving "aid and comfort to the enemy." His implied threat of prosecution was not followed with indictments or efforts to silence the abolitionist press; neither did it intimidate abolitionists. On the contrary, the abolitionist editor William Lloyd Garrison turned the president's charge around by resolving that "all who participate in this war, or who give it any countenance, are the enemies of the country, and traitors to liberty and . . . that the American troops, now occupying Mexican soil, ought immediately to be withdrawn, and full

John Quincy Adams. John Frost, *Pictorial History of Mexico and the Mexican War*, 1862

reparations made to Mexico." Abolitionist lecturer Stephen S. Foster, speaking at the New Hampshire Anti-Slavery Society, instructed the president that "there was a wide difference between treason to the country, and treason to the government. Treason to the government may be a duty. Such is the case now." He compounded the affront by adding that "Every true friend of the country . . . will be found fighting in defense of freedom—under the banners of Mexico."

Such sentiments, so at odds with conventional patriotism, probably did little to impede prosecution of the war. They did, however, reveal abolitionists' deep alienation from prevailing values and governmental policy. Military victory and acquisition from Mexico of vast territory in the path of Southern expansion confirmed abolitionist conviction that slaveholding interests ruled the nation. The war inaugurated a decade in which a faction of abolitionists, despairing of ending slavery by persuasion, became increasingly receptive to the use of violent means, while others of them, certain that the traditional political parties were hopelessly immune

to antislavery influence, played central roles in forming the Free-Soil Party (1848) and the Republican Party (1854), both of which adopted the venerable abolitionist aims of halting the spread of slavery and diminishing the "slave power."

Merton L. Dillon

BIBLIOGRAPHY

Dillon, Merton L. *Benjamin Lundy and the Struggle for Negro Freedom.* 1966.

Dillon, Merton L. *Slavery Attacked: Southern Slaves and Their Allies, 1619–1865.* 1990.

Kraut, Alan M., ed. *Crusaders and Compromisers: Essays in the Relationship of the Antislavery Struggle to the Antebellum Party System.* 1983.

Merk, Frederick. "Dissent in the Mexican War." In *Dissent in Three American Wars,* by Samuel Eliot Morison, Frederick Merk, and Frank Freidel. 1970.

Schroeder, John H. *Mr. Polk's War: American Opposition and Dissent, 1846–1848.* 1973.

Sewell, Richard H. *Ballots for Freedom: Antislavery Politics in the United States, 1837–1860.* 1976.

See also **Slavery**

Adams, John Quincy

U.S. president John Quincy Adams (1767–1848) was born in Massachusetts on 11 July into a distinguished family. His father, John Adams, was the second president of the United States. Before the U.S.–Mexican War, John Quincy had a distinguished public career, serving as minister to several European nations, secretary of state from 1817 to 1825, president from 1825 to 1829, and congressman from Massachusetts from 1831 until his death in 1848.

Regarded as one of the nation's greatest secretaries of state, Adams tried in the 1840s and during the U.S.–Mexican War to prevent U.S. expansion into some of the same areas he had tried to acquire when he was secretary of state. This reversal is explained by slavery and its spread, issues that had become important by the 1840s. As a fervent antislavery Whig, Adams led the fight in the House of Representatives against the "gag rule," the slave trade, and slavery in the District of Columbia. "Old Man Eloquent," as he became known, opposed the annexation of Texas and the acquisition of the Mexican territories as aggressive schemes of the South to extend slavery. In May 1846, Adams was one of only fourteen antislavery Whigs to vote against the bill recognizing war against Mexico. From then until his death he fought stubbornly in Congress against the war. However, because he was in his late seventies and much less active than in previous years, Adams was no longer as effective an antislavery Whig leader as he had once been. Adams died 23 February 1848, after suffering a stroke on the floor of the House of Representatives while delivering a speech protesting the "most unrighteous war" with Mexico.

John H. Schroeder

BIBLIOGRAPHY

Bemis, Samuel Flagg. *John Quincy Adams and the Union.* 1956.

Richards, Leonard L. *The Life and Times of Congressman John Quincy Adams.* 1986.

Adams-Onís Treaty

During the decade of the 1810s, a combination of filibusters by U.S. citizens and activities by U.S. troops resulted in a U.S. challenge to Spanish authority in West Florida (the area between Baton Rouge and the Perdido River), East Florida, and Texas. Filibustering, or cross-border invasions by individuals, eventually led to the acquisition of the Floridas by the United States from Spain. After the U.S.–Mexican War, filibustering would be a major theme in U.S.–Mexican history between 1849, when José María Carvajal established the "Republic of Sierra Madre" in northeastern Mexico and South Texas, and the 1870s, when U.S. bandits created an unstable environment in northern Mexico.

In 1818, while French insurgents and British adventurers were creating chaos in the Floridas and Texas, Gen. Andrew Jackson seized Pensacola. Although he eventually withdrew his forces, the message was clear: Spain either would cede the Floridas to the United States or lose them by force.

On 22 February 1819, U.S. negotiator John Quincy Adams and his Spanish counterpart, Luis de Onís, signed a Treaty of Amity that gave the United States authority over East Florida and tacitly recognized U.S. control of West Florida. The treaty, ratified on 10 July 1821, enabled Spain to secure its hold over Texas.

The boundary line established by the Adams-Onís Treaty (also called the Transcontinental Treaty) began at the Gulf of Mexico at the Sabine River, extended along the west bank to 32° north latitude, then north to the Red River and west to the 100th meridian. From this point, the boundary extended north to the Arkansas River and its headwaters, then due west to the Pacific Ocean along the 42d parallel.

Article III of the treaty relinquished U.S. claims to Texas and in effect meant that Mexico would inherit Texas from Spain "as delimited by the Transcontinental Treaty." U.S. citizens in Louisiana and other western states were angered by the failure of the United States to obtain Texas. Dissatisfied with the treaty terms, they eventually decided to settle in the disputed territory and resolve the Texas question by force.

W. Dirk Raat

BIBLIOGRAPHY

Brooks, Philip Coolidge. *Diplomacy and the Borderlands: The Adams-Onís Treaty of 1819.* 1939.

"Treaty of Amity, Settlement and Limits between Spain and the United States, signed at Washington, 22 February 1819." In *The Consolidated Treaty Series,* edited and annotated by Clive Parry, vol. 70, pp. 1–30. 1969.

African Americans

Fewer African Americans participated militarily in the U.S.–Mexican War than in any declared war in U.S. history. When the war broke out, there were more than three million blacks living in the United States. Of this population, more than four hundred thousand were free blacks. Of the free black population, approximately 55 percent lived in the South and about 45 percent lived in the North. However, U.S. Army regulations of 1820 and 1821 banned blacks from the service, and state laws excluded African Americans from the nation's militia system. As a result, U.S. regular and volunteer army units in Mexico were white, except for a handful of blacks who joined the army under unusual circumstances. Records of the Department of War reveal, for instance, that at least one mulatto convinced an army recruiter that he was white and subsequently served in Mexico. In a few instances, black servants of white officers shouldered arms in Mexico. One such servant, Jacob Dodson, was granted pay by Congress in 1856 for his wartime duty with Col. John C. Frémont's California Battalion. African Americans were permitted in the U.S. Navy at the time of the U.S.–Mexican War but were restricted by quota to 5 percent of naval enlistments. Historians have yet to relate how many African Americans actively participated in the navy's effort in Mexico or what their wartime experiences were like.

Although few blacks served in a military capacity in the army's ground campaigns in Mexico, slaves and hired free blacks did accompany army units as officers' servants. Federal statutes granted commissioned officers, depending on their rank, reimbursement for from one to four servants. African Americans, as a result, accompanied virtually all large U.S. Army units in Mexico. These servants played an important role in the army's day-to-day routine. African Americans cooked, washed clothes, groomed horses, and performed other camp duties such as procuring fresh fruit from Mexican markets. They also served as teamsters, nursed wounded officers, ran errands during battles, and sometimes risked their lives in the performance of their assignments. There are no mortality statistics to document how many African Americans died while serving as servants, soldiers, and sailors in the U.S.–Mexican War.

African Americans encountered discriminatory military justice and racially inspired prejudice while in the wartime army. However, service in Mexico also provided economic and social opportunities for some African Americans. For instance, one of Gen. William J. Worth's former servants operated a restaurant in Mexico City when it was under U.S. occupation. Surviving documents indicate instances of fraternization between officers' African American servants and white U.S. Army soldiers as well as female Mexican civilians. Most important, some officers' slaves capitalized on their wartime situation by escaping to freedom behind Mexican lines.

While some blacks toiled for the army and navy in Mexico, prominent African Americans back in the United States attacked the U.S. government for waging the war and called for its end. In public letters and speeches, black leaders such as Frederick Douglass and Henry Highland Garnet concurred with white abolitionists that the war was a slave power conspiracy to spread Southern involuntary servitude into Mexico. Well after the war ended, African American speakers continued to criticize the conflict in remarks to black state conventions.

Although relatively few blacks served militarily in the U.S.–Mexican War, the conflict was profoundly significant for the future of African Americans in the United States. Nationwide debate over whether slavery ought to be permitted in territory acquired by the United States from Mexico almost disrupted the Union following ratification of the Treaty of Guadalupe Hidalgo. The various enactments that made up the Compromise of 1850 temporarily resolved this dispute. However, provisions within these laws, most particularly their application of the principle of "popular sovereignty" to the new territories of Utah and New Mexico and their clauses concerning the recovery of fugitive slaves, had much to do with the continued friction between the North and the South throughout the 1850s, which culminated in the Civil War.

Robert E. May

BIBLIOGRAPHY

Foner, Philip S., and George E. Walker, eds. *Proceedings of the Black State Conventions, 1840–1865.* 2 vols. 1979–1980.

May, Robert E. "Invisible Men: Blacks and the U.S. Army in the Mexican War." *The Historian* 49 (1987): 463–477.

Records of the General Accounting Office. Records of the Paymaster (1846–1848). Record Group 217. National Archives. Washington, D.C.

Ripley, C. Peter, ed. *The Black Abolitionist Papers.* 5 vols. 1985–1992.

Agriculture

Agriculture was the most important economic endeavor of both the United States and Mexico in the nineteenth century. The success of agricultural progress in the United States and the failure of these advancements in Mexico helped bring these two nations to war in 1846.

From its beginning the United States was an agrarian nation, and many early leaders envisioned it as a country with great opportunities for expansion. Most U.S. farmers cultivated grain crops, such as corn and wheat, on small, self-sufficient farms. Many others owned herds of livestock that thrived on the open range. The most expansion-minded agriculturalists, however, were the southern plantation owners. The 1793 invention of the cotton gin and the development of short-staple varieties of the fiber meant that the slavery-based plantation system could produce massive quantities of cotton to meet the growing demand of the thriving textile industry in the northern United States and abroad.

Southerners, both subsistence farmers and herders and large planters, became the staunchest supporters of territorial expansion. Southern slaveowners and livestock herders considered U.S. land acquisitions such as the Louisiana Purchase and the procurement of Florida as natural developments for the United States. This Manifest Destiny of an expanding country worked in favor of the southern agrarian economy and became the ultimate catalyst for the U.S. war with Mexico.

Mexico failed to participate in the agricultural revolution. Slavery was illegal in Mexico, but large estates, known as haciendas, did exist based on the labor of *peones*. In practice, these peasants' lives mirrored those of slaves in the United States. Both groups of laborers worked from sunrise to sunset for the estate owner. *Peones* did receive wages, but in the form of certificates redeemable only at the hacienda's company store (*tienda de raya*). *Peones,* therefore, stayed in perpetual debt and remained legally bound to the hacienda to which they were indebted. Similarities between Mexican haciendas and U.S. plantations end, however, when comparing productivity. Mexican estate owners (*hacendados*) were apparently more interested in the status afforded them by their position than in making their operations productive. Most Mexican agriculture in the first half of the nineteenth century functioned on a small scale, with farmers using only primitive technology, such as digging sticks and ox-drawn plows.

Mexico's main agricultural production consisted of corn, chili peppers, beans, and cattle. Shortly after independence there were some attempts to make cotton a profitable crop, but poor transportation limited the fiber's production viability. By the 1840s the only major cotton areas of Mexico were near textile mills in Puebla and Guadalajara. As a result, Mexico produced only about one-third of the cotton necessary to meet domestic demand.

The United States and Mexico started down the path to war with the Mexican allowance of U.S. immigration into Texas. Initially, the Mexican government believed the immigrants from the United States would be an asset to the northern Mexican region, especially with regard to agricul-

Mexican herdsman. John Frost, *Pictorial History of Mexico and the Mexican War*, 1862

tural development. The formal papers from the Monterrey Provincial Council transferring Moses Austin's grant to his son, Stephen, specifically stated that the government's "most flattering hopes" were that Texas would receive from these new citizens "an important augmentation in agriculture." With enticements of cheap land, U.S. citizens poured into Mexico; many of these immigrants were southern planters who brought their slaves with them in hopes of spreading the southern U.S. cotton prosperity. By the late 1820s the number of U.S. immigrants in Texas was nearly twice that of Mexican nationals, and tensions with the Mexican government resulted in revolution. Texas gained a tenuous independent status in 1836, and many in the United States believed that this action meant that Texas was soon to become part of the United States. The U.S. annexation of Texas in 1845 not only added a significant agricultural region to its holdings but also opened the door for access to the agricultural richness of California, another reason for war against Mexico.

The U.S.–Mexican War brought changes to both countries through the pressures of an invading army on Mexico's limited agricultural resources, and ultimately with the large areas of land ceded to the United States as a result of the Treaty of Guadalupe Hidalgo. U.S. soldiers ravaged the sparse agriculture of Mexico during the war, and often complained of

the foraging selections being limited to beans, corn, and chili peppers, with occasional cattle. The only reprieve from this menu came during Gen. Winfield Scott's campaign, where soldiers found large quantities of bananas growing wild in the tropics near Vera Cruz. When the war came to an end, the United States gained vast territories for the expansion of agriculture but soon became embroiled in the slavery issue and, ultimately, civil war. For Mexico, the agricultural revolution failed to come. Subsistence farmers and ranchers dominated the agrarian economy, and Mexican agriculture still failed to fulfill the country's needs for food.

Robert F. Pace

BIBLIOGRAPHY

Cumberland, Charles C. *Mexico: The Struggle for Modernity.* 1968.

Ferenbach, T. R. *Lone Star: A History of Texas and the Texans.* 1968.

Gates, Paul W. *The Farmer's Age: Agriculture, 1815–1860.* 1960.

Gray, Lewis Cecil. *A History of Agriculture in the Southern United States to 1860.* 1933.

Ruiz, Ramón Eduardo. *Triumphs and Tragedy: A History of the Mexican People.* 1992.

Siemens, Alfred H. *Between the Summit and the Sea: Central Veracruz in the Nineteenth Century.* 1990.

Alamán y Escalada, Lucas

Mexican politician and historian Lucas Alamán y Escalada (1792–1853), was born in Guanajuato. Alamán survived the capture of that city in 1810 by insurgent troops during the Wars of Independence, after which he traveled and studied in Europe. Ten years later he represented New Spain in the Spanish Parliament. When Spanish authorities refused to grant any autonomy to the colonies, Alamán returned to New Spain and occupied various governmental posts after Mexico won its independence in 1821.

Alamán served as minister of foreign relations between 1823 and 1825, and again from 1830 to 1832. In this capacity he sought, but failed, to strengthen the Mexican presence in Texas by prohibiting further U.S. immigration to the region and bringing in colonists from other countries. Eight years later, as a member of the Council of State, Alamán recommended that Mexico recognize the independence of Texas to avoid a major conflict. His proposal was rejected and Alamán was accused of treason.

In late 1845, after the United States had annexed Texas, Alamán, along with the Spanish minister to Mexico, Salvador Bermúdez de Castro, orchestrated a monarchist plot to obtain European aid to fight the United States and to eliminate the internal political turmoil in Mexico. Although they preferred to avoid an open confrontation with the United States, the military leader chosen to carry out the plot, Mariano Paredes y Arrillaga, advocated a military demonstration against the United States. Paredes overthrew President José Joaquín de Herrera, accusing him of trying to avoid a "glorious and necessary war." That action forced Alamán and Bermúdez to support the warlike attitude of their leader, as they did in the newspaper *El Tiempo*, where they also advocated monarchy as the solution for Mexico's problems.

After the military defeats of the Mexican army at Palo Alto and Resaca de Guerrero, Minister Bermúdez put an end to the monarchist plot. Much to Alamán's disappointment the European powers left Mexico alone to fight the United States. When the Paredes government was overthrown, as he had done before, Alamán went into hiding and three years later reappeared publishing *El Universal,* in which he presented previews of his cathartic *Historia de Méjico.* In it, he condemned the movement for independence of Hidalgo and Morelos and favored the one of Agustín de Iturbide. His message was to give preeminence to "law and order" rather than to popular insurrection like that of the first insurgent leaders. Another major trait of his ideas was that without the aid and assistance of Europe, Mexico would disappear to U.S. expansionism. Justly, Alamán can be considered one of the "spiritual fathers" of Maximilian's monarchist adventure in Mexico. Alamán died in 1853, in charge, once more, of the Ministry of Foreign Relations, this time during President Antonio López de Santa Anna's last administration.

Miguel Soto

BIBLIOGRAPHY

Green, Stanley C. *The Mexican Republic: The First Decade, 1823–1832.* 1987.

González Navarro, Moisés. *El pensamiento político de Lucas Alamán.* 1952.

Hale, Charles. *Mexican Liberalism in the Age of Mora, 1821–1853.* 1968.

Soto, Miguel. *La conspiración monárquica en México, 1845–1846.* 1988.

Soto, Miguel. "Texas en la Mira: política y negocios al iniciarse la gestión de Anthony Butler." In *Política y negocios. Ensayos sobre la relación entre México y los Estados Unidos en el Siglo XIX,* coordinated by Marcela Terrazas and Ana Rosa Suárez. 1997.

Lucas Alamán y Escalada. Fayette Robinson, *Mexico and Her Military Chieftains*, 1851

Alamo

The siege of the Alamo (23 February–6 March 1836) was one of the key events of the Texas war for independence from Mexico. The Alamo was the former Spanish mission of San Antonio de Valero, founded near the headwaters of the Río San Antonio in 1718 by Father Antonio Olivares, a Franciscan attached to the Querétaro College. Between 1719 and 1724 the mission was moved twice before construction commenced at a permanent location on the east side of the Río San Antonio opposite the villa and *presidio* of San Antonio. A series of buildings and workshops enclosed a three-acre plaza that included quarters for the Indian converts, a granary, a two-story *convento* (Long Barracks), and a church, which was never completed. An irrigation or *acequia* system supplied water to the mission as well as the surrounding fields. The mission primarily served various tribes of the Coahuilican language group, but missionary activity ceased in 1795 when the mission was secularized. In 1801 the site was turned into a *presidio* and villa for the Segunda Compañía de Volante de San Carlos de San José y Santiago de Parras del Alamo, hence it became known as the Alamo. In 1810, as part of improvements made to deter invasion from Anglo-American filibusters, a one-story jail, guardhouse, and barracks were erected on the south side of the compound, which contained the main gate. The Alamo remained a military installation under both the Spanish and the Mexican armies. In the fall of 1835, Gen. Martín Perfecto de Cos began fortifying the Alamo in preparation for a possible attack by Texian rebels. These improvements included erecting earthen ramps for artillery, expanding the mission *acequia* system, and constructing a palisade to close a gap between the Alamo church and the south barracks. A Texian army did attack the Alamo and San Antonio during the siege of Béxar, but the military actions against the Alamo were primarily Texian artillery fire. Cos's surrender on 10 December 1835 placed the Alamo under control of the Texian provisional government.

In January 1836 Col. James C. Neill was in command of the Alamo and San Antonio. Col. James Bowie of the Texian volunteers was dispatched by Gen. Sam Houston, commander of the Texian army, to reinforce Neill. Houston ordered Bowie to destroy the military fortifications in the town and recommended that the Alamo be blown up and the garrison retired to Gonzales. Henry Smith, the governor of the provisional government, did not support Houston's recommendation and dispatched William B. Travis, a lieutenant colonel in the regular army, to help coordinate Neill's cavalry operations. Neill and Bowie also disagreed with Houston's recommendations and began to strengthen the garrison. Soon after Travis's arrival on 2 February, Colonel Neill took a leave of absence to attend to family matters and collect supplies and funds for the garrison. His departure created a strain between Bowie and Travis. In an election the volunteers selected Bowie as commander. A split in command developed but was soon resolved when both officers agreed to a joint command. The garrison was soon reinforced by a small detachment of volunteers from the United States that included former U.S. representative David Crockett. The overall garrison was a mixture of colonists, volunteers from the United States, and at least nine Tejanos.

On 23 February 1836 elements of the Mexican Army of Operations arrived within three miles of San Antonio. Travis and Bowie quickly ordered the garrison to the Alamo. Later that afternoon, the first elements of the Mexican army occupied the town. This included Mexican general and president Antonio López de Santa Anna, who assumed direct control of all military operations: Santa Anna demanded that the Texians surrender at the discretion of the Mexican government. Travis responded to the surrender demand with a cannon shot. Using light artillery and howitzers, the Mexican army quickly established a series of batteries and commenced a bombardment against the Alamo defenses. Bowie, troubled by illness, soon collapsed, and turned full command over to Travis.

The siege of the Alamo became a waiting game by both commanders to see who could bring in enough reinforcements to tip the balance. The Mexican army started the siege with approximately 1,500 troops, while the Texians had probably mustered fewer than 150. Santa Anna ordered additional infantry battalions be force-marched to San Antonio. Only a small detachment of volunteers, primarily from Gonzales, organized quickly enough and were close enough to arrive during the siege on 1 March. The Texian garrison at Goliad under Col. James Fannin also commenced a relief effort, but following the breakdown of wagons and carts and intelligence of Gen. José Urrea's movement toward Goliad, it was abandoned. Santa Anna was reinforced on 2 March, bringing his force to an estimated 3,000 to 4,000 men.

On 3 March, Santa Anna held a senior officers' meeting in which he detailed the plans for storming the Alamo. The first column under General Cos would consist of the *fusilero* and *cazadore* companies of the Permanente Aldama and the three right *fusilero* companies of the Activo San Luis. This column was to attack the northwest corner of the Alamo defenses. The second column, commanded by Col. Francisco Duque and comprising the three left *fusilero* companies of the Activo San Luis and the *fusilero* and *cazadore* companies of the Activo Toluca, was to attack the center of the Alamo's north wall. The third column under command of Col. José Maria Romero, comprising the *fusilero* companies of the Permanente Matamoros and Jimenez, was to attack the northeast and east section of the defenses. The fourth column, commanded by Col. Juan Morales and made up of the *cazadore* companies of the Permanente Matamoros and Jimenez and that of the Activo San Luis, was to skirmish with the southern defenses. The reserves consisted of the *grenadero* companies of all five battalions and the Zapadores. A total of 1,400 *soldados,* including reserves, was assigned to the assault.

Shortly after midnight on 6 March, 1,400 to 1,800 Mexican troops were moved into position around the Alamo. The attack commenced about 5 A.M. The concentration of troops at the north proved too much for the defenders, who evacuated the wall line as Mexican troops climbed over. Despite this success, Santa Anna also committed the battalion reserves comprising the grenadier companies of each battalion and the Zapadores.

Morales's column at the south took cover in the ruins of homes outside the southwest corner. The *cazadores* attached to this unit then moved against the Alamo's largest cannon, the 18-pounder, securing it and that section of the wall.

As Mexican troops took control of the outer walls and plaza, the Texians took up secondary defense positions inside the Long Barracks, which had been fortified with cowhide barricades. The Mexicans responded by turning the captured Alamo cannon inward, blasting out doorways and starting a systematic assault against each room. The heaviest hand-to-hand fighting occurred within the Long Barracks rooms. By 6:30 A.M. the Alamo was in Mexican hands.

Estimates of the number of dead and wounded vary. Texian sources put the number of their dead at between 180 and 189; Mexican sources say around 250. Likewise, estimates of the number of Mexicans killed and wounded vary from 370 to 1,600; it is probable that there were about 600 Mexican casualties. At least five Texian wounded were executed after the battle, one of these reported by Mexican officers as being David Crockett. One Tejano convinced Mexican officers he had been a prisoner and was spared, as were Travis's slave, Joe, and 14 to 16 women and children.

The Mexican army repaired the Alamo as a cavalry station but evacuated it and destroyed its defenses in June 1836 following the Texian victory at San Jacinto. The Catholic church retained title to the plaza and the three principal buildings, while the rooms along the compound were reclaimed by their owners. The U.S. Army rented the property from the Catholic church, and from 1846 to 1876 it was used as a quartermaster's depot. In 1850 repairs were made by the army that included the placement of the now famous parapet or "hump" over the church facade. The church was purchased by the state of Texas in 1880 and the Long Barracks eventually purchased for preservation due to the efforts of Adina de Zavala and Clara Driscoll of the Daughters of the Republic of Texas. The property, now owned by the state of Texas with custodianship to the Daughters of the Republic of Texas, is operated as a museum, historic site, and "Shrine to Texas Liberty."

The long-term results of the siege of the Alamo have been debated. The event did not buy Houston and the Texian army time to organize as claimed but did give the convention at Washington-on-the-Brazos time to declare Texas independence, form a government, and pass a constitution. Like so many frontier military events, the defeat at the Alamo and the destruction of its garrison gave the rest of Texas a battle cry that was used at the battle of San Jacinto on 21 April. The Alamo had far-reaching emotional consequences, as it became not only the most famous clash between Anglo-Americans and Mexicans, but also a symbol of sacrifice and the desire for freedom. Myth and legend quickly took the place of historical fact, and today they still dominate the interpretation of the Alamo as both historical event and site.

Kevin R. Young

BIBLIOGRAPHY

Almonte, Juan N. "The Private Journal of Juan Nepomuceno Almonte." *Southwestern Historical Quarterly* 48 (1945): 10–32.

Castaneda, Carlos E. *The Mexican Side of the Texas Revolution.* 1928.

Hard, Robert J. *A Historical Overview of Alamo Plaza and Camposanto.* 1994.

Jenkins, John H., gen. ed. *The Papers of the Texas Revolution, 1835–1836.* 10 vols. 1973.

Alcorta, Lino José

Mexican general Lino José Alcorta (1794–1854) was a native of Vera Cruz. He entered military service on 19 July 1813 as a cadet in the Cazadores de América Regiment. He participated in the royalist counterinsurgency campaigns until seconding the Plan of Iguala in March 1821. In the new republic, Alcorta played a key role in the campaign that drove the Spanish expeditionary army from Tampico in 1829. Thereafter, he held successive positions of increased authority.

As second-in-command of the capital military garrison on 15 July 1840, Alcorta helped crush Brig. Gen. José Urrea's attempt to overthrow the centralist regime of President Anastasio Bustamante. Despite a head wound sustained early in the destructive twelve-day contest that ensued, he continued to direct loyalist artillery fire that progressively wore down the insurrectionists. The outbreak of war with the United States found Alcorta serving as chief of the general staff. After the Battle of Cerro Gordo in 1847, he took over as minister of War and Marine, a position he retained throughout the valley campaign and subsequent peace negotiations. In the wake of the Chapultepec, Belén, and San Cosme defeats, he was one of three senior Mexican generals who advised Santa Anna to yield Mexico City, thereby sparing the capital needless destruction. In 1851, Alcorta was elected vice president of the prestigious Mexican Society of Geography and Statistics. He died in Mexico City in 1854, while serving as minister of war in Santa Anna's final cabinet.

William A. DePalo, Jr.

BIBLIOGRAPHY

Andrade, Vicente de P. "Biografía de Lino José Alcorta." *Boletín de la Sociedad Mexicana de Geografía y Estadística*, vol. 2. p. 165. 1856.

Carreño, Alberto M., ed. *Jefes del Ejército Mexicano en 1847: Biografías de generales de división y de brigada y de coroneles del ejército por fines del año 1847*, pp. 95–97. 1914.

Diccionario Porrúa: De história, biografía, y geografía de México. 6th ed., p. 99. 1995.

Alleye de Cyprey, Baron

Isidore-Elisabeth-Jean-Baptiste Alleye (de Billon) de Cyprey (1784–18??), minister plenipotentiary of the French legation to Mexico, was born in Basse-Terre, Guadeloupe, in the French West Indies.

A recently ennobled career diplomat, Alleye de Cyprey was transferred (in effect, demoted) by the monarchy of King Louis Philippe (1830–1848) from a post in Frankfurt to Mexico, where he served from February 1840 to October 1845. The pattern of quarrelsome, tactless, and indiscreet behavior displayed by Alleye de Cyprey in Frankfurt continued in Mexico. Ignorant of Mexican affairs, he derided the Mexicans as "spoiled and obstinate children" unfit for republicanism. He campaigned in his dispatches to Paris for the establishment of a monarchy (preferably Bourbon) by force of French arms, even if it meant conflict with the United States. Although King Louis Philippe's foreign minister, François Guizot, was determined to avoid such conflict, the baron ignored instructions and provoked a succession of petty disputes over protocol that he hoped would prod the French government into military action.

This culminated on 25 May 1845 in the affair of the "Baño de las Delicias," a livery stable that provided the setting for a brawl between the baron's grooms and Mexican stable boys. This later escalated into gunfire between the minister himself and an angry crowd. The baron then broke off relations, called on the embarrassed Guizot to invade, and eventually fled Mexico for his own safety in October. This mission, Alleye de Cyprey's last, left France despised and without a presence in Mexico City as the U.S.–Mexican War approached. Alleye de Cyprey was by no means atypical of French representatives to Mexico, which indicates how casually France took relations with that country.

James R. Munson

BIBLIOGRAPHY

Barker, Nancy N. *The French Experience in Mexico, 1821–1861: A History of Constant Misunderstanding.* 1979.

Peña y Reyes, Antonio de la, ed. *El Baron Alleye de Cyprey y el Baño de las Delicias.* Archivo Histórico Diplomático Mexicano, No. 18. 1926.

Pletcher, David M. *The Diplomacy of Annexation: Texas, Oregon, and the Mexican War.* 1973.

All of Mexico Movement

In 1845 President James K. Polk was anxious to set the border of Texas at the Río Grande and obtain New Mexico and California from Mexico. He offered $30 million for these lands, but Mexico was not willing to sell.

When war broke out there was an initial patriotic flurry of U.S. newspaper editorials calling for the United States not only to defeat Mexican forces but also to take over the entire country, but this sentiment soon subsided. Early U.S. successes on the battlefields suggested that the war would be short and that Mexico must soon cede at least the lands that President Polk desired. Instead, the war dragged on with an ever lengthening cost in both dollars and lives. Many U.S. citizens began to demand even greater amounts of Mexican territory—perhaps to as far south as the Sierra Madre—as compensation.

The desire to acquire all of Mexico was strongest in the fall and winter of 1847, after Mexico City had been occupied by U.S. forces. The turbulent state of Mexican politics caused the U.S. State Department's Nicholas P. Trist to have a difficult time working out an acceptable peace treaty with Mexican officials. Many feared that if peace were not attained soon, the war must continue until the entire country was conquered, occupied, and annexed.

Despite these developments there was still no U.S. public consensus; the lines of disagreement formed along regional as well as party lines. Although President Polk's Democratic supporters thought that Mexican land should be considered an indemnity, most Whigs deplored the idea of taking large amounts of land from Mexico. Most New Englanders, apparently feeling that their region's influence in national politics would be diluted by such an acquisition, also opposed it. South Carolina senator John C. Calhoun and other slave owners of the southeast opposed wholesale annexation; they recognized that slavery probably would not flourish on Mexican lands, and that their very possession might even sap the strength of slavery elsewhere. Some observers pointed out that annexing all of Mexico meant assuming some $100 million in debt. Others feared the effects of the sudden influx of dark-skinned Mexicans to U.S. citizenship, since they believed that only those with fair skins were capable of understanding and benefitting from republican government. But Western expansionists, both North and South, embracing the concept of Manifest Destiny, eagerly sought more land. They cited the proven wealth of Mexican silver mines and the potential value of transit rights across the isthmus of Tehuantepec, and they played on the fear that unless the United States annexed all of a weakened Mexico a European power would step in and do so. Some saw Mexican lands as a possible haven for ex-slaves when that institution finally ended. Others saw American hegemony as the only hope that Mexican peons had of rising above their present state of squalid poverty. Ironically, now that the outcome of the war was no longer in question, some radical liberals and a few moderates in Mexico favored U.S. annexation as a way for Mexico to rid itself of the influence of the Catholic church and the army and offering a chance to progress toward political stability.

Nicholas Trist and Mexican authorities finally hammered out the Treaty of Guadalupe Hidalgo, which called for the Mexican cession of Upper California and New Mexico, as well as recognition of the Río Grande as the Texas boundary.

This accomplishment reduced the impetus of the All of Mexico Movement, because it meant that the only way more territory could be obtained was if the United States refused to ratify the proposed treaty and continued to prosecute the war. War weariness in the United States, as well as growing disillusionment in Congress, might well have made it impossible to continue the war.

James M. McCaffrey

BIBLIOGRAPHY

Fuller, John Douglas Pitts. *The Movement for the Acquisition of All Mexico, 1846–1848.* 1936.

Lambert, Paul F. "The Movement for the Acquisition of All Mexico." *Journal of the West* 11 (1972): 317–327.

Lander, Ernest M., Jr. *Reluctant Imperialists.* 1980.

Merk, Frederick. *Manifest Destiny and Mission in American History.* 1963.

Pletcher, David M. *The Diplomacy of Annexation: Texas, Oregon, and the Mexican War.* 1973.

Almonte, Juan Nepomuceno

Mexican general and politician Juan Nepomuceno Almonte (1803–1869) was the son of the famous independence leader José Mariá Morelos y Pavón. Almonte's lengthy public career found him involved in some of the most important events in Mexican history and U.S.–Mexican relations. As a youth Almonte went to the United States to seek recognition and military supplies for the independence movement. Later he studied in New Orleans. After diplomatic and military service in the 1820s, Colonel Almonte was assigned to Texas in 1834 to determine the boundary between Mexico and the United States. He later filed a "secret report" evaluating the grievances of the Anglo-American settlers and the strength of the independence party in Texas. After the outbreak of the Texas Revolution in late 1835, Almonte participated in the battles at the Alamo and at San Jacinto, where he was taken prisoner by the victorious Texian forces.

Almonte's involvement in the loss of Texas did little damage to his political and military career. In 1839 he was made a brigadier general and served as secretary of war between 1839 and 1841. In 1842 he became Mexican ambassador to the United States. He was serving in that position in March 1845 when the U.S. Congress passed the resolution providing for the annexation of Texas. Mexico had warned the United States that annexation would be considered an act of war, and Almonte responded to this action by breaking relations and returning to Mexico.

With war threatening, Almonte became a candidate for the presidency of Mexico; in elections held in August 1845, he lost to Provisional President José Joaquín de Herrera. The process of annexing Texas was coming to a conclusion in December 1845 when Almonte joined with other Mexican generals to overthrow Herrera, whose search for a peaceful settlement with the United States had cost him domestic political support. The new administration of Gen. Mariano Paredes y Arrillaga rewarded Almonte by appointing him secretary of war in January 1846. Almonte served as secretary of war from 5 January to 20 February and then again from 28 August to 23 December 1846. Almonte tried to organize the nation's defenses and cope with the U.S. blockade of Vera Cruz, Mexico's principal port, which had begun in September 1846. Almonte also briefly held the position of minister of the treasury; he resigned both positions in December 1846. Almonte held no national leadership positions during the rest of the war but did run again for the presidency in Mexico's first postwar election in May 1848, losing again to José Joaquín de Herrera.

Almonte continued to play an important role in Mexican history after the war with the United States. He served the liberal government as ambassador to Great Britain and France in 1856 but sided with the losing conservatives in the three-year civil war that lasted from 1858 to 1860. Almonte went into exile in Europe, where he played a central role in bringing about the French intervention in 1862 and the establishment of Maximilian's empire in Mexico in 1864. Almonte was in France on a diplomatic mission for Maximilian when the empire collapsed in 1867. Almonte remained in Paris until his death two years later.

Don M. Coerver

BIBLIOGRAPHY

Asbury, Samuel E. "The Private Journal of Juan Nepomuceno Almonte, February 1–April 16, 1836." *Southwestern Historical Quarterly* 48 (1944): 10–32.

Cotner, Thomas Ewing. *The Military and Political Career of José Joaquín de Herrera, 1792–1854.* 1949.

Gutiérrez Ibarra, Celia. *Como México perdió Texas: Analisis y transcripción del informe secreto (1834) de Juan Nepomuceno Almonte.* 1987.

Harris, Helen Willits. "The Public Life of Juan Nepomuceno Almonte." Ph.D. diss., University of Texas at Austin, 1935.

Alvarado, Juan Bautista

California governor and politician Juan Bautista Alvarado (1809–1882) was born in Monterey, Alta California. He belonged to one of that province's most distinguished Mexican families. By the mid-1830s, he had, by virtue of his own personal talents, education, and family ties, become a prominent figure in California politics. In August 1836, the Californios (Mexicans born in California), resentful of the central government's indifference and neglect as well as its repudiation of the federalist Constitution of 1824, ousted Governor Mariano Chico. Control of the province devolved to the Spanish-born former governor Nicolás Gutiérrez. In October, Alvarado, an enemy of Gutiérrez and an opponent of centralist rule, led an army of 150 Californios, Indians, and foreign volunteers against the regional capital in Monterey, which fell after a brief struggle and ended with the expulsion of Gutiérrez. Alvarado persuaded the *diputación* (local legislature) to proclaim a form of home rule.

When Chico and Gutiérrez arrived at Mexico City, the government there was too preoccupied with the consequences of the defeat of Gen. Antonio López de Santa Anna and his army in Texas to devote attention to affairs in California. In the meantime, Alvarado, realizing that California could not exist as an independent entity, proclaimed on 9 July 1837 his allegiance to the national government. On 7 August 1839 he was confirmed by the central government as governor of California, with his uncle, Mariano Guadalupe Vallejo, as *comandante general* (commander general).

In late December 1842, Alvarado was replaced as governor by José Manuel Micheltorena, who, together with a troop of convict settlers (*cholos*), had been sent to California by the national government in a desperate attempt to bolster the province's defenses against foreign encroachments. Mexican direct rule over California ended forever in November 1844, when Alvarado led a revolt that unseated Micheltorena. The Treaty of San Fernando, signed on 22 February and which ended the struggle, designated Pío Pico of Los Angeles as governor, with José Castro, Alvarado's associate, as *comandante general*. Alvarado spent much of the period between the transfer of California to U.S. rule in 1848 until his death at *rancho* San Pablo on 13 July 1882 in litigation against U.S. settlers who tried to confiscate his lands.

Lawrence D. Taylor

BIBLIOGRAPHY
Bancroft, Hubert Howe. *History of California.* 7 vols. 1888–1890.
Hittel, Theodore H. *History of California.* 4 vols. 1885–1897.
Mathes, W. Michael, ed. *Vignettes of Early California: Childhood Reminiscences of Juan Bautista Alvarado.* 1982.

Alvarado Expedition

On 16 October 1846 the U.S. Navy attempted to capture the Mexican Gulf port of Alvarado some thirty miles south of Vera Cruz. Soon after the war began the U.S. Navy had blockaded Mexico's Gulf Coast, but the easiest way to enforce the blockade was to capture the Mexican ports. With the exception of Vera Cruz, however, all the ports were upriver with bars at the river mouths that made it too shallow for the large U.S. warships. Alvarado was three miles up the Río Papaloapán, and even if the U.S. ships crossed the bar, they still had to pass three river forts to reach the port itself.

A number of Mexican gunboats had taken refuge at Alvarado and Commo. David Conner was determined to take the port. A 7 August attempt failed because the river current was too swift for the small steam vessels towing a landing force in boats. After he secured two shallow-draft revenue cutters, Conner ordered a second attempt. The Mexicans, meanwhile, had reinforced Alvarado, adding additional breastworks and strengthening its garrison.

The U.S. Navy expedition arrived off the river mouth on 16 October. The steamer *Mississippi* tried to engage the outer fort while the other warships crossed the bar, but its draft was too great and it could not get close enough to inflict much damage. In addition, heavy surf unnerved the pilots aboard the smaller vessels.

That afternoon when the surf subsided Conner ordered an attempt to cross the bar in two columns. He took command in the *Vixen*, which towed two schooner-gunboats; the revenue cutter *McLane* towed three others and the *Mississippi* provided gunfire support. Conner's column crossed the bar safely but the *McLane* soon went aground. Reluctantly Conner canceled the operation and the *McLane* was floated free. Conner then ordered the expedition to return to Antón Lizardo. No men were killed on either side, but a few were wounded.

The failure of the Alvarado Expedition boosted Mexican morale and falsely convinced the government that it could successfully defend the coast against the U.S. Navy.

Alvarado finally fell on 31 March 1847, in what was to have been a joint U.S. Army–Navy operation to secure horses and cattle, which the army needed for its advance on Mexico City. Commo. Matthew Perry, who had replaced Conner, ordered Charles G. Hunter in the USS *Scourge*, a converted iron-screw steamer, to blockade Alvarado until an army expedition could arrive there from Vera Cruz. Hunter exceeded his instructions and took Alvarado. The ease of the capture remains a mystery. Hunter claimed afterward that some men came out in a boat under a white flag and offered to surrender. Although Alvarado was defended by some sixty artillery pieces, few Mexican troops were available and that may have been the reason for the surrender.

Hunter then garrisoned Alvarado with two midshipmen and sailed upriver to Tlacotalpán, firing his guns as he went and capturing that town also. Hunter's actions alerted the Mexicans, however, and they drove off the horses and cattle to keep them from falling into U.S. hands. When Perry arrived the next day at Alvarado with twelve vessels he had Hunter court-martialed for disobeying orders. The court found Hunter guilty, dismissed him from the squadron, and sent him back to the United States. Later Hunter made much of his capture of "a second Gibraltar" and managed to secure reinstatement.

Spencer C. Tucker

BIBLIOGRAPHY
Bauer, K. Jack. *Surfboats and Horse Marines. U.S. Naval Operations in the Mexican War, 1846–48.* 1969.

Knox, Dudley W. *A History of the United States Navy*. 1936.
Morison, Samuel Eliot. *"Old Bruin": Commodore Matthew Calbraith Perry*. 1967.

Álvarez, Ángel Trías

See **Trías Álvarez, Ángel**

Álvarez, Juan

Mexican general and politician Juan Álvarez (1790–1867) was born to a wealthy family in Santa María de la Concepción Atoyac in the present-day state of Guerrero. He began his military career as a volunteer in the insurgent forces under José María Morelos y Pavón. Álvarez rose quickly through the insurgent ranks and became the commander general of Acapulco in 1821. After Mexico gained independence, he distinguished himself as a liberal partisan on the battlefield and developed into one of the principal military figures in the liberal political movement. His military service earned him promotion to *general de brigada* in 1830 and *general de división* eleven years later.

Álvarez served in few formal political positions. His stature as a political figure, however, was formidable due to his relationship with the rural inhabitants of southern Mexico, who increasingly trusted him to both represent and protect their interests. During the three decades between independence and the war with the United States, he gradually cultivated a powerful base of support among the peasantry in the present-day state of Guerrero and surrounding areas. By the 1850s, peasants inhabiting a zone that included Guerrero, Morelos, Oaxaca, the southern section of México State, and part of Michoacán looked to him as their political leader. Moreover, they provided him with loyal troops in his frequent rebellions against conservative political initiatives that threatened his growing regional power throughout the 1830s and 1840s.

In light of his political prominence and popular image, Álvarez's lackluster performance in the war with the United States has been a matter of contention. Gen. Antonio López de Santa Anna awarded him command of the Mexican cavalry operating against the U.S. forces in the Basin of Mexico in 1847, charging him with cutting U.S. communications with Puebla and harassing the U.S. rear. Álvarez's activities, however, proved largely ineffectual. At the Battle of El Molino del Rey on 8 September 1847, he failed to lead the four thousand cavalry under his command into the fray to press the Mexicans' temporary advantage. His inaction allowed the U.S. troops to regroup and attack another, weaker section of the Mexican line and significantly contributed to the eventual Mexican loss. The explanation for Álvarez's behavior in that engagement remains a matter of dispute.

Despite his apparently poor performance at El Molino del Rey, Álvarez enjoyed considerable success as a soldier and politician for the rest of his life. He was elected governor of the newly created state of Guerrero and concurrently served as its commander general. Safe among his power base in Mexico's southern mountains, he launched the Ayutla Revolution in 1854, which ended Santa Anna's dictatorial regime and swept the liberals to power the following year. Álvarez served briefly as Mexico's president from September to November 1855 and remained a primary military leader among the liberal ranks right up to his death. He died at his hacienda, La Providencia, Guerrero, on 25 December 1867.

Daniel S. Haworth

BIBLIOGRAPHY
Bauer, K. Jack. *The Mexican War, 1846–1848*. 1974.
Bushnell, Clyde Gilbert. *La carrera política y militar de Juan Álvarez*. Translated by Mario Melgar Adalid. 1988.
Díaz Díaz, Fernando. *Caudillos y caciques: Antonio López de Santa Anna y Juan Álvarez*. 1972.
Guardino, Peter. *Peasants, Politics, and the Formation of Mexico's National State: Guerrero, 1800–1857*. 1996.
Jones, Oakah L., Jr. *Santa Anna*. 1968.

American Blood, American Soil

See **War Message, Polk's**

American Peace Society

Founded in 1828, the American Peace Society was one of many reform societies that made up the broad social, political, and utopian antebellum reform movement. The small organization was centered in New England and was always more earnest than influential. Moreover, for years its members disagreed over whether the society should attempt to abolish international war or should advocate antigovernment activity and the abolition of capital punishment.

Just as the U.S.–Mexican War began in 1846, an extreme group led by Elihu Buritt, President Samuel E. Coues, and Amasa Walker withdrew from the society. Subsequently, during the war, Buritt's followers condemned the war and urged noncooperation with government war efforts. In contrast, the moderate pacifists led by George Beckwith refused to counsel or sanction antigovernment activity. They held no demonstrations, did not try to prevent volunteers from enlisting, and did not urge citizens to withhold the payment of their taxes. Instead, they petitioned and appealed to President James K. Polk's administration to end the war while also working to undermine the national war spirit through a campaign of antiwar propaganda. Their publication, *The Advocate of Peace,* carried a steady stream of speeches, sermons, poems, and petitions as well as eyewitness accounts attesting to the horrors of the war. The society also petitioned both the 29th and the 30th Congresses to end the war and offered a $500 prize for the best book on the war. In its literature, the society argued that since the United States was both the invader and the stronger nation, it should initiate peace negotiations by withdrawing from Mexico. Despite its considerable efforts to mobilize antiwar public opinion, the American Peace Society had little effect on mainstream public opinion or on the conduct of the war.

John H. Schroeder

BIBLIOGRAPHY

Brock, Peter. *Pacifism in the United States: From the Colonial Era to the First World War.* 1968.

Ziegler, Valerie H. *The Advocates of Peace in Antebellum America.* 1992.

Ampudia, Pedro de

Born in Havana, Cuba, Mexican general and politician Pedro de Ampudia (1805–1868) entered the Spanish military as a young cadet. As a lieutenant in 1821, he arrived in Mexico as part of the retinue of Juan O'Donoju, the last viceroy of New Spain. In the negotiations between O'Donoju and Gen. Agustín de Iturbide that resulted in the Plan de Iguala and the formation of the Army of the Three Guarantees, Ampudia joined Iturbide's cause and fought against the Spaniards at San Juan de Ulúa. Two decades later, in 1840, he was promoted to general by Antonio López de Santa Anna. Soon after, he participated in the 1840 to 1842 campaign against Texas, commanded by Mexican general Adrian Woll. During the campaign, a Texan army under Gen. Alexander Somervell attempted to attack Mier, a town held by Ampudia. Feigning surrender, Ampudia deceived the Texians and took them prisoner. Shortly thereafter, under orders from Santa Anna, every tenth man was executed.

In the summer of 1844 Ampudia was assigned to Yucatán where he participated in the siege of Campeche against separatists who rebelled against the central government of Mexico. The rebels, after failing later to take Tabasco, were captured, and Ampudia ruthlessly carried out their executions, after which he displayed their heads in public as object lessons.

As the United States and Mexico prepared for war, Ampudia was reassigned to the Texas frontier, where he had served previously. In 1846 he was general-in-chief of the Army of the North, but he was replaced by Gen. Mariano Arista a few weeks before the Battle of Palo Alto.

Just before that battle began, Ampudia, still beseiging Fort Texas, was recalled by Arista to join his force on the battlefield. By 12:15 P.M. on 8 May 1846, Ampudia, with the 4th Regiment of Infantry, was on his way. Concerned that he would not reach Palo Alto in time to reinforce Arista, Ampudia forced his men forward. About 1:15 in the afternoon, Arista's Army of the North met Gen. Zachary Taylor's force and both armies maneuvered into their respective battle lines. A cannonade from the U.S. line, nearly a thousand paces away, soon began to take its toll. Anticipating a bayonet charge, Ampudia impatiently watched the devastating effect of the U.S. artillery on the Mexican line. During the most violent barrage of cannonry, Ampudia dashed across the rear to Arista's command position and demanded that the general act at once. The order, however, was not given, and Ampudia returned to his command. Later that afternoon, he reported to Arista that if the order were not given to charge, the men would disband and all would be lost. Finally, near sunset, Ampudia formed his men for the charge, but they were still too far from the U.S. line, which continued its barrage on the Mexican line. Nightfall ended the battle and both armies camped on the battlefield. The next day the Mexican Army of the North, which had moved a few miles south to Resaca de Guerrero (also known as Resaca de la Palma), was caught by Taylor's army and overrun before they could set up their defenses.

Ampudia led Mexican forces to their surrender at the battle for Monterrey in 1846 and commanded light infantry at the Battle of La Angostura (Buena Vista) in 1847.

In 1854 he was appointed general-in-chief and governor of Nuevo León. In the 1857 Three Year War, or War of the Reform, Ampudia sided with the liberals. Ampudia died 7 August 1868 and is buried in the Panteón de San Fernando in Mexico City.

Joseph P. Sánchez

BIBLIOGRAPHY

DePalo, William A., Jr. *The Mexican National Army, 1822–1852.* 1997.

Roa Barcena, José María. *Recuerdos de la invasion Norteamericana (1846–1848).* 3 vols. 1883. Reprint, 1993.

Anaya, Pedro María

Born in Huichapán (Intendency of Guanajuato), Mexican general and politician Pedro María Anaya (1795–1854) began his military career as an independence fighter at the early age of sixteen. A staunch liberal-federalist, Anaya achieved the rank of brigadier general in 1833, during the first *puro* liberal government of Valentín Gómez Farías. During this brief *puro* interregnum, Anaya also served as minister of war and the navy.

In January 1847, he belonged to a group of *moderado* liberals horrified by the Gómez Farías government's seizure of church resources. Gómez Farías had hoped to use church assets to finance the war against the U.S. invaders. Led by Mariano Otero, Anaya and other deputies signed a decree condemning the seizure, and he later supported the Polkos Revolt in early February. After removing Gómez Farías from power, Gen. Antonio López de Santa Anna appointed Anaya interim president of the republic, while Santa Anna led Mexican forces to face Gen. Winfield Scott's army in the east. Anaya remained president for only two months, however, a post he relinquished when, on 20 May, he assumed direct command of Mexico City's perimeter defenses. Despite his role in the divisive *polkos* affair, Anaya remained a dedicated patriot. He was one of the principal defenders of the convent of Churubusco on 20 August, where his under-equipped, half-trained troops withstood a combined U.S. artillery barrage and infantry charge for more than half a day. Anaya was taken prisoner by Gen. David E. Twiggs following that battle. In 1847 Anaya again served as interim president. He died in December 1854 while serving as postmaster general under the last Santa Anna government.

M. Bruce Colcleugh

BIBLIOGRAPHY

Carreño, Alberto María. *Jefes del Ejército Mexicano en 1847: Biografías de generales de división y de brigada y de coroneles del Ejército Mexicano por fines del año de 1847.* 1914.

Roa Bárcena, José María. *Recuerdos de la invasión Norte-Americana: Por un joven de entonces.* 1902.

Santoni, Pedro. *Mexicans at Arms: Puro Federalists and the Politics of War, 1845–1848.* 1996.

Andrade, Juan José

Like many of his contemporaries and peers, Juan José Andrade (1796–1843) exemplifies the hybrid general-politician of Mexico's Age of Caudillos. Born in Mexico City, Andrade enlisted in the Durango Regiment at age thirteen and served in twenty-seven skirmishes and four major battles against the insurgents during Mexico's War for Independence. In 1821, the twenty-five-year-old veteran turned against the Spanish and endorsed the Plan de Iguala, thus becoming a founder of independent Mexico. His decision led him into three more battles and seven skirmishes, this time against his former comrades-in-arms.

The new government awarded Andrade the rank of major general of cavalry. He also served as the military and political governor of Puebla in the 1820s before accepting the post of commandant general of San Luis Potosí. In 1835 Andrade served as commander of a cavalry brigade in the invasion of Texas. After the Battle of the Alamo in March 1836, Gen. Antonio López de Santa Anna left Andrade in charge of the garrison at San Antonio. Following the Mexican defeat at San Jacinto, Andrade received orders to demolish the Alamo and to concentrate his command with that

of Gen. Vicente Filisola at Goliad. Despite orders from Gen. José Urrea to the contrary, Andrade and Filisola followed instructions conveyed from the captive General Santa Anna and abandoned Goliad and by 18 June, had led their commands to Matamoros, thus ending the campaign.

After his service in Texas, Andrade left the North to assume the position of commandant general of the state of México. In late 1842 Andrade moved to his last assignment, this time as governor and commandant general of the Department of Sinaloa. He died the next year in Mazatlán.

Donald S. Frazier

BIBLIOGRAPHY

Bancroft, Hubert Howe. *History of the North Mexican States and Texas.* 1886.

Hardin, Stephen. *Texian Iliad.* 1994.

Andrade, Manuel

Mexican general Manuel Andrade (1800–18??) was born in Puebla. Andrade began his military career in 1814 as a cadet in Spain's *Escuadrón de Tulancingo*. He was a cavalry officer by 1823 and supported Antonio López de Santa Anna. During the war with the United States, Andrade commanded a cavalry division under the overall control of Gen. Juan Álvarez. His role in the Mexican loss of the battle of El Molino del Rey caused great controversy. U.S. infantry and artillery had taken up positions around El Molino del Rey and the nearby garrison of Casa Mata. On the morning of 8 September 1847, a large company of U.S. heavy siege guns opened fire on the solid stone fortifications at El Molino del Rey, while a battery of field artillery attempted to soften the positions of the Mexican defenders inside Casa Mata. Solidly entrenched inside this supposedly soft target were remnants of the Mexican 3d and 4th Light Infantry Battalions, as well as some national guard troops. When the U.S. infantry, led by Lt. Col. James McIntosh, began its assault on the garrison, the Mexican cavalry was ordered to scatter the U.S. charge. After twice disobeying these orders, Andrade's column did make a movement toward the U.S. forces, but his division retreated in complete disarray after a single burst from the U.S. cannons. The disorder of Andrade's retreat, General Álvarez later complained, caused panic among the other cavalry columns, and they too fled the field. Musket fire from the garrison defenders, meanwhile, slowed the U.S. advance. Ultimately jumping the parapets to engage the U.S. troops with bayonets, the Casa Mata forces repulsed the first U.S. attacks, but only at an unnecessarily high cost. After the war, President Mariano Arista appointed Andrade to head a commission of senior officers to recommend measures to reform the Mexican army and to raise professional standards in the officer corps.

M. Bruce Colcleugh

BIBLIOGRAPHY

Balbontín, Manuel. *La invasión Americana, 1846 á 1848: Apuntes del subteniente de artillería Manuel Balbontín.* 1883.

Riva Palacio, D. Vicente, ed. *México a Través de los Siglos.* 1967.

Roa Bárcena, José María. *Recuerdos de la invasión Norteamericana: Por un joven de entonces.* 1902.

Anesthesiology

In October and November 1846 the first public demonstrations of anesthesia to relieve surgical pain were made by dentist William T. G. Morton at Massachusetts General Hospital in Boston. Within a few months Morton's vaporous agent letheon—sulfuric ether—appeared on the battlefield for the first time. In mid-December surgeon Edward H. Barton urged in a letter to Thomas Lawson, U.S. Surgeon General, that ether be used for pain relief in wounded soldiers. By early spring, Barton, attached to the 3d Dragoons cavalry brigade in Gen. David E. Twiggs's Division, arrived in Vera Cruz. In late March or early April the first documented case of anesthesia administered in a military setting occurred. A German teamster with a U.S. supply train had both legs crushed in an accident. One leg was amputated immediately, without anesthesia. A few days later Barton appeared with ether and an inhaler—a device to administer the vapor to the patient. The teamster's second leg was amputated painlessly. After the war one of Barton's assistants on this case, surgeon John B. Porter, published a series of five lengthy articles in the *American Journal of Medical Sciences*. These articles discussed various medical aspects of the conflict including anesthesia administration. Although ether was available and was at first used frequently for wounded soldiers, its use in such cases was eventually discontinued. "In gunshot wounds, anesthetic agents are almost universally unnecessary, and are almost universally injurious," Porter wrote. "It is for this reason that they were entirely given up in the hospital at Vera Cruz." Porter thought the "obstinate" bleeding of wounded soldiers was due to ether inhalation, which he believed was ineffective anyway. Porter did not know about the rapid vaporization of ether in the warm temperatures of a Mexican summer or the rapid metabolization of ether in profusely bleeding patients. Nevertheless, these U.S. surgeons were responsible for the first anesthesia administered in an armed conflict.

A. J. Wright

BIBLIOGRAPHY

Aldrete, J. Antonio, G. Manuel Marron, and A. J. Wright. "The First Administration of Anesthesia in Military Surgery: On Occasion of the Mexican-American War." *Anesthesiology* 61 (1984): 585–588.

Duncum, Barbara M. *The Development of Inhalation Anesthesia.* 1947.

Angostura, La

See **Buena Vista, Battle of**

Apaches

This entry consists of four articles: **Chiricahua Apaches;** **Gileño and Mimbreño Apaches;** **Lipan Apaches;** *and* **Mescalero Apaches.** *For information on other native peoples, see* **Caddo Indians;** **Cherokees;** **Comanches;** **Indian Policy;** **Indians;** *and* **Pueblo Indians.**

Chiricahua Apaches

Members of the Athapaskan linguistic family, the Chiricahua Apaches migrated from the Pacific Northwest and reached the Southwest by the sixteenth century. One of seven major Apache groups, the Chiricahua consisted of four bands: the Chihennes, who ranged through southwestern New Mexico; the Chokonens, whose home was southeastern Arizona; the Nednhis, who lived in northern Mexico; and the Bedonkohes, whose base was the Mogollon Mountains in southwestern New Mexico. By 1840, the tribe's population was nearly three thousand. The term *Chiricahua* first became synonymous with the Chokonens who lived in the Chiricahua Mountains of southeastern Arizona. Their economy consisted of hunting and gathering and the loot and livestock they captured while raiding.

The Chiricahuas resisted Spanish authority for more than 200 years, until the government's military forces compelled them to make peace about 1790. For the next forty years a fragile armistice prevailed as the Spanish, and later the Mexicans, provided rations and spiritual guidance to prevent Apache raiding. With Mexico's independence from Spain in 1821, the balance provided by this precarious equation was threatened because the Mexican government, strapped for money, systematically reduced its assistance. In 1831, the Chiricahuas rebelled. A bloody cycle of revenge and retaliation followed an intense period of warfare, relieved occasionally by shaky armistices. The Chiricahuas consummated treaties with the state government of Chihuahua at Santa Rita del Cobre on 21 August 1832 and 31 March 1835, and with the state of Sonora at Fronteras in October 1836. None endured, however, because even though peace was attractive, the desire for revenge was strong among the Chiricahuas; the sanguinary fighting split the Apache bands into war and peace factions. As the conflict escalated during the 1830s and 1840s, Sonora adopted a militant stance based on extermination and scalp bounties. Chihuahua, however, favored humane policies, preferring to make treaties to control the Chiricahuas. In July 1842, Chihuahua consummated an important pact with Chiricahua Apache tribal leader Pisago Cabezon, one that appealed to the bellicose Chiricahua

Apache war chief Mangas Coloradas and his followers the next year. That truce continued through early 1844, when the Apaches left the Chihuahuan frontier because of a smallpox epidemic. Mangas Coloradas led several war parties against the state of Sonora in 1844 and early 1845. Sonora responded militarily and surprised Chiricahua camps at Janos, Chihuahua, in August 1844, killing 100 Apaches. Two years later Chihuahua hired mercenary James Kirker to hunt Apaches. In the early morning of 7 July 1846, he butchered and scalped 148 Chiricahuas who were living peacefully near Galeana, Chihuahua. These incidents left indelible impressions on the Chiricahuas, who waged a fierce war against Sonora throughout the 1840s. Mangas Coloradas warmly received U.S. troops when they entered New Mexico in October 1846, even offering assistance against their common enemy. During the U.S.–Mexican War in 1847–1848, the Chokonens, under Miguel Narbona and Cochise, launched several incursions against Sonora, forcing the abandonment of ranches and small settlements: Cuquiarachi in December 1847; Chinapa in February 1848; Fronteras in August 1848; and Tubac in December 1848. In the spring of 1849 they assaulted Sonora's three northern *presidios*—Santa Cruz, Bavispe, and Bacoache. The Chiricahua Apaches dominated Mexico's northern frontier until the mid-1850s, and some bands raided until 1886, when Geronimo surrendered to U.S. troops.

Edwin R. Sweeney

BIBLIOGRAPHY

Griffen, William B. *Apaches at War and Peace: The Janos Presidio, 1750–1758.* 1988.

Moorhead, Max L. *The Apache Frontier: Jacobo Ugarte and Spanish-Indian Relations in Northern New Spain, 1769–1791.* 1968.

Sweeney, Edwin R. *Cochise: Chiricahua Apache Chief.* 1991.

Gileño and Mimbreño Apaches

The Gileños and Mimbreños were two of four Chiricahua Apache bands. They took their names from the geographic locations near which they lived. The Gileños, known to the Chiricahuas as the Bedonkohes, camped along the Gila River and in the Mogollon Mountains. The Mimbreños, known among the Apaches as the Chihennes, ranged from the Burros Mountains east to the Río Grande; the Mimbres River in southern New Mexico was their principal base. Together the two bands numbered about fifteen hundred individuals in 1840. They had fought the Spanish until 1790, when they made peace in exchange for economic assistance. By 1820 a powerful thirty-year-old Apache chief, Mangas Coloradas, led both bands, conspicuously during times of conflict. In 1830, faced with declining economic assistance from Mexico, the Gileños and Mimbreños went to war against Mexico, for livestock and revenge. In May 1832 a ferocious

three-day battle occurred near the Mogollon Mountains between Mexicans and the allied Gileños and Mimbreños, who were soundly routed with a loss of twenty-two dead and fifty wounded. This defeat compelled the two bands to make peace in August 1832. The calm lasted only a few months, however, and a state of war, occasionally relieved by temporary truces, prevailed into the 1840s. When U.S. troops under Brig. Gen. Stephen W. Kearny arrived in Apacheria in 1846, they encountered a friendly Mangas Coloradas, who offered to join forces with Kearny to fight their common enemy. During the U.S.–Mexican War these bands continued to make incursions into Mexico. These hostilities continued until Mangas Coloradas's death in 1863 at the hands of U.S. troops.

Edwin R. Sweeney

BIBLIOGRAPHY

Griffen, William B. *Apaches at War and Peace: The Janos Presidio 1750–1758.* 1988.

Sweeney, Edwin R. *Cochise: Chiricahua Apache Chief.* 1991.

Lipan Apaches

The Lipan Apache Indians were a relatively small but significant tribe. During the early 1700s the Lipans migrated southward from the panhandle of Texas to escape constant raids by the Comanches. They settled in the region of San Antonio, which they raided off and on for the next century. The Spanish attempted to create missions for the Lipans and encouraged them to adopt a sedentary lifestyle but had little success. The Spanish eventually adopted a policy of extermination regarding the Lipans but failed to accomplish that goal as well. When Mexico won its independence from Spain in 1821, the new republic signed two treaties with the Lipans promising annual gifts of gunpowder and corn in exchange for peace. The treaties led to a decrease in the Apache raids but did not eliminate them.

When Anglo-American settlers began arriving in Texas, the Lipans cultivated a friendly relationship toward them. This friendship endured, with some minor breaks, throughout the revolution and the early years of the republic. During the 1840s Lipans often served as scouts or as auxiliaries for Texas raiding parties. In 1842, however, the murder of a popular young Lipan chief (Flacco the younger) caused a breakdown in Apache-Texian relations. More than one-half of the approximately four hundred Lipans moved to Mexico as a result. The others remained in the area between the San Marcos and San Antonio rivers. For the rest of the decade the Lipans raided both Mexican and Texian settlements, often selling their plunder to the opposing side. The Lipans do not appear to have taken an active part in the U.S.–Mexican War, perhaps because of the split in the tribe. In 1873 Col. Ranald Mackenzie attacked the Lipan villages in Mexico, killing or capturing virtually all of the Lipans there. The survivors were deported to the Mescalero Reservation in the Sacramento Mountains of New Mexico.

Jeffrey D. Carlisle

BIBLIOGRAPHY
Reeve, Frank D. "The Apache Indians in Texas." *The Southwestern Historical Quarterly* 50 (1946): 189–219.
Schilz, Thomas F. *Lipan Apaches in Texas.* 1987.

Mescalero Apaches

The Mescalero Apaches, "mescal eaters," were mountain people who lived in and around the Sierra Blanca, the Sacramento, the Guadalupe, and the Davis mountains, which were located between the Pecos River and the Río Grande in northern Chihuahua. This band of Apaches frequented the desert and the high plains as well, as they were hunter-gatherers who migrated when their food supplies moved. They roamed the open country from the Sierra Blanca east to the present-day Texas Panhandle, south to the Big Bend region, and into central Chihuahua.

The Mescalero Apaches were fierce warriors who were almost constantly at war with many of the other Indian tribes. The Mescalero homeland was the Apacheria, the enormous area of plains, deserts, and mountains covering much of present-day southwestern United States and northern Mexico. When the Spanish began to settle in the Apacheria, the Mescaleros realized that they had a new and more dangerous enemy than they had previously encountered. After many years of intense fighting between the Spanish and the Mescaleros, a series of treaties was signed to end the violence. The Spanish agreed to provide goods and rations to the Mescaleros as an act of appeasement in hopes that the Mescaleros would stop raiding and killing Spanish citizens who inhabited the Apacheria. The Spanish and the Mescaleros abided by the treaties.

In 1821 Mexico gained independence from Spain, and this altered the way the Mescaleros would live the rest of their lives. The Republic of Mexico had no obligation to continue the Spanish policy of appeasement and thus did not, primarily out of economic necessity. The Mescaleros in response renewed their raids on farms and travelers throughout the Apacheria.

Through their raids, the Mescaleros obtained horses, captives, and other commodities, which they traded to agents in Mexico and the United States in return for food and weapons. The Mexican army did little to stop the raiding. No roads were safe, and Mexican settlers were forced to move into the cities for security.

When Texas gained independence from Mexico in 1836, the Mescaleros continued to pillage the trade routes through their homeland, occasionally confronted by Texas Rangers, who, like the Mexican army, could rarely locate the elusive Mescaleros. In 1845 the United States annexed Texas, and by the spring of 1846 the United States and Mexico were at war. The Mescaleros took advantage of the situation; as the Mexican and U.S. forces were preoccupied with fighting each other the Mescaleros continued their raids. Mescalero attacks on U.S. troops slowed the execution of operations in New Mexico and Chihuahua and forced the United States to rethink its military strategy. The U.S. punitive raids against the Mescalero raiders were seldom any more successful than the raids by Mexicans or Texians.

The Mescalero Apaches, who viewed the Mexicans as enemies, believed that a partnership with the United States would be mutually beneficial and tried to establish a treaty with the United States. The U.S. government, however, did not hold the same view, and Gen. Stephen W. Kearny warned the Mescalero chief Mangas Coloradas (at an 1846 meeting requested by the Apaches at San Lucia Springs, New Mexico) that if they continued to raid within the borders of the United States they would have to suffer the consequences. Kearny warned that the United States, more powerful than both Mexico and Spain, would not hesitate to prove its might and would annihilate the Mescaleros. Even so, the Mescaleros continued to torment settlers living on the Apacheria. The resulting warfare in the Apacheria helped inspire Article XI of the Treaty of Guadalupe Hildalgo, which made the United States responsible for protecting the citizens of Mexico from the Apaches or any other Indian raiders residing in the area ceded to the United States.

Josh Lee Winegarner

BIBLIOGRAPHY
Sonnichsen, C. L. *The Mescalero Apaches.* 1973.
Terrell, John Upton. *Apache Chronicle.* 1972.
Worcester, Donald E. *The Apaches: Eagles of the Southwest.* 1979.

Archives

See **Museums and Archives**

Arista, Mariano

Mexican general and president Mariano Arista (1802–1855) was born in San Luis Potosí on 26 July. At age fifteen he served as a cadet in the Regimiento Provincial de Puebla. By 1821 he was a rising officer in Agustín de Iturbide's army, and by 1821 he had been promoted to lieutenant colonel. At age twenty-nine Arista served as a brigadier general in the Mexican army. In 1833, after siding with Antonio López de Santa Anna in a failed rebellion against the liberal-federalist government, he was sentenced to exile in the United States. He returned in 1836 when the conservatives were

Mariano Arista. John Frost, *Pictorial History of Mexico and the Mexican War*, 1862

restored to power with the Plan de Cuernavaca under the dictatorship of Santa Anna. That year he was restored to the rank of general and subsequently named to the Supreme Tribunal of War. In the next three years he served on the Committee of Military and Civil Codes, as inspector of the militia, and as commandant general of Tamaulipas. In 1838 he was taken prisoner by the French, who had invaded Vera Cruz during the Pastry War.

After a brief retirement, Arista was recalled to service by President Mariano Paredes y Arrillaga in 1846. In response to invading U.S. forces led by Gen. Zachary Taylor in South Texas, Paredes y Arrillaga named Arista to command the Army of the North as general-in-chief. In that campaign Arista fought the U.S. Army under Taylor to a standstill on 8 May at Palo Alto, the first major battle of the U.S.–Mexican War; he was defeated the next day at Resaca de Guerrero (also known as Resaca de la Palma). Arista then retreated to Matamoros where he left Gen. Francisco Mejía in command while he continued his march southward to Mamulique, Linares, and Tetecala, south of Mexico City, with the remains of the shattered Army of the North.

In 1846 Arista petitioned the Supreme Tribunal of War to review his merits and efforts in the campaign, including his participation in the Battle of Palo Alto. In his *Campaña Con-*

tra los Americanos (1846), Arista explained the principles of war he followed to fight Taylor; these were a checklist of basic requirements for the strategy and tactics he used against the U.S. Army. They included his objectives, intelligence reports, plan for offensive action, security of his forces, morale, mobility, and administration of his command. Arista described the action at Palo Alto in South Texas and explained why he moved his Army of the North to Resaca de Guerrero. At the Battle of Palo Alto, Arista arrayed his forces in a double battleline extending nearly a half mile. As a typical nineteenth-century commander, he had anticipated a bayonet charge across the field. Instead, Taylor opened fire with cannons and kept up the barrage for more than four hours. Meanwhile, Arista attempted several flanking movements that failed to dislodge the U.S. troops. Toward the end of the day, Arista shifted his battleline, hoping this maneuver would create a weakness he could exploit in the U.S. line, but the U.S. forces held their positions. Night ended the first day's battle. The next day, 9 May, Arista moved his forces southward a few miles to an area filled with high chaparral. His hope was that the brushy terrain would conceal his forces against Taylor's artillery and hamper any cavalry maneuvers against his men. Still, the U.S. troops were able to exploit the Mexican weaknesses. At Resaca de Guerrero the Army of the North was routed and its morale broken. At the board of inquiry Arista's men presented mixed testimony regarding how Arista had conducted himself on the battlefield against the U.S. forces. In the end, the tribunal absolved him with the words *"perdío peleando"* (he went down fighting).

Following the war with the United States, Arista was named secretary of war and marine affairs in 1848. His report, *Proyecto para el arreglo del Ejército*, advocating the reform of the military, was published in 1848. Three years later, on 8 January 1851, the national congress declared him the constitutional president of Mexico. He was rudely accepted as president by opposing political factions, but the government during his tenure as president was characterized as one that respected the law. For example, he worked to establish honesty in the treasury. Although he attempted to establish morale and discipline in the military, he was forced to step down in January 1853 after the army pronounced against him. Soon after, suffering ill health, Arista departed for Europe, where he lived for a while in Sevilla, Spain. Leaving Spain for France he boarded an English steamship at Lisbon and, en route, died aboard the *Tagus* on 7 August 1855. He was buried in Lisbon's San Juan Cemetery. According to his wishes, his heart was taken to Mexico and buried there. In 1880 the Mexican government proclaimed Arista *Benemérito de la Patria* (national hero) and requested that his remains be cremated and returned to Mexico, where, in 1881, they were placed in a chapel in the Colegio de Minería.

Joseph P. Sánchez

BIBLIOGRAPHY

DePalo, William A., Jr. *The Mexican National Army, 1822–1852.* 1997.

Esposito, Matthew. "Memorializing Modern Mexico: The State Funerals of the Porfirian Era, 1876 to 1911." Ph.D. diss., Texas Christian University, 1997.

González Navarro, Moisés. *Anatomía del poder en México (1848–1853).* 1977.

Haecker, Charles M. *A Thunder of Cannon: Archaeology of the Mexican-American War Battlefield of Palo Alto.* 1994.

Arizona

Unlike New Mexico and California, Arizona was not a distinct political subdivision of Mexico when war broke out between that country and the United States early in 1846. Rather, the Mexican state of Sonora claimed the region south of the Gila River and New Mexico exercised vague jurisdiction over most of the remainder. The indigenous population, comprising Indians of at least fourteen distinct cultural groups, was large and widespread, whereas persons of Mexican and Spanish descent numbered in the low hundreds and lived only in Tubac and Tucson—two small *presidios* (military posts) on the Santa Cruz River. Apaches roamed the area and it was hazardous for any others to reside elsewhere.

Gen. Stephen W. Kearny headed the first U.S. military unit to enter Arizona during the U.S.–Mexican War. On 21 October 1846 he led a contingent of one hundred soldiers along the Gila River from southwestern New Mexico. California was Kearny's destination and, at Kit Carson's suggestion, he took the Gila route in order to avoid contact with Mexican military personnel from Tucson and Tubac. After passing successfully down the river without opposition and spending a few days in the Pima Indian villages along the way, the U.S. soldiers arrived at the Colorado River crossing on 22 November.

Close behind Kearny and following a different, and potentially more dangerous, route were members of the Mormon Battalion under the direction of Lt. Col. Philip St. George Cooke. Recruited mainly in Iowa, the members of this unit had enlisted both to demonstrate their patriotism and to secure safe passage to California. More than three hundred strong, including five women, the Mormons left Santa Fe on 19 October 1846, marching down the Río Grande, then turning southwestward. They entered Arizona through Guadalupe Pass in the extreme southeastern corner of the present-day state of Arizona. Famed mountain men Pauline [sic] Weaver and Antoine Leroux, who had visited Tucson fifteen years earlier, guided them over much of this route.

Later, while traveling northward along the banks of the San Pedro River, the Mormons encountered problems with herds of wild cattle but were thankful for the ready source of fresh meat. Most of the cattle were bulls from herds that had once grazed on nearby ranches, now abandoned due to the Apache danger. Members of the battalion left the San Pedro near present-day Benson and marched overland toward Tucson.

Approaching the Mexican fort, Lieutenant Colonel Cooke sought to persuade Capt. Antonio Comadurán, the commanding officer of the garrison, to grant safe passage through the town while the Mormons replenished their supplies. Comadurán refused. Nonetheless, as the battalion's members prepared to enter the *presidio*, the Mexican commander withdrew his troops south to San Xavier del Bac. Early on the morning of 17 December 1846, the Mormons entered Tucson without opposition and raised the U.S. flag over the settlement. They remained in the vicinity overnight, then departed the following morning in the direction of the Gila River. Three days later they picked up Kearny's trail and followed it to California.

In addition to the passage of the Kearny and Cooke parties through Arizona during the U.S.–Mexican War, a third group from the United States may have visited the area while the war was still in progress. A California resident visiting Tucson in 1889 informed a reporter for the *Tucson Citizen* that he had belonged to a company of soldiers carrying dispatches from El Paso to General Kearny in November 1847. He stated that, while in the vicinity of Tucson, the U.S. soldiers attempted to seize the Mexican fort but failed. They remained in the area overnight. The following day messengers reached them from El Paso with orders to return to that post.

During the late years of the war, the Mexican citizens of southern Arizona suffered from a severe shortage of military goods, food, and clothing. In October 1847, U.S. warships had blockaded the port of Guaymas on the west coast of Mexico and prevented the entry of Mexican vessels carrying much-needed supplies for Sonorans. This blockade continued until June 1848, shortly after the Mexican congress ratified the Treaty of Guadalupe Hidalgo. Under terms of the treaty, Arizona north of the Gila River became part of the United States. Six years passed, however, before the Gadsden Purchase of 1854 brought southern Arizona into U.S. hands.

James E. Officer

BIBLIOGRAPHY

Cooke, Philip St. George. *The Conquest of New Mexico and California in 1846.* 1964.

Emory, William H. *Notes of a Military Reconnaissance from Fort Leavenworth, in Missouri, to San Diego, California.* 1848.

Officer, James E. *Hispanic Arizona, 1536–1856.* 1988.

Sheridan, Thomas E. *Arizona: A History.* 1995.

Wagoner, Jay J. *Early Arizona: Prehistory to Civil War.* 1975.

Arizpe, Miguel Ramos

See **Ramos Arizpe, Miguel**

Armijo, Manuel

Born in Albuquerque, governor of New Mexico Manuel Armijo (1801–1854) rose from humble *mestizo* origins. He held the position of governor off and on from 1837 until Gen. Stephen W. Kearny took New Mexico for the United States in 1846. A man of power and wealth, Armijo reportedly harbored aspirations to emulate Texas and make New Mexico an independent country. In 1841 Armijo intercepted and defeated the Republic of Texas's Santa Fe Expedition, led by Gen. Hugh McLeod. He trumpeted this unimpressive defeat of inadequately prepared intruders as a great victory, receiving praise from Mexico City. Armijo possessed a reputation for ambition, opportunism, and profiteering. By 1846 he had accumulated most of the lands in and around Albuquerque as his personal property.

In 1846 the United States marched on New Mexico. On 14 August, under a flag of truce, an envoy from Armijo contacted U.S. troops led by Kearny. The envoy's message conveyed the governor's intention of offering resistance. Armijo took up a strong defensive position at Apache Pass on the road leading to Santa Fe. After troops promised from neighboring Mexican states failed to arrive, however, Armijo, with his command divided on whether to oppose Kearny, suddenly abandoned his position and retreated. Fearing for his life from threats by members of the New Mexican militia and by the encroaching U.S. forces, he fled to Albuquerque protected by his personal troops. Kearny marched into Santa Fe 16 August without opposition. Although not exactly a traitor, as accused by some of his countrymen, Armijo cannot be described as either a patriot or a hero.

Robin Robinson

BIBLIOGRAPHY

Diccionario Porrúa: De história, biografía y geografía de Mexico. 6th ed. 1995.

Eisenhower, John S. D. *So Far from God: The U.S. War with Mexico, 1846–1848.* 1989.

Lecompte, Janet. "Manuel Armijo, George Wilkins Kendall, and the Baca-Caballero Conspiracy." *New Mexico Historical Review* 59, no. 1 (January 1984): 55.

Smith, Justin H. *The War with Mexico.* 2 vols. 1919. Reprint, 1963.

Army, Mexican

This entry consists of three separate articles: **Overview; Organization of the Mexican Army;** *and* **Postwar Reforms.** *See also* **Army Life,** *article on* **Life in the Mexican Army; Guerrillas; Lancers; Military Academy, Mexican; Militia, Mexican Civic; Recruitment,** *article on* **Mexican Recruitment; San Patricio Battalion;** *and* **Appendix** *for a chart of Mexican army units.*

Overview

Over the four decades following Mexican independence (1821), the army played an influential role in the history of the republic. Mexico's army, initially derived directly from the largely Creole (of European descent but born in the Americas) colonial army of New Spain, and their former insurgent adversaries, who had rallied behind Lt. Col. Agustín de Iturbide to end Spanish colonial rule. From independence forward a succession of generals occupied the presidency. Perceived threats of foreign occupation further ensured the army a prominent position in Mexican society. The Mexican army's legacy, however, derives primarily from its political activities and its inability to defend the nation from the United States.

The regular army should not be confused with the civic militia, even though at times the two organizations could be difficult to distinguish from one another. They shared similar command structures, identical titles of rank, and a propensity to intervene in politics. Militiamen and regulars often served side-by-side in times of national emergency, as during the U.S.–Mexican War, when militia units were routinely integrated into regular army battalions. The militia, however, was not a professional organization. Militiamen were activated only for the duration of a given crisis and were administered and paid by the government of the state in which they lived. In contrast, the regular army represented an institutional branch of the national government and was composed of professional, full-time soldiers. Neither did the militia enjoy the legal protection of the *fuero militar*. The army was, therefore, distinct from the civic militia.

A daunting set of weaknesses diluted the Mexican army's professionalism and compromised its effectiveness. Pay was irregular, recruitment depended on conscription rather than voluntary enlistment, and a wide social gulf separated officers and men. Aside from the half-hearted Spanish attempt to reconquer Mexico in 1829, the so-called Pastry War with the French in 1838, and the war with the United States, the army was never called on to defend the nation from a foreign aggressor. Commanders focused their attentions in the meantime on the contentious arena of domestic politics. All of these factors combined to produce an army in which morale was generally low, desertion commonplace, and institutional cohesiveness practically unknown.

Ineffective civilian control of the standing army and the prevalence of political alliances between private citizens and military commanders complicated the army's relationship with the national government. Soldiers enjoyed a legal guarantee of immunity from civil prosecution, the *fuero militar,* which obviated effective civilian authority over the army. Commanders, particularly generals, operated with a great deal of autonomy in the locales in which they were based. The ties they and members of their command cultivated with local elites and other groups compromised the loyalty of the troops to the government and allowed the army to position itself as an intermediary between local polities and the national state.

Politically motivated barracks revolts, or *pronunciamientos,* proliferated during Mexico's early years as a republic. Such rebellions generally erupted over disputes between local leaders and the national government. Ambitious army officers frequently harnessed *pronunciamientos* as vehicles to obtain promotion or political office, particularly the presidency. Soldier-presidents such as Anastasio Bustamante, Antonio López de Santa Anna, Nicolás Bravo, and Mariano Paredes y Arrillaga came and went in a recurring cycle of military rebellion during the two decades preceding the U.S.–Mexican War.

Mexico's inability to wage a defensive war against the United States showcased all of the handicaps outlined above. Problems of transport, supply, and communication during the conflict, coupled with the Mexican army's pre-existing weaknesses, aided the U.S. war effort immensely. All in all, the Mexican army of the first half of the nineteenth century cannot be characterized as a particularly effective fighting force, especially when compared with the French army after which it was patterned or the U.S. army that it faced on the battlefield.

Daniel S. Haworth

BIBLIOGRAPHY

Costeloe, Michael P. *The Central Republic in Mexico: Hombres de Bien in the Age of Santa Anna.* 1993.

Jones, Oakah L., Jr. *Santa Anna.* 1968.

Samponaro, Frank Nichols. "The Political Role of the Army in Mexico, 1821–48." Ph.D. diss., State University of New York–Stonybrook, 1974.

Vázquez, Josefina Zoraida. "Political Plans and Collaboration Between Civilians and the Military, 1821–1846." *Bulletin of Latin American Research* 15 (January 1996): 19–38.

Organization of the Mexican Army

The Mexican army of 1846 rostered 18,882 permanent troops (*permanentes*) organized into twelve infantry regiments (of two battalions each), eight regiments and one separate squadron of cavalry, three brigades of artillery, one dragoon brigade, and one battalion of sappers (engineers specializing in laying mines and digging saps). Supplementing the *permanentes* were 10,495 active militiamen (*activos*) apportioned into nine infantry and six cavalry regiments.

Commanded by permanent army officers, the militia was supposed to be activated only in times of emergency; in reality, however, most units were retained on active duty indefinitely. Posted along the northern periphery, presidial companies (*presidiales*) reported 1,174 additional troops. Poorly trained and inadequately outfitted, these frontier units were too far removed to affect the correlation of forces in the main theaters of war.

These standing formations were allocated among five territorially delineated military divisions and five *commandancies-general*. A general staff was in place to coordinate the concentration of brigade- and division-size units to practice the linear tactics necessary for conventional battlefield success. The regional dispersal of forces, however, minimized centralized military authority and abetted localism. The advantages of regrouping scattered permanent army formations into single garrison divisions where units could train routinely under the supervision of experienced officers were not realized before the outbreak of hostilities with the United States.

This regional force distribution scheme compelled the war ministry to confront foreign aggression with extemporaneous armies assembled from the most readily available formations. Generally, the ranks of these hastily assembled composite armies were filled with conscripts impressed into service via the detested levy (*leva*), an arbitrary process that rounded up eligible males and marched them off to the nearest training center. Prone to desertion, mutiny, and larceny, such draftees were difficult to train and discipline but fought well when resolutely led. The repetitive creation of improvised armies kept Mexican units from acquiring the cohesion and esprit necessary to persevere under trying circumstances. On battlefields where small unit leadership and individual initiative were keys to success, such melded organizations were decidedly disadvantaged.

The lone exception to such improvisation was Div. Gen. Mariano Arista's 5,200-man Army of the North. Created in the wake of the loss of Texas to guard the extended Río Grande frontier, it was Mexico's most experienced military formation and the one that engaged Gen. Zachary Taylor's Army of Occupation in all four major battles of the northern campaign. Redeployed to the Valley of Mexico in July 1847, under the command of Div. Gen. Gabriel Valencia, the Army of the North bore the brunt of the action at Padierna (Contreras) and thereafter ceased to exist as an effective fighting force.

Gen. Winfield Scott's imminent advance into the Mexican heartland prompted the war ministry to activate the Army of the East in March 1847. Commanded by President Gen. Antonio López de Santa Anna, this 11,000-man force was an amalgamation of units posted in central Mexico, fragments from the Army of the North, and remnants of the defeated Vera Cruz garrison. After its disintegration at Cerro

Gordo, the Army of the East was reconstituted under the command of Brig. Gen. Manuel María Lombardini with the survivors of that battle and selected national guard (*guardia nacional*) battalions. These national guard troops, comprising both middle- and lower-class residents of the Valley of Mexico, had a vested interest in preserving their homes and fought tenaciously to defend the capital's perimeter strongpoints.

Responsibility for interdicting General Scott's communications with Puebla and guarding the line from Acapulco to Mexico City was entrusted to the 3,000-man Army of the South. Commanded by the impetuous regional warlord (*cacique*) Div. Gen. Juan Álvarez, this predominantly cavalry formation had minimal influence in the war until El Molino del Rey, when Álvarez's refusal to commit his cavalry likely affected the outcome of that engagement. A 3,800-man contingent under the nominal leadership of Div. Gen. Nicolás Bravo rounded out the valley campaign's force structure. Designated the Army of the Center, this ad hoc organization was initially positioned to protect the Mexicalzingo–San Antonio line. Thereafter, elements of the Army of the Center participated in the Churubusco bridgehead fight and the defense of Chapultepec.

In the absence of established government depots, Mexican soldiers routinely procured supplies from nearby communities or foraged off the land. Because local purchases were habitually compensated with unredeemable drafts on the treasury, troops often went hungry. The army's systemic logistical deficiencies were recompensed in part by soldiers' wives and girlfriends (*soldaderas*) who invariably accompanied each campaign. By performing essential sewing, cooking, maintenance, and foraging duties, and ministering to the sick and wounded of both armies, *soldaderas* made a significant contribution to the Mexican War effort.

William A. DePalo, Jr.

BIBLIOGRAPHY

Balbontín, Manuel. *Estado militar de la República Mexicana en 1846*, pp. 12–18, 25. 1890.

Decreto que arregla los cuerpos de caballería, July 27, 1846. Archivo General de la Nación (AGN), Guerra y Marina (GM), vol. 27.

DePalo, William A., Jr. *The Mexican National Army, 1822–1852*, pp. 120–130. 1997.

Martínez Caraza, Leopoldo. *La intervención Norteamericana en México, 1846–1848*, pp. 45–47. 1981.

Memoria de los ramos de Guerra y Marina, 1845, pp. 17, 30–31.

Memoria del Ministerio de Estado y del despacho de Guerra y Marina, 1846, p. 6 and estado 1.

Reestablecimiento de la plana mayor de ejército, September 17, 1846, AGN, GM, vol. 145.

Reglamento para el corso de particulares contra los enemigos de la nación, pp. 3–20. 1846.

Salas, Elizabeth. *Soldaderas in the Mexican Military: Myths and History*, pp. 29–30. 1990.

Postwar Reforms

Proliferating regional challenges to federal authority in postwar Mexico prompted President José Joaquín de Herrera to propose a series of comprehensive military reforms intended to professionalize the army and institutionalize civilian primacy. To build the professionally socialized officer corps so desperately needed, War Minister Mariano Arista reopened the Colegio Militar on 17 June 1848, using the Cuartel del Rastro as an interim facility until Chapultepec could be repaired from damage suffered during the U.S.–Mexican War. The three-year curriculum was revised to incorporate scientific and mechanical courses and more intensified tactical and gunnery instruction. Additionally, entrance exams regulated admission while successful completion of standardized proficiency tests determined advancement.

Legislation enacted on 4 November 1848 reduced statutory permanent army strength to 10,000 men, increased salaries, and revamped recruiting procedures so that army units would no longer be regarded as *presidios* of impressed criminals. The government endeavored to generate interest and attract suitable volunteers by awarding a ten-peso enlistment bonus, furnishing uniforms, and paying entry-level salaries ranging from fifteen to seventeen pesos per month for infantrymen and sappers (engineers specializing in laying mines and digging saps), respectively.

To help maintain public order, the national guard was restructured into mobile and local militia formations. The former could be deployed for up to six months outside the confines of its home state, while the latter was restricted to service within its territorial boundaries. All physically fit men between the ages of eighteen and fifty-five, except doctors, servants, police, federal employees, and members of the permanent army were subject to conscription by lottery.

These reforms improved military education and training, reduced the officer-to-enlisted ratio, attenuated some of the more egregious inequities, curtailed special privileges, and made the entire military establishment more affordable. Even cumulatively, however, these well-intentioned measures ultimately failed to engender a cohesive national army. While the army was in fact leaner and more efficient, it remained scattered in small garrisons subject to the caprices of regional warlords and resurgent ideological factionalism. Preoccupied with the perceived need to safeguard institutional prerogatives, political considerations quickly superseded the military's reform agenda.

William A. DePalo, Jr.

BIBLIOGRAPHY

DePalo, William A., Jr. *The Mexican National Army, 1822–1852*, pp. 146–151. 1997.

Fuentes, Gloria. *El ejército mexicano,* pp. 145–146. 1983.

Ley de 4 de noviembre de 1848 sobre arreglo del ejército, Archivo General de la Nación (AGN), Guerra y Marina (GM), vol. 15.

Ley de 22 de abril de 1851 sobre arreglo del ejército, AGN, GM, vol. 16.

Ley orgánica de la guardia nacional. AGN, GM, vol. 27. 1848.

Memoria del Secretarío de Estado y del despacho de Guerra y Marina, 1848, pp. 8–10.

Memoria del Secretarío de Estado y del despacho de Guerra y Marina, 1850, pp. 20–30 and estados 4, 11, 16–18, 20, and 24.

Memoria del Secretarío de Estado y del despacho de Guerra y Marina, 1851, pp. 29–32.

Army, Texas

During the Texas Revolution of 1835 to 1836, the army consisted primarily of volunteers organized into companies with elected officers. Although various interim governments made provisions for a regular army, both the residents of Texas and recruits from the United States rejected the discipline, longer enlistment, and loss of democratic privileges it required. Therefore, its commander, Sam Houston, had no men serving under him until after the crisis that was brought on by the fall of the Alamo, and these were all short-term volunteers. The ranks of the army of Texas swelled after the Battle of San Jacinto and by the summer of 1836 it was 2,500 men strong, with nearly three-fourths having arrived from the United States after Texas declared its independence. By December the army numbered 3,600, the largest force ever assembled by the Republic of Texas. As president, Houston furloughed most of these soldiers in spring 1837 because of the expense and because such a large organized force threatened to undermine the principles of civilian control.

Thereafter the Republic of Texas generally scrambled for its defense without benefit of an organized body of troops serving specified terms, accepting military discipline, and obeying commands of superior officers chosen by the political authority. This state of military uncertainty was a product of circumstance rather than choice. The Texas congress passed legislation for a regular army—organized into brigades, regiments, battalions, and companies—in 1837 and at the end of 1838, but these units never attracted sufficient enrollment or received sufficient appropriations and supplies to be fully operational. Nor did the army attain the necessary discipline. Efforts to organize a force of mounted troops also fell short. A June 1837 law provided for six hundred horsemen with six-month enlistments, but calls to enroll in this unit went largely unheeded. In May 1838 congress again established a corps of regular cavalry, this time for 280 men enlisting for a minimum of one year for frontier service; however, this unit was never at full strength and disbanded a year later.

When Mirabeau B. Lamar became president in December 1838 he found military destitution—Texas lacked arms, soldiers, and the revenue and credit to correct these weaknesses. The army also never had standardized uniforms, supplies, or equipment. Discipline was weak; desertion was chronic and mutiny commonplace. One strength was that the high-level staff positions were filled by capable, trained, and diligent leaders. Congress again passed legislation to establish a line of frontier posts to defend against both Mexicans and Indians and authorized the president to raise additional companies. A frontier regiment of seventeen companies with a combined strength of 840 men, recruited largely in New Orleans, served between 1839 and 1841 but it was hard pressed to defend a line extending from the Red River to the Gulf of Mexico. Further, this force never achieved more than half its authorized size. Likewise, recruitment fell short of another mounted volunteer unit authorized in January 1839. In 1841 congress failed to appropriate funds to maintain the regular army, and Lamar ordered it officially disbanded. This ended the last significant effort in the Republic of Texas to establish a regular army.

Houston returned to the presidency at the end of 1841 to find the same basic conditions that Lamar had complained of three years earlier—a paper army, defense by ad hoc volunteerism, and inadequate supplies in the government arsenals. This situation left the republic without an army to repel the two Mexican expeditions that reached San Antonio in 1842, although Texas once again fielded hastily assembled volunteers. Earlier that year congress had devised a scheme to establish a chain of frontier colonies supported by fortresses manned by regular army soldiers, but this was another initiative that failed.

Many Texas leaders believed that the defense of the republic would be spread more equitably among the population if militia service were required. A December 1837 law required all men between ages 17 and 50 to enroll in one of four militia brigades; however, the system of enlistment, assembly, and drills never became regular. Militia units did take the field during the Córdova Rebellion of 1838 and 1839, but they had the characteristics of irregular, short-term volunteer units. Another congressional attempt to revive the militia in March 1840 also failed.

The Republic of Texas had much need for a system of defense because of the repeated challenges posed by its relations with Mexico and with Indians, but it never found the financial resources or political methods to establish a viable regular army. Although the government experimented repeatedly, the citizens closest to the trouble spots provided most of their own protection through volunteer units. Whatever was provided by law, the defense of the Republic of Texas always rested in fact with citizen-soldiers who became institutionalized in the Texas Rangers tradition.

Paul D. Lack

BIBLIOGRAPHY
Cutrer, Tom. "Army of the Republic of Texas." In *The New Handbook of Texas*, pp. 247–250. 1996.
Lack, Paul D. *The Texas Revolutionary Experience: A Political and Social History, 1835–1836.* 1992.
Nance, John Milton. *After San Jacinto: The Texas-Mexican Frontier, 1836–1841.* 1963.

Army, U.S.

This entry consists of three separate articles: **Organization**; **Army of Observation and Occupation**; *and* **Army of the West**. *See also* **Army Life**, *article on* **Life in the U.S. Army**; **Militia, U.S.**; **Recruitment**, *article on* **U.S. Army Recruitment**; **Uniforms**, *article on* **U.S. Uniforms**; **Voltigeurs and Foot Riflemen, U.S.**; **Volunteers**; *and* **Appendix** *for a chart of U.S. Army units.*

Organization

During formation of the United States a debate arose over the nature of the young republic's military. There was a strong mistrust of a standing army, which prompted a call for a limited force of regulars. Several safeguards were instituted to ensure the military remained subservient to the civilian government. First, the president was made commander-in-chief. Second, a cabinet-level position (secretary of war) was created to oversee the War Department. Finally, Congress was empowered to control important aspects of the army; it regulated its size and the pay rates and confirmed all appointments to the officer corps. Thus, civil authorities controlled the army's organization.

The U.S. Army underwent numerous changes after its inception in 1789. A cost-conscious Congress maintained only enough troops to garrison the nation's permanent installations and to guard frontier outposts. Congress traditionally responded to each new national emergency by increasing the size of the army, only to slash personnel and units after the danger had passed. In 1846 the authorized manpower level

U.S. Army Staff Departments, 1846

Department	Incumbent
Adjutant General's Department	Col. Roger Jones
Inspector-General's Department	Col. George Croghan
Quartermaster's Department	Brig. Gen. Thomas S. Jesup
Ordnance Department	Col. George Bomford
Subsistence Department	Col. George Gibson
Medical Department	Col. Thomas Lawson
Pay Department	Col. Nathan Towson
U.S. Engineers	Col. James G. Totten
Topographical Engineers	Col. John J. Abert

was 8,613 officers and enlisted men, but desertion, illness, and vacancies had reduced the number below 5,500.

The army was organized into staff departments and permanent regiments. The staff departments were responsible for logistical and administrative duties; they formed the bureaucratic framework that was necessary for effective operations. These included the Adjutant General's, Inspector General's, Commissary, Medical, Ordnance, Pay, Quartermaster's, and Subsistence Departments, the Corps of Engineers, and the Topographical Engineers.

The regular army consisted of fourteen permanent regiments on the eve of the war with Mexico. These included the 1st, 2d, 3d, 4th, 5th, 6th, 7th, and 8th Infantries, the 1st, 2d, 3d, and 4th Artilleries, and the 1st and 2d Dragoons. In May 1846 Congress voted to create a company of engineers and an additional mounted unit (U.S. Mounted Rifles). Together these troops were designated the Old Establishment to distinguish them from others raised during the war. The Old Establishment formed the backbone of Gen. Zachary Taylor's and Gen. Winfield Scott's armies, participating in every major action in northern and central Mexico. War Department records indicate that 15,736 officers and men served with this corps during the U.S.–Mexican War.

On 11 February 1847, Congress passed the Ten Regiment Bill, which authorized the War Department to raise ten regiments of regulars to serve for the duration of the war. These regiments were the 9th through the 16th Infantries, a regiment of Foot Riflemen and Voltigeurs, and the 3d U.S. Dragoons. These 11,186 troops were designated the New Establishment because they were not intended as permanent regiments. Although some of these units were raised in time to serve with Major General Scott in his Mexico City campaign, others arrived after the fighting had ended.

As president of the United States, James K. Polk was the army's commander-in-chief, and he took an active role in formulating strategy and managing the army. He and Secretary of War William L. Marcy formed an effective team that directed five armies across North America. Their relations with the army's high command, however, were often contentious. Polk believed the general-in-chief of the army, Major General Scott, and the department chiefs were too slow and bound by tradition to prosecute the war swiftly. He and Marcy frequently ignored advice from these generals, who were almost all Whigs, and proceeded to run the war as they saw fit.

The War Department grouped regiments into larger formations called brigades and divisions for wartime operations. A brigade was composed of two or more regiments under the command of a brigadier general. A division was composed of two or more brigades commanded by a major general. Brigades or divisions operating in one theater of war formed an army (e.g., the Army of Observation, Army of Occupation, Army of the West, and Army of the Center) and

U.S. Commanders: Army, Division, and Brigade

	Name	Date of Commission	Original Date of Appointment	Rank
Major generals	Winfield Scott	25 June 1841	3 May 1808	Captain, U.S. light artillery
	J. P. Henderson	11 May 1846	11 May 1846	Major general, Texas Volunteers
	Zachary Taylor	29 June 1846	3 May 1808	1st lieutenant, 7th U.S. Infantry
	William O. Butler	29 June 1846	29 June 1846	Major general of volunteers
	Robert Patterson	7 July 1846	7 July 1846	Major general of volunteers
	Gideon J. Pillow	13 April 1847	1 July 1846	Brigadier general of volunteers
	John A. Quitman	14 April 1847	1 July 1846	Brigadier general of volunteers
Brigadier generals	Persifor F. Smith	15 May 1846	15 May 1846	Brigadier general of Louisiana Volunteers
	John E. Wool	25 June 1841	14 April 1812	Captain, 13th U.S. Infantry
	David E. Twiggs	30 June 1846	12 March 1812	Captain, 8th U.S. Infantry
	Stephen W. Kearny	30 June 1846	12 March 1812	1st lieutenant, 13th U.S. Infantry
	Thomas Marshall	1 July 1846	1 July 1846	Appointed from civil life
	Gideon J. Pillow	1 July 1846	1 July 1846	Appointed from civil life
	Thomas L. Hamer	1 July 1846	1 July 1846	Appointed from civil life
	Joseph Lane	1 July 1846	1 July 1846	Appointed from civil life
	John A. Quitman	1 July 1846	1 July 1846	Appointed from civil life
	James Shields	1 July 1846	1 July 1846	Appointed from civil life
	Franklin Pierce	3 March 1847	3 March 1847	Appointed from civil life
	George Cadwalader	3 March 1847	3 March 1847	Appointed from civil life
	Enos D. Hopping	3 March 1847	3 March 1847	Appointed from civil life
	Caleb Cushing	14 April 1847	14 April 1847	Appointed from civil life
	Sterling Price	20 July 1847	20 July 1847	Appointed from volunteer service
Brevet major generals	William I. Worth	23 September 1846	19 March 1813	1st lieutenant, 23rd U.S. Infantry
Brevet brigadier generals	William J. Worth	1 March 1842	19 March 1813	1st lieutenant, 23rd U.S. Infantry
	Persifor E. Smith	23 September 1846	27 May 1846	Colonel, U.S. Mounted Rifle Regt.
	John Garland	20 August 1847	31 March 1813	1st lieutenant, 35th U.S. Infantry
	William S. Harney	18 April 1847	13 February 1818	2d lieutenant, 1st U.S. Infantry

	Name	Command Rank	Original Date of Appointment	Original Commissioned Rank
Acting brigade commanders	James S. McIntosh	Lieutenant colonel, 5th U.S. Infantry	13 November 1812	2d lieutenant
	William Whistler	Colonel, 4th U.S. Infantry	6 June 1801	2d lieutenant
	John Garland	Lieutenant colonel, 4th U.S. Infantry	13 March 1813	1st lieutenant
	Henry Wilson	Lieutenant colonel, 1st U.S. Infantry	17 May 1814	Ensign
	Thomas Staniford	Major, 5th U.S. Infantry	12 October 1814	Ensign
	Newson S. Clarke	Colonel, 6th U.S. Infantry	12 March 1812	Ensign
	Bennett Riley	Lieutenant colonel, 2d U.S. Infantry	12 March 1813	Ensign
	Samuel E. Wilson	Lieutenant colonel, U.S. Marine Corps		

SOURCE: Francis B. Heitman, *Historical Register and Dictionary of the United States Army, from Its Organization, September 29, 1789, to March 2, 1903.* 2 vols. (Washington: Government Printing Office, 1903; Gaithersburg, Md.: Olde Soldiers Book, Inc., 1988).

An unidentified infantry noncommissioned officer. Daguerreotype, c. 1846. From the collection of William J. Schultz, M.D.

were placed under the command of the most senior general officer present.

The army's rank structure contained several levels. The highest rank was general, with two separate grades recognized: brigadier and major. The next category, field officers, included colonels, lieutenant colonels, and majors. Field officers commanded regiments. Each regiment was subdivided into ten companies; each company was commanded by a captain, first lieutenant, and second lieutenant. Each company also had five sergeants and eight corporals, called noncommissioned officers (NCOs). Unlike their superiors, NCOs did not receive a commission from Congress but were instead appointed by their colonels. The lowest rank in the army was private.

Several issues confused the matter of rank. The first was a division between staff officers, those assigned to the various departments, and line officers, those serving with regiments. Both staff and line officers claimed seniority over the other with neither side willing to recognize the other's claim. Second, the brevet (an honorary rank created by Congress during the War of 1812) inflated some officers' ranks several grades above their actual ranks. Congress originally intended the brevet to serve as a reward for gallant actions or meritorious service. Officers who earned a brevet were not automatically entitled to the title, pay, and other amenities associated with the higher rank. They could assume the po-

sition, however, if no officer with that actual rank were present for duty. A serious problem had developed before the war when some officers, led by Winfield Scott, claimed brevet was superior to actual rank. President Polk settled the debate, declaring brevet rank inferior to actual rank.

Some personnel fulfilled special needs within the army. Musicians (e.g., drummers and fifers for the infantry and buglers for the artillery and dragoons) directed the army through its activities whether in camp or field. Teamsters hauled rations and other supplies. Surgeons, hospital stewards, and nurses cared for sick and injured soldiers. Farriers did the same for the army's horses. Sutlers (government-licensed traders) accompanied the army and sold luxuries not provided by the quartermaster or commissary. Laundresses (at a rate of four per company) kept the army looking as presentable as possible.

While not prepared for war, the U.S. Army proved capable of meeting the changing circumstances. Organization undoubtedly was a major factor in its ability to dominate the Mexican forces.

Richard Bruce Winders

BIBLIOGRAPHY

Callan, John F. *Military Laws of the United States.* 1863.

Coffman, Edward M. *The Old Army.* 1986.

Robinson, Fayette. *An Account of the Organization of the Army of the United States of America.* 2 vols. 1848.

Scott, Henry L. *Military Dictionary.* 1864. Reprint, 1984.

2d Lt. John Reynolds, 3d Artillery. Daguerreotype, c. 1846. From the collection of William J. Schultz, M.D.

Skelton, William B. *An American Profession of Arms.* 1992.

War Department. *General Regulation for the Army of the United States.* 1841.

Winders, Richard Bruce. *Mr. Polk's Army: The American Military Experience in the Mexican War.* 1997.

Army of Observation and Occupation

In April 1844 President John Tyler ordered Brev. Brig. Gen. Zachary Taylor to take command of the "Corps of Observation" forming at Fort Jesup, Louisiana, near the eastern border of the Republic of Texas. The mission of this force of 2d Dragoons and 3d and 4th Infantry Regiments was to be prepared to move into Texas in the event of a Mexican-inspired uprising of the Native American tribes or in the event that the annexation of Texas became a reality. In anticipation of Texas's acceptance of annexation, President James K. Polk on 29 June 1845 ordered Taylor's small Army of Observation to the Texas coast as a show of force in the political dispute over the official boundary of Texas.

Taylor sent his dragoons overland and his infantry by sea, landing on the Texas coast 31 July 1845, in effect becoming the "Army of Occupation" of Texas. During the next seven months on the beach at Corpus Christi, Taylor built and trained his 3,400-man army consisting of the 3d, 4th, 5th, 7th, and 8th Infantry, 2d Dragoons, and batteries from the 2d and 3d Artillery. Establishing a supply depot on St. Joseph's Island, he sent engineers to survey the coast and had the dragoons establish camps in San Antonio and Austin.

In January 1846 President Polk ordered Taylor across the Nueces River into the disputed territory. While the supply depot moved by sea to Brazos Santiago, the 2d Dragoons advance guard of the three brigades of the Army of Occupation led off from Corpus Christi on 8 March 1846 toward the Río Grande, Matamoros, and war.

Thomas Tyree Smith

BIBLIOGRAPHY

Ferrell, Robert H., ed. *Monterrey Is Ours: The Mexican War Letters of Lieutenant Dana, 1845–1847.* 1990.

Grant, Ulysses S. *Personal Memoirs of U.S. Grant: Selected Letters, 1839–1865.* 2 vols. 1885.

Hitchcock, Ethan Allen. *Fifty Years in Camp and Field: Diary of Major General Ethan Allen Hitchcock, U.S.A.* Edited by W. A. Croffut. 1909.

Meade, George, ed. *The Life and Letters of George Gordon Meade, Major General, United States Army.* 2 vols. 1913.

Army of the West

The Army of the West, a combination of Missouri Volunteers and regular U.S. troops, was organized in May and June 1846. Commanded by Col. (later general) Stephen W. Kearny, the army consisted of the 1st Regiment Missouri Mounted Volunteers under Col. Alexander W. Doniphan (eight companies, totaling 850 men), the Battalion Missouri Light Artillery (two companies, totaling 232 men), Battalion Infantry (two companies, totaling 275 men), Laclede Rangers (100 men), and various companies of the 1st U.S. Dragoons (300 men). The artillery counted twelve six-pounders and four twelve-pounders. A small unit of Topographical Engineers was also attached to the army.

Kearny's orders were to occupy the Mexican Department of New Mexico, but these were subsequently modified to include the conquest of California as well. The Army of the West left Fort Leavenworth in sections, rendezvousing at Bent's Fort on the Arkansas River at the end of July, and occupying Santa Fe without a fight on 18 August. After establishing a U.S. civil government for New Mexico, Kearny proceeded on his march to California on 25 September. Estimating that he had a surplus of troops in his force, Kearny ordered Colonel Doniphan's 1st Regiment Missouri Mounted Volunteers to march south and join Gen. John E. Wool, who was supposed to be advancing on Chihuahua. The rest of the Missouri Volunteers were to remain as an occupation force in New Mexico.

Doniphan received additional instructions to conduct a campaign into the Navajo country before starting for Chihuahua, his Missourians finally setting out on the Chihuahua Trail in December 1846. Unaware that Wool's Chihuahua campaign had been abandoned, Doniphan and his Missourians ended up conquering the populous Mexican state themselves, winning the battles of Brazito (25 December 1846) and Sacramento (28 February 1847) in the process. Doniphan's command eventually returned to Missouri via Monterrey and New Orleans.

Another splintering of Kearny's army occurred on 6 October 1846, after the general learned from Kit Carson that California was under U.S. control. Kearny detached about two hundred of his dragoons to remain in New Mexico, leaving him with one hundred men plus some topographical engineers and guides. Reaching California after an exhausting march, Kearny's small force, with the addition of some fifty men from San Diego under Lt. Archibald Gillespie, was mauled by Andrés Pico's Mexican lancers at the Battle of San Pasqual (6 December 1846). After receiving reinforcements, the Army of the West arrived in San Diego on 12 December. Kearny and his men subsequently participated with other U.S. troops and sailors in the Battle of San Gabriel (8 January 1847) and the Battle of Los Angeles (9 January 1847).

Other units of the Army of the West included the 2d Regiment Missouri Mounted Volunteers under Col. Sterling Price, and the Mormon Battalion, both of which were organized as reinforcements for Kearny's California expedition. Price's regiment remained as an occupation force in New Mexico, however, participating in the campaign against the Taos insurgents in January and February 1847. The

Mormon Battalion followed Kearny to California, charged with opening a wagon road to the Pacific. Generally, all those troops that occupied New Mexico until the end of the war, including the replacement volunteer regiments of Missouri and Illinois, received the appellation Army of the West.

Mark L. Gardner

BIBLIOGRAPHY

Clarke, Dwight L. *Stephen Watts Kearny: Soldier of the West.* 1961.

Connelley, William E., ed. *War with Mexico, 1846–1847: Doniphan's Expedition and the Conquest of New Mexico and California.* 1907.

Cutts, James Madison. *The Conquest of California and New Mexico.* 1847.

Emory, William H. *Lieutenant Emory Reports: A Reprint of Lieutenant W. H. Emory's Notes of a Military Reconnoissance.* Edited by Ross Calvin. 1951.

Harlow, Neal. *California Conquered: War and Peace on the Pacific, 1846–1850.* 1982.

Army Life

This entry includes two articles: **Life in the Mexican Army** *and* **Life in the U.S. Army.**

Life in the Mexican Army

The Mexican army of 1821 to 1854 was composed largely of peasants who were either drafted or dragooned into service. Thus, the culture and social life of the Mexican rank and file while under arms reflected that of Mexico as a whole. Like their civilian counterparts, the *soldados* of Mexico enjoyed music, paid dutiful attention to Catholic ritual, if not tenets, were self-reliant in terms of medicines and food, maintained a healthy cynicism toward their government, and pursued various forms of recreation including talking, drinking, and games of skill and chance. Largely illiterate, the common soldiers who fought for Mexico spent little time keeping diaries, writing letters, or reading books; rather, these were activities that distinguished the officer corps. One of the aspects that had the most profound effect on the culture of the Mexican army in the first three decades of independence was the large number of women accompanying the troops.

Music abounded. From the fairly sophisticated brass bands that accompanied every army to the simple wooden flutes of the privates, the tunes of Castilian marches and Indian *corridos* floated from the midst of every encampment. In 1836 when Gen. Antonio López de Santa Anna marched north to suppress the rebellion in Texas, his advance guard of 2,000 men was accompanied by a band numbering 150 members. The band book included tunes inherited from the Spanish army, revolutionary airs like the *Marseillaise*, and

campesino waltzes that reminded them of home. One observer from the early stages of the siege of the Alamo noted that the band frequently played selections from the opera *The Barber of Seville*.

For a Catholic army, priests were required on the march. These men were more than the obligatory chaplains of the U.S. armies and served the dual role of confessor and enforcer. The Catholic calendar was respected in the field to varying degrees depending on the forcefulness of the army's clerics. Before battle, priests offered prayers and blessings; after the fight, they offered rites and absolution.

The true keepers of the soldiers' morale, however, were the ubiquitous *soldaderas*. These women had no official role in the army but tagged along with their husbands, brothers, customers, and lovers as they had since the earliest days. These women served a variety of useful roles, including those of laundress, cook, nurse, and maid. This informal relationship became such a part of Mexican war planning that logistics often were neglected by military officials with the expectation that the *soldaderas* would make up for any deficiencies.

Mexican soldiers had to endure the effects of a poor system of logistics and medical care. Food was often scarce and had to be pressed from local residents as the army passed. Animals, too, were often requisitioned. As a result, troops often spent time away from camp foraging for supplies. In combat, the rank and file's weapons and ammunition were unreliable. Powder and shot were often in short supply throughout the Mexican military, and *soldados* often faced U.S. forces with less than a full cartridge box. Men wounded in battle faced a grim future. The medical corps of the Mexican army was virtually nonexistent, and even a modest injury could result in weeks of agony and death. Soldiers who did not receive attention from relatives or friends were often abandoned by their officers.

A reality of the Mexican army was the gulf that separated the enlisted ranks from their officers. Considered a bastion of wealth and privilege, the officer corps was filled with aristocrats who had little concern for the welfare of their men. These leaders, more often than not, saw their position as an opportunity for personal glory and financial gain. As a result, payrolls disappeared, phantom soldiers remained on rolls for pay and supply purposes, and food and ammunition often became "lost." While on campaign, Santa Anna referred to his men as "mere chickens" and viewed their lives simply as tools for advancing his career. Military justice was often arbitrary, and punishments in camp, for crimes real and imagined, were severe, ranging from execution by hanging or firing squad to flogging, branding, and cropping. Even so, when called on by these same officers to perform heroically, the *soldados* did their duty to the best of their ability.

Another feature of the Mexican army of 1821 to 1854 is that it spent more time fighting other Mexicans in the various coups and in the service of the various *caudillos* than it did fighting foreigners. As a result, battles were not as lethal and campaigns not as protracted as those that would be experienced when fighting the United States, Texas, France, Spain, or Indians.

When out of the watchful eye of priests and officers, the men of the Mexican army enjoyed the universal pastimes pursued by soldiers worldwide. Gambling was commonplace, from cards to dice to horse races in mounted regiments. Mexican soldiers often composed poems and songs as satire of their plight. *Fandangos,* impromptu dances accompanied by drinking, were favorites in an army in the field.

Donald S. Frazier

BIBLIOGRAPHY

Hefter, J. *Cronica del Traje Militar en Mexico.* 1968.

Hefter, J. *The Mexican Soldier.* 1958.

Olivera, Ruth R., and Lillian Crété. *Life in Mexico under Santa Anna, 1822–1855.* 1991.

See also **Camp Followers**, *article on* **Mexican Camp Followers; Music**, *article on* **Mexican Music**; *and* **Soldaderas**

Life in the U.S. Army

At the outbreak of war with Mexico the U.S. Army had only 8,600 officers and men, and almost half were assigned to frontier defense. In addition, more than thirty years had elapsed since the last war, and, except for those with experience fighting Indians, most of the soldiers had no combat experience. In response to the manpower shortage Congress authorized the president to call up 50,000 volunteers, who, after receiving a bare minimum of training, left for Mexico.

These additional troops were necessary for victory, but even though they were subject to the same regulations as those in the regular army their arrival caused friction with the regulars. During peace time, many saw the army as simply a place of refuge for those men who were unable to earn an honest living anywhere else. Although most of the regular officers were professionally educated, the enlisted men came from the low end of the socioeconomic ladder; approximately 40 percent were immigrants and a third of them were illiterate. Now, suddenly, it was fashionable to be in the army, and the regulars resented these newcomers for their absence of training and their appalling lack of discipline.

The volunteers quickly learned that soldiering was not all flag waving and martial glory. The food was often bad, the housing primitive, and the threat of disease always present. The soldier's basic ration consisted of beef or pork, hard bread (or flour or cornmeal with which to bake bread), peas, beans, or rice, and a little salt, sugar, and coffee as available. Each member of a squad took his turn in preparing the food. Often the various articles were put into a camp kettle and

A camp kitchen. John Frost, *Pictorial History of Mexico and the Mexican War,* 1862

boiled for hours into an easily digestible soup. There were ways to supplement this meager fare. Some men sampled the local cuisine, but many found it too spicy. Others patronized civilian sutlers who set up shop wherever the army was. Many raided local gardens and orchards, although army regulations strictly forbade all uncompensated foraging. The volunteers soon earned an unsavory reputation for this practice.

Upon arrival in Mexico most of the troops lived in canvas tents. These simple affairs, each designed to accommodate six men and their bedrolls, offered far less protection against the wind and rain than even the rudest log cabins back home. As the war progressed and U.S. forces occupied towns, Mexican government buildings served as barracks.

Yellow fever, malaria, dysentery, smallpox, measles, and various other diseases prevalent in Mexico were a constant scourge to the U.S. soldiers and killed far more than did Mexican bullets. The lack of attention to hygiene exhibited by many of the volunteers left them particularly susceptible to illness. Treatment of the sick and wounded in army hospitals was probably comparable to what was available in the United States. Army doctors were, on average, as capable as their civilian counterparts, but the general state of medical knowledge was such that treatments offered were not always beneficial to the patient. When the overworked surgeons encountered a wounded soldier with a limb shattered by a heavy musket ball, they often did not have time to do much more than amputate it quickly before moving on to the next patient.

On the march the U.S. soldier traveled as lightly as possible, since every ounce of extra weight made it that much more difficult to continue in the heat and dust. Still, with a nine-and-a-half pound musket, ammunition, a bayonet, a canteen of water, a haversack in which to carry food and small personal items, and a blanket, even soldiers carrying the bare essentials often plodded along with thirty or more pounds of gear.

Soldiers in camp sought various means by which to reduce their boredom. Some attended Mexican fandangos where they sought the company of young women. Some found solace in drink, and this often led to violations of military rules. Soldiers committing offenses faced court martial proceedings, but the Articles of War gave the courts considerable leeway in assessing penalties. Consequently, two soldiers committing identical crimes but tried by different courts might receive vastly different sentences. These sentences ran the gamut from a few hours in the guardhouse for drunkenness to death by hanging for desertion.

In many ways the U.S. soldiers who fought in Mexico were the same as their brothers in arms of other periods. They complained about their food, they groused about incompetent officers, they belittled the ethnic character of their enemies, and they believed in their ultimate military success.

James M. McCaffrey

BIBLIOGRAPHY

Coffman, Edward M. *The Old Army: A Portrait of the American Army in Peacetime, 1784–1898.* 1986.

Cunliffe, Marcus. *Soldiers and Civilians: The Martial Spirit in America, 1775–1865.* 1968.

Irey, Thomas R. "Soldiering, Suffering, and Dying in the Mexican War." *Journal of the West* 11 (1972): 285–298.

McCaffrey, James M. *Army of Manifest Destiny: The American Soldier in the Mexican War, 1846–1848.* 1992.

Payne, Darwin. "Camp Life in the Army of Occupation: Corpus Christi, July 1845 to March 1846." *Southwestern Historical Quarterly* 73 (1970): 326–342.

Smith, George W., and Charles Judah. *Chronicles of the Gringos: The U.S. Army in the Mexican War, 1846–1848. Accounts of Eyewitnesses and Combatants.* 1968.

U.S. War Department, *General Regulations for the Army of the United States, 1841.* 1841.

Winders, Richard Bruce. *Mr. Polk's Army: The American Military Experience in the Mexican War.* 1997.

Arrillaga, Mariano Paredes y

See **Paredes y Arrillaga, Mariano**

Art

Numerous contemporary artists from both countries produced images related to the war between the United States

and Mexico. U.S. artists of the period were especially prolific. This was the first foreign war of the United States, and many artists have been credited with a desire to create a sense of national unity to counter separatist tendencies fueled by sectionalism and expansionism.

U.S. lithographers provided the first images shortly after war began in May 1846. As the New York *Sun* and *Herald* and others of the "penny press" reported on the battles of Palo Alto and Resaca de la Palma, eastern lithographers such as Nathaniel Currier, James Bailley, and Sarony and Major published hand-colored lithographs of imaginary images—copied from European prototypes by Epinal, Pellerin, and others—intended to provide visual counterparts to the news reports. Eventually, the newspapers, such as the *Herald* and *Brother Jonathan*, published crude engravings derived from eyewitness drawings sent by correspondents.

The first eyewitness images appeared in the works of the war correspondents who followed Gen. Zachary Taylor's army into northern Mexico. Thomas Bangs Thorpe, an artist and writer and correspondent for the New Orleans *Tropio*, published engravings of the northern campaign in his book, *"Our Army" on the Rio Grande* (1846). Capt. William Seaton Henry of the 3d Infantry included engravings after Joseph H. Eaton and Alfred Sully (son of the famous Philadelphia artist Thomas Sully) in his *Campaign Sketches of the War with Mexico* (1847). Several other books also contain eyewitness images, such as those made from the drawings of veteran George C. Furber in his *The Twelve Months Volunteer; or, Journal of a Private in the Tennessee Regiment of Cavalry, in the Campaign in Mexico, 1846–1847* (1857).

More impressive were the hand-colored lithographs made from the paintings of Pvt. Stephen G. Hill, Lt. Daniel Powers Whiting, Sgt. Angelo Paldi, and Maj. Joseph Horace Eaton, who were among the soldier-artists under General Taylor's command. Whiting documented Taylor's encampment at Corpus Christi, Texas, as well as his occupation of Monterrey and his march to Saltillo. Paldi witnessed the events at Palo Alto and Resaca de la Palma, publishing two images in the Cincinnati-based German literary journal *Fliegende Blätter*. Hill's lithographs include a view of the cathedral in Monterrey, with the distinctive El Cerro de la Silla mountain in the background. Major Eaton, Taylor's aide, composed the clearest depiction of the events at Buena Vista, which were published by H. R. Robinson of New York City. Other artists such as William Garl Brown Jr. and daguerreotypist J. H. William Smith joined Taylor at his camp in Monterrey to produce portraits of the general.

Other artists accompanied Gen. John E. Wool on his march from San Antonio to Saltillo. Edward Everett got as far as San Antonio, but injury forced him to remain there, where he produced watercolors of the Spanish missions, including an unusual view of the interior of the ruined Alamo. Samuel E. Chamberlain provided extensive documentation of the war, also in watercolor, from a private's point of view; he participated in the Battle of Buena Vista as a member of Wool's 1st U.S. Dragoons. John Mix Stanley and James W. Abert documented Gen. Stephen W. Kearny's occupation of New Mexico and his march to the Pacific.

Lt. Henry Walke recorded the events of the naval war on Mexico's east coast after Gen. Winfield Scott's capture of Vera Cruz in 1847, while David W. Haines, a member of the 6th Infantry, Company F, documented his march with Scott's force toward Mexico City. Also with Scott was James Walker, an Englishman who had taught art at the military academy in Tampico. When the war broke out, he risked his life to join the U.S. troops at Puebla and served as an interpreter on General Worth's staff. After the war, he produced several pictures, including a study of the U.S. attack on Chapultepec Castle that was chromolithographed in the United States by Sarony and Major in New York.

Perhaps the most important visual images of the war were produced as collaboration between war correspondent George Wilkins Kendall, editor of the New Orleans *Picayune,* and Carl Nebel, a German artist who had spent a number of years in Mexico and had published *Voyage pittoresque et archéologique dans la partie la plus intéressante du Mexique* (Paris, 1836). Kendall had written extensively about Mexico in his *Narrative of the Texan Santa Fé Expedition* (New York, 1844) as well as in his dispatches on the war. He and Nebel collaborated to produce two books— one a short history of the war accompanied by large, hand-colored lithographs, and the other, a full history that Nebel would illustrate with smaller pictures.

Kendall wrote thumbnail histories of the battles to accompany Nebel's twelve pictures and the pair employed the best lithographers in Paris to produce the prints. Both the text and the pictures were printed in Paris; the book, *The War between the United States and Mexico, Illustrated,* was issued in 1851 and distributed by Appleton's in New York. It includes images of all the major battles of the war, including Palo Alto, Monterrey, Buena Vista, Vera Cruz, Cerro Gordo, Contreras, Churubusco, El Molino del Rey, Chapultepec, and General Scott's entrance into the *zócalo* (central city plaza) of Mexico City. Critics declared that the artist and author had accomplished their goals—that the book represented the "natural scenery . . . with the faithfulness of a daguerreotype reflection" (New York *Knickerbocker*), that it "far exceeds . . . anything of the kind that I have ever before seen" (Boston *Atlas*), and the truthfulness of the pictures "creates the impression that [one] . . . is a spectator of the 'shock of armies' " (New York *Spirit of the Times*).

Other artists interpreted the war retrospectively from the home front. Richard Caton Woodville compared it with the American Revolution in his painting *Old '76, Young '48.* German-American Emanuel Leutze condemned the cultures of both the Spaniards and Indians in his painting *The Storm-*ing of the Teocalli by Cortez and His Troops* (1848). William T. Ranney, George Caleb Bingham, John Mix Stanley, and Leutze illustrated the U.S. belief in Manifest Destiny in paintings like *Boone's First View of Kentucky* (1849), *The Squatters* (1850), *Scouts in the Tetons* (c. 1854–1863), and *Westward the Course of Empire Takes Its Way [Westward Ho!]* (1861).

Several Mexican artists and lithographers produced scenes from the war which were published in collection such as Julio Michaud y Thomas, *Album pintoresco de la República Méxicana.* (México, 1850). [One of the works reproduced as a lithograph in this collection is the painting *United States Assault on the Convent of Churubusco* by Gregorio Marmolejo (1847), which appears on the front cover of this encyclopedia.] These artists included Cumplido, Joaquín Heredia, Abraham López, H. Mendez, and Reinaldo, but the war was not one of their favorite subjects.

Ron Tyler

BIBLIOGRAPHY

Chamberlain, Samuel E. *My Confession: Recollections of a Rogue.* Edited by William H. Goetzmann. 1996.

Kendall, George Wilkins, and Carl Nebel. *The War between the United States and Mexico, Illustrated.* Edited by Ron Tyler. 1995.

Sandweiss, Martha A., Rick Stewart, and Ben W. Huseman. *Eyewitness to War: Prints and Daguerreotypes of the Mexican War, 1846–1848.* 1989.

Tyler, Ron. *Prints of the West.* 1994.

Tyler, Ron. *The Mexican War: A Lithographic Record.* 1973.

Ashmun Amendment

In early 1848 George Ashmun, a Whig representative from Massachusetts, offered an amendment to a resolution praising Gen. Zachary Taylor for his able command of U.S. forces in northern Mexico. Ashmun moved that the commendation be modified to indicate that General Taylor had served "in a war unnecessarily and unconstitutionally begun by the President of the United States." The House passed the measure by a vote of 85 to 81, a sharp reprimand for President James K. Polk. Ashmun sincerely deplored the war, but he and other Whigs also sought to embarrass the Democratic president. Ashmun had suspected Polk's course from the start. "The mask is off; the veil is lifted," he warned in mid-1846, "and we see . . . *invasion, conquest,* and *colonization* emblazoned upon our banners." In 1847 Ashmun lamented "an abyss of national debt" and a "bankrupt" treasury caused by "a war of conquest on a foreign soil." The Senate did not pass Ashmun's 1848 amendment, but the House approval of the measure reflected the Whigs' gains in the 1846 and 1847 elections, the growing antiwar sentiment in the

House, and mounting suspicion about Polk's methods and motives in his conduct of foreign relations with Mexico.

Thomas R. Hietala

BIBLIOGRAPHY

Schroeder, John H. *Mr. Polk's War: American Opposition and Dissent, 1846–1848.* 1973.

U.S. Congress. *Congressional Globe.* 29th Cong., 1st and 2d sess.; 30th Cong., 1st sess.

Atocha, Alexander J.

An occasional resident of New Orleans and a U.S. citizen of Spanish birth, "Colonel" Alexander J. Atocha (1???–1???) won President James K. Polk's attention by virtue of his friendship with Antonio López de Santa Anna. The latter, in exile in Cuba, reportedly instructed Atocha to offer the U.S. president a deal. In February 1846, Atocha told Polk that Santa Anna could guarantee Mexican acceptance of the Río Grande as the southern boundary of the United States, and this boundary could be extended westward to include San Francisco Bay within U.S. territory. All that Santa Anna required was U.S. assistance in returning to Mexico, where Atocha had promised that Santa Anna would be welcomed as a savior by the Mexican people. Thirty million dollars was specified as the sum that Santa Anna would need to consummate the settlement.

In February meetings with the president, Atocha praised Polk's aggressive move in ordering Gen. Zachary Taylor's army to move from the Nueces River to the Río Grande. Mexico, he said, respected only force, and Polk had laid the essential groundwork for a successful negotiation. Polk was suspicious, however. "He is evidently a man of talents and education," Polk wrote of Atocha in his diary, "but his whole manner and conversation impressed me with a belief that he was not reliable." Nevertheless, Polk committed his administration to pursuing Atocha's scheme.

In August, U.S. officials escorted Santa Anna through the U.S. naval blockade of Mexico as the first step of the former Mexican leader's return to power. Landing at Vera Cruz, Santa Anna publicly denounced all attempts at negotiating with the *norteamericanos.* By the end of the year he resumed the Mexican presidency, yet nothing happened to bring about the promised settlement. In early 1847, Atocha continued to reassure Polk and his associates that Santa Anna's real intentions had not changed, no matter what his words or actions suggested. But by that time Polk concluded that his investment of time and energy in Atocha had been a mistake. In his last diary entry on the man, Polk referred to Atocha as "a great scoundrel."

Ward M. McAfee

BIBLIOGRAPHY

Pletcher, David M. *The Diplomacy of Annexation: Texas, Oregon, and the Mexican War.* 1973.

Quaife, Milo Milton, ed. *The Diary of James K. Polk during His Presidency, 1845 to 1849.* 4 vols. 1910.

Atrocities

The conflict between Mexico and the United States was extremely bitter and marked by brutal acts on all sides. Murder and reprisal dated back to the Mexican struggle for independence more than thirty years before the outbreak of hostilities in 1846.

Father Miguel Hidalgo's 1810 uprising in Mexico fueled the revolutionary fervor of republicans on both sides of the Sabine River. In 1812 a force of several hundred rebels crossed into Texas from Louisiana and confronted Spanish officials. The leaders of the revolutionaries were Bernardo Gutíerrez de Lara, a Mexican national, and Augustus W. Magee, a former U.S. Army officer. When Magee died from a sudden illness at Presidio La Bahía, another U.S. citizen, Samuel Kemper, assumed command of the U.S. contingent. Gutíerrez, following his victory over the Spanish at Salado Creek near San Antonio in 1813, held a number of prisoners. When he condoned the execution of some of the Spaniards, including the governor of Texas, Manuel María de Salcedo, Kemper and his countrymen were shocked, and some of the men from the United States gave up the cause and returned to the United States. The revolution ended when a Spanish army under Gen. José Joaquín Arredondo routed the republican force on the Río Medina. Several hundred retreating revolutionaries were captured and executed on the spot. Serving under Arredondo on the battlefield that day was Antonio López de Santa Anna, then a lieutenant in the Spanish army.

Some of the most noted atrocities of the period occurred more than twenty years later, during the Texians' struggle for independence from Mexico. The Mexican government attributed much of the unrest to outsiders from the United States and issued an important order to its army and navy. The Tornel Decree, named after Minister of War José María Tornel, proclaimed that armed foreigners caught on Mexican soil participating in the revolution were "pirates" and were to be executed. This is the context in which the brutality exhibited at the Alamo and Goliad took place. These deeds convinced many Texians and Anglo-Americans that Mexicans were savages and deserved no mercy. The Texians in turn wrought havoc on the Mexican army at the Battle of San Jacinto on 21 April 1836, where more than six hundred Mexican soldiers were killed, many as they tried to surrender.

Bloody reprisals and retaliation continued throughout the ten-year existence of the Republic of Texas. In 1841, Mexicans forced the members of Republic of Texas Governor Mirabeau B. Lamar's ill-fated Santa Fe Expedition to march from New Mexico to Mexico City over mountains and through deserts. The following year, the Mexican army twice captured San Antonio, Texas. On Christmas Day, 1842, a Texian force that had crossed into Mexico to retaliate surrendered to an overwhelming Mexican force at Mier, south of the Río Grande. On the way to prison in Mexico City, 176 Texians attempted a mass escape but were recaptured. Mexican officials ordered every tenth man involved in the breakout executed and made the Texians draw beans from an earthen jar: life for those who drew white beans and death for seventeen who drew black beans.

Atrocities continued after war broke out between the United States and Mexico. Texians hunted down Mexicans from previous conflicts to settle old scores. Mexicans also killed a significant number of Anglo-Americans off the battlefield. Mexican horsemen frequently lassoed U.S. soldiers who lagged behind on the march, dragging them through the chaparral at a gallop and then leaving them to die. The best documented case of mass murder committed against Mexican civilians occurred near Parras in February 1847, where Arkansas volunteers, angered over the murder of one of their men, rounded up the inhabitants of Hacienda del Patos and killed more than twenty men before Illinois volunteers interceded to halt the massacre. Later that month, in an unrelated incident, Mexican guerrillas attacked a U.S. quartermaster train consisting of 110 wagons and 300 pack mules on the road between Camargo and Marín. Accounts from survivors say forty to fifty teamsters were murdered, many tied to the wheels of their wagons and burned alive when the entire train was put to the torch. On 9 October 1847, angry U.S. volunteers sacked the town of Huamantla in retaliation for the death of Capt. Samuel H. Walker. While these episodes serve as examples of large-scale atrocities, the number of individual murders committed during this period can never be known.

Richard Bruce Winders

BIBLIOGRAPHY

Bauer, K. Jack. *The Mexican War, 1846–1848.* 1974.

Brackett, Albert G. *General Lane's Brigade in Central Mexico.* 1854.

Engelmann, Adolph. "The Second Illinois in the Mexican War: Mexican War Letters of Adolph Engelmann, 1846–1847." *Journal of Illinois State Historical Society* (January 1934): 357–452.

Giddings, Luther. *Sketches of the Campaign in Northern Mexico in 1846–1847.* 1853.

Smith, S. Compton. *Chile Con Carne; Or, The Camo and Field.* 1857.

[Tornel Decree]. *Texas Telegraph and Register.* March 12, 1836.

Austin, Stephen F.

Stephen Fuller Austin (1793–1836), known as the Father of Texas, was born in Virginia on 3 November, the son of Moses and Maria Brown Austin. In 1798 the Austins moved to Missouri, where Moses opened a lead-mining operation and founded the towns of Herculaneum and Potosi. Stephen Austin was educated at Bacon Academy in Connecticut and Transylvania University in Kentucky. In 1810 he returned to Missouri to work for his father. He soon took over management of the mines. In 1815 he won a seat in the Missouri territorial legislature and served four one-year terms. When the mining business failed in 1819, Austin moved to Arkansas Territory, where he plunged into high-risk land speculation. Failing at this, in 1820 he moved to New Orleans and began studying law under former U.S. representative Joseph H. Hawkins.

Moses Austin also was financially ruined by 1820, so he traveled to San Antonio and successfully applied for permission to introduce three hundred families from the United States into Spanish Texas. The elder Austin died upon his return to the United States, and Stephen Austin, with financial backing from Hawkins, took over the venture, thus becoming the first Anglo-American *empresario* (colonization agent) in Texas.

When Mexico won independence from Spain in 1821, Austin was forced to travel to Mexico City to secure the new government's approval of his colonization plan. This errand kept Austin in Mexico City for a year, but by 1824 the first three hundred families had arrived in Texas, and Austin had essentially completed his first colonization contract.

Over the next decade, Austin signed four more colonization contracts with the Mexican government. By 1835 the Anglo-American population of Austin's colonies was more than eight thousand. The efforts of some forty other *empresarios,* though far less successful than Austin's, brought the number of Texians in Texas to more than twenty thousand, far outnumbering the native Mexican population.

Until 1835 Austin pursued an accommodationist policy toward the Mexican government, encouraging his colonists to remain loyal to their adopted country. But in 1833, after traveling to Mexico City to petition the government for political reforms, he was imprisoned for more than a year on sedition charges. Finally released, he returned to Texas in 1835 and took command of the Texas independence movement. After he briefly commanded Texas volunteers besieging San Antonio de Béxar, the provisional government sent him to the United States to raise funds for the revolution. Returning to Texas after the Texian victory over Gen. Antonio López de Santa Anna at San Jacinto, he ran for president of the Republic of Texas but was defeated by Sam Houston, and then accepted the position of secretary of state. In that position he made annexation by the United States his top priority, but he died on 27 December 1836.

Austin did not live to see the annexation of Texas by the United States, but his successful colonization efforts led to the peopling of Texas by Anglo-Americans and thus to the Texas Revolution. U.S. annexation of Texas a decade later set in motion the forces that triggered the U.S.–Mexican War.

Gregg Cantrell

BIBLIOGRAPHY
Barker, Eugene C. *The Life of Stephen F. Austin*. 1925.
Barker, Eugene C., ed. *The Austin Papers*. 3 vols. 1924–1928.

Ayala, S. Tadeo Ortiz de

See **Ortiz de Ayala, S. Tadeo**

Ayutla Revolution

The movement known as the Revolution of Ayutla had its roots in the decades of political turmoil that followed the Mexican War of Independence. The defeat and occupation of their country as a result of the war with the United States caused Mexican intellectuals to search for underlying reasons for the political and social ills affecting the republic.

Whereas some federalists continued to blame the Spanish colonial legacy, conservatives, headed by Lucas Alamán, advocated the idea of a monarchical government. In April 1853 Alamán brought Antonio López de Santa Anna back from exile to govern temporarily, while conservative envoys searched Europe for a royal prince to rule as a monarch. With the death of Alamán in June, however, Santa Anna's regime degenerated into a dictatorship. This situation led the federalists to close ranks in an effort to oust Santa Anna from power.

The rebellion commenced on 24 February 1854 when Gen. Juan Álvarez, ruling *cacique* (headman) of the Department of Guerrero, declared himself in revolt against the central government. The insurgent plan, penned principally by Ignacio Comonfort, Álvarez's chief lieutenant, was proclaimed on 1 March in the town of Ayutla, Guerrero. The rebellion grew into a national insurrection as guerrilla groups in other departments, especially that led by Santiago Vidaurri of Nuevo León, joined the insurgent cause. On 12 August 1855 Santa Anna, fearful that his escape route might soon become blocked by the rebels, abdicated and, a few days later, set sail from Vera Cruz into exile. On 16 September the *insurrecto* leaders signed a convention at Lagos, Guanajuato, in which they promised to abide by the terms of the Ayutla agreement, to recognize Álvarez as their commander-in-chief, and to obey Comonfort as his representative. In early October, Álvarez, upon being chosen provisional president by a junta of his own designation, convoked elections for a special congress.

Many of the issues involved in the Ayutla movement had been debated and discussed by Valentín Gómez Farías and the *puros*, or radical federalists, during the mid-1840's. The U.S.–Mexican War helped shape their response to problems concerning the structure of national power, the relationship between the state, the church, and the military, and the nation's association with the United States. The Juárez law of 1855 abolished military and ecclesiastical *fueros* (privileges), while the Lerdo Law of the following year disentailed all church property not used in daily operations. Although the Constitution of 1857, the culminating place of *Reforma* legislation, provided for a federal republic, certain key powers were granted to the national government. A program of economic reform and modernization was also undertaken, in which the United States played a significant role.

Lawrence D. Taylor

BIBLIOGRAPHY
García, Genaro, ed. *Documentos inéditos o muy raros para la historia de México*. Volume 26, *La revolución de Ayutla según el archivo del General Doblado*. 1913.
Hale, Charles A. "The War with the United States and the Crisis in Mexican Thought." *The Americas* 14 (1957): 153–175.
Johnson, Richard A. *The Mexican Revolution of Ayutla, 1854–1855: An Analysis of the Evolution and Destruction of Santa Anna's Last Dictatorship*. 1939.
Santoni, Pedro. *Mexicans at Arms: Puro Federalists and the Politics of War, 1845–1848*. 1996.
Scholes, Walter V. "A Revolution Falters: Mexico, 1856–1857." *Hispanic American Historical Review* 32 (1952): 1–21.

Aztec Club

The Aztec Club of 1847 was a fraternity of U.S. officers who marched with Gen. Winfield Scott to Mexico City. Intended to provide camaraderie and social diversion for its members, the society first met at the Mexico City home of Señor J.M. Boca Negra, former minister to the United States, on 13 October 1847. Enrollment initially to 160 members, mainly officers of the Old Establishment, the regular army before the war. Although Gens. George Cadwalader, Robert Patterson, John A. Quitman, Winfield Scott, and David E. Twiggs belonged to the club, high rank was not a requirement; members included officers of all grades. General Quitman served as the club's first president.

The members, wishing to make their organization permanent, adopted a constitution, instituted an initiation fee, and published a list of members in the *American Star*. On the eve of the U.S. Army's departure from Mexico in May 1848, members voted to preserve the club in "perpetuity" to maintain their "bonds of friendship and brotherhood." Postwar garrison and frontier duty, however, curtailed the club's activities.

Many members of the Aztec Club later gained fame as generals during the Civil War, including Robert E. Lee, Ulysses S. Grant, Pierre Gustave Toutant Beauregard, George B.

McClellan, Simon B. Buckner, Joseph Hooker, William J. Hardee, and Earl Van Dorn. The club experienced a revival in 1867 under the leadership of Gen. Robert Patterson, one of President Polk's thirteen Democratic officer appointees. Membership soared after the club was opened in 1871 to all officers who had served in Mexico, and in 1882, to their closest surviving male blood relatives. Operated by approximately 350 descendants of the original members, the Aztec Club of 1847 still exists, making it the second oldest patri-otic organization (the Society of the Cincinnati is the oldest) in the United States.

Richard Bruce Winders

BIBLIOGRAPHY

The Aztec Club of 1847, Military Society of the Mexican War. 1972.

Constitution of the Aztec Club of 1847 and the List of Members, 1893. 1893.

B

Baja California

The mountainous, arid, thousand-mile-long peninsula of Baja California resisted European settlement from its discovery in 1533 until 1697 when Juan María Salvatierra, S.J., established the first of twenty-nine missions, which sought acculturation of the marginal hunting-foraging seminomadic groups of Pericúes, Guaycuras, and Cochimíes who sparsely populated the peninsula. These missions were successively administered by Jesuits, Franciscans, and Dominicans for over a century and a half. Civilian settlement began in 1754, attracted by silver strikes and pearl fishing; at Mexico's independence (1821) small settlements were located in Mulegé, Loreto, Comondú, La Paz, San Antonio, Todos Santos, and San José del Cabo.

Baja California was a territory of the Mexican Republic administered by a *jefe político* (civil administrator-governor), initially from Loreto and subsequently from La Paz. Its geographic isolation made it virtually autonomous and self-sufficient. Its economy was based on cattle raising and silver mining, and its homogeneous population allowed it to avoid the mainland's internecine conflicts. Exempted from the secularization decrees of 1833, Dominican missionaries continued their labors throughout the peninsula.

During the U.S.–Mexican War, the United States carried out a strategic naval blockade in the Golfo de (Gulf of) California. Troops from the USS *Cyane* under Comdr. Samuel F. DuPont occupied La Paz on 14 September 1846, and Jefe Político Col. Francisco Palacios Miranda agreed to maintain neutrality toward U.S. forces. The *Cyane* on 11 November and the *Dale* on 16 November were peacefully received at San José del Cabo. In 1847 troops from the USS *Portsmouth* under Comdr. John B. Montgomery raised the U.S. flag there on 30 March and at La Paz on 14 April; and Lt. Col. Henry S. Burton with Companies A and B, New York Volunteers,

landed without resistance at La Paz on 21 July. However, Capt. Manuel Pineda, after initiating armed resistance and repelling troops from the *Dale* at Mulegé on 2 October, attacked Burton's forces at La Paz on 16 November. Pineda sent volunteer commanders Vicente Mejía, José Matías Moreno, and José Antonio Mijares against Marine forces under Lt. Charles Heywood at San José del Cabo on 20 November. Although unsuccessful in forcing a quick U.S. withdrawal, the resistance forced the United States to divert troops from Alta California to the peninsula, producing casualties, logistical problems, and constant military engagement until U.S. withdrawal on 19 June 1848. Notwithstanding President James K. Polk's desire to control the Pacific Coast by acquisition of both Californias, this popular active resistance discouraged U.S. interest in the peninsula, permitted its retention by the Mexican republic, and thus gave the Golfo de California status as territorial sea.

W. Michael Mathes

BIBLIOGRAPHY

Mathes, Miguel, ed. *Textos de su Historia. Baja California.* 2 vols. 1988.

Nunis, Doyce B., Jr., ed. *The Mexican War in Baja California: The Memorandum of Captain Henry W. Halleck Concerning His Expeditions in Lower California, 1846–1848.* 1977.

See also **Lower California Campaign**

Bancroft, George

The career of George Bancroft (1800–1891) as a cabinet officer and U.S. diplomat followed years as an educator. He cofounded Round Hill School outside Cambridge, Massachusetts; the school, for males from nine to twelve years old, was patterned on the German gymnasium. Bancroft taught most of the courses in Greek, Latin, German, history, and logic from 1823 to 1830. He authored several articles on German literature while teaching and later published the first volume of *History of the United States from the Discovery of the American Continent*.

Bancroft supported James K. Polk for the Democratic nomination for president and convinced delegates from key states to do the same. He later wrote Polk, explaining his role at the convention and pledging New England's support in the election in hopes of future rewards. As Polk's newly appointed secretary of the Navy, Bancroft sought to replace naval promotion based solely on seniority with advancement based on ability. His major contribution was the establishment of the U.S. Naval Academy at Annapolis to ensure the necessary officer training. Bancroft served for only a few days in William L. Marcy's stead as acting secretary of war as of 31 May 1845. On the following day, in anticipation that Texas would accept the U.S. invitation to join the Union, Bancroft ordered Gen. Zachary Taylor, in command of U.S. troops in Texas, to move across the Nueces River into land claimed by Mexico. As secretary of the Navy, he also ordered Commo. John Sloat to avoid provocation, but to seize Yerba Buena (present-day San Francisco) and other California ports if hostilities did commence and Mexico declared war first. When Polk considered asking Congress for a declaration of war on 9 May 1846, Bancroft voiced the only negative opinion in the cabinet. He preferred to wait for word of a Mexican attack on Taylor's forces, which had moved by that time to the Río Grande. However, Bancroft approved the president's decision when word arrived later that day of such an attack.

Bancroft's desire to serve in a diplomatic post was fulfilled when Polk appointed him minister to Great Britain from 1846 to 1849. Bancroft then continued his work as a historian until his next post as minister, to Berlin in 1867. He spent the remainder of his life completing numerous volumes in his history of the United States, almost until his death on 17 January 1891.

Carol Jackson Adams

BIBLIOGRAPHY

Bancroft, George. *History of the United States, from the Discovery of the American Continent*. 6 vols. 1888.

Handlin, Lilian. *George Bancroft: The Intellectual as Democrat*. 1984.

Nye, Russel B. *George Bancroft: Brahmin Rebel*. 1944.

Bandini, Juan

The son of a Spanish sea captain, Juan Bandini (1800–1859) came to California as a young man from his native Peru. He settled in San Diego and became a ranchero and a political leader, representing his region in the province's *diputación* (governor's advisory council) from 1827 to 1828. He then held a variety of minor political posts during the Mexican period of California's history. During the U.S.–Mexican War he readily collaborated with the U.S. invading force, supplying it with needed provisions. For this service, he was rewarded by being made *alcalde* (mayor) of San Diego at the war's end. Despite the fact that he had three sons-in-law who were U.S. citizens, Bandini eventually lost his properties under the new order.

An opportunist rather than pro-Yankee, Bandini allowed Commo. Robert Stockton, the U.S. naval commander in conquered California, to establish his headquarters in Bandini's San Diego residence. Bandini supplied Stockton with sheep, needed to feed his men. Andrés Pico, who led the Californios' major military resistance against the invaders in the Los Angeles area, identified Bandini as one who early had gone over to the enemy and facilitated an easy conquest.

Ward M. McAfee

BIBLIOGRAPHY

Bancroft, Hubert Howe. *History of California*. Vol. 5. 7 vols. 1886–1890.

Harlow, Neal. *California Conquered: War and Peace on the Pacific, 1846–1850*. 1982.

Banditry

Civil strife (including war) fuels banditry as individuals and groups take advantage of the turmoil to settle scores, redress grievances, improve their lot, and stake out claims for a place in the new order that will emerge from the struggle. Mexico's War of Independence from Spain spawned a rash of bandits who were led by those with nicknames such as "The Crate," "The Castrator," and "Colonel of Colonels." These bandits ran amok through the war for independence and late into the nineteenth century, when the strengthened central government of Mexico finally began to control them, although it was not able to eliminate them entirely.

These brigands frequently were hired by regional strongmen to maintain their hegemony in the countryside. When local conflict escalated into widespread strife, contenders hired bandits who knew the territory to guide their troops and to rampage guerrilla-style behind enemy lines. For their services bandits frequently earned the right to rape and pillage as they foraged and to keep all the booty they acquired. Bandits sold their services to the highest bidder, but they also were known to switch sides, as did the brigand García, who fought first for the Spaniards around Orizaba and later supported the Mexican cause. When authorities complained about his brutality, he responded by burying his victims alive. García was eventually captured and sent to California, where he continued his activities. When bandits chose sides, their intent was to side with the political victors, from whom they subsequently demanded protection and jobs. Many bandits eventually became involved in public security organizations, where they provided protection services for the government even while continuing to carry out criminal activities. The general populace both feared and sympathized with these outlaws. People who fed and sheltered kinsmen who were outlaws could also impale the severed head of an executed brigand on a pike as an example of punishment for others. Both U.S. and Mexican authorities learned that to label someone "outlaw" could bring the public response, "Whose law?" Calling an individual and his gang "bandits" might raise their status among the public. People disdained bandits for their depredations and admired them for their courage, singing folk ballads that praised their deeds and decried their demise.

Bandit life was hard; they were always on the run, hiding out in forsaken terrain, and persistently in fear of being betrayed by one of their own. Most died quite young, often at the end of a rope or in a hail of bullets. Many left their mark; for example, during the U.S.–Mexican War (perhaps because of it), Eleuterio Quiróz ignited a caste war in the rugged Sierra Gorda of north central Mexico.

After the war the newly established international boundary gave bandits a shield. The region, especially along the Lower Río Grande Valley, had always been a haven for bandits, but the new line enabled them to raid in one country and hide in the other. Not until the late nineteenth century did Mexico and the United States agree to allow their police forces to chase fleeing bandits into the other's territory. But such diplomacy hardly slackened banditry, however. It only made it more sophisticated, as brigands developed new techniques to thwart the law and to forward their ambitions.

Paul J. Vanderwood

BIBLIOGRAPHY

Hobsbawn, Eric J. *Bandits*. 1969.

Joseph, Gilbert M. "On the Trail of Latin American Bandits: A Re-examination of Peasant Resistance." *Latin American Research Review* (1990): 7–53.

Vanderwood, Paul J. *Disorder and Progress: Bandits, Police, and Mexican Development*. 1992.

See also **Caudillos; Guerrillas; Sierra Gorda Revolt**

Bankhead, Charles

As British minister to Mexico on the eve of the U.S.–Mexican War, Charles Bankhead (1???–18??) repeatedly told Mexican leaders that they should not expect British aid in a military conflict with the United States. In conversations with Manuel de la Peña y Peña, the Mexican foreign minister in the autumn of 1845, Bankhead emphasized the hopelessness of Mexico's dream of reconquering Texas and offered Great Britain's good offices for negotiating a settlement between Mexico and the United States. The British government's fear was that Mexico's passionate feelings about Texas, left unchecked, would result in the loss of not only Texas but also California, a province that England did not want to see come into the possession of the United States. Bankhead's instructions from the British foreign secretary made it clear that his role was to prevent, if at all possible, the outbreak of war between the United States and Mexico because Mexico, if not allied with Great Britain, would inevitably lose territory to the United States.

Bankhead's position was difficult. In urging Mexico to negotiate, he might easily be interpreted as indicating British approval of the U.S. annexation of Texas. Indeed, some months later Bankhead was chastised by his superiors for pushing too zealously for negotiation and creating just that impression. He was admonished to be more guarded in his language and behavior, an instruction that hampered his attempts to prevent war.

Once the war was under way, Bankhead continued to push for a negotiated settlement, behavior that was most appreciated by the United States. In October 1847, illness forced his retirement and departure from Mexico. He was replaced by Percy W. Doyle.

Ward M. McAfee

BIBLIOGRAPHY

McAfee, Ward M., and J. Cordell Robinson, eds. *Origins of the Mexican War*. 2 vols. 1982.

Pletcher, David M. *The Diplomacy of Annexation: Texas, Oregon, and the Mexican War*. 1973.

Barragán, Matías de la Peña y

See **Peña y Barragán, Matiás de la**

Battle of

See under the place name of the battle; for example, **Brazito, Battle of**

Baz, Juan José

Mexican politician Juan José Baz (1820–1887) was an energetic and lifelong advocate of the *exaltado* liberalism of Valentín Gómez Farías. Born in Guadalajara, Baz began his political career at the precocious age of eighteen. Both as a *jefe político* for Taxco, and as a *puro* partisan in Mexico City, Baz pushed for radical liberal reforms of education and the state. In 1846 he published a pronouncement calling for the disamortization of ecclesiastical wealth to aid in the struggle against the U.S. invaders. Subsequently, at the age of twenty-seven, he was named governor of the Federal District by Gómez Farías. In 1847 he was one of just a handful of local politicians to sign the congressional decree relieving the church of more than 20 million pesos for the war effort.

Baz participated in the defense of the capital as the Governor of the Estado Mayor and head of the National Guard of the Federal District. He remained in Mexico City throughout the U.S. occupation and was a member of the *ayuntamiento* during the presidency of Mariano Arista.

Following the return of Antonio López de Santa Anna in 1853, Baz was first embraced and then exiled by the dictator. Throughout the Reform he continued to struggle for *exaltado* issues. From Morelia he published the famous *Bandera Roja*, which championed liberal concerns, and he corresponded regularly with Benito Juárez, Manuel Payno, and Melchor Ocampo. During the French intervention he fought as an artillery commander under Porfirio Díaz. During the Restored Republic he served as interior minister, a post he used to implement a capital beautification program. The opening of streets such as Cinco de Mayo, and the founding of several schools and orphanages such as the Escuela Industrial de Huérfanos, were the result of his efforts. Baz died in October 1887.

M. Bruce Colcleugh

BIBLIOGRAPHY

Carreño, Alberto María. *Jefes del ejército Mexicano en 1847: Biografías de generales de división y de brigada y de coroneles del ejército Mexicano por fines del año de 1847.* 1914.

Robinson, Fayette. *Mexico and her Military Chieftains: From the Revolution of Hidalgo to the Present Time.* 1847. Reprint, 1970.

Santoni, Pedro. *Mexicans at Arms: Puro Federalists and the Politics of War, 1845–1848.* 1996.

Beach, Moses Y.

Agent of the U.S. State Department and newspaperman Moses Yale Beach (1800–1868) was born in Connecticut and apprenticed to a cabinetmaker at the age of fourteen. After he married Nancy Day in 1819, he spent the next decade of his life as a machine inventor and craftsman. In 1834, he went to work for the New York *Sun* in New York City as a reporter; by 1838, he owned the newspaper. This venture turned out to be a great success for Beach, and in the ten years that he ran the paper it expanded its size and circulation and became a major booster of the Democratic Party.

After the battles of Palo Alto and Resaca de la Palma in 1846, President James K. Polk commissioned Beach as an agent of the U.S. government to go to Mexico to arrange a peace treaty. He and his wife went via Cuba under the cover of false British passports, claiming newspaper and personal financial reasons. Jane McManus Storm Cazneau, a clever newspaper woman in her own right, accompanied them. The Mexican authorities, watching for suspicious foreigners from the United States, detained Beach on two different occasions but never imprisoned him. Although successful in convincing Mexican church officials that they would be rewarded by the United States for their efforts on behalf of peace, overall his mission ended in failure. He and his entourage returned to New York in 1847.

In 1848, he turned the paper over to two of his sons and the business remained in the family for the next twenty years. Beach died in Wallingford, Connecticut, in 1868 at the age of sixty-eight.

Amy M. Wilson

BIBLIOGRAPHY

Eisenhower, John S. D. *So Far from God: The U.S. War with Mexico, 1846–1848.* 1989.

Smith, Justin H. *The War with Mexico.* 2 vols. 1919. Reprint, 1963.

Bear Flag Revolt

The Bear Flag Revolt of 1846 was a short-lived rebellion of U.S. and other foreign settlers living in Alta California against Mexican rule. For several years before the revolt, many U.S. citizens were moving into Alta California, adding to the U.S. interest in California. Although the United States had tried several times to purchase the territory, Mexico had refused. Meanwhile, the settlers' resentment of Mexican rule was exacerbated by the injustice shown to them on many occasions. The Mexican officials seldom listened to the settlers' ideas about how they should be governed, and when the officials did listen, it took several months, even years, for them to act. Emboldened by these sentiments, Ezekiel Merritt and William B. Ide led a group of thirty-two settlers to capture the town of Sonoma and the local Mexican official, Gen. Mariano Guadalupe Vallejo, on 14 June 1846. They sent General Vallejo to Sutter's Fort, where he was held for two months by Col. John C. Frémont. Gen. José María Castro, the Mexican military commander of California, sent fifty Mexican soldiers to put down the rebellion, but they were defeated on 24 June at the Battle of Olompali. The growing group of rebellious settlers marched into San Francisco on 1 July. Three days later, Colonel Frémont gave a speech declaring a free California republic and adopted a ragged flag of a large star and a grizzly bear. From that day on, the rebels were referred to as the Bear Flaggers. The next day, Colonel Frémont organized the California Battalion. On 7 July 1846, Commo. John D. Sloat ordered Capt. William Mervine to raise the U.S. flag over Monterey, thereby declaring California part of the United States.

There is a great deal of debate about how much the U.S. government was involved in the California revolt. Reports claim that President James K. Polk told Thomas Larkin, the U.S. consul in Monterey, and Colonel Frémont to support any California movement against Mexico, although Polk denied such allegations. Even so, Captain Mervine and a small party of troops, plus Commodore Sloat and five ships, were close to the California border at the time of the revolt. Although the California republic lasted less than a month, it provided an excuse for the United States to intervene in California.

Carlyn E. Davis

BIBLIOGRAPHY

Connor, Seymour V., and Odie B. Faulk. *North America Divided: The Mexican War, 1846–1848.* 1971.

Eisenhower, John S. D. *So Far from God: The U.S. War with Mexico, 1846–1848.* 1989.

Bell, Peter H.

Peter Hansborough Bell (1812–1898), lieutenant colonel and governor of Texas, was born 12 May in Spotsylvania County, Virginia. Bell moved to Texas to fight in the Texas Revolution, serving as a private in the cavalry company of Capt. Henry W. Karnes at the Battle of San Jacinto on 21 April 1836. After serving as assistant adjutant general and then inspector general of the Republic of Texas from 1837 to 1840, he joined the Texas Rangers under the command of Col. John C. "Jack" Hays and held the rank of major for the Somervell Expedition of 1842. Bell resigned his commission as a captain in the Rangers in 1845 to join the U.S. Army as a volunteer at the onset of the U.S.–Mexican War. He served as a lieutenant colonel in Hays's command on the Río Grande. Under the command of Gen. Zachary Taylor, Bell fought with distinction at the Battle of Buena Vista.

A strong advocate for frontier defense against nomadic Indians, Bell was elected governor of Texas in 1849 and 1851. In 1850 he called for three thousand Texas Rangers to suppress rebellion in eastern New Mexico. He resigned in 1853 to fill a vacancy in the U.S. Congress, in which he served until 1857. After marrying Ella Reeves Eaton Dickens in 1857, he moved to North Carolina. Although offered a commission of colonel in the Confederate Army, he refused to serve. He died 8 March 1898 in North Carolina. His remains were moved to the State Cemetery in Austin in 1930.

Jodella K. Dyreson

BIBLIOGRAPHY

Biographical Directory of the American Congress, 1774–1989. 1989.

Kittrell, Norman. *Governors Who Have Been and Other Public Men of Texas.* 1921.

Bennett, James Gordon

James Gordon Bennett (1795–1872) was the controversial editor whose *New York Herald* lent a strident voice in support of the expansionist clamor of the 1840s. Born and educated in Scotland, he migrated to the United States in 1819, learned the news business in various cities, and in May 1835 founded the *Herald* as a nonpartisan penny daily. His aggressive news-gathering techniques and unconventional, often sensationalized coverage of popular subjects both redefined U.S. journalism and, in the opinion of Horace Greely and others, debased its character.

To report the war with Mexico, Bennett in 1846 joined the *Baltimore Sun* and *Philadelphia Public Ledger* in reviving an overland courier system, which regularly defeated a frustrated U.S. postal service by as much as five days. Bennett alone among New York editors dispatched a reporter to cover the conflict, and his paper frequently bedeviled President James K. Polk's administration with disclosures of confidential information. These included details of Nicholas P. Trist's secret mission to Mexico, which made public Polk's territorial objectives. In February 1848 *Herald* Washington correspondent John Nugent, to the government's consternation and in a fashion still unexplained, procured the Treaty of Guadalupe Hidalgo and related documents then under consideration in the Senate. That the *Herald,* hitherto in the forefront of the All of Mexico Movement, shortly supported the treaty's provisions, raises the possibility that Bennett's shrill expansionism had more to do with circulation than conviction.

Bennett remained editor of the *Herald* until his retirement in 1867. He supported the Union cause through the Civil War despite his well-known southern sympathies and died in New York City on 1 June 1872.

L. Marshall Hall

BIBLIOGRAPHY

Carlson, Oliver. *The Man Who Made News: James Gordon Bennett.* 1942.

Seitz, Don C. *The James Gordon Bennetts.* 1928.

Bent, William

Born at St. Louis, Missouri, William W. Bent (1809–1869) followed his older brother, Charles, into the Rocky Mountain fur trade at the age of nineteen. As a member of Bent, St. Vrain & Co., Santa Fe and Indian traders, William Bent supervised construction of Fort William, later known as Bent's Fort, on the north bank of the Arkansas River (near present-day La Junta, Colorado) in 1833. From this adobe stronghold, Bent managed the extensive trade of the firm with such tribes as the Arapaho, Cheyenne, Lakota Sioux, and others. During the U.S.–Mexican War, the private trad-

Bent's Fort. John Frost, *Pictorial History of Mexico and the Mexican War*, 1862

ing post served as a rendezvous point and supply base for the U.S. Army of the West under Col. (later general) Stephen W. Kearny. Shortly after Kearny's arrival at the fort on 29 July 1846, Bent agreed to captain a "spy company" that would scout in advance of the army on its march to Santa Fe. Bent and his command of six men (including Frank P. Blair Jr., future Civil War general and U.S. senator) entered the service on 2 August, and most were discharged at Santa Fe on 14 September. Charles Bent, senior member of Bent, St. Vrain & Co., was appointed territorial governor of New Mexico by Kearny; he was killed during the Taos Revolt of 1847. William Bent abandoned Bent's Fort in 1849, moving approximately forty miles down the Arkansas River to an area known as Big Timbers, where he established Bent's New Fort in 1853 (later leasing the post to the military in 1860). In addition to his Indian trade, Bent received government freighting contracts. In 1859 he was appointed Indian agent for the Upper Arkansas Agency; he resigned the position a year later. One of the most influential whites among the var-

ious plains tribes, Bent was often involved in treaty negotiations between those tribes and the U.S. government. He died of pneumonia at his ranch on the Purgatoire River near present-day Las Animas, Colorado, on 19 May 1869.

Mark L. Gardner

BIBLIOGRAPHY

Lavender, David. *Bent's Fort*. 1954.

Mumey, Nolie. *Old Forts and Trading Posts of the West: Bent's Old Fort and Bent's New Fort on the Arkansas River*. 1956.

Benton, Thomas H.

Born in North Carolina, Thomas Hart Benton (1782–1858) attended the University of North Carolina and William and Mary before beginning a legal practice in Tennessee in 1806. He served in the state senate from 1809 to 1811 and as a colonel during the War of 1812. After the war Benton moved to St. Louis and in 1821 was elected the first U.S. Senator from Missouri—a position he held for thirty years. As a loyal Democrat and strong unionist, Benton championed Jacksonian domestic policy and strongly endorsed Manifest Destiny.

When James K. Polk assumed the presidency in March 1845, he solicited the views and support of this senior senator. Commencing in October, the two men met frequently to discuss foreign affairs. They generally agreed on the goals—both coveted Oregon and California. Benton, however, feared conflict and was drawn to compromise. He supported a negotiated 49° north latitude settlement with Great Britain over the Oregon territory boundary and purchase of Mexican lands in the southwest. When hostilities along the Río Grande doomed the latter, Benton voted reluctantly for the declaration of war.

Benton provided Polk with military advice and much-needed political support. They agreed that the war should be won with Democratic leaders, both in Washington, D.C., and on the battlefield. Benton teamed with Secretary of War William L. Marcy in May to draft legislation to supplant rising Whig military stars—especially Maj. Gen. Winfield Scott. A bill to create four new brigadier generals and two new major generals, one position intended for Benton himself, passed the Senate, but was defeated by the Whig opposition in the House. Congress passed an amended version in June providing for one position—destined for victorious commander Brig. Gen. Zachary Taylor.

Benton continued to counsel Polk, however, on the progress of the war. By November, Benton, frustrated by the inactivity on the battlefield, urged Polk to launch a new offensive against Vera Cruz and Mexico City. Benton would lead a commission accompanying the army to negotiate a peace settlement. Because both Polk and Benton feared the political impact of a successful Whig-led military expedition, however, they resurrected the idea of creating a high-level (lieutenant general) command for the senator. The realization of congressional reluctance on the subject temporarily sidetracked the plan and forced the selection of Scott. Polk unwisely returned to the issue in January 1847 where the new rank was defeated in the Senate by a coalition of Democrats who supported John C. Calhoun and Whigs. Benton subsequently declined a commission as a major general in March when he realized that he would not hold overall field command in Mexico.

The court-martial for insubordination of Benton's son-in-law, Col. John C. Frémont, had soured the Benton-Polk relationship by February 1848. Frémont had played an integral part in the capture of California but incurred the wrath of his commanding general, Stephen W. Kearny. Polk approved the proceedings, and although he later pardoned the guilty Frémont, Benton remained angry. The senator manifested his bitterness by opposing the ratification of the Treaty of Guadalupe Hidalgo in March.

Opposed to the free-soil extremism of the Wilmot Proviso and the proslavery guarantees of Calhoun, Benton lost his reelection bid to the Senate in 1850. He returned briefly to Congress (1853–1855) but lost a bid for the governorship (1856). Benton opposed the repeal of the Missouri Compromise and endorsed Democrat James Buchanan over Republican Frémont for the presidency in 1856. He moved to Washington, D.C., to write and died there of cancer in April 1858.

John M. Belohlavek

BIBLIOGRAPHY

Benton, Thomas H. *Thirty Years' View.* 1856.

Chambers, William N. *Old Bullion Benton: Senator from the New West.* 1956.

Eisenhower, John S. D. *So Far from God: The U.S. War with Mexico, 1846–1848.* 1989.

Smith, E. B. *The Magnificent Missourian.* 1958.

Benton-Brown Compromise

The victory of the proexpansion Democrats in the election of 1844 reenergized President John Tyler and the champions of Texas annexation. Whig representative Milton Brown of Tennessee presented resolutions that called for the immediate annexation of Texas but left unresolved the prickly issues of the boundary, public lands, and debts. Although the measure passed the Democratic-dominated House by a vote of 128 to 98 on 25 January 1845, the issue faced a tougher challenge in the Whig-controlled Senate.

Democrat Thomas Hart Benton of Missouri had earlier advocated annexation with the consent of Mexico, but he reversed himself under pressure from his Democratic colleagues and recommended a $100,000 appropriation to fund a five-member presidential commission to conduct new negotiations. Mexican approbation of Benton's measure was noticeably absent. Forces led by Senators Robert John Walker of Mississippi and William Allen of Ohio, and quite possibly by President James K. Polk, lobbied, pleaded, and cajoled in an effort to avoid a congressional impasse. Senators were persuaded to endorse a compromise that allowed Benton's proposal to amend the Brown bill. The president could then choose either immediate admission or renewed negotiations. The Senate passed the measure by a vote of 27 to 25 on 27 February and the House concurred the next day. Tyler signed the compromise on 1 March. As one of the last acts of his term, Tyler, on 3 March, surprised the nation by instructing Andrew Jackson Donelson, the U.S. chargé d'affaires to Texas, to offer the Lone Star Republic immediate annexation under the House terms. On 4 July, the Texas convention accepted the proposal.

John M. Belohlavek

BIBLIOGRAPHY

Eisenhower, John S. D. *So Far from God: The U.S. War with Mexico, 1846–1848.* 1989.

Smith, E. B. *Old Bullion Benton: Senator from the New West.* 1956.

Bermúdez de Castro, Salvador

Born in Jerez de la Frontera, Spain, Salvador Bermúdez de Castro y Díez (1814–1883), Duke of Ripalda and Marquis of Lema, was a poet and diplomat. His longest diplomatic station was in the court of Naples (1853–1864). In 1840 he published *Ensayos poéticos.*

Bermúdez de Castro was minister to Mexico from March 1845 to 1848. During his mission, in compliance with instructions he received before his departure, he participated in a plot to establish a monarchy in Mexico with a Spanish prince on the throne. In his effort to carry out these instructions, he joined forces with the Mexican ideologue and conservative politician Lucas Alamán and with the ambitious Gen. Mariano Paredes y Arrillaga. As it turned out, the idea of establishing a monarchy proved to be highly controversial politically, and Paredes y Arrillaga displayed more political independence than was expected.

In 1846, when war broke out with the United States and as defeats of the Mexican army at the hands of U.S. forces began, Minister Bermúdez de Castro decided to postpone enacting the monarchist plan.

Now that the complete documentation of this monarchist scheme is available, it is clear that Bermúdez magnified his own role and downplayed the participation of others, such as Alamán. While it is true that the Spanish minister (just like the British) tried to assist Mexico during early negotiations with the United States, it is clear that to save his plot and back the hawkish Paredes he pushed for the war, and when the conflict began he backed off and let Mexico suffer the consequences alone. Even though this responsibility was pointed out at the time in the Spanish Parliament, Mexican authorities asked only reluctantly for diplomatic satisfaction from Madrid, without the intention of worsening their already difficult international relations.

Miguel Soto

BIBLIOGRAPHY

Alborg, Juan Luis. *Historia de la literatura Española.* 4 vols. 1980.

Delgado, Jaime. *La monarquía en México (1845–1847).* 1990. (It contains the complete documentation of the monarchist plot).

Pletcher, David. *The Diplomacy of Annexation: Texas, Oregon, and the Mexican War.* 1973.

Soto, Miguel. *La conspiración monárquica en México, 1845–1846.* 1988.

Béxar, Siege of

The Siege of San Antonio de Béxar during the Texas Revolution continued from late October to 9 December 1835. Four hundred Texians, with Stephen F. Austin as commander in chief, advanced from the east on San Antonio, held by 750 Mexican troops under Gen. Martín Perfecto de Cos. Cos fortified the town west of the San Antonio River and the Alamo mission east of the stream. On 28 October Texians at Concepcion mission south of the town drove off a Mexican counterattack. After reinforcements arrived in November, the Texians numbered more than 600 men, but 150 soon left because of cold weather and limited supplies. In late November Edward Burleson became commander in chief when Austin left to represent Texas in the United States. On 26 November the Texians captured fodder intended for Mexican horses in the so-called Grass Fight.

Burleson called off an attack on San Antonio in early December, when it seemed the Mexicans had been alerted, and considered withdrawing to winter quarters. But more than 300 volunteers under Col. Ben Milam attacked the town from the north on 5 December after learning that Mexican morale was low. Burleson with 400 men guarded the Texian camp and threatened the Alamo, which kept Mexican troops divided. Col. Frank Johnson directed the attack following Milam's death on 6 December. Texians with their rifles inflicted heavier losses than they suffered, while capturing houses on the north side of town through the 8th. That day Mexican reinforcements arrived, but most were untrained recruits with no provisions for an army already low on supplies. That night four Mexican cavalry companies abandoned Cos, who surrendered on 9 December. Burleson, who lacked enough supplies for both armies, allowed Cos to take his men south, while many Texians departed to see their families. Texian control of the town led to the battle of the Alamo, less than three months later. The siege of Béxar resulted in one of two major victories that helped create the Texas Republic, whose annexation in 1845 by the United States led to the U.S.–Mexican War.

Alwyn Barr

BIBLIOGRAPHY

Barr, Alwyn. *Texans in Revolt: The Battle for San Antonio, 1835.* 1990.

Jenkins, John H., and Kenneth Kesselus. *Edward Burleson: Texas Frontier Leader.* 1990.

Santos, Richard G. "The Siege and Storming of Bexar." In *Six Flags of Texas.* 1968.

Black, John

John Black (1???–18??) was U.S. consul in Mexico City in 1845. He was the official U.S. representative in the Mexican capital at the time Secretary of State James Buchanan wrote him an important letter, dated 17 September 1845, requesting Black to "ascertain from the Mexican government whether it would receive an envoy from the United States entrusted with full power to adjust all the questions in dispute between the two governments." Effectively, the U.S. consul was to ask if the Mexican government was ready to renew full diplomatic relations or if it would at least deal with a U.S. envoy with all the powers of a minister.

On the evening of 11 October, Black met with Manuel de la Peña y Peña, Mexican minister of foreign affairs, who requested that Black put Buchanan's query in writing. Two days later, Black wrote to the Mexican official, quoting verbatim the crucial segment of Buchanan's letter. On 15 October, Peña y Peña replied that although his government remained "deeply injured" by U.S. annexation of Texas earlier in the year (the incident that had led to the break in official diplomatic relations with the United States), Mexico was "disposed to receive the commissioner of the United States." His letter continued that Mexico understood that this commissioner would come "with full powers from his government to settle the present dispute." Two days later, Black wrote to Buchanan that he had achieved "a favorable result" in his communications with Peña y Peña. He used Peña's term *commissioner* when referring to the proposed U.S. envoy. In his communication to Buchanan, however, Black neither hinted nor stated directly that the precise question (whether the Mexican government was willing to negotiate "all the questions in dispute") had not been agreed to by the Mexican government. Apparently, this miscommunication was not intentional but simply the result of carelessness. Similar to Black's letter to Buchanan, Peña's written communication to Black also evidenced lack of directness and clarity of expression, failing to explain that "the present dispute" meant something other than the matter presented by Buchanan. Neither Buchanan nor President James K. Polk had any reason to believe that Black had either failed to understand his clear instructions or execute them faithfully. Accordingly, Polk appointed John Slidell U.S. minister to Mexico in order to negotiate a variety of matters, including U.S. claims against Mexico and the purchase of California and New Mexico.

Only when Slidell arrived in Mexico did it become clear that a terrible misunderstanding had occurred. Mexico was willing to negotiate only about one issue—Texas—and only with a low-level commissioner, not a full-fledged minister plenipotentiary. Black later blamed his superiors for what he regarded as their brash assumptions. In any case, his own sloppy handling of Buchanan's important query had done nothing to discourage those assumptions, which produced the impasse between the two nations.

Mexico's humiliating rejection of Slidell and refusal to negotiate under the conditions that the U.S. government be-lieved it had agreed to in October stiffened U.S. resolve to occupy Texas down to the Río Grande. As U.S. military forces marched toward the Río Grande, war became inevitable.

Black remained in Mexico after the commencement of hostilities, but when Vera Cruz fell to U.S. forces Mexican authorities expelled him. At war's end, he returned to serve as the U.S. consul in Mexico City. His subsequent history is unknown.

Ward M. McAfee

BIBLIOGRAPHY

McAfee, Ward M., and J. Cordell Robinson, eds. *Origins of the Mexican War.* 2 vols. 1982.

McAfee, Ward M. "A Reconsideration of the Origins of the Mexican-American War." *Southern California Quarterly* 62 (1980): 49–65.

Black Bean Episode

In the years preceding the outbreak of the U.S.–Mexican War, racial antagonisms between Anglo-Americans and Mexicans were occasionally inflamed by border clashes between Mexico and Texas and by the alleged mistreatment of Texas prisoners incarcerated in Mexico. Two such events were the Mier Expedition and the so-called Black Bean Episode that followed. In December 1842 an army of Texians invaded the lower Río Grande valley and was defeated at Ciudad Mier. The Texians were marched to Matamoros, then south en route to prisons in the interior of Mexico. Along the way the prisoners resolved to escape, and on 11 February 1843 they overpowered the Mexican escort guard at the Hacienda del Salado, a way station located between Saltillo and San Luis Potosí. Unable to find food and water, 176 prisoners were soon recaptured and returned to Salado. As punishment for the escape attempt, the Mexican government ordered the execution of all the Texian prisoners, a decree that was later amended to every tenth man after the intercession of the U.S. and British ministers in Mexico City. On 25 March 1843 the prisoners drew from an earthen jar containing white and black beans; the seventeen Texians who drew black beans were promptly executed. Although intended as an act of clemency, the Black Bean Episode was condemned as arbitrary and inhumane by the U.S. expansionist press and created much anti-Mexican feeling in the United States.

During the U.S.–Mexican War the bodies of the executed Texians were exhumed and brought back to Texas, where they were interred in a vault overlooking the Colorado River at LaGrange. The obelisk monument that stands today was added a century later.

Sam W. Haynes

BIBLIOGRAPHY
Haynes, Sam W. *Soldiers of Misfortune: The Somervell and Mier Expeditions.* 1990.
Stapp, William Preston. *The Prisoners of Perote.* 1845.

Blanco, Santiago

Mexican general Santiago Blanco (1815–1883) was born in Campeche. He was among the first generation of graduates of Mexico's Colegio Militar, where he also taught mathematics until 1832. After the Battle of Buena Vista (La Angostura) on 22–23 February 1847, where he distinguished himself under the command of Gen. Ignacio Mora y Villamil, he was promoted to general and given command of the Battalion of Army Engineers. In that post he participated in the battle of the Padierna (Contreras) on 20 August. There he was responsible for directing the artillery barrage that slowed the advance of the U.S. forces across the lava fields of El Pedregal toward Gen. Gabriel Valencia's poorly planned defensive position. During the battle he was seriously wounded. Following the war, Blanco continued to command the Engineers. He later became a conservative deputy for Campeche under Antonio López de Santa Anna and director of the Colegio Militar. He opposed the liberals throughout the Reform, the Three Years' War, and the French intervention. Consequently, he was tried, convicted and sentenced to two years' imprisonment following the restoration of the Republic. His sentence was commuted, however, and he spent the remainder of his years in Mexico City, where he died in 1883.

M. Bruce Colcleugh

BIBLIOGRAPHY
Carreño, Alberto María. *Jefes del ejército Mexicano en 1847: Biografías de generales de división y de brigada y de coroneles del ejército Mexicano por fines del año de 1847.* 1914.
Riva Palacio, D. Vicente, ed. *México a través de los siglos.* 1967.

Bliss, William W. S.

William Wallace Smith Bliss (1815–1853), chief of staff to Gen. Zachary Taylor, was born 17 August in Whitehall, New York, the son of Capt. John Bliss, an 1811 graduate of West Point. Highly motivated and intellectually gifted, Bliss was only fourteen years old when he gained an appointment from New Hampshire to enter West Point in 1829. He graduated ninth in his class in 1833 and joined the 4th U.S. Infantry as a second lieutenant, serving in Alabama from 1833 to 1834 and then returning to West Point to teach mathematics from 1837 to 1840. Promoted to lieutenant in 1836 and brevet

William W. S. Bliss. John Frost, *Pictorial History of Mexico and the Mexican War,* 1862

captain in 1839, Bliss served as a headquarters staff officer from 1840 to 1841 in Florida during the Seminole War.

On a frontier assignment from 1842 to 1845 as assistant adjutant general to Brig. Gen. Zachary Taylor in Indian Territory, Arkansas, and Louisiana, the handsome, mannerly Bliss impressed Taylor greatly and vice versa. A serious student of philosophy and poetry, fluent in six foreign languages and with a reading knowledge of another thirteen, Bliss became an expert on the Cherokees and assisted Taylor in his difficult dealings with the Native American tribes on the frontier. Garnering the utterly apt nickname "Perfect" Bliss, he provided Taylor "trustworthy information, honest and competent advice, a friendly hand to supplement or subtract, and a skillful pen to report, explain and, if necessary, discreetly color the facts." Bliss proved nearly indispensable to Taylor for the remainder of his life.

To bolster what he perceived as Taylor's weaknesses as a commander, Gen. Winfield Scott ensured Bliss's assignment as Taylor's chief of staff in 1845 when Taylor's army was stationed in south Texas. Bliss usually edited and clarified Taylor's written communications and often delivered orders during battle. Bliss was promoted to brevet major for gallant and meritorious conduct (delivery of Taylor's orders under heavy Mexican fire) at the Battles of Palo Alto and Resaca de la Palma in May 1846 and received promotion to captain in July. Following Taylor's victory at Buena Vista, Bliss was breveted lieutenant colonel. Throughout the war, Taylor's official letters and reports reflected Bliss's ability to emphasize the general's strengths and successes while downplaying or ignoring his lapses.

After the war, Bliss assisted Taylor in deliberations with Whig politicians who convinced him to become the party's presidential candidate. On 5 December 1848 Bliss married Taylor's vivacious daughter Betty, who would grace the White House as surrogate first lady for her reclusive mother. Bliss served Taylor as personal secretary during his brief presidency and was with him when he died in July 1850. Bliss served as adjutant general of the army's Western Division, with headquarters in New Orleans, from November 1850 until his death on 5 August 1853. Only 38 years old, he died of yellow fever at his home in East Pascagoula, Mississippi.

T. Michael Parrish

BIBLIOGRAPHY

Bauer, K. Jack. *Zachary Taylor: Soldier, Planter, Statesman of the Old Southwest.* 1985.

Cullum, George W. *Biographical Register of the Officers and Graduates of the U.S. Military Academy.* 3 vols. 1879.

Dyer, Brainerd. *Zachary Taylor.* 1946.

Hamilton, Holman. *Zachary Taylor: Soldier of the Republic.* 1941.

Hamilton, Holman. *Zachary Taylor: Soldier in the White House.* 1951.

Bocanegra, José María

Mexican lawyer and politician José María Bocanegra (1787–1862) was born in La Troge, Aguascalientes. He received his law degree from El Colegio de San Ildefonso in Mexico City. Bocanegra originally supported the regime of Agustín de Iturbide against the imposition of a Bourbon monarchy and was later appointed a member of the Junta Nacional Instituyente. In 1823, he sponsored the Constitutional Plan and was instrumental in forcing Iturbide to restore the constitutional congress, thus limiting the power of the monarchy. Bocanegra later opposed the Iturbide monarchy and was instrumental in his downfall when the emperor centralized political power. Bocanegra allied himself with Yucatecan liberal Lorenzo de Zavala throughout much of his career and remained a strong federalist in his attitudes toward the construction of the national state. He served as first deputy from Zacatecas to the congress between 1827 and 1828.

Bocanegra served as minister of foreign relations twice, from 27 October 1837 until 6 November 1837 and from 18 November 1841 until 24 July 1844. During his tenure, re-

lations between the United States and Mexico deteriorated significantly. On 20 October 1842, thinking that war between the United States and Mexico had begun, U.S. commodore Thomas ap Catesby Jones occupied the Mexican port of Monterey, California. Bocanegra protested the "Catesby Affair" vigorously to U.S. minister Waddy Thompson, insinuating that the U.S. government had authorized the invasion. On 31 May 1842, Bocanegra again protested private actions, this time the Mier Expedition in which raiders from the Republic of Texas invaded the Mexican province of New Mexico. Bocanegra, a staunch Mexican nationalist, constantly protested attempts by the United States to annex Texas, threatening that such actions would lead to war between the two nations. He resigned as minister of foreign relations in August 1844. In the late 1840s Bocanegra wrote a book about the early years of Mexico's national history.

Mark Saad Saka

BIBLIOGRAPHY

Anna, Timothy E. *The Mexican Empire of Iturbide.* 1990.

Bocanegra, José María. *Memorias para la historia de Mexico Independiente, 1822–1846.* 2 vols. 1892, 1897.

Pletcher, David M. *The Diplomacy of Annexation: Texas, Oregon, and the Mexican War.* 1973.

Bomb Brigs

Bomb brigs were shallow-draft sailing vessels with only two masts and mounting heavy mortars or cannon for shore bombardment. In 1846 the U.S. Navy purchased four brigs, or schooners, and fitted them out as shore bombardment vessels: the *Etna* (the third of that name in the U.S. Navy), *Stromboli*, *Vesuvius* (the second of that name), and *Hecla*. They ranged in length from 182 feet to 239 feet and weighed from 182 to 239 tons. The first two were purchased and fitted at Boston, the second two at New York. A National Archives drawing shows the internal arrangements of the *Etna* as modified at the Boston Navy Yard in February 1847 to carry a 10-inch columbiad gun on pivot.

Columbiads were short, large-bore guns specifically designed to fire shell in flat trajectory. In 1844 the U.S. Army tested new 8- and 10-inch columbiads. The 10-inch type, weighing 15,400 pounds, was the one used in pivot mounts in the four bomb brigs during the war. Trials were also conducted with a 12-inch columbiad that fired a 172-pound shell and had a range of 5,761 yards, but its great weight (25,000 pounds) rendered it too heavy for sea service.

All four of the bomb vessels served with the Home Squadron during the war. They participated in the April 1847 capture of Tuxpan and in blockade duties along the Gulf Coast. All were sold out of the Navy in 1848.

Spencer C. Tucker

BIBLIOGRAPHY

Emmons, George F. *The Navy of the United States. From the Commencement, 1753 to 1853; With a Brief History of Each Vessel's Service and Fate as Appears Upon Record.* 1853.

Jeffers, William M. *A Concise Treatise on the Theory and Practice of Naval Gunnery.* 1850.

Tucker, Spencer C. *Arming the Fleet: U.S. Navy Ordnance in the Muzzle-loading Era.* 1989.

Borden, Gail

Surveyor and newspaper publisher Gail Borden Jr. (1801–1874), son of Gail and Philadelphia Wheeler Borden, was born 9 November in Norwich, New York, later moving to Indiana. Borden married Penelope Mercer in 1828. While visiting New Orleans from his home in Mississippi with his brother Thomas, he decided to try his luck in Texas, arriving there on 24 December 1829. In addition to farming, Borden surveyed for Stephen F. Austin's colony. He was named a member of the San Felipe Committee of Correspondence in 1832 and represented the district of Lavaca for the Convention of 1833. When Stephen F. Austin left on a trip to Mexico City in 1833, from which he did not return until 1835, Borden assisted Austin's secretary and partner left-in-charge, Samuel May Williams.

Borden, in partnership with his brother Thomas and Joseph Baker, began publishing the *Telegraph and Texas Register* on 10 October 1835, coinciding with the advent of the Texas Revolution. Although Borden sold his interest in 1837, the newspaper he founded published for more than forty years. Borden became the first collector of the port of Galveston for the Republic of Texas. From 1839 to 1851 he was secretary and agent for the Galveston City Company, which owned most of the island. He began experimenting with commercial inventions in the 1840s, but his greatest achievement, a process for condensing milk, was not a success until after the Civil War. He died 11 January 1874 in Borden, Texas, and is buried in Woodlawn Cemetery in New York.

Jodella K. Dyreson

BIBLIOGRAPHY

Frantz, Joe B. *Gail Borden: Dairyman to a Nation.* 1951.

Wharton, Clarence R. *Gail Borden: Pioneer.* 1941.

Border Cultures

Though the Spaniards established settlements in the borderlands as early as 1598, their occupation of the region that today embraces the states of Arizona, California, New Mexico, and Texas did not become permanent until the eighteenth century. Villages (among them Santa Fe and Albu-

Gail Borden. Daguerreotype, c. 1845. From the collection of William J. Schultz, M.D.

querque) and several *ranchos* already existed in New Mexico, as did numerous missions in present-day southern Arizona, when in the 1710s the Spaniards claimed California and Texas. During the 1710s and 1720s, the Spanish founded the towns of Nacogdoches, San Antonio, and La Bahía (present-day Goliad) in Texas; in California, civilian settlements (among them Los Angeles) developed near Franciscan missions that had been established during the latter decades of the eighteenth century.

Rule by Spain came to an end when Mexico gained independence in 1821. Following independence, Mexican citizens in the north developed a loose relationship with the Mexican government in the interior. The Constitution of 1824, a liberal document that established a federalist system for Mexico, was in effect from 1824 until 1835, when a coup led by Antonio López de Santa Anna imposed a centralist political structure on the country. Many in the borderlands disliked such a system, and in 1836 Mexico lost Texas to an Anglo-American separatist rebellion. Expressions of discontent against centralist rule surfaced about the same time in New Mexico and in California.

Mexico did not neglect these northern territories, however, and in fact sought new ways to strengthen its hold on those regions. In Arizona, Mexico attempted to induce immigration by Mexicans during the 1820s and 1830s by granting lands to soldiers. In California, similarly, it undertook a settlement plan (which did not succeed) to relocate people from the interior, while also enacting a land grant policy that attracted new settlers, among them Anglo-Americans from the United States. Another land grant program was used in New Mexico, but mainly New Mexicans took advantage of it.

Generally, the *pobladores* during the Mexican period continued to live in the areas their ancestors had inhabited since the colonial era. In Texas, Mexican-Americans resided in and around San Antonio and Goliad, and south from there to the Río Grande. In Arizona, the *pobladores* were subject to frequent attacks by Apaches, so the Tucson area was the only viable settlement in the province. Californios found the coastal plain the area most conducive to survival, and so lived primarily around the towns that stretched from San Diego to Yerba Buena (later San Francisco). Most New Mexicans stayed primarily in the upper Río Grande area, from villages south of Albuquerque to others just above Taos. Although it is impossible to determine the exact number of Mexican *pobladores* in these four regions, estimates put the total population at about 14,000 Tejanos, 7,300 Californios, 60,000 Nuevo Mexicanos, and some 1,000 in Arizona, most of the latter in the Tucson area.

For the most part, the *pobladores* of the far north developed a quasi-autonomous accommodation with the Mexican government, which was frequently entangled in political imbroglios and generally ruled the far north through military officials who often were indifferent to local problems. The *pobladores* both lamented and appreciated this neglect. On one hand, it forced settlers to fend for themselves in contending with the indigenous tribes and with other frontier issues. On the other hand, it meant minimal government intervention in their affairs. Political activity in the north frequently involved ignoring official directives or adjusting them to make them relevant to immediate circumstances.

The economy in the far north during the 1820s through the 1840s revolved around ranching, farming, commerce, and small manufacturing endeavors. Ranching constituted the main avenue toward profits, although such wealth did not extend outside the major landholders, and certainly did not help the poverty-stricken labor force. Commerce, another avenue that brought dividends to the upper classes, became tied to the capitalist economy of the United States after the Santa Fe Trail was established in the 1820s as New Mexicans acted as middlemen for merchants in the United States and the interior of Mexico. In California, merchants looked toward the Pacific, where by the 1820s U.S. and other foreigners arrived along the California coast to exchange manufactured goods for hides, tallow, and otter pelts.

The war between the United States and Mexico disrupted life for the Mexican *pobladores* of the far north. In both California and New Mexico, there were those who welcomed the prospect of joining the United States, but the U.S. settlers faced resistance from many who wanted to defend the homeland. In California, guerrilla fighters defeated U.S. forces in late 1846 in battles at Los Angeles and Santa Barbara, although better equipped U.S. soldiers later subdued them. In Taos, local resistance led to the death of Governor Charles Bent in January 1847, and the insurgents held out, albeit briefly, against superior military forces sent to quell the rebellion.

The settlers of the conquered regions that became the U.S. southwest were subject to the Treaty of Guadalupe Hidalgo, which stated that residents living in the Mexican Cession were to become citizens of the United States (unless they elected to relocate to Mexico) and were guaranteed their liberty, properties, and religion. Thus, citizens who once lived as Spaniards and then as Mexicans, became Mexican-Americans.

The border culture influenced by the presence of Mexican Americans in the U.S. Southwest displayed itself in numerous ways after 1848. Many residents retained the Spanish language and a love for delectable Mexican foods. The vaquero heritage of Mexico persisted and is seen in the vocabulary still used on the ranch or in modern-day range management techniques. The legal influences of Spain and Mexico are evident in the Southwest's adherence to the principles of common law and in the way it governs water rights. In the border ambient, many residents are bicultural and bilingual. They operate with ease on both sides of the border, engage in cross-border commerce, and celebrate the traditions (including holidays) of both countries. But the survival of border culture has also affected race relations. Racism, segregation, and violence against Mexicans has been a tradition in the Southwest, as have been bitter struggles over land grants between the original Mexican-American grantees and Anglo-American claimants.

Arnoldo De León

BIBLIOGRAPHY

Deutsch, Sarah. *No Separate Refuge: Culture, Class and Gender in an Anglo-Hispano Frontier in the American Southwest, 1880–1940.* 1987.

Gutiérrez, Ramón. *When Jesus Came, the Corn Mothers Went Away: Marriage, Sexuality, and Power in New Mexico, 1500–1846.* 1991.

Monroy, Douglas. *Thrown among Strangers: The Making of Mexican Culture in Frontier California.* 1990.

Sandoval, David. "Gnats, Goods, and Greasers: Mexican Merchants on the Santa Fe Trail." *Journal of the West* 28 (1989): 22–31.

Sheridan, Thomas E. *Los Tucsonenses: The Mexican Community in Tucson, 1854–1941.* 1986.

Weber, David J. *The Mexican Frontier, 1821–1846: The American Southwest under Mexico.* 1992.

Borderlands

The historian Herbert Eugene Bolton first used the term *borderlands* in reference to the areas along both sides of the boundary between Spanish territories and the United States. This region—between New Spain (Spanish Mexico) and the provinces of Texas, New Mexico (including Arizona), and California—was a sparsely populated land of brush country, deserts, mountains, and plains. From Mexico's perspective the borderlands allowed for trade but needed to be defended in case of invasion. U.S. interest in Texas was aroused in 1790 when Philip Nolan traveled there to acquire Spanish mustangs to sell in Louisiana. In 1798 Thomas Jefferson wrote to Nolan inquiring about the mustangs, and Nolan visited him in Philadelphia.

After the 1803 Louisiana Purchase the United States garrisoned Natchitoches (in present-day Louisiana), and in response Spain sent troops and militia to Nacogdoches (in present-day Texas). To prevent conflict, U.S. general James Wilkinson and the commander at Nacogdoches, Simón de Herrera, agreed to keep their troops out of the neutral ground between the Arroyo Hondo in western Louisiana and the Sabine River. Spain closed the border except to Spanish subjects in Louisiana, while the neutral ground became a haven for outlaws.

Under Spanish rule, Texas had no open ports, and the only legal commerce, which was small, came by the Camino Real from Monclova, Coahuila, to the Río Grande at Presidio del Norte, then to San Antonio and Nacogdoches. Another route was via Laredo to La Bahía (present-day Goliad), then on to the Camino Real at the Trinity River.

In 1810 Padre Miguel Hidalgo launched the war for Mexican independence. He was captured and executed while fleeing to the province of Texas, which one Spanish official observed "was the key to all New Spain." One of Hidalgo's followers, Juan Bautista de las Casas, staged a short-lived revolt in Texas. Another, Bernardo de Gutiérrez, raised a force of Mexicans and U.S. adventurers and seized Texas in 1812, but in 1813 Gen. Joaquín Arredondo crushed the invaders, took no prisoners, and executed more than three hundred Tejanos on suspicion, leaving Texas weaker than ever. Other attempts to revive the revolution in Texas also failed.

The Adams-Onís Treaty of 1819, which ceded Florida to the United States, also established the previously undefined western boundary of Louisiana. The U.S. abandoned its claim to eastern Texas, which it had asserted was part of the Louisiana Purchase. Dr. James Long of St. Louis led a small army of outraged citizens to "restore" Texas to the United States, but Spanish troops dispersed them. With fifty men, Long later attacked La Bahía but was defeated and captured.

When in 1821 Mexico became independent under Agustín de Iturbide, filibustering in Texas ended. Warfare and flight had reduced the Texas population by two-thirds, but no other borderland area suffered similarly. In 1824 Texas was attached to the state of Coahuila y Texas, while New Mexico and California became territories of the new Republic of Mexico.

Mexico confirmed Stephen F. Austin's *empresario* grant inherited from his father. It allowed him to bring three hundred families to Texas in the expectation that immigrants would create a barrier to U.S. expansion. Other *empresario* grants were made, and many U.S. families settled in Texas on their own. By 1834 the Texas population was estimated at 21,000, mostly U.S. immigrants and their slaves.

Immediately after Mexican independence, William Becknell opened the lucrative Missouri–Santa Fe trade, which expanded rapidly after he and others began using large freight wagons. After supplying the New Mexico market the traders continued south to Chihuahua, Sonora, Durango, and Zacatecas, claiming a large share of the commerce there.

In 1835 President Antonio López de Santa Anna established a dictatorship, abolished the federal constitution, and reduced the states to departments ruled by officials he appointed. At first only Zacatecas, Coahuila y Texas, and California resisted. Santa Anna crushed Zacatecas and in 1836 turned on Texas. His invasion led to the Texas declaration of independence on 2 March, the battle at the Alamo on 6 March, and the massacre at La Bahía (Goliad) on 27 March. His own carelessness caused his capture at San Jacinto, which saved the Texas Republic from destruction. While held prisoner Santa Anna accepted the Texan claim to the Río Grande from its mouth to its source, but the Mexican government repudiated his treaties with Texas. Most of New Mexico's population was east of the river, in the area claimed by Texas.

During the decade that Texas waited for annexation, Comanche and Apache raids became increasingly common in New Mexico and Arizona, and large numbers of raiders also devastated widespread areas of northern Mexico.

Early in 1840 federalists in northern Mexico rebelled against Anastasio Bustamante's centralist regime and established the Republic of the Río Grande. Texas was unable to aid them, however, and the revolt was put down. By the end of the year Santa Anna was again in power.

In the summer of 1841 Texas president Mirabeau Buonaparte Lamar sent a commercial expedition to New Mexico in hopes of sharing in the Santa Fe trade and to offer to extend the Texas government to Santa Fe. Those involved were seized, forced to endure a brutal march to Mexico City, and imprisoned in Perote Castle.

In 1842, President Santa Anna sent two forces briefly into Texas. In retaliation, about three hundred Texans under William S. Fisher invaded Mexico at Mier, but they surrendered and were imprisoned at Perote. When Texas accepted the U.S. offer of annexation in July 1845, President James K. Polk ordered Gen. Zachary Taylor to the Nueces River, which had been the southern boundary of Texas under Spanish rule. In January 1846 President Polk ordered General Taylor to take a defensive position at the Río Grande, which Texans then claimed as their southern border, and war ensued. About five thousand Texans, including a regiment of Texas Rangers, enlisted. After the war the Río Grande was accepted as Texas's southern boundary, but Texan efforts to claim the Río Grande as the western boundary ended with the Compromise of 1850, which established the present-day border between Texas and New Mexico.

With the 1854 Gadsden Purchase the United States added all of Arizona south of the Gila River for the purpose of acquiring a southerly railroad route to California. One provision in the agreement also canceled the clause in the Treaty of Guadalupe Hidalgo that required the United States to prevent Native Americans from raiding into Mexico, which had proved impossible. One last filibustering expedition occurred in 1856 when Henry A. Crabb of California led a disastrous attempt to take over Sonora. Apache and Comanche raids into Mexico continued for several decades.

Donald E. Worcester

BIBLIOGRAPHY

Bannon, John Francis. *The Spanish Borderlands Frontier, 1513–1821.* 1970.

Bolton, Herbert Eugene. *The Spanish Borderlands: A Chronicle of Old Florida and the Southwest.* 1921.

John, Elizabeth. *Storms Brewed in Other Men's Worlds: The Confrontation of Indians, Spanish, and French in the Southwest, 1540–1795.* 1975.

Weber, David J. *The Mexican Frontier, 1821–1846: The American Southwest under Mexico.* 1982.

Weber, David J. *The Spanish Frontier in North America.* 1992.

See also **Arizona; Boundary Disputes; New Mexico;** *and* **Texas**

Borginnis, Sarah

Born as Sarah Knight (1812–1866) in either Tennessee or Missouri, this remarkable woman, often called "the heroine of the Mexican War," spent most of her life in the company of soldiers. She held little regard for formal marriage, and held several surnames during her life, including Borginnis, Bourdette, Davis, and Bowman. Knight evidently married a soldier in the 7th Infantry young in life and cooked and washed for several of the regimental officers, paying for her quarters and rations from the income. Sarah became known as "the Great Western" for her size, an obvious comparison with the famous steamship of that name. One contemporary described her as "a remarkably large [six feet, two inches tall], well proportioned, strong woman, of strong nerves, and great physical powers."

She accompanied Gen. Zachary Taylor's army to Texas and at the bombardment of Fort Texas she displayed great courage by administering to the wounded and setting up a tent near the center of the fort, where she provided food and hot coffee for the soldiers despite having shell fragments pierce her bonnet and knock a bread tray from her hands. Later she was present on the battlefield of Buena Vista, again tending to the wounded.

While in Mexico, Sarah took a new husband, this time a soldier in the 5th U.S. Infantry, and purchased a hotel in Saltillo that catered to the needs of the soldiers; by 1848 she had amassed a sizable fortune. At the close of hostilities, Sarah accompanied yet another soldier, this time a dragoon, on the march to New Mexico Territory, where she operated several hotels as his nominal wife. In 1852 she accompanied a fourth husband to Fort Yuma, California, working as "an admirable pimp." Later, Sarah moved by herself to the vicinity of Tucson. She fled that region in 1861 at the beginning of the U.S. Civil War; one contemporary refugee referred to her as "a notorious whore." She returned to Fort Yuma and died in 1866 from complications of a tarantula bite. She was buried with full military honors in the post cemetery.

Donald S. Frazier
Summer J. Lamb

BIBLIOGRAPHY

Elliott, J. F. "The Great Western: Sarah Bowman, Mother and Mistress to the U.S. Army." *Journal of Arizona History* 30 (Spring 1989).

Sandwich, Brian. *The Great Western: Legendary Lady of the Southwest.* 1990.

Boundary Commissions

The Treaty of Guadalupe Hidalgo (2 February 1848) ended the U.S.–Mexican War and required drawing a new boundary. Work began in San Diego, California, in July 1849 and was completed in Nogales, Arizona, in October 1855. Scientific survey work proceeded in stages: California, 1849 to 1851; Bartlett–García Conde compromise line, 1851; Gila River, 1851; Río Grande, 1851 to 1853; and Gadsden Purchase, 1855. The joint commission included commissioners John B. Weller (1849–1850), John Russell Bartlett (1850–1853), Gen. Robert Blair Campbell (1853), Maj. William H. Emory (1854–1855), Brig. Gen. Pedro García Conde (1849–1851), and José Salazar Ilarregui (1852–1855). Surveyors were Andrew B. Grey (1849–1851), Emory (1851–1853), and Salazar (1849–1852). Hiram H. Robinson (1849–1850), Thomas H. Webb, M.D. (1850–1853), Lucius Campbell (1853), Charles Radziminski (1855), Capt. Francisco Martínez Chavero (1849–1850), and Capt. Francisco Jiménez (1850–1855) were secretaries.

A surveyor of the period. Daguerreotype, c. 1846. From the collection of William J. Schultz, M.D.

In California Emory collected astronomical data, Lt. Edmond Hardcastle led reconnaissance, and Gray and Salazar established the initial point on the Pacific coast. Salazar and Lt. Amiel Weeks Whipple located the Gila and Colorado rivers junction. Politics, internal dissension, and logistical difficulties plagued both commissions and work stopped in March 1850. The reorganized commissions met in El Paso, Chihuahua, in December 1850.

A dispute over New Mexico's southern and western boundary, caused by errors in John Disturnell's map, which was affixed to the treaty, allowed each country to claim boundaries reflecting national interests. Bartlett was instructed to be fair, but he lacked understanding of the complex geographic issue and was handicapped because Gray and the chief astronomer, Lt. Col. James D. Graham, were not present. García Conde, an engineer, argued the Mexican position. Bartlett agreed to Mexico's claim to a boundary at 32°22′ north latitude, but only if Mexico gave up its claim to a longitude beginning about 1 degree west of the Río Grande for a line 3 degrees west of the river.

The Bartlett–García Conde compromise caused the Mesilla crisis when Bartlett's principal advisors, Gray and Graham, refused to accept the agreement after they arrived in July 1851 and stopped the U.S. work. The United States never completed the compromise line. Congress suspended work in December 1852 pending resolution of the New

Mexico issue. García Conde claimed his compromise a victory while his engineers, Salazar, Capt. Juan B. Espejo, and Lt. Agustín Díaz, surveyed the line in the summer of 1851. Lt. Hardcastle and Lt. Ricardo Ramirez completed the California boundary in July 1851.

Operations moved to the Gila River's intersection with New Mexico's western boundary and to the Río Grande's intersection at 32°22′ north latitude. Whipple and Gray worked at the Gila River intersection, while Capt. Francisco Jiménez led a Mexican team between the junction of the Salt and Gila Rivers to the Colorado River in the fall and winter of 1851. Physical and financial hardships plagued the teams. García Conde died in Arizpe, Sonora, 19 December 1851, while Bartlett traveled a route through Sonora to Guaymas, Mazatlán, and Acapulco, before reaching California and returning to El Paso in August 1852.

The Río Grande survey began under Lt. Col. Graham and Salazar. The Mexicans hoped the river, which had moved south in the El Paso area because of flooding, would move its channel to the north, but in November 1851 an agreement divided work on the river into six sections: (1) initial point to San Ignacio, (2) San Ignacio to Presidio del Norte, (3) Presidio del Norte to Agua Verde, (4) Agua Verde to Laredo, (5) Laredo to Matamoros, and (6) Matamoros to the Gulf of Mexico. Both teams would survey the first and sixth sections, Mexico the third and fifth, and the United States the second and fourth.

Emory returned as surveyor in November 1851 replacing Graham and Gray, who had been dismissed for failing to sign the Bartlett–García Conde agreement. Emory put teams in the field under Lt. Nathaniel Michler, Moritz von Hipple, and Marine T. W. Chandler. Despite financial problems, physical duress, difficult terrain, and complex geography, they surveyed the upper river. Lt. Agustín Díaz surveyed section one, and Salazar finished the section between El Paso and Presidio in May 1853. Financial and logistical problems and Indian raids slowed progress but work stopped when New Mexico governor William Lane threatened to invade and take control of the Mesilla.

In November 1852 Capt. Jiménez went to Matamoros via Mexico City and surveyed the river from the Gulf to Laredo, while Lt. Díaz did the topographic work. U.S. teams on the lower Río Grande were led by Lt. Michler, Radziminski, Clinton Gardner, and Arthur Schott. Jiménez and Radziminski met in November 1853 to finalize the lower Río Grande border.

The Gadsden Treaty (1853–1854) established a new boundary in New Mexico. Emory and Salazar began the scientific work in El Paso in January 1855 and worked westward to Nogales. Capt. Jiménez and Lt. Michler met in March 1855 and worked eastward from the Colorado River south of Yuma. The fieldwork was completed in October 1855.

Emory and the U.S. engineers deserve credit for accomplishing an extraordinary scientific work that included mapping the new boundary and collecting a wide range of geological, botanical, and zoological data. The Mexican scientists did more than "re-observe and recompute" the U.S. work, however, and have not been given credit for their accomplishments. Their work was important in locating the initial point in California. There they surveyed independently the southernmost part of San Diego Bay and forced a small compromise with Gray in locating the point from which a marine league was measured to the south. The U.S. surveyors were not familiar with a marine league, so Emory accepted Salazar's figure. On the Río Grande, Salazar surveyed the initial point independently and his teams completed the Bartlett–García Conde compromise line. The work of Jiménez on the Gila has never been recognized, nor have the Mexican scientists received much credit for surveying portions of the Río Grande and completing the Gadsden Purchase line.

Harry P. Hewitt

BIBLIOGRAPHY

Bartlett, John Russell. *Personal Narrative of Exploration and Incidents in Texas, New Mexico, California, Sonora, and Chihuahua.* 2 vols. 1854. Reprint, 1965.

Comisión internacional de límites entre México y los Estados Unidos. *Memoria documentada del juicio de arbitraje del Chamizal.* 3 vols. 1911.

Emory, William H. *Report on the United States and Mexican Boundary Survey.* 3 vols. 1857–1859. Reprint, 1987.

Faulk, Odie. *Too Far North, Too Far South.* 1967.

Garber, Paul Neff. *The Gadsden Treaty.* 1923.

Goetzmann, William H. *Army Exploration in the American West, 1803–1863.* 1959. Reprint, 1979.

Hewitt, Harry P. "The Mexican Boundary Survey Team: Pedro García Conde in California." *The Western Historical Quarterly* 21 (1990), 171–196.

Hewitt, Harry P. "The Mexican Commission and Its Survey of the Rio Grande River Boundary, 1850–1854." *Southwestern Historical Quarterly* 94 (1991): 555–580.

Lesley, Lewis B. "The International Boundary Survey from San Diego to the Gila River, 1849–1850." *Quarterly of the California Historical Society* 9 (1930): 1–15.

See also **Boundary Disputes; Emory, William H.**

Boundary Disputes

During the rapid expansion of the United States in the nineteenth century, establishing an exact western and southern boundary for the country plagued the nation and its neighbors alike. The original western border of the Mississippi River, established in 1783 at the conclusion of the American Revolution, stood for twenty years. In 1803, the Louisiana Purchase put the U.S. boundary back into question by doubling the size of the federal domain but describing its limits in only the vaguest language. Based on original French claims, the United States, under the leadership of Thomas Jefferson, attempted to press a claim on portions of Texas, but to no avail. A compromise with Spanish officials created a neutral ground between the two domains. Even so, illegal border incursions occurred on a regular basis, starting with Lewis and Clark's expedition to the Pacific from 1803 to 1806, which established a claim of joint tenancy with Great Britain over the Columbia River region—this despite a previous Spanish claim. The United States annexed Spanish West Florida in 1810 after U.S. settlers there staged an insurrection and declared their independence from Spain. Andrew Jackson's invasion of Florida (1817–1818) and several filibustering expeditions into Texas exacerbated the boundary question. Finally, in 1819, the ratification of the Adams-Onís Transcontinental Treaty clearly defined the frontiers of Spanish and U.S. lands and ended a decade and a half of bellicose posturing.

Upon achieving independence in 1821, Mexico's inheritance included this legacy of boundary disputes. When U.S. immigrants began to settle in Texas in the 1820s, the government in Mexico City quickly became aware of the potential threat looming on their northern and eastern border, with the possibility that these new citizens might in fact serve as clandestine agents of U.S. expansion. Andrew Jackson, his appetite for territorial acquisition well established, enlarged this image of U.S. territorial aggrandizement by repeatedly attempting to purchase Texas from Mexico. Failing this, many observers suspected him of sending agents, including his friend Sam Houston, into the region to agitate for Texas independence on the West Florida model. By 1836, Texan independence had changed the boundary of the United States and Mexico.

The ten-year existence of this sovereign state further complicated the disputed border. Mexico never recognized the independence of Texas and therefore claimed the 1819 borders as intact. The United States, as well as Great Britain and France, however, did approve of Texas's claim to nationhood. The question remained as to the precise western and southern borders of the nation. In 1836, Texas pressed a frontier claim south to the Río Grande and west to its source, in spite of the lack of historical precedent. This put into dispute the Trans-Nueces region, or the Seno Mexicano, long a part of the Mexican state of Tamaulipas, as well as most of Nuevo Mexico. In subsequent years, Texas legislatures claimed even more Mexican territory, eventually laying claim to the Californias. Starting in 1841, Texas attempted to press its claim to eastern New Mexico militarily, but without success.

Diplomacy would intervene to settle the issue, or so it appeared. An armistice between Texas and Mexico in 1844 hinted at recognition of Texas independence, but the boundaries remained at issue. Meanwhile, Lone Star agents worked for annexation to the United States, a goal sought by the vast majority of Texans. Their efforts, however, were themselves retarded by the vagueness of Texas borders as the issue aggravated fears of abolitionists that slavery would be extended across the continent.

In 1845, the United States had worked out its own reluctance regarding the expansion of slavery and intervened in the question of national boundaries once again by annexing Texas through a joint resolution of Congress. That same year, it settled its dispute with Great Britain over the Oregon country. When Gen. Zachary Taylor's army moved from U.S. territory to Corpus Christi, Texas, all observers realized that the issue of borders between the United States and Mexico would be resolved at the point of the bayonet. Indeed, by the end of the U.S.–Mexican War, not only had Texas been secured, but so had a large swath of territory including Alta California, Nuevo Mexico, and large portions of the Mexican states of Chihuahua and Sonora in a vast tract known simply as the Mexican Cession. Even with this enormous acquisition, many in the United States advocated the annexation of all of Mexico and grumbled at their government's failure to do so.

This latest adjustment of frontiers led to further conflict. The boundary commissioners of both nations could not agree on an exact starting point from which to begin their surveys. Eventually, officials settled this issue through negotiation and compromise. The territorial claims of Texas, however, were not as easily settled. Opposed by abolitionists and stunned by the creation of a territorial government in Santa Fe, New Mexico, by occupying U.S. forces, Texas politicians threatened war to bring back the "rebellious counties" it had organized, at least on paper, from eastern New Mexico. The rhetoric of President Zachary Taylor and Governor Peter H. Bell waxed hot, but the two sides never came to blows. Instead, politicians settled the issue peacefully as part of the Compromise of 1850.

Three years later, the Gadsden Purchase settled most of the remaining issues regarding the disputed border between the United States and Mexico. The need for a southern transcontinental railroad route and the inability of the United States to control Apache raids into Mexico led to a modification of the Treaty of Guadalupe Hidalgo. The resulting agreement, negotiated by James Gadsden and Antonio López de Santa Anna, sold additional Mexican territory to the United States and established the borders as they exist to the present day. Surprisingly, the final arrangements were for the least amount of territory requested by the United States at the maximum price authorized by Gadsden's instructions.

Donald S. Frazier

BIBLIOGRAPHY

Brooks, Philip Coolidge. *Diplomacy and the Borderlands: The Adams-Onís Treaty of 1819.* 1939.

Goetzmann, William H. *Army Exploration in the American West, 1803–1863.* 1959. Reprint, 1979.

Hietala, Thomas R. *Manifest Design: Anxious Aggrandizement in Late Jacksonian America.* 1985.

Merk, Frederick. *Manifest Destiny and Mission in American History: A Reinterpretation.* 1963.

See also **Adams-Onís Treaty; Boundary Commissions; Gadsden Purchase;** *and* **Mexican Cession**

Bowie, James

A land speculator and soldier, Jim Bowie (1796–1836) personified the type of adventurer who inhabited the U.S.–Mexican borderlands in the early nineteenth century. One of the most famous characters of Texas history, Jim Bowie was born in south central Kentucky, relocated with his family to Spanish-held Missouri in 1800, and then moved to central Louisiana the following year. Bowie grew up as a frontiersman, becoming a skilled hunter and a fearsome six-foot, 180-pound brawler. As an adult, Bowie went into the Caribbean slave smuggling business with his brothers, earning a reputation as a deadly knife fighter among the denizens of the lower Mississippi River. By the late 1820s he began speculating in land backed by financial partners in Natchez.

The land speculation business led Bowie to Texas in 1830. After ingratiating himself with the leading families of San Antonio, he began to work the Mexican immigration laws to his advantage, amassing grants of thousands of acres under suspicious terms. In 1831 he married Ursula Veramendi, the daughter of a local notable. Rarely at home, Bowie spent the next year traveling to and from Natchez on business or scouting the frontier for new sources of wealth. In 1832 Bowie was lured into anti–Mexican government violence at Nacogdoches, and a year later fought in Mexico for the cause of Monclova as state capital against the forces of Saltillo. The new state government rewarded his allegiance by allowing him access to lucrative land deals. In 1835 Bowie's good fortune ended as the new policies of Antonio López de Santa Anna criminalized most land speculation.

As a result, Bowie became a leading proponent of Texas independence, and in the fall of 1835 he led Texian forces in several early engagements with Mexican troops. A natural leader, Bowie held the rank of colonel and was active in planning Texian strategy. In early 1836 Bowie arrived in San Antonio, where he decided, against orders, to fortify and hold the mission called the Alamo. He died in its defense on 6 March 1836.

Donald S. Frazier

BIBLIOGRAPHY

Bowie, Walter. *The Bowies and Their Kindred: A Genealogical and Biographical History.* 1899.

Dobie, J. Frank. "James Bowie." *American West* (Spring 1965).

Lord, Walter. *A Time to Stand.* 1961.

Bradburn, Juan Davis

Juan (John) Davis Bradburn (1787–1842) was a U.S. citizen who served most of his life as a career Mexican army officer. Born in Virginia, Bradburn grew up in Kentucky and spent his early adult life in the mercantile and trading business, which eventually took him to the lower Mississippi River. He joined the 18th Louisiana Militia Regiment during the 1814 to 1815 New Orleans campaign against the British. Although the regiment did not participate in the battle, Bradburn's service influenced his future career, as other members of the regiment included James and Rezin Bowie, former Texas filibusters, and Mexican revolutionaries. Mustered out of service 11 March 1815, Bradburn joined Henry Perry on an expedition into Texas, then joined Francisco Xavier Mina and Guilford Dudley Young's expedition against the Spanish in Mexico. In 1817 the expedition captured Soto la Marina and marched inland to Fort Sombrero in Guanajuato.

Bradburn took command of the non-Mexican volunteers upon Young's death during the Spanish siege of the fort, then escaped and joined the revolutionary forces of Gen. Vicente Guerrero. In 1820 friction with Guerrero compelled Bradburn to join the Spanish Royalist forces under Gen. Agustín de Iturbide. Following Iturbide's Plan of the Three Guarantees and the establishment of Mexican independence, Bradburn became a trusted aide of Iturbide, emperor of Mexico.

The collapse of Iturbide's empire and establishment of the federalist Constitution of 1824 placed Bradburn as a centralist. His alliance with Manuel de Mier y Terán kept him in good favor with the new government however, and when Mier y Terán became commandant-general of the Eastern Interior States, he appointed Bradburn, then a colonel, commandant of a new customs house and fort proposed for Galveston Bay. Under the Law of April 6, 1830, the Mexican congress enacted new regulations for the colonization and administration of Texas, and Bradburn was to enforce these laws in the area between Galveston and the Sabine River.

In October 1830, Bradburn established a customs house, town, and fort on the lower Trinity River at a site named Anáhuac. Bradburn's attempt to enforce the new law placed him at odds with both the Texan colonists and the Mexican land commissioner for the State of Coahuila. These difficulties and Bradburn's arrest of two local lawyers (one of whom was William Barret Travis) erupted in violence in June 1832.

The colonists forced the surrender of Anáhuac, Velasco, and the Mexican garrison at Nacogdoches, declaring that the action was taken in support of the federalist revolution of Gen. Antonio López de Santa Anna. Bradburn escaped to Louisiana and returned to Mexico to join the centralist forces of Gen. Anastasio Bustamante. Following Bustamante's defeat, Bradburn retired to his ranch Puertas Verde (near present-day Mission, Texas), upriver from Matamoros.

In January 1836 Gen. José Urrea reinstated Bradburn as a colonel under the condition that Bradburn would not have to participate in military actions against Anglo-Americans. He was placed in command of Copano until the Mexican defeat at San Jacinto forced his retreat to Matamoros. He once again retired to his ranch, and, while there, was interviewed by Ruben Potter, a former Mexican customs agent. This material was a source for Potter's *The Fall of the Alamo* (1860), the first true history of that battle. Bradburn died at his ranch on 20 April 1842 and is buried in an unmarked grave.

Kevin R. Young

BIBLIOGRAPHY

Henson, Margaret Swett. *Juan Davis Bradburn: A Reappraisal of the Mexican Commander of Anahuac.* 1982.

Bravo, Nicolás

Mexican rebel leader and politician Nicolás Bravo Rueda (1787–1854) was born in Chilpancingo, in the present-day state of Guerrero. Together with his family, he fought as an insurgent in the War of Independence. He was given the honorary title of national hero (*Benemérito de la Patria*) in 1822. He later participated in Agustín de Iturbide's overthrow, and afterward he was part of the Supreme Executive (*Supremo Poder Ejecutivo*). On establishment of the republican system Bravo was twice named vice president of the Republic, from 1824 to 1828 and in 1846. He also functioned as interim and substitute president during three brief periods: 1839, 1842 to 1843, and 1846. He held other posts as well, such as commander-in-chief and governor of the District of México in 1843, governor of the state of Puebla in 1848, and as local representative of the recently formed state of Guerrero in 1850.

Some sources say that between October 1836 and March 1837, during the campaign against Texas, Bravo was named Division Chief in the Army of the North, but it is not clear how he performed in that post.

In 1847, Antonio López de Santa Anna named Bravo general-in-chief of the Army of the East to defend the country against the U.S. invasion. In August that year, he commanded the line from Mexicalzingo to Churubusco to San Antonio and in September, was named military commander of Chapultepec Castle, which was attacked and taken on 12 and 13 September. In his official report, he stated that the castle's fortifications were incomplete, that his forces were insufficient, and that he had no reinforcements. Santa Anna accused him of abandoning the castle and surrendering shamefully. Charges were brought against Bravo, but he was acquitted.

Bravo died under mysterious circumstances in April 1854, one day after Santa Anna, on his way to Acapulco to combat the Ayutla Revolution, was in Chilpancingo.

María Teresa Pavía Miller
Translated by The Horse's Mouth Lanaguage Services

BIBLIOGRAPHY

Noticia biográfica del general d. Nicolás Bravo, vicepresidente de la república mexicana. Biblioteca Nacional, Colección Lafragua, vol. 125.

Parrish, Leonard. "The Life of Nicolás Bravo." Ph.D. diss., University of Texas at Austin. 1951.

"Sumaria en aberiguacion de la conducta obserbada por el Exmo. Sor. Gral. Benemerito de la Patria D. Nicolas Brabo como Gefe de la fortificacion de Chapultepec el día 13 de Septiembre del año pp. en que fue asaltada por el Ejército N. Americano." Archivo general de la nación, Guerra, vol. 273, exp. 2672.

Brazito, Battle of

The Battle of Brazito was fought on Christmas Day 1846 on the Río Grande's east bank, approximately thirty miles upstream of El Paso del Norte (present-day Juaréz, Mexico), between the forces of Col. Alexander W. Doniphan and Bvt. Lt. Col. Antonio Ponce de León. Doniphan and his command, most of whom were from the 1st Regiment Missouri Mounted Volunteers, were on their now-famous march to Chihuahua City. The vanguard of Doniphan's small army, approximately five hundred men, reached the camping place of Brazito at about 3 P.M. on 25 December; they had begun gathering firewood and water when a large dust cloud appeared on the horizon, followed shortly by the intelligence that a Mexican force was rapidly approaching. De León, with five hundred to one thousand troops (accounts vary), both regulars and national guard, and a two-pound howitzer formed a line of battle about a half mile from the Missourians. Doniphan quickly drew up his men as infantry (only a very few were mounted), the river at their backs. After de León's request that Doniphan meet with him was rebuffed, the Mexican line advanced, opening fire at about four hundred yards. The Mexican volleys were high. Doniphan ordered his men to kneel and hold their fire until the Mexicans were within sixty paces. The first volley from the Missourians routed most of de León's force, and a small group of Doniphan's men rushed the howitzer and captured it. A charge of Mexican dragoons on the left of Doniphan's line was also soundly repulsed. The Mexicans fled the field, hav-

ing lost over forty killed and many more wounded; Doniphan's loss was seven wounded and none killed. The battle, more properly a skirmish, lasted about thirty minutes. Doniphan's victory resulted in his subsequent occupation of El Paso del Norte without opposition.

Mark L. Gardner

BIBLIOGRAPHY

Armstrong, Andrew. "The Brazito Battlefield." *New Mexico Historical Review* 35 (1960): 63–74.

Connelley, William E., ed. *War with Mexico, 1846–1847: Doniphan's Expedition and the Conquest of New Mexico and California.* 1907.

Gallaher, F. M., trans. "Official Report of the Battle at Temascalitos (Brazito)." *New Mexico Historical Review* 3 (1928): 385–389.

Brazos Santiago

Brazos Santiago, literally "the arms of Saint James," is a narrow inlet between Brazos Island and Padre Island, barrier islands off the coast of south Texas. At the time of the U.S.–Mexican War, this shallow inlet provided six to eight feet of clearance, connecting the Laguna Madre to the Gulf of Mexico. About four miles west of the inlet and across the laguna on a bluff overlooking the water was an official Mexican port of entry known as Frontón (El Frontón de Santa Isabela), which consisted of a few thatched customs shacks.

Frontón was occupied by the forces of Gen. Zachary Taylor on 24 March 1846, and shortly thereafter U.S. ships began unloading supplies for Taylor's army. The village, renamed "Point Isabel" by the U.S. soldiers, became a bustling port throughout the remainder of the U.S.–Mexican War.

In early May 1846, a hastily constructed earthwork, known as Fort Polk, was thrown up to protect Point Isabel against an anticipated Mexican attack. Five hundred sailors and marines from the Home Squadron, anchored offshore, were ferried ashore to bolster the manpower of the defenders, but the attack never materialized. The old lighthouse currently at Port Isabel sits on the remnants of one wall of Fort Polk.

By July 1846, one observer reported that the harbor off Point Isabel contained "50 to 60 vessels of every class from ships down to sloops" and that the inlet and beaches were littered with the wreckage of many ships. Supply ships entering Brazos Santiago often got stuck on the shallow bar and then broke up under the relentless pounding of the surf.

Brazos Island became a rendezvous site for thousands of state volunteer soldiers on their way to service in northern Mexico. Their white tents dotted the island as they awaited orders in the heat of the south Texas sun, often without adequate supplies or medical facilities. Many volunteers, falling victim to the cramped quarters of the transport ships and the harsh environment of the beach, sickened, died, and were buried in a sand hill on the island.

To alleviate the critical shortage of quarters on the island, a steamboat was driven ashore at full steam during the high water of a norther, becoming beached on land when the high waters receded. The cabins and galley of the steamer became known as the Greenwood Saloon, a unique boardinghouse that counted Gen. Winfield Scott as one of its guests.

By early 1847 there were commercial establishments on Brazos Island and at Point Isabel. Private warehouses, a customs house, and a post office were built on the island, while at Point Isabel the Palo Alto House and Traveller's Hall accepted guests. By May 1847, a large military hospital was under construction on the bluffs of the city, and by May 1848, the pioneer printer and publisher Samuel Bangs had under construction a large and commodious brick hotel.

Joseph E. Chance

BIBLIOGRAPHY
The American Flag. Matamoros, Mexico. 1846–1848.
Chance, Joseph E. *Jefferson Davis's Mexican War Regiment.* 1991.
Chance, Joseph E. *Mexico under Fire.* 1994.
Coker, Caleb, ed. *The News from Brownsville.* 1992.

Brown, Jacob

U.S. Army major Jacob Brown (1788–1846) was originally from Massachusetts. Brown enlisted at the onset of the War of 1812. Elevated from the ranks for gallantry, he served as

first lieutenant (1815–1825) and captain in the 6th Infantry (1825–1843) before promotion to major in the 7th Infantry on 27 February 1843.

Following the death of regimental commander Lt. Col. William Hoffman the previous winter, Brown led the 7th from Corpus Christi to Matamoros in the spring of 1846. When Gen. Zachary Taylor found it necessary to withdraw toward Point Isabel to protect the army's supply route, the highly regarded Brown and his regiment were selected to defend the fortifications across from Matamoros. According to Lt. Napoleon J. T. Dana, a young officer under Brown's command, Taylor, aware of the strong Mexican military presence in the area, stated that Fort Texas would be renamed in honor of the first officer to fall in its defense. On the third day of the ensuing siege (6 May), Brown was mortally wounded while observing the Mexican works. After his shattered leg was amputated, Brown's condition worsened in the heat of the fort's magazine. He died on 9 May 1846 and was buried in the fort the next day. Upon Taylor's return, the fort was renamed Fort Brown in his honor. Present-day Brownsville, Texas, was also named in remembrance of the fallen officer.

Robert P. Wettemann, Jr.

BIBLIOGRAPHY
Heitman, Francis B. *Historical Register and Dictionary of the United States Army.* 2 vols. 1903.
Ferrel, Robert H. *Monterrey Is Ours!: The Mexican War Letters of Lieutenant Dana, 1845–47.* 1990.

Buchanan, James

Secretary of State James Buchanan (1791–1868) entered President James K. Polk's cabinet in 1845 after two decades in Congress as a representative (1821–1831), and a senator (1834–1845), and brief service as U.S. minister to Russia (1832–1833). He served afterwards as minister to Great Britain (1853–1856) and in 1856 carried the Democratic banner in defeating Republican John C. Frémont to become the nation's fifteenth president. A courtly Pennsylvania lawyer born near Mercersburg and educated at Dickinson College, his penchant for caution, moderation, and compromise left him open to charges of vacillation and weakness.

Buchanan was never comfortable as secretary of state; he hated the pressures and long hours, and his relationship with Polk was tenuous. The president thought Buchanan able but distrusted him and rightly suspected that presidential ambitions tempered his conduct. As secretary, Buchanan supported Texas annexation and worked effectively for the 1846 Oregon Compromise despite eleventh-hour cabinet posturing to retain credibility with the extremist "fifty-four-forty" Democrats. At the opening of the U.S.–Mexican War, he counseled that Polk abjure territorial objectives but thereafter altered his position. He worked quietly in 1848 for the

Treaty of Guadalupe Hidalgo, but only after refusing in the cabinet to recommend its submission to the Senate because it provided insufficient territorial compensation. A disgusted Polk, sensing political calculation, lamented that presidential candidates made unsafe advisors.

After his own presidency disintegrated in the secession crisis of 1860 to 1861, Buchanan retired from public life. He died at his Pennsylvania estate, Wheatland, on 1 June 1868.

L. Marshall Hall

BIBLIOGRAPHY

Klein, Philip S. *President James Buchanan.* 1962.

Pletcher, David M. *The Diplomacy of Annexation: Texas, Oregon, and the Mexican War.* 1973.

Buena Vista, Battle of

The Battle of Buena Vista, fought on 22 and 23 February 1847 near Saltillo, Mexico, was one of the most important U.S. victories of the U.S.–Mexican War.

Following Maj. Gen. Zachary Taylor's capture of Monterrey in September 1846 and his armistice with the Mexicans until mid-November, Taylor began to establish a defensive line along the Sierra Madre. He first occupied Saltillo on 16 November, then garrisoned the coastal city of Tampico shortly afterward. U.S. forces occupied the town of Parras, west of Saltillo, on 5 December, and finally Taylor directed troops to Victoria, between Saltillo and Tampico, where they arrived on 29 December. To Taylor's great annoyance, however, his army was sharply reduced in January 1847, when most of his regulars and some volunteers were ordered to join Maj. Gen. Winfield Scott for the invasion of central Mexico. By early February, Taylor's remaining troops were concentrated in the Saltillo area.

Gen. Antonio López de Santa Anna, based at San Luis Potosí, about 250 miles south of Saltillo, planned to march north to defeat Taylor's numerically inferior army and drive the U.S. forces to the Río Grande, allowing the Mexicans to return south unmolested to meet General Scott's drive on Mexico City. A victory in northeastern Mexico would also enhance Santa Anna's prestige in the capital. In late January, Santa Anna began his advance toward Saltillo with approximately 20,000 men, but only about 15,000 survived the difficult march to Buena Vista.

Taylor, unconvinced that a Mexican force was advancing toward him, nonetheless ordered his army to advance about seventeen miles south of Saltillo to Agua Nueva. There, on 21 February, Taylor finally received reliable word from his scouts that Santa Anna was nearby, and the U.S. general wisely ordered his men to retire to the more defensible Angostura Pass, near the hacienda Buena Vista, about seven miles from Saltillo. There, Taylor left his subordinate, Brig. Gen. John E. Wool, to deploy most of the U.S. forces, while he fell back to Saltillo with several units to protect his supplies from a rumored Mexican attack on that city.

The battlefield of Buena Vista had several unique topographical features. Angostura Pass and the Saltillo Road running through it were the key landmarks in the area. There were impassible gullies to the west of the pass, while a wide plateau, cut by several deep ravines and bordered by a mountain, lay to the east. The rugged terrain left Santa Anna with few options if he wished to continue his advance northward. He would be forced to march against the pass itself, drive over the plateau, or move across the mountain. Wool deployed Capt. John M. Washington's artillery battery to guard the pass, supported there and along the plateau by various volunteer and regular units of infantry and cavalry.

Taylor returned from Saltillo early on the morning of 22 February, in time to watch the Mexicans deploy and to receive a surrender demand from Santa Anna, which he promptly refused. It was about mid-afternoon before the main action of the day commenced, as Mexican light infantry under Gen. Pedro de Ampudia climbed the mountain on the U.S. left and were met by dismounted Kentucky cavalrymen and Indiana riflemen. By nightfall, the skirmishing between these forces had resulted in no significant gain for either side, and Taylor left once more for Saltillo with his escort.

Despite a light rain that soaked the armies that night, Wool and Santa Anna both changed the positions of their troops in the expectation of renewed fighting at dawn. The U.S. commander reinforced his riflemen and cavalrymen on the heights, while his opponent likewise increased the number of light infantrymen on the mountainside, emplaced artillery to target Washington's battery at the pass, and massed assault columns and artillery to turn the U.S. left flank.

Early on the morning of 23 February, Santa Anna began his onslaught. A Mexican column moved up the Saltillo Road and was stopped by Washington's battery. The Mexican right fared better, however. Two of Santa Anna's divisions advanced against the U.S. flank, held primarily by the vastly outnumbered 2d Indiana Regiment and three artillery pieces under Capt. John Paul Jones O'Brien. After a brief but determined stand, the 2d Indiana's commander, Col. William Bowles, became confused and ordered his unit to retreat. The panicked Hoosiers fled, O'Brien was forced to retire, and the troops on the mountainside withdrew as well, as Wool's left flank began to disintegrate.

Fortunately for the U.S. forces, some Illinois and Kentucky reinforcements Wool had dispatched earlier to assist the Hoosiers arrived to slow the Mexican advance. Bolstered by artillery, Wool's center made a fighting withdrawal, and Taylor soon arrived again on the field. He set about rallying his routed men, directing troops to reinforce the hacienda (where the supply wagons were parked), and putting reinforcements into the fight. A Mexican cavalry attack on the

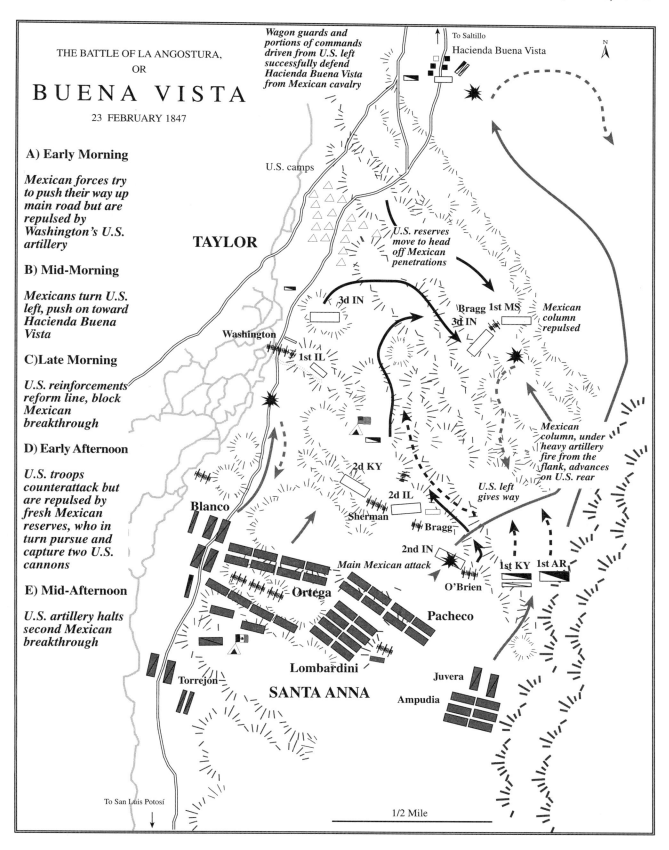

THE BATTLE OF LA ANGOSTURA,
OR

BUENA VISTA

23 FEBRUARY 1847

A) Early Morning

Mexican forces try to push their way up main road but are repulsed by Washington's U.S. artillery

B) Mid-Morning

Mexicans turn U.S. left, push on toward Hacienda Buena Vista

C) Late Morning

U.S. reinforcements reform line, block Mexican breakthrough

D) Early Afternoon

U.S. troops counterattack but are repulsed by fresh Mexican reserves, who in turn pursue and capture two U.S. cannons

E) Mid-Afternoon

U.S. artillery halts second Mexican breakthrough

Wagon guards and portions of commands driven from U.S. left successfully defend Hacienda Buena Vista from Mexican cavalry

To Saltillo
Hacienda Buena Vista

U.S. camps

TAYLOR

U.S. reserves move to head off Mexican penetrations

3d IN

Washington

1st IL

Bragg 1st MS
3d IN

Mexican column repulsed

Mexican column, under heavy artillery fire from the flank, advances on U.S. rear

U.S. left gives way

2d KY

2d IL

Sherman

Bragg

2nd IN

1st KY 1st AR

O'Brien

Main Mexican attack

Blanco

Ortega

Pacheco

Lombardini

Torrejón

SANTA ANNA

Juvera

Ampudia

To San Luis Potosí

1/2 Mile

**Battle of Buena Vista
Order of Battle
22–23 February 1847**

Mexican Forces

Commander
Gen. Antonio López de Santa Anna

Infantry
1st Light Regiment
2d Light Regiment
3d Light Regiment
1st Line Regiment
3d Line Regiment
4th Line Regiment
5th Line Regiment
10th Line Regiment
11th Line Regiment
12th Line Regiment
Battalion of Mexico
Tampico Guardacostas
1st Regiment, Mexico Activo Militia
2d Regiment, Mexico Activo Militia
Celaya Battalion, Activo Militia
Gudalajara Battalion, Activo Militia
Lagos Battalion, Activo Militia
Puebla Battalion, Activo Militia
Querétaro Regiment, Activo Militia

Cavalry
Hussars of the Supreme Powers
Light Regiment
1st Regiment
3d Regiment
4th Regiment
7th Regiment
8th Regiment
5th Regiment
Mounted Rifles Squadron
Tulancingo Cuirrasiers
Jalisco Lancers
Puebla Light Squadron, Activo Militia
Guanajuato Regiment, Activo Militia
San Luis Potosí Regiment, Activo Militia
Michoacan Regiment, Activo Militia
Oaxaca Regiment, Activo Militia

Artillery
13 pieces (manned in part by the San Patricio Battalion)

U.S. Forces

Commander
Gen. Zachary Taylor

Infantry
1st Illinois Volunteers
2d Illinois Volunteers
2d Kentucky Volunteers
2d Indiana Volunteers
3d Indiana Volunteers
1st Mississippi Rifles
Independent Company Texas Volunteers (Galveston Invincibles)

Cavalry
1st U.S. Dragoons
2d U.S. Dragoons
1st Arkansas Cavalry
1st Kentucky Cavalry
McCulloch's Spy Company, Texas Mounted Volunteers

Artillery
Company C, 3d U.S. Artillery (Bragg's battery)
Company B, 4th U.S. Artillery (Washington's battery)
Company E, 4th U.S. Artillery (Sherman's battery)

hacienda was repulsed, and the tide began to turn in favor of Taylor's army.

One of the fresh units that the U.S. general brought into the battle was the 1st Mississippi Regiment. Joined by many members of the reorganized 2d Indiana and the 3d Indiana, this combined U.S. force assembled in a rough *V* configuration on the new U.S. left flank and shattered a Mexican lancer attack. On the verge of destruction by the advancing U.S. forces, these Mexicans were allowed to withdraw safely under a truce flag.

Despite his losses, Santa Anna gathered his forces for one more assault, this time against the U.S. center. Unfortunately for Taylor, several of his units advanced at the same time, hoping to pursue what they believed to be a Mexican retreat. These isolated and outnumbered Illinois and Kentucky infantrymen and regular artillerymen were decimated by the Mexicans, and only the timely appearance of more U.S. artillery and the Mississippi and Indiana regiments saved them from annihilation.

The Mexican army slowly withdrew and the fighting was over by late afternoon. Santa Anna's forces had suffered more than 3,400 dead, wounded, and missing, and although the Mexican common soldiers had shown courage under fire, their superior numbers had failed to destroy Taylor's army. That night the Mexicans began a slow retreat, which eventually led them back to San Luis Potosí.

Taylor's victorious army camped on the field of battle, counted their losses (more than 650 casualties from approximately 4,700 men engaged), and prepared for another attack by Santa Anna the following morning. The numerous dead and wounded were evidence that, despite occasional panics, the U.S. volunteers could fight extremely well under desperate circumstances, although victory would have been doubtful without the aggressive actions of the regular artillery batteries. Nonetheless, it was fortunate for Taylor that the sequence of Santa Anna's assaults had allowed Taylor to shift troops from one critical sector of the field to another and that reinforcements had been available when needed.

The Battle of Buena Vista. A nineteenth-century engraving depicts the battle, the results of which were crucial to the following months of the war (Benjamin Perley Poore, *Perley's Reminiscences*, vol. 1, 1886).

The results of the Battle of Buena Vista were crucial to the subsequent conduct of the war. U.S. forces had turned back a Mexican thrust, which, if successful, could have forced a U.S. withdrawal from that portion of northern Mexico and the loss of important territory. In addition, because of his success at Buena Vista, Taylor's standing as a potential presidential candidate in 1848 was greatly enhanced.

Although Mexican morale was damaged by the U.S. victory and valuable troops were lost, Santa Anna was able to raise another army to face Scott's invaders marching inland from Vera Cruz. After Buena Vista, the war in the north was essentially over, and the focus shifted to the campaign for Mexico City.

Jeffrey L. Patrick

BIBLIOGRAPHY

Carleton, James Henry. *The Battle of Buena Vista, with the Operations of the "Army of Occupation" for One Month.* 1848.

Gibson, J. [T.] W. *Letter Descriptive of the Battle of Buena Vista.* 1847.

Lavender, David. *Climax at Buena Vista: The American Campaigns in Northeastern Mexico, 1846–47.* 1966.

McIntosh, James T., ed. *The Papers of Jefferson Davis, Volume III.* 1981.

Nichols, Edward J. *Zach Taylor's Little Army.* 1963.

Scribner, Benjamin F. *Camp Life of a Volunteer.* 1847.

Smith, Isaac. *Reminiscences of a Campaign in Mexico.* 1848.

Smith, Justin H. *The War with Mexico.* 2 vols. 1919. Reprint, 1963.

U.S. House. *House Executive Document 60. Mexican War Correspondence.* 30th Cong., 1st sess., 1848.

U.S. Senate. *Senate Executive Document 1, Message from the President . . . at the Commencement of the First Session of the Thirtieth Congress.* 30th Cong., 1st sess., 1847.

Burleson, Edward

Edward Burleson (1798–1851), U.S. Army major and president pro tempore of the Texas Senate, was an experienced Indian fighter and Texas frontier hero. He led forces against the Mexican armies of Gen. Antonio López de Santa Anna in the Texas Revolution as commanding general of volunteer forces at the Siege of Béxar. A few months later he was elected colonel by volunteers in the campaign that led to victory at San Jacinto, and at the battle he served as second-in-command to Gen. Sam Houston.

After retiring from military service in 1840, Burleson served as vice president of Texas, and after statehood, he was serving in the Texas senate when Gov. James P. Henderson called for Texan volunteers to join U.S. regulars in Mexico. Burleson enlisted as a private on 19 May 1846 and arrived at Gen. Zachary Taylor's headquarters in Matamoros in early July. He was appointed major and named senior aide by Henderson, now a commissioned major general. Henderson's command included twenty-two Tonkawa warriors, probably led by Burleson's friend and longtime ally, Chief Placido.

Burleson's primary contribution to the U.S.–Mexican War took place at the Battle of Monterrey on 20 September 1846. To overcome the strong Mexican fortifications, Gen. William Worth's command was dispatched to the enemy's rear at the base of Independence Hill where the Bishop's Palace stood. Unwilling to stand in the background as aide to Henderson, Burleson took about twenty Texan volunteers to scout the enemy's strength. After making his report to Worth, Burleson was ordered to lead a charge, since he was familiar with the ground and had been well-tested against Mexican forces during engagements in Texas. With Edward Burleson in the front, his unit charged a formidable force of Mexican calvary and artillery. After intense engagement, they took the hill, an important success in the three days of fighting that led to the Mexican surrender of the city. For his actions in this battle, Burleson was cited for bravery by General Henderson. Burleson returned to Texas with many other volunteers after 2 October 1846, when Taylor discharged them. The general noted his appreciation of Burleson's valuable contributions.

Kenneth Kesselus

BIBLIOGRAPHY

Jenkins, John H., and Kenneth Kesselus. *Edward Burleson: Texas Frontier Leader.* 1990.

Reid, Samuel C., Jr. *The Scouting Expedition of McCulloch's Texas Rangers.* 1847.

Burnet, David G.

Texas land speculator and politician David Gouverneur Burnet (1788–1870) was born in New Jersey, the fourteenth child of Dr. William Burnet and his second wife. He was raised by his older brothers, U.S. senator Jacob Burnet (Ohio Whig) and Isaac Burnet, mayor of Cincinnati. In 1806 he joined Francisco Miranda's ill-fated Venezuela expedition; in 1817 he became an Indian trader in Spanish Texas based in Natchitoches, Louisiana; and in 1820 he returned to Ohio to study law with his brother. Aided by *empresario* Stephen F. Austin, Burnet received a six-year colonization contract from the state of Coahuila y Texas in December 1826 to settle three hundred families in the Nacogdoches area. Un-

able to attract immigrants because of unsettled Mexican politics, he sold his contract in 1830 to the New York–based Galveston Bay and Texas Land Company. He used the proceeds to move his bride, Hannah Este, to Austin's colony, settling in present-day Harris County.

Hoping for a Mexican judgeship, Burnet's conservative Toryish politics made him unpopular, and he was not elected as a delegate to the Anglo-Texan protest meetings that took place between 1832 and 1836. On the pretext of seeking amnesty for a client accused of murder, Burnet traveled to Washington-on-the-Brazos to attend the meeting anyway. Carrying a petition against independence, he did not arrive until after the Texas declaration of independence was adopted on 2 March 1836. The delegates, unaware of his petition and unable to agree on a president for the newly created Republic of Texas, narrowly chose as interim president nondelegate Burnet on 16 March. He proved unpopular and inept and resigned in October after the presidential election in September elevated his rival Sam Houston to the presidency. In the 1838 election, Burnet became vice president under Mirabeau B. Lamar, but in a bid for the presidency in 1841 he was again defeated by Sam Houston. Although Burnet argued against annexation to the United States in 1845, he was appointed secretary of state by the first governor, James Pinckney Henderson, in 1846. A penniless, childless widower, he lived with friends in Galveston when the state legislature named him a U.S. senator in 1866, but the Texans were not seated. Four years later friends buried him in Galveston.

Margaret Swett Henson

BIBLIOGRAPHY

Clarke, Mary Whatley. *David G. Burnet.* 1969.

Henson, Margaret Swett. "David G. Burnet." *The New Handbook of Texas.* 1996.

Hobby, A.M. Hobby. *Life and Times of David G. Burnet.* 1871.

Bustamante, Anastasio

Mexican general and politician Anastasio Bustamante (1780–1853) was born to Spanish parents at Jiquilpan, Michoacán, and briefly studied medicine in Mexico City as a young man. When the Mexican War for Independence began in 1810, he enlisted in the Spanish army with the rank of lieutenant. He switched sides in 1821 and joined fellow Creole officer Lt. Col. Agustín de Iturbide's rebellion, which finally achieved Mexico's independence. Iturbide and Bustamante subsequently developed a close relationship. During Iturbide's short tenure as emperor he awarded Bustamante with senior military commands. Bustamante retained his military position after Iturbide's fall in 1823 and entered politics. His political career formally began with his election as Vicente Guerrero's vice president in 1829. The political

Anastasio Bustamante. John Frost, *Pictorial History of Mexico and the Mexican War*, 1862

partnership between Bustamante, a staunch conservative, and Guerrero, a committed progressive and a champion of Mexico's liberals, was doomed to failure. Bustamante led a conservative coup that ousted Guerrero in December 1829 and served as chief executive until 1833, when he himself was overthrown by Antonio López de Santa Anna, then a liberal, and sent into exile.

Bustamante returned to Mexico in 1836 in the aftermath of the loss of Texas and was elected president. His second presidential term did little to remedy the mounting political antagonism between liberals and conservatives and perpetuated the internal problems that would eventually render Mexico unable to defend itself against the United States. A chronically empty treasury frustrated Bustamante's administrative efforts, and armed rebellions against his government challenged his presidency at every turn. Bustamante complicated matters by adopting an ambiguous stance on the political issues of the day. Though personally conservative, he hesitated to fully enact the conservatives' agenda. Moreover, Bustamante never publicly declared his support for one side or the other in the highly contentious debate between liberals and conservatives over whether Mexico was to be a federal republic or a central republic. This behavior may have ensured his political survival in the short term but

did little to establish a coherent policy that could address Mexico's considerable needs. His inability to impose order on the mounting chaos made him increasingly unpopular with liberals and conservatives alike. Bustamante's failure to exert decisive leadership congruent with the conservative agenda resulted in a conservative coup d'état that toppled him from power in 1841.

Bustamante returned to Mexico in 1844 after a three-year European exile and was serving as a congressman when the war with the United States broke out. His role in that conflict was minor. In 1847 he was appointed to command a military expedition to California, but he never got any closer to his destination than Guadalajara. The troops charged with breaking the U.S. blockade of Mazatlán so that Bustamante's forces could embark began fighting among themselves when a dissident colonel led an attempt to seize control of the state government. With Mazatlán embroiled in civil war, Bustamante's mission was aborted, and his role in the U.S.–Mexican War ended.

Bustamante never again entered politics. His military career came to a close shortly after the end of the war with the United States. He suppressed a political rebellion by Manuel Doblado and Gen. Mariano Paredes y Arrillaga in 1848, then retired to San Miguel de Allende, Guanajuato, where he died five years later.

Daniel S. Haworth

BIBLIOGRAPHY

Costeloe, Michael P. *The Central Republic in Mexico, 1835–1846: Hombres de Bien in the Age of Santa Anna.* 1993. (Chapter 7 includes "The Triangular Revolt.")

Costeloe, Michael P. "The Triangular Revolt in Mexico and the Fall of Anastasio Bustamante, August–October 1841." *Journal of Latin American Studies* 20, no. 2 (1988): 337–360.

Cotner, Thomas E. *The Political and Military Career of José Joaquín de Herrera, 1792–1854.* 1949.

Green, Stanley. *The Mexican Republic: The First Decade, 1823–1832.* 1987.

Hamnett, Brian R. "Anastasio Bustamante y la guerra de independencia, 1810–1821." *Historia Mexicana* 28, no. 4 (1979): 515–545.

Zamacois, Nicieto. *História de Méjico.* Vol. 12. 1880.

Bustamante, Carlos María de

Mexican politician and writer Carlos María de Bustamante (1774–1848) was born in Oaxaca. He studied jurisprudence in Mexico City and obtained a degree in law in the city of Guadalajara. In 1812 he began working as a journalist and made a career out of criticizing the Spanish government. Fearing for his safety, Bustamante joined the rebel army commanded by José María Morelos y Pavón, with whom he had a close friendship.

He joined Agustín de Iturbide's movement that consummated the independence of the country in 1821. From that moment on, he was politically active and participated in eight different legislatures. In congress, he defended the rights of Mexico over Texas and predicted the inevitable clash with U.S. expansionism, although by the time of the war he had retired from public life.

Bustamante was a prolific author, writing 117 works in which he defended the heroes of independence, centralism, and the Catholic Church. His work on the Anglo-American invasion of Mexico, *El nuevo Bernal Díaz del Castillo*, published in 1847, is one of the least structured he ever wrote. His narration begins with the exile of Gen. Antonio López de Santa Anna in 1845 and ends with the occupation of the city of Puebla by the U.S. Army. The central idea of the book is the alleged betrayal of General Santa Anna, the injustice of the war, and the ineptitude of the Mexican rulers, in contrast to the courage and virtues of the Mexican people. Bustamante planned to write another book to end the account of the war, but he had no time to do it. He died in 1848, and it has been said that his death was due in part to the suffering he endured during the military invasion of his country.

Reynaldo Sordo Cedeño

BIBLIOGRAPHY

(Alamán, Lucas). *Noticias biográficas del licenciado Don Carlos María de Bustamante, y juicio crítico de sus obras, escritas por un amigo de D. Carlos y mas amigo de la verdad.* 1849.

Salado Alvarez, Victoriano. *La vida azarosa y romántica de D. Carlos María de Bustamante.* 2d ed. 1968.

Butler, Anthony W.

Serving under President Andrew Jackson, Anthony Wayne Butler (1787–1849) was U.S. minister to Mexico from 1829 to 1835. When Andrew Jackson became president of the United States in 1829, his primary diplomatic objective was to secure possession of the Mexican state of Coahuila y Texas. This territory was populated largely by former U.S. residents, who were considered a potential problem—indeed a threat—by leading Mexican authorities. President John Quincy Adams's administration had broached the subject of annexation to Mexico but failed to acquire the territory. In fact, the first U.S. minister to Mexico, Joel Roberts Poinsett, between 1825 and 1829 was unable to persuade Mexican officials that acquisition of Coahuila y Texas actually would benefit Mexico. By 1829, Poinsett was persona non grata in Mexico and was recalled.

President Jackson turned to a longtime acquaintance, Anthony Wayne Butler, as his replacement for Poinsett. Born in South Carolina in 1787, Butler met Jackson as a youth and served under Jackson during the War of 1812. At war's end the adventurous Butler moved to Mississippi, then to Coahuila y Texas where he became a land speculator; it was in this capacity that he became reacquainted with Jackson.

Contacting Jackson and convincing him that he was an authority on Mexico, Butler secured the ministerial appointment to Mexico. Jackson urged Butler to obtain Coahuila y Texas and possibly other territory, and during his tenure as minister from 1829 to 1835 this brash, rather unprincipled individual attempted to coerce, cajole, and bribe Mexican officials in his efforts to acquire territory. Butler's persistence enraged Mexican officials and convinced them of U.S. perfidy. The groundwork was effectively laid for conditions that culminated in war in 1846.

Curt Lamar

BIBLIOGRAPHY

Lamar, Curt. "A Diplomatic Disaster: The Mexican Mission of Anthony Butler, 1829–1835." *The Americas* 45 (1988): 1–17.

Mayo, Bernard. "Apostle of Manifest Destiny." *American Mercury* 33 (1929): 420–426.

Butler, William O.

U.S. general and politician William Orlando Butler (1791–1880) won praise as one of the more successful volunteer

William O. Butler. John Frost, *Pictorial History of Mexico and the Mexican War,* 1862

officers of the U.S.–Mexican War. A native of Kentucky, Butler first saw military service during the War of 1812. Enlisting as a sergeant in the Kentucky volunteers, he was captured at the River Raisin. After exchange he received a commission and rose to brevet major for gallant conduct at New Orleans under Andrew Jackson. The Kentuckian resigned his commission in 1817, thereafter practicing law and becoming active in Democratic politics. Butler served two terms in the U.S. House of Representatives and ran unsuccessfully for governor in 1844.

On the outbreak of war with Mexico, Butler obtained a major general's commission from President James K. Polk. He commanded Gen. Zachary Taylor's 3d Division, composed of volunteer regiments from Kentucky, Mississippi, Ohio, Tennessee, and Texas, during the attack on Monterrey. On 21 September 1846, while personally leading a portion of his command (the 1st Ohio Regiment) during its assault against Fort Diablo on the town's eastern outskirts, Butler suffered a severe leg wound. The Kentuckian subsequently commanded garrisons at Monterrey and Saltillo, but his wound had not healed by early 1847 and he was ordered home for recuperation. In March 1847 the U.S. Congress passed a resolution honoring Butler's gallantry at Monterrey and presented the general with a sword. President Polk briefly considered Butler, a loyal Democrat, for command of the Vera Cruz expedition, but he reluctantly chose the more experienced, yet politically questionable, Gen. Winfield Scott instead. Butler returned to Mexico in late 1847, after the capture of Mexico City, with reinforcements for Scott. Early the next year, after learning of Scott's prior dealings with Nicholas P. Trist in a scheme to bribe Gen. Antonio López de Santa Anna, Polk ordered the removal of the Whig general, replacing him with Butler. The Kentuckian commanded the U.S. forces in Mexico for several months and directed the evacuation of the capital in June 1848.

Discharged from the service in August 1848, that same year Butler ran unsuccessfully on the Democratic ticket for vice president. Active in politics during the 1850s and loyal to the Union in the Civil War, he died in Carrollton, Kentucky, on 6 August 1880.

David J. Coles

BIBLIOGRAPHY

Eisenhower, John S. D. *So Far from God: The U.S. War with Mexico, 1846–1848.* 1989.

Nichols, Edward J. *Zack Taylor's Little Army.* 1963.

The Life and Public Services of Gen. Lewis Cass . . . to Which Is Added, the Military and Civil Life of Gen. William O. Butler, Comprising His Services in the War of 1812 in Various Civil Capacities and in the War with Mexico Which Has Recently Terminated. 1848.

Cabinet, U.S.

With the news that James K. Polk had won the election of 1844, the president-elect came under intense pressure from the various factions of the Democratic Party who sought to influence his selection of the six-member cabinet. Anxious to avoid antagonizing any of the major power blocs that made up the party, Polk chose his cabinet-level advisors with great care.

Polk chose Pennsylvania senator James Buchanan for secretary of state. A rising star in the Democratic Party, Buchanan would bring to the administration much-needed support in his home state, where manufacturing interests remained decidedly wary of Polk's views on a lower tariff. To gain favor with the supporters of Martin Van Buren, Polk initially offered cabinet-level posts to two of the New Yorker's top lieutenants, Silas Wright and Benjamin Butler, but both men declined. Polk then asked William L. Marcy, a former governor of New York, to serve as secretary of war. To satisfy southern Democrats, Polk appointed as treasury secretary Mississippi senator Robert J. Walker, an expansionist whose support for the former Tennessee governor had helped pave the way for Polk's dramatic "dark horse" nomination in the 1844 convention. New Englander George Bancroft, who had placed Polk's name in nomination, was named secretary of the navy. Two men well known to Polk rounded out the cabinet. Tennessee congressman Cave Johnson, perhaps Polk's closest friend, accepted the job of postmaster general. John Y. Mason, a North Carolinian and college classmate of the president who had served as President John Tyler's secretary of the navy, was tapped to serve as attorney general.

Inevitably, the appointments failed to meet with the approval of all segments of the party. Buchanan's appointment caused friction with Vice President George M. Dallas, the two men being rivals for control of Democratic forces in Pennsylvania. Van Buren and his supporters, long considered the dominant wing of the party, were particularly unhappy with the president's cabinet appointments. The Van Burenites regarded William Marcy as the leader of an opposing faction within the New York party organization, while Walker had played a pivotal role in denying their candidate the presidential nomination at the 1844 convention.

Polk made most important executive decisions only after he had consulted with his cabinet, which met twice a week, more frequently in times of political crisis. Although his cabinet had been selected based on political considerations rather than on talent, the president relied heavily on the collective and individual wisdom of its six members. Because the executive staff consisted only of a private secretary, Polk's nephew J. Knox Walker, the president called on his cabinet to assist him in writing presidential messages to Congress. During cabinet meetings each of his advisers was encouraged to express his views freely, even on matters that did not pertain to his departmental responsibilities. More often than not the group of six like-minded Democrats managed, with the president's prodding, to reach a consensus.

During the U.S.–Mexican War, the president generally received the full support of his cabinet on most major decisions. However, Polk's relationship with Secretary of State Buchanan was frequently strained as a result of the secretary's desire to position himself as a candidate for the Democratic presidential nomination in 1848. At the outset of the war, Buchanan asked the president to publicly forswear all territorial demands against Mexico, a stand Polk refused to adopt, having already decided to take California and New Mexico if the United States won the war. Two years later Buchanan was among the most zealous champions of U.S. expansionism. No doubt mindful of the growing popularity of the All of Mexico movement, Buchanan opposed the

Polk and His Cabinet

Position	Years	Incumbent	Lifespan
President	1845–1849	James Knox Polk	1795–1849
Vice President	1845–1849	George Mifflin Dallas	1792–1864
Secretary of State	1845–1849	James Buchanan	1791–1868
Secretary of Treasury	1845–1849	Robert J. Walker	1786–1857
Secretary of War	1845–1849	William L. Marcy	1786–1857
Attorney General	1845–1846	John Y. Mason	1799–1859
Attorney General	1846–1848	Nathan Clifford	1803–1881
Attorney General	1848–1849	Isaac Toucey	1792–1869
Secretary of the Navy	1845–1846	George Bancroft	1800–1891
Secretary of the Navy	1846–1849	John Y. Mason	1799–1859
Postmaster General	1845–1849	Cave Johnson	1793–1866

Treaty of Guadalupe Hidalgo on the grounds that it did not give the United States a large enough territorial indemnity. The president wrote of Buchanan in his diary: "He cares nothing for the success or glory of my administration further than he can make it subservient to his own political aspirations."

Polk's cabinet underwent few personnel changes during the president's four years in office. In the summer of 1846 Bancroft resigned to accept the post of minister to Great Britain and was replaced as navy secretary by Attorney General Mason. To fill the vacant post of attorney general, the president appointed Nathan Clifford of Maine. Clifford served for fifteen months before being appointed as a special commissioner delegated to take the Treaty of Guadalupe Hidalgo to Mexico after its ratification by the U.S. Senate. Clifford was replaced by Isaac Toucey, the governor of Connecticut.

Sam W. Haynes

BIBLIOGRAPHY
Bergeron, Paul H. *The Presidency of James K. Polk.* 1987.
Haynes, Sam W. *James K. Polk and the Expansionist Impulse.* 1996.

See also biographies of figures mentioned herein

Caddo Indians

The Caddo Indians of northwest Louisiana and northeast Texas, mound builders governed by priest-chiefs during the Mississippian Cultural Tradition (c. 800–1550 A.D.), had sustained contact with the Spanish in Texas and the French in Louisiana around the turn of the eighteenth century. The Caddos participated in the hide and horse trade with these European colonies and often served as their military allies. By the late 1700s, depopulation from disease and from raids by the Osages and Choctaws had weakened the Caddos. After the Louisiana Purchase in 1803, U.S. settlers flooded onto Caddo land in western Louisiana. In 1835 after ceding their land in Louisiana to the United States, the Louisiana Caddos split up—most joined their kinspeople in Texas, some briefly moved to Mexico, and others relocated to Indian Territory.

The Texas Revolution in 1836 created a hostile environment for the Indians of Texas. Relations between the Caddos and the Texians alternated between war and peace. By the time of the U.S.–Mexican War, most Caddos lived in small villages on the upper Brazos River where they grew corn and hunted buffalo. On 15 May 1846 the Caddos and other Texas Indians made peace with the United States by signing the Treaty of Council Springs.

While the Caddos did not actively participate in the war against Mexico, many Caddo warriors served as scouts for the Texas Rangers and the U.S. Army in battles against the Comanches, Kiowas, and Wichitas. In 1859 the Caddos were moved from Texas to Indian Territory.

David La Vere

BIBLIOGRAPHY
Carter, Cecile E. *Caddo Indians: Where We Come From.* 1995.
Smith, F. Todd. *The Caddo Indians: Tribes at the Convergence of Empires, 1542–1854.* 1995.

Cadwalader, George

George Cadwalader (1806–1879) of Pennsylvania commanded as brigadier general the 1st Brigade of Maj. Gen. Gideon Pillow's division in Gen. Winfield Scott's drive on Mexico City. A wealthy, brash, flamboyant Philadelphia socialite of Welsh lineage, Cadwalader was an 1823 University of Pennsylvania graduate and in private life a lawyer and businessman who served many years as president of Philadelphia's Mutual Assurance, or "Green Tree," Company. Militia service constituted his military experience before engagement in Mexico, but he rose to the rank of brigadier general in the Pennsylvania militia and played a decisive role in suppressing Philadelphia's violent anti-Catholic riots of 1844.

President James K. Polk's administration commissioned Cadwalader a brigadier general of volunteers in March 1847. He arrived at Vera Cruz in June and marched troops over the guerrilla-plagued National Highway to join Gen. Scott at Puebla in July. Thereafter his brigade—the 11th and 14th Infantries and the gray-clad Voltigeurs—with a light company of the 1st Artillery, fought at Contreras, Churu-

ultepec Castle, and in
aisals of Cadwalader's
deed, historian Justin
veteran of Chestnut
nd not a gifted com-
portant blunders and
itorious actions on the

rvice as a Union gen-
ly limited duty in the
ty, 3 February 1879.

L. Marshall Hall

towicz. *Catalogue of*

vols. 1919. Reprint,

a Perspective: The
the Years 1834–1871.

Calhoun, John C.

John C. Calhoun (1782–1850), U.S. secretary of state, vice president, and South Carolina senator, was the youngest surviving child of South Carolina backcountry farmers. Calhoun attended Yale and displayed a remarkable intellectual gift. He then practiced law and served a term in the state legislature prior to his 1810 election to Congress. An ardent patriot, Calhoun emerged a leader of the War Hawks who successfully maneuvered a poorly prepared country into war with the British in 1812. Five years later, he joined James Monroe's cabinet as secretary of war and reorganized and enlarged the army. Calhoun maintained war was necessary to fulfill the nation's destiny and that the country must prepare for war during times of peace.

In 1824 Calhoun began serving the first of two terms as U.S. vice president, but political rivalries, philosophical differences, and his allegiance to sectionalism and states' rights resulted in his resignation in 1832. Upon his election to the Senate the following year, he emerged as the leading spokesman for slavery and the plantation system in the antebellum South. His *Exposition and Protest* (1828) and *Disquisition on Government* (1848) developed a political ideology to protect the interests of the southern states. Calhoun maintained that states had the right to nullify federal laws that they deemed unconstitutional.

Appointed secretary of state for the John Tyler administration in 1843, he supported an annexation treaty with the Republic of Texas. Calhoun warned that failure to bring Texas into the Union might result in British interference and abolition of slavery in the Lone Star Republic. He then sent a diplomatic note to the British minister, Richard Pakenham, admonishing the British not to interfere in Texas or force their abolitionist views on the United States. He concluded the letter with an explanation that African Americans fared better under slavery and that servitude was beneficial to their development. The correspondence caused a storm of controversy by identifying annexation explicitly as a sectional issue. Calhoun may have hoped the debate would unite southern Whigs and Democrats around the cause with him as its leader. For Calhoun, expansion without slavery was not only unwise for southern interests but also unacceptable. Sectional strife helped to defeat the treaty, although the Tyler administration managed to obtain Texas by a joint resolution of Congress in 1845.

In 1845 Calhoun was reelected to the Senate, where he attempted to protect southern interests by opposing war with Mexico. He anticipated a long and costly conflict that would expand the size and power of the federal government and increase the corrupting influence of the spoils system. Calhoun also expected protectionists to impose high tariffs, destroying the economy of the South. Most troubling for him, however, was the growing strength of the antislavery movement, which threatened the expansion of slavery. He maintained Congress had no authority to prohibit settlers from taking their slaves into any territory. He reasoned the exclusion of slavery in lands acquired through war would diminish the South's influence.

At the beginning of the war Calhoun abstained from voting on James Polk's war message and remained a critic of the Polk administration. He advocated a negotiated settlement and warned against an invasion of central Mexico, instead favoring a defensive policy with limited territorial gains. He thought escalation of the war could result in defeat and that the people of Mexico would not make suitable citizens of the United States. The course of the war and the support it received in the South doomed Calhoun's presidential hopes.

While his antiwar efforts did little to dissuade, they served as a harbinger of the perils of peace. Calhoun vehemently opposed David Wilmot's proposal to ban slavery in territories acquired from Mexico. He urged southern Whigs and Democrats to resist the proviso, even at the cost of disunion. He argued that such a proviso would permanently relegate the South to minority status.

Calhoun was a dominant figure in American political life from 1810 to 1850. Though the presidency he coveted eluded his grasp, he articulated the case for minority rights under majority rule. Calhoun died in Washington, D.C., on 31 March 1850, preventing him from witnessing the disruption of the Union and the adoption of his arguments by the Confederacy.

Dallas Cothrum

BIBLIOGRAPHY

Bartlett, James. *John C. Calhoun.* 1993.

Current, Richard. *John C. Calhoun.* 1963.

Lander, Ernst McPherson. *Reluctant Imperialists: Calhoun, the South Carolinians, and the Mexican War.* 1980.

Niven, John. *John C. Calhoun and the Price of Union.* 1988.

California

This entry consists of two articles: an **Overview** *and an article on* **U.S. Occupation**

Overview

Hernán Cortés, the most famous of Spanish conquistadores, inspired the first European expedition to Baja California in the 1530s. But credit for full-scale exploration that led to mapping of both Baja (Lower) and Alta (Upper) California belongs to Juan Rodriguez Cabrillo, whose 1542 to 1543 trek produced the first written account of the topography and inhabitants of Alta California. Cabrillo's report actually discouraged further exploration because it described the region as stark and remote. During the seventeenth century Jesuit missionaries established a network of missions in Baja California, but the Spanish showed little interest in Alta California, the area that would in 1850 become the thirty-first state of the United States.

Following the Seven Years' War (1756–1763), a conflict among the major European empires, the Peace of Paris led Spain to change its priorities in California. The treaty shifted the power among the empires, and Spain felt that if it did not take steps to solidify its position in Alta California, it would be challenged in the area by Great Britain, Russia, or both. Spain decided to establish a network of missions similar to that it had created in Baja California. Some officials balked at the plan initially because it would place substantial control of the settlements in the hands of the Catholic Church. These fears were reduced in 1767 when King Carlos II expelled the Jesuits from the Spanish Empire and, in California, replaced them with Franciscan friars, who were perceived to be less politically established and more likely to comply with government directives.

The missions were intended to integrate the native peoples into the religious and economic life of the Spanish Empire. (In fact, they often proved brutal and insensitive to the culture of the proposed converts.) Each mission was to be the precursor of a Spanish town. Alongside the missions, Spain planned to develop a network of *presidios*, or military forts, that would extend from San Diego to San Francisco. These would make Spain's claim to the Pacific Coast of the North American continent clear to competing nations. The *presidios* would serve two purposes: to defend the missions and to function as base camps for further exploration of the vast territory. The final component of the settlement plan was the pueblo, or experimental civilian community. Three were strategically placed at Branciforte (present-day Santa Cruz), Los Angeles, and San Jose. The latter two survived into the Mexican period.

Two experienced settlement professionals, Gaspar de Portola and Fray Junípero Serra, led land and sea contingents into San Diego in the spring of 1769. Between them they had almost sixty years of experience on the Spanish American frontier. Over the next thirty years, the Spanish concentrated most of their efforts on establishing a network of communities along the Pacific Coast from San Diego to San Francisco.

Progress was slow and success spotty. Less than 10 percent of the native population could be induced into the mission system, and contact with the new settlers proved lethal to thousands of California Native Americans, both within and outside the missions. Spanish settlers were reluctant to follow military and church leaders into the new province. In fact, in four decades fewer than 3,500 Spanish colonists left their homes in Baja, Sinaloa, and Sonora and made the passage into Alta California.

When Mexican independence was asserted in 1810, Spanish rule in both Alta and Baja California began to crumble. Supplies intended to reinforce those missions and *presidios* that were not self-sufficient were stolen by guerrillas in the struggle for independence. The Napoleonic Wars destroyed Spain's ability to retain control of California, leaving the area in economic and political isolation. By 1821 when Mexico achieved its independence, the missions had become the dominant institution in Alta California.

Mexico learned from the Spanish experience in California that a more varied and imaginative approach would be needed to actually settle the area. The new Mexican government embraced a liberal land grant policy that enticed thousands to develop the area. The secularization of the missions, which began in the 1830s, opened the most attractive grazing areas in Alta California to prospective settlers.

In the ensuing years Mexico would have to face the challenge of expansionist politicians in the United States who viewed the Pacific Coast of California as the staging ground for a two-ocean economy. That challenge would ultimately lead to the 1846 war between the United States and Mexico.

Ronald J. Quinn

BIBLIOGRAPHY

Bancroft, Hubert Howe. *History of California.* 7 vols. 1890.

Chartkoff, Joseph L., and Kerry Kona. *The Archaeology of California.* 1984.

Crosby, Harry W. *Antigua California.* 1994.

Gibson, Charles. *Spain in America.* 1966.

Kelsey, Harry. *Juan Rodríguez Cabrillo.* 1986.

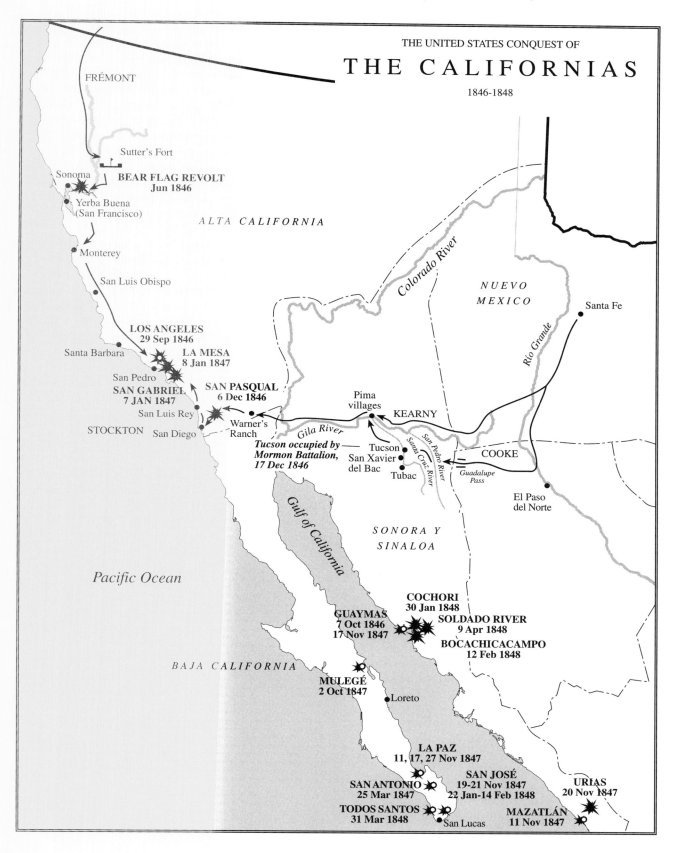

THE UNITED STATES CONQUEST OF

THE CALIFORNIAS

1846-1848

FRÉMONT

Sutter's Fort

Sonoma

BEAR FLAG REVOLT
Jun 1846

Yerba Buena
(San Francisco)

ALTA CALIFORNIA

Monterey

San Luis Obispo

LOS ANGELES
29 Sep 1846

Santa Barbara

LA MESA
8 Jan 1847

San Pedro

SAN GABRIEL
7 JAN 1847

SAN PASQUAL
6 Dec 1846

San Luis Rey

STOCKTON

San Diego

Warner's
Ranch

Gila River

KEARNY

Tucson occupied by
Mormon Battalion,
17 Dec 1846

Pima
villages

Tucson

San Xavier
del Bac

Tubac

COOKE

Guadalupe
Pass

Colorado River

NUEVO
MEXICO

Santa Fe

Rio Grande

San Pedro River

Santa Cruz River

El Paso
del Norte

SONORA Y
SINALOA

Gulf of California

Pacific Ocean

BAJA CALIFORNIA

COCHORI
30 Jan 1848

GUAYMAS
7 Oct 1846
17 Nov 1847

SOLDADO RIVER
9 Apr 1848

BOCACHICACAMPO
12 Feb 1848

MULEGÉ
2 Oct 1847

Loreto

LA PAZ
11, 17, 27 Nov 1847

SAN JOSÉ
19-21 Nov 1847
22 Jan-14 Feb 1848

URIAS
20 Nov 1847

SAN ANTONIO
25 Mar 1847

TODOS SANTOS
31 Mar 1848

San Lucas

MAZATLÁN
11 Nov 1847

Schutz, John A. *Spain's Colonial Outpost.* 1985.

Weber, David J. *The Spanish Frontier in North America.* 1992.

See also **Missions; Presidios**

U.S. Occupation

By 1846 California had captured the imagination of the United States. Many U.S. citizens, embodying the spirit of Manifest Destiny, decided to start a new life in this utopia of the Pacific Coast. In the decades preceding the U.S.–Mexican War, thousands headed for the Oregon Territory, but hundreds of U.S. settlers also moved into the Mexican province of California. With the annexation of Texas by the United States and war looming between the United States and Mexico, these settlers feared for their safety.

Many of the people who inhabited California, New Mexico, and Arizona were Anglo-Americans who had entered these territories illegally. They had not become citizens of Mexico and thus were voiceless in the dealings of their local governments. They feared reprisal by the Mexican government if war broke out, but they refused to leave their property.

In June 1846, a group of Californios, who were unhappy with rule by the central government of Mexico, and a group of U.S. settlers organized a rebellion to overthrow the Mexican government in northern California. With the help of Col. John C. Frémont, a U.S. Army officer who was in the region on an exploration and surveying mission, the rebels were successful in their coup. The "Bear Flaggers," as they became known, set up their own government in Sonoma and declared independence from Mexico.

Meanwhile, U.S. naval forces offshore, who had heard nothing official about a declaration of war against Mexico, assumed that because Frémont was aiding the rebels in California he must have received authorization from Washington, D.C. In response to Frémont's actions, Commo. John D. Sloat devised a plan to blockade all of the major ports along the California coast. U.S. sailors and marines occupied both San Francisco and Monterey without incident on 7 July 1846. The ports of Santa Barbara, San Pedro, and San Diego fell a short time later. Commo. Robert F. Stockton replaced Sloat later that month and continued naval operations in and along the coast of California, capturing Los Angeles on 13 August in a joint operation with Frémont's Bear Flaggers, now reorganized as the California Battalion. By this time U.S. forces controlled most of the important towns, and the naval officers set up local governments and established garrisons to defend the U.S. gains.

While U.S. troops built forts and set up governments in the occupied towns, Governor Pío Pico and Gen. José María Castro were assembling an army to resist the further occupation of California, with the center of the pro-Mexico supporters in Los Angeles. José María Flores led fewer than one hundred Californios and captured and paroled Lt. Archibald H. Gillespie's forty-eight-man garrison on 29 September, reclaiming the "city of angels" for Mexico.

Brig. Gen. Stephen W. Kearny and the Army of the West, with Christopher "Kit" Carson as guide, reached California in early December 1846, unaware of the actions that had taken place in the territory before his arrival. Kearny's troops had left Santa Fe, which they had captured without firing a single shot, on 25 September. Kearny sent couriers to Stockton's San Diego headquarters to announce his arrival in California and to request an escort. Kearny's reinforcements, a detachment of sailors and marines under Lieutenant Gillespie, joined the Army of the West at Warner's Ranch on 4 December. He carried with him a suggestion from Stockton that Kearny and his troops try to surprise the rebels near San Diego. Kearny agreed.

The Army of the West was unprepared to go into battle, as Kearny's troops and horses were exhausted from their overland march. Kearny successfully located the Californio camp at the Indian village of San Pasqual and attacked on 6 December. The soldiers' poor execution of Kearny's orders and their fatigue made the attack a disaster for the Army of the West. Gen. Andrés Pico's seventy-five lancers counterattacked, killing eighteen U.S. soldiers and wounding thirteen more, including Kearny and Gillespie, while suffering only twelve casualties of their own.

Kearny's troops retreated, arriving in San Diego on 12 December where they regrouped and joined the garrison of sailors and marines under the command of Commodore Stockton. On 29 December, Stockton abandoned San Diego and moved his command to San Luis Rey from where he could coordinate an attack to regain Los Angeles, again with the aid of Frémont.

On the night of 7 January 1847, as Stockton conducted his change of base, Flores's band of three hundred *rancheros* ambushed the U.S. forces while they were trying to cross the San Gabriel River. The Californios started with good position on the soldiers, but superior U.S. discipline and firepower fended off the attack, and the U.S. soldiers were able to drive Flores's men from the field.

The next day the U.S. forces confronted the Californios again on a strip of ground between the San Gabriel and Los Angeles rivers known as La Mesa. The U.S. troops once more handily defeated the demoralized rebels, and Flores's troops fled the field. Stockton's column continued toward Los Angeles and, on 10 January, they entered the city with no further resistance. The United States had regained control over a vital point in California, and the U.S. flag returned to the city.

On his way south to Los Angeles, Frémont encountered the remnants of the Californio contingent and sent Pío Pico, who had become a guide for Frémont after his capture at

San Luis Obispo, to the camp to convince them to surrender. Flores abdicated his command to Andrés Pico and left for Mexico. Andrés Pico agreed to surrender; a truce was negotiated and signed on 12 January 1847. The terms of the Treaty of Cahuenga were generous, and although Frémont had no authority to grant a truce Commodore Stockton had no choice but to accept the terms that Frémont had declared.

Although the U.S. occupation of California was complete and resistance crushed, both Kearny and Stockton laid claim to presiding over the new government of California. They both had orders from President James K. Polk to occupy California and set up a military government.

Commodore Stockton was preparing to leave California for a campaign against Acapulco. He refused to consider Kearny's claim as the leader of California and instead commissioned Frémont as governor of California on 16 January. Kearny conceded the post for the time being in order to avoid conflict.

Reinforcements continued to arrive in California to help maintain peace. Commo. Branford Shubrick, Stockton's replacement, arrived with instructions from Washington, D.C., that settled the issue as to who would govern California. Disregarding Frémont's claims to the office, Shubrick authorized Kearny to exercise the role of governor until California was declared pacified. In this role, Kearny took control of the California Battalion, Frémont's base of power, and reorganized it according to military regulations, driving many of the men to leave the ranks and return to civilian life, effectively disbanding the organization. In summer of 1847, Frémont returned to Washington, D.C., in a rage and faced dismissal from the army for insubordination; Kearny returned at the same time to receive acclaim as the conqueror of California and promotion to brevet major general.

Josh Lee Winegarner

BIBLIOGRAPHY

Bauer, K. Jack. *The Mexican War, 1846–1848.* 1974.

Cutts, James M. *The Conquest of California and New Mexico, 1846–1848.* 1965.

Weems, John Edward. *To Conquer a Peace: The War Between the United States and Mexico.* 1974.

Californios

The term *Californios* (or *Californianos*), indicating Californians of Mexican descent, is generally used to refer to Mexicans who were living in Alta California when the United States seized the territory in 1846; the term refers to their descendents as well. In the more restrictive sense, it is also sometimes applied to the upper class of California landowners of the period as well as members of their families.

Economically, Californio society was based on the production of cattle for the hide and tallow trade. The majority of *rancheros* (ranchers) also grazed sheep and horses or, alternatively, cultivated grain crops or wine grapes. Industry was limited to the fabrication of soap, wine, and cloth. The increase in shipping in the late eighteenth and early nineteenth centuries enabled the *rancheros* to acquire a wide range of manufactured and luxury goods.

Many Anglo-American travelers and merchants, as well as Mexicans from the south who visited the northern borderlands, considered the Californios slothful and indolent. Other observers regarded them as a robust people with a strong and resilient culture. While educational facilities were limited, some Californios, such as Mariano Guadalupe Vallejo and Juan Bautista Alvarado, became highly educated men through their own efforts and initiative.

Although Alta California played a minor role in the Mexican independence struggle from 1810 to 1821, by the beginning of the 1830s the local inhabitants had begun to chafe under Mexican rule. Discontent with the central government's imposition of a series of overbearing and inept governors, as well as its general indifference with regard to local concerns, led to several revolts against national authority. By 1845, with the expulsion of Manuel Micheltorena, the last Mexican governor, the Californios achieved their goal of autonomy. They also possessed a practical knowledge of self-government because hundreds of them had previous political or administrative experience.

While many Californios, especially among the landowning class, favored independence, they almost unanimously opposed attempting to achieve it by means of foreign armed intervention. Although U.S. forces occupied Alta California in the summer of 1846 almost without encountering resistance, the Californios in the southern district soon revolted against the despotic administration headed by Archibald H. Gillespie. The rebels defeated the U.S. forces on two occasions before being decisively beaten in the battle of Los Angeles in January 1847.

The great influx of settlers from the United States and other countries into California following the discovery of gold in 1848 left the Californios a minority group. Over the next few decades they experienced a steady loss of political and economic influence. Although the U.S. settlers held the wealthier Californios in higher esteem than other persons of Mexican origin, prejudice and discrimination restricted many of the poorer groups to performing manual labor. Anglo-American dominance over the state's political and judicial institutions led to the loss of a large portion of Californio lands to U.S. speculators, financiers, and railroad constructors. By the mid-1870s, Anglo-American power and culture had become so firmly entrenched that the Californio and Mexican population had become reduced to a substratum within Californian society.

Lawrence D. Taylor

BIBLIOGRAPHY

Blew, Robert Willis. "*Californios* and American Institutions: A Study of Reactions to Social and Political Institutions." Ph.D. diss., University of Southern California, 1973.

Campbell, Leon G. "The First *Californios*: Presidial Society in Spanish California." *Journal of the West* 11 (1972): 582–595.

Hutchinson, C. Alan. *Frontier Settlement in Mexican California: The Híjar-Padrés Colony, and Its Origins, 1769–1835.* 1969.

Langum, David J. "*Californios* and the Image of Indolence." *The Western Historical Quarterly* 9 (1978): 181–196.

Langum, David J. "*Californio* Women and the Image of Virtue." *Southern California Quarterly* 59 (1977): 245–250.

Pitt, Leonard. *The Decline of the* Californios: *A Social History of the Spanish-Speaking Californians, 1846–1890.* 1966.

Camargo

Nuestra Señora de Santa Ana de Camargo is a Mexican town in the state of Tamaulipas, situated on the east bank of the Río San Juan about four miles above its junction with the Río Grande. The town was founded in 1749 by Spanish colonist José de Escandón, and construction of the church, Parroquia Señora Santa Ana, still in use, was begun on that date. Camargo is about 140 miles northwest of Matamoros but more than 300 river miles if approached along the Río Grande. Camargo had a population of two thousand in early 1846, but many fled after a flood in June 1846 destroyed many of the adobe buildings.

During the U.S.–Mexican War, Camargo, located at the head of navigation on the Río Grande, became a vast supply depot. The town was first occupied by U.S. troops (two companies of the 7th U.S. Infantry under Capt. Dixon Miles) on 14 July 1846. It was in Camargo that the U.S. forces assembled to march on Monterrey, located about one hundred miles to the southwest.

The camps of the U.S. soldiers who were left behind to garrison Camargo lined the Río San Juan for many miles on both sides of the river. Communicable diseases swept through these camps, then wholesale death. Military bands so often struck up the chords of the death march in funeral services that the mockingbirds of the area learned to repeat the refrain. One U.S. volunteer referred to Camargo as "a yawning grave," and it is estimated that more than one thousand unmarked graves of U.S. volunteers line the banks of the Río San Juan.

Joseph E. Chance

BIBLIOGRAPHY

Chance, Joseph E., ed. *The Mexican War Journal of Captain Franklin Smith.* 1991.

Frost, John. *Pictorial History of Mexico and the Mexican War.* 1849.

Livingston-Little, D. E., ed. *The Mexican War Diary of Thomas D. Tennery.* 1970.

Cameron, Ewen

The Texan adventurer Ewen Cameron (1811–1843) was born in Scotland. Trained as a stonemason, Cameron emigrated to the United States in the 1830s, and in 1835 he joined a company of Kentucky volunteers for service in the Texas Revolution. After the Battle of San Jacinto, Cameron led a band of cattle rustlers in the Trans-Nueces region, stealing Mexican cattle that they would then drive to Goliad for sale. Cameron served as a captain on the Somervell Expedition in the fall of 1842 and, after the breakup of the campaign, participated in the Mier Expedition under the command of Capt. William Fisher. After the battle at Mier, Cameron and the other Texan prisoners were separated from their commanding officers and marched south, en route to prisons in the interior of Mexico. Cameron emerged as a leader of the Texans, and on 11 February 1843 he led an escape attempt at the Hacienda del Salado, a ranch house where the Texas prisoners had been quartered for the night. Several days later, unable to find food and water, the Texans surrendered. By order of the Mexican government every tenth man was executed, an event known in Texas history as the Black Bean Episode. Cameron was one of the survivors, but his role as the leader of the escape attempt and his earlier marauding activities in the Trans-Nueces region led the Mexican government to order his execution. On 25 April 1843 Cameron was separated from the Texas prisoners at Huehuetoca, near Mexico City, and executed by firing squad.

Sam W. Haynes

BIBLIOGRAPHY

Green, Thomas Jefferson. *Journal of the Texian Expedition Against Mier.* Edited by Sam W. Haynes. 1993.

Haynes, Sam W. *Soldiers of Misfortune: The Somervell and Mier Expeditions.* 1990.

Camp Followers

This entry consists of two separate articles: Mexican Camp Followers *and* U.S. Camp Followers.

Mexican Camp Followers

Since the days of the Spanish conquistadores, women "corn grinder" camp followers had become an established tradition in the armies of Mexico. Women of all ages, whether they were mothers with children, wives, sisters, daughters, or single unattached women, did follow armies. Their presence, estimated at between 20 and 30 percent of any given Mexican army, was acknowledged by military officials as a "necessary evil" to help prevent soldiers from deserting the ranks due to starvation or limited food rations.

When Mexican armies went on the march, the women camp followers added foraging to their key duties as cooks, laundresses, nurses, and servants to the soldiers. They carried on their backs bedding, clothes, food, utensils, arms, and ammunition.

Living conditions for women were rudimentary at best and consisted of only what bedding, clothing, food, and cooking utensils they could carry from one campsite to another. Some camp followers were prostitutes or spies or engaged sporadically in combat if they decided to fight in the ranks. Many women participated in the battles of Cerro Gordo and Monterrey. A U.S. soldier noted that among the dead at Cerro Gordo were a number of Mexican camp followers. In the Battle of Monterrey, Maria de Jesús Dosamantes served as a lancer in the ranks, while Maria Josefa Zozaya rallied the Mexican troops in Monterrey. An unidentified woman camp follower, "the Maid of Monterrey," incorrectly identified as Maria Zozaya, was killed on the battlefield while tending to wounded Mexican and U.S. soldiers.

Elizabeth Salas

BIBLIOGRAPHY

Chamberlain, Samuel E. *My Confession, 1855–1861.* 1956.
Salas, Elizabeth. *Soldaderas in the Mexican Military: Myth and History.* 1990.

See also **Soldaderas**

U.S. Camp Followers

Scores of women—wives, sweethearts, cooks, nurses, seamstresses, laundresses, and ladies of easy virtue: actresses, mistresses, saloon keepers, prostitutes—and their children followed the U.S. Army during the U.S.–Mexican War. Army regulations allowed each company of men "four laundresses" and made allowance for hospital "matrons." The majority of women officially attached to the army were married to soldiers and were foreign born, the majority Irish or German, as were many of the enlisted regulars. No firsthand accounts of camp followers' experiences have been uncovered. What is known of their lives comes from secondary sources and from general knowledge of camp life. While most camp followers justified their presence by cooking, cleaning, sewing, washing, or nursing, a significant number sold sexual favors or provided other forms of ribald entertainment to the men.

Evidence indicates that there were Anglo-American women and children at the battles of Palo Alto, Resaca de la Palma, Monterrey, and Buena Vista and at every major U.S. encampment thereafter, despite Gen. Zachary Taylor's and Gen. Winfield Scott's orders banning U.S. Army–related women and children from the interior of Mexico. Living conditions were extremely harsh for women who insisted on accompanying the troops. When a fever epidemic ravaged Fort Brown, seventeen army children were buried in a single week, and data indicate that more U.S. children were buried during the march to Mexico City.

The most famous and colorful camp follower was Sarah Borginnis, "The Great Western," a tall, large-boned woman of Irish descent whose flowing red hair and bawdy nature made her a favorite with the troops. She is particularly remembered for ministering to the soldiers during the bombardment of Fort Brown and for nursing them after the battles of Monterrey and Buena Vista.

Linda D. Vance

BIBLIOGRAPHY

Bloom, John Porter. "With the American Army into Mexico, 1846–1848." Ph.D. diss., Emory University, 1956.
Cashion, Peggy. "Women and the Mexican War, 1846–1848." Master's thesis, The University of Texas at Arlington, 1990.
Sandwich, Brian. *The Great Western: Legendary Lady of the Southwest.* 1991.
Vance, Linda. "Women and the Mexican War." *Mexican War Journal* 3, no. 3 (1994): 5–11.

Canales Rosillo, Antonio

Soldier and political leader of Tamaulipas, Antonio Canales Rosillo (1802–1869), was born in Monterrey, but made his home in Camargo from the 1820s onward. He married Refugio Molano, the sister of Juan Nepomuceno Molano, thus beginning a familial political group joined later by Jesús Cárdenas, Antonio Zapata, José María Carvajal, and others that had a great influence in Tamaulipas until 1852. Beginning in 1829, Canales practiced law under the authorization of the local congress, and was a state's official surveyor. As head of the militias of the northern towns of Tamaulipas, he fought against the Apaches and Comanches. Between 1838 and 1840, he led a federalist rebellion against the centralist regime in Mexico City, forming a provisional government of the Eastern Departments. Because the rebellion received support in Texas, the central government in Mexico City viewed it as a separatist movement whose objective was to create a Republic of the Río Grande. The Texas support later ended, and Canales made peace with Gen. Mariano Arista in 1840. In Mier in 1842, Canales and Gen. Pedro de Ampudia defeated a Texian force led by Capt. W. S. Fisher and sent by President Sam Houston in retaliation for Mexican attacks against Texas and the defeat of another Texian force in New

Mexico. Four years later Canales participated in the battles of Palo Alto and Resaca de la Palma, as a military commander of the northern towns of Tamaulipas. After the defeat of Mexico's Army of the North, he organized a guerrilla force to harass Taylor's troops. After the U.S.–Mexican War, Canales served as a local representative, as senator of the republic, and as governor of Tamaulipas in 1851. In 1852, he helped put down the rebels who proclaimed the Plan of La Loba. The uprising was linked to U.S. filibusters and to Brownsville businessmen interested in introducing contraband into Mexico. He died in the town of Miquihuana.

Octavio Herrera

BIBLIOGRAPHY
Cavazos Garza, Israel. *Diccionario Biográfico de Nuevo León*, vol. 1, p. 71. 1984.
Zorrilla, Juan Fidel, and Carlos González Salas. *Diccionario Biográfico de Tamaulipas*, pp. 76–77. 1984.

Canalizo, Valentín

Mexican general and president Valentín Canalizo (1794–1850) was born in Monterrey, Nuevo León, on 14 January. He entered military service in August 1811 as a cadet in the Celaya Infantry Regiment. Like most of his contemporaries, Canalizo participated in the royalist counterinsurgency campaigns before embracing the Plan of Iguala in 1821. Subsequently, he served as commandant-general and military governor of Oaxaca, military prefect of Cuernavaca, and governor of the Department of Mexico. A political disciple of Antonio López de Santa Anna, Canalizo was elevated to brigade general in return for seconding the *caudillo*'s litany of pronouncements. On 4 October 1843, Canalizo became interim chief executive, retaining the post until Santa Anna reclaimed it eight months later.

In September 1844, while at San Luis Potosí preparing the Army of the North for a projected campaign to recover Texas, Canalizo was again summoned by Santa Anna to assume the interim presidency. He occupied that position only until 6 December 1844 when the bloodless "three-hour revolution" instigated by Div. Gen. Mariano Paredes y Arrillaga removed him. Exiled to Cádiz in October 1845, Canalizo returned to Mexico in December 1846 and served as Santa Anna's minister of war until 23 February 1847, when he was appointed commander of the newly activated Army of the East. Relinquishing that post to Santa Anna in April, Canalizo led the cavalry corps into battle at Cerro Gordo, where he was routed by Brig. Gen. James Shields's volunteer brigade on the second day of that engagement. Retreating to the safety of Perote, Canalizo abandoned his mentor and withdrew from subsequent military and political activity.

William A. DePalo, Jr.

BIBLIOGRAPHY
Carreño, Alberto M., ed. *Jefes del Ejército Mexicano en 1847: Biografías de generales de división y de brigada y de coroneles del ejército por fines del año 1847*, pp. 38–40. 1914.
Costeloe, Michael P. *The Central Republic in Mexico, 1835–1846: Hombres de Bien in the Age of Santa Anna*, 243. 1993.
Orozco Linares, Fernando. *Gobernates de México: Desde la época prehispánica hasta nuestros días*, pp. 262–263 and 268–269. 1985.

Cañoncito, Battle of

No actual combat took place at Cañoncito (little canyon) fifteen miles southeast of Santa Fe, New Mexico. With three thousand troops, mostly militia, at his disposal, New Mexico governor Manuel Armijo prepared to resist the advance of the U.S. Army of the West in the narrow passage, also known as Apache Canyon, a naturally strong defensive position. Commanding the U.S. forces, Brig. Gen. Stephen W. Kearny planned a frontal assault and flanking maneuver to dislodge the New Mexicans. At the last minute, however, Governor Armijo sent his militia troops home, and he and his few regulars fled southward to Chihuahua. When the U.S. troops sallied forth into Apache Canyon on 18 August 1846, they found only abandoned earthworks. That same day, the Army of the West marched unopposed into Santa Fe under light summer showers.

A skillful defense would have sorely bloodied the Army of the West, but Governor Armijo, both a fiery gentleman and a cagey diplomat, doubted that he could win the war in New Mexico, although he might triumph in the opening battle. His regular force was small in number, and his militia was poorly armed and trained. As the Army of the West approached Santa Fe, Armijo concluded that a bloody battle was senseless, that U.S. conquest was inevitable, and that aborting the battle would benefit himself and New Mexico in the long run.

Durwood Ball

BIBLIOGRAPHY
Gardner, Mark L. Foreword to *A Campaign in New Mexico with Colonel Doniphan*, by Frank S. Edwards. 1847. Reprint, 1996.
Tyler, Daniel. "Governor Armijo's Moment of Truth." *Journal of the West* 11 (April 1972): 307–316.

Carbajal, Francisco

Although little information is available regarding Mexican politician Francisco Carbajal's early life and postwar activities, several sources make clear that he was an active participant in Mexican public affairs during the war with the United States.

In the spring of 1845, the *puros*, a prowar faction, set about rallying support for a combined policy advocating the recovery of Texas and a return to federalism under the auspices of the Constitution of 1824. Carbajal, who belonged to this political bloc, helped fuel these sentiments as a writer for *El Estandarte Nacional*. At the time he also served on the Mexico City *ayuntamiento* (city council) and in that capacity vigorously supported development of a civic militia to repel the expected U.S. invasion. One year later Carbajal was appointed to a special committee that helped draw up the 11 September 1846 decree, which established the civic militia in Mexico's states, districts, and territories.

By October 1847, however, Carbajal became convinced of the futility of carrying on the war. He feared that Mexico would lose its sovereignty if hostilities continued. Carbajal broke ranks with *puro* leader Valentín Gómez Farías, whose bellicose disposition remained steadfast, and became the editor of *La Razón*, a newspaper that clamored for peace. Carbajal also promoted establishment of a U.S. protectorate. He wanted the U.S. Army to remain in Mexico to provide a guardianship that would promote establishment of trial by jury and freedom of religion and help to abolish internal customs duties and the military and ecclesiastical *fueros* (privileges). These reforms, Carbajal believed, would regenerate Mexico and enhance social progress.

Pedro Santoni

BIBLIOGRAPHY

Baker, George Towne. "Una propuesta Mexicana para la ayuda militar Norteamericana, o sea, un recuerdo del liberalismo Mexicano desconocido." *Anuario de historia*. Mexico City: Universidad Nacional Autónoma de México, Year VII, 1976.

Pletcher, David. *The Diplomacy of Annexation: Texas, Oregon, and the Mexican War*. 1973.

Santoni, Pedro. *Mexicans at Arms: Puro Federalists and the Politics of War, 1845–1848*. 1996.

Carson, Christopher ("Kit")

Trapper, guide, Indian agent, and soldier Christopher "Kit" Carson (1809–1868) was born 24 December in Madison County, Kentucky. Illiterate until the last few years of his life, at sixteen Kit ran away from an apprenticeship to a saddler and spent the rest of his life in the West. In the summer of 1846, Carson was a hunter and guide in Bvt. Capt. John C. Frémont's third exploring expedition, which had been in California for some months. After the outbreak of the Bear Flag Revolt in June, Carson was included, but held no rank, in the citizen-soldier brigade formed under Frémont. Later that month, when three Californians thought to be spies were captured near San Rafael by Carson's three-man guard unit, Carson sought Frémont's instruction. Fré-

mont responded, "Mr. Carson, I have no use for prisoners, do your duty," and the three were summarily shot by Carson and his two companions.

When the California Battalion was organized at Monterey on 23 July (the records were subsequently backdated to 7 July), Carson was appointed second lieutenant, probably in Company A. The new battalion sailed to San Diego a few days later to raise the U.S. flag there, then proceeded overland back north to effect the first U.S. occupation of Los Angeles on 13 August 1846.

During his California service, Carson was ordered out on three express trips across the continent to Washington, D.C. On his first trip, which commenced 5 September 1846, Carson encountered westbound Brig. Gen. Stephen W. Kearny and his forces in central New Mexico. Kearny ordered Carson to reverse course and return to California, while others went on to Washington. Kearny's forces were badly beaten by Gen. Andrés Pico's Californian lancers at San Pasqual on 6 December and were surrounded and besieged at San Bernardo the next day. On learning that Carson was with Kearny, General Pico warned his sentinels to be vigilant or *"se escapara el lobo"* (the wolf will escape). Despite Pico's warning, Carson, together with Midshipman Edward F. Beale and Chemuctah, a Delaware Indian, crept through the lancers' lines under cover of darkness and escaped to San Diego, thirty miles away, where U.S. troops were dispatched for Kearny's relief.

When the regrouped U.S. forces moved northward from San Diego, Carson participated in the action at San Gabriel on 8 January, and in the second occupation of Los Angeles on 10 January 1847, where Carson rejoined Frémont, now officially a lieutenant colonel in the Regiment of Mounted Rifles, U.S. Army.

On 25 February, with Midshipman Beale and a small escort, Carson commenced his second express trip to Washington, D.C., arriving there in late May. President James K. Polk received Carson on three occasions, once privately to discuss the state of affairs in California. On 9 June 1847, Polk appointed Carson a second lieutenant in the Regiment of Mounted Rifles. When Carson arrived back in California in October he found Frémont had been taken east by Kearny to face charges of mutiny, disobedience, and prejudicial conduct. Carson was assigned to a unit of dragoons and passed the winter on patrol at Tejón Pass.

Carson departed on his last express trip on 4 May 1848, accompanied by Lt. George D. Brewerton. Passing through Santa Fe in June, Carson learned that his lieutenancy had been negated by the U.S. Senate because of his association with the discredited Frémont, which terminated his official relationship with the military establishment. Despite this disappointing news, Carson continued to Washington, D.C., to deliver the dispatches entrusted to him in August 1848, thus ending his involvement in the affairs of the U.S.–Mexican War.

Lee Burke

BIBLIOGRAPHY

Bonsal, Stephen. *Edward Fitzgerald Beale: A Pioneer in the Path of Empire, 1822–1903.* 1912.

Carter, Harvey L. *'Dear Old Kit': The Historical Christopher Carson.* 1968.

Hine, Robert V., and Savoie Lottinville, eds. *Soldier in the West: Letters of Theodore Talbot During His Services in California, Mexico, and Oregon, 1845–53.* 1972.

Jackson, Donald, and Mary L. Spence, eds. *The Expeditions of John Charles Frémont.* Volume 2, *The Bear Flag Revolt and the Court Martial.* 1973.

Rogers, Fred B., ed. *Filings From An Old Saw: Reminiscences of San Francisco and California's Conquest by "Filings"—Joseph T. Downey.* 1956.

Thompson, Gerald. *Edward F. Beale and the American West.* 1983.

Cartography

The U.S.–Mexican War had a major impact on the mapping of the Greater Southwest. Before the war, much of this region was largely terra incognita on U.S. and, to a lesser degree, Mexican maps of the early nineteenth century. With Texas's independence and subsequent annexation and with U.S. expansion across North America to Oregon and California under the ideology of Manifest Destiny, by 1846 the Southwest, although still considered a vast and boring wasteland, had become of greater interest to the United States. While the region was perhaps better known in Mexico, there, too, it was emerging from a period of neglect dating back to the late Spanish period. This geographic and cartographic ignorance of the Southwest by both countries began to be rectified as a result of the troop and naval movements and military campaigns during the war and the accompanying maps such as the U.S. Army Corps of Topographical Engineers' *Battle of Cerro Gordo April 17th & 18th 1847* (Washington, 1847), the postwar U.S.–Mexican Boundary Survey, and newspaper maps during and after the war.

By the 1840s the increasing use of paper made from wood pulp and the adoption of the relatively new technology of lithography allowed maps to be printed more cheaply and in greater volume. At the outbreak of the U.S.–Mexican War, several important maps covering the region—to varying degrees of accuracy—were already in wide circulation to feed the expansionist appetite of a public still largely without information about the Southwest. One example was Henry Scheck Tanner's *A Map of the United States of Mexico . . .* (Philadelphia, 1845), based in part on the earlier manuscript cartography (1823–1829) of the "Father of Texas," Stephen F. Austin. Charles Preuss's *Map of Oregon and Upper California from the surveys of John Charles Frémont . . .* (Washington City, 1845) and Samuel Augustus Mitchell's *A New Map of Texas, Oregon and California . . .* (Philadelphia, 1846) were real "Manifest Destiny maps."

Perhaps the most significant of these maps was John Disturnell's *Mapa de los Estados Unidos de Méjico . . .* (New York, 1846), which because of its popularity (twenty-three editions during the period from 1846 to 1858) rather than its accuracy was used during the peace negotiations and was attached to the Treaty of Guadalupe Hidalgo. The misplacement of El Paso thirty miles too far north and the location of the Río Grande two degrees too far to the west on this "Treaty Map" necessitated the Gadsden Purchase (1854) of the subsequently disputed Mesilla tract from Mexico to ensure U.S. control of that area's mineral wealth and of the potential southern transcontinental railroad route. This crisis probably spurred the further interior surveying of the new lands of the North American West. Article V of the treaty also called for the accurate surveying of the boundary, which was carried out by a joint U.S.–Mexican commission from 1849 to 1857.

After the war and during the demarcation of the U.S.–Mexican boundary, all of those maps produced immediately before and during the conflict and others in official reports—such as 1st Lt. William H. Emory's *Map of the United States and Their Territories Between the Mississippi and the Pacific Ocean and Part of Mexico . . .*, published in the *Report of the United States and Mexico Boundary Survey . . .* (Washington, 1851)—were used to further explain and understand the war. This cartography also greatly facilitated U.S. continental expansionism before and especially after the U.S. Civil War.

Dennis Reinhartz

BIBLIOGRAPHY

Garrett, Jenkins. *The Mexican-American War of 1846–1848: Bibliography of the Holdings of the Libraries of The University of Texas at Arlington.* 1995.

Martin, James C., and Robert Sidney Martin. *Maps of Texas and the Southwest, 1513–1900.* 1984.

Martin, Robert Sidney, and James C. Martin. *Contours of Discovery: Printed Maps Delineating the Texas and Southwestern Chapters in the Cartographic History of North America, 1513–1930. A User's Guide.* 1982.

Reinhartz, Dennis, and Charles C. Colley. *The Mapping of the American Southwest.* 1987.

Ristow, Walter W. *American Maps and Mapmakers: Commercial Cartography in the Nineteenth Century.* 1985.

See also **Boundary Commissions**

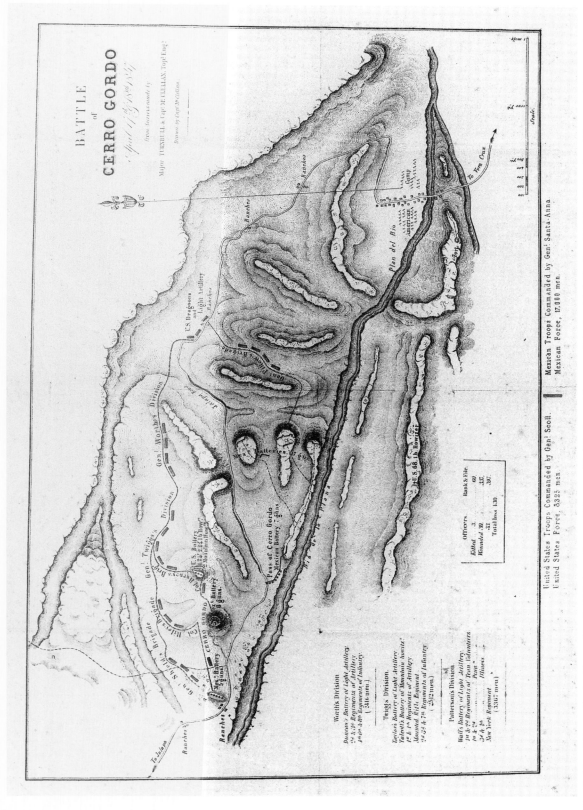

The Battle of Cerro Gordo. Mapped by the U.S. Army Corps of Topographical Engineers (Courtesy of the Special Collections Division, University of Texas at Arlington Libraries).

79

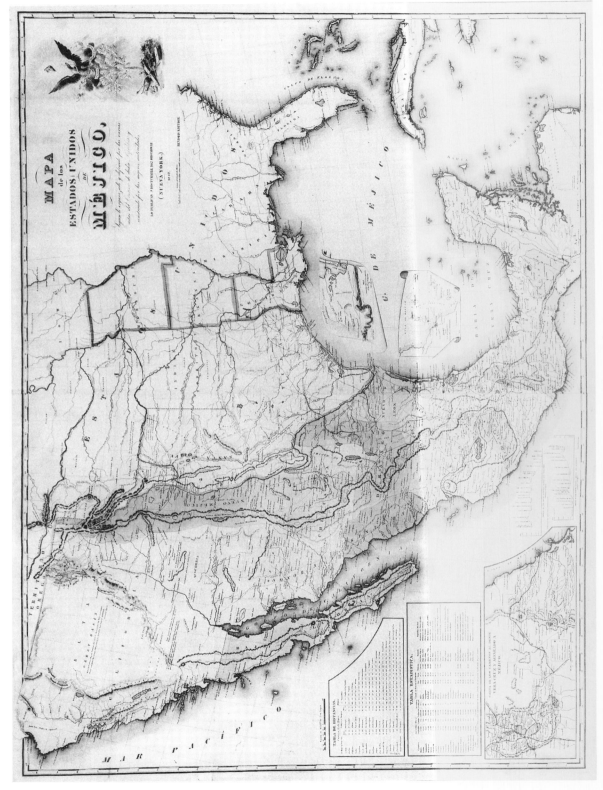

The Disturnell Map. Courtesy of the Special Collections Division, University of Texas at Arlington Libraries

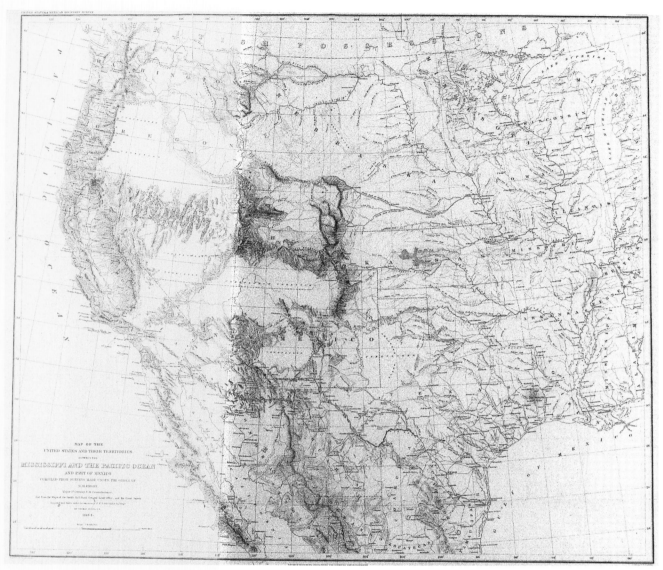

Map of the United States and Their Territories. . . . Mapped by William H. Emory (Courtesy of the Special Collections Division, University of Texas at Arlington Libraries).

Castes

Loosely defined ethnic groups, castes made up colonial Mexico's social hierarchy and continued to influence nineteenth-century Mexican politics. The reconquest of Spain from Muslim occupation (711–1492) instilled in the Spanish a concern for racial purity; only "old Christians," people who claimed—often erroneously—no trace of Muslim or Jewish ancestry, were considered trustworthy. Purity of blood became even more important, and more problematic, in the New World where the shortage of European women led to widespread intermarriage. Settlers took Native American wives and mistresses, producing large numbers of mestizo children. The Crown divided New Spain into separate Eu-

ropean and Indian societies; in theory, children claimed by their European fathers entered Spanish society, while the others remained with their mothers' Indian communities. Nevertheless, large numbers of illegitimate mestizos, together with African slaves and mulattoes, formed an urban underclass known collectively as *castas*.

Unlike the rigid Hindu caste system of India, enterprising individuals of mixed blood could "whiten" themselves with money and marriage. Elites drew elaborate charts containing more than fifty racial categories, but only the most basic labels—Spaniard, mestizo, mulatto, black, and Indian—applied in practice. José María Morelos, a mulatto priest and independence leader, abolished Mexico's caste system in November 1810. But the urban underclass remained, known derisively as *léperos,* and the Mexican government's hesitation in arming them during the U.S.–Mexican War had a detrimental effect on national defense efforts. Moreover, the Caste War in Yucatán, both a secessionist movement and a racial war between Spanish Mexicans and Maya Indians, raged intermittently through the 1840s and 1850s, further undermining Mexico's political stability.

Jeffrey M. Pilcher

BIBLIOGRAPHY

Morner, Magnus. *Race Mixture in the History of Latin America.* 1967.

Reed, Nelson. *The Caste War of Yucatán.* 1964.

See also **Class Structure in Mexico**

Castro, José

A native Californio, José Castro (c. 1810–1860), was military commander of the Mexican province during the war with the United States. During his prior political career, he had worked for California's independence, but unlike some of the other Californios who also supported separation of California from Mexico, Castro remained hostile to any plan that would allow a U.S. takeover of the province. With the Californio expulsion in 1845 of the last Mexican-appointed governor of California, Manuel Micheltorena, Colonel Castro exhibited fierce patriotism in his role as California's military commander. When Capt. John C. Frémont led a well-armed party of Anglo-Americans into the vicinity of Monterey in early 1846 (ostensibly to keep an eye on British intrigues to take control), Castro brought a superior Californio force against him, forcing him to retreat into California's interior valleys.

Regional jealousies divided the small Californio community, just when it needed to unite to resist a foreign enemy. Also a Californio, Governor Pío Pico, housed in Los Angeles, viewed Castro's raising of a military force with suspicion, believing that Castro intended to use it to seize all power. Thus, with the news that Anglo-American settlers near Sutter's Fort had risen in the Bear Flag Revolt against the Californios, the latter were at each others' throats. The Bear Flaggers' excuse for their own behavior was their fear that Castro would forcibly expel them from the province. Shortly thereafter, U.S. naval forces landed at Monterey and demanded Castro's surrender. Although Castro refused, he could not effectively resist. He disbanded his small force and fled to Sonora, where he pleaded to the Mexican government for military assistance, which was not forthcoming. At war's end, Castro returned to Monterey, only to depart for Baja California in 1853, where he was a Mexican official until his death in 1860.

Ward M. McAfee

BIBLIOGRAPHY

Bancroft, Hubert Howe. *History of California.* 7 vols. 1886–1890.

Harlow, Neal. *California Conquered: War and Peace in the Pacific, 1846–1850.* 1982.

Castro, Salvador Bermúdez de

See **Bermúdez de Castro, Salvador**

Casualties

See **Numbers and Losses**

Catholic Church

The Roman Catholic Church was the center of Mexican towns, geographically and spiritually. For almost three hundred years, the church had held a virtual monopoly on Mexico's spiritual life. Catholicism was the only faith permitted by law. Religious freedom was considered almost immoral even though the Catholic priests earned a reputation for debauchery. Most of the Mexican clergy were barely literate enough to read the mass. The Catholic Church enjoyed political and economic privileges guaranteed by law including *fueros* and an exemption from taxes. *Fueros* guaranteed that clergymen were exempt from having to stand trial in civil courts even if they were charged with a violation of civil law; they were literally guaranteed a trial by their peers. Many joined the clergy solely to enjoy these privileges, not for religious reasons.

The church was the largest single property owner in Mexico and thus supported conservative governments because this faction protected their rights and privileges. This protection came at the cost of public policies that favored the rich and widened the gulf between prosperity and poverty among Mexicans.

The Catholic Church seemed indifferent to the U.S. settlers in Texas even though it was a part of Mexico. The leader of the settlement in Texas, Stephen F. Austin, wrote several letters asking the church to send a priest to perform sacraments such as marriage and baptism. The visits of any priest were infrequent at best. The unresponsiveness of the Catholic Church contributed to increasing hostility toward Mexico.

The Catholic Church in the United States differed greatly from its Mexican counterpart. Catholic priests in the United States were some of the most highly educated people in the

Mexican priests. Robert A. Wilson, *Mexico: Its Peasants and Its Priests*, 1856

country. Religious institutions, including the Catholic Church, gave up their political and economic privileges as separation of church and state continued to develop. When the U.S.–Mexican War began, the United States was in the middle of the Second Great Awakening, a revivalistic fervor that swelled the membership of many Christian churches. The Protestant denominations were the most popular, and many started political and social reforms to improve the lives of the poor.

Before the U.S.–Mexican War began, many U.S. Protestants were becoming increasingly hostile toward the Catholic Church. There were violent anti-Catholic riots in Boston and Philadelphia. These feelings resulted from resentment of the large number of Catholic immigrants, feelings that the war did not help alleviate. The United States was at war with a nation whose people were predominantly Catholic. Some Southern Baptists and Methodists even justified the war as a Protestant crusade against the Roman Catholic faith.

During the war, some U.S. soldiers were less than complimentary about the Catholic Church. Many volunteers said that Catholicism was a misdirected and misbegotten Christian heresy, and they wrote letters home that contained degrading comments about Mexican churches, including comments about the lack of pews and that the people had to kneel or stand on the bare floor. These circumstances made the often rich church furnishings seem ridiculous. Many churches had gold, silver, jewels, tapestries, statues, and pic-

tures of the saints, which seemed out of place in congregations of paupers.

Many U.S. soldiers were openly anti-Catholic. Some even mocked or mimicked the services and practices of the Catholic Church. Most of these anti-Catholic feelings resulted from a simple lack of appreciation for the devotions and traditions of the church. The soldiers did not respect the Mexican priests either.

Not all U.S. troops were anti-Catholic. Many enlisted soldiers were Catholics of Irish or German descent. Some soldiers even attended the services while they were in Mexico. Others were stationed in monasteries, and some drank and gambled with monks. On the home front, U.S. Roman Catholics were some of the most loyal and vocal war supporters. Some reasons for this support were their traditional obedience to authority, eagerness to demonstrate patriotism against a Catholic enemy, and sensitivity to anti-Catholicism. The U.S. Catholic Church also hoped to increase its numbers if any territory were gained from Mexico.

President James K. Polk, hoping to offset anti-Catholicism in the military, asked the U.S. Catholic bishops to send priests with the U.S. soldiers into Mexico. During the war, a proclamation from Washington, D.C., was sent with Gen. Zachary Taylor, guaranteeing the safety of Catholics and their churches and trying to dispel the fear and distrust of Protestants held by most Mexicans.

As the conflict deepened, the Mexican government increasingly resented the Catholic Church because of its huge influence over the economy of Mexico. The Catholic Church could have supplied the financial resources needed for the war efforts, but refused. The government tried to persuade the church to help by pointing out that the war was against a Protestant nation and urged the church to supply more money and fewer prayers, but to no avail.

Betsy Wingert

BIBLIOGRAPHY

Bauer, K. Jack. *The Mexican War, 1846–1848.* 1974.

Callcott, Wilfrid Hardy. *Church and State in Mexico, 1833–1857.* 1965.

Johannsen, Robert W. *To the Halls of the Montezumas: The Mexican War in the American Imagination.* 1985.

McCaffrey, James M. *Army of Manifest Destiny: The American Soldier in the Mexican War, 1846–1848.* 1992.

Santoni, Pedro. *Mexicans at Arms: Puro Federalists and the Politics of War, 1845–1848.* 1996.

Schroeder, John H. *Mr. Polk's War: American Opposition and Dissent, 1846–1848.* 1973.

Caudillos

The *caudillo* was a regional chieftain who derived his power from control of local resources of men and supplies. Classical *caudillismo* took the form of armed patron-client bands, held together by personal ties of dominance and submission and by a common desire to obtain wealth by force of arms. The *caudillo*'s domain could expand from a local to a national scale, but in making the transition his power remained personal, not institutional, and was directed less toward policy making than to seizure of offices and resources.

The *caudillo* was a product of the War of Independence, when the colonial state was disrupted, institutions were destroyed, and rural people grouped into bands under leaders who promised plunder and subsistence. *Caudillos* gradually grew into war leaders who could assemble irregular forces and place them at the service of liberation. *Caudillismo* was then perpetuated by postwar conflicts between center and periphery, between rival *caudillos,* or between political enemies. In some cases the *caudillo* was representative of a large kinship elite, acting on behalf of landowners or regional interests, often defending local economies against the policy of the center. The *caudillo* was seen as a benefactor, or distributor of patronage. *Caudillos* attracted clients by promising their followers office, land, or other rewards when they reached power; and clients attached themselves to a powerful patron in the expectation of preferment when he reached the top.

The *caudillo* fulfilled a further role: he was the "necessary gendarme" in the service of the republican elites. Constitutions alone could not guarantee life and property; the militancy of urban mobs and rural rebels could be contained only by a personal power more effective than a constitution. For the elites the *caudillo* was the strongman, with enough influence over the popular classes to keep them in order. The *caudillos* were not populists, however; they manipulated the popular sectors and gave them an illusion of participation without altering their position in the existing structure. While the *caudillos* led a coalition of interest groups, they were not mere agents of the elite. Their indispensibility gave them leverage and enabled them to act with independent sovereignty. As private landowners and patrons they had their own power base, and this was usually stronger than that of any single component of the coalition.

The War of Independence in Mexico called for *caudillos,* men who as heads of client networks already possessed local bases of power and resources and could be recruited to fight or raise supplies. The practice survived into the republic. Mexico inherited not only insurgent *caudillos* but also a professional military previously loyal to Spain. The majority of Mexican military personnel were not of a landed class or the recipients of any income independent of their salaries. The army was therefore tempted to seek shortcuts to riches by periodically intervening in politics to secure its share of the budget. In searching for a power base, therefore, the Mexican *caudillo* had to deal not only with landowners and financiers but also with the military.

Antonio López de Santa Anna learned these lessons early in his career. In Vera Cruz, the province of his birth, he had an extended network of friends and relations. From his service in the royal army he acquired military contacts that he was able to bring to the cause of independence. He cultivated his regional base, and when he made his push for power at the center, he had behind him the support, and the expectations, of his provincial followers. Santa Anna exemplified a number of trends in contemporary Mexico: the bias toward regional autonomy, the ability of local chieftains to act independently, and the strength of personal networks. The size of the country, the underdevelopment of the economy, and the weakness of infrastructure all favored the existence of regional *caudillos,* who often acted in open defiance of the central government, if not in complete rebellion. Yet *caudillismo* of this kind was not mere anarchy: through their influence, derived from military reputation and economic position, regional chieftains became spokesmen of the rights of their countrymen; at the same time they channeled a modicum of government authority into their state, acting in effect as power brokers between the center and the periphery.

Santa Anna also fulfilled the role of prime protector. His followers in Vera Cruz and occasional allies among bureaucrats, clergy, and financiers gave him a civilian support base. But his principal source of power was the regular army, and the military in turn looked to him for patronage and promotion. It was Santa Anna's ability to recruit, assemble, and motivate the military to meet particular crises that preserved his reputation with the politicians and explains their repeated readiness to forget the past and recall him to power. Santa Anna was regarded as the last resort against anarchy, the ultimate *caudillo*. Nevertheless, the *caudillo* system did not serve Mexico well during the war with the United States. Then the regional *caudillos* held back from Santa Anna; personal influence and client allegiance proved to be poor substitutes for strong institutions and an effective national army.

John Lynch

BIBLIOGRAPHY

Díaz Díaz, Fernando. *Caudillos y caciques: Antonio López de Santa Anna y Juan Alvarez.* 1972.

Lynch, John. *Caudillos in Spanish America, 1800–1850.* 1992.

Slatta, Richard W., ed. *Bandidos: The Varieties of Latin American Banditry.* 1987.

Wolf, Eric R., and Edward C. Hansen. "*Caudillo* Politics: A Structural Analysis." *Comparative Studies in Society and History* 9 (1966–1967): 168–179.

Causes of the War

This entry includes two articles, which examine the causes of the conflict from two different perspectives: that of Mexico and that of the United States. See also **Claims and Damages; Expansionism and Imperialism.**

Mexican Perspective

Mexico became an independent nation in 1821 with many of its colonial structures intact and persistent doubts about its own identity. The new country's leaders had recently been royalists, and their allegiance to Spain had been among the most resolute in Spanish America. The Mexican elite at independence was a political hybrid, divided by many interests and split by numerous loyalties. Social and racial divisions were accompanied by a distinct lack of national unity. From Yucatán to California, individual states defied the constitution and mocked the federal government. Conservatives blamed the national disorder on the Constitution of 1824, a federal document modeled on that of the United States and influenced by Spanish liberalism and Mexico's own regionalist experience. Liberals blamed the persistence of corporate rights, which guaranteed a privileged position to the army and the clergy. While Mexicans fought each other, they were united in one thing: a determination to preserve intact the territory claimed from Spain and won in the War of Independence.

Mexican statesmen were deeply suspicious of the intentions of the United States, which was heir to a different political tradition, home of a different culture and religion, and openly interested in undefended and uncolonized frontier provinces. Texas, the scene of growing conflict between Anglo-American settlers and Mexican institutions, became the first test of U.S. intentions and Mexican reactions. The restoration of centralism by Antonio López de Santa Anna and his associates in 1835, while it did little to further the cause of national unity, destabilized the distant provinces of Mexico and left them vulnerable to external threat. Destruction of states' rights was more keenly felt by the frontier societies that did not conform to the Mexican model. The Mexicans were not intransigent over the issues of religion and slavery, and the clash of cultures was not in itself a cause of war. But Mexican rule in Texas was threatened by sheer weight of numbers; by 1835 there were thirty-five thousand Anglo-Americans in Texas and fewer than eight thousand Mexicans. In 1830 the Mexican government decided to stop further immigration, to enforce Mexican laws, and to place higher duties on foreign imports. At the same time Mexico offered residents of Texas a reformed administration, greater representation in the state legislature, and access to a form of common law and trial by jury. But Mexico did not have the power or the presence in Texas to enforce a policy of either repression or conciliation. In any case, positions on both sides were hardening. There was a war party in Texas that went beyond defense of local autonomy, rejected consensus, and prepared for rebellion. In Mexico the rise to power of Santa Anna was a warning to all federalists that only the center ruled, and this was followed by his decision to impose a military solution in the name of a centralized state and a nationalist policy.

Aggression caused further problems for Mexico. When, in February 1836, Santa Anna led an army of six thousand across the Río Grande to crush the rebellion in Texas, he changed the terms of the dispute, even for moderate Texians, from defense of states' rights against central government into one of independence against a foreign enemy. Observing that resistance came not only from native Texians but also from volunteers from outside Texas, he issued a decree that all foreigners caught under arms on Mexican soil were to be shot. The subsequent killing of prisoners helped convince Texians that they were at war to save themselves from military despotism and to increase support for their cause in the United States. In the end Santa Anna was defeated and the Texians won their independence by force of arms. The Mexican congress refused to recognize Texas independence but was powerless to prevent it. A greater danger would arise if the Republic of Texas were annexed by the United States. This did not happen immediately—it was delayed by the issue of slavery—but the trend had begun: the United States was defined as an expansionist state and Mexico was its victim.

Political opinion in Mexico was divided over Texas. No one was prepared to fight or to be taxed for a campaign of reconquest. To this extent nationalism was an expression of internal politics rather than foreign policy. Conservatives argued that the incorporation of the rebel state into the United States would bring that powerful neighbor too close to central Mexico and should be interpreted as an act of war. The liberals were split. While radicals favored war, moderates argued that Mexico could not win a war with the United States and should negotiate over Texas. When annexation came in 1845, it was regarded by the Mexicans as a declaration of war. On its own this would appear an insufficient cause for conflict; but in the context of U.S. expansion along the whole of northern Mexico it was one that Mexicans could no longer ignore. If Texas were taken, could California be retained?

California was important to Mexico not only for its potential wealth but also as the western fortress of a long frontier. Many residents of California wanted space to manage their own affairs free of interference by a government in a remote metropolis. In this case, California viewed Mexico as an imperial power, while Mexico viewed California as a distant colony. Mexico did not send an army to California because, with turmoil nearer home and expenditure out of control, it had no troops to spare; this allowed California considerable autonomy without being propelled into revolt or, necessarily, into the grasp of the United States. But Mexicans saw this as a possibility. The U.S. seizure of Monterey, California, in 1842, attempts to buy California, and rising immigration alerted Mexicans to the intentions of the United States. By 1845 the Mexican press had completely fused the annexation of Texas with the danger to California. And again the double weakness of Mexico, unable either to colonize or to garrison the state, was manifest. Meanwhile, in New Mexico the failure of the Mexican government either to devolve or to reform its administration provoked a revolt in 1837, one with elements of class conflict but not to the immediate advantage of the United States. The Mexican government, however, was convinced that New Mexico was another victim of U.S. subversion and that the whole of the Mexican north was now at risk unless the United States was halted. The Mexican press did not hesitate to invoke culture and religion, to suggest that Mexicans, along with blacks and Native Americans, were perceived as inferior beings by their northern neighbor and to dispute the suggestion that the United States would make better use of these great territorial resources. But these were subsidiary arguments. In the final analysis the war with the United States was viewed by most Mexicans as a just war in defense of Mexican rights and Mexican interests.

John Lynch

BIBLIOGRAPHY
Barker, Eugene C. *Mexico and Texas, 1821–1835.* 1928.
Binkley, William C. *The Texas Revolution.* 1952.
Brack, Gene M. *Mexico Views Manifest Destiny, 1821–1846: An Essay on the Origins of the Mexican War.* 1975.
Castañeda, Carlos E. *The Mexican Side of the Texas Revolution.* 1928.
Weber, David J. *The Mexican Frontier, 1821–1846: The American Southwest under Mexico.* 1982.

U.S. Perspective

Although the U.S. decision for war against Mexico resulted from a clash of arms along the Río Grande in April 1846, the antagonisms that rendered the war acceptable to the U.S. public were long in developing. Still, those antagonisms did not define any U.S. interests whose resolution dictated war. Mexico's divided and ineffective regimes were unable to protect the possessions and rights of individual U.S. citizens in Mexico from robbery, theft, and other illegal actions, resulting in numerous claims against Mexico; however, U.S. citizens were under no obligation to do business in Mexico and understood the risks of transporting goods and money in that country. Even as the United States, after 1842, attempted futilely to collect from Mexico the $2 million awarded its citizens by a claims commission, it was more deeply in debt to England over speculative losses. Thus, if President James K. Polk decided to sacrifice human and material resources in a war against Mexico, his objectives would be far more than the enforcement of claims.

For Polk, in 1845, the immediate source of U.S.–Mexican tension—and possible war—was Texas. The Mexican government had repeatedly warned that it would not tolerate that province's annexation to the United States. Congress voted annexation by joint resolution during President John Tyler's final days in the White House. By the time Polk, after taking office in March, completed the annexation process, Gen. Juan Almonte, the Mexican minister in Washington, D.C., had departed for Vera Cruz to sever his country's relations with the United States. To defend Texas from a possible Mexican invasion, Polk ordered Gen. Zachary Taylor to move from Fort Jesup, Louisiana, down the Gulf Coast to Corpus Christi on the Nueces River. What Polk desired of Mexico was the acceptance not only of the loss of Texas but also of Texas's claims to the Río Grande boundary. Polk's pressure on Mexico would bring either a negotiated boundary settlement or war, depending on the acceptability of his demands to the insecure and distraught Mexican government.

When Congress, in December 1845, prepared to accept Texas into the Union, Polk's attention had shifted from the Río Grande to his major objective, Mexican California, especially the bays of Yerba Buena (later San Francisco) and San Diego. During the summer of 1845, Thomas O. Larkin, a U.S. merchant in Monterey, warned the U.S. government of apparent British and French designs on the region. Polk appointed Larkin a special agent to report British and French activities and to encourage the California populace to cast its destiny with the United States. Mexican officials, recognizing California's vulnerability to U.S. encroachment by land and sea, approached British minister Charles Bankhead for help, but the British government was not prepared to contest U.S. expansionism in California.

Polk aggravated Mexican fears when in November 1845 he sent John Slidell of Louisiana to Mexico City to offer as much as $40 million if Mexico would agree to a boundary along the Río Grande to New Mexico, then westward to the Pacific Ocean. Slidell's mission to Mexico seemed to offer Mexico the choice between acceptance of a body of concrete diplomatic demands or eventual war. Although Slidell's instructions included a settlement for the Río Grande boundary alone in exchange for the cancellation of claims, Mexican officials understood that such an arrangement would merely postpone confrontation over California. The Mexican government thus refused to recognize Slidell's presence. By early 1846, writers and officials who shared Polk's impatience were prepared to deny Mexico the luxury of further delay. In January, the Washington *Union* publicly threatened Mexico with war if it rejected the demands of the United States: "The result of such a course on her part may compel us to resort to more decisive measures . . . to obtain the settlement of our legitimate claims." As Slidell prepared to leave Mexico in March, he reminded the U.S. administration: "Depend upon it, we can never get along well with them, until we have given them a good drubbing." Members of the Democratic press began to clamor for war.

Such sentiment, widespread and threatening, placed Mexico under intense diplomatic pressure to negotiate away its territories, although Mexico was under no moral obligation to do so. For Mexican editors and officials the U.S. offer of money for California was, in reality, a demand for capitulation. Polk could easily have reduced his demands on Mexico to obtain an immediate settlement or permitted U.S.–Mexican relations to drift until a more propitious time. Instead, backed by the vast superiority of U.S. military power and burgeoning anti-Mexican sentiment, Polk escalated pressure on Mexico. What drove his program of escalation to the point of war was his determination to gain objectives that lay outside the possibilities of peaceful negotiations.

In January 1846 Polk instructed Taylor to advance from the Nueces River, through contested territory, to the Río Grande. In March, Taylor established his headquarters on the north bank of the Río Grande, opposite the Mexican village of Matamoros. In response, Mexican general Pedro Ampudia arrived at Matamoros on 11 April and ordered Taylor to withdraw to Corpus Christi. When Taylor refused,

Mexican officials again approached Bankhead for support. The British minister, suspecting that Mexican patience was wearing thin, warned the Mexicans to avoid any show of force along the Río Grande. Polk anticipated a clash but did nothing to avoid it. On 6 May he received a dispatch from Taylor dated 15 April, that reported no action. He confided to his diary: "No actual collision has taken place, though the probabilities are that hostilities might take place soon."

On 9 May the U.S. cabinet agreed that the president should respond to any Mexican attack on Taylor's forces with an immediate war message to Congress. On 23 April the Mexican government had issued a proclamation declaring a defensive war against the United States. One day later Mexican soldiers fired on a detachment of U.S. dragoons. Taylor's report reached Washington, D.C., on Saturday, 9 May. Polk drafted his war message on Sunday and sent it to Congress the following day. With U.S. forces directly engaged with Mexican forces on the Río Grande frontier, Polk's assertion that U.S. blood had been shed on U.S. soil ensured an immediate and overwhelming congressional acceptance of his war against Mexico.

Norman A. Graebner

BIBLIOGRAPHY

Bauer, K. Jack. *The Mexican War, 1846–1848.* 1974.

Graebner, Norman A. *Foundations of American Foreign Policy: A Realist Appraisal from Franklin to McKinley.* 1985.

Pletcher, David M. *The Diplomacy of Annexation: Texas, Oregon, and the Mexican War.* 1973.

Singletary, Otis A. *The Mexican War.* 1960.

Smith, Justin H. *The War with Mexico.* 2 vols. 1919. Reprint, 1963.

Cazneau, Jane McManus Storm

Journalist Jane McManus Storm [later Cazneau] (1807–1878) was born in Troy, New York, and attended Emma Willard's Troy Female Seminary. She married, gave birth to a son, and separated from her husband. In December 1832 she came to Texas on the advice of Aaron Burr and planned a German settlement on her land grant near the Waco Indian village. Unsettled politics discouraged settlers, however, and the few Germans who returned with her to Matagorda in 1834 settled near the Colorado River. Named as a correspondent in the Aaron Burr divorce case, she deeded away her headright to cover debts and left Texas in 1839. Storm wrote to supplement her income and contributed to several newpapers, sometimes using the pseudonym "Montgomery." In 1844 she promoted Texas annexation in the New York *Sun* and *U.S. Magazine and Democratic Review.*

In December 1845 Moses Y. Beach, publisher of the *Sun,* hired her as Washington correspondent under the signature of Montgomery. Fluent in Spanish, she was sent to Mexico with Beach by President James K. Polk in December 1846. Traveling under British passports, Beach and Storm contacted clergy and peace factions in Mexico to bring an end to the war and made secret arrangements more favorable to the United States than those later negotiated at Guadalupe Hidalgo. The United States would capture Vera Cruz to display its superior power and its readiness to march to the capital, then a "crisis" could be declared that would allow Mexican capitulation on honorable terms. From 11 December 1846 to 26 March 1847 the New York *Sun* printed dispatches written by Montgomery from 1 December to 13 January.

On 27 February elite National Guard units, called the *polkos,* began a revolt in Mexico City to depose acting president Valentín Gómez Farías. Leaving Mexico City in upheaval, Storm traveled alone to Vera Cruz and told Gen. Winfield Scott of the peace plan. Meanwhile, with no "crisis" because of the invasion's delay, Gen. Antonio López de Santa Anna returned to Mexico City and quelled the revolt, and the peace plan failed. Beach fled Mexico City and arrived in Tampico on 10 April; he immediately steamed to Vera Cruz and informed Scott of the conditions for peace and the most favorable route inland. When queried about his disregard of Storm's message, Beach later said that Scott cursed and lectured, "Never send messages of such importance by a plenipotentiary in petticoats." From 15 April to 24 May the New York *Sun* published twenty articles by Montgomery as she recorded events in Mexico City and Vera Cruz from March 8 through April 20. Scott began the siege of Vera Cruz on 9 March.

In 1848 Storm edited *La Verdad,* a bilingual paper financed by the Havana Club. About 1850 she married William L. Cazneau, and they settled in Eagle Pass, Texas. Beginning in 1853, the Cazneaus were special agents for Presidents Franklin Pierce, James Buchanan, and Andrew Johnson in an unsuccessful attempt to gain recognition of the Dominican Republic as a homeland for freed slaves. They later became involved with the scandals of the Ulysses S. Grant administration. Storm published eight books on U.S. territorial and commercial expansion into Texas and the Caribbean before drowning in a shipwreck 12 December 1878.

Linda Sybert Hudson

BIBLIOGRAPHY

Beach, M. S. "A Secret Mission to Mexico." *Scribner's Monthly* 18 (May 1879): 136–140.

May, Robert E. "'Plenipotentiary in Petticoats': Jane M. Cazneau and American Foreign Policy in the Mid-Nineteenth Century." In *Women and American Foreign Policy: Lobbyists, Critics, and Insiders,* edited by Edward P. Crapol. 2d ed. 1992.

Reilly, Tom. "Jane McManus Storms: Letters from the Mexican War, 1846–1848." *Southwestern Historical Quarterly* 85 (July 1981): 21–44.

Cerralvo

An ancient Mexican town in the state of Nuevo León, Cerralvo was founded in 1578 by Don Luis Carvajal de la Cueva, viceroy of El Nuevo Reyno de León. The town, whose name is thought to have been derived from the Spanish words *cerro* and *alba,* lies on the slopes of a white limestone foothill of the Sierra Madre Oriental. During colonial times more than twenty-seven major silver mines located in the Cerralvo district furnished a vast supply of coinage for Spain. About fifty miles southwest of Camargo, the town had a population of about eighteen hundred at the time of the U.S.–Mexican War. Most buildings were made of stone, and many private residences had flowing water via a system of canals from a vast spring south of town.

Cerralvo was on the main line of advance of the U.S. Army from Camargo to Monterrey and thus became a forward supply base. By February 1847, the Mexican army initiated offensive operations to drive U.S. forces from northern Mexico. Gen. Antonio López de Santa Anna's main forces marched north from San Luis Potosí to attack U.S. forces at Saltillo. The second prong of this attack was to be Gen. José Urrea's division of light cavalry, which entered northern Mexico through Tula Pass, near Victoria. General Urrea's goal was to sever the U.S. lines of supply and communication to Saltillo from the Río Grande, which extended through Cerralvo. Mexican forces recaptured Cerralvo and held the town for more than a month, while an anxious U.S. public awaited word on the fate of U.S. forces at Saltillo. In March 1847 a force of Ohio and Kentucky volunteers were dispatched from Monterrey with a train of 160 empty wagons to resupply U.S. forces. After a spirited skirmish with Mexican defenders, supply lines were reopened. This wagon train pushed on to Camargo, bringing the first official news of the U.S. victory at Buena Vista and much needed supplies to Gen. Zachary Taylor's army on a return trip to Saltillo.

The U.S. garrison at Cerralvo continued to be a target for Mexican guerrilla raids throughout the remainder of the war.

Joseph E. Chance

BIBLIOGRAPHY

Giddings, Luther. *Sketches of the Campaign in Northern Mexico in Eighteen Hundred Forty-Six and Seven.* 1853.

Scribner, Benjamin Franklin. *Camp Life of a Volunteer: A Campaign in Mexico, or a Glimpse at Life in Camp by "One Who Has Seen the Elephant."* 1847.

Wood, Conan T. "Cerralvo as the Mother City of the Valley."

Selections from the Collected Papers of the Lower Rio Grande Valley Historical Society, 1949–1979.

Cerro Gordo, Battle of

The Battle of Cerro Gordo occurred 17 and 18 April 1847 when a Mexican army under Gen. Antonio López de Santa Anna attempted to block the march of Gen. Winfield Scott's army from Vera Cruz to Jalapa.

With the fall of Vera Cruz Scott needed to move his force into the Mexican highlands before the onset of the yellow fever season. Hoping to trap Scott on the coast, Santa Anna established a strong defensive position along the National Road, outside the village of Plan del Río, three days' march from Vera Cruz. Just beyond the village the road entered a long, narrow defile. Three artillery batteries commanded the defile from the south, and two elite infantry regiments, supported by more artillery, blocked any exit from the defile. The summit of El Telégrafo, a large hill locally known as Cerro Gordo, dominated the entire battlefield.

On 11 April elements of Brig. Gen. David E. Twiggs's division of regulars surprised Mexican lancers in the village of Plan del Río, and it quickly became clear that the Mexicans were deployed in force beyond the village. Twiggs's engineer, Lt. Pierre G. T. Beauregard, scouted the Mexican works and reported that possession of a second hill, El Atalaya, just short of El Telégrafo, would allow U.S. troops to flank the entire Mexican line. Twiggs, however, decided to force the Mexican positions head-on, sending a report of his situation to Scott, estimating the Mexican force at four thousand.

Maj. Gen. Robert Patterson's division of volunteers arrived the next day, and his brigade commanders, Brig. Gen. Gideon Pillow and Brig. Gen. James Shields, persuaded Twiggs to delay his attack for twenty-four hours. On 14 April Patterson, bedridden by fever, took himself off the sick list and suspended the attack until the arrival of General Scott. Scott ordered a more complete reconnaissance, and Capt. Robert E. Lee reported that Santa Anna had established no significant positions on his left, relying on the difficulty of the terrain to keep Scott's troops on the road. Lee believed it was possible to swing around the Mexican left and seize the Jalapa road behind El Telégrafo, at the village of Cerro Gordo. Scott ordered the trail Lee had blazed widened and planned an attack for the morning of 18 April. Twiggs's division, supported by Shields's brigade, would

---

**Battle of Cerro Gordo
Order of Battle
17–18 April 1847**

Mexican Forces

Commander
    Gen. Antonio López de Santa Anna

Infantry
    Grenadier Guards of the Supreme Powers
    1st Light Regiment
    2d Light Regiment
    3d Light Regiment
    4th Light Regiment
    3d Line Regiment (destroyed)
    4th Line Regiment (destroyed)
    5th Line Regiment
    6th Line Regiment (destroyed)
    11th Line Regiment
    Puebla Regiment, Activo Militia (destroyed)

Cavalry
    Hussars of the Supreme Powers
    Light Regiment
    5th Regiment
    9th Regiment
    Tulancingo Cuirrasiers
    Oaxaca Regiment, Activo Militia

Artillery
    32 pieces

U.S. Forces

Commander
    Gen. Winfield Scott

Infantry
    2d U.S. Infantry
    3d U.S. Infantry
    4th U.S. Infantry
    7th U.S. Infantry
    8th U.S. Infantry
    1st U.S. Artillery (serving as infantry)
    2d U.S. Artillery (serving as infantry)
    3d U.S. Artillery (serving as infantry)
    4th U.S. Artillery (serving as infantry)
    1st U.S. Regiment of Mounted Rifles (dismounted)
    Company A, U.S. Engineers
    3d Illinois Volunteers
    4th Illinois Volunteers
    1st New York Volunteers
    1st Tennessee Volunteers
    2d Tennessee Volunteers
    1st Kentucky Volunteers
    1st Pennsylvania Volunteers
    2d Pennsylvania Volunteers
    1st South Carolina Volunteers
    William's Independent Company of Kentucky Volunteers

Cavalry
    2d U.S. Dragoons (part)
    1st Tennessee Volunteer Cavalry

Artillery
    Ordnance Department Siege Train

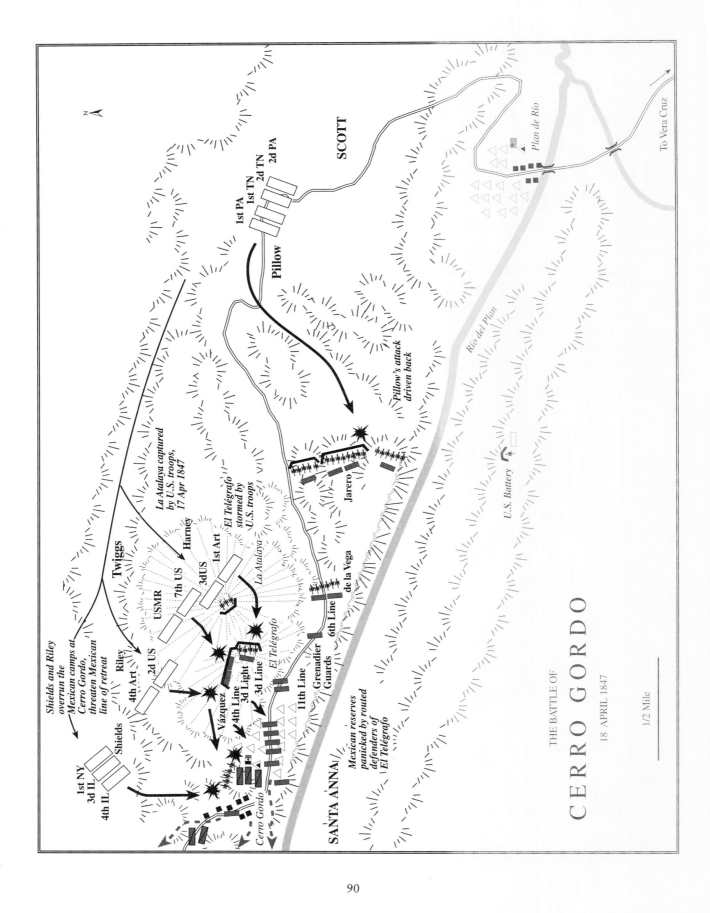

THE BATTLE OF

CERRO GORDO

18 APRIL 1847

1/2 Mile

*Shields and Riley
overrun the
Mexican camps at
Cerro Gordo,
threaten Mexican
line of retreat*

1st NY
3d IL
4th IL
Shields

*La Atalaya captured
by U.S. troops,
17 Apr 1847*

Twiggs
Riley
4th Art
2d US
USMR
7th US
3dUS
1st Art
Harney

*El Telégrafo
stormed by
U.S. troops*

La Atalaya

El Telégrafo

Vázquez
4th Line
3d Light
3d Line
11th Line
Grenadier
Guards
6th Line
de la Vega

Jarero

El Telégrafo

SANTA ANNA

*Mexican reserves
panicked by routed
defenders of
El Telégrafo*

Cerro Gordo

N

Pillow

1st PA
1st TN
2d TN
2d PA

SCOTT

*Pillow's attack
driven back*

Rio del Plan

U.S. Battery

Plan de Rio

To Vera Cruz

swing around the Mexican line, while Pillow's brigade attacked the main Mexican positions south of the road.

Twiggs moved to occupy attack positions on 17 April but soon ran into Mexican pickets, provoking Twiggs to order Col. William S. Harney to take the summit of El Atalaya. Harney's regulars cleared the top and pursued the retreating Mexicans down the far side and half way up El Telégrafo before being pinned down by Mexican fire. His men withdrew after dark, but the attack and the defection of a German-born U.S. soldier alerted Santa Anna to Scott's plan. Twiggs's attack, however, suggested that Scott's objective was El Telégrafo, not the Jalapa road, and Santa Anna reinforced his positions around El Telégrafo.

The next morning Harney's men stormed the summit of El Telégrafo, while Shields's men, supported by a brigade commanded by Col. Bennett Riley, swung to the right around the base of the hill into the Mexican camp at Cerro Gordo. Briefly stopped by a blast from a battery that severely wounded Shields, the volunteers regrouped under Col. Edward Baker of the 4th Illinois and stormed through the camp, seizing the village of Cerro Gordo and the Jalapa road. Pillow's attack stalled in confusion, but as soon as the Mexicans on Santa Anna's right realized they were cut off, they surrendered. Scott lost 63 killed and 353 wounded. His men killed or wounded an estimated 1,000 Mexicans, captured 3,000, and seized forty-three heavy guns. Santa Anna and his senior commanders escaped the battlefield, abandoning their personal effects and baggage, and 8,000 Mexican troops fled in disorder up the road to Jalapa.

The Cerro Gordo victory allowed Scott to move out of the coastal yellow fever zone and reorganize his army for its eventual descent into the Valley of Mexico.

Ronald L. Spiller

BIBLIOGRAPHY

Balentine, George. *Autobiography of an English Soldier in America.* 1853.

Brooks, Nathan C. *A Complete History of the Mexican War: Its Causes, Conduct, and Consequences, Comprising an Account of the Various Military and Naval Operations, from Its Commencement to the Treaty of Peace.* 1849. Reprint, 1965.

Furber, George C. *The Twelve Month Volunteer; or, Journal of a Private, in the Tennessee Regiment of Cavalry, in the Campaign in Mexico, 1846–7.* 1857.

Grant, Ulysses. *Ulysses Grant: Memoirs and Selected Letters.* Edited by Mary D. McFeely and William S. McFeely. 1990.

Peskin, Allan, ed. *Volunteers: The Mexican War Journals of Private Richard Coulter and Sergeant Thomas Barclay, Co. E, Second Pennsylvania Infantry.* 1991.

Tennery, Thomas. *The Mexican War Diary of Thomas Tennery.* Edited by D. E. Livingston-Little. 1970.

Weems, John. *To Conquer a Peace: The War between the United States and Mexico.* 1974.

Chapultepec, Battle of

A brief and bitter battle for a fortified hill, the last major obstacle to U.S. capture of Mexico City, was fought on 13 September 1847 between U.S. troops under Maj. Gen. Win-

**Battle of Chapultepec
Order of Battle
13 September 1847**

Mexican Forces

Commander
Gen. Nicolás Bravo

Infantry
1st Light Regiment
2d Light Regiment
3d Light Regiment
10th Line (destroyed)
Mexico Battalion
Corps of Cadets
Querétaro Battalion, Activo Militia
Toluca Battalion, Activo Militia
Hidalgo Battalion National Guard
Mina Battalion, National Guard
Unión Battalion, National Guard
Patria Battalion, National Guard
Matamoros de Morelia Battalion, National Guard
San Blas Battalion, National Guard

Artillery
7 pieces

U.S. Forces

Commander
Maj. Gen. Winfield Scott

Infantry
5th U.S. Infantry
6th U.S. Infantry
8th U.S. Infantry
9th U.S. Infantry
11th U.S. Infantry
12th U.S. Infantry
14th U.S. Infantry
15th U.S. Infantry
U.S. Voltigeur Regiment
U.S. Regiment of Mounted Rifles
U.S. Marine Battalion
1st New York Volunteers
2d Pennsylvania Volunteers
1st South Carolina Volunteers

Artillery
Company I, 1st U.S. Artillery (Magruder's Mounted Battery)
Company H, 3d U.S. Artillery (Steptoe's Battery)

Cavalry
Company C, 3d U.S. Dragoons

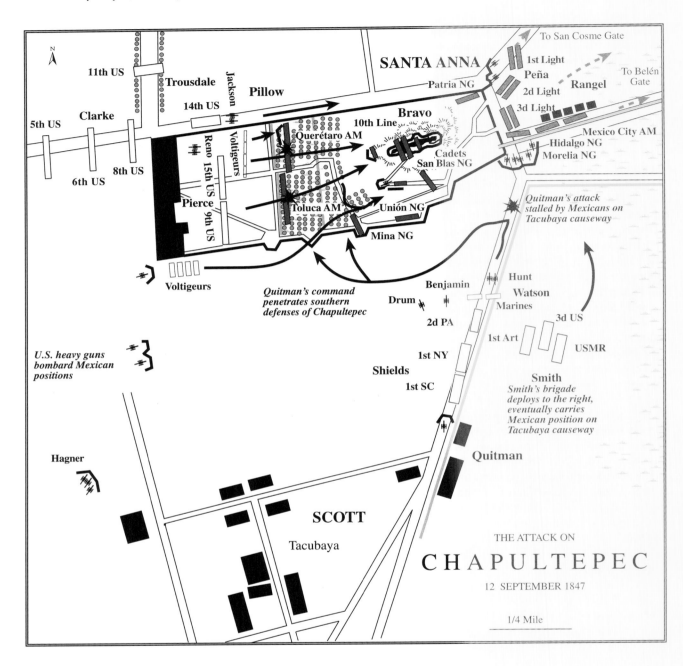

THE ATTACK ON

CHAPULTEPEC

12 SEPTEMBER 1847

1/4 Mile

field Scott and the Mexican forces of Gen. Antonio López de Santa Anna. Scott's forces totaled 7,180; Santa Anna had some 15,000, of whom about 1,000, including some 50 military academy cadets, defended Chapultepec under the command of Gen. Nicolás Bravo.

Chapultepec, with its old summer palace and the buildings of the Mexican military academy, towered two hundred feet over the surrounding plain and the two main causeways that led into the city from the west. Terrain made the hill unassailable from the north and east. Only from the south and

west did a gradual slope allow any possibility of an infantry attack. Although Santa Anna recognized Chapultepec's importance in defending the capital, he lacked time and materials to complete all preparations. Moreover, Bravo needed at least 2,000 troops to man the extensive works.

Scott's artillery bombarded Chapultepec throughout 12 September and resumed at dawn the following day. At 8 A.M. the bombardment lifted, and Brig. Gen. Gideon J. Pillow's division, supported by Brig. Gen. William J. Worth's division, attacked eastward through a swampy grove of cypress trees up the rocky slopes through a rain of Mexican artillery and musket fire. From the south Brig. Gen. John A. Quitman's division charged along the causeway. Farther to the east Brig. Gen. David E. Twiggs's division launched a diversionary attack. Halfway up the hill Pillow's assault seized a redoubt and reached the ditch at the castle's retaining wall. The canvas powder trains leading to mines were also cut, thus preventing them from exploding. Meanwhile, Quitman's attack burst through the southern defenses and linked up with its storming party under the castle wall. After some delay, scaling ladders arrived and were used to bridge the ditch and scale the wall. Despite the heavy fire from the parapet, so many ladders arose that fifty men could climb abreast. Soon the attackers rushed over the walls and swept into the castle. By 9:30 A.M. all opposition on Chapultepec had ended. The heroic and gallant young Mexican cadets—some no older than thirteen—would be immortalized as los Niños Héroes, the heroic children. Mexican soldiers not killed or captured fell back over the causeways to the city.

The loss of Chapultepec was a serious blow to Mexican resistance and set the stage for the U.S. capture of the Mexican capital and negotiations to end the war. In all, the Mexicans lost 1,800 men that morning. U.S. losses were one-quarter as many.

Adrian G. Traas

BIBLIOGRAPHY

Bauer, K. Jack. *The Mexican War, 1846–1848.* 1974.

Eisenhower, John S. D. *So Far from God: The U.S. War with Mexico, 1846–1848.* 1989.

McCaffrey, James M. *Army of Manifest Destiny: The American Soldier in the Mexican War, 1846–1848.* 1992.

Nevin, David. *The Mexican War.* 1978.

Smith, Justin H. *The War with Mexico.* 2 vols. 1919. Reprint, 1963.

See also Los Niños Héroes; Military Academy, **Mexican**

Chapultepec, Military Academy

See Military Academy, Mexican

Chase, Ann

A spy for the United States during the U.S.–Mexican War, Ann McClarmonde Chase (1809–1874) was born in Northern Ireland and moved to the Mexican gulf port of Tampico in 1834 after ten years' residence in the United States. She married the U.S. consul Franklin Chase at Tampico and together they operated a mercantile business. When an 1846 decree forced U.S. citizens to leave Mexican ports, Chase—

a British subject—remained in the city to manage the family store.

Between July and November 1846 she also became a spy for the United States. Living on the same plaza as the military barracks, Chase overheard important pronouncements by Tampican military officials. She began forwarding this information through letters to the U.S. Navy Gulf Squadron as early as July. Her ability to smuggle intelligence improved after a Mexican-approved visit with her husband on a British ship in August 1846, because she then believed that the British were allies on whom she could depend. No sources have indicated exactly how she conveyed her reports, but she likely smuggled them out via British soldiers.

Chase proved instrumental to the U.S. occupation of Tampico in November 1846, drawing a plan of the port that provided the U.S. Navy with important information about the city's fortifications. Chase may also have prompted the Mexican evacuation of Tampico by informing Mexican spies that between 25,000 and 30,000 U.S. soldiers were approaching the port. Most important, she informed the U.S. squadron of the Mexican withdrawal. That information persuaded the navy to capture the city without loss of life, allowing the port to become a staging point for troops from Gen. Zachary Taylor's army who joined Gen. Winfield Scott's expedition against Vera Cruz.

Shannon L. Baker

BIBLIOGRAPHY

The Franklin and Ann Chase Collection, Dallas Historical Society, Dallas, Texas.

Cherokees

A small branch of the Cherokee people, in the process of a lengthy, and sometimes forced, movement of the Cherokee Nation from the southeastern United States, migrated to Spanish Texas from 1819 to 1820. They were led by a chief named Duwali (commonly known as Bowl). In November 1822 the new Republic of Mexico gave them citizenship, naming them "Hispano Americans, and entitled to all the rights and privileges granted to such," and gave them permission to occupy land in the northeastern part of the Mexican province of Texas, where they peacefully farmed, traded, and raised families for almost twenty years. Within three years of the establishment of the Republic of Texas in 1836, however, a Texian army had driven the "Texas Cherokees"—nominally Hispano Americans—from their lands. Most of the Cherokees fled northward to Indian Territory, but several Cherokee leaders maintained allegiance to Mexico and established camps on the upper Brazos River. In 1840 a group of them joined a contingent of Cherokees from Indian Territory in an excursion south of the border to Monclova, Coahuila, where they petitioned Mexico for a land grant. Although the grant was denied, some, including Sequoyah (George Guess, creator of the Cherokee syllabary), relocated south of Texas along the lower Río Grande, in San Fernando, Coahuila.

The Cherokees' determination to regain their east Texas lands led them to ally with Mexican troops and other Native American groups for a series of minor military engagements during Mexican operations and invasions to recapture Texas from 1839 to 1842. The last skirmish occurred when Mexican general Adrian Woll captured San Antonio in the summer of 1842; ten or eleven Cherokees perished in battle at Salado Creek. Subsequently, the Republic of Texas took steps to mollify the Cherokees. In September 1843 and October 1844 the Cherokees and a number of other tribes signed treaties of friendship with the republic. Among the signatories was Duwali's son, Standing Bowls. During the period 1845 to 1848 Cherokees still resided in both Texas and Mexico and some migrated back and forth from Indian Territory to Texas to Mexico. Despite treaties made with the then defunct Republic of Texas, potential Cherokee hostility was worrisome to U.S. military officials. When the U.S.–Mexican War erupted in 1846, the Cherokees' Mexican settlements in Monclova were in the same Mexican state that was invaded by Gen. John E. Wool's troops as they marched from San Antonio to Saltillo, and also near the 1846 actions in which Gen. Zachary Taylor laid seige to Monterrey and captured Saltillo, the capital of Coahuila. There is no documentary evidence, however, that indicates Texas–Mexican Cherokee participation in actions against the United States during the war with Mexico.

Dianna Everett

BIBLIOGRAPHY

Everett, Dianna. *The Texas Cherokees: A People between Two Fires, 1819–1840*. 1990.

Foreman, Grant. "The Story of Sequoyah's Last Days." *Chronicles of Oklahoma* 12 (1934): 255–341.

Kendall, George. *Narrative of the Texan Santa Fe Expedition.* 1944.

Muckleroy, Anna. "The Indian Policy of the Republic of Texas." *Southwestern Historical Quarterly* 26 (1923): 188–196.

Sanchez Lamego, Miguel A. *The Second Mexican-Texas War.* 1972.

Smither, Harriet K., ed. "Diary of Adolphus Sterne." *Southwestern Historical Quarterly* 31 (1931): 262.

Winfrey, Dorman, and James M. Day, eds. Vol. 1 of *The Texas Indian Papers*. 1965.

Chihuahua, State of

Located on the northwestern frontier of Mexico, Chihuahua had long held political, economic, and military significance. Harsh in desert climate but rich in mineral wealth, this vast province also hosted grand haciendas with massive herds of cattle, sheep, and horses controlled by a clique of powerful families that drew their patrimony from the earliest days of the Spanish Empire. The principal cities in Chihuahua were its capital, Chihuahua City, and the Río Grande outpost of El Paso del Norte, the last true settlement before entering the vastness of New Mexico. The Camino Real ran from Mexico City through Chihuahua to Santa Fe and was later linked by a trail to St. Louis, Missouri, enhancing Chihuahua's position as a crossroads of commerce. Always a frontier province, Chihuahua had developed a sense of *patria chica* early in its development, relying on its own resources and leadership instead of those of Spain or, later, the Republic of Mexico. By 1821 Chihuahua had fallen onto hard times. The Mexican Wars of Independence had damaged or ruined many of its mines and haciendas, and a lack of military protection had laid its northern frontier open to Indian attack. Before long, politicians and patricians in Chihuahua began to set policy for the northwest Mexican frontier regardless of the intentions of Mexico City.

A critical influence on Chihuahua's sense of independence came in the 1820s and 1830s with the frequent arrival of trade caravans from the United States. These merchants not only boosted the Chihuahuan economy but also introduced its people to U.S. republican principles and to individual citizens of the United States. As tension between the United States and Mexico mounted in the early 1840s, Chihuahuans were torn between loyalty to Mexico and their economic interests with the United States. As a result, a perceptible lack of enthusiasm marked Chihuahua's mobilization for war.

This changed under the leadership of Governor Ángel Trías. Soldiers from Chihuahua City's Activo Battalion and its militia (Guardia Nacional) moved north to El Paso del Norte in the fall of 1846 to counter an invasion by Col. Alexander W. Doniphan's Missourians. On Christmas Day, units from Chihuahua City lost a skirmish with U.S. troops on the banks of the Río Grande at Brazito, a few miles north of El Paso. These Mexican troops then abandoned the region and moved across the wastes of the Chihuahuan Desert and, reinforced by additional militia, regulars, and active battalions from surrounding states, prepared positions near the Río Sacramento on the road leading to the capital. On 28 February 1847 Doniphan and his Missouri Mounted Rifles routed this sizable force, inflicting severe casualties on the Mexican defenders. The U.S. troops continued on to capture Chihuahua City on 1 March unopposed.

Entering the nearly deserted city, the Missourians simply appropriated homes and belongings. Within days an English-language newspaper appeared, and Doniphan's troops conducted pursuits of Apache marauders. Trade wagons loaded with goods from the United States rumbled in from the north, and local leaders made political accommodations with the U.S. officers, promising to carry on civil government and to protect the lives and property of U.S. citizens after the troops left on 28 April.

After the departure of U.S. troops, life in Chihuahua slowly returned to its prewar tempo. Many in Mexico City accused Chihuahuans of collaborating with U.S. forces. In 1848, as terms for a final peace treaty were discussed, a small faction of Chihuahuans actively but unsuccessfully campaigned to be annexed to the United States. In the later decades of the nineteenth century, Chihuahua continued to hold its semi-autonomous place in the Mexican nation and would maintain its role of shaping the national destiny while maintaining favorable ties to the United States.

Donald S. Frazier

BIBLIOGRAPHY

Eisenhower, John S. D. *So Far from God: The U.S. War with Mexico, 1846–1848*. 1989.

Magoffin, Susan S. *Down the Santa Fe Trail, 1846–47*. 1926.

China

A Mexican town in the state of Nuevo León about seventy-five miles southwest of Camargo, San Felipe de Jesús de China was founded about 1776. The village was known as "China" because the church built in the town was named for Saint Phillip de las Casas, a Jesuit martyred in 1697 at Nagasaki, Japan. China received its first mention in U.S. newspapers when the Texas Mounted Division, led by Maj. Gen. J. Pinckney Henderson, passed through on 17 September 1846. The Texans were covering the left flank of Gen. Zachary Taylor's advance on Monterrey. General Taylor had thought the route through China might be a way to reach Monterrey, but the road proved to be rocky and difficult for wagons.

During the U.S.–Mexican War, the town became important as a center for guerrilla resistance to the U.S. occupation of northern Mexico and at times was the headquarters of the noted Mexican guerrilla leaders Antonio Canales and Jesús Romero. On 22 February 1847 a raid on a U.S. supply train was launched from the town; the action involved guerrilla forces and the cavalry division of Brig. Gen. José Urrea. Mexican forces overtook the train near Ramos, burning the wagons and killing the teamsters. A company of Texas volunteers, led by the infamous Mabry B. "Mustang" Gray, attacked Rancho Guadalupe near China on the evening of 28 March 1847 and murdered twenty-four civilians in retaliation for the wagon train attack.

China was never burned in retaliation for harboring guerrillas, as was the fate of the nearby villages of Puntiagucla, Ramos, and many *ranchos* in northern Mexico accused of such activity during the war. On 13 April 1847, to pacify the town, six companies of the 1st Virginia Volunteer Regiment and one piece of artillery were ordered to garrison China.

The battalion of Virginians remained in China until 1 June 1847 when ordered to Buena Vista to replace the departing regiments of one-year volunteers whose terms of enlistment had expired. On 20 May 1847, two members of the Virginia regiment stationed in China, Lt. Washington L. Mahan and Lt. Carlton R. Munford, fought a duel that resulted in the death of both officers.

Joseph E. Chance

BIBLIOGRAPHY

Chance, Joseph E., ed. *Mexico under Fire*. 1994.

Wallace, Lee A., Jr. "The First Regiment of Virginia Volunteers, 1846–1848." *Virginia Magazine of History and Biography* 77 (1969): 46–77.

Churubusco

See **Contreras and Churubusco**

Civil War Generals

There were only fifteen years between the commencement of the U.S.–Mexican conflict and the commencement of the U.S. Civil War. Thus, the experience in Mexico provided valuable training to many of the U.S. officers who later participated in the Civil War.

In 1861 both the North and South sought experienced military leaders, and heroes of the U.S.–Mexican War were likely candidates. Appointments to the Confederate States Army included veteran generals Gideon J. Pillow and David E. Twiggs. Other senior officers who received commissions from the Confederate congress were Joseph E. Johnston, Albert Sidney Johnston, and Robert E. Lee. For the North, Generals James Shields and Robert Patterson returned to the military to lead troops, but like Pillow and Twiggs, they were quickly replaced by younger and more able men.

The field and company officers who had served in Mexico found places in both armies. More than 160 of these veteran officers had West Point training; nearly 350 had served in the volunteer corps. George B. McClellan, who as a young lieutenant had served under Gen. Winfield Scott in central Mexico, replaced Scott as general in chief of Union forces in 1861, illustrating the rise of men who had first experienced war on the battlefields of Mexico to the command of the Civil War armies.

Officers who had served together in Mexico sometimes found themselves facing former comrades, making the conflict especially difficult for those who had once shared hardship and danger together. After the war, many veterans of Mexico renewed acquaintances in the resurrected Aztec Club.

Richard Bruce Winders

BIBLIOGRAPHY

The Aztec Club. *Constitution of the Aztec Club of 1847 and List of Members*. 1928.

Bill, Alfred Hoyt. *Rehearsal for Conflict: The War with Mexico, 1846–1848*. 1947.

Waugh, John C. *The Class of 1846: From West Point to Appomattox*. 1994.

Waugh, John C. "The Proving Ground." *Civil War Times Illustrated* (April 1996).

See also **Aztec Club**

Claims and Damages

This entry includes two separate articles: **Mexican Claims** *and* **U.S. Claims**.

Mexican Claims

In 1826, the U.S. government began pressing Mexico for compensation for injuries suffered or financial losses caused by the Mexican government or by its citizens. Although Mexico acknowledged its responsibility for such injuries and losses, political instability and the continual bankrupt state of the treasury hindered its ability to pay.

Over the years, the United States aggressively pressed its claims. A U.S.–Mexican treaty signed in 1843 modified the form in which Mexico was to pay the $2.5 million in claims that an international board of arbitration had awarded the United States in 1839. The treaty also promised the negotiation of a later agreement to deal with still-pending U.S. claims as well as with claims of Mexico and its citizens against the United States.

Mexican claims for damages included those resulting from the filibuster expeditions led by James Long and others into Texas during the Mexican War of Independence; the seizure by U.S. ships, on several occasions during the 1830s, of Mexican naval craft in Mexican territorial waters and the auctioning of these vessels in New Orleans; and filibuster and Native American incursions of the late 1830s and early 1840s.

The issue of claims, particularly concerning those put forward by the United States, embittered relations between the two countries in the period prior to the U.S.–Mexican War. In 1845 President James K. Polk proposed the declaration of war against Mexico on that account should the latter refuse to settle U.S. claims by ceding a portion of its territory to the United States.

Following its victory in the subsequent conflict, the U.S. government linked the settlement of its claims to the question of war spoils. The Treaty of Guadalupe Hidalgo of February 1848 specified that the United States would pay $15 million to Mexico as indemnity for its cession to the United States of the territories of New Mexico and California and would also assume claims of U.S. citizens against Mexico to the amount of $3.25 million. Although the question of Mexican claims against the United States was not addressed, Article XI of the treaty provided a source for future claims by Mexico in that it held the United States responsible for preventing Indian incursions into Mexico and for punishing the offenders.

A Joint Claims Commission created in 1868 to settle outstanding claims presented by the United States and Mexico allowed the latter, out of 998 claims totaling $86,661,891.15, only $150,498.41, corresponding to 167 cases. Mexican claims relating to losses from Indian depredations and from filibuster incursions during the period between 1848 and the Gadsden Treaty of 1853 (366 claims totaling over $31 million) were dismissed on the grounds that the latter accord had released the United States from "all liability." Also dismissed were claims relating to the loss of Mexican-owned lands situated in the territories ceded to the United States in 1848, as well as claims made by Mexicans residing in these same territories who had subsequently become U.S. citizens. The bulk of the approved claims (a total of 150) were awarded to the inhabitants of Piedras Negras, whose town had been burned by troops under the command of Capt. James H. Callahan and Capt. William R. Henry in October 1855. A further $24,000 was awarded to Mexican claimants for losses incurred from a raid by a group of Texas volunteers against Sabinas Hidalgo, Coahuila, shortly after the signing of the treaty of 1848.

Lawrence D. Taylor

BIBLIOGRAPHY

Callahan, James Morton. *American Foreign Policy in Mexican Relations*. 1932.

Chavezmontes, Julio. *Heridas que no cierran*. 1988.

Conmy, Peter Thomas. *A Centennial Evaluation of the Treaty of Guadalupe Hidalgo, 1848–1948*. 1948.

Griswold del Castillo, Richard. *The Treaty of Guadalupe Hidalgo: A Legacy of Conflict*. 1990.

Kohl, Clayton C. *Claims as a Cause of the Mexican War*. 1914.

Reeves, Jesse S. *American Diplomacy under Tyler and Polk*. 1907.

Rippy, J. Fred. *The United States and Mexico*. 1926.

Rives, George Lockhart. *The United States and Mexico, 1821–1848*. 2 vols. 1913.

Zorrilla, Luis G. *Historia de las relaciones entre México y los Estados Unidos de América, 1800–1958*. 2 vols. 1965.

U.S. Claims

The claims for monetary compensation of U.S. citizens against the Mexican government arose from the destruction of property in Mexico during the chaotic conditions that followed the War of Independence (1810–1821) and the

Texas Revolution (1835–1836). By 1839 they amounted to $11,850,589. On 11 April 1839 the two governments signed a convention agreeing to submit the U.S. claims to a mixed commission with a judge, Baron von Roenne, the Prussian minister in Washington, D.C., to rule on those cases where there was no agreement. The commission met in August 1840 and deliberated for more than a year, finally awarding $439,393 to eleven cases; von Roenne was left to award $1,586,745 to fifty-three remaining claims, but many were left unresolved, particularly those involving commercial matters and the Texas Revolution.

Finally, on 20 November 1843 the two governments signed a new treaty agreeing to adjust the outstanding damages. Mexico insisted that the new commission meet in Mexico City, and as a result the U.S. Senate refused to ratify the treaty. This was the unsettled state of affairs in the years just before the outbreak of war between the two countries. Beginning in 1842 various U.S. administrations had suggested trading the claims for adjustments in the Texas boundary. In 1846 U.S. minister John Slidell was given instructions by President James K. Polk to offer $5 million and the assumption of the claims obligation in return for Mexico's recognizing the Río Grande as an international boundary. He also was given the authority to "purchase" California for various sums of money along with the U.S. government's assuming Mexico's claims debt. The Mexican government's refusal to recognize Slidell's credentials offered President Polk further reason to consider war as an alternative. In his declaration of war, read to Congress on 11 May 1846, the issue of the outstanding claims figured prominently. Ultimately, the fact that both England and France had outstanding claims against the Mexican government made it unlikely that they would intervene against the United States in the war against Mexico. Thus, indirectly, the claims issue figured in the U.S. government's consideration of war.

On 2 February 1848 the United States and Mexico signed the Treaty of Guadalupe Hidalgo, which included special articles dealing with the outstanding claims in addition to claims that had arisen since 1840. Article XIII committed the United States to pay all the claims of its nationals against the Mexican government. Article XV of the treaty promised to establish a board of commissioners to adjudicate the outstanding damages. After deliberating several years, from 1849 to 1851, the U.S. government settled all the outstanding claims against Mexico. The amount paid was approximately $5 million.

Richard Griswold del Castillo

BIBLIOGRAPHY

Jonas, Peter M. "William Parrott, American Claims, and the Mexican War." *Journal of the Republic* 12 (Summer 1992): 211–240.

Kohl, Clayton Charles. *Claims as a Cause of the Mexican War.* 1914.

Pletcher, David M. *The Diplomacy of Annexation: Texas, Oregon, and the Mexican War.* 1973.

Class Structure in Mexico

Mexico's class structure was a notable weakness during its war with the United States. As in the colonial period, there was limited social mobility, which retarded the sense of national patriotism that had developed at the end of the eighteenth century. The inability of the early republic to maintain political order, promote economic growth, and reform social problems fragmented, rather than united, society during the U.S.–Mexican War.

The upper class enjoyed traditional privileges but had little concern for the masses. The *gente de razón* (people who reasoned) believed that they were superior to the mestizo and indigenous majority. The Spanish colonial caste system ideology did not die away after independence.

Political exclusion widened the gap between upper and lower classes in the years leading up to 1846. Virtually all the upper class believed that only respected, educated, and moneyed males (*hombres de bien*) should exercise the full rights of citizenship. Therefore *hombres de bien* devised electoral laws that excluded the vast majority of Mexican men from voting and public affairs. But the upper class split regarding political ideology because while many championed the conservative cause, others were moderates or federalists.

Many of the upper class also resisted anticlericalism and patronized the church. Able to establish wealthy *capellanías* (chapels), which served as trust funds secure from confiscation until 1859, powerful landowners and merchants also supported convents and monasteries, which allowed their sons and daughters to live comfortably above the level of the masses. Because the church opposed government intervention into its vast landholdings, wealth, and privileges, conservatives and clerics often worked together.

The upper class became urbanized and discriminatory; an aristocracy still existed in Mexico City after creation of the republic. One reason for upper class urbanization was that many of the upper class were merchants. A major factor differentiating the classes was the identification of the upper class with its Spanish roots; it resented efforts by the Vicente Guerrero regime to exile Spaniards in the 1820s. Even white reformers such as Lorenzo de Zavala were incapable of shedding their racist views; like many Mexicans of Spanish descent, de Zavala referred to the indigenous population as a nuisance. Conservative whites were even more critical of the masses.

Although the middle class outnumbered the upper class, it lacked wealth and connections and thus settled into a life of financial uncertainty. Nevertheless, the middle class expanded by serving in the national as well as regional bureaucracies. Many middle class Mexicans established themselves as physicians, militia members, and educators. Entrepreneurs operated dozens of textile factories, while a rural middle class developed hundreds of ranches.

The masses comprised the great majority of Mexicans. Most lived miserably because the earnings of most workers were so low that they could barely support their families. The only thing that prevented a total economic collapse was that wages were stable and corn production doubled during the early republic. But a sack of corn, nevertheless, required four to five days of work. Often hungry, ill-clothed, and illiterate, the masses became increasingly desperate. Most laborers also amassed high debts, which employers encouraged. Landowners, particularly, loaned to field workers sums they would never be able to pay back because their wages were less than the standard of living. In practice, this resulted in peons being bought and sold for the price of their debts.

The working class became increasingly anticlerical. Most Mexicans supported liberal legislation in 1833 that allowed all citizens not to pay the tithe (the tax to support the church), but the high fees charged by parish priests for weddings, baptisms, and funerals were often beyond the means of workers and peasants. When the liberals returned to power during the U.S.–Mexican War, the church responded by doing little to support Mexico's war effort.

The class structure also had a strong racial connotation that weakened national unity during the war. The indigenous population, which comprised one-third of Mexican society, often lived in a state of legalized servitude like the mestizos who toiled on plantations and haciendas. Few Indians spoke Spanish. Denied political representation from their villages and suffering the loss of their communal lands to hostile legislators, the indigenous population had little reason to support any Mexican government. In fact, the Maya revolted in Yucatán and nearly drove the whites out by 1848. Similar caste wars, which resulted in the deaths of hundreds of thousands, broke out in the Bajío region. The sale of communal lands in Querétaro, Puebla, and in the state of México also mobilized indigenous communities against the national government while U.S. armies were advancing into the interior.

Douglas W. Richmond

BIBLIOGRAPHY

Calderón de la Barca, Frances. *Life in Mexico.* 1973.

Costeloe, Michael P. *The Central Republic in Mexico, 1835–1846: "Hombres de Bien" in the Age of Santa Anna.* 1993.

Reed, Nelson. *The Caste War of Yucatán.* 1964.

See also **Castes; Peonage; Yucatecan Revolt**

Clay, Henry

U.S. secretary of state and U.S. senator from Kentucky Henry Clay (1777–1852) was born on a Virginia farm on 12 April. At the age of twenty he moved to Kentucky to practice law and developed an interest in politics.

In 1811, Clay was elected speaker of the House of Representatives and soon gained national exposure as a leading War Hawk, maintaining that war against Great Britain was necessary to protect U.S. political and economic sovereignty. In 1820 he authored the Missouri Compromise in an effort to resolve the slavery debate. A proponent of economic nationalism, Clay advocated an "American System" with a national bank, a protective tariff, and federally funded internal improvements.

Widely recognized as the leader of the Whig Party in the 1830s and 1840s, Clay ran for president in 1844 but was defeated by the lesser-known Democratic nominee, James K. Polk. Clay's opposition to the annexation of Texas hampered his chances. He concluded the annexation of the Lone Star Republic would result in war with Mexico, significant debt, and heightened sectional rivalries, a position which cost him political support in the southern states. At the same time, Clay's refusal to rule out the possibility of annexation at a later date angered many northern Whigs, enabling Polk to carry the crucial state of New York.

Throughout the hostilities between Mexico and the United States, Clay denounced the Polk administration. Aiming for the presidency in 1848, he claimed that if he had been elected war would have been averted. He criticized Polk's prosecution of the "most unnecessary and horrible war," claiming that the war was too costly—in lives and dollars.

Clay also argued against the war from a practical standpoint; he believed that fighting a war so far from the U.S. population and supply base would be difficult. He noted that Gen. Zachary Taylor's army lacked provisions and reinforcements and that U.S. supply lines were dangerously long. Clay became more embittered when one of his sons was bayoneted to death at the Battle of Buena Vista. The U.S. victory at Buena Vista, however, solidified Taylor's hold on the Whig nomination for the upcoming presidential election. Clay condemned the choice of Taylor, a military chieftan and slaveholder, as a desertion of Whig principles.

Returning to the Senate in 1849, Clay hoped to forge a lasting compromise that would defuse the arguments in Congress regarding the Western territories and slavery. Concerned about Sen. John C. Calhoun and other Southern politicians who favored disunion if slavery were banned in the territories, he drafted a compromise calling for the admission of California as a free state, the organization of New Mexico as a territory without restrictions on slavery, and the payment of the debts incurred by the Republic of Texas in exchange for a significant reduction of eastern lands claimed by the state. The compromise, however, passed only as separate measures, revealing the disparate interests of North and South. Continuing to speak out in defense of the union, Clay died of tuberculosis on 29 June 1852.

While Clay never enjoyed the public approval of his rival Andrew Jackson, his economic vision for the future of the United States and steadfast unionism were incorporated by the Republican Party, and Abraham Lincoln declared Clay the ideal statesman and his guiding influence.

Dallas Cothrum

BIBLIOGRAPHY

Eaton, Clement. *Henry Clay and the Art of American Politics.* 1957.

Peterson, Merrill. *The Great Triumvirate: Webster, Clay, and Calhoun.* 1987.

Remini, Robert. *Henry Clay: Statesman of the Republic.* 1991.

Schroeder, John H. *Mr. Polk's War: American Opposition and Dissent, 1846–1848.* 1972.

Clayton-Bulwer Treaty

The Clayton-Bulwer Treaty, signed 19 April 1850, was an agreement between the United States and Great Britain designed to prevent conflict between the two nations over Central America, especially regarding construction of an isthmian canal. The interest of the United States in developing an interoceanic canal became acute in the mid-1840s as the U.S. role in the Pacific increased, with the opening of China to international trade, and especially after the acquisition of California in 1848. In 1849 Cornelius Vanderbilt, with the help of American diplomatic officials, secured exclusive rights for his Atlantic and Pacific Ship Canal Company to build a canal across Nicaragua. Great Britain already was a commercial power in the region; it had a territorial foothold in Belize and the Bay Islands and had established a protectorate over the Mosquito Coast of Nicaragua in 1843. Each power feared that the other might acquire exclusive control over an isthmian canal, but neither wanted a crisis in U.S.–British relations. The United States and Great Britain entered negotiations to ensure equal access to the construction and use of an isthmian canal. U.S. Secretary of State John Clayton and British minister Sir Henry Bulwer signed a treaty in Washington, D.C., containing the following provisions: both nations agreed to cooperate in the construction of a canal in which neither could acquire exclusive transit rights, and each nation pledged not to exercise dominion over any part of Central America and to guarantee the neutrality of the canal once built.

Soon after the treaty was signed, however, a new crisis emerged when William Walker, an American filibuster, seized control of the Nicaraguan government. The U.S. government disavowed Walker's actions, but his intention to seize the Mosquito Coast strained U.S.–British relations. Walker was driven out of Nicaragua in 1857, but problems lingered on as expansionists in Congress, who viewed the treaty as a surrender to the British, insisted that the noncolonization provision of the treaty covered established British possessions. Great Britain retreated by 1860 when it became clear that the construction of a canal across Nicaragua was not feasible. Great Britain reduced the size of the Mosquito protectorate, transferred the Bay Islands to Honduras, and settled the boundaries of Belize.

Lelia M. Roeckell

BIBLIOGRAPHY

Bourne, Kenneth. *Britain and the Balance of Power in North America, 1815–1908.* 1967.

Braver, Kinley J. "Economics and the Diplomacy of American Expansionism, 1821–1860." In *Economics and World Power: An Assessment of American Diplomacy since 1789,* edited by William H. Becker and Samuel F. Wells. 1984.

Rodríguez, M. *A Palmerstonian Diplomat in Central America: Frederick Chatfield, Esq.* 1964.

Coahuila y Texas

Texas first became attached to its southern neighbor Coahuila under Governor Alonso de Leon in the 1690s. After briefly sharing joint jurisdiction (1694–1715) administered from the capital in Monclova, the two provinces entered an on-again, off-again association as parts of various Spanish military districts. After Mexico gained independence in 1821 and opened Texas to Anglo-American colonization, it became imperative to provide effective government to the still sparsely settled northern frontier, and the two provinces once again were united.

On 7 May 1824, a newly adopted constitution created the state of Coahuila y Texas with its capital at Saltillo, located in the southeastern corner of the state. The next year the legislature created a Department of Texas presided over by an official at Béxar, present-day San Antonio. Additional departments were created in 1833 at Nacogdoches and San Felipe. That same year the more centrally located city of Monclova replaced Saltillo as the state capital. The progressive regime that assembled there enacted sweeping legislation favorable to the rapidly increasing population of U.S. settlers called Texians. The measures included increased local representation in state government, approval to use English in public life, and a revised judicial system that included trial by jury.

At Saltillo, the loss of power coupled with xenophobic concerns—sharpened by the way state officials were squandering public lands through sales to speculators—moved a conservative faction to install an extralegal government the next year. That body annulled the laws passed by the Monclova legislature. With tensions mounting, the rival factions submitted their cases to officials in Mexico City for arbitration, and, in July 1834, President Antonio López de Santa Anna declared that Monclova would remain the capital until an upcoming election set for February 1835 could determine otherwise. When the election went in favor of Monclova, the government in Saltillo swiftly contested the vote and again revolted. In the meantime, Santa Anna, busy consolidating his dictatorship, was backed by opportunistic supporters at Saltillo. Monclova's open opposition to Santa Anna provoked military commandant Martín Perfecto de Cos to intercede on behalf of Santa Anna, which resulted in dissolution of the Monclova legislature.

Deposed governor Agustín Viesca first, by force of arms, then secretly, twice failed to remove the Monclova archives to Béxar. Ben Milam and John Cameron were among a handful of Texians who participated in the effort. On 28 June 1835, on the appointment of Ramón Músquiz as governor at Saltillo, constitutional government in Coahuila y Texas came to an end.

In November 1835, fifty-eight representatives from a dozen Texian settlements met at San Felipe de Austin for a convention that would later be called the Consultation, where they voted to separate from Coahuila. While affirming the Mexican Constitution of 1824, the representatives also set up a provisional government that dispatched a delegation to the United States to seek aid and appointed Sam Houston commander of the army. With the outbreak of revolution, Texas's association with its sister province was finally and irrevocably severed.

Ty Cashion

BIBLIOGRAPHY

Alessio Robles, Vito. *Coahuila y Texas en la época colonial.* 1978.

Bancroft, Hubert Howe. *History of the North Mexican States and Texas.* 2 vols. 1886, 1889.

Chipman, Donald. *Spanish Texas, 1519–1821.* 1992.

Lack, Paul. *The Texas Revolutionary Experience.* 1992.

Weber, David J. *The Spanish Frontier in North America.* 1992.

Colegio Militar

See **Military Academy, Mexican**

Coleto Creek, Battle of

The Battle of Coleto Creek (19–20 March 1836), also known as Encinal del Perdido, was the climactic battle of the 1836 Goliad campaign and the catalyst for the Goliad massacre. Following his victory over Texian forces at Agua Dulce and Refugio, Mexican general José Urrea, with a force of approximately 1,400, advanced toward Goliad. Texian

colonel James Walker Fannin commanded 340 men—some regular infantry, a few cavalrymen, and volunteers—at the Presidio La Bahía, which had been refortified and renamed Fort Defiance.

On 11 March Sam Houston, commander of the Texian army, after receiving word of the fall of the Alamo, ordered Fannin "as soon as practical after receipt of this order" to retreat to Victoria. Fannin began preparing for the retreat the morning of 18 March, but after learning that the Mexican army was nearby, he prepared to defend his position. Finally it was decided to proceed with the twenty-eight-mile retreat to Victoria, but it did not begin until the following morning.

When Urrea, who had sent men to scout the Texian position in preparation for a siege against La Bahía, heard that the Texians were retreating, he left a force in La Bahía and, with an advance guard of approximately 360 men, followed the Texians. Elements of the advance guard caught up with the Texians while they were crossing a six-mile stretch of prairie. Fannin deployed two artillery pieces to fire on the Mexicans while his main force continued toward Victoria. When more Mexican cavalry and infantry appeared from the north and west, Fannin recalled his artillery, formed a square with the artillery at the corners, and prepared for battle, surrounded by Mexican forces. Although the Texians successfully repelled the Mexican assaults that day, they suffered from lack of water and a dwindling ammunition supply.

The next day, 20 March, Urrea opened fire with his artillery only 160 yards from the Texian position, and a truce was called. What transpired between the Texian and Mexican representatives is still debated. Urrea met with the wounded Fannin, who agreed to surrender, but it is disputed whether he agreed to do so with terms or at discretion. The surrender was signed and the Texian prisoners were marched to Goliad; Urrea continued with the majority of his force to Victoria. Both forces believed that, despite the Tornel Decree, the behavior of civilized nations would be observed in the treatment of the prisoners. Subsequent orders from Gen. Antonio López de Santa Anna, however, insisted on enforcing the Tornel Decree, and many of the prisoners were executed one week later at Goliad.

The surrender at Coleto Creek not only represented the loss of the second largest Texian fighting force but also gave the Mexican army control of the port of Copano and the coastal region from the Brazos River south.

Kevin R. Young

BIBLIOGRAPHY

Castaneda, Carlos E. *The Mexican Side of the Texas Revolution.* 1928.

Ehrenberg, Herman. *Texas und Seine Revolution.* 1843.

Jenkins, John, ed. *The Papers of the Texas Revolution, 1835–1836.* 10 vols. 1973.

O'Connor, Kathryn Stoner. *The Presidio La Bahía.* 1966.
Wharton, Clarence. *Remember Goliad.* 1931.
Young, Kevin R. *Texas Forgotten Heroes.* 1986.

Collaboration in Mexico

Collaboration in Mexico during the U.S.–Mexican War took three forms: a few hundred Mexicans performed intelligence tasks that facilitated U.S. military operations; Mexican women frequently aided U.S. soldiers; and Mexicans in the regions along the northern, eastern, and southern boundaries of Mexico often cooperated with U.S. forces.

Because many citizens of northern Mexico resented President Antonio López de Santa Anna's centralism, they often aided U.S. military operations. Particularly notable is Chapita Sandoval, who reported the strength of Gen. Mariano Arista's forces at Matamoros to Gen. Zachary Taylor in August 1845. Also, Gen. William J. Worth received valuable information about the defenses of Monterrey from Mexican spies.

After arriving in Puebla from Vera Cruz, Gen. Winfield Scott hired bandits to spy for him and paid other highwaymen to protect U.S. forces moving into Puebla. Eventually Scott's intelligence officer formed about two hundred Mexican criminals into five companies of spies, paying them twenty dollars a month. These men were deserters, robbers, vagrants, and ruffians, as well as political dissidents. From them, Scott received accurate information about Mexico City's defenses. These spies also fought Mexican guerrillas and skirmished with Santa Anna's forces near Mexico City.

Mexican women also collaborated actively with U.S. forces. Mexican women washed laundry and cooked for U.S. soldiers, and sexual liaisons between them and the soldiers were common. Other women nursed sick, wounded, and dying U.S. soldiers. Many wealthy Mexican women, recognizing the potential economic rewards of doing business with U.S. forces, provided hospitality and supplies to the invaders.

Regional cooperation with U.S. forces weakened Mexican hopes for victory. Undoubtedly the most notable example was in the state of Yucatán. After negotiating a December 1843 autonomy agreement with the central government, the Yucatecan elite angrily declared their independence when the national government continued to impose trade restrictions. Santa Anna once again promised autonomy, and Yucatán declared its readmission into the republic in November 1846.

One month later residents of the city of Campeche, who insisted on remaining neutral during the war in order to protect their merchant fleet from action by U.S. naval forces, revolted successfully against Mérida, the capital city of Yucatán. After U.S. forces occupied the port of Ciudad del Car-

men, the Campeche faction, then in charge of Yucatán, simply requested from the U.S. occupational forces lighter customs duties. In 1847, however, when a ferocious Maya revolt nearly succeeded, Yucatán offered its sovereignty in return for foreign assistance from the United States in crushing the revolt. Although President James K. Polk supported the Yucatán proposal, Congress voted it down.

The Yucatán example is indicative of the overall lack of internal unity during the war, especially along Mexico's periphery. The Chiapas and Tabasco governments considered union with Guatemala. Governors in Chihuahua, Coahuila, and Tamaulipas considered establishing close ties with the United States. Governor Manuel Armijo surrendered New Mexico without firing a shot. The Sierra Gorda Revolt, which began with agrarian resistance to government land confiscation, became so intense that the central government lost control of large portions of central Mexico to local insurrections for two years, from 1847 to 1849.

Because the regional economies of the north and east of Mexico depended greatly on international trade, economics motivated many to cooperate with the United States for financial gain. During the U.S. occupation of Mexico City, General Scott, while waiting for the Treaty of Guadalupe Hidalgo to be negotiated and signed, obtained the administrative and managerial services of a member of the Mexico City municipal government for thirteen weeks. There is no doubt that such collaboration affected Mexico adversely before the peace treaty was signed. Collaboration meant that resistance to U.S. military operations became weaker; undoubtedly it encouraged more acceptance of U.S. proposals for acquisition of Mexican territory.

Douglas W. Richmond

BIBLIOGRAPHY

Caruso, A. Brooke. *The Mexican Spy Company: United States Covert Operations in Mexico, 1845–1848.* 1991.

Cashion, Peggy Jeanne. "Women and the Mexican War, 1846–1848." Master's thesis, University of Texas at Arlington, 1990.

Chamberlain, Samuel E. *My Confession: Recollections of a Rogue.* 1996.

Richmond, Douglas W. "Yucatán's Struggle for Sovereignty during the Mexican–U.S. Conflict, 1836–1848." In *La ciudad y el campo en la historia de México,* edited by Richard Sánchez, Eric Van Young, and Gisela von Wobeser. 1992.

See also **Yucatecan Revolt**

Colt Revolver

Designed by Samuel Colt, the Paterson No. 5 and Walker Model revolvers saw significant service in the U.S.–Mexican War. Rejected by the military in favor of the single-shot muzzleloaders then in service, the five-chambered Paterson first won fame in the hands of Texas Rangers. Such widely publicized incidents as an 1844 skirmish in which fifteen Paterson-armed Rangers routed eighty Comanches proved the revolver's effectiveness as a cavalry weapon. By 1846 its reputation was such that a number of U.S. volunteers carried privately purchased Patersons into Mexico.

The Paterson, however, had its drawbacks. It was relatively fragile, and loading required special tools and disassembly, a complicated procedure on horseback. Still, Gen. Zachary Taylor recognized its potential and ordered Capt. Samuel H. Walker of the U.S. Mounted Rifles to procure an improved arm for army issue.

Walker consulted with Colt, who drew on the captain's field experience to add several improvements to his earlier design. He solved the loading problem by adding an integral loading mechanism and using a new fixed cartridge. Colt also enhanced the firepower by increasing the cylinder capacity to six chambers and the caliber from .36 to .44. The resulting four-pound, nine-ounce monster, christened the Colt Walker Model, featured an engraved cylinder scene commemorating the 1844 Ranger-Comanche fight.

In midsummer 1847, the U.S. Army distributed one thousand Walker revolvers among five companies of U.S. Dragoons. An instant success, the Walker assured Colt's future. Captain Walker, however, was killed in early October during the battle of Huamantla while carrying a brace of Walkers, gifts from Samuel Colt.

Jeff Kinard

BIBLIOGRAPHY

Flayderman, Norm. *Flayderman's Guide to Antique American Firearms*. 1987.

Hosley, William. *Colt: The Making of an American Legend*. 1996.

Russell, Carl P. *Guns on the Early Frontiers*. 1957.

Wilson, R. L. *Colt: An American Legend*. 1985.

Comanches

The term *Comanche* refers to the culturally related but politically independent groups of Shoshone-speaking people on the Southern Plains. In the eighteenth century there were three such tribes or divisions, each composed of a number of local residential bands. By the mid-nineteenth century, there were four (one of the earlier groups had disappeared, and two others had coalesced), and other groups coalesced in later years. The total Comanche population, as well as the size of each division, is unclear. In the eighteenth century, estimates ranged as high as twenty thousand for the entire population, but because no Euroamerican individual had contact with all the groups, such estimates are suspect.

In the mid-nineteenth century, the Comanche domestic economy was based around horse-mounted buffalo hunting and the trade in buffalo products, captives, and horses—the latter two taken in increasing raids through Texas and into Mexico. Comanches traded with the surrounding peoples: other Indians, Mexicans in New Mexico and Texas and below the Río Grande, and Anglo-Americans in Louisiana, Missouri, New Mexico, and Texas. At the same time, in efforts to maintain the Comanches' good will in wider political arenas, the governments of the United States, the Republics of Texas and Mexico, as well as several northern Mexican states, provided political gifts, both subsistence items and prestige goods; the redistribution of those gifts became a major source of political capital among Comanche leaders. Treaties between various Comanche groups and various Euroamerican governments had been made since 1785. Although many Euroamericans, particularly the Anglo-Americans and Anglo-Texans, considered those treaties to be binding on all Comanches, the Comanche signatories represented only specific groups, and often other groups had no knowledge of the proceedings.

Direct Comanche involvement in U.S.–Mexican War hostilities was minimal; however, by their very presence, the Comanches exerted an influence on policy. Moreover, there were constant rumors that "renegade" Mexicans were stirring up Comanche antagonism against the Anglo-Americans and indeed were fighting alongside Comanches.

There were two primary theaters of Comanche relations during 1846 and 1847: in lower Texas and along the Arkansas River. In the spring of 1846, in anticipation of possible Mexican reaction to the U.S. annexation of Texas, as well as in hopes of recovering captives, the U.S. government arranged a treaty with the Hois (later known as Penateka) Comanches of Texas, and a Comanche delegation went to Washington, meeting President James K. Polk in the White House.

To the north, rumors and tall tales of Comanche barbarity and hostility were a constant feature of campfire gossip along the Santa Fe Trail; but few of those rumors have any substance. Only two hostile incidents were reported along the Santa Fe Trail in 1845 and 1846. The record for 1847 was very different, if confused. One report claimed that during the summer of 1847, forty-seven Americans were killed, 330 wagons destroyed, and 6,500 animals stolen by Apaches, Comanches, Kiowas, and Pawnees. However, tabulation of the incidents reported in contemporary newspapers suggests that only twenty-seven whites were killed, with comparably reduced numbers of wagons and animals stolen. While one report said that the Comanches and Kiowas themselves claimed sixty scalps, only one incident can be reliably attributed to the Comanches.

Article XI of the Treaty of Guadalupe Hidalgo declared it illegal for U.S. citizens to purchase or acquire Mexican nationals held captive by the Indians and called on the United States to rescue and return any such captives. While the taking of captives in Mexico continued through the 1860s—

several Mexicans taken captive in the 1860s were still living with the Comanches in the 1930s—there were only two incidents of the ransoming of Mexican captives in line with the treaty, in 1850 and 1874 to 1875.

Thomas W. Kavanagh

BIBLIOGRAPHY

Kavanagh, Thomas. *Comanche Political History: An Ethnohistorical Perspective, 1706–1875.* 1996.

Communications

The war between the United States and Mexico witnessed the first sizable use of technological innovations at the strategic level. Nowhere was this more evident than in communications. Mounted couriers still carried battle reports and dispatches tucked safely inside saddlebags, but in the period from 1821 to 1854, steamboats, railroads, and telegraphs advanced critical communications at speeds before unimagined.

Tactical communications for all armies in this era remained unchanged from communications in the earliest days of warfare. Generals conducted their battles from central locations in proximity to the frontlines, within eyesight and earshot of the actual fighting. Drums, bugles, and flags marked the progress of units in combat. Units at distant locations received written or verbal orders delivered by officers and couriers who, as often as not, held their position on the general staff not because of formal training or particular expertise but because of their connections to the commanding officer. The age of professional staff training was far in the future. Even so, these volunteer messengers provided the critical link between the commander and his command. For many armies of this period, including Mexico's, this hand-carried method of information exchange extended to strategic communications as well.

The United States increasingly gained a clear advantage over its adversaries in its application of technology to the issue of communications. In the United States, mechanical devices replaced reliance on bone, muscle, and sinew. When a dispatch arrived at a depot or supply base far to the rear of the army in the field, it often found its way to fast steamships or courier vessels that in turn moved the message to an inland port, rail terminal, or telegraph post. Steamboats had plied U.S. inland waters since 1807. This technological conquest of river currents allowed for relatively rapid transfer of materials and information both upstream and downstream, turning streams and waterways into natural highways. After 1826 railroads began to augment riverine communications.

In 1844 Samuel Morse sent the message "What hath God wrought" over the copper wires of a device he dubbed the telegraph. With the perfection of this invention, communi-

cations took a major leap forward, with corresponding implications for strategic and commercial applications. One military observer noted that, in the past, innovation had occurred slowly and at intervals, while in the first half of the nineteenth century, changes occurred at an alarming rate. Now, ten years' time marked "an epoch in the onward progress of modern invention and improvement. Even five years may modify, materially, plans of defense now reputed wisest and most indispensable." One sound strategic plan could be compromised or undone by the rapid transfer of information. By 1850 writer Richard S. Fisher exclaimed, "We travel by steam and converse by lightning."

The implications these innovations held for the U.S.–Mexican War were profound. In the United States, news from the front arrived in just a few days, and politicians and generals alike could react rapidly to changing circumstances. The public kept abreast of news and supported the war to a greater or lesser degree based on the latest reports from the front. Ultimately, materials and manpower arrived from remote locations in the United States at a steady and reliable pace. All of these advantages allowed the nation to conduct a foreign war far removed from its centers of population.

Donald S. Frazier

BIBLIOGRAPHY

Millett, Allan R., and Peter Maslowski. *For the Common Defense: A Military History of the United States of America.* 1994.

Johannsen, Robert W. *To the Halls of the Montezumas: The Mexican War in the American Imagination.* 1985.

Winders, Richard Bruce. *Mr. Polk's Army: The American Military Experience in the Mexican War.* 1997.

See also **Newspapers; Photography; Railroads; Steamships;** *and* **War Correspondents**

Congress

This entry consists of three separate articles: **Mexican Congress; Texas Congress;** *and* **U.S. Congress.**

Mexican Congress

In nineteenth-century Mexico, most political activity took place in the congress. From 1821 to 1853, there were twenty-two congresses, formed by different constitutions. The military *caudillos* usually in charge of the executive power often conflicted with congress. In December 1844, for example, congressmen's position against the government was decisive in the fall of Gen. Antonio López de Santa Anna's administration.

The Plan de la Ciudadela, proclaimed by Gen. José Mariano Salas on 4 August 1846 in Mexico City, summoned a popular congress in order to restructure the nation and resolve issues related to the war against the United States. This plan also invited General Santa Anna to become chief of the forces involved in the revolution that overthrew the government of Gen. Mariano Paredes y Arrillaga, who was accused of promoting a monarchy and deceiving the nation by assembling an antipopular congress. The main leaders of the revolution were the *puros,* who had made an agreement with Santa Anna and other important military officials to overthrow Paredes.

General Salas was appointed chief of the executive. His first task in the government was to call, in August 1846, for the election of deputies to the constituent congress in a sole chamber that was to meet in December. Furthermore, Salas reestablished the federal Constitution of 1824 and extended the powers of the future congress by the decrees of 22 August 1846. Thus, the liberals were able to take power, reestablish the Constitution of 1824, and see the centralists defeated and monarchists totally discredited. At that point, the situation seemed promising for the people and for the defense of the country against the U.S. invasion.

The liberals, however, were divided into *puros* and *moderados,* two antagonistic and irreconcilable factions, especially with regard to the position of the church in society. From September to November 1846 the elections of deputies were accomplished. During and after the elections, the fight between the two factions began, and when congress gathered on 6 December 1846, it was evenly divided between *puros* and *moderados.* Prominent among the *puros* were Manuel Crescencio Rejón and Benito Juárez; the *moderados* included Mariano Otero and José María Lafragua. The Sovereign Constituent Congress had two main issues to address: drawing up a new constitution and facing the problems associated with war against the United States. As in all issues discussed by this congress, there was no basis of agreement; on the contrary, congress was the focal point of division, antagonism, and dissolution of both morale and public spirit.

Congress appointed General Santa Anna interim president and Valentín Gómez Farías, leader of the *puros,* as interim vice president. Gómez Farías had charge of the executive power and Santa Anna commanded the army. In late 1846 and early 1847, Santa Anna asked congress for funding to supply the army, which was languishing in San Luis Potosí. On 11 January 1847 Congress issued a decree authorizing the government to mortgage or sell the estates of "dead hands" (i.e., estates that had been willed to the Catholic Church) to provide 15 million pesos to pursue the war against the United States. Opposition to the decree by both the church and the *moderados* was so strong, however, that the government could not raise the economic support needed for the war. Santa Anna thus commanded the army with bare-minimum resources. Congress tried again with the law

of 4 February, which granted the government power to obtain up 5 million pesos to defend the nation's territory.

The *moderados,* unable to defeat the *puros* in congress, called for a revolution, with help from members of the national guard commanded by Gen. Matías de la Peña y Barragán, on 27 February 1847, a few days after the Battle of La Angostura. These units included the sons of the wealthiest families in Mexico City, called *polkos,* some historians believe, because the polka was the fashionable dance among high society. The Polkos Revolt served only to worsen the instability of the government. In early April, congress, in the midst of another debate, removed Gómez Farías and appointed the candidate of the *moderados,* Gen. Pedro María Anaya, as "substitute president."

In early April, Santa Anna had moved his army east to fight against Gen. Winfield Scott's army, which had disembarked in Vera Cruz and was heading toward Mexico City. On 18 April 1847, the Mexican army was defeated again, this time at Cerro Gordo, Vera Cruz. Congress assembled immediately and on 20 April approved, almost unanimously, a law granting the government power to take the necessary measures to continue the war. The law did not, however, authorize the executive to make peace with the United States, to conclude negotiations with foreign powers, or to cede Mexican territory, because both factions, *puros* and *moderados,* feared that Santa Anna would make a deal with the United States, ignoring the wishes of the legislative branch.

Congress also debated from late April to middle May 1847 several constitutional reforms that were proposed to modify the Constitution of 1824. The final document was called *Acta de Reformas.* It permitted the enforcement of the constitution with reforms that the congress approved on 18 May 1847, by the promotion of the *moderados,* and especially, Mariano Otero's activity.

From late May to September 1847, congress rarely gathered for lack of a quorum. Congress neither granted the necessary resources to the executive to fight the war nor allowed Santa Anna to make peace by means of negotiation. The congress, therefore, became totally discredited. As it was a constituent congress and the constitution had already been submitted, the congress was dismissed in early September 1847.

After the occupation of Mexico City by U.S. troops, Manuel de la Peña y Peña, on 27 September, seized executive power and removed the Mexican government to the city of Querétaro. The congress was then called to meet in Querétaro. The deputies traveled to that city, and in early November the congress convened the necessary quorum. On 11 November they elected interim president Gen. Pedro María Anaya, who was to serve until 8 January 1848. The congress declared that, if a new congress had not been seated by that date, Manuel de la Peña y Peña again should take the executive office. In Querétaro, the congress was divided once more: the *puros* continued to refuse any possible settlement with the United States; the *moderados* wanted peace between the two nations. The constituent congress concluded its sessions and was dismissed on 6 December 1847.

Meanwhile, from September to November 1847, the Mexican states that the U.S. Army had not occupied had elected deputies and senators for the new congress that was to begin sessions in January 1848. To end the war, the governments of Manuel de la Peña y Peña and Pedro María Anaya negotiated a peace treaty with the United States. Its ratification, according to the Mexican constitution, fell to congress. The new congress, meeting in Querétaro, was divided into two chambers and took a long time to assemble. The *moderados* controlled the majority. The first deputies and senators arrived in January, but the congress did not come to order until 7 May 1848. The main task of congress was to address the Treaty of Guadalupe Hidalgo, signed on 2 February of that year, with all the amendments made by the government and the senate of the United States. In the deputy chamber, the treaty was approved by a vote of 51 to 35 on 19 May. The issued passed to the senate, which approved the treaty by a vote of 33 to 3. Prominent members of this congress were Manuel Gómez Pedraza, Guillermo Prieto, Mariano Riva Palacio, José Ramón Malo, Ignacio Comonfort, and Fernando Ramírez. On 30 May 1848 the ratified treaty was exchanged in Querétaro, thus ending the war between the two countries.

Reynaldo Sordo Cedeño

BIBLIOGRAPHY

Bauer, K. Jack. *The Mexican War, 1846–1848*. 1992.

Costeloe, Michael P. "The Mexican Church and the Rebellion of the Polkos." *Hispanic American Historical Review* 46, no. 2 (1966): 170–178.

Escudero, José Antonio de. *Memoria del diputado por el estado de Chihuahua. Lic. J.A. Escudero, con documentos justificativos que pueden servir para la historia del Congreso constituyente mexicano del año de 1847*. 1848.

Ramírez, José Fernando. *México durante la guerra con los Estados Unidos*. 1991.

Santoni, Pedro. *Mexicans at Arms: Puro Federalists and the Politics of War, 1845–1848*. 1996.

Sordo Cedeño, Reynaldo. "El Congreso y la formación del Estadonación en México, 1821–1855." In *La Fundación del Estado Mexicano*, by Josefina Z. Vázquez. 1994.

Texas Congress

The congress played an important and independent-minded, if often ineffective, role in the politics of the Republic of Texas. This pattern existed for three basic reasons. First, formal political parties did not develop; rather, election results generally turned on factions centered around leadership personalities, namely whether candidates favored or opposed Sam Houston. The absence of an ideological or structural foundation meant also that congressmen followed irregular patterns of legislation. Second, governing the infant republic posed a dilemma—how to establish a successful system of defense while operating within a budget limited by a small tax and uncertain credit base. As a result, the congress tended to express popular dissatisfaction that presidential administrations could not both provide security and correct fiscal weaknesses. Third, annual elections of new members of the house of representatives provided immediate expressions of public discontent with government policies. Senators served for only three years. Even when a majority of legislators initially shared a factional identity with the sitting president, such support for the executive tended to dissipate in a brief period. The congress, then, often played the role of obstructing presidential initiatives, overriding vetoes of legislation that could not be implemented for practical reasons, and carping at failures in leadership.

The congress of Texas included at one time or another most of the outstanding political leaders of the republic. Even Sam Houston served a term in the house, from 1840 to 1841, between his two presidential administrations. Another feature of the composition of the congresses was the commonality of military experience. One study indicates that in the Texas conventions and congresses of the republic period (including those that met during the period of the revolution), all but 15 of the 482 members had some military record and a majority had significant experience in the army.

The first congress (1836–1837) reflected military influences in that most of its members favored compensation to veterans of military service. Like most of its successors, this body also sought annexation to the United States. Another consistent theme was to frame moderate land laws. Legislators verified grants made under Mexico and also promoted growth by making tracts available to all immigrants who settled on their land. The congress broke with Houston in passing over his veto a measure to organize a land office to begin distribution, a policy that the president delayed implementing because of concern over speculation.

Despite being elected initially on strong grounds of consensus with the popular Houston, the first congress eventually broke with him on many issues. Similarly, the third congress began by augmenting the military and financial powers of President Mirabeau B. Lamar, but it ended on hostile notes of disappointment and criticism. The reaction against him was so strong that it resulted in a 3 to 1 anti-Lamar majority in the next congress, but reversals of fortune in Houston's second presidency also led to a legislative-executive split.

The congresses of the Republic of Texas followed some lines of coherence on matters of policy. The abundant public domain became bait to secure debt, reward service, and promote settlement. By the 1840s Texas had reestablished a system comparable to the Mexican *empresario* tradition of making large grants to colonizing agents or companies. Various congresses also acted repeatedly to establish improved military systems—a formal militia, a regular army, lines of forts—but the absence of funding or other issues of impracticality limited implementation of these measures. In matters of diplomacy the congress sometimes took the lead, but generally it deferred to the executive. The first congress voted to set the southern boundary at the Río Grande and refused to ratify a treaty with the Cherokees, which had been negotiated in good faith by Houston. The legislature split on geographic lines over location of the capital and delegated the matter to a special commission, which eventually chose a site on the frontier named for Stephen F. Austin. Houston strongly disliked this solution but had no choice.

On matters of finance, the congress found no solutions to the spiral of borrowing and inflation. The debt stood at $1.25 million at the inception of the republic, grew by an additional $2 million in three years, more than doubled under the more aggressive military policies of the Lamar administration, and increased by more than 50 percent thereafter (to $12 million in 1845), despite policies of retrenchment in Houston's second term. A financial low occurred in 1842 when the congress suspended payment on the public debt. Various forms of paper currency—including land scrip and promissory notes—circulated at deep discounts. Import taxes remained difficult to collect despite efforts at reform, including lowering duty rates.

On balance the nine Congresses of the Texas Republic provided vigorous public policy debates and enough criticism and vetoing to counterbalance presidential whims. In essence the major political test was survival while Texas drifted toward annexation.

Paul D. Lack

BIBLIOGRAPHY

Nackman, Mark. "The Making of the Texan Citizen Soldier, 1835–1860." *Southwestern Historical Quarterly* 78 (January 1975): 239.

Siegel, Stanley. *A Political History of the Texas Republic, 1836–1845.* 1956.

U.S. Congress

President James K. Polk, a Democrat, viewed his 1844 election as a mandate for his policies, but legislators often guarded their constitutional prerogatives and thwarted his agenda. Whigs understandably opposed him, but dissident Democrats such as Sen. John C. Calhoun also thought him reckless in the disputes with Great Britain about Oregon and with Mexico about the Texas border. Domestic issues also divided Congress. The lowered Walker Tariff, for example, passed the Senate by only one vote in 1846. Whigs (and protectionist Pennsylvania Democrats) disapproved. Polk's appointments also strained his party; he seemed to favor the South in patronage as well as policy.

However divisive these issues, no event riled Congress and the nation more than the war against Mexico. Democrats held a solid majority in the House and an edge in the Senate when Polk took office in 1845; but by 1848 Whigs controlled the House and Polk faced a majority coalition of Whigs and dissident Democrats in the Senate. Tensions also increased within the parties, not just between them. In August 1846, Rep. David Wilmot, a Pennsylvania Democrat, proposed an amendment to a war appropriations bill specifying that "neither slavery nor involuntary servitude" should be permitted in any territory acquired from Mexico. The House passed the measure, but the Senate rejected it. Rep. Abraham Lincoln introduced the "Spot Resolutions" in late 1847, challenging Polk to identify the precise "spot" where Mexican troops had "shed American blood" upon U.S. "soil." In early 1848, Rep. George Ashmun, a Massachusetts Whig, offered an amendment calling the ongoing war "a war unnecessarily and unconstitutionally begun by the President of the United States." The House approved it by a vote of 85 to 81. These amendments epitomized the growing rift in national politics. Some condemned "Mr. Polk's war"; others, whatever their views of Polk, opposed the extension of slavery. Rising sectional tensions complicated the customary partisan rivalry.

Polk informed Congress on 11 May 1846 that despite his precautions Mexico had "invaded our territory and shed American blood upon the [sic] American soil." He requested funds to avenge the attack. Polk's floor leaders stifled debate and denied lawmakers time to scrutinize the documents accompanying the message. Both chambers hastily passed the bill, with only two "nay" votes in the Senate, fourteen in the House. Senators Lewis Cass, Ambrose Sevier, and William Allen defended Polk against criticism from Senators Thomas Clayton, John Davis, John Crittenden, and John C. Calhoun. Rep. Stephen Douglas vindicated the president in the House; but Rep. Columbus Delano, a Whig from Ohio, regarded Polk's course as "illegal, unrighteous, and damnable." Some who voted for the bill did so reluctantly. "Never was so momentous a measure adopted," Calhoun confided to a friend, "with so much precipitancy; so little thought; or forced through by such objectionable means."

Despite Polk's assurances that he did not seek territory, his strategy betrayed him. U.S. forces seized California and New Mexico, and commanders set up governments there. A war ostensibly to repel aggression seemed instead a war for empire. The prospect of new land incited fierce debate over whether the president and his advisers intended to extend slavery to the Pacific Ocean. Delano waved the free soil banner in early 1847. "Conquer Mexico and add the territory," he warned, "but we will make it *free;* if not with the politicians we have now, the people of the North will bury these, and send honest men in their places." Sen. Arthur Bagby of Alabama spoke for the South when he objected that he could "never consent that territory, acquired by common blood and common treasure," would be open to one section and its "property" but not to the other. Radicals threatened to dissolve the Union rather than acquiesce to free-soil demands. This crisis alarmed the Whigs. "Will the North consent to a treaty bringing in territory subject to slavery?" Sen. Daniel Webster queried in 1847. "Will the South consent to a treaty bringing in territory from which slavery is excluded? Sir, the future is full of difficulties and full of dangers."

Most Democrats defended Polk. They blamed the war on Mexico, demanded a vast indemnity, and argued that Anglo-Americans had a right to the borderlands because Mexico's "motley races" did not use them. Whigs refuted these views, but their position was tenuous. With U.S. soldiers already under fire, they had little choice but to provision the army. They chafed at their dilemma, voting men and money for a war they deplored. Democrats labeled them traitors. Rep. Anthony Kennedy of Indiana, for example, told the House that "the Mexican Government may have, on this floor, men of greater talent than they have in the field at home." With peace restored, editor Thomas Ritchie repeated the refrain. "The great difficulty which we have had to encounter is not the enemy abroad," he grumbled, "but the opposition at home." Neither party found solace in the outcome of the war. Democrats lost the White House, and the Whigs won it by running Zachary Taylor. The U.S.–Mexican War fomented discord in the United States, not unity.

Thomas Hietala

BIBLIOGRAPHY

Brauer, Kinley. *Cotton Versus Conscience: Massachusetts Whig Politics and Southwestern Expansion, 1843–1848.* 1967.

Hietala, Thomas. *Manifest Design.* 1985.

Morrison, Chaplain. *Democratic Politics and Sectionalism: The Wilmot Proviso Controversy.* 1967.

Schroeder, John. *Mr. Polk's War: American Opposition and Dissent, 1846–1848.* 1973.

Conner, David

U.S. Navy officer David Conner (1792–1856) directed the U.S. Navy's efforts in the Gulf of Mexico during the first year of the U.S.–Mexican War. Born in Harrisburg, Pennsylvania, David Conner began his career as a midshipman in 1809. During the War of 1812 he served aboard the USS *Hornet* and was awarded two congressional medals for bravery. He then held various overseas and stateside commands, including service on the Board of Navy Commissioners and as the first chief of the Construction, Equipment and Repair Bureau.

At the time of the U.S.–Mexican War, Conner was a commodore in command of the Home Squadron (naval forces in the Gulf of Mexico and the Caribbean). He assisted Maj.

Gen. Zachary Taylor's army in the opening weeks of the war by landing marines and sailors to reinforce Taylor's supply base at Point Isabel. Conner's forces then instituted a successful blockade of Mexico's Gulf port cities, and despite receiving harsh (but largely unfair) criticism for two failed attacks on the town of Alvarado, he captured the port of Tampico in November 1846.

Conner's greatest triumph was successfully landing more than 8,500 troops of Maj. Gen. Winfield Scott's invasion force south of Vera Cruz on 9 March 1847. The landing was accomplished in the space of a few hours without a single loss. Conner remained off Vera Cruz during Scott's siege of that city, but as part of routine Navy procedure he transferred his command to Commo. Matthew C. Perry on 21 March 1847. The ailing Conner returned to the United States and, after his recuperation, was placed in command of the Philadelphia Navy Yard. He died in Philadelphia in 1856.

Jeffrey L. Patrick

BIBLIOGRAPHY

Bauer, K. Jack. *Surfboats and Horse Marines: U.S. Naval Operations in the Mexican War.* 1969.

Conner, David. Personal Papers. Library of Congress, Washington, D.C.; New York Public Library, New York, N.Y.; Franklin D. Roosevelt Library, Hyde Park, N.Y.

Conner, Philip S. P. *The Home Squadron under Commodore Conner in the War with Mexico; Being a Synopsis of His Services, 1846–7.* 1896.

Smith, Justin H. *The War with Mexico.* 2 vols. 1919. Reprint, 1963.

Conservatives, Mexican

Mexican conservatives favored a society based on hierarchy, authority, and tradition. They opposed liberal innovations that threatened to weaken class differences, the military, and the Catholic Church. The conservative alliance between the cross and the sword was inherently unstable because the national army was the principal consumer of government funds and the church was Mexico's wealthiest corporation.

Conservatives considered liberalism a foreign doctrine ill-suited to Mexico's conditions and traditions. They believed that liberty, individual rights, and religious toleration would lead to social dissolution and that democracy and federalism would lead to chaos and anarchy. Conservatives identified liberal principles and Enlightenment doctrines as the fundamental causes of the French Revolution of 1789 and what they regarded as the anarchy and destruction of the Reign of Terror. Conservatives maintained their traditional belief that monarchy was the ideal form of government, and they were reluctant to accept a republican form of government after Emperor Agustín de Iturbide relinquished the crown in 1823. Afterward many conservatives continued to hope for a restoration of monarchy; some conspired and even acted to return Mexico to control by a king.

In the mid-1840s Mexican conservatives, including former cabinet minister Lucas Alamán and Gen. Mariano Paredes y Arillaga, conspired with Salvador Bermúdez de Castro, Spain's minister to Mexico, to bring an heir to the Spanish throne to rule Mexico. Knowing that a deal with the United States would discredit President José Joaquín de Herrera (a *moderado*), the monarchical conspirators hoped that President Herrera would resolve the Texas dispute with the United States peacefully and accept the compensation that was offered for Mexican territory. When Herrera declined the U.S. offer, General Paredes led a successful movement against him that was known as the Revolution of the Ciudadela. Once in power, President Paredes y Arillaga had to take a more bellicose posture toward the United States in order to maintain his support among military officers and the public. A peaceful resolution that ceded Mexican territory to the United States was politically impossible. The Paredes regime was discredited by a combination of Mexican defeats at the battles of Palo Alto and Resaca de la Palma in May 1846 and vigorous political opposition in Mexico City. Within seven months of taking power, Paredes was overthrown by a coalition that returned Gen. Antonio López de Santa Anna and Valentín Gómez Farías to power. Political instability continued with control of the national government shifting from one coalition to another.

Defeat in the war convinced conservatives of the accuracy of their diagnosis of Mexico's weakness and the necessity of a monarchy to preserve national integrity. Mexican politics became increasingly polarized between conservatives and radical liberals (known as *puros*). After the Ayutla Revolution returned the liberals to power in 1855, conservative revolt led to the Three Years War (1857–1860). Although the liberals triumphed again, conservatives sought foreign allies and a European prince to take the throne of Mexico. The wars of the French Intervention ended in victory for the liberal armies and President Benito Juárez in 1867. This defeat ended the conservatives' political pretensions, but it did not significantly diminish their control of the economy.

Donald F. Stevens

BIBLIOGRAPHY

Hale, Charles A. *Mexican Liberalism in the Age of Mora, 1821–1853.* 1968.

Santoni, Pedro. *Mexicans at Arms: Puro Federalists and the Politics of War, 1845–1848.* 1996.

Scholes, Walter V. *Mexican Politics during the Juárez Regime, 1855–1872.* 1957.

Soto, Miguel. *La conspiración monárquica en México, 1845–1846.* 1988.

Stevens, Donald F. *Origins of Instability in Early Republican Mexico.* 1991.

Constitution, Mexican

This entry consists of four separate articles: **Constitution of 1824;** **Constitution** *of* **1836;** Constitution *of* 1842; *and* **Constitution of 1843.**

Constitution of 1824

After the fall of the first Mexican empire in 1823, a temporary government secured a loan of 16 million pesos from Great Britain and recommended a constituent congress to draft a new plan of government for Mexico. At the same time, centralist and federalist factions began to form based on conservative and liberal political ideology. In January 1824, these opposing groups adopted thirty-six articles to serve as the blueprint for a future constitution. To a large extent the strongly federalist constitution that emerged was patterned after the U.S. constitution. In the minutes of the constituent congress, delegates made almost daily reference to the United States. However, there was also a heavy Spanish influence. The delegates took the wording of Spain's constitution of 1812 and combined it with that of the U.S. Constitution as a model for federalism. The congress approved the new constitution in October 1824 with Mexico divided into nineteen states and four territories. Each state had its own elected governor and legislature, a tribunal of justice, and the power to oversee its own revenues. Like the United States, the territories were governed by the federal government.

The only thing required of the states by the Constitution of 1824 was that they provide for separate executive, legislative, and judicial systems in their individual constitutions. Each state had the power to decide if it would respect the national constitution or not, and legislative bodies of the states elected the president and the vice president for four-year terms. The candidate with the highest number of votes became president and the one with the second highest number of votes became vice president.

The constitution placed many limitations on the powers of the president. Congress was to be bicameral and to meet annually from 1 January to 15 April. Members of the chamber of deputies (the lower house) served for two years on the basis of population (1 per 80,000). Senators were elected by their state legislators for four-year terms. Judicial power was vested in a supreme court that was made up of eleven judges and the attorney general elected by the state legislatures. Concerning religion, the constitution designated Catholicism as the state religion, prohibited the practice of all other religions, and provided for the church to be supported by the public treasury.

Despite overwhelming popular support, the constitution lasted only eleven years. The possibility for putting opposing political parties together in office as a presidential and vice presidential team was one of the reasons for many of the later violent transfers of power. Other shortcomings of the Constitution of 1824 were that military and ecclesiastical *fueros* (or privileges) continued unchanged, and legal procedures included no trial by jury.

The era following the passage of the Constitution of 1824 was marked by political instability, financial chaos, and difficulty in foreign relations. In part, this was due to the lack of experience in self-government, the introduction of democratic government to a people unaccustomed to representative rule, an extremely high national illiteracy rate, and the exodus of Spaniards from the country, including many of the most educated and talented.

The Constitution of 1824 was revived when Texians declared loyalty to its republican principles as a part of their declaration of independence in 1835. Also, in 1847 the Constitution of 1824 was temporarily in effect until a new constitution could be written, but that was the last time it would dictate the nation's policies.

Virginia Doggett

BIBLIOGRAPHY

Green, Stanley C. *The Mexican Republic: The First Decade, 1823–1832.* 1987.

Miller, Robert Ryal. *Mexico: A History.* 1985.

Noll, Arthur Howard. *The Story of the Struggle for Constitutional Government in Mexico.* 1903.

Priestley, Herbert Ingram. *The Mexican Nation: A History.* 1924.

Simpson, Lesley Bird. *Many Mexicos.* 1941.

Constitution of 1836

The centralist movement of the 1830s was formed in the wake of a reaction against the liberal reforms of the government of Valentín Gómez Farías and the congress of 1833 and 1834. The Plan of Cuernavaca of 1834 achieved consensus among the moderates from various factions in order to overthrow Gómez Farías and the radical congress and to call for elections for a new legislature. The legislature convened in January 1835, with the attendance of centralists, moderates, and federalists as well as the followers of Gen. Antonio López de Santa Anna. The centralist party succeeded in imposing its aims by means of alliances with other political groups.

Congress spent more than a year writing the Constitution of the Seven Laws—as it is commonly known—because of the cumbersome way the document was arranged. It was approved and published in December 1836 and remained in effect until 1841. In that year, General Santa Anna led a military rebellion and took over the government, and the Constitution of the Seven Laws ceased to be in effect.

This constitution was the first one in Mexico that explicitly consecrated the individual rights of the citizens. It also established a fourth power, known as the Supreme Conservative Power, to regulate the acts of the other branches of government. The Seven Laws limited the privileges of the executive and legislative powers and enhanced those of the judicial power. These laws had republican, representative, and popular characteristics but restricted political participation to those with substantial property or income. The constitution maintained a strong national power and divided the Republic into departments with restricted responsibilities and subject to central control; however, it allowed the regions some political autonomy. The Constitution of the Seven Laws was not welcomed by the public and was regarded with suspicion by both federalists and the army.

Reynaldo Sordo Cedeño

BIBLIOGRAPHY

Costeloe, Michael P. *The Central Republic in Mexico, 1835–1846: "Hombres de Bien" in the Age of Santa Anna.* 1993.

Macneil, A. W. S. "The Supreme Harmonizing Power (El Supremo Poder Conservador) 1837–1841." Master's thesis, University of Texas at Austin, 1969.

Sordo Cedeño, Reynaldo. *El congreso en la Primera República Centralista.* 1993.

Constitution of 1842

In 1841 a military rebellion overthrew the government of President Anastasio Bustamante and annulled the 1836 centralist Constitution of the Seven Laws. Gen. Antonio López de Santa Anna took power. The military, by means of Article 4 of the *Bases de Tacubaya,* committed itself to summon a new constituent congress in order to write another constitution.

The constituent congress gathered in June 1842; the majority in this congress were politicians with liberal ideas who desired a federalist system. The final draft of the constitution they prepared called for a representative, federal, popular republic, and it established the rights and duties of citizens. This constitution kept the three classic powers, with a weak executive, a strong legislative, and a judicial body acting as an interpreter of the constitution and creating an electoral power. The departments were given ample autonomy to organize their own government as states belonging to a federation.

Santa Anna's administration and the army had expected a compromise between the constitutions of 1824 and 1836. The draft discussed at this congress maintained two radical principles, in the view of the government and the army: universal suffrage and complete autonomy of the departments. Santa Anna stepped down, and Gen. Nicolás Bravo, as provisional president, closed congress's sessions before it finished discussions on the draft. The government, closing the congress, was unable to conciliate the political groups. In the long term, the positions were radicalized and the liberals attempted to take over the government by force.

Reynaldo Sordo Cedeño

BIBLIOGRAPHY
Herrera y Lasso, Manuel. "Centralismo y Federalismo (1814–1843)." In *Los Derechos del Pueblo Mexicano. México a través de sus Constituciones,* vol. 1, pp. 595–637. 1978.
Noriega Elío, Cecilia. *El Constituyente de 1842.* 1986.

Constitution of 1843

In December 1842, Gen. Nicolás Bravo's provisional government appointed an assembly of prominent men (Legislative National Assembly) to replace the recently closed constituent congress and to draw up guidelines for the country's political organization (*Bases Orgánicas*). During the debates, the assembly opted to make a constitution rather than simply promote guidelines for a political reorganization.

The *Bases Orgánicas* were approved on 12 June 1843. They established a representative, popular, and centralist republic and guaranteed individual rights. The *Bases* included the three classic powers but gave ample freedom of action to the executive by means of a veto that was hard for congress to override. This met the needs of both Gen. Antonio López de Santa Anna and the military, who had retained power since 1841. The *Bases* proposed a centralism that gave more liberties to the departments than did the Constitution of the Seven Laws of 1836. However, they restricted popular suffrage and specified property as a condition for holders of popularly elected positions. The *Bases* established that congress could reform the constitution at any time and with minimum restraints.

In June 1843 General Santa Anna jured this Constitution, but he did not obey it. In December 1844 a political movement overthrew Santa Anna's government, giving as cause that Santa Anna had not respected the *Bases Orgánicas.* Gen. José Joaquín de Herrera was named provisional president; he maintained the *Bases Orgánicas* in order to avoid another constitutional change. Still, political bickering and instability continued, exacerbated by the U.S. annexation of Texas. In December 1845, Gen. Mariano Paredes y Arrillaga took over the government in a military rebellion, and he suspended the *Bases Orgánicas.*

Reynaldo Sordo Cedeño

BIBLIOGRAPHY
Costeloe, Michael P. *The Central Republic in Mexico, 1835–1846: "Hombres de Bien" in the Age of Santa Anna.* 1993.
Urbina, Manuel. "The Impact of the Texas Revolution on the Government, Politics and Society of Mexico, 1836–1846." Master's thesis, University of Texas at Austin, 1976.

Constitution, Texan

The constitution of the Republic of Texas was written from 1 to 17 March 1836 by a harried set of delegates at a convention called to declare independence and construct a government. As they labored, two hundred miles away a poorly organized and feebly led Texas army was unsuccessfully trying to fend off five times its number of Mexican troops under President Antonio López de Santa Anna at the Alamo.

The constitution of Texas incorporated the basic features of the U.S. Constitution, modified slightly by a few democratic features of U.S. state governments and by the Spanish-Mexican legal tradition. The Texas version provided for shorter terms of office for legislators (one year for House members and three years for Senators) and for a three-year term for the executive with the added restriction that he could not succeed himself. All elections were to be by ballot, separation of church and state were guaranteed by denying national office to clergymen, the declaration of rights included prohibition of monopolies, and imprisonment for debt was abolished.

Reflecting concern for the emergency of war, the constitution allowed quartering of troops, public impressment of property, and forfeiture of citizenship for those who fled to avoid "participation in the present struggle." The constitution endorsed slavery, set forth a slave code, and explicitly denied equal rights to free blacks, although it did prohibit the international slave trade in a sop to U.S. public opinion. The delegates struggled more with balancing the various land interests than with any other issue. In the end the document recognized most of the large holdings accumulated by *empresarios* and smaller plots granted to settlers under Mexican policy during the previous fifteen years. Soldiers in the war for Texas independence received special constitutional protection, and a specific, though noninclusive, antispeculator provision also passed.

The constitution operated under an interim government until a public referendum overwhelmingly approved it and elected officials in September 1836. In the same election the people almost unanimously expressed their preference for annexation by the United States.

Paul D. Lack

BIBLIOGRAPHY
Lack, Paul D. *The Texas Revolutionary Experience: A Political and Social History, 1835–1836.* 1992.
Richardson, Rupert N. "Framing the Constitution of the Republic of Texas." *Southwestern Historical Quarterly* 31 (January 1932): 209.

Contreras and Churubusco

Two significant engagements were fought on Friday, 20 August 1847—one near the villages of Contreras and Padierna, about ten miles southwest of Mexico City, the other around the town of Churubusco some seven miles northeast of Contreras. The battles, fought within a few hours of each other

Battle of Contreras
Order of Battle
20 August 1847

Mexican Forces

Commander
Maj. Gen. Gabriel Valencia

Infantry
1st Line Regiment (decimated)
10th Line Regiment
12th Line Regiment (destroyed)
Tampico Guardacostas (destroyed)

Cavalry
2d Regiment
3d Regiment
7th Regiment
8th Regiment
Guanajuato Regiment, Activo Militia (destroyed)

Artillery
5 pieces

U.S. Forces

Commander
Maj. Gen. Winfield Scott

Infantry
11th U.S. Infantry
14th U.S. Infantry
1st U.S. Artillery (serving as infantry)
3d U.S. Infantry (serving as infantry)
1st U.S. Regiment of Mounted Rifles (dismounted)
U.S. Voltigeur Regiment
U.S. Marine Battalion
1st New York Volunteers
1st South Carolina Volunteers

Artillery
Company I, 1st U.S. Artillery (Magruder's mounted battery)

Battle of Churubusco
Order of Battle
20 August 1847

Mexican Forces

Commander
Gen. Antonio López de Santa Anna

Infantry
1st Light Regiment
2d Light Regiment
4th Light Regiment
11th Line Regiment
San Patricio Battalion
Bravo Battalion, National Guard
Independencia Battalion, National Guard
Victoria Battalion, National Guard
Hidalgo Battalion, National Guard

Cavalry
Hussars of the Supreme Powers
9th Regiment
Tulancingo Cuirrasiers

Artillery
5 pieces (manned by the San Patricio Battalion)

U.S. Forces

Commander
Maj. Gen. Winfield Scott

Infantry
2d U.S. Infantry
3d U.S. Infantry
4th U.S. Infantry
5th U.S. Infantry
6th U.S. Infantry
7th U.S. Infantry
8th U.S. Infantry
9th U.S. Infantry
11th U.S. Infantry
12th U.S. Infantry
14th U.S. Infantry
15th U.S. Infantry
U.S. Voltigeur Regiment
1st U.S. Regiment of Mounted Rifles (dismounted)
Company A, U.S. Engineers
1st U.S. Artillery (serving as infantry)
2d U.S. Artillery (serving as infantry)
3d U.S. Artillery (serving as infantry)
4th U.S. Artillery (serving as infantry)
U.S. Marine Battalion
1st New York Volunteers
1st South Carolina Volunteers

Artillery
Company I, 1st Artillery (Magruder's Mounted Battery)
Company K, 1st Artillery (Taylor's Light Battery)
Company A, 2d Artillery (Duncan's Light Battery)
Ordnance Company

between the armies of Maj. Gen. Winfield Scott during his advance on the Mexican capital and Gen. Antonio López de Santa Anna, could be considered two parts of one battle. Both battles were decisive victories for the U.S. forces, setting the stage for the climactic battle for Mexico City.

On 11 August, Scott's army reached Ayotla, fifteen miles from the Mexican capital. His force numbered 10,000 men organized in four divisions. Santa Anna had gathered an army of 36,000 men and 100 cannon to defend the city. He fortified the approaches to the city and took advantage of the natural obstacles in the surrounding valley, especially the lakes and marshy tableland that limited the approaches to several built-up roads and causeways.

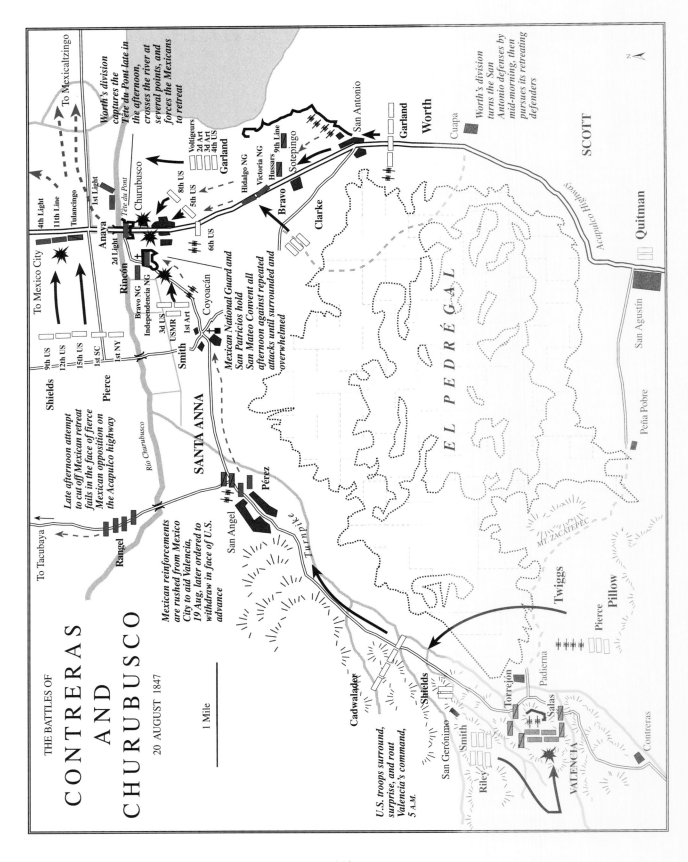

THE BATTLES OF

CONTRERAS
AND
CHURUBUSCO

20 AUGUST 1847

1 Mile

Shields

9th US
12th US
15th US
1st SC
1st NY

Pierce

Smith

3d US
USMR
1st Art

SANTA ANNA

Rangel

To Tacubaya

To Mexico City

Late afternoon attempt to cut off Mexican retreat fails in the face of fierce Mexican opposition on the Acapulco highway

Mexican reinforcements are rushed from Mexico City to aid Valencia, 19 Aug, later ordered to withdraw in face of U.S. advance

Río Churubusco

Pérez

San Angel

Cadwalader

Shields

San Gerónimo

Riley

Smith

U.S. troops surround, surprise, and rout Valencia's command, 5 A.M.

Contreras

VALENCIA

Salas

Torrejón

Padierna

MT. ZACATEPEC

Pillow

Pierce

Twiggs

Turnpike

EL PEDRÉGAL

Peña Pobre

San Agustín

To Mexicaltzingo

To Mexicaltzingo

Worth's division captures the Tête du Pont late in the afternoon, crosses the river at several points, and forces the Mexicans to retreat

4th Light
11th Line
Tulancingo

1st Light

Anaya

2d Light

Rincón

Bravo NG
Independencia NG

Coyoacán

Mexican National Guard and San Patricios hold San Mateo Convent all afternoon against repeated attacks until surrounded and overwhelmed

Tête du Pont

Churubusco

8th US

5th US

6th US

Voltigeurs
2d Art
3d Art
4th US

Garland

Hidalgo NG
Victoria NG
Hussars
9th Line
Sotepingo

Bravo

Clarke

San Antonio

Garland

Worth

Cuapa

Worth's division turns the San Antonio defenses by mid-morning, then pursues its retreating defenders

SCOTT

Acapulco Highway

Quitman

112

Scott moved his army along a muddy but passable route skirting the two lakes south of Ayotla. Over the next two days he completed the twenty-five-mile trek, reaching San Agustín, less than nine miles from the city's gates. Santa Anna countered Scott's flanking movement by shifting the bulk of his defenses to fortified areas between Contreras and Churubusco. About two miles above San Agustín the heavily fortified hacienda at San Antonio blocked the road to Churubusco. Scott's engineers also reported that the causeway road leading to Churubusco was flanked by obstacles, on the right by swamps and on the left by a rugged lava field called El Pedregal.

On 18 August Scott dispatched Capt. Robert E. Lee of the engineers to find a way around El Pedregal. Lee found a path, and Scott ordered Maj. Gen. Gideon J. Pillow's division to build a crude road across the lava field. Brig. Gen. David E. Twiggs's division was to follow and, the path once open, was to pass through and protect the work parties as they improved the route for the artillery. Brig. Gen. William J. Worth's division remained opposite San Antonio, and Brig. Gen. John A. Quitman's division protected the supply train and depot at San Agustín. By early the next afternoon Pillow reached the western edge of the lava field overlooking the Mexican army's right flank under Maj. Gen. Gabriel Valencia, who had impulsively advanced about four miles south of his assigned position. Pillow impetuously led his and Twiggs's divisions in an attack, but Santa Anna deployed a large force to support Valencia. As night fell, Pillow faced the possibility of being crushed by two much larger Mexican forces.

Meanwhile, 1st Lt. Zealous B. Tower of the engineers had found a ravine that gave a hidden avenue for an attack behind Valencia's camp. That night Brig. Gen. Persifor F. Smith sent Lee across El Pedregal during a driving rainstorm to get Scott's approval for the surprise assault. About 1 A.M. on 20 August, Lee guided a diversionary force through El Pedregal into position. The main assault forces, guided by Tower, set out at 3 A.M. The diversionary attack began at 5 A.M., and just as the Mexican troops awakened to the threat to their front, they were attacked from the rear by Smith's force, which fired one volley and charged with fixed bayonets. Within seventeen minutes the Mexicans broke and fell back toward Churubusco.

Santa Anna positioned delaying forces and ordered his garrison at San Antonio, in danger of encirclement, to withdraw to Churubusco. About the same time Worth's division found a path across El Pedregal. Before the Mexican troops could execute an orderly withdrawal from San Antonio, they realized they were cut off and fled north in disorder. The U.S. forces pursuing from Contreras hastily attacked a fortified convent manned by other Mexican forces, whose spirited defense momentarily halted this advance. About the same time Worth's troops faced strong opposition at a fortified bridge crossing the Río Churubusco near the convent. Another U.S. flanking force north of Churubusco also met stiff Mexican resistance. Worth's persistent attacks, resulting in much hand-to-hand fighting, succeeded nonetheless. The convent was heavily bombarded, and the defenders surrendered, among them a group of U.S. deserters fighting for Mexico, called the San Patricio Battalion. By that afternoon both U.S. forces linked up on the road north of Churubusco, and the hard fighting turned into a pursuit as the dispirited Mexicans fled northward to Mexico City.

Scott could have continued the pursuit into the city but decided to pause. He became concerned because his men had fought two battles simultaneously, and he arranged an armistice to allow for negotiations. Scott's losses in the two battles were significant for the size of his force: 133 killed (1.5 percent) and 865 wounded (10.5 percent) of his 8,500 men engaged. Santa Anna lost almost one-third of his force or roughly 10,000 men in the two actions.

Adrian G. Traas

BIBLIOGRAPHY

Bauer, K. Jack. *The Mexican War, 1846–1848.* 1974.

Eisenhower, John S. D. *So Far from God: The U.S. War with Mexico, 1846–1848.* 1989.

McCaffrey, James M. *Army of Manifest Destiny: The American Soldier in the Mexican War, 1846–1848.* 1992.

Nevin, David. *The Mexican War.* 1978.

Traas, Adrian G. *From the Golden Gate to Mexico City: The U.S. Army Topographical Engineers in the Mexican War, 1846–1848.* 1993.

Conventions of 1832 and 1833

The conventions of 1832 and 1833 in the Anglo-American colonies of Texas resulted from events in 1831 and 1832 that included aggressive colonists defying and attacking Mexican port officials in conflicts over taxes and a strong military presence. Many Anglo colonists, immigrants from the United States to Mexico, decided that the time was ripe to voice their grievances because the new Mexican government was liberal. The colonists held a convention at San Felipe de Austin in October 1832, violating laws for political meetings in Mexico. Although Stephen F. Austin, founder of the vast majority of Anglo colonies, did not fully approve of the meeting, he accepted election as president so that he could control some of its activities. The official call for the meeting made it clear that the convention's purpose was to dispel rumors that questioned the fidelity of Anglo colonists to the Republic of Mexico.

William H. Wharton wrote a forceful memorial, or petition, requesting the repeal of Article 11 of the Law of April 6, 1830, which prohibited immigration from the United States. He stated that, in addition to the detrimental effect it had on settling the region, the law implied a suspicion of the Anglo colonists' loyalty to Mexico. The most controversial decision at the convention was a motion to request separate statehood from Coahuila, to which Texas had been joined under the Constitution of 1824. Other issues included tariff collection, public education, protection from Indians, and the organization of militia companies. Convention participants also agreed to appoint a Central Committee of Vigilance, Safety, and Correspondence with subcommittees in all districts in Texas to disseminate news quickly in case of an emergency. Mexican law, however, did not allow the organization of committees for such purposes.

Austin sought to present the convention's views through the strictly legal channels of petitions arising from the *ayuntamientos,* a type of town council, and was concerned that the decision to hold a second convention in March 1833 would exacerbate the Mexican government's distrust of the Anglo colonists in Texas.

Wharton, more belligerent than Austin, presided over the second convention. This convention also requested repeal of Article 11 of the Law of April 6 but framed the document more delicately than Wharton had in 1832. It also drew up a constitution for the proposed State of Texas, modeled after the Massachusetts constitution of 1780, a copy of which was on hand. Austin, Dr. James B. Miller, and Erasmo Seguín were to take the petitions to Mexico City. Because Miller and Seguín were unable to go, Austin went alone and was imprisoned there for eighteen months on a number of charges.

In the end convention leaders never presented the petitions to the Mexican congress or the state legislature, however, because of the absence of support from Tejanos in San Antonio de Béxar and uncertainties regarding leadership and direction in Mexican politics. The conventions of 1832 and 1833 confirmed the suspicions of many Mexican officials of the Anglo colonists' disrespect for Mexican laws.

Jodella K. Dyreson

BIBLIOGRAPHY

Barker, Eugene C. *The Life of Stephen F. Austin.* 1925.

Barker, Eugene C., ed. *The Austin Papers.* 1924–1928.

Edward, David B. *The History of Texas.* 1836. Reprint, 1967.

Gammel, H. P. N., comp. *The Laws of Texas, 1822–1897.* 1898.

Córdova Rebellion

The affair known as the Córdova Rebellion occurred in Nacogdoches in eastern Texas, closer to the United States–Texas border than to the more common flash points in the ongoing tensions between Mexico and Texas during this period. This 1838 to 1839 revolt against the Republic of Texas, although traditionally viewed by U.S. historians as originating with Mexican designs against Texas, had its origins in the experience of the Tejano residents.

The rebellion stemmed from their years of declining influence and increasing isolation and the growing disrespect of Anglo-Americans for the native Mexican residents. Tejanos for the most part withheld support from the Texas Revolution in favor of a form of armed neutrality designed to protect their homes and families from any and all threats. Rumors in the spring of 1836 held that the Tejanos were plotting an alliance with neighboring Cherokee Indians to support the Mexican forces heading toward Nacogdoches. The Tejano leader, former town official Vicente Córdova, never acknowledged the legitimacy of the new Texas Republic.

After 1836 the native Mexicans found themselves under constant suspicion and without legal protections for their persons, property, or political participation. Early in the summer of 1838 agents from Mexico had brought encouragement, arms, promises of military support, and promises to gain alliances with a variety of Indian tribes. The official proclamation of rebellion by Córdova and his followers, on 10 August 1838, stated that the Tejanos, "having gathered together with their weapons in hand, are determined to shed their last drop of blood in order to protect their individual rights and those of the Nation to which they belong."

Hostilities had actually begun a week earlier in conflicts involving small numbers of Anglo-Texans and Tejanos over horse-thieving allegations and retaliations. Texas president Sam Houston, visiting in Nacogdoches at the time, made last-ditch promises to ameliorate conditions but also prepared for war and for diplomacy with his Cherokee friends to keep them from supporting Córdova. No Indian tribe as a group joined in the rebellion, although individual Cherokee, Kichai, and Coshatto did fight with the rebels. Outnumbered by as many as eight to one, Córdova's men nevertheless repeatedly eluded Texas militia and mounted volunteer units. He managed to move around in remote areas until 15–16 October when a pitched battle occurred between 230 militia under Gen. Thomas J. Rusk and a smaller number of Tejano, Indian, black, and Anglo-Texan rebels.

This indecisive engagement ended in Rusk's return to Nacogdoches, while Córdova's force remained together but away from population centers on the northeastern frontier. In March 1839 Córdova received word from Mexico that no army was being sent to assist him and that he should move westward with only seventy-five men, and they suffered from attacks by Texas Ranger companies on the upper Colorado and Guadalupe Rivers. Only a wounded Córdova and a few followers made it to safety in Matamoros.

The Tejanos who remained in Nacogdoches fared only slightly better. Many had property confiscated or lost through neglect, while 33 were imprisoned for four months awaiting a trial that found all but 3 innocent. They were all released later because of procedural irregularities. The Córdova Rebellion hastened the decline and isolation of Tejanos, provided a rationale for Texas president Mirabeau B. Lamar's efforts to remove Indians from the region by force, and provoked more animosity between Mexico and Texas.

Paul D. Lack

BIBLIOGRAPHY

Lack, Paul D. "The Córdova Revolt." In *Tejano Journey, 1770–1850.* 1996.

Nance, Joseph Milton. *After San Jacinto: The Texas-Mexican Frontier, 1836–1841.* 1963.

Wunder, John R., and Rebecca Herring. "Law, History, Turner, and the Cordova Rebellion." *Red River Valley Historical Review* 5 (Summer 1982): 51–67.

Corona, Antonio

Mexican general and politician Antonio Corona (1808–1863) was born in Guadalajara and received his education in France. He joined the Mexican army in 1831 as a second lieutenant and in 1840 joined the forces of Antonio López de Santa Anna, who promoted him to lieutenant colonel. Corona participated in Mexico's various civil wars, specializing in artillery. In mid-1846, he was governor at the fort of San Juan de Ulúa. A year later he served as Chief of Artillery in the army established at San Luis Potosí, which was defeated at the Battle of La Angostura. His service in this campaign earned him the rank of general.

Corona supported Santa Anna's return to the presidency in 1853, and the same year Santa Anna named him military commander of Vera Cruz, with the mission to suppress all political movements against Santa Anna. After the Ayutla Revolution in 1855, Corona was stripped of military rank. During the War of Reform he joined the conservatives, and in 1859 President Miramón made him a major general and named him military commander of the Federal District as well as minister of war. After the ultimate defeat of the conservatives in 1860, Corona left the country. He died in Nice, France, in 1863.

Faustino A. Aquino Sanchez

BIBLIOGRAPHY

Cárdenas de la Peña, Enrique. *Mil personajes en el México del siglo XIX.* 1979.

Diccionario Porrúa: De história, biografía y geografió de México. 6th ed. 1995.

Corpus Christi

Located on the Gulf of Mexico at the mouth of the Nueces River, this small village of two hundred was transformed by the arrival of Gen. Zachary Taylor and the Army of Observation in August 1845. Close enough to observe Mexican activities, yet far enough to allow ample warning of any Mexican invasion force, the protected bay made Corpus Christi an ideal logistical base for operations in the disputed territory. By March 1846, 2,000 sutlers and traders had relocated there, providing liquor, lumber, and dry goods to the 4,300 U.S. soldiers encamped on the beaches, as well as entertainment at newly constructed bars, bowling alleys, billiard halls, and theaters.

Letters from U.S. officers spoke about pleasant weather conditions upon their arrival. However, fall thunderstorms, in conjunction with lower temperatures, flimsy tents, firewood shortages, and a plague of insects and venomous snakes, made conditions in the army's encampment miserable. The elements, coupled with primitive sanitary conditions and brackish water, rendered as much as 13 percent of Taylor's force unfit for duty.

Despite such difficulties, the seven-month period at Corpus Christi was valuable for the U.S. Army. Prior to 1845 regular units were divided among many posts, with few locations occupied by more than one company. While isolation and combat experience during the Second Seminole War bred quick-thinking and independent company commanders, few field officers had the opportunity to gain experience directing large formations of soldiers. At Corpus Christi, Taylor and his unit commanders drilled troops on the beaches, refamiliarizing both officers and men with regimental and brigade maneuvers. As a result of this training and the presence of competent commanders at the company and regimental levels, U.S. forces at the beginning of the U.S.–Mexican War were among the most well trained and disciplined to enter battle under U.S. colors.

Robert P. Wettemann, Jr.

BIBLIOGRAPHY

Patch, Joseph Dorst. *The Concentration of General Zachary Taylor's Army at Corpus Christi, Texas.* 1962.

Payne, Darwin. "Camp Life in the Army of Occupation: Corpus Christi, July 1845 to March 1846." *Southwestern Historical Quarterly* 73 (1970): 326–342.

Cortina, José Gómez de la

The son of a wealthy and well-known Spanish family from Mexico City, José Gómez de la Cortina (1799–1860) was a respected politician and man of letters in nineteenth-century Mexico. A member of several scientific and literary societies, Cortina authored works of fiction, collaborated with newspapers, and founded the Mexican Geographic and Statistical Society. Cortina's political views leaned to the conservative and *moderado* (moderate liberal) camp. He served as minister of finance between December 1838 and March 1839 and in 1840 headed a group that favored establishment of a monarchy (Cortina's daughter was married to José María Gutiérrez Estrada, who at the time published a controversial pamphlet supporting that form of government). Cortina subsequently was a member of the Assembly of Notables, which drafted the 1843 charter known as the *Bases Orgánicas,* and of the senate that spearheaded the *moderado*-led 6 December 1844 rebellion.

Appointed governor of the Federal District shortly after the August 1846 rebellion of the Ciudadela, Cortina tried early in October to curtail the political ascendancy of the *puros,* a more radical, anticlerical faction. Acting on the grounds that domestic tranquility was threatened, Cortina apprehended *puro* partisan Francisco Próspero Pérez, tried to disband a *puro*-led civic militia battalion, and organized a militia unit supported by a merchant group to protect *moderado* interests. The uproar that followed not only brought *puros* and *moderados* to the brink of civil war during the U.S. invasion but also forced Cortina to resign his post. Cortina, nonetheless, continued to plot against the *puros* and helped organize the February 1847 rebellion of the *polkos.* He died a pauper in the Mexican capital nearly twenty years later.

Pedro Santoni

BIBLIOGRAPHY

Bustamante, Carlos María. *El nuevo Bernal Díaz del Castillo, o sea, historia de la invasión de los Anglo-Americanos en México.* Reprint, 1949.

Diccionario geográfico, histórico y biográfico de los Estados Unidos Mexicanos. 5 vols. 1888.

Santoni, Pedro. *Mexicans at Arms: Puro Federalists and the Politics of War, 1845–1848.* 1996.

Cortina, Juan

Mexican military leader and Texas folk hero Juan Nepomuceno Cortina (1824–1894) was born in Camargo, Tamaulipas, on 16 May. At age twenty-two as a corporal in the Defensores de la Patria, a company of the Guardia Nacional de Tamaulipas, Cortina served as a scout in the Tamaulipas Brigade during the battles against U.S. forces at Palo Alto and Resaca de la Palma. Cortina's whereabouts following the U.S. occupation of Matamoros cannot be determined with certainty. As Gen. Zachary Taylor moved upriver to establish a supply base at Camargo before pushing into the interior toward Monterrey, Mexican irregulars remained active in the area, and Cortina may have been with these units. He may also have served with Mexican guerrillas that preyed on U.S. supply lines before and after the battles of Monterrey and Buena Vista. Years later he would remember being forced to live a life of "proscription" and to "wander about," either fighting isolated units of the U.S. Army or "fleeing in the deserts."

After the war, Cortina signed on with Capt. John J. Dix

of the U.S. Army Quartermaster's Department at Fort Brown. For $25 dollars per month, he and other Tejanos and Mexicanos worked to recover equipment and draft animals that had been left in northeastern Mexico. In the following years, Cortina established a small ranch at San José, near his mother's large Rancho del Carmen, upriver from Brownsville. During this period Cortina developed a burning hatred for a group of judges and unscrupulous Brownsville attorneys who he accused of expropriating land from Tejanos unfamiliar with the U.S. judicial system. Although largely illiterate, Cortina became a charismatic leader to many of the Mexicans who lived along both banks of the Río Grande.

On 13 July 1859 Cortina witnessed Brownsville city marshal Robert Shears's brutal arrest of a Tejano from Rancho del Carmen. Cortina shot the marshal and rode out of town with the prisoner, igniting the so-called Cortina War. On 28 September Cortina rode back into Brownsville with seventy-five men and seized control of the town. Five men, including the city jailer, died during the raid, as Cortina and his men raced through the streets shouting "Death to the Americans" and "Viva Mexico." For three months Cortina, at the head of several hundred revolutionaries, successfully eluded the Texas Rangers before being defeated by the Rangers and U.S. Army at Río Grande City on 27 December 1859.

During the French intervention in Mexico, Cortina became a powerful *caudillo,* a general in the army of President Benito Juárez, and twice governor of Tamaulipas. During the early 1870s Cortina was accused by U.S. authorities of masterminding the theft of thousands of cattle in South Texas; some of his men raided as far north as Corpus Christi. In retaliation, Texas Rangers invaded Mexico, burned, plundered, and indiscriminately hanged Mexicans. In May 1875 U.S. diplomatic pressure resulted in Mexican president Sebastian Lerdo de Teja ordering Cortina's arrest and confinement at the prison of Santiago Tlatelolco in Mexico City. Two months later Cortina pronounced for Gen. Porfirio Díaz and fled Mexico City. Back on the border, Cortina was again arrested, this time by orders of Díaz, and imprisoned in Mexico City. He died of pneumonia at Azapotzalco on the outskirts of the city on 30 October 1894. He was buried with military honors in the Panteon de Dolores.

Jerry Thompson

BIBLIOGRAPHY

Douglas, James Ridley. "Juan Cortina: El Caudillo de la Frontera." Master's thesis, University of Texas at Austin, 1987.

Goldfinch, Charles W., and Jose T. Canales. *Juan N. Cortina: Two Interpretations.* 1974.

Thompson, Jerry. *Juan Cortina and the Texas-Mexico Frontier, 1859–1877.* 1994.

Corwin, Thomas

The antiwar Whig senator Thomas Corwin (1794–1864) had been an Ohio lawyer, state legislator, U.S. representative in the 1830s, and a one-term governor. He served in the Senate from 1844 to 1850, maintaining a low profile until early 1847, when he sharply rebuked fellow senator Lewis Cass and other prowar and expansionist Democrats. Annoyed with mere rhetoric critical of President James K. Polk, Corwin declared that he would oppose the president's request for more money and men—a bold step other antiwar senators refused to take. Although Corwin had voted for previous appropriations, he then changed course, accusing Polk of "bold usurpation" when he "made war" on Mexico "without the advice or consent of Congress." Corwin believed Polk was responsible for starting the war because "Mexico, and not Texas, possessed this territory [east of the Río Grande] to which your armies marched."

He resented Democrats who insisted that Congress must blindly support the Polk administration. "If it be my duty to grant whatever the President demands," he queried, "for what am I here?" Corwin refuted Cass's plea for a vast indemnity of land. "Sir, look at this pretense of want of room," he protested.

> "With twenty millions of people, you have about one thousand millions of acres of land, inviting settlement by every conceivable argument. . . . If I were a Mexican I would tell you, 'Have you not room in your own country to bury your dead men? If you come into mine we will greet you with bloody hands, and welcome you to hospitable graves.'"

Corwin urged senators to "call home our armies . . . [to] our own acknowledged limits." After the war Corwin held the post of secretary of the treasury in Millard Fillmore's cabinet, then returned to Congress as a Republican in the late 1850s. In 1861 President Abraham Lincoln appointed him minister to Mexico, where he served until 1864. Corwin died in Washington, D.C., in 1865.

Thomas Hietala

BIBLIOGRAPHY
Congressional Globe, 11 February 1847, pp. 211–218.
Morrow, Josiah, ed. *Life and Speeches of Thomas Corwin.* 1896.

Cos, Martín Perfecto de

Born in Vera Cruz, Martín Perfecto de Cos (1800–1854) joined the army in 1820 as a cadet, received promotion to lieutenant the following year, and was responsible for building fortifications on Mexico's east coast. He supported Antonio López de Santa Anna in the 1823 uprising against Agustín de Iturbide and had advanced to the rank of general of brigade by 1833. Two years later, Cos participated in the campaign against federalist rebels in Zacatecas. He then

Martín Perfecto de Cos. John Frost, *Pictorial History of Mexico and the Mexican War*, 1862

marched with his command to Monclova, where he shut down the profederalist legislature of the state of Coahuila y Texas, and then on to Texas to investigate anticentralist disturbances in that region.

Cos landed near Goliad with three hundred men in September 1835, intending to arrest all critics of the Santa Anna government. Instead, his arrival helped stoke antigovernment sentiment, and he found himself besieged at San Antonio by several hundred Texian insurgents. He surrendered to them in December and was paroled.

In February 1836 Cos returned to Texas as part of Santa Anna's army and participated in the attack on the Alamo. His command pursued Texian forces past the Brazos River, but was attacked and defeated, along with Santa Anna's detachment, at the Battle of San Jacinto on 21 April. During this Mexican military disaster, he surrendered yet again and was later released.

His military career stagnated until the U.S.–Mexican War. In 1847 he unsuccessfully defended the port of Tuxpan. After the war, Cos assumed the position of political chief and commandant general of the Territory of Tehuantepec. He died at Minatitlán, Vera Cruz, on 1 October 1854.

Donald S. Frazier

BIBLIOGRAPHY
Bancroft, Hubert Howe. *History of the North Mexican States and Texas.* 1889.
DePalo, William A., Jr. *The Mexican National Army, 1822–1852.* 1997.

Hardin, Steve. *Texian Iliad.* 1994.
Smith, Justin. *The War with Mexico.* 2 vols. 1919. Reprint, 1963.

Cosío, Manuel González

See González Cosío, Manuel

Coups, Mexican

See Elections and Coups, Mexican

Couto, José Bernardo

Born in the city of Orizaba, Vera Cruz, Mexican politician José Bernardo Couto (1803–1862) earned a law degree in 1827 from the Colegio de San Ildefonso in Mexico City. During the next twenty years Couto figured prominently in Mexican political circles. A member of the *moderado* party, Couto served in various congresses during the 1830s and 1840s, and for two months in late 1845 he joined Gen. José Joaquín de Herrera's cabinet as minister of justice.

Couto played a major role in the negotiations that ended the conflict with the United States. During the August 1847 armistice arranged by Generals Antonio López de Santa Anna and Winfield Scott, Couto was one of the four commissioners charged with negotiating a peace with U.S. envoy Nicholas P. Trist. Although the talks were unsuccessful and the U.S. Army occupied Mexico City in mid-September, two months later then-president Gen. Pedro María Anaya again appointed Couto peace commissioner. Shortly thereafter, Couto urged Trist to disregard instructions from Washington, D.C., that ordered Trist to break off diplomatic talks.

In late spring 1848 Couto defended the Treaty of Guadalupe Hidalgo when the *puros,* a prowar faction, agitated against ratification. Couto noted that the treaty, while a painful necessity, was neither a national disgrace nor a permanent setback to Mexican development. He likened the territorial cessions to an amputation performed to save a patient's life. By ending the war, the treaty had saved Mexico from possible obliteration as a nation.

Couto retired from politics after the war. At the time of his death in Mexico City, Couto was devoting his energies to various literary and educational pursuits.

Pedro Santoni

BIBLIOGRAPHY
Costeloe, Michael P. *The Central Republic in Mexico, 1835–1846: Hombres de Bien in the Age of Santa Anna.* 1993.
Griswold del Castillo, Richard. *The Treaty of Guadalupe Hidalgo: A Legacy of Conflict.* 1990.

Pletcher, David. *The Diplomacy of Annexation: Texas, Oregon, and the Mexican War.* 1973.

Crabb, Henry

Henry Alexander Crabb (c. 1821–1857) was a lawyer, politician, newspaper editor, and filibuster. Little is known of Crabb's early life in Tennessee, but he practiced law and perhaps engaged in politics. He journeyed to California in 1849, served in the California senate during 1853 and 1854, briefly edited the *Stockton Argus,* and in 1855 and 1856 ran unsuccessfully for the U.S. Senate. Crabb had known William Walker when the two were boys in Tennessee, and the two met again in California and discussed Walker's filibustering aims. Both men believed the U.S. acquisition of considerable Mexican territory that resulted from the U.S.–Mexican War left Mexico vulnerable to additional ventures from north of the border. Crabb married into a Californio family with political influence in Sonora, which put him in touch with the leading political faction there led by Ignacio Pesqueira. Allegedly with Pesqueira's encouragement, Crabb agreed to lead a group of "colonizers" into Sonora.

Crabb organized a venture, The Arizona Colonization Company, that was actually a filibustering expedition into Sonora, possibly under the disguise of helping Pesqueira win power over an opposing political faction. There is no proof that Crabb was actually invited to colonize in Sonora, but circumstantial evidence indicates that originally he may have believed so.

By late 1856 Pesqueira was firmly in power in Sonora, and he distanced himself from Crabb's group. Crabb and approximately one hundred men arrived in Los Angeles in January 1857, preparatory to entering Sonora, only to learn that Pesqueira had denounced the venture. Despite hearing this, Crabb and his men marched into northern Sonora. Pesqueira called on Sonorans to arm themselves to repel the invaders, and on 6 April a Mexican militia force captured the Crabb party. The day after the surrender Mexican troops executed the filibusters. They severed Crabb's head and placed it in a jar of mescal as a warning to all U.S. citizens who might aspire to filibustering in Mexico.

Joseph A. Stout, Jr.

BIBLIOGRAPHY
Ainsa, J. Y. *History of the Crabb Expedition into N. Sonora.* 1951.
Forbes, Robert H. *Crabb's Filibustering Expedition into Sonora, 1857: An Historical Account with Map, Illustrations and Bibliography.* 1952.
Stout, Joseph A., Jr. *The Liberators: Filibustering Expeditions into Mexico, 1848–1862, and the Last Thrust of Manifest Destiny.* 1973.

Crockett, David

Frontiersman David Crockett (1786–1836), hero of the battle of the Alamo, was born on 17 August in what is now Green County, Tennessee. Crockett spent his youth on the frontier working various jobs. During his military service, from 1813 to 1815, he fought against the Creek Indians and was a scout in West Florida.

Following his first wife's death in 1815, Crockett married Elizabeth Patton and settled in Shoal Creek, Lawrence County, Tennessee, where he served as a magistrate, justice of the peace, town commissioner, and colonel of the 57th Militia Regiment. Crockett was elected to represent Lawrence and Hickman Counties in the Tennessee state legislature, serving from 1821 to 1823. He ran unsuccessfully for Congress in 1825 but in 1827 was elected U.S. representative from the 9th Congressional District. Crockett's politics originally were in line with those of Andrew Jackson, but Crockett's determination to vote his own mind and not that of a party soon caused him to oppose Jackson; in particular, Crockett strongly opposed the Indian Removal Act. Crockett was defeated in the 1835 election.

That November, Crockett and two companions left Memphis to explore Texas, traveling down the Arkansas River to Little Rock, overland through present-day Oklahoma, and south across the Red River. Crockett explored north and central Texas before arriving at Nacogdoches in early January 1836, where he swore allegiance to the Texian government and enlisted as a private in Captain Harrison's company of Tennessee Mounted Volunteers.

The company arrived on 3 February at San Antonio, where it joined the garrison commanded by Col. James Bowie and Lt. Col. William B. Travis. On 23 February 1836, Mexican troops under Gen. Antonio López de Santa Anna arrived and forced the Texians into the Alamo mission, which they defended for thirteen days. Santa Anna's army took the Alamo on 6 March 1836, killing all of its male defenders.

Crockett's activities and role in the Alamo siege and battle are uncertain. Dr. John Sutherland, who claimed to have been sent out as a courier on the first day of the siege, stated that Crockett had requested to be considered a "high private" and that Travis had assigned the Tennessee Mounted Volunteers to defend the palisade wall between the Alamo church and south barracks. Susannah Dickinson, one of the female survivors, gave testimony that Crockett was sent out during the siege to bring in reinforcements. Mexican accounts, the best of which is in a memoir written by Lt. Col. José Enrique de la Peña, identify Crockett as one of the five to seven prisoners executed after the battle. Some modern writers have tried to discount the authenticity of de la Peña and other Mexican sources in regard to Crockett's probable execution, but author James Crisp has effectively discredited these latter-day challenges.

David Crockett. Benjamin Perley Poore, *Perley's Reminiscences,* vol. 1, 1886

Crockett was the most famous member of the Alamo garrison, and the strong popular image of Davy Crockett has continued in folklore, literature, theater, and motion pictures.

Kevin R. Young

BIBLIOGRAPHY

Crockett, David. *A Narrative of the Life of David Crockett of the State of Tennessee.* 1834.

de la Peña, Enrique. *With Santa Anna in Texas.* Edited and translated by Carmen Perry. Introduction by James E. Crisp. 1997.

Lofaro, Michael A. *Davy Crockett: The Man, the Legend, the Legacy, 1786–1986.* 1986.

Shackford, James Atkins. *David Crockett: The Man and the Legend.* 1956.

Cuba

Throughout the nineteenth century, Cuba loomed large in the U.S. public's imagination. Just ninety miles off the Florida coast, many observers in the United States assumed that Cuba naturally belonged to the United States and would some day be added to the national territory. Nations around the Caribbean basin remained suspicious of this last important Spanish remnant in the New World.

In Latin America most leaders viewed Cuba as the last outpost of Spanish authority, which evoked fear or confidence depending on liberal or conservative proclivities. Mexican nationalists were uncomfortable with this presence, and the Spanish invasion of Tampico in 1829, staged from Havana, reinforced their distrust. In addition, political exiles from Mexico, including Antonio López de Santa Anna, often made their way to asylum in Cuba where they plotted their comebacks with tacit Spanish approval.

On 18 October 1854 Pierre Soule, U.S. minister to Spain, recommended to Secretary of State William L. Marcy that the United States acquire Cuba from Spain. This Ostend Manifesto, as it came to be known, advocated the peaceful purchase of the island for $130 million. The document also recommended, however, that if the offer were rejected, that the United States should invade, evoking the spirit of Manifest Destiny. The climate in the United State after the U.S.–Mexican War was different, however, and Marcy correctly sensed that the addition of Cuba to the nation would exacerbate issues regarding the expansion of slavery, and thus he dropped the matter completely. The attention of the nation had clearly changed from unbridled expansionism to increasingly bitter sectionalism.

Donald S. Frazier

BIBLIOGRAPHY

May, Robert E. *The Southern Dream of a Caribbean Empire, 1854–1861.* 1973.

May, Robert E. "Young American Males and Filibustering in the Age of Manifest Destiny: The United States Army as a Cultural Mirror." *The Journal of American History* 78 (1991–1992): 846–874.

Potter, David M. *The Impending Crises, 1848–1861.* 1973.

Smith, Justin H. *The War with Mexico.* 2 vols. 1919. Reprint, 1963.

Cuevas, Luis Gonzaga

Mexican politician Luis Gonzaga Cuevas (1800–1867) was born in Lerma, state of México. He received a formal education at the College of San Ildefonso, where he graduated with high honors. He served in various capacities within the Mexican government starting in 1825. In 1826, 1837, and 1838 Cuevas was foreign minister, mostly under centralist presidents. During difficult negotiations with France, President Anastasio Bustamante named him minister plenipotentiary to bring about a favorable solution to the conflict that later would be known as The Pastry War. In 1838, on the eve of his temporary retirement from public service, Cuevas issued a report denouncing the expansionist tendencies of

the United States, stopping just short of predicting a war between the two North American republics.

Cuevas briefly returned to government as secretary of foreign relations under President José Joaquín de Herrera in 1844 and 1845 and urged that leader to follow a conciliatory role in his negotiations with the United States and Texas. After Herrera was removed from power, Cuevas retired to his home. When U.S. troops occupied Mexico City in 1847, Cuevas fled with the government to Querétaro where he helped negotiate an end to hostilities. He ultimately drafted portions of the Treaty of Guadalupe Hildago.

After the war, Cuevas wrote *Porvenir de México: Juicio sobre su Estado Politico en 1821 y 1851,* in which he took a critical view of the problems that had beset Mexico. He maintained his conservative views during the War of the Reform, and aided the imperialists during the French intervention. Cuevas died in Mexico City in 1867.

Donald S. Frazier

BIBLIOGRAPHY

Cárdenas de la Peña, Enrique. *Tiempo y tarea de Luis Gonzaga Cuevas.* 1982.

Cuevas, Luis Gonzaga. *Porvenir de México: Juicio sobre su Estado Politico en 1821 y 1851.* 1851.

Cushing, Caleb

Born in Massachusetts, Caleb Cushing (1800–1879) graduated from Harvard and practiced law before his election to the legislature in 1825 and then the U.S. House (1835–1843). Appointed by President John Tyler as minister to China, he negotiated a commercial treaty in 1844.

A former Whig turned Democrat and an ardent expansionist, Cushing organized a company for the 1st Massachusetts Volunteers in January 1847. He was elected colonel of the entire regiment, but denial of state funds forced him to provide $12,000 to place the unit in the field. By 6 April Cushing had assumed command of the town of Matamoros on the Río Grande. The stern measures he implemented to deal with vice in the community damaged his popularity with his men, but did not affect his promotion to brigadier general by President James K. Polk.

Cushing desperately sought combat, but to no avail; his brief tenures in Monterrey under Gen. Zachary Taylor (June–July) and under Gen. Winfield Scott in Mexico City (December 1847–February 1848) brought only garrison duty. In February the War Department appointed Cushing to a court of inquiry to investigate charges by General Scott against three of his subordinates. After two months of hearings in Mexico City and Washington, D.C., the court exonerated the defendants.

Following the U.S.–Mexican War, Cushing returned to

politics, running unsuccessfully as the Democratic candidate for governor of Massachusetts in 1847 and 1848. Recognized for his political and diplomatic skills, he served in a variety of appointed legal and diplomatic posts, including attorney general to President Franklin Pierce (1853–1857) and minister to Spain (1874–1877) under President Ulysses S. Grant.

Cushing remained active in national and state affairs until his death in Newburyport in January 1879.

John M. Belohlavek

BIBLIOGRAPHY

Fuess, Claude. *The Life of Caleb Cushing.* 1923.

Smith, Justin H. *The War with Mexico.* 2 vols. 1919. Reprint, 1963.

Daguerreotypes

See Photography

Dallas, George M.

The well-born son of Philadelphia lawyer and politician Alexander James Dallas, U.S. vice president George Mifflin Dallas (1792–1864) graduated from Princeton College in 1810, studied law, and was admitted to the bar in 1813. He entered politics as a Jeffersonian Republican and formed the Philadelphia-based Family Party, a conservative, business-oriented faction that supported John C. Calhoun's presidential ambitions before an opportunistic "eleventh-hour" switch to Andrew Jackson in the mid-1820s. Over the years Dallas held numerous local and state offices, filled a vacancy in the U.S. Senate (1831–1833), and served as President Martin Van Buren's minister to Russia (1837–1839).

Dallas was elected vice president of the United States in 1844 as the Democratic running mate of James K. Polk. His failure to block the selection of Pennsylvania rival James Buchanan as secretary of state muted his influence in the Polk administration, but he nevertheless remained loyal to the president. He faithfully supported Polk's expansionist agenda, and cast a key tie-breaking Senate vote that sent the administration's low-tariff Walker Bill of 1846 to a third reading and subsequent approval. Although Dallas, who opposed the bill, took the high ground that national interests outweighed state and personal considerations, his action outraged his protectionist constituents in Pennsylvania.

President Franklin Pierce returned Dallas to public service in 1856 as minister to Great Britain, a post he held through the presidency of his old foe James Buchanan. He afterward retired to private life and died in Philadelphia on New Year's Eve, 1864.

L. Marshall Hall

BIBLIOGRAPHY

Belohlavek, John M. *George Mifflin Dallas: Jacksonian Patrician.* 1977.

Klein, Philip S. *President James Buchanan: A Biography.* 1962.

Quaife, Milo M., ed. *The Diary of James K. Polk during his Presidency, 1845 to 1849.* 1910.

Sellers, Charles G. *James K. Polk: Continentalist, 1843–1846.* 1966.

Davis, Jefferson

Colonel of the 1st Mississippi Volunteer Regiment (the Mississippi Rifles), later president of the Confederate States of America, Jefferson Davis (1808–1889) was born in Kentucky on 3 June and was raised in Mississippi. He attended Transylvania University and graduated from the United States Military Academy in 1828. Davis served at Fort Crawford, near the present-day city of Prairie du Chien, Wisconsin, under the command of Col. Zachary Taylor, and while there fell in love with Sarah Knox Taylor, Taylor's eldest daughter. Davis resigned his commission in 1835, eloping with Sarah over the protests of her father. The couple moved to Davis's new plantation, Brierfield, near Vicksburg, Mississippi, where both fell victim to malaria. Davis's wife died on 15 September 1835, and the grief-stricken Davis retired to the solitude of his plantation until 1845, when he married Varina Howell on 26 February. That same year he was elected to Congress but resigned his term to serve as colonel of the 1st Mississippi Volunteer Regiment, the famous Mississippi Rifles.

Jefferson Davis. Engraving. John Frost, *Pictorial History of Mexico and the Mexican War*, 1862

The regiment arrived in south Texas in July 1846, and Davis was then warmly welcomed there in a letter from his old commander and former father-in-law, Gen. Zachary Taylor, who stated, "I am more than anxious to take you by the hand." Davis set about training his inexperienced regiment, and their military bearing soon caught the eye of Taylor, who was then planning the attack on Monterrey, Mexico. Davis and his Mississippians were ordered to be moved by steamboat up the Río Grande to Camargo, a staging site for the attack on Monterrey, ahead of seven other volunteer regiments who had arrived in south Texas before Davis and his men.

The Mississippians' first action occurred on 21 September 1846, against the fortifications on the eastern side of Monterrey. Advancing through a deadly cross fire, the 1st Mississippi, led by Davis, and the 1st Tennessee Regiment attacked and captured Fort Tenería. On 23 September Davis led the 1st Mississippi into Monterrey again, this time in a house-to-house battle, which ended at nightfall near the main square. A cease-fire was proposed the next day, and U.S. forces occupied Monterrey by 28 September 1846. A bitter controversy arose after the capture of Monterrey as to which unit first entered Fort Tenería during the battle. Davis claimed the honor for his Mississippians, while Col. William

Bowen Campbell argued that the fort had first been entered by his regiment, the 1st Tennessee. Letters from both claimants to the honor appeared in U.S. newspapers, but the issue was never decided.

Davis's most significant service during the U.S.–Mexican War occurred on 23 February 1847 at the battle of Buena Vista. Davis and the men of the Mississippi Rifles, who had accompanied Taylor from Saltillo on that morning, discovered when they reached the battlefield that a large force of Mexican infantry and cavalry had turned the left flank of the U.S. defenses and were advancing along the North Plateau toward Saltillo. The attacking force consisted of the two infantry divisions of Maj. Gen. Manuel María Lombardini and Maj. Gen. Francisco Pacheco and the cavalry brigade of Brig. Gen. Julián Juvera. Davis immediately advanced his force of about 370 Mississippians against an estimated force of more than 4,000 Mexicans. Although their losses were severe (40 killed, 56 wounded, 2 missing), stiff resistance by the Mississippians gave U.S. forces time to bring up reinforcements, which, with the aid of artillery, drove the Mexicans back. Wounded in the right foot by a musket ball, Davis remained on the field leading his regiment.

By midday, a large force of Mexican cavalry, Juvera's brigade, advanced onto the North Plateau in another attempt to force a passage into Saltillo. Davis organized his men and the forces of the 3d Indiana into a V formation, with the mouth of the V facing the advancing Mexicans. Volleys of converging fire repulsed the Mexican lancers, who were again driven off the North Plateau. In Taylor's official report on the Battle of Buena Vista, he praised the significant role played by Davis and his regiment but had little to say about the 3d Indiana Volunteers, who had also served with distinction. Newspapers from Indiana accused Taylor of showing favoritism to his former son-in-law. A bitter opposition to Taylor developed in that state, which contributed to his defeat in Indiana during the presidential election of 1848.

Davis and the regiment completed their year of service by serving in garrison at Monterrey and returned to Vicksburg on 12 June 1847. Jefferson Davis's distinguished military service in Mexico attracted public attention throughout the United States and resulted in his rise from regional to national prominence.

Joseph E. Chance

BIBLIOGRAPHY

Carleton, James Henry. *The Battle of Buena Vista, with the Operations of the "Army of Occupation" for One Month.* 1848.

Chance, Joseph E. *Jefferson Davis's Mexican War Regiment.* 1991.

McElroy, Robert. *Jefferson Davis, The Unreal and the Real.* 1937.

McIntosh, James T., ed. *The Papers of Jefferson Davis.* Vol. 3. 1981.

Dawson Fight

See Woll's Expedition

de

For most names containing de and de la, see under the following element of the name: for example, Herrera, José **Joaquín de**

Decree of 1830

Known in Mexico and Texas as the Law of April 6, 1830, this Mexican law restricting immigration into Texas from the United States was the first manifestation of Mexican suspicion about the expansionist intent of the United States during Andrew Jackson's presidency. Some Texas historians believed it was a stimulus to the Texas Revolution as the Stamp Act was a stimulus to the American Revolution. After the Mexican conservative centralist party seized power in 1829, Secretary of State Lucas Alamán initiated the act to stop immigration into Texas from the United States. A multipurpose expedition across Texas in 1828 led by Gen. Manuel de Mier y Terán revealed that while the Anglo-Texan population was peaceful, it was not being assimilated into Mexican culture and was much larger than supposed. His recommendations became the framework for the law, which closed immigration from the United States and encouraged Mexican and European settlement in the eastern half of the state. Furthermore, Texas residents were not permitted to import more black slaves. In addition, because the special temporary exemption from the national tariff granted to Stephen F. Austin's colony was expiring and, therefore, customs duties would resume, military garrisons were to be established at the ports of entry to assist customs officials and enforce immigration laws. These military installations would become the nucleus for Mexican communities. For the first time, the coastal maritime trade was open to foreign ships to encourage trade between Texas and Mexican ports instead of New Orleans.

From the Mexican point of view these steps were taken to preserve the integrity of the motherland. Anglo-Texans, however, suddenly faced with radical change and a Mexican military presence within some of their communities, viewed the law as unreasonable oppression that was similar to what Great Britain had imposed on its Atlantic colonies. They believed that the exemption from the tariff was a right, not a special privilege; agrarian Anglo-Texans hated any tariff. Austin, however, found a vague phrase in the law that allowed immigrants from the United States to enter "established" colonies—which meant his and that of Green De Witt—an interpretation that was allowed to stand.

The new law, however, slowed overall immigration from the United States and remained in effect until 1834, when it was repealed. The collection of the tariff was suspended and the troops were withdrawn after the settlers' disturbances, later called the Texas Revolts, at Velasco, Anáhuac, and Nacogdoches between June and August 1832.

Margaret Swett Henson

BIBLIOGRAPHY

Henson, Margaret Swett. *Juan Davis Bradburn: A Reappraisal of the Mexican Commander of Anahuac.* 1982.

Morton, Ohland. *Terán and Texas.* 1948.

Wallace, Ernest, and David M. Vigness, eds. *Documents of Texas History.* 1963.

de la Peña, José Enrique

Mexican military officer José Enrique de la Peña (1807–1842) is best remembered for his memoirs concerning the Alamo and the Texas Revolution. Born in Jalisco, de la Peña trained as a mining engineer but joined the Mexican navy in 1825. After several years of service he transferred to the army, joining the Zapadores Battalion. He was present at the defeat of the Spanish invasion force at Tampico in 1829.

In January 1836 de la Peña, then a lieutenant colonel, took part in the campaign against Texas. He arrived at San Antonio with the Zapadores and Mexican reinforcements during the siege of the Alamo. From 2 to 5 March de la Peña participated in siege operations against the Texian position and was present for the final assault on 6 March. De la Peña then moved with the army into East Texas, was at the Brazos River when word came of Gen. Antonio López de Santa Anna's defeat at San Jacinto, and retreated with the army to Matamoros.

Imprisoned in November 1839 because of his support for Gen. José Urrea and federalism, de la Peña wrote and published a sixteen-page pamphlet, *Una victima del despotismo.* Sometime thereafter, he completed his memoirs of the Texas campaign, a work that drew not only on his own observations but also on material gathered from official and private sources, as well as newspapers. Highly critical of Santa Anna, José María Tornel, and Vicente Filisola, the work was suppressed. When released from prison, de la Peña left military service. He died in 1842.

In 1955, Jesús Sánchez Garza published the de la Peña memoirs under the title *La Rebellion de Texas.* Twenty years later, Carmen Perry translated them into English and published them under the title *With Santa Anna in Texas.* The Perry translation caused controversy because of a single passage in which de la Peña described the execution of some Texian prisoners immediately after the battle of the Alamo, naming David Crockett as one of these men. Alamo buffs and Crockett fans have challenged the account; one theory posits that the de la Peña memoirs are a forgery. James Crisp, in his new introduction to the Perry translation, has countered these claims.

Kevin R. Young

BIBLIOGRAPHY
Crisp, James E. "The Little Book That Wasn't There." *Southwestern Historical Quarterly.* Texas State Historical Association 98 (2 Oct. 1994): 261–296.
de la Peña, Enrique. *With Santa Anna in Texas.* Edited and translated by Carmen Perry. Introduction by James E. Crisp. 1997.
Sanchez-Lamego, Miguel A. *Apuntes para la historia del Arma de Ingenieros en Mexico: Historia del Battalion de Zapadores.* 1943.

de la Rosa, Luis

A member of the *moderado* party, Mexican politician Luis de la Rosa (1804–1856) was born in Mineral de los Pinos, Zacatecas. He studied law in the 1820s at Guadalajara's Colegio de San Juan Bautista and later served in the Zacatecas legislature. De la Rosa moved to Mexico City in 1841 and wrote for several liberal newspapers. He also belonged to the national congress that in December 1844 led a coup that removed Gen. Antonio López de Santa Anna from power.

De la Rosa served as minister of finance between March and August 1845. Early in 1846 he joined other *puros* and *moderados* in their efforts to overthrow the government of Gen. Mariano Paredes y Arrillaga. But in late September, approximately seven weeks after the *puros* ousted Paredes y Arrillaga, de la Rosa sought to limit their influence by refusing to take his seat in the council of state, an organ designed to showcase Mexico's newly fashioned domestic harmony.

As minister of foreign relations in late September 1847 and again in January 1848, de la Rosa oversaw the peace negotiations that led to the Treaty of Guadalupe Hidalgo. Before the exchange of ratifications, he requested a meeting with the two U.S. commissioners that resulted in the Protocol of Querétaro, a document that sought to clarify the intentions of the U.S. government in modifying the original treaty by altering Article IX and deleting Article X.

De la Rosa remained active in postwar politics. Appointed minister to the United States in 1848, he ran for the presidency three years later, and in December 1855 he was again chosen minister of foreign relations. He had been named supreme court chief justice just before his death in Mexico City.

Pedro Santoni

BIBLIOGRAPHY
Griswold del Castillo, Richard. *The Treaty of Guadalupe Hidalgo: A Legacy of Conflict.* 1990.
Pletcher, David. *The Diplomacy of Annexation: Texas, Oregon, and the Mexican War.* 1973.
Santoni, Pedro. *Mexicans at Arms: Puro Federalists and the Politics of War, 1845–1848.* 1996.

de la Vega, Rómulo Díaz

See **Díaz de la Vega, Rómulo**

Democratic Party

By the mid-1840s, the Democratic Party, which had dominated national politics since the election of Andrew Jackson in 1828, was in disarray. New Yorker Martin Van Buren, Jackson's heir as the party's principal standard-bearer, had been soundly defeated in the 1840 election, and opposition to his candidacy as the party nominee had been growing steadily as the 1844 election approached. Never especially popular in the Southern states, Van Buren had refused to endorse the annexation of Texas, a matter of great concern to slaveowners as well as to other Democrats who favored a policy of vigorous territorial expansion.

These intraparty antagonisms were brought to the fore by the controversial circumstances surrounding the presidential nomination of James K. Polk in 1844. At the Baltimore convention, the expansionist wing of the party, in an effort to deny Van Buren a place at the head of the ticket, engineered a rules change requiring a two-thirds majority for nomination. Deadlocked, the delegates turned on the ninth ballot to James K. Polk, a former Tennessee governor, as a compromise candidate.

Aware that the unexpected outcome at the Baltimore convention had alienated the Van Buren supporters as well as other party leaders, Polk promised in his letter accepting the nomination that if elected he would serve only one term. In so doing, Polk sought to unite all factions behind his candidacy; those dissatisfied with the choice could pin their hopes on the next election.

Once in office, however, Polk was unable to bring the party's disparate groups into line. Committed to a laissez-faire economic agenda, the president favored a sweeping reduction of tariff rates and opposed all forms of federally funded internal improvements, angering many party leaders who preferred a more active role for the federal government in the nation's economic affairs.

The president's expansionist policies placed similar strains on party solidarity. In the 1844 campaign, Polk had called for the United States to assert its control over the entire

Oregon Territory, a position favored by many expansion-minded northern and midwestern Democrats. As president, however, Polk reached a compromise with Great Britain that divided the Oregon Territory at 49 degrees north latitude. With the outbreak of the U.S.–Mexican War in 1846, northern Democrats were quick to accuse the administration of using the conflict as a pretext to enlarge the South's slave empire. In August 1846 Pennsylvania representative David Wilmot proposed an amendment to an appropriations bill that would have prohibited slavery in any of the territories acquired from Mexico. Although the proviso was never adopted, it continued to gather support from Whigs and northern Democrats as the war dragged on, thereby driving a wedge between the Southern and Northern wings of the Democratic Party over the slavery issue.

In keeping with his pledge to serve only one term, Polk stepped aside in the 1848 presidential contest, leaving the Democrats to nominate another expansionist, Michigan senator Lewis Cass. The nomination prompted a group of disaffected northern Democrats to bolt the party and create the Free-Soil Party. Garnering 10 percent of the popular vote in 1848, the Free-Soil Party cost the Democrats much-needed votes in key northern states, thus ensuring the victory of Whig candidate Gen. Zachary Taylor.

Sam W. Haynes

BIBLIOGRAPHY

Haynes, Sam W. *James K. Polk and the Expansionist Impulse.* 1997.

Paul, James C. N. *Rift in the Democracy.* 1957.

Deserters

Desertion plagued the U.S. military establishment throughout the early nineteenth century as soldiers tired of army life and left before the expiration of their enlistment. Before the U.S.–Mexican War, the desertion rate during some years was as high as 20 percent. In the age when a private earned seven dollars per month, the government offered thirty dollars plus expenses to any citizen who apprehended and turned over a deserter to military authorities. The measure failed as an effective means for returning deserters to the ranks, however. Punishment for desertion, as stipulated by Congress, was meted out by a court-martial that reviewed each case. While flogging was the most serious punishment that could be given to soldiers found guilty of the crime during peacetime, deserters during wartime could be put to death.

The war with Mexico posed a new problem for the U.S. military as the army's advance to the Río Grande provided soldiers with a chance to escape to a foreign country. The problem became so serious for Gen. Zachary Taylor's Army of Occupation that sentinels were permitted to fire on deserters they spotted swimming across the river to Matamo-

ros. A fair number of regulars deserted before the declaration of war, a factor that worked in their favor when they were finally apprehended.

Desertion became a major issue following the Battle of Churubusco in August 1847 when Gen. Winfield Scott's army captured Mexico's famed San Patricio Battalion, a unit composed largely of fugitives from the U.S. Army. In the case of these men, the lives of those who had deserted before the opening of hostilities were spared, a decision that angered many U.S. soldiers and citizens.

The Old Establishment, the units of the regular army that existed before the war, had the highest desertion rate in the U.S. military: 12.5 percent. The rate for the New Establishment was 5.1 percent. The overall desertion rate for all volunteers was 5 percent, but the rate for volunteers who enlisted specifically "for the war" was 7.5 percent.

There were several reasons soldiers deserted. The harsh discipline of the Old Establishment drove many soldiers from the ranks. For volunteers, especially those who had enlisted for the war, service failed to meet their expectations, and they therefore felt little obligation to stay. Some soldiers deserted just before their units returned to the United States so they could stay with their Mexican wives and sweethearts. News of the discovery of gold in early 1848 prompted many regulars and volunteers alike to head for California.

Desertion plagued the Mexican army, too. Added to the familiar complaint of harsh discipline were several reasons not found among U.S. soldiers. A poor supply system that failed to adequately feed and clothe them caused great dissatisfaction among Mexican soldiers. In addition, the Mexican army relied on conscripts from the countryside who, taken from their rural homes and unmotivated by a sense of nationalism, slipped away when the opportunity arose.

Richard Bruce Winders

BIBLIOGRAPHY

Ballentine, George. *Autobiography of an English Soldier in the United States Army.* 1853.

Coffman, Edward M. *The Old Army: A Portrait of the American Army in Peace Time, 1784–1898.* 1986.

McCaffrey, James M. *The Army of Manifest Destiny.* 1992.

Olivera, Ruth R., and Liliane Crété. *Life in Mexico under Santa Anna, 1822–1855.* 1989.

Scott, Henry L. *Military Dictionary.* 1864.

Winders, Richard Bruce. *Mr. Polk's Army: The American Military Experience in the Mexican War.* 1997.

See also **San Patricio Battalion**

Díaz de la Vega, Rómulo

Mexican general Rómulo Díaz de la Vega (c. 1804–1877) was a Mexico City native born about 1804 to Pedro Díaz de la Vega and Monica Fuentes Carrion de Díaz de la Vega. He supported independence in 1821, entered the School for Cadets in 1822, joined the engineers in 1825, and constructed fortifications at Coatzacoalcos and Alvarado, Vera Cruz. He supported conservatives during his career, participated in the 1836 campaign against the Texian rebels and fought at the Alamo. He was promoted to lieutenant colonel in 1838, fought the French at Vera Cruz in 1838 and was promoted to colonel. He participated in border skirmishes with Mexican rebels and Texians between 1839 and 1843 and was promoted to general in 1843. In 1845 he became commander of the 4th Brigade in the Army of the North stationed in Monterrey.

During the U.S.–Mexican War, Díaz de la Vega fought in Texas at Palo Alto on 8 May and at Resaca de la Palma (Guerrero) on 9 May 1846. Before the hostilities he represented Gen. Francisco Mejía in discussions with Gen. William Worth about the nature and presence of U.S. troops on the Río Grande. He commanded the Mexican center defending Resaca de la Palma and was credited with strong resistance, but he was captured, refused parole, and sent to New Orleans; he was then permitted to spend time in Kentucky. He was exchanged at the end of the year for the crew of the steamship *Funston* captured in the Río Tuxpan. He became commandant general of the Plaza de México, then second chief of the Division of the East, and he fought at Cerro Gordo, Vera Cruz, on 17 and 18 April 1847. He was captured when he refused to retreat, held at San Juan de Ulúa and Perote, Vera Cruz, and was freed in December.

Following the U.S.–Mexican War, Díaz de la Vega was commandant general and governor of several states and his campaign in the Yucatán caste war gained him a promotion to general of division in 1854. When Antonio López de Santa Anna left office in 1855, Díaz de la Vega was made interim president from 12 September to 15 November, until Gen. Juan Álvarez arrived. He was exiled to the U.S. in 1856 but returned in 1859 supporting conservative general Miguel Miramón. During the War of the Reform he was wounded and captured in battle at Loma Alta, Zacatecas, in 1860. He joined Emperor Maximilian in 1863 and served as prefect of Jalisco. After the French intervention, he was confined in Puebla and died in poverty.

Harry P. Hewitt

BIBLIOGRAPHY

Brooks, N. C. *A Complete History of the Mexican War.* 1849. Reprint, 1965.

Diccionario Porrúa: De historia, biografía, y geografía de México. 5th ed., vol. 1, pp. 646–647. 1986.

Dufour, Charles L. *The Mexican War: A Compact History, 1846–1848.* 1968.

Frost, J. *The Mexican War and its Warriors.* 1848.

Garza, Israel Cavazos. *Diccionario biografico de Nuevo León.* Vol. 1, p. 120. 1984.

Johannsen, Robert W. *To the Halls of the Montezumas: The Mexican War in the American Imagination.* 1985.

The New Handbook of Texas. Vol. 5, pp. 26–27, 550. 1996.

Peskin, Allan, ed. *Volunteers: The Mexican War Journals of Private Richard Coulter and Sergeant Thomas Barclay, Company E. Second Pennsylvania Infantry.* 1991.

Sanchez Lamego, Miguel A. *Generales de ingenieros del ejército Mexicano, 1821–1914.* 1952.

Smith, Justin H. *The War with Mexico,* 2 vols. 1919. Reprint, 1963.

Tennery, Thomas D. *The Mexican War Diary of Thomas D. Tennery,* edited by D. E. Livingston-Little. 1970.

Zorrilla, Juan Fidel. *Gobernadores, obispos y rectores.* 1989.

Diplomacy

This entry consists of three separate articles: Mexican Diplomacy; Texan Diplomacy; *and* U.S. Diplomacy.

Mexican Diplomacy

Between 1835 and 1848, Mexico's manifold internal and external problems greatly impeded its effort to confront U.S. expansion. For most of the period, conflicts between centralists and federalists wracked Mexico, and a rapid succession of coups d'état prevented the stabilization of a central government. Furthermore, the authority of the central government rarely extended beyond the area surrounding Mexico City. Most of the real political power lay in the hands of the regional *caudillos,* strongmen who had emerged as the greatest winners of the Wars of Independence. To make matters worse, the Mexican economy had never recovered from the ravages of these wars. The country remained deeply in debt to European banks and thus (as the 1838 Pastry War with France showed) prone to foreign intervention.

In light of these circumstances, and considering the demonstrated U.S. resolve to settle first Texas and then the rest of the Mexican north, the principled Mexican refusal to sell or cede national territory needs explanation. After all, European powers such as France and Spain, conscious of their inability to prevent U.S. settlers from pushing westward, had sold similarly vast and sparsely colonized areas to the United States, making a small profit in the process. Nevertheless, the Mexican case was different because the country's own territory, and not just a colony, was at stake. Moreover, the integrity of national territory served an important symbolic function. The fact that the territory of Mexico represented almost the entire former viceroyalty of New Spain served as one of the few common denominators that kept the sprawling and heterogeneous country from disintegrating. Mexican politicians feared that the secession of Texas could set a bad precedent for Chiapas and Yucatán, two other states plagued by secessionist movements.

As a result, Mexican diplomacy had to be completely inflexible on the subject of territorial cessions. To invite Roman Catholic settlers willing to abide by Mexican law into the country's northern expanses—as both the Spanish crown and President Guadalupe Victoria had done—meant bowing to geographical and demographic realities. To permit the secession or even the U.S. annexation of Texas, however, was something no Mexican politician could even appear to countenance.

Even before the beginning of the rebellion in Texas, the Mexican government actively opposed U.S. expansion. The Mexican government rejected a variety of proposals put forward by U.S. diplomatic representatives Joel R. Poinsett and Anthony Butler to amend the Adams-Onís Treaty of 1819, and it placed increasing yet futile strictures on immigration into Texas (for instance, the 6 April 1830 Law of Colonization). Due to the country's difficulties with the European powers, however, the Mexican government could not approach Great Britain or France for help against expansionist U.S. designs. While Anglo-American settler families came to outnumber Tejanos in Texas, the Mexican government had to content itself with hoping that the new arrivals—who accepted land grants that were far more generous than those available in the United States—would not desire a secession. During this period of rapidly changing presidents and cabinet members, one leader was particularly instrumental in formulating Mexican foreign policy: Lucas Alamán, the longtime secretary of foreign relations, whose dislike of the United States rivaled only his fear of liberal modernization in Mexico in any form. After 1833, Alamán obtained an ally in the Mexican strongman Antonio López de Santa Anna, a *caudillo* who served eleven stints as president between 1833 and 1853 and whose overthrow of the federalist government of Valentín Gómez Farías ultimately contributed to the rebellion of the Texians in 1835.

Because the United States supported this rebellion, the Mexican government saw its fear of the United States justified. By giving support to the rebels, President Andrew Jackson blatantly violated U.S. neutrality laws. The protests of Manuel de Gorostiza, the Mexican minister in Washington, D.C., accomplished nothing, however, as U.S. assistance continued and the rebels ultimately defeated Santa Anna's Mexican army. Faced with defeat, Mexican diplomacy shifted toward denial, the only available policy choice at the moment. Any official acknowledgment of Texas independence would have encouraged secessionist elites in Chiapas and Yucatán. Instead, the Mexican government held out hope that it might recover Texas. Aware of strong opposition within the U.S. Congress to the annexation of another slave state, it rejected a series of British and French proposals to recognize the independence of Texas in return for an assurance that the new republic would not join the United States. This policy was based on three calculations: the erroneous assumption that Mexico could resist a potential U.S. military invasion, the fallacious notion that sectional interests would delay or forestall U.S. annexation of Texas, and an accurate reading of opinion within Mexico.

In 1845, however, U.S. efforts to annex the Lone Star Republic changed the Mexican diplomatic position. When the Mexican government realized that the United States would offer admission to Texas, it finally recognized Texas as an independent nation. Nevertheless, President José Joaquín de Herrera steadfastly refused to discuss further territorial cessions. Unlike his predecessors, Herrera realized that a U.S. invasion posed a grave threat to Mexico: in 1842 Commo. Thomas ap Catesby Jones had briefly seized the port of Monterey, California, and a group of Texians had invaded the town of Santa Fe, New Mexico. Moreover, Texas and Mexico found themselves embroiled in a border controversy: while the Texians claimed the Río Grande (Río Bravo in Mexico) as their state's southern border, Mexico would only concede the Nueces River, a river much farther north. Alarmed, Herrera attempted to strengthen the administration of the northern provinces and bolster Mexican defenses along the U.S. border in an effort to stave off hostilities. While he made progress in both areas, his policies speeded up rather than prevented the coming of war between the United States and Mexico. His steadfast refusal to receive U.S. emissary John Slidell to discuss the Texas border question led to U.S. President James K. Polk's deployment of Gen. Zachary Taylor's troops beyond the Nueces River—a deployment viewed by Mexicans as an act of invasion.

The coup by Mariano Paredes y Arrillaga in December 1845 ushered in another period of chaos in Mexican politics, one that served as the backdrop for the country's failures in the war with the United States. Paredes y Arrillaga waged a war against corruption and inefficiency in the Mexican government, but he never commanded enough authority throughout Mexico to rule effectively. Indeed, during his rule, the autonomy of regional warlords further increased, which in effect weakened the country's prospects of withstanding a foreign invasion. Most significant, however, Paredes y Arrillaga presided over one of the most fateful moments in Mexican history: the Río Bravo incident, also known as the Thornton affair, of 25 April 1846 that ushered in the U.S. invasion. During the next weeks, the inability of the Mexican government to resist the advancing U.S. troops once again led to a coup in Mexico. In June 1846, a federalist uprising ousted Paredes y Arrillaga's government, and Santa Anna returned to power two months later.

Santa Anna's return, however, did not improve the fortunes of the Mexicans. During most of the war, the veteran *caudillo* misread the dismal situation of his armies and expected an eventual triumph. Even as Gen. Winfield Scott's troops pushed toward Mexico City, Santa Anna refused to offer territorial concessions. From 27 August to 6 September,

1847, with Scott's army just outside the capital, Mexican representatives maintained this strict position during armistice talks with U.S. commissioner Nicholas P. Trist. As a result, negotiations failed, Scott occupied Mexico City, and the resultant Treaty of Guadalupe Hidalgo validated most of the U.S. demands. Mexican negotiators stood their ground as much as they could, saving Baja California and a sliver of land linking that territory to Sonora from U.S. annexation. But they could not prevent the loss of present-day Arizona, California, Nevada, New Mexico, and Utah as well as parts of Colorado, Oklahoma, and Wyoming.

Like that of any country victimized by foreign expansion, Mexican policy regarding the Texas secession and the war with the United States was understandably rigid and inflexible. From the Mexican perspective, the U.S. annexation of half of the country's territory amounted to theft, and the events of the 1835 to 1853 period remain a searing memory. Even today, Mexicans take exception to the nationalist U.S. nomenclature of these events—the "Texas Revolution" (which implies Texian heroism) as well as the "Mexican War" (a name that supposes that Mexico caused the war). To Mexicans, U.S. annexation and invasion constitute the defining characteristics of this period.

Jurgen Buchenau

BIBLIOGRAPHY

Benson, Nettie Lee. "Territorial Integrity in Mexican Politics, 1821–1833." In Jaime Rodríguez, ed. *The Independence of Mexico and the Creation of the New Nation*, pp. 275–310. 1989.

Brack, Gene M. *Mexico Views Manifest Destiny, 1821–1846: An Essay on the Origins of the Mexican War.* 1975.

Castañeda, Carlos. *The Mexican Side of the Texas Revolution.* 1928.

Ramírez, J. F. *Mexico during the War with the United States.* Walter V. Scholes, ed., E. B. Scherr, trans. 1950.

Vázquez, Josefina Z. *Mexicanos y norteamericanos ante la Guerra del 47.* 1978.

Texan Diplomacy

The Texian victory at San Jacinto on 21 April 1836 ensured Texas's independence. Disguised as a common soldier, Gen. Antonio López de Santa Anna was captured the next day, presenting the Republic of Texas with its first diplomatic dilemma. The rank and file of the Texas army wanted to execute the Mexican dictator as atonement for the massacres at the Alamo and Goliad, but Gen. Sam Houston (later president of the Texas republic) insisted on sparing his life. Santa Anna was compelled to sign the Treaties of Velasco, which recognized Texas's independence, set the international boundary at the Río Grande, and pledged Texas to return Santa Anna to Mexico. This promise proved difficult to keep, however, as factions in the first congress of the Texas republic demanded that Santa Anna be tried by a military court for his war crimes. The issue was resolved when congress made President Houston solely responsible for the treatment of Santa Anna.

Stephen F. Austin, Houston's secretary of state, conceived the idea of sending Santa Anna to Washington, D.C., to meet with departing President Andrew Jackson. While Austin had little faith in U.S. mediation, at the least the United States would become responsible for Santa Anna's safety. When Jackson suggested to Texas officials that the United States should purchase Texas from Mexico, the proposal was quickly rejected. Such a negotiation would imply that Texas was still part of Mexico, which was unacceptable to President Houston. A few brief meetings were held between Jackson and Santa Anna, but no substantial agreements resulted. When Santa Anna landed at Vera Cruz after being returned on a U.S. ship, he claimed that he had been tortured and promptly repudiated the Treaties of Velasco.

Houston's successor as president, Mirabeau B. Lamar, had little faith in the annexation process. He favored independence and realized that a diplomatic agreement with Mexico was essential to that end. Lamar had not been in office very long when France declared war on Mexico to secure payment of claims owed to French citizens residing in Mexico. Although the abortive Pastry War ended quickly, Lamar believed the time was opportune to press Mexico for recognition of independence. Barnard E. Bee resigned as Texas secretary of state to journey to Mexico City, and Richard Dunlap was sent to Washington, D.C., to press for mediation between Texas and Mexico. As a special agent Bee was bound by only two provisions of his instructions. He was to sign no treaty that did not unconditionally recognize Texas's independence and locate the boundary at the Río Grande rather than the Nueces River. In the interim, Powhatan Ellis, the U.S. minister to Mexico, announced the readiness of his country to mediate if Mexico would request it.

On arriving in Mexico City, Bee was informed that if he represented a "rebellious province" in Mexico, negotiations could commence. If, however, his object was the recognition of independence, he would not be granted a hearing and should immediately return to Texas. Bee, realizing that no Mexican administration could withstand the political damage attendant on negotiating with Texas, returned to New Orleans. A letter awaited him there from Col. Juan N. Almonte, a close friend of Santa Anna, indicating that Mexico was willing to parley after all. Pursuant to that end, President Lamar then sent James Treat to Mexico with an offer of $5 million for the settlement of the boundary at the Río Grande, but this proposal was also rejected.

In June 1840 the Federalist party in the state of Yucatán rebelled and captured the Yucatán Peninsula from the centralists. Proclaiming their fidelity to the 1824 Constitution, the situation of the Yucatecan rebels was akin to that of

Texas on the eve of the revolution. As assistance from the United States was decisive for Texas then, Yucatán sought aid from the Lone Star Republic. Lamar, eager to foment discord in Mexico, decided to send the small Texas navy into the Gulf of Mexico. Commo. Edwin W. Moore, the highest ranking Texas naval officer, was ordered to prevent a Mexican blockade of Texas ports and to contact the Yucatecan dissidents. As Moore set sail, Martin Peraza, minister from Yucatán, was in Austin to formalize an alliance with Texas.

The treaty, signed 17 September 1841, pledged Texas naval assistance in preventing a centralist invasion of Yucatán. Texas would provide three or more vessels for the defense of Yucatán's coast, and any prizes taken would belong to the country that made the capture. Finally, Yucatán would advance the costs of readying the Texas fleet for service and $8,000 monthly for as long as the fleet patrolled the Yucatán coast. In January 1842 Moore entered the Yucatán port of Sisal, but the political situation had altered dramatically since the treaty was signed. Santa Anna had been returned to power and begun talks with Miguel Barbachano, governor of Yucatán. Accepting a promise of greater autonomy for the states, Yucatán abandoned its opposition to the central government, which nullified the Texas treaty and signaled final failure for Lamar's Mexican policies.

In 1837, France granted diplomatic recognition to Texas. Alphonse Dubois de Saligny, who was serving at the French embassy in Washington, D.C., was then appointed the first minister to the Republic of Texas. Once established at Austin, he outlined a project to locate colonies of French immigrants along the republic's frontier. The Franco-Texienne bill, submitted to the Texas congress, would grant a corporation of French investors three million acres of land on which the company would settle at least eight thousand French colonists by January 1849. The company was granted exclusive trading rights with the towns of upper Mexico and agreed to build at least twenty forts on a line from the Red River to the Río Grande and maintain them for a period of twenty years.

As de Saligny had feared, the bill was immediately attacked in Texas as permitting too great a French influence in Texas affairs. Accusations by Texas newspaper editors that certain legislators had been bribed for their votes also nettled the French envoy. When it became apparent that the measure would fail, de Saligny, in a fit of pique, broke off diplomatic relations and demanded his passports. Although relations were later restored, the incident destroyed all prospects of a French loan. Another factor was Great Britain's failure to financially sustain Texas in any meaningful way, which made annexation by the United States all the more imperative. Antislavery sentiment in the North was principally responsible for the failure of Texas to gain quick admission to the Union. In the presidential election of 1844, the Democratic candidate, James K. Polk, made the annexation of Texas the

centerpiece of his campaign. His victory over the Whig nominee, Henry Clay, and a growing awareness of the economic value of Texas to the Union ensured success for the partisans of annexation. Until it was successfully achieved, that issue dominated the diplomacy of the Republic of Texas.

Stanley E. Siegel

BIBLIOGRAPHY

Nackman, Mark E. *A Nation within a Nation: The Rise of Texas Nationalism.* 1975.

Schmitz, Joseph W. *Texan Statecraft, 1836–1845.* 1941.

See also **Texas**, *article on* **Conflicts with Mexico, 1836–1845**

U.S. Diplomacy

The diplomatic origins of the U.S.–Mexican War can be traced back a quarter of a century before the conflict began. In 1819 Secretary of State John Quincy Adams and Luis de Onís, Spanish minister to the United States, negotiated the Adams-Onís (Transcontinental) Treaty. The pact fixed the Sabine River as the northern boundary of Spanish Texas and established 42° north latitude as the boundary between Spanish and U.S. claims in North America. Florida became U.S. territory at 31° north latitude, and the United States assumed the monetary claims of its own citizens against Spain.

The acquisition of Florida only served to whet the U.S. appetite for Texas and California. When Mexico won its independence from Spain in 1821, its hold on the former Spanish colonial empire was tenuous. Far removed from the seat of government in Mexico City, the provinces of Texas and California were ripe for U.S. intrigue and intervention. Manifest Destiny was the operative theme of the era, and Mexican statesmen knew that Texas independence could never have been realized without volunteers and substantial financial assistance from the United States. Although Mexico consented, under protest, to accept U.S. diplomatic recognition of Texas in 1837, it warned the U.S. government that annexation would result in war. Three weeks after the annexation resolution was passed in the U.S. Congress in 1845 Mexico suspended diplomatic relations and prepared for conflict.

A year passed from the time of annexation until the outbreak of war. During that time, President James K. Polk sought a diplomatic solution by sending John Slidell as a one-time negotiator to Mexico. The U.S. diplomat would insist on the demarcation line at the Río Grande in return for the assumption by the United States of claims held by U.S. citizens against Mexico. An earlier mediation by the king of The Netherlands had established the property damage claims at $5 million, but Mexico refused to pay. Slidell was also empowered to offer $25 million for the purchase of New Mexico and California. Some historians believe that Polk would have offered as much as $40 million.

Before Slidell left for Mexico City, Polk received assurances from the Mexican foreign minister that a U.S. "commissioner" would be welcomed in friendly fashion. Upon arriving, however, Slidell was told that his credentials as a "minister plenipotentiary" implied resumption of regular diplomatic relations, which Mexico could not sanction. In truth, the Mexican people were so aggrieved over the annexation and boundary issues that no Mexican president could long remain in office if he did not defy the United States. President José Joaquín de Herrera recognized this and broke off the talks, leaving Polk free to pursue a more adventurous policy toward Mexico.

After Slidell's rejection, Polk ordered Gen. Zachary Taylor to move his forces from the Nueces River to the Río Grande. By occupying this 165 miles of disputed territory, the president seemed to foreclose any reasonable chance for peace. Mexican troops were massed on the other side of the Río Grande, and the inevitable incident occurred on 25 April 1846. A U.S. patrol was surprised by a Mexican force, and there were casualties on both sides. Mexico had already declared a "defensive war" against the United States, and Polk now sought a declaration of war from Congress. Responding to the president's famous phrase that, "American blood had been shed upon American soil," war was quickly declared. Northern antislavery opposition to the war was disquieting to the administration, however, and intensified the president's desire to end it quickly.

On 27 March 1847 Vera Cruz fell to Gen. Winfield Scott's combined military and naval assault. Nicholas P. Trist, the chief clerk in the State Department, now began talks at Vera Cruz seeking a cessation of hostilities. The United States insisted on the boundary at the Río Grande, the acquisition of New Mexico and California, and the right of free transit across the Isthmus of Tehuantepec, a potential interocean canal route. When Mexican diplomats rejected these terms as too harsh, Scott lifted the armistice and resumed his march to Mexico City.

After a hard-fought campaign, Mexico City surrendered to U.S. forces on 17 September 1847. When Charles Bankhead, the British minister to Mexico, declined to participate in the talks, Mexico agreed to negotiate directly with the United States. On 2 February 1848, at a small village outside Mexico City, the Treaty of Guadalupe Hidalgo was signed. In accordance with its terms, the Texas boundary was placed at the Río Grande, and the United States acquired New Mexico and California for $15 million and assumed the claims of U.S. citizens against Mexico.

Faced with a threat by Polk to end the armistice and renew the war, the Mexican congress accepted the distasteful treaty. After a spirited debate, the U.S. Senate also ratified the treaty, by a vote of 38 to 14. The annexation of Texas and the consequent U.S.–Mexican War increased the territory of the United States by almost 65 percent.

Stanley E. Siegel

BIBLIOGRAPHY

Ruiz, Ramon Eduardo, ed. *The Mexican War: Was It Manifest Destiny?* 1963.

Singletary, Otis. *The Mexican War.* 1960.

Diseases and Epidemics

See Health and Medicine

Domeco de Jarauta, Celestino

See Jarauta, Celestino Domeco de

Donelson, Andrew Jackson

Andrew Jackson Donelson (1799–1871) was the last chargé d'affaires from the United States to the Republic of Texas. Donelson was born in Nashville, Tennessee, on 25 August. He was graduated second in his class from West Point and became private secretary and aide to his uncle by marriage and foster father, President Andrew Jackson. Accepting the diplomatic appointment to Texas, Donelson noted that three of his predecessors had died of yellow fever in Galveston. However, he took up his duties and arrived in Texas 10 November 1844.

Donelson was instructed to present the U.S. offer of annexation when it was approved. The proposal, admitting Texas into the Union as the twenty-eighth state, was in the form of a joint resolution ratified by Congress in February 1845. The resolution protected slavery, allowed Texas to keep its public lands, and stipulated that Texas might later be divided into as many as five states, with slavery not allowed north of a line at 36° 30′ north latitude.

Meeting with Texas president Anson Jones, Donelson suggested that a convention be called to approve the U.S. offer. However, Jones countered with a second proposal for the convention. In addition to the U.S. proposal for annexation, the delegates would consider a Mexican pledge of Texas independence, guaranteed by Great Britain and France, in which all disputed territorial questions would be negotiated by the European powers. The action taken by Great Britain and France was prompted by the prospect of war between the United States and Mexico over annexation.

On 4 July 1845 the convention overwhelmingly endorsed annexation, and in January 1846 Donelson closed the legation and returned to the United States. During the U.S.–Mexican War, Donelson served as a U.S. diplomat in Prussia. In 1856 he surfaced again as Millard Fillmore's vice presidential candidate on the Know-Nothing ticket. A bitter critic of secession, he died in Memphis on 26 June 1871, faithful to the Union.

Stanley E. Siegel

BIBLIOGRAPHY

Middleton, Annie. "Donelson's Mission to Texas in Behalf of Annexation." *Southwestern Historical Quarterly* 24 (1921): 279–291.

Schmitz, Joseph W. *Texan Statecraft, 1836–1845.* 1941.

Doniphan, Alexander W.

Leader of "Doniphan's March," U.S. volunteer colonel Alexander W. Doniphan (1808–1887) was born near Maysville, Mason County, Kentucky, on 9 July. Doniphan graduated from Augusta College, at Augusta, Kentucky, in 1826. He studied law, settled in Missouri in 1830, established a law practice, and was elected to the Missouri legislature in 1836 and 1840. An advocate of Manifest Destiny, Doniphan helped raise one thousand soldiers for the 1st Regiment of Missouri Mounted Volunteers at the outbreak of war with Mexico in 1846. Enlisting as a private, he was elected the regiment's colonel and became one of the most successful U.S. volunteer colonels in the war.

Serving under Brig. Gen. Stephen W. Kearny, Doniphan led his regiment from Fort Leavenworth (in present-day Kansas) to the capture of Santa Fe, New Mexico, on 18 August 1846. At Santa Fe, Doniphan became one of the first military government administrators in U.S. history. Acting through his authority as the commander of U.S. troops in the territory, Doniphan, and not the new civil governor, Charles Bent, drafted a constitution and laws, inappropriately called the Kearny Code, and made a treaty with the Navajo Indians.

Doniphan led his regiment to victory against twelve hundred Mexican forces under Col. Antonio Ponce de León at Brazito on 25 December 1846, which enabled him to capture El Paso del Norte (present-day Juárez, Mexico). He then led his soldiers deep into Mexico and fought again on 28 February 1847 north of Chihuahua City on the Río Sacramento, defeating three thousand Mexicans under Gen. José Heredia. U.S. forces took possession of the city of Chihuahua on 2 March. Doniphan and his men proceeded to Matamoros and took steamboats home to Missouri. "Doniphan's March" of 5,500 total miles on foot and by sea became legendary, prompting U.S. writers to compare him with Xenophon, a Greek military officer of ancient times.

After the war Doniphan practiced law and was reelected to the Missouri legislature. He died in Richmond, Missouri, on 8 August 1887.

Joseph G. Dawson III

BIBLIOGRAPHY

Connelley, William E. *Doniphan's Expedition.* 1907.
Duchateau, Andre P. "Missouri Colossus: Alexander William Doniphan." Ed.D. diss., Oklahoma State University, 1973.

Doniphan's March

From June 1846 to June 1847 Col. Alexander W. Doniphan led his regiment of Missouri volunteers on a 5,500-mile trek over land and water from Fort Leavenworth to Santa Fe and on to El Paso del Norte, across Chihuahua, and eventually to Matamoros, where steamers transported them to New Orleans and then back to Missouri. During the U.S.–Mexican War, U.S. forces conducted several long marches. Doniphan's March was the most notable, leading to comparisons between the colonel and Xenophon, an Athenian officer who led Greek soldiers on a thousand-mile march across Asia Minor during the Persian War (c. 400 B.C.)

A well-recognized Missouri lawyer with little military experience, Doniphan was elected colonel by the recruits of the 1st Regiment of Missouri Mounted Volunteers. Comprising one thousand citizen-soldiers, Doniphan's regiment received a few days of rudimentary training supervised by regular U.S. Army officers at Fort Leavenworth, in present-day Kansas. A regiment in Brig. Gen. Stephen W. Kearny's Army of the West, the 1st Missouri set out in June 1846 for Santa Fe, New Mexico, which fell to Kearny and Doniphan without a battle on 18 August. On the 850 miles from Leavenworth to Santa Fe, Doniphan's soldiers subsisted on half rations, and water for men and horses was scarce. Such rations and lack of water became routine features of Doniphan's March. Kearny departed for California but ordered Doniphan to draft laws for the New Mexico Territory.

On 14 December the colonel set out toward El Paso del Norte (present-day Juárez, Mexico). Accompanying him were dozens of merchants driving wagons loaded with trade goods, some of which were used to support his regiment. To reach El Paso del Norte the Missourians traversed 250 miles of poorly watered and almost woodless terrain, including the *Jornada del Muerto*—the Journey of Death—perhaps the roughest one hundred miles of the entire march. Doniphan spread out his regiment to make a wider search for water and wood for campfires. On 25 December 1846, several miles from El Paso del Norte, 1,200 Mexican soldiers led by Col. Antonio Ponce de León encountered about half of the Missouri regiment. During the ensuing fight at Brazito, in less than one hour, Doniphan's volunteers won the battle, inflicting casualties of about 50 killed and 150 wounded while suffering only 7 wounded. The Mexicans retreated and the Missourians entered El Paso del Norte on 27 December.

After Maj. Meriwether Lewis Clark's artillery battalion reinforced them, Doniphan's soldiers began the third leg of

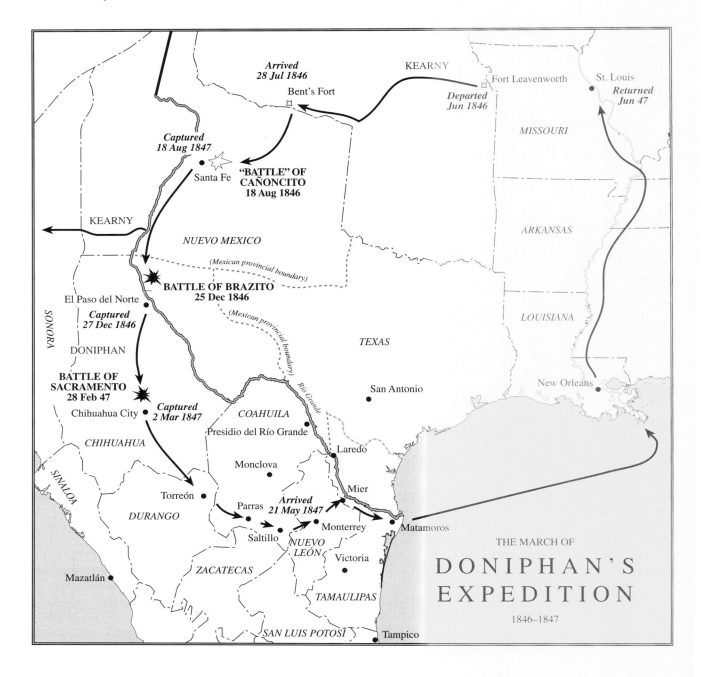

Arrived
28 Jul 1846

KEARNY

Fort Leavenworth   St. Louis
                                            Returned
Bent's Fort   Departed   *Jun 47*
               Jun 1846

MISSOURI

Captured
18 Aug 1847

"BATTLE" OF
CAÑONCITO
18 Aug 1846

Santa Fe

ARKANSAS

KEARNY

NUEVO MEXICO

(Mexican provincial boundary)

BATTLE OF BRAZITO
25 Dec 1846

LOUISIANA

El Paso del Norte

SONORA

Captured
27 Dec 1846

(Mexican provincial boundary)

TEXAS

DONIPHAN

San Antonio

BATTLE OF
SACRAMENTO
28 Feb 47

Chihuahua City   *Captured*
                  2 Mar 1847

COAHUILA

CHIHUAHUA

Presidio del Río Grande

Laredo

New Orleans

Monclova

Río Grande

Mier

SINALOA

Torreón   *Arrived*
           21 May 1847

Parras

Matamoros

DURANGO

Saltillo   Monterrey

NUEVO
LEÓN

THE MARCH OF

DONIPHAN'S
EXPEDITION

1846–1847

Victoria

Mazatlán

ZACATECAS

TAMAULIPAS

SAN LUIS POTOSÍ   Tampico

their march on 8 February 1847, moving south toward Chihuahua City. The merchants organized themselves into an informal military company to assist the expedition. They trekked some 250 miles in the winter from El Paso del Norte, across difficult, almost waterless land. Fifteen miles north of Chihuahua City, along the Río Sacramento, Gen. José A. Heredia's Mexican army of three thousand waited behind cannons and redoubts. Doniphan consulted with other officers, including Capt. Philip Thompson, a regular U.S. Army officer assigned as an adviser to the expedition, and they decided to attack the Mexican fieldworks. The resulting Battle of Sacramento on 28 February lasted for three hours. Doniphan achieved tactical surprise by striking the left flank of the Mexican defensive line. Using their artillery to advantage, the colonel and his subordinates led assaults that routed the Mexicans, who suffered 169 killed, 300 wounded, and 79 made prisoner. U.S. losses were only 4 killed and 8 wounded. Heredia's army dispersed, leaving the provincial capital open. Doniphan entered Chihuahua City on 2 March and remained there for a month. In the vicinity of Chihuahua, Doniphan's patrols skirmished with Apache Indians.

The last leg of Doniphan's March covered 750 inhospitable miles from Chihuahua to Matamoros near the Gulf of Mexico. Along the way the Missourians fought another skirmish with Indians. From Matamoros, several steamers transported the Missouri regiment to New Orleans. Most of Doniphan's soldiers looked like scarecrows when they arrived in New Orleans; one newspaper writer likened them to the fictional character Robinson Crusoe, who had been stranded for years on a desert island. After a few days in Louisiana, the Missourians boarded steamboats going up the Mississippi River to St. Louis, where they landed in early June 1847. Excited crowds cheered their arrival. In twelve months Doniphan and his men had traveled 5,500 miles, some 2,500 miles overland through unmapped regions, and fought two battles with Mexican armies as well as skirmishes with Indians. Contemporary politicians and journalists hailed Doniphan as the "American Xenophon" for leading his regiment on that adventurous march.

Doniphan's campaign for Chihuahua and the Battle of Sacramento were not as important as Gen. Zachary Taylor's triumph at Buena Vista (Angostura) on 22 and 23 February 1847, but Doniphan's victory did contribute to the overall U.S. military effort. The defeat at Sacramento drove Mexican regular units south of Chihuahua City and dashed Mexican hopes of mounting a counteroffensive to retake Santa Fe. Moreover, the fall of Chihuahua City lowered Mexican morale and emphasized that the Mexican army was unable to turn back any of the U.S. incursions into its northern states. Doniphan's victory over a well-entrenched army also deprived the Mexicans of the intangible yet potentially significant uplift that a victory over any U.S. force would have provided. Finally, a few weeks after the event, Doniphan's victory at Sacramento was reported widely by newspapers in the United States. Those reports came at about the same time as coverage of the U.S. victory at Buena Vista and Gen. Winfield Scott's capture of Vera Cruz, further confirming the trend of the war toward U.S. victory.

Joseph G. Dawson III

BIBLIOGRAPHY

Bauer, K. Jack. *The Mexican War.* 1974.

Connelley, William E. *Doniphan's March.* 1907.

Dawson, Joseph G. III. "Volunteer Soldiering and the Service of Colonel Alexander Doniphan in the Mexican-American War." In *Military Power,* edited by Brian Holden Reid. 1997.

Eisenhower, John S. D. *So Far from God: The U.S. War with Mexico.* 1989.

Douglas, Stephen A.

Stephen Arnold Douglas (1813–1861), U.S. representative and senator from Illinois, was born in Vermont and educated in upstate New York. He migrated to Illinois in 1833, where he held a number of state offices before his election as a Jacksonian Democrat to the U.S. House of Representatives in 1843. A strong supporter of westward expansion and the extension of democratic government, he called for the acquisition of all of Oregon and the immediate annexation of Texas, both of which were included in the 1844 Democratic Party platform. With the outbreak of the U.S.–Mexican War, Douglas briefly considered seeking a commission in the army, but was persuaded by President James K. Polk to remain in the House, where he became a principal defender of the administration's war policies. A spirited and powerful debater, Douglas argued that the United States had ample cause for war against Mexico, and he branded those who opposed it as traitors. His speeches attracted widespread attention, as when he mustered maps, history books, and official documents to show that the lower Río Grande was the true boundary of Texas.

In 1847 Douglas was elected to the U.S. Senate, where he continued to defend the war as just and necessary and as demonstrating the superiority of republican institutions over military dictatorship.

As chairman of the committee on territories, first in the House and then in the Senate, Douglas focused attention on the need for provisional governments in the occupied areas of Mexico and later wrote the bills admitting California as a state and creating Utah and New Mexico territories. He vigorously opposed the Wilmot Proviso, which would ban slavery in the lands taken from Mexico, and argued that the introduction of the slavery question was a dangerous distraction from more important national issues. Douglas was one of fourteen senators who voted against the Treaty of Guadalupe Hidalgo, believing that the United States should have exacted more territory from Mexico than the treaty provided. Douglas's response to the U.S.–Mexican War was an important stage in the development of his vision of a dynamic, expanding, and perpetual Union.

Robert W. Johannsen

BIBLIOGRAPHY

Johannsen, Robert W. *Stephen A. Douglas.* 1973.

Johannsen, Robert W. "Stephen A. Douglas and the American Mission." In *The Frontier, The Union, and Stephen A. Douglas.* 1989.

Durango, State of

The city of Durango was established as a town on 8 July 1563. During a great part of the colonial period, it served as the capital of a vast territory called Nueva Vizcaya comprising what are the present-day Mexican states of Sinaloa, Sonora, Chihuahua, and part of Coahuila. In 1731 its territorial jurisdiction began to contract. With the constitution of the Mexican Federation in 1824, it became part of the Northern Internal State together with Chihuahua, Nuevo México; governmental power was seated in Chihuahua.

However, Durango's provincial delegation demanded that it be designated an autonomous territory, and this demand was realized on 22 May 1824, with the creation of the Federal Republic. In the past as in the present day, Durango's principal economic activities consist of agriculture, livestock, and mining.

Since the colonial era, Durango's most important population centers have been Durango (the state capital), Nombre de Dios, San Juan del Río, Santiago Papasquiaro, Canatlán, Cuencamé, Mapimí, Peñón Blanco, Tamazula, Gómez Palacio, Ciudad Lerdo, Guadalupe Victoria, Vicente Guerrero, El Salto, and Tayoltita. The accompanying table represents the population of Durango at the end of the Spanish regime and during the period from 1821 to 1841.

In 1835 the Texians declared the right to secede from the Mexican union. With the rebellion under way at the outset of 1836, a group of Durangan patriots commanded by Gen. José Urrea, who had been governor of Durango at the end of the previous year, went to Texas to fight the rebels. Among the best-known battles at which Urrea fought are Goliad and San Patricio. At Juntas he defeated Col. Ward and a hundred men, who were led to the fort at Goliad and shot on orders from above. Later Urrea headed for Matagorda, where he captured Texian artillery and food supplies. He then went on to Columbia and Brazoría, the former of which he occupied until 22 April. General Urrea opposed the retreat of Mexican troops ordered by Gen. Antonio López de Santa Anna.

Various Durangan contingents enlisted during the U.S. invasion of 1847. Col. Alexander W. Doniphan's account indicates that a force of twelve hundred cavalry troops from Durango and Chihuahua had assembled by the month of February. At this time, Gen. Vicente Filisola left for the front with three hundred soldiers to combat the U.S. troops along a line between Saltillo and Matamoros. Later, by a decree issued on 26 April by Pedro María Anaya, the interim president of Mexico, one thousand men were enlisted from Durango to replace casualties in the army battling the invaders. These men became reinforcements in Chihuahua and Nuevo México under General Filisola.

At the end of March 1847, reports of a party of ten or more U.S. troops spotted near Aguaje de San José in the Mapimí district, as well as seventeen others in the environs of the district seat, caused alarm in that area and in the state capital. The government sent forces and ordered an auxiliary company from Cuencamé to march on Mapimí to apprehend the U.S. parties, but there was no encounter and the U.S. soldiers moved on to Chihuahua. The state of Durango was not within the strategic plans of expansion by the U.S. government. Had U.S. forces occupied Durango, the consequences would have been disastrous for the state due to the internal weakness it was undergoing as a result of the war being waged against nomadic Indians.

José de la Cruz Pacheco Rojas
Translated by The Horse's Mouth Language Services

BIBLIOGRAPHY

Escudero, José Agustín de. *Noticias estadísticas del Estado de Durango reunidas y presentadas a la Comisión de Estadística Militar.* 1849.

Pacheco Rojas, José de la Cruz. "Durango entre dos guerras, 1846–1847." Ensayo inédito. Seminario "La Guerra del 1847" que coordina la Dra. Josefina Z. Vázquez. El Colegio de México. 1996.

Ramírez, José Fernando. *Noticias históricas y estadísticas de Durango, 1849–1850.* 1851.

Urrea, José. *Diario de las operaciones militares de la división al mando del general José Urrea, hizo la Campaña de Tijos.* 1838.

Records of the Population of Durango

Year	Source	Population
1793	Count of Revillagigedo (Durango was known as "Nueva Vizcaya")	122,866
1804	Baron of Humboldt	157,970
1804	Don Fernando Navarro y Noriego	177,400
1833	Don Lucas Alamán	155,793
1836	Don Juan N. Almonte	179,121
1841	Convention of 1841	162,618

SOURCE: The Mexican War Heritage Foundation

Elections, U.S.

This entry includes seven articles: Election of 1824; **Election of 1828**; Election of 1836; Election of 1840; **Election of 1844;** Election of 1848; *and* Election of 1852.

Election of 1824

The House of Representatives decided the outcome of the U.S. presidential election of 1824 because none of the four candidates of the only political party, the Republican, won a majority of the electoral votes. Gen. Andrew Jackson of Tennessee, the military hero of the War of 1812, gained the most popular votes and 99 electoral votes. Secretary of State John Quincy Adams of Massachusetts and Secretary of the Treasury William H. Crawford of Georgia garnered 84 and 41 electoral votes, respectively. Winning only 37 votes, Speaker of the House Henry Clay of Kentucky had no chance for election because only the names of the top three candidates were sent to the House of Representatives. This election was the first in which most voters actually chose presidential electors, as only six states still allowed their legislatures to do so.

Clay viewed Adams as the least objectionable of the remaining candidates, although years before Clay had denounced Secretary of State Adams's role in negotiating the Adams-Onís Treaty (or Transcontinental Treaty) of 1819, which recognized the Sabine River as the western U.S. boundary with Spanish Texas. Expansionists claimed that Texas was part of the original Louisiana Purchase from France in 1803 and that Onís would have conceded more territory during the negotiations. Under President James Monroe's instructions, however, Adams had not pushed the issue. During the election of 1824, Clay dismissed Jackson as a military figure with no political experience and as a rival in the West. Crawford had been stricken, possibly with a stroke, in the fall of 1823 and remained seriously ill through-

out the next year. Therefore, despite his earlier sentiments, Clay supported Adam's selection by the House of Representatives. When Adams subsequently named Clay secretary of state, Jackson and his supporters cried "corrupt bargain," believing that the presidency had been stolen from him.

During Adams's presidency, U.S. relations with Mexico deteriorated as tensions grew over U.S. settlers immigrating to Texas and the U.S. administration's push for a U.S.–Mexico boundary revision at the Sabine River.

Carol Jackson Adams

BIBLIOGRAPHY

Bemis, Samuel Flagg. *John Quincy Adams and the Foundations of American Foreign Policy.* 1965.

Hargreaves, Mary W. M. *The Presidency of John Quincy Adams.* 1985.

Mooney, Chase C. *William H. Crawford, 1772–1834.* 1974.

Remini, Robert V. *Henry Clay: Statesman for the Union.* 1991.

Election of 1828

In the 1828 election Andrew Jackson launched a presidential campaign unprecedented in U.S. history. Nominated by the Tennessee legislature in October 1825 to run against the incumbent, John Quincy Adams, Jackson directed a vigorous anti-Adams movement, organizing national politicians, newspaper editors, and local leaders in his effort to gain the executive office.

Adams's supporters organized only later in the campaign to meet the challenge of the "Hero of New Orleans," and with few real issues on the table, the two sides resorted to scurrilous personal attacks. The Jacksonian Democrats asserted that Adams had stolen the presidency in 1824 with a "corrupt bargain," and they portrayed him as an elitist aristocrat. Adams's National Republicans countered with charges that Jackson was an ignorant "military chieftain," unfit for the highest office in a republic. They supported this claim with descriptions of Jackson's violent past and accusations of immorality in his private life.

Disillusionment with the 1824 election had also led all states but South Carolina and Delaware to allow the voting populace to choose the presidential electors. These changes resulted in a 56.3 percent voter turnout in 1828, nearly tripling the 1824 results. Jackson won 56 percent of the popular vote and 178 of the 261 electoral votes, gaining all electoral votes from the West and the South and Pennsylvania, and the majority in New York. This election, with the victory of a Tennessean, marked the arrival of the West as a potent political force, and it foreshadowed a West-South coalition that would ultimately focus the nation toward an expansionist agenda that became known as Manifest Destiny.

Robert F. Pace

BIBLIOGRAPHY
Boller, Paul F., Jr. *Presidential Campaigns*. 1984.
Watson, Harry L. *Liberty and Power: The Politics of Jacksonian America*. 1990.

Election of 1836

The election of 1836 served to fashion the two-party system in the United States. President Andrew Jackson announced in 1835 that he would not run for a third term, and he supported Vice President Martin Van Buren of New York to be his successor with Richard M. Johnson of Kentucky as his running mate. The infant Whig Party chose to field three presidential candidates: Hugh Lawson White of Tennessee, Daniel Webster of Massachusetts, and William Henry Harrison of Indiana. Each Whig held strong support in his respective region.

Although no major issues dominated the campaign, the protection of slavery and states' rights dominated the political rhetoric. Southern Whigs accused Van Buren supporters of favoring abolitionism and a powerful central government; Southern Democrats defended Van Buren's record of opposition to abolitionism. Both parties avoided discussion of the new Republic of Texas and its desire for U.S. recognition.

The Democratic Party's organization and methods eventually paid off against the divided Whigs. Van Buren won 50.9 percent of the popular vote and 170 electoral votes, while his opponents split the other 124 electoral votes.

With Van Buren's election, Jackson recognized the Republic of Texas on 3 March 1837, his last day in office. The Whig Party then regrouped behind its 1836 front-runner Harrison, a Westerner cut from the Jackson mold. The growing U.S. interest in Texas, the ascension of the two-party system, and the developing influence of the West all emerged from this election as issues that would dominate the decade leading to the U.S.–Mexican War.

Robert F. Pace

BIBLIOGRAPHY
Freehling, William W. *The Road to Disunion: Secessionists at Bay, 1776–1854*. 1990.
Van Deusen, Glyndon G. *The Jacksonian Era, 1828–1848*. 1959.

Election of 1840

The 1840 election, which produced the highest voter turnout in U.S. history (80 percent), also carried momentous consequences for slavery. With the economy depressed following the Panic of 1837, Democratic incumbent Martin Van Buren was a weak candidate, mocked as "Van Ruin." But the Whigs' opposition was divided between proslavery Southerners and reform-minded Northeasterners. To maximize their appeal, the Whigs nominated William Henry Harrison, victor over an Indian alliance at the 1811 Battle of Tippecanoe, and chose Virginia Democrat John Tyler for vice president.

The Whigs embraced populist politics. After a Democrat said that Harrison (who was born on a plantation with two hundred slaves and was college educated) would be happiest on his backwoods farm sipping hard cider, the Whigs turned this insult to their advantage by portraying him as the "log cabin" candidate. The party even distributed log-cabin–shaped whiskey bottles, filled by the E. C. Booz distillery, adding the word *booze* to the language. Meanwhile, the Whigs called Van Buren an aristocrat who dined on golden plates and wore a corset.

The election introduced the first campaign slogans (including "Tippecanoe and Tyler Too") and the first speeches ever delivered by a presidential candidate. It directly involved voters through barbecues and torchlight parades. Although Harrison won an overwhelming electoral college victory (234 to 60), the popular vote was close (53 percent to 47 percent). A shift of 8,000 votes would have elected Van Buren.

The election marked the first time an antislavery candidate ran for president. Although Liberty Party nominee James Birney received only 7,000 votes, his party won 60,000 votes in 1844, enough to throw the election to James K. Polk. When Harrison died only thirty days after taking office, Tyler became president. He promoted annexation of Texas by arguing that Great Britain wanted to make Texas an antislavery satellite state.

Steven Mintz

BIBLIOGRAPHY
Gunderson, Robert Gray. *The Log-Cabin Campaign*. 1957.
Wilentz, Sean. "1840." In *Running for President: The Candidates and Their Images*, edited by Arthur Schlesinger Jr. Vol. 1, pp. 143–161. 1994.

Election of 1844

The U.S. presidential contest of 1844 resulted in the election of James K. Polk, a Democrat whose program of vigorous

A Tippecanoe Procession. Supporters of William Henry Harrison roll a giant ball covered with campaign slogans at a rally during the 1840 presidential campaign (Benjamin Perley Poore, *Perley's Reminiscences*, vol. 1, 1886).

territorial expansion would lead to the U.S.–Mexican War. Martin Van Buren, who had won the presidency in 1836 and been defeated in 1840, was regarded as the likely nominee as the Democratic Party convention approached in the spring of 1844. The course of the upcoming election took a dramatic turn, however, as a result of President John Tyler's Texas annexation treaty then pending before the U.S. Senate. Mindful of the passions that the prospect of expanding the institution of slavery generated in the North and South, both Van Buren and Whig leader Henry Clay were anxious to defuse the explosive issue before it irreparably damaged the unity of their respective parties. Accordingly, the two leaders issued separate statements on 27 April opposing the treaty.

Although Henry Clay won the Whig Party's nomination by acclamation, Martin Van Buren's refusal to endorse the annexation of Texas infuriated slaveowners as well as other Democrats who favored vigorous territorial expansion. When Democratic Party delegates assembled in Baltimore on 27 May, expansionists led by Mississippi senator Robert J. Walker secured the election of a convention chairman hostile to Van Buren supporters, then lobbied successfully for a rules change requiring a two-thirds majority for nomination. Despite their strong delegate majority, Van Buren's supporters could not command the two-thirds majority needed to win the nomination on the first ballot. Michigan senator Lewis Cass, an avowed expansionist, picked up strength as the balloting continued, but like Van Buren he could not muster enough votes to win the nomination. Turning to a compromise candidate on the ninth ballot, party leaders threw their support to former Tennessee governor James K. Polk. Although in recent years Polk's political career had faltered—he had tried unsuccessfully to regain the governorship in

1841 and 1843—his candidacy offered certain advantages. Having taken an unequivocal stand in favor of annexation, he was acceptable to the expansionist wing of the party. Equally important he had played no part in the effort to sabotage Van Buren's candidacy and remained on good terms with the New York delegation. Finally, Polk was the choice of former president Andrew Jackson, an endorsement that carried considerable weight for many Democrats.

Running on a platform that included the usual planks on behalf of limited government and a low tariff, Polk took a strong stand on Texas annexation and, in an effort to attract western voters to the expansionist cause, called for the United States to establish control over the entire Oregon Territory, an area that had been occupied jointly with Great Britain for more than twenty-five years.

As the campaign got under way, Clay began to qualify his earlier statements on the Texas issue in an effort to placate Southern Whigs. The Whig nominee now averred that he favored annexation, but only if it could be achieved without a war with Mexico. The gambit angered antislavery Whigs in key Northern states, many of whom then bolted to the abolitionist Liberty Party. Clay was compelled to issue yet another statement on the subject, which, far from clarifying his position, only confused matters, leaving him vulnerable to charges of inconsistency and vacillation on the eve of the election.

Clay's inept handling of the Texas issue cost him much-needed votes in New York and turned out to be his greatest blunder of the race. Annexation was not, however, the only issue of the campaign. In an effort to allay fears that he might reduce the tariff, a matter of great concern to manufacturing interests in such key states as Pennsylvania, Polk issued a

Virtuous Harry, or Set a Thief to Catch a Thief! Lithograph with watercolor. Published in 1844, this political cartoon satirizes the Whig party's anti-annexation platform. Texas, personified as a beautiful woman, stands between presidential candidates Henry Clay and James K. Polk. At Polk's left stands his running mate, George M. Dallas; a Quaker, possibly an abolitionist, stands at Clay's right (Library of Congress).

carefully worded statement in which he opposed protectionism on principle, but pledged his support for a tariff high enough to raise revenue for the federal government. The presidential contest was also affected in northern urban centers by the strident nativism and anti-Catholicism of local Whig candidates, which prompted large numbers of immigrants to vote Democratic.

The election was one of the closest in history, with Polk receiving less than 40,000 votes more than Clay out of some 2,700,000 cast. In some states, the winner was decided by narrow margins. Amid allegations of election fraud, Polk failed to carry his home state of Tennessee by a mere 113 votes, although he edged out his Whig opponent in enough key states to give him a comfortable 170 to 105 lead in the electoral college. On 4 March 1845 James K. Polk—at forty-nine the youngest chief executive up to that time—took the oath of office as the eleventh president of the United States.

Sam W. Haynes

BIBLIOGRAPHY

Paul, James C. N. *Rift in the Democracy.* 1957.

Sam W. Haynes. *James K. Polk and the Expansionist Impulse.* 1997.

Election of 1848

A major issue in the election of 1848 was the fate of lands recently acquired from Mexico as a result of the U.S.–Mexican War. Citizens and politicians were divided over whether these lands would become slave territories as a part of the South, or maintain their current status as free territories. The third party Free-Soil movement supported maintaining these areas as free territories, while the Democrats supported the South and the Whigs remained silent on this issue.

Gen. Zachary Taylor, the most famous military figure of the war, was chosen to be the Whig candidate. Because Taylor was a slaveholder, Southerners saw him as a potential supporter of the institution of slavery. As the Whig candidate, however, Taylor in his platform largely ignored the issue, refusing to commit to either side of the debate. The Democratic Party ran Sen. Lewis Cass of Michigan on a platform of "squatter sovereignty." Later called popular sovereignty, this policy determined that each individual territory would determine its own slavery status. The Free-Soil movement, an antislavery third party, ran Martin Van Buren on a policy of upholding the conditions of the Wilmot Proviso. The party attracted supporters of the proviso itself, including New York Democrats and antislavery Whigs who were disheartened by their party's refusal to take a stand on the issue of slavery. Although Taylor won the election by thirty-five electoral votes, his victory was cemented not by support for the Whig party itself, but most likely because Free-Soilers split New York State's popular vote.

Karen L. Archambault

BIBLIOGRAPHY

Bauer, K. Jack. *Zachary Taylor: Soldier, Planter, Statesman of the Old Southwest.* 1985.

Rayback, Joseph G. *Free Soil: The Election of 1848.* 1971.

Election of 1852

Having won the 1848 presidential election with U.S.–Mexican War general Zachary Taylor, the Whig Party selected Gen. Winfield Scott as its candidate for president and Secretary of the Navy William A. Graham for vice president in 1852. The Democrats nominated New Hampshire senator and U.S.–Mexican War general Franklin Pierce for president and Alabama senator William King for vice president. Both parties had endorsed the Compromise of 1850, eliminating the slavery question as a major controversy in the race.

Scott's reputation as a military hero was not sufficient to ensure his election because he was so pompous that he had been nicknamed "Old Fuss and Feathers." The Democrats depicted him as foolish and conceited, with no talent for leadership outside the military. Pierce also had a distinguished U.S.–Mexican War record, but he was not nationally known. During the war Pierce's horse had fallen on rocks, and Pierce lost consciousness in the accident. Thus, the Whigs nicknamed him "The Fainting General" and during the campaign accused him of cowardice.

Pierce won the election with 50.9 percent of the popular vote, but with 254 electoral votes to Scott's 42. Pierce's strongest support came from the South, where slaveholders believed that he had backed the Compromise of 1850, including the Fugitive Slave Law, with more vehemence than Scott. Pierce also garnered most of the Free-Soil Party's vote, although the dying party had nominated John Hale of New Hampshire on an antislavery ticket. The Whigs' failure to deal with the slavery issue in this campaign combined with passage of the Kansas-Nebraska Act in 1854 resulted in the formation of the Republican Party.

Robert F. Pace

BIBLIOGRAPHY

Boller, Paul F., Jr. *Presidential Campaigns.* 1984.

Potter, David M. *The Impending Crisis, 1848–1861.* 1976.

Elections and Coups, Mexican

During the first half of the nineteenth century, Mexico failed to construct a peaceful and stable means for the transfer of national political power. From independence in 1821 until the triumph of the liberal Ayutla Revolution in 1855, the executive office changed hands almost fifty times. The constitutional bases of governance fluctuated between federalist and centralist republican models, with regular lapses into military dictatorship and an occasional monarchist resurgence. Rebellions, coups, and attempted coups were the common, although not the only, political currency. Traditional explanations for this instability often stressed the population's unpreparedness for self-rule after three hundred years under Spanish colonial authority and the deleterious effects of personality conflicts among regional strong men. Recent research has examined Mexico's instability in material and ideological terms rather than individual or group psychology. New interpretations emphasize that Mexico shared with other new nations of Latin America a legacy of militarization during the late eighteenth and early nineteenth centuries and a difficult relationship with a changing international political economy. Further, conflicts based on regional political, economic, and social interests played a large role in the arduous process of state formation throughout the region. These disputes encompassed, but were not limited to: the relationship between former colonial capitals and provincial centers; the role of the church and other corporate structures and the privileges invested in them; the direction of government economic and fiscal policy, particularly taxation; and the construction of a new body politic, which engendered struggle over the nature of citizenship and political participation. In addition to these, Mexican politics were complicated by a particularly high degree of popular mobilization and numerous foreign military interventions.

While these issues contributed to conflict and turnover in national political office, it is important to contrast regime instability with the constancy of many protagonists who first rose to power during the War for Independence and played important roles in these internecine struggles until mid-century. Perhaps the best known is Antonio López de Santa Anna, who began his military career as a royalist officer fighting against the insurgency before joining the rebels late in the struggle for independence. From his base in Vera Cruz, Santa Anna achieved the presidency nine times between 1833 and 1855, raising the banner of almost every political faction at one time or other during his career. Santa Anna's interludes as president were always brief, however. He never served longer than two years, four months at any one time before being driven out of office or voluntarily retiring to his hacienda. Juan Álvarez presents an interesting contrast to Santa Anna. Álvarez took up the insurgent cause during the early days of the War for Independence and built strong and lasting political, military, and economic connections in the region southwest of Mexico City. He remained a stalwart federalist republican power broker for decades, although he served as president only once, for about one month in 1855, after leading the rebellion that overthrew the last of Santa Anna's regimes.

In the first decades after independence, executive authority was rarely transferred without armed struggle. Agustín de Iturbide, a royalist military officer, joined the rebel forces in 1821 and proved decisive in securing independence. The following year Iturbide engineered a military coup, accompanied by popular manifestations to proclaim him emperor. This Creole empire was short-lived, however, as Iturbide was driven into exile in 1823, and Mexico's status as a federal republic was codified in the Constitution of 1824. The republic's first president, Guadalupe Victoria, had the unique distinction of being the only executive in the first half-century after independence to serve his full term. In 1828 his successor, Manuel Gómez Pedraza, was selected according to constitutional stipulation by a majority vote of the state legislatures, but he never took office. Instead, a rebellion that decried the lack of popular support for the president-elect swept Vicente Guerrero, hero of the War for Independence, to power. In addition to Guerrero's popular support in the countryside and among key military factions, the urban masses in several towns joined the rebellion. In Mexico City, Guerrero's impending victory set off an attack on the Parián market, for many a symbol of continued ethnic and class inequities in the new nation. For several days afterward, looting continued in the city's center. The triumph of Guerrero's supporters, who flexed their military muscle while appealing to the "will of the people," became a pattern repeated through the following decades.

The speed with which leaders occupied and vacated the presidential palace accelerated during the 1830s and 1840s. A centralist, conservative constitution was promulgated in 1836, only to be overturned in the early 1840s. The federalist aspirations of the constituent congress of 1842 were frustrated, however, by Santa Anna, who closed this congress and developed the *Bases Orgánicas*, another centralist constitution that placed power clearly in the hands of the elites. The alternation between centralist and federalist principles of governance continued into the 1850s, depending on which faction controlled the capital at the time. During these decades, foreign governments attempted to capitalize on the perceived weakness of the Mexican state. A brief war with France in 1838, called the Pastry War, preceded the more consequential confrontation with the United States in the 1840s. This international warfare in turn contributed to

even greater turnover in the executive office. In fact, between the outbreak of war with the United States and the ratification of the Treaty of Guadalupe Hidalgo, seven men rotated through the presidency, three of them more than once. Soul-searching in the wake of the war led to mutual recriminations and continued conflict. Civil war in the 1850s, a second French intervention in the 1860s that briefly revived European monarchy in the Americas, and accelerating changes in the international political economy after mid-century set the stage for the rise of a stable authoritarian state under Porfirio Díaz beginning in the 1870s, which lasted until 1910.

Finally, the political upheavals of the nineteenth century were not simply squabbles within the elite or between the obedient foot soldiers of men like Santa Anna and Álvarez. Rather, rural and urban popular interest in and mobilization around issues such as taxation and municipal autonomy formed the synapses between local and national politics, and account to a great degree for the nature of conflict during the period. Within this panorama, where armed struggle formed one pole of action, elections also served a complex and oscillating role in the transfer of power. Popular support was the sine qua non of legitimacy at the discursive level, if not in reality, and every political movement of the era produced and executed plans for the discovery of the popular will, usually through an electoral process. Any generalizations about these elections must be tempered by spatial, institutional, and temporal caveats.

Focus on disputes over the presidency obscures the fact that elections served as a regular means for the transfer of authority at the local and state levels. Study of the electoral process is made difficult, however, by variations in state legislation and between centralist and federalist models. Early federalist laws, often based on the 1812 Spanish constitution, were vague about the requirements for the suffrage, stipulating only that voters and officeholders had to be adult males with an "honest" living. A number of states instituted minimum property or income requirements for the suffrage and officeholding in the late 1820s, and these changes were incorporated into the centralist constitutions of the 1830s and 1840s. Centralist programs also tended to reduce the number of elected offices. One common electoral theme unified the era: prior to the liberal reforms of the mid-century, all elections for local, state, and national office were indirect; that is, popular elections designated a number of delegates who would meet at a later date to select officeholders.

The variety of legislation and the distinct histories of Mexico's regions preclude any generalizations about the frequency or effectiveness of elections in determining who would govern and how. In theory at least, a citizen of a town or city voted regularly in elections for municipal council members and for state and national legislators. Existing research, while incomplete, indicates that these elections often were contested and formed an important part of the era's political dynamic. Further research will no doubt elaborate the local and regional logics of this complex issue.

Richard Warren

BIBLIOGRAPHY

Annino, Antonio. "El pacto y la norma: Los orígenes de la legalidad oligárquica en México." *Historias* 5 (1984): 3–31.

Berge, Dennis E. "A Mexican Dilemma: The Mexico City Ayuntamiento and the Question of Loyalty, 1846–1848." *Hispanic American Historical Review* 50 (1970): 229–256.

Costeloe, Michael P. "Generals Versus Politicians: Santa Anna and the 1842 Congressional Elections in Mexico." *Bulletin of Latin American Research* 8 (1989): 257–274.

Guardino, Peter. *Peasants, Politics, and the Formation of Mexico's National State: Guerrero, 1800–1857.* 1996.

Guedea, Virginia. "The First Popular Elections in Mexico City, 1812–1813." In *The Evolution of the Mexican Political System*, edited by Jaime E. Rodríguez O. 1993.

Mallon, Florencia E. *Peasant and Nation: The Making of Postcolonial Mexico and Peru.* 1995.

Noriega Elío, Cecelia. *El Constituyente de 1842.* 1986.

Rodríguez O., Jaime E., ed. *Mexico in the Age of Democratic Revolutions, 1750–1850.* 1994.

Safford, Frank. "Politics, Ideology and Society in Post-Independence Spanish America." In *The Cambridge History of Latin America*, vol. 3, edited by Leslie Bethell. 1984.

Stevens, Donald Fithian. *Origins of Instability in Early Republican Mexico.* 1991.

Tenenbaum, Barbara A. *The Politics of Penury: Debts and Taxes in Mexico, 1821–1856.* 1986.

Warren, Richard. "Elections and Popular Political Participation in Mexico, 1808–1836." In *Liberals, Politics and Power: State Formation in Nineteenth-Century Latin America*, edited by Vincent C. Peloso and Barbara A. Tenenbaum. 1996.

Elliot, Charles

Charles Elliot (1801–1875), British minister to the Republic of Texas, was born in Dresden when his father was serving as the British envoy there. He entered the British navy in 1815 and served in the East Indies, resigning in 1834 to go to Hong Kong as a British trade commissioner. There he represented the interests of British opium traders in negotiations with the Chinese that preceded the first Opium War.

In 1838 Great Britain extended diplomatic recognition to the Republic of Texas. A trade convention was signed and Charles Elliot was appointed chargé d'affaires. Elliot soon became involved in attempts to foil President Sam Houston's efforts to achieve annexation. Vigorous British abolitionist sentiment precluded any true rapprochement with slaveholding Texas, but Houston, in order to whet the U.S. government's appetite, stressed his friendship with Great Britain. Much alike in personality, the president and the British envoy became fast friends.

In a last-minute gambit to prevent U.S. annexation, Elliot journeyed to Mexico City. Due principally to Elliot's efforts, Mexico signed the Diplomatic Act acknowledging Texas independence. Boundary and other questions were to be negotiated by Great Britain and France. However, as an alternative to annexation, this proposal was rejected by the Lone Star Republic.

Following his tour in Texas, Elliot served as governor of Bermuda (1846–1854) and held administrative posts in Trinidad (1854–1856) and on the island of St. Helena (1863–1869). He died at Witteycombe, Exeter, on 9 September 1875.

Stanley E. Siegel

BIBLIOGRAPHY

Adams, Ephraim Douglass. *British Diplomatic Correspondence Concerning the Republic of Texas, 1838–1846.* 1917.

Pletcher, David M. *The Diplomacy of Annexation: Texas, Oregon, and the Mexican War.* 1973.

Emory, William H.

U.S. Army general and boundary commissioner William Hemsley Emory ("Bold Emory"; 1811–1887) was born on 7 September at Poplar Grove estate in Queen Anne's County, Maryland, of Thomas and Anna Maria (Hemsley) Emory.

He graduated from West Point in 1831, held the ranks of lieutenant, captain, and major in the Topographical Engineers, and made an indelible stamp on the history of topography, cartography, and the scientific study of the southwestern United States. He distinguished himself as the most important individual in the Mexico–United States boundary survey from 1849 to 1857.

Emory entered the territory that consumed a decade of his life in 1846 as a first lieutenant in the Topographical Engineers assigned to Gen. Stephen W. Kearny's California expedition during the U.S.–Mexican War. He is remembered for his report *Notes of a Military Reconnaissance from Fort Leavenworth in Missouri to San Diego in California.* He was with Kearny when Santa Fe was occupied, participated in the battles of San Pasqual and San Gabriel, California, and was breveted twice for gallantry.

Emory joined the U.S. Boundary Survey team under Commissioner John B. Weller as chief astronomer in 1849. Emory resigned in 1850 but served as interim commissioner when Weller was relieved. The commission was reorganized in 1850 under Commissioner John Russell Bartlett; Emory chose not to serve but returned in November 1851 as surveyor and chief astronomer, replacing Andrew B. Gray and Lt. Col. James D. Graham. Under Emory's direction the survey was completed in 1855. Culminating the work was the publication of his three-volume *Report on the United States and Mexican Boundary Survey* in 1857 and 1859. He was responsible for most of the topographic observations and the maps produced were an important part of his personal accomplishments. He also oversaw the collection, preservation, and identification of a significant amount of botanical, zoological, and other scientific data that were analyzed by prominent scientists of the day. A naturalist in the tradition of Baron von Humboldt, his work greatly increased the scientific knowledge of the Southwest.

Emory's other work included surveying the Mexico-Texas and the Canada–United States borders. In the Civil War he commanded troops withdrawn from Fort Cobb, Indian Territory, in 1861, served in the Army of the Potomac in 1862 and as a division commander in the Port Hudson and Red River operations in 1863 and 1864, and returned east in 1864. He held several commands in the South during Reconstruction and retired in 1876. Emory died on 1 December 1887 in Washington, D.C.

Harry P. Hewitt

BIBLIOGRAPHY

Calvin, Ross. *Lieutenant Emory Reports.* 1968.

Emory, William H. *Notes of a Military Reconnaissance, from Fort Leavenworth, in Missouri to San Diego, in California.* 1848.

Emory, William H. *Report on the United States and Mexican Boundary Survey.* 3 vols. 1857–1859. Reprint, 1987.

Goetzmann, William H. *Army Exploration in the American West, 1803–1863.* 1959. Reprint, 1979.

The New Handbook of Texas. 6 vols. 1996.

Empresarios

Known as land contractors, land agents, and colonization agents, *empresarios* were individuals who received land grants, first from Spain and then from Mexico, to distribute to settlers. After U.S. acquisition of the Louisiana Territory in 1803, Texas became the northern outpost of the Spanish Empire in the Americas. After neglecting Texas for more than two centuries, Spain tried to secure this region by encouraging immigrants to settle in Texas. As in Louisiana in the eighteenth century, Spain wanted to create a buffer zone (mainly with European immigrants like French and Irish settlers) against filibusters from the United States. The Spanish government also had in mind Catholic settlers who had lived under Spanish rule in Louisiana, as it generally mistrusted the Protestants from the United States. In 1820 the liberal Constitution of 1812 came into effect once more in Spain, making it much easier for municipalities and governors to grant land to settlers. Individuals could apply for land just for themselves or as land contractors—*empresarios*—for a large area to distribute to prospective settlers. Before news of this change in Spanish policy reached possible interested parties, however, Mexico became independent in 1821. The first person to be granted an *empresario* contract—still under the old Spanish law—was Moses Austin from Missouri.

On 17 January 1821 he received permission to settle three hundred families in Texas. Although he died soon after, his son Stephen F. Austin was recognized by Mexico as his father's successor. This marked the beginning of Anglo-American settlement of Texas and, at the same time, of the *empresario* system as the major form of colonizing Texas. Between 1823 and 1835, twenty-seven different parties concluded forty-one *empresario* agreements with the Mexican government. The most important condition of these agreements was that the land assigned to the *empresario* must be settled within six years by one hundred to eight hundred families, depending on the size of the area. A family was entitled to a *labor* (177 acres) for farming and a *sitio* (4,428.4 acres) or league for ranching. For a *labor*, the family had to pay $3.50 and for a *sitio* $30.00, payable during the first six years. In comparison, the 177 acres of a *labor* would have cost $221.25 in the United States and a *sitio* $5,310. As compensation for his efforts, the *empresario* could keep for himself five *labores* and five *sitios* for every one hundred families that settled on his land. According to Mexican law, the *empresario* was also granted judicial power over his colony. Only two *empresarios* were able to fulfill their contracts: Stephen F. Austin and Green De Witt. Fourteen *empresarios* or parties were successful in part, and the rest either made no attempt to fulfill their contracts or did not succeed. Most of the 24,700 inhabitants of Texas in 1834 had received their land from an *empresario*. The Mexican government used the *empresario* system in various provinces, although never with as much political and economical importance as in Texas. Because it proved easier for most settlers to deal with their *empresario* than with the Mexican bureaucracy directly, Anglo-American settlers never became familiar with Mexican laws. The *empresario* system therefore was instrumental in bringing about the separation of Texas from Mexico and at the same time opened the door for extensive land speculation in Texas.

Andreas V. Reichstein

BIBLIOGRAPHY

Barker, Eugene Campbell. *The Life of Stephen F. Austin, Founder of Texas, 1793–1836.* 1925. Reprint, 1969.

Reichstein, Andreas V. *Rise of the Lone Star: The Making of Texas.* 1989.

Tijerina, Andrés A. *Tejanos and Texas under the Mexican Flag, 1821–1836.* 1994.

Weber, David J. *The Mexican Frontier, 1821–1846.* 1982.

Encarnación, Hacienda de

Located along the road connecting Saltillo and San Luis Potosí, Hacienda de Encarnación was the site of several important episodes in early 1847 that led to the Battle of Buena Vista, or La Angostura.

Rumors of the imminent arrival of Gen. Antonio López de Santa Anna's army reached Maj. Gen. William O. Butler at Saltillo. Needing information about the Mexican army's whereabouts, Butler ordered several patrols to Encarnación, fifty miles to the south. Maj. Solon Borland led fifty men of the 1st Arkansas Cavalry to the hacienda, where he was joined by Maj. John P. Gaines and a thirty-man detachment from the 1st Kentucky Cavalry. On 22 January 1847, Borland and Gaines exceeded their orders and marched their party farther south. Rain changed their plans, and the volunteers returned to Encarnación for the night. They failed to post an adequate guard, however, and in the morning found themselves surrounded by at least three thousand Mexican lancers commanded by Gen. José Vicente Miñon. Overwhelmingly outnumbered, Borland and Gaines surrendered when promised they and their men would be treated as prisoners of war. One of the prisoners, former Texas Ranger Daniel Drake Henrie, escaped and notified General Butler of the incident.

The rumor of imminent attack persisted, and Gen. Zachary Taylor, who replaced Butler as commander at Saltillo, sent more reconnaissance parties to Encarnación. On 20 February 1847, he ordered Capt. Ben McCulloch to the hacienda. The Texan, accompanied by six of his command, reached the hacienda at night where he found Santa Anna's army camped along the valley floor. Wrapping himself in a Mexican blanket, McCulloch entered the camp alone to gather information. McCulloch's scouting mission to Encarnación and his subsequent report to Taylor confirmed that Saltillo was about to be attacked.

Following the Battle of Buena Vista on 22 to 23 February, Santa Anna's army retreated through Encarnación, leaving behind several hundred wounded soldiers in its retreat to San Luis Potosí. Encarnación served as a field hospital while these soldiers recovered. They were later paroled.

Richard Bruce Winders

BIBLIOGRAPHY

Bauer, K. Jack. *The Mexican War, 1846–1848.* 1974.

Cutrer, Thomas W. *Ben McCulloch and the Frontier Military Tradition.* 1993.

Scott, John A. *Encarnación Prisoners.* 1848.

England

See Great Britain

Espionage

Both the U.S. and Mexican governments used spies to gain information about the other nation before and during the U.S.–Mexican War. Although neither government established intelligence services during the conflict, ad hoc espionage operations occurred at the national, or strategic, level and at the operational, or theater, level. Although it is not well documented, various political factions in Mexico, including those supporting Gen. Antonio López de Santa Anna, used secret agents to gain strategic information from U.S. officials and to influence policy. For example, Santa Anna used Col. Alexander Atocha (who claimed to be a U.S. citizen) as a confidential agent in Washington, D.C., to report information to Santa Anna at his residence while he was in exile in Havana, Cuba. At the operational level, Mexican commanders used guerrilla forces, such as those led by Gen. José Urrea and Gen. Antonio Canales, against Gen. Zachary Taylor's army in the northern campaign to harass Taylor's units and report on U.S. troop positions.

U.S. president James K. Polk also used espionage to further his strategic objectives. Although a pious man, Polk enjoyed intrigue (his detractors, when in a benevolent mood, accused him of being cunning, devious, and underhanded) and often used secret agents, normally sent for ostensibly diplomatic purposes, to gain information on which to base national policy. Immediately after his inauguration in March 1845, Polk successively sent Archibald Yell, Charles Wickliffe, and Commo. Robert F. Stockton to Texas with secret instructions to further his plans to influence politicians in the Lone Star Republic to accept annexation by the United States. They also had orders to report back on local political conditions and attitudes. In the fall of 1845, Polk decided to give the U.S. consul at Monterey, California, Thomas Larkin, a second mission as a secret agent to counteract British influence, encourage anti-Mexican, pro–U.S. attitudes, and generally to work toward the administration's hidden objective of gaining California for the Union. To deliver Larkin's highly sensitive instructions, Polk personally briefed a Marine lieutenant, Archibald Gillespie, before dispatching him on a clandestine journey to California to deliver the order. Gillespie traveled in civilian clothes under the cover of being a businessman representing a Boston trading company. Fearing detection as a spy in Mexico at a time when relations with the United States were strained over annexation of Texas, Gillespie memorized his confidential message and then destroyed it. His circuitous route took him to Vera Cruz and Mazatlán in Mexico, the Hawaiian Islands, and finally to Monterey where he delivered Polk's instructions to Larkin.

One clandestine intelligence source for U.S. forces early in the war was the British wife of the U.S. consul in Tampico, Anne McClarmonde Chase. After Mexican authorities ordered Consul Franklin Chase to depart Tampico in 1846, Anne Chase remained in the port city. Under the protection of her immunity as a British subject, she continued to circulate in the city, using her contacts to gain information that she passed to U.S. naval officers. She forwarded the strategically important plan of the Mexicans to abandon the city and passed false rumors in Tampico that exaggerated the size of U.S. naval forces in adjacent waters in the Gulf of Mexico.

When Commo. David Conner's forces took Tampico on 14 November, 1846, they marched in under the banner of the U.S. flag, hoisted on a rooftop by the fearless and patriotic Chase. After the war, Anne Chase submitted a claim to Congress for compensation for her work as a U.S. spy, but there is no record that she received payment from the U.S. government.

In November 1846 Polk instructed the wealthy publisher of the *New York Sun*, Moses Y. Beach, to go to Mexico City as a confidential agent and peace emissary. Traveling via Cuba, Beach obtained a false British passport to use on his journey. Although on a presidential mission, Beach was briefed in detail and paid by Secretary of State James Buchanan (Beach did meet on one occasion with Polk). When Gen. Winfield Scott's forces landed at Vera Cruz in March 1847, Beach was accused by the Mexicans of being an agent provocateur—a reward of $1,000 was offered for him, dead or alive. Beach covered his sudden departure by paying his hotel bill in advance, leaving most of his personal belongings, and fleeing by carriage in the dead of night to Tampico on the Gulf Coast. Because his activities made the Polk administration appear duplicitous (a diplomat supposedly seeking peace in the capital while an army was invading on the coast), the self-righteous Polk denied to the Senate that Beach had any diplomatic powers, claiming instead that he was simply a secret agent sent to collect useful information for the government.

Polk sent other secret agents to Havana, Cuba, to influence General Santa Anna to work for a settlement of U.S.–Mexican disputes favorable to the U.S. administration. The first, sent in early 1846, was William Linn Brown, who was instructed by Secretary of State Buchanan to report on Santa Anna's attitude. A more serious attempt to influence Santa Anna occurred later when Polk sent a naval commander, Alexander Slidell Mackenzie, as an undercover agent to Havana, ostensibly to check on privateers operating from Cuban waters. His real mission, given verbally by Polk, was to inform Santa Anna that he would be allowed to pass through the U.S. blockade and return to Mexico if, after assuming power, he would work to secure a peace favorable to the United States. Mackenzie infuriated Polk by putting his verbal instructions in writing and showing them to Santa Anna. The mission did pave the way for Santa Anna's return, but he did not work toward peace once back in Mexico.

In the northern theater of war, General Taylor rarely used operational espionage in his campaign. Although he occasionally sent out advance scouting parties, notably after Gen. John E. Wool joined him as second-in-command before the Battle of Buena Vista, Taylor normally paid little heed to the need for operational intelligence. On two occasions he failed to act after being given authority by Secretary of War William L. Marcy and General Scott to build up an operational intelligence capability. Marcy authorized him to hire Texas

Rangers as reconnaissance troops and Scott advised him to hire Mexican nationals as spies.

Scott, on the other hand, used espionage at both the strategic and operational levels. Before opening the second front in Vera Cruz, Scott sent emissaries to Havana to recruit secret agents to send to Mexico to gain intelligence for his army. During his campaign in southern Mexico, he made superb use of engineer officers to gain operational and tactical intelligence on Mexican forces, routes of advance, and local attitudes and conditions. Scott authorized one of his senior staff officers, Lt. Col. Ethan Allen Hitchcock, to recruit a spy company of approximately one hundred Mexicans (mostly highway brigands) to infiltrate Mexican cities and military strongholds and report vital information to his headquarters before his army marched on Mexico City. Although Scott's efforts gave engineer officers such as Capt. Robert E. Lee and Lt. Pierre G. T. Beauregard practical training in collecting information on enemy forces, little of lasting institutional value emerged in the field of intelligence from the U.S. war with Mexico.

Paul Coe Clark, Jr.

BIBLIOGRAPHY

Ameringer, Charles D. *U.S. Foreign Intelligence: The Secret Side of American History.* 1990.

Bauer, K. Jack. *The Mexican War, 1846–1848.* 1974.

Bryan, George S. *The Spy in America.* 1943.

Hitchcock, Ethan Allen. *Fifty Years in Camp and Field*, edited by W. A. Croffut. 1909.

Nelson, Anna K. "Mission to Mexico—Moses Y. Beach, Secret Agent." *New York Historical Quarterly* 59 (1975): 234–238.

Ramsey, Albert C., trans. *The Other Side: Or, Notes for the History of the War between Mexico and the United States.* 1850.

Santa Anna, Antonio López de. *The Eagle: The Autobiography of Santa Anna.* 1967.

Smith, Justin H. *The War with Mexico.* 2 vols. 1919. Reprint, 1963.

Wriston, Henry Merritt. *Executive Agents in American Foreign Relations.* 1967.

See also **Mexican Spy Company** *and biographies of figures mentioned herein*

Expansionism and Imperialism

The United States experienced its most rapid territorial growth during the mid-1840s. The nation annexed Texas in 1845, acquired Oregon south of 49° north latitude in a treaty with Great Britain in 1846, and conquered and held California and New Mexico during the U.S.–Mexican War. The nation also obtained vast cessions from Native American tribes, which were relocated to remote and unwanted regions, a process begun in the seventeenth century.

Journalist John L. O'Sullivan attributed this remarkable expansion to "Manifest Destiny," a label scholars still use to describe the decade. But O'Sullivan did not formulate a clear or coherent definition of Manifest Destiny. In 1845 he interpreted the phrase to mean that the United States was predestined to control the entire continent because God wanted it that way. But O'Sullivan soon abandoned his original doctrine. In 1846 he supported a war of conquest against Mexico and in 1848 he urged that Cuba and Yucatán be made a part of the United States, by purchase or by force. O'Sullivan coined a catchy phrase for the expansionism of the 1840s, but his concept does not explain the motives, means, and goals behind aggrandizement.

The historical evidence on this topic is abundant, contradictory, and often misleading. Presidents John Tyler and James K. Polk, their advisers, and their partisans in Congress supported territorial acquisitions, but their reasons for doing so varied widely. Although they sometimes invoked the idea of Manifest Destiny to justify expansion, they primarily sought land, markets, and ports for materialistic, not idealistic, ends. Like other empires, the United States sought power, wealth, security, and mobility for a fast growing population. Scholars generally agree that the United States rivaled other modern empires in the rapidity and degree of its enlargement. They differ, however, on the extent of similarity between the United States and traditional imperial powers such as Great Britain, France, Spain, and Russia. The United States, like its rivals, obtained territory by means both fair and foul. The chief difference, however, was that U.S. leaders in the 1840s eschewed colonialism and militarism. They intended to transform acquisitions into states equal in status to those already in the Union.

When O'Sullivan introduced Manifest Destiny in 1845, he predicted his country would acquire California in the same way it had just acquired Texas. Pioneers would venture to California, eclipse Mexicans and Native Americans, win independence, and then seek admission to the Union. Before the U.S.–Mexican War, Thomas Ritchie, summoned to Washington, D.C., by President James K. Polk to edit a newspaper favorable to his administration and policies, stressed the purity of previous cessions. "Our government is not extended by the sword," he wrote. "By its own merits it extends itself." Polk and his cabinet, however, lacked the patience to rely on the nation's "own merits," its pioneers, or providence to obtain California. Instead, they ordered Gen. Zachary Taylor and his troops into disputed territory between the Nueces River and the Río Grande.

Both the United States and Mexico miscalculated in 1846. Contemptuous of Mexico's government and army, Polk and his advisers tried to intimidate Mexican officials into ceding California and other provinces to the United States to pay outstanding claims owed to U.S. citizens. Mexico, for its part, erred in assessing its northern neighbor's ability to raise

and equip an effective military. Moreover, Mexican leaders miscalculated their nation's capacity to rally the church, the army, and the people to repel the invaders. Still stung by the loss of Texas, Mexican leaders vowed to resist further dismemberment. But in trying to avenge a previous defeat, they lost California and New Mexico.

Some scholars contend that Polk purposely goaded Mexico into war. Though he acted provocatively, he apparently hoped to realize his goals without war. The bloodshed in 1846 signified failure, not success, in his strategy. Polk deployed the army to gain territory, a move that alarmed the Whigs. Two months into the war, U.S. representative George Ashmun, from Massachusetts, rebuked the president. "It is no longer pretended that our purpose is to repel invasion," he protested. "The mask is off; the veil is lifted; and we see . . . *invasion, conquest,* and *colonization,* emblazoned upon our banners." Ashmun and other Whigs could not reconcile Polk's course with ideals of innocence and exceptionalism. Democrats, however, replied that Polk was beyond reproach. When the war ended, Sen. Sidney Breese of Illinois argued that his country's historic commitment to peace and national honor had been maintained. "We have never, sir, since the birth of our nation, given occasion for war, not even with the barbarous tribes upon our borders," he insisted. "It is our pride . . . that our whole history may be explored, and no single act of national injustice can be found upon its page—no blot of that kind upon our national escutcheon."

Politicians, editors, soldiers, and citizens, wanted new territory for various reasons. In the case of Texas, the Tyler administration sought to prevent the abolition of slavery there, control a potential rival in cotton production, provide a haven for masters and their slaves, thwart Great Britain from keeping Texas independent, and comply with the wishes of most Texians to join the United States. In the Oregon dispute, Democrats hoped to dominate Asian commerce, provide land for future pioneers, and safeguard citizens already settled there. The war with Mexico and the strategy of conquest revealed a desire to secure a border at the Río Grande, satisfy claims against Mexico, and acquire California to monopolize trade with Asia. Democrats wanted to supply abundant land to the nation's poor and to future immigrants. To attain this laudable goal, however, they relied on bribery, bullying, and warfare to wrest land from Native Americans and Mexicans. Often idealistic, they were also racist and materialistic.

Without opinion polls and single-issue elections from this era, scholars have limited data for measuring the popularity of expansionism. Each state was different, and attitudes changed with time. The war, for example, aroused far greater enthusiasm in mid-1846 than it did one year later. Polk won in 1844 on a strident party platform demanding the "rean-

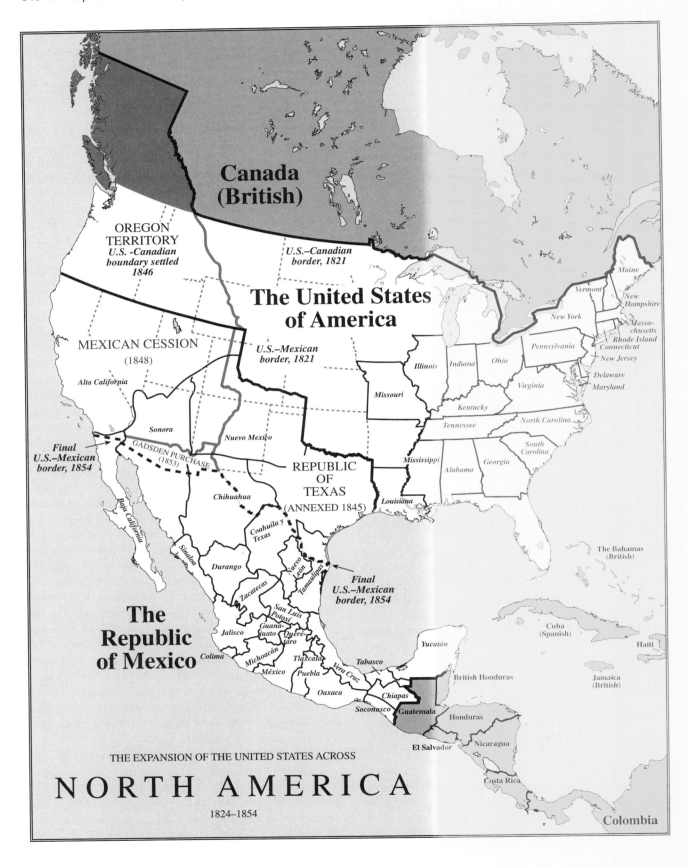

THE EXPANSION OF THE UNITED STATES ACROSS

NORTH AMERICA

1824–1854

nexation" of Texas and the "reoccupation" of Oregon. But his party lost clout in Congress after the war began and lost the presidency in 1848.

No subsequent decade matched the expansion of the 1840s, but leaders and private groups continued to seek more land from Native Americans, Central American countries, and European governments. Some adventurers resorted to filibustering expeditions to Cuba and Nicaragua. Among those who supported these private armies was John L. O'Sullivan. With the national government deadlocked over slavery and its extension after the U.S.–Mexican War, adventurers who sought new slave territories, commercial opportunities, or personal glory planned, financed, and occasionally conducted private invasions and occupations of Latin American nations and colonies. These filibusters generally hailed from the South and the best known among them was William Walker, whose execution in Honduras in 1860 marked the inglorious end of these unofficial efforts to extend Southern slavery below the Río Grande.

Thomas Hietala

BIBLIOGRAPHY

Graebner, Norman. *Empire on the Pacific.* 1955.

Hietala, Thomas. *Manifest Design.* 1985.

Horsman, Reginald. *Race and Manifest Destiny.* 1981.

May, Robert. *The Southern Dream of a Caribbean Empire, 1854–1861.* 1973.

Price, Glenn. *Origins of the War with Mexico.* 1967.

Weinberg, Albert. *Manifest Destiny.* 1935.

See also **Filibustering**; **Manifest Destiny**

Fannin, James

Texas colonel and slave trader James Walker Fannin Jr. (1804–1836) was born in Georgia on New Year's Day. He entered the United States Military Academy at West Point in July 1819 under the name James F. Walker but left the institution in November 1821. He moved in 1834 to Velasco, Texas, where he traded slaves and joined the War Party, a faction agitating for Texas independence.

On 2 October 1835, Fannin fought at the Battle of Gonzales, and on 28 October he served as co-commander of a Texas detachment during the Battle of Concepcion. On 7 December, Fannin won appointment as a colonel in the Texas regular army.

On 9 January 1836, Fannin began mustering volunteers for the Matamoros Expedition. With Gen. Sam Houston on furlough, Fannin acted as commander-in-chief from 12 February to 12 March. After learning that Gen. José Urrea was leading a superior Mexican force toward Goliad, Fannin abandoned his Matamoros scheme and took up a defensive position inside the Presidio La Bahía. On 14 March, Fannin received orders from Houston to withdraw his command to Victoria. Delaying retreat until he confirmed that Urrea had captured Texian units at Refugio, Fannin began a sluggish withdrawal toward Victoria on 19 March. Later that day, however, vanguard units of Urrea's division overtook and surrounded the Texian contingent near Coleto Creek. The rebels repelled repeated assaults. Without provender or the means to treat his wounded, Fannin surrendered to Urrea on 20 March.

Obeying Gen. Antonio López de Santa Anna's categorical directive against taking any rebel prisoners, Mexican soldiers executed Fannin and most of his Goliad command on 27 March.

Stephen L. Hardin

BIBLIOGRAPHY

Davenport, Harbert. "Men of Goliad." *Southwestern Historical Quarterly* 43 (1939–1940): 1–41.

Hardin, Stephen L. *Texian Iliad: A Military History of the Texas Revolution.* 1994.

Smith, Ruby Cumby. "James W. Fannin, Jr., in the Texas Revolution." *Southwestern Historical Quarterly* 23 (1919–1920): 79–90, 171–203, 271–284.

Farias, Valentín Gómez

See **Gómez Farias, Valentín**

Filibustering

The word *filibuster* derives from the Dutch *vrijbuiter,* meaning freebooter (pirate). When used in Latin America the term usually refers to U.S. citizens leading illegal expeditions into various countries with the aim of taking some of their territory. Spain and later Mexico both suffered loss of territory as a consequence of filibustering that originated in the United States.

In 1806 Francisco de Miranda, a Venezuelan, and Aaron Burr, former U.S. vice president, led the first filibustering expeditions into Spanish territory. Miranda hoped to overthrow the Spanish government in Venezuela. He failed and some of his men were either executed or imprisoned for their actions. During the same year Burr allied with Gen. James Wilkinson, who commanded U.S. troops in New Orleans, to lead a filibustering expedition into Spanish territory, hoping to seize Florida and Texas and establish a new republic. Although Burr led a group of men into Mississippi, Wilkinson double-crossed him, and the effort collapsed before any territory was captured. Between 1810 and Mexican independence from Spain in 1821, several other filibustering attempts were launched from the United States into Mexico's Texas frontier. José Bernardo Maximiliano Gutiérrez de Lara and Augustus W. Magee entered Texas from Louisiana in 1812 but suffered defeat the next year. In 1819 and 1820 James Long led an expedition into Texas. Spanish officials captured him and shot him in 1821.

After Mexico won its independence from Spain, filibustering efforts declined until the 1840s. By the time of the election of U.S. president James K. Polk in 1844, the idea of expanding the borders of the United States had taken form in what was called *Manifest Destiny*, a term used to describe the United States's supposed God-given destiny to expand its democratic institutions and culture. From this period into the twentieth century, individuals planned or led expeditions to take control of several Latin American countries.

Beginning in 1847 John L. O'Sullivan and Moses Y. Beach promoted a scheme for the United States to annex Cuba. Other entrepreneurs suggested that the United States should annex the Yucatán, which was then in rebellion against Mexico. Filibustering, particularly into Mexico, became more pronounced in the era after the U.S.–Mexican War (1846–1848). As a consequence of the war, the United States acquired Arizona, California, New Mexico, and parts of several other present-day western states. Although this territorial acquisition was considerable, many people in the United States believed that more Mexican territory should have been acquired. Some of these individuals wished to annex parts of the northwestern Mexican frontier to the United States. Others wanted to establish themselves as president of a new republic at the expense of Mexico.

During 1850 and 1851, U.S.–Mexican War veteran Joseph C. Morehead led an expedition to capture Baja California. Poor organization, insufficient funding, and bad luck thwarted this attempt. Morehead had just launched his scheme when several others began planning similar ventures. Charles de Pindray, a Frenchman living in California, led a group to Sonora ostensibly to work mines, but in reality to set himself up as the leader of a new country. He died under mysterious circumstances during the expedition, and most of his party fled the country. Another Frenchman, the so-called Count Raoussett de Boulbon, led a group of French and U.S. adventurers into Sonora two times between 1852 and 1854, failing to win a foothold. As his second venture got under way, Raoussett proclaimed himself the Sultan of Sonora and leader of the region. The Mexicans captured him, tried him for violation of Mexican sovereignty, and executed him.

By the time Raoussett was organizing his expeditions, William Walker had organized a party of U.S. citizens to take over Baja California, and possibly Sonora. The Walker expedition traveled by ship to La Paz, where Walker proclaimed himself president of the Republic of Lower California. Pursued overland by the Mexican army, Walker fled to the United States, where he and his party narrowly escaped capture. While Walker survived this episode, he was executed in 1860 in Honduras after leading a temporarily successful filibustering expedition to Nicaragua.

Another filibuster, Henry Crabb of California, also schemed after the U.S.–Mexican War to take away part of Mexico. In 1857 Crabb led a party overland from Arizona into the Sonoran frontier. At the Sonora Mexican village of Caborca, after being surrounded by Mexican troops, the Crabb group surrendered. The Mexicans executed all but a sixteen-year-old boy who was with the men. Crabb's head was severed and preserved in a bottle of mescal as a warning to all U.S. citizens who thought there was filibustering opportunity in Mexico.

Filibustering continued into the twentieth century. During the reign of Porfirio Díaz (1877–1911), despite the stability of Mexico, several individuals planned, organized, and even crossed the border hoping to take over the Mexican frontier. None of these individuals succeeded. As late as the final years of the Mexican Revolution (1911–1921), such schemes were still under way. From San Diego, California, an erstwhile actor named Dick Ferris, along with other consipirators, attempted to invade Baja California. They, too, failed, however, and Ferris later claimed he had not been involved. Although filibustering has received little attention from U.S. scholars, and most believe that it was insignificant, the opposite is true in Mexico. Mexican historians study the phenomenon, and a few believe that the U.S. government supported the efforts to destabilize the Mexican frontier and thus to annex more Mexican territory.

Joseph A. Stout, Jr.

BIBLIOGRAPHY

Brown, Charles H. *Agents of Manifest Destiny: The Lives and Times of the Filibusters.* 1980.

Forbes, Robert H. *Crabb's Filibustering Expedition into Sonora, 1857: An Historical Account with Maps, Illustrations, and Bibliography.* 1952.

Scroggs, William O. *Filibusters and Financiers, William Walker and His Associates.* 1916.

Stout, Joseph A., Jr. *The Liberators: Filibustering Expeditions into Mexico 1848–1862, and the Last Thrust of Manifest Destiny.* 1973.

Wyllys, Rufus K. *The French in Sonora.* 1932.

Filisola, Vicente

An Italian-born soldier who came to Mexico with the Spanish army in 1811, Vicente Filisola (1789–1850) was the first general in the Army of the Three Guarantees to enter Mexico City at the end of the War for Independence. He held several significant military posts through the 1820s and 1830s and was promoted to division general in 1833.

As Gen. Antonio López de Santa Anna's second-in-command, Filisola led the withdrawal of forces from Texas after the Mexican defeat at San Jacinto in 1836. Pulling his troops south to Matamoros on the right bank of the Río Grande gave sustenance to Texian claims of the river as the new international boundary. Filisola was accused of treason and cowardice for leading the retreat, and he published the *Memorias para la historia de la guerra de Tejas* in 1848 to exonerate himself.

Filisola's role in the war between Mexico and the United States was generally unremarkable. After Chihuahua fell to U.S. forces in March 1847, Filisola prepared to lead the reconquest of the state. Because U.S. forces abandoned Chihuahua before Filisola's force was assembled, Gen. Gabriel Valencia ordered him to organize an attack against the occupied cities of Saltillo and Monterrey. The northern campaign was cancelled altogether in August after Filisola's division suffered through a desperate summer in Durango, plagued by staggering supply shortages and high desertion rates. In early 1848 President Manuel de la Peña y Peña appointed Filisola commander of the Division of Querétaro, the largest of the three remaining divisions of the Mexican army. His short-lived command was ineffective due to continued soaring desertion rates and resource scarcity. A victim of the cholera epidemic of 1850, Filisola died in Mexico City shortly after he was named president of the Supreme War Tribunal.

Aaron P. Mahr Yáñez

BIBLIOGRAPHY

Filisola, Vicente. *Memoirs for the History of the War in Texas.* 2 vols. Translated by Wallace Woolsey. 1986.

Smith, Justin. *The War with Mexico.* 2 vols. 1919.

Fillmore, Millard

Millard Fillmore (1800–1874) served as U.S. representative from New York and was elected U.S. vice president under Zachary Taylor; upon Taylor's death, he became the thirteenth president of the United States. During the mid-1830s Fillmore had evolved into a conservative antislavery Henry Clay Whig. As early as 1838 he spoke out against the annexation of Texas and later opposed President James K. Polk and the U.S.–Mexican War.

Fillmore perceived the 1844 presidential election as a watershed in the question of whether slavery or free white labor would reign supreme in the future, but after he and Clay both lost elections that year, Fillmore returned to his law practice and did not participate in national politics during the U.S.–Mexican War. In a 2 October 1846 article in the *Buffalo Express,* Fillmore averred that the war would "sac-

Millard Fillmore. Benjamin Perley Poore, *Perley's Reminiscences,* vol. 1, 1886

rifice" the "interests of the North" by wasting "100 million dollars for the wild and wicked scheme of foreign conquest" simply to add "another slave territory to the United States."

Fillmore became vice president under Zachary Taylor in 1849, and while he supported the principle of the Wilmot Proviso (1846) he would not back it openly. Instead, his method of blocking slavery was more subtle, less openly antagonistic to the South. This became evident after Fillmore acceded to the presidency following Taylor's death on 9 July 1850. Later that year he signed the substance of Henry Clay's 1850 Compromise measures into law. Intended to settle sectional questions about the disposition of the territories acquired from Mexico through the Treaty of Guadalupe Hidalgo in 1848, Clay's proposals were designed to secure the nonextension of slavery through the concept of popular sovereignty (i.e., because the North had received the overwhelming number of foreign immigrants it had an obvious advantage in the number of potential free settlers in the West). The Compromise of 1850, by not mentioning slavery in the New Mexico and Utah Territories, laid the basis for popular sovereignty (i.e., when these areas became states they could omit mention of slavery in their state constitutions and let the settlers decide).

While some viewed the Compromise of 1850 as pro-South, the contrary appears to be the case: (1) popular sovereignty favored the North; (2) the South lost a guarantee of slavery south of 36 degrees 30 minutes north latitude (i.e., the Missouri Compromise of 1820); (3) the South received none of California (which under the Compromise of 1850 came in as a free state), not even southern California, sought in the Bright Amendment (which would have been possible with the westward extension of the Missouri Compromise line); (4) Texas, a slave state, gave up 72,000 square miles of territory claimed by New Mexico (and Fillmore ordered federal troops to New Mexico to reinforce those claims), receiving $10 million in U.S. bonds; (5) the South agreed to abolish the slave trade in the District of Columbia; and (6) while the South was pleased with passage of the Fugitive Slave Law of 1850, it proved costly and troublesome to slaveholders, and the South already had a fugitive slave clause in the Constitution plus the 1793 Fugitive Slave Law.

It was this 1850 Fugitive Slave Law that spurred the Whig Party's disintegration, which began in New York State in 1850, pitting the Fillmore and Francis Granger Clay-Compromise Whigs (Silver Grays) against the Thurlow Weed and William Henry Seward Radical Whigs (Woolies). Nationally the Whig Party was all but dead by 1856, followed four years later by the weakening of the Democratic Party and civil war. Fillmore, still true to his Clay-Compromise Whig principles, refused to join the newly formed Republican Party and ran as the presidential candidate of the American Party in 1856. Thereafter, Fillmore spent his remaining years as a private citizen, devoting most of his efforts toward improving the city of Buffalo. Although he entertained President-elect Lincoln in his home in February 1861 he was critical of the conduct of the Civil War and maintained that the Republicans were a "corrupt proscription radical party that now curses the country."

James D. Bilotta

BIBLIOGRAPHY

Bilotta, James D. "Western New York and the Sectional Controversy, 1840–1860." Master's thesis, State University College of New York at Buffalo, 1972.

Fillmore, Millard. Manuscript Collection, Buffalo and Erie County Historical Society. Buffalo, New York.

Rayback, Robert J. *Millard Fillmore: Biography of a President.* 1959.

Smith, Elbert B. *The Presidencies of Zachary Taylor & Millard Fillmore.* 1988.

Finances

This entry includes two articles: **Mexican Finances** *and* **U.S. Finances.** *See also* **Claims and Damages.**

Mexican Finances

One of the most critical concerns facing Mexico in the early nineteenth century was the establishment of a stable financial system for its government. The Wars for Independence had disrupted the economy, and this crisis was exacerbated by the trend among revolutionaries to provide widespread tax relief to attract supporters. When Agustín de Iturbide took power in 1821 as head of newly independent Mexico, he saw revenues dwindle at the same time the nation inherited a huge war debt. To return order to Mexico's finances, he ordered issuance of paper money and made forced loans against wealthy merchants and, ultimately, the Catholic Church. In addition, he contracted for two loans from Great Britain at high interest rates. The reaction against Iturbide's "tyrannies" led to revolution, and he abdicated in 1823. The pattern for future Mexican fiscal government, however, had been set.

The republic that emerged had no more success putting its finances in order. A period of relative calm evaporated in 1827 when congress, to curry favor with supporters and to reduce Spanish influence in Mexico, expelled all Spaniards still residing in the nation. These people—the wealthiest and most influential element in Mexican society—took their skills and money with them. The unsettled nature of Mexican affairs led Spain to intervene, leading to the failed invasion of Tampico in 1829. These conflicts added to Mexico's debt, which gave pause to European financiers as to the stability of the Mexican Republic.

The cycle of revolutions that marked the "Age of Caudillos" also required huge expenditures to cover the costs of war and to purchase the loyalty of the army and its generals. The crisis became acute in 1837 when, for six months, no one in Mexican government received pay, leading many officials to resign from office. Within a year, observers from the United States and Europe declared Mexico in a state of anarchy. The French acted on this assumption in 1838 by blockading and then capturing Vera Cruz until all debts owed to French citizens were paid. The ensuing conflict, known as the Pastry War, resulted in some satisfaction for the French, who withdrew their troops under pressure after a battle in the streets of the city.

For Mexico, however, it marked one of the many political comebacks of Antonio López de Santa Anna, who had led his nation to victory. With the endorsement of the country, Santa Anna took control of the government in 1841. He immediately began a program to refill the public treasury by imposing forced loans on the church and private individuals and by suspending payment of public debts. He also spent lavishly—on himself, his entourage, and his army—until his attempts at financial recovery were negated. He used Mexico's treasury to perpetuate his power instead of promoting the common good, and Mexico again approached default on all of its foreign loans. By 1845, with relations between the United States and Mexico deteriorating, the treasury of Mexico was virtually empty and the government found itself entitled to a mere 13 percent of its 16.5 million pesos in annual revenues due to outstanding obligations.

In 1846 fighting between the United States and Mexico led to emergency measures by President Mariano Paredes y Arrillaga aimed at funding a successful conclusion to what most believed would be a limited conflict. The clergy contributed 1 million pesos to support a campaign against the U.S. invaders and to subsidize the costs of refitting and equipping the army. Other efforts to raise revenues fell flat and the suspension of payments of salaries, pensions, and treasury obligations all ended in agitation against the government and a lack of credit overseas. The U.S. blockade of Mexico cut public revenues in half. By the end of the summer, only 1,839 pesos remained in the treasury. Mexican patriots rallied and sought voluntary loans from towns, states, businessmen, and the church, but gathered only an additional 90,000 pesos.

On 11 January and 4 February 1847 Mexico resorted to laws that amounted to a wholesale attack on the long-held privilege of the church. To raise 15 million pesos for prosecution of the war, the government pledged church property as collateral on loans. The result was civil war as defenders of the church overthrew the government and called on Santa Anna to save the nation again. He responded by assuming the presidency on 23 March and demanding a contribution of 2 million pesos from the church and access to 20 million pesos in church property. He then turned to other means including the levying of special war taxes on the population, discounting government bonds and securities, turning control of Mexico's mint over to British contractors, and even door-to-door solicitations. When these efforts fell short, money and materials of war were often seized. Despite these serious financial handicaps, Mexico maintained a stout resistance for the rest of the year on a very thin budget.

Mexico emerged from its war with the United States in dire financial straits. The war had cost more than 100 million pesos. Mexicans were therefore ready to negotiate, and the Treaty of Guadalupe Hidalgo provided $15 million from the United States and an assumption of an additional $3 million in debts owed to U.S. citizens. In 1854 Mexico received another boost from the sale of its national territory when Santa Anna, chief executive of the nation for the eleventh time, traded a 45,000-square-mile area in present-day Arizona, known as the Gadsden Purchase, to the United States for $10 million. Ironically, this last attempt to raise money led to accusations of selling out to the United States, and the resulting Ayutla Revolution removed Santa Anna from power for good.

Donald S. Frazier

BIBLIOGRAPHY

Ramirez, J. F. *Memorias, negociaciones y documentos de la Guerra con los Estados Unidos.* 1853.

Ramirez, J. F. *Mexico durante su Guerra con los Estados Unidos.* 1905.

Smith, Justin H. *The War with Mexico.* 2 vols. 1919. Reprint, 1963.

U.S. Finances

Financing the war with Mexico was a significant struggle for the United States. Burdened with a lackluster economy, declining federal revenues, and limited international credit, the U.S. Congress found itself with limited means to finance what proved to be an expensive war.

Long before the declaration of war in May 1846, the U.S. economy had foundered under the pressures of currency inflation and declining stock prices. The government itself suffered from falling revenues because of decreased land sales and reduced customs receipts. The tariffs of 1842 had proved too high and the resulting decline in imports adversely affected the federal coffers. At the state level, international debt, in excess of $200 million, meant that the states, too, were strapped for money. Delinquent payments and European scepticism about the financial stability of the United States severely limited the country's borrowing power. By the spring of 1846, a surplus of only $7 million was in the federal treasury.

Securing financing for the war proved as tenuous for President James K. Polk as securing support for the war itself. Although able to convince Congress to attach $10 million to the declaration of war, Polk struggled to maintain federal revenues as the democratic leadership in Congress worked to lower the tariff. Once the new Walker Tariff passed in August 1846, trade all but stopped as importers waited for December, when the lower tariff was slated to take effect. Revenues plummeted so dramatically that the president suggested to the House of Representatives that it impose duties on tea and coffee and create a system for graduated public land prices. The House rejected both recommendations. In the fall of 1846, Secretary of the Treasury Robert J. Walker estimated a federal deficit of $12 million. In response, Congress authorized a $10-million loan in treasury notes and bonds. Walker not only found it difficult to sell these notes but also, in December, had to report to Congress that the deficit would actually amount to more than $23 million.

The U.S. economic picture brightened in 1847, when U.S. victories increased support for the war. Moreover, famine in Ireland and to a lesser degree in Germany swelled demand for U.S. agricultural goods. Immigrants fleeing the famine brought $24 million in specie to the country. Most significant, the reduced tariff dramatically boosted trade. Customs duties totaled some $11 million for the third quarter of 1847 alone, half the revenue for the entire previous year. Treasury receipts also increased in 1847 because the U.S. military began collecting taxes and duties from Mexicans in occupied towns. Mexican merchants offered little resistance to the U.S. tariffs because they were much less than the Mexican tariffs had been.

At the close of the war, U.S. military expenditures totaled almost $64 million, including a $16-million loan authorized by Congress in the spring of 1848. Pensions, damage claims, and other liabilities brought the total to $98 million. Additionally, the United States agreed to pay Mexico $15 million for new territory in the West and to assume claims of U.S. citizens against Mexico of $3 million. Although the war was costly to the U.S. treasury, the economic prosperity resulting from increased agricultural exports to Europe, the concurrent influx of immigrants, and the western territorial expansion kept the United States in a period of relative prosperity for several years afterward.

Kevan D. Frazier

BIBLIOGRAPHY

Connor, Seymour V., and Odie B. Faulk. *North America Divided: The Mexican War, 1846–1848.* 1971.

Schroeder, John H. *Mr. Polk's War: American Opposition and Dissent, 1846–1848.* 1973.

Smith, Justin H. *The War with Mexico.* 2 vols. 1919. Reprint, 1963.

Fisher, William S.

A noted Texas adventurer during the 1830s and 1840s, William S. Fisher (18??–1845) was born in Virginia and settled in Texas in 1834. During the Texas Revolution he participated in the battles of Gonzales, San Antonio, and San Jacinto. After the war he served briefly in President Sam Houston's cabinet as interim secretary of war and was later appointed by Mirabeau B. Lamar to command a frontier regiment that fought against the Comanches in the Council House Fight of 1840. In that same year Fisher was recruited by leaders of the Republic of the Río Grande, a separatist movement in northern Mexico, to organize an army of Texas mercenaries to assist them in the their struggle against the Mexican government.

After the defeat of separatist forces and the collapse of the Republic of the Río Grande, Fisher returned to Texas, and in 1842 he entertained hopes of leading a filibuster expedition into the lower Río Grande valley. In the fall of that year, however, in retaliation for Mexican raids upon the Texas frontier, President Houston appointed Alexander Somervell to lead an army into northern Mexico. Fisher joined the so-called Somervell Expedition as a captain. Bad weather, meager supplies, and a lack of discipline among his men convinced Somervell to terminate the expedition at the Río Grande near Guerrero, on 19 December 1842, but the bulk of his force, slightly more than three hundred men, disobeyed the order to return home. Subsequently named the Mier Expedition, the renegade army elected Fisher as its commanding officer. On the night of 25 December, the Texans attacked a Mexican army at the town of Ciudad Mier. Fisher, like Somervell before him, proved unable to control his fractious troops. After renewed fighting on 26 December, a large number of Texans decided to lay down their arms. Realizing that these defections made further resistance futile, Fisher surrendered. The Texas commander later attributed the outcome to his troops' inability to act in concert, noting that "we were utterly defeated, not by the enemy, but by ourselves."

During the early months of 1843 the Texans were marched under heavy escort into the interior of Mexico. Fisher and his second-in-command, Thomas Jefferson Green, were separated from the main body of prisoners and taken to Mexico City, then sent to the fortress San Carlos de Perote, a military installation on the National Road located midway between the capital and Vera Cruz. Although Green escaped in the summer of 1843 and made his way back to Texas, Fisher chose to remain at Perote, unwilling to abandon his men to Mexican captivity. The main body of Mier Expedition prisoners joined Fisher at Perote in September. One year later, in an attempt to repair deteriorating relations with the United States, Mexican president Antonio López de Santa Anna ordered the release of Fisher and the remaining prisoners. Fisher returned to Texas, where he died in 1845.

Sam W. Haynes

BIBLIOGRAPHY

Dixon, S. H., and Louis Kemp. *The Heroes of San Jacinto.* 1932.

Green, Thomas Jefferson. *Journal of the Texian Expedition against Mier.* 1845.

Haynes, Sam W. *Soldiers of Misfortune: The Somervell and Mier Expeditions.* 1990.

Flacco the Elder

A Lipan Apache chief, Flacco (fl. 1840) was one of the leaders of the Lipan Apache Indians during the years of the Texas Republic and early statehood. He was generally friendly with the Texians and joined them on several raids against hostile Indian tribes and Mexicans. Flacco's son, also called Flacco, was killed returning from a Texian expedition into Mexico in 1842. Two of the white men on the expedition apparently murdered the younger Flacco to steal his horses. The Texians, fearing that Flacco the Elder and the Lipans would launch retaliatory raids if they learned the truth, blamed Mexican bandits for the warrior's death. President Sam Houston sent gifts to the bereaved parents and promised to investigate the cause of young Flacco's death, although he, too, later indicated that Mexicans had been responsible. Flacco became despondent over his son's loss, and a few months later he led approximately 250 of the 400

Texas Lipans into Mexico, where he joined forces with a band of Mescalero Apaches. Later raids into Texas by Lipans might have been carried out by this band; they apparently continued to raid Mexican settlements as well. It is unknown if Flacco actually led or encouraged Lipan raids on Texians or Mexicans.

Jeffrey D. Carlisle

BIBLIOGRAPHY

Schilz, Thomas F. *Lipan Apaches in Texas*. 1987.

Smithwick, Noah. *The Evolution of a State or Recollections of Old Texas Days*. 1983.

Flags

This entry consists of four separate articles: **Mexican Flags**; **Texan Flags**; **U.S. Flags**; *and* **Militia Flags**.

Mexican Flags

In 1822, the Mexican empire adopted a *pabellón nacional* consisting of a tri-color with three equal vertical bars of green, white, and red. In the center of the white bar the *escado de armas* was placed, which consisted of a rampant eagle standing on a cactus with a snake in its mouth. The *escado de armas* was taken from the Aztec legend that an eagle killing a snake upon a cactus would be a sacred sign marking the island site of the future Aztec capital. A crown was placed over the eagle's head as a symbol of Emperor Agustín de Iturbide. Following the overthrow of the emperor and the creation of the Mexican republic, the crown was removed. The new design remained the Mexican *pabellón nacional* until the twentieth century.

Mexico's military units carried variations of the *pabellón nacional* as regimental and battalion colors. Most of the infantry flags were made from silk and were 68″ × 52″. Cavalry standards were smaller. While regulations called for the *escado de armas* in the white center and the name of the regiment or battalion inscribed, it is apparent from surviving examples that no standard form was in fact followed. Most of the military flags lack the cactus, and the direction the eagle faces also varies. In one case, the word *Activo* is misspelled as *Activa*. The *ligero* regiments created in 1839 had their own distinctive colors and guide flags with the regimental number embroidered with the *cazadore* hunting horn. Surviving Mexican unit flags are made of silk with embroidered inscriptions and *escado de armas*.

Despite changes in battalion and regimental distinctions during the period from 1833 to 1839, units often hung onto their old colors. In some cases, relics of the Spanish period were used. One cavalry regiment carried a guidon complete with skull and crossbones and the motto in Spanish, "Liberty or Death."

Mexican flag, 1825

Texas flag, 1839

U.S. flag, 1846

Militia flag, 1835

Mexican *soldados* often fought hard to keep their flags out of enemy hands, as exemplified by the legendary actions of a young cadet at Chapultepec who, tradition says, wrapped himself in the garrison colors and jumped from the rampart to his death rather than be captured. A well-documented event during the same battle occurred when Lt. Col. Santiago Xicotencatl, the commander of the San Blas Battalion, wrapped his unit colors around his waist in an effort to keep them safe from U.S. forces. Not a single Mexican standard bearer is reported to have survived the Battle of Palo Alto.

During the 1836 Texas Revolution and the 1846 to 1848 U.S.–Mexican War, several Mexican flags came into Texan and U.S. possession. While many remain in local historical collections, in 1950 the U.S. Government under the administration of President Harry Truman returned some sixty-six Mexican flags taken between 1846 and 1848. Three Mexican flags captured in the 1836 battle of San Jacinto by Texian forces remain in the charge of the Texas State Archives.

Kevin R. Young

BIBLIOGRAPHY
Brown, A.S., J. Hefter, and A. Neito. *El Soldado Mexicano, 1837–1847.* 1958.

Texan Flags

The first official flag of the Republic of Texas was adopted by the convention held at Washington-on-the-Brazos in the spring of 1836. Conflicting sources claim both 9 April and 11 May as the official date. Designed by Gen. Lorenzo de Zavala, the first vice president of the Republic of Texas, the first Texas flag bore a white five-pointed star in the center of a blue field. The letters *T-E-X-A-S* encircled the star. This flag was similar to other designs used by nineteenth-century revolutionaries.

Only a few months later, the first congress of the new republic chose to simplify the design. David G. Burnet proposed that the star's color be changed to gold and the surrounding letters dropped completely. Burnet had been the first Texas president but his successor Sam Houston had already taken office, and signed the new design bill on 10 December 1836. Both Burnet and Houston hoped Texas would soon join the United States and this design was similar to other state flags. There is no authentic written evidence that either of these early Texas flags was ever displayed, however.

Mirabeau B. Lamar succeeded Sam Houston and was not in favor of joining the Union. Lamar favored a flag that was distinctly different from any of the state flags and so he assigned a committee of six to begin a search for a Texas national flag. These six had signed the Texas declaration of independence and included Lorenzo de Zavala, designer of the first official Texas flag. The Lone Star Flag was designed by Dr. Charles B. Stewart and was adopted in 1839. It preserved the original white star, this time in a vertical blue bar on the flag's left, with a white stripe above a red stripe on the right. Under this flag, Texas was an active free nation, recognized by the United States, France, and Great Britain.

When Texas was annexed by the United States in 1845, the red, white, and blue Lone Star Flag was retained as the state flag.

Lee Ann Woodall

BIBLIOGRAPHY
Conner, John Edwin. *The Flags of Texas.* 1964.
Gilbert, Charles E., Jr. *Flags of Texas.* 1989.

U.S. Flags

During the U.S.–Mexican War, all regular U.S. infantry and artillery regiments were allowed to carry both a national and a regimental flag, also called colors. By regulation they were to be made of silk, were to measure six feet on the pole and six feet six inches on the fly, and were to be displayed on a staff nine feet ten inches in length measuring from spearpoint to ferrule. Both were fringed in yellow silk. A set of cords, blue and white for infantry, red and yellow for artillery, completed the stand.

The U.S. national flag was the Stars and Stripes, with 13 stripes and stars numbering from 26 to 28. It was not until 1834 that army regiments had been issued national flags, which by regulation were not to be carried into battle. The name and number of the regiment were embroidered on the center stripe, in gold for artillery and silver for infantry. The stars were also embroidered in the appropriate color.

Infantry regimental flags were blue silk and featured the arms of the United States, an eagle with arrows and olive branches in its talons. Below the eagle was a scroll with the name of the regiment. Clutched in the eagle's beak was a smaller scroll with the motto, "E Pluribus Unum." Above the eagle's head was a galaxy of stars representing the current union, varying from 26 in the old line regiments to 28 in the new establishment. The flag was designed to be readable from either side, and the artwork was to be embroidered. This embroidery was not done, however; all surviving colors, national and regimental, are painted on the silk.

Artillery regiments carried yellow silk colors with crossed cannon barrels painted in the center, the letters *U.S.* above, and the regiment's name in a scroll beneath.

Garrison flags were the national color, on stars and stripes, and were constructed of wool bunting. They were twenty feet on the pole and forty feet on the fly. Like the silk national, the width of the union was one-third the length of the flag, the bottom of the union butting against the lower edge of the fourth red stripe from the top.

Dragoon regiments had a much smaller national standard to make it easy to carry while mounted. The same pattern as the infantry regimental, it was only two feet three inches on the lance and two feet five inches on the fly. Dragoons also were issued a silk swallow-tailed guidon divided red and white, with the red uppermost. The red section featured the letters *U.S.* in white paint while the white bottom bore the company designation in red paint.

The colors were the pride of the regiments who carried them. The highest honor an enlisted man could receive was to carry the colors, followed by being a member of the guard to protect it. Always in the thick of combat these flags became the rallying point of the small regular force and a symbol of the respect they earned for their actions during battle.

Steve Abolt

BIBLIOGRAPHY

Johannsen, Robert W. *To the Halls of the Montezumas: The Mexican War in the American Imagination.* 1985.

Katcher, Philip R. N. *The Mexican-American War 1846–1848, Osprey Men-At-Arms Series.* Colour Plates by G. A. Embleton. 1976. Reprint 1989.

Nevin, David. *The Mexican War.* Time-Life Old West Series. 1978.

U.S. War Department. *General Regulations for the Army, 1847,* pp. 156–157. 1847.

Militia Flags

Throughout the U.S.–Mexican War, the use and display of state and local flags served as a source of pride to men enlisted in the militia, and as tangible links to their families and homes back in the States. Although the style of the flags carried by regular units of the U.S. Army was specified by U.S. Army regulations, and these flags were made at a central depot, flags carried by state volunteer forces were another matter.

Since the first militia adaptation of *Scott's Tactics* in 1815, provisions had been made for state regiments to carry their colors into battle, but nowhere in the regulations were allowances made for carrying a national color. While technically prohibited from displaying the national emblem, however, many volunteer regiments marched into battle under the Stars and Stripes.

When calling the militia into service, the U.S. government made no provision for the presentation or procurement of state or regimental flags. This task generally fell to the women of the town. Depending on their skill, these flags were ornate works of art or simple, straightforward displays of patriotism.

Flag presentations were occasions of high solemnity. Amid the playing of patriotic music and lofty speeches these homemade symbols were presented to the troops from a local district, often during ceremonies held as the troops left their community for the state rendezvous.

As these units, each with its own color, met at the rendezvous point, it became a difficult task to decide which flag a regiment would carry when completely organized. This often was solved by using a large silk color similar to that carried by the regular infantry regiments, but emblazoned with the state seal rather than the national seal. Like those of the regulars, the volunteers' flags were generally six feet on the pole and six feet six inches on the fly. Although some flags were embroidered, most were painted because it was a more efficient method of procurement. A great source of pride, these colors were returned to the state capitols to be displayed at the war's conclusion.

Many U.S. Army regular enlisted soldiers, whose units did not carry a state or local flag, spent their idle hours sewing them, or adorning personal belongings with the national symbol. Some soldiers displayed the stars set in a variety of fashions, some included an eagle with its wings spread surrounded by a galaxy of stars, some, claiming artistic license, inverted the order of the stripes.

The greatest honor an enlisted soldier, whether volunteer or regular, could receive was to carry the regiment's colors. Many of these banners, whatever their design, were carried by men intent on seeing their state or community's pride floating in the breeze above the Halls of Montezuma.

Steve Abolt

BIBLIOGRAPHY

U.S. Department of War. *Abstract of Infantry Tactics; including Exercises and Maneuvers of Light-Infantry and Riflemen, for the Use of the Militia of the United States.* Under the Authority of an Act of Congress of the 2d of March, 1829. 1830.

Johannsen, Robert W. *To the Halls of the Montezumas: The Mexican War in the American Imagination.* 1985.

Nevin, David. *The Mexican War.* Time-Life Old West Series. 1978.

Wilcox, Cadmus M. *History of the Mexican War.* 1892.

Flores, José María

José María Flores (1???–1???) was a Mexican military commander in California. Flores came to California four years before the outbreak of the U.S.–Mexican War, serving as secretary to Manuel Micheltorena, the last Mexican-appointed governor of the province. When the latter was expelled in 1845 by Californio rebels opposed to Mexican rule, Flores remained in California and worked as an assistant to José Castro, California's military commander when the war began. When Castro fled to Mexico before apparently invincible U.S. forces, again Flores remained behind, himself later to become *comandante.*

On 4 November 1846 Flores successfully mounted a southern California revolt against U.S. authority, which had been established only superficially by a weak military force under Lt. Archibald Gillespie in Los Angeles. Even during this brief hiatus of Californio resurgence, however, the Californios' internal divisiveness weakened the effort. Native Californios distrusted Flores because he was a Mexican, which led to his being temporarily put under arrest at the very time his leadership was needed to organize his forces. Commo. Robert Stockton, the commander of U.S. forces in California, quickly moved troops southward to crush all resistance. Flores fled to safety in Sonora. He could not remain in California because he had broken his pledge to Stockton not to carry on resistance, and Stockton had threatened to execute him for reneging on his word. Flores went on to serve in the Mexican army during the war with the United States.

Ward M. McAfee

BIBLIOGRAPHY

Bancroft, Hubert Howe. *History of California,* vol. 5. 7 vols. 1886–1890.

Harlow, Neal. *California Conquered: War and Peace on the Pacific.* 1982.

Flying Artillery

U.S. Army artillery companies during the U.S.–Mexican War that were armed with light field guns and practiced highly mobile tactics and firing techniques were called "flying artillery." The terms *flying artillery, mounted artillery,* and *horse artillery* often are used interchangeably, but incorrectly so.

The vast majority of artillerymen in the four U.S. artillery regiments of ten companies manned fixed fortifications along the U.S. coast. When these regiments went to the field, the artillerymen often fought as light infantry. The few guns taken to the field were large, unwieldy, and not very mobile. They were moved by heavy draft animals—often oxen—and the cannoneers walked alongside the guns. In September 1838, Secretary of War Joel R. Poinsett exercised a long-dormant provision of the 1821 Army Reorganization Act to equip one company in each regiment as light artillery.

The first of these units was Capt. Samuel Ringgold's Company C, 3d Artillery. This unit was armed with new bronze 6-pounder guns, and every cannoneer was mounted. The other three units were Capt. Francis Taylor's Company K, 1st Artillery; Lt. James Duncan's Company A, 2d Artillery; and Capt. John Washington's Company B, 4th Artillery. The cannoneers in these three units were not all mounted. They usually walked alongside the guns, and during rapid maneuvering they rode on the caissons or the limbers (both two-wheeled vehicles, mounting, respectively, double or single ammunition chests).

Strictly speaking, only Ringgold's unit was horse artillery, while the other three were mounted artillery. Although the mounted artillery companies were faster and more maneu-

verable than normal artillery in the field, Ringgold's was faster still. Because of its speed, only Ringgold's company could properly be called flying artillery. Just before hostilities, Capt. Braxton Bragg's Company E, 3d Artillery also received light field guns. These five companies were the primary source of battlefield firepower for the U.S. Army during the U.S.–Mexican War.

Despite the relative light weight of their guns, American mounted and horse artillery was able to maneuver faster and fire at a much higher rate than the conventional field artillery of the day. This gave them a considerable tactical advantage in field operations against their heavier Mexican opponents. At Palo Alto, the guns of Capt. Samuel Ringgold fired eight rounds for every one fired by the Mexican gunners. At Buena Vista, the unparalleled mobility of the American guns was the decisive factor in the battle. Despite the long-accepted myth, Gen. Zachary Taylor did not order the guns of Capt. Braxton Bragg to fire more grape shot. What Taylor actually ordered was double canister.

David T. Zabecki

BIBLIOGRAPHY

Birkhimer, William E. *Historical Sketch of the Artillery, United States Army.* 1884.

Dillon, Lester R., Jr. *American Artillery in the Mexican War, 1846–1847.* 1975.

Downey, Fairfax. *The Sound of the Guns: The Story of the American Artillery.* 1955.

Foraging

Technically, according to military usage, the term *foraging* means the organized gathering of forage for horses. Equipped with reaping hooks and cord for binding sheaves, soldiers were sent into the countryside to collect hay for the army's mounts and draft animals. Guards accompanied these details during wartime when they operated in hostile territory and were subject to attack. One officer who served under Gen. Winfield Scott noted the term was used incorrectly to indicate marauding or the unauthorized seizure of property. U.S. generals in the field, who recognized the need to gain the good will of the Mexican people, routinely issued orders against plundering and insisted that quartermasters pay for items taken by the army. According to the U.S. Articles of War, an officer or soldier convicted of leaving "his post or colors to plunder or pillage" faced death or any other punishment ordered by a general court-martial.

Many U.S. soldiers, however, were undeterred by the threat of punishment and took produce and fresh beef from Mexican fields and orchards to supplement their army rations. The constant diet of coffee, hard bread, salt pork, and stringy beef drove many soldiers to view Mexican crops and livestock as their personal larder. Corn fields, citrus groves, and grazing herds were too tempting to pass by without sampling. Euphemisms such as "capturing" were used to describe acts of thievery. Officers, who shared the same hunger as their men, often ignored infractions in return for a share of the spoils. Soldiers also frequently bought food from Mexican markets and traveling vendors.

Richard Bruce Winders

BIBLIOGRAPHY

Furber, George C. *The Twelve Month Volunteer: Or, Journal of a Private in the Tennessee Regiment of Cavalry, in the Campaign, in Mexico, 1846–7.* 1848.

Kenly, John R. *Memoirs of a Maryland Volunteer.* 1873.

Scott, Henry L. *Military Dictionary: Comprising the Technical Definitions: Information on Raising and Keeping Troops: Actual Service, Including Makeshift and Improved Matériel; And Law, Government, Regulation, and Administration Relating to Land Forces.* 1864.

Winders, Richard Bruce. *Mr. Polk's Army: The American Military Experience in the Mexican War.* 1997.

Ford, John Salmon

John Salmon Ford (1815–1897), adjutant in the 1st Texas Mounted Volunteers, was born in South Carolina on 26 May to William Ford and Harriet Salmon. Ford grew to maturity in Tennessee. He studied medicine and moved to Texas to ply his trade at San Augustine. He served in the Texas army and in the last congress in which he introduced the resolution to accept the terms of annexation to the United States. In 1845 Ford became editor of the Austin *Texas Democrat* but left that post to join Col. John C. Hays's second regiment of Rangers as adjutant, serving under Gen. Joseph Lane, fighting guerrillas around Mexico City and on the Vera Cruz road. Ford participated in skirmishes at Galaxa Pass, San Juan Teotihuacán, and Zacualtipán. He earned his sobriquet "RIP" from the abbreviation of "rest in peace," which he signed on letters to deceased soldiers' families. After the war, he returned to Texas and fought with several Ranger units against Indians, especially the Comanche. Ford edited papers at Austin and Brownsville, served in several legislatures and participated in the Texas secession convention in 1861. He led Confederate forces at Palmito Ranch (11 May 1865), considered the last battle of the Civil War. He died at San Antonio on 3 November 1897.

Jimmy L. Bryan, Jr.

BIBLIOGRAPHY

Ford, John Salmon. *Rip Ford's Texas.* 1963.

Hughes, W. J. *Rebellious Ranger: Rip Ford and the Old Southwest.* 1964.

Forts

Fortifications during the U.S.–Mexican War represented the full range of military engineering skill, from elaborate permanent forts to hastily prepared fieldworks. Both the U.S. and Mexican armies had achieved a high degree of technical expertise and were thoroughly versed in principles of fortifications, such as those of French military engineer Sébastien Le Prestre de Vauban (1633–1707), the most influential designer of European forts in the age of gunpowder. Vauban's sieges were a clockwork system of approach trenches; his defensive methods relied on detailed terrain analysis and the careful geometry of mutually supporting positions with interlocking fires and outworks, which were designed to catch the attacker in a web of shot and shell.

Mexican military engineers were masters at converting the natural strength of existing Spanish architecture into formidable temporary defensive positions, adding reinforcing earthworks and tying into local permanent fortifications. For example, at the city of Monterrey in September 1846, attacking U.S. forces faced western approaches guarded by two hilltop stone redoubts, El Soldado and Fort Libertad, backed by the Bishop's Palace. Completed in 1790, the stone palace had high, thick walls with musket loopholes, which lent readily to defense when reinforced by sandbags and frontal earthworks for a four-gun battery *en barbette* (i.e., firing over a parapet without embrasures). To the north of Monterrey was the Citadel, an unfinished cathedral converted into a permanent fort with four arrow-shaped extended-corner bastions (projecting gun towers) protected by ditches. The southern flank of the city was guarded by a river and a head-high stone wall with loopholes. Smaller forts, Tenería and Diablo, protected the eastern approaches to narrow barricaded streets lined by square rooftops sandbagged and transformed into elevated infantry fighting positions.

The southern approach to Mexico City had a similar combination of permanent, temporary, and field fortifications to create a defense in depth. Four miles from the city gates in the fortified village of Churubusco was the Convent San Pablo, which had massive walls and battlements, square bastions, and firing loops reinforced by seven guns and by frontal earthworks. The convent served as a forward position to the earthwork *tête du point*, or strongpoint, of three heavy guns guarding the Río Churubusco crossing. Two miles from the city was the converted position El Molino del Rey (Mill of the King), a stone compound that served as an outwork controlling the approaches to Chapultepec. Chapultepec (Grasshopper Hill) had angled four-foot-thick walls encasing a castle-like structure on the terrace of a two-hundred-foot hill. Constructed in 1783 as a viceroy's summer palace, it had been a military academy since 1833 and commanded the two elevated causeways to the western gates. The fortified *garitas*, or gates, of San Cosmé and Belén were backed by a permanent barracks called the Ciudadela and reinforced by forward artillery batteries and earthen redoubts.

The highest expression of the art of permanent formal masonry fortification in the U.S.–Mexican War was in the walled seaport of Vera Cruz. The city walls had angled bastions on curtain walls cornered by two square forts, Concepción and Santiago. One thousand yards into the harbor was the island fortress of San Juan de Ulúa. Completed by the Spanish in 1790, it contained two towers surrounded by smooth-faced stone walls with batteries positioned in protective encasements.

U.S. Army fortifications in the war consisted exclusively of earthen fieldworks, temporary fighting positions, and the nine-thousand yards of siege trenches at Vera Cruz. The most complex and ambitious U.S. field fortification was Fort Texas on the Río Grande opposite Matamoros. Completed in May 1846 after one month of work by a thousand soldiers, it was renamed Fort Brown for Maj. Jacob Brown, the commander who died of wounds in its defense. Capt. Joseph K. F. Mansfield supervised the star fort design, which had gun positions on the points of sharp traverse angles to allow cannon to sweep the eight hundred yards of fifteen-foot-thick parapets and the twelve-foot-wide protective ditch. In this classic example of a Vauban-style star fort, four hundred men of the 7th Infantry Regiment, with four eighteen-pound cannon, three six-pounders, and one mortar, withstood a one-week Mexican artillery barrage of 2,800 rounds starting 3 May 1846.

In the final analysis, no fortification of the U.S.–Mexican War held against direct assault by infantry, and only one, Fort Texas, withstood prolonged artillery bombardment without significant casualties. In this final twilight of the age of smoothbore short-range artillery and muskets, it proved practically impossible to retain permanent or field fortifications against a determined ground attack, thus spurring the development of accurate long-range rifled weapons adopted by modern armies in the following decade.

Thomas Tyree Smith

BIBLIOGRAPHY

Duffy, Christopher. *Fire and Stone: The Science of Fortress Warfare, 1660–1860.* 1975.

Floyd, Dale E. *Military Fortifications: A Selective Bibliography.* 1992.

Hogg, Ian V. *Fortress: A History of Military Defence.* 1975.

Hogg, Ian V. *The History of Fortification.* 1981.

Vocabulario Arquitectó Illustrado. 1975.

Fort Texas

Constructed on an exposed peninsula on the north bank of the Río Grande opposite Matamoros, Mexico, Fort Texas (also known as Fort Taylor) was built to protect the U.S. presence along the southern border of Texas. Under the direction of Capt. Joseph K. F. Mansfield of the Corps of Engineers, work began on this six-pointed, star-shaped fortification following the arrival of the Army of Occupation at the Río Grande on 28 March 1846. In response, Mexican general Mariano Arista assembled 5,700 Mexican troops in Matamoros to construct gun emplacements to oppose the U.S. earthworks. For the next month, soldiers from both armies labored in view of each other. The Mexican works were completed by late April, and on 3 May, Gen. Pedro de Ampudia (who took command when General Arista led the remainder of the Mexican army in an attempt to sever the U.S. supply line to the coast) ordered his men to open fire on the U.S. fort, initiating a seven-day siege.

In addition to its strategic value, the construction of Fort Texas served as a productive outlet for the labors of desertion-prone U.S. regulars. Tempted by Mexican women and by official Mexican circulars that promised them land and privileges in exchange for desertion, a large number of soldiers swam the river to escape military service. Some of these men later served in the Mexican army. Orders to shoot deserters, coupled with fatigue duties at the fort, reduced these attempts after late April 1846.

Following the siege of 3 to 10 May 1846, the post was renamed Fort Brown, in honor of Maj. Jacob Brown, its fallen commanding officer. During the U.S.–Mexican War, the fort served as a logistical base, and it remained in possession of the U.S. Army until 1946. Although structures built during later years of the fort's operation remain in use, only one of the original earthen bastions remains, and it is presently part of the Brownsville, Texas, municipal golf course.

Robert P. Wettemann, Jr.

BIBLIOGRAPHY

Marcum, Richard Tandy. "Fort Brown, Texas: The History of a Border Post." Ph.D. diss., Texas Technical College, 1964.

Sides, Joseph C. *Fort Brown Historical: History of Fort Brown, Border Post on the Rio Grande.* 1942.

Fort Texas, Siege of

On 1 May 1846, Gen. Zachary Taylor and the Army of Occupation withdrew from Matamoros to protect the supply route from Point Isabel, leaving Maj. Jacob Brown, the 7th Infantry, four eighteen-pound guns commanded by Capt. Allen Lowd, 2d Artillery, and Lt. Braxton Bragg's mortar and three six-pound field pieces from the 3d Artillery (in all about five hundred men) to defend Fort Texas. Two days later, Mexican artillery emplaced across the river and fourteen hundred Mexican soldiers on the northern side of the Río Grande began firing on the fort in efforts to dislodge the U.S. forces from their strategic position overlooking the river

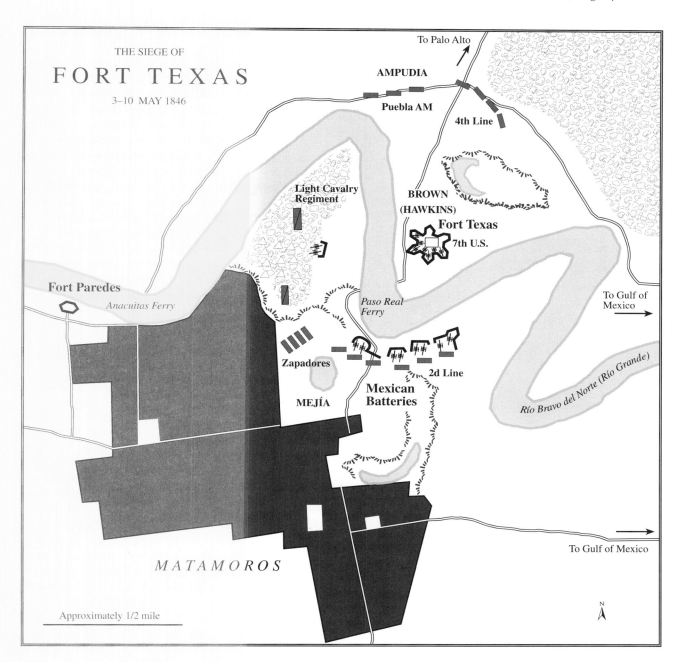

THE SIEGE OF
FORT TEXAS
3–10 MAY 1846

To Palo Alto

AMPUDIA

Puebla AM

4th Line

BROWN (HAWKINS)
Fort Texas
7th U.S.

Light Cavalry Regiment

Fort Paredes
Anacuitas Ferry

Paso Real Ferry

To Gulf of Mexico

Río Bravo del Norte (Río Grande)

Zapadores

MEJÍA

Mexican Batteries

2d Line

MATAMOROS

To Gulf of Mexico

Approximately 1/2 mile

N

crossing. On 6 May, Capt. Edgar S. Hawkins of the 7th, who had assumed command earlier that day when Brown was mortally wounded, received a request from Mexican general Mariano Arista to surrender the fort. Having received orders from General Taylor that the fort must be defended at all costs, Hawkins, anticipating reinforcements, declined Arista's request.

Between 3 and 10 May, U.S. forces held out despite almost continual bombardment, returning fire sparingly to conserve ammunition for an expected assault. During the course of the seven-day siege, 2,800 Mexican shells landed in and about the earthworks, killing one and wounding thirteen soldiers in addition to the fort's original commander.

Having heard the rumble of guns from the Battles of Palo Alto and Resaca de la Palma (8 and 9 May), the defenders of Fort Texas learned of the U.S. victories when they saw Mexican infantry and cavalry retreating across the Río Grande in chaos. The next day, elements of General Taylor's

Siege of Fort Texas
Order of Battle
3-10 May 1846

Mexican Forces

Commanders
Gen. Pedro de Ampudia
Gen. Francisco Mejía

Infantry
4th Line Regiment
Battalion de Puebla
2 companies of sappers
Auxiliaries from towns in northern Mexico

Cavalry
7th Line Regiment (detachment)
8th Line Regiment (detachment)
Presidials
Light Regiment (detachment)

Artillery
approximately 10 pieces

U.S. Forces

Commanders
Maj. Jacob Brown
Capt. Edgar S. Hawkins

Infantry
7th Infantry

Artillery
Company I, 2d Artillery (heavy battery)
Company E, 3d Artillery (Bragg's mounted battery)

victorious army returned to relieve the beleaguered garrison. Although overshadowed by the more impressive battles of 8 and 9 May, the successful defense of Fort Texas raised the morale of U.S. forces.

Robert P. Wettemann, Jr.

BIBLIOGRAPHY

Thorpe, Thomas Bangs. *Our Army on the Río Grande.* 1846.

U.S. Senate. *Message of the President of the United States Relative to the Operations and Recent Engagements on the Mexican Frontier.* 29th Cong., 1st sess., 1846. Senate Document 388, 30–37.

France

From Mexico's independence in 1821 until the end of the U.S.–Mexican War in 1848, France was governed by two royal houses. The Bourbons, restored after Napoléon Bonaparte's final defeat in 1815, were overthrown in the July Revolution of 1830 and replaced by the Duke of Orléans, who as King Louis Philippe, "the citizen king," promised to rule constitutionally.

The French Restoration government withheld recognition from Mexico because of the Family Compact with the Spanish Bourbons, who were unreconciled to the loss of their former colony. Louis Philippe's regime immediately granted recognition in 1830 but, like the Bourbons, soon ran afoul of the penurious Mexican government. The main issue was the latter's habit of using various taxes, forced loans, and confiscations to extract revenue from foreign retailers, among whom French nationals were a leading presence. This policy prompted the July Monarchy to launch a naval bombardment and blockade of Mexico's principal Gulf Coast port, Vera Cruz, in 1838 and 1839. This so-called Pastry War (after one of the leading claimants, a pastry chef) was a Pyrrhic victory for the French because yellow fever forced the French invaders to accept terms that left the original claims virtually unsettled. The incident also raised suspicions in the United States about European intervention in the Americas, especially because France and Great Britain were making similar moves in the Río de la Plata region of South America throughout the 1830s and 1840s. For Louis Philippe, it reinforced a growing aversion to military actions.

This aversion was shared by his foreign minister and leader of the cabinet after 1840, François Guizot. Guizot sought to dissociate France from aggressive adventurism as most recently embodied by Napoléon Bonaparte. He thus pursued an entente cordiale with Great Britain, made possible by the presence of a kindred spirit, the Tory Earl of Aberdeen, in the British Foreign Office. Guizot's policy was loudly attacked in France. His bitter rival Adolphe Thiers saw the entente as abandoning France's historic friendship with the United States, an attitude shared by many in the United States. Yet Guizot had no intention of using more than words to help the British prevent U.S. expansion to the Río Grande or to the Pacific Coast at Mexico's expense. In June 1844, Lord Aberdeen sought to forestall U.S. annexation of the Republic of Texas, which France was among the first to recognize in 1839, by proposing the "Diplomatic Act": Great Britain and France would jointly guarantee the independence of Texas and its border with Mexico in return for Mexican recognition of the breakaway state. Guizot agreed with the aim in principle, but balked at guarantees. He instructed his representatives in the region to use "moral suasion" alone in preventing U.S. annexation, and to do so in a way that gave no offense to the U.S. government.

Guizot clearly irritated the new administration of President James K. Polk by proclaiming in a parliamentary speech of June 1845 that the balance of power applied to American republics as well as to European monarchies, in effect reiterating France's rejection of the Monroe Doctrine. Guizot also offered French support to the secret and ultimately futile attempts of the British chargé d'affaires to Texas, Charles

Elliot, to forestall annexation by mediating an agreement between Texas and Mexico in early 1845. Such actions, combined with an anti–United States element in the French press and the almost insubordinate bellicosity of French agents like Baron Alleye de Cyprey in Mexico and Alphonse Dubois de Saligny in Texas, kept alive fears of French intervention. President Polk, however, was better informed by his envoy to Paris, William R. King, who correctly gauged Guizot's deep reluctance to clash with the United States.

French refusal even to consider joint military action eventually doomed Great Britain's attempts to restrain U.S. ambitions. In truth, the French had no interest in backing what they considered a contemptuously inept and corrupt Mexican government against the United States, however much they feared Mexico's dismemberment and the dwindling European presence in the Western Hemisphere. Guizot lost all influence over events when the hugely unpopular Baron Alleye de Cyprey ruptured relations with Mexico in the summer of 1845 because of a private skirmish with a Mexican crowd. Fearing to back down before a weak power and preoccupied by domestic affairs, Guizot still had not resumed direct relations with Mexico when he and Louis Philippe were overthrown in the February Revolution of 1848. This moved the U.S.–Mexican War from the stage. French interest and influence in the region revived only when Napoléon III (reigned 1852 to 1871) tried to establish Austrian Archduke Maximilian as ruler of Mexico in the 1860s.

James R. Munson

BIBLIOGRAPHY

Barker, Nancy N. *The French Experience in Mexico, 1821–1861: A History of Constant Misunderstanding.* 1979.

Johnson, Douglas. *Guizot: Aspects of French History, 1787–1874.* 1963.

Pletcher, David M. *The Diplomacy of Annexation: Texas, Oregon, and the Mexican War.* 1973.

Price, Glenn W. *Origins of the War with Mexico: The Polk-Stockton Intrigue.* 1967.

See also **Pastry War of 1838**

Freaner, James L.

A native of Hagerstown, Maryland, U.S. war correspondent James L. Freaner worked as a printer's apprentice in Tallahassee, Florida, before relocating to New Orleans in 1845. At the outbreak of war with Mexico, he enlisted in the Louisiana Volunteers, but that unit's precipitate disbandment thrust the tall, raw-boned, slow-talking Freaner into the role of war correspondent for the *New Orleans Delta.* Using the pseudonym "Mustang," he covered the entire conflict from the opening battles on the Río Grande through the final treaty negotiations.

After the fall of Vera Cruz, Freaner established a close friendship with Nicholas P. Trist, the chief clerk of the State Department, who had been appointed to negotiate an end to the war. Trist strayed significantly from his official instructions and was recalled by Secretary of State James Buchanan on 16 November 1847. As Trist prepared to leave Mexico, Freaner attempted to persuade his friend to reconsider. Arguing that Trist's departure not only would prolong the war but also might eventuate in annexation of the entire country of Mexico, a possibility condoned by neither man, Freaner convinced the chief negotiator to stay on. Disregarding his summons to Washington, D.C., Trist reopened a dialog with the Mexican peace commission that on 2 February 1848 yielded the Treaty of Guadalupe Hidalgo. Freaner, who had remained in Mexico with Trist, personally delivered the signed document to Secretary Buchanan on 19 February. After the war, Freaner joined the rival *New Orleans Picayune* and covered the California gold rush story for that newspaper.

William A. DePalo, Jr.

BIBLIOGRAPHY

Copeland, Fayette. *Kendall of the Picayune,* p. 210. 1943.

Farnham, Thomas J. "Nicholas Trist & James Freaner and the Mission to Mexico." *Arizona and the West* 2 (Autumn 1969): 247–260.

Mahin, Dean B. *Olive Branch and Sword: The United States and Mexico, 1845–1848,* pp. 145, 169–171. 1997.

Reilly, Tom. "The War Press of New Orleans, 1846–1848." *Journalism History* 13 (Autumn–Winter 1986): 86–95.

Fredonia Rebellion

Centered in Nacogdoches, Texas, in 1826, the Fredonia Rebellion alarmed Mexican centralists who feared that immigrants from the United States would seize Texas from Mexico. In reality, the rebellion amounted to little more than Haden Edwards's attempt to retain his empresarial land grant in eastern Texas.

Edwards had supported Stephen F. Austin's effort to obtain permission from the central government and from the Mexican state of Coahuila for U.S. citizens to become colonists in Mexican Texas. In 1825 Edwards received a grant to the area around Nacogdoches. Like all *empresarios,* he had to honor previous individual grants from Spain or Mexico, but only Edwards's grant contained a significant number of such grants.

When Edwards arrived in Nacogdoches he had no way to determine who had valid grants, so he announced that he would regard all lands as available to him unless current landholders could show proof of ownership. Few could do so, since they had lost their patents in fires, floods, or during the forced evacuation of the area in 1773. Edwards seized only one prior grant, but that one threatened all, so the previous settlers protested to the political chief in San Antonio.

Benjamin Edwards, brother of the *empresario,* handled the colony's affairs while Haden Edwards recruited settlers in the United States. Benjamin's intemperate letters offended the political chief, who declared the entire Edwards grant forfeit. In response, Haden Edwards declared the Nacogdoches area to be the Fredonia Republic.

No other Anglo-Americans supported Edwards, and his "republic" dissolved even before Mexican troops arrived. The importance of the Fredonia Rebellion lies in the reaction to it among Mexican centralists: thereafter, they regarded virtually every activity in Texas as a plot to seize territory from Mexico.

Archie P. McDonald

BIBLIOGRAPHY

McDonald, Archie P. "The Fredonia Rebellion." In *Nacogdoches: Wilderness Outpost to Modern City, 1779–1979,* pp. 33–39. 1980.

Partin, James G., Carolyn Reeves, Joe Ericson, and Archie P. McDonald. *Nacogdoches: The History of Texas' Oldest City.* 1995.

Freemasonry

Mexico's first post-independence political parties evolved from Masonic organizations. Principal leaders in the early republic were officials of one of three Masonic rites. First to appear, during the 1810 to 1821 Wars for Independence, was *escocés,* or Scottish Rite Masonry, allegedly brought to Mexico by Spanish expeditionaries. Scottish Masons, or *escoceses,* were influential in the brief empire of Agustín de Iturbide, especially its congress; they led the military revolt that forced him to resign and proclaimed a republic. Their voice in Mexico City was the periodical *El Sol.* Scottish Masons also were prominent in congress during the government of President Guadalupe Victoria (1824–1829), but by 1825 they faced a challenge from the *yorkinos,* or York Rite Masonry. Unlike the Scottish Rite Masons, the York Rite Masons admitted men of all races and classes, and soon emerged as the more popular party, although their propertied opponents considered them Jacobins. The Yorkists in turn viewed the Scottish Rite Masons as aristocrats and disguised monarchists. Yorkists were Mexican nationalists who offered equality of opportunity to the racially mixed majority. Supported by the Mexico City daily *Correo de la Federación,* the Yorkists advocated the expulsion of all Spanish-born males from Mexico.

Hostility between the two organizations escalated to armed conflict and the two Masonic orders met on the battlefield at Tulancingo in January 1828. Gen. Vicente Guerrero (York Grand Master) with two thousand men forced the surrender of Gen. Nicolás Bravo (Scottish Grand Master), who arrived with just three hundred men. Its leaders were exiled, and the Scottish Rite in Mexico subsequently collapsed. The Yorkists then gained political dominance over the existing Victoria government in 1828 when the results of national elections were undermined by a popular revolt (La Acordada). General Guerrero assumed the presidency in January 1829, advised by Lorenzo de Zavala, a fellow Yorkist and future vice president of the Republic of Texas.

Such destabilizing conflicts had led congressional moderates in 1828 to outlaw political intervention by Masonic bodies. In 1825 moderates such as José María Mateos founded a new Masonic order, the Mexican National Rite (*Rito Nacional Mexicano*), whose voice in Mexico City was *El Aguila Mexicana.* Future liberal leaders such as Valentín Gómez Farías, Benito Juárez, and Mexican presidents into the twentieth century would be affiliated with this enduring National Rite.

The Guerrero government collapsed in December 1829 when confronted by its unpaid soldiery led by Vice President Anastasio Bustamante, an anti-Yorkist. Yorkists chose either exile or guerrilla warfare in the south, where many, including Guerrero, perished.

Political conflict refocused on the liberal-conservative dichotomy; the National Rite Masons aligned themselves with the liberal faction. Excluded from power, the Mexican National Rite's opportunity came when Gen. Antonio López de Santa Anna toppled the Bustamante government in 1833 and turned authority over to his vice president, Gómez Farías. The vice president launched Mexico's first wide-ranging anticlerical reforms—so extensively that President Santa Anna was forced to return in April 1834, proclaiming an *autogolpe* (self-coup), which precipitated a revolt in Zacatecas and the Texas Revolt. Santa Anna then formed the first of a series of conservative governments that were anti-Masonic. Political instability became endemic then, with liberal Masons such as Gómez Farías primarily in opposition.

Harold Dana Sims

BIBLIOGRAPHY

Ayala, Jaime. *Introducción a la Masonería.* n.d.

Mateos, José María. *Historia de la Masonería en Mexico de 1806 a 1884.* 2 vols. 1884.

Navarrete, Félix. *La masonería en la historia y en las leyes de Mexico.* 1957.

Sims, Harold D. "The Expulsion of the Spaniards from Mexico, 1827–1828." Ph.D. diss. 1968.

Free-Soil Party

When it became clear that the United States would acquire territory as a consequence of war with Mexico, the venerable abolitionist demand to confine slavery to states where it already existed found expression first in the Wilmot Proviso and then in formation of the Free-Soil Party. Organized in Buffalo, New York, in August 1848 by a coalition of "Barnburner" Democrats, "Conscience" Whigs, and Liberty Party members, its most ardent proponents were Gamaliel Bailey, Salmon P. Chase, and Henry B. Stanton. It nominated Martin Van Buren, the former president, and Charles Francis Adams as its candidates on a platform of "No more slave states and no more slave territory." The party also called for free homesteads, internal improvements, and tariff reform. Because the platform was silent on the issue of equal rights for African Americans, some historians branded Free-Soilers racists, but most black leaders at the time supported the party as an antislavery organization. Although Van Buren received only 291,804 popular votes, the party elected twelve congressmen, a bloc that sometimes wielded the balance of power. In 1852 Free-Soilers, reorganized as Free Democrats, nominated Sen. John P. Hale for president and adopted a platform that was more resolutely antislavery than that of 1848. In 1854 the party was swept into the Republican Party, the new coalition formed in response to the Kansas-Nebraska Act, which, by opening the northern part of the Louisiana Purchase to slavery, defied the central plank in the Free-Soil platform.

Merton L. Dillon

BIBLIOGRAPHY

Blue, Frederick J. *The Free Soilers: Third-Party Politics, 1848–54.* 1973.

Sewell, Richard H. *Ballots for Freedom: Antislavery Politics in the United States, 1837–1860.* 1976.

Frémont, John C.

John Charles Frémont (1813–1890), born in Savannah, Georgia, was educated at the College of Charleston in South Carolina. In 1838 he joined the U.S. Army Corps of Topographical Engineers and subsequently led several exploring expeditions to the West. During 1846, on the third of these, as tensions mounted between the United States and Mexico, young Lieutenant Frémont became one of the chief actors in California's conquest by U.S. forces.

Frémont repeatedly asserted that cartography alone had been his original goal, denying that he had gone to the Mexican province under the pretext of heading up a scientific expedition. Yet some historians maintain that Frémont carried secret instructions, either from his powerful father-in-law, Sen. Thomas Hart Benton, or from President James K. Polk, anticipating the outbreak of war with Mexico.

Frémont soon was in the midst of political turmoil. Ostensibly merely a visitor to California, in January 1846, six months before the arrival of U.S. naval forces, Frémont took his guide, Kit Carson, and a small group across the bay at Yerba Buena, present-day San Francisco. There they spiked

John C. Frémont. John Bigelow, *Memoir of the Life and Public Service of John Charles Frémont,* 1856

the Mexican shore artillery pieces at Fort Point, located below the old Spanish *presidio.* Members of Frémont's party, meanwhile, killed several Californios in retaliation for the murder of several of Frémont's men.

Early in March 1846, outside Monterey, the California provincial capital, Frémont defied Mexican officials by building a rude log fort. When he faced opposition, however, Frémont led his party northward, as if to continue his topographical assignment. Near Sonoma, Frémont met a band of disgruntled U.S. settlers who were alarmed by rumors of an impending attack on them by Mexican troops. These frontiersmen were part of a floating population of immigrants mostly from the United States who would become known as "Bear Flaggers." They thought that California might well come under U.S. rule. This was expressed in a letter of 9 March 1846 from Charles Weber (a German who had settled in the Sacramento Valley) to John March, a neighbor:

> Great News! War! War! Captain Frémont . . . with sixty or more riflemen has fortified himself on the heights between San Juan and Don Joaquin Golmero's rancho, the Stars and Stripes flying over their camps. José Castro and two or three hundred Californians [Californios] with artillery are besieging their position. Captain [Isaac] Graham and sixty or more boys are moving to their rescue. Spaniards [actually Mexicans] and foreigners are enlisting under their respective banners.

On 10 June, the Bear Flaggers captured a band of horses being driven to the Santa Clara Valley by resident Californios and took them to Frémont's field headquarters. The rebellious "Bears" next raided Sonoma, the largest settlement in northern California, and incarcerated Gen. Mariano Guadalupe Vallejo, its commandant. A day later they hoisted an improvised Bear Flag, creating what has come to be called the Bear Flag Republic. Frémont gave these "Bears" mixed signals of support, well before he knew that war would break out between the United States and Mexico.

In response to these events, in July Frémont reorganized his topographical engineers into a military unit later called the "California Battalion" at Sutter's Fort, present day Sacramento. Prepared to do battle with Mexican forces, he guarded his scarce supplies behind the fort's ten-foot walls and began to sign papers as "Military Commander of U.S. Forces in California." A member of his party boasted, "Capt. Frémont is the only man who can command the California foreigners . . . needed to subdue the Spanish Californians."

On 7 July 1846, Commo. John D. Sloat of the U.S. Pacific Squadron ordered the Stars and Stripes to be raised at Monterey. He planned to occupy California's ports in order to establish U.S. rule. On 9 July Sloat hoisted his standard at Yerba Buena. Throughout the province the U.S. flag soon displaced both the crudely made device of the Bear Flag Republic and the Mexican flag.

During this period there was much confusion over command of U.S. forces in California. Commodore Sloat, in charge of the Pacific Squadron, took his orders from Secretary of State James Buchanan—as did Consul Thomas Oliver Larkin at Monterey. President Polk, however, had encouraged only a subtle defiance of Mexico by U.S. residents in California. If it was impossible to buy Alta California, he and Buchanan hoped for a quiet revolt by native Californios, encouraged by Consul Larkin.

After the U.S. Navy arrived in California, Frémont was no longer the only U.S. military figure there, and he reported to Commodore Sloat, then the senior commander in California. When Sloat returned to Washington, D.C., Commo. Robert F. Stockton, his successor, cajoled Frémont into reforming his unit as the "Regiment of Mounted Volunteer Riflemen," later shortened to California Battalion. The army's topographical engineers, to which Frémont belonged, had meanwhile named him a captain. But the Pathfinder, as he had come to be called, had already risen in rank from lieutenant to lieutenant colonel—appointed by Stockton to this position (and with dubious authority), courtesy of the Navy.

Frémont moved south to capture, on 17 July 1846, the mission-pueblo of San Juan Bautista. Two days later, after also subduing San José, his battalion re-entered Monterey. On 26 July 1846, Commodore Stockton dispatched Frémont's force southward to San Diego on the sloop *Cyane*, hoping to cut off a Mexican retreat southward. By midday of 29 July, Frémont and Commodore Stockton raised the U.S. flag at San Diego without firing a shot. Next, their united forces entered Los Angeles on 13 August, ran up the U.S. flag, and received pledges of allegiance from its citizens. Stockton then sailed on to Santa Barbara and to Monterey while Frémont marched his men back toward the northern Sacramento Valley. Both men then thought the war in California was over.

A revolt at Los Angeles, however, forced Frémont again to march on that pueblo from the north. After the locals signed the Cahuenga Capitulation, thereby surrendering Los Angeles to Frémont, Commodore Stockton, like Sloat before him, departed for the East Coast. Frémont then began to call himself the military governor of California.

Meanwhile, on 6 December 1846 Brig. Gen. Stephen W. Kearny had arrived overland to assume command of military operations in the new U.S. province; he deeply resented Frémont's assumption of command. The general established his headquarters at Monterey and requested Frémont to report there for duty. When the latter repeatedly refused to heed Kearny's orders, the general arrested and pressed charges of insubordination and mutiny against Frémont. There followed a famous court-martial in Washington, D.C. Although Frémont's conviction of mutiny was ultimately commuted by President Polk, Frémont resigned his Army commission.

Frémont became a mining and railroad investor before being appointed in 1849 as one of California's first two U.S. senators. Seven years later the Republican Party chose him as its first, and unsuccessful, presidential candidate. He was also a highly controversial major general during the Civil War, and later governor of Arizona. His biggest booster was his wife, Jessie, whose writings exaggerated his role in the American conquest of California from Mexico. On 13 July 1890 Frémont died in New York City.

Andrew Rolle

BIBLIOGRAPHY

Hague, Harlan, and David J. Langum. *Thomas O. Larkin: A Life of Patriotism and Profit in Old California.* 1990.

Harlow, Neal. *California Conquered: War and Peace on the Pacific, 1846–1850.* 1982.

Hawgood, John A. "John C. Frémont and the Bear Flag Revolution." *Southern California Quarterly* 54 (March 1962): 67–96.

Larkin Papers. Bancroft Library. University of California at Berkeley.

Marti, Werner H. *Messenger of Destiny: The California Adventures, 1846–1847, of Archibald H. Gillespie, U.S. Marine Corps.* 1960.

Rolle, Andrew. *John Charles Frémont: Character as Destiny.* 1991.

Stenberg, Richard R. "Polk and Frémont." *Pacific Historical Review* 27 (May 1938): 211–227.

Tays, George. "Frémont Had No Secret Instructions." *Pacific Historical Review* 9 (June 1940): 159–171.

Frontera, José

Born in Jalapa, Vera Cruz, Mexican general José Frontera (1798–1847) began his military career on 6 August 1814 as a cadet in the provincial militia company of his native city. He participated in the royalist counterinsurgency campaigns until embracing the independence cause in 1821. Thereafter, Frontera held a variety of increasingly responsible positions in the Puebla Dragoon and 7th Cavalry Regiments. Following assignments as aide-de-camp to Division Generals Manuel Rincón and José Rincón, he was designated to help activate the Comercio Cavalry Regiment and organize two squadrons of the Querétaro Cavalry Regiment.

In the federalist uprising of 15 July 1840, Frontera remained loyal to the centralist regime of President Anastasio Bustamante. The following year, however, he threw the support of his regiment behind Div. Gen. Mariano Paredes y Arrillaga's movement for the "Political Regeneration of the Republic" that finally drove Bustamante from office on 8 October 1841. Assigned to the Army of the North during the latter stages of the war with the United States, Frontera commanded the 2d Cavalry Regiment of Gen. Anastasio Torrejón's cavalry brigade. On 19 August 1847, during the Battle of Padierna (Contreras), Torrejón ordered Frontera's regiment to counterattack U.S. units who were moving through a grove of trees in an attempt to flank the left wing of the Mexican defense. Hit in the chest by musket fire, Frontera died shortly after that ill-conceived engagement.

William A. DePalo, Jr.

BIBLIOGRAPHY

Alcaraz, Ramón, et al. *Apuntes para la historia de la guerra entre México y los Estados Unidos*, pp. 236–238. 1848.

Balbontín, Manuel. *La invasión Americana, 1846 á 1848: Apuntes del subteniente de artillería Manuel Balbontín*, pp. 112–116. 1883.

Carreño, Alberto M., ed. *Jefes del Ejército Mexicano en 1847: Biografías de generales de división y de brigada y de coroneles del ejército por fines del año 1847*, pp. 242–243. 1914.

DePalo, William A., Jr. *The Mexican National Army, 1822–1852*, p. 129. 1997.

Diccionario Porrúa: De história, biografía, y geografía de México. 6th ed., p. 1340. 1995.

Fueros

Fueros were special privileges granted to Mexican institutions, including the military and the Catholic Church. Each group was granted particular *fueros,* with special privileges that included trial by jury and freedom from civil legal proceedings. These privileges were often abused or used as recruiting incentives. Many Mexicans joined the military and the priesthood to take advantage of the protecting *fueros.* The resulting corruption hurt the effectiveness of the Mexican military during the U.S.–Mexican War.

During the colonial period, the Spanish crown had expanded the military *fueros* to include the militia members to make service more appealing. The poorly written and vague statutes were easily exploited and officers, especially the low-ranking officers, abused the law to the extreme, which resulted in a judicial system that was in complete disarray. Soldiers who were tried by their own units had sympathetic juries and usually were exonerated. Most of the time, militia members remained at home and enjoyed the benefits of the *fuero militar* without suffering the hardships or dangers of active campaigning. Eventually the crown reversed its position and limited *fueros* to the regular units, leaving the status of the rights of the militia ambiguous.

Fueros granted to the church produced a similar situation. In criminal cases the clergy were tried by a selection of clerical and secular authorities; they usually were acquitted of a wide range of crimes, which included rape and murder.

After Mexican independence in 1821, the liberal Constitution of 1824 guaranteed the continuance of the *fueros* to the military and the clergy but did not extend trial by jury to the general population, thus ensuring that abuses would continue.

By 1846, the effects of the long-held *fueros* on Mexican society were evident. A bloated officer corps reduced the efficiency of the military and crowded the ranks with men of little martial talent, while church leaders suffered the humiliation of priests tainted by constant scandal. As a result, the Mexican public developed a cynicism toward public institutions that undermined the emerging sense of nationalism during the first decades of the Republic of Mexico.

Amy M. Wilson

BIBLIOGRAPHY

MacLachlan, Colin M., and Jamie E. Rodriguez O. *The Forging of the Cosmic Race: A Reinterpretation of Colonial Mexico.* 1990.

Olivera, Ruth R., and Liliane Crété. *Life in Mexico under Santa Anna, 1822–1855.* 1991.

G

Gadsden Purchase

By 1853, when the government of the United States appointed railroad contractor James Gadsden to represent it in talks with the Mexican government, a variety of incidents had disturbed relations between the two nations. These included claims of Mexican citizens who had remained in the ceded territories concerning their property and political rights under Articles VIII and IX of the Treaty of Guadalupe Hidalgo, which ended the U.S.–Mexican War. There were also disagreements over the rights of U.S. contractors to build a railroad across the Isthmus of Tehuantepec. Most important was the boundary dispute, especially for the Chihuahua–New Mexico section of the international border.

Article V of the Treaty of Guadalupe Hidalgo provided for surveying and marking of the boundary by commissions of the two nations. A line had been surveyed from the mouth of the Río Grande westward to San Diego. Although most of the boundary along Texas and California was not controversial, the section defining the Chihuahua–New Mexico area was contested. Unfortunately, the original commissions lacked precise information about the true location of El Paso del Norte (present-day Juárez), placing the city north and east of its actual location. Because the Treaty of Guadalupe Hidalgo vaguely stipulated that the international border would extend west from El Paso del Norte, its location was critical.

To complicate matters, in 1850 approximately two thousand settlers from New Mexico and the El Paso area founded the town of Mesilla on the Río Grande north of El Paso, thinking that they were in Chihuahua. Armed confrontation between military personnel in Chihuahua and New Mexico became a real possibility.

To resolve these difficulties, James Gadsden, representing the United States, and Manuel Díez de Bonilla, Mexico's minister of foreign relations, negotiated a settlement. President Franklin Pierce, Gadsden, and other southern railroad expansionists sought to include Baja California in the final agreement. A treaty was signed at Mexico City on 30 December 1853. Known in U.S. history as the Gadsden Purchase, it was called the *Tratado de la Mesilla* in Mexico. In 1854 the U.S. Senate amended the treaty; the government of President Antonio López de Santa Anna, needing funds to fight an insurrection in Guerrero and fearing that nonacceptance could lead to another war with the United States, reluctantly accepted the terms in June 1854. These included the payment of $10 million to Mexico for the Mesilla tract, an area of thirty thousand square miles of barren Sonoran desert that included both the presidio of Tucson and the town of Mesilla; transit and other privileges across the Isthmus of Tehuantepec, including a license to intervene on behalf of U.S. investors; and abrogation of Article XI of the Treaty of Guadalupe Hidalgo.

Acquisition of the Mesilla tract was a victory for U.S. expansionists, especially railroad promoters, and left Mexico with the fear of further dismemberment. Abrogation of Article XI meant that Mexicans could not seek relief from raids by nomadic Indians living in the United States. As for Santa Anna, his acceptance of the Gadsden Purchase provided his enemies with political ammunition, and he was overthrown and retired from Mexican politics within the year.

W. Dirk Raat

BIBLIOGRAPHY

Faulk, Odie B. *Too Far North, Too Far South.* 1967.

Martínez, Oscar J. *Troublesome Border.* 1988.

"Treaty between Mexico and the United States, signed at Mexico City, 30 December 1853." In *The Consolidated Treaty Series,* edited by Clive Parry. Vol. 111, pp. 235–245. 1969–1981.

Vázquez, Josefina Zoraida, and Lorenzo Meyer. *The United States and Mexico.* 1985.

Edmund P. Gaines. Daguerreotype, c. 1848. From the collection of William J. Schultz, M.D.

Gaines, Edmund P.

The U.S.–Mexican War took place at the end of a long and distinguished, if somewhat controversial, military career for U.S. general Edmund P. Gaines (1777–1849). A Virginia native, Gaines joined the regular army in 1799. Eight years later, while commanding a post in the Mississippi Territory, he arrested Aaron Burr for conspiracy. During the War of 1812 Gaines rose to the rank of brigadier general and received a brevet to major general for his defense of Fort Erie. After the war he served along the southern border and participated in Andrew Jackson's invasion of Spanish Florida.

Over the next two decades Gaines alternately commanded both the Western and Eastern departments of the army. Passed over for army command in 1828, by the time of the U.S.–Mexican War Gaines's influence had been much reduced. The year 1845 found the general commanding the Western Department with his headquarters in New Orleans. To Gaines's chagrin his military rivals, Gen. Zachary Taylor and Gen. Winfield Scott, were chosen for active command during the conflict with Mexico.

When the war began, Gaines became embroiled in controversy. Without authority he called for troops from the southern states to reinforce Taylor's army. Ultimately, some twelve thousand troops enlisted for three or six months' service, although the government had neither the need for them at that time nor supplies nor equipment. Gaines's actions led to unnecessary expense and embarrassment, and by the end of May the general had been ordered to stop the requisitions. In early June, President James K. Polk relieved him of command. A board of inquiry in Washington, D.C., found Gaines guilty of exceeding his authority but recommended no punishment. Placed in command of the Eastern Department, his appeals to serve in Mexico were denied. In late 1848 Gaines returned to the Western Department, but he developed cholera and died the following June.

David J. Coles

BIBLIOGRAPHY

Silver, James W. *Edmund Pendleton Gaines: Frontier General.* 1949.

Smith, Justin H. *The War with Mexico.* 2 vols. 1919. Reprint, 1963.

Gaona, Antonio

A native of Havana, Cuba, Antonio Gaona (1793–1848) first entered military service in 1801 as an underage cadet in the Regiment of New Spain. He fought for the royalist cause during the Mexican War for Independence until embracing the Iguala manifesto in 1821. After seconding the Plan of Casa Mata that precipitated Agustín de Iturbide's abdication in 1823, Gaona went on to hold diverse positions of increasing authority, culminating in promotion to brigade general in 1832.

Appointed to command the Army of Operations' 1st Infantry Brigade in the Texas campaign of 1835 to 1836, Gaona participated in the assault on the Alamo and conducted follow-on operations as far as Bastrop before being ordered to withdraw from Texas. During the French intervention in 1838 and 1839, Gaona governed the fortress of San Juan de Ulúa, which he surrendered to Adm. Charles Baudin after a brief naval bombardment. Although court-martialed for his role in that ignominious episode, he was cleared of culpability.

The outbreak of war with the United States found Gaona serving as commandant-general of Puebla and governor of the Perote fortress. At the outset of the valley campaign in August 1847, he was reassigned as second-in-command of the Army of the Center. Initially positioned at Mexicalzingo to protect the capital's southern approaches, Gaona redeployed his forces to the Candelaria Garita (Candelaria Gate) following the Churubusco defeat but saw little action. He died in 1848 during the U.S. occupation of Mexico City.

William A. DePalo, Jr.

BIBLIOGRAPHY

Carreño, Alberto M., ed. *Jefes del Ejército Mexicano en 1847: Biografías de generales de división y de brigada y de coroneles del ejército por fines del año 1847*, pp. 88–89. 1914.

Diccionario Porrúa: De história, biografía, y geografía de México. 6th ed., p. 1380. 1995.

Filisola, Vicente. *Memorias para la historia de la guerra de Téjas, por el Sr. General de división y actual presidente de Supremo Tribunal de guerra y marina de la República.* Vol. 2, pp. 333–341. 1849.

Rives, George L. *The United States and Mexico, 1821–1848: A History of the Relations between the Two Countries from the Independence of Mexico to the Close of the War with the United States.* Vol. 1, pp. 438–441. 1913.

Santa Anna, Antonio López de. *Detall de las operaciones occurridas en la defensa de la capital de la república, atacada por el ejército de los Estados Unidos del Norte en el año de 1847*, pp. 15–16. 1848.

Garay, Francisco de

Born in the city of Jalapa, Vera Cruz, Francisco de Garay (1796–1865) was a general and one of Mexico's first diplomats. He served as consul to Gibraltar from 1824 to 1828 during the presidency of General Guadalupe Victoria. Little is known about Garay's early military career except that in 1841 he earned a promotion to the rank of general.

After the fall of Tampico in November 1846, Mexican government leaders set up a military line centered around Huejutla (located in the present-day state of Hidalgo, about 120 miles from Tampico) to watch the movement of U.S. troops and to guard the Huasteca. The position, manned by approximately 800 national guardsmen from the area, was under Garay's command. In May 1847 the Mexican government sent Garay 200 U.S. prisoners who believed they were to be exchanged for Mexican soldiers captured at the Battle of Cerro Gordo. The U.S. commander at Tampico, after failing to arrange for their release, organized a rescue mission the following month. On 12 June Garay posted his forces (sources disagree on the exact number, ranging from 170 to 550 men) on the bank of the Río Calabozo. Garay's troops repelled the U.S. advance and pursued the retreating U.S. troops vigorously. In reward for his efforts, Garay received a hero's welcome on returning to Huejutla.

In 1859 Garay again took on consular duties, this time in New York. He subsequently supported the government of Benito Juárez during the French intervention. Juárez's regime appointed Garay Mexican consul in New Orleans, a position he hold until his death.

Pedro Santoni

BIBLIOGRAPHY

Alcaraz, Ramón, ed. *The Other Side; or, Notes for the History of the War between Mexico and the United States.* Translated by Albert C. Ramsey. 1970. Originally published as *Apuntes para la historia de la Guerra entre México y los Estado Unidos,* 1848.

Roa Bárcena, José María. *Recuerdos de la invasión norteamericana (1846–1848).* 3 vols. 1947.

García Conde, Pedro

Mexican general and border survey commissioner Pedro García Conde (1805?–1851) was born in Arizpe, Sonora. He became a cadet with the Presidential Company of San Carlos in 1817, attended the Colegio de Minería from 1822 to 1826, and served as minister of war in 1845 and as senator in 1846. When war broke out with the United States, Gen. Antonio López de Santa Anna banished him to the northern state of Chihuahua, where he assisted Governor Ángel Trías Álvarez against the invading column of Col. William A. Doniphan. García Conde established a strong defensive position for Gen. José Heredia on the Río Sacramento north of the state capital. When U.S. forces launched a flanking assault on 28 February 1847, García Conde personally commanded a cavalry counterattack but failed to stop the invaders.

In 1849 he was appointed Mexican commissioner to survey the border established by the Treaty of Guadalupe Hidalgo. The boundary between Upper and Lower California was drawn without controversy, but a map error caused a dispute over the southern limit of New Mexico. García Conde proposed a line from the Río Grande to the Gila River; his U.S. counterpart, John Russell Bartlett, wanted a boundary farther south to allow a railroad route to the Pacific. A compromise was reached on a line beginning forty miles north of El Paso and leaving much of the Mesilla Valley in Mexico. García Conde died while completing the survey, but the line was rejected by U.S. politicians. In 1853 Santa Anna sold the disputed territory, known as the Gadsden Purchase, to the United States for $10 million.

Jeffrey M. Pilcher

BIBLIOGRAPHY

Bauer, K. Jack. *The Mexican War, 1846–1848.* 1974.

Diccionario Porrúa: De história, biografía, y geografía de México. 6th ed. 1995.

Martínez, Oscar. *Troublesome Border.* 1988.

Garza, Carlos de la

Carlos de la Garza (1801–1882), a Mexican Texan who faced the dilemma of changing allegiances from Mexican to

Texan to United States governments, remained a supporter of law and order under all three. De la Garza was born the son of a presidial soldier at the fort of La Bahía del Espíritu Santo (present-day Goliad, Texas) on the San Antonio River. In 1829, Carlos married Tomasita and established a ranch on the San Antonio River known as Carlos Rancho. De la Garza helped Irish settlers brought in by James Powers and James Hewetson in 1829 and protected them from Karankawa Indian raids. During the Texas Revolution in 1836, de la Garza supported Gen. Antonio López de Santa Anna and the centralist cause and scouted for Mexican general José Urrea, but when his Irish neighbors were captured and threatened with execution, de la Garza helped them escape.

During the Comanche raids of the 1840s, de la Garza's Carlos Rancho became a safe haven for Refugio County residents, a ferry crossing, part-time county seat, and headquarters for a Texas Ranger company. During the U.S.–Mexican War, Gen. Albert Sidney Johnston used the ranch as his headquarters in forming the 1st Texas Rifle Volunteers. Throughout 1846 and 1847, Carlos de la Garza sold cattle to the U.S. Army and supplied ox carts and mule teams to carry supplies for the U.S. Army into Mexico. He remained an influential cattle rancher on the San Antonio River until his death in 1882.

Carolina Castillo Crimm

BIBLIOGRAPHY

Huson, Hobart. *Refugio: A Comprehensive History of Refugio County from Aboriginal Times to 1953.* 1953.

Grimes, Roy, ed. *300 Years in Victoria County.* 1968.

Geography and Climate

At the beginning of the U.S.–Mexican War, Mexico covered more than one-third of the North American continent, extending as far northwest as the present-day California-Oregon border at 42° north latitude and northeast to the Missouri River. Texas independence (1836) and statehood (1845) had substantially reduced Mexico's territory by moving Mexico's eastern border to the Nueces River, which Mexico claimed as the border, while Texas and the United States claimed the Río Grande (or Río Bravo del Norte) as the border. To U.S. expansionists, northern Mexico blocked the natural course of U.S. extension westward because it lay athwart a possible railroad route to the Pacific Ocean. Thus, on the eve of the war, Mexico's northern frontier was disintegrating under the pressure of Anglo-American intrusion and the difficulties in managing a frontier so distant from Mexico City.

The remainder of Mexico stretched southward well into the tropics—its southernmost tip about 14° north of the equator. South of the disputed boundary rivers at the Texas border, Mexico was limited on the east by the Gulf of Mex-

A Mexican hut in the *tierra caliente*. Brantz Mayer, *Mexico As It Was and As It Is*, 1844

ico and on the west by the Pacific Ocean. Thus Mexico was a huge, geographically diverse country essentially bounded by water on its east and west flanks—a condition that made it vulnerable to attack from the sea. Its northern frontier with the expansionist United States occupied a generally arid to semiarid land of relatively low population density and hence was also easy for invading troops to penetrate because they would not face well-defended and well-fortified population centers.

Extending from the tropics to the mid-latitudes and featuring highly extreme topography (e.g., high mountains of 18,700 feet [5,700 meters] near Mexico City and areas below sea level in the California deserts), Mexico was geographically and climatically varied and diverse. The northern and more elevated portions of Mexico in 1846 (e.g., the city of Santa Fe in the province of New Mexico) are characterized by large seasonal temperature variations and extreme winter cold, while the southern and lowland reaches of the country are tropical in climate. Whereas the prevailing tradewinds blow from the Gulf toward tropical Mexico in the vicinity of Vera Cruz, especially in July when they are most noticeable, the northern part of Mexico reaches well into the mid-latitudes, where westerly winds prevail, as in coastal California. Correlated with both elevation and latitude, precipitation varies from the humid tropical lowlands, which are characterized by wet summers, fairly dry winters, and dense jungle growth, to the mild coast of California, with its characteristically mild, wet winters and dry summers typical of Mediterranean climates. Between the tropics and the mid-latitudes is a huge area of elevated basins and tablelands that are characterized by prolonged drought. Most of this interior upland area has dry winters and hot summers, which are occasionally mitigated by afternoon thundershowers as moisture finds its way inland from either the Gulf of California or the Gulf of Mexico. This huge and climatically and physiographically diverse country was the setting for the U.S.–Mexican War of 1846 and 1847. So widespread were the hostilities in this war, and so distinctive the geography, that virtually every battle was characterized by the geographic environments encountered there by U.S. troops or defended by Mexican forces.

EASTERN COASTAL LOWLANDS

The vicinity of Vera Cruz in southeastern Mexico is characteristic of the Eastern Coastal Lowlands, which are situated on a coastal shelf at the base of mountains and exemplify the *tierra caliente* (hot country) of the tropical coast, with its high humidity and heavy precipitation, especially in the summer. To the north, the Gulf's subtropical lowlands widen in the vicinity of Corpus Christi, Texas, an area that witnessed the buildup of troops in May 1846 and provided many U.S. soldiers with their first look at the Mexican countryside. There the troops under Gen. Zachary Taylor first praised the invigorating onshore summer breezes, or "tradewinds" as they were erroneously called, but by late fall they cursed the "northers" that brought cold temperatures and rain—weather conditions that debilitated the troops with diseases. The battlefronts along the lower Río Grande Valley in the vicinity of Resaca de la Palma were adjacent to the coast and had a similar climate. In that area, standing water contributed to its "miasmatic" reputation as mosquitoes bred so readily there. In general, the eastern coastline of Mexico featured a broad coastal shelf and shallow waters less than ten feet deep that made access by sea difficult.

CENTRAL PLATEAUS AND INTERIOR MOUNTAINS

Troops entering Mexico in the vicinity of Monterrey and Buena Vista ascended into starkly mountainous terrain that was arid for much of the year, with most of the rainfall occurring as summer thunderstorms. This vast area of mountain ranges whose bases are buried in deep alluvial valleys (the drier or more interior of which drain into dry lakes or *playas*) contained relatively isolated cities, such as Chihuahua and Saltillo. This high semiarid physiographic area was penetrated by U.S. forces on several fronts. For example, Col. Alexander W. Doniphan's troop movements into central Mexico traversed broad basins (or *bolsónes*) punctuated by rugged mountains that trended north to south as part of the basin and range topography of this part of North America. Farther north, the Mormon Battalion traversed similar parts of the basin and range country in southern Arizona, especially in the vicinity of the San Pedro River, where the summer rains are supplemented by an occasional winter rain storm, or snow storm at the higher elevations.

The Mormons began to settle the Great Basin in 1847, when the area was still nominally Mexican territory, and the experience of the Mormon Battalion provided a better understanding of the region's geography and potential for settlement, as they hoped to create a theocratic empire called "Deseret." The surveyor and military commander John C. Frémont and others traversed Nevada on their way to California as they crossed the formidable Great Basin. Subsequent exploration revealed that all of these varied locations were physiographically part of the basin and range province, which includes the desert states of present-day Arizona, Nevada, and Utah in the United States and Chihuahua and Sonora in Mexico.

VOLCANIC HIGHLAND REGION

Mexico City, the country's largest single population center, is situated in the Volcanic Highland Region, also known as the Sierra Volcánica Transversal. The soil is rich, the climate mild, and the precipitation dependable, conditions that have helped sustain agriculture and large, densely settled populations there since prehistoric times. During the U.S.–Mexican War this region was the site of important battles such as those at Contreras, Churubusco, El Molino del Rey, and Chapultepec. Rimmed by tall volcanoes, the valley is situated approximately 7,800 feet (2,600 meters) above sea level. Given its upland subtropical location, the climate is mild despite the altitude and the region is known as *tierra templada,* or temperate country. When in the Valley of Mexico, U.S. troops found well-watered areas, and the topography made for relatively easy travel. To reach the valley, however, troops had to ascend the precipitous eastern face of the eastern Sierra Madres. The climate of the higher mountains is perpetually cold in this *tierra fria* (cold country), and snow covers the tallest peaks all year.

COASTAL CALIFORNIA

Extending from Alta California into Baja California, the coast was readily accessible to maritime troop movements despite the mountainous country that lay just inland. The numerous harbors provided easy entry for naval forces such as those under the command of Commo. John D. Sloat and Commo. Robert F. Stockton, although the weather conditions (including strong winds and fog) often made for rough going. The coastal portion of California, especially of Alta California, was well populated, having been settled in a series of missions by the Spanish and later the Mexicans. Significantly, most of the population centers that were captured by U.S. forces during the war were close to the sea. Baja California, although less populated, was also easily invaded from the sea because most of the settlements of any size (e.g., Ensenada and La Paz) were coastal ports; the population of the more interior mission communities had dwindled before the war.

EASTERN GREAT PLAINS

Although not part of the battlefront proper, the plains of extreme northeastern Mexico (present-day eastern Colorado and New Mexico) were important for troop movements. Even by the time of the war they had earned the name "Great American Desert," although in fact the area was covered, at least in part, by prairie grasses. On this front, too, Mexico was vulnerable; invading troops could move deeper into the country from the east traversing the longitudinal river valleys, which provided water, wood, and shelter, as witnessed by the invasion of Santa Fe by troops under Gen. Stephen W. Kearny.

SUMMARY

So dominant is the topography and physiography of Mexico that many of the battles in the war gained their logistical character based on the physiographic conditions. For example, the coast in the vicinity of Texas was particularly difficult for maritime operations due to shallow water, and special vessels with shallow draft had to be acquired. In addition, fresh water was so difficult to acquire that on several occasions vessels had to return to Pensacola, Florida, from the Texas and Mexican coasts to replenish water supplies.

Troop movements into the various physiographic areas also included reconnaissance operations, which helped chart the countryside for future settlement and development that, it was widely believed, would occur after the war. Exemplary in this regard were the explorations of Bryant P. Tilden Jr. on the steamboat *Major Brown*, which ventured more than two hundred miles up the Río Grande on an ostensibly military reconnaissance until reaching rapids beyond Laredo. The expedition then continued overland to Presidio del Norte where Tilden noted carefully the prospects for settling the countryside.

At the conclusion of the war in 1848, Mexico lost nearly one-half of its territory to the United States, and the border was formally established along the Río Grande to El Paso del Norte and thence roughly in a line due west to the Gila River, and then to the west coast. This border in effect cut across the countryside from the coastal subtropical lowlands of Texas to the Pacific coastal lowlands in the vicinity of San Diego, California. Surveying errors and the later realization by the United States that the Gila River did not represent a feasible transcontinental railroad route led to the Gadsden Treaty and Purchase of 1853, which placed the U.S.–Mexican border in its present location, about one hundred miles south of the Gila River. After the war, this arbitrary military boundary became an important zone of contact between the United States and Mexico, the Great Borderlands, which extends along the Río Grande to El Paso, thence westward along southern New Mexico and Arizona, thence to the coast just south of San Diego, where it divides Alta and Baja California politically. During the war many residents of Baja California had supported the United States, and when the current border was established they were permitted to relocate to Alta California for fear of retribution.

One major geographic consequence of the U.S.–Mexican War was that the United States possessed a well-defined Southwest that reached to the Pacific Ocean as an outcome of the Manifest Destiny sentiments that had been voiced before the war. Mexico, on the other hand, was left with an arid northern frontier ("el Norte"), which remains a developing zone in the 1990s. Two other geographic consequences of the war should be noted. The first relates to the Southern Transcontinental Railroad, which was constructed some thirty years later (1879–1881) as the Southern Pacific Railroad's "Sunset Route" was built from California to New Orleans by way of Yuma, Tucson, El Paso, and San Antonio. Farther north, predecessors of the Santa Fe Railroad were completed across New Mexico and Arizona by 1881 and 1882. The second geographic consequence relates to mining. Despite various reconnaissance missions, Mexico had done little to exploit or develop the mineral resources of its far northern frontier, which was taken by the United States in the war. The discovery of placer gold in California by James Marshall (a Mormon who accompanied the Mormon Battalion) and subsequent placer and hardrock mining ventures by Anglo-Americans revealed that the area Mexico had lost to the United States was a virtual El Dorado of gold, copper, and silver mines.

Richard V. Francaviglia

BIBLIOGRAPHY

Beck, Warren. *Historical Atlas of the American West.* 1989.

Beck, Warren, and Ynez Haase. *Historical Atlas of New Mexico.* 1969.

Description of the Republic of Mexico: Including its Physical and Moral Features, Geography, Agriculture, Products, Manufactures, etc. Illustrated by a map, in which is included smaller maps of the Valley of Mexico, and the fields of Palo Alto, and Resaca de la Palma. 1846.

Ewing, Russell C., ed. *Six Faces of Mexico: History, People, Geography, Government, Economy, Literature and Art.* 1966.

Farnham, Thomas Jefferson. *Mexico: Its Geography, its People, and its Institutions with a map containing the result of the latest explorations of Fremont, Wilkes, and others.* 1846.

Halls of the Montezumas; or Mexico, in Ancient and Modern Times; Containing a . . . History of the Ancient and Modern Races, Antiquities, and especially its splended Palaces and Halls of State; also its Geography, Government, Institutions, Mines, Minerals and Churches . . . with the Conquest by Cortes and a Sketch of the late War with the United States, including the Treaty of Peace. 1848.

Lander, Ernest M., Jr. *The Reluctant Imperialists: Calhoun, the South Carolinians, and the Mexican War.* 1980.

Naufal, Victor M. Ruiz, Ernesto Lemoine, and Arturo Gálvez

Medrano. *El territorio mexicano.* Volume 1, *La nación;* Volume 2, *Los Estados;* folio, "Planos y Mapas." 1982.

Van Young, Eric, ed. *Mexico's Regions: A Comparative History and Development.* 1992.

Walker, Henry P., and Don Bufkin. *Historical Atlas of Arizona.* 1979.

West, Robert, and John Augelli. *Middle America: Its Lands and Peoples.* 1966.

West, Robert Cooper. *Sonora: Its Geographical Personality.* 1993.

Giddings, Joshua

Abolitionist and antislavery congressman Joshua Reed Giddings (1795–1864) was born 6 August in Bradford County, Pennsylvania. The family moved to New York and then to the Western Reserve of Ohio where Joshua was raised. He received little formal schooling but studied law and was admitted to the bar in 1821. He entered politics, served a term in the Ohio legislature, was elected to the U.S. House of Representatives as an antislavery Whig in 1838, and served until 1858.

Before the U.S.–Mexican War, Giddings opposed a whole series of measures put forth by the alleged Southern slave power. He lobbied incessantly in Congress against the "gag rule," the slave trade, slavery in the District of Columbia, and the annexation of Texas. When war with Mexico began in May 1846, he was the natural leader of the radical opposition and was one of only fourteen antislavery Whigs to vote against the war bill. The day after the vote, Giddings denounced the war as a war of aggression and conquest to expand slavery. Giddings continually tied the immoral expansion of slavery to the war effort, thus making it difficult for prowar legislators to defend the war in Northern antislavery circles. Although his group of radical Whigs was too small to be effective and did not represent the mainstream of the Whig opposition party, Giddings and his compatriots embarrassed the administration of President James K. Polk at every opportunity and on occasion combined with more moderate antiwar congressmen to defeat administration proposals.

Throughout his career, Giddings was a fervent, radical antislavery politician. He became a Free-Soiler in 1848 and a Republican in 1854. He later served as President Abraham Lincoln's consul-general to Canada and died in Montreal on 27 May 1864. Giddings's politics embodied a powerful personality and strong moral convictions.

John H. Schroeder

BIBLIOGRAPHY

Stewart, James Brewer. *Joshua R. Giddings and the Tactics of Radical Politics.* 1970.

Gillespie, Archibald H.

Archibald H. Gillespie (c. 1812–1873), a lieutenant in the U.S. Marine Corps, was sent to California as a U.S. secret agent disguised as a merchant to work with Capt. John C. Frémont, who had arrived in the Mexican province months before to observe British activity. Gillespie reached Frémont in May 1846 in southern Oregon.

Gillespie informed Frémont of the preparations for war that he had observed while passing through Mexico, and he delivered messages from both administration officials and Frémont's father-in-law, Sen. Thomas Hart Benton of Missouri. This news persuaded Frémont to turn southward in order to be present in California should war break out. Frémont's return to the Sacramento Valley helped put the U.S. settlers there into a revolutionary mood, resulting in the Bear Flag Revolt.

Once the news of war with Mexico arrived, the Bear Flaggers, Frémont, and Gillespie were all mustered into service by the U.S. Navy and formed the California Battalion, which marched down the coast and, with the help of naval forces under Commo. Robert F. Stockton, easily secured California for the United States. Gillespie was put in charge of a small garrison to control Los Angeles, but his arbitrary regulations, threats of punishment, and humiliation of several citizens sparked a local Californio rebellion in September 1846. Gillespie called for reinforcements before he was forced to surrender his post. Help sent by Commodore Stockton arrived just as Gillespie was leading his defeated garrison out of the city. Nevertheless, U.S. authority was not completely reestablished in the Los Angeles area until January 1847.

In August 1847, Gillespie left California, taking the overland route. Back in Washington, D.C., Gillespie testified in the famous trial of John C. Frémont, by then a lieutenant colonel. Frémont was charged with violating the orders of his superior, Brig. Gen. Stephen W. Kearny. Subsequently, Gillespie played no significant historical role.

Ward M. McAfee

BIBLIOGRAPHY

De Voto, Bernard. *The Year of Decision, 1846.* 1943.

Harlow, Neal. *California Conquered: War and Peace on the Pacific, 1846–1850.* 1982.

Marti, Werner. *Messenger of Destiny: The California Adventures, 1846–1847, of Archibald H. Gillespie, U.S. Marine Corps.* 1960.

Gilmer, Thomas W.

U.S. politician Thomas Walker Gilmer (1802–1844) had been elected to the Virginia legislature and to the governorship before entering Congress in 1841. A close friend of both President John Tyler and Senator John C. Calhoun, Gilmer wrote a letter, which appeared in the Washington *Madisonian* on 23 January 1843, supporting the U.S. annexation of Texas. He asserted that the free states would benefit from the annexation and that it was in the national interest. He claimed that the United States must annex Texas or watch Great Britain gain influence there. Great Britain sought to abolish slavery in Texas and in the southern United States in order to raise the cost of production of cotton so that British colonies would be more competitive. Gilmer's letter prompted Representative John Quincy Adams and eleven other antislavery members of Congress to respond that the United States had intervened in Texas unlawfully and to warn that if annexation occurred, the North would secede from the Union.

Confirmed as secretary of the Navy in mid-February 1844, Gilmer joined President Tyler, cabinet members, senators, and representatives to inspect the newly commissioned USS *Princeton* on a cruise of the Potomac on 28 February. The ship's guns were fired successfully throughout the day. On the return trip to Washington, D.C., that afternoon, a new twelve-inch gun with a fifteen-foot barrel, the "Peacemaker" was fired a final time. The largest wrought-iron gun forged at the time, the Peacemaker exploded, sending metal fragments into the crowd, killing Gilmer, Secretary of State Abel Upshur, and others.

Carol Jackson Adams

BIBLIOGRAPHY

Hall, Claude H. *Abel Parker Upshur: Conservative Virginian, 1790–1844.* 1964.

Pletcher, David M. *The Diplomacy of Annexation: Texas, Oregon, and the Mexican War.* 1973.

Wiltse, Charles M. *John C. Calhoun: Sectionalist, 1840–1850.* 1951.

Gold Rush

On 24 January 1848, as the U.S.–Mexican War was winding down and only a few days before the Treaty of Guadalupe Hidalgo was signed, James Marshall discovered gold at Sutter's Mill, in what is present-day Coloma, California. Although its existence and value were at first disbelieved, this discovery of a small amount of gold in the hills of what would become the state of California changed the development of the land acquired from Mexico during the war.

After the discovery was confirmed, people from across the new territories flocked to the hills of California. Word spread rapidly along the Pacific coast and eventually across the United States. Although those in the East were initially uninterested and doubtful of the value of the claim, President James K. Polk's December 1848 declaration acknowledging the abundance of gold in the West electrified the nation.

Men traveled to the mines, flooding the hills in and around San Francisco. Some came across the Oregon Territory from the East; others came by boat around Cape Horn or through the jungles of Central America. Some simply sought a new experience. Many were U.S.–Mexican War veterans who deserted their units in hope of a new adventure rather than return home. Most miners, however, sought only to get rich quick and return home to their families, homes, and way of life.

Marshall's original gold discoveries and the subsequent mining experiences did seem to provide the opportunity for instant riches. Those who had no hope of fortune in the East could have not only the adventure of western travel but also the dream of possible wealth at their final destination. Only a few actually discovered gold, however; most who made the trip to California rarely found enough gold even to cover their expenses. Often, these former miners became permanent citizens of California, not because they remained in the goldfields, but because they did not make enough money from mining to return home.

Settlers from the United States discriminated against natives of the land, Mexican settlers, and various immigrant groups, especially the Chinese, in their search for wealth. The treaty signed by the United States and Mexico was largely forgotten by squatters who claimed the land of Mexican settlers. Although the treaty had claimed property and other rights for Mexicans in the area, the forty-niners practiced the frontier policy of "squatting" for property and overran the land. Native Californians were hunted down and eventually wiped out by those who felt they were in the way of the "progress" of the gold miners.

The gold rush forever changed California. On formerly free and relatively vacant territory, a state was declared in 1850. California, established out of former Mexican lands, gained statehood not because of what it offered, but because of dreams left unfulfilled in the forty-niners' search for gold and riches.

Karen L. Archambault

BIBLIOGRAPHY

Kelly, Leslie A. *California's Gold Rush Country.* 1997.

Marks, Paula Mitchell. *Precious Dust: The American Gold Rush Era, 1848–1900.* 1994.

Parke, Charles Ross. *Dreams to Dust: A Diary of the California Gold Rush, 1849–1850.* 1989.

Seidman, Laurence I. *The Fools of '49: The California Gold Rush, 1848–1856.* 1976.

Goliad Massacre

The Mexican massacre of Texians at Goliad on 27 March 1836 was the aftermath of the 1836 Goliad campaign and was the largest single loss of Texian lives during the Texas Revolution.

Following the surrender of his command at the battle of Coleto Creek, Col. James Walker Fannin and nearly 320

Texians were marched back to their former garrison, the Presidio La Bahía at present-day Goliad, as prisoners of the Mexican army. There has been debate about the terms of the surrender. Mexican general José Urrea insisted that the Texians surrendered at discretion while surviving Texians insisted they were given honorable terms including parole.

Learning of the surrender, Mexican president and commander Antonio López de Santa Anna ordered that the terms of the Tornel Decree of 30 December 1835 be enforced. Because the majority of Fannin's command were volunteers from the United States, they fell within the provision that stated, "All foreigners who may land in any port of the republic or who enter it armed and for the purpose of attacking our territory, shall be treated and punished as pirates, since they are not subjects of any nation at war with the republic nor do they militate under any recognized flag." Santa Anna interpreted this as an order for execution. Col. Nicolás Portilla, commander at Goliad after General Urrea departed, received Santa Anna's order on the night of 26 March.

The Coleto prisoners had been joined by others who had been captured at Victoria and Copano. The majority of the prisoners were crammed into the small presidio chapel, but some were allowed into the yard.

On the morning of 27 March 1836, Palm Sunday, the prisoners were mustered, divided into three groups under the commands of Capt. Agustín Alcerrica, Capt. Luis Balderas, and Capt. Antonio Ramírez, and marched out of the fort. The wounded were left in quarters. About a half mile from the fort, the groups were halted and the Mexican guards opened fire. The wounded were shot in the streets.

Spared from the massacre were all of the U.S. medical personnel who were needed to care for Mexican wounded, and carpenters, blacksmiths, and wheelwrights. About eighty men were spared; about twenty escaped the massacre by running to safety during the executions; and more than three hundred were killed.

The bodies were stripped and placed in pyres, but their remains were still exposed when, following the Battle of San Jacinto and the Mexican retreat, the Texian army returned to Goliad on 3 June 1836. Texian general Thomas J. Rusk led the burial services.

The Goliad massacre, designed to frighten those who would support the Texas cause, did just the opposite and became a battle cry used at the Battle of San Jacinto and to recruit more U.S. volunteers. The massacre continued to be used as a source of vengeful inspiration during recruitment of U.S. volunteers for the U.S.–Mexican War.

Kevin R. Young

BIBLIOGRAPHY

Barnard, Joseph Henry. *Dr. J. H. Barnard's Journal: A Composite of Known Versions of the Journal of Dr. Joseph H. Barnard.* Edited by Hobart Huson. 1949.

Jenkins, John H. *The Papers of the Texas Revolution, 1835–1836.* 10 vols. 1973.

O'Connor, Kathryn Stoner. *The Presidio La Bahía.* 1966.

Urrea, José. *Diario de las operaciones militares de la division que al mando del General José Urrea.* In *The Mexican Side of the Texas Revolution,* edited by Carlos E. Castaneda, 1970.

Gómez, Gregorio

There is little information about the early life, military career, and postwar activities of Mexican general Gregorio Gómez (1???–1???). It is clear, however, that Gómez's comportment during the 1830s exacerbated tensions between Mexico and the United States.

Gómez was commander of the Mexican garrison at Tampico when Gen. José Antonio Mejía's expedition (which was intended to aid the Texas rebels in the belief that they supported federalism) arrived on 14 November 1835. Mejía's troops retreated after a brief skirmish, leaving behind several prisoners, of whom thirteen were U.S. citizens, nine English or Irish, seven German, and two French. Three of these men died of their wounds; the others were court-martialed and shot in December on Gómez's orders.

During the following spring Gómez quarreled with the U.S. consul at Tampico. When a lieutenant from the U.S. revenue cutter *Jefferson* went ashore at Tampico to see the U.S. consul, Gómez had him arrested and his crew imprisoned. The Mexican government apologized, disavowed Gómez's actions, and removed him from his command. Soon afterward, however, Gómez was promoted to a higher post at Vera Cruz and again became embroiled in controversy after arresting several seamen from the U.S. sloop-of-war *Natchez.* Sources do not state how authorities resolved the incident.

In March 1847 Gómez commanded a district in the state of Vera Cruz extending from Corral Falso to Las Vigas. At the Battle of Cerro Gordo he was in charge of the second line of defense at La Hoya, but, on hearing of the rout, Gómez fled after sending word to the rear that all had been lost.

Pedro Santoni

BIBLIOGRAPHY

Rives, George Lockhart. *The United States and Mexico, 1821–1848.* 2 vols. 1913.

Smith, Justin H. *The War with Mexico.* 2 vols. 1919. Reprint, 1963.

Gómez de la Cortina, José

See **Cortina, José Gómez de la**

Gómez Farías, Valentín

Born to a middle-class Guadalajara family, Mexican politician Valentín Gómez Farías (1781–1857) became a physician in 1807 and practiced medicine until 1820. He then became involved in politics, serving in the Aguascalientes town council and subsequently in the national legislature. By the end of the decade Gómez Farías had assumed a leadership position among radical liberals (known as *puros*). As provisional president in 1833 and 1834 he sponsored legislation designed to weaken the army and the clergy. The reforms were short-lived, however, and Gómez Farías spent much of the following decade in exile. During that time he became convinced that armed rebellion was a legitimate means to fulfill the political agenda of the *puros*.

Gómez Farías returned to Mexico early in 1845 with two objectives: to restore the 1824 federal constitution as the basic law of the land and to launch a military campaign to recover the former Mexican territory of Texas. He believed that achieving both objectives would solve the country's domestic problems and halt U.S. expansionism. The administrations of Generals José Joaquín de Herrera and Mariano Paredes y Arrillaga, however, did not intend to implement Gómez Farías's program. The former wanted to keep the *Bases Orgánicas* (with reforms) as Mexico's constitution while the latter intended to establish a monarchy; neither desired to wage war against the United States.

Gómez Farías thus became a political agitator and organized numerous plots to overthrow both regimes. His efforts did not meet with success, however, until he struck an alliance with the *moderados* and Gen. Antonio López de Santa Anna in the spring of 1846. When the unwieldy coalition toppled the Paredes y Arrillaga regime in early August, it seemed that Gómez Farías's hopes would finally come true. The *puros* held the reins of government and Santa Anna, who was exiled in Cuba, would return to lead military resistance against the United States.

During the next eight months, however, numerous obstacles dashed Gómez Farías's expectations. Although the *puro* leader strove to reconcile the various political groups, his domestic rivals saw traces of demagoguery in *puro* activities, and Santa Anna often tried to break his ties with Gómez Farías. In January 1847 Acting President Gómez Farías issued a decree authorizing the government to raise 15 million pesos by mortgaging or selling ecclesiastical property. Designed to finance the war effort, the law instead fostered public animosity toward Gómez Farías. His political enemies began to plot against him and their intrigues culminated in the 27 February 1847 rebellion of the *polkos*. The uprising, which erupted just a few days before Gen. Winfield Scott and the U.S. Army landed in Vera Cruz, led to the ouster of Gómez Farías as chief executive in late March.

During the next fifteen months, Gómez Farías assisted *puro* statesmen in their efforts to continue hostilities against the United States and invalidate the Treaty of Guadalupe Hidalgo. But ill health and disappointment over the *puros*' inability to achieve these goals led him to withdraw from public life during the early 1850s. By the time of his death in Mexico City in June 1858, Gómez Farías's position had been reduced to that of respected *puro* elder statesman.

Pedro Santoni

BIBLIOGRAPHY

Costeloe, Michael P. *The Central Republic in Mexico, 1835–1846: Hombres de Bien in the Age of Santa Anna*. 1993.

Fowler, Will. "Valentín Gómez Farías: Perceptions of Radicalism in Independent Mexico, 1821–1847." *Bulletin of Latin American Research* 15, no. 1 (1996): 39–62.

Hutchinson, Cecil Allan. *Valentín Gómez Farías: La vida de un republicano*. 1983.

Santoni, Pedro. *Mexicans at Arms: Puro Federalists and the Politics of War, 1845–1848*. 1996.

Gómez Pedraza, Manuel

Born to a prominent family from the state of Querétaro, Manuel Gómez Pedraza (1789–1851) became one of the foremost statesmen of early republican Mexico. He served as a royalist officer during the Wars of Independence and as a deputy to the 1820 Spanish parliament, and subsequently received a succession of military commands during the empire of Agustín de Iturbide. Following Iturbide's abdication, he made the ideological switch to federalism and occupied several high government offices between 1825 and 1845. However, the political skirmishes of this epoch fostered a deep antagonism between Gómez Pedraza and Valentín Gómez Farías, the respective leaders of the *moderado* and *puro* political blocs. This rivalry heated up during the U.S.–Mexican War and compromised Gómez Pedraza's capacity to cooperate with the national defense effort.

Gómez Pedraza exerted considerable influence over Mexican domestic affairs in the mid-1840s. Although he did not occupy an official cabinet post during the regime of President José Joaquín de Herrera, contemporaries believed that Gómez Pedraza held considerable sway throughout 1845 over Herrera and his ministers. Therefore, the *puros* held him personally responsible for devising and implementing what they considered to be the government's ill-advised policies of attempting to reach an amicable accord with the United States over the Texas question and preserving the *Bases Orgánicas* (with reforms) as Mexico's constitution.

The unmerciful tirades that *puro* newspapers subjected Gómez Pedraza to surely remained vivid in his memory and influenced his conduct once the *puros* assumed power in August 1846. Over the next eight months, Gómez Pedraza, sometimes in conjunction with Gen. Antonio López de Santa

Anna and other times in association with conservative and *moderado* politicians, feverishly worked to sabotage the *puros'* efforts to achieve national unity as Mexico tried to fend off the U.S. invasion. He participated in intrigues such as the February 1847 revolt of the *polkos* that ousted Gómez Farías from the presidential chair and ended the *puros'* political ascendancy.

Gómez Pedraza shied away from public posts that might have compromised his political reputation for the rest of the year. He refused to join the peace commission that entered into negotiations with the United States in August 1847, and after the occupation of Mexico City in mid-September he retreated to a nearby hacienda to avoid an active role in a *moderado* government whose foremost priority was to end the war. In the spring of 1848, however, Gómez Pedraza was elected to the national legislature, and he twice addressed the senate to argue in favor of ratifying the Treaty of Guadalupe Hidalgo. In his initial speech—the more significant of the two—Gómez Pedraza tried to vindicate his support of Herrera's foreign policy in 1845 and also pointed out the immense benefits that Mexico could accrue if it settled for peace. Although this discourse received little publicity at the time, the speech probably strengthened the convictions of those senators who needed further reassurance that Mexico could begin to put its internal affairs in order only by settling for peace with the United States.

Like many of his peers, after the war Gómez Pedraza came to believe that Mexico needed the patronage of a strong foreign country to survive. He signed an agreement in January 1850 (later annulled by congress) with U.S. minister plenipotentiary Robert P. Letcher to build a canal through the Isthmus of Tehuantepec. Gómez Pedraza also was a presidential candidate later that year and, until his death in 1851, served as director of the national pawnshop (*Monte de Piedad*).

Pedro Santoni

BIBLIOGRAPHY

Alcaraz, Ramón, et al. *The Other Side; or, Notes for the History of the War between Mexico and the United States.* 1970.

Costeloe, Michael P. *The Central Republic in Mexico, 1835–1846: Hombres de Bien in the Age of Santa Anna.* 1993.

de la Peña, Antonio, ed. *Algunos documentos sobre el tratado de Guadalupe y la situación de México durante la invasión norteamericana.* 1930.

Santoni, Pedro. *Mexicans at Arms: Puro Federalists and the Politics of War, 1845–1848.* 1996.

Gonzaga Cuevas, Luis

See **Cuevas, Luis Gonzaga**

González Cosío, Manuel

Born in Mexico City but educated in Zacatecas, Mexican politician Manuel González Cosío (1790–1849) joined the ranks of the Liberal Party during the 1820s and entered state politics. His first term as governor of Zacatecas (January–May 1835) coincided with an attempt by conservative and *moderado* leaders to remodel Mexico from a federal to a centralist republic. To achieve this goal, supporters of centralism in the national congress issued a March 1835 decree restricting the size of the civic militia in the states to one militiaman for every five hundred inhabitants. González Cosío mustered a force to resist the measure, but it was defeated in May.

During the war with the United States, González Cosío (who was appointed state governor in August 1846) supported *puro* leader Valentín Gómez Farías and counseled him on the issues of the day. For example, González Cosío shared with Gómez Farías his frustrations with the domestic and foreign policies of Gen. José Joaquín de Herrera's government, his hopes and concerns regarding the consequences of an alliance with Gen. Antonio López de Santa Anna, and his insights on the best way to organize the civic militia.

After the U.S. Army captured Mexico City in September 1847, González Cosío pledged to support *moderado* president Manuel de la Peña y Peña. However, once the *moderados* made it clear that they did not intend to prosecute the war, González Cosío, like other *puros* who believed that national honor was at stake, protested against the peace negotiations and the Treaty of Guadalupe Hidalgo. He also plotted to overthrow the *moderado* governments so that hostilities might continue. González Cosío was elected in December 1848 to a third term as state governor and held that post until his death.

Pedro Santoni

BIBLIOGRAPHY

León, Andrés, ed. *Diccionario enciclopédico de México ilustrado.* 4 vols. Reprint, 1990.

Roa Bárcena, José María. *Recuerdos de la invasión norteamericana (1846–1848).* 3 vols. 1947.

Santoni, Pedro. *Mexicans at Arms: Puro Federalists and the Politics of War, 1845–1848.* 1996.

Gorostiza, Manuel de

Manuel Eduardo de Gorostiza (1794–1851) was Mexico's minister to the United States in Washington, D.C., at the end of the Texas Revolution in 1836. Gorostiza protested the U.S. involvement in this rebellion. Before his appointment he had served in London, where he publicly warned against U.S. ambitions in Texas, writing several articles in *The Times*.

Spanish-born, Gorostiza had a promising career as an internationally known playwright and writer before his immigration to Mexico and his government service for that country. He published a number of works in Spain and Mexico and his plays were performed in the major capitals of Europe. He fled Spain in 1823 for political reasons and in Mexico helped establish a secular theater movement that led to the establishment of the Gran Teatro Nacional. His comedy *Indulgencia para todos* (*Tolerance for All*) was his greatest work.

Gorostiza served in various Mexican government posts in the 1830s and 1840s. In his communiques to the Mexican government while he was minister to the United States, he warned of the U.S. government's support for the Texas Revolution, despite the official U.S. position of neutrality. When the U.S.–Mexican War broke out in 1846, he organized a battalion for the defense of Mexico City. He fought alongside his men at the Convento de San Mateo at the Battle of Churubusco, surrendering only after a ferocious battle. He died in 1851 and his bust was given a special place within the National Theater building.

Richard Griswold del Castillo

BIBLIOGRAPHY

Aguilar, María Esperanza. *Estudio bio-bibliográfico de D. Manuel Eduardo de Gorostiza.* 1932.

Spell, Lota M. "Para la biografía de Gorostiza." *Historia Mexicana* 8, no. 2 (1958).

Great Britain

In the years preceding the U.S.–Mexican War, Great Britain was the dominant external power opposed to U.S. annexation of Texas. Several factors provide the context for Great Britain's response to events. First, Great Britain maintained extensive commercial and financial links with Mexico. Mexico owed a substantial debt to British bondholders (the majority of foreign merchants resident in Mexico were British) and a significant portion of Mexico's customs receipts were pledged as payment for the debt. Also, British capital dominated Mexican mining. The secession of Texas in 1836 did not affect these interests directly, but continued warfare threatened to further weaken Mexico, already beset by fiscal problems and intense civil conflict that had strained British-Mexican relations since Mexico had achieved independence. Second, under no circumstances would Great Britain actively assist Mexico in recovering Texas or challenge the United States directly in resisting annexation. Although British diplomats openly supported Mexican attempts to ban further U.S. immigration into the province after 1830, Great Britain viewed the Texas–Mexico separation as complete and Texan independence as sustainable if Mexico could conclude a peace settlement with Texas before the United States could

overcome its domestic differences in regard to annexation. Third, as leader of the international effort to suppress the slave trade, Great Britain could not discount the possibility that a new North American slave trade might go unchecked and thus demanded from Texas a treaty prohibiting the slave trade as the price of formal recognition. Convinced that Mexico could not recover Texas, Great Britain signed treaties with Texas in 1840 providing for British mediation between Mexico and Texas.

British policy had two main objectives. One was to secure Mexico's northern frontier against further encroachment by the United States. Texan independence, once established permanently, might sustain a regional stability that a weak Mexico seemed incapable of providing. The other aim, closely associated with the first, was the expectation that Texas would be a great cotton producer and thus reduce Great Britain's dependence on the United States. In this context, abolitionist pressure played an important role. Although Great Britain's foreign secretary, Lord Palmerston, refused the abolitionist demand to make emancipation a prerequisite for formal diplomatic relations with Texas, British leaders could not ignore the antislavery argument that there was little to distinguish Texas from the Southern United States and that proslavery expansionists would covet Texas for as long as slavery existed there. At abolitionist prompting, Lord Aberdeen, Palmerston's Tory successor as foreign secretary, placed emancipation into a proposed peace equation between Texas and Mexico in 1843. Aberdeen abandoned the policy, however, when it began to fuel annexationist agitation in the United States.

A more aggressive and interventionist policy developed in 1844 in which European considerations played a role. Eager to strengthen relations with France, Great Britain proposed a plan committing Texas to permanent independence with fixed boundaries guaranteed by France and Great Britain. This would deter the United States from pursuing annexation further in the face of united European opposition, while providing external security to Mexico as an incentive to recognize Texas. Fearing a loss of leverage with the United States, France backed down on a direct commitment to Texan independence in 1845, supporting instead a policy of informal mediation. European agents did secure a commitment from Mexico to recognize Texan independence in 1845, but when presented with a choice between annexation and independence, Texas opted for the former.

Success of Great Britain's policy depended on a number of independent variables: Mexico had to relinquish its claim to Texas, and Texas had to accept the alternative to annexation. British policy failed on both counts. Despite external pressures, Mexico could not overcome internal resistance to an independent Texas. Texas was willing to consider an independent future only if there were no alternative. Once the U.S. annexation of Texas was an accomplished fact, Great

Britain abandoned further efforts to resist U.S. expansion, rejecting several opportunities to acquire California in 1845 and 1846.

British public opinion accused the United States of deliberately provoking an unjust war for the extension of slavery, and British commercial interests expressed concern over the deleterious consequences to British trade and investments in Mexico. However, Great Britain remained officially neutral, rejecting repeated pleas for aid by the Mexican government while assuring the United States that it would not intervene on behalf of Mexico. Both sides turned down the British offer to mediate. British diplomatic agents and merchants in Mexico, who maintained close ties with political and commercial elites, played a crucial role in facilitating communication between the belligerents. Official British policy approved of these efforts, and it was largely due to British urging that Nicholas P. Trist remained in Mexico despite President James K. Polk's recall. British agents assisted in the negotiations that followed, leading to the Treaty of Guadalupe Hildago in 1848.

Lelia M. Roeckell

BIBLIOGRAPHY

Adams, Ephraim D. *British Interests and Activities in Texas, 1838–1846.* 1910.

Bourne, Kenneth. *Britain and the Balance of Power in North America, 1815–1908.* 1967.

Merk, Frederick. *The Monroe Doctrine and American Expansionism, 1843–1849.* 1966.

Pletcher, David M. *The Diplomacy of Annexation: Texas, Oregon, and the Mexican War.* 1973.

Roeckell, Lelia M. "British Interests in Texas, 1825–1846." D. Phil. diss., University of Oxford, 1993.

Tenenbaum, Barbara. "Merchants, Money, and Mischief: The British in Mexico, 1821–1867." *The Americas* 25 (1979): 317–339.

Varg, Paul. *United States Foreign Relations.* 1979.

Great Western

See Borginnis, Sarah

Green, Duff

Duff Green (1791–1875) was an attorney, entrepreneur, editor, politician, propagandist, and U.S. secret agent. Born in Kentucky, Green fought in the Northwest Territory during the War of 1812 and then settled in frontier Missouri, where he practiced law, speculated in real estate, participated in Missouri territorial politics, edited a newspaper that supported Andrew Jackson for president, and promoted a proslavery coalition of states-rights southerners and westerners.

Green moved to Washington, D.C., in 1825 to run a newspaper devoted to Jackson's nomination in 1828. When President Jackson and John C. Calhoun later split over both political and personal matters, however, Green sided with Calhoun.

President John Tyler sent Green to London in 1841 as a confidential agent, where he lobbied for lower tariff rates, reported on British abolitionists, and monitored British relations with the Republic of Texas. Green believed the slave South had to expand and hoped his nation would first annex Texas, then California, New Mexico, and other provinces. As early as 1844 Green urged war with Mexico. "We have no means of regaining the trade of Mexico," he advised Secretary of State Calhoun, "but by chastising them into decent behavior." A war, he argued, would allow the United States to "indemnify" itself while also "show[ing] other nations what we can and will do" to "command their respect." Believing the gains would far outweigh negligible losses, he assured Calhoun that "a war with Mexico will cost us nothing and [will] reinstate us in the estimation of other nations."

In 1844 and 1845 Green anticipated renewed warfare between Mexico and Texas, a turn of events that he believed might give the United States a pretext to intervene. He considered raising his own army to invade Mexico, but Texas president Anson Jones rebuffed him. During the U.S.–Mexican War Green tried but failed to win command of a company of Texas volunteers.

From the 1830s through the 1860s Green organized or advanced many business enterprises, mostly in coal, iron, and railroads. He managed iron works in Alabama and Tennessee for the Confederacy during the Civil War. After the war he promoted industrialization in the South. He died at his home near Dalton, Georgia, in 1875. "He was a man of impulse, of keenness, of ability," the journalist Frederic Hudson observed. "His ideas were large, and his schemes expansive."

Thomas Hietala

BIBLIOGRAPHY

Green, Duff. *Facts and Suggestions, Biographical, Historical, Financial and Political.* 1866.

Green, Duff. Papers. Library of Congress.

Hietala, Thomas. *Manifest Design.* 1985.

Green, Thomas Jefferson

Born into a prominent tidewater planting family in North Carolina, Thomas Jefferson Green (1802–1863) was an adventurer, entrepreneur, and politician who migrated to Texas on the eve of its independence from Mexico. As a senator from Béxar County in the first Texas congress, Green in 1836 sponsored a bill claiming the Río Grande as the southern and western boundary of the new republic. Although Mexico continued to regard the Nueces River as the boundary of Texas, passage of the bill would lead the James K. Polk administration to claim the Trans-Nueces region as U.S. territory when Texas was annexed in 1845. One year later, when Mexican troops fired on U.S. dragoons, precipitating the U.S.–Mexican War, President Polk would insist that "American blood has been spilled on American soil."

In the fall of 1842 Green joined the Somervell Expedition and emerged as a leader of the expedition's malcontents who were determined to push on into Mexico after Brig. Gen. Alexander Somervell ordered the army to return to Texas. As second-in-command of the Mier Expedition that followed, Green took part in the battle at Mier on 25–26 December 1842 and after the defeat of the Texians was incarcerated in Mexico. In 1843 Green escaped from the fortress San Carlos de Perote and returned to Texas. He later wrote a book of his experiences, *Journal of the Texian Expedition against Mier,* a scathing polemic against Mexico published in 1845. Green later traveled to California to mine for gold and speculate in land, but after a series of failed business ventures he returned to North Carolina, where he died in 1863.

Sam W. Haynes

BIBLIOGRAPHY

Green, Thomas Jefferson. *Journal of the Texian Expedition against Mier.* Edited by Sam W. Haynes. 1993.

Haynes, Sam W. *Soldiers of Misfortune: The Somervell and Mier Expeditions.* 1990.

Gregg, Josiah

U.S. trader and newspaper correspondent Josiah Gregg (1806–1850) recorded his experiences on the Santa Fe Trail while prospering as a trader in the 1830s. His *Commerce of the Prairies,* published in 1844, was the first to describe in detail Mexican society and culture in the Santa Fe region. It served as a guide to future travelers.

When the U.S.–Mexican War began in 1846, Gregg's knowledge of Spanish, Mexican culture, and the geography of the southern plains attracted the U.S. military. Initially, Gregg rejected an appeal to go to Texas with Arkansas volunteers and joined a wagon train heading to the plains, but he reconsidered when approached again while on the trip. He was unsure of his role, for he was neither military nor civilian. Soldiers did not accept him despite his position as guide and interpreter during campaigns of 1846 and early 1847. His accounts of the Battle of Buena Vista were published in Arkansas and Kentucky newspapers. The situation so frustrated Gregg that he left the position on 9 April 1847 and joined a Santa Fe trader to reclaim his possessions in Chihuahua. Later that spring, he visited Philadelphia to purchase merchandise to sell in Monterrey and Saltillo, but the venture failed when his partner considered it too risky financially. In the fall, Gregg traveled overland through Texas to Saltillo, where he practiced medicine, which he had studied in Kentucky before the war. After visiting Mexico City, Gregg embarked for San Francisco in April 1849. He died of starvation and exposure in February 1850 while leading an expedition on the Trinity River in search of a northwestern bay.

Carol Jackson Adams

BIBLIOGRAPHY

Connor, Seymour V., and Jimmy M. Skaggs. *Broadcloth and Britches: The Santa Fe Trade.* 1977.

Gregg, Josiah. *Diary and Letters of Josiah Gregg: Southwestern Enterprises, 1840–1847.* Edited by Maurice Garland Fulton. 1941.

Gregg, Josiah. *Diary and Letters of Josiah Gregg: Excursions in Mexico and California, 1847–1850.* Edited by Maurice Garland Fulton. 1944.

Horgan, Paul. *Josiah Gregg and His Vision of the Early West.* 1941.

Guadalupe Vallejo, Mariano

See **Vallejo, Mariano Guadalupe**

Guerrero, Vicente

Mexican revolutionary leader Vicente Guerrero (1783–1831) was born at Tixtla in present-day Guerrero, the uneducated son of a rural laborer. He became a muleteer, then joined the revolt for independence from Spain led by José María Morelos. Following Morelos's capture by Spanish forces in 1814, Guerrero conducted guerrilla operations, rallying a largely indigenous population. He refused Spanish pardons, keeping alive demands for the abolition of slavery and for legal equality for *castas* (racially mixed persons). With the 1820 liberal revolution in Spain, congenial to Mexican *criollos* (native-born whites), the cause of independence suffered dwindling support.

By 1821, compromise with conservative rebel forces seemed the surest route to independence, and Guerrero and the republicans came to terms with Col. Agustín de Iturbide. The resulting rebel Plan of Iguala promised to create a Catholic monarchy with legal equality for all. Republicans and monarchists then united against the colonial regime, and their military and political campaign finally succeeded with the fall of Mexico City in 1821.

When Spain rejected an agreement with the rebels, Iturbide declared himself emperor, challenging both Masonic liberals and republicans like Guerrero. These opposing camps eventually toppled the empire and then conspired against each other to determine which should govern republican Mexico. Division General Guerrero played a key role, primarily as an influential peace emissary between rebel forces and the federal government. He served in the interim government (triumvirate) of 1823 to 1824, then as regional commander during President Guadalupe Victoria's term (1824–1828).

In 1825, Guerrero's former sponsor, Vice President Nicolás Bravo, became a political rival, backed by the *escoceses*, Scottish rite Masons. In response, Guerrero's supporters and the U.S. minister, Joel Poinsett, founded the York Rite. (Poinsett's cooperation may have resulted, in part, from instructions that urged him to work for the U.S. acquisition of Texas.) The *escoceses* backed the December 1827 Montaño revolt, in which Bravo was captured by Guerrero at Tulancingo. Exiling the *escocés* leadership advantaged the Yorkists (*yorkinos*) and Guerrero. When 1828 general elections produced a narrow presidential victory for Gen. Manuel Gómez Pedraza over General Guerrero, Yorkists were disinclined to accept the outcome. The revolt of La Acordada in December 1828 placed the popular party (*yorkinos*) in power, and Guerrero became minister of war. Congress elevated him to the presidency in January 1829.

The successful popular revolt of La Acordada paved the way for the first attempt by the government to address fundamental social issues. Slavery was abolished (except in Texas, the northern extension of the state of Coahuila y Texas), but an attempt by Minister Lorenzo Zavala (later, vice president of the Republic of Texas) to introduce an income tax was defeated, sharpening the fiscal crisis that would bring down the government. Guerrero and the Yorkists were soon pressured into requesting the recall of his friend, U.S. minister Poinsett, for meddling in Mexico's internal politics. (Poinsett had failed to acquire Texas.)

In the summer of 1829, Ferdinand VII of Spain ordered an expeditionary force against Tampico. Guerrero's forces defeated Gen. Isidro Barradas's Spaniards, but the effort, combined in 1829 with a *yorkino*-sponsored nationwide expulsion of Spaniards, exhausted the treasury. As a result, the government was toppled in December 1829 by its own unpaid reserve army, which marched toward Mexico City from Jalapa under Vice President Anastasio Bustamante.

Guerrero fled south, initiating a guerrilla war in which hundreds of his compatriots were killed. The rebel leader, kidnapped while dining (by his host, a Genoan ship captain), was sold to his enemies at Huatulco. The former president received a summary court-martial in Oaxaca and was executed at Chilapa on 14 February 1831. Guerrero's populist identification with Mexico's impoverished former *castas* had presented a threat to the *criollo*-Spanish elite, and he symbolized to the wealthy the dangers of unrestricted democracy and jacobinism. This fear remained alive in later nineteenth-century Mexico, hindering efforts to consolidate democracy and stability prior to the war with the United States.

Harold Dana Sims

BIBLIOGRAPHY

Lafragua, J. N. In *Hombres ilustres mexicanos,* edited by Eduardo L. Gallo. Vol. 4. [1873–1874].

Magaña Esquivel, Antonio. *Vicente Guerrero.* 1946.

Sims, Harold Dana. *The Expulsion of Mexico's Spaniards, 1821–1836.* 1990.

Sprague, William R. *Vicente Guerrero, Mexican Liberator.* 1939.

Guerrillas

The role of guerrilla resistance during the U.S.–Mexican War has received little attention. It is clear, however, that by late 1847 and early 1848, as Mexico's regular army sustained defeat after defeat at the hands of the well-equipped U.S. forces, Mexicans were divided over the issue of continued resistance. Added to the usual domestic, social, and political cleavages were rancorous disputes over whether to negotiate a treaty with the occupying U.S. forces or to continue hostilities by means of irregular insurgent warfare.

On the one hand were despondent and disillusioned patriots who believed that to continue hostilities was madness and would result only in the loss of more, if not all, of the

Mexican guerrillas. John Frost, *Pictorial History of Mexico and the Mexican War,* 1862

nation's remaining territory. Full of self-recrimination, some wondered how they could ever have fancied that Mexico might emerge victorious. Included in this group were both conservatives, such as José Fernando Ramírez and Luis Cuevas, and moderate liberals, such as José Joaquín de Herrera and Manuel de la Peña y Peña. Having placed their hope in the regular army, they saw no recourse for the nation but to resign itself to defeat and to obtain whatever advantages were possible from a peace treaty.

Conversely, many leaders began to call for a reorganized resistance using classic guerrilla tactics. Zealous patriots such as Mariano Otero, Carlos María de Bustamante, Manuel Crescencio Rejón, and Melchor Ocampo, advocated resistance to the U.S. forces. Mexico, according to these militant intellectuals, struggled not for honor, territory, or riches, but for its very existence as an independent nation. "The issue of Texas," *La Voz del Pueblo* had written before the outbreak of hostilities, "is the issue of our independence, of our nationality, of the honour of our motherland." They believed that it was imperative that they reconstitute and channel the nation's energies into guerrilla forces to resist the foreign occupiers. Outside of the Department of Mexico this was a popular and well-received suggestion as early as April 1847. Indeed, following Gen. Winfield Scott's landing and capture of Vera Cruz, hastily organized bands of insurgents soon set about harassing the entrenched invasion force using classic hit-and-run tactics. Throughout the summer of 1847, as General Scott moved his army inland to surround the capital, guerrilla patriots successfully harassed the U.S. supply lines between Mexico City and Vera Cruz. "It is well known," wrote Carlos María Bustamante in September, "that it is our guerrillas who have truly opposed and tenaciously resisted the enemy, attacking and diminishing his forces and cutting his supply convoys."

Following the fall of Mexico City, many continued to urge resistance and denounced peace negotiations. "Let us make war, then," wrote Melchor Ocampo, "but in the only fashion that is possible for us. Let us organize a system of guerrillas . . . " Official circulars from late 1847 suggest that state governors throughout the country had, in fact, begun to organize, equip, and recruit volunteers for such forces. By early 1848, however, the treaty protagonists dominated both the central executive and what remained of the main army. The enthusiasm of the militants turned dour when within a few months, defeatist elements negotiated the substance of the Treaty of Guadalupe Hidalgo. The provisional congress quickly approved the document by a narrow margin. By September 1848 the withdrawal of all U.S. forces was complete and the national government had returned to the capital.

M. Bruce Colcleugh

BIBLIOGRAPHY

Smith, Justin H. *The War with Mexico.* 2 vols. 1919. Reprint, 1963.

Spurlin, Charles. "Ranger Walker in the Mexican War." *Military History of Texas and the Southwest* 9 (1971): 259–279.

Guizot, François

French historian and statesman François-Pierre-Guillaume Guizot (1787–1874) led the French government and guided foreign affairs from October 1840 until the overthrow of King Louis Philippe's July Monarchy in February 1848. A Protestant with an intellectual and reserved manner, Guizot became identified with the regime's plodding centrism (the *juste milieu*).

In foreign policy, Guizot's philosophical opposition to adventurism appealed to Louis Philippe. The king was displeased with aggressive predecessors such as Guizot's archrival, Adolphe Thiers, who had precipitated a war scare with Great Britain over Mideast affairs in 1840. Guizot thus pursued an entente cordiale with the like-minded British foreign secretary, the Tory Lord Aberdeen (George Hamilton-Gordon), and avoided potential conflicts. Led by Thiers, Guizot's opponents relentlessly attacked his inaction and presumed subservience to British policy, although the entente between France and Great Britain was often far less cordial than it appeared.

While genuinely concerned about U.S. expansion and Mexico's possible dismemberment, Guizot deemed friendly relations with the United States too important, French interests in North America too slight, and Mexico too unstable an ally to lend anything but verbal support to Lord Aberdeen's more strenuous efforts to forestall U.S. penetration into Texas and California. As sensible as this caution was (compared with earlier and later interventions in the region), Guizot's evasions earned him mistrust both in Great Britain and the United States. His failure to curb insolent and outspoken agents such as Alphonse Dubois de Saligny in Texas and Alleye de Cyprey in Mexico made France despised in places where it might have exerted some influence.

James R. Munson

BIBLIOGRAPHY

Barker, Nancy N. *The French Experience in Mexico, 1821–1861: A History of Constant Misunderstanding.* 1979.

Johnson, Douglas. *Guizot: Aspects of French History, 1787–1874.* 1963.

Pletcher, David M. *The Diplomacy of Annexation: Texas, Oregon, and the Mexican War.* 1973.

Hacienda de Encarnación

See Encarnación, Hacienda de

Hamer, Thomas L.

U.S. brigadier general Thomas Lyon Hamer (1800–1846) was born in Northumberland County, Pennsylvania, and moved with his family to Ohio in 1817. Hamer taught school, became a lawyer, and in 1825 was elected to the first of three terms in the Ohio legislature. He later served three terms (1832–1838) as a Democrat in the U.S. House of Representatives. Soon after the U.S. declaration of war on Mexico, Hamer joined an Ohio volunteer company as a private. On 1 July 1846, President James K. Polk appointed him one of six newly authorized brigadier generals of volunteers. All were loyal Democrats.

Although organized too late to participate in the battles at Palo Alto and Resaca de la Palma, General Hamer and the Ohio volunteers played a large part in the Battle of Monterrey. While Brig. Gen. William J. Worth's division of regulars attempted to envelop the city from the west, Hamer's brigade was part of a force that attacked the eastern end of the heavily fortified city on 21 September 1846. When defending Mexican major general Pedro de Ampudia decided to ask Maj. Gen. Zachary Taylor for surrender terms on 24 September, General Hamer accepted the request and forwarded it on to Taylor.

After the Battle of Monterrey, Hamer was kept busy with routine garrison duties there. Ohio voters once again elected him to Congress, but his health failed suddenly; he died of disease on 2 December 1846. The army was stunned by the death of this popular general. General Taylor mourned the loss of what he considered the "balance wheel" of his vol-

unteers, and 2d Lt. Ulysses S. Grant, who owed his West Point appointment to Representative Hamer, stated that the country had been denied a future president.

James M. McCaffrey

BIBLIOGRAPHY

Giddings, Luther. *Sketches of the Campaign in Northern Mexico by an Officer of the First Regiment of Ohio Volunteers.* 1853.

Michael, Steven Bruce. "Ohio and the Mexican War: Public Response to the 1846–1848 Crisis." Ph.D. diss., Ohio State University, 1985.

Winders, Richard Bruce. *Mr. Polk's Army: The American Military Experience in the Mexican War.* 1997.

Hamilton-Gordon, George

British statesman and politician George Hamilton-Gordon (1784–1860), fourth Earl of Aberdeen, was foreign secretary from 1841 to 1846. Aberdeen led an attempt by Great Britain to maintain Texan independence through a mediated peace settlement with Mexico. He tried to make abolition of slavery in Texas the basis for negotiations in 1843, then abandoned this policy when the U.S. administration of President John Tyler began to agitate for annexation.

Aberdeen was the architect of an ambitious plan in 1844 to place an Anglo-French guarantee on both Texan independence and the Texas-Mexico boundary. His plan was designed in part to facilitate British diplomatic cooperation with France and to promote political stability in the region by establishing Texan independence on a permanent basis before the United States made tangible steps toward annexation. France favored the plan initially, but abandoned a material commitment to Texan independence in 1845 when it became apparent that cooperation with the British risked jeopardizing friendly relations with the United States. Aberdeen continued to press for a mediated peace settlement, with partial success; European agents secured Mexico's recognition of Texan independence, but only after the United States had offered Texas the option of annexation in 1845–1846. Aberdeen was never willing to resist Texan annexation to the point of war (although no British action short of war could have prevented it), yet he viewed U.S. policy as aggressive. Thus, he would not allow use of Great Britain's "good offices" in reconciling the differences between the United States and Mexico, so as not to give formal approval for annexation. Aberdeen maintained a policy of strict neutrality also to ease ongoing negotiations with the United States over the Oregon boundary. War broke out between the United States and Mexico shortly before Great Britain reached a settlement with the United States over the Oregon boundary and Aberdeen offered mediation informally as a measure of this neutrality. Aberdeen left the foreign office in June 1846 and was succeeded by Lord Palmerston.

Lelia M. Roeckell

BIBLIOGRAPHY

Chamberlain, Muriel. *Lord Aberdeen: A Political Biography.* 1983.

Jones, Wilbur Devereux. *Lord Aberdeen and the Americas.* 1958.

Hannegan, Edward A.

Edward A. Hannegan (1807–1859), an Indiana Democrat, served in the U.S. Senate from 1843 to 1849. Born in Ohio and raised in Kentucky, Hannegan moved to Indiana where he practiced law, won a seat in the state legislature, and then in 1832 was elected to Congress as an ardent Jacksonian. Like many Democrats from the Old Northwest, Hannegan was nationalistic, Anglophobic, and belligerent. He urged the annexation of Texas; the acquisition of all Oregon ("Fifty-four Forty or Fight!"); and a punitive war against Mexico to obtain indemnity and territory. Hoping to exclude Great Britain from the Pacific Coast of the continent, Hannegan told the Senate in 1844 that he "would take the hazards of a war which should end only in the destruction of the one or the other" rather than divide Oregon at 49° north latitude. Although outraged by the compromise with Great Britain on the Oregon boundary, he defended President James K. Polk's policy toward Mexico, absolving him of blame for the war. Hannegan advised that his nation seize and hold the borderlands, perhaps even take control of all Mexico. But he wanted its land and ports, not its population. "Mexico and the United States are peopled by two distinct and utterly unhomogeneous races," he declared in 1847. "In no reasonable period could we amalgamate. . . . [T]hey are utterly unfit for the blessings and restraints of rational liberty." Typical of most expansionists, Hannegan frequently disparaged the British, Mexicans, Natives, and African

Americans. The Indiana legislature did not elect Hannegan to a second term in the Senate. But Polk showed his gratitude by appointing him envoy to Prussia. Hannegan's long struggle with alcohol and the Whigs' triumph in the election of 1848 led to his recall from Berlin in 1850. He then settled in St. Louis and pursued his extensive business interests until his death in 1859.

Thomas Hietala

BIBLIOGRAPHY

Congressional Globe, 28th Cong., 1st sess., 1844, Appendix 243–45; 29th Cong., 2d sess., 1847, vol. 16, 515–17; 30th Cong., 1st sess., 1848, vol. 17, 231–233.

Harney, William S.

Col. William S. Harney (1800–1889), U.S. 2d Dragoons, was born at Haysborough, Davidson County, Tennessee, on 2 August, a son of Margaret Hudson and Thomas Harney. On 13 February 1818, he received a commission as second lieutenant in the 1st Infantry. He served on the staff of Andrew Jackson during his governorship of Florida and participated in the Black Hawk War in 1832. On 15 August 1836, Harney was promoted to lieutenant colonel of the 2d Dragoons and fought with that unit during the Second Seminole War, 1835 to 1842.

Harney received the rank of colonel on 30 June 1846 at San Antonio, and he led an unauthorized expedition to Presidio del Río Grande to open the U.S.-Mexican War. Gen. John E. Wool forced Harney to return under arrest but released him. Gen. Winfield Scott, however, used this episode to remove Harney from command of the cavalry on the eve of the Vera Cruz campaign. President James K. Polk viewed this as an improper attempt by Scott, a Whig, to demote a Democratic officer. After a formal inquiry, Harney apologized to Scott, who received a reprimand from the Polk administration. Colonel Harney returned to his command and participated in the Mexico City campaign, leading a successful charge up El Telégrafo at Cerro Gordo on 18 April 1847, which earned him a commendation as brevet brigadier general, and fighting at Contreras on 19 to 20 August and Churubusco on 20 August. On 13 September 1847, Harney presided over the execution of thirty deserters of the San Patricio Battalion.

After the war, Harney served in various departments in the western United States. He commanded federal forces during the Kansas crisis of 1857 and 1858, attaining the rank of brigadier general on 14 June 1858. Harney retired 1 August 1863 after being removed from command because of suspected Southern loyalties. He died at Orlando, Florida, 27 November 1889.

Jimmy L. Bryan, Jr.

BIBLIOGRAPHY

Adams, George Rollie. "General William Selby Harney: Frontier Soldier, 1800–1889." Ph.D. diss., University of Arizona, 1983.

Reavis, L. U. *The Life and Military Services of General William Selby Harney.* 1878.

Hawkins, Charles E.

U.S., Mexican, and Texan naval officer Charles Edward Hawkins (1802–1837) was a native of Kingston, New York. Hawkins joined the U.S. Navy in 1818, serving on board the *Guerriere, Washington,* and the *Constellation.* Hawkins's service included a tour in the Mediterranean and in 1825 a transfer to the newly formed West India Squadron under the command of able, yet controversial, Capt. David Porter. When in 1826 Porter resigned his commission to become the ranking officer in the newly formed Mexican navy, Hawkins and a handful of other officers joined him. As commander of the Mexican schooner *Hermon,* Hawkins harassed Spanish shipping, often using Key West as a base for his operations against Cuba. Though effective, Hawkins resigned his commission in the Mexican navy and worked for a time on the Chattahoochee River as a steamboat captain. In 1835 while in New Orleans, Hawkins became involved with José Antonio Mexía, a disaffected Mexican general who was plotting a filibustering expedition to Tampico for a triumphal return to Mexico. The expedition failed miserably, but Hawkins escaped to Texas and immediately volunteered his services for the Texian cause. Given command of the newly commissioned *Independence* and appointed first commodore of the Texas navy, Hawkins helped sustain the Texas cause against Mexico by transporting troops and supplies and by disrupting commercial relations between Mexico and the United States. Thus Hawkins was a major irritant to Mexican–U.S. relations. He was still in command of the Texas navy when he died of smallpox in New Orleans on 12 February 1837.

James M. Denham

BIBLIOGRAPHY

Denham, James M. "Charles E. Hawkins: Sailor of Three Republics." *Gulf Coast Historical Review* 5 (Spring 1990): 92–103.

Denham, James M. "New Orleans, Maritime Commerce, and the Texas War for Independence, 1836." *Southwestern Historical Quarterly* 97 (January 1994): 511–538.

Hays, John C.

Texas Ranger John Coffee (Jack) Hays (1817–1883) was born 28 January in Wilson County, Tennessee. He moved to Mississippi in 1832 and to Texas in 1836, although too late to participate in the Texas Revolution. Assigned to the Texas Rangers with the help of his father's friend, Sam Houston, Hays earned a reputation as an outstanding military leader in skirmishes with Comanches, Mexicans, and bandits. In 1840 Texas president Mirabeau B. Lamar promoted Hays to captain. Hays and Samuel H. Walker are credited with introducing the Colt revolver to the Western frontier.

In 1842 Hays led the Texian resistance to the raids on San Antonio by Mexican generals Rafael Vásquez and Adrian Woll. Promoted to major in 1842, he commanded the Ranger detachment that accompanied the ill-fated Mier Expedition, but he and his company left before the Texian force surrendered in December.

On the outbreak of the U.S.–Mexican War, Hays recruited a force of mounted volunteers, which was mustered into Gen. Zachary Taylor's army at Fort Brown on 24 May 1846 as the 1st Regiment of Mounted Volunteers. His unit served as scouts and guards during Taylor's advance into northern Mexico and played a decisive role, as part of Gen. William J. Worth's division, in the capture of Monterrey in September. Hays's unit spearheaded Worth's interdiction of the Saltillo Road and was instrumental in the capture of Federation Hill, Independence Hill, and the Bishop's Palace. Although both Taylor and Worth praised Hays's unit, Taylor was relieved to see them leave in mid-October as they reportedly committed several atrocities against civilians in Monterrey.

While in Texas in 1847, Hays married Susan Calvert of Seguin in April, but by July he had recruited another mounted force, which President James K. Polk assigned to disperse the guerrilla bands that were threatening to sever Gen. Winfield Scott's line of communication between Vera Cruz and Mexico City. Hays's four-hundred-man unit landed at Vera Cruz on 17 October and was assigned to Brig. Gen. Joseph Lane's brigade, which proceeded toward Jalapa and Puebla. On 23 and 24 November Hays and his men distinguished themselves in a battle at Izúcar de Matamoras near Puebla, and at Galaxara, against a force led by Brig. Gen. Joaquín Rea.

On 6 December Hays and his regiment entered Mexico City. As was the case in Monterrey, Hays's men were accused of atrocities against civilians, and Scott on 10 January 1848 ordered him to leave the city in search of a band of partisans led by Padre Cenobia Jarauta. Hays and his regiment engaged Jarauta's *guerrilleros* at Zacualtipán on 25 February 1848, reported killing 150 of the estimated 450 *rancheros* in what was said to be the last military engagement of the U.S.–Mexican War. Hays and his unit were mustered out of service in Vera Cruz on 30 April.

After the discovery of gold in California, Hays led a group of Texans to the West Coast, where he served as sheriff of San Francisco County. In 1853 he was appointed surveyor general of California by President Franklin Pierce. He died near Piedmont, California, on 25 April 1883.

Thomas W. Cutrer

BIBLIOGRAPHY

Brackett, Albert G. *General Lane's Brigade in Central Mexico.* 1854.

Ford, John Salmon. *Rip Ford's Texas,* edited by Stephen B. Oates. 1963.

Greer, James Kimmins. *Colonel Jack Hays: Texas Frontier Leader and California Builder.* 1952. Rev. ed., 1987.

Reid, Samuel C. *Scouting Expedition of McCulloch's Texas Rangers.* Reprint, 1970.

Webb, Walter Prescott. *The Texas Rangers: A Century of Frontier Defense.* 1935.

Health and Medicine

As U.S. troops and civilians traveled west in the 1840s, they brought with them many of the illnesses and unhealthy conditions that plagued them in the eastern cities. The average life expectancy for both sexes was only forty years, with as many as 20 percent of infants and mothers dying at childbirth from puerperal fever and infection. New immigrants and Native Americans were particularly devastated by epidemics due to their lack of acquired immunity. One out of every ten U.S. soldiers died while in Mexico, with the volunteer troops suffering the greatest share of loss. It is estimated that close to eleven thousand men died from infectious disease whereas approximately fifteen hundred officers and men died from wounds sustained in battle. Among the survivors, ten thousand men were discharged home on surgeon certificates, many of whom died later from their illnesses.

The rugged terrain of the western United States, Texas, and Mexico caused many physical hardships for inexperienced troops or unprepared travelers. These were intensified by extremes in temperature, limited water supplies, isolation, unavailability of fresh food, and overcrowding. The coastal areas of Mexico were extremely unhealthy in the late summer and early fall when the mosquito-borne fevers of malaria (ague), dengue, and yellow fever (black vomit) reached a peak. It was thought that "bad vapors," or miasmas, from decaying vegetable matter were responsible, and some efforts were made to camp in well-ventilated areas away from the swamps. The mosquito's role in yellow fever was just being considered as the war came to a close. It was fear of yellow fever and malaria in the coastal lowlands of Mexico during the "sickly season" that prompted Gen. Winfield Scott to send his volunteer troops home early before he continued onward to Mexico City.

Cholera and typhoid fever were contracted from polluted water supplies and resulted in death from severe diarrhea

An unidentified naval surgeon. Daguerreotype, c. 1846. From the collection of William J. Schultz, M.D.

and dehydration. Cholera in particular was dreaded for its agonizing death and for a series of epidemics in the United States, starting in the 1830s and peaking around the time of the U.S.–Mexican War. A typhoid epidemic in Puebla after the fall of Mexico City contributed to the four thousand sick out of the fifteen thousand troops awaiting departure from Mexico via Vera Cruz. Typhus fever spread by body lice appeared on board overcrowded ships and in prisons, but like many fevers with a similar course and symptoms, it was often misdiagnosed or confused with typhoid fever or other diseases. Measles and mumps were extremely virulent and spread rapidly among confined populations of soldiers in camp. In the adult, the measles virus attacked the respiratory system and was often fatal. Smallpox, another viral illness, was most common among the immigrant population and the volunteer troops who, unlike soldiers in the regular U.S. Army, were not vaccinated. Venereal disease struck hardest in Saltillo and Mexico City but generally followed the army, with reports of some volunteer troops bringing it into Mexico and others acquiring it during the occupation. Tuberculosis was also spread by living in close quarters and would linger on to cause years of debilitation back home. In distant outposts and settlements, such as New Mexico, where fresh fruit and vegetables were unavailable, outbreaks of scurvy would appear from vitamin C deficiency; in areas plentiful in produce, such as inland from Vera Cruz, many soldiers

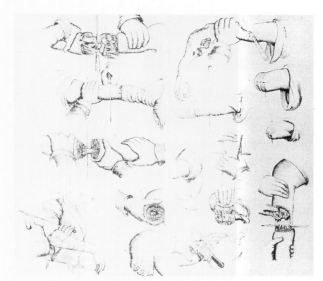

Flap and circular amputations. An illustration from a surgical manual of the era demonstrates amputation procedures (Richard Upton Piper, *Operative Surgery*, 1852).

contracted dysentery from poor food handling and lack of hygiene. Diarrhea and dysentery were critical problems throughout Mexico but were most incapacitating and fatal in Puebla, where they affected some two thousand troops. Apart from infectious disease, alcohol abuse in the military was a major health problem that was impossible to curb, despite severe punishments and the positive effects of temperance societies.

Treatment for most diseases was nonspecific and directed at symptoms of an illness, since the underlying cause was often not known. The pharmacy of active drugs was limited, and their use varied from case to case. Quinine sulfate extracted from cinchona bark was used in malaria as well as nonmalarial fevers. Opiates were used to relieve pain and, in the form of laudanum, used to treat diarrhea and dysentery. Calomel, a mercurial, was used as a purgative and emetic. Venereal disease was treated with both internal and external use of mercurial, which also poisoned many of the afflicted. Venesection, or bleeding, was still common practice, though its use was starting to wane during the time of the war. In cases of serious illness, such as cholera and smallpox epidemics, a combination of treatments called "heroic therapy" would be used, which included bloodletting, emetics and purgatives, blistering of the skin, and a starvation diet. In many cases these drastic measures actually hastened the patient's death.

Medical training in the 1840s was far from standardized. As frustration with mainstream allopathic medicine grew, competing disciplines sprung up, such as Thomsonianism and naturopathy, each with its own schools. Few states had

any licensing requirements, and the majority of practicing physicians never graduated from medical school. Because of the great variability in training and competence of physicians, and in order to prevent political patronage in selection, the U.S. Army Medical Department required all new physician applicants to appear before an examining board after 1839. Over half of the applicants were found unqualified or morally unfit and would be taken off the eligibility roll if they failed reexamination in two years. Beside their role in caring for the sick, the army surgeons also were required to keep a daily journal at their post, recording the temperature, climate, and environmental features that could affect the troops; thus in many ways they acted as naturalists in recording the local flora and fauna. Before the U.S.–Mexican War, there were 71 physicians in the regular army caring for approximately 7,500 soldiers. The war would see an increase in the regular army to approximately 30,000, along with around 64,000 volunteers. A legislative act in February 1847 allowed for an increase in regular army medical staff to 115 and 135 for volunteers; however, not all of these positions would be filled. It also granted military rank to medical officers. Though the volunteer forces had to supply physicians to their troops, these physicians did not have to pass a qualifying exam and were on the whole inferior to the medical staff of the regular army. Their general lack of competence was seen in the large number of physically unfit volunteers enlisted after a cursory medical exam and the disproportionate number of volunteers who succumbed to disease.

During the war, the Medical Department was headed by Surgeon General Thomas Lawson, who held the rank of colonel until later breveted brigadier general. Lawson was often criticized for being outspoken, yet he was farsighted enough to advocate for an ambulance service, the training of designated hospital stewards, and the use of hospital ships. Though unsuccessful in realizing these dreams, he was able to have his officers granted military rank, which strengthened their status and authority. The hospital staff of hospital stewards, nurses, cooks, and wardmaster were by regulation drawn from the ranks and rarely had any prior medical training. Many of the attendants were convalescing patients or were in some way deemed unfit for combat service. Hospitals in occupied Mexico could be any local building appropriated for that purpose and were many times ill-lit with poor ventilation and dirt floors. A preferred site was in a church or convent, where care was often aided by the nuns.

Surgical treatment of battle injuries was complicated by a general disregard for sanitary conditions. Overwhelmed by the continuous carnage, the surgeons could rarely stop to clean their instruments between patients. Amputations taking a couple of minutes were performed as a last resort on crushed or torn extremities, using either a circular cut or flap technique. Operative speed was the surgeon's gift to his patients. Anesthetics, specifically sulfuric ether, were briefly tried in Vera Cruz, but surprisingly, they were met with opposition for being too dangerous. Surgeon John Porter blamed anesthetics for poisoning the blood and delaying the healing process. Along with amputations, other procedures included removing gunshot and shrapnel, repair of lacerations, and on occasion trephining, a process whereby a hole was bored into the skull to relieve intracranial pressure from bleeding. Even if the surgery was successful, thousands died from the complications of infection, including "hospital gangrene," sepsis, and crysipelas.

The time of the U.S.–Mexican War saw little progress in medical care, as centuries-old dogma was just beginning to be challenged with scientific reasoning and observation. During the war, several medical advances were tried in the field, such as the use of anesthetics and the refinement of some surgical techniques. These, however, saw limited use and would not be further developed until the Civil War. Overall, the Medical Department was ill-prepared to handle the massed numbers of casualties resulting from major military engagements.

William J. Schultz, M.D.

BIBLIOGRAPHY

Gillett, Mary C. *The Army Medical Department, 1818–1865.* 1987.

Rothstein, William G. *American Medical Schools and the Practice of Medicine: A History.* 1987.

Winders, Richard Bruce. *Mr. Polk's Army: The American Military Experience in the Mexican War.* 1997.

Henderson, James P.

James Pinckney Henderson (1808–1858), secretary of state of the Republic of Texas and architect of annexation, was born in Lincolnton, North Carolina. Educated at the University of North Carolina, he was licensed as an attorney in 1829. He practiced briefly in Mississippi and then recruited a company of volunteers to fight in the Texas Revolution. Although they arrived in May 1836 after hostilities had ceased, Henderson decided to remain and seek his fortune. He settled first in San Augustine, then moved to San Antonio in 1840.

Henderson served for a short time as attorney general in Texas president Sam Houston's first cabinet and then, upon the death of Stephen F. Austin, as secretary of state. In 1844 he was sent to Washington, D.C., to work for annexation. Following rejection of one proposal, Henderson devised the strategy of a joint resolution to effect the same end. His fellow Texans, grateful for their admission to the Union, elected Henderson the first governor of the state in 1846.

Shortly after his election, Henderson resigned to lead

Texas volunteers in the war against Mexico. Cited for bravery, he returned from the battlefield and finished his term. In 1857 the Texas legislature appointed him to the U.S. Senate to succeed Thomas J. Rusk. Poor health dogged him from the inception of his term, and he died in Washington, D.C., in 1859.

Stanley E. Siegel

BIBLIOGRAPHY

Schmitz, Joseph W. *Texan Statecraft: 1836–1845.* 1941.

Smith, Justin H. *The Annexation of Texas.* 1911. Reprint, 1971.

Henrie, Daniel Drake

After serving as a midshipman in the U.S. Navy, Ohio native Daniel Drake Henrie (18??–18??) moved to Texas to fight in the revolution. In 1842 he enlisted in the Somervell Expedition, which had been authorized by Texas president Sam Houston to invade Mexico, and following the breakup of the campaign he joined the Mier Expedition under the command of William Fisher. After the battle of Mier he was imprisoned in Mexico. In July 1843 Henrie escaped with expedition second-in-command Thomas Jefferson Green and several others from Perote Castle and returned to Texas.

Daniel Drake Henrie. John Frost, *Pictorial History of Mexico and the Mexican War,* 1862

During the U.S.–Mexican War, owing to his fluency in Spanish and knowledge of the terrain, he served as a scout for Gen. John E. Wool's division. Captured at Encarnación, he feared he would be shot when Mexican authorities learned of his role in the Mier Expedition and escape from Perote. Borrowing a particularly fleet horse from a fellow prisoner, he succeeded in making yet another daring escape. This widely publicized exploit made him one of the most renowned regular soldiers of the war.

Sam W. Haynes

BIBLIOGRAPHY

Green, Thomas Jefferson. *Journal of the Texian Expedition Against Mier.* Edited by Sam W. Haynes. 1993.

Johanssen, Robert W. *To the Halls of the Montezumas: The Mexican War in the American Imagination.* 1985.

Herrera, José Joaquín de

Mexican general and president José Joaquín de Herrera (1792–1854) was born in Jalapa. Little is known about Herrera's early life other than that he began his military career while very young. By 1811 he was a captain in the Spanish army. After participating in numerous campaigns as a Mexican insurgent during the Wars of Independence, he was promoted to lieutenant colonel in 1820 and shortly thereafter retired from the military. He came out of retirement after Agustín de Iturbide proclaimed the Plan de Iguala, was reinstated in his previous rank, and quickly rose to the rank of brigadier general. In 1824 Herrera participated in the overthrow of Iturbide. Between 1832 and 1834 he served as minister of war between the presidencies of Manuel Gómez Pedraza and Antonio López de Santa Anna.

For the next ten years, Herrera served in various positions and, in 1844, after Santa Anna had been overthrown and exiled, Herrera was elected interim president of Mexico. Although he tended to play both ends of the centralist-federalist split, his administration was marked by the continual struggle for control of the national government by both sides. During his administration the United States annexed Texas, placing Herrera in a difficult position in Mexico. When he sought to negotiate with the United States, riots broke out, for the majority of the people favored war. Using Herrera's diplomacy as an excuse, Gen. Mariano Paredes y Arrillaga pronounced against him and took over the government. Paredes y Arrillaga's administration lasted for a year, during which time he took a hard stance against the U.S. annexation of Texas. Frustrated by Paredes y Arrillaga's inability to stop the United States from occupying Texas with a large military force, conservative forces overthrew him. Offering strong military leadership as war against the United States was declared by the Mexican national congress, General Santa Anna was brought back as president. After losing the war with the United States, Mexicans bitterly resented the conditions of the Treaty of Guadalupe Hidalgo.

Disillusioned and exhausted by war and years of revolutions, the Mexican people, seeing their country in shambles, looked to General Herrera to restore order. Elected as president by the national congress, Herrera at first refused to serve but soon realized the perilous situation of the country. To begin with, Mexico had no money to run the government. The only funds available were the $15 million the United States had given in payment for nearly half of Mexico's territory, which was taken in the war. Herrera also had to deal with a major rebellion, known as the Caste War, in Yucatán and other uprisings in Xichú in Guanajuato, Vera Cruz, Misantla, and Huasteca.

Meanwhile, in 1850, the first peaceful transfer of power since independence took place as Herrera handed over the government to Mariano Arista, the duly elected president of Mexico. Arista's administration continued many of Herrera's policies, particularly reducing the annual budget of the Mexican army from ten million pesos to three million; negotiating an agreement with British bondholders by agreeing to mortgage three quarters of Mexico's customs duties in order to pay off debts owed them; and consolidating the national debt by using the money paid Mexico by the United States. But Mexico's problems were too great to be overcome by the administrative plan established by Herrera and carried out by Arista. Herrera died at Tacubaya 10 February 1854.

Joseph P. Sánchez

BIBLIOGRAPHY

DePalo, William A., Jr. *The Mexican National Army, 1822–1852.* 1997.

Santoni, Pedro. *Mexicans at Arms: Puro Federalists and the Politics of War, 1845–1848.* 1996.

Historiography

The literature on the causes, conduct, and consequences of the U.S.–Mexican War is extensive. Many primary sources, however, are currently out of print, giving the impression the war was not well documented. Finding aids can help historians locate scarce material. Norman E. Tutorow's *The Mexican-American War: An Annotated Bibliography* (1981) has been a great asset to researchers. Several institutions with large holdings on the subject, the University of Texas at Arlington and the United States Military Research Center to name two, have published guides to their collections. Many modern scholars, spurred on by new attention on U.S. and Latin American history and the 150th anniversary of the U.S.–Mexican War, have chosen to concentrate on this once neglected field. New works on the war lately have appeared with regularity, adding to an already rich historiography.

Participants produced the first accounts, as soldiers' journals and letters became the basis of initial publications about the war. William Seaton Henry, a captain in the 3d U.S. Infantry, was one of the first to publish his wartime experiences in a volume entitled *Campaign Sketches of the War with Mexico* (1847). Many regular officers followed Henry's lead and published their own accounts. One important work of note by George Ballentine, *Autobiography of An English Soldier in the United States Army* (1853), is valuable because it described the experiences of an enlisted man in the regular army. Numerous volunteers told the war from the citizen-soldier's point of view. Some of the better-known volunteer accounts include George C. Furber's *The Twelve Months Volunteer* (1848), Luther Giddings' *Sketches of a Campaign in Northern Mexico, in 1846, and 1847* (1853), John Reese Kenly's *Memoirs of a Maryland Volunteer* (1873), and J. Jacob Oswandel's *Notes of the Mexican War, 1846–47–48* (1885). While diaries and memoirs tend to be narrowly focused, describing the daily experiences which the author witnessed, they are extremely valuable for the detail they provide.

General histories of the war appeared shortly after its conclusion. Many came from the pens of men who had already made a career of publishing history, such as Edward D. Mansfield, John Frost, and John S. Jenkins. Others, like Nathaniel C. Brooks, produced histories after being moved by the events of their day. Roswell S. Ripley's *The War with Mexico* (1849) stood out because it was written by an officer of the regular army who had participated in the Mexican campaigns. Although a serious analysis of the war, critics have largely ignored the two-volume work, categorizing it as a partisan attempt to boost the career of Maj. Gen. Gideon Pillow. Most of these early histories of the war generally present either Gen. Winfield Scott or Gen. Zachary Taylor as the hero of the conflict, depending on the author's bias.

A strong antiwar sentiment exists in literature dating back to the period of the war. The American Peace Society, celebrating its eighteenth year in 1846, sponsored a contest for the best analysis of the war based on Christian principles and enlightened statesmanship. The $500 prize went to a Unitarian minister, Abiel Abbot Livermore, for a work entitled *The War with Mexico Reviewed* (1850). Livermore contended that a spirit of militarism existed in the United States that gave force to the drive for more land. Furthermore, ardent republicans (eager to chastise perceived despots), and slave owners (eager to spread the institution), had worked together to create the pretext for war. William Jay, another contestant whose entry gained wide acceptance, also blamed the war on the Slave Power and their alleged agent, President James K. Polk, in *A Review of the Causes and Consequences of the Mexican War* (1849). Both Livermore and Jay were expounding on a well-established theme that was also used to explain the revolt in Texas and to block annexation.

Many of New England's intellectual elites expressed their opposition to the war in their writings. Ralph Waldo Emerson viewed the fall of Mexico to the United States as inevitable but deplored war as the means. Poets John Greenleaf Whittier and James Russell Lowell published antiwar works. Lowell's *Biglow Papers* (1847) used sarcasm to make the point that the war was immoral. The most famous antiwar piece of the period, *On Civil Disobedience* (1849) by Henry David Thoreau, was written after authorities jailed the author for refusing to pay a poll tax. Thoreau's contention that passive resistance or noncompliance was an effective tactic to oppose government action laid the cornerstone for future protest movements. Nevertheless, these antiwar authors have had a much greater effect on the modern peace movement than they did on events during their own day.

Books on the war continued to be written long after the last participant passed away. For many years Justin Smith's two-volume work, *The War with Mexico* (1919), reigned supreme. Smith spent twenty years writing his magnum opus, and even today scholars are amazed at the amount of research that went into this seminal work. Criticized for its jingoistic style, Smith's work still remains an important study. A lesser known but important work was John D. P. Fuller's *The Movement for the Acquisition of All of Mexico* (1936), which examined the unsuccessful drive to seize the entire country of Mexico as an indemnity for the war. The war's centennial caused renewed interest, resulting in a new round of general histories of the war. These include Alfred Hoyt Bill's *Rehearsal for Conflict* (1947) and Robert S. Henry's *The Story of the Mexican War* (1950). Both authors highlight the roles of young officers who later rose to prominence as Civil War commanders. The notion of the U.S.–Mexican War as a training ground for the Civil War remains a popular theme today.

The U.S. experience in Vietnam created interest in the U.S.–Mexican War for historians who saw similarities between events in Southeast Asia and Mexico. Many writers of this period used the war to make the point that the United States government was merely continuing imperialistic policies it had first demonstrated in its war against Mexico. However, several significant contributions appeared during that period that were free of polemics. One work, *Chronicles of the Gringos* (1969), was an extensive compilation of primary accounts of the war. K. Jack Bauer's *Surfboats and Horse Marines* (1969) remains a valuable study of naval operations of the war while his later work, *The Mexican War, 1846–1848* (1974), provided an excellent overview of the war. Another important study that appeared during this period was David M. Pletcher's *The Diplomacy of Annexation: Texas, Oregon, and the Mexican War* (1973), which examined the role of annexation as a cause of the war between the United States and Mexico.

Several significant works have appeared recently that prove interest in the war still exists and is even growing. Robert W. Johannsen's *To the Halls of the Montezumas* (1985) was a groundbreaking work that examined the war on an intellectual level, analyzing contemporary literature to determine how Americans living in the 1840s perceived their war. John S. D. Eisenhower's *So Far from God* (1989) provided students of the war with another general history. The current trend, however, seems to be moving away from general histories toward more specific areas of the war. Ernest McPherson Lander's *Reluctant Imperialists: Calhoun, the South Carolinians, and the Mexican War* (1980) not only chronicled the career of the Palmetto Regiment, but looked at Calhoun's opposition to the "All of Mexico Movement." The year 1985 marked the appearance of Robert A. May's *John A. Quitman: Old South Crusader* and K. Jack Bauer's *Zachary Taylor: Soldier, Planter, and Statesman of the Old South*, indicating a revival of biography as scholars began to reexamine the lives of Mexican War commanders. John S. D. Eisenhower's *Winfield Scott: Agent of Destiny* (1997) is the first of several new biographies that are currently in various stages of development. Scholars have continued to locate, edit, and publish soldiers' journals, letters, and diaries, as evidenced by Joseph E. Chance's *The Mexican War Journal of Captain Franklin Smith* (1991) and *Mexico Under Fire: The Diary of Samuel Ryan Curtis* (1994), and Robert Ryal Miller's *The Mexican War Journal and Letters of Ralph W. Kirkham* (1991) and *An Immigrant Soldier in the Mexican War* (1995).

The military has also come under recent scrutiny as scholars apply new research methods to this field. Robert Ryal Miller's *Shamrock and Sword: The Saint Patrick's Battalion in the U.S.–Mexican War* (1989) examined a well-known unit of the Mexican Army composed of deserters from the U.S. Army. James M. McCaffrey's *Army of Manifest Destiny: The American Soldier in the Mexican War, 1846–1848* (1992) was the first real published attempt to examine the U.S. Army in detail. Richard Bruce Winders analyzed the U.S. military during the war in *Mr. Polk's Army: The American Military Experience in the Mexican War* (1997), examining the effect of U.S. politics on the army. This trend, if continued, has the potential to dramatically increase our understanding of this period as authors examine the war in terms of cultural, societal, and gender history.

On the other hand, the war's traumatic impact on the national psyche, the partisan bias of Mexican historiography, and the chronic turmoil that afflicted the republic during its infancy have obscured Mexican interpretations of the events of 1845 to 1848. As a result, in the words of Josefina Zoraida Vázquez (in *Mexicanos y Norteamericanos ante la Guerra del 47*, 1977), Mexican historians have proven "in-

capable of assimilating the war of [18]47." Although Professor Vázquez's judgment remains largely true today, during the past twenty years a new generation of scholars has examined previously unexplored aspects of the war. Their efforts have added to the existing body of knowledge about the conflict and will surely lead to new interpretations of the war's meaning.

Shortly after the conclusion of hostilities, a number of Mexican authors tried to explain why the country had failed to respond to the challenge of national defense. The first publication of this type, probably authored by the rising *moderado* politician Mariano Otero, was entitled *Consideraciones sobre la situación política y social de la república mexicana en el año 1847* (1848). The essay analyzed the ills that afflicted Mexican society and concluded that Mexico's military fiasco in 1847 could only be attributed to the fact that the country had not achieved a sense of nationhood.

Three other contemporary accounts of the events of 1845–1848 also attempted to explain the military defeat. Fifteen men, many of whom figured prominently in Mexican public affairs during the second half of the nineteenth century, divided the labors of writing a survey of the war. Their work, *Apuntes para la historia de la guerra entre México y los Estados Unidos* (1848), edited and republished in 1850 by Albert C. Ramsey as *The Other Side: or Notes for the History of the War between Mexico and the United States* (reprint, 1970), indicted the U.S. as the aggressor and identified U.S. expansionism as a cause of the war. Conservative statesman Carlos María Bustamante authored *El nuevo Bernal Díaz del Castillo, o sea, historia de la invasión de los anglo-americanos en México* (1847). Bustamante wrote as an anguished patriot who was haunted by the political intrigues and armed coups that shook Mexico as U.S. troops pushed deeper into the national territory. He also blamed Gen. Antonio López de Santa Anna for his treachery and ineptness in losing the war. Finally, José Fernando Ramírez, a distinguished intellectual and devoted public servant from the state of Durango, wrote lengthy notes and numerous letters about politics in Mexico City during the war that were published posthumously as *Mexico during the War with the United States* (1905). He, too, believed that Mexico's disordered political factions were largely to blame for the country's failure to offer a more stubborn resistance to the foreign threat.

Several books, conceived at the time of the war, did not see publication until late in the nineteenth century. These works include Manual Balbontín's *Recuerdos de la invasión americana* (1883) and José María Roa Bárcena's three-volume work, *Recuerdos de la invasión norteamericana (1846–1848)* (1887). Balbontín, an artillery lieutenant during the war who had risen to the rank of colonel by the 1880s, made a number of judicious observations about the military errors that led to the debacle of 1847. Roa Bárcena's account provided a generally objective summary of the various military campaigns and frequently praised the Mexican troops. He emphasized that the conflict was caused by U.S. expansionism and that Mexico, once at war, was bound to lose because of the weaknesses of its social, political, and economic systems.

Few significant studies on the U.S.–Mexican War appeared during the period of the 1910 Mexican Revolution and its aftermath. In fact, between 1890 and 1947 only two works directly linked to the conflict were published in Mexico. But in the 1940s, coinciding with a conservative political resurgence in Mexico and a period of relative harmonious relations between the two countries, historians once again sought to interpret the meaning of the war. Eight books were published to commemorate the centennial of the conflict. Perhaps the two most noteworthy were Vicente Fuentes Díaz's *La intervención norteamericana en México* (1947) and José Valadés' *Breve historia de la guerra con los Estados Unidos* (1947). These works were notable for their objectivity and impartiality. Valadés', for example, praised Santa Anna for his intelligence and cunning and judged him undeserving of the charges of treason. Books written during the 1950s, such as Carlos Bosch García's *Historia de las relaciones entre México y los Estados Unidos, 1819–1848* (1961), continued this pattern.

But the turbulent 1960s and 1970s, which witnessed the outbreak of revolutions in Cuba and other Latin American nations, influenced the way in which some Mexican historians interpreted the conflict with the United States. Agustín Cue Canovás' *Los Estados Unidos y el México olvidado* (1971) and Gastón García Cantú's *Las invasiones norteamericanas en México* (1971) were openly critical of the United States. Other books, however, did not follow this trend and presented a more optimistic assessment. Both César Sepúlveda's *La frontera norte de México, historia, conflictos, 1762–1975* (1980), and the multi-author work *Historia general de México* (1976) pointed out the advantages gained by the Mexican diplomats who negotiated the Treaty of Guadalupe Hidalgo. Also worthy of note is Luis Zorrilla'a two-volume *Historia de las relaciones entre México y los Estados Unidos de América, 1800–1958* (1977), which reflected the view of a diplomatic historian interested in chronicling rather than interpreting the political process.

Historians have shed light on specific aspects of the conflict during the last twenty years. Jesús Velasco Márquez's *La guerra del 47 y la opinión pública (1845–1848)* and Gene M. Brack's *Mexico Views Manifest Destiny, 1821–1846: An Essay on the Origins of the Mexican War,* both of which were published in 1975, provided a much-needed overview of the origins and nature of Mexican attitudes and public opinion toward the U.S. from about the 1820s until after the war. Richard Griswold del Castillo's *The Treaty of Guada-*

lupe Hidalgo: A Legacy of Conflict (1990) analyzed the interpretations given to that settlement by U.S. courts, intellectuals and diplomats in both countries, and Mexican-American activists.

Three other books have helped fill the widest gap in the historiography of the war, that of Mexican domestic affairs during the conflict. Miguel Soto's *La conspiración monárquica en México, 1845–1846* (1988) and Jaime Delgado's *La monarquía en México (1845–1847)* examined a Spanish intrigue to restore monarchy in Mexico during the mid-1840s, while Pedro Santoni's *Mexican at Arms: Puro Federalists and the Politics of War, 1845–1848* (1996) offered a detailed analysis of the political factionalism that plagued Mexico at the very time U.S. armies invaded the national territory, focusing on Valentín Gómez Farías, leader of the *puro* political bloc. Another fresh contribution to the historiography of the U.S.–Mexican War was William A. DePalo Jr.'s *The Mexican National Army, 1822–1852* (1997). The book, which examined the institutional development of the Mexican army during its first thirty years as a national force, devoted several chapters to an analysis of the army's performance in the Texas Revolution and the war with the United States.

More fresh works have recently brought attention to numerous heretofore neglected aspects of the war. The conflict's impact on Mexico's regions has been scrutinized by Angela Moyano Pahissa's *La resistencia de las Californias a la invasión norteamericana (1846–1848)* (1992), and by the collection of essays in Laura Herrera Serna's (coord.) *México en guerra (1846–1848): Perspectivas regionales* (1997). María Elena García Muñoz and Ernesto Fritsche Aceves, "Los niños héroes, de la realided al mito," B.A. thesis in history, Universidad Nacional Autónoma de México (1989), and Enrique Plascencia de la Parra's article, "Conmemoración de la hazaña épica de los Niños Héroes: Su origen, desarrollo y simbolismos" (1995) shed light on the cultural dimensions of the conflict by probing the way in which Mexicans manufactured heroic symbols and figures. In addition, Cecilia Autrique's "La misión diplomática del Dr. Mora en Londres, 1846–1850," B.A. thesis in history, Universidad Nacional Autónoma de México (1996), and Raúl Figueroa Esquer's *La guerra de corso de México durante la invasión americana, 1845–1848* (1996) have offered new insights into the diplomatic history of the war. In conclusion, it is to be hoped that these and other innovative scholarly endeavors will ensure that the war between Mexico and the United States finally receives the thorough examination and even-handed appraisal it deserves.

Pedro Santoni
Richard Bruce Winders

BIBLIOGRAPHY

Alcaraz, Ramón, ed. *The Other Side; or, Notes for the History of the War between Mexico and the United States.* Translated by Albert C. Ramsey. 1970. Originally published as *Apuntes para la historia de la Guerra entre México y los Estados Unidos, 1848.*

Brack, Gene M. *Mexico Views Manifest Destiny, 1821–1846: An Essay on the Origins of the Mexican War.* 1975.

Garrett, Jenkins. *The Mexican–American War of 1846–1848: A Bibliography of the Holdings of the Libraries, the University of Texas at Arlington.* 1995.

Herrera Serna, Laura, coord. *México en guerra, 1846–1848: Perspectivas regionales.* 1997.

Johannsen, Robert W. *To the Halls of the Montezumas: The Mexican War in the American Imagination.* 1985.

Tutorow, Norman E. *The Mexican–American War: An Annotated Bibliography.* 1981.

Houston, Sam

President of the Republic of Texas and U.S. senator Sam Houston (1793–1863) did not play a vital part in the U.S.–Mexican War; however, he had a major role in creating the circumstances that led to the conflict and in responding to the issue of slavery extension that arose concerning the territory acquired from Mexico. Born on 2 March 1793 in Virginia, Houston moved with his family to Tennessee in 1807. He showed no interest in school or work and left home in 1809 to live with the Cherokee Indians. In 1812 he left the Cherokees and soon enlisted in the U.S. Army. He fought in Andrew Jackson's campaign against the Creek Indians in Alabama and was wounded severely at the Battle of Horseshoe Bend in March 1814.

Houston remained in the army until 1818, then moved to Middle Tennessee, became a lawyer, and began a political career. A strong Jacksonian, Houston served as a U.S. representative from 1823 to 1827 and ran successfully for governor of Tennessee in 1827.

In April 1829, Houston's wife of less than three months, Eliza Allen, left him. Neither he nor Eliza ever gave an explanation for the breakup of their marriage, but the separation caused such a public furor that he resigned the governorship and went into exile with the Cherokees in present-day Oklahoma. He remained with the Cherokees for more than three years before going to Texas in December 1832 as an agent of the U.S. government to negotiate with the Comanche Indians about sharing hunting grounds with tribes being moved west of the Mississippi River. Some historians claim that Houston intended to create a revolution in Texas, but there is no reliable evidence to support such a charge.

Legal migration by U.S. settlers into Mexican Texas had begun about 1821. By the early 1830s, U.S. settlers dominated Texas, and cultural differences with their Mexican hosts virtually ensured conflict. Minor disturbances arose in 1832 and 1833, and a full-scale independence movement developed in 1835. From the settlers' point of view, Mexican authorities, especially President Antonio López de Santa Anna, caused the revolution by imposing a centralized government on Texas rather than allowing Texas to become a separate state within Mexico's federal system, which had been established in 1824.

Sam Houston did not play a leading role in the events that led to the outbreak of fighting in October 1835, but the convention that declared independence and wrote a constitution for the Republic of Texas in March 1836 made him commander in chief of the Texas army. In the meantime, Santa Anna invaded Texas, took the Alamo, and advanced eastward into the heart of the province. Houston's small army retreated for nearly a month, but then took advantage of several miscalculations by Santa Anna to win an overwhelming victory at the Battle of San Jacinto on 21 April 1836. Houston was among the few Texian casualties; a musket-ball shattered the front part of his tibia just above the right ankle.

In September 1836 Houston became the first popularly elected president of the Republic of Texas. He held office a little more than two years and then, constitutionally ineligible for reelection, gave way to Mirabeau B. Lamar. Houston returned to the presidency in 1841 and during his second administration began a major effort to achieve annexation to the United States. Playing on fears within the U.S. government about British influence in an independent Texas, Houston was rewarded with a treaty of annexation in April 1844. To his chagrin, sectional politics in the United States prevented approval of the treaty, and his second term ended in December 1844 with Texas still independent. He continued to work for annexation in an unofficial capacity, however, and Texas became part of the United States in 1845.

Elected early in 1846 as one of Texas's first U.S. senators, Houston strongly supported President James K. Polk's administration in its move toward war with Mexico. In May, when some senators were requesting more evidence that war existed by act of Mexico, he argued that Texas had been under attack by Mexico for ten years and that annexation had put the United States in the place of the Lone Star Republic. Houston considered going "out with the army" in 1846, but at age fifty-three, with a young wife and growing family back home, decided against volunteering. The next year, he claimed to have declined a command offered him by President Polk because he differed with the president about the sort of campaign to be waged in Mexico.

Senator Houston did not like the terms of the Treaty of

Guadalupe Hidalgo, believing that it did not take enough territory from Mexico. He saw the futility of trying to gain more land or extend the war, however, and simply did not vote when the Senate approved the treaty. In any case, the war vindicated Texas's claim to the Río Grande as the southern boundary and ended any serious threat to Texas from Mexico.

The successful completion of the U.S.–Mexican War raised an issue—the extension of slavery into new territories—that would bedevil Houston for the rest of his career. Seeking an evenhanded approach, he opposed both the Wilmot Proviso for keeping slavery out of the Mexican Cession and the demands of Southerners for protection of slavery in all territories. He begged both sides to avoid passionate extremes and to allow the passage of time and reasonable men to find a solution that would preserve the Union.

Houston's unionism eventually cost him his senate seat and brought defeat in an effort to win the governorship of Texas in 1857. He won the gubernatorial election of 1859, but his opposition to secession and refusal to take an oath of loyalty to the Confederacy led to his removal from office in 1861. Upon leaving the governorship Houston retired to Huntsville, where he died on 26 July 1863.

Randolph B. Campbell

BIBLIOGRAPHY

Campbell, Randolph B. *Sam Houston and the American Southwest.* 1993.

De Bruhl, Marshall. *Sword of San Jacinto: A Life of Sam Houston.* 1993.

Friend, Llerena B. *Sam Houston: The Great Designer.* 1954.

James, Marquis. *The Raven: A Biography of Sam Houston.* 1929.

Williams, Amelia, and Eugene C. Barker, eds. *The Writings of Sam Houston, 1813–1863.* 8 vols. 1938–1943.

Huamantla, Battle of

The U.S. Army's entrance into Mexico City on 14 September 1847 by no means ended the fighting. Mexican forces under Gen. Joaquín Rea had invested the U.S. garrison at Puebla, threatening to strand Gen. Winfield Scott's army in the Mexican capital. Without control of the road to the coast, U.S. forces in the interior could not receive much needed supplies and reinforcements. Hoping to make the most of the situation, Gen. Antonio López de Santa Anna took the remnants of his army eastward following his defeat at Mexico City in an attempt to capture Puebla.

News of the garrison's plight had reached U.S.–held Vera Cruz. Gen. Joseph Lane moved westward along the National Road, picking up reinforcements at Perote. Hearing of Lane's approach, Santa Anna planned to ambush the relief column before it reached Puebla. He took his troops to Huamantla, a town northeast of Puebla situated along the north-

ern branch of the National Road. Lane, who had learned of the proposed ambush, left his supply train under a strong guard and proceeded to Huamantla, hoping to surprise Santa Anna instead. Capt. Samuel H. Walker's company of U.S. Mounted Rifles led the advance, entering the town well ahead of any support. Walker and his men captured several cannon and briefly forced the Mexican troops from the town. Regrouping, the Mexicans mounted a spirited counterattack in which Walker was killed. The death of the popular officer outraged Lane's men, who not only drove the Mexican forces from the vicinity, but sacked the town in retaliation. U.S. officers watched while volunteers, who made up the bulk of Lane's command, broke into public buildings and private dwellings, committing acts of violence against both people and property.

In the days immediately following the action at Huamantla, General Lane relieved the U.S. garrison at Puebla. The Mexican government, which had accepted Santa Anna's resignation as president on 16 September, relieved him of all command.

Richard Bruce Winders

BIBLIOGRAPHY

Alcaraz, Ramón, ed. *The Other Side; or, Notes for the History of the War between Mexico and the United States.* Translated by Albert C. Ramsey. 1970. Originally published as *Apuntes para lat historia de la Guerra entre México y los Estado Unidos,* 1848.

Department of War. "Report for General Lane to the Adjutant General of the U.S. Army, Puebla, Mexico, October 18, 1847." Report of the Secretary of War to the President of the United States.

Oswandell, J. Jacob. *Notes on the War With Mexico, 1845–46–47.* 1885.

Huasteca Revolts

From 1846 to 1848, during the U.S. occupation of the Mexican gulf ports of Tampico and Tuxpan, a series of rural uprisings broke out that had their antecedents in Mexico's past. In 1821, its principal economic activities diminished after long years of war, Mexico faced large external and internal debts. In order to function in the midst of political anarchy and bankruptcy, the government was forced to depend on speculators, who loaned money at enormous rates of interest and demanded Mexican ports' customs revenues as guarantees. As if this were not enough, the country was struggling with its sociocultural, linguistic, and political heterogeneity. This is perhaps the best explanation for the fact that, throughout the first half of the nineteenth century, public figures defended in their writings, debates, and projects of colonization the notion of Catholicism as the only permissible religion. It would seem that even the most radical politicians saw Catholicism as the only common thread capable of uniting all Mexicans.

The diverse political projects undertaken to shape the Mexican state were evidence of this heterogeneity, which more noticeably manifested itself in the political realm than it did in the social or linguistic ones. In addition to this situation were the hostilities between Mexico and the United States, whose immediate antecedent had been the war over the secession of Texas from the Mexican Republic. The intent by Mexicans to arrive at a suitable political system led them to adopt in August 1847, while at war with the United States, the federalist policies of the Constitution of 1824. This meant that the states that belonged to the federation reassumed political autonomy and control of their own armed forces. At the moment hostilities broke out, with U.S. forces advancing on various fronts, the nation seemed to be lost. Not only did several distinct armies suddenly appear—without training, officers, or arms—but several parts of the Republic (the Huasteca, the Isthmus of Tehuantepec, Sierra Gorda, and Yucatán) witnessed armed uprisings, which political figures of the time categorized as "caste wars," or wars of Indian against white.

From November 1846 to March 1848, the United States occupied two of the three most important ports on the Gulf of Mexico, Tampico and Tuxpan. During this period, in the Huasteca, a series of rural uprisings took place that were generally considered to be the result of the loss of lands. The Huasteca is located in Mexico's northeast and is made up of the current states of Hidalgo, Puebla, Querétaro, San Luis Potosí, Tamaulipas, and Vera Cruz. The uprisings that took place during the war with the United States encompassed the areas of Hidalgo and Vera Cruz.

Since 1845 military and public officials had informed their respective superiors that a certain air of "rebellion" had been noted among the indigenous, mulatto, and mestizo populations north of Vera Cruz. The apparent immediate cause was a search by one Lucio Velázquez for property deeds pertaining to some Indian villages. The situation reached a critical point when the Indians rebelled in Ozuluama because questions over boundaries of their territory and private properties were not clarified. The Indians were put down militarily but rebelled again in March 1847. This time the rebellion involved Indians from villages within the jurisdiction of Tuxpan. This is not to say that social conflicts did not exist between 1845 and 1847.

In order to deal with U.S. advances, smuggling, and Indian conflicts, Gen. Francisco de Garay reported moving military combat headquarters from Huejutla to Ozuluama in February 1847. He set up a line of observation and defense comprising guerrillas located in Huejutla and Ozuluama and along the course of the Río Pánuco. In November 1847 a rural rebellion broke out in the district of Tampico, Vera Cruz. Months later, the military commander at Huejutla reported that the rebels were the Indian, black, white, and mulatto tenants of the haciendas surrounding Ozuluama.

During the most intense moments of the war with the United States, the Huasteca region again became a trouble spot. In this period, the grievances of the rebels no longer centered on land rights or rent issues, but rather they reflected the existing conflict between members of the oligarchy in the Huasteca over control of the principal towns of the region. As a result, the Amatlán Plan was announced on 30 December 1847 and the Tantoyuca Plan on 7 January 1848. Both of these plans, announced by Juan Llorente, a prominent member of the elite, called for the defense of the country against the "invader," the distribution of lands on the haciendas among the peasants, and a change in political authorities in the region. The rebellion grew in strength when it was joined by people from the towns of Chicontepec, Ozuluama, San Nicholás, and Tantoyuca, almost all located to the north of Vera Cruz. In February and March 1848, the Mexican minister of war received reports from the generals in the Huasteca that the rebels of San Nicolás had offered to place themselves beneath the protection of the flag of the United States. Some governors, such as the governor of Puebla, were of the opinion that the rebellion's very origin was in the occupation of the country by the U.S. forces.

Passions between the mestizos and the white political rulers rose to such a point that in April 1848 Cristóbal Andrade, the political prefect of Huejutla (Hidalgo), was accused of soliciting U.S. troops still stationed in Tampico to aid in pacifying the region, Mexican troops being almost nonexistent by that time. The U.S. commander did not consider Andrade's request, since by then the U.S. troops were in the process of withdrawing from Tampico.

With the signing of the Treaty of Guadalupe Hidalgo, the Mexican government was able to pay more attention to the various rebellions in the country. In the case of the Huasteca, a pact was signed with Llorente, but it did not result in the disarmament of the Indian and mestizo peasants. By the middle of 1848 the movement no longer represented the interests of the oligarchy who had put it together in the first place. Local authorities agreed on an important point: the rebellion had other leaders now and no longer involved a considerable number of Indians; rather, it comprised mestizos, blacks, and mulattos, and now ranchers and tenants were in rebellion over the "imprudent" levying of taxes. The rebellion finally died out between August and September 1848, when forces from the states of México, Puebla, and Vera Cruz were sent to attack the rebels.

Antonio Escobar Ohmstede
Translated by The Horse's Mouth Language Services

BIBLIOGRAPHY

Ducey, Michael T. "From Village Riot to Regional Rebellion: Social Protest in the Huasteca, México, 1760–1870." Ph.D. diss., University of Chicago, 1992.

Escobar Ohmstede, Antonio. "De cabeceras a pueblos sujetos. Las continuidades y transformaciones de los pueblos indios de las Huastecas hidalguense y veracruzana, 1750–1853." Ph.D. diss., ET Colegio de Mexico, 1994.

González Navarro, Moisés. "Las guerras de castas." *Historia Mexicana* 26 (no. 1, 1976): 70–106.

Huejutla Expedition

In May 1847 Mexican authorities sent two hundred U.S. prisoners of war to Huejutla, a town 120 miles from Tampico, to prevent the prisoners, who had been taken captive the previous February at Encarnación, from being recaptured by U.S. forces. The captives, held originally in Mexico City, were to have been exchanged but were instead confined at Huejutla by local commander Gen. F. de Garay. Six prisoners escaped and reported the condition of their comrades to Col. William Gates, commanding at Tampico, who decided to mount an expedition to release the prisoners.

The expedition consisted of troops from Col. L. G. De Russey's Louisiana Regiment, a company from the 3d Artillery with one cannon, and a dragoon detachment, totaling about 120 men. The expedition left Tampico on 7 July, traveling by steamboat up the Rió Pánuco and then marching overland toward Huejutla. On 12 July, as the troops were about to cross a river seven miles from Huejutla, they were attacked by a large Mexican force lying in ambush. The initial fire killed or mortally wounded several members of the advance party and forced the remainder to withdraw.

Over the next three days, De Russey conducted a fighting retreat toward Tampico. At Tantoyuca an estimated one thousand or more Mexican infantry and lancers blocked the retreat. In a sharp skirmish De Russey's force scattered them and then occupied and sacked part of the town. After rejecting a surrender demand, De Russey's men slipped out of town early the next morning during a rainstorm and continued their withdrawal.

De Russey sent word of his predicament to Gates, who immediately dispatched a relief force of 160 men and two cannon. The reinforcements reached the Pánuco by steamboat, and both detachments then withdrew back to Tampico. A contemporary account in the *Niles National Register* described the expedition as "one of the most brilliant affairs, for the numbers engaged . . . which has taken place this war." Estimates of U.S. casualties ranged from 19 to 30, while newspaper accounts listed Mexican losses at 150. Ironically the U.S. prisoners, objects of the expedition, were later released on parole.

David J. Coles

BIBLIOGRAPHY

Encarnacion Prisoners: Comprising an Account of the march of the Kentucky Cavalry from Louisville to the Rio Grande, together With an Authentic History of the Captivity of the American Prisoners, Including Incidents and sketches of Men and things on the Route and in Mexico. By a Prisoner. 1848.

Niles National Register, 7 August 1847.

Smith, Justin H. *The War with Mexico.* 2 vols. 1919. Reprint, 1963.

Huston, Felix

Felix Huston (1800–1857) was a Mississippi lawyer and commanding general of the army of the Republic of Texas. Huston led a large mounted force from Natchez, Mississippi, to Texas in 1836, but he arrived too late to participate in the revolutionary fighting. He quickly rose to prominence in a Texas volunteer army, which often defied civilian control. In a duel on 5 February 1837 Huston shot and severely wounded Albert Sidney Johnston, whom President Sam Houston had named to replace Huston as army commander. Huston yearned to mount a major offensive invasion of Mexico, but President Houston undermined these plans of conquest when he furloughed most of the volunteer army in May 1837.

As major general of the Texas militia, Huston nominally commanded a highly successful counterattack against a large Comanche raiding party at the Battle of Plum Creek in August 1840. In the fall of that year he returned to the United States, where he became a champion of the U.S. annexation of Texas and a fierce supporter of James K. Polk's election in 1844. Ironically, Huston did not join the U.S. army that actually defeated Mexico. Following the U.S.–Mexican War, Huston bitterly opposed the Compromise of 1850, and in his last years he advocated Southern secession.

James E. Crisp

BIBLIOGRAPHY

May, Robert E. *John A. Quitman: Old South Crusader.* 1985.

McIntosh, James T., ed. *The Papers of Jefferson Davis.* Vol. 2. 1974.

Ide, William B.

William B. Ide (1796–1852), a carpenter, schoolteacher and Bear Flag Revolt leader, was born in Rutland, Massachusetts, on 28 March. Ide, a delegate to the Mormon Presidential Convention of 1844, lived in Kentucky, Ohio, and Illinois before moving his family to California the following year. The Ides arrived in the upper Sacramento Valley and settled within the Josiah Belden *rancho*, Barranca Colorada.

On 14 June 1846, Ide participated in the capture of the Mexican pueblo at Sonoma. Assuming leadership of the conquerors, he issued the famous Bear Flag proclamation, a declaration of rebellion against Mexican rule. Fearing a Mexican counter assault, Ide organized the defenses of the fort. Mexican forces made no attempt to retake the garrison, however, and by 9 July the U.S. flag waved over Sonoma. Ide then became a private in Granville P. Swift's company of the California Battalion. In 1847 a committee comprising Ide, John H. Nash, and John Grigsby wrote an extensive report on the Bear Flag Revolt entitled "The Revolution in California." *Niles National Register* and the *Illinois Journal* published this account.

That same year, Ide was appointed land surveyor for the Northern Department of California. Beginning in 1851 he became a public servant in Colusi County, filling such positions as justice of the peace, county judge, county recorder, and county auditor. On 19 December 1852, Ide died of smallpox at the age of fifty-six in Monroeville, California.

S. Kirk Bane

BIBLIOGRAPHY

Parker, Jerry L. "William B. Ide: A Re-examination of His Life and Role in California History." M.A. thesis, California State University, Chico, 1993.

Rogers, Fred Blackburn. *William Brown Ide: Bear Flagger.* 1962.

Immigration

This entry consists of three separate articles: **Immigration to California***;* **Immigration to Texas***; and* **Immigration to New Mexico***.*

Immigration to California

Spain made the initial European contact with California at San Diego Bay in 1542. During Spanish control, military personnel and clergy accounted for the majority of immigrants. Their primary concern was not to settle the area, but to protect Spain's interest and Christianize the indigenous peoples. California's population of Spanish soldiers and priests was 3,270 in 1820.

Mexico gained its independence from Spain in 1821 and claimed the territory of California shortly thereafter. Adventurers and trappers from the United States were some of the immigrants attracted to the Mexican territory. By 1830, the immigrant population had increased to 4,250 with Mexican soldiers counting as the majority of the growth.

A more sizable migration occurred during the years 1841 to 1846. During this period, approximately eight hundred settlers traveled west from the United States by covered wagon; most settled inland rather than on the coast. Since the Californios were so removed from the central Mexican government they welcomed the U.S. arrivals. Immigration was at such a small level that relations between the U.S. and Mexico were not adversely affected. On the eve of the U.S.–Mexican War, the future state of California boasted a population of only several thousand settlers, almost equally divided between immigrants from the United States and immigrants of Spanish and Mexican origin. After 1846 and during the U.S.–Mexican War, more than five hundred settlers came to California making their homes in the valleys.

While they had made their plans during the time Mexico controlled California, the immigrants reached their new home after the U.S. flag had been raised at Monterey.

Before the U.S.–Mexican War, California was settled primarily by soldiers and offered limited interest for new settlers, but in 1848, shortly after the end of the war, the discovery of gold in northern California initiated a flood of immigrants from all over the world. California's immigrant population increased from 90,000 in 1849 to 220,000 in 1852.

Tracy M. Shilcutt

BIBLIOGRAPHY

Bean, Walter. *California: An Interpretive History.* 1973.
Nava, Julian, and Bob Barger. *California: Five Centuries of Cultural Contrasts.* 1976.

See also **Gold Rush**

Immigration to Texas

Mexico attracted foreign immigrants in the 1820s and 1830s because of its liberal land policy and its seeming lack of problems encountered in other countries, such as military conscription and debt. Many immigrants came from the United States into the borderlands, particularly Texas. The population of Texas had been seriously decimated during the Mexican Wars of Independence, and most people lived in San Antonio de Béxar (present-day San Antonio), La Bahía (present-day Goliad), and Nacogdoches, the only settlements. The Spanish and then Mexican governments were eager to populate the region so that it would serve as a buffer zone for the interior, but Mexican citizens were reluctant to move into the vast, unfamiliar territory.

In 1821 the government turned to controlled introduction of foreigners through *empresarios,* the most famous being Stephen F. Austin of the United States. Although the law demanded that the immigrants observe Mexican law, many U.S. settlers refused to accept Mexican laws and traditions, including the prohibition on slavery. The government, perceiving this lack of respect and fearing trouble, passed the Law of April 6, 1830, which prohibited further immigration from the United States. Although this slowed U.S. immigration, U.S. settlers by this time heavily outnumbered the Tejanos in the province of Texas. Estimates of the Texas population at the time of the Texas Revolution vary, but a reasonable estimate is approximately 34,000, including slaves. By 1850, after independence and statehood, this region had a population of 212,000, including 58,000 slaves. Nearly one-third of the 154,000 white persons and free blacks had been born in Texas, under Spanish, Mexican, or U.S. control, or when it was independent.

Jodella K. Dyreson

BIBLIOGRAPHY

Almonte, Juan N. "Statistical Report on Texas." *Southwestern Historical Quarterly* 28 (1925): 177–221.
Hogan, William Ransom. *The Texas Republic: A Social and Economic History.* 1946.
Kite, Jodella D. "A Social History of the Anglo-American Colonies in Mexican Texas." Ph.D. diss., Texas Tech University, 1990.

See also **Empresarios; Land Grants**

Immigration to New Mexico

Immigration to New Mexico from the United States in the period of the U.S.–Mexican War (1846–1848) was limited to Santa Fe Trail merchants who settled primarily to engage in commerce, and a very small number of military personnel who remained or returned after service in New Mexico. Some Santa Fe traders, such as the Bent brothers, had local connections that antedated the war and included marriage into local families of Spanish origin, affiliation with the Catholic Church, and acquisition of Mexican citizenship, making real estate ownership legally possible. Some traders who settled did not remain long.

No immigrant of this period engaged primarily in agriculture. Absent new, expensive irrigation, arable land was already occupied, and markets were too distant for profitability. Soldiers who remained in or returned to New Mexico are now identifiable in some instances only by their grave markers. Some of these were men left behind by their units because of illness or accident. Others were deserters and adventurers who had been drummed out of service.

Postwar immigration continued to be minimal in the face of New Mexico's challenging geography. A few settlers dropped out from groups of forty-niner travelers and from troops operating in New Mexico during the U.S. Civil War. Some "California Column" volunteers settled in the Mesilla Valley. Other than a very thin scattering of merchants, miners, and cattlemen, non-Hispanic settlers were hardly seen until the railroads came in the years from 1879 to 1881. New Mexico retained a predominant Hispanic–Native American population and its economic development was also slow. For both reasons, Congress viewed New Mexico as a poor candidate for statehood, and it was not admitted to the union until 1912.

John Porter Bloom

BIBLIOGRAPHY

Callon, Milton W., "The Merchant-Colonists of New Mexico." In *Brand Book of the Denver Westerners,* edited by A. L. Campa.
Lang, Herbert H. "The New Mexico Bureau of Immigration, 1880–1912." *New Mexico Historical Review* 51, no. 3 (1976): 193–214.
Meketa, Jacqueline Dorgan. "A Soldier in New Mexico, 1847–1848." *New Mexico Historical Review* 66, no. 1 (1991): 15–32.

Tobias, Henry J., and Charles E. Woodhouse. "New York Investment Bankers and New Mexico Merchants: Group Formation and Elite Status among German Jewish Businessmen." *New Mexico Historical Review* 65, no. 1 (1990): 21–48.

Immortal Fourteen

The fourteen antislavery Whigs who voted against the war bill in the House of Representatives on 11 May 1846 were called the "Immortal Fourteen." The war bill recognized that a state of war already existed by virtue of a previous Mexican attack on U.S. soldiers and provided for the initial volunteers and funds necessary to fight the war.

All of the fourteen representatives were from congressional districts in Maine, Massachusetts, New York, Ohio, Pennsylvania, and Rhode Island. The most prominent were 78-year-old John Quincy Adams and Joshua R. Giddings. These antislavery Whigs believed that the U.S.–Mexican War was a device of a Southern president and the Southern slave power to expand slavery. To them, Mexico had been provoked into war for the purposes of rendering slavery secure in Texas and conquering New Mexico and California. Considering it a shameful war of aggression and conquest, Adams, Giddings, and their radical colleagues refused to support or implicate themselves in what they regarded as a national crime. Other Whigs denounced the war, criticized the administration, and demanded that no Mexican territory be taken, but they also voted for the appropriations, supplies, and men necessary to fight the war. To do so, these moderate Whigs argued, was patriotic because the war once begun had to be won to preserve U.S. honor. The Immortal Fourteen disagreed. Because of their moral outrage, they regularly voted against war appropriations, supplies, and additional men. To them, true patriotism rested in preserving the republican virtue of the nation. Despite their vehemence, they had little, if any, effect on the war effort. They did, however, have a political impact by effectively linking the war to slavery.

John H. Schroeder

BIBLIOGRAPHY

Schroeder, John H. *Mr. Polk's War: American Opposition and Dissent, 1846–1848.* 1973.

Stewart, James Brewer. *Joshua R. Giddings and the Tactics of Radical Politics.* 1970.

Imperialism

See Expansionism and Imperialism

Indian Policy

This entry consists of three separate articles: **Mexican Policy;** **Texan Policy;** *and* **U.S. Policy.** *See also* **Indians.**

Mexican Policy

Throughout the period of Spanish rule in Mexico, the Indians constituted a group that was ethnically and juridically separate from the governing elite. During the early national period, Mexico remained institutionally a Hispanic nation, except at the local and rural levels. Although the Indians made up approximately 60 percent of the population of the new republic, they had almost no voice in national affairs.

The *criollo* (Creole) rulers of the postindependence period, who were of Spanish descent, tried to avoid use of the term *Indian* in the formulation of governmental policy. In attempting to implement the doctrine of equality under the law, tribute payments were suppressed. Racial, caste, and class distinctions were legally abolished. Yet, although the Indians were by law free citizens, little progress was made to provide them with education and thus a means of upward social mobility. Moreover, their exploitation by landowners and moneylenders continued as in previous epochs.

While the liberals were conscious of the Indians' plight, they attributed it to the paternalistic nature of Spanish colonial rule. Lorenzo de Zavala, for example, criticized the Laws of the Indies for keeping the Indians segregated from Europeans and thus hindering their acculturation. The liberals particularly blamed the colonial regime for having perpetuated the notion of communal property among the Indians.

The liberals could or would not acknowledge, however, that they had substituted their own paternalistic views of the Indian for those of their predecessors. Both liberal and conservative thinkers believed that the Indian was inferior to the white and that the future of Mexico lay with the latter. They held that the numerical superiority of the Indians could be reduced by a concerted program of European colonization: white settlers would be induced to settle in Mexico by granting them lands or economic concessions.

The Maya revolt in Yucatán, which commenced in July 1847 during the advance of Gen. Winfield Scott's army on Mexico, together with the Indian rebellion in the Sierra Gorda region in 1848 and 1849, were assumed by many contemporaries to have been caused by the U.S. invasion. The uprisings provoked fears among the governing elite of social upheaval and race war. For some liberals, such as José María Luis Mora and Bernardo Couto, the Indian rebellions constituted a more serious national security problem than did the U.S. invaders. Despite such preoccupations, the consensus of liberal opinion favored a continuation of paternalistic "civilizing" efforts and colonization over a war of extermination against the indigenous peoples.

Mexican policy toward the nomadic Indian peoples, the so-called *indios bárbaros,* of the northern border regions, differed from the treatment accorded the more settled indigenous groups of the country's interior. In the north, raids carried out by Comanches, Apaches, and other tribes against agricultural and mining communities induced national and state authorities to implement a policy of extermination and expulsion toward the U.S.-based tribes.

Lawrence D. Taylor

BIBLIOGRAPHY

González Navarro, Moisés. "Instituciones indígenas en México independiente." In *Métodos y resultados de la política indigenista en México.* 1954.

Hale, Charles A. *Mexican Liberalism in the Age of Mora, 1821–1853.* 1968.

Smith, Ralph A. "Indians in American-Mexican Relations before the War of 1846." *Hispanic American Historical Review* 43 (1963): 34–64.

Villoro, Luis. *Los grandes momentos del indigenismo en México.* 1950.

Texan Policy

From the time of Spanish entrance into the largely unsettled province of the area of Texas, relations with the Native Americans in the region were characterized by almost continuous conflict. Following the Louisiana Purchase of 1803, Spanish (and later Mexican) authorities, who wanted to limit the entrance of Anglo-Americans into Texas, granted lands to the tribes that were being forced out of the Louisiana Territory and the Trans-Appalachian region.

This was the situation when Stephen F. Austin and other U.S. *empresarios* began establishing colonial enclaves in Texas in the 1820s. The relative size of the populations of the Anglo-American settlers (approximately 3,500) and the Indians (approximately 20,000) during this time dictated a conciliatory policy toward the Indians. Both the central Mexican and the Coahuila y Texas state governments assured the "civilized" tribes title to their lands.

Because Mexico offered no protection against the warlike nomadic tribes, Austin and the colonists organized militia units and established treaties with some of the tribes to minimize conflict. In four conventions, held between 1832 and 1836, the colonists addressed two issues related to the Indians: one was to establish peace with the nearby sedentary tribes and the other was to provide protection from the nomadic tribes. Treaties were established with some of the immigrant tribes in 1836 and a border ranger force was established to provide protection.

When Sam Houston assumed the presidency of the newly established Republic of Texas in 1836, he instilled an Indian policy of peace, friendship, and commerce, but also determined to provide adequate frontier protection. A December 1836 law authorized Houston to send agents among the Indians, make treaties and distribute gifts, establish blockhouses and trading posts, provide a battalion of mounted riflemen to patrol the frontier, and to call out the militia when necessary. Houston, recognizing the nomadic Plains tribes' superiority in horsemanship and knowledge of the region, erected trading posts on the perimeter of the "Comanchería" rather than send untrained, inexperienced troops against them.

Problems were complicated by the increasing flow of immigrant Indians from the United States, the influence of Mexican agents, and the activities of private land companies that extended their surveys into the Indians' domains, as well as by racial antagonisms between Indians and the Anglo-American settlers. In the summer of 1838 some Indians in east Texas allied themselves with Mexican agents under Vicente Córdova in the short-lived Córdova Rebellion, which occurred near Nacogdoches.

President Houston held councils at various locations to conclude treaties with the different tribes, including the Lipan Apaches, the Penateka Comanches, and the Wichita confederacy. Having been closely associated with the Cherokees from his youth, the "Raven," as Houston was known among them, was sympathetic to the Indians' position in Texas. Even so, no completely satisfactory solution to the Indian problem was achieved. Isolated bands continued to steal horses and harass the settlements, thus making clashes with Texian citizens and militia units inevitable.

Mirabeau B. Lamar, who succeeded Houston as president in December 1838, had neither experience with nor sympathy for the Indians. Instead, he advocated a policy of total destruction or expulsion from Texas. Lamar argued that the Cherokees had no just claims to their lands because the promises of the still-hostile centralist-controlled Mexican government had induced them to make war on Texians. He also repudiated the treaty of 23 February 1836, declaring that it had never been ratified and that the collaboration of Indians with Córdova and Mexican agents nullified it.

Lamar's attitude was shared by the third congress, particularly after a Ranger unit attacked Manuel Flores's camp and discovered documents that assured the Cherokees valid title to their East Texas holdings in exchange for cooperating with the Mexicans. Lamar, with congressional approval, strengthened the armed forces. The subsequent Texas Cherokee War culminated in their expulsion from Texas. Similar actions were taken against the Penateka Comanches, who also had been in contact with Mexican agents.

Two efforts at conciliation tempered Lamar's policy of Indian extermination. One was a treaty with the Shawnees in 1839, who agreed to leave Texas peacefully if the government would provide supplies and transportation and pay for improvements to their land. The Texas senate did not approve this treaty. The other conciliatory measure was provision of land to the Alabama and Coushatta tribes and a strip of land thirty miles square on the frontier to which all friendly Indians should eventually be removed.

Lamar's stern policy had severe financial consequences. Whereas during Houston's first term Indian affairs had cost the republic $190,000, Lamar's expenditures soared to $2,500,000, more than one-half of the total expenditures of the government during his administration. Lamar's policy thus contributed greatly to the republic's rapidly growing public indebtedness and weakened financial condition.

With the start of Sam Houston's second administration in December 1841, the policy of peace toward Indians returned. Houston reinstated his plan to send agents among the tribes, establish frontier posts and trading posts to meet their needs, and hold councils with tribal representatives to establish treaties. In 1842 several tribes agreed to cease hostilities and to attend a grand council with all Texas tribes at Bird's Fort on the Trinity River. At the council, nine tribes signed a permanent treaty, which was ratified by the senate on 31 January 1844. Other tribes followed suit, and the Witchitas' signing of the treaty on 16 November 1844 brought the Indian affairs of the Republic of Texas to a close. Overall, the total amount expended for Indian affairs was $94,092 during Houston's second term, and only $45,000 during Anson Jones's administration.

Following annexation and statehood, U.S. federal authorities assumed control of Indian affairs, including all debts arising from Indian depredations since 1836.

H. Allen Anderson

BIBLIOGRAPHY

Anderson, H. Allen. "The Delaware and Shawnee Indians and the Republic of Texas, 1820–1845." *Southwestern Historical Quarterly* 94 (October 1990): 231–260.

Brice, Donaly E. *The Great Comanche Raid*. 1987.

Castaneda, Carlos E. *Our Catholic Heritage*. 5 vols. 1936–1942.

Clarke, Mary Whatley. *Chief Bowles and the Texas Cherokees*. 1971.

Connor, Seymour V. *Adventure in Glory: The Saga of Texas, 1836–1849*. 1965.

Fehrenbach, T. R. *Comanches: The Destruction of a People*. 1974.

Handbook of Texas. 3 vols. 1952, 1976.

Muckleroy, Anna. "The Indian Policy of the Republic of Texas." *Southwestern Historical Quarterly* 25 (January 1923), 26 (October 1925).

Newcomb, W. W. *The Indians of Texas from Prehistoric to Modern Times*. 1961.

Newlin, Deborah Lamont. *The Tonkawa People*. 1982.

Richardson, Rupert N. *The Comanche Barrier to South Plains Settlement*. 1933.

Winfrey, Dorman H., and James M. Day, eds. *The Indian Papers of Texas and the Southwest, 1825–1916*. 5 vols. 1966.

Winkler, Ernest W., ed. *Secret Journals of the Senate, Republic of Texas, 1836–1845*. 1911.

U.S. Policy

Conquest of the frontier and economic progress were the two key ideologies of the westward expansion of the United States. Both ideas—(1) that the frontier wilderness should give way to farms, factories, and towns, and (2) that the new land should promote economic riches—were central to U.S. Indian policy. Because the Indians were part of the frontier, by definition the Indian tribes had to give up their way of life and be incorporated into the new nation as economically responsible citizens.

Originally, U.S. Indian policy had been defined by Thomas Jefferson, who sought to civilize the Indians through Christianization, allotment in severalty, and education. More important, Jefferson wanted the tribal lands so they could be thrown open to settlers. Sometimes these lands were acquired by fraud, such as with the Treaty of Fort Stanwix in 1784, in which the New York Iroquois had sold lands in Ohio and Indiana that they had never owned. Sometimes the acquisition was accompanied by bloodshed, as with Andrew Jackson's defeat of the Creek Red Sticks in 1815 and the massacre of Black Hawk's Sauk and Fox followers in 1832.

By the end of the War of 1812 the line of U.S. settlement was advancing so fast that the United States sought to move Indians far enough west so that the process of civilization could be carried on without Indians and whites coming into conflict over land claims. Although U.S. policymakers recognized Indian sovereignty on tribal lands east of the Mississippi River, the simple arithmetic of politics—settlers could vote and Indians could not—dictated that the Indians must go. In 1832 Congress passed the Removal Act, which directed President Andrew Jackson to buy out the tribal lands coveted by settlers and remove the eastern tribes to a huge western "Indian Territory," which extended from the Red River to the Platte River. By a combination of promises of perpetual peace and protection in new homes in the west, bribery, and brute force, the removal process was largely completed by 1840.

The U.S.–Mexican War had barely begun when U.S. officials recognized the need for a new Indian policy. This policy revision was necessitated in part by the experience of the Republic of Texas, whose incorporation into the Union in 1845 had precipitated the war with Mexico. Texas settlers had carried on bloody wars with most of the Texas tribes, which the United States sought to end. Indian policy also had to be changed because westward removal was no longer practical. Finally, while the army proposed to build and man a line of forts on the frontier, the War Department could never promise adequate protection to settlers nor could it define where the frontier was.

The new policy, formulated by William Medill (Commissioner of Indian Affairs under President James K. Polk) and Luke Lea (his successor under President Zachary Taylor) proposed that tribes sell their lands in exchange for reservations away from the main lines of westward immigration and settlement. Medill and Lea offered the tribes payments for their lands in the form of goods as well as seeds, tools, and other implements of Jeffersonian civilization, and schools and churches were to be built for the Indians. U.S. officials believed that the Indians, isolated on small tracts of land, could be "civilized" slowly by missionaries and federal agents, away from the contaminating influence of the white frontier, until they were Christianized Jeffersonian farmers.

Thomas F. Schilz

BIBLIOGRAPHY

Berkhofer, Robert F., Jr. *The White Man's Indian: Images of the American Indian from Columbus to the Present.* 1978.

Gibson, Arrell Morgan. *The American Indian: Prehistory to the Present.* 1980.

Prucha, Francis Paul. *American Indian Policy in the Formative Years: The Indian Trade and Intercourse Acts, 1790–1834.* 1962.

Prucha, Francis Paul. *The Great Father: The United States Government and the American Indians.* 1984.

Satz, Ronald N. *American Indian Policy in the Jacksonian Era.* 1975.

Sheehan, Bernard W. *Seeds of Extinction: Jeffersonian Philanthropy and the American Indians.* 1973.

Trennert, Robert A., Jr. *Alternative to Extinction: Federal Indian Policy and the Beginnings of the Reservation System, 1846–51.* 1975.

Utley, Robert M. *The Indian Frontier of the American West, 1846–1890.* 1984.

Indians

This entry includes two articles: **Overview** *and* **Indian Raids**. *For an account of government policies concerning native peoples, see* **Indian Policy**. *See also articles on specific tribes.*

Overview

The Indian tribes of the southwestern rim of the United States had been in contact with European civilization since Francisco Coronado had clashed with the Zunis in 1540. The Mexican territories coveted by the United States contained approximately 150,000 indigenous people in 1846.

The Pueblos of the upper Río Grande valley in New Mexico had the most elaborate civilization in northern Mexico. Although subject to Spanish missionary activity, the Pueblo tribes never abandoned their ancient culture, instead incorporating what they found useful from the whites who settled near them.

East of the Río Grande were the Shoshonean-speaking Comanches, able buffalo hunters, warriors, and traders. To the west were the Apaches and Navajos, who practiced a mixed economy of hunting and gathering and agriculture. Enemies of Mexicans, Pueblos, and Comanches, they had lived for six centuries on the periphery of Pueblo civilization and had borrowed most of their culture from their sophisticated neighbors. Like the Comanches they raided the Mexican residents for horses, cattle, and captives, as well as in retaliation for Mexican attacks on them.

Like the Pueblos, the Caddos of Texas had evolved a sophisticated urban and agrarian culture, but much of their culture had disappeared by 1846. On their periphery were the Tonkawas and Lipans, small tribes who sought U.S. protection from the Mexicans and Comanches.

Indians of the Great Basin and the interior of California were mainly small, nomadic bands of hunter-gatherers. The California coastal tribes south of San Francisco Bay had been missionized in the 1770s, and their population had decreased more than 80 percent by 1846.

Thomas F. Schilz

BIBLIOGRAPHY

Gibson, Arrell Morgan. *The American Indian: Prehistory to the Present.* 1980.

Keilman, Chester. *Guide to the Microfilm Edition of the Bexar Archives, 1717–1803.* 1967.

Kenner, Charles. *A History of New Mexican–Plains Indian Relations.* 1969.

Smithwick, Noah. *The Evolution of a State.* 1983.

Swanton, John R. *The Indian Tribes of North America.* 4th ed. 1984.

Utley, Robert M. *The Indian Frontier of the American West, 1846–1890.* 1984.

Indian Raids

The Indians located north of the Río Bravo (also known as the Río Grande), called *indios bárbaros* by non-Indian Mexicans, were primarily seminomadic peoples, more opposed than their Mesoamerican counterparts (Nahuas, Mayas, Zapotecos, Tarascos, etc.) to the sedentary lifestyles and cultural absorption that nineteenth-century Mexican society attempted to impose on them. Some groups (Apache, Navajo, Ute) originated in the mountains; others (Comanche, Kiowa) came from the North American plains. When not subjected to mission life or confined to the garrisons that were their legacy from the colonial period, they attacked, terrorized, and abducted the inhabitants and animals of settlements in northern Mexico. The gradual disappearance of the garrisons and missions in the early period following Mexican independence in 1821 made the situation worse for the northern settlements. The changes brought about by independence played an important role in weakening the frontier systems

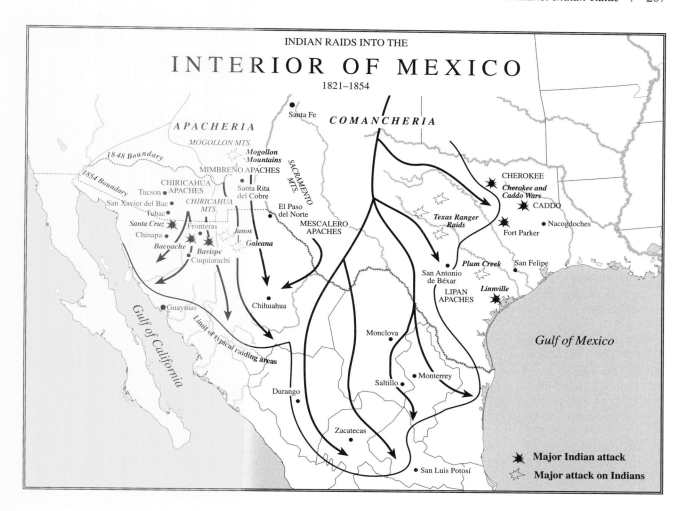

INDIAN RAIDS INTO THE
INTERIOR OF MEXICO
1821–1854

that had been developed by the Spanish, especially during the eighteenth century. In addition to Mexico's ever more pressing problem regarding its border with the United States, the Spanish had bequeathed to Mexico a sparsely populated northern territory that had always been characterized by weak ties to the viceroyalty. Mexico had also inherited the territorial conflict with the nomadic Indians, which became no less than a prolonged war.

In the early years of independent Mexico, the national press so strongly criticized the government for the lack of attention and resources devoted to lessening attacks in the so-called Internal Provinces that there was some consideration of excluding the nomads from national territory. These journalistic attacks took on a political hue, since they spread the suspicion that the nomads received support from the new settlers in Texas.

During the war with Texas, in 1836, the Mexican press published news reports of alliances between Gen. Antonio López de Santa Anna and the Indians in order to attack the

Texians. Santa Anna's defeat at San Jacinto and signing of the Treaties of Velasco, in which the "independence" of Texas was recognized, altered the situation for Mexico. On one hand, the retreat of Mexican troops to the Río Bravo after Santa Anna's capture by the Texians caused the border to be established there, and as a result some nomadic groups were left outside of Mexican jurisdiction. On the other hand, land was offered to Indians who had collaborated in the attempted "retaking" of Texas. After the Mexican defeat, incursions into Mexican territory by nomadic groups becamse more aggressive. The northern states constantly solicited arms and funds from the central government in order to assemble troops to halt Indian raids. The use of mobile companies of soldiers was tried, but they were outmaneuvered and outgunned by the Indians who, it was thought, obtained their arms from Texians in exchange for stolen cattle. Mexican politicians of the first half of the nineteenth century were of the opinion that the great efforts necessary to deal with the "restless" Texians were the result of a deliberate attempt by them to further destabilize the political scene in Mexico.

The frequency of raids by Indians diminished during the war with the United States, or so available documentation makes it appear. It may be that military and other officials were more preoccupied with the war than with Indian attacks. In any event, news reports about Indian raids dropped sharply during the period, from 416 such reports between 1844 and 1845 to only 59 between 1845 and 1848, most of which concerned stolen animals and attacks on isolated ranches.

After the signing of the Treaty of Guadalupe Hidalgo, the establishment of military outposts was proposed, along with the organization of thirty-four companies of mobile guards. This project was to be financed with a portion of the war compensation funds that were to be received from the United States. In addition, some believed that Article XI of the treaty would cause Indian incursions to diminish. Unfortunately for the inhabitants of the north, the project proved ineffective.

Mexico's defeat had several results apart from the loss of an important piece of territory. After 1848, Indian attacks on northern Mexico intensified as the Lipan Apaches and Comanches abandoned their peace treaties with Chihuahua, Sonora, and Durango. Another grave result was that the majority of the most warlike groups based themselves on the U.S. side, organizing raids into Mexico and then returning to the United States, leaving Mexican forces unable to prevent such attacks or pursue the attackers. In addition, U.S. settlers were driving the Indians toward the southwest of the United States, and the contrast between the strong state to the north and the weak Mexican state, between a U.S. border that was advancing and a Mexican border that was retreating, made it more attractive for the nomadic groups to conduct raids against Mexico.

Antonio Escobar Ohmstede

Translated by The Horse's Mouth Language Services

BIBLIOGRAPHY

Aboites Aguilar, Luis. "Poblamiento y Estado en el norte de México, 1830–1835," in Antonio Escobar Ohmstede (coord.), *Indio, nación y comunidad en el México del siglo XIX*, pp. 303–314. 1993.

Escobar Ohmstede, Antonio, and Teresa Rojas Rabiela (coords.). *La presencia del indígena en la prensa capitalina del siglo XIX. Catálogo de Noticias.* 4 vols. 1992–1993.

Rodríguez, Martha. *Historias de resistencia y exterminio: Los indios de Coahuila durante el siglo XIX.* 1996.

Velasco Avila, Cuauhtemoc. "Historiografía de una frontera amenazada: Los ataques comanches y apaches del siglo XIX," in Antonio Escobar Ohmstede (coord.), *Indio, nación y comunidad en el México del siglo XIX*, pp. 315–328. 1993.

J-K

Jackson, Andrew

A veteran of the Battle of New Orleans during the War of 1812, Andrew Jackson (1767–1845) was the seventh president of the United States and a proponent of U.S. expansionism. The son of Scotch-Irish immigrants, Jackson was born on 15 March and was raised in the Waxhaw area straddling the border between North and South Carolina. At the tender age of thirteen, young Andrew became a prisoner of war during the Revolution, the first war of his long military career.

Following the first Seminole War, Spain ceded East and West Florida to the United States, while retaining Texas. Northeast Texas and its panhandle were considered by some Americans, including Jackson, to be a part of the Louisiana Purchase. Andrew Jackson had a fierce desire to spread U.S. control from the Atlantic Ocean to the Pacific Ocean. As president of the United States during the 1830s Jackson continually tried to annex Texas. Following Texas independence in 1836, Jackson kept in close contact with Texian and Mexican leaders. His retirement from the presidency in 1837 did not end U.S. efforts to regain Texas. Great Britain's efforts to develop an alliance with Texas strengthened Jackson's belief that U.S. annexation of Texas was vital to U.S. national security. He believed that a Texas alliance with Great Britain would restrict U.S. migration to California. On behalf of President John Tyler's administration, Jackson encouraged Sam Houston, president of the Republic of Texas, to pursue annexation with the United States. Jackson's involvement, although small, did influence both sides and on 12 April 1844 a treaty of annexation was signed.

The annexation treaty was condemned by the potential Democratic Party presidential candidates. Secretary of State John C. Calhoun interpreted the treaty as a document that protected the institution of slavery in the United States from British efforts to bring universal abolition to the North

Andrew Jackson. Benjamin Perley Poore, *Perley's Reminiscences*, vol. 1, 1886

American continent. This view aroused the eastern states against annexation. Other candidates, such as Henry Clay and Martin Van Buren, stated that annexation would create sectional rancor and increase the probability of war with Mexico. Because neither favored annexation, Jackson felt that another man should be selected to represent the Democratic Party in the election of 1844. Jackson wanted a candidate who supported annexation of Texas for U.S. national security and who could unite the party together on this one issue. Jackson looked to James K. Polk because Polk supported annexation. This particular election was considered a mandate for the annexation of Texas, especially with the Senate's rejection of the treaty in June 1844. Polk won the presidential election of 1844 by a small margin, and Jackson, who had dreamed of acquiring all of Spanish North America, saw the beginnings of this dream fulfilled. The election of Polk meant that Texas must be annexed, even if it meant war with Mexico. Although Jackson was dying, he continued to focus his energies on the annexation of Texas. When Congress reconvened in December 1844 annexation was again a topic of priority. By February 1845 Congress had approved the annexation of Texas, much to Jackson's delight. The Mexican response to annexation was hostile and U.S. relations with Mexico continued to decline after this point. Suffering from tuberculosis, Jackson spent his remaining days at his plantation, the Hermitage, located near present-day Nashville. It was here that he died on 8 June 1845, less than a year before James K. Polk declared war against Mexico.

Cassandra Britt

BIBLIOGRAPHY

Marquis, James. *Andrew Jackson: Portrait of a President*. 1967.

Remini, Robert V. *Andrew Jackson and the Course of American Democracy, 1833–1845*. Vol. 3. 1984.

Jacksonianism

See **Republicanism, U.S.**

Jalapa

Capital city of the state of Vera Cruz, Jalapa is 4,680 feet above sea level and is shrouded year-round in clouds coming in from the Gulf Coast 75 miles to the east. Misty rains bathe the countryside, giving it an emerald color and rich agricultural produce, including coffee, oranges, avocados, and the famous jalapeño peppers.

During the colonial period the city was the site of trade fairs, as merchants sought refuge from the yellow fever that plagued the port city of Vera Cruz. By the mid-nineteenth century, Jalapa's population had fallen from a peak of forty thousand to about ten thousand people as a result of declining trade. After the seaborne landing of U.S. troops under Gen. Winfield Scott at Vera Cruz City on 9 March 1847, Gen. Antonio López de Santa Anna planned to stop the invasion at nearby Cerro Gordo, holding the invaders in the tropical lowlands where disease would cripple their operations. Nevertheless, on 18 April General Scott successfully flanked the Mexican defenses, and the next day his soldiers occupied Jalapa.

Justin H. Smith, in *The War with Mexico* (1919), claimed that the citizens of Jalapa were prone to collaboration with the U.S. forces, but Mexican authors such as Carmen Blázquez Domínguez (*Veracruz*, 1988) have refuted this accusation. Mexican irregular forces certainly continued to operate in the area, disrupting U.S. supply lines. Two of these guerrillas, Lt. Antonio García and Lt. Ambrosio Alcalde, when captured after receiving an amnesty, were shot in the city on 24 November 1847. A month later, Jalapeños witnessed two more executions, this time of U.S. teamsters who had murdered a local boy. U.S. forces evacuated the city on 12 July 1848.

Jeffrey M. Pilcher

BIBLIOGRAPHY

Blázquez Domínguez, Carmen. *Veracruz: Una historia compartida*. 1988.

Siemens, Alfred H. *Between the Summit and the Sea: Central Veracruz in the Nineteenth Century*. 1990.

Jarauta, Celestino Domeco de

Born in the city of Zaragoza, Spain, Celestino Domeco de Jarauta (1814–1848) joined the priesthood and fought on behalf of Carlos María Isidro de Borbón in Spain's First Carlist War (1833–1839). Afterward Jarauta sailed for Cuba and in 1844 reached the Mexican city of Vera Cruz, where his sermons and demeanor in the confessional made him a popular figure.

Jarauta was one of the most efficient guerrilla leaders to emerge in the state of Vera Cruz after the April 1847 Battle of Cerro Gordo. Active along the Vera Cruz-Jalapa route, his troops set fire to the small ranches around the area and harassed U.S. convoys. During the street fighting that followed the U.S. Army's occupation of Mexico City on 14 September 1847, Jarauta led the residents of the *barrios* of Santa Catarina and Santa Anna in spirited attacks against U.S. soldiers. At least one historian indicates that as of mid-February 1848 Jarauta's guerrillas remained operational north and northeast of the Mexican capital.

Jarauta moved to Aguascalientes later that spring, where his popularity increased as he praised the Mexicans' valor and the beauty of their women; he also repeatedly stated that his only ambition was to kill many U.S. soldiers in order to free Mexico. On 1 June 1848 Gen. Mariano Paredes y Arrillaga rebelled against the *moderado* government in Querétaro because of its willingness to sign a peace treaty with the United States. Jarauta joined the uprising but on 18 July was captured in Valenciana, a town near the city of Guanajuato. He was executed following a summary court-martial that found him guilty of treason.

Pedro Santoni

BIBLIOGRAPHY

González Navarro, Moisés. *Anatomía del poder en México. 1848–1853.* 2d ed. 1983.

Roa Bárcena, José María. *Recuerdos de la invasión norteamericana (1846–1848).* 3 vols. 1947.

Smith, Justin. *The War with Mexico.* 2 vols. 1919. Reprint, 1963.

Jarero, José María

Born in Jalapa, Vera Cruz, Mexican general José María Jarero (1801–1867) entered military service on 1 January 1816 as a soldier in the Urban Infantry Regiment of his native city. Initially a royalist, he joined the Army of the Three Guarantees (*Ejército Trigarante*) in 1821. He was promoted to brigade general in 1832. In 1839 he succeeded Antonio Gaona as governor of San Juan de Ulúa after the French returned that harbor fortress to Mexican control.

In December 1833 a court-martial convicted him of dereliction for having led government forces to defeat at Chilpancingo the preceding month. Briefly incarcerated, Jarero regained favor by supporting the prevailing side in subsequent political adversarialism. As a reward, he received successive commandancies-general in Aguascalientes (1841), Jalisco (1842), Sonora (1846), and México (1847).

At Cerro Gordo in 1847, Jarero commanded one of three brigades that made up the right wing of the Mexican defense. His brigade's destructive fire routed Brig. Gen. Gideon Pillow's inept attack on 18 April, leaving that segment of the defense virtually unscathed. But the loss of El Telégrafo isolated his position, compelling Jarero to surrender his largely intact command. His capitulation put him out of favor with Santa Anna, and thereafter he played an insignificant role in the war. With the advent of peace in 1848, Jarero became commandant-general of Querétaro, seat of the provisional Mexican government. Appointed commandant-general of Puebla in 1849, Jarero ended his lengthy military career at that post in 1857, with the rank of division general. He died in Mexico City at the age of 66.

William A. DePalo, Jr.

BIBLIOGRAPHY

Carreño, Alberto, M. ed. *Jefes del Ejército Mexicano en 1847: Biografías de generales de división y de brigada y de coroneles del ejército por fines del año 1847,* pp. 126–127. 1914.

DePalo, William A., Jr. *The Mexican National Army, 1822–1852,* pp. 121, 124, 226. 1997.

Paz, Eduardo. *Reseña histórica del estado mayor mexicano, 1821–1860,* vol. 2, p. 141. 1907.

Sumario averiguación contra el Sr. General graduado de Brigada José María Jarero . . . December 5, 1833. Archivo General de la Nación (AGN), Archivo de Guerra (AG). Vol. 86, expediente 914, pp. 220–400.

Jesup, Thomas S.

U.S. quartermaster general Thomas Sidney Jesup (1788–1860) was born in Berkeley County, Virginia. Jesup entered the army in 1808, serving with distinction in the War of 1812. In 1818 Jesup was appointed quartermaster and though he remained at the head of that service for the next forty-two years, Jesup was assigned a number of other important commands as emergencies arose. In 1836 he saw service against the Creeks near the Alabama-Georgia border. After a public quarrel with Gen. Winfield Scott following Scott's ineffectual performance in the first year of the Second Seminole War (1836–1842), Jesup himself received the Florida command. Jesup's career took a turn for the worse when he ordered Seminole chief Osceola seized under a flag of truce, citing Osceola's broken promises and the need to bring the rebellion to a close. Nevertheless, Jesup's act, his critics charged, violated the honor of the United States; the issue haunted him throughout his life. Before he was relieved of command by Gen. Zachary Taylor in May 1838, Jesup developed a system of base and advance depots that enhanced his ability to pursue the Seminoles. These methods later proved valuable in the U.S.–Mexican War.

As quartermaster general in that conflict Jesup played a key role in supplying the two U.S. armies invading Mexico in 1846 and 1847. Jesup's first duty was to supply Zachary Taylor's troops massing at various camps opposite Matamoros. There were numerous shortages, especially of wagons, tents, horses, harnesses, saddles, boats, and barges. Jesup advised that pack mules rather than baggage trains be used in General Taylor's trek through northern Mexico—an innovation that was used to good effect. Jesup's next major task was to oversee the supply of Scott's expedition against Vera Cruz, which began in earnest near the end of 1846. Jesup personally procured transport vessels and oversaw the construction of specially made landing craft used to deliver men from the transport vessels. These craft, sometimes called flatboats or surfboats, proved vital to the success of Scott's amphibious landing. Although Taylor, Scott, and other commanders blamed Jesup for shortages, most historians credit Jesup's efforts as outstanding—especially in the face of uncertain and inadequate congressional appropriations. After the war with Mexico Jesup continued to lead the Quartermaster's Department until his death at his home on 10 June 1860.

James M. Denham

BIBLIOGRAPHY

Kieffer, Chester L. *Maligned General: A Biography of Thomas S. Jesup.* 1979.

Smith, George Winston, and Charles Judah, eds. *Chronicles of the Gringos: The U.S. Army in the Mexican War, 1846–1848. Accounts of Eyewitnesses and Combatants.* 1968.

Joaquín de Herrera, José

See **Herrera, José Joaquín de**

Johnston, Albert Sidney

Texas secretary of war and officer in the Texas and U.S. armies, Albert Sidney Johnston (1803–1862) was born in Kentucky. He was educated at Transylvania College and graduated from West Point in 1826. Adopting Texas as his second home, Johnston enlisted as a private in the army of the Republic of Texas in 1836 and advanced within a year to the rank of brigadier general and control of the Texas army. Gen. Felix Huston had temporarily commanded the army, and Johnston's appointment wounded Huston's pride. In February 1837 Huston responded by challenging Johnston to a duel. Johnston chose pistols. Both men fired and missed, reloaded and fired again up to six times; Johnston finally caught a ball in the hip. Huston apologized and pledged his loyalty to Johnston. As Texas secretary of war from 1838 to 1840 Johnston urged strong military preparations and promoted Texas independence.

Johnston was in Kentucky in 1846 when he heard news of the U.S. declaration of war with Mexico. He rushed back to Texas where Gen. Zachary Taylor recommended him for a position in the U.S. Army. Johnston did not receive an appointment, however, because of a long-standing personality conflict with Sam Houston. Houston, at this time a U.S. senator from Texas, opposed granting Johnston a commission, leaving him to seek his own assignment.

The volunteers of the First Regiment of Foot Riflemen of Texas elected Johnston as their colonel, and they performed so well in training under his strict discipline that General Taylor gave Johnston command of the U.S. advance base in Camargo. In August 1846 Johnston took a portion of his regiment to Camargo, where disease and death were so prevalent that his volunteers voted to disband, despite Johnston's fierce objections.

In late August Taylor then assigned Johnston inspector general of Gen. William O. Butler's division, where he served until after the battle of Monterrey. At Monterrey Johnston ordered retreating U.S. troops to turn and hold against the Mexican attack, quite possibly saving them from a massacre. Following his actions at Monterrey, Johnston's fellow officers recommended him for a regular army command, but no position was offered.

After the war, Johnston retired to his Galveston plantation to be with his family. He reentered the U.S. Army in 1849 but resigned in 1861 to become a general in the army of the Confederacy. He was killed at the Battle of Shiloh in 1862.

Tracy M. Shilcutt

BIBLIOGRAPHY

Johnston, William Preston. *The Life of General Albert Sidney Johnston.* 1878.

Roland, Charles P. *Albert Sidney Johnston.* 1964.

Jones, Anson

Anson Jones (1798–1858), last president of the Republic of Texas, was born in Massachusetts and educated as a physician. Jones arrived in Texas in 1833. He served as a regimental surgeon at the Battle of San Jacinto and was elected to the Texas congress in 1836. In 1842, Republic of Texas president Sam Houston appointed Jones his secretary of state. Endorsed by Houston and campaigning on a platform of annexation, Jones was elected as the last president of the Republic of Texas in 1844.

The work of negotiating the annexation agreement with the U.S. government fell to James P. Henderson and Isaac Van Zandt, both appointed by Houston before he left office. Jones also strongly advised Texians to accept annexation rather than the belated Mexican offer of independence. In February 1846 Jones resigned as president when Texas was formally admitted to the Union.

After statehood, Jones prepared a history of the Republic and annexation, a work that was published after his death and garnered much acclaim. He was a candidate for the U.S. Senate in 1857, but the Texas legislature selected John T. Hemphill, chief justice of the Texas Supreme Court. Beset by financial difficulties and depressed over the senatorial contest, Jones committed suicide on 7 January 1858.

Stanley E. Siegel

BIBLIOGRAPHY

Gambrell, Herbert. *Anson Jones: The Last President of Texas.* 1948.

Jones, Anson. *Memoranda and Official Correspondence Relating to the Republic of Texas, Its History and Annexation— Including a Brief Autobiography of the Author.* 1859.

Jones, Thomas ap Catesby

U.S. naval officer Thomas ap Catesby Jones (1790–1858) was born 24 April in Westmoreland County, Virginia. He entered the navy in June 1807. During the War of 1812 he gained recognition for his spirited gunboat defense to the east of New Orleans at Lake Borgne against overwhelming British odds. He later served in the Mediterranean, in December 1814 in the Hawaiian Islands, and was the first commander for the South Seas Surveying and Exploring Expedition in 1836.

While commander of the Pacific Squadron during the summer of 1841, Jones received reports of an impending war between the United States and Mexico. Compounding the issue was the British fleet's mysterious departure from Callao, Peru, in early September amid rumors that Great Britain intended to seize California for debts owed by Mexico to Great Britain. Using the Monroe Doctrine as his justification, Jones proceeded to Monterey, California, where on 19 October 1842 he seized the town to forestall British designs. Upon learning that no war existed, he promptly returned the town to Mexican authorities. He then traveled to Hawaii to thwart British occupation of the islands. Jones returned to Washington, D.C., in October 1843 to face a congressional censure for his actions in Monterey.

During most of the U.S.–Mexican War, Jones served on the Board of Examiners for the newly established Naval Academy, and as inspector of ordnance. Near the end of the war he again commanded the Pacific Squadron. He arrived off California to find a chaotic situation as the gold rush had stripped San Francisco of its civil government and most of its inhabitants. While the navy was needed for order, it, too, faced many problems, including desertion by seamen. To stop desertions Jones resorted to courts-martial, and this illegal action in national waters helped bring about his downfall. Jones was recalled and in 1852 suspended from the service for five years. He spent the remainder of his life trying to exonerate himself and regain his commission. He died 30 May 1858 in Fairfax County, Virginia.

Gene A. Smith

BIBLIOGRAPHY

Bradley, Udolpho Theodore. "The Contentious Commodore: Thomas ap Catesby Jones of the Old Navy, 1788–1858." Ph.D. diss., Cornell University, 1933.

Jones, Walter, et al. *Review of the Evidence, Findings, and Sentence of the Naval Court Martial in the Case of Comm. Thomas ap Catesby Jones.* 1851.

O'Neil, Dan. "From Forecastle to Mother Lode: The U.S. Navy in the California Gold Fields." *Southern California Quarterly* 71 (1989): 69–88.

Jordan, Samuel W.

Samuel W. Jordan (c. 1810–1841) was typical of the adventurous men who infested the border during the days of the Republic of Texas. Sam Houston called Jordan "the abandoned man" for his mysterious past. He arrived in Texas in 1836 too late to participate in the battles of the revolution but quickly advanced to the rank of captain in the Texas army. In 1839 he fought against the East Texas Cherokees but resigned his commission on 2 September to pursue larger ambitions.

Allying himself with Mexican federalist Gen. Antonio Canales, Jordan received the rank of colonel in an insurgent army operating in the northern Mexican states of Tamauli-

pas, Nuevo León, and Coahuila. Leading approximately two hundred Texians and other adventurers, Jordan, Texas Ranger captain Rueben Ross, and several hundred Mexican federalists under Canales, participated in the Battle of Alcantra on 3–4 October 1839. Claiming to be part of Canales's Republic of the Río Grande, Jordan and the other Texians helped occupy Río Grande towns on both sides of the river. That winter the federalist insurgents sought safety within the borders of Texas.

The following year Jordan's troops preceded Canales's army on a raid into the Mexican interior. After capturing Victoria, Tamaulipas, Jordan moved toward San Luis Potosí before realizing that he was unsupported by Canales and heading for the main concentration of centralist forces. On 25 October 1840 Jordan's command fought its way past a centralist force at Saltillo under Gen. Raphael Vasquez, and barely escaped to the Río Grande, where Jordan disbanded his unit.

That December Jordan was in Austin, where he attempted to kill Sam Houston over a harsh exchange of words. By the summer of 1841 Jordan had drifted to New Orleans, where he attempted unsuccessfully to join a campaign against Yucatecan insurgents. Distraught over missing this latest adventure, Jordan killed himself with an overdose of laudanum on 22 June 1841.

Donald S. Frazier

BIBLIOGRAPHY

Nance, Joseph Milton. *After San Jacinto: The Texas-Mexican Frontier, 1836–1841.* 1963.

Pierce, Gerald S. "The Texas Army Career of Samuel W. Jordan." *Texas Military History 5* (Summer 1966).

Vigness, David M. "A Texas Expedition into Mexico, 1840." *Southwestern Historical Quarterly* 62 (July 1958).

Journalism

See **Newspapers**

Juárez, Benito

Born to a Zapotec peasant family in the state of Oaxaca, Mexican politician Benito Juárez (1806–1872) was raised by an uncle after becoming an orphan at the age of three. He moved to the state capital when he turned twelve and in 1831 earned a law degree from the state's Institute of Sciences and Arts. During the next fifteen years Juárez came to identify with the liberal party and entered political life, serving both as a city councilman and state legislator.

Juárez made the transition from provincial to national politics in August 1846 after the restoration of the 1824 federal constitution. As one of Oaxaca's ten deputies to the national legislature, Juárez belonged to a congressional committee that shaped the controversial January 1847 law—designed to finance the war with the United States—that authorized the government to raise 15 million pesos by mortgaging or selling ecclesiastical property.

After returning to Oaxaca, Juárez served as governor from October 1847 until August 1852. Like other liberals, he believed that Mexico could win a protracted guerrilla war and opposed the Treaty of Guadalupe Hidalgo. Juárez also did not grant asylum to Gen. Antonio López de Santa Anna in March 1848 because he feared that Santa Anna's presence in the state might provoke a rebellion. Five years later, shortly after assuming power for the last time, Santa Anna exacted revenge on Juárez, forcing him into exile in New Orleans.

Juárez returned to Mexico in 1855 and served as president between 1857 and 1867. He led Mexican liberals against foreign and domestic enemies in the War of the Reform and the French Intervention, and many thus consider Juárez as the greatest of Mexico's presidents. He remained in office until a heart attack took his life in 1872.

Pedro Santoni

BIBLIOGRAPHY

Cavenhead, Jr., Ivie E. *Benito Juárez y su época. Ensayo histórico sobre su importancia.* 1975

Griswold del Castillo, Richard. *The Treaty of Guadalupe Hidalgo: A Legacy of Conflict.* 1990.

Hamnett, Brian. *Juárez.* 1994.

Juvera, Julián

Mexican general Julián Juvera (1784–1860) was born in Atitaliquia. Early in the U.S.–Mexican War, Juvera commanded cavalry in northern Mexico, screening and scouting against U.S. forces during the Buena Vista campaign. Julián Juvera was the commander of the Querétaro Lancers with whom he saw action at the Battle of El Molino del Rey. On the morning of 8 September 1847, the U.S. 2d Army, under the command of Gen. William J. Worth, began its attack on El Molino del Rey where, Gen. Winfield Scott had been informed, a Mexican cannon foundry was housed. After a brief artillery barrage, Worth ordered an infantry assault. In anticipation of this point in the battle, Gen. Antonio López de Santa Anna's defense plan had called for a flanking charge by the four thousand cavalry troops bivouacked at the nearby Hacienda de Morales. This was to be followed by a reserve-led counteroffensive. The cavalry, however, failed to advance at the right moment. The overall commander of the cavalry, Juan Álvarez, later claimed that his subordinates, who included Juvera, failed to carry out his orders to advance. The leading formation (under Gen. Manuel Andrade) had, in fact, begun to advance, but this vanguard movement

was easily pushed back by the U.S. field artillery. Panic ensued among the other cavalry columns, and the entire force retreated in disarray. Unaided by reinforcements, the Mexican defenders were subsequently reduced by a remounted U.S. artillery barrage and then overcome by a second infantry assault. Despite his association with this bloody battle, Juvera was later appointed commander general of the army in Querétaro and was later elected governor of that state. He died in the city of Querétaro in 1860.

M. Bruce Colcleugh

BIBLIOGRAPHY

Balbontín, Manuel. *La invasión Americana, 1846 á 1848: Apuntes del subteniente de artillería Manuel Balbontín.* 1883.

Roa Bárcena, José María. *Recuerdos de la invasión Norte-Americana, por un joven de entonces.* 1902.

Kearny, Stephen W.

U.S. general and commander of the Army of the West Stephen Watts Kearny (1794–1848) was born in New Jersey.

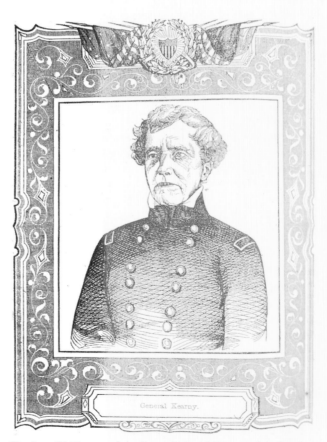

Stephen W. Kearny. John Frost, *Pictorial History of the Mexican War,* 1862

He was commissioned in 1812, served on the first and second Yellowstone expeditions, built Jefferson Barracks near St. Louis, and reestablished Fort Townsend. He became the second-in-command of the new Dragoon Regiment in 1833 and its commander in 1836. In 1846 he traveled the Santa Fe Trail to take possession of New Mexico. The 1st Dragoons regiment formed the nucleus of Kearny's Army of the West. President James K. Polk issued orders promoting Kearny to brigadier general and ordering him on to California after he secured New Mexico. Kearny entered Santa Fe unopposed, proclaiming that the United States would protect the New Mexican citizens' property and religion. He established a law code for New Mexico and installed Charles Bent as its first U.S. civilian governor.

As Kearny started on to California, Kit Carson brought him false news that Col. John C. Frémont had already secured the area. Kearny went on with a single Dragoon company as escort, but when he arrived in California, he discovered the U.S. settlers holed up due to a popular revolt in San Diego and Los Angeles. Kearny fought the battle of San Pasqual en route to San Diego, suffering severe losses. Philip St. George Cooke altered the balance of power in favor of the U.S. forces when he arrived with the Mormon Battalion. Frémont refused to turn over California to Kearny despite presidential orders, and Kearny arrested him for insubordination. Sen. Thomas Hart Benton, Frémont's father-in-law, turned Frémont's court-martial into a trial of Kearny and the Dragoons. Kearny died in St. Louis of malaria contracted at Vera Cruz.

J. Patrick Hughes

BIBLIOGRAPHY
Clark, Dwight L. *Stephen Watts Kearny: Soldier of the West.* 1961.
Hughes, William Boldt, "The Army and Stephen Watts Kearny in the West, 1819–1846." Ph.D. diss., University of Minnesota, 1975.
Kearny, Stephen Watts. Kearny Papers, Missouri Historical Collection, St. Louis, Missouri.

Kendall, George Wilkins

The most celebrated war correspondent of the U.S.–Mexican War, George Wilkins Kendall (1809–1867) was born in Mount Vernon, New Hampshire and first entered journalism as a printer in Vermont. He later served on Horace Greeley's *New Yorker* before relocating to New Orleans, where he cofounded the *Picayune* in 1837.

Soon after the U.S.–Mexican War broke out, Kendall attached himself to Gen. Zachary Taylor's command. In the process of covering most of the important battles of the war, Kendall suffered a gunshot wound to the leg at Chapultepec and captured the Mexican flag at the fall of Monterrey,

which he sent home to his paper as a war souvenir. Kendall is credited with inventing Taylor's famous order, "A little more grape, Captain Bragg."

In order to scoop his competitors Kendall organized his own pony express in Mexico, which doubled as a courier service for official dispatches as well. His fleet of couriers became known as "Mr. Kendall's express." He witnessed the capture of the San Patricio flag at the Battle of Churubusco and the carnage at Cerro Gordo, and he covered the peace negotiations following the fall of Mexico City. At Churubusco he recorded one of the most controversial episodes of the war when, as the lone witness for the press corps, he reported the desertion trial of the San Patricio Battalion.

Following the war Kendall covered revolutions in Europe before returning to Texas and a ranching career. He died on 21 October 1867. Besides his newspaper reports Kendall wrote *Narrative of the Texan Santa Fe Expedition* (1844) and collaborated with Carl Nebel on *War Between the United States and Mexico* (1851).

Mitchel Roth

BIBLIOGRAPHY
Copeland, Fayette. *Kendall of the* Picayune. 1943. Reprint, 1970.
Sandweiss, Martha, Rick Stewart, and Ben. W. Huseman. *Eyewitness to War: Prints and Daguerrotypes of the Mexican War, 1846–1848.* 1989.

Knights of the Golden Circle

The Knights of the Golden Circle was a post–U.S.–Mexican War expansionist organization whose goals included the extension of slavery via military occupation of Latin American countries and creation of a Southern Nationalist Empire.

In the wake of Narcíso Lopez's Cuban expedition in 1850 and William Walker's 1854 attempt to occupy Mexican territory, a Virginia doctor named George Bickley formed a secret organization whose goals included "the expansion of Anglo-Americanism: to strengthen the South and thereby the whole scheme of American civilization." The name, Knights of the Golden Circle, or KGC, was derived from the planned Southern Empire that was to extend from Florida to Panama and back through Latin America to Texas. Bickley apparently had the KGC organized, at least on paper, by 1858.

The KGC had three levels of active membership: military, financial, and political. It was organized in local chapters, or castles, established throughout the South, with elaborate secret codes and rituals. As the organization grew, Bickley's role diminished. A general convention of the KGC was held in Raleigh, North Carolina, from 7 to 11 May 1860. Bickley then moved his headquarters to San Antonio, Texas, to oversee KGC activities there.

The Texas castles, due to their proximity to Mexico, became the most active. Almost every major community in

Texas had a KGC castle, and members included prominent civic leaders. Elkanah Bracken Greer of Marshall, Texas, a lawyer and veteran of the 1st Mississippi Volunteers during the U.S.–Mexican War, became state leader. In February 1860, Greer called on the KGC castles to provide a regiment of mounted volunteers to march into Mexico. Greer's plans were initially supported by Gov. Sam Houston. Robert E. Lee, then colonel of the 2d Cavalry and acting commander of the Department of Texas, was approached to help lead the expedition. Lee turned down the request, and Houston later ordered the assembled volunteers to disband.

As the election of 1860 dominated national affairs, KGC activities shifted to support of the secession movement. KGC castles made up the majority of Col. Ben McCulloch's forces, which forced the surrender of Gen. David E. Twiggs and the U.S. Army Department of Texas at San Antonio in February 1861. The outbreak of the Civil War placed most KGC members in the Confederate Army, ending the organization's plans for conquest of Mexico and Latin America. Various Southern sympathizer groups used the KGC name during the war. Bickley himself was arrested in Indiana and held in a federal prison. He died on 20 August 1867.

Kevin R. Young

BIBLIOGRAPHY

Crenshaw, Ollinger. "The Knights of the Golden Circle: The Career of George Bickley." *American Historical Review* 47: 23–50.

Dunn, Roy Sylvan. "The KGC in Texas, 1860–1861." *Southwestern Historical Quarterly* 70: 543–573.

Knights of the Golden Circle. *Rules, Regulations & Principles of the KGC.* 1859.

Young, Kevin R. *To the Tyrants Never Yield: A Texas Civil War Sampler.* 1992.

Lafragua, José María

Mexican politician José María Lafragua (1813–1875) was born into poverty in the city of Puebla, the son of a retired army officer. He received his law degree from the State University of Puebla in 1835 and entered public service. A Mexican of pure Spanish ancestry, Lafragua joined the *moderados,* or moderate liberal party, and served in the 1842 constitutional congress. In an attempt to form a stable government, Valentín Gómez Farías chose Lafragua as minister of foreign and internal affairs in 1846 under the provisional government. When Antonio López de Santa Anna became president in 1846, Lafragua served as minister of finance but resigned when he disagreed with the president over the excise tax. His critics also accused Lafragua of stealing from the treasury.

During the treaty negotiations of 1848 at the conclusion of the U.S.–Mexican War, he was a secret adviser to the Mexican delegation. He later helped lead the Ayutla Revolution in 1855. He then served as a cabinet member under such presidents as Ignacio Comonfort and Benito Juárez and helped write the Constitution of 1857.

Throughout his career, Lafragua was an extreme nationalist. He sought to place the government as the supreme authority in Mexico while working to weaken the power of the military and the Roman Catholic Church. As a means of limiting the army's power, he worked to establish national guard units. Like most liberals, Lafragua blamed the aristocracy for Mexico's political turmoil, yet he feared social disorder and strongly distrusted the Indians, who he viewed as barbarians.

Randall C. Presley

BIBLIOGRAPHY

Ramírez, José Fernando. *Mexico during the War with the United States.* 1970.

Sinkin, Richard N. *The Mexican Reform, 1855–1876: A Study in Liberal Nation-building.* 1979.

Lamar, Mirabeau B.

Republic of Texas president Mirabeau B. Lamar (1798–1859) was born 16 August near Louisville, Georgia, then the capital of the state. He was the second child in a family that was later to include four sons and five daughters. The Panic of 1819 prevented him from enrolling at Princeton and, after failing at mercantile ventures in Alabama, Lamar returned to Georgia. Through an older brother he met George W. Troup, and when the latter was elected governor in 1823, Lamar became his private secretary. In 1826 he married Tabitha Jordan, and in 1828, when Troup was defeated for reelection, Lamar turned to journalism. He moved to Columbus, Georgia, and founded the *Columbus Enquirer,* a newspaper still in publication.

These busy and happy years were soon marred by tragedy. In 1829, after giving birth to a daughter the previous year, his wife died of tuberculosis at the age of twenty-one. Two poetic elegies, written by Lamar and dedicated to his wife's memory, "Thou Idol of my Soul," and "At Evening on the Banks of the Chattahoochee," date from this period of turmoil and grief. In 1833 Lamar was defeated in a race for the U.S. House of Representatives, and in 1834 the suicide of a brother acted as the capstone to his misfortunes. Recognizing a strain of melancholia in his own personality, Lamar heeded the pleas of James W. Fannin, a friend from Columbus, and agreed to visit Texas. Attracted by the opportunities he perceived in this new society, Lamar returned to Georgia to settle his affairs. The outbreak of the revolution brought him back to Texas in time to learn of Fannin's defeat and death at La Bahía (present-day Goliad). Lamar joined Gen.

Sam Houston's army at San Jacinto and was cited for bravery following the battle there. Politics beckoned and Lamar was ready.

Lamar was elected vice president in the first election held in Texas in 1836. Far from running on the same ticket with the president-elect, Sam Houston, Lamar differed with "Old Sam" on virtually every major issue. Lamar favored an aggressive campaign against the Apaches and Comanches, the execution of captured Gen. Antonio López de Santa Anna, and continued independence rather than admission to the United States. As Houston grappled with financial difficulties and vexing land legislation questions, Lamar put together a political organization looking to the election of 1838. The constitution of the republic forbade a president from serving consecutive terms; with Houston ineligible, Lamar was an easy winner in 1838.

Lamar's presidential term of 1838 to 1841 was marked by both victories and defeats. After talks broke down over compensation for their land claims in East Texas, Lamar harried the Cherokees across the Red River and into Arkansas. At the Battle of Plum Creek near San Antonio in 1841, he reduced the Comanches to an insignificant force in Texas. In accordance with his desire to place the Republic's capital in a more central location, the seat of government was moved from Houston to Austin in 1841. The Homestead Act (1838) and the Education Act (1839) were Lamar's greatest legislative victories. The former guaranteed an owner's rural homestead against seizure for indebtedness, which reflected earlier Spanish and Mexican legislation in Texas. The latter immediately established the Texas public school system and provided for the creation of a "University of the first class" at a later date, which is why Lamar is referred to as the "Father of Education" in Texas.

There were also disappointments during his term. Adamantly opposed to annexation to the United States, Lamar sought direct recognition from the Mexican government of Texas independence. Three separate diplomatic missions to Mexico City failed before Lamar turned to the use of force. The ill-fated Santa Fe Expedition was the greatest failure of his administration. The Texas Boundary Act (1836) claimed the Río Grande as the rightful boundary, but Lamar's attempt to validate the claim by conquering Santa Fe ended in disaster. Some of the Texans starved to death on the march to New Mexico, and the remainder were captured at the gates of Santa Fe. The Republic's financial condition also grew worse under Lamar, exacerbated by the president's profligate spending habits. Sam Houston's overwhelming return as chief executive in 1841 reflected the judgment of most Texans on the Lamar administration.

Lamar's opposition to annexation, combined with the failures of his administration, tarnished his standing in Texas. Although eager for appointment to the U.S. Senate, he received scant attention when the legislature named Houston and Thomas Jefferson Rusk the first two senators from Texas. Lamar fought in the U.S.–Mexican War and received a citation for bravery at the Battle of Monterrey. He was promoted to the rank of lieutenant-colonel and organized the "Laredo Guards," a company of Texas volunteers charged with protecting the border against raiding Comanches. Following the war he returned to his plantation at Richmond, Texas, and fitfully worked on a history of Texas, which he never completed. In 1857 President James Buchanan named him U.S. minister to Nicaragua and Costa Rica. His two-year tour of duty was spent mainly in forestalling the granting of an exclusive contract to a French company to build an interoceanic canal. Worn down and in ill health when he returned to Texas, Lamar suffered a fatal heart attack at his home in Richmond and died 19 December 1859.

Stanley E. Siegel

BIBLIOGRAPHY

Graham, Philip. *The Life and Poems of Mirabeau B. Lamar.* 1938.

Gulick, Charles A., Jr., et al., eds. *The Papers of Mirabeau Buonaparte Lamar.* 6 vols. 1921–1927.

Hogan, William R. *The Texas Republic: A Social and Economic History.* 1946.

Siegel, Stanley. *The Poet President of Texas: The Life of Mirabeau B. Lamar, President of the Republic of Texas.* 1977.

La Mesa, Battle of

On the plains known as La Mesa, outside the pueblo of Los Angeles, Alta California, in the present-day city of Commerce, the last battle of the U.S.–Mexican War in California occurred on 9 January 1847. Gen. José María Flores, leading some five hundred or six hundred Californios, battled U.S. forces under the command of Commo. Robert F. Stockton with Gen. Stephen W. Kearny in tactical command. The U.S. force of some six hundred was made up of dragoons, sailors, marines, California Battalion volunteers, and local volunteers.

The Californios opened fire with a cannonade along the line of march of the U.S. troops. Commodore Stockton advised the men to fall flat when they saw flashes from the Mexican guns, which they did, thus avoiding casualties. An artillery duel ensued for several hours without any serious consequence. The Californios then arrayed themselves in a horseshoe formation and made a charge to attack General Kearny's defensive formation on all sides. The U.S. troops formed a square, with the front rank kneeling with pikes and fixed bayonets, the second rank firing weapons, and repulsed the Mexican cavalry. General Flores then broke off the battle, turned his command over to Maj. Andrés Pico, and departed for Mexico with a number of his followers. This

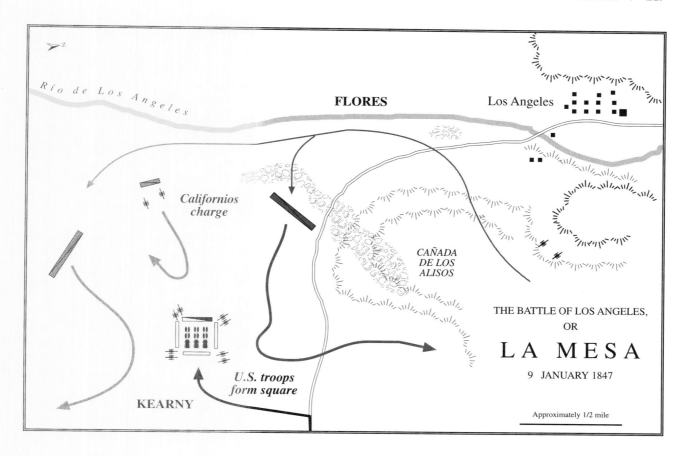

FLORES

Los Angeles

Río de Los Angeles

Californios charge

CAÑADA
DE LOS
ALISOS

U.S. troops form square

KEARNY

THE BATTLE OF LOS ANGELES,
OR

LA MESA

9 JANUARY 1847

Approximately 1/2 mile

ended the fighting in California and led to the capitulation in Cahuenga Pass on 13 January 1847, which was signed by Andrés Pico, chief of the National Forces, for the Californios, and Lt. Col. John C. Frémont, military commandant, for the United States.

Ron Hinrichs

BIBLIOGRAPHY

Duvall, Robert C. "Extracts from the Log of the U.S. Frigate, *Savannah.*" *California Historical Society Quarterly* 3 (July 1924): 105–125.

Emory, William H. *Notes of a Military Reconnaissance from Fort Leavenworth, in Missouri, to San Diego, in California, in 1846.* 1848.

Gillespie, Archibald H. "Gillespie and the Conquest of California, from Letters dated February 11, 1846, to July 8, 1848, to the Secretary of the Navy." *California Historical Society Quarterly* 17 (1938): 123–140, 271–184, 325–350.

Griffin, John S. "A Doctor Comes to California, the Diary of John S. Griffin, Assistant Surgeon with Kearny's Dragoons, 1846–1847." *California Historical Society Quarterly.* Special Publication no. 18 (1943).

Lancers

Mexican lancers held an almost mythical place in the minds of most nineteenth-century writers. Their dramatic uniforms, fearsome weapons, elaborate drill, and supposed discipline suggested that these troopers were the elite of the Mexican army. The lancer military tradition supported this perception. When Hernán Cortés first arrived in Mexico, his well-trained lancers held a military advantage over their Indian opponents far out of proportion to their numbers. Later, Spanish presidial troops used the lance as the weapon of choice against hostile Indians, or *indios bárbaros,* as they were called. As military descendants of the medieval Spanish *Genitours,* these light troops excelled at scouting and skirmishing. In Mexico's Wars of Independence, Royalist lancers had proven especially effective at pursuing routed insurgent armies, the reach of the nine-foot weapon enabling the galloping horsemen to skewer retreating enemies even if the targets crouched or fell to the ground.

On independence, the lance continued to hold a special mystique among mounted troops. Most line regiments of Mexican cavalry carried the instrument as their primary shock weapon. The lance's eight-inch tip, designed to have

A Mexican lancer. John Frost, *Pictorial History of Mexico and the Mexican War*, 1862

three or four cutting edges and a sharpened point, inflicted a nasty wound, while its swallow-tailed pennant frightened enemy mounts. Against disorganized, undisciplined, and poorly trained infantry, such as the Texian revolutionaries, Mexican lancers proved devastating.

In the U.S.–Mexican War, the weapon had an uneven career. Early in the war, Mexican lancers enjoyed notable successes against U.S. dragoons along the Río Grande. Irregular *ranchero* cavalry also used the weapon with good effect as guerrillas and, most notably, at the Battle of San Pasqual, California, against Gen. Stephen Kearny's U.S. regulars. When facing infantry or horsemen armed with reliable firearms and in position to receive a charge, however, the Mexican lancers suffered high casualty rates and often found themselves routed and pursued. After large numbers of U.S. mounted troops began carrying revolvers, the lancers' uncontested domination of the cavalry battlefield ended. Even so, lancers remained a useful and much-feared component of the Mexican military establishment for the rest of the century.

Donald S. Frazier

BIBLIOGRAPHY
Dupuy, R. Ernest, and Trevor N. Dupuy. *The Encyclopedia of Military History from 3500 B.C. to the Present.* 1986.
Hefter, Joseph. *El Soldado Mexicano, 1837–1847.* 1958.
Smith, Justin H. *The War with Mexico.* 2 vols. 1919. Reprint, 1963.

Landero, Juan José

Born in Vera Cruz, Juan José Landero (1802–1869) achieved the rank of general in 1842 by supporting the political ambitions of Antonio López de Santa Anna. On 31 July 1846, shortly after the start of the U.S.–Mexican War, Landero led the garrison of Vera Cruz, aided by Gen. Francisco Pérez, in pronouncing in favor of Santa Anna, allowing him to return from exile. Landero, under the command of Gen. Juan Morales, defended Vera Cruz against Gen. Winfield Scott's March 1847 invasion. Under orders to hold the town to the last, Morales simply turned command over to Landero, forcing him to take the blame for the outcome. When Landero subsequently surrendered the city after running out of ammunition, Santa Anna reacted by imprisoning both Landero and Morales in Perote Castle. Landero was liberated by U.S. troops when they captured the fortress a few weeks later.

His treatment by Santa Anna evidently caused Landero to change his loyalties to the cause of federalism. After the U.S.–Mexican War, he supported Benito Juárez and the liberals in the War of the Reform from 1854 to 1857. He also fought against the imperialists during the French intervention. Landero died in Vera Cruz in 1869.

Donald S. Frazier

BIBLIOGRAPHY
Smith, Justin H. *The War with Mexico.* 2 vols. 1919. Reprint, 1963.
Eisenhower, John S. D. *So Far from God: The U.S. War with Mexico, 1846–1848.* 1989.

Land Grants

Land grants are a form of legal disposition of land by the government. Between 1791 and 1819 Spain issued land titles in Texas to Spanish individuals and families who promised to improve the land, covering some estimated 10 million to 20 million acres. When Texas was opened to foreign settlement by Spain in 1820, land was its only asset and attraction. In contrast to the $1.27 that an acre cost in the United States in 1820, an acre of farmland in Texas cost less than $0.02. This made land speculation in Texas highly attractive. Between 1821 and 1835, when Texas belonged to Mexico, the central and local Mexican governments issued land grants covering 26,280,000 acres either to individuals for personal use or to *empresarios* for further distribution.

After the war of independence in 1835 and 1836, the government of the Republic of Texas had to offer nothing but land to attract prospective settlers. Under a provision of the constitution of 1836, everybody who had been in Texas at the time of the declaration of independence on 4 March 1836 was entitled to extensive headrights: the head of a family was entitled to a league and one *labor* (4,605.4 acres), whereas a single man over seventeen could receive one-third of a league. Those who immigrated to Texas after this date received 1,280 acres if they had a family or 640 acres if they were single. This was changed again for immigrants arriving after 1 October 1837. Then, heads of families received 640 acres and single men only 320 acres. All in all, the Republic of Texas issued land titles for a total of 36,876,492 acres. As the Republic had no money, it also established a donation system for rewarding service in the military. Both the Republic and later the state of Texas issued land titles for this purpose. Everyone who had engaged in the Battle of San Jacinto on 21 April 1836, as well as those who had participated in all previous campaigns of this war, was entitled to a certificate of 640 acres. All the bounty and donation grants for various military campaigns and later for disabled veterans of the Confederate Army totaled 3,149, 234 acres.

The policy to grant premium lands to *empresarios* was discontinued in 1844. The various ways of distributing land titles caused considerable trouble, though, as many who came to Texas after 1830 had bought worthless land titles in the United States or Europe. Others purchased fraudulent land scrip between 1837 and 1839 with the connivance of corrupt local boards of land commissioners and found their choice lands had been occupied already. The Republic of Texas also granted vast areas of Texas for internal improvements. The settlement of the frontier was complicated by conflicting claims that arose from the various *empresario* contracts. Although they often caused problems, land grants were instrumental in the development of Texas.

Andreas V. Reichstein

BIBLIOGRAPHY

Hogan, William Ransom. *The Texas Republic: A Social and Economic History.* 1946.

Lack, Paul D. *The Texas Revolutionary Experience: A Political and Social History, 1835–1836.* 1992.

Miller, Thomas Lloyd. *The Public Lands of Texas, 1519–1970.* 1972.

Reichstein, Andreas V. *Rise of the Lone Star: The Making of Texas.* 1989.

Weber, David J. *The Mexican Frontier, 1821–1846.* 1982.

See also **Empresarios; Land Speculation**

Land Speculation

Land speculation was one of the major economic factors in the early development of Texas. The foundation for the immense land speculation in Texas was laid by the Adams-Onís treaty of 1819, named for the lead negotiaters—John Quincy

Adams of the United States and Luis de Onís of Spain. This treaty, which regulated the cession of Florida to the United States by Spain, set a precedent in regard to Texas, especially Article VIII, which stipulated that all existing land titles would be recognized by the United States. The United States had purchased the vast Louisiana Territory from France in 1803, and many in the United States regarded Texas as having belonged to that territory originally. Thus, as soon as ratification of the Adams-Onís treaty and the new Spanish liberal land policy of 1820 became publicly known in the United States, individuals who assumed eventual U.S. acquisition of Texas formed companies to profit from land speculation in Texas.

The first company was the Texas Association, founded in 1822 by businessmen and professionals from Kentucky and Tennessee. Their representative, Robert Leftwich, received an *empresario* contract in 1825 in his own name to settle eight hundred families in the east of Texas (north of the first settlement area, which had been granted to Stephen F. Austin). Unable to fulfill his contract, it was later transferred to Austin. Haden Edwards also received an *empresario* contract for eight hundred families, but when his brother Benjamin led a rebellion against Mexico in 1826, Mexico annulled the contract and divided it among David G. Burnet, Joseph Vehlein, and Lorenzo de Zavala. These three men brought their contracts and legal positions (as *empresarios*) into a speculation enterprise: in 1830 they participated in establishing the Galveston Bay and Texas Land Company, the most prominent land speculation company in the history of Texas.

Numerous other companies were formed in the United States to speculate in Texas lands, all based on various *empresario* contracts. James Prentiss from New York became the most successful individual in this business. Speculating in Texas lands was not confined to groups and citizens from the United States; Europeans and Mexicans too bought land in Texas that they never intended to settle on themselves.

The most infamous speculation in Texas lands was known as the Monclova speculation, which some historians such as Richard Stenberg believe was a major cause of the Texas Revolution. Representatives of Texas in the parliament of the Mexican state of Coahuila y Texas at Monclova had been instrumental in passing a law in 1835 that disposed of up to four hundred leagues of land to anyone who had enough cash. In this way, sixteen hundred leagues of Texas public lands were sold at prices between fifty and one hundred dollars per league. All the purchasers were speculators, many of them parliamentary representatives, who defended themselves with the argument that the cash was needed to raise an army against Mexican dictator Antonio López de Santa Anna. This sign of disloyalty caused Santa Anna to send an army against Texas, beginning the war that would lead to the independence of Texas in 1836. Most people believed this war was Santa Anna's response to the federal opposition of Coahuila y Texas. This political issue was only part of Santa Anna's reason, however. Santa Anna also had financial interests in Texas and realized how valuable Texas was.

Since 1821, when Mexico had won independence from Spain, the U.S. government had tried to buy Texas from Mexico. Santa Anna and other members of his government as well as members of the Mexican congress were manipulated by individuals, some of whom were U.S. government officials, and others who worked for speculation companies in the United States. They tried to secure as many land grants as possible before Texas became part of the United States. The most notorious agent, other than the U.S. chargé d'affaires, Anthony Butler, who worked secretly for James Prentiss, was John T. Mason, agent for the Galveston Bay and Texas Land Company.

Before all these men succeeded with their schemes, however, Texas won independence from Mexico. Their efforts were not completely in vain, though. Many of the land titles were declared valid, and most of the speculators made enormous profits. In addition, after the U.S.–Mexican War, the Commission for the Settlement of Claims by American Citizens against the Republic of Mexico compensated many for losses they had never suffered. James Prentiss, for example, received nearly $123,000, which was more than double what the Galveston Bay and Texas Land Company received, by handing in fictitious bills.

Andreas V. Reichstein

BIBLIOGRAPHY

Barker, Eugene Campbell. "Land Speculation as a Cause of the Texas Revolution." *Southwestern Historical Quarterly* 10 (1906): 76–95.

Henson, Margaret Swett. *Samuel May Williams: Early Texas Entrepreneur.* 1976.

Reichstein, Andreas V. *Rise of the Lone Star: The Making of Texas.* 1989.

Stenberg, Richard Rollin. "The Texas Schemes of Jackson and Houston, 1829–1836." *Southwestern Social Science Quarterly* 15 (1935): 229–250.

Weber, David J. *The Mexican Frontier, 1821–1846.* 1982.

Williams, Elgin. *The Animating Pursuits of Speculation: Land Traffic in the Annexation of Texas.* 1949.

See also **Empresarios**

Lane, Joseph

U.S. brigadier general of volunteers Joseph Lane (1801–1881) was born in Buncombe County, North Carolina, on 14 December. He moved with his family to Kentucky three years later. Leaving home at age fifteen, Lane moved to Indiana, where he worked at a variety of occupations before winning election to the state legislature at the age of twenty-one.

With the outbreak of war with Mexico in 1846, Lane resigned from the state senate to enlist in the 2d Indiana Volunteers. The men of the regiment elected him colonel, and President James K. Polk soon appointed him a brigadier general of volunteers. Lane's brigade performed with mixed results. At Buena Vista in February 1847, where he was wounded, Lane failed to keep all of his subordinate commanders apprised of changing battle conditions, and one of his regiments broke and fled in the face of a powerful Mexican assault. But in central Mexico, where Lane earned the nickname "Rough and Ready No. 2," his men were instrumental in lifting the siege of Puebla in October 1847. Even after the siege they remained relentless in their pursuit of roving bands of guerrillas, thus earning for General Lane another nickname, that of the "Francis Marion of the Mexican War." The U.S. War Department recognized Lane's outstanding service with a brevet promotion to major general.

President Polk named Lane governor of Oregon Territory in August 1848. Lane also served four terms in Congress and was Oregon's first U.S. senator after statehood in 1859. Lane's stance in support of secession ended his political career with the outbreak of the Civil War. He died at Roseburg, Oregon, on 19 April 1881.

James M. McCaffrey

BIBLIOGRAPHY

Brackett, Albert G. *General Lane's Brigade in Central Mexico.* 1854.

Kelly, M. Margaret Jean. *The Career of Joseph Lane, Frontier Politician.* 1942.

Viola, Herman J. "Zachary Taylor and the Indiana Volunteers." *Southwestern Historical Quarterly* 72 (1969): 335–346.

Winders, Richard Bruce. *Mr. Polk's Army: The American Military Experience in the Mexican War.* 1997.

Laredo and Nuevo Laredo

Spanish settlers established Laredo in 1745 at a crossing of the Río Grande. The village became an assembly point for campaigns north of the river, including Antonio López de Santa Anna's invasion of Texas in 1836. The town supposedly passed to the control of the Republic of Texas later that year when it declared independence, but the new government made no effort to extend its jurisdiction over the town. The residents of Laredo continued to behave as citizens of the Mexican state of Tamaulipas and remained loyal to the government of Mexico.

This changed in 1840, when federalists in the region proclaimed the Republic of the Río Grande with Laredo as its capital. Centralist forces crushed the rebellion and captured the leaders, Antonio Canales Rosillo and Antonio Zapata;

Canales Rosillo recanted and proclaimed himself a centralist while Zapata was executed.

Laredo suffered during the ongoing border war between the Republic of Texas and Mexico. In 1842 troops under the nominal command of Brig. Gen. Alexander Somervell looted the city, but Laredo was not placed under Texas civil jurisdiction. In March 1846 Texas Rangers under Capt. Richard A. Gillespie passed through Laredo and claimed the region for the United States, followed several months later by a military force under the command of Capt. Mirabeau B. Lamar.

In 1848 Laredo became the county seat of Webb County, Texas, but establishing the Río Grande as the international border divided the city of Laredo both politically and physically. Many of its citizens moved across the river to what became the village of Nuevo Laredo, Tamaulipas. The following year, U.S. troops established Fort McIntosh a mile west of Laredo to guard the Río Grande frontier.

Josh Lee Winegarner

BIBLIOGRAPHY

Green, Stan, ed. *A Changing of Flags: Mirabeau B. Lamar at Laredo.* 1990.

Wilkinson, J. B. *Laredo and the Rio Grande Frontier.* 1975.

Larkin, Thomas O.

U.S. consul (1843–1848) to Mexican Alta California, Thomas O. Larkin (1802–1858) was born in Charlestown, Massachusetts. Larkin worked in the Boston area as a bookbinder before moving to North Carolina in 1822. In June 1831, because of unprofitable business ventures in the East, he moved to Monterey, Alta California, where he worked as a bookkeeper for his half-brother John Bautista Rogers Cooper, and then opened his own general merchandise store.

While Larkin prospered as a businessman and had ample opportunities to secure land grants and other concessions from the Mexican government, he chose to remain a U.S. citizen and favored U.S. acquisition of California. Following Thomas ap Catesby Jones's abortive seizure of Monterey in October 1842, Larkin began a prolific correspondence with friends, relatives, and Eastern newspapers encouraging U.S. immigration and annexation. In May 1843, Larkin's business and propaganda activities resulted in his being named U.S. consul to California. He later received government appointments as confidential agent, naval agent, and naval storekeeper and served in an official U.S. capacity through five of the most turbulent years of California's history.

In October 1845, the James K. Polk administration received an urgent letter from Larkin warning Washington of British activities in California. This letter prompted Polk to add the purchase of California to John Slidell's instructions, along with a warning that the U.S. would not allow Mexico

to sell its Pacific coastline to a foreign power. This news was leaked to the Mexican press, which doomed Slidell's mission. Ironically, in the meantime Larkin had sent another letter, which arrived in Washington, D.C., in December, indicating that California was not in any immediate danger after all. Polk promptly instructed Secretary of State James Buchanan to modify his instructions to Slidell, but Slidell was already in Mexico, the news of his initial instructions had leaked to the press, and the damage had been done.

Prior to June 1846, Larkin tried to secure peaceful annexation of California by creating a feeling of mutual trust between U.S. citizens and native non-Indian California-born Mexicans. During the Bear Flag Revolt and U.S. occupation, he served in a civilian capacity, making useful suggestions to army and navy commanders. After the conquest and subsequent annexation he functioned only as an influential businessman and speculator, and his importance diminished. He died in San Francisco of a fever. Throughout his years on the Pacific Coast Larkin promoted the region's growth and painted an unparalleled picture that encouraged immigration and ultimately helped bring California into the Union.

Gene A. Smith

BIBLIOGRAPHY

Hague, Harlan, and David J. Langum. *Thomas O. Larkin: A Life of Patriotism and Profit in Old California.* 1990.

Hammond, George P., ed. *The Larkin Papers: Personal, Business, and Official Correspondence of Thomas Oliver Larkin, Merchant and United States Consul in California.* 10 vols. 1951–1968.

Thomas O. Larkin. Papers. Bancroft Library, University of California, Berkeley.

Legacy of the War

This entry consists of two separate articles: **Legacy of the War in Mexico** *and* **Legacy of the War in the United States.**

Legacy of the War in Mexico

The U.S.–Mexican War has been a crucial event in the two countries' relationship that has left ineffaceable marks. The most obvious and physical mark is the border that separates the United States and Mexico. Mexico was forced to cede a considerable portion of its original territory, which in turn reduced its opportunities for future economic development. The loss of that territory also deprived Mexico of a safety valve for demographic growth in years to come. Hence, the asymmetries between Mexico and the United States in economic growth, resources, and population that existed before the war became even more pronounced, and continue to the present day. Thus, some of the social and economic problems that both governments and societies confront today had their roots in the final outcome of the U.S.–Mexican War.

The war also left its mark on Mexican perceptions about the United States. Even after peace was achieved, the military occupation had ended, and normal diplomatic relations had been resumed, Mexicans did not believe that the territorial ambitions of the United States had been completely satisfied. Hence, the United States remained a potential enemy of Mexico's interests and prosperity. Yet, Mexicans also believed that the U.S. victory was due in large part to U.S. social and political cohesiveness and to the strength of its institutions. Therefore, after the war and to the late twentieth century, the Mexican perception of the United States has been ambivalent; the United States was a kind of model, but also an undependable neighbor. In fact, the United States became an important catalyst for Mexican nationalism. Social, ideological, and cultural differences among Mexicans were attenuated by the sense of danger that the United States represented for Mexico. As Mexican historian Daniel Cosio Villegas said, "The war with the United States, the loss of territory itself, contributed, as did few other events, to consolidate a genuine nationalism [in Mexico]—through the perception of danger, a fatalistic but tremendously effective feeling in a powerless country." (*La guerra con Estados Unidos, la perdida misma del territorio, ayudó, como pocos hechos, a consolidar nuestra nacionalidad—a travis de la fuerza negativa, pero tremendamente eficaz cuando se trata de pueblos débiles, de la sensación del peligro.*)

During the months following the withdrawal of U.S. forces from Mexico, Mexican political parties began to consolidate, and the war and its consequences were determining factors in how the parties reformulated their platforms. The Conservative Party believed that the only way Mexico would be able to resist the expansionism of the United States was to restore the monarchical form of government and strengthen its ties with the European powers. The Liberal Party, however, reasserted the need to maintain the republican and federal system and also proposed a new program of radical social reforms. The conservatives maintained that Mexico must reaffirm its European, particularly its Spanish, legacy and distance itself from the ideological influences of the United States. The liberals, on the other hand, believed that the only way Mexico could confront the challenge that the United States represented was to be as similar to the United States as possible. Paradoxically, the most important leaders of both parties, and the editorials published in the papers that supported them, reached the conclusion that regardless of the painful and humiliating results of the war, these had presented Mexico with the opportunity to review its errors and correct them in search of a more promising future. The Mexican defeat thus aroused the national consciousness.

Between 1858 and 1867 these two political forces confronted each other in a civil war, during which the Conservative Party invited the intervention of the French government, and with it succeeded in restoring a precarious monarchy under the rule of Maximilian of Hapsburg. The war with the United States had prepared Mexicans to confront foreign intervention, however, a factor that helped the liberals defeat the conservatives and their French allies. The victory of the Liberal Party resulted in policies designed to emulate U.S. social, economic, and political institutions, yet conservative ideology did not disappear completely; both the triumphant liberals and the defeated conservatives maintained a strong distrust of the United States.

This distrust arose again during the years of the Mexican Revolution (beginning in 1910) and its aftermath, when renewed U.S. intervention (which included the 1914 U.S. occupation of the port of Vera Cruz and the 1916 Punitive Expedition, when U.S. troops again entered Mexico) made Mexicans recollect the war of 1846 to 1848. More recently, in the 1990s, under the new climate of cooperation symbolized by the North American Free Trade Agreement (NAFTA) of 1993, Mexican authorities tried to diminish the importance of the U.S.–Mexican War in elementary school textbooks. This decision caused heated debate among Mexican intellectuals and the public; most opposed the government officials' decision. This decision also contradicted the fact that the second most important memorial in Mexico City is the one dedicated to the defenders of Chapultepec, los Niños Héroes; this monument is symbolically named the Altar to the Fatherland (*el Altar a la Patria*).

The caution and distrust that sprang from the war was also evident in the way Mexican diplomacy was carried out with respect to the United States. Mexico, lacking comparable resources of power, developed a legalistic approach. Thus, the Mexican style of conducting its diplomatic affairs has emphasized legal grounds over practical ones. The main doctrinal principles of Mexican foreign policy—nonintervention, self-determination, and peaceful resolution of international conflict—reflect the painful experiences of the early years of its history, particularly its war with the United States.

The war's shadow continues to fall on the Mexican national consciousness. The war was the first evidence of the asymmetry between Mexico and the United States, and its results deepened their differences. The war, though not an unhealed wound, remains a painful scar. Above all, in addition to being an important part of the bilateral diplomatic history, the war also is part of a mutual, shared history. Since the Treaty of Guadalupe Hidalgo in 1848, it has been evident that what occurs in one of the two countries has some consequence in the other; in this way, the national destinies of Mexico and the United States have ever since been linked.

Jesús Velasco-Márquez

BIBLIOGRAPHY

Cosio-Villegas, Daniel. "El Porfiriato, era de consolidacion." *Historia Mexicana* 12 (1963).

Vazquez, Josefina Zoraida, and Lorenzo Meyer. *México frente a Estados Unidos: Un ensayo historico, 1776–1993*. 1994.

Velasco-Márquez, Jesús. *La Guerra del 47 y la opinion publica, 1845–1848*. 1975.

Velasco-Márquez, Jesús, and Thomas Benjamin. "La Guerra entre México y los Estados Unidos." In *Mitos en las relaciones México–Estados Unidos*, compiled by Ma. Esther Schumacher. 1994.

Legacy of the War in the United States

In 1848, as a result of the U.S.–Mexican War, the United States added more than 500,000 square miles of former Mexican territory in exchange for $15 million and the assumption of Mexican obligations to U.S. citizens. The war also settled the issue of the boundaries of Texas. The new territory comprised the present-day states of Arizona, California, Colorado, Nevada, New Mexico, and Utah. The acquisition of these rich new lands insured that the United States would become a major continental power and enter the industrial age with vast new natural resources. Additionally, the conquest of new populations of Mexican origin would create new currents of ethnic conflict.

The U.S.–Mexican War was a catalyst in intensifying sectional rivalries between the North and South that led eventually to the outbreak of the Civil War. The acquisition of the Mexican Cession by the Treaty of Guadalupe Hidalgo reopened the issue of slavery in the territories. During the war, New England antislavery spokesmen such as Ralph Waldo Emerson and James Russell Lowell had intensified their anti-Southern rhetoric. They saw in the war a conspiracy of slave owners to acquire more slave territory. The Wilmot Proviso, a statement that slavery would be excluded from the conquered territories, had been added to many bills in Congress during the war and then defeated by Southern senators. By the end of the war the issue of slavery in the territories had become a bitter issue of debate between Northern and Southern interests.

When California applied for admission to the union in 1850 as a free state, the public discussion reached new levels of intensity. Sen. Henry Clay offered a compromise to settle the issue: California would be admitted as a free state, and the territories of New Mexico and Utah would be allowed to decide for themselves whether slavery would be allowed. This arrangement violated the spirit of the Missouri Compromise of 1820, which protected slavery in territories south of the line 36°30′ north latitude and excluded it north of that line. The concessions to Southern interests such as allowing slavery to continue to exist in Washington, D.C., and the national recognition of the internal slave trade intensified sectional conflict over slavery. But the passage of a national Fugitive Slave Law by Congress, part of the Compromise of 1850, provided fuel for a larger fire. The Fugitive Slave Law, which required the return from the North of escaped slaves, became a constant source of irritation for abolitionists in the North and created the emotional and political climate that made *Uncle Tom's Cabin* by Harriet Beecher Stowe a bestseller. This book more than anything else popularized the antislavery cause among nonabolitionists.

Another legacy of the U.S.–Mexican War was the forcible incorporation of almost one hundred thousand people within the United States: former Mexican citizens including Spaniards, mestizos, and large Native American populations in Arizona and New Mexico. These groups soon suffered under the change of sovereignty as their lands were taken by corporations, land speculators, railroads, and the government and as their constitutional rights were violated. In the years following the signing of the Treaty of Guadalupe Hidalgo in 1848, the promises the U.S. government made in Articles VIII and IX with respect to the U.S. citizenship and property rights of the conquered Mexican populations remained largely unfulfilled, providing a source of bitterness and moral outrage that lasts into the late twentieth century.

Further, because of the war and the Treaty of Guadalupe Hidalgo, many Mexican Americans born in the twentieth century feel that they have a special status within the United States by virtue of their interpretation of the treaty as a human rights document. As a conquered people the Mexicans within the United States have been given special considerations under an international treaty. Although these considerations proved to be quite illusory when the U.S. government undermined the intent of the original document, U.S. citizens of Mexican descent continue to have a historical claim on the collective moral conscience of the United States.

The legacy of the war extends to international relations. The Treaty of Guadalupe Hidalgo is the oldest international agreement still in force between Mexico and the United States. Those portions of the original treaty still binding on their relations in the late 1990s are included in Articles VIII and IX (land and citizenship provisions), Article XVI (the right to fortify ports), and Article XXI (renouncing war as a means of settling future disputes and providing for arbitration of conflicts).

Another legacy of the U.S.–Mexican War has been to engender a number of conflicts between the two countries. The first and most serious had to do with the specification of the new international boundary between the two countries. The treaty, in effect, created new boundary disputes in its designation of the southern border between the territory of New Mexico (including Arizona) and the Mexican state of Chihuahua. Article V in the treaty had specified a new dividing line for this region, but a serious controversy arose over the exact southern boundaries of New Mexico. The map used by the treaty makers, Disturnell's 1847 *Map of Mexico*, had several errors, placing El Paso del Norte one-half degree too far south and the Río Grande two degrees too far north, meaning that the United States would lose about six thousand square miles of territory along with about three thousand persons. After lengthy disputes the United States sent James Gadsden to Mexico in 1853, and eventually Mexico signed the Gadsden Treaty or Tratado de Mesilla. As eventually modified by the U.S. Congress, the United States agreed to pay $10 million, and Mexico ceded the territory the U.S. interests wanted for a railroad while allowing the United States to abrogate Article XI in the Treaty of Guadalupe Hidalgo and granting the rights of transit across the Isthmus of Tehuantepec. The new treaty granted the United States an additional 29,142,000 acres (45,539 sq. mi.) of Mexican territory and released the United States from the obligation of policing the border Indians (as provided in Article XI).

Another legacy of international conflict engendered by the U.S.–Mexican War included the Pious Fund controversy, a dispute over the rights to a Mexican investment fund earmarked for the California missions. This dispute was not resolved until 1967. Another dispute was the ownership of a tract of desert land in El Paso, Texas, the Chamizal. This conflict also lasted more than one hundred years and was not settled until 1968.

The U.S.–Mexican War has assumed more importance as the population of those of Mexican origin within the United States has increased and as U.S.–Mexican economic relations have become more significant, especially with the signing of the North American Free Trade Agreement between the two countries in December 1993. The contemporary issues of Mexican immigration and the Mexican national debt are indirect legacies of the U.S.–Mexican War. The war is a defining event for the history of the Mexican-Americans within the United States, providing a just claim on the conscience of the country.

Richard Griswold del Castillo

BIBLIOGRAPHY

Griswold del Castillo, Richard. *The Treaty of Guadalupe Hidalgo: A Legacy of Conflict.* 1990.

Mawn, Geofry. "A Land Grant-Guarantee: The Treaty of Guadalupe Hidalgo or the Protocol of Queretaro?" *Journal of the West* 14, no. 4 (October 1975): 49–63.

Pletcher, David M. *The Diplomacy of Annexation: Texas, Oregon, and the Mexican War.* 1973.

León, Antonio

Mexican general Antonio León (1794–1847) was born in Huajuapam, Oaxaca, on 4 June. He entered military service in May 1811 as an ensign in his provincial militia company. León participated in the royalist counterinsurgency campaigns before embracing the independence movement in March 1821. Appointed commandant-general of Oaxaca in postindependence Mexico, León was subsequently elected a deputy to the constituent Congress of 1824 and the national Congress of 1832 (which never convened). In 1838 León assumed the added responsibility for governing the unruly state of Chiapas, which he had previously helped pacify.

A federalist, León supported Div. Gen. Mariano Paredes y Arrillaga's August 1841 movement for the "Regeneration of the Republic" that ultimately brought down the centralist regime of President Anastasio Bustamante. He also played a key role in the incorporation of the Soconusco region (part of present-day Chiapas) into the Republic of Mexico (1842), a military achievement that earned him promotion to brigade general in January 1843.

During the war with the United States León commanded a Oaxacan brigade assigned to the reserve forces at Cerro Gordo. Following that disastrous engagement, his largely intact brigade formed the core around which the Army of the East was reconstituted for the ensuing valley campaign. On 8 September 1847, León was mortally wounded while leading his brigade at El Molino del Rey and died a few hours after that bloody contest subsided. Elevated posthumously to division general, León is still revered in the pantheon of Mexican war heroes.

William A. DePalo, Jr.

BIBLIOGRAPHY

Carreño, Alberto, M., ed. *Jefes del Ejército Mexicano en 1847: Biografías de generales de división y de brigada y de coroneles del ejército por fines del año 1847,* pp. 185–187. 1914.

DePalo, William A., Jr. *The Mexican National Army, 1822–1852,* pp. 124, 133, 171, 232. 1997.

Roa Bárcena, José María. *Recuerdos de la invasión norteamericana, 1846–1848,* vol. 2, p. 80n. 1947.

Sosa, Francisco. *Biografías de mexicanos distinguidos (doscientos noventa y cuatro),* pp. 349–352. 1985.

Léperos

The term *léperos,* of unknown derivation, was used as a pejorative to describe the lower class in Mexican cities in the nineteenth century. The wealthy and socially prominent also used the terms *populacho* or *chusma* to express their distaste for and purported moral superiority to the drifters, beggars, criminals, and unemployed people who inhabited the streets. The elite regarded the *léperos* as particularly vice-ridden and immoral and thought that they could be distinguished from the honest, working poor. Historians who have studied arrest records and other documentation have determined that these were not precise sociological categories but rather evidence of social prejudices. The terms *lépero, chusma,* and *populacho* lumped together most of a city's working poor, underemployed laborers, and out-of-work artisans with criminals and vagrants. The cities' intermittent political and economic disturbances frequently resulted in economic disruption and forced more people into occasional criminal activity. The largest breakdown in civil order during the early republican period was the Mexico City Parián Riot of 1828, but looting commonly resulted from the disruption of civil authority and the intermittent political instability that characterized early republican Mexico. During the U.S.–Mexican War period conservatives and *moderados* feared that the *puros'* plans to organize civic militias would result in arms falling into the hands of the *léperos*.

Donald F. Stevens

BIBLIOGRAPHY

Arrom, Silvia M. "Popular Politics in Mexico City: The Parián Riot, 1828." *Hispanic American Historical Review* 68 (May 1988): 245–268.

Di Tella, Torcuato S. "The Dangerous Classes in Early Nineteenth Century Mexico." *Journal of Latin American Studies* 5 (May 1973): 79–105.

Santoni, Pedro. "A Fear of the People: The Civic Militia of Mexico in 1845." *Hispanic American Historical Review* 68 (1988): 269–288.

Shaw, Frederick J., Jr. "Poverty and Politics in Mexico City, 1824–1854." Ph.D. diss., University of Florida, 1975.

Warren, Richard Andrew. "Vagrants and Citizens: Politics and the Poor in Mexico City, 1808–1836." Ph.D. diss., University of Chicago, 1994.

Lerdo de Tejada, Miguel

The eldest son of a merchant family from the city of Vera Cruz, Miguel Lerdo de Tejada (1812–1861) pursued business as a career until entering the government bureaucracy at a low level. He joined the ranks of the liberal party at an early age but remained a largely unknown political figure at the time of the U.S.–Mexican War.

During the U.S. occupation of the Mexican capital, Lerdo belonged to a group of twenty-one liberals, mostly *puro*, who secured election to the *ayuntamiento* with the help of U.S. authorities. Lerdo and his associates cooperated with the invaders, using the situation to launch a number of radical social, political, and economic reforms. Their agenda included the creation of a loose political system in which Mexico City and the Federal District would be almost sovereign. Members of the public, however, interpreted Lerdo's program as being indicative of his desire to annex Mexico to the U.S. Such cooperation earned him the label of traitor.

After the war Lerdo became the most influential economic theorist for Mexican liberalism. He served various regimes in the 1850s both as minister of development and of finance. Perhaps his most important legacy was authoring the Lerdo Law of 1856. The decree, which forced the church to sell all its urban and rural real estate not directly used in day-to-day operations, sought to end church economic power and hence reduce its political and social influence. Lerdo was

running for president at the time of his death in Mexico City in 1861.

Pedro Santoni

BIBLIOGRAPHY

Berge, Dennis B. "A Mexican Dilemma: The Mexico City Ayuntamiento and the Question of Loyalty, 1846–1848." *Hispanic American Historical Review* 50, no. 2 (May 1970): 229–256.

Blázquez, Carmen. *Miguel Lerdo de Tejada: Un liberal veracruzano en la política nacional.* 1978.

Olliff, Donathon. *Reforma Mexico and the United States: A Search for Alternatives to Annexation, 1854–1861.* 1981.

Liberty Party

The Liberty Party grew out of the antislavery movement and functioned as its adjunct. In the 1830s politically oriented abolitionists adopted the tactic of questioning candidates on issues crucial to their cause, especially the prospect of annexing Texas, and then publicizing their support for the least objectionable aspirant. Because neither Whigs nor Democrats often met abolitionists' standards, many concluded that independent, third-party nominations were essential.

In 1839 a group dedicated to abolition and to severing the national government from all support for slavery organized the Liberty Party. Backing for the new party was particularly strong in western New York, where the lawyer Alvan Stewart and Myron Holley, a former Anti-Masonic Party activist, were leading proponents. In 1840 the party's presidential candidate, James G. Birney of Ohio, a former slaveholder, received scarcely 7,000 votes. The poor showing did not discourage party loyalists, for they viewed their party more as a vehicle for abolitionist propaganda than as an instrument of political power. In 1844 Birney was nominated again and this time received 62,000 votes. In that election enough Whigs in New York deserted their party's candidate, Henry Clay, in favor of Birney to give the state's electoral votes to James K. Polk, thereby assuring his election.

In 1848 Liberty Party voters generally supported the new Free Soil Party, although one faction, led by Gerrit Smith of New York, believing that a separate identity was essential, continued its independent course as the Liberty League in the elections of 1848 and 1852, but it received only minuscule support.

Merton L. Dillon

BIBLIOGRAPHY

Kraditor, Aileen S. *Means and Ends in American Abolitionism: Garrison and His Critics on Strategy and Tactics, 1834–1850.* 1969.

Sewell, Richard H. *Ballots for Freedom: Antislavery Politics in the United States, 1837–1860.* 1976.

Linden, Pedro Vander

See **Vander Linden, Pedro**

Literature

When the United States went to war against Mexico, momentous changes were altering the ways people in the United States viewed themselves and their nation and the ways they lived their everyday lives. Technology was bringing them more closely together, as steam power facilitated mobility on land and water and the magnetic telegraph revolutionized the dissemination of news. The expansion of public education and one of the highest literacy rates in the world led to an insatiable demand for inexpensive reading material. The populace became known as a reading people. Steam-powered cylinder presses and new techniques in papermaking made possible the mass production of low-priced books, newspapers, and magazines. Railroads provided the means for distribution to all parts of the country. It was an age of steam in matters literary and intellectual, as well as in the material aspects of life.

Romanticism was at its height in the United States, a circumstance nowhere more evident than in the character of the nation's literature. The generation that fought the U.S.–Mexican War had been nurtured on the medieval and border romances of Sir Walter Scott and his imitators. Mexico, an ancient, strange, and mysterious land, seemed to exhibit vestiges of the romantic past described by Scott. The epic struggle between sixteenth-century Spain and the Aztec empire captivated the U.S. public imagination, and when the war with Mexico came, such fictional accounts as Robert Montgomery Bird's *Calavar; or, The Knight of the Conquest* (1834) and Charles Maturin's *Montezuma: The Last of the Aztecs* (1845) played a part in stimulating a popular war spirit. William Hickling Prescott's monumental *History of the Conquest of Mexico* (1843) more than any other single work influenced the popular response to the U.S.–Mexican War.

The first battles of the war heralded a new direction for literature in the United States, as works of fiction, poetry, biographies of the military leaders, and histories flooded the market for reading material. Many predicted that the war would form a distinct epoch in the nation's literary history, that it would provide writers with all the elements of romance and drama they would need for years to come. Some believed the war would prove to be an important step toward the development of a national literature that would faithfully reflect the country's ideals, aspirations, and mission.

One of the innovations fostered by the war was the appearance of inexpensive paperbound adventure stories, the precursors of dime novels. Commonly called novelettes, the stories were bound in bright yellow paper covers, printed on rough paper in double columns, rarely exceeding one hundred pages in length, and were published in editions of as many as sixty thousand copies. Soldiers bought them to break the monotony of camplife and of the long sea voyages from eastern ports; they also were eagerly read by the folks back home. The Mexican settings and the simple plots were embellished by sentimental and Gothic characteristics. Bearing such titles as *The Chieftain of Churubusco; or, The Spectre of the Cathedral* (1848); *The Mexican Ranchero; or, The Maid of the Chapparal* (1847); *The Texan Ranger; or, The Maid of Matamoras* (1847); and *Magdalena, the Beautiful Mexican Maid: A Story of Buena Vista* (1847), the stories revealed a familiarity with Mexico and the war that was derived from travel narratives, campaign accounts, and soldiers' letters that filled the newspapers and magazines. Their portrayal of the war reflected the way many in the United States perceived the conflict: the contrast between the wholesome patriotic volunteer and the dark, skulking Mexican rancheros; the deeds of heroism on the battlefield and the volunteers' generosity to the vanquished foe; the rescue of Mexican maids from the clutches of villainous Mexican soldiers and priests; and the love that overcame all national and cultural differences. With a few exceptions, the authors are now lost to history.

Three of the most popular writers of fiction in midcentury America, Henry William Herbert, George Lippard, and James Fenimore Cooper, exploited U.S.–Mexican War themes: Herbert, whose fiction ranged from ancient Rome through medieval knighthood to the American Revolution, in *Pierre, The Partisan: A Tale of the Mexican Marches* (1848); Lippard, who was best known for his sensational exposé of urban life, in his *Legends of Mexico: The Battles of Taylor* (1847) and *'Bel of Prairie Eden: A Romance of Mexico* (1848); and Cooper in his novel of the war at sea, *Jack Tier; or, The Florida Reef* (1848).

Those writers who are now considered to be the major literary spokesmen of the mid-nineteenth century United States contributed little toward a U.S.–Mexican War literature. Nathaniel Hawthorne later wrote a biography of Franklin Pierce (1852), who served as a brigadier general of volunteers, in which he saw in the volunteers the spirit of young knights; Herman Melville published only a series of satirical sketches of Zachary Taylor in a humor magazine. Walt Whitman, in his Brooklyn newspaper editorials, strongly supported the war as a fulfillment of U.S. destiny and mission. Ralph Waldo Emerson was ambivalent about the war, while Henry David Thoreau protested the war on the mistaken assumption that it was brought about by a conspiracy to extend slavery into western lands.

The nation's midcentury years have often been called an age of poetry, when poems filled the columns of newspapers and periodicals and when publishers announced new books of poetry almost daily. The U.S.–Mexican War provided the impetus for a remarkable outpouring of verse that captured all the moral drama and romantic pathos of clashing armies, of heroism and self-sacrifice, patriotism and devotion to the country's cause, and the glory of death in battle. Some looked for a new *Iliad* that would provide the country with a national epic, and indeed some efforts were made to tell the war's story in long narrative poems, including the *Siege of Monterey* in 493 stanzas (1851) by William C. Falkner, great-grandfather of the twentieth-century novelist. William Gilmore Simms honored South Carolina's volunteers in his *Lays of the Palmetto* (1848); Charles Fenno Hoffman's popular poem "Monterey" (1846) was widely reprinted; the abolitionist John Greenleaf Whittier expressed his opposition to the war in a number of poems, including his most enduring war poem "The Angels of Buena Vista" (1847); and James Russell Lowell, a dedicated abolitionist, viewed the war as a national crime committed on behalf of slavery in his harsh political satire, *The Biglow Papers* (1848).

The U.S.–Mexican War cannot be said to have inspired a great literature, as so many thought it would, nor did it provide the distinctive national literature for which "Young America" yearned. The war aroused a new interest in earlier wars, particularly Wellington's Peninsular War and the American Revolution (with which the U.S.–Mexican War was often linked), and publishers were quick to meet the demand with fiction, biographies, and historical works. Nonetheless, the war, through the novelettes, the fiction, and the poetry, as well as the music (the first U.S. war in which music played an important, patriotic role) and the art, complemented by the timely reports of war correspondents, the soldiers' letters and their campaign accounts, entered the national consciousness as no other major episode in U.S. history had to that time.

Robert W. Johannsen

BIBLIOGRAPHY

DeLeon, Edwin. *The Position and Duties of "Young America," An Address Delivered Before the Two Literary Societies of the South Carolina College, December, 1845.* 1845.

Johannsen, Robert W. *To the Halls of the Montezumas: The Mexican War in the American Imagination.* 1985.

Somkin, Fred. *Unquiet Eagle: Memory and Desire in the Idea of American Freedom, 1815–1860.* 1967.

Stafford, John. *The Literary Criticism of "Young America": A Study in the Relationship of Politics and Literature, 1837–1850.* 1952.

Lithographs

See Art

Lombardini, Manuel María

One of Mexico's "kingmakers" during the age of the *caudillos,* Manuel María Lombardini (1802–1853) entered Spanish military service at age twelve. After independence, he rose through the ranks, generally by supporting Antonio López de Santa Anna, and commanded a brigade that opposed an uprising in Puebla in 1834. In 1836 Lombardini rushed north to the Río Grande to reinforce Santa Anna's army after the disaster at San Jacinto. In 1838 the veteran soldier helped fight the French in Vera Cruz during the Pastry War.

By 1846 he was a general of division and commanded the Mexican Army of the East, headquartered at Vera Cruz. In 1847 he led the 1st Division of Santa Anna's army at the Battle of Buena Vista on 22 February. While leading the assault that would eventually turn the U.S. left flank, Lombardini fell wounded, passing command of his troops to Gen. Francisco Pérez.

By summer Lombardini had recovered enough to resume command and participated in the defense of Mexico City, particularly at the Belén Garita (Belén Gate). When the fall of that city appeared inevitable, Santa Anna gave command of the Mexican army to Lombardini and ordered him to evacuate the capital. In 1848, after the reinstallation of José Joaquin de Herrera as president, Lombardini defended the government against an attempted coup.

Lombardini led the entire Mexican army in 1853 as head of the headquarters, or *Plana Mayor.* During a series of political disturbances that year, Lombardini took over the government as interim president from February through April, before passing control of the government to Santa Anna. Lombardini took over as head of the state of México and commandant general of the Federal District, thus ensuring Santa Anna loyalty from the local garrison. Lombardini died suddenly shortly thereafter.

Donald S. Frazier

BIBLIOGRAPHY

Carreño, Alberto M., ed. *Jefes del ejército Mexicano en 1847: Biografías de generales de división y brigadad y de coroneles del ejército Mexicano por fines del año de 1847.* 1914.

DePalo, William A., Jr. *The Mexican National Army, 1822–1852.* 1997.

Smith, Justin H. *The War with Mexico.* 2 vols. 1919. Reprint, 1963.

Los Niños Héroes

On 13 September 1847 the battle of Chapultepec began when U.S. forces stormed the fortified hill of Chapultepec Castle, which was defended by about one thousand Mexican troops inside the fortifications and another four thousand nearby. Housed within the castle was the Colegio Militar, the Mexican military academy, and its teenage cadets, who participated in the battle. Six of these cadets—Juan de la Barrera, Juan Scutia, Francisco Márquez, Agustín Melgar, Fernando Montes de Oca, and Vicente Suárez Ferrer—became known as los Niños Héroes, or the heroic children, because they preferred to die rather than surrender to U.S. forces. Their actions during the battle and how they died were described in detail in notes made by Antonio Sola, a cadet who was taken prisoner.

In subsequent years the story of los Niños Héroes became part of a nationalist cult. The cadets were invested with the ideal virtues of defenders of the country: loyalty to the government and to the army. In the early years the former cadets of the Colegio Militar met to commemorate the deaths of their compatriots. Poems and songs elaborated their deeds and virtues. According to many accounts, the cadet Fernando Montes de Oca had wrapped himself in the Mexican flag, then leaped to his death rather than surrender. Other cadets who died were invested with heroic motives and actions. During the presidency of Porfirio Díaz, the Niños Héroes became prototypes of good citizens who were willing to die to support the country's institutions. Since Chapultepec Castle was at that time the presidential palace, the legend of the Niños Héroes was put in service of the status quo. In recent times the symbolic importance of los Niños Héroes has become more anti-American, antiforeign, and even antigovernment. In debunking the mythology surrounding los Niños Héroes, its critics have attacked the official control of national loyalties.

In 1947 the remains of the six heroes were discovered in Chapultepec Park, at the base of the hill. They were moved to the Colegio Militar until 1957, when they were laid to rest in the new Monumento a los Niños Héroes at the end of the Paseo de la Reforma, near the Colegio. The monument consists of six massive columns flanking the heroic-sized figures of a woman and two cadets; she cradles the limp body of one, while the other stands proudly at her side. The Colegio Militar continues to honor los Niños Héroes in a retreat ceremony still conducted daily by the corps of cadets.

Richard Griswold del Castillo

BIBLIOGRAPHY

Carreño, Alberto Maria. *El Colegio Militar de Chapultepec, 1847–1947.* 1972.

Plasencia de al Parra, Enrique. "Conmemoración de la hazaña épica de los niños héroes: Su origen, desarrollo y simbolismos." *Historia Mexicana* 45, no. 2 (Oct.–Dec. 1995): 241–279.

See also **Chapultepec, Battle of; Military Academy, Mexican;** *and* **Monuments and Memorials**

Louisiana Purchase

Although France had ceded the Louisiana Territory to Spain in 1763, Napoléon Bonaparte regained the region with the Treaty of San Ildefonso, dated 1 October 1800. Napoléon expected Louisiana to supply his envisioned Caribbean empire based in Santo Domingo and to attract the allegiance of U.S. citizens west of the Appalachian Mountains. President Thomas Jefferson learned of this treaty in May 1801 and, because of the commercial importance of U.S. trade on the Mississippi River, sent his new minister to France, Robert R. Livingston, to negotiate with Napoléon.

In 1802 Napoléon sent thirty thousand troops to begin his new western empire by reconquering the former slaves of Santo Domingo, but to his surprise this campaign failed. In January 1803 Jefferson appointed James Monroe a minister extraordinary and plenipotentiary and sent him to join Livingston with a $2 million congressional appropriation (with secret congressional approval to go as high as $10 million) and instructions to negotiate for New Orleans and as much of Florida as possible. In April 1803 Napoléon decided to cut his losses and offered a treaty ceding the entire Louisiana Territory to the United States for $15 million in bonds and property claims.

The Louisiana Purchase increased the country's geographical area by about 140 percent and added nearly two hundred thousand people to the population. Because the treaty did not delineate a southwestern boundary, the United States would later maintain that the purchase also included Texas. Although the Monroe administration relinquished this claim in 1819, many expansionists continued to clamor for the "reannexation" of Texas in the years that followed. Finally, the Louisiana Purchase reinforced Jefferson's republican vision that expansion was necessary to create an "empire for liberty." This expansionism continued to dominate the U.S. political sphere, becoming a major factor in the causes and outcomes of the U.S.–Mexican War.

Robert F. Pace

BIBLIOGRAPHY

Smelser, Marshall. *The Democratic Republic, 1801–1815.* 1968.

Tucker, Robert W., and David C. Henderson. *Empire of Liberty: The State Craft of Thomas Jefferson.* 1990.

Lower California Campaign

In the summer of 1846 the U.S. Navy, Army, and U.S. settlers worked together to secure Alta (Upper) California, but Baja (Lower) California remained under Mexican control. Determined to take it and southern Mexican ports, Pacific Squadron commander Commo. Robert F. Stockton on 19 August 1846 proclaimed a blockade of the entire western Mexican coast, although he did not have the ships to enforce it. Concerned about the illegality of a paper blockade, Stockton sent the sloop *Cyane* (20 guns, commanded by Samuel F. DuPont) to blockade San Blas and another sloop, the *Warren* (with 24 guns, Cmdr. Joseph B. Hull), to blockade Mazatlán, Mexico's largest Pacific port, located directly east of the tip of Baja California, and second in Mexico only to Vera Cruz. In February Stockton replaced the *Warren* off Mazatlán with the *Portsmouth* (22 guns, Cmdr. John B. Montgomery).

By January 1847 operations in Alta California had ended, and the navy was able to turn its full attention to Baja California. Stockton wanted to take Acapulco; he believed it would be the main base for any privateers Mexico might commission against U.S. Pacific commerce. It would also offer the enterprising Stockton an operational base for a land assault against Mexico City from the west. Such an effort would require more resources, and Stockton reorganized his remaining forces and enjoined Lt. Col. John C. Frémont to raise men for the coming western land assault on Mexico City.

Stockton hoped to seize Mazatlán and San Blas in addition to Acapulco. However, he had a falling out with Brig. Gen. Stephen W. Kearny, whose Army of the West had linked up with Stockton at Los Angeles; both men claimed to be governor of California. In January U.S. Navy reinforcements arrived at Monterey in the form of the frigate *Independence* (54 guns, Commo. W. Branford Shubrick) from the east coast of the United States. Shubrick was to replace Stockton, but he had held his command only six weeks when on 2 March Commo. James Biddle aboard ship-of-the-line *Columbus* (74 guns), returning from an Asian cruise, assumed command of the Pacific Squadron. Stockton remained in California until June, when he left for home overland.

In an order dated 24 December 1846 Secretary of the Navy John Y. Mason, while not disavowing Stockton's blockade, reasserted that "a lawful maritime blockade requires the actual presence of a sufficient force, stationed at the entrance of the port, sufficiently near to prevent communication." This did not mean that Mason, or President James K. Polk for that matter, were uninterested in Baja California. In May 1847 orders from Mason reached Monterey for the Pacific Squadron to take and hold at least one port there. Secretary of War William L. Marcy also instructed General Kearny to occupy at least one port in Baja California so there should be no question about the U.S. claim to the peninsula. The Pacific Squadron was short of supplies and provisions, however; operations involving the entire squadron had to wait until summer and the arrival of the storeship *Southampton* (8 guns).

Biddle, who had been at sea aboard the *Columbus* since June 1845, allowed Shubrick to carry out the campaign against Baja California. Shortly after his arrival Biddle had lifted the paper blockade, enforcing it only at Mazatlán and Guaymas. In March and April Commander Montgomery of the *Portsmouth* landed shore parties at San José del Cabo and San Lucas but held these places only briefly. In July, knowing that his ship-of-the-line was useless in such operations, Biddle turned over his command to Shubrick.

That fall Shubrick began operations against Baja California. His plan was to leave two sloops to protect Alta California, sail to the Gulf of California in the *Independence*, extend the blockade to Guaymas, then go south and seize Mazatlán, San Blas, and Acapulco.

On 19 October Capt. Elie La Vallette in the frigate *Congress*, supported by the sloop *Portsmouth*, demanded the surrender of Guaymas. The next day the two ships began a bombardment of the port. The Mexican garrison had withdrawn during the night and the town authorities soon surrendered. On 8 November the sloop *Dale* (16 guns, Cmdr. Thomas O. Selfridge) arrived at Guaymas to relieve the *Portsmouth*. Several weeks later some 250 Mexican troops made a determined effort to recapture the town but were repulsed by naval forces under Selfridge, who was seriously wounded in the engagement.

On 4 November Commodore Shubrick issued a proclamation announcing the beginning of active operations in Baja California and that the United States intended to retain that territory after the war. The latter statement was designed to encourage a separatist movement from Mexico. On the evening of 10 November Shubrick arrived off Mazatlán with the *Independence, Congress, Cyane,* and storeship *Erie* (4 guns), and the next day he demanded the town's surrender. On the 11th Shubrick landed a force of 730 seamen and marines, who occupied Mazatlán without opposition. Mexican forces retreated to Urias, ten miles from Mazatlán, where on the 20th they were routed in a combined land and water attack commanded by Capt. La Valette (Lt. George L. Selden had charge of the land force and Lt. Stephen Rowan led the men sent into the bay in boats). U.S. losses in the assault were one killed and twenty wounded; four Mexicans were killed and an unknown number wounded. On 12 January 1848, a landing party from the storeship *Lexington* (6 guns, Capt. T. Bailey) took the town of San Blas without opposition.

There were other U.S. Navy landings, and Shubrick's forces also attacked Mexican merchantmen when they could be found. Shubrick's requests to Gen. Winfield Scott at Mexico City for land reinforcements, however, were met with the response that no troops could be spared. Shubrick lacked manpower for effective occupation of Baja California, and therefore its cession was not included in instructions to U.S. negotiator Nicholas P. Trist. The 2 February Treaty of Guadalupe Hidalgo left Baja California in Mexico's possession.

Spencer C. Tucker

BIBLIOGRAPHY

Bancroft, Hubert H. *History of California.* 1963.

Bauer, K. Jack. *Surfboats and Horse Marines: U.S. Naval Operations in the Mexican War, 1846–48.* 1969.

Hagan, Kenneth J. *This People's Navy: The Making of American Sea Power.* 1991.

Harlow, Neal. *California Conquered: War and Peace on the Pacific.* 1982.

Knox, Dudley W. *A History of the United States Navy.* 1936.

Smith, Justin H. *The War with Mexico.* 2 vols. 1919. Reprint, 1963.

Mackenzie, Alexander Slidell

A U.S. naval officer and brother of diplomat John Slidell, Alexander Slidell (1803–1848) was born in New York City; he took the surname Mackenzie in 1837 to honor a maternal uncle. In 1815 he entered the U.S. Navy as a midshipman. Promoted to lieutenant in 1825 and commander in 1841, Mackenzie saw a variety of assignments and traveled widely. A prolific writer, he published several well-received volumes, including travel accounts and biographies of John Paul Jones and Oliver Hazard Perry, and formed close associations with Washington Irving and Henry Wadsworth Longfellow.

In 1842, while commanding the training ship *Somers*, Mackenzie hanged Midshipman Philip Spencer, son of Secretary of War John Spencer, and two others on dubious mutiny charges. Although exonerated, he retired from the navy to devote his attentions to writing, farming, and his family.

Recalled to duty as a special emissary by President James K. Polk in 1846, Mackenzie met in Havana with exiled Mexican dictator Antonio López de Santa Anna. Mackenzie, who spoke fluent Spanish, relayed Polk's willingness to support Santa Anna's return to power in exchange for an end to military operations, a peaceful (but favorable) resolution of the border issue, land concessions, and friendly relations between the two countries. Santa Anna apparently accepted Polk's proposal and even offered advice to facilitate U.S. operations, all of which Mackenzie shared with Gen. Zachary Taylor during a meeting in South Texas.

Commander Mackenzie served throughout the U.S.–Mexican War, most notably during the naval operations against Vera Cruz and Tabasco. In declining health, he returned home in April 1848 and died later that year. His son, Ranald Slidell Mackenzie, became a Civil War general and an accomplished Indian fighter.

David Coffey

BIBLIOGRAPHY

Robinson, Charles M., III. *Bad Hand: A Biography of General Ranald S. Mackenzie.* 1993.

Smith, Justin H. *The War with Mexico.* 2 vols. 1919. Reprint, 1963.

Magoffin, James

Longtime trader to Chihuahua and former U.S. consul at Saltillo, Mexico, James Wiley Magoffin (1799–1868) offered his services to President James K. Polk in June 1846, agreeing to accompany the Army of the West under Col. (later general) Stephen W. Kearny and use his influence with Mexican officials in New Mexico and Chihuahua to help bring about a peaceful occupation by U.S. forces. Magoffin joined Kearny at Bent's Fort and was sent ahead of the army with a small dragoon detachment on 1 August. At Santa Fe, Magoffin met with New Mexico governor Manuel Armijo and other leaders. Armijo subsequently mobilized his forces and made defensive preparations at Apache Canyon, fifteen miles from Santa Fe, but then disbanded his army and fled south on 16 August, thus allowing Kearny to march into the capital unopposed. Magoffin later claimed sole reponsibility for the "bloodless conquest" of New Mexico, yet his exact contribution to that result remains clouded. Magoffin was taken prisoner while on his way to Chihuahua in September 1846 and held until the following summer. He later submitted a claim to the U.S. government, requesting compensation for his services as special agent; he eventually received $30,000. In 1849, across the Río Grande from El Paso del Norte (present-day Juarez), Magoffin established a large residence and business headquarters, which became known as Magoffinsville (now part of El Paso, Texas). Magoffinsville became the site of Fort Bliss in 1854, and Magoffin served for a period as the post sutler. A strong supporter of the South, Magoffin actively cooperated with Confederate military leaders in their efforts to conquer the Southwest during the Civil War. He died on 27 September 1868 at San Antonio, Texas, and was buried there.

Mark L. Gardner

BIBLIOGRAPHY

Benton, Thomas Hart. *Thirty Year's View; or, A History of the Working of the American Government for Thirty Years, from 1820 to 1850 . . . by a Senator of Thirty Years.* 2 vols. 1854, 1856.

Keleher, William A. *Turmoil in New Mexico, 1846–1868.* 1952.

Strickland, Rex W. *Six Who Came to El Paso: Pioneers of the 1840's.* 1963.

Timmons, W. H. *El Paso: A Borderlands History.* 1990.

Magoffin, Susan

Susan Shelby Magoffin (1827–1855) was the daughter of a prominent Kentucky family, the wife of trader Samuel Magoffin, and the sister-in-law to President Polk's special agent James Magoffin. As an eighteen-year-old bride and a dedicated diarist she wrote one of the most historically valuable and entertaining eyewitness accounts of a phase of the U.S.–Mexican War. Her diary covers the months June 1846 to September 1847, when she accompanied her husband and his supply wagons from Independence, Missouri, down the Santa Fe trail and into Mexico. A keen observer of people and customs, she left descriptions of Bent's Fort, Santa Fe, Saltillo, Monterrey, and Matamoros, and perceptive impressions of Generals Taylor, Cushing, Wool, Kearny, and Colonel Doniphan. Her accounts of Indian tribes, traders, teamsters, government officials and of fandangos, balls, and political intrigues are considered classics. Of particular interest, because of their rarity, are her descriptions of women—Native American, Hispanic, Anglo—that she met, including the Señoras Barcelo, Juliana, and Ortis, and Maria Hunter, wife of Maj. David Hunter, who apparently was the only U.S. officer's wife to accompany her husband on the campaign trail during the war. Susan Magoffin died in St. Louis, Missouri, in 1855.

Linda D. Vance

BIBLIOGRAPHY

Drumm, Stella M., ed. *Down the Santa Fe Trail and into Mexico: The Diary of Susan Shelby Magoffin, 1846–1847.* 1982.

Manifest Destiny

A term attributed to New York journalist John L. O'Sullivan, *Manifest Destiny* became a slogan of U.S. expansionists in the period immediately before, during, and after the U.S.–Mexican War. O'Sullivan, cofounder and editor of both the *Democratic Review* and the New York *Morning News,* first applied the words *Manifest Destiny* to the issue of U.S. annexation of Texas in the July–August 1845 issue of the *Review,* and then to the U.S. dispute with Great Britain over possession of Oregon in the 27 December 1845 *Morning News.* Although neither column was signed, O'Sullivan did write about Manifest Destiny in a signed 5 January 1846 letter on Oregon in the *Morning News* and is generally credited by historians with coining the phrase. Scholars note, however, that most of the concepts attached to the phrase Manifest Destiny had been espoused by O'Sullivan in only slightly different language before his 1845 and 1846 pieces; that his arguments drew on the ideology of earlier U.S. expansionists such as John Quincy Adams; and that many of his ideas can be traced back even further—to, for instance, the sense of destiny of the Puritans who settled in colonial New England and the thoughts about empire taking a westward course in the early eighteenth-century writings of the British philosopher George Berkeley.

Manifest Destiny, as O'Sullivan explained it, described the United States's providential mission to extend its systems of democracy, federalism, and personal freedom, as well as to accommodate its rapidly growing population by ultimately taking possession of the entire North American continent. O'Sullivan argued that this U.S. "true title" superseded any competing claims to the continent that European states might have on the basis of prior discovery or prior settlement. Further, he emphasized that the way to continental hegemony was to be peaceful, achieved primarily through the work of "Anglo-Saxon emigration." Unlike imperial European nations that conquered their empires, the United States would wait for peoples living elsewhere to realize the advantages of annexation and voluntarily seek incorporation into the Union.

After the U.S.–Mexican War began, U.S. expansionists invoked the phrase Manifest Destiny to rationalize imperialistic demands that their country use the opportunity provided by the conflict and conquer and retain much or all of Mexico. Even O'Sullivan, who had stressed Manifest Destiny's peaceful nature, claimed that the United States deserved an indemnity such as California from Mexico. Many wartime proponents of Manifest Destiny fused into the ideology a belief that the United States had a mission to regenerate Mexico by bringing progress and Protestantism southward: U.S. troops would liberate what was described as a benighted Mexican population from the control of despotic rulers and Catholic priests. In answer to racialist arguments against absorbing Mexicans into the Union, some wartime expansionists, using a primitive form of Darwinian logic, responded that through superior breeding abilities or other means U.S. Anglo-Saxons would gradually displace Mexicans, and that there was nothing to fear from expansion southward.

After the U.S.–Mexican War, U.S. expansionists broadened Manifest Destiny's scope, applying the slogan increasingly to areas beyond the continent including Cuba, Hawaii, and South America. The term remained in use throughout the late nineteenth century.

Robert E. May

BIBLIOGRAPHY

Hietala, Thomas R. *Manifest Design: Anxious Aggrandizement in Late Jacksonian America.* 1985.

Horsman, Reginald. *Race and Manifest Destiny.* 1981.

Merk, Frederick. *Manifest Destiny and Mission in American History: A Reinterpretation.* 1963.

Weinberg, Albert K. *Manifest Destiny: A Study of Nationalist Expansionism in American History.* 1935.

Marcy, William L.

A native of Massachusetts, U.S. secretary of war William Learned Marcy (1786–1857) graduated from Brown University in 1808. He then read law and was admitted to the bar in Troy, New York, where he became a member of Martin Van Buren's increasingly influential faction, known as the Albany Regency, in New York politics. Under its sponsorship, Marcy served as New York state comptroller, as associate justice to the state supreme court, and as a U.S. senator. After leaving the senate, Marcy served three terms as governor of New York before his appointment as President Polk's secretary of war in 1845, a crucial position on the eve of the U.S.–Mexican War.

The War Department in 1845 consisted of nine clerks directing the activities of 14 regiments (8 infantry, 2 dragoons, and 4 artillery). The authorized strength of the army at 7,883 would soon prove insufficient to the needs of a country confronting two separate border crises. In addition to the dispute with Mexico over Texas annexation, the administration inherited a dispute with Britain over the Oregon Territory. Thus, in his first annual report, Marcy urged a substantial army expansion that would increase the number of regiments and the size of companies from 42 to 80. A budget-conscious Congress rejected Marcy's proposals.

On 9 May, news of the Mexican attack on a party of Taylor's dragoons reached Washington. Marcy added his voice to the unanimous Cabinet decision to ask that Congress declare war on Mexico. Polk also asked Congress to authorize the muster of volunteers for six- or twelve-month terms. Congress now responded with alacrity. It provided for fifty thousand volunteers and raised company strengths to one hundred. It also voted to create a regiment of mounted riflemen and a company of engineers. These moves essentially adopted Marcy's plan of the previous winter.

Despite U.S. victories at Palo Alto and Resaca de la Palma, the administration's plans for the war had not made much of a start. No strategic vision guided policy in the opening weeks of the conflict, and Marcy spent most of his time fending off glory-seekers coveting commissions in the volunteer forces.

In a 14 May conference between Polk, Marcy, and Gen. Winfield Scott, the rough contours of a plan finally emerged. The administration would call up twenty thousand volunteers to seize northern California and New Mexico. In two more days, the administration added another objective by directing Taylor to secure the Río Grande valley, calling up the remainder of the authorized fifty thousand volunteers to act as reserves. Yet these ideas remained daunting prospects in actual application.

While Marcy labored with Polk and Scott to construct strategic plans, he also dealt with the Committees on Military Affairs in the House and Senate and conducted interviews with numerous applicants for commissions, all the while beset by frequently abrasive political jealousies. In late May, Marcy found himself entangled in a political dispute with Scott. Slated to take command in the lower Río Grande valley, Scott insisted that the volunteers needed more training before the campaign. Marcy and Polk, both impatient for a speedy resolution of the war, chafed at the delay, causing Scott to complain that politics rather than military necessity was guiding policy. Scott asked to be removed from command and Polk obliged him. Taylor took command of the campaign with Monterrey as his objective.

In spite of the president's insistence on haste, hopes for a quick end to the contest by fall were illusory. Marcy renewed his efforts to augment the army, settling for a compromise of fifteen thousand regulars, but only ten thousand volunteers for the duration of the war. Nobody yet knew how the army should use these men. Although the administration had decided early to target Vera Cruz, Marcy opposed any advance into the interior toward Mexico City. The secretary did urge, however, that Winfield Scott command the campaign regardless of its objective. During the Mexico City campaign, Scott would not only direct operations, he would enjoy the wide latitude that aided their success, all thanks to Marcy's efforts.

At the war's conclusion, Marcy stood firm for reason and political sensibility. When Polk took exception to the activities of his emissary Nicholas Trist and contemplated rejecting any treaty negotiated by him, Marcy urged the president to accept the treaty and send it to the Senate. It was advice that Polk ultimately followed.

After the war, Marcy continued a long run of public service, especially as Franklin Pierce's secretary of state. Yet his time at the War Department equaled any of his civic labors before or after. Although he lacked a broad strategic vision—he wrongly judged the Mexico City campaign as too perilous—Marcy's talents lay in his capacity as a careful administrator and as a good judge of character and temperament. He handled political disputes with aplomb and tact, administering his department with nonpartisan fairness. He was thus able to save Polk, who fed on partisanship, from the greater excesses of his political appetites. Marcy died on 4 July 1857 at Ballston Spa, New York.

Jeanne T. Heidler
David S. Heidler

BIBLIOGRAPHY

Scott, Winfield. *Correspondence between General Winfield Scott and the Secretaries of War, William L. Marcy and Peter B. Porter: From the Evening Post, June 10th, 1846.* 1852.

Spencer, Ivor Debenham. "William L. Marcy and the Albany Regency." Ph.D. diss., Brown University, 1940.

Spencer, Ivor Debenham. *The Victor and the Spoils: A Life of William L. Marcy.* 1959.

United States War Dept. *Correspondence between the Secretary of War and Generals Scott and Taylor, and between General Scott and Mr. Trist. Message from the President of the United States, transmitting reports from the Secretary of State and Secretary of War, with the Accompanying Documents, in Compliance with the Resolution of the House of Representatives, of the 7th February, 1848.* 30th Congr., 1st sess. House. Ex. doc. 56.

Mariano Salas, José

See Salas, José Mariano

Lt. Daniel Sutherland, U.S. Marines. Daguerreotype, c. 1846. From the collection of William J. Schultz, M.D.

Marines, U.S.

Much to the chagrin of Col. Comdt. Archibald Henderson, neither Congress nor Secretary of the Navy George Bancroft saw a special role for the U.S. Marine Corps in the war with Mexico. The mobilization of a wartime army and navy in 1846 excluded the Marines despite Henderson's proposal to add 21 temporary officers and double the size of the enlisted force. For the first year of the war the Marine Corps retained its prewar strength of 40 officers (47 authorized) and around 1,200 enlisted men, divided evenly between Marine security detachments at navy yards and ships guards aboard men-of-war. In March 1847 Congress authorized Henderson to recruit enough temporary officers to bring the officer corps to 75, easily reached, but an authorized increase of the enlisted force to over 2,000 produced an actual force in 1847–1848 of only 1,700 Marines. Deprived of any special bonuses or incentives for enlistment, potential volunteers ignored the golden-tongued recruiting sergeants that prowled the immigrant and harbor neighborhoods of East Coast cities.

The most useful contributions Marines made to the war came from the ships guards of navy warships that blockaded and raided Mexico's two long and vulnerable coasts. On the Pacific coast Marines helped secure the U.S. enclaves at San Francisco, Monterey, the Los Angeles area, and San Diego during the conquest of California. Lt. Archibald H. Gillespie, USMC, served with Capt. John C. Frémont's California battalion. Ships guards then rescued Gillespie and his unruly soldiers—and Gen. Stephen W. Kearny's 1st Dragoons—from a Californio counterrevolution, fighting small battles at San Gabriel and La Mesa (8–9 January 1847) that allowed the U.S. reoccupation of Los Angeles. With Alta California firmly under Anglo rule, the ships of the U.S. Navy Pacific squadron spent the rest of the war raiding along the Mexican coast as far south as Mazatlán. Marine landing parties made several raids and defended two towns against Mexican counterattacks. In all these operations the Marines performed with consistent but unpublicized discipline and skill.

The companion operations of the U.S. Navy's Home Squadron in the Gulf of Mexico gave the Marine ships guards more ambitious opportunities for amphibious raids. Under the direction of Commo. David Conner and Commo. Matthew C. Perry, the Home Squadron blockaded Mexico's six major unoccupied Gulf Coast port cities. (Vera Cruz, of course, was occupied as a base of U.S. operations against Mexico City.) The navy conducted major raiding operations against Tuxpan and Tabasco (twice) in order to cut coastal and riverine commerce. Except for some minor skirmishing, the U.S. landing parties did not face serious Mexican resistance; weather and hydrographic conditions constrained the raids, not bullets. In fact, the larger Marine contingents in Gulf waters did far less fighting than their Pacific comrades.

Colonel Henderson, however, wanted more Marine Corps participation in the war than the navy could provide, and he successfully lobbied to include a Marine regiment in Gen. Winfield Scott's expeditionary army. Scott, a fellow Virginian, welcomed the Marines, not least because he had so few regular regiments in his army. Henderson's effort, however, produced only a small battalion of 22 officers and 324 enlisted men, slightly enlarged at Vera Cruz with ships guards. The Marine battalion, commanded by Bvt. Lt. Col. Samuel E. Watson, joined Gen. John Quitman's division, the Marines conspicuous in their tall shakos and white crossbelts. At the rear of Scott's army, Watson's battalion guarded the wagon and mule trains and did not participate in any of the engagements that brought Scott's army to the gates of Mexico City.

The Marine Corps' claim to fame in the campaign "to the Halls of Montezuma" rests on one day's dubious battle in the storming of Chapultepec castle and the seizure of two of the city's western gates (13 September 1847). Scott's plan for a general assault on the castle did not include a major role for Quitman's division, which was supposed to provide a diversion by attacking a Mexican artillery position blocking the roads to the San Cosme and Belén gates. Quitman redefined his mission to include an assault on the southeast slope of Chapultepec and assigned Marine Corps major Levi Twiggs the command of an Army-Marine storming party. Watson remained in command of his weakened battalion, assigned a reinforcing mission.

The actual operation, like much else that day, did not go as planned. Twiggs's force disintegrated in the face of Mexican fire, and Twiggs was killed. Watson's battalion went to ground until Quitman ordered a general assault against the Mexican positions along the Tucabayo highway and the castle's southeast corner. One party of Marines under Lt. John S. Devlin joined the climb up Chapultepec hill without orders. Capt. George S. Terrett took five other officers (including Charles Henderson, the commandant's teenaged son) and twenty-six men on another freelance charge all the way to the approaches to the San Cosme gate, fighting with elements of the army's 4th and 11th Infantry. Most of the Marines advanced under Watson's command (and with Quitman's blessing) to the Belén Gate, where they had a hot fight with the Mexicans until the gate fell to a mixed force of army regulars, South Carolina volunteers, and the remnants of

Watson's battalion. Marine casualties for the day were seven dead and twenty-four wounded. The next day Scott made the Marine battalion his provost-guard (their uniforms still looked presentable), which meant that they raised the U.S. flag over the surrendered city. The honor had nothing to do with their performance the day before.

Commandant Henderson tried to make much in Washington over the heroic performance of Watson's battalion, but even his inventive mind could not produce a better story. Instead, he had to cope with a wretched feud among Watson's officers, with two warring camps led by Devlin and Terrett. Charges and countercharges ranged and spilled into the press over Watson's timid leadership, Twiggs's incompetence, and Maj. William Dulaney's drunken confusion and looting. Only one Marine officer, Capt. John Reynolds, emerged from the fray with his reputation intact, thus establishing a position that made him the Marine Corps' field leader in the Civil War. The public furor encouraged Congress to reduce the corps quickly to its prewar strength. However, Congress did recognize that a wartime Marine Corps needed the same recruiting advantages as the army, and in 1855 it authorized the corps to offer land and monetary reward to wartime veterans and recruits. On the margin, then, the U.S.–Mexican War experience contributed to the Marines' institutional development.

During the course of the war about 2,500 men served as officers or enlisted men in the U.S. Marine Corps. Of this force, 11 died in battle, 47 suffered wounds, and 107 died of disease, accidents, and unofficial violence.

Allan R. Millett

BIBLIOGRAPHY

Bauer, K. Jack. *Surfboats and Horse Marines: U.S. Naval Operations in the Mexican War, 1846–48.* 1969.

Collum, Richard S. *History of the United States Marine Corps.* Rev. ed., 1903.

Eisenhower, John S. D. *So Far from God: The U.S. War with Mexico, 1846–1848.* 1989.

Millett, Allan R. *Semper Fidelis: The History of the United States Marine Corps.* 1991.

Wilcox, Cadmus. *History of the Mexican War.* 1892.

Winders, Richard Bruce. *Mr. Polk's Army: The American Military Experience in the Mexican War.* 1996.

Marshall, Thomas

Thomas Marshall (1793–1853), brigadier general of the Kentucky volunteers, was born in Mason County, Kentucky, on 13 April, son of Thomas and Frances Maitland Marshall. He served as a lieutenant in the War of 1812. On 19 April 1812, Marshall, who had taken offense to disparaging statements made by Charles S. Mitchell about Marshall's father, challenged Mitchell to a duel. In the resulting exchange,

Marshall was severely wounded in the hip. Marshall served six terms as a Democrat in the Kentucky legislature, one as Speaker of the House.

With the onset of the U.S.–Mexican War, President James K. Polk rewarded Marshall for his Democratic Party loyalty by appointing him a brigadier general of Kentucky volunteers, to serve in northern Mexico under the command of General Zachary Taylor. Marshall arrived in south Texas at Brazos Santiago on 4 August 1846. He travelled from there to Camargo, where a U.S. force was being organized for the march on Monterrey. But Marshall was left behind with Brig. Gen. Gideon Pillow to command the garrison at Camargo. Marshall remained at Camargo until December 1846, when rumor of an impending attack on Saltillo caused him to be ordered forward to Monterrey.

As Gen. Zachary Taylor and Gen. Orlando Butler were absent from Monterrey during January 1847, Marshall, by virtue of his rank, commanded this major U.S. garrison. He raised the ire of Gen. Winfield Scott by opening secret orders addressed to Generals Taylor and Butler and reading the contents aloud to officers and civilians present. These were crucial orders from Scott to Taylor that stripped Taylor's command of the regular troops, which Scott needed for his upcoming campaign in central Mexico. The resealed orders were then sent on to General Taylor at Victoria. The dispatch courier, sent with an inadequate escort, was ambushed and murdered by Mexican guerrillas. The importance of these dispatches was immediately recognized by the Mexicans, and they were forwarded to General Santa Anna in San Luis Potosí. Many believe that this captured dispatch, which contained information on Taylor's weakened condition, prompted Santa Anna to march against Taylor at Buena Vista. An angry General Scott attempted unsuccessfully to prefer charges against Marshall for these actions.

By the middle of February 1847, General Taylor, suspecting that a Mexican attack on Saltillo was imminent, ordered Marshall to bring the heavy 18-pounder artillery forward from Monterrey to Saltillo. The artillery was ordered to halt at Rinconada Pass but was ordered forward to Saltillo on the evening of 23 February 1847, arriving the next day, too late to participate in the Battle of Buena Vista.

Marshall resigned his military commission on 20 July 1848, having served honorably but without having participating in any battles—an untested general. He was murdered on his estate in Kentucky on 28 March 1853 by one of his tenant farmers.

Joseph G. Chance

BIBLIOGRAPHY
French, Samuel G. *Two Wars: An Autobiography.* 1901.
Scott, Winfield. *Memoirs of Lieutenant-General Scott, Written by Himself.* 1864. Reprint, 1970.

Martínez, Antonio José

Born to an affluent New Mexican family, Antonio José Martínez (1793–1867) was ordained a Roman Catholic priest in Durango, Mexico, in 1822 and became the parish priest at Taos, New Mexico, his former place of residence, in 1826. An educator, large landowner, and powerful political leader, Martínez has often been charged with being one of the prime instigators of armed resistance to the U.S. occupation of New Mexico during the U.S.–Mexican War, including the Taos Revolt of January 1847. Such a charge appears to be unfounded. During the revolt in Taos, Martínez was responsible for saving Elliott Lee of Missouri from the same angry crowd of Mexicans and Pueblo Indians that brutally killed Territorial Governor Charles Bent and others. According to one biographer (Pedro Sánchez), Martínez sent word of the revolt to Col. Sterling Price at Santa Fe. When Price (commander of U.S. forces in New Mexico) and his army marched into Taos in early February, Price made Martínez's home his headquarters. After the defeat of the insurgents, Martínez's residence served as the site of the court-martial of one of their leaders, Pablo Montoya; the Taos priest was a witness for the prosecution. Following the Treaty of Guadalupe Hidalgo, Martínez worked to bring about the formation of a territorial government for New Mexico. He was president of the council at the first session of New Mexico Territory's first Legislative Assembly in June 1851. Martínez was elected to three additional terms on the council (not all consecutive). During the 1850s Martínez and other native priests came into increasing conflict with their reform-minded superior, Bishop Jean Baptiste Lamy, who had arrived in New Mexico in 1851. What one authority has described as a "head-on collision between two strong personalities" came to a bitter end with Lamy's excommunication of Martínez in 1857. However, Martínez continued to say Mass and perform other religious functions for loyal parishioners out of his own home. He died at Taos on 27 July 1867.

Mark L. Gardner

BIBLIOGRAPHY
Chavez, Fray Angelico. *But Time and Chance: The Story of Padre Martínez of Taos, 1793–1867.* 1981.
Francis, E. K. "Padre Martínez: A New Mexican Myth." *New Mexico Historical Review* 31 (1956): 265–289.
Sánchez, Pedro. *Memories of Antonio José Martínez.* Translated by Guadalupe Baca-Vaughn. 1978.

Masons

See **Freemasonry**

Mata, José María

The son of a soldier in the Spanish army, José María Mata (1810–1895) was born in Jalapa, Vera Cruz, and studied medicine in Mexico City. After graduation he returned to Jalapa as a surgeon and joined the national guard.

On 23 March 1847, during the U.S. siege of Vera Cruz, Mata made a daring entrance by sea through the U.S. blockade to bring desperately needed assistance from the state government. In the following weeks, Mata led several guerrilla bands that patrolled the National Road between Vera Cruz and Perote. Mata was captured by U.S. forces at the Battle of Cerro Gordo while he served as chief of the civic militia of Jalapa and was brought to New Orleans. He was released in a prisoner exchange at the end of the war.

During the U.S. withdrawal in 1848, Mata was appointed military prefect of Jalapa. Like many young men of his generation and social position, Mata was disillusioned by Mexico's war experience and past politics. He became an ardent critic of the regime of President Antonio López de Santa Anna in 1853 and was expelled from the country. While in exile in the United States, he rose in prominence among the exiled community of reformists. After Santa Anna's ouster, Mata represented Vera Cruz and Mexico states in the constituent congress and was praised as one of the primary authors of the Constitution of 1857. In 1861 he became treasury minister in President Benito Juárez's cabinet. During the French Intervention (1852–1866) Mata became a general in the republican army. He served as ambassador to the United States in 1877, but dictator Porfirio Díaz forced him into obscurity, and he died while a member of the city council of Martínez de la Torre, Vera Cruz.

Aaron P. Mahr Yáñez

BIBLIOGRAPHY

Murillo Vidal, Rafael. *José María Mata: Padre de la constitución de 1857.* 1966.

Roa Barcena, José María. *Recuerdos de la invasion Norteamericana (1846–1848).* 3 vols. 1883. Reprint, 1993.

Matamoros

Matamoros was given its name in 1826, in honor of Independence hero Mariano Matamoros Guridi. The future city, originally a few scattered ranches, was founded in 1782 as San Juan de los Esteros and renamed the Congregación de Nuestra Señora del Refugio de los Esteros in 1793.

The 1846 city of Matamoros, in the state of Tamaulipas, had major importance for both Mexico and the United States during the U.S.–Mexican War. This importance derived from several factors, including its location on the Río Grande, its port, its fortifications, its jurisdiction in the disputed territory between the Nueces River and the Río Grande, its large population (16,372 in 1837), its prominence in the trade between inland northeast Mexico and the Gulf of Mexico, and its symbolic value as Mexico's northeast frontier bastion. Militarily, the fortified city evolved in response to Indian attacks, internal conflicts, the 1835–1836 Texas Revolution, and Mexico's perception of U.S. intentions.

Assessments of the city's defensive capability helped shape the early course of the U.S.–Mexican War. On 6 October 1845 Matamoros garrison commander Gen. Francisco Mejía told the Northern Division commander Gen. Mariano Arista in Monterrey that Matamoros could not be defended against a U.S. attack—despite the central government's belief that the city was impregnable—and he recommended that the U.S. Army be attacked in the field. On 4 April 1846, the minister of war, Gen. José María Tornel y Mendivil, ordered Arista to attack Gen. Zachary Taylor's army, which had fortified the left or northern bank of the Río Grande, opposite Matamoros. Six days later, Arista ordered Gen. Pedro de Ampudia, his second-in-command, to hold the town at all costs until Arista arrived from Monterrey. Arista's attack against Taylor in the disputed territory began in Matamoros. As part of his plan, Arista arranged for the city's northeastern fortifications to be used in the siege of Fort Texas. Before and after hostilities began, officials from the two armies met in Matamoros. After determining that Taylor had no interest in an armistice, and taking into account the weaknesses of the city's fortifications, his one-day supply of cannonballs, and the reduced size of his dispirited army after the battles of Palo Alto and Resaca de la Palma, Arista evacuated Matamoros on 17 May. The U.S. Army occupied the city the next day, and U.S. forces remained until 9 August 1848.

Thomas B. Carroll

BIBLIOGRAPHY

Carroll, Thomas B. "Heroica Matamoros, Tamaulipas, Mexico: Where Were the Fortifications of the Walled City?" In *Studies in Brownsville and Matamoros History,* edited by Milo Kearney, Anthony Knopp, and Antonio Zavaleta. 1995.

Thorpe, T. B. *Our Army on the Río Grande.* 1846.

Maverick, Samuel

Texas businessman and politician Samuel Augustus Maverick (1803–1870) was born 23 July at Pendleton, South Carolina, and graduated from Yale University in 1825. His antisecession and antinullification politics caused him to leave South Carolina for Alabama before moving to Texas in April 1835. As a resident of San Antonio de Béxar, he participated in the successful Texian siege of Béxar in December 1835. He served as a delegate to the independence convention at Washington-on-the-Brazos in March 1836, having left a besieged Alamo garrison to do so. He left for Alabama in the late spring of 1836, married Mary Ann Adams there, and returned to San Antonio with his new wife and son in 1838. He obtained a Texas law license, engaged in land speculations, and served as San Antonio's mayor before fleeing the city in 1842 upon rumors of a Mexican invasion. Upon his return he was captured by Mexican general Adrian Woll and imprisoned in Perote Castle until 1843. He then was elected a congressman in the Republic of Texas, supporting annexation to the United States, and served in the state legislature from 1851 to 1863.

Because of a permanent move to San Antonio in 1847, he left behind with slaves a herd of cattle, which was allowed to roam free on the Matagorda Peninsula to which he had moved in 1844. From this came the term *maverick*, denoting unbranded cattle. Maverick amassed huge holdings of land, particularly in West Texas, through the purchase of headright, bounty, and donation certificates. Maverick County, Texas, is named for him. He died 2 September 1870 and was buried in City Cemetery Number One in San Antonio.

Jodella K. Dyreson

BIBLIOGRAPHY

Green, Rena Maverick, ed. *Samuel Maverick, Texan.* 1952.

Marks, Paula Mitchell. *Turn Your Eyes toward Texas: Pioneers Sam and Mary Maverick.* 1989.

May, Charles

U.S. Dragoon officer Charles Augustus May (1819–1864) was born in Washington, D.C. In 1836 he caught the attention of President Andrew Jackson, who observed May vaulting onto his horse. That display of horsemanship won him a commission in a new regiment of Dragoons, the 2d U.S. Dragoons, which participated in the Seminole War in Florida. Charles May was the image of a dashing cavalry officer. Over six feet tall, on campaign he wore a full beard and his hair long. His hair streamed behind him as he charged on his favorite horse, Black Tom.

In the U.S.–Mexican War, May's regiment accompanied Gen. Zachary Taylor as part of the campaign on the Río Grande that commenced the hostilities. During the Battle of Palo Alto, May's actions won him a brevet promotion to major. On the next day, at the Battle of Resaca de la Palma, he again distinguished himself as he led his dragoons in a charge on the Mexican guns. He was credited with capturing the Mexican general Rómulo Díaz de la Vega and breveted to lieutenant colonel. He received his final brevet, to full colonel, at the Battle of Buena Vista. Contemporaries raised questions about May's conduct at Resaca de la Palma, however, accusing him of taking credit for General Vega's capture from one of his enlisted men. He also was accused of hiding his troops in a ravine during the heat of the action at Buena Vista. May resigned from the U.S. Army on 20 April

Charles May. John Frost, *Pictorial History of Mexico and the Mexican War,* 1862

1861 to enter business in New York, and he died 24 December 1864.

J. Patrick Hughes

BIBLIOGRAPHY

The Mexican War and Its Heroes, pp. 217–221. 1860.

Rodenbough, Theo F. *From Everglade to Canon with the Second Dragoons.* 1875.

McCulloch, Ben

Ben McCulloch (1811–1862), an officer in the Army of the Republic of Texas, was born in Rutherford County, Tennessee, on 11 November, the elder brother of Henry Eustace McCulloch. In 1835 Ben McCulloch followed his boyhood mentor, David Crockett, to Texas, but a case of measles prevented him from reaching the Alamo before its fall. After recovering, McCulloch joined Sam Houston's army as a private on its retreat into East Texas. At the Battle of San Jacinto he commanded one of the pieces of Texian artillery—the famed "Twin Sisters"—and won a battlefield commission as first lieutenant. He soon left the army to become a surveyor on the Texas frontier. There he joined the Texas Rangers and served as first lieutenant under Capt. John C. (Jack) Hays, winning a considerable reputation as an Indian fighter.

At the battle of Plum Creek on 12 August 1840, McCulloch distinguished himself as a scout and as commander of the right wing of the Texian army. When, in February 1842, the Mexican government launched a raid against San Antonio, McCulloch scouted the Mexican positions and played a prominent role in the fighting that harried Brig. Gen. Raphael Vásquez's raiders back beyond the Río Grande. On 11 September 1842 a second Mexican expedition occupied San Antonio. McCulloch again rendered valuable scouting service and joined in the pursuit of Mexican general Adrian Woll's raiders to the Hondo River, where Hays's Rangers engaged them on 21 September. After the repulse of Woll's incursion, McCulloch remained with the Ranger company that formed the nucleus of the army with which the Texians planned to invade Mexico. The so-called Somervell expedition was poorly managed, however, and he left it on the Río Grande only hours before the remainder of the Texians were captured at Mier, Mexico, on 25 December 1842.

With the outbreak of the U.S.–Mexican War, McCulloch raised a command of rangers that became Company A of Col. Jack Hays's 1st Regiment, Texas Mounted Volunteers. Reporting to the U.S. Army on the Río Grande, McCulloch was soon named Gen. Zachary Taylor's chief of scouts and won his commander's praise and the admiration of the nation with his exciting reconnaissance expeditions into northern Mexico. The presence in his company of George Wilkins Kendall, editor of the New Orleans *Picayune*, and Samuel Reid, who was to write a popular history of the campaign, *The Scouting Expeditions of McCulloch's Texas Rangers*, propelled McCulloch's name into national prominence. McCulloch's "Spy Company" was constantly in the vanguard of Taylor's army as it drove into northern Mexico from Matamoros, scouting for passable roads, sources of water and forage, and concentrations of Mexican soldiers. Leading his dismounted company at the Battle of Monterrey, McCulloch distinguished himself at the storming of Federation and Independence hills on 21 and 22 September, respectively.

Discharged from service after the Monterrey campaign, McCulloch returned to Texas to recruit a second ranger company, which he led in the Buena Vista campaign. There his astute and daring reconnaissance work saved Taylor's army from disaster when, on 20 February 1847, he discovered the presence of Gen. Antonio López de Santa Anna's 15,000-man army at Encarnación, within fifteen miles of Taylor's advanced and vulnerable position at Agua Nueva. After a night with a single companion inside Mexican lines, McCulloch reported their proximity and strength in time for the U.S. Army to fall back to defensible ground at Buena Vista. During the battle, McCulloch's small company fought

as mounted cavalry. These exploits won McCulloch promotion to the rank of major of U.S. Volunteers.

McCulloch set out in September 1849 for the gold fields of California. Although he failed to strike it rich, he was elected sheriff of Sacramento. He later served as U.S. Marshal for Texas during the Franklin Pierce and James Buchanan administrations and in 1858 was appointed one of two peace commissioners to negotiate with Brigham Young, helping to prevent armed hostilities between the U.S. government and the Latter-day Saints in Utah.

With his state's secession from the Union, McCulloch was commissioned a colonel in the Texas army, and on 11 May 1861 Jefferson Davis appointed McCulloch a brigadier general. Assigned to the command of Indian Territory, he built the Army of the West with regiments from Arkansas, Louisiana, and Texas. On 7 March 1862, McCulloch was killed at the battle of Pea Ridge in northwest Arkansas. First buried in the field, his body was later moved to the cemetery at Little Rock and then to the Texas State Cemetery in Austin.

Thomas W. Cutrer

BIBLIOGRAPHY

Cutrer, Thomas W. *Ben McCulloch and the Frontier Military Tradition.* 1993.

Reid, Samuel C. *Scouting Expedition of McCulloch's Texas Rangers.* 1847. Reprint, 1970.

Rose, Victor M. *The Life and Services of Gen. Ben McCulloch.* 1888. Reprint, 1958.

McLane-Ocampo Treaty

Signed on 14 December 1859, this unratified treaty resulted from the territorial designs of President James Buchanan's administration and the serious financial problems of Mexican president Benito Juárez's government. U.S. minister to Mexico Robert M. McLane and Mexican foreign minister Melchor Ocampo negotiated for the better part of a year before coming to terms. Before their formal exchanges, U.S. agents believed that if the U.S. government extended recognition to the Juárez government, affirmative discussions would follow on the sale of Baja California to the United States.

McLane's initial assessment of Mexican politics and of the liberal government's willingness to bargain led him to extend recognition in April 1859. Melchor Ocampo, perhaps the leading liberal intellectual, remonstrated against territorial exchange on the basis of the impossibility of gaining congressional approval. Discussions then centered on transferral of rights of transit and police to the United States for financial considerations. The Juárez government acceded to measures that threatened national sovereignty because of its severe need for funds.

The diplomats agreed to the following treaty terms on 14 December 1859: (1) the United States would receive perpetual rights of transit across the Isthmus of Tehuantepec and from Texas and Arizona to the Gulf of California; (2) the United States could intervene at will to defend the security of its citizens and property along these transit routes; (3) the United States would gain free ports of entry at the terminus of each route; and (4) Mexico would receive $2 million for these concessions.

The treaty, debated in the U.S. Senate Executive Session in May 1860, failed to gain even a simple majority in a largely sectional vote, with Northerners overwhelmingly opposed. In Mexico the agreement was criticized severely by members of both parties as surrendering a right of intervention that amounted to the territory becoming a U.S. protectorate. Thus, it never came to a vote in the Mexican congress.

Paul D. Lack

BIBLIOGRAPHY

Callahan, James Morton. *American Foreign Policy in Mexican Relations.* 1932.

Findling, John E. *Dictionary of American Diplomatic History.* 1980.

Rippy, J. Fred. *The United States and Mexico.* 1926.

Schmitt, Karl M. *Mexico and the United States, 1821–1973: Conflict and Coexistence.* 1974.

Scholes, Walter V. *Mexican Politics during the Juárez Regime, 1855–1872.* 1969.

McLeod, Hugh

Hugh McLeod (1814–1862), Texas pioneer, attorney, politician, and military officer, was born in New York City on 1 August 1814. He graduated from the U.S. Military Academy at West Point in 1835 but resigned his commission on 30 June 1836 and moved to Texas, where he served in the army of the Texas Republic from July 1836 to 21 December 1837. In December 1837 the Texas congress named him adjutant general.

In 1838 McLeod served as an aide to Gen. Thomas J. Rusk in Rusk's campaign against Capt. Vicente Córdova's Mexican and Indian insurgents. Texas president Mirabeau B. Lamar appointed McLeod adjutant general of the Texas army on 30 January 1839, and later inspector general, with the rank of colonel. In that capacity McLeod again served with Rusk in the war against Chief Bowles's Cherokees and was involved in the Council House Fight against the Penateka Comanches in March 1840. McLeod also was involved in the clandestine events surrounding the short-lived Republic of the Río Grande, from 1839 to 1840.

On 17 June 1841 Lamar breveted McLeod to brigadier general and made him commander of the ill-advised and ill-fated Texian Santa Fe Expedition. Captured with his men in eastern New Mexico on 5 October by Governor Manuel Armijo's militia under Col. Juan Andrés Archuleta, McLeod was among those forced to march overland through the torturous Jornada del Muerto and across northern and central Mexico to Perote Castle. There he was held prisoner until summer 1842, when he was released through the intercession of the U.S. government.

Late in 1842, soon after his return to Texas, McLeod married Rebecca Johnston Lamar, a first cousin of former president Lamar. By 1844 the couple had moved to Galveston, where he established himself as an attorney, cotton planter, and land speculator; the couple had two children.

McLeod was elected to the Texas house of representatives of the seventh congress in 1842 to succeed Samuel A. Maverick, who had been taken prisoner during Gen. Adrian Woll's raid in September of that year. From 1 December 1844 to 28 June 1845 McLeod was returned to the ninth congress. Throughout the U.S.–Mexican War, McLeod served in an administrative capacity as adjutant general of Texas, following its annexation to the United States.

After the war, McLeod devoted his time to his law practice, business, and community interests and was involved in early efforts to survey and construct a transcontinental railroad line across Texas to the Pacific Coast.

At the outbreak of the Civil War, McLeod joined the Confederate cause. He died of pneumonia while in camp as colonel of the 1st Texas Infantry on 3 January 1862.

H. Allen Anderson

BIBLIOGRAPHY

Biographical Directory of Texas Conventions and Congresses. 1941.

Gulick, Charles Adam, et al., eds. *The Papers of Mirabeau Buonaparte Lamar.* 1968.

Heitman, Francis B. *Historical Register and Dictionary of the United States Army.* 1903.

Kendall, George Wilkins. *Narrative of an Expedition from Texas to Santa Fe.* 1845.

Loomis, Noel M. *The Texan-Santa Fe Pioneers.* 1958.

Winkler, Ernest W., ed. *Secret Journals of the Senate, Republic of Texas, 1836–1845.* 1911.

Medicine

See **Health and Medicine**

Mejía, Francisco

A native of Ixtapan, Francisco Mejía joined the Spanish Tulancingo squadron in 1811. He joined Agustin de Iturbide's Army of the Three Guarantees in 1821. In 1829 he helped defend Tampico from a Spanish invasion and supported Antonio López de Santa Anna's 1832 revolution. In 1840 he again fought against Anastasio Bustamante before moving north the following year to serve under Gen. Mariano Arista at Saltillo. In June 1842 Mejía commanded the department of Coahuila and in that capacity received the Texian Mier Expedition prisoners. When Gen. Nicolás Bravo ordered Mejía to execute many of the Texians, the governor refused and resigned his command. Mejía was later forgiven and assigned to command of the garrison at Matamoros where he continually threatened Texas by dispatching irregulars across the Río Grande and by organizing a planned offensive. Although his projected campaign never occurred, his belligerence caused Texas and the United States much concern.

In April 1846 the aggressive general opposed Gen. Zachary Taylor's march from Corpus Christi and threatened battle at Arroyo Colorado before retreating to Matamoros. Mejía fortified the town and commanded its garrison after being superseded in command of the army by Generals Pedro de Ampudia and Mariano Arista. Illness caused Mejía to miss the Battles of Palo Alto and Resaca de la Palma, but he was left in charge of Matamoros and the army after the recall of General Arista. Mejía abandoned the border to Taylor's army and fell back to Monterrey, where he was credited with rebuilding the morale of the army. Although ordered to abandon that strategic city, he refused, and instead laid plans to conduct guerrilla warfare against U.S. troops. Again superseded by Ampudia, Mejía resumed control of the 1st Infantry Brigade, but he convinced his superiors that Monterrey should, indeed, be held to keep the mountain passes to the interior out of U.S. hands. Mejía fought at the Battle of Monterrey, then again at Buena Vista. After withdrawing with the army, he served again at the Battle of Contreras, where his command was decimated. After the war, Mejía commanded the departments of Durango in 1849 and San Luis Potosí in 1852.

Donald S. Frazier

BIBLIOGRAPHY
Carreño, Alberto M., ed. *Jefes del ejército Mexicano en 1847: Biografías de generales de división y brigadad y de coroneles del ejército Mexicano por fines del año de 1847.* 1914.
De Palo, William A., Jr. *The Mexican National Army, 1822–1852.* 1997.
Smith, Justin H. *The War with Mexico.* 2 vols. 1919. Reprint, 1963.

Memorials

See Monuments and Memorials

Mesilla Valley

The Río Grande's Mesilla Valley, in present-day southern New Mexico, extends north-south about fifty-five miles, from Radium Springs to Sunland Park. The valley's width varies greatly, a narrow area of fertile bottomland rimmed east and west by arid foothills. It was a well known, favorably regarded segment of the Camino Real, the Spanish-Mexican roadway from Mexico City to Santa Fe. Northbound travelers entered the valley where the Río Grande broke through mountains at El Paso del Norte (Pass of the North). When they left the valley they entered the dread *Jornada del Muerto* for several days of usually waterless travel made especially dangerous by frequent Indian attacks.

Before United States possession, few persons lived permanently in the valley bottom. In addition to the problem of isolation, there was annual flooding by the Río Grande, often changing the river's course. The earliest documented settlement, Doña Ana, was on an 1839 Mexican government land grant to José María Costales and 116 other settlers. Flooding continued to impede development until a multipurpose dam was completed to the north in 1916.

On Christmas Day 1846 in the Battle of Brazito, at a Mesilla Valley camping place familiar to travelers, Col. Alexander W. Doniphan's Missouri volunteers defeated a larger Mexican force that had marched about thirty miles up from El Paso. As described by men of the Doniphan Expedition, Doña Ana clearly was languishing. After the Treaty of Guadalupe Hidalgo, many of the settlers moved to the newer village of Mesilla, because it was still in Mexico. Others, with Anglo newcomers, established Las Cruces in 1849. Population increased significantly after the Gadsden Purchase of 1853, by which the entire valley came under United States jurisdiction.

John Porter Bloom

BIBLIOGRAPHY
Harris, Linda G. *Las Cruces: An Illustrated History.* 1993.
Price, Paxton P. *Pioneers of the Mesilla Valley.* 1995.

Mexía, José Antonio

The date and place of birth of Mexican general and politician José Antonio Mexía (1800?–1839) is a matter of controversy among historians. Mexía himself claimed to have been born in Jalapa, Mexico, while some historians list him as a native of Cuba. Mexía fought in the Mexican War of Independence against Spain, and as early as 1823 he had dreamed of establishing a colony of settlers from Louisiana in Texas.

By the 1830s Mexía had become a proponent of establishing a liberal federalist system of sovereign states in Mexico. His opposition to centralism pitted him against those who favored terminating the liberal colonization plan inaugurated in Texas in the 1820s. A prominent legislator with vast interests in Texas, Mexía favored continued U.S. immigration into Texas. These policies brought him into increasing conflict with Gen. Antonio López de Santa Anna, who had taken over the government and launched a war against Texas after that northern province declared independence in 1836. Exiled to New Orleans, Mexía, Valentín Gómez Farís, and other federalists bided their time for a return. They sometimes interacted with Texas revolutionaries during the Texas Revolution. Although it appeared that they had a common goal—to overthrow Santa Anna—Mexía, Farías, and other exiled Mexican leaders in New Orleans opposed Texas independence; they rarely collaborated closely with the revolutionaries because they and the Texians distrusted each other.

Nevertheless, in the fall of 1835, some U.S. citizens participated in Mexía's filibustering expedition from New Orleans against Tampico. The objective was to land a force, gain support from the local populace, overthrow Santa Anna, and install in his place exiled leader Goméz Farías. The mission failed miserably. The majority of the party was killed or captured, but Mexía escaped to Texas, eventually rejoining Gómez Farías in New Orleans.

Mexía remained in New Orleans until December 1838 when he returned to Mexico. Though the exact date and place of the event cannot be determined, Mexía was shot in 1839 during an attempt to overthrow President Anastasio Bustamante's government.

James M. Denham

BIBLIOGRAPHY

Barker, Eugene C. "The Tampico Expedition," *Quarterly of the Texas State Historical Association* 6 (January 1903): 169–186.

Hutchinson, C. Alan. "General José Antonio Mexía and His Texas Interest." *Southwestern Historical Quarterly* 82 (October 1978): 117–142.

Hutchinson, C. Alan. "Mexican Federalists in New Orleans and the Texas Revolution." *Louisiana Historical Quarterly* 39 (January 1956): 1–47.

Mexican Cession

On 2 February 1848, at the Villa de Guadalupe Hidalgo, a treaty was signed ending the U.S.–Mexican War and ceding Texas and the territories of New Mexico and Alta California to the United States. The agreement, known in the United States as the Treaty of Guadalupe Hidalgo, was signed by Nicholas P. Trist for the United States and José Bernardo Couto, Miguel Atristain, and Luis Gonzaga Cuevas for Mexico. By May 1848, both countries had ratified the cession, which transferred over 500,000 square miles, or close to half of Mexico's national territory, to the United States.

The Mexican Cession defined the international boundary as the Río Grande to Paso del Norte (present-day Juárez), from there westward to the Gila River, and then to the Pacific coast along the thirty-second parallel. Controversies concerning disputed territory were to be resolved by two separate commissions of both nations. What was not disputed was that the port of San Diego belonged to the United States. U.S. expansionism had cost Mexico nearly half of its territory, including Texas, New Mexico, Arizona, California, Nevada, and Utah, and portions of Oklahoma, Colorado, and Wyoming. The United States paid Mexico an indemnity of $15 million and assumed more than $3 million in claims that U.S. citizens had against the Mexican government. Mexico retained Baja California and a land link to Sonora.

Articles VIII and IX of the Guadalupe treaty guaranteed to the Mexicans living in the ceded territory the protection of their property and "free exercise of their religion." Article XI committed the United States to control the Native Americans in the ceded area.

The harsh terms of the treaty led to rebellions and some *pronunciamientos* (barracks revolts) in Mexico. It also did not satisfy the desires of extreme expansionists in the United States, who continued filibustering expeditions into Mexico throughout the next decade. While Mexicans who remained in the areas ceded to the United States lost much of their land to fraud and outright confiscation, in general the U.S.–Mexican War marked the transition of the economy of the conquered provinces from subsistence cultivation to market production. In Mexico, moral outrage stimulated national cohesion, while the spoils of war increased the national domain of the United States, creating a market that sustained economic growth throughout the nineteenth century.

W. Dirk Raat

BIBLIOGRAPHY

Griswold del Castillo, Richard. *The Treaty of Guadalupe-Hidalgo: A Legacy of Conflict.* 1990.

Martínez, Oscar J. *Troublesome Border.* 1988.

Raat, W. Dirk. *Mexico and the United States: Ambivalent Vistas.* 1992.

"Treaty of Peace, Friendship, Limits and Settlement between Mexico and the United States, signed at Guadalupe Hidalgo, 2 February 1848." In *The Consolidated Treaty Series*, edited and annotated by Clive Parry, vol. 102, pp. 29–59. 1969.

Zoraida Vázquez, Josefina, and Lorenzo Meyer. *The United States and Mexico.* 1985.

Mexican Spy Company

Not all Mexicans opposed the U.S. invasion of their country. One group of Mexicans from Puebla was recruited to gather intelligence along the National Road for Gen. Winfield Scott. Called the Mexican Spy Company, the band was organized

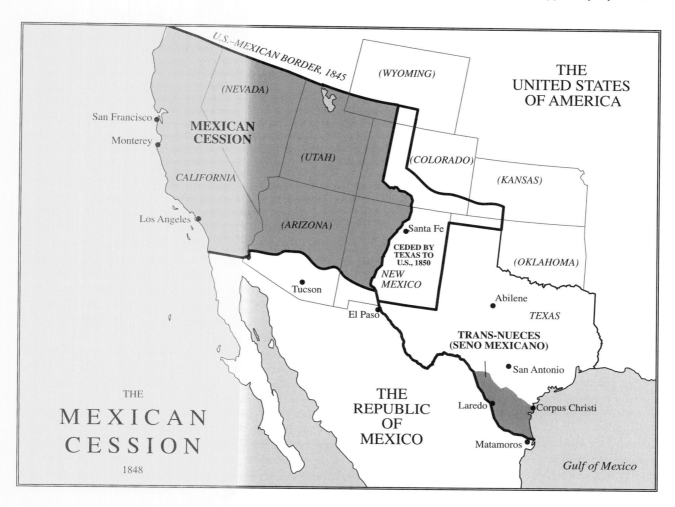

THE

MEXICAN CESSION

1848

by Lt. Col. Ethan Allen Hitchcock, Scott's inspector general, and operated from the spring of 1847 until U.S. forces left Mexico in July 1848. It gathered information and helped secure the roads in central Mexico against insurgents. Little known, the Mexican Spy Company contributed to Scott's success.

The band's leader, Manuel Dominguez, was a Puebla native who had been imprisoned by Gen. William J. Worth for banditry. Freed from jail, Hitchcock authorized the reputed bandit chieftain to raise two companies of his associates to work for him, although only one company was formed. Paid $20 per month, members of the company disguised themselves as market vendors and traveled to Mexico City before battles there to obtain information about Mexican troop movements and road conditions. One U.S. volunteer stated that Dominguez's men wore red scarfs around their hats so that they could identify each other. The company later reportedly had "parrot green" jackets trimmed in red. When

they were not incognito, the officers and noncommissioned officers wore the same insignia as U.S. soldiers.

Dominguez, who feared retribution from the Mexicans at the end of the war, left Mexico and settled near New Orleans. Hitchcock, aided by Sen. Jefferson Davis, tried to secure a pension for Dominguez, but Congress did not approve it. The fate of his men, who were left behind, is not known.

Richard Bruce Winders

BIBLIOGRAPHY

Brackett, Albert G. *General Lane's Brigade in Central Mexico.* 1854.

Croffut, W. A., ed. *Fifty Years in Camp and Field: Diary of Major-General Ethan Allen Hitchcock.* 1971.

Katcher, Philip R. N. *The Mexican-American War, 1846–1848.* 1989.

Smith, Justin. *War with Mexico.* 2 vols. 1919. Reprint, 1963.

Mexico, 1821–1854

Though one of the most eventful periods in Mexican history, the early national period has received relatively little attention and scholarly study in comparison to both the colonial period and the twentieth century. As a consequence there is, as yet, an incomplete view of Mexico during the first thirty years of its independence. While substantial agreement exists on the actual events that occurred, a useful explanation of their significance still eludes us. What follows is a brief interpretive summary of the major events.

Instability in Mexico during the early national period was a continuation of the instability of the late colonial era. Although Mexicans had high expectations for the future, few fully realized the extent to which the traditional economy and infrastructure had been devastated by the Wars of Independence (1810–1821). When Gen. Agustín de Iturbide entered Mexico City on 27 September 1821, no one realized how difficult it would be to muster the national will, unity, and purpose necessary to rebuild the economy and government. The new nation's elite felt momentarily buoyed by the hope that Iturbide's Plan of Iguala had resolved old tensions between church and state, between regional and central authority, and between ethnic castes. The initial calm, however, belied the persistence of these deeply entrenched divisions that hampered the construction of a coherent national policy for decades to come.

One of the most vexing problems to follow Mexico into independence was the dispute over whether political authority should reside in the provincial capitals or remain concentrated in Mexico City. The Cádiz Constitution of 1812 had granted provincial deputations to several of Mexico's far-flung regions, and many regional leaders hoped that independence would herald a return to the process of the devolution of central authority and powers. Indeed, the abrogation of the Cádiz Constitution (and all subsequent Cortes legislation based on it) by Spanish monarch Ferdinand VII had so frustrated localist ambitions that many royalist Creoles (Mexicans of European descent) subsequently supported the independence movement.

Unfortunately, Iturbide showed no intention of addressing regional issues. Shortly after his coronation as Emperor Agustín I, Iturbide confirmed the centralization of political authority in Mexico City and muted resistance by closing all opposition newspapers. Saddled with a massive debt inherited from the Wars of Independence, Iturbide believed that centralization was necessary to rationalize taxation, pacify the lower classes, and prevent regional fragmentation. He hoped that Mexico's mineral resources, which had long supported the Bourbon monarchs, would now resuscitate the economy and mitigate antagonisms.

Mexico's great silver mines would not be put back into production easily, however. Expensive and crucial mining machinery had been destroyed by insurgent armies or left to rust, and mine owners had been terrorized or killed by rebel and royalist armies alike. The internal production of grains and textiles was directly dependent on mining and thus declined in equal proportion to the decline in mineral production. Rebel and royalist forces had routinely burned fields and looted or destroyed *obrajes* (mills) and the wealthy were wary of investing in any activity requiring substantial capital or expanded production. What remained of the nation's manufactures, moreover, now faced increased competition from cheap imports championed by foreign governments.

When Iturbide introduced a series of direct taxes to meet the debt problem, many provincial leaders grew cynical. It seemed preposterous to them that their leader would engage in imperial pageantry while resorting to onerous taxation. They denounced Iturbide's measures as arbitrary and rallied their forces within the army and the legislature. When the emperor responded by dissolving the congress and jailing his shrillest critics, regional leaders quickly secured the support of ambitious and influential young army officers to overthrow the empire.

One such individual was Antonio López de Santa Anna, whose energy and talent allowed him to rise from cadet in the royalist army to the rank of lieutenant colonel and military governor of Vera Cruz. Like many other political and military luminaries of his day, Santa Anna was flexible and ready to switch his allegiance from one faction to another as expediency demanded. Once a supporter of Iturbide's push for independence, Santa Anna now perceived an opportunity for personal gain and promotion by opposing him. On 2 December 1822, Santa Anna pronounced against Iturbide's empire and declared Mexico a republic. Santa Anna's revolt received the endorsement of generals Nicolás Bravo and Guadalupe Victoria, but within a few months the original plan had been revised and renamed as the Plan de Casa Mata. The amended version was distributed to all thirteen Mexican provinces where it was acclaimed by the regional military commanders, whose salaries were now seriously in arrears. Iturbide abdicated on 19 March 1823 and went into exile in Europe. Upon his return to Mexico the next year, Iturbide was arrested and executed as a traitor.

Santa Anna's defection symbolized another problem inherited by independent Mexico: a powerful, politicized military. During the Wars of Independence regional military commanders were directly responsible to the Spanish viceroy, although in fact they usually ruled by decree within their respective regions. With limited resources allocated by the central government, royalist commanders regularly resorted to arbitrary taxes and levies on local populations to subsidize (they claimed) the army's counterinsurgent operations. In reality, many royalist commanders abused their authority and amassed large personal fortunes. These abuses helped to crystallize mass and elite support for the insurgent cause.

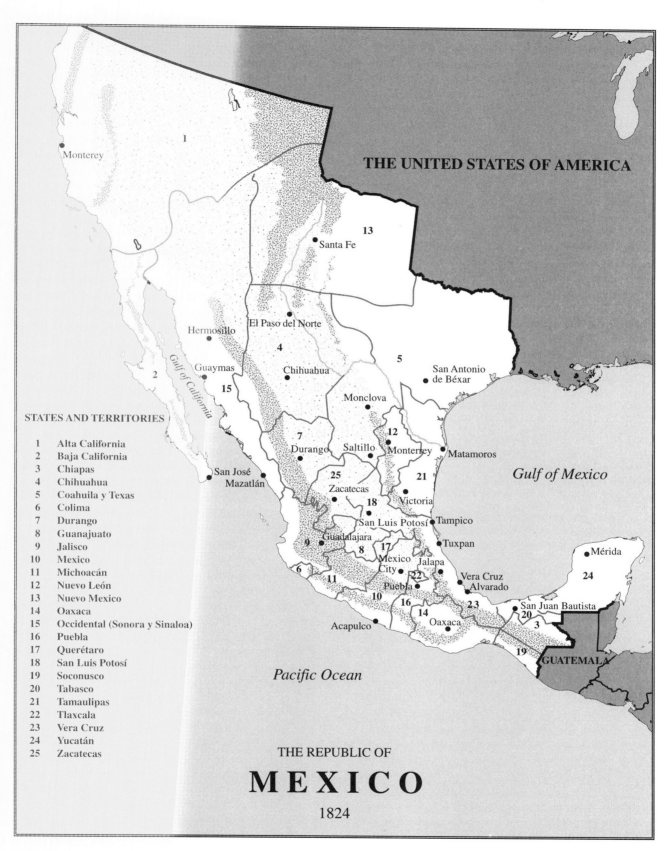

THE UNITED STATES OF AMERICA

Monterey

Santa Fe

13

Hermosillo

El Paso del Norte

4

5

Guaymas

Chihuahua

San Antonio
de Béxar

15

Monclova

Gulf of California

STATES AND TERRITORIES

12

7

Durango   Saltillo   Monterrey

Matamoros

Gulf of Mexico

1	Alta California
2	Baja California
3	Chiapas
4	Chihuahua
5	Coahuila y Texas
6	Colima
7	Durango
8	Guanajuato
9	Jalisco
10	Mexico
11	Michoacán
12	Nuevo León
13	Nuevo Mexico
14	Oaxaca
15	Occidental (Sonora y Sinaloa)
16	Puebla
17	Querétaro
18	San Luis Potosí
19	Soconusco
20	Tabasco
21	Tamaulipas
22	Tlaxcala
23	Vera Cruz
24	Yucatán
25	Zacatecas

San José
Mazatlán

25

21

Zacatecas

18

Victoria

San Luis Potosí

Tampico

9   Guadalajara

8

Tuxpan

Mérida

17

24

6

Mexico
City

Jalapa

11

22

Vera Cruz

Acapulco

Puebla

Alvarado

10

16

23

San Juan Bautista

14

20

Oaxaca

3

19

GUATEMALA

Pacific Ocean

THE REPUBLIC OF

MEXICO

1824

248 / Mexico, 1821–1854

Personnel of the Presidency, Mexico*

Period of the First Federal Republic: 1824–1837

10 Oct. 1824–1 Apr. 1829, Guadalupe Victoria
1 Apr. 1829–18 Dec. 1829, Vicente Guerrero
18 Dec. 1829–23 Dec. 1829, José Maria Bocanegro, ad interim
23 Dec. 1829–31 Dec. 1829, Pedro Velez, Luís Quintana, Lucas Alamán

Provisional Government

31 Dec. 1829–14 Aug. 1832, Anastasio Bustamante
14 Aug. 1832–24 Dec. 1832, Melchor Musquiz, ad interim
24 Dec. 1832–1 Apr. 1833, Manuel Gómez Pedraza
1 Apr. 1833–16 May 1833, Valentín Gómez Farías, acting
16 May 1833–3 June 1833, Antonio López de Santa Anna
3 June 1833–18 June 1833, V. Gómez Farías, acting
18 June 1833–5 July 1833, A. López de Santa Anna
5 July 1833–27 Oct. 1833, V. Gómez Farías, acting
27 Oct. 1833–15 Dec. 1833, A. López de Santa Anna
16 Dec. 1833–24 Apr. 1834, V. Gómez Farías, acting
24 Apr. 1834–28 Jan. 1835, A. López de Santa Anna
28 Jan. 1835–27 Feb. 1836, M. Barragán
27 Feb. 1836–19 Apr. 1837, José Justo Corro

Period of the Centralized Republic; 1837–1846

19 Apr. 1837–18 Mar. 1839, Anastasio Bustamante
18 Mar. 1839–10 July 1839, A. López de Santa Anna
10 July 1839–17 July 1839, Nicolás Bravo
17 July 1839–22 Sept. 1841, A. Bustamante
22 Sept. 1841–10 Oct. 1841, J. Echeverría
10 Oct. 1841–26 Oct. 1842, A. López de Santa Anna, dictator
26 Oct. 1842–5 Mar. 1843, N. Bravo, substitute
5 Mar. 1843–4 Oct. 1843, A. López de Santa Anna
4 Oct. 1843–4 June 1844, Valentín Canalizo
4 June 1844–20 Sept. 1844, A. López de Santa Anna
20 Sept. 1844–6 Dec. 1844, V. Canalizo
6 Dec. 1844–30 Dec. 1845, José Joaquín de Herrera
4 Jan. 1846–28 July 1846, Mariano Paredes y Arrillaga
29 July 1846–4 Aug. 1846, N. Bravo

Period of the Second Federal Republic; 1846–1858

5 Aug. 1846–23 Dec. 1846, Mariano Salas
23 Dec. 1846–21 Mar. 1847, V. Gómez Farías, acting
21 Mar. 1847–2 Apr. 1847, A. López de Santa Anna
2 Apr. 1847–20 May 1847, Pedro María Anaya
20 May 1847–16 Sept. 1847, A. López de Santa Anna
20 Sept. 1847–13 Nov. 1847, Manuel de la Peña y Peña
13 Nov. 1847–8 Jan. 1848, P. María Anaya
8 Jan. 1848–3 June 1848, M. de la Peña y Peña
3 June 1848–15 Jan. 1851, José Joaquín de Herrera
15 Jan. 1851–6 Jan. 1853, Mariano Arista
6 Jan. 1853–7 Feb. 1853, Juan de Ceballos
7 Feb. 1853–20 Apr. 1853, Manuel de Lombardini, dictator
20 Apr. 1853–12 Aug. 1855, A. López de Santa Anna
15 Aug. 1855–12 Sept. 1855, Martin Carrera
4 Oct. 1855–11 Dec. 1855, Juan Álvarez
11 Dec. 1855–14 Jan. 1858, Ignacio Comonfort

*The exact dates vary with the authorities, but those given above appear to be the most reliable.
SOURCE: Wilfred Hardy Calcott. *Church and State in Mexico, 1822–1857.* (Duke University Press, 1926), pp. 341–342.

As a reward for the conversion to the independence camp, many former royalists now expected promotion, or at least that they retain their *fueros* (special privileges, such as immunity from civilian prosecution) and prestige. Whenever these privileges were challenged by Mexico City, the army was sure to rebel. Localized military rebellions and even national coups d'etat became frequent events in Mexico, bringing the potential for rapid promotion to junior officers who carefully cultivated relationships with a patron commander. Thus, despite directives and administrative reorganizations prescribed by the war ministry in Mexico City, army operations throughout the early republic remained subject to decentralized, irregular rules.

Following Iturbide's fall, Mexico's elite fragmented into two mutually antagonistic constitutional factions, organized loosely around the Scottish (*escocés*) and York (*yorkino*) rite Masonic lodges. As exclusive, semisecret societies, the Masonic lodges were appropriate focal points for the conspiratorial politics of the period. Federalists (often called liberals) tended to congregate in the York lodge, while centralists (often called conservatives) were usually Scottish-rite Masons. By 1824, when a new federalist constitution was introduced, the *yorkinos* were spread more widely throughout the country and had elected a majority of deputies in the congress. The wealthy and influential landowners of Mexico's central valley, however, as well as the higher ranking members of the clergy, continued to support the Scottish rite.

The 1824 constitution brought a degree of relative stability and peace, if for only a few years. While the dominant *yorkinos* sought to introduce efficient government and to breathe life into the dormant mining sector, the *escoceses* regrouped and waited for an opportunity to seize control. That opportunity presented itself in 1827 when a new *yorkino*-dominated congress passed the first of a series of laws expelling Spaniards from the country. A leading centralist and Grand Master of the Scottish-rite Masons, General Bravo joined with other *escoceses* to lead an ultimately unsuccessful coup d'etat that was put down by the federalist, York-rite general Vicente Guerrero.

The *yorkinos* soon showed themselves equally ready to engage in violence to achieve political objectives. When *escocés* minister of war Manuel Gómez Pedraza was elected president in 1828, *yorkinos* quickly issued charges of gerrymandering. General Santa Anna was the first to decry the results and pronounce in favor of Gomez Pedraza's opponent, Guerrero. Others joined General Santa Anna in December, including the radical federalist politician Lorenzo de Zavala. Known as the Movimiento de la Acordada, the rebellion precipitated the Parián riot in the capital during which several shops near the *zócalo* (central plaza) were sacked and looted by a mob of rioters. Horrified at the prospect of a mobilized populace and fearful of more rioting, the

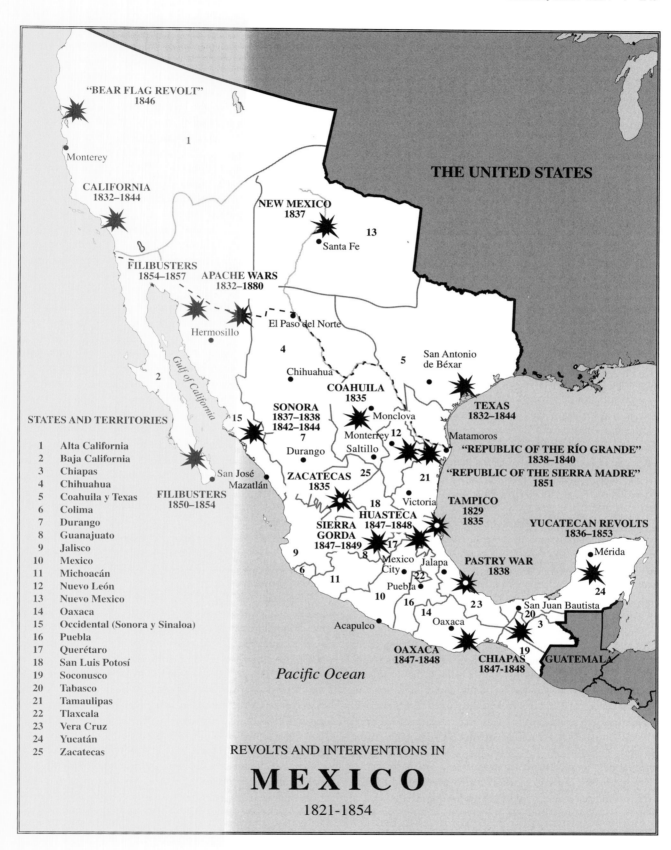

"BEAR FLAG REVOLT"
1846

1

Monterey

CALIFORNIA
1832–1844

THE UNITED STATES

NEW MEXICO
1837

13

Santa Fe

FILIBUSTERS
1854–1857

APACHE WARS
1832–1880

El Paso del Norte

Hermosillo

4

Chihuahua

San Antonio
de Béxar

5

COAHUILA
1835

SONORA
1837–1838
1842–1844

Monclova

TEXAS
1832–1844

STATES AND TERRITORIES

15

7

Monterrey 12

Matamoros

"REPUBLIC OF THE RÍO GRANDE"
1838–1840

1   Alta California
2   Baja California
3   Chiapas
4   Chihuahua
5   Coahuila y Texas
6   Colima
7   Durango
8   Guanajuato
9   Jalisco
10   Mexico
11   Michoacán
12   Nuevo León
13   Nuevo Mexico
14   Oaxaca
15   Occidental (Sonora y Sinaloa)
16   Puebla
17   Querétaro
18   San Luis Potosí
19   Soconusco
20   Tabasco
21   Tamaulipas
22   Tlaxcala
23   Vera Cruz
24   Yucatán
25   Zacatecas

Durango

Saltillo

"REPUBLIC OF THE SIERRA MADRE"
1851

San José
Mazatlán

FILIBUSTERS
1850–1854

ZACATECAS
1835

25

21

TAMPICO
1829
1835

YUCATECAN REVOLTS
1836–1853

Gulf of California

18

Victoria

Mérida

HUASTECA
1847–1848

SIERRA
GORDA
1847–1849

8

17

9

Mexico
City

Jalapa

22

PASTRY WAR
1838

24

6

11

Puebla

10

16

14

Oaxaca

23

20

San Juan Bautista

3

Acapulco

19

Pacific Ocean

OAXACA
1847-1848

CHIAPAS
1847–1848

GUATEMALA

REVOLTS AND INTERVENTIONS IN

MEXICO

1821-1854

federalist congress quashed the elections and, within a month, named Guerrero president.

Guerrero did not last long in office. Suspicious of his non-white, lower class background, the Creole elites, federalists and centralists alike, lost all confidence in the administration when Zavala, Guerrero's minister of finance, introduced a series of progressive property and income taxes. By the end of the year Guerrero's own vice president, Gen. Anastasio Bustamante, pronounced against the regime and Guerrero fled the capital. Bustamante moved quickly to suppress the federalists. Once in power he carried out a series of purges in the state and national legislatures with the aid of his chief minister, Lucas Alamán. Without officially annulling the 1824 constitution, Bustamante and Alaman used army intimidation and threats to oust all federalist governors and their legislators, while regional military commanders ensured that centralists were elected to replace them. Guerrero was apprehended and executed. Within two years, however, Bustamante and the centralists were themselves chased out of government, and the federalists, supported by Santa Anna, carried out their own campaign of suppression.

Temporarily pushed from power in 1832, the centralists regained control of both the executive and the legislature in 1835. Between 1836 and 1845, centralist regimes dominated the government under a new constitution known as the *Siete Leyes* (Seven Laws) until 1843, followed by the *Bases Orgánicas* in 1843–1845. With Santa Anna a converted proponent of the new political framework, constitutional debates now eschewed the issue of federalism (within the government at least) and instead focused on whether Mexico would be governed by a republican-centralist or an authoritarian-centralist regime (i.e., a Santa Anna dictatorship).

Having temporarily silenced his erstwhile federalist allies, Santa Anna marched north in early 1836 on an ultimately unsuccessful punitive mission to crush the Texas bid for independence, and was himself captured at the Battle of San Jacinto. It was an odyssey that temporarily eclipsed his presidential career but was far from marking an end to either his newly acquired centralist orientation or his dictatorial pretensions. Leaving his brooding retirement in 1838 to defeat a ragtag French invasion force at Vera Cruz (the so-called Pastry War), Santa Anna's reputation was rehabilitated and his star again on the rise. Anointing himself the "supreme" authority in Mexico, in 1841 and 1853, in the intervening years the dictator experienced both acclaim and admonition.

Although rebellions were a familiar feature of Mexico's politics, the nation overall remained relatively stable. Insurrections were the territory of the politically active (no more than about 10 percent of the population) in the state and national urban centers. Many rural areas returned to agricultural subsistence as a consequence of the mining depression, but recent research has shown that the peasantry did not remain completely passive. The Wars of Independence had politicized peasants across New Spain and had mobilized them into active guerrilla groups. Insurgent leaders had used emotive rhetoric such as "emancipation," and "justice" to stir peasant communities into action. This type of language implied that independence would deliver direct political participation to the formerly compliant mass of the population. Even the first national elections, in which the deputies were chosen through universal male suffrage, seemed a generous effort toward inclusion. A decree of 17 November 1821 had stipulated, "Citizens of all classes and ethnic castes, even foreigners, in keeping with the Plan of Iguala, may vote provided they have attained eighteen years of age." Some deputies, such as Carlos María de Bustamante, even argued that the lands of the largest haciendas should be distributed among the poor Indians of the nation. The more liberal federalist deputies in Congress (for whom property was sacrosanct) were aghast.

By 1824, however, there was no longer any talk of universal suffrage among centralists or federalists. Creole *hombres de bien* (men of property) had consummated independence to enhance control over and protection of their properties. The Constitution of 1824 represented the fruition of the post-independence reform effort to retie the hierarchical social bonds of Mexican society. In general, political participation was to be limited, the Catholic Church was to be protected, and the military heroes of independence were to be venerated. José Luis Mora articulated an elite consensus when he wrote in 1830 that citizenship itself ought to depend on the possession of property. One of the most odious consequences of the Wars of Independence had been, he believed, the dangerous and regrettable spread of the notion of literal equality of condition, as opposed to the more sensible equality of opportunity. To check the shameful spread of rights to that execrable class of *léperos* (Mexico City's underclass), he proposed stricter limits on voting and that all political rights be directed toward the protection of private property.

One split that did emerge among Mexico's republican leaders was over the issue of reform for institutions such as the church. Secularism had predated independence. Largely as the result of the reform policies of the Bourbon monarchies, the church had declined in power and prestige. The new parties to emerge from the Scottish and York-rite Masonic lodges, though they shared an overall esteem for the church, were convinced that sovereignty had transferred regal authority and patronage for the institution to the national government. While nearly all of the elite shared this view, the anticlerical reasoning of the French Enlightenment also had its influence on various individuals in both the *yorkino* and *escocés* lodges.

By the 1830s these men had found each other, and in 1833, under the leadership of Valentín Gómez Farías, they maneuvered their agenda into the presidential palace. With the support of Santa Anna, federalists swept the Bustamante government from power in 1832. As Santa Anna's interim president, Gómez Farías hoped to purge Mexico of the influence of all colonial institutions and thereby heralded the emergence of an enlightened, eventually democratic, secular society. In implementing his anticlerical program, however, Gómez Farías alienated the majority of the still-devout, upper-middle-class elite. Removing from office or exiling all dissenters, the Gómez Farías government also initiated encumbrances against church mortmain and raised taxes to pay for new education policies and the recently reorganized civic militias. The strengthening of the militias and the elimination of military, clerical, and other *fueros* spawned hostility among the regional strongmen. Church leaders combined with these chiefs in 1834 to convince Santa Anna to dismiss Gómez Farías and rescind many of the reforms.

Aside from class issues, periodic threats to the nation's sovereignty and territorial integrity tended to eclipse any internal constitutional wrangling. Between 1821 and 1853 Mexico was invaded three times—by Spain, France, and the United States. In 1829 a Spanish expeditionary force landed in Tampico in a vain attempt to reconquer the former colony. A decade later, France landed a small invasion force at Vera Cruz in an ill-fated effort to seize Mexico's principal customs house and recover delinquent debt payments. Throughout the 1820s, 1830s, and 1840s, British, Russian, and U.S. warships surveyed California's rich coastline. Though there were exceptions in each case, most of Mexico's leaders closed ranks in the face of these external pressures. U.S. support for the Texas rebels, however, was perceived to be the greatest threat yet to Mexico's national sovereignty.

Indeed, the Texas issue had been a source of major concern in Mexican politics even before the Texian declaration of independence in 1836. In the years between 1836 and 1845, as *santanistas*, federalists, and centralists vied for the command of public opinion and the government, the patriotic goal of recapturing the rebellious department became one of the central issues around which political leaders and parties defined themselves. It was the principal gauge against which adversaries publicly measured and assailed the patriotism of their political opponents.

Most ordinary Mexicans prior to 1821 knew little and cared less about the United States. Aside from vague notions that it was a nation of Protestants and that it had, like Mexico, waged a war for national independence from Europe, the United States was terra incognita. By the end of the first two decades of Mexican independence, however, ignorance and indifference about the United States had changed first to admiration, then to ambivalence, and finally to distrust and suspicion.

Early U.S. recognition of Mexico's independence had been gratefully received in Iturbide's empire and had helped to allay the worry among the new rulers regarding U.S. expan-

sionism. It also aroused an acute curiosity about their northern neighbor and its institutions. Hailing from Mexico's far-flung regions, many of the new nation's provincial elite came to openly admire the U.S. federal system, which they believed delegated significant powers to men just like themselves.

Gradually, however, admiration for the United States first waned and then evaporated as the aggressively stated U.S. policy objectives began to clash with Mexico's perceived national interests. The first U.S. ambassador to Mexico, Joel R. Poinsett, had made clear to Mexico's leaders his country's intention to acquire at least Texas, and perhaps California and New Mexico as well. In his first diplomatic instructions to Poinsett, Secretary of State Henry Clay directed the new ambassador to promote U.S. influence in the country at the expense of British interests, to insist on "most favored nation" commercial status for the United States, and most important, to demand a northern boundary resolution that would have resulted in the virtual cession of the Texas territory to the United States. In short, Poinsett was instructed to pursue objectives that were sure to alienate all but the most dedicated admirers of the United States.

Mexicans were outraged when the United States assisted the Texian rebels in their independence efforts throughout 1836 and then rewarded them with prompt diplomatic recognition in March 1837. Accompanied as they were by numerous and increasingly cacophonous U.S. claims against the Mexican government, these acts seemed to prove bad faith. By 1844, when President John Tyler's administration negotiated the annexation of Texas, Mexican opinion of the United States had evolved from general suspicion to fear and open animosity. In May, the U.S. chargé d'affaires in Mexico City informed Foreign Minister Francisco González Bocanegra that such a treaty did exist and had been submitted to Congress for approval. The Mexican government's response was vitriolic. Bocanegra roared that the United States, despite Mexico's forbearance and good faith, had proven itself to be a "usurper" and an "aggressor" nation.

A December 1844 coup brought moderate federalist Gen. José Joaquín de Herrera to power. When rumors circulated in the fall of 1845 that Herrera's regime was negotiating with the United States for the sale of Texas, New Mexico, and the Californias, Gen. Mariano Paredes y Arrillaga, the leader of a secret monarchist conspiracy, declared himself in rebellion against the government. The main justification for the uprising was the Herrera administraion's failure to recapture Texas. Marching into the capital on 1 January 1846, Paredes y Arrillaga was soon anointed president with Nicolás Bravo named his vice president. This also was a short-lived government. Within seven months Mexico and the United States had declared war on each other, Mexico's large Northern Division had been humiliated in the opening battles of the conflict, and the Paredes government had fallen to a coup. Politics, however, could not be laid aside even in the face of impending disaster, and the hatreds between the various factions hindered the organization of cohesive resistance against the United States. As a result, the U.S. army captured Mexico City in September 1847 and negotiators reached a peace settlement approximately five months later.

The end of hostilities did not bring immediate unity to Mexico. A new generation of radical and moderate federalist thinkers concluded that Mexico's main problem had been the failure to extirpate the Spanish colonial legacy, while conservatives argued that monarchy was the best means of restoring national well-being. Debate grew increasingly rancorous and turned to open conflict in 1854. Only thirteen years later, after overcoming a new round of civil war and a foreign intervention orchestrated by French emperor Napoleon III, did radical federalist leaders, led by Benito Juárez, manage to establish a new republic and greater national consensus.

M. Bruce Colcleugh and Colin MacLachlan

BIBLIOGRAPHY

Costeloe, Michael P. *The Central Republic in Mexico, 1835–1846: Hombres de Bien in the Age of Santa Anna.* 1993.

Di Tella, Torcuato S. *National Popular Politics in Early Independent Mexico, 1820–1847.* 1996.

Fowler, Will. *The Liberal Origins of Mexican Conservatism, 1821–1832.* 1997.

González Navarro, Moisés. *Anatomia del poder en Mexico, 1848–1853.* 2d ed. 1983.

Guardino, Peter. *Peasants, Politics and the Formation of Mexico's National State: Guerrero, 1800–1857.* 1996.

Hale, Charles. *Mexican Liberalism in the Age of Mora, 1821–1853.* 1968.

Stevens, Donald F. *Origins of Instability in Early Republican Mexico.* 1991.

Mexico City

Founded in the early 1520s by the Spanish conquerors over Tenochtitlán, capital of the Aztec empire, Mexico City (*Ciudad de Mexico*) lies on a plateau in central Mexico at an elevation of about 7,800 feet. By the 1840s, during the U.S.–Mexican War, the city occupied about four square miles, had a population of 200,000, and was the locus of much of the nation's wealth. In 1846, when Gen. Winfield Scott was named commander of the campaign against Mexico, the U.S. government's objective was to force Mexico to capitulate by taking the capital city.

Historically, the capital was the center in which national political disputes were settled; local affairs were considered of secondary importance. Criticism against the national government increased in February 1847 when the Polkos Revolt (*rebelión de los polkos*) broke out in response to the U.S.

invasion in the north and rumors of the imminent attack on Vera Cruz.

Though the municipal government and the populace of the capital cooperated in the national defense from the outset of the war, some other states that might have supported the city refused to send assistance, arguing that the war was an affair between the capital and the United States. Once Chapultepec and the city gates had been lost, Mexican leaders evacuated the city, and the municipal government negotiated the peaceful entry into the capital by U.S. troops. However, when U.S. forces took the National Palace and raised their flag there on 14 September, the enraged population began *"la guerra pública"* (the public war). Street-fighting ensued until 16 September, when it became clear that the Mexican army was not going to take part. The federal government had evacuated to Querétaro, and for the first time Mexico City was not the capital. Isolated, the city was just one of many forced to endure nine months of U.S. occupation.

As in other invaded cities, a military–civilian government, in which municipal authorities were subordinate to the military, was established to maintain order, collect new taxes, and make the arrangements necessary to accommodate the occupying U.S. soldiers, who in Mexico City numbered 8,000 to 14,000. Although the policy of the military government initially was to respect the civilian population and prevent abuses by the troops, occupied towns were obliged by the end of 1847 to pay the costs of the war. In November 1847 General Scott ordered each state to pay U.S. authorities a given amount of money, and decreed that U.S. forces would no longer pay any rent for the houses and buildings they occupied. These measures were designed to pressure the federal government—which was in Querétaro at the time—into signing the peace treaty. Security was the top priority at all times, to which end police bodies and special courts were created, the Federal District's boundaries were extended, and efforts were made to control Mexican officials.

The presence of U.S. troops changed the profile of the city from an economic standpoint also. The surge of currency benefited businesses that offered goods and services, especially those concerned with lodging, food, and entertainment. This influenced the types of relationships that developed between the soldiers and the different portions of the population. The public's reaction to the U.S. occupation varied from attitudes favoring collaboration and annexation to outright rejection and clandestine resistance, which continued throughout the occupation.

On 12 June 1848, after ratification of the peace treaty in May, U.S. forces withdrew from the city, leaving in their wake the residue of war: feelings of defeat and discouragement. When U.S. forces left the capital, the Mexican federal government returned to Mexico City. As a result, the capital, as always, again became the most important stage for political affairs in the country. The new government had to face

Mexico City. This engraving depicts the city's main plaza and the cathedral (Fayette Robinson, *Mexico and Her Military Chieftains*, 1851).

a grave economic crisis caused, among other factors, by the breakdown of trade, the increased cost of goods, and smuggling. In addition, a number of social problems, such as criminality and an increasing number of unemployed (to mention but two), forced the Mexico City *ayuntamiento* (municipal authorities) to invest more resources in an attempt to restore public security.

Laura Herrera Serna

BIBLIOGRAPHY

Alcaraz, Ramón, et al. *Apuntes para la historia de la guerra entre México y los Estados Unidos.* 1970.

Berge, Dennis E. "A Mexican Dilemma: The Mexico City Ayuntamiento and the Question of Loyalty, 1846–1848." *Hispanic American Historical Review* 50 (1970): 229–256.

Gayón, María. *La ocupación yanqui de la Ciudad de México, 1847–1848.* 1997.

Roa Bárcena, José María. *Recuerdos de la invasión Norteamericana, 1846–1848.* 1947.

Sánchez de Tagle, Esteban. "La asamblea municipal de la ciudad de México durante la ocupación norteamericana." *Historias.* Dirección de Estudios Históricos-INAH, México, Instituto Nacional de Antropología e Historia, Octubre 1991–Marzo, pp. 115–119. 1992.

Mexico City Campaign

This entry consists of three separate articles: **The March to Mexico City;** **Assault on Mexico City;** *and* **Defending the Road to Mexico.**

The March to Mexico City

The surrender of Vera Cruz on 29 March 1847 secured Maj. Gen. Winfield Scott's base of operations to prepare the four divisions of his Army of the South for the 225-mile march inland to Mexico City. Scott, anxious to depart the low Mexican coast before the onset of yellow-fever, or *vómito*, season, but frustrated by the lack of adequate mule and wagon transportation to move his 10,000-man army, decided to leave the sick and wounded in Vera Cruz.

Col. William S. Harney led the cavalry brigade advance guard northwestward on the National Road on 2 April, followed on 8 April by the 2d Division, commanded by Brig. Gen. David E. Twiggs, and on the following day by the Division of Volunteers, under Maj. Gen. of Volunteers Robert Patterson. Lacking transportation, the 1st Division, under Maj. Gen. William J. Worth, remained temporarily in Vera Cruz. Scott's intermediate objective was the higher, and healthier, city of Jalapa, seventy-five miles inland. Mean-

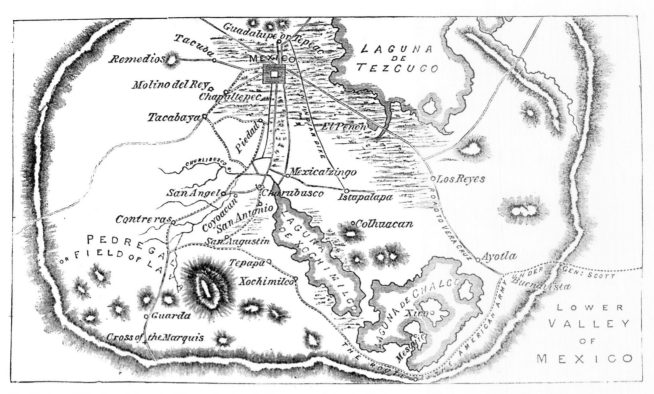

The Valley of Mexico. Robert A. Wilson, *Mexico: Its Peasants and Priests,* 1856

while Mexican general Antonio López de Santa Anna had reorganized his forces after the battle at Buena Vista and intended to confine Scott's army to the unhealthy coastal plain by blocking its approach to the Sierra Madre. Santa Anna chose the narrow pass at Cerro Gordo for his defense.

After attacking and defeating Santa Anna at Cerro Gordo on 17 and 18 April, Scott resumed his advance to Jalapa, which his army occupied without a fight on 19 April. Worth's division continued on thirty miles to Perote, which it reached on 22 April. Scott paused at Jalapa for one month to gather local supplies, establish amicable relations with the indigenous population, and attempt to stem the guerrilla activity that threatened his supply line to Vera Cruz. Scott's situation was further complicated by the need to send home his seven regiments of twelve-month volunteers, whose terms of enlistment expired in April. Their departure left him with a field strength of 7,100. While waiting for reinforcing volunteer regiments sent by the War Department, Scott ordered Worth, at Perote, to advance sixty-five miles and seize the key city of Puebla. Worth took Puebla on 15 May with only a minor skirmish during the approach march.

Scott advanced his main force forward into Puebla on 29 May. To increase his strength Scott ordered the garrisons at Jalapa and Perote to join him at Puebla, thus leaving virtually unguarded his lines of communication with the coast.

Scott did not, as is sometimes claimed, completely cut his line of supply. In a bountiful agricultural region, Scott relied for his rations on local procurement and forage and on occasional heavily escorted wagon convoys from Vera Cruz for military supplies. Thus, Scott, in an economy of force measure, focused his combat power, directly protecting his rolling supply convoys rather than dispersing that power to guard the entire road along which his supplies traveled.

The Army of the South enjoyed a two-month interlude at Puebla until two columns of reinforcements arrived the first week in August. With his field strength increased to 10,738, Scott immediately ordered the army forward to the capital, leaving behind in Puebla a small 400-man garrison and 1,800 hospitalized soldiers.

Marching by divisions at one-day intervals, Scott's army set out on 7 August, averaging twelve to fifteen miles per day. Descending from a high plateau above Ayotla on 11 August 1847, the advance guard of the Army of the South entered the Valley of Mexico, its goal of Mexico City now in sight. In the final advance to the capital the staff of Scott's Army of the South consisted of Scott's personal staff of six and a military staff of sixty-three officers including nine engineers, four topographical engineers, nine quartermasters, three ordnance officers, two commissary or subsistence officers, four paymasters, and thirty-two doctors.

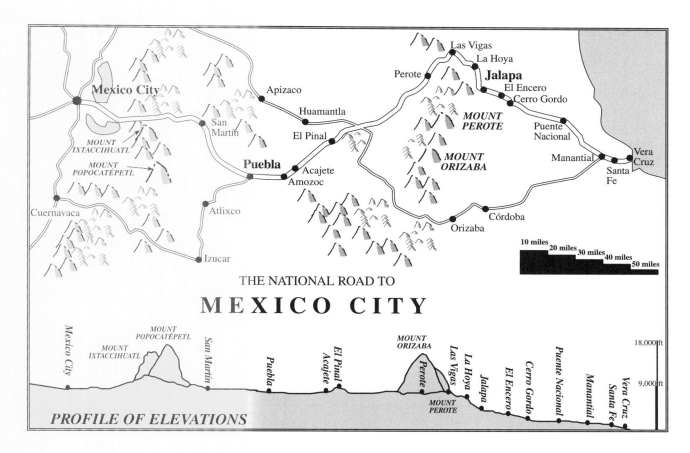

THE NATIONAL ROAD TO

MEXICO CITY

PROFILE OF ELEVATIONS

The combat units were divided into a separate cavalry brigade and four infantry divisions of two brigades each. Colonel Harney commanded the cavalry, composed of the 2d and 3d Dragoons and one company each of the 1st Dragoons and Mounted Rifles. Major General Worth commanded the 1st Division, which contained the 4th, 5th, 6th, and 8th Infantry and the 2d and 3d Artillery. The 2d Division, commanded by Brigadier General Twiggs, consisted of the 2d, 3d, and 7th Infantry, the Mounted Rifles Regiment, and the 1st and 4th Artillery. Maj. Gen. of Volunteers Gideon J. Pillow, a southern Democratic political appointee and former law partner of President James K. Polk, commanded the 3d Division of the 9th, 11th, 12th, 14th, and 15th Infantry and the Regiment of Voltigeurs. Brig. Gen. of Volunteers John A. Quitman, a political appointee, Mississippi lawyer, and model citizen-soldier, commanded a division of Volunteers composed of the Marine Corps detachment, the New York and South Carolina Volunteer Regiments, and the 2d Pennsylvania Volunteers.

As Scott's army approached Mexico City from the east on the National Road, his engineers, while conducting route reconnaissances from 12 to 14 August, discovered a formidable Mexican position obstructing direct approach to the capital. The 7,000-strong Mexican Army of the North, under Maj. Gen. Gabriel Valencia, and a fortified 450-foot hill, El Peñon, with sixty cannon in three lines of works with a fifteen-foot ditch, blocked access to the seven-mile causeway leading to the city's eastern gate. One alternative to a head-on assault was for Scott to march to the north, around Lake Texcuco to the Tampico Road. Such a move, however, would mean a march of more than fifty miles and would have placed Scott between two lakes and far out of position to regain his line of communication with Puebla to the southeast, thus leaving his rear vulnerable to Mexican cavalry attacks.

On the advice of his engineers, Scott decided against both a head-on assault of El Peñon and the northern detour, instead maneuvering his army south on 15 August with Worth's 1st Division in the lead. The twenty-five-mile southern route from Chalco to San Augustín kept Lakes Chalco and Xochimilco on his right as security against a potential flank attack, by Mexican general Nicolás Bravo at Mexicalzingo, that could catch Scott's columns dispersed on the march. The most vulnerable part of the route, a muddy stretch near the village of Chalco, was negotiated without interference from Santa Anna. In the two days Scott required to round the lakes and reach San Agustín, Santa Anna used his advantage of interior lines to shift part of his force of 25,000 to positions at San Antonio, Churubusco, and San Angel. From San Angel Mexican general Valencia moved his units farther south to a hill position near Contreras.

Scott, from his new depot and base of operations at San Agustín, controlled the southern road into Mexico City, now seven miles distant, and had several avenues of approach that Santa Anna would be forced to defend. The direct approach to the north through the strong defenses at San Antonio and Churubusco was constricted in the east by marshes, ditches, and lakes and to the west by the rough terrain of a lava field called the Pedregal.

On 18 August, engineers Capt. Robert E. Lee and Lt. P. G. T. Beauregard reported a practical five-mile route west on the southern edge of the jagged lava to Contreras and the San Angel Road. Lee subsequently supervised a five-hundred-man detail to widen the footpath into a road that could accommodate artillery. On 19 August Scott decided to envelop San Antonio from the west by sending part of Pillow's and Twiggs's divisions across the lava fields. This force encountered Major General Valencia near Contreras, and the three U.S. brigades turned that position on the north by capturing the village of San Gerónimo. Lee spent the night carrying messages and guiding reinforcing units across the jagged paths and chasms of the Pedregal from San Agustín to the vicinity of Valencia's position. At dawn on 20 August 1847, four months and three weeks after departing Vera Cruz, Scott's Army of the South was in position to attack Contreras and Churubusco. Thus, the march to Mexico City ended and the final fight for the capital began.

Thomas Tyree Smith

BIBLIOGRAPHY

Bauer, K. Jack. *The Mexican War, 1846–1848.* 1974.

Eisenhower, John S. D. *So Far from God: The U.S. War with Mexico, 1846–1848.* 1989.

Miller, Robert Ryal, ed. *The Mexican War Journal and Letters of Ralph W. Kirkham.* 1991.

Scott, Winfield. *Official List of Officers Who Marched with the Army under the Command of Major General Winfield Scott.* 1848.

Smith, Justin H. *The War with Mexico.* 2 vols. 1919. Reprint, 1963.

Trass, Adrian George. *From the Golden Gate to Mexico City: The U.S. Army Topographical Engineers in the Mexican War, 1846–1848.* 1993.

Assault on Mexico City

Following U.S. victories at El Molino del Rey and Casa Mata on 8 September 1847, Gen. Winfield Scott met with his staff and senior officers to discuss plans for the final assault on Mexico City. Scott elected to make a feint on the city's heavily defended and fortified southern approaches in favor of attacking from the west and southwest. Blocking the U.S. advance was the Chapultepec Castle, which contained a series of rectangular structures that included the Colegio Militar, perched on an eminence two hundred feet above the valley floor. Chapultepec was connected via a network of roads and viaducts with protective ditches, stone walls, parapets, and breastworks to protect against attack. Despite its imposing presence the fortress was not without flaws. Gen. Antonio López de Santa Anna had failed to complete all of the ditches and supporting works, and the structures were not artillery-proof. Worst of all, Santa Anna committed only eight hundred soldiers under Maj. Gen. Nicolás Bravo for its defense, when two thousand soldiers were required. Other troops, which could have been used to defend Chapultepec, were positioned to the southeast to meet other U.S. threats.

On 12 September the division of Maj. Gen. John A. Quitman demonstrated southeast of Chapultepec. Under cover of darkness Quitman's and Maj. Gen. Gideon J. Pillow's divisions marched to the village of Tacubaya, one mile south of Chapultepec. On the morning of 13 September U.S. batteries bombarded the Chapultepec fortifications for more than two hours before the infantry advanced. Quitman's division at Tacubaya drove toward the southeast corner of the fortress while Pillow attacked the western flank. Passing through the ruins of El Molino del Rey, Pillow's men reached the foot of the hill but not before taking heavy casualties. A portion of Gen. William J. Worth's division reinforced Pillow. To the south, Quitman's division raced across open ground to the base of the bluffs. The divisions of Quitman and Pillow, united and under the protective cover of the bluff, placed scaling ladders into position for the final push to capture Chapultepec. General Bravo surrendered at 9:30 A.M., about two hours after the assault started.

The fall of Chapultepec did not signal an end to the fighting. Quitman and Worth's divisions regrouped for the assault on the heavily fortified gates of Belén and San Cosme. Quitman's troops met stiff resistance but captured the Garita de Belén southwest of the city. To the northwest, Worth's men dislodged Mexican forces at the gates of San Cosme. Scott called a halt to the attacks before dark. U.S. casualties were approximately 850 killed, wounded, and missing. Mexican losses amounted to 3,000, including 800 prisoners.

During the evening Scott consolidated his forces, believing that 14 September would result in heavier house-to-house fighting to dislodge the Mexican army. Mexico City officials, however, persuaded Santa Anna to evacuate the city, thus saving it from destruction and loss of civilian lives. Santa Anna withdrew with the remnants of his army to Guadalupe Hidalgo. In the predawn hours of 14 September Scott ac-

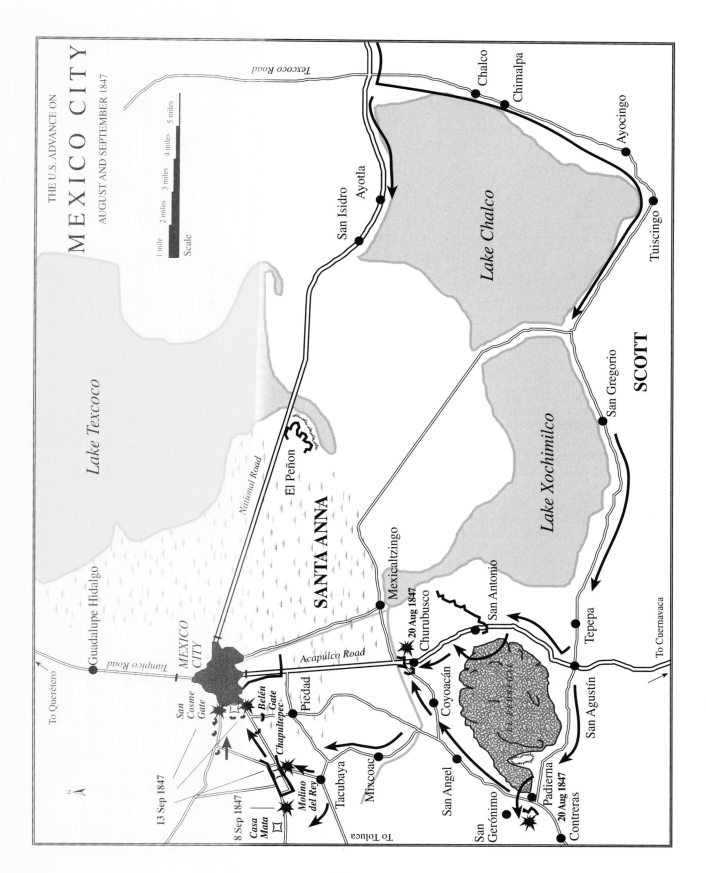

THE U.S. ADVANCE ON

MEXICO CITY

AUGUST AND SEPTEMBER 1847

Scale

1 mile 2 miles 3 miles 4 miles 5 miles

Lake Texcoco

Lake Chalco

Lake Xochimilco

Chalco

Chimalpa

Ayocingo

Tuiscingo

Ayotla

San Isidro

Texcoco Road

San Gregorio

SCOTT

To Cuernavaca

Tepepa

San Agustín

National Road

El Peñon

SANTA ANNA

Guadalupe Hidalgo

To Querétero

Tampico Road

MEXICO CITY

San Cosme Gate

Belén Gate

Chapultepec

Piedad

Acapulco Road

Mexicaltzingo

Churubusco

20 Aug 1847

San Antonio

Coyoacán

13 Sep 1847

8 Sep 1847

Casa Mata

Molino del Rey

Tacubaya

Mixcoac

San Angel

San Gerónimo

Padierna
20 Aug 1847
Contreras

To Toluca

N

257

Assault on Mexico City
Order of Battle
Belén & San Cosme Gates
13–14 September 1847

Mexican Forces

Commander
Antonio López de Santa Anna

Infantry
Grenadier Guards
1st Light Regiment
2d Light Regiment
3d Light Regiment
11th Line Regiment
Invalid Battalion
1st Regiment, Mexico Activo Militia

Cavalry
Hussars of the Supreme Powers
2d Regiment
3d Regiment
5th Regiment
7th Regiment
8th Regiment
9th Regiment
Tulancingo Cuirrassiers
Michoacan Regiment, Activo Militia
Oaxaca Regiment, Activo Militia

Artillery
2 pieces (at Belén Gate)

U.S. Forces

Commander
Gen. Winfield Scott

Infantry
2d U.S. Infantry
3d U.S. Infantry
4th U.S. Infantry
5th U.S. Infantry
6th U.S. Infantry
7th U.S. Infantry
8th U.S. Infantry
9th U.S. Infantry
11th U.S. Infantry
14th U.S. Infantry
15th U.S. Infantry
1st U.S. Artillery (serving as infantry)
2d U.S. Artillery (serving as infantry)
3d U.S. Artillery (serving as infantry)
4th Artillery (serving as infantry)
U.S. Regiment of Mounted Rifles (dismounted)
U.S. Voltigeur Regiment
Company A, U.S. Engineers
U.S. Marine Battalion
2d New York Volunteers
2d Pennsylvania Volunteers
1st South Carolina Volunteers

Artillery
Company I, 1st Artillery (Magruder's mounted battery)
Company K, 1st Artillery (Taylor's battery)
Company H, 3d U.S. Artillery (Steptoe's battery)
Company A, 2d Artillery (Duncan's battery)
Ordnance Company

Cavalry
Company F, 1st U.S. Dragoons
2d U.S. Dragoons
Company C, 3d U.S. Dragoons

cepted the unconditional surrender of the capital and marched triumphantly into the National Plaza.

Neil Mangum

BIBLIOGRAPHY

Bauer, K. Jack. *The Mexican War, 1846–48*. 1974.

Eisenhower, John S. D. *So Far from God: The U.S. War with Mexico, 1846–1848*. 1989.

Defending the Road to Mexico

The 250-mile National Road, Gen. Winfield Scott's link to the coast, had to be defended if U.S. victories in the interior were to have lasting significance. The Duke of Wellington, who vanquished Napoléon Bonaparte at Waterloo, recognized Scott's precarious situation, predicting disaster for the U.S. forces with the terse comment, "Scott is lost." Only the successful defense of the National Road prevented the prediction from coming true.

Scott landed at Vera Cruz on 9 March 1847 knowing that a large segment of his 10,000-man army had less than four months left on their enlistment. He wasted little time marching inland once the city fell on 29 March. On 18 April he successfully turned the Mexican position at Cerro Gordo,

opening the way to the capital. Pausing briefly at Jalapa in early May, Scott released his twelve-month volunteers. Their departure left him with slightly more than 7,000 troops. He moved the bulk of his forces on to Puebla, where he spent the summer waiting for promised reinforcements and rebuilding his army. By August, enough new troops had arrived to allow him to advance on Mexico City at the head of a 10,738-man column.

Scott had stationed troops at Vera Cruz, Jalapa, Perote, and Puebla to secure these strategic points as well as to guard hospitals and depots there. At Puebla alone more than 2,000 invalids were left behind, too ill to continue on with Scott's column. The line of communication, stretched to the limit, proved fertile grounds for guerrilla activity.

Prompted by Gen. Antonio López de Santa Anna's loss at Cerro Gordo on 18 April 1847, Mexican officials called for a guerrilla war against the invaders. With no regular army

The National Bridge. Fayette Robinson, *Mexico and Her Military Chieftains*, 1851

to defend them, inhabitants along the National Road had to rely on themselves. They hoped to imitate the Spanish, whose guerrilla bands had helped drive French forces from Spain thirty years earlier. Several leaders helped organize the Mexican bands, including Gen. Joaquín Rea. The lower clergy also was particularly active, especially Father Caledonio Domeco Jarauta. Men under Rea, Jarauta, and others took up the cry, "War without pity unto death!"

The movement of U.S. reinforcements inland sparked serious guerrilla activity along the road from Vera Cruz to Puebla. In early August Maj. Folliot T. Lally left the coast with sixty-four supply wagons and an escort of approximately one thousand men. He encountered a determined force of nearly fifteen hundred guerrillas under Jarauta who had prepared entrenchments along the route. From 10 to 19 August Lally's command fought sharp engagements at Paso de Ovejas, National Bridge, Cerro Gordo, and Las Animas, losing a total of 105 men killed, wounded, and missing in these battles. Two companies sent from Vera Cruz to reinforce Lally were attacked and sustained losses but made it through. Commands under Lt. George W. Hughes and Capt. Samuel P. Heintzleman also had to fight their way into the interior. On 19 September Gen. Joseph Lane led a large column up from the coast; resistance was lighter, but it was still noticeable in the area of the National Bridge.

At Plan del Rio Lane learned that a large force of Mexicans under Rea had laid siege to the U.S. garrison at Puebla. He marched forward, attaching Lally's command to his own. Lane also collected the garrison at Perote, which consisted of a regiment of Pennsylvania volunteers and Capt. Samuel H. Walker's company of U.S. Mounted Rifles. News reached Lane en route to Puebla that Santa Anna had thrown the remnants of his army into the siege and planned an attack on his column. On 9 October Lane left his baggage train under strong guard and headed twelve miles north to Huamantla where spies told him the location of Santa Anna's forces. A brief but fierce engagement dispersed the combined force of Mexican regulars and guerrillas but at the cost of Walker's life. After sacking the town in retaliation for the popular officer's death, Lane's force resumed the march and entered Puebla on 12 October, lifting the siege.

With the major population centers under their control, U.S. officials turned their efforts to the countryside. Lane began an antiguerrilla campaign around Puebla, finding and punishing Rea and his men at Atlixco on 19 October. Scott ordered the garrisons along the National Road strengthened, ensuring each had a mounted force assigned to it. In November Col. John C. Hays's regiment of Mounted Texas Volunteers (popularly called Texas Rangers) arrived in central Mexico, adding to Scott's anti-insurgent force. Lane earned the title of "The Francis Marion of the Mexican War" for his part in curbing guerrillas. While small raids continued throughout the U.S. occupation, guerrilla activity never again reached the level of late summer and early fall of 1847.

Guerrilla activity posed a serious threat to U.S. forces in central Mexico, but it failed to free Mexico of the U.S. invaders. Scott's policy of paying for supplies proved an important factor in diminishing public support for the insurgents. Without support from the populace, the guerrilla bands could not function effectively. The November execution of two Mexican officers, who a U.S. military tribunal found guilty of breaking their paroles, also deterred many Mexicans from taking up arms against the U.S. forces again. Another measure, the creation of special military courts to try brigands, gave the army an additional tool in the war against guerrillas.

The guerrilla war along the National Road has received scant historical attention. The spectacular battles for Mexico City overshadowed the action between the guerrillas and Lally, Lane, and the U.S. garrison along the line connecting Scott to the coast. Both U.S. and Mexican scholars have failed to fully comprehend the situation. In addition, the issue is further confused because many contemporary observers lumped guerrillas and bandits into the same category, making no distinction between the two.

Richard Bruce Winders

BIBLIOGRAPHY
Brackett, Albert G. *General Lane's Brigade in Central Mexico.* 1854.
Henry, Robert S. *Story of the Mexican War.* 1950.
Kenly, John R. *Memoirs of a Maryland Volunteer.* 1873.
Oswandel, J. Jacob. *Notes of the Mexican War, 1846–47–48.* 1885.
Ramsey, Albert C. *The Other Side.* 1850. Reprint, 1970.
Smith, Justin. *War with Mexico.* 2 vols. 1919. Reprint, 1963.

Micheltorena, Manuel

Born in the city of Oaxaca, Mexican general Manuel Micheltorena (1802–1850) fought on the royalist side during Mexico's wars of independence and in 1821 rallied behind the banner of Agustín de Iturbide. Two years later, Micheltorena withdrew his support of Iturbide and adhered to the Plan of Casa Mata. He then served as an aide in Oaxaca's military commandancy and formed part of an 1828 expedition led by Gen. Manuel Mier y Terán that carried out an extensive investigation of conditions in Texas. Micheltorena saw action in the Texas campaign of 1836 and in 1840 was promoted to brigadier general.

In 1842, alarmed at the rapid increase in the number of foreigners in California, the Mexican government sought to reassert control over the province and appointed Micheltorena as governor. He arrived in San Diego that September with three hundred ill-disciplined troops. Micheltorena remained favorably disposed toward foreigners during his tenure. In 1844, for example, he issued a decree forbidding the import of foreign goods from Mexico without payment of duties, thus protecting shippers from New England and the commercial basis of California's economy.

Micheltorena's rule did not endure, however, as resentment against his troops, who stole from the residents, and the ambitions of local leaders provoked a November 1844 rebellion headed by former governor Juan Bautista Alvarado. On 20 February 1845 the contending forces met at Cahuenga Pass and engaged in a nearly bloodless two-day artillery duel. Micheltorena's resistance collapsed when the settlers who supported him withdrew their support after the battle. He then resigned and returned to Mexico with his troops. Micheltorena's departure signified the end of Mexican direct rule over California.

Micheltorena served as chief of staff of the Mexican army during the February 1847 Battle of Buena Vista. After the war he defended and won an acquittal for Gen. Andrés Terrés, who was being tried by a military court to determine his responsibility for the fall of the Belén Gate in September 1847. Micheltorena then served as Yucatán's military commander general from 1850 to 1851. He died in Mexico City two years later.

Pedro Santoni

BIBLIOGRAPHY
Pletcher, David. *The Diplomacy of Annexation: Texas, Oregon, and the Mexican War.* 1973.
Roa Bárcena, José María. *Recuerdos de la invasión Norteamericana (1846–1848).* 3 vols. 1947.
Rolle, Andrew F. *California: A History.* 1978.

Mier Expedition

In retaliation for Mexican raids on the Texas frontier in 1842, Texas president Sam Houston sanctioned in the fall of that year an invasion of the lower Río Grande valley under the command of Gen. Alexander Somervell. Bad weather, meager supplies, and a lack of discipline among his men convinced Somervell to terminate the expedition at the Río Grande near Guerrero on 19 December, but the bulk of his force, slightly more than three hundred men, disobeyed the order to return home. Subsequently called the Mier Expedition, the renegade army elected Capt. William Fisher as their commanding officer and followed the course of the river toward Ciudad Mier. There, on the night of 25 December, the Texians attacked a Mexican army and then were forced by a Mexican counterattack to barricade themselves in a block of houses on the outskirts of the town. After fierce fighting the Texians surrendered the following day. The battle at Mier proved to be the most serious clash between Anglo-American and Mexican forces between the Battle of San Jacinto in 1836 and the U.S.–Mexican War a decade later.

The prisoners were marched into the interior of Mexico, and along the way they managed to overpower their guards and escape into the mountains below Saltillo. Most were later recaptured, and as punishment for the escape one out of every ten men was executed. Seventeen Texians were chosen by lottery, in what came to be known as the Black Bean Episode. The main body of prisoners was then marched to the environs of Mexico City, where they were forced to labor on public works projects. In the fall of 1843 they were transferred to the fortress of San Carlos de Perote, located in the mountains east of Jalapa. Disease and the rigors of captivity took the lives of many Texians, while a few managed to escape or obtained their release through the intercession of friends and relatives in the United States. Their travails received considerable attention in the U.S. expansionist press, creating much anti-Mexican feeling on the eve of the U.S.–Mexican War. Finally, in an attempt to repair deteriorating relations with the United States, President Antonio López de Santa Anna ordered the release of the 104 remaining Mier Expedition prisoners on 16 September 1844.

Sam W. Haynes

BIBLIOGRAPHY

Green, Thomas Jefferson. *Journal of the Texian Expedition Against Mier.* 1845.

Haynes, Sam W. *Soldiers of Misfortune: The Somervell and Mier Expeditions.* 1990.

Mier y Terán, Manuel de

Mexican general and patriot Manuel de Mier y Terán (1789–1832) was born in Mexico City on 18 February. Terán rose to prominence in the struggle for Mexican independence. The eldest of three brothers, he studied engineering at the College of Mines in Mexico City where he applied his mathematical abilities to the science of ballistics.

Terán graduated from the College of Mines in 1811 and joined rebel forces commanded by Ignacio Rayón. In 1812, while training recruits and manufacturing ammunition in the army of the parish priest-turned-rebel, general José María Morelos y Pavón, he was appointed captain of artillery. Terán demonstrated remarkable ability as a commander and soon achieved the rank of lieutenant colonel. Promoted to brigadier general in the Mexican army after the revolution, Terán trained engineers and artillerymen. Selected as the military deputy from Chiapas to the first Constituent Congress in 1822, Terán carefully avoided involvement in factional strife between Bourbonists, who desired a constitutional monarchy, and republicans, who sought a federal

republic. He was one of a small group of deputies who proposed a compromise measure which had great popular support and to which Congress yielded.

Prompted by U.S. migration and interest in Texas, Mexican officials ordered Terán to make an extensive inspection of the region. While completing his inspection during 1828–1829 Terán foresaw problems in the region. Many in the United States viewed Texas as a part of the Louisiana Purchase of 1803. The initial trickle of U.S. settlers entering Texas was becoming a flood, and Terán feared the loss of this territory if adequate measures were not taken. Ongoing factional strife in Mexico ensured that no official response would be made. Even as commandant general of the Eastern Internal Provinces, Terán was unable to move his government to action. Beset by despondency, Terán established his headquarters at San Antonio de Padilla. There on 3 July 1832, Terán slipped behind a wall of the old San Antonio churchyard and thrust his sword through his heart.

Fred Dominguez

BIBLIOGRAPHY

Fehrenbach, T. R. *Lone Star.* 1985.

Morton, Ohland. *Terán and Texas.* 1948.

Stephenson, Nathaniel W. *Texas and the Mexican War.* 1921.

Military Academy, Mexican

Founded in October 1823, the Mexican Military Academy (Colegio Militar) was intended to provide an institutionalized environment for the professional socialization of the army officer corps. First set up in the fortress of San Carlos de Perote, the Colegio was relocated to Mexico City in August 1828 and lodged in the former convent of Betlemitas. Studies were frequently interrupted as cadets took leaves of absence to participate in the various politically inspired uprisings that plagued Mexico during the early republican era.

Col. Ignacio Mora y Villamil served as director from 1833 to 1838. A talented engineer, he introduced a relevant three-year curriculum, increased enrollment capacity to two hundred cadets, and moved the Colegio to the Casa de Arrecogidas in September 1838. Brig. Gen. Pedro García Conde succeeded Mora y Villamil, administering the institution until 1844 when he became minister of war and marine. Also an engineer of considerable ability, García Conde restructured the curriculum to incorporate mathematics, chemistry, physics, artillery, fortifications, modern tactics, architecture, astronomy, and land surveying, and required cadets to study French and English. The expanded technical curriculum reflected the influence of the French military educational system where artillery and field fortifications had traditionally received primacy. At the end of García Conde's tenure in 1844, the Colegio boasted an enrollment of 120 students and a new home in the Castillo de Chapultepec.

By 1846, the Colegio had commissioned more than four hundred officers whom field commanders considered their best junior leaders. Despite expanded enrollment, however, the number of new ensigns (*alférezes*) graduated remained insufficient to satisfy the army's growing needs. Moreover, while successful completion of the Colegio's three-year program was supposed to be a commissioning prerequisite, political influence still enabled unqualified persons to receive officer appointments, weakening the institution's prestige and significance. This dearth of trained junior officers impaired the Mexican army's tactical performance throughout the war with the United States.

The Colegio Militar suspended operations in September 1847 following the U.S. bombardment, assault, and capture of Chapultepec, during which six cadets were killed, three wounded, and thirty-seven taken prisoner. Classes resumed on 17 June 1848 in the Cuartel del Rastro on the Plaza de San Lucas, where the Colegio remained until repairs permitted reoccupation of Chapultepec in August 1849. Today, the heroism of the six youths who died defending Chapultepec (Los Niños Héroes) is celebrated in a moving retreat ceremony conducted daily by the corps of cadets.

William A. DePalo, Jr.

BIBLIOGRAPHY

Decreto separando el Colegio Militar y la Escuela de Aplicación, January 20, 1842, Archivo General de la Nación (AGN), Guerra y Marina (GM), volume 27.

DePalo, William A., Jr. *The Mexican National Army, 1822–1852*, pp. 30, 73, 89, 133, and 137–138. 1997.

Fuentes, Gloria. *El ejército Mexicano*, pp. 135–146. 1983.

Memoria del Secretarío de Estado y del despacho de Guerra y Marina, pp. 39–40. 1823.

Memoria de los ramos de Guerra y Marina, pp. 31–32. 1845.

Sánchez Lamego, Miguel A. *El Colegio Militar y la defensa de Chapultepec en Septiembre de 1847*, pp. 23–34. 1947.

Torrea, Juan Manuel. *La vida de una institución gloriosa: El Colegio Militar, 1821–1930*, pp. 12–63. 1931.

See also **Chapultepec, Battle of**; *and* **Los Niños Héroes**

Military Academy, United States

On 16 March 1802 the administration of President Thomas Jefferson created a separate U.S. Army Corps of Engineers to be headquartered at the remote Hudson River army post of West Point, New York, and ordered the corps to form the United States Military Academy (commonly known as West Point) for the formal study of engineering. Some historians argue that the antimilitarist Jefferson, by forming a broad-based national military school, attempted to erode the Federalists' control of the officer corps by providing a path to higher education for all classes. Other historians view the visionary Jefferson as motivated to create a body of officers trained in the engineering skills necessary for nation building and national expansion.

Led from 1802 to 1812 by Superintendent Maj. Jonathan Williams, a science-oriented senior engineer officer, the academy began in 1802 with two cadets and an informal course of two years. By 1812 the West Point senior class had eighteen cadets graduating after four years of study. As an institution West Point was criticized for its narrow technical focus and an apparent admissions bias in favor of the New England educated elite.

Encouraged by Secretary of War John C. Calhoun and the era of military reform in the wake of the War of 1812, West Point's greatest transition occurred under the leadership of Bvt. Lt. Col. Sylvanus Thayer, an engineer from the class of 1808 and the academy's formidable superintendent from 1817 to 1833. Thayer's reforms transformed the school into a national university by the introduction of systematic administrative procedures, comprehensive regulations, strict academic and discipline standards, and a formal four-year curriculum.

Although he did not serve as superintendent, Thayer's brilliant protégé, Dennis Hart Mahan, class of 1824, inherited the mantle of academic leadership from Thayer and taught at West Point for forty years. Heavily influenced by the writings of Antoine Henri Jomini and French military methods, Mahan's course "Engineering and the Science of War" was the most significant intellectual trial for senior cadets. Mahan's books, particularly *Out-Posts* (1847), formed the basic literature of professional military thought in North America in the pre–Civil War period.

By the era of the U.S.–Mexican War the United States Military Academy was the preeminent engineering school in the nation; the average graduating class provided forty commissioned officers for the army, the top few graduates assigned to the prestigious Corps of Engineers. The curriculum of the period featured for the freshmen, or plebes, mathematics and French; for the sophomores, or third classmen, mathematics, French, and drawing; for the second classmen, or juniors, natural philosophy, chemistry, mineralogy, and drawing; and for the first class, rhetorical, moral, and political science, chemistry, infantry and artillery tactics, and a series of demanding military and civil engineering courses.

At the beginning of the U.S.–Mexican War about 60 percent of the regular army officer corps were graduates of West Point, the majority serving as company-grade line officers, such as Lt. Ulysses S. Grant and Lt. James Longstreet. However, with many of the regimental colonels too old or infirm to campaign, the younger officers took field command of the regiments. During Maj. Gen. Winfield Scott's final battles for Mexico City one-quarter of his regimental commanders were West Point graduates, of whom two-thirds were killed or wounded in the last battles. In all, 714 graduates of the U.S. Military Academy served in the war; 48 were killed and 100 were wounded.

Additionally, because of the system of assigning top graduates to technical fields, West Pointers completely dominated the more scientific branches of the army such as artillery, engineers, and the topographical corps. For example, Bvt. Maj. Samuel Ringgold introduced innovative tactical techniques for mobile artillery before his death at Palo Alto, and Capt. Robert E. Lee earned renown as an engineer for his daring battlefield reconnaissances.

In the era of the U.S.–Mexican War the rigorous mathematics and engineering-based education of the military academy provided a solid foundation for the mental discipline and competence required of an emerging professionalism among the army officer corps. Likewise, the strong bond shared by West Point classmates became an important element in the *esprit de corps* and cohesion of the officer corps in the antebellum army. Finally, as West Point graduates began to fill the majority of leadership positions, the rigid code of honor instilled at the military academy helped form the core of U.S. Army ethics.

An eyewitness reported that at a speech in Mexico City after his successful campaign General Scott observed, "but for the science of the military academy this Army, multiplied by four, could not have entered the capital of Mexico."

The United States Military Academy came of age during the U.S.–Mexican War. The reputation of its graduates' wartime service solidified the national respect for the institution and enhanced the self-esteem of the emerging military professionals of the regular army.

Thomas Tyree Smith

BIBLIOGRAPHY

The Centennial of the United States Military Academy at West Point, New York, 1802–1902. 2 vols. 1904.

Crackle, Theodore J. *The Illustrated History of West Point.* 1991.

Forman, Sidney. *West Point: A History of the United States Military Academy.* 1950.

Morrison, James L. *"The Best School in the World": West Point, the Pre–Civil War Years, 1833–1866.* 1986.

Skelton, William B. *An American Profession of Arms: The Army Officer Corps, 1784–1861.* 1992.

Military Colonies, Mexican

Beginning in the mid-eighteenth century, the Spanish colonial government pursued military colonization to achieve dual objectives: defending Mexico's northern frontier against nomadic raiding Indians and foreign interlopers, and encouraging Hispanic population growth in the isolated northern provinces. In their various guises, military colonization policies were founded in the belief that peasants who owned and farmed their land were the most reliable defenders of it. To this end, modest land grants around frontier communities were given to peasant families, generally regardless of ethnicity, in exchange for a commitment to serve in the frontier army and assist in frontier defense duties.

The military colonies supplemented the *presidios,* the frontier forts garrisoned by special mobile forces that were the premier element of Mexico's frontier defense system. But after Mexican independence, the presidios deteriorated due, in part, to Mexico's intensifying political and economic instability. Increasingly, the frontier communities, including many that were strengthened by military colonization policies, bore a greater burden of frontier defense responsibilities.

During the U.S.–Mexican War, the military colonies and frontier militia played significant roles as accessory irregular forces in battles such as Palo Alto, Resaca de la Palma, and Sacramento, and as guerrilla forces that threatened U.S. supply lines from the Río Grande to Monterrey and Saltillo and along other routes in northern Mexico.

Mexican military attention focused on the northern frontier after the U.S.–Mexican War, a response to not only the persistent dangers posed by raiding Indian bands but the conviction that a strong Hispanic cultural barrier on the frontier was the best defense against further U.S. expansion into Mexico. As part of the broad postwar military reform program, in 1848 President José Joaquín de Herrera eradicated the decrepit *presidios* and replaced them with military colonies. The eighteen colonies stretched along the new international border from Camargo in Tamaulipas, along the Río Grande to El Paso in Chihuahua, and then across the Chihuahuan and Sonoran deserts to Rosales in Baja California.

The military colonies faced insurmountable obstacles. Apache and Comanche raiding increased after 1848. The burdensome life of a soldier-farmer attracted few recruits to the precarious colonies. In 1849, the program's most successful year, only 1,070 troops were distributed among the eighteen colonies, which by regulation required 2,614 soldiers. The program also suffered from erratic funding from the federal and state governments. Nor did it enjoy strong support on the frontier, where the control of defense resources became a divisive issue that kindled local political conflict. In one of his first actions after returning to the presidency in 1853, Antonio López de Santa Anna abolished the military colonies and reinstated the *presidio* companies. Nevertheless, the principle of military colonization continued to influence frontier defense policy into the twentieth century.

Aaron P. Mahr Yáñez

BIBLIOGRAPHY

Cotner, Thomas. *The Military and Political Career of José Joaquín de Herrera, 1792–1854.* 1949.

Faulk, Odie, ed. and trans. "Projected Mexican Military Colonies for the Borderlands, 1848." *Journal of Arizona History* 9 (Spring 1968): 39–48.

Nugent, Daniel. *Spent Cartridges of Revolution: An Anthropological History of Namiquipa, Chihuahua.* 1993.

Military Contractors, U.S.

As thousands of volunteers swelled the ranks of the U.S. Army during the U.S.–Mexican War, its Quartermaster, Ordnance, and Subsistence Departments found it necessary to improvise to fulfill their roles. As a result, numerous civilian contractors performed a vital function in supplementing army logistics. The resulting supply system, however, proved ripe for inefficiency and corruption. Despite the government's efforts to appeal to citizens' patriotism, war profiteers often resorted to patronage and graft to obtain lucrative military contracts. Also, the lack of standardization between diverse manufacturers and their failure to provide interchangeable replacement parts plagued the military throughout the war.

In 1846 army ordnance was in transition. Artillery standardization was incomplete, and a number of private gunshops were slowly converting small arms from the flintlock to the percussion system. The subsequent confusion often led to shortages and a lack of uniformity in weapons issues. To augment federal production, the government utilized civilian firms holding existing military contracts with quasi-official status as government arsenals, such as Whitney, Remington, and North. Under the supervision of ordnance officers, these companies produced some of the most advanced weapons of the war. The most commonly issued weapons, however, were smoothbore, flintlock muskets.

Government workshops as well as private companies also manufactured other essential equipment such as uniforms and accoutrements. Some fly-by-night firms, anxious to realize quick profits, obtained government contracts through questionable means. Their use of substandard materials and workmanship often led to defective products such as leaking tents and ill-fitting shoes. Food supply and quality also suffered for similar reasons as the Subsistence Department searched for ration sources both domestically and in Mexico.

Transportation proved the most difficult obstacle. Lacking sufficient watercraft and wagons for the campaign, the army leased, bought, and built them on an unprecedented scale. While some government agents procured steam-powered and sail-driven coasting vessels to ferry troops to Mexico, others searched the Mississippi River for light-draft steamboats to navigate the shallow Mexican rivers. For special-purpose pontoon and surfboats, purchasing agents signed orders with firms as distant as Philadelphia.

A lack of standardization in wagon construction led to the loss of innumerable vehicles on rough Mexican roads. Built in such diverse sites as New York, Ohio, and Georgia, little effort was expended to provide wagons with interchangeable repair parts. Moreover, the army often found it expedient to replace its own independent-minded civilian teamsters with more cooperative Mexicans. As the war progressed, the army's supply train gradually became more and more reliant on Mexican pack mules and hired local drovers.

Jeff Kinard

BIBLIOGRAPHY

Bauer, K. Jack. *The Mexican War, 1846–1848.* 1974.

Flayderman, Norm. *Flayderman's Guide to Antique American Firearms.* 1987.

Risch, Erna. *Quartermaster Support of the Army: A History of the Corps, 1775–1939.* 1962.

Winders, Richard Bruce. "Mr. Polk's Army: Politics, Patronage, and the American Military in the Mexican War." Ph.D. diss., Texas Christian University, 1994.

Militia, Mexican Civic

Established during the 1820s to preserve domestic order and security, the Mexican civic militia fell victim to the turmoil that plagued the country between independence in 1821 and the mid-1850s. *Puro* and *moderado* leaders tried to build up the militia to offset the regular army's role as arbiter in national politics and to protect state autonomy, but their efforts were opposed by high-ranking military chiefs and conservative politicians, who feared that a strong militia would destroy the privileged position they held in society. The militia force was suppressed and reorganized on several occasions and did not flourish as it might have under more stable conditions.

The year 1845, however, seemed to promise the dawn of a new era for the militia. Having just overthrown Gen. Antonio López de Santa Anna with the aid of the civic militia, the government of Gen. José Joaquín de Herrera had the opportunity to firmly establish the militia as a military force. But Herrera and his advisers believed that the militia might just as easily bring about their downfall and opted to disband it. The U.S. annexation of Texas in 1845 paved the way for reestablishment of the militia later that summer, but restrictive legislation excluded most Mexicans from militia service. Thus, the civic militia remained but a fantasy as the year ended.

Despite this turn of events, the defeats suffered by the Mexican army at the battles of Palo Alto and Resaca de la Palma in the late spring of 1846 reawakened public demands for a powerful civic militia. It was popularly believed that mobilization of such a military force would help save Mexico from a humiliating defeat at the hands of the United States. Much like Herrera, however, then-president Gen. Mariano Paredes y Arrillaga did not develop a militia because he feared that his rivals would use it to topple the government.

Valentín Gómez Farías and the *puros* revived the civic militia shortly after deposing Paredes in August 1846. Over the following eight months, however, several factors that had contributed to Mexico's postindependence instability obstructed organizational efforts. These factors included political strife, scarcity of funds, regionalism, flawed legislation, disagreement over the social groups that would compose the militia, and the generalize disdain that Mexicans held for military service. As a result, Mexican political leaders had little to show for their endeavors to turn the civic militia into a nonpartisan institution capable of contributing to the national defense effort as Gen. Winfield Scott and the U.S. expeditionary army prepared to move against Mexico City in April 1847.

Notwithstanding these obstacles, the Mexican government managed to develop the semblance of a militia system by the time Scott's troops reached the outskirts of the Mexican capital in early August. The elite militia battalions that spearheaded the February 1847 "revolt of the *polkos*" fought valiantly in the defense of the convent of Churubusco and at the battle of El Molino del Rey. Their heroics renewed the faith of public-spirited Mexicans in the promise of the civic militia as a bulwark of civilian government, and this military force became a bastion of Mexican liberalism in the 1850s and 1860s.

Pedro Santoni

BIBLIOGRAPHY

Alcaraz, Ramón, et al. *The Other Side: or Notes for the History of the War Between Mexico and the United States.* 1970.

Escalante Gonzalbo, Fernando. *Ciudadanos imaginarios: Memorial de los afanes y desventuras de la virtud y apología del vicio triunfante en la república mexicana: Tratado de moral pública.* 1992.

Santoni, Pedro. "The Failure of Mobilization: The Civic Militia of Mexico in 1846." *Mexican Studies/Estudios Mexicanos* 12, no. 2 (1996): 169–194.

Santoni, Pedro. "A Fear of the People: The Civic Militia of Mexico in 1845." *Hispanic American Historical Review* 68 (1988): 269–288.

Santoni, Pedro. *Mexicans at Arms: Puro Federalists and the Politics of War, 1845–1848.* 1996.

Thomson, Guy P. C. "Bulwark of Patriotic Liberalism: The National Guard, Philharmonic Corps and Patriotic Juntas in Mexico, 1847–88." *Journal of Latin American Studies* 22 (1990): 31–68.

Militia, U.S.

At the time the U.S.–Mexican War began, the largest military arm of the United States was not the army or navy but rather the state militias, which on paper numbered in the hundreds of thousands. However, the militia system in 1846 was moribund. Most Northern states had ended compulsory militia training entirely, relying on volunteer militia companies that in some states constituted an effective militia and in others did not. Compulsory militia training was still on the books in the South, but in reality Southern militias were no better than their Northern counterparts.

Nevertheless, militiamen did serve in the U.S.–Mexican War. In the spring of 1846 President James K. Polk authorized Gen. Zachary Taylor to call on Gulf states for short-term militia. Polk, significantly, did not promise states that their militia would not be used in Mexico (a use that probably would have been unconstitutional), but Taylor left 6,000 of these troops behind when he moved south into Mexico. About 12,500 militia entered federal service during the war, 12 percent of the total U.S. military manpower.

Those states that had functioning militia systems used them to accept or recruit volunteers for federal service. Militia officers canvassed for volunteers and forwarded their names to their adjutant general's office, or volunteers did so directly, usually by company. The militia also produced some of the most prominent U.S. commanders, including Gen. Robert Patterson and Gen. John A. Quitman, both former high-ranking militia officers.

If the militia played a peripheral but noteworthy part in the history of the U.S.–Mexican War, so too did the war play such a part in the militia's history, as opposition to the war in New England states such as Massachusetts caused militia membership to decline considerably.

Mark Pitcavage

BIBLIOGRAPHY

Mahon, John K. *History of the Militia and the National Guard.* 1983.

Pitcavage, Mark. "An Equitable Burden: The Decline of the State Militias, 1783–1858." Ph.D. diss., The Ohio State University, 1995.

Winders, Richard Bruce. *Mr. Polk's Army.* 1997.

Miñón, José Vincente

Although born in Cádiz, Spain, Mexican general José Vincente Miñón (1802–1878) was brought to Mexico as an infant. He became a cadet in the colonial army as a youth and fought notably in several battles against the insurgents before joining the Army of the Three Guarantees in 1821.

General Miñón was an ally in the failed plot led by Valentín Gómez Farías in June 1845 to overthrow President

José Joaquín de Herrera. In early 1847 Miñón commanded one of four cavalry brigades in Gen. Antonio López de Santa Anna's Army of the North. Part of the advance guard used to screen the army's march north from San Luis Potosí, Miñón's sixteen-hundred-man brigade arrived at the foothills outside the Buena Vista *hacienda* on 22 February and moved east toward Saltillo. The maneuver threatened Gen. Zachary Taylor's supply lines and communication with Saltillo and put Miñón's brigade behind Taylor's army, which was engaging Santa Anna's at La Angostura (Buena Vista) a few miles east. U.S. artillery batteries at Saltillo saw the danger, however, and dispersed Miñón's cavalry. Thus, when Gen. Julian Juvera's cavalry broke through the U.S. far left flank and nearly reached Buena Vista, the anticipated joining of Juvera's and Miñón's cavalries failed to materialize, forcing Juvera to retreat.

Santa Anna was harshly critical of Miñón's failure to attack Taylor's rear guard and blamed him for Juvera's unsuccessful cavalry flank attack. After the army withdrew from Buena Vista, Santa Anna arrested Miñón at Matehuala. In a published defense, Miñón protested that Santa Anna's orders were haphazard and ambiguous and that his brigade had lacked sufficient numbers to assault the U.S. position.

Miñón became an important military ally of Mexico's postwar moderate regimes. He supported Maximilian and the imperialists during the French Intervention. He died in Mexico City in 1878.

Aaron P. Mahr Yáñez

BIBLIOGRAPHY

Carleton, James. *The Battle of Buena Vista, with the Operations of the "Army of Occupation" for One Month.* 1848.

Santoni, Pedro. *Mexicans at Arms: Puro Federalists and the Politics of War, 1845–1848.* 1996.

Missions

The mission was a frontier institution designed to civilize the Spanish borderlands. Together with the *presidio*, or fort, the mission spread Spanish influence throughout the Southwest.

The Catholic Church formed an integral part of the effort to settle the frontier, working in connection with the military and royal authorities. Each mission supposedly formed a self-sufficient community complete with missionaries and neophytes. The mission's purpose was three-fold: to convert the region's indigenous inhabitants to Christianity; to teach them the skills needed to become loyal Spanish subjects; and to integrate them into the Spanish economic system.

Various religious orders—Jesuits, Franciscans, and Dominicans—were assigned responsibilitiy for different geographical regions. Each location was ordinarily allotted at least three missionaries, augmented by a support staff of con-

verts from older missions. The missions were most successful in areas where the natives already led agrarian and sedentary lives. Missions in areas with nomadic bands usually fell prey to periodic raids on their livestock. The nearby *presidio* too often lacked the military manpower needed to punish the perpetrators, let alone round up converts who decided to forsake mission life.

Historians hold differing views on the success of the mission in settling the frontier. Once established, the line of missions failed to routinely advance as planners had envisioned. The missions were costly to run, a factor that eventually led to their demise. Spanish missionaries did, however, successfully establish their culture and religion throughout the region. Without a doubt, the legacy of the missions has lasted long after the last mission was secularized in 1845.

Richard Bruce Winders

BIBLIOGRAPHY

Bolton, Herbert E. "The Missions as a Frontier Institution in Spanish American Colonies." *American Historical Review* 23 (1917): 42–61.

Weber, David J. "Failure of a Frontier Institution: The Secular Church in the Borderlands under Independent Mexico, 1821–1846." *Western Historical Quarterly* 12 (April 1981): 125–143.

Weber, David J. *The Mexican Frontier, 1821–1846: The American Southwest under Mexico.* 1982.

Mississippi Rifle

The U.S. Model 1841 Percussion Rifle as it was officially known, called by the troops the Mississippi rifle, Windsor rifle, Harpers Ferry rifle, and Jager rifle, weighed 10 pounds, fired a .525 caliber patched ball with an effective battle range of 200 yards, and was the first regulation muzzle-loading percussion rifle adopted for use by U.S. forces. Designed during the years from 1840 to 1841 by a team of U.S. Army officers at the Harpers Ferry Arsenal as an accurate and reliable rifled weapon for issuance to infantry rifle companies and for use on the frontier, it had no provision for a bayonet. It offered a vast improvement in reliability (percussion) of ignition and accuracy but was not intended for general issuance to the regulars or state militias. The rifle's reputation resulted primarily from its early issuance in August of 1846 to the 1st Mississippi Rifle Regiment under the command of Col. Jefferson Davis at Brazos Santiago on the Texas–Mexico border. Davis specifically requested that this weapon be issued to his unit, which used it with great effectiveness at the battles of Monterrey and Buena Vista. The U.S. Mounted Rifles, the Voltigeur Regiment, and various infantry rifle companies along with some Texas Rangers carried the Mississippi rifle during the U.S.–Mexican War, and it subsequently became the favorite weapon of Confederate forces during the Civil War. The rifle was superior in quality of manufacture, accuracy, and dependability to any other weapon in either the U.S. or Mexican forces.

David Jackson

BIBLIOGRAPHY

Butler, David F. *United States Firearms: The First Century, 1776–1875.* 1971.

Chance, Joseph E. *Jefferson Davis's Mexican War Regiment.* 1991.

Flayderman, Norman. *Flayderman's Guide.* 5th ed. 1987.

Hicks, James E. *Notes on United States Ordnance.* Vol. 1. 1936.

Reilly, Robert M. *United States Military Small Arms, 1816–1865.* 1970.

Missouri Compromise

The Missouri Compromise of 1820 resolved the first of several crises in the U.S. Congress to arise over the question of slavery in the territories acquired by the United States west of the Mississippi River. In 1819 Missouri, part of the Louisiana Purchase territory, petitioned Congress for admission to the Union as a slave state. Representatives and senators from free states objected, fearing a tilt in the balance of power in Congress toward the slave South. On numerous occasions the country had split along sectional lines over such matters as the tariff and foreign relations. Now slavery exacerbated those divisions, seriously threatening the Union. With Congress deadlocked, Speaker of the House Henry Clay, from Kentucky, orchestrated a compromise.

In 1821 Missouri was admitted as a slave state. To maintain the sectional balance of power Congress also admitted Maine, then a part of Massachusetts, as a free state. In an effort to prevent further crises from arising over the remaining western territories, Congress extended a line at 36°30' north latitude, the southern border of the new state of Missouri, westward to the U.S. territorial limit, and prohibited slavery north of the line, Missouri excepted. Slavery was neither barred nor permitted in the small remaining territory south of the 36°30' line. A relieved but still fearful Thomas Jefferson exclaimed that the Missouri Compromise rang "like a fire bell in the night." He was right, for it proved to be but a temporary settlement. In 1846 the Wilmot Proviso resurrected the debate over the expansion of slavery, this time into territory won in war with Mexico, much of it lying below the 36°30' line.

Christopher Morris

BIBLIOGRAPHY

Freehling, William W. *The Road to Disunion.* Volume 1, *Secessionists at Bay, 1776–1854.* 1990.

Moore, Glover. *The Missouri Compromise, 1819–1821.* 1953.

Moderados

Meaning "moderates," *moderados* is a term used to denote one of two major divisions among liberals in nineteenth-century Mexico; the others are called *puros.* Mexican liberals favored constitutional government and the rights to a free press, free speech, and free association. The *moderados* were liberals who were less anticlerical than the *puros.* Moderados favored a gradual reduction in the power and wealth of the Catholic Church, which at the time was the only legal religion in Mexico. The church monopolized registration of births, marriages, and deaths and owned vast amounts of real estate in Mexico City. While *puros* preferred to use political power as a tool to transform Mexican society, *moderados* believed that liberty and equality were ends in themselves. Moderates preferred cautious change in church–state relations and the gradual sale of church property, while the *puros* pushed for more rapid and radical changes. *Moderados* often had significant legislative experience before moving into cabinet positions in the executive branch of government. President José Joaquín de Herrera (1844–1845) and his minister of foreign relations, Manuel de la Peña y Peña, were prominent *moderados* who demonstrated a conciliatory attitude toward the United States. The 1845 goals of the *moderados,* including to preserve the *Bases Orgánicas* with some reforms as the Mexican constitution, and their flexible Texas policy, fueled dissent.

Rivalry and dissension between *puros, moderados,* and conservatives led to a series of rapid changes in Mexican governments during this period. The division between *puros* and *moderados* was evident early in 1847 when Vice President Valentín Gómez Farías attempted to mortgage church property to raise funds for the war against the United States. *Moderados* first tried to block the legislation in Congress. When this failed, they allied with conservatives, clergy, and some militia units in an uprising known as the Polkos Revolt. As a result, the decree was withdrawn, Vice President Valentín Gómez Farías was removed from power, and the church made a loan to the government of President Antonio López de Santa Anna. After the war ended, *moderados* negotiated the Treaty of Guadalupe Hidalgo with the United States. The treaty, which ceded Arizona, California, New Mexico, and Texas to the United States in return for $15 million, was opposed by the *puros.*

The division between *moderados* and *puros* was rooted in decades of conflict before the war, and their differences persisted for decades after the war as well. Moderates generally opposed explicit religious toleration during the Constitutional Convention of 1856 and 1857. During the French Intervention in the 1860s, *moderados* such as Pedro Escudero y Echánove and José Fernando Ramírez supported Emperor Maximilian (who, despite his title, was himself a liberal).

Donald F. Stevens

BIBLIOGRAPHY

Costeloe, Michael P. "The Mexican Church in the Rebellion of the Polkos." *Hispanic American Historical Review* 46 (May 1966): 170–178.

Hale, Charles A. *Mexican Liberalism in the Age of Mora, 1821–1853.* 1968.

Santoni, Pedro. *Mexicans at Arms: Puro Federalists and the Politics of War, 1845–1848.* 1996.

Scholes, Walter V. *Mexican Politics during the Juárez Regime, 1855–1872.* 1957.

Stevens, Donald F. *Origins of Instability in Early Republican Mexico.* 1991.

Molino del Rey, Battle of

Located two miles southwest of the gates of Mexico City was a group of low, stone structures known as El Molino del Rey. These fortifications formed a link in Gen. Antonio López de Santa Anna's defensive works around Mexico City, barely one thousand yards from the Castle of Chapultepec. Because El Molino de Rey was rumored to be a factory for casting Mexican cannon, Maj. Gen. Winfield Scott ordered a daylight assault on 8 September 1847. Brig. Gen. William J. Worth's 3,400-man division was the attack force. In the fierce charge, Worth's three attacking columns suffered huge losses from undetected Mexican artillery and small arms fire under the direction of Brig. Gen. Antonio León. U.S. troops recoiled under the barrage only to be reinforced and sent back into the chaos. Worth's men eventually breached El Molino del Rey's defense, forcing the Mexicans to also abandon the nearby bastioned earthworks protecting Casa Mata.

The U.S. forces gained little from their hard-fought victory. The action at El Molino del Rey, originally planned as a large raiding party to destroy the foundry, proved costly and empty as there were no cannon there. U.S. dead and wounded approached 800, 23% of Worth's aggregate. U.S. casualties at El Molino del Rey were the highest for any single battle during the U.S.–Mexican War. Mexican casualties exceeded 2,000. The heavy losses at El Molino del Rey and Casa Mata caused recriminations, especially at Worth for poor planning and faulty reconnaissance, which failed to detect the Mexican artillery positions. General Scott learned from this oversight in his own preparations for battle, and in later engagements around Mexico City, he devoted time and effort to planning before launching assaults.

Neal Mangum

Molino del Rey. Chapultepec Castle appears in the distance (John Frost, *Pictorial History of Mexico and the Mexican War*, 1862).

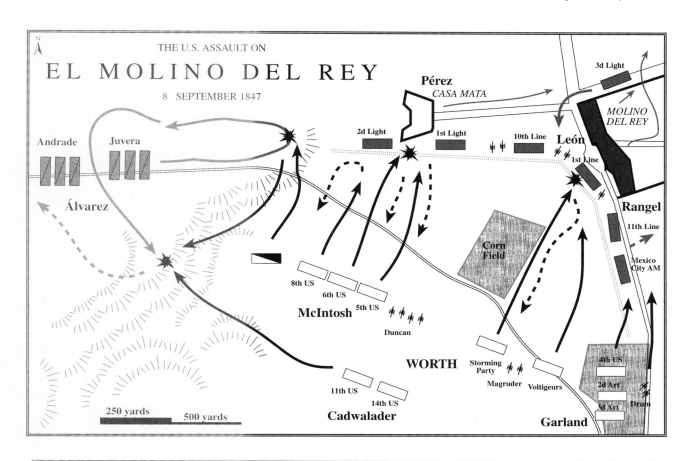

THE U.S. ASSAULT ON

EL MOLINO DEL REY

8 SEPTEMBER 1847

Battle of Molino del Rey
Order of Battle
8 September 1847

Mexican Forces

Commander
  Gen. Antonio López de Santa Anna

Infantry
  1st Light Regiment
  2d Light Regiment
  3d Light Regiment
  1st Line (Destroyed)
  10th Line Regiment
  11th Line Regiment
  Mexico Battalion

Artillery
  6 pieces

U.S. Forces

Commander
  Gen. William J. Worth

Infantry
  2d U.S. Infantry

  4th U.S. Infantry
  5th U.S. Infantry
  6th U.S. Infantry
  8th U.S. Infantry
  11th U.S. Infantry
  14th U.S. Infantry
  2d U.S. Artillery (serving as infantry)
  3d U.S. Artillery (serving as infantry)
  Company A, U.S. Engineers
  U.S. Voltigeur Regiment

Artillery
  Company I, 1st Artillery (Magruder's battery)
  Company A, 2d U.S. Artillery (Duncan's battery)
  Company G, 4th U.S. Artillery (Drum's battery)
  Ordnance Department siege train

Cavalry
  2d U.S. Dragoons
  3d U.S. Dragoons
  1st U.S. Regiment of Mounted Rifles (one company)
  1st South Carolina Volunteers

Artillery
  Company I, 1st U.S. Artillery (Magruder's mounted battery)
  Company H, 3d U.S. Artillery (Steptoe's battery)

Cavalry
  Company C, 3d U.S. Dragoons

BIBLIOGRAPHY

Copeland, Fayette. *Kendall of the* Picayune. 1997.

Eisenhower, John S. D. *So Far from God: The U.S. War with Mexico, 1846–1848.* 1989.

Weems, John Edward. *To Conquer a Peace.* 1974.

Monroe Doctrine

When eight Spanish colonies in Latin America rebelled and gained their independence, the United States sought to prevent further European encroachment into the Western hemisphere. To aid in making U.S. policy clear, President James Monroe and Secretary of State John Quincy Adams created the Monroe Doctrine, presenting it before Congress on 2 December 1823. The document revolved around three central concepts: noncolonization of the Western hemisphere by European nations, noninterference by Europe or the United States in the internal affairs of independent nations, and noninterference of the United States in European affairs.

The United States government verbally supported the Monroe Doctrine between 1824 and 1841 but failed to consider the doctrine when formulating and enacting policy. In 1836, Texas declared its independence from Mexico and championed a call for annexation by the United States. On 2 December 1845, President James K. Polk revived the doctrine in his first presidential message. In regard to Texas, Polk asserted that the United States was in no way violating the Monroe Doctrine with the annexation of the area, because Texas was independent and therefore free to choose its own course. Polk held that the annexation of Texas, which quickly led to war with Mexico, was undertaken to thwart the British and French influence over the area. Both during the war and at its conclusion, Polk confiscated large tracts of land. While many felt that Polk took the doctrine out of context, he justified his claims on the land citing the Monroe Doctrine. Polk's December 1845 presidential message marked a watershed for the doctrine and its use in U.S. policy, albeit not always in the context that President Monroe had implied.

Angela D. Moore

BIBLIOGRAPHY

May, Ernest R. *The Making of the Monroe Doctrine.* 1992.

Perkins, Dexter. *The Monroe Doctrine: 1826–1867.* 1965.

Monterey, California

This entry consists of two separate articles: **City of Monterey** *and* **Monterey Incident of 1842**.

City of Monterey

The capital and the major town in northern California, Monterey was the site of many events of the U.S.–Mexican War, including the brief U.S. takeover in 1842 and the 1846 proclamation claiming California for the United States.

Monterey, established near the mouth of the Salinas River in 1770, became the civil and military headquarters for colonial California. It blossomed, especially after Mexican independence in 1821, which brought more open trade (and a significant number of Anglo-American settlers), and the development of the *rancho* land system, which led to the establishment of many wealthy *ranchos* in the Salinas Valley. Mexican officials, *rancho* families, and Anglo commercial families intermingled socially and in marriage, producing in Monterey a lively, liveable, and fairly wealthy community.

In the mid 1840s, the population of nearly one thousand, most of whom were male, consisted of government officials, traders, ranchers, artisans, and laborers (mostly Indian). The majority lived along dirt lanes that radiated out from the waterfront, custom house, and government headquarters. Most buildings were adobe, but the Anglos added some features of New England wooden architecture to create a unique Monterey building style. By the time of the U.S.–Mexican War, the Hispanic population (over 90 percent in 1836) was being overtaken by Anglo-Americans, who by 1849 accounted for 40 percent of the population.

After the California gold rush of the late 1840s, Monterey was displaced by San Francisco as the leading town of California, and after hosting the California constitutional convention of 1849, Monterey declined in size and importance.

Raymond Starr

BIBLIOGRAPHY

Fink, Augusta. *Monterey County: The Dramatic Story of Its Past.* 1972.

Johnson, David. *Founding the Far West: California, Oregon, and Nevada, 1840–1890.* 1992.

Van Nostrand, Jeanne. *Monterey: Adobe Capital of California, 1770–1847.* 1968.

Monterey Incident of 1842

The Monterey Incident (19–21 October 1842), in which the town was seized from Mexico by Thomas ap Catesby Jones, commander of the U.S. Pacific Squadron, resulted from a mistaken belief that the United States and Mexico were at war. Jones had been appointed commander of the seven-vessel Pacific Squadron in September 1841. He was instructed to protect commerce, improve the discipline of his men, and gain useful information on the actions of foreign agents or forces, orders that reflected the uncertainty surrounding the future of the Pacific region. When Jones arrived at Callao, Peru, in May 1842, he and the British admiral there believed that a French squadron, which had departed three months

Monterey. A view of the city and harbor (John Frost, *Pictorial History of Mexico and the Mexican War*, 1862).

earlier, was headed for a California colonization venture. The subsequent mysterious departure of the British fleet in early September prompted Jones to believe that war had begun between Mexico and the United States and that Great Britain intended to seize California for debts owed by Mexico to British capitalists. Using the Monroe Doctrine as his justification, Jones proceeded to California to forestall British designs.

Jones arrived at Monterey on 19 October 1842 and demanded the town's surrender; Mexican officials capitulated the following morning. Jones soon realized his mistake, and on 21 October the Mexican flag was rehoisted, all seized property was returned, U.S. troops reembarked, and a formal salute was fired to the Mexican government.

Jones remained on the California coast for several months, meeting with the Mexican governor and leading citizens in an attempt to reestablish favorable relations. Jones surrendered his command in October 1843 and returned to the United States to face a congressional censure for his actions at Monterey, although the Navy Department did not punish him. The Monterey incident demonstrated that the United States would have little difficulty taking California when and if hostilities did commence, thus adding force to the expansionist movement under the banner of Manifest Destiny.

Gene A. Smith

BIBLIOGRAPHY

Bancroft, Hubert H. *History of California.* Vol. 4. 1886.

Harlow, Neal. *California Conquered: War and Peace on the Pacific, 1846–1850.* 1982.

Smith, Gene A. "The War that Wasn't: Thomas ap Catesby Jones's Seizure of Monterey." *California History* 66 (1987): 104–113, 155–157.

Monterrey, Mexico, Battle of

The Battle of Monterrey (spelled Monterey at the time) ended in both victory and controversy for Gen. Zachary Taylor, commander of the U.S. forces. The capture of Monterrey strengthened U.S. control of northern Mexico and set the stage for the Battle of Buena Vista five months later.

Taylor's 6,640 men reached the northern outskirts of Monterrey on 19 September 1846, where they camped at Walnut Springs and spent the day scouting Mexican positions. The following day Taylor detached Gen. William J. Worth's division to the southwest with orders to sever the road connecting Monterrey to Saltillo. After they had accomplished that, Worth's men were to seize several fortified heights, which permitted the Mexicans a commanding view of the city. Taylor held the rest of his army in reserve.

An army of more than five thousand Mexican regulars commanded by Maj. Gen. Pedro de Ampudia awaited the attack, which came early on the morning of 21 September.

Monterrey Plaza. Daguerreotype of a sketch made by Capt. John R. Vinton during the occupation of Monterrey. Note that the writing is reversed because of the daguerreotype image (*see* **Photography**). From the collection of William J. Schultz, M.D.

Worth's column moved into position, severed the road to Saltillo to prevent reinforcements from reaching the city, and launched assaults on Federation Hill, capturing two redoubts in quick succession. Taylor had planned a diversion on the eastern side of the city to draw attention away from Worth's force. He sent Gen. David E. Twiggs's division (minus its general, who was ill) to probe the eastern approach, but Twiggs's regulars met stiff resistance and were pinned down. Gen. William O. Butler's volunteer division, ordered to assist the regulars, captured fortified positions at Purísima Bridge and La Tenería before Taylor withdrew the bulk of his forces from eastern Monterrey for the night.

As dawn broke on 22 September, Worth's men had captured yet another position as a party of regulars and Texians succeeded in scaling Independence Hill and capturing the Opispado, or Bishops Palace. The eastern area remained quiet as Taylor kept Twiggs's and Butler's troops at Walnut Springs, except for a small contingent guarding the Mexican positions captured the previous day. During the night of 22 September, Ampudia reacted to his losses by abandoning his outworks (except the impregnable Black Fort) and redeploying his forces around the central plaza and cathedral.

On the morning of 23 September, Taylor learned of Ampudia's retrograde movement and sent U.S. forces back into Monterrey from the east. Hearing the renewed fighting, Worth ordered his column to advance. Both wings of Taylor's army converged on the central plaza. That evening, Taylor again ordered his forces out of the city, angering volunteers and regulars alike who had fought their way to within two blocks of their objective.

During the night, shells from a 10-inch mortar fired from Worth's lines landed around the plaza, causing much concern in the Mexican ranks that ammunition stored in the cathedral would be hit. Ampudia sent a messenger to Taylor's headquarters proposing to surrender the city if his troops were allowed to leave. Fighting was halted while commissioners from both sides worked out the terms of the agreement. Mexican officials turned Monterrey over to Taylor on 25 September and marched away. Taylor's armistice, which included a cessation of fighting for eight weeks, was strongly criticized by President James K. Polk and caused the president to lose confidence in Taylor.

U.S. losses were 120 killed and 333 wounded; General Ampudia claimed 430 killed, wounded, or missing among his forces. According to Mexican officers, this defeat was more due to infighting in their ranks than the ability of the U.S. army to capture the city.

Richard Bruce Winders

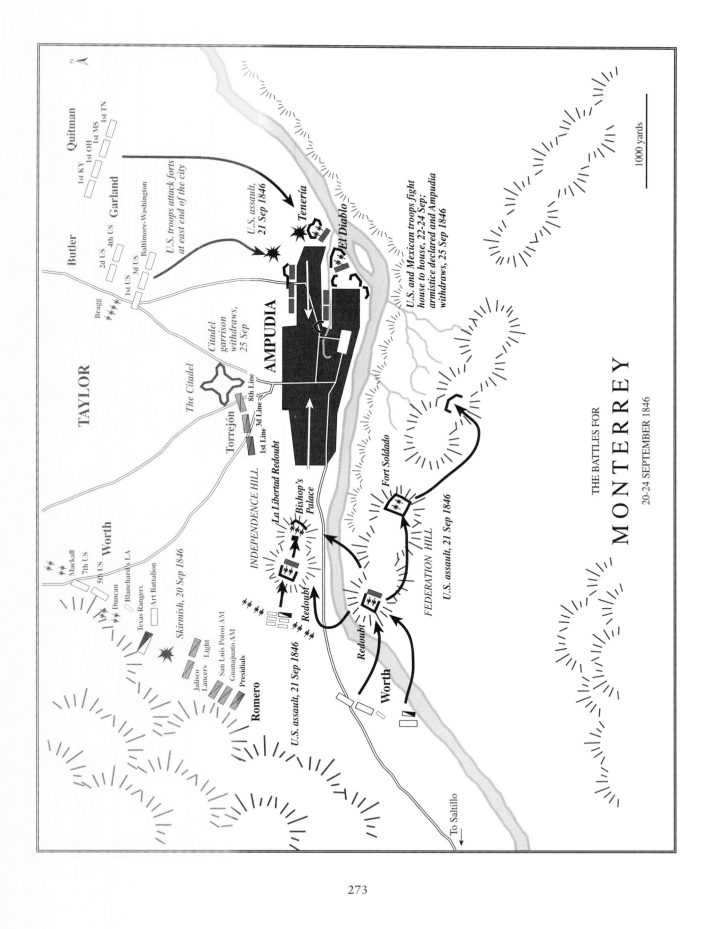

N

TAYLOR

Quitman

1st KY
1st OH
1st MS
1st TN

Butler

Garland

2d US
4th US
1st US
3d US
Baltimore-Washington

Bragg

U.S. troops attack forts
at east end of the city

*U.S. assault,
21 Sep 1846*

Tenería

El Diablo

U.S. and Mexican troops fight
house to house, 22-24 Sep;
armistice declared and Ampudia
withdraws, 25 Sep 1846

*Citadel
garrison
withdraws,
25 Sep*

AMPUDIA

The Citadel

Torrejón

8th Line
3d Line
1st Line

La Libertad Redoubt

INDEPENDENCE HILL

Bishop's
Palace

Fort Soldado

Mackall
7th US
5th US
Duncan
Blanchard's LA
Texas Rangers
Art Battalion

Worth

Skirmish, 20 Sep 1846

Redoubt

FEDERATION HILL

U.S. assault, 21 Sep 1846

Jalisco
Lancers
Light
San Luís Potosí AM
Guanajuato AM
Presidials

Romero

U.S. assault, 21 Sep 1846

Redoubt

Worth

To Saltillo

THE BATTLES FOR

MONTERREY

20-24 SEPTEMBER 1846

1000 yards

Battle of Monterrey
Order of Battle
21–23 September 1846

Mexican Forces

Commander
Gen. Pedro de Ampudia

Infantry
2d Light Regiment
3d Light Regiment
4th Light Regiment
1st Line Regiment
3d Line Regiment
4th Line Regiment
6th Line Regiment (part)
7th Line Regiment (part)
8th Line Regiment (part)
Zapadores
1st Regiment, Mexico Activo Militia
Morelia Regiment, Mexico Activo Militia
San Luis Potosí Regiment, Mexico Activo Militia
Querétaro Regiment, Mexico Activo Militia
Aguascalientes Regiment, Mexico Activo Militia
Monterrey Battalion National Guard

Cavalry
1st Regiment
3d Regiment
7th Regiment
8th Regiment
Jalisco Lancers
Béxar Presidials
La Bahía Presidials
Tamaulipas Presidials
Lampazos Presidials
Guanajuato Regiment, Activo Militia
San Luis Potosí Regiment, Activo Militia
Nuevo León Militia Company
Nuevo León Defensores Militia Battalion

Artillery
32 pieces

BIBLIOGRAPHY

Alcaraz, Ramón, ed. *The Other Side; or, Notes for the History of the War between Mexico and the United States.* Translated by Albert C. Ramsey. 1970. Originally published as *Apuntes para la historia de la Guerra entre México y los Estado Unidos,* 1848.

Balbontin, Manuel. "The Siege of Monterey." *Journal of the Military Service Institution of the United States.* (1887):325–354.

Henry, Robert S. *The Story of the Mexican War.* 1950.

Henry, William S. *Campaign Sketches of the War with Mexico.* 1847.

Kenly, John R. *Memoirs of a Maryland Volunteer.* 1873.

U.S. Forces

Commander
Gen. Zachary Taylor

Infantry
1st Infantry
2d Infantry
3d Infantry
4th Infantry
5th Infantry
7th Infantry
8th Infantry
1st Artillery (serving as infantry)
2d Artillery (serving as infantry)
3d Artillery (serving as infantry)
4th Artillery (serving as infantry)
1st Baltimore, Washington, D.C. Battalion of Volunteers
1st Ohio Volunteers
1st Kentucky Volunteers
1st Mississippi Volunteers
1st Tennessee Volunteers
Blanchard's Company, Louisiana Volunteers
Shivor's Independent Company of Mississippi and Texas Volunteers

Artillery
Company C, 1st Artillery (one 10-inch mortar & two 24-pdr. howitzers)
Company K, 1st Artillery (Mackall's light battery)
Company A, 2d Artillery (Duncan's light battery)
Company C, 3d Artillery (Ridgley's light battery)
Company E, 3d Artillery (Bragg's light battery)

Cavalry
2d Dragoons (part)
Hays' Regiment of Mounted Texas Volunteers
Wood's Regiment of Mounted Texas Volunteers

Monuments and Memorials

Unlike most of the wars in which the United States has been involved, the U.S.–Mexican War has been little remembered in the form of monuments or memorials on either side of the border. In the United States there is no national U.S.–Mexican War memorial, but a few monuments have been erected by states and local governments as well as by veterans organizations and other patriotic societies. Perhaps the oldest of these monuments is located in Lawrenceburg, Tennessee. It commemorates the citizens who enlisted in 1846 in a company of volunteers who styled themselves the "Lawrenceburg Blues." In 1849 work began on the monument, which consists of a tall white marble shaft and a base on which the names of both those killed in battle and those who died of disease are inscribed.

Another U.S. monument stands in Baltimore, Maryland. Erected in 1903 by the Maryland Association of Veterans of the Mexican War as a memorial to all the Marylanders killed in the U.S.–Mexican War, it consists of a tall granite pedestal surmounted by a statue of Lt. Col. Henry Watson, who was killed during the Battle of Monterrey, Mexico. Bronze plaques attached to the sides of the pedestal list the names of those killed in battle, the names of the monument committee members, and the names of surviving and deceased association members.

In California, a monument commemorating the July 1846 "conquest" of California by Commo. John Sloat stands on a bluff overlooking Monterey. Forty states, as well as the U.S. Army, the U.S. Navy, and President Theodore Roosevelt donated materials for its construction. A bronze statue of an eagle was the gift of the federal government.

In Austin, Texas, a bronze plaque inside the state capitol memorializes all the U.S. officers killed in battle during the U.S.–Mexican War. It was placed there in 1910 by the National Society of the Colonial Dames in the State of Texas.

In Mexico, the best-known memorial to the war is the Monumento a los Niños Héros, formally dedicated in 1952. It stands in Mexico City at the base of the hill on which Chapultepec Castle stands. The monument consists of six tall marble columns, forming a semicircle around a massive stone pedestal on which the words "A Los Defensores de la Patria 1846–1847" are spelled out in large bronze letters. This impressive memorial honors the six young cadets who were killed during the battle of 13 September 1846. Atop the pedestal are the heroic-sized figures of a woman and two young men, one of whom stands proudly beside her. With her left arm, the woman cradles the limp body of the other, a cadet who is said to have wrapped himself in the Mexican tricolor before leaping from the castle ramparts rather than be captured alive.

Another group remembered in Mexico is the San Patricio (Saint Patrick) Battalion, a collection of mostly Irish-American deserters from the U. S. Army who served in the Mexican army during the war. In 1847 a large number of the San Patricios were captured, and many were hanged. The remainder were branded with the letter D on their cheeks. A bronze plaque on the wall of a building in the public square in San Angel, a southern suburb of Mexico City, lists the names of those who were hanged.

Alongside the highway that runs through the battlefield of Buena Vista, near Saltillo, Mexico, stands a small granite marker commemorating the February 1847 Battle of Buena Vista or La Angostura. It is a simple monument, upon which the words "La Angostura" (the Narrows) are engraved, along with the date of the battle.

Today, the location of the graves of U.S. soldiers in Mexico, from the time of the U.S.–Mexican War, are long forgotten. One notable exception is the mass grave of 750 U.S. soldiers who are interred in the one-acre U.S. National Cemetery in Mexico City, created by an act of the U.S. Congress in 1851. A discreet white marker, inscribed with gold letters, makes no mention of the war or how the soldiers came to be there. Nor does it identify them as soldiers. It reads simply: "TO THE HONORED MEMORY OF 750 AMERICANS KNOWN BUT TO GOD WHOSE BONES COLLECTED BY THEIR COUNTRY'S ORDER ARE HERE BURIED."

It could be argued that U.S. frontier forts named for veterans of the U.S.–Mexican War were memorials of a sort, although they honored individuals rather than a group of soldiers. Perhaps the best known of these outposts was Fort Brown, formerly Fort Texas, named in honor of its commanding officer, mortally wounded during the siege of May 1846. Another was Ringgold Barracks in South Texas, named for the famed artillery officer who received a fatal wound at the Battle of Palo Alto. Both Fort Inge and Fort Chadbourne, in Texas, were named for junior officers killed at the Battle of Resaca de la Palma.

Steven R. Butler

BIBLIOGRAPHY

Bond, Peggy, and Mike Bond. *The Insider's Guide to Mexico.* 1992.

Butler, Steven R. *Historic Sites of the Mexican War in the United States, Part One: Texas.* 1995.

Butler, Steven R. "Mexico City National Cemetery." *Mexican War Journal* 5, no. 1 (1995): 15–17.

Carpenter, Viola, and Mary Maude Carter. *Our Hometown.* n.d.

Corder, Jim W. *Hunting Lieutenant Chadbourne.* 1993.

Fehrenbach, T. R. *Lone Star.* 1968.

Fisher, John. *The Real Guide to Mexico.* 1989.

Miller, Robert Ryal. *Shamrock and Sword: The Saint Patrick's Battalion in the U.S.–Mexican War.* 1989.

Rusk, William Sener. *Art in Baltimore: Monuments and Memorials.* 1929.

Moore, Edwin Ward

U.S. and Texas naval officer Edwin Ward Moore (1810–1865) was born in Alexandria, Virginia. Moore entered the U.S. Navy in 1825. Serving in the West India squadron on board the *Hornet,* and later in the Mediterranean on board the *Fairfield,* Moore was promoted to lieutenant in 1835. In 1839 Moore resigned from the U.S. Navy and assumed overall command of the Republic of Texas navy. After traveling to New York and Baltimore in an effort to recruit sailors and procure ships, Moore sailed with five vessels off the coast of Mexico. During ongoing clashes between the governments of Texas and Mexico from 1840 to 1842, Moore harried Mexican shipping, captured Tabasco, and assisted Mexican federalists in the Yucatán who were revolting against the Mexican central government.

In early 1843 Moore, against the orders of his superiors who were contemplating selling off the Texas navy, took his fleet out of New Orleans and in two separate encounters that April and May defeated the Mexican squadron blockading the Yucatán. Ordered home by President Sam Houston to face charges of mutiny and disobedience, Moore ably defended himself in *To the People of Texas,* a pamphlet defending his controversial activities. Moore was eventually prosecuted on sixteen counts in court-martial proceedings, but was convicted of only four minor charges. Moore spent the rest of his life writing pamphlets vindicating his activities in both the Texas and U.S. navies.

Following Texas's annexation to the United States in 1845, the ships of the Texas navy, but not its officers, were incorporated into the U.S. Navy. Frustrated in his attempt to secure requisite rank in the U.S. Navy, Moore spent his last years in New York City as an inventor, dying there in 1865.

James M. Denham

BIBLIOGRAPHY

Carter, Robert Foster. "The Texan Navy." *United States Navy Institute Proceedings* 59 (July 1933): 1032–1038.

Hill, Jim Dan. *The Texas Navy in Forgotten Battles and Shirt Sleeve Diplomacy.* 1937.

Jenkins, John H. "The Texas Navy: Los Diablos Tejanos on the High Seas." In *The Republic of Texas,* edited by Stephen B. Oates. 1968.

Wells, Tom Henderson. *Commodore Moore and the Texas Navy.* 1960.

Mora, José María Luis

Mexican politician, journalist, and historian José María Luis Mora (1794–1850) was one of the leading liberal thinkers in Mexico during the early nineteenth century. His influence is evident in the laws he drafted, in the newspapers he founded, and the histories he wrote in the first critical decades of the Republic of Mexico. Born in Chamacuero, Guanajuato, Mora's family suffered great hardships during the War for Independence. After receiving his primary education in Querétaro, Mora attended the College of San Ildefonso where he earned a doctorate of theology in 1829. At the same time, he became politically active.

Mora was a vocal opponent of the Mexican Empire declared by Agustín de Iturbide, and he soon became a leading champion and shaper of liberal and federalist ideology. In 1823 he served in the legislature of the state of México and was influential in the formation of its state constitution. Later he became a leading writer and pamphleteer for federalist causes and often published in *El Observador,* an important newspaper. Mora was infamous in federalist circles for his advocacy of state ownership of Church property as a tool for building Mexican self-sufficiency. In 1833 Mora founded *El Indicador,* a paper soon famous for its attacks against centralism. This earned him the enmity of the Santa Anna government, forcing him to flee to Paris, France, in 1834.

In Paris, Mora found himself having to apologize for his nation, as he reported France's doubts over Mexico's ability to govern itself. In 1836, he chronicled the story of his troubled nation in *Mexico y sus Revoluciones,* the first important history of the republic. Two years later, he followed this important work with *Obras Sueltas,* marking him as one of the most important thinkers of his time. During the U.S.–Mexican War, he served as minister plenipotentiary to the government of Great Britain. While in London, Mora attempted to sway British opinion in favor of Mexico, but with little success. After the passage of the Treaty of Guadalupe Hidalgo, Mora sought to gain promises from Great Britain that the new U.S.–Mexico boundary would be defended diplomatically into the future, but he received no assurances from Lord Palmerston. In 1847, he returned to Paris in poor health. He died there three years later.

Donald S. Frazier

BIBLIOGRAPHY

Flores D., Jorge. *José María Luis Mora: Un constructor de México.* 1963.

Hale, Charles. *Mexican Liberalism in the Age of Mora, 1821–1853.* 1968.

Mora, José María Luis. *Mexico y sus revoluciones.* 1856. Reprint, 1950.

Morales, Juan

Born in the city of Puebla, Juan Morales (1802–1849) became a leading soldier in the struggle for Mexican independence in 1820 and 1821. He also helped establish the Mexican Republic in 1823. In 1835 he commanded troops in Antonio López de Santa Anna's campaign in Zacatecas. The following year he participated in the invasion of Texas and was instrumental in the Mexican victories at the Alamo on 6 March and at Coleto Creek on 20 March.

After Texas, Morales received the rank of general of brigade in 1839. In August 1842 Morales again served Santa Anna by leading a brigade against Yucatecan insurgents. In 1846 Morales, a *puro* federalist, helped overthrow the government of Mariano Paredes y Arrillaga.

Described as "brave, active, and popular," Morales was responsible for the defense of Vera Cruz against Gen. Winfield Scott's 1847 invasion. In late March, when Vera Cruz appeared doomed to fall to U.S. forces, Morales abandoned his post and passed command to a subordinate, Gen. Juan José Landero, a well-known Santa Anna crony. When the U.S. forces paroled the garrison, Santa Anna ordered both Morales and Landero imprisoned in Castle Perote pending investigation of their actions. Both were freed within weeks when Scott's army captured that place. Morales died soon after in Atlixco, Puebla.

Donald S. Frazier

BIBLIOGRAPHY

Bancroft, Herbert Howe. *History of the North Mexican States and Texas.* 1889.

DePalo, William A., Jr. *The Mexican National Army.* 1997.

Hardin, Steve. *Texian Iliad.* 1994.

Smith, Justin H. *The War with Mexico.* 1919. 2 vols. Reprint, 1963.

Mora y Villamil, Ignacio

A native of Mexico City, Ignacio Mora y Villamil (1791–1870) was one of Mexico's premier military engineers. With the independence of Mexico in 1821, General Mora y Villamil created a comprehensive plan of fortifications and defenses for the republic. He served as secretary of war and navy for a month in late 1837. He also served as military inspector for all of Mexico's fortifications and fretted over the readiness of his nation's defenses in the event of war, constantly arguing for a tighter control of the peripheral holdings of the nation, including California. At the outbreak of war between the United States and Mexcio, Mora y Villamil tried in vain to get his government to finance renovations of the defenses at Vera Cruz and San Juan de Ulúa.

After the fall of Vera Cruz, Gen. Antonio López de Santa Anna appointed Mora y Villamil to the command of the tattered Army of the North at San Luis Potosí, and he led it south to the Battle of Cerro Gordo where that command was virtually destroyed. Mora y Villamil next served in laying out the defenses of Mexico City and worked as one of the peace commissioners that negotiated the final armistice with U.S. general Winfield Scott. Following the war, Mora y Villamil wrote an engineering treatise dealing with the construction, attack, and defense of fortifications. He served in the Mexican Imperial Army during the French Intervention and died in 1870 in Mexico City.

Donald S. Frazier

BIBLIOGRAPHY

DePalo, William A., Jr. *The Mexican National Army.* 1997.

Smith, Justin H. *The War with Mexico.* 2 vols. 1919. Reprint, 1963.

Mormon Battalion

On 5 June 1846 President James K. Polk authorized the military recruitment of five hundred Mormons encamped in the Iowa Territory. Historian Daniel Tyler has claimed the recruitment was meant as a test of loyalty for the Mormons, but there is no evidence that was Polk's intention. Brigham Young, leader of the Mormon faith, endorsed the recruitment, exclaiming, "Let the Mormons be the first to set their feet on the soil of California." On 16 July 1846 an estimated

543 men were mustered into the Mormon Battalion at Council Bluffs, Iowa Territory. They were accompanied on the march by 33 women, 20 of whom served as laundresses, and 51 children.

The battalion trekked from the bluffs to Fort Leavenworth and then to Santa Fe. After reaching Santa Fe, the sick were detached to Fort Pueblo (present-day Pueblo), while the able soldiers continued on to the San Diego mission. These soldiers completed a march that spanned nearly two thousand miles. On 30 January 1847 Lt. Col. Philip St. George Cooke penned, "History may be searched in vain for an equal march of infantry. Half of it has been through a wilderness where nothing but savages and wild beasts are found, or deserts where, for lack of water, there is no living creature."

The Mormon Battalion soldiers were mustered out of the military on 16 July 1847 in Ciudad de los Angeles (present-day Los Angeles). Although they never saw combat, they are remembered for their unprecedented march from Council Bluffs to California, for building Fort Moore in Los Angeles, for making the first southern wagon road from California to Utah, and for strategically strengthening the U.S. position in the newly claimed southern portion of Alta California.

Following their discharge, many battalion veterans helped build flour mills and saw mills in northern California. Some of them were among the first to discover gold at Sutter's Mill. Henry Bigler's journal entry for 24 January 1848 reads, "This day some kind of mettle [sic] was found in the tail race that looks like goald, first discovered by James Martial."

Susan Easton Black

BIBLIOGRAPHY

Golder, Frank Alfred. *The March of the Mormon Battalion from Council Bluffs to California: Taken from the Journal of Henry Standage.* 1928.

Tyler, Daniel. *A Concise History of the Mormon Battalion in the Mexican War, 1846–1847.* 1969.

Mormonism

The Church of Jesus Christ of Latter-day Saints is commonly, but unofficially, referred to as the Mormon Church and its members as Mormons because of their belief in the Book of Mormon.

Mormonism traces its roots to nineteenth-century New York State, where founder Joseph Smith claimed that God the Father and Jesus Christ appeared to him. He further stated that the fullness of the gospel as known by ancient prophets was restored to him. On 6 April 1830 in upstate New York, Smith organized the Mormon Church. From its beginnings, violent persecution and mobocracy raged against its members, and led directly to the death of Smith in 1844.

The Mormons, under Smith's successor, Brigham Young,

continued to suffer from persecution in Illinois. Newspaper editors reported, "Anti-Mormons still thirst for blood and are laying plans for driving [Mormons] from the country, or destroying their lives and property." Illinois governor Thomas Ford advised Mormon leaders, "I do not foresee the time when you will be permitted to enjoy quiet."

In 1846 Mormons fled from their enemies to the Iowa territory. Their flight does not mirror the westward-bound settler seeking greener pastures in Oregon, or the adventurous forty-niner rushing to California. Instead, it was a migration to find a location where they could live their religion in peace.

Charges of disloyalty to the U.S. government were rumored as Mormons fled from the borders of the United States. Brigham Young answered the charges by encouraging five hundred Mormon volunteers to join the Mormon Battalion and fight for the United States in the war with Mexico. He said to the recruits, "Hundreds would eternally regret that they did not go, when they had the chance." His actions not only dispelled the charges but also directly led to U.S. government support of the Mormon pioneer expedition to the Great Basin.

Susan Easton Black

BIBLIOGRAPHY

Black, Susan Easton, and Larry C. Porter. *Lion of the Lord: Essays on the Life and Service of Brigham Young.* 1995.

The Book of Mormon. 1995.

Ludlow, Daniel H., ed. *Encyclopedia of Mormonism.* 5 vols. 1992.

Mountain Men

The mountain men were beaver trappers and fur traders operating in the Rocky Mountain West from roughly 1807 to 1840. These included both freemen (free trappers) and those employed to trap and hunt for various fur companies. Beginning in 1825, annual rendezvous were held at preselected locations in the mountains where trappers and Indians traded in their season's catch of furs for supplies and money. The rendezvous system allowed the mountain men to remain in the beaver-rich country year-round. A decline in the price of beaver pelts, from nearly $6.00 per pound in the early 1830s to less than $3.00 ten years later, brought a close to the era of the mountain men (the last rendezvous was held in 1840). However, many mountain men remained on the frontier, becoming Indian traders, Santa Fe traders, meat hunters, and guides for government exploring expeditions.

With the outbreak of the U.S.–Mexican War, the mountain men's firsthand knowledge of the geography of the West and intimate acquaintance with its native inhabitants was of especial value to the U.S. military, which was charged with occupying and holding New Mexico and California. Several former beaver trappers served as guides, interpreters, and

dispatch carriers, including Christopher "Kit" Carson, Thomas Fitzpatrick, James Beckwourth, Richens Lacy "Uncle Dick" Wootton, James Kirker, and William Bent. A number of mountain men were among the American insurrectionists who formed California's Bear Flag Revolt of June and July 1846. In New Mexico, in January 1847, when news of the Taos Revolt reached Santa Fe, trader Ceran St. Vrain quickly formed a volunteer company, nicknamed the "avengers," which included several mountain men in its ranks. Captained by St. Vrain, a former fur trapper himself, this company served throughout Col. Sterling Price's campaign against the Taos insurgents.

Mark L. Gardner

BIBLIOGRAPHY

Carter, Harvey L., and Marcia C. Spencer. "Stereotypes of the Mountain Man." *Western Historical Quarterly* 6 (1975): 17–32.

Hafen, LeRoy R., ed. *The Mountain Men and the Fur Trade of the Far West.* 10 vols. 1965–1972.

Mounted Rifles, U.S.

Congress created the U.S. Mounted Rifles on 19 May 1846. Originally intended for service on the Oregon Trail, the regiment was instead sent to Mexico as soon as it was raised. Pay and allowances were the same as for the dragoons. The enlisted men wore the same dark blue jackets trimmed in yellow as dragoons except with the letter *R* on their buttons instead of *D*. Unlike the dragoons, their trousers were dark blue instead of sky blue. The regiment was armed with sabers and the M1841 rifle (and later Colt revolving pistols) so that they could fight both mounted and on foot. President James K. Polk's appointments of officers to the regiment angered Whigs, who charged that he offered commissions only to western Democrats. Only one of the field officers, Maj. William W. Loring, served with the regiment, as both Col. Persifor F. Smith and Lt. Col. John C. Frémont held other commands during the war and this had no associations with the regiment they nominally commanded.

The regiment saw extensive service in central Mexico and was present at the Battle of Cerro Gordo and the battles for Mexico City. Although nominally "mounted," all but two companies served on foot because most of the regiment's horses were lost at sea. Two companies, however, were mounted and used against guerrillas on the National Road. The most celebrated member of the U.S. Mounted Rifles was Capt. Samuel W. Walker, the former Texas Ranger and co-designer of the Colt Walker revolver, whose death at Huamantla, Mexico, so shocked the U.S. Army. After the war, the regiment was reorganized and sent to Oregon. The regiment became the 3d U.S. Cavalry in 1861.

Richard Bruce Winders

2d Lt. George M. Gordon, U.S. Mounted Rifles. Daguerreotype, c. 1846. From the collection of William J. Schultz, M.D.

BIBLIOGRAPHY

Frost, Daniel M. "The Memoirs of Daniel M. Frost: Part III, The Mexican War Years." *Missouri Historical Bulletin* 26 (1970): 200–226.

Winders, Richard Bruce. "Mr. Polk's Army: Politics, Patronage, and the American Military in the Mexican War." Ph.D. diss., Texas Christian University, 1994.

Mulegé, Battle of

On 2 October 1847, at Mulegé on the Gulf of California, successful defense by Mexican forces against superior U.S. forces inspired active resistance to U.S. occupation of Baja California. Following reports of Dominican mission president Fray Gabriel González marching from Loreto to fortify Mulegé, Commo. Thomas Oliver Selfridge in the corvette USS *Dale* sailed from La Paz 26 September 1847 to "neutralize" the town. Anchoring off Río Mulegé under British colors on 30 September, Lt. Tunis A. M. Craven led a detachment ashore under a flag of truce to inform Subteniente Jesús Avilez that California was U.S. territory. After being told by Judge Tomás Zúñiga and Capt. Manuel Pineda that the town would be defended, Craven retired to the *Dale* towing the captured Mexican sloop *Magdalena*. On 1 October, while Craven repeated U.S. demands, which were again re-

jected, Selfridge planned a landing. At the same time Pineda prepared a defense, dispatching civilian Vicente Mejía with thirty infantry north to Cerro Amarillo, Avilez to occupy hills south of the arroyo, Guardia Nacional ensign Francisco Fierro as lookout on the beach, and civilian Jesús Rodríguez to command the sole artillery piece in the plaza. At 9 A.M. on 2 October, Craven returned with four boats under a flag of truce and again had his demands rejected by Pineda. At 2 P.M. Craven landed at El Sombrerito at the river mouth with Lt. William Taylor Smith and Lt. Robert Tansill commanding seventy-one troops and assaulted the plaza, while *Dale* bombarded it and fired 135 rounds of canister against defenders on the beach. Craven was recalled at 5 P.M. with two wounded; the 140 defenders suffered some casualties. At daylight on 3 October, the *Dale* sailed, reaching La Paz on 8 October. As Comandante en Jefe de la Guerrilla Guadalupana, Pineda allied with Jefe Político Mauricio Castro and led strong resistance to a U.S. presence. Their success was substantially responsible for subsequent U.S. disinterest in incorporating Baja California into territorial demands of the Treaty of Guadalupe Hidalgo.

W. Michael Mathes

BIBLIOGRAPHY

Mathes, Miguel, ed. *Textos de su Historia: Baja California*. 2 vols. 1988.

Nunis, Doyce B., Jr., ed. *The Mexican War in Baja California: The Memorandum of Captain Henry W. Halleck Concerning His Expeditions in Lower California, 1846–1848*. 1977.

Museums and Archives

The largest museum and archival collections relating to the U.S.–Mexican War are housed at a few key national depositories and research universities in the United States and Mexico. Numerous states and municipalities also have U.S.–Mexican War collections. These holdings, although significant, are usually localized, and researchers should begin their work in the U.S. and Mexican national collections.

In the United States, extensive holdings are at the National Archives and Records Administration and the Library of Congress in Washington, D.C. Most of the U.S. government's official records, such as documents of the Office of the Secretary of War as well as a substantial collection of maps and photographs, are at the National Archives. The Library of Congress has an extensive collection of maps and photographs as well as early prints and personal correspondence. The library's collection of secondary literature and published contemporary accounts and analyses is unmatched.

In Mexico City three national facilities house most of the collections relating to the Mexican side of the war. The Archivo General de la Nación houses the country's largest collection of manuscripts. The Archivo de Relaciones Exteriores has documents covering the Foreign Relations Ministry since independence, and the Archivo de Defensa provides coverage of the Mexican military. Like the Library of Congress in the United States, the Biblioteca Nacional houses a substantial collection of manuscripts and published secondary works on the U.S.–Mexican War.

Beyond the federal holdings, extensive collections covering political, military, and social aspects of the war are held at a small group of universities and independent research centers. Five collections stand out. Significant holdings are found in the Mexican War Collection of the Jenkins Garret Library at the University of Texas at Arlington. The collection includes government records, Mexican imprints, manuscripts and family papers, diaries, works of art, maps, and a unique collection of patriotic sheet music. Equal to the collection at Arlington are the collections of Yale University and the United States Military Academy at West Point. The Beinecke Library at Yale and the research center at West Point house substantial collections of books, pamphlets, manuscripts, and music. Yale also has a unique collection of daguerreotypes. The Mexican Archives in the Nettie Lee Benson Latin American Collection at the University of Texas at Austin houses one of the strongest collections of personal and family papers. The Genaro Garcia Collection there provides valuable insight into the personal and professional lives of many Mexican political figures. In California, the Latin Americana materials of the Bancroft Collection at the University of California at Berkeley offers extensive holdings describing California's relationship to Mexico in the prewar and wartime eras as well as numerous holdings relating to the war.

While an exhaustive list of archival resources is not possible, other collections of significance include the Southern Historical Collection at the University of North Carolina at Chapel Hill; the Huntington Library in San Marino, California; the Ohio Historical Society; the Texas State Archives; the University of Texas at San Antonio; and the Center for Southwest Research at the University of New Mexico. In Mexico, the municipal archives of Coahuila and Saltillo provide valuable information outside the federal holdings. Many of these centers, large or small, often hold microform copies of other collections.

Kevan D. Frazier

BIBLIOGRAPHY

Bancroft Library, University of California at Berkeley. *Manuscripts Relating Chiefly to Mexico and Central America.* Edited by George P. Hammond. 1972.

Benson Latin American Collection, University of Texas at Austin. *Catalog of the Nettie Lee Benson Latin American Collection.* 1977.

Library of Congress. *Handbook of Latin American Studies.* 1– (1935–).

Mañé, Jorge Ignacio Ruio. *El archivo general de la Nación, México, D.F.* 1940.

Patterson, Jerry. "The Mexican War, 1846–1848: A Collection of Contemporary Material Presented to the Yale University Library by Frederick W. Beinecke, 1909." *The Yale University Library Gazette* 34 (January 1960).

Stampa, Manuel Carrera. *Archivalia Mexicana.* 1952.

Ulibrari, George S., and John P. Harrison. *Guide to Materials on Latin America in the National Archives of the United States.* 1987.

Music

This entry includes two separate articles: **Mexican Music** *and* **U.S. Music**.

Mexican Music

The war between Mexico and the United States left few obvious musical traces on Mexico. Humiliating defeat and dismemberment in 1848 left Mexicans with little cause to match the multitude of anthems, battle pieces, patriotic marches, and battle songs composed to commemorate the U.S. victory. Yet, the trauma of defeat had important musical consequences in Mexico.

During the early 1840s travelers Brantz Mayer and Frances Calderon de la Barca were impressed by the progress of Mexican music, comparing military and village bands and church and secular orchestras favorably with their U.S. and European counterparts and commenting on Italian opera's dominance of the repertoire. Earlier Spanish and Moorish influences were evident in the popular *sones* (rhyming couplets set to undulating rhythms), played by small guitar and harp ensembles of the type that was formed initially for the fanfare at bullfights. During the late 1700s these *sones* inspired the development of a sensual (and initially prohibited) popular dance—the *jarabe*—that the Mexican upper classes adopted during the early Republic. Pre-Columbian influences were also still evident, especially in the drum and flute ensembles, known as *chirimías* or *conjuntos aztecos*, that played outside churches and at village festivals. These defining features of Mexican music—Italianized cultivated music, popular *sones* and *jarabes*, and indigenous *chirimías*—were observed from 1846 to 1848 by U.S. war diarists and by Guillermo Prieto in his *Memorias de Mis Tiempos*. Prieto described how "bands of music" were attached to most Mexican battalions to instill patriotism and bravery. On the eve of the Battle of Buena Vista in February 1847, the emotional power and virtuosity of Gen. Antonio López de Santa Anna's military bands inspired both the Mexican and the U.S. forces. The repertoire of these bands was mostly European.

Organized musical life in Mexico City was disrupted (there was no operatic company or concert orchestra in the capital between 1846 and 1848), first by civil war, then by the U.S. invasion and the sudden defeat. These conditions explain why no new patriotic marches or overtures were engendered, with the solitary exception of "Marchemos, niños polkos." This proclerical, monarchist march was adapted from a Spanish ballad in 1847 by the *polkos*, who were rebelling against Vice President Valentín Gómez Farías's anticlerical decrees. (The term *polkos* referred to upper-class militia regiments known for their love of dancing the fashionable polka, or may have been a derisive epithet alleging loyalty to U.S. president Polk.) The sentiments of the *polkos* confirm how factional loyalties sometimes prevailed over the calls of patriotism during the U.S.–Mexican War. Only during the protracted resistance to the French intervention (1862–1867) were Mexicans inspired to compose patriotic military marches of their own.

In the aftermath of the war with the United States, several musical developments are noteworthy. In July 1849 Anne Bishop, an English soprano and future director of the Conservatorio Nacional (Mexican national conservatory), performed to great acclaim at a concert in Mexico City a fantasia of *sones y aires mexicanos*, composed by the French harpist Charles Bochsa. In August, Bishop took this vernacular theme to the provinces, delighting audiences in Guadalajara, Puebla, and Querétaro with renditions of popular patriotic songs such as "Oh Patria!," "La Mexicana," and "La Pasadita."

Apart from sparking an interest in vernacular and patriotic songs, the war also acted as a spur to the thirty-year search for a national anthem and to the organization of military music. In 1849 Austrian Henry Herz composed "Marcha Nacional dedicada a los Mexicanos," delivered in the Teatro Nacional (national theater) in September by twenty pianos, two full orchestras, a military band, and a male choir. However, renewed political instability frustrated this and several other attempts by foreign and Mexican musicians until 1854, when a march composed by a Catalan, Jaime Nunó, set to verse by Francisco González Bocanegra, was decreed by President Santa Anna as Mexico's first national anthem. Nunó's anthem survives today, entirely unchanged. Santa Anna had invited Nunó to Mexico in 1852 to direct an academy of military music to train the Republic's military bands. By the fall of Santa Anna's conservative regime in 1854, these bands numbered more than 230.

Quite as significant as these developments in cultivated music was the impact of the U.S.–Mexican War on the vernacular tradition. When, on a moonlit night at Buena Vista in February 1847, a U.S. sentry listened to the songs of the Mexican soldiers nearby, he judged the music to be the "dirge of souls in bondage, the cry of an oppressed race." Yet, it is only in popular song that direct musical traces of

the war are found. While the cadets of the Colegio Militar (military academy) at Chapultepec adapted Spanish songs to reflect Mexican circumstances, such as "Clarín de la Campaña," conscripts revived ballads of the Insurgency (1810–1815) such as the "Canción de Morelos" or devised *sones* such as "La Campana," "Las Margaritas," (women who consorted with "Yanqui" soldiers), and "La Pasadita." The last song is the best known of the war, with lyrics that suggest a well of popular patriotism that Mexico's military leaders failed to tap. The xenophobic theme of "La Pasadita" was later manifested in the border ballad "El General Cortina," which recounts the tale of a veteran of the war who led an abortive uprising of smallholders in southern Texas in 1859. Anti-U.S. sentiment stemming from the war also surfaces repeatedly in the *corridos* (ballads) that sprang from the revolution of 1910 to 1917.

Guy P. C. Thomson

BIBLIOGRAPHY

Calderon de la Barca, Frances. *Life in Mexico.* 1843. Reprint, 1973.

Johannsen, Robert W. *To the Halls of the Montezumas.* 1985.

Mayer, Brantz. *Mexico as It Was and as It Is.* 1847.

Mendoza, Vicente T. *La canción Mexicana.* 1982.

Orta Velázquez, Guillermo. *Breve historia de la música en Mexico.* 1970.

Paredes, Américo. *A Texas-Mexican Cancionero: Folksongs of the Lower Border.* 1976.

Prieto, Guillermo. *Memorias de Mis Tiempos.* 1876. Reprint, 1970.

Saldívar, Gabriel. *Historia de la música en México.* 1934.

Simmons, Merle E. "Attitudes toward the United States Revealed in Mexican *corridos*." Hispania 36 (1953): 34–42.

Stevenson, Robert. *Music in Mexico, A Historical Survey.* 1952.

Thomson, Guy P. C. "The Ceremonial and Political Roles of Village Bands, 1846–1974." In William H. Beezley, et al., *Rituals of Rule, Rituals of Resistance: Public Celebrations and Popular Culture in Mexico,* pp. 307–341. 1995.

U.S. Music

Music formed a significant component of the overall effort of the United States during the U.S.–Mexican War, both within the military—from providing signals to sustaining morale among soldiers—and without—in helping recruit volunteers and creating public consensus for military involvement. In turn, the war and surrounding issues of the period provided textual material for both folk songs and for a growing industry of music publishing.

There were two distinct types of military music, field music and band music. The field musicians included the company drummers and fifers (infantry) and trumpeters (cavalry) who signaled troops during operations and in daily routine. At times, the infantry musicians came together to

Sheet music cover. The song "On to the Charge," 1846, memorialized Maj. Samuel Ringgold (Library of Congress).

form regimental fife-and-drum corps. The "band of music" was an ensemble of up to sixteen instrumentalists, usually attached to a regiment and often paid by the unit's officers. The brass-and-percussion bands of the U.S.–Mexican War differed from those of the Civil War in that the brass instruments were of an older, often keyed, type; some, such as the ophicleide, were superseded by the over-the-shoulder saxhorns in the mid-1850s. In addition to performing as troops marched into battle, bands entertained during periods of recreation and supplied music for ceremonies and special events. The repertoire of U.S.–Mexican War bands consisted of marches and popular airs, including "Hail Columbia" and "Yankee Doodle." A number of the bandsmen also served in the Civil War; an example is James B. Smith, cornetist of the band of the 2d U.S. Artillery Battalion, who later led the band attached to the 1st Virginia Infantry of the Confederate army.

In addition, the U.S. troops enjoyed singing and dancing to music provided by peers (soldier-fiddlers and fifers) or by Mexican musicians. Numerous reports exist of off-duty soldiers, such as some of Col. Alexander W. Doniphan's Missourians at Chihuahua, attending local dances (fandangos) and dancing African-American, Anglo-Celtic, and Mexican steps. One folk song of the period, "Green Grow the Lilacs" (cf. "Green Grows the Laurel"), became so identified with the Irish-American troops that it is sometimes said to have given rise to the term *gringo* among the Mexican populace.

At home, music served to support patriotism. Civic brass bands performed martial airs at recruiting rallies as well as at welcoming ceremonies for returning units. Published sheet music of the period—generally songs or works for piano—often reflected themes associated with the war. Some songs, like "The Heroine of Monterey" (composed by James G. Lyon, published in 1847) captured the romance of the exotic locale. Many pieces glorified war heroes, such as the "Old Rough and Ready Quickstep," composed by Charles Grobe and published for piano in 1846, and "General Persifor F. Smith, The Hero of Contreras' March," composed by Thomas J. Martin and published, also for piano, in 1848. The U.S.–Mexican War also contributed material to a musical genre popular since the time of the American Revolution: the "battle-piece," an extended instrumental work that depicted the progression of a specific battle. Examples include Grobe's *The Battle of Buena Vista*, Op. 101 (piano, 1847) and Francis Buck's *Fall of Vera Cruz . . . 29 March 1847*, composed for piano (1847) and dedicated to "the officers and men of the U.S. Army and Navy engaged in that glorious achievement."

Charles E. Kinzer

BIBLIOGRAPHY

Camus, Raoul. "Military Music." In *The New Grove Dictionary of American Music*, edited by H. Wiley Hitchcock. 1986.

Higham, C. L. "Songs of the Mexican War: An Interpretation of Sources." *Journal of the West* 28 (July 1989): 16–23.

Hitchcock, H. Wiley. *Music in the United States: A Historical Introduction*. 3d ed. 1988.

McCaffrey, James M. *Army of Manifest Destiny: The American Soldier in the Mexican War, 1846–1848.* 1992.

National Road, Mexico

The National Road, which connects the port city of Vera Cruz to Mexico City, was used by Gen. Winfield Scott as a route to the interior in his campaign to conquer central Mexico.

The 250-mile road passes through three climatic zones, offering travelers a variety of experiences and sights. The journey through the *tierra caliente*, or hot country, was made difficult for Scott's men by the tropical heat, high humidity, sandy soil, and an increasingly steep ascent. The *tierra templada*, or temperate country, offered relief, as the road leveled off and the tropics were left behind. Farther on they reached the *tierra frio*, or cold country, and emerged onto Mexico's central plateau. The eastern and western branches of the Sierra Madre provided a backdrop for much of the route, with the road crossing mountain passes at several points. Cities along the way included Jalapa, Perote, and Puebla, and numerous haciendas lined the important highway. Stone bridges built by the Spanish spanned broad valleys and deep chasms, reminding the U.S. forces that other conquerors had marched along the same route three hundred years earlier.

The National Road played a major role in Scott's invasion of central Mexico. Scott's advance guard left Vera Cruz for Mexico City on 8 April 1847 and encountered and defeated Gen. Antonio López de Santa Anna near Plan del Rio at the Battle of Cerro Gordo on 18 April, opening the way to Mexico City, which U.S. troops entered on 14 September 1847. Mexican resistance along the road was at times fierce and took on the form of a guerrilla war against the small garrisons Scott left at key points. Although U.S. forces occupied Jalapa, Perote, and Puebla, communication with the coast was severed for weeks at a time. Nevertheless, U.S. forces eventually gained control of the highway, but only after a vigorous antiguerrilla campaign.

Richard Bruce Winders

BIBLIOGRAPHY

Alcaraz, Ramón, ed. *The Other Side; or, Notes for the History of the War between Mexico and the United States.* Translated by Albert C. Ramsey. 1970. Originally published as *Apuntes para la historia de la Guerra entre México y los Estado Unidos,* 1848.

Smith, Justin. *The War with Mexico.* 2 vols. 1919. Reprint, 1963.

Naval Blockade

At the end of 1843 Commo. David Conner became commander of the U.S. Navy Home Squadron, operating in the Gulf of Mexico. U.S. Secretary of the Navy George Bancroft clearly envisioned a war of aggression and, well before the start of hostilities, warned Conner to be ready to seize or blockade Mexican ports. The Mexican navy posed no threat; it had only two warships of consequence—the steamers *Guadalupe* and more powerful *Moctezuma*—and both were repossessed by the British at the start of the war. On the eve of hostilities Conner had the powerful steamer *Mississippi*, two frigates, three sloops, and three brigs. He requested small shallow-draft vessels to complete his force, but without success.

When the war began Bancroft ordered that Conner "effectively blockade the principal Mexican ports, protect our commerce from the depredations of privateers, [and] assist the operations of our army." The navy successfully met all these goals. While it played a leading role in securing California and putting the army ashore in a brilliant operation at Vera Cruz and keeping it supplied, the navy's most important contribution in the war and its principal task was to blockade the Mexican coasts, chiefly the Gulf Coast.

The blockade not only applied significant political and economic pressure on the Mexican government but also pro-

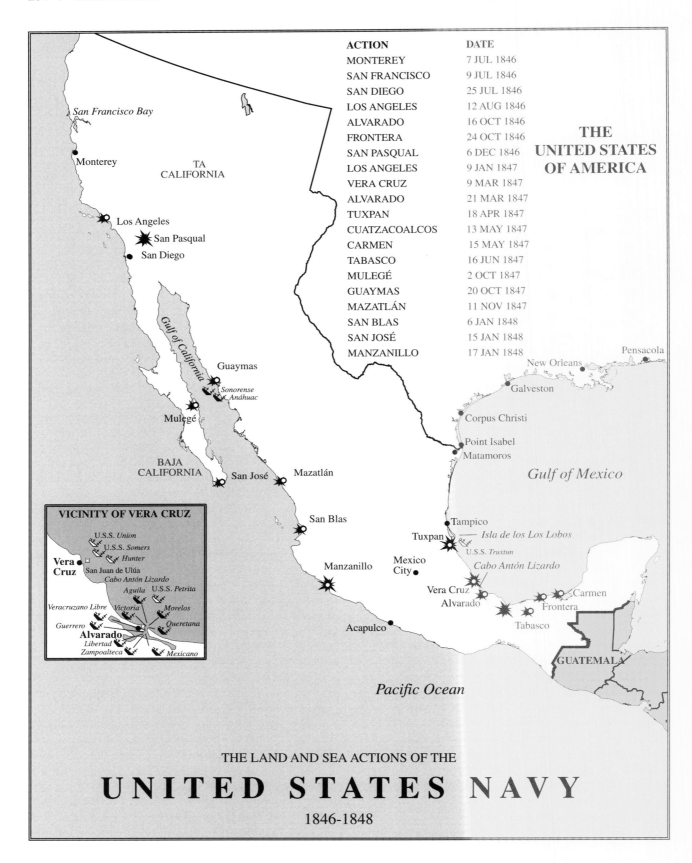

ACTION	DATE
MONTEREY	7 JUL 1846
SAN FRANCISCO	9 JUL 1846
SAN DIEGO	25 JUL 1846
LOS ANGELES	12 AUG 1846
ALVARADO	16 OCT 1846
FRONTERA	24 OCT 1846
SAN PASQUAL	6 DEC 1846
LOS ANGELES	9 JAN 1847
VERA CRUZ	9 MAR 1847
ALVARADO	21 MAR 1847
TUXPAN	18 APR 1847
CUATZACOALCOS	13 MAY 1847
CARMEN	15 MAY 1847
TABASCO	16 JUN 1847
MULEGÉ	2 OCT 1847
GUAYMAS	20 OCT 1847
MAZATLÁN	11 NOV 1847
SAN BLAS	6 JAN 1848
SAN JOSÉ	15 JAN 1848
MANZANILLO	17 JAN 1848

THE LAND AND SEA ACTIONS OF THE

UNITED STATES NAVY

1846-1848

tected U.S. commerce against privateers, which Mexico tried to commission in Cuba. (Only one privateer with a Mexican commission is known to have seized a U.S. vessel, which the Spanish government subsequently returned.)

The blockade was a considerable achievement, given the distances involved (the nearest U.S. Navy base was at Pensacola, Florida, nine hundred miles from Vera Cruz) and the severe conditions, which included disease (especially yellow fever), a lack of accurate coastal charts, and extremes of weather from summer heat to the sudden and violent winter "norther" storms. After one bad storm off Vera Cruz, Commo. Matthew C. Perry reported twenty-three merchant ships blown ashore, several boats lost, and the steam-frigate *Mississippi* had parted its anchor cable.

There were few natural harbors on the Mexican Gulf Coast, and most of those had shallow bars that were passable only in calm conditions. This necessitated operations in shoal waters too shallow even for the smallest sloops. Indeed, a goal of some later U.S. Navy coastal operations was to capture vessels suited to coastal conditions.

Initially Conner had available the powerful steamers *Mississippi* and *Princeton*, two heavy frigates, three sloops, five brigs, and a schooner. One of Bancroft's first steps was to purchase five small fast-sailing schooners. Commanded by senior lieutenants, each was equipped with a single heavy gun and additional armament. Other warships were added later.

Conner soon established a floating advance base near Vera Cruz. At this time according to international law, for a blockade to be legal the blockaders had to be stationed at the ports to be blockaded. In conformity with the traditional U.S. position toward neutral rights, the U.S. Navy confiscated only those ships flying the Mexican flag. All such seizures were later upheld by admiralty courts. Foreign flag vessels were allowed to pass freely.

Despite the difficulties maintaining the blockade, it was effective. It is impossible to measure its importance with precision because there is no complete list of all the blockade runners that were taken. Some ships got through—at least six got into Vera Cruz in the five months before it was captured. But no large quantities of war matériel reached Mexico during the war.

Spencer C. Tucker

BIBLIOGRAPHY

Bauer, K. Jack. *Surfboats and Horse Marines. U.S. Naval Operations in the Mexican War, 1846–48.* 1969.

Smith, Justin H. *The War with Mexico.* 2 vols. 1919. Reprint, 1963.

Navarro, José Antonio

José Antonio Baldomero Navarro (1795–1871) was a Tejano leader and commissioner of the Texas–Santa Fe Expe-

dition. Born 27 February in San Antonio de Béxar, Navarro was the son of Maria Josefa Ruiz y Peña and Angel Navarro. From early adulthood, Navarro espoused republican ideals and supported José B. Gutiérrez de Lara's effort to establish a republic in Texas. He fled with Gutiérrez's defeated forces in 1813, returning after three years. He supported the introduction of U.S. citizens into Texas and assisted in several colonization projects. Navarro sympathized with the Texas Revolution. He and his uncle José Francisco Ruiz were the only Tejanos to sign the Texas declaration of independence. He served in the legislative bodies of Mexico, Coahuila y Texas, the Texas Republic, and the state of Texas, often as the sole Tejano representative. In 1841 Navarro participated in the Texas–Santa Fe Expedition, and when that force surrendered, Mexican officials singled him out as a traitor and condemned him to death. President Antonio López de Santa Anna commuted his sentence to life imprisonment, but after three years of incarceration he escaped. In 1845 Navarro participated in the Texas conventions that accepted annexation to the United States and that framed the first state constitution. In the latter, he defeated an effort to disenfranchise Tejanos. Historians have often described Navarro as an "Americanized" Mexican and overlooked him as a champion of Tejano rights. He died 31 January 1871 and was buried in San Antonio.

Jimmy L. Bryan, Jr.

BIBLIOGRAPHY

Dawson, Joseph Martin. *José Antonio Navarro: Co-Creator of Texas.* 1969.

McDonald, David R., and Timothy M. Matovina, eds. *Defending Mexican Valor in Texas: José Antonio Navarro's Historical Writings, 1853–1857.* 1995.

Navy, Mexican

Most of the military expenditures in the early decades of Mexican independence went toward the creation of armies that could, and often did, support or suppress domestic rebellions and their sponsoring *caudillos* (regional strongmen). As a result, Mexico spent only a small fraction on the navy. When Mexico did acquire warships, the event occurred under the steady hand of a strong centralist administration. By 1835, only a few dilapidated warships defended Mexican territorial waters. When President Antonio López de Santa Anna declared himself a centralist in 1834, he tripled the budget for the navy and authorized the purchase of six new vessels, which eventually bore the names *Iturbide, Vencedor del Alamo, Libertador Mexicano, General Bravo, General Cos,* and *General Urrea.* The fact that four of these warships would bear the names of past or contemporary centralist army officers reveals that the Mexican leadership considered the navy an adjunct of the army.

Many of these ships had not been delivered from their foreign shipyards by the time of the Texas Revolution in 1835, and this lack of naval support allowed the rebels to contest supremacy on the Gulf of Mexico. On 1 September 1835 the insurgent sloop *San Felipe* and steamer *Laura* fought and captured the Mexican warship *Correo Mexicano* in one of the first actions of the Texas Revolution. Within weeks, the *General Bravo* arrived off the coast of Texas and began capturing merchant vessels loaded with supplies for the rebels and keeping Texan privateers in port. When it departed that winter, the rebels returned. In early March, as Santa Anna besieged the Alamo and Gen. José Urrea marched up the Texas coast from Matamoros, the Texan sloop *Invincible* surprised and disabled the aging *Moctezuma* and captured a Mexican supply ship off the mouth of the Río Grande. Santa Anna's surrender at San Jacinto on 19 April brought only a temporary end to the Mexican navy's campaign off Texas.

The next few years brought new ships and new battles to Mexico's navy. On 17 April 1837 the *Vencedor del Alamo* and *Libertador Mexicano* captured the *Independence* after a four-hour battle off Velasco, Texas, and, after sending the Texan ship back to Vera Cruz with a prize crew, added it to the naval inventory. These same two Mexican warships, patrolling near Galveston on 27 August 1837, surprised and destroyed the Texan sloop *Invincible*. Soon after, the French captured Vera Cruz in the so-called Pastry War, capturing the Mexican fleet virtually intact and ending its operations in the Gulf. At the close of that conflict, a greatly weakened Mexican navy had to contend with insurgents in Tamaulipas, Nuevo León, and Yucatán. In 1841 Mexico's naval problems intensified when a revitalized Texan Navy began sailing for the cause of Yucatecan independence. To counter these threats, Mexico ordered a large iron-hulled steam frigate, the *Guadalupe,* and the wooden-hulled steam frigate *Moctezuma* (the second so-named) constructed in Great Britain. On 30 April 1843 these powerful vessels confronted the Texan sloops *Wharton* and *Austin* off Vera Cruz but broke off the engagement after experiencing mechanical troubles. Later that year, these ships and several others in the fleet sailed to the United States for complete overhauls before returning to Mexico in 1845.

When war began with the United States in 1846, the Mexican Navy counted its two newly refitted steam frigates, seven older schooners, and three brigantines as their most powerful warships, supported by more than a dozen gunboats. Most of the vessels served in the Gulf of Mexico in the Departemento del Norte from the ports of Vera Cruz and Tampico while two schooners and four gunboats served the Departemento del Sur from their base in Acapulco. While no match for the U.S. Navy in a fleet action, these Mexican ships, especially the two frigates, posed a potential threat as commerce raiders and caused U.S. planners some concern.

Their speed and armament made the *Guadalupe* and *Moctezuma* a match for any of the steam frigates in the U.S. Navy.

Despite its apparent strengths, the Mexican navy, plagued by a shortage of supplies, money, leadership, and manpower, could contribute little to the defense of Mexico. The first serious blow came when the United States seized six Mexican gunboats under construction in New York and Baltimore shipyards. Unwilling to risk their remaining gunboats and larger ships in combat, Mexican naval officers instead ordered their vessels into secure ports or transferred them to foreign owners. Under new names, the powerful *Guadalupe* and *Moctezuma* sailed uncontested to Havana, Cuba. The brigs and sloops sailed to Alvarado where Mexican commanders immediately ordered three sunk to block the channel. When U.S. Navy lieutenant C. G. Hunter captured that port in April 1847, Mexican officers ordered the remainder burned at anchor. The gunboats of the Mexican Departemento del Norte fell prey to U.S. attacks on the ports of Vera Cruz, Tampico, Tuxpan, and Frontera. Without ships, most Mexican sailors served on land as cannon crews in forts and redoubts. By the end of the U.S.–Mexican War, the once robust Mexican navy had disintegrated into a mere shadow from which it was slow to recover.

Donald S. Frazier

BIBLIOGRAPHY

Bonilla, Juan de Dios. *Historia maritima de México.* 1962.

Scheina, Robert L. "The Forgotten Fleet: The Mexican Navy on the Eve of War, 1845." *The American Neptune* 30 (1970): 46–53.

See **Appendix** *for chart*

Navy, Texan

Although Texas did not formally declare its independence from Mexico until 2 March 1836, conflict on land and sea between the two began somewhat earlier. In fact, the first skirmish between Mexico and its territory to the north occurred at the mouth of the Brazos River in the fall of 1835 when the Texas schooner *San Felipe* fell in with the *Correo.* In a battle that lasted several hours the *Correo* struck its colors, and the matter was adjudicated in New Orleans.

By November discussions of the Texas "Consultation," a makeshift decision making body established to oversee both land and sea defenses, had selected Sam Houston commander-in-chief of its military forces. Discussions also involved naval preparedness, and Governor Henry Smith advocated the commissioning of letters of marque to privately owned vessels against Mexican shipping, a stratagem often used by needy Latin American republics, including Mexico, in their struggle for independence against Spain. A naval affairs committee was also formed calling for the creation of a regular Texan navy. Soon, commissioners were on their way to New Orleans to raise troops, purchase supplies, and acquire vessels for the navy. Offering liberal land grants for service in the Texas conflict against Mexico, the commissioners were soon swamped with U.S. volunteers for both the army and naval service.

One of the most impressive of these was Charles E. Hawkins. Though only thirty-four years of age, Hawkins had already served in the U.S. Navy (1818–1826) and the Mexican Navy (1827–1829). An experienced naval professional familiar with the Gulf of Mexico, Hawkins's talents were well-suited to Texan needs. His enthusiasm for the Texian cause was also proven by his participation in the ill-fated expedition against Tampico led by José Antonio Mexía only months earlier. Armed with a number of personal recommendations, including Sam Houston's, Hawkins was selected commodore of the Texas navy. Within days Hawkins and the Texas commissioners in New Orleans had created a fleet consisting of four vessels: Hawkins's command, the *Independence,* the *Brutus,* the *Invincible,* and the *Liberty*—each manned by a crew of about forty men. Though U.S. neutrality laws forbade the use of its ports for the conduct of the Texas insurgency, circumstances dictated that Hawkins and the others operate out of the Crescent City. Critical in this work were the efforts of Texas purchasing agents William Bryan and Thomas Toby.

The mission of the Texan Navy was threefold. First, the ships were to transport men, supplies, and ammunition to Texas. Second, the vessels would guard Texan ports against invasion. Third, Texan vessels would attack and seize all manner of Mexican craft on the high seas. This would damage Mexico's commerce and perhaps provide a booty of food, arms, and other supplies to the insurgents. Hawkins proved an aggressive and skilled naval commander. From January to March 1836 Hawkins and the Texan Navy launched a series of successful raids against Mexican shipping. In July and August three vessels blockaded Matamoros in the wake of the Battle of San Jacinto on 21 April.

On 12 February 1837, Charles E. Hawkins's brief but impressive career as founding commodore of the Texas navy came to an end, when he died of disease in New Orleans. Hawkins's death and the Texian victory over the Mexicans at San Jacinto pushed the Texan navy into a new phase. Though naval skirmishes did transpire in the next two years, the Panic of 1837 and Mexico's Pastry War with France in 1838 kept operations to a minimum.

By 1839 the Republic of Texas had reconstructed its navy. Newly elected president Mirabeau Lamar appointed Edwin W. Moore, late lieutenant of the U.S. Navy, commodore. If anything, Moore was even more aggressive in his operations than Hawkins. Moore moved first to support Mexican insurrectionists in the Yucatán but soon ran short of funds.

Operating independently to raise money, Moore used his own personal credit and also secured funds from the insurrectionists themselves. Moore soon fell into disfavor with President Sam Houston, who was elected to a second term in 1841. Despite Houston's recall of the navy, and even the Texan congress's secret vote to sell off his fleet, Moore convinced a three-man commission sent to New Orleans by Houston not to carry out their orders. Arguing that a Mexican invasion was imminent, Moore defied Houston's instructions and set out toward the Yucatán, where he attacked and severely damaged two Mexican warships. When Moore returned to Galveston in the summer of 1843, Houston and Moore clashed continually until Moore was court-martialed late in 1844. The court determined that Moore had disobeyed orders but imposed no punishment.

Meanwhile, events were proceeding toward the annexation of Texas by the United States. The joint resolution of the United States Congress, passed 1 March 1845, provided that all Texan "Navy, Navy-yards, Docks, Magazines, Arms armaments," be ceded to the United States. Thus the *Austin, Wharton, Archer,* and *San Bernard* were received by U.S. authorities at Pensacola. All but the *Austin* were sold immediately. At that point, many of the officers of the Texan Navy expected to be incorporated into the U.S. Navy. It was not to be. Moore and the others pressed their claims in Congress for over ten years. In 1857 the matter was finally resolved when Congress passed a law providing that the "surviving officers of the Navy of the Republic of Texas, who were duly commissioned as such at the time of annexation, shall be entitled to the pay of officers of the like grades when waiting orders."

James M. Denham

BIBLIOGRAPHY

Denham, James M. "New Orleans, Maritime Commerce, and the Texas War for Independence, 1836." *Southwestern Historical Quarterly* 97 (January 1994): 511–38.

Hill, Jim Dan. *The Texas Navy in Forgotten Battles and Shirtsleeve Diplomacy.* 1937.

Jenkins, John H. "The Texas Navy." In *The Republic of Texas,* edited by Stephen B. Oates. 1968.

Subject File—U.S. Navy, 1776-1910, National Archives, RG 45, Office of Naval Records and Library, Box 689, folder entitled "Texas Navy."

See **Appendix** *for chart*

Navy, U.S.

Mexico had only two major warships when the U.S.–Mexican War began. Realizing that it could not challenge the United States for command of the sea with such a small

U.S. sailor. Daguerreotype, c. 1845. From the collection of William J. Schultz, M.D.

force, the Mexican government sold both vessels to British commercial firms. As a result the United States exercised naval supremacy over both coasts throughout the war. This not only kept Mexico isolated from potential allies but also allowed U.S. seaborne forces to move virtually at will: to interrupt Mexican trade, to attack coastal cities, and to transport and supply friendly forces. Secretary of the Navy George Bancroft ordered Commo. David E. Connor, the U.S. naval commander in the Gulf of Mexico, to "blockade the principal Mexican ports, protect our commerce from the depredations of privateers, [and] assist the operations of our army. . . . " The U.S. Navy successfully fulfilled all three of these missions.

Within days of the U.S. declaration of war, Connor established a naval blockading force at Antón Lizardo, midway between the important coastal cities of Vera Cruz and Alvarado, and he dispatched the sloop *St. Mary's* to blockade Tampico. Maintaining the blockade was generally tedious work, interrupted only by occasional expeditions to capture Mexican port cities. It also presented a number of logistical problems. Food and coal had to be shipped regularly in

transports from Pensacola, Florida; fresh fruit and water had to be obtained ashore. The elements were also a threat. Antón Lizardo and Tampico provided some security against severe weather, but many ships had to ride out storms at anchor in open roadsteads; and in December 1846, the brig *Somers* capsized and sank in a sudden squall off Vera Cruz with the loss of thirty-two men.

Connor's squadron consisted of eleven vessels—two frigates, two steamers, four sloops, and three brigs—but he lacked a sufficient number of small craft for effective inshore work. All of the Mexican ports on the east coast except Vera Cruz were located up rivers that were protected by sandbars, and many of the larger U.S. warships could not close to effective range. At Alvarado, for example, U.S. naval forces tried three times in 1846 to advance up the Papaloapan River only to be turned back each time because none of the larger vessels could cross the bar. (Alvarado eventually fell to a combined army–navy force in 1847.) The need for small, steam-powered, inshore craft led to the purchase of the *Vixen* and *Spitfire*, each 188 feet in length and carrying three guns.

With these new vessels attached to his command, Commo. Matthew C. Perry, Connor's second in command, led an expedition against San Juan Batista (called Tabasco by U.S. forces) in October 1846. Leaving the deep-draft sidewheel steamer *Mississippi* off the entrance to the Grijalva River, Perry raised his flag on the smaller *Vixen*, which towed two schooners over the bar, although another vessel, the *McLane*, went aground. Once across the bar, the U.S. squadron captured a Mexican brig and three gunboats and compelled the surrender of Frontera near the river's mouth. Then, after steaming seventy miles up river, Perry landed his marines and seized Tabasco, although his force was too small to hold it and he soon withdrew. In November Connor won a bloodless victory by seizing Tampico, two hundred miles north of Vera Cruz, and in December Perry captured the port city of Carmen two hundred miles to the east.

The navy's most important operation of the war was to cover the landing of the army under Gen. Winfield Scott at Vera Cruz in March 1847—the largest amphibious landing in history up to that time. Connor and Scott proved to be an effective team, and many of their innovations became established amphibious doctrine that lasted into the next century. Army transports brought ten thousand soldiers and sixty-four specially designed surfboats (constructed in three different sizes so that they could nest inside one another) to a rendezvous off the island of Lobos near Tampico. From there the armada sailed down the coast to Antón Lizardo, where it arrived on 4 March. Five days later, the soldiers clambered into the boats, which navy personnel maneuvered into a line abreast off the landing beach near Sacrificios Island. The surfboats each carried forty soldiers to the beach, where two thousand men splashed ashore more or less simultaneously. The boats then returned to the waiting transports for the next wave of soldiers. The landings were a great success, and Scott had his foothold for the conquest.

The naval war on Mexico's west coast was more modest in scale. When war broke out, the small U.S. Pacific squadron of two vessels under the command of Commo. John Sloat was at Mazatlán. Four years earlier, Sloat's predecessor, Thomas ap Catesby Jones, had earned an official censure for his rashness in prematurely seizing Monterey, California, when he had heard rumors that war had begun. Determined not to make the same mistake, Sloat delayed making any movement until mid-summer of 1846 after the battles of Palo Alto and Resaca de la Palma had been fought. He arrived at Monterey on 5 July to find that Lt. Col. John C. Frémont had already raised the flag of the California Republic at Sonoma. Sloat's marines seized Monterey on 7 July and Yerba Buena (present-day San Francisco) on 9 July. Not long afterward, Commo. Robert F. Stockton arrived in the frigate *Congress* to supercede Sloat. Stockton absorbed Frémont's small force into his own command and carried it to San Diego and Los Angeles in August. At that point, he discovered that he had taken on more than his force could handle. Only when Brig. Gen. Stephen W. Kearny's column arrived in southern California in December after a ten-week march from Santa Fe did U.S. forces succeed in pacifying California. Stockton was reluctant to grant Kearny the command authority he claimed, and the two men quarreled until Commo. William B. Shubrick arrived in January 1847. Shubrick and Kearny reached an agreement, but Kearny preferred charges against Stockton and Frémont, both of whom left the territory to plead their cases in the political arena.

Although the role of the U.S. Navy in the war with Mexico was secondary to that of the army, its unchallenged command of the sea ensured complete freedom of movement for U.S. forces on both coasts, made possible the amphibious landing that initiated the decisive land campaign, and helped to solidify the U.S. claim to California confirmed in the Treaty of Guadalupe Hidalgo.

Craig L. Symonds

BIBLIOGRAPHY

Bauer, K. Jack. *Surfboats and Horse Marines: U.S. Naval Operations in the Mexican War.* 1969.

Morison, Samuel Eliot. *"Old Bruin": Commodore Matthew Calbraith Perry.* 1967.

Parker, William H. *Recollections of a Naval Officer, 1841–1865.* 1883. Reprint, 1985.

Semmes, Raphael. *Service Afloat and Ashore during the Mexican War.* 1851.

See **Appendix** *for chart*

Nepomuceno Seguin, Juan

See **Seguin, Juan Nepomuceno**

New Mexico

This entry includes three separate articles: **Overview**; **Revolt of 1837**; *and* **U.S. Occupation**.

Overview

New Mexico was the first western province created by imperial Spain in its North American borderlands. Watered by the Río Grande and Río Pecos, New Mexico was an arid region of plains, mountains, and mesas. In the mid–sixteenth century, Spanish conquistador Francisco Vásquez de Coronado observed Pueblo tribes raising corn, beans, and squash, principally in irrigated fields. These town-dwelling farmers traded their crops to nomadic Plains tribes, who offered dried meat and hides in return.

The Spanish founded their first settlement on the upper Río Grande in 1598 and established the capital at its present-day location of Santa Fe eleven years later. Exacting labor, food, and tribute from the Pueblos, the colonists built haciendas and missions from Socorro in the south to the pueblos in the north. In 1680, after eight decades of colonial tyranny, the Pueblos violently expelled the Spanish settlers. Fourteen years later, however, the determined Spanish reoccupied Santa Fe and crushed the rebellion.

After the reconquest, New Mexico came under assault from horse-mounted Comanches, Apaches, Navajos, and Utes, who raided settlements, missions, and pueblos for horses, plunder, and honor. By the mid–eighteenth century the Spanish and Pueblos, outgunned and impoverished, were hard-pressed to defend their settlements and mount offensive operations. Worried about the security of valuable silver mines in northern Mexico, the Spanish crown unified New Spain's borderland provinces from California to Texas under the *Provincias Internas* (Internal Provinces) in the 1770s. The commandant general reorganized and strengthened the antiquated *presidial* system and brought modest stability to the borderlands frontier. Benefitting as well, New Mexicans and Pueblos defeated the western Comanches, than allied with them against the Apaches, resulting in a modest peace for thirty years.

The Mexican independence movement of the 1810s eroded the stability of the borderlands frontier. Preoccupied with rebellion closer to Mexico City, the Spanish colonial government failed to keep up the *presidial* system and let relations with the Native American tribes deteriorate. New Mexico settlements again were subject to constant raids by nomadic tribes. Conditions for the Mexican military did not improve after Mexican independence from Spain in 1821.

In fact, the deterioration crept deeper into political institutions, the mission system, and frontier militia. Unhappy with the central government and higher taxes, northern New Mexicans expressed their discontent in the Rebellion of 1837, which Mexican authorities violently suppressed.

In the nineteenth century, New Mexico became a critical defensive buffer against the expanding United States. After the Louisiana Purchase in 1803, the United States and New Spain shared a frontier border from eastern Texas to the Pacific Northwest. From the Missouri frontier, U.S. merchants and fur trappers began operating illegally in New Mexico. Spanish officials tried to check their economic activities, but trade-starved New Mexicans wanted a competitive alternative to their suppliers in Chihuahua. With Mexican independence, New Mexican authorities welcomed William Becknell and other Missouri traders, who inaugurated the Santa Fe trade. By the end of the decade, U.S. and Mexican traders were carrying $145,000 worth of merchandise per year over the Santa Fe–Chihuahua Trail. These lucrative economic ties between New Mexico and Missouri helped neutralize the loyalty of New Mexicans to the Mexican central government. Consequently, when the U.S. Army of the West entered New Mexico in August 1846, residents then mounted no armed resistance to the invasion.

Throughout the Spanish and Mexican periods, New Mexico was a poor society of subsistence farmers and pastoralists. Importing far more goods than they exported, they were the beneficiaries of royal financial support, albeit at the poverty level. At first growing slowly, the Spanish population increased gradually from a few hundred persons in 1600 to eight hundred in 1680, and accelerated to 16,358 in 1790, approximately 32,000 in 1830, and 58,415 in 1850. The Pueblo Indian population fluctuated between 8,000 and 9,000 throughout the eighteenth and early nineteenth centuries.

At the top of New Mexican society was a small number of privileged elite who held large grants of land and sold wool and sheep to Chihuahua. The advent of the Santa Fe trade substantially expanded their wealth and consequently their landholdings. Although they became more impoverished as the eighteenth century progressed, Franciscan missionaries enjoyed prestige and respect in New Mexican society. At the bottom of society were the *pobladores,* or common farmers and shepherds, who raised crops in their irrigated fields and tended the flocks of the elite for a portion of the profits. During the first two hundred years the hard frontier life, shared by rich and poor alike, minimized class divisions in colonial New Mexico. During the Mexican period, however, economic fissures cracked New Mexico's social foundations. The *pobladores* became more impoverished and more indebted to wealthy landowners, whose fortunes multiplied through trade with the United States and Chihuahua. Life for these poor farmers and pastoralists remained difficult and precarious into the twentieth century.

Durwood Ball

BIBLIOGRAPHY

Bannon, John Francis. *The Spanish Borderlands Frontier, 1513–1821.* 1963. Reprint, 1974.

Beck, Warren A. *New Mexico: A History of Four Centuries.* 1962.

Gutiérrez, Ramon. *When Jesus Came, the Corn Mothers Went Away: Marriage, Sexuality, and Power in New Mexico, 1500–1846.* 1991.

Simmons, Marc. *Spanish Government in New Mexico.* 1968.

Weber, David J. *The Mexican Frontier, 1821–1846: The American Southwest Under Mexico.* 1982.

Revolt of 1837

Mexico's liberal federal Constitution of 1824 created a weak central government and granted the states political autonomy, while conservatives blamed the Republic of Mexico's chronic instability on the weak constitution. In 1834 President Antonio López de Santa Anna and his conservative allies launched the centralization of the Mexican republic. They reduced the size of state militias and eliminated state and local representative government. Under a new departmental plan, the president directly appointed the state and territorial governors, under whom prefects, subprefects, and justices of the peace served. Rebellions expressed the outrage at this radical political change.

On Mexico's northern frontier, New Mexicans aimed their discontent at Col. Albino Pérez. A conservative appointee and an outsider who arrived in Santa Fe in 1835, he represented the evil of conservative centralization. Insurrection festered in the Río Arriba mountain communities, particularly Chimayó, Santa Cruz de la Cañada, and Taos. On 3 August 1837 the Río Arribaños openly rebelled at Santa Cruz de la Cañada, formed a "canton" government, and demanded local autonomy. Five days later the rebels smashed Colonel Pérez's demoralized troops at La Mesilla near San Ildefonso Pueblo and executed the governor and several *ricos,* wealthy upperclass New Mexicans. The following day the insurrectionists peacefully occupied Santa Fe, the territorial capital.

Rebel leaders proclaimed José Angel Gonzales, an illiterate buffalo hunter from Taos, New Mexico governor and, on 27 September convened a *junta popular* in Santa Fe. Representatives swore allegiance to Mexico and to Gonzales, who represented the faceless *pobres*—the small farmers, shepherds, and ranchers—frontier New Mexico's backbone. Without food or pay, they waged frequent militia campaigns against the nomadic Native American tribes and endured the ridicule of unappreciative *rico* leadership.

From the Río Abajo south of Albuquerque, the *ricos* finally denounced the canton. On 8 September at Tomé they issued the "Plan de Tomé," advocating restoration of the conservative system. Assembling an army, the loyalists put former governor Manuel Armijo in command. On 9 September in Santa Fe, conservative Capt. José Caballero reorganized his regular troops, took control of Santa Fe in Gonzales's absence, and invited the Río Abajeños to campaign against the rebels. On 11 September when Gonzales returned from Taos where he had soothed exercised rebels, he was jailed by the Caballero faction. After Governor Manuel Armijo's army reached Santa Fe three days later, the loyalist governor quickly negotiated a treaty with rebel leader Pablo Montoya of Taos and released Gonzales as a goodwill gesture. In return, Montoya turned over four instigators of the August rebellion.

The mountain inhabitants, however, still defied Governor Armijo and demanded his resignation. In response the governor beheaded the four rebel prisoners and marched his army into the Río Arriba area. With the addition of regulars from Chihuahua, the loyalists thrashed rebel forces near Santa Cruz de la Cañada on 27 January 1838. Armijo's rival, Gonzales, was captured, then confessed and was executed.

Unlike rebellions in Texas and California, the Revolt of 1837 in New Mexico emerged from deep class divisions. The conservative Constitution of 1836 stripped the *pobres* of their political power and concentrated it in hands of the *ricos*. Already economically and militarily overstretched, New Mexico's poor foresaw no benefit in Santa Anna's centralization of Mexico, resenting the central government's new taxes and its callousness toward their plight. Rebellion seemed their only recourse.

Durwood Ball

BIBLIOGRAPHY

Lecompte, Janet. *Rebellion in Río Arriba, 1837.* 1985.
Reno, Philip. "Rebellion in New Mexico, 1837." *New Mexico Historical Review* 40 (July 1965): 197–210.
Weber, David J. *The Mexican Frontier, 1821–1846: The American Southwest under Mexico.* 1982.

U.S. Occupation

After the outbreak of the U.S.–Mexican War, one of President James K. Polk's first objectives was the military conquest of New Mexico. An army eventually numbering 1,657 men, about 80 percent of these Missouri Volunteers, was quickly organized in May and June 1846 and sent down the Santa Fe Trail to capture the capital city of Santa Fe. Commanding this force, designated the Army of the West, was Col. (later general) Stephen W. Kearny of the 1st U.S. Dragoons. Because Polk intended to retain New Mexico after the war ended, Kearny was instructed to seize the Mexican department peaceably, if possible. Kearny's expedition left Fort Leavenworth in detachments of varying size and, at the end of July, rendezvoused near Bent's Fort on the Arkansas River.

From there, Kearny issued a conciliatory proclamation to the New Mexican people and sent special agents ahead to Santa Fe and Taos in an attempt to smooth the planned takeover. The main body of the Army of the West crossed the Arkansas River into Mexican territory on 2 August and, nearly two weeks later, reached the first New Mexican settlement, Las Vegas, without any fighting. At Las Vegas, Kearny made a speech absolving the inhabitants of their allegiance to Mexico and promising them the protection of "their property, their persons and their religion" as well as protection from Navajo, Ute, and Apache depredations. The local *alcalde* and two militia captains were then required to take an oath of allegiance to the United States. A similar public demonstration was made at other villages.

Fifteen miles southeast of Santa Fe, at Apache Canyon, New Mexico governor Manuel Armijo had assembled a force of three to four thousand militia and Pueblo Indians to contest Kearny's invasion, but Armijo abruptly disbanded his army on 16 August and fled south. Two days later the Army of the West made a "bloodless" entrance into Santa Fe, and Kearny claimed New Mexico for the United States. In a proclamation of 22 August, Kearny went so far as to proclaim the inhabitants of New Mexico U.S. citizens

(Kearny did not have the authority to confer U.S. citizenship on New Mexicans, and this act had significant ramifications later when several Taos insurgents were tried for treason against the United States).

To defend the new U.S. possession, Kearny ordered the construction of a fort, which he named Fort Marcy, on a hill overlooking the New Mexican capital. Following earlier instructions from the War Department, he began the process of establishing a civil government for New Mexico. A new set of laws for the territory, known as the Kearny Code, was drafted by Col. Alexander W. Doniphan and Pvt. Willard Hall of the Missouri Volunteers. On 22 September, Kearny appointed several territorial officials; merchant Charles Bent was named governor. Kearny left Santa Fe for California on 25 September, taking with him three hundred dragoons (he later sent two hundred of these back to New Mexico). Colonel Doniphan's 1st Regiment Missouri Mounted Volunteers conducted a brief campaign against the Navajos and then marched south to Chihuahua in search of Gen. John E. Wool's army. Remaining members of the Army of the West came under the command of Col. Sterling Price, who had arrived in Santa Fe with the 2d Regiment Missouri Mounted Volunteers in early October.

Not all New Mexicans were content with the change of power, and in December a plot involving several prominent citizens was formed to overthrow U.S. forces in Santa Fe. The plot was discovered, and a number of participants were arrested although all of these eventually went free. New Mexican resistance was far from suppressed, however, and on 19 January 1847 a mob of Mexicans and Pueblos in Taos killed Governor Bent (then in Taos visiting his family) and other U.S. citizens and U.S. sympathizers in the town and surrounding area. Colonel Price marched north from Santa Fe with an army of 353 men (479 with later reinforcements) and defeated the insurgents in fights at Cañada, Embudo, and finally Taos Pueblo, forcing their surrender. Several participants in the revolt were subsequently tried and hanged. No major uprising occurred after the Taos revolt, but guerrilla activity persisted in eastern New Mexico until near the war's end.

New volunteers from Missouri and Illinois arrived in New Mexico in late summer 1847 to replace those Missouri Volunteers whose one-year enlistments had expired. Col. Edward W. B. Newby of the 1st Regiment Illinois Volunteer Infantry became the temporary military commander of New Mexico (the Ninth Military Department) in the absence of Colonel Price, who had traveled back to Missouri with his regiment in August. Price, promoted to brigadier general, returned to Santa Fe that winter and resumed command of the department. In February 1848 Price led an army of volunteers and regulars under his command on a campaign to Chihuahua, remaining there until July, the Ninth Department again reverting to Newby. Colonel Newby conducted a campaign against the Navajos in May 1848.

With the ratification of the Treaty of Guadalupe Hidalgo, New Mexico officially became part of the United States, although its civil administration continued under military control. An attempt was made in 1850 to gain New Mexico's admission to the Union as a state, but Congress instead organized it as a territory. U.S. military control of New Mexico, which dated to Kearny's 1846 conquest, finally ended with the inauguration of Territorial Governor James S. Calhoun on 3 March 1851.

Mark L. Gardner

BIBLIOGRAPHY

Cutts, James M. *The Conquest of California and New Mexico.* 1847.

Gardner, Mark L., and Marc Simmons, eds. *The Mexican War Correspondence of Richard Smith Elliott.* 1997.

Lieutenant Emory Reports: A Reprint of W. H. Emory's Notes of a Military Reconnaissance. 1951.

McNitt, Frank. "Navajo Campaigns and the Occupation of New Mexico, 1847–1848." *New Mexico Historical Review* 43 (1968): 173–194.

Twitchell, Ralph Emerson. *The History of the Military Occupation of the Territory of New Mexico from 1846 to 1851.* 1909.

New Orleans

Long considered the gateway to Texas and the Southwest, New Orleans was founded in 1718 by Frenchman Jean Baptiste Le Moyne. The prize of the Louisiana Purchase, possession of the city, located ninety-four miles up the Mississippi River from the Gulf of Mexico, gave the United States control of the Mississippi basin. Named capital of Louisiana at statehood (1812), New Orleans witnessed Gen. Andrew Jackson's victory over the British on 8 January 1815. After the war the city grew rapidly, profiting from the sale of cotton, slaves, and consumer goods shipped down the Mississippi. By 1840, it boasted a population of 102,193 inhabitants, placing it behind New York (312,710) and Baltimore (102,313) as the third largest city in the United States.

Despite the ever-present threat of yellow fever, the Crescent City earned a reputation as the cultural center of the South between 1815 and 1845, housing a cosmopolitan population that hosted numerous operatic and dramatic performances, balls, and receptions. Entertainment such as horse and steamboat racing, cock and dog fighting, and gambling were popular among the working classes. During the Texas Revolution, volunteers passed through the city en route to Texas in the fall of 1835. Most of the locally raised 1st Company of Texas Volunteers, popularly known as the "New

Orleans Grays," died either at the Alamo or at the Goliad massacre.

Anticipating conflict with Mexico, in August 1845 Gen. Edmund P. Gaines, commander of the Western Division, ordered two volunteer artillery companies from New Orleans to Corpus Christi to strengthen Gen. Zachary Taylor's forces. Although the city was initially divided over the prospect of war with Mexico, the rejection of John Slidell's mission by the Mexican government galvanized local support for the war's vigorous prosecution. After the battles of Palo Alto and Resaca de la Palma, the city became the principal point of embarkation for volunteers and regulars from throughout the United States. Awaiting transport by sea, troops encamped at Jackson Barracks, Place d'Armes, or Armory Hall, spending their leisure hours touring the city. Many volunteers visited the site of Jackson's 1815 victory, anticipating the perpetuation of the citizen-soldier tradition.

Because it was the principal U.S. port on the Gulf of Mexico, Secretary of War William L. Marcy named New Orleans as base of military operations in November 1846. Throughout the war with Mexico, weapons, ammunition, and other supplies arrived from Baton Rouge and other federal arsenals for shipment to the Army of Occupation. From New Orleans, locally based steamships hired by the U.S. Quartermaster Corps transported supplies to Brazos Santiago and Mexican ports. Profits from military shipping and foreign trade made 1847 the most prosperous year to date for local exporters. In addition to serving as a military depot, New Orleans was the chief source of war-related news. Innovative local editors (most notably George Wilkins Kendall of the New Orleans *Picayune*) took advantage of newspapers published by the occupation forces, reporters with the U.S. Army, post riders, and the telegraph to make war news available to the people of the United States on an unprecedented scale.

New Orleans served as the chief point of discharge for veterans of the U.S.–Mexican War, both during and after the conflict. Despite celebrations hailing the conquering heroes, many local speculators profited from the unscrupulous purchase of government land warrants issued to the returning veterans.

Robert P. Wettemann, Jr.

BIBLIOGRAPHY

Boyett, Gene W. "Money and Maritime Activities in New Orleans during the Mexican War." *Louisiana History* 17 (Fall 1976): 413–430.

Copeland, Fayette. *Kendall of the Picayune.* 1943.

Kennedy, Bertha B. "Louisiana in the Mexican War." Master's thesis, Louisiana State University, 1930.

Rogan, Bernadette. "Louisiana's Part in the Mexican War." Master's thesis, Tulane University, 1939.

Newspapers

This entry includes two separate articles: **Mexican Press** *and* **U.S. Press.** *See also* **War Correspondents.**

Mexican Press

A typical Mexican newspaper during the war with the United States followed a standard format. First, there were the sections of local, national, and international news, which were obtained from official communiqués or were taken from other national or international newspapers. Second, there were letters written by the public to the editors, informing about or commenting on the news and editorials. Third, there was the editorial page.

Following Mexico's independence in 1821, the Mexican press was an instrument of the various political factions. The press was conceived more as a means to form public opinion in favor of the diverse political factions than to provide objective or unbiased information. Hence, the press was clearly aligned with political parties or factions, which between 1830 and 1840 consisted of the radical liberals or *puros,* the moderate liberals or *moderados,* and the conservatives. The primary differences among those parties were mostly in regard to the type of government and the extent to which social reforms should be carried out.

During 1845, when the possible U.S. annexation of Texas was the central issue, one of the most important newspapers was *El Siglo XIX,* which had been founded in 1841 by Ignacio Cumplido and expressed the point of view of the *moderados.* This paper originally supported the measures taken by President José Joaquín de Herrera favoring a negotiated settlement with the government of the Republic of Texas to avoid its annexation. Opposing this view were *La Voz del Pueblo* and *El Amigo del Pueblo,* which expressed the opinions of the *puros* and demanded an immediate military campaign against Texas. After the Republic of Texas agreed to annexation by the United States, *El Siglo XIX* joined the opposition, asking for military action to prevent annexation and rejecting the Mexican government's acceptance of John Slidell as U.S. commissioner to negotiate the annexation.

In December 1845 President Herrera was forced to resign and was replaced by Mariano Paredes y Arrillaga, whose political aim was to establish a monarchical government. His effort was supported by the newspaper *El Tiempo,* which was founded and directed by Lucas Alamán. This paper not only pushed for the government's design but also denounced both the U.S. attempt to acquire Texas and the U.S. demand for cession of more territory from Mexico. It did not, however, support a military solution until Slidell's mission was finally rejected in April 1846.

The political view (i.e., establishment of a monarchical government) expressed by *El Tiempo* was opposed by the liberals—both *puros* and *moderados*—in early 1846 through papers such as *El Republicano* (which was the continuation of *El Siglo XIX*) and *El Monitor Republicano,* whose names indicated their political orientation. Joining these was *Don Simplico,* which was founded by two young liberals: Guillermo Prieto and Ignacio Ramírez. This paper was a satirical tabloid that criticized almost all political leaders. The liberal press asked the Paredes y Arrillaga administration for immediate deployment of army troops to defend the border. By June 1846 both the liberal and the conservative press were denouncing the U.S. invasion of Mexican territory and requesting an effective governmental response.

In August 1846 Paredes y Arrillaga was overthrown, and *El Tiempo* was shut down. Liberal journals then dominated the country. In Mexico City they pushed for restoring the federal republican Constitution of 1824 and favored the return of Antonio López de Santa Anna, who had been banished from Mexico in 1844. They hoped that these actions would enable Mexico to resist the advance of the U.S. army into Mexican territory. They also supported the creation of the *guardias nacionales,* or civil regiments, to resist the U.S. invasion.

With news of the Battle of La Angostura, the fall of Vera Cruz, and the defeat at Cerro Gordo, the press accused Santa Anna of lack of judgment and even treason, and at the same time demanded a public uprising against U.S. forces in those places that had been occupied. Yet by May 1847, when the arrival of Nicholas P. Trist as peace commissioner was reported, the paper *El Razonador* started a campaign favoring negotiations with the United States, a view that was strongly attacked by other newspapers. By that time also, some newspapers were being edited by U.S. writers in places that were under U.S. control, among these papers were *The American Eagle, The American Star,* and *The North American.* Their goal was to convince the residents of the need to accept the U.S. terms for peace. *The North American* even pursued a propaganda campaign favoring annexation of all of Mexico by the United States.

With the approach of Gen. Winfield Scott's army to Mexico City, the Mexican government closed all the papers in July 1847 with the sole exception of *El Diario del Gobierno,* the official journal. Nevertheless, after the fall of Mexico City the liberal press resumed its activities in September 1847, mainly through *El Monitor Republicano* and *El Eco de Comercio,* which concentrated on refuting the U.S. press in Mexico and campaigned in favor of peace negotiations.

Jesús Velasco-Márquez

BIBLIOGRAPHY

Brack, Gene M. *Mexico Views Manifest Destiny, 1821–1846: An Essay on the Origins of the Mexican War.* 1975.

Bravo-Urgarte, José. *Periodistas y periódicos Mexicanos.* 1966.

Carrasco-Puente, Rafael. *La prensa en México: Datos históricos.* 1962.

Santoni, Pedro. *Mexicans at Arms: Puro Federalists and the Politics of War, 1845–1848.* 1996.

Velasco-Márquez, Jesús. *La guerra del 47 y la opinion pública (1845–1848).* 1975.

U.S. Press

The U.S.–Mexican War provided the emerging penny press in the United States with an excellent opportunity to demonstrate news enterprise. It was the first foreign war to be covered extensively by U.S. correspondents, and key penny press newspapers made expensive, elaborate arrangements to have their reports carried back to the United States. By combining pony express, steamships, railroads, and the fledgling telegraph, the press established a two-thousand-mile communications link that repeatedly beat military couriers and the U.S. mail with the Mexico news. So effective was the express system maintained by the press that President James K. Polk learned of the U.S. victory at Vera Cruz via a telegram from the *Baltimore Sun.*

The goals of the war, however, left a number of editors perplexed. Even though they reported the U.S. victories with enthusiasm and financial profit, some worried about the moral consequences of the conflict. To Horace Greeley of the *New York Tribune,* it was a war "in which Heaven must take part against us." James Gordon Bennett of the *New York Herald,* meanwhile, was an adamant supporter, arguing, "We are on the verge of vast and unknown changes in the destiny of nations."

Most penny press leaders threw their editorial support behind the war and at the same time established a New York–to–New Orleans express system to deliver news from the battle zones. The express system "is a creature of modern times," Bennett explained to his readers, "and is characteristic of the American people." Led by the New York morning dailies, a number of papers participated, including the *Philadelphia North American* and *Public Ledger,* the *Baltimore Sun,* the *Charleston Courier,* and the New Orleans *Picayune.* During the final six months of the war these papers pooled their efforts to operate the delivery system on a daily basis.

The prowar New Orleans press, closest to the combat zones, led the coverage of the conflict. Because newspapers of the day depended heavily on news from their "exchanges"—free copies they received of other newspapers—the reporting by the New Orleans correspondents was widely reprinted throughout the United States. One of the innovative New Orleans papers was *La Patria,* the nation's first Spanish-language daily. Many U.S. dailies reprinted the letters from *La Patria*'s correspondents and liberally used its translations of Spanish-language papers in Mexico, Cuba, and Latin America.

The star reporter of the war was George Wilkins Kendall, coeditor of the New Orleans *Picayune.* Kendall covered ma-

MATAMOROS REVEILLE.

"WE MUST EVER MAINTAIN THE PRINCIPLE, THAT THE PEOPLE OF THIS CONTINENT, ALONE HAVE THE RIGHT TO DECIDE THEIR OWN DESTINY."

VOL. 1, MATAMOROS, JULY 15, 1846. NO. 7.

MATAMORAS REVEILLE

Published Wednesdays and Saturdays.

SAMUEL BANGS, G. K. LEWIS

☞ Persons desirous of sending the "REVEILLE" to any portion of the United States, can have it done for any length of time they may designate by applying to the publishers, and leaving the name and address of the parties to whom they wish the paper forwarded.

CAPT. SAM'L. H. WALKER

Head Quarters Army of Occupation,
Camp opposite Matamoros, July 9th, 1846

Mr. Editor—Sir, according to promise, I send you an account of the different engagements and actions, that Capt. Sam'l H. Walker has been engaged in, since his arrival at Point Isabel. I should not have taken the liberty of doing so, had it not have been for your strong solicitations for the particulars of his actions, and the different number of contradictory notices, that I have seen published in the news papers, particularly in some of the northern journals, when the accounts have often been such as might be termed ridicule, and that upon as noble and as brave a man as Texas or any other country ever produced. As I know that it must be both unpleasant and disagreeable for Captain Walker or his friends, to have seen or heard of such accounts written entirely regardless of truth. I therefore submit the following [illegible] as well as the gratification of the public.

I was informed by Capt. Walker upon his arrival at Point Isabel, that he had came down merely as a looker on, with the intention of acting as a private in a company; should any opportunity offer for revenge, (which he had such good cause to seek) as in that capacity he could gratify his secret wish and desire, better than in any other. He used every exertion to get Gen. Taylor to order down Maj. Hays' company from St. Antonio, but without success. A few Texians that came down directly after the army, insisted upon his asking the permission of Gen. Taylor to raise a company; he did so, and was refused. Shortly after this, was the murder of Col. Cross, and in a few days more Lieut. Porter was attacked and defeated, himself being killed. It was immediately after this, that he received permission to raise a company, and pitch his camp half way between the point and Matamoros, which he did. We were mustered into the service on the 21st April, 1846, numbering in all about twenty five men; he then received orders to build a picket fence around his encampment, as a protection against surprise, in five days we had this completed. The material we had to build this stockade or enclosure, was of course, as in all parts of this country, very limited, both in size and quality; we built it, however, in obedience to orders, and made it as strong and substantial as the nature of the case would admit of. On the 25th April, Capt Thornton, a brave and gallant officer, with a squadron of dragoons, was captured by the enemy; the same day we entered Gen. Taylor's camp opposite Matamoros. On his returning to his own camp, in company with one man, he was attacked by a party of frontier Mexicans, armed with rifles; he was at the time mounted on a fine war steed, presented to him I believe by Mr Harrison. He endeavoured to draw their shots by getting them to fire upon him or bring them out of the timber, but knowing him as they did, he could not succeed in either case, and therefore did not get to use Colt's revolvers with any effect. He made his way to his camp, and immediately prepared to evacuate it, finding orders to that effect from Gen. T., in case the enemy should approach with a large force.

He sent out Lieut. Jos. Wells with seven men, to the Little Colarou, in search of Col. Canales, who he supposed was there, with a party of Rancheros. He then took thirteen men, after using every precaution to secure the fifteen he left in camp from surprise, and went in search of the main body of the enemy, intending to reconoitre them, and give them a fight or run, as might be thought most prudent; but not finding them were he expected, he started for Gen. T's camp, supposing that they were on the main road in that direction but they were not to be found.

After communicating with Gen. T., he started back for his old camp at which place he arrived about 9 o'clock A. M., and found that it had been surprised by a party of four hundred Mexicans, and six men killed, and four taken prisoners, the remaining five had made their escape. This loss may be said to be the fault of the men themselves, for if they had obeyed his orders, which was to sleep in a ravine close by, and not in this fortification, they could not have been surprised. This Mexican party was still in the thicket, and of course from the number of men that he had with him, he could not think of giving them a fight, unless they should think fit to follow us into the prairie, then we might have got them scattered so as to have done them some injury. The whole force followed us to the edge of the timber, and as we moved on at a slow and steady gait, which showed them, that we were not badly frightened, they returned; this was on the 28th April. On the 29th, in the afternoon he returned with his little squad, and on the same night he buried the dead, after which, he ordered back to the point, all of his men, with the exception of one, which he kept with him, and started for Gen T's camp, at which place he arrived in safety, reported what had transpired, and returned on the next day, the enemy being in full force all the while between the two points.

On the 1st of May, he sent out Lieut. Wells as brave and as gallant an officer as ever took the field, with a small party to reconnoitre the enemy; he returned on the morning of the 2d, and reported them at La Burita or near that point. He fell in with several small parties of Mexicans while out, all of which he whipped or drove back into the main camp. He then made his way into Gen T's camp, and gave him the information, and immediately returned to the Point. I have often heard Capt. Walker say, that he could not recommend him too highly for his numerous acts of coolness and bravery.

On the 2nd May, Gen. Taylor with his army arrived at Point Isabel. On the same evening, Capt Walker and Lieut Wells started out with eighteen men, for the purpose of attacking the enemeys picket guard. After advancing about eight miles towards the place that Lt Wells had reported them the evening before, we fell in with their scouts, who were following Gen. T., for the purpose of reconnoitering his position. After discovering them, he divided us into two parties, so as to have entirely cut off their retreat, but night closed upon us before we could act, the low palmetto's favoring them as they did to avoid us; they soon reached their camp in safety, which we discovered to be on our right some four or five miles, at a place called the Palo Alto, the ground that Gen. T. had had that morning. He made it his first business of course, to gain all the information he could respecting their force and positions; he passed entirely around their camp with his men, after which he dismounted, and with one man went sufficiently close to their main lines to satisfy himself in regard to their numbers. He then returned and with his men managed to get between their camp and picket guard. Their picket numbered in all about 45 or 50 men. We come in contact with six of them that were on post, and killed five out of the six. The first shot that he fired, five of his men deserted him; three Germans, one Englishman, and one American, this left him rather too weak to attack the main body, he then [illegible] returned immediately to the point, and made his report to Gen T. He immediately discharged the men that left him in the stack: the Englishman is at present with the Mexicans, having voluntarily joined them.

He was ordered by Gen T. to take as many efficient men as he could get, to accompany Capt. May with a squadron of dragoons for the purpose of carrying communications to the fort opposite Matamoros. As his horses were very much worn down, he could find only Lieut Wells and four men, whom he considered sufficiently well mounted to undertake the hazardous duty. The bombardment on the fort had commenced about day-break and they had continued a constant fire until the time we started, which was about 3 o'clock P. M. We passed the enemies camp in the night; according to orders, Capt May halted in the chapparel, about seven miles from the Fort, to await our return. At daylight he was discovered, and the Mexicans collected their forces immediately, and caused him to retreat to the point. By fast travelling, Capt Walker managed to reach the ground upon which he had left Capt May, by sunrise. The Mexican scouts had in the mean time discovered the trail by which he had left the party, and anticipating his return, between two and three hundred were in their saddles, waiting for him. He made several attacks with men upon small parties of them, although they invariably gave way and joined the main body, which was rapidly advancing from their camp, and forming between him and the point. It was then we found out how much we all stood in need of good horses [I forgot to state that Captain Walker lost his fine horse when his camp was taken, as he left him there to rest.] As he found that it was a matter of impossibility to reach the point at that time, he started back for the fort, driving a party of Mexicans that were on his trail ahead of him, into the timber. He reached the fort in safety with his men.

After changing his horses, for some of those of the Artillery, and receiving an addition to his party of one man, Wm A Caldwell Esq., who on this occasion he made his guide, he again started for the point, taking by-paths through the chapparel, the enemy had entirely surrounded the fort with their pickets, and were advancing with their main body directly for it, at the time that he left, which was about dusk. Shortly after he started, some of the enemys' pickets discovered us, but no sooner did they do so, than they put spurs to their horses, and were soon out of sight of us in the thicket. About half an hour after we had seen the [illegible] that allowed us to pass without firing a gun, several thousand rounds of musketry were fired into the chapparel, which we supposed was an attack upon the fort, but which we afterwards learnt was to drive us back, and they never knew but what they had accomplished their ends, until the morning of the 8th.

Mr Caldwell succeeded in taking us past all the prominent points of defence that we thought the enemy would guard most strictly. We had considerable difficulty in working our way through the thick chapparel, and also to cross a Lagoon, which was about as wide, and fully as difficult to pass as the Rio Grande. We reached the prairie about 2 o'clock, it became very cloudy at that time, and there being no land marks to travel by, he made Mr Creed Taylor the guide, he being an experienced frontier man, to travel by the south-east wind, that was blowing at the time. We stopped about half an hour to rest our horses, and then continued our march. At day break we found ourselves directly on our course, and reached Point Isabel on the 5th, at 8 o'clock A. M., bringing full details of what had transpired at the Fort.

On the 7th, he was again on the march, having had all his men well mounted, with a few recruits, numbering in all 28 men. Gen. T. moved with his forces on the same evening six miles. During the night Capt. Walker, with his company scoured all the country as far as Palo Alto, and and reported no enemy to be found. That night he slept near to where the Mexicans had formerly encamped; in the morning at daybreak, started for his old camp to hunt some forage, which had been hid in the chapparrel the day previous to the attack, which had been made on his camp. As he was proceeding, his scouts on the right, composed of the celebrated frontier men, familiarly known all over Texas as the "*Taylor Boys*" and several others, discovered the enemies spies in the point of the chapparel, gave them chase and dismounted one of them. This was reported to Gen. Taylor, who was advancing on the main road, and within seven or eight miles. Capt Walker returned to his old camp, and fed his horses with the forage which had been previously hid there; he then sent all of his men except seven of the best mounted back to the command. With these he proceeded to Palo Alto, and discovered several small parties of the enemy, which he reported and continued to advance and drove in all their scouts. It was now evident that a fight would take place, as the enemeys forces were in sight and rapidly advancing.

[*To be continued.*]

The brig P. Soule, Capt. Delaville, arrived yesterday from Havana. We have received files of papers by her to the 20th inst, but find nothing in them of more than local interest.

Gen. Gaines, we perceive by the correspondence of the New York Herald, was received at Coleman's Hotel in Washington, with three hearty cheers from the assembled crowd.

The West Boston Bridge has been sold to a company in Cambridge for seventy five thousand dollars.

Congress.—In the House on the 20th, nearly the whole day was consumed in the debate on the tariff bill. Several ineffectual efforts were made to appoint a day for closing the debate. It will probably continue a week or or two longer. The Senate did not sit on the 20th.

An occupation newspaper. The *Matamoros Reveille*, one of the newspapers published by U.S. occupation forces in Mexico. Courtesy of the Special Collections Division, University of Texas at Arlington Libraries.

jor battles from Monterrey to Chapultepec and Mexico City and gave long accounts of the military and political strategy involved. At least ten other "special correspondents" followed Kendall into the field, led by Christopher Mason Haile of the *Picayune,* John Peoples for the New Orleans *Bee, Delta,* and *Crescent,* and James L. Freaner of the New Orleans *Delta.* Haile, a West Point dropout, matched Kendall's reporting ability and provided readers with detailed lists of battle casualties. Freaner and Peoples, former New Orleans printers, became accomplished writers and gained national reputations under their respective pseudonyms of "Mustang" and "Chaparral." Freaner capped his successful career as an army correspondent by personally delivering the peace treaty from Mexico City to Washington, D.C., in a then-record seventeen days. Other U.S. correspondents in Mexico were Francis A. Lumsden, Daniel Scully, Charles Callahan, and John E. Durivage of the *Picayune;* George Tobin, the *Delta;* William C. Tobey ("John of York"), *Philadelphia North American;* and John Warland, *Boston Atlas.* The reports from the correspondents with the army often supported U.S. involvement in the war and the idea of Manifest Destiny. The correspondents also empathized with the plight of the invading U.S. forces, which often were isolated in the interior of Mexico; reflected attitudes of distrust and bias against the Mexicans; and promoted and reinforced the popular war hero images of Gen. Zachary Taylor and Gen. Winfield Scott. Taylor, benefiting from a wave of favorable newspaper publicity resulting from his battlefield exploits, was elected president in 1848.

A quixotic chapter in the war was provided by the colorful publisher of the New York *Sun,* Moses Yale Beach. Accompanied by Jane McManus Storm, an editorial writer for the *Sun,* Beach arrived in Mexico City in 1847 on a secret U.S. peace mission. The effort failed and Beach, suspected of assisting antiwar forces in Mexico, barely escaped arrest. Storm, a strong advocate of Manifest Destiny, wrote prowar commentaries to the *Sun* and *New York Tribune* from Havana, Vera Cruz, and the Mexican capital under her pseudonym "Montgomery." Storm made one of the war's more memorable observations about the press coverage when she wrote, "Truth always goes home in clothes of American manufacture."

Also important to the war's coverage, a large number of U.S. printers followed in the wake of the army and established "occupation newspapers" in Mexico. Before the conflict was over, enterprising U.S. printers and publishers had established twenty-five such publications in fourteen occupied cities. Serving both the troops at the front and the public at home, these papers provided considerable war coverage. The occupation newspapers proved valuable for the U.S. military occupation of Mexico. In many instances, order was maintained only through the strict use of martial law, and many of the war papers were encouraged and funded by the

U.S. military authorities because they helped the army maintain local control by publishing official decrees and regulations.

Another valuable function of the occupation newspapers was to keep the public, at home and in Mexico, aware of conditions and issues in the expeditionary army. The U.S. press often was the channel by which officials in Washington, D.C., and Mexico City learned of actions in the other capital. For the general public, it was the only communication link.

Tom Reilly

BIBLIOGRAPHY
Copeland, Fayette. *Kendall of the Picayune.* 1943.
Eisenhower, John S. D. *So Far from God: The U.S. War with Mexico, 1846–1848.* 1989.
Johannsen, Robert W. *To the Halls of the Montezumas: The Mexican War in the American Imagination.* 1985.
Reilly, Tom. "The War Press of New Orleans: 1846–1848." *Journalism History* 13, nos. 3–4 (Autumn–Winter 1986): 86–95.
Schroeder, John H. *Mr. Polk's War: American Opposition and Dissent, 1846–1848.* 1973.

Niños Héroes

See **Los Niños Héroes**

Novels

See **Literature**

Nuevo Laredo

See **Laredo and Nuevo Laredo**

Nuevo León

Nuevo León, which is located in northeastern Mexico between the states of Coahuila and Tamaulipas, was one of the Mexican states most affected by the U.S. invasion; it endured a long occupation which lasted from 24 September 1846 until June 1848.

The inhabitants of Nuevo León, a state whose economy was based on agricultural production and livestock, encountered diverse political and social problems in the years preceding the war. Periodic droughts parched the region and made life difficult for a population dependent on what their fields could produce. Fatal illnesses such as cholera wreaked havoc among families, and constant invasions by nomadic Indians endangered the lives of settlers in the region.

One of the most serious political problems was maintaining the state's peace and stability in the face of dramatic and frequent changes brought about by the ongoing struggle between the country's centralists and federalists. The pragmatism of local leaders was crucial to maintaining Nuevo León at a distance from these internal conflicts.

The centralist coup led by Mariano Paredes y Arrillaga in late 1845 had military and political repercussions in Nuevo León. Governor Juan N. de la Garza Evia resigned in January 1846 and was replaced by Gen. Rómulo Díaz de la Vega, who also assumed the regional command of the Army of the North, a post formerly held by Gen. Mariano Arista, a much beloved military figure in Nuevo León.

Díaz de la Vega failed to govern the state effectively, however, and Garza Evia returned to the government in February. Arista, too, was recalled from his brief retirement in late April in order to march to the border and confront Gen. Zachary Taylor's army.

Deficiencies in Arista's forces quickly became evident. The regular army suffered shortages of munitions and transportation, and the auxiliary forces, made up of civilians, lacked horses, arms, and the most rudimentary training required to defend the country. A commanding officer of the auxiliary in Cerralvo complained, "Many of those making up the squadron must be discounted as useless since they possess no skills as soldiers."

Arista's defeat at Palo Alto and Resaca de la Palma in May 1846 brought about other changes in military leadership. Francisco Mejía assumed control, but after Valentín Gómez Farías's federalist coup on 6 August, Mejía was replaced by Pedro de Ampudia, another imposition from the central government.

Ampudia's appointment was greeted with anger by the local government and not a few military officials. Garza Evia and another prominent local politician and former governor, Manuel María de Llano, wrote to Gómez Farías rejecting Ampudia and requesting that a different officer take his place. These petitions were denied.

Ampudia arrived in Monterrey in late August, implemented changes in the city's defense and took political leadership of the state from Garza Evia. His changes in strategy and in the plans for fortifying the city caused doubt and confusion among the populace. As in all wars, the civilian population was divided, responding with a diversity of reactions that alternated between fear and patriotic fervor, confusion and clarity of purpose, cowardice and heroism, and rejection of and collaboration with the invaders.

Monterrey marked its 250th anniversary on 20 September 1846, the day that U. S. forces arrived and surrounded the city. The battle began the following day, and after three days of heavy combat, Ampudia surrendered the plaza on the morning of 24 September.

Some, like Nuevo León's governor Francisco de Paula Morales, blamed Ampudia for the defeat. Manuel Balbontín, a witness from among the Mexican army, wrote that instability and disorganization contributed to the fall of Monterrey. These were no doubt important factors; in the five months preceding the battle, military control had changed hands four times and in a thirty-day period before the battle there had been four governors, three of them appointed by the central government.

The impact of the U. S. occupation varied throughout the state of Nuevo León. Monterrey and other towns suffered destruction, but the majority were unaffected. The main problem stemmed from the presence of volunteers in Taylor's army. Many of these, especially the Texians, came to Mexico seeking revenge for the atrocities committed by Santa Anna's army during the Texas Revolution a decade before. They abused the population to such an extent that Governor Morales wrote to Taylor protesting civilian deaths "at the hands of these very volunteers who, without pity or reasonable motive of any kind, take lives simply because it is in their power to do so."

Life was difficult for the inhabitants of the ranches and *haciendas* of the countryside as well. They fell victim not only to the depredations of the U.S. forces but also to guerrilla bands, who, rather than attacking the U.S. troops, dedicated themselves to antagonizing and looting their fellow Mexicans.

This problem could not be resolved by a state government that virtually disappeared during the chaotic year of 1847. In March, Governor Morales, who had abandoned the capital and tried to establish his government in the southern part of the state, decided that conditions made it impossible to govern, and so he abandoned his office and left the municipalities to their fate. He attempted to return in September, but conditions did not greatly improve and he was replaced by José María Parás in January 1848. Parás also found governance impossible until late February, when the Treaty of Guadalupe Hidalgo established the basis for the reorganization of the state government.

Not all of the towns in the state suffered equally from the war. Some of them—Cerralvo, Marín, and Monterrey in particular—were greatly affected while the peace and tranquility of others, especially in the south and southeast, was hardly disturbed as they managed to maintain normal rythms of labor and production. In fact, some of the state's growers and cattle ranchers benefited by selling their products to the U.S. Army. After almost two years, the occupation of Nuevo León ended in June 1848 when the U.S. Army abandoned the state.

Miguel Angel González Quiroga
Translated by The Horse's Mouth Language Services

BIBLIOGRAPHY

Alcaraz, Ramón, ed. *The Other Side; or, Notes for the History of the War between Mexico and the United States.* Translated by Albert C. Ramsey. 1970. Originally published as *Apuntes para la historia de la Guerra entre México y los Estado Unidos,* 1848.

Balbontín, Manuel. *Año de 1846: Capitulación de la ciudad de Monterrey.* Reprint, 1974.

Cossío, David Alberto. *Historia de Nuevo León.* Vol. 6. 1925.

Nuevo Mexicanos

Juan de Oñate brought the first permanent Spanish colonists to the province of New Mexico in 1598. A bloody uprising orchestrated by the Indian Pueblos drove the Spaniards from New Mexico in 1680, but the colonists returned in force and reoccupied the province twelve years later. By the 1820s the population of New Mexico was more than forty thousand, including the Pueblos. *Mestizos,* those of mixed Spanish and Indian parentage, made up the largest percentage of the population. The principal settlements were at El Paso del Norte, Santa Fe (the capital), Santa Cruz de la Cañada, and Albuquerque, and there were dozens of small *ranchos* and villages (called *plazas*), primarily along the valley of the Río Grande. Sheep raising and subsistence farming were the main occupations of the settlers. Manufactured items, with the exception of locally woven rugs and *serapes,* were scarce and expensive, as there were no factories in New Mexico. Before Mexican independence in 1821, the trade of the province was tightly controlled by Chihuahua merchants to the south (Spanish law forbade trade with foreigners). With independence, however, came the inauguration of legal trade with the United States along the Santa Fe Trail. This commerce had a dramatic impact on New Mexico. The material culture of the New Mexicans, or at least that of the *ricos,* underwent a revolution as cotton and woolen textiles and numerous manufactured goods virtually flooded the market. Also, a rising class of New Mexican merchants soon competed equally in the trade with their U.S. counterparts, and their annual caravans employed many New Mexican teamsters and herders. Additionally, customs duties collected on the trade goods helped pay the salaries of officials and soldiers in the capital.

Still, the majority of New Mexicans remained poor and, being far removed from Mexico City, had several legitimate reasons for feeling neglected by their government. The most pressing problem was the depredations on the settlements by various Indian tribes, including the Apaches, Utes, and Navajos. The presidial garrisons in the Department of New Mexico were grossly undermanned, lacked adequate mounts, and were poorly armed. Some frustrated New Mexicans suggested that they should join the United States, rumblings that

did not go unnoticed by U.S. traders. It is no surprise that in his invasion of New Mexico, Gen. Stephen W. Kearny promised the citizenry that for their "allegiance, they would be protected by the United States government from the Indians."

Because of the ties that New Mexico had developed with the United States, opinions about the U.S. conquest were mixed. Governor Manuel Armijo had gathered a large force in August 1846 to resist the U.S. invasion but then abruptly disbanded it (there is considerable controversy over this episode), thus allowing Kearny to take Santa Fe without firing a shot. Some New Mexicans filled political offices under the new U.S. regime. Yet a plot was hatched in December 1846 to overthrow U.S. forces in the capital, which was discovered before it could be implemented, and a deadly revolt erupted in Taos in January 1847, which was put down only after hard fighting.

Although annexation came with the Treaty of Guadalupe Hidalgo in 1848, the situation of most New Mexicans, especially in remote settlements, did not noticeably improve. And while an increased military presence in the territory brought additional jobs and the opportunity to market livestock, grains, and hay to various forts, Indian depredations that Kearny had promised to keep in check remained a problem for another four decades.

Mark L. Gardner

BIBLIOGRAPHY

Boyle, Susan Calafate. *Los Capitalistas: Hispano Merchants and the Santa Fe Trade.* 1997.

Carroll, H. Bailey, and J. Villasana Haggard, eds. *Three New Mexico Chronicles.* 1942.

Gonzales, Manuel G. *The Hispanic Elite of the Southwest.* 1989.

Vigil, Donaciano. *Arms, Indians, and the Mismanagement of New Mexico.* Edited by David J. Weber. 1986.

Weber, David J. *The Mexican Frontier, 1821–1846: The American Southwest under Mexico.* 1982.

Numbers and Losses

By percentage, the U.S.–Mexican War was the most deadly war in the history of the United States. The most common cause of death was dysentery, followed by various types of camp fever. Out of an average regiment of 1,000 men, 110 did not live to return home. Some units were struck harder than others. The 1st South Carolina Infantry had the sad distinction of having the highest casualty rate, losing slightly more than 400 out of 1,007 officers and enlisted men. Conversely, some regiments had relatively low death rates, losing fewer than ten men to enemy action, disease, or accident. Location and duty assignment (combat vs. garrison) were contributing factors to a unit's casualty rate.

Statistics show that the regulars, who made up a smaller percentage of the total number of U.S. troops employed in the war, bore the brunt of the fighting, losing 935 in action. Battle deaths for the volunteers amounted to 613. The figures also indicate that the rate of death by disease was higher for volunteers, 6,256 as compared to 4,714 for the regulars. Most observers attributed the difference in the rate of disease to the fact that volunteers and their officers—fresh from civil life—did not know how to care for themselves properly in camp or on campaign, often eating their food half cooked or fried and sleeping directly on the damp ground. Regulars, however, seemed to fare better under the watchful eye of their officers, whose strict discipline ensured a higher level of health.

Mexican casualty rates are more difficult to ascertain. Writing at the war's conclusion, however, Abiel Abbot Livermore considered the question, saying "we set the estimate of the number of soldiers no doubt within very moderate bounds, if we should say, that three times the number compared with our troops were in the field, and that the loss in battle averaged three times as much; and that the loss in battle and sickness together was as much or more than that of the Americans."

Richard Bruce Winders

BIBLIOGRAPHY

Livermore, Abiel Abbot. *The War with Mexico Reviewed.* 1850.

Winders, Richard B. *Mr. Polk's Army: The American Military Experience in the Mexican War.* 1997.

Ocampo, Melchor

Born in the town of Peteo, Michoacán, politician Melchor Ocampo (1814–1861) spent his childhood in Mexico City. He returned home to study at the Colegio San Nicolás in the city of Morelia and then went to law school but never earned his degree. An amateur naturalist and student of Indian languages, Ocampo traveled to Europe in 1840 and became fascinated with the writings of French anarchist Pierre Proudhon. Upon returning to Mexico in 1842, Ocampo joined the ranks of *puro* liberals and served in the constituent congress of that year.

Ocampo held the post of governor of Michoacán from September 1846 to March 1848 and in that capacity raised troops and money to support the war effort against the United States. He opposed, even after the fall of Mexico City in September 1847, any peace settlement with the invaders. Ocampo also took up the cry for continued resistance relying on the hit-and-run tactics of guerilla warfare to drive out the U.S. occupation. He lent his assistance to the June 1848 uprising led by Father Celedonio Jarauta, which called for a renewal of hostilities with popular forces.

After the war with the United States Ocampo became one of the luminaries of the Mexican Reform. Exiled from Mexico soon after Gen. Antonio López de Santa Anna began his last presidency in April 1853, Ocampo became the leader of the revolutionary clique in New Orleans that sought to overthrow that regime. He returned to Mexico, held various cabinet posts between 1855 and 1859, and served as a deputy to the congress that drafted the 1857 constitution. Ocampo's reputation was damaged when in 1859 he negotiated the McLane-Ocampo treaty—never ratified by the U.S.—which gave that country transit rights across the Isthmus of Tehuantepec and along Mexico's northern border. His place in the pantheon of Mexican heroes, however, was salvaged by the brutal death he suffered at the hands of conservative guerrillas on 3 June 1861.

Pedro Santoni

BIBLIOGRAPHY

Obras completas de D. Melchor Ocampo. 5 vols. 1985–1986.

Olliff, Donathon C. *Reforma Mexico and the United States: A Search for Alternatives to Annexation.* 1981.

Valadés, José C. *Don Melchor Ocampo, reformador de México.* 1954.

Occupation of Mexico

Despite the doubtful legitimacy of the U.S. war against Mexico, in general the regular U.S. Army behaved with respect toward the institutions and the populace of the country it occupied. This was exemplified in Matamoros, where Gen. Zachary Taylor recognized the city council in office at the time and defended its continuance based on the right of jus gentium. This became a pattern in other Mexican towns, although in some municipalities, such as Tampico and Vera Cruz, the councils dissolved and the U.S. forces became military authorities with civil functions.

While in Jalapa before advancing into central Mexico, Gen. Winfield Scott calmed the population by assuring local authorities that private property, civil liberties and guarantees, as well as the church and religious freedom would be respected and that crime—even that committed by U.S. troops—would be punished. He did, however, declare martial law in order to control relations between his army and the Mexican authorities and population.

Nevertheless, in its military actions, the U.S. Army did not hesitate to use its force to the fullest, even if it brought devastating consequences to the civilian population, as was observed in Monterrey, New Mexico, and Vera Cruz. The siege

301

of Monterrey involved ferocious combat that inflicted great material losses on the population. When the inhabitants of New Mexico, led by the native Tomás Ortiz, rebelled and killed Governor Charles Bent and five Anglo-Americans, Col. Sterling Price reacted quickly, attacking the rebels at Taos. The principal leaders were killed and the rest of the rebels dispersed. In confronting resistance and fortifications at the port of Vera Cruz, the U.S. Army and marines implemented an intense bombardment of the city from 22 to 26 March 1847, causing about five hundred civilian deaths and five million pesos of damage to homes, buildings, and merchandise. General Scott and Commo. Matthew C. Perry capitalized on this civilian suffering; by refusing to allow the consulates of Spain and France to assist in civilian evacuation, they pressed Gen. Juan Morales to negotiate surrender.

The civilian population suffered as well under attacks by guerrilla forces against the U.S. invaders because the U.S. Army, as a warning to cities, townships, and whole vicinities, held them responsible for damages and losses to its war machine. One such case occurred in the township of Guadalupe, near Mexico City, when the town council was arrested for divesting a U.S. soldier of his weapons and his horse.

After Mexico City was occupied, General Scott officially recognized the city council, which was headed by Reyes Veramendi. He also allowed the continued functioning of the local police and granted that the civil administration continue to take charge of routine court cases, except when U.S. forces were involved or when they took on a political nature. He appointed Gen. John A. Quitman military governor. In consideration for its protection, the U.S. Army charged the city council 150,000 pesos, which was used to care for U.S. soldiers wounded during the campaign. To cover this cost, the city council pledged money from district revenue sources that remained under its control such as customs, the post, tobacco, and direct contributions. As the occupation continued, the U.S. Army increased its authority in some towns by assuming control of public works, jails, and judicial administration and by taking over the collection of various public revenues. In Mexico City, the U.S. military governor authorized gambling and assessed one thousand pesos per table per month.

At the end of 1847, U.S military authorities allowed for the renovation of city hall in Mexico City. This went against Mexican laws and was done purposely to cultivate a city government that would collaborate or accept peace terms, thereby putting pressure on the national government of Mexico, which was headquartered in Querétaro. Some Mexican politicians were under the impression that if the country were not to lose its autonomy altogether, it must submit to the new U.S. order. One of these was Francisco Suárez Iriarte, who began the movement for renovation of Mexico City's city hall. He was named president of the new municipal assembly, one of the first functions of which was to change the city's political definition to that of state. These advantages did not prevent the U.S. occupiers from demanding a new loan of 668,000 pesos, which the municipal assembly was obliged to pass on to the people in the form of a 6-percent tax on revenues and other payments.

Foreign trade, formerly heavily taxed under the Mexican fiscal system, was simplified under U.S. control of maritime customs. The U.S. military levied a low tax, which helped the U.S. invaders finance war costs and as a byproduct stimulated contraband. The state monopoly on tobacco was also abolished, as well as the tax on domestic trade. During the occupation, the U.S. forces paid for their provisions, which caused a flow of dollars in occupied areas and facilitated the circulation of foodstuffs and merchandise.

U.S. soldiers developed a taste for tropical fruits, which they ate peels and all. They consumed candle tallow as a substitute for butter and traded salt pork and flour for local products, especially rum. Rum was heavily taxed, and restrictions were placed on its distribution because it not only caused soldiers to "lose their heads" but also sometimes their lives, as Mexican peasants used it to lure them away from their companions. Nevertheless, U.S. forces caused little disturbance among the locals and comported themselves well in the churches. They developed a curious language to make themselves understood, especially with the peddlers of fruit and trinkets. They respected women, dealing with the prostitutes and marrying some of them, who at the war's end accompanied their new husbands back to the United States.

Nevertheless the conduct of the U.S. volunteers left much to be desired. After an area was occupied, and there was little left to do, they often resorted to theft and treated the Mexicans abusively. This was plain from the outset of the war, when Texas volunteers preyed on the ranches in northern Tamaulipas and Nuevo León. The U.S. Army installed public pillories in Mexico City to punish soldiers and volunteers who disobeyed the law. There, U.S. culprits were flogged along with Mexican offenders.

To amuse themselves in the Mexican capital, U.S soldiers enjoyed the shows at the Nuevo México Teatro and frequented the dance halls on Coliseo and Betlemitas Calles. In the Hotel Bella-Unión they set up a canteen where there were gambling tables and prostitutes. U.S. citizens published various newspapers during the U.S occupation of Mexico, in which they reported the progress of the war, promoted factionalism among Mexicans, and advertised various businesses and shows.

Octavio Herrera

Translated by The Horse's Mouth Language Services

BIBLIOGRAPHY

Roa Bárcena, José María. *Recuerdos de la invasión americana 1846–1848 por un jóven de entonces.* 1888.

O'Hara, Theodore

U.S. Army officer, poet, newspaper editor, adventurer, and political activist Theodore O'Hara (1820–1867) received his army commission as captain and assistant quartermaster as a reward for faithful service to the Democratic Party. During the fall of 1846 he was stationed in Cerralvo, Mexico, midway between Monterrey and Camargo, engaged in stockpiling supplies and dispatching essential equipment, ordnance, and food to Gen. Zachary Taylor's army. In December 1846 he took charge of Brig. Gen. John A. Quitman's wagon train during a dangerous transfer of base to Tampico.

O'Hara accompanied Quitman's brigade to Vera Cruz and took part in the siege of that fortress. In June 1847 he was promoted to chief quartermaster of Maj. Gen. Gideon J. Pillow's division. Pillow tended to use O'Hara as an aide-de-camp, and it was in this capacity at Contreras that O'Hara won commendation for gallantry and promotion to major.

Following the U.S.–Mexican War O'Hara became deeply involved in an ill-fated 1850 invasion of Cuba, where he commanded a company in the 2d Cavalry. He later edited newspapers in Louisville and New Orleans. During the Civil War he served as a staff officer under John C. Breckinridge and Albert Sidney Johnston. He died in Alabama in 1867.

What permanently links O'Hara's name to the U.S.–Mexican War, however, is the poem he wrote soon after the war ended to honor the war dead of Kentucky. "Bivouac of the Dead" became a celebrated nineteenth-century poem in the United States, appearing in national cemeteries from Arlington, Virginia, to Little Bighorn in present-day Montana, and in anthologies well into the twentieth century.

> On Fame's eternal camping ground
> Their silent tents are spread
> And Glory guards with solemn round
> The bivouac of the dead.

Nathaniel C. Hughes, Jr.

BIBLIOGRAPHY

Hughes, Nathaniel Cheairs, Jr., and Thomas C. Ware. *Theodore O'Hara.* Forthcoming.

Ranck, George Washington. *The Bivouac of the Dead and Its Author.* 1898.

Oregon Territory

Disputed by rival powers since its "discovery" in the late eighteenth century, Oregon Territory extended from the Pacific Ocean to the continental divide and, after Spanish (1819) and Russian (1824–1825) concessions, from California to 54°40′ north latitude. The United States and Great Britain remained antagonistic claimants, each citing respective explorations and fur-trading ventures. With no agreement on division, conventions between Great Britain and the United States in 1818 and 1827 accepted joint occupation.

The Oregon question dangerously intensified in the mid-1840s. U.S. commercial demand for Puget Sound harbors rose with confirmation that the Columbia River could not service hoped-for Asian trade. Land-hungry westerners, meanwhile, flowed along the Oregon Trail into the fertile Willamette Valley as "Oregon fever" gripped the popular imagination. Accordingly, the expansionist 1844 Democratic platform sought cross-sectional support by pairing an all-Oregon demand with that for Texas.

President James K. Polk brazenly reasserted the U.S. title to Oregon as "clear and unquestionable," but fears of British–Mexican cooperation moved him to renew a U.S. offer to divide Oregon at the 49th parallel. The premature rejection by British minister Richard Pakenham angered Polk, who then fueled passionate congressional debate by calling for the abrogation of joint occupation.

By 1846, Manifest Destiny and "Fifty-four forty or fight" bombast appeared to be rushing the United States headlong into simultaneous wars. Soberly, however, Polk hinted openness to an Oregon compromise, an opportunity then also welcome in London. Foreign Secretary Lord Aberdeen cooperatively reproposed the 49th parallel, except retaining all of Vancouver Island. The Oregon Treaty, signed 15 June in Washington, D.C., removed a long-standing source of friction between Great Britain and the United States and freed U.S. leaders to conduct war with Mexico unhindered.

David Alan Greer

BIBLIOGRAPHY

Goetzmann, William H. *When the Eagle Screamed: The Romantic Horizon in American Diplomacy, 1800–1860.* 1966.

Merk, Frederick. *The Oregon Question: Essays in Anglo-American Diplomacy and Politics.* 1967.

Pletcher, David M. *The Diplomacy of Annexation: Texas, Oregon, and the Mexican War.* 1973.

Sellers, Charles Grier. *James K. Polk: Continentalist, 1843–1846.* 1966.

Ortega, José María

Born in Mexico City, José María Ortega (1793–1871) joined the Spanish army around 1810. In the War for Independence, he fought against the Mexican insurgents in a dragoon regiment but in 1821 changed sides. Ortega rose to the rank of colonel and commanded the artillery of Gen. Anastasio Bustamante. In 1822 Ortega assumed command of the Provincias Internas in the north of Mexico, but by 1830 he commanded the artillery of Gen. Nicolás Bravo in southern Mexico.

In 1835 Ortega participated in Antonio López de Santa Anna's Texas campaign. After the fall of the Alamo, Colonel Ortega briefly commanded at that post before being ordered to destroy the old mission and fall back at the conclusion of the campaign. In 1841 Ortega was promoted to general of brigade.

From 1844 to 1846 General Ortega served as commandant general of Nuevo León and held that same position for San Luis Potosí in 1847. He commanded the 3d Division of Gen. Antonio López de Santa Anna's army at the Battle of Buena Vista on 22 February 1847. Ortega's commander noted that he "performed his duties to my satisfaction."

After the battle, he resumed his post in San Luis Potosí. In 1853 General Ortega assumed command as commandant general of the district of Jalisco. He subsequently retired from the military and died in Mexico City in 1871.

Donald S. Frazier

BIBLIOGRAPHY

Carreño, Alberto M., ed. *Jefes del ejército Mexicano en 1847: Biografías de generales de división y brigadad y de coroneles del ejército Mexicano por fines del año de 1847*. 1914.

Mansfield, E. O. *The Mexican War*. 1848.

Smith, Justin H. *The War with Mexico*. 2 vols. 1919. Reprint, 1963.

Ortiz de Ayala, S. Tadeo

Born 18 October in Mascota in the intendancy of Guadalajara (present-day Jalisco), Mexican economist and colonizer Tadeo Ortiz (1788–1833) studied Latin and philosophy in Mexico City before journeying to Spain in 1809 to complete his formal education. While there, he became committed to the cause of Mexican independence. Ortiz spent much of the following decade traveling throughout the Americas and Europe as a revolutionary agent in an effort to obtain foreign aid for the insurgents' cause.

Returning to Mexico in 1821, Ortiz dedicated himself to the economic development of the new nation. Between 1824 and 1831 he surveyed the Isthmus of Tehuantepec to assess its potential as a future interoceanic transportation route and made a largely unsuccessful attempt to set up colonies in the region. In 1832 he was commissioned by the Mexican government to inspect and report on conditions in Texas. In his reports and a book, *México considerado como nación independiente y libre,* published that same year, Ortiz urged the development and defense of Mexico's northern border regions to halt U.S. expansionism. In addition to legislation prohibiting further Anglo-American immigration to Texas, he recommended that Mexico undertake counter-colonization programs, which involved the settling of Mexican and European families in the region. Appointed director of colonization in Texas in 1833 by the liberal administration of President Valentín Gómez Farías, Ortiz died as a result of a cholera epidemic six days after embarking at Vera Cruz for New Orleans to assume his new position.

Lawrence D. Taylor

BIBLIOGRAPHY

Ortiz de Ayala, Simón Tadeo. *México considerado como nación independiente y libre*. 1832.

Timmons, Wilbert H. "Tadeo Ortiz and Texas." *Southwestern Historical Quarterly* 72 (1968): 21–33.

Timmons, Wilbert H. *Tadeo Ortiz: Mexican Colonizer and Reformer*. 1974.

Ostend Manifesto

The Ostend Manifesto of 1854 was connected with the annexationist movement in Cuba—a Spanish possession—whose aim was to join that island to the United States. In the middle of the nineteenth century the annexationists were searching for support within the United States, and they found it among several Southern politicians. Among them were Pierre Soulé, a "Young American" and U.S. senator from Louisiana, and John A. Quitman, a supporter of Mexico's annexation to the United States, who had taken part in the Mexican campaign. An invasion force composed chiefly of veterans of the U.S.–Mexican War actually sailed for Cuba from New Orleans. Although it failed to achieve the aims of the annexationists, it seriously damaged relations between the United States and Spain. The Spanish government, aware of the U.S. government's support for the annexation of Texas in the mid-1840s, feared the possibility of open support by the U.S. government for annexationist goals in Cuba, and thus sought support from Great Britain and France, which in turn provoked resentment in the United States. There, especially in the South, there was once again talk of the danger of Cuba falling under the control of a European power more powerful than Spain. Thus, President Franklin Pierce in 1853 named Pierre Soulé U.S. minister to Madrid, his mission to persuade the Spanish government to sell the colony to the United States. Soulé was unsuccessful, and his rude behavior worsened relations between the two countries. The tension reached a peak at the beginning of 1854, when action by the Spanish authorities in Havana, the capital of Cuba, against the captain of the U.S. ship *Black Warrior* sparked a diplomatic conflict. Secretary of State William L. Marcy thereupon instructed the U.S. ministers in London, Paris, and Madrid to meet in order to assess the prospect for U.S. acquisition of Cuba and to gauge the reactions of European powers to such a move. The ambassadors began their meetings on 9 October in Ostend, Belgium, and in Aix-la-Chapelle, Prussia, on 18 October they signed the document, whose main author appears to have been Pierre Soulé.

At the outset the signatories expressed their conviction

that the U.S. government should make every effort to conclude an agreement with Spain for the purchase of Cuba. In their view this question was of equal importance for both sides, so that eventual failure of the project must be attributed to the intervention of foreign powers, who had no right to meddle in the affair. According to the authors of the manifesto, the natural market of U.S. goods on the Atlantic and Pacific coasts could never be guaranteed except by control of the island, and control of Cuba by any European power would pose a permanent threat to the United States. So long as Cuba was not part of the United States, it would be impossible to speak of "guaranteed security" of the Union. For Spain, the project offered a financial resource, while rejecting it brought the risk of losing not only the offered sum but also the colony itself, where a "successful revolution" might lead to liquidation of the Spanish colonial government. Should any of the powers extend aid to Spain, nothing could prevent the United States from helping its neighbors and friends in Cuba in their civil war. Refusal of the U.S. offer would expose Spain to the danger that the United States, vitally interested in acquiring the island, might consider any means to achieve its aims. In conclusion the signatories warned of the "Africanization" of Cuba and the danger of a repetition of the events in St. Domingue, which would represent a grave threat to the security of the United States. The ministers' view was that events were in fact moving in that direction, and that the United States must be prepared for the worst.

The Ostend Manifesto was widely seen as a direct threat not only to Spain but also to the stability of a sensitive region of the Americas. Therefore it was roundly rejected in Madrid, and also in London and Paris. Fears of international complications and the opposition to the activities of the expansionists from within the United States prompted President Pierce and Secretary Marcy to adopt a critical stance toward the manifesto. Marcy did not accept the recommendations of his ministers, and Pierre Soulé resigned his post in Madrid before the end of the year. He did not abandon his expansionist attitude toward the regions south of the United States, however, as was shown by his later activities in connection with the Isthmus of Tehuantepec.

Josef Opatrný

BIBLIOGRAPHY

Commager, Henry S., and Milton Cantor, eds. *Documents of American History*, vol. 1, pp. 333–335. 10th ed. 1988.

Ettinger, Amos. *The Mission to Spain of Pierre Soulé, 1853–1855.* 1932.

Manning, William R., ed. *Diplomatic Correspondence of the United States: Inter-American Affairs, 1831–1860.* 1932–1939.

May, Robert E. *The Southern Dream of a Caribbean Empire, 1854–1861.* 1973.

Opatrný, Josef. *U.S. Expansionism and Cuban Annexationism in the 1850s.* 1990.

O'Sullivan, John L.

Democratic editor and political operative John L. O'Sullivan (1812–1895) was one of the most eloquent spokesmen for radical Jacksonian Democracy. He was a friend and promoter of Nathaniel Hawthorne and a leading foe of capital punishment. Editor of two influential publications, the *United States Magazine and Democratic Review* and the New York *Morning News,* O'Sullivan in 1845 coined the phrase *manifest destiny,* which came to symbolize the physical expansion of the United States. In his "Annexation" article in the July–August 1845 issue of the *Democratic Review* (volume 7, pp. 5–10), he wrote that the annexation of Texas was "the fulfillment of our manifest destiny to overspread the continent allotted by Providence for the free development of our yearly multiplying millions." He repeated the phrase in the *Morning News* (27 December 1845) while addressing the issue of the Oregon boundary dispute. Reluctant to resort to arms, O'Sullivan believed territory could be acquired by the United States through a voluntary, evolutionary process rather than through war. Some of his last editorials in the *Morning News* (11 and 13 May 1845), reacting to the first shots of the U.S.–Mexican War, questioned the circumstances that brought Gen. Zachary Taylor's troops into conflict with Mexican forces.

Forced out of the newspaper in May 1846 by disgruntled backers, O'Sullivan then sold the magazine, which he had founded in 1837, the following month. He later was involved in Narciso Lopez's attempts to liberate Cuba from Spain and served as the U.S. diplomatic representative to Portugal from 1854 to 1858. A supporter of the Confederacy during the Civil War, he returned to the United States in the 1870s, dabbled in spiritualism, and lived in obscurity until his death in New York City.

Robert D. Sampson

BIBLIOGRAPHY

Harris, Sheldon H. "The Public Career of John Louis O'Sullivan." Ph.D. diss., Columbia University, 1958.

Pratt, Julius W. "John L. O'Sullivan and Manifest Destiny." *New York History* 14 (July 1933): 213–234.

Sampson, Robert D. " 'Under the Banner of the Democratic Principle': John Louis O'Sullivan, the Democracy and the *Democratic Review*." Ph.D. diss., University of Illinois, 1995.

Otero, Mariano

Mexican politician Mariano Otero (1817–1850) was born in the city of Guadalajara. Otero received his baccalaureate at the age of eighteen and later developed a unique brand of romantic liberalism through the study of writers such as Sismonde de Sismondi, Benjamin Constant, Thomas Jefferson, and Alexis de Tocqueville. After his election to congress in 1842, Otero influenced and was influenced by several of

Mexico's political luminaries, including Manuel Gómez Pedraza and Ignacio Cumplido. It was through Cumplido that Otero began to write for Mexico City's most prominent liberal newspaper, *El Siglo XIX*, producing several essays in which he announced his particular strain of socially conscious, constitutional liberalism.

By 1846 Otero, a *moderado* federalist, had become one of the most outspoken and influential members of Mexico's Chamber of Deputies. Along with many of his political and ideological associates, he admired various aspects of the liberal republic to the north. However, he was not oblivious to the open solicitation toward Texas by the United States. Far from harboring a divided loyalty, Otero vehemently condemned the U.S. invasion and called for national unity to face the invaders. Following the fall of Mexico City, he repeatedly called for continued resistance against the U.S. forces by means of guerilla warfare and urged rejection of the Treaty of Guadelupe Hidalgo.

Even in the face of the U.S. invasion, however, Otero was not prepared to surrender his domestic political agenda. He is said to have been the chief organizer of the 1847 Polkos Revolt in which factions of the civic militia sought to overturn the *puro* government of President Valentín Gómez Farías at the very moment that U.S. forces were poised to open a new front on Mexico's eastern coast. Otero died prematurely of cholera three years later.

M. Bruce Colcleugh

BIBLIOGRAPHY

Hale, Charles. *Mexican Liberalism in the Age of Mora, 1821–1853.* 1968.

Otero, Mariano. *Consideraciones sobre la situación política y social de la República mexicana en la año 1848.* 1848.

Otero, Mariano. *Essayo sobre el verdadero estado de la cuestión social y política que se agita en la República mexicana.* 1842.

Otero, Mariano. *Obras. Recopilación, Selección, Comentario y Estudio Preliminar de Jesús Reyes Heroles.* 2 vols. 1967.

Oury, William Sanders

A soldier, businessman, and politician, William Sanders Oury (1817–1887) was born 13 August. Oury lived in Abingdon, Virginia, and Missouri, until 1834, when he migrated to Texas. He served as a private at the Alamo from 23 to 29 February 1836, when William B. Travis sent him to Sam Houston with dispatches. He then fought in Houston's army, and was present at the 21 April 1836 Battle of San Jacinto. On 30 December 1837 he left the Republic of Texas army, remaining in Texas until joining the Texas Rangers in 1839, probably as a corporal. In 1842 he participated in the Mier Expedition into northern Mexico, where the Mexican army captured him and imprisoned him at Perote in Mexico City until his release on 16 September 1844. Returned to Texas, Oury joined the 1st Regiment of Texas Mounted Volunteers. He fought Mexican forces on 8 and 9 May 1846 at the battles of Palo Alto and Resaca de la Palma and on 22 to 24 September at the Battle of Monterrey. Discharged at the end of 1846, he joined Ben McCulloch's spy company (January–February 1847).

Oury lived in San Antonio, Texas, during 1848 and 1849, where he married Inez Garcia. They lived in San Francisco and Sacramento, California, from 1849 to 1856, when he journeyed to Tucson, Arizona. Although originally a Confederate sympathizer during the Civil War, upon Union occupation he helped organize a civil government. He held several public offices, including that of the first mayor of Tucson (1863), an alderman, and sheriff of Pima County. He also was an organizer of and participant in the Camp Grant Massacre of Apache Indians on 30 April 1871. He died in Tucson 31 March 1887.

Joseph A. Stout, Jr.

BIBLIOGRAPHY

Smith, Cornelius C., Jr. *William Sanders Oury: History Maker of the Southwest.* 1967.

Wagoner, Jay J. *Arizona Territory 1863–1912, A Political History.* 1970.

P-Q

Pakenham, Richard

Richard Pakenham (1797–1868) was born on 19 May into a distinguished family, his father an admiral and his uncle a famous general. Pakenham attended Trinity College in Dublin, Ireland, and became an attaché in October 1817 at the Hague. In 1824 he was transferred to Switzerland, where he served until his appointment as foreign minister to Mexico in March of 1825.

While in Mexico he enjoyed close working relations with that country's most prominent political leaders, but was unable to obtain Mexico's recognition of the Texas Republic, which had declared its independence in 1836. Pakenham argued that Texas would serve as a buffer state, protecting Mexico from territorial encroachment by the United States.

His next appointment came as the British foreign minister to the United States, a post which he held from 1843 to 1847. Pakenham's correspondence with Secretary of State John C. Calhoun sparked an international controversy over the British government's role on behalf of the abolition movement. Calhoun, a staunch advocate of southern interests, suspected that the British were seeking the abolition of slavery in Texas. Any effort by Her Majesty's government to undermine slavery in the Lone Star Republic, Calhoun warned, would impinge directly upon the stability of the institution in the American South. The secretary of state went on to lecture the British minister on the advantages of slavery to both races, which created a firestorm of protest among abolitionists in the United States when his correspondence with Pakenham was published in the national press.

By far the most important of Pakenham's duties during his tenure as British minister to the United States was the resolution of the Oregon boundary dispute. Great Britain and the United States had signed a joint occupation agreement in 1818, but the question threatened to bring the two countries to the verge of war in the mid-1840s when Democratic expansionists insisted that the United States had a valid claim to the entire Pacific Northwest. Soon after his inauguration, U.S. president James K. Polk offered to divide the territory at the 49th parallel, a proposal which represented a marked retreat from his "All Oregon" position during the 1844 presidential campaign. Without consulting his superiors in London, Pakenham promptly rejected the offer on the grounds that it did not grant the British navigation rights on the Columbia River, a point which the Tyler administration had conceded one year earlier. Anxious to defuse tensions with the United States, British foreign secretary Lord Aberdeen ordered Pakenham to reopen negotiations, but Polk, ever suspicious of the British, refused to resubmit the compromise proposal. In a move that was widely regarded on both sides of the Atlantic as an ominous first step toward hostilities, Polk in December 1845 urged Congress to end the joint occupation of Oregon and assume full control of the territory, British claims to the region notwithstanding. Determined to "look John Bull straight in the eye," Polk refused to consider an offer by Pakenham to submit the Oregon dispute to international arbitration. Washington soon abandoned its policy of brinkmanship, however, unwilling to risk a war with Great Britain as it moved closer to a conflict with Mexico. Once again adopting a conciliatory posture, the Polk administration in 1846 agreed to accept the 49th parallel compromise line. The Oregon treaty was ratified by the Senate by a wide margin in June, one month after Washington's declaration of war against Mexico.

In 1847 Pakenham returned to Britain. He was appointed minister to Portugal in 1851, a position which he held for four years. Retiring from public life, he lived at Castle Pollard, Ireland, until his death on 28 October 1868.

Clay Cothrum

BIBLIOGRAPHY

Niven, John. *John Calhoun and the Price of Union: A Biography.* 1988.

Peterson, Merrill. *The Great Triumvirate: Webster, Clay, and Calhoun.* 1987.

Pletcher, David M. *The Diplomacy of Annexation: Texas, Oregon and The Mexican War.* 1973.

Sidney, Lee, ed. *Dictionary of National Biography.* 1895.

Padierna

See **Contreras and Churubusco**

Paintings

See **Art**

Palmerston, Lord

See **Temple, Henry John**

Palo Alto, Battle of

Fought on 8 May 1846 between U.S. forces led by Gen. Zachary Taylor and the Mexican Army of the North under Gen. Mariano Arista, the Battle of Palo Alto was the first major engagement of the U.S.–Mexican War (1846–1848). Although the Mexican army suffered many casualties, the battle was indecisively fought as darkness ended the battle. The immediate factor leading to the battle was the U.S. buildup of forces on the north bank of the Río Grande near Matamoros and at Corpus Christi as well as at Point Isabel on the Texas coast. The U.S. occupation of the lower Río Grande resulted from the U.S. annexation of Texas in 1845, which Mexico considered a violation of its sovereignty.

For several months the U.S. forces had occupied Fort Texas opposite Matamoros, which had been besieged by Mexican troops. On 1 May 1846 General Taylor, at Fort Texas, exploited an opportunity to break through Mexican lines and raced across the plain of Palo Alto to his arsenal at Point Isabel. Taylor's objective was to resupply Fort Texas before Mexican troops could take it. He reached Point Isabel on 2 May after a twenty-four-hour march and gathered supplies and every available cannon the arsenal could spare. Taylor's reinforced army comprised 2,200 men.

Meanwhile, Arista, on the north bank of the Río Grande, learned that the U.S. troops had left Point Isabel heading for Palo Alto. The Mexican objective was to cut Taylor's road to Fort Texas. About 1:15 P.M. on 8 May the two armies

Battle of Palo Alto
Order of Battle
8 May 1846

Mexican Forces

Commander
Gen. Mariano Arista

Infantry
2d Light Regiment
1st Line Regiment
2d Line Regiment
4th Line Regiment
6th Line Regiment
10th Line Regiment
Tampico Guardacostas
Zapadores

Cavalry
Light Regiment of Mexico
7th Line Regiment
8th Line Regiment
Presidial Companies
Matamoros Auxiliary

Artillery
approximately 13 pieces

U.S. Forces

Commander
Gen. Zachary Taylor

Infantry
3d U.S. Infantry
4th U.S. Infantry
5th U.S. Infantry
8th U.S. Infantry
2d U.S. Dragoons
1st U.S. Artillery (serving as infantry)
2d U.S. Artillery (serving as infantry)
3d U.S. Artillery (serving as infantry)
4th U.S. Artillery (serving as infantry)

Cavalry
2d U.S. Dragoons
Walker's Company of Texas Rangers

Artillery
Company A, 2d U.S. Artillery (Duncan's Light Battery)
Company C, 3d U.S. Artillery (Ringgold's Light Battery)
3d U.S. Artillery (Churchill's Section of two 18-pdr. siege guns)

sighted each other, and each maneuvered its units into a battleline. Arista looked over the U.S. line and observed that Taylor had a mix of guns: two 18-pound siege guns, four 12-pound howitzers, and several 6-pound howitzers

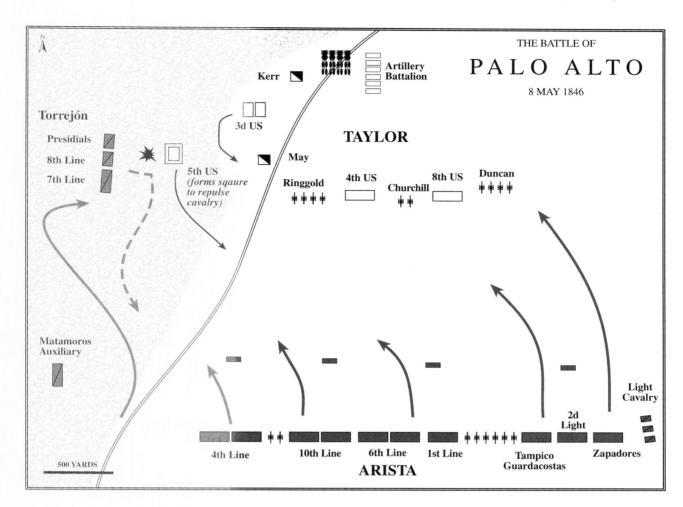

mounted on large-wheel caissons. The latter, an innovation of Maj. Samuel Ringgold, came to be called the "flying artillery," as it increased firepower and could be quickly maneuvered. No one realized the significance of the flying artillery at that time, however, as it was yet untested. This battle was to be decided by the effective use of such artillery.

The Mexican line appeared formidable to U.S. forces at first sight, but its vulnerabilities soon became apparent: its artillery was of poor quality, the gunpowder and shot inferior, and the musketry antiquated. Arista's cavalry, equipped with lances and carbines, comprised the most effective arm of the Army of the North. The Mexican horses had been in the field for several days and lacked the stamina that would be needed in the next few hours of battle. What Arista did have to his advantage was superior numbers, 3,300 men, and the choice of terrain; he had earlier decided to force a battle at Palo Alto because it was a flat piece of land with low, shrubby mesquite with a slight rise favoring the Mexican army's position.

About 2:00 P.M. the U.S. Army advanced to a point eight hundred yards from the Mexican line. The Mexican artillery opened fire first, hitting the U.S. line, but the U.S. troops sidestepped the solid shot that came their way. Shortly, the U.S. artillery fired on the Mexican line. During the most violent barrage of U.S. artillery, Arista's officers demanded a bayonet charge, but Arista thought better of it. Instead, he ordered attacks against the U.S. flanks, but they failed to quiet the artillery.

By 5:00 P.M. the Mexican army had advanced but little and was pinned down by the U.S. guns. Frustrated and unable to advance, Arista continued to use flanking tactics but was unable to turn the U.S. line. By 6:00 P.M. the U.S forces had advanced and caught a good part of Arista's troops in a deadly cannonade. As the sun set, the battle ended and a truce was called for the night. Both armies camped on the battlefield.

Arista's commissary report indicated 102 men killed, 129 wounded, and 26 men lost. His casualties totaled 257 men. U.S. reports indicated that Mexican casualties numbered closer to 400. The Mexicans estimated that the U.S. forces had suffered 200 dead and wounded. U.S. estimates were a small fraction of that. Despite the Mexican casualties, the Army of the North still numbered at least 2,900 men, including 400 men on the Mexican extreme right flank, which never entered the battle.

The Battle of Palo Alto proved to be the beginning of the end for the effective military use of the Army of the North; it was decisively defeated on 9 May 1846 at Resaca de Guerrero, also known as Resaca de la Palma. Thereafter, Mexican resistance to the U.S. advance proved futile, and Taylor's army occupied much of northeastern Mexico.

Joseph P. Sánchez

BIBLIOGRAPHY

Haecker, Charles M. *A Thunder of Cannon: Archaelogy of the Mexican-American War Battlefield of Palo Alto.* 1994.

Lavender, David. *Climax at Buena Vista: The American Campaigns in Northeastern Mexico, 1846–7.* 1966.

Smith, Justin H. *The War with Mexico.* 2 vols. 1919. Reprint, 1963.

Paredes y Arrillaga, Mariano

Mexican general Mariano Paredes y Arrillaga (1797–1849) was born in Mexico City. Paredes y Arrillaga fought on the royalist side during the Wars of Independence. Only when the Plan of Iguala was issued in 1821 did he support independence. Like many followers of Emperor Agustín de Iturbide, Paredes y Arrillaga turned against him in 1823. In the following years he participated in various political conflicts, particularly against any federalist aims. By 1832 he was a brigade general, and in 1838 for a few days he occupied the ministry of war. In 1841 he started a rebellion against the government of Anastasio Bustamante, which culminated with the issuing of the *Bases de Tacubaya*, allowing the third presidency of Antonio López de Santa Anna to take place. Paredes y Arrillaga rebelled again three years later, this time to remove Santa Anna. As a result of this movement José Joaquín de Herrera became president. Again, at the end of 1845 Paredes y Arrillaga rebelled, overthrew Herrera, and became the new ruler of the country.

In the Plan of San Luis, which was used to oust President Herrera, Paredes y Arrillaga accused Herrera of trying to negotiate the loss of Texas to the United States. In order to gain power the military officer had acted under the monarchist persuasion of the Spanish minister Salvador Bermúdez de Castro and conservative ideologue Lucas Alamán. In truth, Paredes y Arrillaga was acting on his own, and just as he had offered his support to the pro-European monarchists, he was also playing on the expectations of the republicans of the country.

At any rate, Paredes thought that a military demonstration against the United States would be enough to get a better

Mariano Paredes y **Arrillaga.** Fayette Robinson, *Mexico and Her Military Chieftains*, 1851

indemnization for the loss of Texas as well as dignified treatment from the northern neighbor. Thus, Paredes y Arrillaga was willing to play a war game with the United States, hoping that his overtures to the monarchists would grant him European support. In the event of a war Paredes y Arrillaga hoped that it would be a "little one" in which Mexico would not lose much, in territory or otherwise, and that it would ensure his permanence in power.

In fact, as Mexican military defeats accumulated, Paredes y Arrillaga tried to save his government by asking a newly elected congress in June 1846 to maintain the republican institutions of the country. The petition proved insufficient and he was overthrown two months later. He went into exile in Europe and tried to gather support for a new monarchist attempt in Mexico.

In 1848, along with other politicians such as Manuel Doblado and a Spanish priest, Celedonio Dómeco de Jarauta, he opposed the Treaty of Guadalupe Hidalgo but was defeated. He left Mexico again and returned in 1849, only to die penniless in a convent in Mexico City.

Miguel Soto

BIBLIOGRAPHY

Costeloe, Michael P. "Los generales Santa Anna y Paredes y Arrillaga en México, 1841–1843: Rivales por el poder, o una copa más." *Historia Mexicana* 39, no. 2 (October–December 1989): 417–440.

Costeloe, Michael P. *The Central Republic in Mexico. 1835–1846: Hombres de Bien in the Age of Santa Anna.* 1993.

Robertson, F. D. "The Military and Political Career of Mariano Paredes y Arrillaga, 1797–1849." Ph.D. diss., University of Texas, 1949.

Soto, Miguel. *La conspiración monárquica en México, 1845–1846.* 1988.

Parker, Theodore

Abolitionist and editor Theodore Parker (1810–1860) was one of the leading liberal theologians and social reformers of the antebellum United States. Trained for the Unitarian clergy at Harvard Divinity School in the 1830s, his controversial but path-breaking theology and biblical criticism drew fire from orthodox Protestants and even Unitarians, but earned the praise of Ralph Waldo Emerson and the Transcendentalists. In 1846 Parker became the minister of the Twenty-Eighth Congregational Society in Boston where he preached to audiences of more than two thousand people, supported the antislavery movement, and regularly assisted fugitive slaves. In the late 1850s he became involved in the Secret Six conspiracy to fund John Brown's raid on Harpers Ferry.

From his pulpit in Boston and at various meetings in the city, Parker denounced the U.S.–Mexican War as the product of a "Slave Power" conspiracy designed to extend the influence of slavery across the continent. At Boston's Faneuil Hall in May 1846, he accused the administration of President James K. Polk of duplicity in its negotiations with Mexico and called on the citizens of Massachusetts to take no part in the conflict. Although Parker's religious convictions and antislavery principles led him to oppose the war, his racial views and his distinctive conception of U.S. nationalism were nevertheless compatible with the vast territorial expansion that resulted from the conflict. In his widely reprinted 1848 "Sermon on the Mexican War," for example, he described the westward spread of Anglo-Saxon economic and political life as both inevitable and progressive. While hoping that future expansion could be achieved without violence or the spread of slavery, he confidently predicted that all of North America would eventually fall to the aggressive, democratic, and industrious Anglo-Saxon Americans.

Paul E. Teed

BIBLIOGRAPHY

Commager, Henry S. *Theodore Parker: Yankee Crusader.* 1936.

Teed, Paul E. "Racial Nationalism and Its Challengers: Theodore Parker, John Rock, and the Antislavery Movement." *Civil War History* 49 (1995): 142–160.

Teed, Paul E. " 'A Very Excellent Fanatic, A Very Good Infidel and a First-Rate Traitor.' Theodore Parker and the Search for Perfection in Antebellum America." Ph.D. diss., University of Connecticut, 1994.

Parrodi, Anastasio

Born in Havana, Cuba, Anastasio Parrodi (1805–1867) came to Mexico at an early age and enrolled in the army. Little is known of his career as an officer, but in 1846 he was military commander general of the state of Tamaulipas. This left Parrodi in charge of the garrison at Tampico, Mexico's second most important port after Vera Cruz.

After the commencement of hostilities with the United States, Mexican government officials decided to defend Tampico and instructed Parrodi to fortify the city. By October 1846, however, Parrodi was subject to the orders of the commander-in-chief of all Mexican armies, Gen. Antonio López de Santa Anna, who was attempting to concentrate his men in San Luis Potosí to start new military operations against U.S. general Zachary Taylor. Santa Anna, after determining that Tampico was indefensible, ordered its evacuation. Parrodi tried to dissuade him but in the end obeyed.

On 27 October Parrodi hurriedly evacuated Tampico, leaving behind much valuable military equipment. Recalled to San Luis Potosí and subjected to a court-martial by Santa Anna for having ordered the abandonment of Tampico, Parrodi was acquitted of all charges. He subsequently saw action at the Battles of Buena Vista and Contreras and was wounded at the latter.

After the war Parrodi supported the Ayutla rebellion (1854) against Santa Anna. In the late 1850s he served as governor of the states of Jalisco and Tamaulipas and in 1862 held the same post in the Federal District. Parrodi then withdrew from public affairs. He later endorsed the French intervention (1862–1867) but did not hold office for the regime. Parrodi died in Mexico City.

Pedro Santoni

BIBLIOGRAPHY

Alcaraz, Ramón, et al. *The Other Side: or Notes for the History of the War Between Mexico and the United States.* 1970.

Roa Bárcena, José María. *Recuerdos de la invasión norteamericana (1846–1848).* 3 vols. 1947.

Smith, Justin H. *The War with Mexico.* 2 vols. 1919. Reprint, 1963.

Parrott, William S.

William S. Parrott (1798–1863), U.S. confidential agent to Mexico, was born in Halifax County, Virginia, on 17 September. He grew to maturity in Jackson County, Tennessee. Parrott served in the Tennessee militia during the War of

1812 and suffered a wound at New Orleans (1815) that left him with a permanent limp. Trained as a dentist, he moved to Mexico City in 1822 where he established a mercantile firm, operated a stage line, and worked on several colonization projects in Texas. By 1834 he had become one of the wealthiest merchants in Mexico City. Parrott served as U.S. consul at Mexico City from 1834 through 1836. He became the target of several lawsuits, which left him bankrupt by 1839. He returned to the United States and filed a claim of $470,000 against the Mexican government, which swelled to $986,000 by 1842.

Parrott accepted an administrative position in the Navy Department in 1842 and served in that capacity until President James K. Polk appointed him confidential agent to Mexico on 28 March 1845. Polk instructed him to investigate the possibility of reopening diplomatic relations in order to settle the differences between the two nations (Mexico having recalled its minister after the annexation of Texas). Parrott's appointment, with his large claim, antagonized the Mexican government. Mexico agreed to receive a minister but requested that it not be Parrott. The mission went to John Slidell, and Parrott accompanied him to Mexico as his secretary, serving in that post until 1848. He returned to the Navy Department and retired in 1852. The claims commission awarded Parrott $115,000 of his original suit against Mexico in 1851. He died on 6 September 1863 in York County, Pennsylvania, and was buried there.

Jimmy L. Bryan, Jr.

BIBLIOGRAPHY
Farabee, Ethel. "William Stuart Parrott, Business Man and Diplomat in Mexico." Master's thesis, University of Texas at Austin, 1944.
Pletcher, David M. *The Diplomacy of Annexation: Texas, Oregon, and the Mexican War.* 1973.

Pastry War of 1838

A French war with Mexico, the Pastry War of 1838 was the first European military intervention in Latin America for the purpose of collecting debts. Based on an 1827 commercial agreement, which was not ratified by the Mexican congress, King Louis Philippe demanded payment of 600,000 pesos in compensation to French citizens, including a baker in Tacubaya who claimed 60,000 pesos for certain pastries allegedly eaten by Mexican revolutionaries on 4 December 1828. The French minister in Mexico, Baron Deffaudis, presented the demand in February 1838 and rejected the Mexican proposal of arbitration. On 16 April the French navy declared a blockade of Vera Cruz, and on 26 September an invasion force of twenty-six vessels with 4,300 men under Rear Adm. Charles Baudin arrived off the coast of Mexico. Baudin entered negotiations with the Mexican government for pay-

ment but failed to gain a quick resolution. On 28 November the French bombarded the fortress of San Juan de Ulúa and occupied the port of Vera Cruz. Gen. Antonio López de Santa Anna reached the city on 4 December, and the following day he engaged a column of French troops, forcing them back to their ships. At that point French naval cannon opened fire, killing Santa Anna's horse and severely wounding him in the left leg and right hand. The leg was amputated at the knee, a poor job that caused him considerable pain for the rest of his life. Santa Anna preserved and later enshrined the leg with full military honors as a symbol of his dedication to the national defense. The Pastry War ended on 7 March 1839 with a treaty in which Mexico agreed to pay the 600,000 pesos.

Jeffrey M. Pilcher

BIBLIOGRAPHY
Jones, Oakah L., Jr. *Santa Anna.* 1968.
Robertson, William S. "French Intervention in Mexico in 1838." *Hispanic American Historical Review* 24 (1944): 222–252.

Patria Chica

The term *patria chica,* loosely translated into English, means "the small homeland," and refers to the phenomenon described as localism by modern scholars. Mexican society in the nineteenth century was the product of centuries of societal stratification and geographical isolation. As a result, loyalties to polities larger than family, home, village, or region were difficult to foster. Under Spanish rule, officials considered this highly fragmented society desirable and a useful bulwark against rebellion and unrest. Unlike the experience of the British North American colonies, the idea of a national identity separate and apart from Spain was actively discouraged. As a refuge, Mexicans retreated to the familiar identifiers of their day-to-day lives. This local loyalty was further enhanced by the fact that Mexican society reflected many aspects of native culture, which celebrated clan and community above all else.

Patria chica, while a boon to Spain in controlling its overseas empire, proved a major problem for Mexican leaders attempting to forge a nation in the early 1800s. With no overwhelming experience as "Mexicans," most of the population had difficulty identifying their own interests with those of the nation. Exacerbating this issue was the government's lack of stability. Leaders and politicians could often inspire loyalty from the citizens of their region, but building a national constituency proved an almost insurmountable task, often leading to fragile coalitions in government charged with guiding the national destiny.

Patria chica manifested itself in a number of ways in the period from 1821 to 1854. Taxes and contributions required from areas distant from Mexico City, the seat of power, remained difficult to collect. Fighting men were reluctant to serve far from home. The semiautonomous regions on the periphery of the nation—Yucatán, New Mexico, Texas, Baja and Alta California, Chihuahua, Sonora, Tamaulipas, and Coahuila—proved difficult to govern and prone to rebellion and even, on occasion, attempted to secede. Thus, when Spain, France, and the United States each intervened in Mexican affairs, they faced a fragmented and divided Mexico.

Donald S. Frazier

BIBLIOGRAPHY

MacLachlan, Colin M., and Jaime E. Rodriguez O. *The Forging of the Cosmic Race.* 1990.

MacLachlan, Colin M., and William H. Beezley. *El Gran Pueblo.* 1994.

Ramírez, J. F. *Mexico durante su Guerra con los Estados Unidos.* 1905.

Patronage in the U.S. Military

Political patronage, the policy of appointing members of one's own party to office as a reward, was well entrenched in U.S. politics by the commencement of the U.S.–Mexican War. While most often identified with President Andrew Jackson and his supporters, patronage was a tool that both Democrats and Whigs used to further the goals of their parties.

Patronage is as old as government itself. The system as it developed in the United States during the early nineteenth century, however, had its origins in the presidential campaign of 1828, when Jackson and his followers promoted the idea of "Rotation of Office." They contended that government office was a republican duty that should be open to all men of talent and not reserved for a privileged few. Jackson's opponents predicted mass firings if he were elected, a prediction that failed to come true. Modern historians contend that the number of officeholders ousted because of their political affiliation during Jackson's administration did not exceed 20 percent. Patronage became a part of the U.S. political system, used by both major parties on the national, state, and local levels. One Democratic politician from New York, William L. Marcy, remarked in apparent justification of the practice, "To the victor belongs the spoils." Thereafter the *spoils system* became the catchphrase for patronage.

The U.S. military was not immune to patronage. Jackson and his supporters contended that a small group of officers formed a privileged elite and controlled the regular army. Indeed, since its establishment in 1803, the United States Military Academy at West Point increasingly had become the gateway to the officer corps. Reared in a martial society, many Democrats failed to see what books and classrooms had to do with soldiering. In their minds, great leaders like George Washington and Andrew Jackson were born, not

graduated. The number of West Point–trained officers who left the service to take lucrative civilian jobs did little to dispel the popular notion that West Point was a charitable institution for sons of wealthy and well-connected families. During the Seminole War, Jackson appointed a number of officers from civilian life, a move applauded by opponents of the U.S. Military Academy.

War with Mexico presented President James K. Polk, an ardent Jacksonian, with an opportunity to make hundreds of new officer appointments. While Polk claimed that party politics did not influence his selections, the overwhelming majority of his appointees, including all thirteen volunteer generals authorized by Congress as well as many of the field officers, were active Democrats. Besieged by those seeking to become officers, Polk came to loathe the patronage system. He blamed many of its evils on members of Congress who voted to create offices and then sought to fill them with their friends or even take them for themselves. Polk later claimed that patronage, which had been intended to bind his party together, had actually worked to pull it apart. In his opinion, many Democrats, disappointed at not receiving a political appointment, turned against their party in retaliation.

Patronage was not confined to the Democratic Party. Some Whig governors used their patronage power to appoint officers to command state volunteers. In the case of the 1st North Carolina Infantry, the appointment of a Whig colonel by the Whig governor led to mutiny after the regiment reached Mexico. A court of inquiry into the affair showed that many Democrat volunteers resented the appointment of a Whig to command them.

Richard Bruce Winders

BIBLIOGRAPHY

Polk, James K. *The Diary of James K. Polk during His Presidency, 1845 to 1849.* 4 vols. 1910.

White, Leonard D. *The Jacksonians: A Study in Administrative History, 1829–1861.* 1965.

Winders, Richard Bruce. *Mr. Polk's Army.* 1997.

Patterson, Robert

U.S. general Robert Patterson (1792–1881) was born in Ireland. Patterson moved with his family to the United States in 1798 and settled in Pennsylvania. He served as a young officer during the War of 1812 and thereafter engaged in business in Pennsylvania and was active in the state militia. Prominent in Democratic politics, he was appointed a major general of volunteers by President James K. Polk following the outbreak of the U.S.–Mexican War.

As one of the highest ranking officers in Mexico, Patterson played an important, if unspectacular, role in the war. Under Gen. Zachary Taylor, he commanded U.S. troops on the Río

Grande but was denied by Taylor the assignment to take Tampico. Polk's plan to install Patterson, a Democrat, as commander of the invasion of central Mexico via Vera Cruz backfired when it was revealed that Patterson was not a U.S. native and therefore could not be a presidential candidate. Patterson did, however, participate in the campaign. He commanded a division in the siege of Vera Cruz and during the Battle of Cerro Gordo, after which he spearheaded the pursuit of Mexican forces to Jalapa. In May 1847 Patterson led a group of volunteers whose enlistments had expired back to the United States and then returned to Mexico in November with reinforcements. He remained in Mexico City until May 1848.

Mustered out of service in July 1848, he resumed his various business pursuits. He served briefly at the beginning of the Civil War as major general of Pennsylvania volunteers but failed in his assignment to prevent Confederate forces from concentrating for the Battle of Bull Run and was relieved from his position. Patterson became one of the leading industrialists in the United States, operating more than thirty cotton mills in Pennsylvania as well as several sugar and cotton plantations in Louisiana. He retained an avid interest in the U.S.–Mexican War and was instrumental in reviving the Aztec Club after the Civil War, serving as its president from 1867 until his death on 7 August 1881.

David Coffey

BIBLIOGRAPHY

Singletary, Otis A. *The Mexican War.* 1960.

Smith, Justin H. *The War with Mexico.* 2 vols. 1919. Reprint, 1963.

Pedraza, Manuel Gómez

See **Gómez Pedraza, Manuel**

Peña, José Enrique de la

See **de la Peña, José Enrique**

Peña y Barragán, Matías de la

Mexican general and leader of the Polkos Revolt, Matías de la Peña y Barragán (1800?–1850) was born to a wealthy family in Mexico City and educated in Europe. He pursued a business career while participating in the civic militia. Peña y Barragán gained a regular appointment as brigadier general for his defense of the National Palace during a July 1840 revolt, then served in various campaigns to stifle secessionist movements in Yucatán. In February 1847, liberal vice president Valentín Gómez Farías ordered the conservative general Peña y Barragán and several battalions to leave Mexico City for Vera Cruz, ostensibly to bolster the resistance against the U.S. invasion. Gómez Farías actually wanted to clear the capital of conservative forces that might block his 11 January 1847 decree appropriating church property. Peña y Barragán refused the order, and on 26 February he revolted against the government. The aristocratic rebels became popularly known as the *polkos* because many danced the polka, which had recently become fashionable (or, according to some historians, because their attempted coup played into the hands of U.S. president James K. Polk). An indecisive struggle continued against loyalist forces under Gen. Valentín Canalizo until a truce was arranged on 23 March. President Antonio López de Santa Anna abrogated the appropriation law and abolished the office of vice president, essentially firing Gómez Farías. After U.S. troops captured Chapultepec on 13 September, Peña y Barragán made a defensive stand at San Cosme on the road to Mexico City. He died of cholera in Jalapa while serving as military commander of Vera Cruz.

Jeffrey M. Pilcher

BIBLIOGRAPHY

Costeloe, Michael P. "The Mexican Church and the Rebellion of the Polkos." *Hispanic American Historical Review* 46 (1966): 170–178.

Diccionario Porrúa: De história, biografía y geografía de México. 6th ed. 1995.

Peña y Peña, Manuel de la

Mexican politician Manuel de la Peña y Peña (1789–1850) was born in the village of Tacuba in the Federal District. He earned a law degree in 1811. Peña y Peña joined several scientific, economic, and educational societies and also held numerous public posts during the early republic. A member of the *moderado* party, he served as supreme court justice and minister of the interior, and he helped draw up the 1843 constitution known as the *Bases Orgánicas.*

As minister of foreign relations from August to December 1845, Peña y Peña tried to prevent an armed conflict with the United States. He informed the U.S. consul in Mexico City in October that Mexico would receive special envoy John Slidell to negotiate and settle the boundary dispute with Texas. Early in December, Peña y Peña tried to broaden the public support required by this conciliatory policy and asked departmental authorities to voice their opinion on war or peace. In the end, however, the strategy did not succeed, and Mexico drifted toward war with the United States.

Peña y Peña again took on a leading political role after Mexico City fell to the U.S. Army. Between September 1847 and June 1848 he served as Gen. Pedro María Anaya's minister of foreign relations and twice as chief executive. He worked to negotiate peace with the United States and in May 1848 addressed the Mexican congress in defense of the Treaty of Guadalupe Hidalgo.

After the war Peña y Peña governed the state of México for two months, March to May 1849. He died the following year. In 1895 President Porfirio Díaz ordered Peña y Peña's remains to be transferred to the Rotunda of Illustrious Men.

Pedro Santoni

BIBLIOGRAPHY
Pletcher, David. *The Diplomacy of Annexation: Texas, Oregon, and the Mexican War.* 1973.
Roa Bárcena, José María. *Recuerdos de la invasión norteamericana (1846–1848).* 1947.
Robinson, Cecil, ed. *The View from Chapultepec: Mexican Writers on The Mexican-American War.* 1989.

Pensions, U.S.

In 1846 Congress passed an act approving the raising of volunteers to fight the war with Mexico. The act included a proviso that any volunteer "wounded or otherwise disabled" would be "entitled to all the benefit which may be conferred on persons wounded in the service of the United States." An act approved 21 July 1848 was more specific. It stated that all disabled U.S.–Mexican War veterans, as well as widows or orphans of soldiers, were entitled to the benefits of the act of 4 July 1836, which provided a pension of half-pay. For a private, this amounted to $3.50 per month.

In 1874 the National Association of Veterans of the Mexican War began pressing Congress to approve a U.S.–Mexican War service pension. Opposition was encountered from radical Republican congressmen who objected not only to the projected cost but also to the fact that a large number of U.S.–Mexican War veterans were also former Confederate soldiers, the most notable being Jefferson Davis. Davis's renunciation of any entitlement to a federal pension helped pave the way for the passage of a bill granting a pension of $8 per month to both veterans and their widows. It was signed into law on 29 January 1887. After the turn of the century, the amount was increased to $12 per month, later to $20.

The number of U.S.–Mexican War veterans on the pension rolls peaked at 17,158 in 1890. By 1916, only 513 veterans and 3,785 widows were still drawing a pension. Applications were accepted until 1926.

Steven R. Butler

BIBLIOGRAPHY
Butler, Steven R. "Alexander Kenaday and the National Association of Veterans of the Mexican War." *Mexican War Quarterly* 1 (1992): 10–21.
Glasson, William H. *Federal Military Pensions in the United States.* 1918.
National Archives. *Guide to Genealogical Research in the National Archives.* 1982.
National Association of Veterans of the Mexican War. *Origins and Progress of the National Association of Veterans of the Mexican War.* 1887.
National Association of Veterans of the Mexican War. *Proceedings of the Second Annual Reunion.* 1875.
U.S. Statutes at Large.

Peonage

Debt peonage in Mexico had its roots in the systems known as *encomienda* and *repartimiento*, which were introduced into Spain's territories in the New World almost immediately after their conquest. The *encomienda* did not constitute a land grant, but instead gave to the *encomendero*, or holder, the right to labor services performed by Indians placed under his charge by the crown. Under the system of *repartimiento*, or labor allotment, Indian laborers were to be paid for their work and treated with consideration. In practice, however, they were often compelled to work long hours and were frequently mistreated and cheated of their pay.

By the late sixteenth century, the Indian population had declined so drastically due to disease, ill treatment, and other causes that landowners were forced to seek solutions that would permit them to conserve and continue to use what remained of their limited labor supply. The landholder and merchant groups, especially those who sought to capitalize on the growing demand for grain in the cities and mining centers, required a more permanent labor force than had previously been the case. With the increasing extension of Spanish ownership over lands that had formerly been held in common by Indian groups, the hacienda became established in the early seventeenth century as the dominant institution in many rural areas.

Indian laborers on haciendas, as well as in mines and *obrajes*, or sweatshops, were offered advances on their pay as an inducement to work. A portion of the wages was given to them in the form of food and clothing. In most cases, the wage portion paid in money was not given in cash, but rather in the form of credit at the *tienda de raya* (company store) established on all large haciendas. The *peones acasillados*, or indebted laborers, could not legally leave their place of employment until their debts had been paid off. If they died before liquidating their debts, the debts were inherited by their sons.

During the independence struggle from 1810 to 1821, the proposals of some of the more radical insurgent leaders, such as José María Morelos y Pavón, concerning the breakup of large haciendas and an end to debt peonage, remained unrealized because victory was ultimately achieved by the Mexican creole oligarchy, which sought to protect its vested interests. Subsequent recommendations made by liberal ideologues such as Lorenzo de Zavala and José María Luis Mora regarding the redistribution of large landholdings among small farmers met with resistance among the ruling elite. Instead, *hacendados* were able to expand their properties due to the demand in European urban centers for certain commercial crops such as coffee, cotton, sisal, sugar, and tobacco. In addition, despite the abundance of land in the northern border regions, the perennial lack of government funds and initiative failed to induce peons and other Mexicans to migrate from the south.

The period of conflict between the federalist and centralist factions, which dated from the mid-1820s, resulted in a deterioration of the peons' living standards. The U.S.–Mexican War of 1846 to 1848 left the country prostrate before the U.S. invaders and also imposed additional hardships on the rural population. The latter, however, failed to be goaded into armed rebellion motivated by the desire for land reform or better treatment by landowners. (Rural uprisings in the late colonial and early national periods usually involved inhabitants from free Indian villages attempting to retain or recover their lands from hacienda encroachments or were in protest against elevated taxes, with the peons fighting in defense of their masters.) In the wake of the U.S.–Mexican War, there were Indian rebellions in many states, partially in response to the central government's weakened condition. The largest of these were the Caste War in Yucatán from 1847 to 1855 and the Sierra Gorda Revolt in central Mexico from 1848 to 1849, together with a renewal of attacks by nomadic tribes on settlements in the northern border areas.

Though briefly abolished under the empire of Maximilian, debt peonage was reestablished with the restoration of the liberal republic in 1867. During the rule of Porfirio Díaz (from 1876 to 1880 and 1884–1911) an increasing demand for agricultural products, coupled with large-scale foreign investment, strengthened the system in certain areas, especially in the southeast. In the north, where peonage had been weaker since colonial times, it was further debilitated by the construction of railways linking the capital with the international border and the increase in the demand for labor in mines and industry. Debt peonage was not officially outlawed until the promulgation of the Constitution of 1917, which was followed by similar prohibitions adopted by many regional states.

Lawrence D. Taylor

BIBLIOGRAPHY

Berge, Dennis E., ed. *Considerations on the Political and Social Situation of the Mexican Republic, 1847.* 1975.

Coatsworth, John H. "Obstacles to Economic Growth in Nineteenth-Century Mexico." *American Historical Review* 83 (1978): 80–100.

Florescano, Enrique. *Origen y desarrollo de los problemas agrarios de México, 1500–1821.* 1976.

Gilmore, N. Ray, ed. "The Condition of the Poor in Mexico, 1834." *Hispanic American Historical Review* 37 (1957): 213–226.

Orozco, Luis Chávez. *Páginas de historia económica de México: Condiciones del trabajo durante la colonia y principios del siglo XX.* 1976.

Zavala, Silvio. *Los orígenes coloniales del peonaje en México.* 1935.

See also **Castes**; Class Structure in Mexico

Pérez, Francisco

Born in Tulancingo (located in the present-day state of Hidalgo), Mexican general Francisco Pérez (c. 1810–1864) joined the Mexican army as a lieutenant in 1826. He participated in the Texas campaign of 1836, and five years later distinguished himself fighting against the secessionist government of Yucatán. Pérez, who was promoted to general in 1846, saw action in several battles during the war with the United States.

Late in the afternoon of 23 February 1847, Gen. Antonio López de Santa Anna made a final effort for victory at the Battle of Buena Vista. He combined the remnants of several detachments and ordered Pérez to lead a new assault against the center of the U.S. line. The main body of Pérez's men initially pushed back the U.S. defenders but failed to dislodge them. That night, after a council of war, the Mexican army withdrew from the field.

Pérez played a controversial role at the Battle of Contreras. When hostilities broke out on the afternoon of 19 August, Santa Anna ordered Pérez's three-thousand-man brigade to reinforce Gen. Gabriel Valencia. Because Santa Anna subsequently determined that it was impossible to aid Valencia, Pérez's troops, although posted nearby, did not engage in the battle, and Valencia blamed Pérez for depriving him of a chance to crush the U.S. forces.

The troops under Pérez fought bravely on 8 September at the Battle of El Molino del Rey. They manned a stone fortress known as the Casa Mata, about five hundred yards to the west of El Molino del Rey, which was said to house a cannon foundry. Pérez's men withstood the initial U.S. assault but had to abandon the Casa Mata when U.S. field pieces opened fire on the position.

Pérez was among the generals who early on the evening of 13 September, after the U.S. Army had breached the defenses of Mexico City, advised Santa Anna that a continued defense of the capital would be futile. Santa Anna then decided to evacuate the city and named Pérez second general-in-chief.

After the war Pérez held a variety of military and civilian posts. He served as governor of Puebla (1853–1855), was promoted to division general in 1855, and during the 1860s he fought against the French invaders. At the time of his death in 1864 Pérez was serving as Tulancingo's military commander general.

Pedro Santoni

BIBLIOGRAPHY

Rives, George Lockhart. *The United States and Mexico, 1821–1848.* 2 vols. 1913.

Roa Bárcena, José María. *Recuerdos de la invasión norteamericana (1846–1848).* 3 vols. 1947.

Smith, Justin. *The War with Mexico.* 1919. 2 vols. Reprint, 1963.

Perfecto de Cos, Martín

See Cos, Martín Perfecto de

Perote Castle

Located on the western slope of the Sierra Madre Oriental, some one hundred winding miles via the National Road from Vera Cruz, the village of Perote formed one of several potential barriers to Gen. Winfield Scott's march to Mexico City. Perote Castle, a formidable stone-walled citadel capable of supporting a two-thousand-man garrison, was built during the 1770s and covered two dozen acres. Its sturdy construction and surrounding moat lent the castle to a variety of uses. Used as an arsenal and shipping depot, it gained infamy as a prison for political prisoners and prisoners of war. During the 1840s the castle housed captured U.S. adventurers and Texians from the failed Santa Fe and Mier Expeditions and from Mexican general Adrian Woll's 1842 attack on San Antonio. The severe treatment of Perote prisoners aroused great indignation in Texas and the United States and left a lasting impression on survivors; the castle became a dark, looming presence in the U.S. and Mexican imagination. Despite its military potential, Perote Castle lacked the resources to seriously deter the U.S. invasion and, if necessary, could have been bypassed by Scott's soldiers.

Following his April 1847 victory at Cerro Gordo and the subsequent occupation of Jalapa, General Scott ordered Gen. William J. Worth's division to pursue the fleeing Mexican troops. After a difficult mountain passage, Worth's men arrived at Perote on 22 April only to find the castle abandoned and its garrison withdrawn. Worth's force occupied the village without resistance. The general then called a halt to the pursuit pending further orders from Scott, who remained at Jalapa.

Even had the Mexicans chosen to fight at Perote, they had little chance of success. Aware that the castle was woefully undermanned, Gen. Valentín Canalizo, commander of the Eastern Division, ordered it abandoned three days before Worth's column arrived. In haste and without adequate transportation, the Mexicans left behind a great deal of valuable ordnance and other equipment. When Worth's command took possession of the castle it claimed among its prizes more than 50 cannon and 25,000 rounds of solid shot and shell as well as some 500 muskets.

U.S. forces maintained a sizable garrison at Perote for the balance of the war. Well situated between Vera Cruz and Puebla, Perote served as a way station for reinforcements bound for Scott's invading army and supplied troops for other operations, including the relief of Puebla.

David Coffey

BIBLIOGRAPHY

Connor, Seymour V. "Perote Prison." In *The New Handbook of Texas.* 1996.

Eisenhower, John S. D. *So Far from God: The U.S. War with Mexico, 1846–1848.* 1989.

Smith, Justin H. *The War with Mexico.* 2 vols. 1919. Reprint, 1963.

Perry, Matthew C.

U.S. naval officer Matthew C. Perry (1794–1858) was born in Newport, Rhode Island, to a prominent naval family. Perry's naval service began in 1809 as a fourteen-year-old

Matthew Perry. Fayette Robinson, *Mexico and Her Military Chieftains,* 1851

midshipman. Over the next thirty-five years he fought Barbary pirates, assisted in the settlement of Liberia, contributed to a treaty with Turkey, served as commandant of the New York Navy Yard, supported advances in steam propulsion and ordnance, and promoted improvements in naval officer education.

Perry began the U.S.–Mexican War as second-in-command of the navy's Home Squadron, then blockading the east coast of Mexico. In addition to blockading duties, the squadron's ships mounted several attacks along the coast. Perry led a raid up the Río Tabasco in October 1846 and the following month participated in the capture of Tampico. He replaced Commo. David Conner as squadron commander in March 1847, in time for Perry to lead the naval forces in the bombardment and capture of Vera Cruz.

Following that action, Perry's squadron continued to blockade the coast and launch raids against Mexican strongpoints. To accomplish this, he organized a landing force from among his squadron's sailors. In April he captured and wrecked Tuxpan, and the next month he took Coatzacoalcos. A second raid against Tabasco took place in mid-June, when U.S. forces routed the Mexican defenders and occupied the town for the next month. Yellow fever, a transfer of his marines to the army, and a shortage of steamers and qualified officers limited the navy's activities for the rest of the war. Perry did, however, provide some support for Mexican antigovernment forces in Yucatán.

After the war Perry earned his greatest fame for his expedition to Japan, which opened U.S.–Japanese relations and began the transformation of the Asian nation into a modern world power. During his final years Perry headed the Navy Efficiency Board and completed a narrative of his expedition. He died in New York City on 4 March 1858.

David J. Coles

BIBLIOGRAPHY

Barrows, Edward M. *The Great Commodore: The Exploits of Matthew Calbraith Perry.* 1935.

Bauer, K. Jack. *Surfboats and Horse Marines: U.S. Naval Operations in the Mexican War, 1846–48.* 1969.

Morison, Samuel Eliot. *"Old Bruin": Commodore Matthew Calbraith Perry, 1794–1858.* 1967.

Spiller, Roger J., and Joseph G. Dawson, eds. *Dictionary of American Military Biography.* 1984.

Photography

Photography was still in its infancy during the U.S.–Mexican War. In 1839, seven years before the war, Frenchman Louis Daguerre invented the first commercially produced photographic image, which he named the daguerreotype. Until this time, all portraiture and scenery had to be interpreted by the artist working in various media. For example, small portraits

Daguerreotype. Before departing for the war, soldiers often had their photographs taken as a memento for those left behind. Here an unknown second lieutenant poses with a loved one. From the collection of William J. Schultz, M.D.

painted on ivory, called miniatures, were popular visual mementos among the wealthy. The daguerreotype was a less costly true-to-life alternative that was affordable to the general public and thus became immediately popular. Its popularity spanned the U.S.–Mexican War years into the mid 1850s, when it was supplanted by the ambrotype and tintype.

The daguerreotype process was extremely cumbersome, requiring many steps to polish and chemically sensitize the silvered copper plate for exposure in the camera. The subject being photographed had to sit motionless for up to a minute, depending on the amount of sunlight available. To reduce body movement, an upright pole stand was placed behind the patron with a metal clamp immobilizing the head. A light-tight plate holder containing a silvered copper plate previously exposed to iodine fumes was placed in the camera. The light-sensitive iodized plate was then exposed and developed in a darkroom by exposure to mercury vapors. The image formed was immersed in cold water and fixed in a bath of hyposulfite of soda and placed under glass in a special protective case. The resulting unique image had a mirrored surface which had to be held to reflect a dark background in order to be viewed. The relatively long exposure time, the need for optimal natural lighting, and the bulky equipment restricted most photography to studios in the larger cities, with the exception of a smaller number of itinerants who travelled throughout the country setting up temporary studios. Before departing for Mexico, soldiers often had their "likeness" taken for friends and relatives to remember them by back home.

The U.S.–Mexican War represents a milestone in that it was the first military campaign to be recorded in photographs. It also provided the earliest photographs of U.S. soldiers going off to war. As public demand for news and visual accounts of the war increased, several enterprising photographers followed the army into Mexico. Among the photographers known to have established temporary studios in Mexico were A. Hurly in Mexico City; G. Palmer in Matamoros; Charles Betts in Matamoros, Monterrey, Vera Cruz, Peubla, and Mexico City; and George Noessel in Vera Cruz. Few images of soldiers taken in Mexico have survived. Outdoor images of the U.S.–Mexican War are rare because of the ideal conditions required for proper lighting and development. One remarkable series of outdoor daguerreotypes was taken in the area of Saltillo, showing the entrance of

Daguerreotype. Probably taken in 1846; an unidentified trapper. From the collection of William J. Schultz, M.D.

Daguerreotype. An unidentified infantry major or lieutenant colonel. From the collection of William J. Schultz, M.D.

Gen. John E. Wool into the city, occupation of volunteer troops, and artillery movements outside the town.

While the pioneering efforts of the itinerant photographers sent a scant visual record back to the United States, newpapers, namely the New Orleans *Picayune,* sent war correspondents into the field of action. Notable among them, George Kendall used his own mounted couriers to relay reports back to New Orleans where they were subsequently rushed to the north by the recently developed telegraph. Contemporary books written about the war often used woodcuts and engravings adapted from or taken directly from daguerreotypes. The direct use of photographs to illustrate breaking news stories did not occur during the U.S.–Mexican War, but the basic elements necessary for the development of photojournalism were established during the war.

William J. Schultz

BIBLIOGRAPHY

Gilbert, George. *Photography: The Early Years.* 1980.

Newhall, Beaumont. *The History of Photography from 1839 to the Present Day: Revised and Enlarged Edition.* 1964.

Sandweiss, Martha A., Rick Stewart and Ben W. Huseman. *Prints and Daguerreotypes of the Mexican War, 1846–1848.* 1989.

Taft, Robert. *Photography and the American Scene*. 1938. Reprint, 1961.

Pico, Andrés

Soldier Andrés Pico (1810–1876) was born in San Diego into a prominent Californio family. He was a customs receiver, politician, and militiaman in the 1830s and 1840s before taking an active part as a militia captain in the defense of California during the U.S. invasion of 1846 to 1847. During the U.S.–Mexican War, he commanded a contingent of about one hundred horsemen, poorly equipped with lances attached to crude willow poles, and successfully defeated U.S. troops at the Battle of San Pasqual in December 1846. Unable to follow up his initial success, Andrés and his troops eventually surrendered to U.S. forces in California. Although his older brother Pío was the governor of California, Andrés took part in the peace talks on behalf of Mexico. As chief of national forces, he signed the Treaty of Cahuenga, ending the war in California.

After the war, Andrés operated a gold mine, served in the assembly, and was a state senator. He was a leading proponent of proposals to divide California into two territories on joining the United States. He campaigned for President Abraham Lincoln's reelection but declined a command in the Civil War due to poor health. He devoted the last twenty years of his life to his two large ranches in southern California. He died in February 1876.

Amy Wilson

BIBLIOGRAPHY

Rosenus, Alan. *General M. G. Vallejo and the Advent of the Americans*. 1995.

Smith, Justin H. *The War with Mexico*. 2 vols. 1919. Reprint, 1963.

Pico, Pío de Jesús

Pío Pico (1801–1894), governor of California, was born 5 May. Despite his family's wealth he received little formal education and was only literate enough to write his name and little else. By his mid-twenties he was an active politician and businessman and became one of the largest landowners in California and his political career included local and provincial government posts. In early 1832, he became acting governor after the overthrow of the new governor from Mexico City, Manuel Victoria.

Irritated by Mexico's lack of attention to California and aggravated by his nation's policy of exiling criminals to its northwest Pacific frontier, Pío, like many Californios, sought separation from Mexico and alliance with an outside power.

Pío Pico strongly favored a British protectorate, although others favored the United States or France.

In 1846 he again undertook the role of governor and tried to organize a defense against the U.S. invasion while actively seeking British intervention. When the strategic situation became impossible, he fled south to Sonora after announcing the hopelessness of the circumstances. Pío returned to California after the Treaty of Guadalupe Hidalgo to become a rancher. He took part in local and county politics and supported the Union during the Civil War. He built and operated the Pico House, the largest hotel in Los Angeles, when he was in his early seventies. Before his death, however, he lost all of his extensive landholdings due to defaulted loans. He moved in with his godson, John J. Warner, after losing his last piece of property and died 11 September 1894, penniless.

Amy Wilson

BIBLIOGRAPHY

Rosenus, Alan. *General M. G. Vallejo and the Advent of the Americans*. 1995.

Smith, Justin H. *The War with Mexico*. 2 vols. 1919. Reprint, 1963.

Pierce, Franklin

President of the United States Franklin Pierce (1804–1869) was born 23 November at Hillsboro, New Hampshire. Before the U.S.–Mexican War, Pierce practiced law, then served as a Democrat in the New Hampshire legislature, the U.S. House of Representatives, and the U.S. Senate. When war broke out he enlisted as a private but was appointed colonel by President James K. Polk, then brigadier general, before going into service with the New England regiment.

After arriving in Vera Cruz on 27 June 1847, Pierce led 2,500 men one hundred fifty miles over difficult terrain to join Gen. Winfield Scott at Puebla. Encounters with Mexican forces resulted in several skirmishes, and his troops suffered widespread illness. Despite these setbacks he reached Scott's headquarters on 6 August with reinforcements, heavy siege artillery, and $85,000 in uncashable drafts.

At the Battle of Contreras on 19 August 1847, Pierce's horse, frightened by artillery fire, threw him against the pommel of his saddle, then stumbled and fell, causing the general to faint from extreme pain. A soldier called out, "General Pierce is a damned coward," a charge the man later retracted. Despite his injury Pierce returned to the field. The next day General Scott urged him to get medical attention, but Pierce insisted on joining the Battle of Churubusco, only to twist his injured knee again and fall to the ground in pain. He remained on the ground for the rest of the battle.

Franklin Pierce. Daguerreotype, c. 1850. Pierce holds a Mexican War presentation sword. From the collection of William J. Schultz, M.D.

When Gen. Antonio López de Santa Anna requested an armistice, Scott asked Pierce and Brig. Gen. Persifor F. Smith, and Brig. Gen. John A. Quitman to arrange it. They met with Mexican negotiators at Tacubaya on 24 August. Peace negotiations fell through, however, and Scott moved into the capital city and resumed fighting on 6 September. Once again Pierce missed a chance for military glory when his brigade arrived at El Molino del Rey after the fighting had ended. Though plagued with illness, Pierce hoped at least to participate in the final battle for Mexico City, but he arrived after the surrender.

While in Mexico, Pierce formed close friendships with many fellow officers who later supported him in his bid for the presidency. Although political enemies used an unjustified claim of a reputation for cowardice against him during the presidential campaign of 1852, Pierce nevertheless was elected to become the nation's fourteenth president.

Larry Gara

BIBLIOGRAPHY

Nichols, Roy Franklin. *Franklin Pierce: Young Hickory of the Granite Hills.* 2d ed., 1958.

Smith, Justin H. *The War with Mexico.* 2 vols. 1919. Reprint, 1963.

Pillow, Gideon

A wealthy and innovative farmer, eminent Tennessee lawyer, and sometime politician, Gideon Johnson Pillow (1806–1878) had the ear and trust of President James K. Polk. Pillow viewed himself as a second Andrew Jackson and welcomed the opportunity to command the Tennessee brigade in Mexico as brigadier general. Regarding both Mexicans and Whigs as enemies, Pillow rushed his troops up the Río Grande in 1846 only to be deprived of his best regiment by Gen. Zachary Taylor and denied a role in the attack on Monterrey. Pillow retaliated with sharp criticism in an attempt to undermine Taylor.

Joining Gen. Winfield Scott's attack on Vera Cruz in March 1847, Pillow acquitted himself well, but in the subsequent fight against Gen. Antonio López de Santa Anna at Cerro Gordo "got badly whipped" (said Lt. D. H. Hill) and was severely wounded. Nevertheless, he was promoted to major general in the regular army and in the expedition against Mexico City ranked second only to Scott. As a division commander, Pillow performed creditably at Contreras and Churubusco and led the assault against Chapultepec, where he was again seriously wounded.

Ignored by Scott and diplomat Nicholas P. Trist in their negotiations with the Mexican government, and feeling that his performance at Contreras had been minimized, Pillow retaliated by organizing a cabal of regular and volunteer officers against Scott, opening up a feud in U.S. newspapers, and appealing directly to Secretary of War William L. Marcy and to President Polk. The charges and countercharges soon led to Pillow's arrest and subsequent court-martial. Of greater importance, the bickering divided and demoralized the U.S. officer corps and resulted in the humiliating recall of Scott by Polk.

Following an inconclusive court of inquiry that further damaged the reputations of both Pillow and Scott, Pillow retired to his home to restore his farming interests. By 1850 he had returned to the political scene in Tennessee, and despite his efforts on the national level on behalf of Franklin Pierce, he was unsuccessful in his bid for the vice presidency and the Senate. In the Civil War Pillow organized and commanded the forces of Tennessee only to meet disaster and humiliation at Fort Donelson. Bankrupt and embittered, Pillow died on his farm in Arkansas in 1878, vainly attempting to escape the yellow fever raging in Memphis.

Nathaniel Cheairs Hughes, Jr.

Self-inflating Pillow. Lithograph, Nathaniel Currier, 1848. This cartoon, published during or shortly after Pillow's court-martial, depicts Gen. Winfield Scott puncturing a pillow with the sword of "truth" (Library of Congress).

BIBLIOGRAPHY

Frost, John. *The Mexican War: Its Warriors*. 1848.

Hughes, Nathaniel Cheairs, Jr., and Roy P. Stonesifer, Jr. *The Life and Wars of Gideon J. Pillow*. 1993.

See also **Polk-Scott Feud**

Poinsett, Joel

As the first official diplomatic representative from the United States to newly independent Mexico, Joel Roberts Poinsett (1779–1851) played a significant role in creating the atmosphere and tenor of diplomacy between the two nations during the 1820s and 1830s. Poinsett's zealous, intense determination to make Mexican officials aware of the advantages of a democratic political system resulted in many becoming apprehensive about the intentions of their northern neighbor toward Mexico.

Born in South Carolina, Poinsett in the early 1800s became familiar with the various Latin American independence struggles that had erupted against Spain. He was appointed a special commercial agent to Buenos Aires by the James Madison administration in 1810, then consul general to sev-

eral provinces in the present-day Argentine region. In 1811 Poinsett was transferred to Chile, remaining there until 1814, when he was ordered back to Buenos Aires. In 1816 Poinsett returned to the United States, recognized for his capable (if somewhat meddling) service in these South American posts and for his understanding of the complex conditions in that area of the hemisphere.

Back in South Carolina, Poinsett inaugurated a state and national political career, securing election to the South Carolina general assembly in 1816 and attaining reelection two years later. In 1821 Poinsett was elected to the U.S. House of Representatives. Because of his earlier service in South America, Poinsett received a presidential appointment in 1822 to visit the new nation of Mexico. He was to assess the state of political affairs there and report his findings to President James Monroe. Poinsett's quick visit to Mexico brought forth a brief monograph, *Notes on Mexico, Made in the Autumn of 1822*, which further enhanced his reputation as an expert on Latin America.

Indeed, Poinsett's reputation for such expertise resulted in his appointment as the first U.S. minister to Mexico. President John Quincy Adams, following his inauguration in early 1825, informed Poinsett of this critical diplomatic appointment. President Adams and Secretary of State Henry

Clay held discussions with Poinsett regarding his duties and objectives as minister, specifically instructions to purchase sizable amounts of Mexican territory to the southwest of the United States. Poinsett arrived in Mexico City in May 1825.

From the beginning, Poinsett's diplomatic tenure was difficult. Poinsett himself was much of the problem. Although earnest and dedicated, Poinsett was a passionate, aggressive advocate of the U.S. democratic system, which he considered nearly flawless. Moreover, he had only contempt for most other political systems, particularly monarchical or conservative systems. Conversely, Lucas Alamán, the Mexican minister with whom Poinsett first negotiated, was an avowed monarchist and conservative, as well as Mexico's most capable political thinker. Alamán, who viewed democracy as anathema and the United States as a threat to Mexico's sovereignty, was determined to thwart any efforts by Poinsett to acquire territory for the United States. The meetings and deliberations between Poinsett and Alamán from July to September 1825 thus set the diplomatic tone—that is, intensified attitudes of mistrust, suspicion, and hostility, one nation toward the other—that eventually would lead to war between the two countries. Unable to achieve anything positive for the U.S. government following the confrontations with Alamán, Poinsett returned to the United States in 1829, bringing along specimens of the plant, the poinsettia, that was later named for him.

Curt Lamar

BIBLIOGRAPHY

Fuentes Mares, José. *Poinsett: Historia de una gran intriga.* 1958.

Lamar, Curt. "Genesis of Mexican–United States Diplomacy: A Critical Analysis of the Alamán-Poinsett Confrontation, 1825." *The Americas* 38 (1981): 1, 87–110.

Rippy, J. Fred. *Joel R. Poinsett, Versatile American.* 1935. Reprint, 1972.

Point Isabel

See **Brazos Santiago**

Politics

This entry consists of three separate articles: **Mexican Politics;** **Texan Politics;** *and* **U.S. Politics.**

Mexican Politics

Faced with not only political discord, in which the contenders were federalism and centralism, but also economic woes (an empty treasury and debts to foreign and national creditors as well as the army and the bureaucracy), the Mexican governments that followed the War of Independence had lit-

tle chance of achieving anything other than a solution to immediate conflicts. Since 6 December 1844 General José Joaquín de Herrera had held the executive power of a centralist republic ruled by the *Bases Orgánicas.* He faced severe internal political strife among the different factions, created largely by the U.S. annexation of Texas. President Herrera wanted to prevent annexation, even if it meant recognizing the independence of the Republic of Texas. His views were supported by moderate liberals; the radicals and the extremist press, however, disagreed with his pacifist stance and demanded that Mexico declare war against the United States. Under such pressure, Herrera refused to meet with John Slidell, President James K. Polk's emissary to Mexico, who had been instructed to negotiate to purchase New Mexico and California and to establish the southwestern boundary of Texas at the Río Bravo. Holding an interview with Slidell would have maintained relations with the United States, but it would not have solved the issues that eventually led to the U.S.–Mexican War.

To make matters worse, while the U.S. Army was approaching the Río Bravo, Gen. Mariano Paredes y Arrillaga, supported by the contingent sent to San Luis Potosí to fight the U.S. troops, rebelled against Herrera, accusing him of treason. Paredes y Arillaga, promising to declare war, marched to Mexico City, where the conservatives helped him assume power on 4 January 1846. After being in power for only a short time he, too, recognized Mexico's weakness and, like his predecessor Herrera, adopted a conciliatory stance toward the United States. He refused to meet with Slidell, and hostilities between the two countries began in May. His attempts to put the nation's treasury in order and to organize the army were in part successful, but his delay in declaring war and his monarchist tendencies deprived him of support from the *puros,* who decided that Gen. Antonio López de Santa Anna, in exile at the time, would be the best person to defend the country. When news of the Mexican defeats at Palo Alto and Resaca de la Palma in northern Mexico reached the capital, Paredes y Arrillaga began to favor the republic openly, which ended his support from the conservatives. Allied with Santa Anna's friends, the *puros* asked Santa Anna to return, overthrew Paredes y Arrillaga in August, and created a temporary government led by Gen. Mariano Salas. Santa Anna returned in September, immediately organized an army, and marched north to stop the U.S. Army's advance. A new congress met in December and reestablished the Constitution of 1824 and the federal republic. Santa Anna was elected president; Valentín Gómez Farías was named vice president, and he led the government while Santa Anna was leading Mexican forces into battle. Gómez Farías, in an attempt to solve the nation's critical economic crisis and acting on the belief that the Catholic Church was the only institution with enough money to fund the war effort, forced Congress to decree that some of the ecclesiastical properties would be sold or mortgaged in January and February 1847. This led to a widespread outcry, and the *polkos*, national guard battalions established to defend Mexico City, supported by the clergy and some of the moderate liberals, revolted. The *polkos* revolt lasted only a few weeks; Santa Anna returned from the military campaign to restore peace. Defense of the country was subsequently funded through a loan from the Catholic Church. Santa Anna, surrounded by moderate liberals, attempted to remove Gómez Farías, who refused to step down; so Santa Anna had Congress abolish the vice presidency. This move led to Santa Anna's loss of support from the *puros*.

In the meantime, the U.S. Army had disembarked at Vera Cruz and was advancing along the National Road toward Mexico City. Santa Anna left for the battle site in April, and Gen. Pedro María Anaya was named president ad interim. The Mexican army was defeated several times in succession. After a short armistice, hostilities were renewed and did not end until Mexico City surrendered on 14 September.

Two days later, Santa Anna resigned the presidency but retained command of the Mexican army. However, after being defeated at Huamantla on 11 October, he received an order to appear before a military court of inquiry; he decided to escape and started his way toward a new exile. The executive power devolved upon the presiding justice of the Supreme Court, Manuel de la Peña y Peña, who moved the government to the city of Querétaro. Peña y Peña and General Anaya then alternated power while the scattered congress reunited. This gave the moderate liberals control for some months, although it still took a great effort on their part to impose their increasingly pacifistic point of view on the other factions. The moderate liberals were themselves divided into two factions: some willing to sacrifice whatever territory was necessary to end the war, others who wanted a less expensive alternative. On 2 February 1848, the moderate liberal government in Querétaro signed the Treaty of Guadalupe Hidalgo, which was approved by the U.S. Congress and signed by President James K. Polk in May. Once peace was achieved, the Mexican legislature started thinking in terms of a constitutional presidency. General Herrera was elected and assumed the presidency on 3 June.

Ana Rosa Suárez Argüello

BIBLIOGRAPHY

Alcaraz, Ramón, ed. *The Other Side; or, Notes for the History of the War between Mexico and the United States.* Translated by Albert C. Ramsey. 1970. Originally published as *Apuntes para la historia de la Guerra entre México y los Estado Unidos,* 1848.

Bosch García, Carlos. *Documentos de la relación de México con los Estado Unidos.* 4 vols. 1983–1985.

Peña y Reyes, Antonio de la, ed. *Algunos documentos sobre el Tratado de Guadalupe y la situación de México durante la invasión americana.* 1971.

Pletcher, David M. *The Diplomacy of Annexation: Texas, Oregon, and the Mexican War.* 1973.

Riva Palacio, Vicente, coord. *México a través de los siglos.* 5 vols. 1887.

Roa Bárcena, José María. *Recuerdos de la invasión norteamericana (1846–1848).* 3 vols. 1947.

Santoni, Pedro. "Los federalistas radicales y la guerra del 47." Ph.D. diss., El Colegio de México, 1987.

Vázquez, Josefina Z., and Lorenzo Meyer. *México frente a Estados Unidos: Un ensayo histórico 1776–1980.* 1982.

Velasco Márquez, Jesús. *La opinión pública y la guerra del 47.* 1975.

Zamacois, Niceto de. *Historia de México desde sus tiempos más remotos hasta nuestros dís, escrita en vist de todo lo que de irrecusable han dado a luz los más caracterizados historiadores, y en virtud de documentos auténticos no publicados todavía, tomados del Archivo Nacional de Méjico, de las bibliotecas públicas, y de los preciosos manuscritos que, hasta hace poco, existían en las de los conventos de aquel país.* 20 vols. 1876–1882.

See also **Conservatives, Mexican**; **Moderados**; *and* **Puros**.

Texan Politics

There were no Whig or Democratic parties in Texas during the period of the republic (1836–1846). Political parties, as they existed in the United States, did not become a factor in Texas until after statehood. Political factions in Texas, however, date back to the colonial era before independence. The peace faction, led by Stephen F. Austin, was loyal to the Republic of Mexico and the Mexican Constitution of 1824. The war faction, dominated by William H. Wharton and Sam Houston, preferred a break with Mexico and complete independence. The climactic victory at San Jacinto and the establishment of the Republic of Texas in 1836 united all these groups and resolved the earlier political differences.

The pro–U.S. annexation faction in the new republic was led by Sam Houston and James Pinckney Henderson. The anti-annexation faction was led by Mirabeau B. Lamar and David G. Burnet. Houston twice served as president of the republic (1836–1838; 1841–1844) and Lamar once (1838–1841). Those in favor of annexation argued that Texas needed the protection of the United States against Indian attacks on the frontier and against a threatened Mexican invasion. They also stressed the financial advantages that would accrue to the state of Texas after annexation. Those opposed to annexation emphasized the economic potential of the Republic of Texas once peace with Mexico was assured. They also argued that as a Southern state, newly admitted to the Union, Texas would suffer from the antislavery prejudice of the Northern states. Both sides used newspaper editorials to sway public opinion, but Texians overwhelmingly favored annexation and admission to the Union.

In the first presidential election in Texas, held in 1836, Sam Houston emerged as a decisive winner. Stephen F. Austin's death a few months later signaled the end of the colonial period and left Houston the dominant political personality in the republic. During his first administration, from 1836 to 1838, the seat of government was located at Houston, the General Land Office was established, and the Customs Act was passed to raise desperately needed money. Most important, the Boundary Act (1836) claimed the Río Grande as the southwestern boundary of Texas. This claim was consistent with the treaty signed with Mexico after the Battle of San Jacinto. The United States was the first nation to extend diplomatic recognition to Texas (1837), but early annexation talks proved inconclusive.

The Republic of Texas constitution forbade consecutive terms for the office of president, thus Houston was ineligible in the 1838 election. The constitution also stipulated that the first presidential term would be two years and all thereafter three years. After a campaign marred by the suicides of his principal opponents, Peter W. Grayson and James Collinsworth, Mirabeau B. Lamar easily defeated Robert Wilson for the first three-year term. Lamar's policies differed radically from those of his predecessor. Not friendly to the Indians as Houston had been, Lamar drove the Cherokees from Texas in 1839. He was less successful against the Comanches, but did blunt their raiding forays on the frontier. Determined to move the capital to a more western location, Lamar persuaded Congress to move the seat of government to Austin in 1841. After diplomatic overtures failed to secure a lasting peace with Mexico, Lamar turned to force. The Santa Fe Expedition, however, resulted in the greatest disaster of his administration. Failure to capture Santa Fe seriously damaged the Texas claim to the Río Grande as the southwestern boundary.

Sam Houston defeated David G. Burnet, Lamar's vice president, in the 1841 presidential campaign. With annexation talks between Texas and the United States gaining momentum, Mexico decided to stake its boundary claims. In April and again in September 1842, Mexican troops raided San Antonio to effectively negate the republic's claim to the Río Grande as the boundary. Although he felt it could not succeed, Houston reluctantly consented to a retaliatory attack on the Mexican side of the river. Mier, a village south of the Río Grande, was briefly held by the invading Texians but was quickly retaken by regular Mexican troops. The captured Texians expected to be exchanged for prisoners held by Texas, but the surrender terms were violated by Mexico. In the course of a forced march to Mexico City, an escape attempt was made at Salado, a small town south of Saltillo. Although Gen. Antonio López de Santa Anna had ordered that all captured prisoners be put to death, the local commander permitted the unfortunate captives to gamble for their lives. Seventeen men drew a fatal black bean and were quickly executed. Of the 159 men who drew a white bean, many perished on the remainder of the march or in Mexican prisons thereafter. Thus, Texas was no more successful under Houston than it had been under Lamar in validating its claim to the Río Grande border.

In the last presidential election in Texas (1844), Anson Jones defeated Edward Burleson by a comfortable margin. Jones owed his triumph to Houston's support and to his promise to continue annexation negotiations that Houston had begun. With the admission of Texas into the Union in 1846, James P. Henderson was elected the first governor of the state. A few months later the United States declared war against Mexico, in part over the unresolved boundary question.

Stanley E. Siegel

BIBLIOGRAPHY

Haynes, Sam W. *Soldiers of Misfortune: The Somervell and Mier Expeditions.* 1990.
Siegel, Stanley. *A Political History of the Texas Republic, 1836–1845.* 1956.

U.S. Politics

Texas and the southwest shaped political debate in the pre–Civil War United States. The issue proved so divisive that it eventually destroyed the old political alliances of the Jacksonian era and led to the new politics of sectionalism.

Two major parties—Democrats and Whigs—dominated U.S. politics throughout the 1830s and 1840s. The Democratic Party had formed around Andrew Jackson during his years on the national scene, and he continued to exert enormous influence on his party even after retiring from public life in 1837. The Whig Party grew out of opposition to Jackson's policies and actions. Borrowing from the British political system, Jackson's opponents called themselves Whigs, the traditional name for the opposition party in Great Britain. Although both parties had a national constituency that cut across all sections, there were factions in each that had different ideas about the fate of Texas.

The Texas issue first came to the forefront of U.S. politics in 1836 when Texas won its independence from Mexico. In July both the House and Senate passed resolutions recognizing the new republic, but President Andrew Jackson, not wanting to antagonize Mexico, did not officially recognize Texas until just before the end of his term. In August 1837 Texas petitioned for annexation to the United States, but the petition was rejected when the antislavery faction in Congress objected to the admission of a new slave state.

The issue of annexation remained dormant for nearly ten years, until it arose in presidential politics and promised to be just as controversial in 1844 as it had been in 1837.

Knowing how volatile the issue was, both front-runners—Democrat Martin Van Buren and Whig Henry Clay—tried to avoid bringing Texas into the campaign. The strategy supposedly had been formulated in 1842 when Van Buren, former protégé of Jackson and former president, visited Clay at his home in Ashland, Kentucky. As the election drew closer, both hopefuls published letters opposing immediate annexation. In doing so, Van Buren lost the support of the expansionist faction of his party, including Jackson, as pro-Texas Democrats backed Tennessean James K. Polk. Running on a platform that promised to "Reoccupy Oregon" and "Reannex Texas," Polk emerged victorious at both the Democratic convention in May 1844 and the national polls the following autumn.

Outgoing president John Tyler used Polk's election to push for immediate annexation. The United States had opened negotiations with the Republic of Texas in 1843, resulting in an annexation treaty in April 1844. The issue seemed dead when the Senate rejected the treaty, but Tyler interpreted the success of the expansionist platform as a mandate for action. He and his allies maneuvered a joint resolution through Congress that annexed Texas to the Union. The move succeeded and Texas formally became the twenty-eighth state on 29 November 1845.

The campaign and the events that followed shattered the Democratic alliance. Shunned by the mainstream party, Van Buren felt betrayed. He and his New York supporters represented the reform branch of the Democratic Party, called Barnburners. Polk passed over Van Buren's colleagues and selected William L. Marcy, member of a rival New York faction called the Hunkers, for secretary of war, angering the Barnburners. In addition, many pro-Oregon Democrats also felt betrayed by Polk's compromise with Great Britain that divided the region in half. The Democratic Party was further rocked when David Wilmot, Democratic representative from Pennsylvania, introduced on 8 August 1846 an amendment to an appropriations bill that, had it passed, would have prohibited slavery in any new territories gained from Mexico. The Barnburner-Hunker feud and the schism over the Wilmot Proviso became national issues and affected the outcome of the 1848 presidential election.

The Wilmot Proviso proved to be a powerful wedge to the Whigs, too, splitting them into two opposing factions. Northern Whigs spoke out openly against slavery as a moral evil, forming a block called Conscience Whigs. Other Whigs, mainly Southerners who supported slavery, were termed Cotton Whigs.

The election of 1848 was a turning point for both national parties. The Whigs had chosen a popular war hero for their candidate, Gen. Zachary Taylor. The Democrats also ran a politician with a military background, Lewis Cass of Michigan. The election, however, turned on dissident Democrats and Whigs who had banded together with members of the old abolitionist Liberty Party to form the new Free Soil Party. While the Free Soil candidate, Van Buren, failed to carry a single state in the November election, he and his party succeeded in drawing enough support away from the Democratic Party to make Taylor's victory possible. The election marked the beginning of the end for the two great Jacksonian parties as factions continued to seek realignment throughout the 1850s.

Richard Bruce Winders

BIBLIOGRAPHY

Binkley, Wilfred E. *American Political Parties: Their Natural History.* 1971.

Cole, Donald B. *Martin Van Buren and the American Political System.* 1984.

Going, Charles Buxton. *David Wilmot, Free Soiler.* 1924.

Morrison, Chaplin W. *Democratic Politics and Sectionalism: The Wilmot Proviso Controversy.* 1967.

Winders, Richard Bruce. *Mr. Polk's Army.* 1997.

Polk, James K.

Eleventh president of the United States James Knox Polk (1795–1849) was born 2 November near Charlotte, North Carolina. The son of a prosperous planter, Polk moved with his family to Columbia, Tennessee, in 1803. After graduating

James K. Polk. John Frost, *Pictorial History of Mexico and the Mexican War*, 1862

first in his class at the University of North Carolina, Polk returned to Columbia to take up a career in law but soon found politics to be his real vocation. In 1825 he was elected to the first of seven consecutive terms in the U.S. Congress.

A loyal supporter of fellow Tennessean Andrew Jackson, Polk rose quickly up the ranks of the Democratic Party hierarchy. As a member of the Ways and Means Committee, he played a key role in President Jackson's war on the Bank of the United States. Elevated to the rank of committee chairman after the election of 1832, Polk emerged as a figure of national prominence, steadfastly defending Jackson against charges of "executive usurpation."

Polk's unswerving devotion to the cause of Jacksonian Democracy was rivaled only by his intense ambition. In 1835 he was elected Speaker of the House, a position that he held for the next four years. Hoping to build a strong, statewide following in his home state and thereby emerge as a contender for his party's vice-presidential nomination, Polk resigned his seat in Congress in 1839 to run for the governorship of Tennessee. After serving one two-year term, Polk was defeated in his bid for reelection; a second attempt to regain the office also failed in 1843. In view of these setbacks, Polk's prospects for winning the second spot on his party's ticket seemed remote, but his political fortunes changed dramatically at the Democratic convention of 1844. Martin Van Buren, the likely nominee, had angered the pro-expansion wing of the party by refusing to endorse a policy of Texas annexation. With Van Buren unable to muster the two-thirds majority needed for nomination, the Democrats after eight ballots turned to the former Tennessee governor as a compromise "dark horse" candidate.

The election was one of the closest in history, with Polk receiving 38,000 more votes than Whig candidate Henry Clay out of 2,700,000 cast, although he edged out his opponent in enough key states to give him a comfortable 170 to 105 lead in the electoral college. The forty-nine-year-old Polk was the youngest chief executive up to that time. From the outset Polk served notice that he intended "to be *myself* president of the U.S." rather than the tool of a particular faction of the Democratic Party. In domestic policy, Polk remained faithful to the laissez-faire economic policies of his mentor, Jackson. Committed to tariff reduction and a hard-money doctrine, Polk pushed Congress to pass in 1846 the Walker Tariff and the Independent Treasury Act. Polk also stood firm against internal improvements, much to the dismay of many northern Democrats, who were beginning to favor a more active role by the federal government in the nation's economic affairs.

In the arena of foreign policy the eleventh president provided similarly determined leadership. Congress presented to the new president the first crisis of his administration by passing in early March a joint resolution offering to annex the Republic of Texas, an initiative that Mexican leaders de-

nounced as grounds for war. Unwilling to wait until the Republic of Texas formally approved the annexation offer, the administration prevailed on Texas leaders to accept U.S. military protection. On 15 June the government ordered fifteen hundred troops under the command of Gen. Zachary Taylor to the Texas frontier. Ignoring the Mexican claim that the Nueces River was the southern boundary of Texas, by the end of July Taylor was ordered to concentrate his forces on the Río Grande.

While tensions between the United States and Mexico escalated, the new administration also faced a growing crisis with Great Britain. The United States had occupied the Oregon Territory with Great Britain by joint agreement since 1818. Although Polk had maintained in his inaugural address that the U.S. claim to the entire Oregon Territory was "clear and unquestionable," he sought to initiate negotiations with Great Britain by offering to divide the territory at the 49th parallel. When Great Britain's minister in Washington, D.C., rejected the offer, Polk ordered Secretary of State James Buchanan to withdraw the proposal, thus bringing negotiations to a standstill. In a move that was widely regarded as the first step toward hostilities, Polk in his first annual message in December 1845 called for an end to the joint occupation of Oregon and asked Congress to give Great Britain one year's notice before terminating the agreement, as the joint occupation treaty required. Anxious to avoid antagonizing the world's reigning naval power, Congress ultimately passed a mildly worded resolution that called for an "amicable settlement" of the dispute. As relations with Mexico continued to deteriorate in the early spring of 1846, Polk also became amenable to a compromise solution with Great Britain, while continuing to insist, at least for the record, on the legitimacy of the U.S. claim. When the British made an offer agreeing to accept the 49th parallel compromise line, the president referred the proposal to the Senate, which ratified the treaty by a vote of 41 to 14.

Polk's policy toward Mexico, meanwhile, remained aggressively confrontational. Convinced that Mexican leaders would submit to U.S. pressure, the president dispatched to Mexico a new U.S. minister, John Slidell, with instructions to settle the Texas boundary dispute and reach an agreement regarding more than $3 million in unpaid U.S. claims against the Mexican government. Slidell was further instructed to see if Mexican leaders would be receptive to the possibility of selling California and New Mexico. The Mexican government refused to receive Slidell as U.S. minister, and in May the U.S. diplomat returned to Washington, D.C., to brief the president on the failure of his mission. Polk maintained that the United States now had grounds for war. Soon afterward the president learned that U.S. troops had been attacked along the Río Grande, and on 11 May he called on Congress for a declaration of war against Mexico.

Polk was the second U.S. president to wage war against a

foreign adversary, but unlike James Madison in the War of 1812, he was the first to exercise fully the powers of commander-in-chief. Although he had no professional military experience, the strong-willed chief executive left no doubt as to who was in charge of the war effort. Rather than wait for the War Department to draft a plan of attack against Mexico, Polk himself developed the broad outlines of an initial strategy that involved striking Mexico at three vital points: Santa Fe, New Mexico; Mexico's northern provinces below the Río Grande; and California.

In the months that followed, Polk supervised every aspect of the war effort, choosing and replacing officers and even taking a direct role in logistical matters. All decisions made at the War Department were subjected to the closest scrutiny. Mindful of government inefficiency, the president insisted on being kept constantly informed by Secretary of War William L. Marcy of military expenditures. Much to his astonishment, Polk discovered that the Quartermaster's Department had ordered thousands of wagons for the campaigns in Mexico, despite the fact that pack mules were better suited to Mexico's rugged terrain. Polk was also annoyed to find that the army was purchasing horses and mules in the United States and transporting them to the theater of operations, when such animals were readily available at a fraction of the cost in Mexico.

From the earliest days of the war, partisan rancor created an atmosphere of distrust between the president and the nation's military authorities. While Polk's powers of appointment allowed him to shape the volunteer regimental command structure to suit his purposes, he did not enjoy similar latitude in the professional army, which was top-heavy with Whig partisans in 1846. Gen. Winfield Scott, the highest ranking officer in the U.S. Army and a prominent Whig, quickly fell into disfavor with the president, who then tapped Gen. Zachary Taylor to serve as field commander of the U.S. forces. Taylor proved equally unsatisfactory from the president's point of view, and Polk's criticism of the general may well have contributed to Taylor's willingness to be drafted by the Whigs as a presidential candidate in 1848. Deciding to open a second front in the fall of 1846, the president turned reluctantly again to Scott to command an invasion of southern Mexico. The president remained suspicious of his general's partisan loyalties, however, and despite a string of impressive victories culminating in the capture of Mexico City, Scott was recalled by the administration.

Polk grew similarly frustrated with his peace commissioner, Nicholas P. Trist, who was sent to negotiate with Mexican leaders after the fall of Vera Cruz. A lifelong Democrat, Trist nonetheless established a close rapport with Scott, which the president interpreted as a sign of his diplomat's untrustworthiness. When peace talks with the Mexican government stalled, Polk recalled Trist, only to find that the diplomat decided to conclude his negotiations in defiance

of Polk's order. Although angered by Trist's insubordination, Polk signed the Treaty of Guadalupe Hidalgo, by which Mexico ceded California and New Mexico to the United States for $15 million.

While the fault for these squabbles was by no means Polk's alone, the president's desire for control of every situation led inevitably to friction with his subordinates. Polk's hands-on style of management worked well enough in Washington, D.C., where a small bureaucracy discharged its duties under the watchful eye of the chief executive, but it was impossible for Polk to supervise the operations of U.S. troops on foreign soil with similar exactitude. Far removed from the seat of government, the nation's military leaders and diplomatic representatives enjoyed a freedom of action that Polk found enormously frustrating. In an atmosphere already poisoned by partisan suspicions, even the most well-intentioned deviation from instructions appeared to the president to be an act of partisanship or betrayal.

While the U.S.–Mexican War established the United States as a hemispheric power, it also exacerbated sectional tensions rooted in Northern fears over the expansion of slavery. Polk remained oblivious to these concerns and, as his term neared its close, continued to press for new territorial acquisitions. The administration briefly considered extending protectorate status over the Yucatán and offered to purchase Cuba from Spain, but these initiatives failed to yield productive results. In the waning months of his administration, the president became preoccupied with the need to establish federal authority over the territories that the nation had recently acquired. An Oregon territorial bill prohibiting slavery passed over the furious objections of Southern politicians; congressional efforts to extend federal jurisdiction over California and New Mexico became hopelessly mired in the growing sectional controversy and did not succeed until the Compromise of 1850.

On 5 March 1849 Polk left Washington, D.C., and embarked on an extensive tour of the Southern states before returning to his native state of Tennessee. The grueling itinerary of speeches and banquets took a severe toll on the former president's already fragile health, and he arrived in Nashville weak and exhausted. With the outbreak of cholera, Polk died on 15 June 1849.

At the time of his inauguration in 1845, few could have predicted that Polk would be a strong chief executive. He had inherited a party apparatus rent by internal discord, and the controversial circumstances surrounding his nomination in 1844 prompted some Democratic leaders to question his legitimacy as the party's standard-bearer. Nonetheless, Polk managed to rise above these limitations. Calling for "a plain and frugal government" and the bold pursuit of U.S. territorial ambitions in his inaugural address, the president could claim significant accomplishments in both areas by the end of his term. With the annexation of Texas, the settlement of the Oregon boundary, and the Mexican Cession, the national domain had grown by 1.2 million square miles, an increase of 64 percent. On the other hand, Polk's expansionist agenda sparked a furious sectional debate, aggravating the tensions that would lead to the Civil War little more than a decade after he left office. In addition, his belligerent policies toward Mexico and his decision to wage war on the dubious grounds of national defense still rank among the more controversial chapters in the annals of U.S. international relations.

Sam W. Haynes

BIBLIOGRAPHY
Bergeron, Paul H. *The Presidency of James K. Polk.* 1987.
Haynes, Sam W. *James K. Polk and the Expansionist Impulse.* 1996.
Quaife, Milo M., ed. *The Diary of James K. Polk during His Presidency, 1845 to 1849.* 1910.
Sellers, Charles Grier. *James K. Polk: Continentalist.* 1966.
Sellers, Charles Grier. *James K. Polk: Jacksonian, 1795–1843.* 1957.

See also **Polk-Scott Feud**

Polkos Revolt

On 11 January 1847 Mexican vice president Valentín Gómez Farías, who had become acting chief executive because Gen. Antonio López de Santa Anna was leading the army in San Luis Potosí issued a decree that authorized the government to raise 15 million pesos by mortgaging or selling ecclesiastical property. Designed to finance the war against the United States, the law instead fostered public animosity toward Gómez Farías. *Moderado* politicians, senior army chiefs, and high-ranking clerical leaders began to plot against him, and their intrigues culminated in the 27 February 1847 "rebellion of the *polkos*."

The principal weapons of the conspirators were the aristocratic civic militia battalions that had been organized during the autumn of 1846. At that time the militia had become divided along factional and social lines because the *puros'* revival of this military force appeared to entail arming the lower echelons of society. Consequently, Mexico City's well-to-do countered by raising their own militia units. Five of these corps (Victoria, Hidalgo, Mina, Bravos, and Independencia) acquired notoriety. Most historians believe they became known as the *polkos* after the polka, which was the most popular dance of elite society; some contend, however, that their name derives from their support of U.S. president James K. Polk. Their commanders included well-known *moderados*, such as Gen. José Mariano Salas and Gen. Pedro María Anaya. The political rivalries and class antagonisms

that afflicted the militia made for a volatile mixture that fueled partisan discord.

Thus, by late February 1847 the Gómez Farías regime not only had to cope with the likelihood of a domestic rebellion, but also faced the expected landing in Vera Cruz of Gen. Winfield Scott and the U.S. expeditionary army. In an attempt to defuse this explosive situation and support Vera Cruz's defense, the acting president transferred three elite militia units to the Gulf Coast, but their leaders used this order as a pretext to rebel. Gen. Matías de la Peña y Barragán put himself at the head of the mutineers, who issued a thirteen-article plan demanding, among other things, Gómez Farías's resignation and the annulment of the 11 January decree. After ten days of sporadic street fighting, on 8 March the rebels tried to reach a settlement by replacing the original plan with one of a single article calling for the removal of Gómez Farías. The modification did not work, however. Hostilities continued and Mexico City found itself immersed in a civil war in the midst of a foreign conflict.

The struggle between *puro* and *polko* militia units ended the *puros'* political ascendancy. On returning to Mexico City in late March following the Battle of Buena Vista, Santa Anna cast his lot with the *moderados*. He persuaded congress to abolish the office of vice president, which effectively removed Gómez Farías, and name General Anaya "substitute president." Santa Anna also agreed to nullify the anticlerical legislation implemented by Gómez Farías in exchange for a donation of 2 million pesos in cash. Even more important, the revolt of the *polkos* weakened the total war effort. It prevented the Mexican government from assisting Vera Cruz (which surrendered on 29 March) and from strengthening the city of Puebla and the fortifications near the coast.

Pedro Santoni

BIBLIOGRAPHY
Alcaraz, Ramón, ed. *The Other Side; or, Notes for the History of the War between Mexico and the United States.* Translated by Albert C. Ramsey. 1970. Originally published as *Apuntes para la historia de la Guerra entre México y los Estados Unidos,* 1848.
Costeloe, Michael P. "The Mexican Church and the Rebellion of the Polkos." *Hispanic American Historical Review* 46 (May 1966): 170–178.
Prieto, Guillermo. *Memorias de mis tiempos.* 1985.
Santoni, Pedro. "The Failure of Mobilization: The Civic Militia of Mexico in 1846." *Mexican Studies/Estudios Mexicanos* 12:2 (Summer 1996): 169–194.

Polk-Scott Feud

The feud between President James K. Polk and Maj. Gen. Winfield Scott, the commanding general of the U.S. Army,

Distinguished Military Operations with a Hasty Bowl of Soup. This lithograph (Edward W. Clay, 1846 or early 1847) satirizes the mercurial nature of President James K. Polk's relationship to his generals. Having been removed from field command, Gen. Winfield Scott protested, stating that he received notice of his removal as he was taking "a hasty plate of soup." When his replacement, Zachary Taylor, began to earn a national reputation for his victories, Polk, hoping to douse Taylor's military reputation and political ambition, turned again to Scott and appointed him to command the invasion of central Mexico.

ran the course of the U.S.–Mexican War and influenced military management at the highest levels. The feud arose from a combination of politics, personality, and ambiguity in the army's command structure. An ardent Whig who had been a candidate for his party's presidential nomination in 1844, Scott incurred from the start the suspicion of the intensely partisan Polk, who viewed him as a potential rival. Moreover, Scott possessed an immense ego and a quarrelsome temperament that were poorly suited for a close relationship with the strong-willed president. Finally, the commanding general's powers and functions were ill-defined by law and precedent, particularly his precise place in the hierarchy of military command and the role he would play in a major war.

On 13 May 1846, the day after passage of the declaration of war, Polk offered Scott command of the field army to be raised to prosecute the war, an assignment that Scott accepted as his due. However, the militarily inexperienced president lacked real confidence in Scott, whom he described as "rather scientific and visionary" in his views on strategy. Polk's dissatisfaction grew when Scott failed to leave immediately for the Río Grande and instead remained at army headquarters, coordinating the general mobilization of forces. For his part, Scott resented the administration's efforts to create new generals' positions, which he believed were intended to supersede himself and other regular army generals with Democratic loyalists. In response to urging by Secretary of War William L. Marcy that he go to the front, Scott composed a letter on 21 May, complaining about undue pressure from "high quarters," explaining the immense work load that he was handling, and suggesting that the administration select another field commander in his place. He did not wish, he wrote, to place himself "in the most precarious of all positions—fire upon my rear, from Washington, and the fire, in front, from the Mexicans."

Polk was furious at what he considered Scott's disloyalty; after consulting with his cabinet, he ordered the general removed from the field command and limited to his stationary duties in Washington, D.C. Shocked by this decision, Scott informed Marcy on 25 May that notification of his removal had arrived while he was taking "a hasty plate of soup," and he went on to insist that his reference to pressure from high quarters had intended no disrespect to the president. Polk refused to revoke the suspension, however, and Democratic editors and cartoonists had a field day with Scott's unfortunate phrasing.

Throughout the summer and fall of 1846, the well-chastened commanding general worked diligently at his Washington desk to support the war effort. Meanwhile, Polk grew increasingly resentful of Maj. Gen. Zachary Taylor, also a Whig, partly because Taylor's victories in Texas and northern Mexico were enhancing his presidential prospects. In November the administration concluded that an invasion of Mexico at Vera Cruz would be necessary to terminate the war. At first Polk favored appointing Sen. Thomas Hart Benton to head the expedition, reestablishing the grade of lieutenant general so that Benton would outrank the two Whig major generals. However, Scott had earlier submitted a detailed and thoughtful plan for attacking Vera Cruz, and Secretary Marcy worked to enhance the general's standing with the president. The cabinet leaned toward Scott's selection, if only because he was the senior officer of the army. On 18 November 1846, Polk reluctantly decided to name Scott field commander of the Vera Cruz expedition.

Ecstatic over his resurrection, Scott promised full cooperation with the administration and agreed to take with him to Mexico any volunteer generals whom Polk desired. However, the aura of reconciliation evaporated as the campaign progressed. Polk continued to push for creation of the lieutenant general's position with the intention of appointing Benton to the overall command—though the proposal eventually died in Congress. Moreover, the president became convinced that Whigs in the high ranks of the army were actively obstructing the war effort. In turn, Scott attributed inevitable shortages of troops and supplies to administration efforts to cripple his campaign against Vera Cruz and Mexico City and thus deprive him of fame. The touchy commander especially resented Polk's appointment of Nicholas P. Trist, chief clerk of the State Department, as diplomatic agent to negotiate with the Mexican government, a move that Scott interpreted as a usurpation of his military powers. Trist and Scott eventually became close friends and collaborators, but Polk was furious at Scott's initial refusal to cooperate with the diplomat and seriously considered removing him from command in the midst of his campaign against Mexico City.

The climax of the long-simmering feud followed Scott's capture of the Mexican capital. During the late fall of 1847, Scott became enmeshed in politically charged quarrels with several high-ranking officers, arising mainly from the publication of reports and anonymous letters intended to inflate the officers' contributions in the battles for Mexico City. One of these commanders, Maj. Gen. Gideon J. Pillow, was the president's close friend and his nephew's law partner. Pillow was responsible for a letter signed "Leonidas" that appeared in the New Orleans *Delta,* attributing the victories at Contreras and Churubusco almost entirely to his own brilliance and disparaging Scott's performance. Learning that Scott had brought charges against Pillow and two other officers, Polk flew into a rage and blamed the matter on the commanding general's "vanity and tyrannical temper, and his want of prudence and common sense." In January 1848, after extended consultation with his cabinet, the president removed Scott as commander in Mexico, replacing him with Maj. Gen. William O. Butler. He also ordered a court of inquiry to examine the web of officers' quarrels and later extended its mandate to include investigation of an unsuccessful attempt by Scott and Trist the previous summer to bribe Gen. Antonio López de Santa Anna into making peace.

Meeting in Mexico City in April 1848 and at Frederick, Maryland, in June and July, the court focused mainly on the dispute between Pillow and Scott and concluded that the evidence did not warrant further proceedings. After reviewing the court's findings, Polk characteristically attributed Scott's treatment of the subordinate general to the fact that Pillow "is a Democrat in his politics and was supposed to be my personal and political friend." With the dissolution of the court of inquiry, Scott went on extended leave because of ill health, and the acrimonious feud petered out in the closing months of Polk's administration. During its course, it had twice led to the removal of the army's highest ranking officer from the war's principal field command.

William B. Skelton

BIBLIOGRAPHY

Bauer, K. Jack. *The Mexican War, 1846–1848.* 1974.

Elliott, Charles W. *Winfield Scott: The Soldier and the Man.* 1937.

Quaife, Milo Milton. *The Diary of James K. Polk during His Presidency.* 4 vols. 1910.

Scott, Winfield. *Memoirs of Lieut.-General Winfield Scott, L.L.D., Written by Himself.* 2 vols. 1864.

Sellers, Charles G. *James K. Polk: Continentalist, 1843–1846.* 1966.

Spencer, Ivor Debenham. *The Victor and the Spoils: A Life of William L. Marcy.* 1959.

Prescott, William Hickling

Historian William Hickling Prescott (1796–1859) was born in Salem, Massachusetts, and moved with his family to Boston in 1808, where he remained for the rest of his life. Following his graduation from Harvard in 1814, he pursued a literary career as an essayist and reviewer before turning to the writing of history. As a historian, Prescott was one of a small group of New England men of letters whose works reflected the prevailing currents of Romantic thought. They were drawn to grand themes and heroic leaders, viewed history as revealing the relentless progress of mankind, and by balancing literary craftsmanship with authenticity of detail sought to invest the past with an immediacy in their own time. The titanic clash of sixteenth-century Spain with the Aztec empire, of Hernán Cortés and Montezuma, of Christianity and "paganism" provided Prescott with a subject of epic proportions. Of all his books, none was more popular or more timely than *The History of the Conquest of Mexico,* published in 1843 (reprinted, 1993), just two and one-half years before the U.S.–Mexican War.

Like many of his generation, Prescott believed that the mission of the United States was to advance what he called "the living principle of freedom," for which an extensive empire was a benefit rather than an evil. As an unwavering antislavery New England Whig, however, he was not prepared to accept the annexation of Texas or the war with Mexico as steps toward fulfillment of the nation's mission. The former was "the most serious shock yet given to the stability of our glorious institutions," while the latter exemplified the "craving for foreign acquisitions" that was fatal to republics (*Biographical and Critical Miscellanies,* pp. 266–268). Prescott attributed the war to a "mad ambition for conquest" that would result only in "barren glory" and the addition of "dirty superfluous acres" to a territory already too vast for a republic (*Correspondence,* pp. 629, 634, 656). Yet, there was an ambivalence in Prescott's attitude toward the conflict, for he expressed growing admiration for the volunteer soldiers. They were made of a "dare-devil sort of stuff which goes ahead in spite of every obstacle . . . the pioneers of civilization" (*Correspondence,* p. 648). He took pride in their victories and judged their triumphant campaign against the Mexican capital to be equally as brilliant as that of Cortés.

It is ironic that the writing of a staunch Whig opponent of the war fostered such a popular war spirit. Prescott's *History of the Conquest of Mexico* turned public attention toward Mexico and kindled a fascination with what was popularly regarded as an exotic and mysterious land. Sales soared, as the book encouraged the enlistment of volunteers who hoped to find in Mexico some of the glory and romance they had found in its pages. Many of the soldiers carried copies with them into Mexico, and for the soldiers in Gen. Winfield Scott's army, following the track of Cortés, Prescott's history served as a guide book. One New England officer, posted near Mexico City, reread the *History,* then assured Prescott, who had never visited Mexico, that his descriptions were accurate. It was not surprising that Prescott was urged by General Scott and some of his Whig friends to write the history of the second conquest of Mexico, as he

had the first. Although tempted, Prescott declined. He was unwilling to interrupt his work on a biography of Philip the Second, but more important, he decided not to "meddle with heroes who have not been under ground—two centuries—at least" (*Literary Memoranda,* 2, p. 181).

Robert W. Johannsen

BIBLIOGRAPHY

Prescott, William Hickling. *Biographical and Critical Miscellanies.* 1845.
Prescott, William Hickling. *Literary Memoranda.* 1898.
Ticknor, George. *Life of William Hickling Prescott.* 1864.
Walcott, Roger, ed. *The Correspondence of William Hickling Prescott.* 1925.

Presidios

In colonial Mexico, a string of military outposts known as *presidios*—a name derived from the Latin *praesidium*—was established to guard the frontiers and coasts against Indian attack, contraband trade, and foreign intrusion. The New Spain viceroy, Martín Enríquez de Almanza, initiated this system of forts in the 1570s, primarily to protect roads and mining camps during the Chichimeco War, which lasted from 1560 to 1600.

As the frontier advanced northward, the *presidio* changed in character and increased in size (to as many as one hundred soldiers in some cases) to deal with sporadic Indian uprisings. The *presidio* often was situated adjacent to a Catholic mission, or group of missions, to which it offered protection and support. By the late eighteenth century a line of *presidios* stretched from La Bahía (present-day Goliad, Texas), near the Gulf of Mexico, to the Gulf of California. Many were walled enclosures, while others comprised a cluster of buildings around an open plaza.

The *presidio* defense system fell apart as the frontiers became settled and as the War of Independence swept Mexico from 1810 to 1821. While some *presidios* continued to serve a military purpose into the 1820s, most were abandoned or formed the nucleus of civilian settlements before the U.S.–Mexican War. Few played a significant military role in that conflict. A minor exception occurred at Presidio del Río Grande (formerly San Juan Bautista), which already had given over its military plaza to the village of Guerrero, Coahuila.

In June 1846, two hundred Mexican soldiers were stationed at this important gateway post, which in colonial times had witnessed the passing of the most important Spanish expeditions into Texas. When Lt. Col. William S. Harney approached the nearby river crossing with six U.S. dragoon companies, the Mexican force withdrew. Harney, receiving orders to return to San Antonio, Texas, left behind three companies, which retreated beyond the Río Grande when the Mexican soldiers returned. The Mexicans subsequently claimed a great victory, having repulsed U.S. forces from Mexican soil.

That autumn, on 12 October, U.S. general John E. Wool's Army of Chihuahua crossed the Río Grande near Guerrero, having been welcomed by the local *alcalde* (mayor) under a flag of truce. As Wool marched on toward Monclova, he passed through other *presidial* towns: San Fernando de Rosas (present-day Zaragoza, Coahuila) and Santa Rosa María del Sacramento (present-day Múzquiz), each with a population estimated at three thousand. But the day of the *presidios* was past. The conflict between two American nations was to play itself out on a grander scale than that of the frontier *presidios*.

Robert S. Weddle

BIBLIOGRAPHY

Fulton, Maurice Garland, ed. *Diary and Letters of Josiah Gregg: Southwestern Enterprises, 1840–1847*. 1941.

Moorhead, Max L. *The Presidio: Bastion of the Spanish Borderlands*. 1975.

Weems, John Edward. *To Conquer a Peace: The War between the United States and Mexico*. 1974.

Price, Sterling

U.S. general Sterling Price (1809–1867) received his initial military experience during the U.S.–Mexican War, commanding a regiment during the U.S. occupation of New Mexico and in operations in northern Mexico. Born and raised in Virginia, Price briefly attended Hampden-Sydney College before moving with his family to Missouri. A planter, he served as a Democrat in both the Missouri legislature and the U.S. House of Representatives. Shortly after the outbreak of the U.S.–Mexican War, Price resigned from Congress. His political connections earned him the colonelcy of a Missouri volunteer regiment then being organized.

Price's unit left Fort Leavenworth in detachments during August 1846, assembling at Santa Fe in late September and early October. In late October, after Gen. Stephen W. Kearny left for California and Col. Alexander W. Doniphan was ordered into Navajo territory, Price was appointed commander of U.S. forces occupying New Mexico. The Missourian was popular with his troops, but he proved a lax disciplinarian and quarrelsome subordinate. In December, learning of a possible revolt against U.S. authority, he arrested several Mexican leaders. Early in 1847 Pueblo Indians and New Mexican insurgents mounted a more serious rebellion. Indians killed Governor Charles Bent and six others at Taos on 19 January, and additional attacks soon followed. Price reacted quickly to the Taos Revolt. On 24 January he defeated a force of approximately 1,500 insurgents near

Santa Cruz. He then advanced with his small force of perhaps 500 men to Pueblo de Taos, which he bombarded on 3 February and assaulted the following day. In a sharp engagement Price lost 7 killed and 45 wounded, while the rebels suffered casualties of perhaps 150 killed and several hundred captured. U.S. officials later tried and hanged Pablo Montoya, one of the revolt's leaders. Price's action had secured control of New Mexico for the United States. The following year, promoted to brigadier general, Price advanced southward without orders and occupied Chihuahua, Mexico. With the Treaty of Guadalupe Hidalgo already signed in February 1848, his forces continued on and captured Santa Cruz de Rosales on 16 March after a brief fight. Price returned to Santa Fe by way of El Paso.

After the war Price engaged again in agricultural and political pursuits, serving as governor of Missouri during the mid-1850s. During the Civil War he rose to the rank of major general in the Confederate army. The old soldier died in St. Louis in 1867 of cholera, a disease he had first contracted during the U.S.–Mexican War.

David J. Coles

BIBLIOGRAPHY

Bauer, K. Jack. *The Mexican War, 1846–1848*. 1974.

Castel, Albert. *General Sterling Price and the Civil War in the West*. 1968.

Shalhope, Robert E. *Sterling Price: Portrait of a Southerner*. 1971.

Twitchell, Ralph Emerson. *The Conquest of Santa Fe*. 1967.

Prisoners of War

This entry consists of three separate articles: **Mexican Prisoners;** **Texan Prisoners;** *and* **U.S. Prisoners.**

Mexican Prisoners

Mexican military prisoners of war were taken by U.S. military forces after almost every battle. The limited resources of Generals Zachary Taylor and Winfield Scott dictated a policy of prisoner exchange often on terms most favorable to the Mexicans. After the battles of Palo Alto and Resaca de la Palma, Taylor and Mexican general Mariano Arista agreed to swap the captured U.S. command of Capt. Seth B. Thornton for all Mexican prisoners held by Taylor with the exception of Brig. Gen. Rómulo Díaz de la Vega and his staff.

The courtly General Díaz de la Vega, probably the most celebrated Mexican prisoner of the war, traveled throughout the United States conferring with political leaders. He first visited Kentucky to meet with Henry Clay, and then traveled to Washington, D.C., for an audience with President James K. Polk before rejoining his command. General Díaz de la Vega was among the more than three thousand Mexican soldiers captured at the Battle of Cerro Gordo, and while

A New Rule in Algebra: Five from Three and One Remains. Lithograph, 1846. A biting satire of the treatment of Mexican prisoners of war by U.S. military surgeons (Library of Congress).

the remainder were paroled, he was retained by U.S. forces until the end of the war.

U.S. soldiers were opposed to the parole system, certain that most Mexican soldiers were being returned to the ranks before an exchange could be effected. The U.S. government finally ordered that no more Mexican officers were to be paroled except for special reasons. Two young Mexican officers were tried by a U.S. military commission and executed at Jalapa on 24 November 1847 for violating their paroles, but punishment for this infraction was rare.

Exact numbers of Mexican prisoners taken in battle were often not determined. After the Battle of Buena Vista, General Taylor reported that a sufficient number of prisoners were taken to ransom all U.S. military personnel then held by Mexican forces. But the trade was a little lopsided: nearly three hundred Mexican prisoners were traded for seven U.S. soldiers. Wounded Mexican prisoners taken at Buena Vista were treated by U.S. Army surgeons and placed in buildings that had been converted to hospitals. After recovery, these troops were paroled and released.

As the guerrilla war intensified in northern and central Mexico, it became a practice of the U.S. military to take civilian prisoners. *Alcaldes* (mayors) of Mexican villages were often held hostage by U.S. forces to guarantee the good conduct of their villages and towns. Mexican guerrillas caught in the act of sabotage or violence were tried before a U.S. military commission and either hanged in public or placed before a firing squad.

U.S. forces reserved their harshest treatment for a battalion of captured American deserters. The San Patricio Battalion, captured under arms against the United States at the Battle of Churubusco on 20 August 1847, was led by John Riley. Riley, who commanded at the rank of brevet major, had deserted while serving as a private in the 5th Infantry with Gen. Zachary Taylor's forces on the Río Grande. The San Patricios manned an artillery battery at the Battle of Buena Vista on 23 February 1847, which caused many casualties among U.S. forces. Resentment against the San Patricios ran high as a court-martial was convened to try the men, charged with desertion. Seventy prisoners were convicted on charges and sentenced to be hanged. However, Gen. Winfield Scott, upon reviewing the convictions pardoned five men, reduced fifteen of the death sentences to a punishment of fifty lashes well laid on, to have each prisoner branded on the cheek with the letter "D" for deserter, and to be drummed out of the service. The punishments were carried out on 10 September 1847 at the Village of San Angel, Mexico, and completed two days later at Mixcoac, Mexico.

Joseph E. Chance

BIBLIOGRAPHY

Bauer, K. Jack. *The Mexican War, 1846–1848.* 1974.

Carleton, James Henry. *The Battle of Buena Vista with Operations of the "Army of Occupation" for One Month.* 1848.

Chance, Joseph E., ed. *Mexico Under Fire: Being the Diary of*

Samuel Ryan Curtis, 3rd Ohio Volunteer Regiment during the American Military Occupation of Northern Mexico 1846–1847. 1994.

Miller, Robert Ryal. *Shamrock and Sword.* 1989.

Texan Prisoners

In the early 1840s the Texas Republic and Mexico clashed in a series of border conflicts that resulted in the capture of many Texians. Numbering approximately four hundred in all, most of these prisoners were taken on three occasions: the capture of the Santa Fe Expedition in September and October 1841; the seizure of San Antonio by Gen. Adrian Woll in September 1842; and the surrender of the Mier Expedition in December 1842. Marched into the interior of Mexico, the Texians were incarcerated in prisons, military installations, and other detention facilities. Ordered to labor on public works projects, the Texians wrote frequently to family members in the United States to complain of the rigors of their captivity.

The plight of these prisoners became a matter of great concern to the U.S. government. Andrew Jackson, Henry Clay, John Quincy Adams, and other prominent U.S. politicians, responding to numerous requests to intercede on the prisoners' behalf, appealed to Mexican president Antonio López de Santa Anna for clemency. The welfare of the imprisoned Texians thus became one of the principal responsibilities of Waddy Thompson during his tenure as U.S. minister to Mexico. When he arrived in the Mexican capital to assume his duties in April 1842, Thompson prevailed on Santa Anna to release the Santa Fe Expedition prisoners (with the exception of José Antonio Navarro who, having signed the Texas declaration of independence, had been sentenced to life imprisonment). As a sign of goodwill toward the U.S. government, the Mexican president occasionally released a small number of prisoners, and in spring 1844, as Thompson was preparing to return to the United States, Santa Anna released to his care the Texians who had been captured during Woll's attack on San Antonio. In September 1844 Santa Anna released the Mier prisoners at the request of Wilson Shannon, Thompson's successor as U.S. minister.

Despite Santa Anna's piecemeal release of the Texians to U.S. diplomats, their imprisonment greatly strained U.S.–Mexican relations during the 1840s. Their travails received considerable attention in the U.S. expansionist press, creating much anti-Mexican feeling on the eve of the U.S.–Mexican War.

Sam W. Haynes

BIBLIOGRAPHY

Green, Thomas Jefferson. *Journal of the Texian Expedition Against Mier.* 1845.

Haynes, Sam W. *Soldiers of Misfortune: The Somervell and Mier Expeditions.* 1990.

U.S. Prisoners

While not unimportant, the issue of prisoners of war lacked the emphasis placed on it by today's modern governments. Exchanging prisoners was usually left to commanders of opposing forces, with arrangements worked out through representatives appointed by the chief of each army. A rate of exchange was frequently determined which placed a higher value on senior officers than on those of lesser rank.

Contrary to the events at the Alamo and Goliad during the Texas Revolution, U.S. soldiers captured in battle by Mexican forces during the U.S.–Mexican War could expect fair treatment considering the circumstances. Capt. Seth Thornton and his men were exchanged on 11 May 1846, only weeks after being captured on the Río Grande in the opening skirmish of the war. Several Mississippi Volunteers, captured in February 1847 at Buena Vista (or La Angostura), returned to their regiment after retreating Mexican forces released them unharmed. The matter of prisoner exchanges is an intriguing topic that has yet been fully explored by historians.

The most celebrated U.S. prisoners of the war were the officers and men of Maj. John P. Gaines's and Maj. Solon Borland's joint command who were captured at Hacienda de Encarnación on 24 January 1847. Marched to Mexico City, the group was incarcerated awaiting their exchange. In May 1847, the Mexican government sent the Encarnación prisoners and other U.S. captives to Huejutla to be exchanged for *soldados* taken at Cerro Gordo. News of their transfer sparked an unsuccessful rescue attempt by U.S. troops stationed at Tampico. The prisoners were later paroled and arrived in New Orleans to a heroes' welcome. Several men, including Major Gaines, had managed to escape their captors in Mexico City and joined Gen. Winfield Scott's advancing column.

Richard Bruce Winders

BIBLIOGRAPHY

Scott, Henry L. *Military Dictionary Comparing Technical Definitions; Information on Raising and Keeping Troops; Actual Service, Including Makeshifts and Improved Matériel; and Law, Government, Regulation, and Administration Relating to Land Forces.* 1864.

Smith, Justin H. *The War with Mexico.* 2 vols. 1919. Reprint, 1963.

Privateers

Privateers were privately owned vessels commissioned by countries through documents known as "letters of marque" to raid enemy shipping. During the U.S.–Mexican War, both belligerent nations investigated the use of privateers. The Mexican consul in New Orleans termed them "terrible weapons" and warned that profit-hungry crews, many of them from the United States, waited at the world's ports to operate against U.S. commerce. The threat of widespread raiding by these vessels caused great concern among U.S. shippers and war planners.

Mexico officially authorized the use of privateers in the summer of 1846, with blank commissions being sent to Cuba, France, Great Britain, Spain, and the West Indies. Within months, the *Carmelita* from Bangor, Maine, became the first victim of Mexico's campaign when it fell prey to *El Unico,* a privateer outfitted in Oran, Algeria, and operated by a predominantly Spanish crew. Weeks later, reports reached the United States that the steamer *La Rosita* had also left Oran, seeking U.S. targets.

The United States, in turn, attempted to head off widespread use of privateers and resorted to military and diplomatic maneuvering. After threatening to commission privateers as well, the United States instead dispatched ships to the Mediterranean and issued diplomatic circulars to France, Great Britain, and Spain. Any citizens of those countries, it read, would be treated as pirates if taken on a Mexican privateer. In addition, the United States would consider prizes sold at ports in those countries as violations of existing accords. The government of France responded promptly by forbidding French citizens to participate in the war. In Great Britain, Lord Palmerston also complied, although there was much pro-Mexican sympathy in his country and British shipowners had made dozens of requests to Mexican officials for letters of marque.

Spain responded by ordering close supervision of Mexican activities in Cuban ports and by actively pursuing privateers in the western Mediterranean. Spanish warships captured *El Unico* and drove *La Rosita* into neutral waters. Thus, the U.S. diplomatic effort to isolate Mexican privateers proved extremely effective and virtually ended the threat to U.S. commerce.

Donald S. Frazier

BIBLIOGRAPHY

Smith, Justin H. *The War with Mexico.* 2 vols. 1919. Reprint, 1963.

Pletcher, David. *The Diplomacy of Annexation: Texas, Oregon, and the Mexican War.* 1973.

Protestantism

Protestantism made remarkable advances in membership during the first four decades of the nineteenth century, in part via the phenomenon called "the second great awakening," or camp meetings. By the 1840s that impulse was subsiding, as the rural areas filled up and towns emerged in the trans-Appalachian region. Revivalism was not dead, but it then began to prosper in more urban settings, led by itinerant evangelists such as Charles G. Finney. The focus on conversion remained strong, for only about 15 percent of the U.S. population yet belonged to a church. Major moral crusades including temperance and abolitionism were added to the mix.

The camp meeting movement released the full implications of the Protestant principle of individual access to God. Out of the turmoil of revivalist emotion and biblical study came a proliferation of new denominations. Among these were the Church of Jesus Christ of Latter-day Saints, the Mormons, whose doctrines were radically at odds with those of traditional Protestantism. The group emerged in upstate New York in the 1820s, but subject to continual persecution, they moved several times before settling in Illinois. In 1844 a mob murdered the founder, Joseph Smith, and by 1846 the Mormons, led by Brigham Young, headed west to find sanctuary in the vastness of the frontier.

The "Restoration movement," led by Alexander Campbell and Barton Stone, sought to restore pristine Christian practice and to end denominational quibbling by adhering strictly to the teachings of the New Testament. It resulted in several new church alliances, grouped around the general description of "Disciples of Christ," especially in Kentucky and Tennessee.

Numerous other "come-outer" groups also developed during the period. One such was Adventism, organized around the idea that the second coming of Christ was imminent. Based on his study of scripture, Adventist founder William Miller preached that 1843 was the time of the end. "The Great Disappointment" that ensued dampened the support of many, but an association of congregations was founded in 1845 to continue the proclamation.

Unitarianism had been on the rise in New England for some time. Profoundly influential because of the adherence of intellectual and political leaders, it called for a reasonable faith that was tolerant of theological differences but founded on solid moral principles, among which was abolition of slavery. Leaders included William Ellery Channing and Ralph Waldo Emerson.

The rising polarization of U.S. life over slavery caused the bonds that held North and South together to fray and break in 1844 and 1845. In those years, the Methodist and Baptist churches both split into northern and southern wings. The Methodists, the largest denomination in the country at the time, split at their General Conference of 1844 over the issue of a slaveholding bishop. Similarly, Baptists in the South, incensed over decisions in 1844 by their home and foreign missions boards to deny support to slaveholding candidates, met in Augusta, Georgia, in 1845 to form the Southern Baptist Convention. Some scholars argue that the New School–Old School Presbyterian split was symptomatic of the same stresses.

Protestant missionary activity within the bounds of the

United States traced back to colonial times, but a new stress on overseas missions began in 1806 as a result of the famous "Haystack Prayer Meeting" at Williams College. In the years following, several denominations founded missions boards. While the principal emphasis before 1846 was on the United States and its probable locus of expansion, these boards were also reaching out to Asia, Africa, and the Pacific islands. Protestant missionaries were largely responsible for the "Oregon fever" of the 1840s.

Increasing immigration from Catholic countries such as Ireland and south Germany made some of the native-born U.S. population concerned about the possibility of a Catholic takeover of the U.S. government and society. Fueled by these concerns, anti-Catholic societies began to form. Riots like the ones in Philadelphia in 1844 suggested that the nation might come apart over the issue. While many Protestants were involved in anti-Catholic agitation, much of it also came from secular sources who feared the end of the separation of church and state.

Thus, when war with Mexico broke out in 1846, Protestantism in the United States contained several threads that could affect the outcome, namely, a sense of U.S. world mission focused on evangelization of non-Christians, a strong suspicion of the Roman Catholic Church, the emergence of autonomous southern branches of the two largest denominations, and a spate of dedicated new groups who were convinced that they knew God's mind.

Robert W. Sledge

BIBLIOGRAPHY

Ahlstrom, Sidney. *A Religious History of the American People.* 1972.

Billington, Ray A. *The Protestant Crusade.* 1952.

Gaustad, Edwin S. *Historical Atlas of Religion in America.* 1976.

Johnson, Charles A. *The Frontier Camp Meeting.* 1955.

Littell, Franklin H. *From State Church to Pluralism.* 1962.

Public Opinion

This entry consists of four articles: Prewar Sentiment in Mexico; Mexican Perceptions during the War; Popular Sentiment in the United States; *and* Political Sentiment in the United States.

Prewar Sentiment in Mexico

To appraise Mexican public opinion during the first half of the nineteenth century it is necessary to bear in mind Mexico's social conditions. A great deal of the rural and urban population was illiterate and poorly educated; hence, they rarely had any information on which to base an opinion. What was considered public opinion was concentrated in the middle and upper classes. On the other hand, there were regional differences; some of the Mexican provinces held positions divergent from those assumed in Mexico City, yet those discrepancies resulted more from internal rivalries and conflicts of interest than from different conceptions of the international milieu. The main sources by which to study Mexican public opinion in that period are newspapers—particularly the editorial pages and the letters addressed to the publishers—pamphlets, political manifestos, and public speeches. From these it is possible to draw some general conclusions.

After Mexico achieved independence in 1821, its political leaders and public opinion makers viewed the United States ambivalently. These views differed depending on ideological orientation. Liberals admired the United States for its progress and vitality and saw in it a clear example of a modern society based on a middle class of proprietors in which there were no special privileges for corporate interest. They also considered it the best example of the benefits of a republican and federalist type of government. Conservatives in Mexico emphasized the historical and institutional continuity that the United States had maintained from colonial times. On the other hand, Mexicans noted some negative features of U.S. society, in particular, the contradiction between the ideals of equality and liberty expressed in the Declaration of Independence and the Bill of Rights and the existence of slavery in the Southern states. But above all, Mexicans feared the expansionist tendencies of the United States, and regarded them as a potential menace to Mexico's security and territorial integrity. This fear increased from 1823 to 1836 as a result of the involvement of U.S. envoy Joel R. Poinsett in the internal political debates in Mexico and the coarse way in which his successor, Anthony Butler, presented the proposals of President Andrew Jackson in an attempt to acquire Texas and the northern part of California.

When Texas seceded from Mexico in 1836 those fears intensified; Mexicans believed that the secession was a result of direct support from U.S. volunteers and covert assistance from the U.S. government. Mexican political leaders and public opinion makers knew through the memoir of Juan de Onís on the negotiations of the Treaty of 1819 that President James Monroe and Secretary of State John Quincy Adams had argued that Texas was part of the Lousiana Territory. Those apprehensions were confirmed nine years later when Texas was annexed by the United States. To Mexico, the U.S. annexation of Texas was unacceptable for legal as well as security reasons. That was why the Mexican government, when it became aware of the treaty of annexation between Texas and the United States, in April 1844 restated its position considering that act a hostile action by the U.S. government and an implicit declaration of war. Later, when the U.S. Congress approved the joint resolution, Mexico suspended diplomatic relations with the United States. From the Mexican point of view, annexation of Texas—either by treaty or by joint resolution—was a violation of the Treaty of Limits signed in 1828, by which the United States acknowledged that Texas was part of Mexican territory. Therefore, both actions were an unacceptable violation of fundamental principles of international law, as well as a clear risk to territorial security of Mexico, because in the same manner other Mexican territory could be incorporated into the United States. Under those circumstances, the government of President José Joaquín de Herrera tried to follow a double-track diplomacy. On one hand, it denounced the joint resolution as unlawful; on the other, it pursued a negotiating approach with the Republic of Texas government. Mexico's goals were to prevent the annexation of Texas and to avoid war with the United States.

While negotiations were being carried out, the Mexican press was divided; some newspapers opposed negotiation, others supported the government. Those who opposed negotiation pressed for an immediate military campaign against the Republic of Texas before annexation could take place. Later, when Texas accepted the U.S. offer, there was a consensus in Mexico that military action was necessary to block it. In both cases, however, it is important to stress that action was intended mainly as military action against Texas and rarely as a declaration of war on the United States. The general opinion was that Mexico had no alternative but to use military force to stop Texas from becoming part of the United States. Such action, they believed, would make it clear that Mexico would not accept U.S. expansion into other territorial possessions of Mexico. When it was evident that Texas would probably accept the U.S. offer, the Mexican congress approved a resolution on 4 June 1845 authorizing the president "with the lawful rights to use all resources to withstand to the last resort such annexation."

By October 1845 the overall feeling was that the recognition of Texas's annexation to the United States was undesirable. Nonetheless, in this critical situation, President Herrera's administration, regardless of the legal and political constraints, remained open to a negotiated solution, which meant acceptance of the Texas annexation. Hence, the U.S. government was informed that Mexico would agree to receive a "commissioner" with full powers to negotiate the issue of Texas. Mexican public opinion in general rejected this approach and continued to demand immediate action against Texas. When the mission of U.S. diplomat John Slidell was rejected by the Mexican governments of José Joaquín de Herrera and Mariano Paredes y Arrillaga, and the terms of Slidell's instructions became known, most Mexicans believed that the mission's main objective had been "to set a gross trap with Machiavellian and outrageous end" ("La Cuestión del Día," *El Tiempo,* México, 5 April 1846, p. 1).

By April 1846, when U.S. forces under Gen. Zachary Taylor advanced to the Río Bravo, the Mexican public, sure that the United States was ready to pursue a war to deprive Mexico of its northern provinces, demanded immediate military action to prevent it. The emphasis was to stop the U.S. advance on the territory between the Nueces River and the Río Bravo. Mexican public opinion always emphasized the need to defend Mexican territorial integrity, first in the case of the Texas annexation, later in the U.S. invasion of Mexican territory. In fact, Mexico *never* declared war against the United States.

When it became known in Mexico that U.S. president James K. Polk had requested and received a declaration of war from Congress, Mexican opinion was that the true intent of the U.S. government was not to protect a questionable claim of its territory or to redress supposed offenses, as it had claimed, but rather to take possession of territory that rightfully belonged to Mexico. As the newspaper *El Tiempo* stated, "The conduct (to) the American government is similar to that of the bandit with the traveler," and in facing that danger the position of Mexico could not be other than to defend itself.

Jesús Velasco-Márquez

BIBLIOGRAPHY

Brack, Gene M. *Mexico Views Manifest Destiny, 1821–1846: An Essay on the Origins of the Mexican War.* 1975.

Santoni, Pedro. *Mexicans at Arms: Puro Federalists and the Politics of War, 1845–1848.* 1996.

Velasco-Márquez, Jesús. *La Guerra del 47 y la opinión pública (1845–1848).* 1975.

Mexican Perceptions during the War

When U.S. diplomat John Slidell left Mexico in 1846 without accomplishing his mission—mostly because of the form in which his credential had been issued and because of the pressure the Mexican press placed on its government in opposition to Slidell's mission—U.S. forces under the command of Gen. Zachary Taylor advanced to the Río Bravo. This act was considered an open transgression on the territorial integrity of Mexico (since Mexico had long considered the Nueces River the border of Texas) as well as a violation of the Treaty of Limits signed on 12 January 1828. Hence, Mexican public opinion demanded the protection of that territory, a stand supported by the government of Mariano Paredes y Arrillaga. This led to the first encounters between the U.S. and Mexican armies, at Palo Alto and Resaca de la Palma. After these battles, U.S. president James K. Polk requested and got a declaration of war by Congress.

When Mexicans learned of the U.S. declaration of war, the U.S. occupation of Matamoros, and the blockade of the Mexican ports of Tampico and Vera Cruz, the Mexican press questioned whether the U.S. government was really pursuing the defense of its territory and the redress of supposed offenses, as President Polk had stated. From Mexico's point of view the U.S. government was using these as excuses to take possession of territory that rightfully belonged to Mexico.

The general opinion among Mexicans was that Mexico was a weaker nation that was in danger of being oppressed by the United States; hence, Mexico was fighting for its survival against the unlawful acts of usurpation and injustice. The war, they said, had been started by the United States, and Mexico had no recourse but to defend itself.

In July 1846, the Mexican congress adopted a resolution for the national defense. By then U.S. occupation of New Mexico had begun and U.S. naval forces had taken strategic positions in California. The opinion in Mexico was not only that justice and law were on its side but also that the integrity and security of Mexico were in danger.

On 8 August 1846, President Polk asked for an appropriation of $2 million to buy the territory in dispute, as well as California and New Mexico; this makes clear that his real purpose in declaring war on Mexico was territorial acquisition. When Polk's appropriation bill became known in Mexico, the newspaper *El Republicano* commented that the statements made by the U.S. government were proof that the real goal was to take more territory from Mexico and that a war initiated with that intent was unjust and barbarous and its promoters should be considered enemies of humanity.

On 3 March 1847 the U.S. Congress approved, after a long debate, an appropriation bill of $3 million to allow the president to conclude a treaty of "peace, limits and borders" with Mexico. One month later Nicholas P. Trist was appointed U.S. commissioner to negotiate with Mexican authorities. By then a new offensive, under the command of Gen. Winfield Scott, had begun to invade the territory between the port of Vera Cruz and Mexico City. Again, the opinion in Mexico, shared by the public and the government, was that Mexico should not sign a peace with ignominy. Even after the first communications had taken place between Trist and Mexican authorities, and despite all the military defeats experienced by Mexican forces, *El Diario del Gobierno* on 8 July 1847 stated,

> . . . [The peace] that now could be accorded between the Mexican Republic and that of North America, would be humiliating to the first, and would gain to her, in the years to come, a dishonor among the rest of the nations, as well as domestic evils of such magnitude, that Mexico soon would be again theater of war and would disappear from the catalogue of the free and independent peoples. . . .

After the Battle of Churubusco, when it became evident that armed resistance was futile, Mexican public opinion started to favor a negotiated end to the war, although it never accepted that the war had been just. The Mexicans always considered that they were fighting for their territorial integrity and their national security against the unjust territorial expansion of the United States. Also some Mexican journalists and political leaders, particularly the moderates and

conservatives, emphasized the cultural and religious differences between Mexico and the United States. Hence, they saw Mexican resistance as a defense of Catholic and Latin culture against Anglo-Saxon Protestant encroachments. Finally, from a legal point of view, Mexican public opinion, during the entire war—even after the signature and approval of the Treaty of Guadalupe Hidalgo—was that Mexico had defended the principles of international law and that the U.S. invasion had been a war of conquest.

Jesús Velasco-Márquez

BIBLIOGRAPHY

Brack, Gene M. *Mexico Views Manifest Destiny, 1821–1846: An Essay on the Origins of the Mexican War.* 1975.

Santoni, Pedro. *Mexicans at Arms: Puro Federalists and the Politics of War, 1845–1848.* 1996.

Velasco-Márquez, Jesús. *La Guerra del 47 y la opinion pública (1845–1848).* 1975.

Popular Sentiment in the United States

By the mid-1840s, most of the U.S. population favored the continued territorial expansion of their nation. The prevailing national mood was captured by the doctrine of Manifest Destiny, which combined pride and confidence with a strong sense of national mission. Attention focused on Texas, California, and Oregon as the nation's next acquisitions, but there was no consensus on how or when these areas should be added to the Union. On the end of the political scale were conservative Whigs who favored a natural process of expansion by which emigrants from the United States would first settle, then control, and later add new territories to the Union. In contrast, Democrats were more aggressive. They were willing to annex a republic such as Texas or to use forceful diplomacy to acquire Oregon. A few expansionists even advocated using the threat of war or war itself to acquire territory. A majority of U.S. citizens and their political leaders favored expansion but preferred means other than war to acquire Texas, California, and Oregon.

The controversial issue that led directly to war with Mexico was the annexation of Texas. On this issue, U.S. public opinion divided sharply. In 1843 southern and western Democrats pressed for annexation. The administration of President John Tyler supported this action and signed an annexation treaty in 1844. Opposition was strong, primarily because of fear of the extension of slavery, and the treaty was soundly defeated by a bipartisan majority in the Senate.

The issue played a significant role in the 1844 presidential contest as James K. Polk used his stance for annexation to help him win the Democratic nomination and then to help upset Whig Henry Clay in a very close election. Polk was an aggressive expansionist who strongly supported annexation while his opponent equivocated on the issue. Although the election cannot be interpreted as a referendum on Texas, public support for annexation grew throughout 1844. After the election, outgoing President Tyler claimed that the issue had been settled and proposed that Congress now annex Texas by a joint resolution. Although the subsequent debate was intense, the measure passed both houses with Democrats and even a few Whigs voting in favor.

Because Mexico considered U.S. annexation of Texas a national insult and had repeatedly warned against its consequences, war became a real possibility. Judging from their politicians and newspapers, most people in the United States willingly accepted annexation but opposed war with Mexico. It is impossible to be certain of public opinion at the time, however, because polls and political surveys were not conducted then. Historians must assess public opinion of that time with the speeches of politicians, the editorials and articles contained in the numerous newspapers of the day, the impressionistic assessments of contemporary observers, the results of elections in which a particular issue played a key role, and key votes in Congress.

Although the nation did not favor war before May 1846, prewar support for hostilities was strong in the frontier states of the Southwest and Northwest, where political hyperbole was intense and Democratic politicians were the most bellicose in their foreign policy views. There, too, contempt for Mexico was strong. Conversely, opposition to the idea of war with Mexico was strongest in the Northeast, where the Whig Party had great influence. Far removed from the potential field of battle, this region was the center of the abolition, antislavery, and peace movements. It was also the commercial center of the nation where businessmen generally opposed war because they believed it would severely disrupt the country's economy.

However, once word spread in May 1846 that U.S. and Mexican soldiers had clashed along the Río Grande, public opinion crystallized quickly. In Congress, while some were concerned that President Polk had provoked the conflict, the Democratic majority united solidly behind the president and permitted little debate on the war bill. In less than 48 hours, Congress approved war by bipartisan margins of 174 to 14 in the House and 40 to 2 in the Senate. Although many Whigs opposed war, only a handful had the courage to vote no. Angry as they were with the president and a war they considered unjust, most Whigs supported the war bill and the subsequent war effort. To them the issue was patriotism. Once U.S. troops had been attacked and the army committed to the field of battle, Whigs praised the courage of U.S. soldiers. They voted the men, money, and supplies to fight the war but continued to blame Polk for the war and attack him politically.

Excitement reigned and war fever swept the nation. Prowar rallies, marches, and meetings were held in large cities and small towns. Large crowds in Baltimore, Indianapolis, New York, and Philadelphia demonstrated overwhelming support for the president's call to arms. Thousands rushed to answer the calls of military recruiters. Most of the population readily agreed with President Polk that Mexico had long provoked the United States and deserved to be quickly and decisively chastised.

The war spirit was most intense in the southwestern and northwestern states closest to the fighting, but public support was also strong in the middle and south Atlantic states and in cities such as Philadelphia and New York. Even in Ohio, a center of western abolitionism and opposition to the annexation of Texas, 2,400 men joined volunteer companies within one month. Enthusiasm lagged only in the Northeast where the business and financial communities joined the politicians in lamenting the outbreak of war. The sharpest dissent was centered in New England, where antislavery Whig politicians and editors joined clergymen, abolitionists, pacifists, and other reformers to denounce Polk's immoral war to extend slavery.

Events in May and June 1846 further strengthened public support for the war. By late May, word of U.S. victories at Palo Alto and Resaca de la Palma reached the East Coast. Then in June, Congress ratified the Oregon Treaty, and the threat of war with Great Britain passed. These events helped set off a new wave of excitement, quickened the public's prowar pulse, and ensured strong support during the early months of the conflict.

Overwhelming popular support for the war did not, however, continue indefinitely. Once the exhilaration of the initial military victories passed, strong opposition emerged from several quarters. The Whig politicians who had reluctantly supported the war bill soon denounced the president's war policies. To them, Mr. Polk's War was a partisan war being waged by a partisan and duplicitous Democratic president. The introduction of the Wilmot Proviso in August 1846 brought the slavery issue openly into the war debate, stimulating strong and sustained opposition from antislavery forces, who saw the war as a blatant attempt by a southern president to expand slave territory to the southwest. Finally, the aggressive, expansionist character of the war outraged various social reformers, clergymen, intellectuals, and idealistic politicans. They charged that the United States was losing its republican soul by waging against a weak and hapless sister republic an imperialistic war to seize New Mexico, California, and other northern Mexican provinces.

As the war persisted into late 1847 and early 1848, public frustration grew. In spite of U.S. military victories, peace was not at hand. In the midterm congressional elections of 1846 and 1847, the Democrats had lost control of the House and had almost lost the Senate. Although the Democratic losses were attributable to numerous factors, the election results weakened support for Polk administration war policies by strengthening the Whig opposition. Moreover, anxiety increased in the business community. With war expenses rising, the government deficit increasing, and another large war loan pending, financial disaster loomed. After twenty months of fighting, the nation was clearly war weary. It is likely that popular support for the war would have continued to decline and political opposition continued to grow, had not the Treaty of Guadalupe Hidalgo been signed unexpectedly and ratified by the Senate in February 1848.

John H. Schroeder

BIBLIOGRAPHY

Bergeron, Paul H., *The Presidency of James K. Polk.* 1987.

Eisenhower, John S.D., *So Far from God: The U.S. War with Mexico, 1846–1848.* 1989.

Horsman, Reginald, *Race and Manifest Destiny: The Origins of American Racial Anglo-Saxonism.* 1981.

Johannsen, Robert W., *To the Halls of the Montezumas: The Mexican War in the American Imagination.* 1985.

Merk, Frederick, *Manifest Destiny and Mission in American History: A Reinterpretation.* 1963.

Pletcher, David, *The Diplomacy of Annexation: Texas, Oregon and the Mexican War.* 1973.

Schroeder, John H., *Mr. Polk's War: American Opposition and Dissent, 1846-1848.* 1973.

Political Sentiment in the United States

In the last U.S. presidential election held before the outbreak of the U.S.–Mexican War, Henry Clay narrowly lost on a platform distinctly cool to the idea of Manifest Destiny. Clay had already compromised two national upheavals directly or indirectly related to the institution of slavery (the Missouri Compromise of 1820 and the Compromise Tariff of 1833). He worried openly that war with Mexico would inevitably reawaken the issue, which had the potential to rend the Union. Nonetheless, many U.S. citizens supported the expansionism of President James K. Polk, the man who defeated Clay in 1844, and looked forward to the fruits of his aggressive policy toward Mexico.

When word of fighting along the Río Grande arrived in May 1846, only fourteen members of the House of Representatives voted against the declaration of war. All of the negative votes were cast by Northern representatives. First-term Whig representative Abraham Lincoln, in his "Spot Resolutions," boldly suggested that Polk himself had started the war by ordering the U.S. Army south of the Nueces River, contesting the president's claim that when Mexican troops attacked U.S. forces just north of the Río Grande they had entered territory rightfully belonging to the United States. However, at the outset, few in the United States were receptive to Lincoln's geography lesson. They knew only that fighting had taken place in Texas and that U.S. troops must be supported. Patriotism and national feeling supported the president in the early months of the war, but this did not last.

The Oregon Treaty in the summer of 1846 altered U.S. perceptions of the war with Mexico. Throughout 1845 and early 1846, Polk's administration had negotiated with Great Britain over settling both nations' claims to the vast Oregon region, which stretched along the Pacific Coast from Mexican California to Russian Alaska. Northern Democrats had backed Polk for the presidency on the expectation that he would prove a tough advocate concerning Oregon. With his unexpected compromise treaty with the British (limiting the U.S. claim at the 49th parallel instead of 54°40′), some of Polk's Northern supporters lost heart in the president's war with Mexico, which increasingly appeared to be a war for Southern preeminence within the nation. It was clear, in Polk's announced strategy of acquiring both Texas and Oregon, that the former took precedence over the latter in his policy of national expansion. It appeared that Polk, himself a Tennessee slaveholder, had pushed an extreme Río Grande boundary claim to the point of war with a weak Mexico, while he compromised with powerful Great Britain on territory desired by Northern expansionists.

The so-called Wilmot Proviso, a House of Representatives resolution introduced in August 1846 (and passed by the House early the next year), reflected Northern anger over a war increasingly perceived as a war to expand slavery. This statement of protest, which passed the House but not the Senate, pledged the government to keep slavery out of any territory taken from Mexico.

While Northern expansionists were upset that the war with Mexico seemingly resulted in a minimization of their interests, Southern expansionists were upset that the House was unwilling to carry the Missouri Compromise line of 36°30′ all the way to the Pacific Ocean. The line had been negotiated in 1820 to limit the northern boundary of slavery in what then had been the westernmost territory of the Union. Yet in 1847, it became apparent that the compromise attitude possible twenty-seven years before had been erased by the U.S.–Mexican War.

Early in 1847, some radical Southerners endorsed four Senate resolutions authored by South Carolina's John C. Calhoun, who suggested that the Missouri Compromise had been unconstitutional and that slavery could not be rightfully kept out of any territories acquired by the United States. The resolutions were not passed by either branch of Congress. Nevertheless, they were indicative of the growing polarizing effect of the war on U.S. politics. Ten years later, the ideas embodied in the Calhoun resolutions would be endorsed by the U.S. Supreme Court in the Dred Scott decision.

Intellectually, the war encouraged new thinking about the nature of democratic government. In Massachusetts, Henry David Thoreau refused to pay taxes on the grounds that his government was seeking to expand slavery in the U.S.–Mexican War. From this episode, which resulted in his being jailed for one night, he developed an applied philosophy of civil disobedience, which later inspired both Mahatma Gandhi and Martin Luther King Jr. But few, other than New England intellectuals, were immediately affected by Thoreau's lonely revolt against the authority of the state.

Of greater immediate impact was the Whig Party's victory in the presidential race of 1848 by running war hero Zachary Taylor on a platform that suggested that the candidate intended to quiet the slavery issue. Although a slaveholder himself, Taylor led a national party increasingly dominated by opponents to slavery's expansion. Antislavery Whigs surrounded the new president, guiding the prospective course of his administration.

In the end, Taylor's policy of calming the slavery issue failed due to news of a gold discovery in California, recently acquired in the war with Mexico. The California Gold Rush forced the slavery issue more to the center of the nation's politics as it became increasingly clear that a rapid increase in California's population would lead to immediate statehood and a necessary choice whether to allow slavery there. The political drama over slavery's expansion had been heightened by the U.S.–Mexican War. And once that conflict was completed, the struggle over slavery was further exacerbated by events emanating from California, so recently a part of Mexico. Sectional polarization over the institution of slavery hardened noticeably during the war, which pushed the nation closer to the national disruption of the Civil War in 1861.

Ward M. McAfee

BIBLIOGRAPHY

Bergeron, Paul H. *The Presidency of James K. Polk.* 1987.

DeVoto, Bernard. *The Year of Decision, 1846.* 1943.

Hamilton, Holman. *Zachary Taylor.* Vol. 2. 1951.

McCormac, Eugene I. *James K. Polk, A Political Biography.* 1922.

Potter, David M. *The Impending Crisis, 1848–1861.* 1976.

Sellers, Charles G. *James K. Polk.* Vol. 2. 1966.

Puebla

This entry consists of two articles: **State of Puebla,** *an overview of the state's strategic importance during the war, and* **Siege of Puebla,** *a discussion of the battle in the city of Puebla, the state's capital.*

State of Puebla

In 1847 the state of Puebla occupied the territory of the colonial province that lay in a broad band extending south from the lowland Department of Tuxpan on the Gulf Coast, across successive mountain barriers and plateaus, to the Department of Tlapa on the Pacific Coast. Second in population only to the state of México, Puebla residents numbered more than 600,000 in 1849, while its capital, Puebla de los Angeles, with 60,000 people, was the second largest city and the leading center of artisan and modern machine industry. The fertile and temperate central tableland was also the breadbasket for southeastern Mexico, regularly exporting surplus wheat and maize to the neighboring states of México, Oaxaca, and Vera Cruz and further afield.

The state was traversed by the principal communication arteries linking Mexico City with the Gulf Coast and the southeast. Hence, taking and holding Puebla became vital strategic objectives for the United States once northern Mexico had been pacified. After the fall of Vera Cruz and the taking of Jalapa in mid-April 1847, Gen. Winfield Scott and Gen. William J. Worth faced little organized opposition to their advance on the tableland, taking the town of Puebla on 15 May, with Mexican forces falling back to defend the Valley of Mexico. Puebla's Gulf port of Tuxpan fell at the same time. Although U.S. forces faced some hostility from the population of the state capital, throughout the summer of 1847 the city of Puebla provided a good location for General Scott to rebuild his disease-stricken army and to organize regular supply lines in preparation for the assault on the Valley of Mexico and Mexico City in late August.

Apart from an abortive attempt by Gen. Antonio López de Santa Anna to retake Puebla in late September 1847, the state of Puebla witnessed no further organized warfare. However, U.S. supply lines were frequently attacked by guerrilla forces led by Gen. Joaquín Rea and Col. Juan Climaco Rebolledo, against whom the U.S. troops applied effective antiguerrilla tactics. U.S. forces were concerned only with policing the central plateau of the state, and throughout the war, the immense northern and southern Sierra regions remained under the control of local units of state of Puebla national guard and guerrilla forces.

Guy P. C. Thomson

BIBLIOGRAPHY

Contreras, Carlos, ed. *Puebla, Una Historia Compartida.* 1993.

Thomson, Guy P. C. *Puebla de los Angeles: Industry and Society in a Mexican City, 1700–1850.* 1989.

Siege of Puebla

Historians traditionally have noted that the fall of Mexico City ended the U.S.–Mexican War, ignoring the numerous military actions that occurred after Gen. Winfield Scott's army entered the Mexican capital. One such battle, the Siege of Puebla, could have altered the war's outcome if the Mexicans had been victorious.

U.S. troops under Gen. William J. Worth entered Puebla in May 1847. The city, established by the Spanish soon after the conquest of the Aztec Empire, lay on the strategic National Road midway between Vera Cruz and Mexico City. Prewar visitors estimated the city's population to be between eighty thousand and one hundred thousand. Scott passed the summer of 1847 at Puebla, rebuilding his army as newly raised regiments of volunteers and regulars arrived from the United States. The rigors of hard campaigning and endemic diseases, however, took a toll on the invaders, causing surgeons to place more than two thousand of Scott's men on the sick list. After deciding that his forces were ready for the battles that lay ahead, Scott marched to Mexico City in August with the greater portion of his army, leaving behind those who could not travel.

A small U.S. garrison was left at Puebla to guard hospitals and depots that had been established in the city. Scott placed Col. Thomas Childs, a veteran of fighting in both Florida and Mexico, in command. The garrison, which numbered slightly more than four hundred, consisted of the following units: Col. Samuel Black's six companies of the 1st Pennsylvania Volunteers; Capt. John H. Miller's company of the 4th U.S. Artillery; Capt. Henry L. Kendrick's company of the 2d U.S. Artillery; Capt. Lemuel Ford's company of the 3d U.S. Dragoons; and some troops of the Mexican Spy Company. In case of an attack Scott and Childs planned to press convalescing soldiers into service and, in fact, several companies of patients were raised from the hospitals once the siege began.

Mexican leaders viewed Scott's departure as the opportunity to regain control of Puebla and trap the force marching against the capital. Gen. Joaquín Rea and several thousand Mexican troops under his command began harassing the garrison soon after Scott left. Some *poblanos* (residents of Puebla) also joined in the attacks. Raids were made on the quartermaster's mule herd and the bakeries supplying the garrison with bread. The aqueduct supplying water to the U.S. sector of the city was destroyed, too. The siege officially commenced on 13 September, when Rea's forces attacked several fortified positions held by Childs's men. Street fighting and sniping, which sometimes reached near-battle proportions, kept the garrison on the alert for the next month. On 22 September, Gen. Antonio López de Santa Anna arrived from Mexico City at the head of his battered army, reinforcing Rea and taking personal command of the operation. The siege was lifted on 12 October when a relief column led by Gen. Joseph Lane reached the city from Vera Cruz. The successful defense of Puebla strengthened U.S. control of central Mexico. U.S. wounded and killed numbered ninety-four; Mexican losses were not recorded.

Richard Bruce Winders

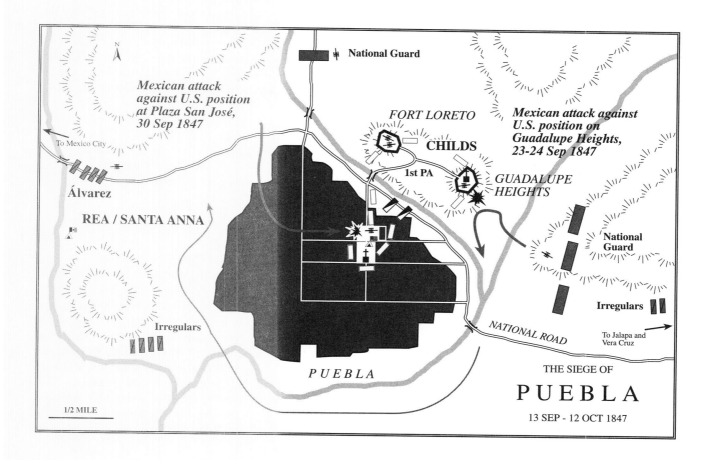

BIBLIOGRAPHY

Alcaraz, Ramón, ed. *The Other Side; or, Notes for the History of the War Between Mexico and the United States.* Translated by Albert C. Ramsey. 1970. Originally published as *Apuntes para la historia de la Guerra entre México y los Estados Unidos,* 1848.

Oswandell, J. Jacob. *Notes of the Mexican War, 1846–7–8.* 1885.

Smith, Justin H. *The War with Mexico.* 2 vols. 1919. Reprint, 1963.

Winders, Richard Bruce. "Puebla's Forgotten Heroes." *Military History of the West* 24 (Spring 1994): 1–23.

Pueblo Indians

When Spaniards first entered the area of the present-day southwestern United States, they encountered Native Americans residing in permanent villages of flat-roofed structures with many rooms, built around a plaza, or square. These reminded them of towns of their homeland, hence they called them *pueblos*. Horticulture provided a large portion of pueblo food requirements and they had storage facilities to keep food for survival during times of shortage. The Pueblo Indians' rights to their land, water, and at least some elements of their culture were guaranteed under Spanish and Mexican rule, and under the 1848 Treaty of Guadalupe Hidalgo, which ended the U.S.–Mexican War. Under Spanish rule no religion but Catholicism was tolerated, however, and in religious and many other ways Pueblo Indian culture was strained and in some ways modified. But the Pueblos still constitute a discrete body of Native Americans and provide interesting contrasts as compared with neighboring nomadic groups such as the Apaches, Navajos, Comanches, Utes, and others.

At the time of the U.S.–Mexican War, the Pueblo Indians of present-day New Mexico and Arizona comprised some twenty-three groups, differentiated by language and other cultural elements. In New Mexico the three major groups were the Tanoan, Keresan, and Zuñian. The Tanoan included the *Tewa* pueblos of Nambé, Pojoaque, San Ildefonso, San Juan, Santa Clara, and Tesuque; the *northern Tiwa* pueblos of Picurís and Taos; the *southern Tiwa* pueblos of Isleta and Sandía; and the *Towa* pueblo of Jémez. The Keresan group included the *eastern Keres* pueblos of Cochití San Felipe, Santa Ana, Santo Domingo, and Zía; and the *western Keres* pueblos of Acoma and Laguna. The Zuñian group included only Zuñi. In Arizona the only group was the Hopi, residing in three "mesa" village clusters and the pueblo of Moencopi. Pueblo and other Native Americans in New Mexico were not counted in the earliest U.S. censuses. A reasonable estimate of the total Pueblo population about 1850 is between ten and fifteen thousand. In 1970 the U.S. Bureau of Indian Affairs determined their number to be

33,569. Alfonso Ortiz, a leading authority, estimated 53,000 in a 1997 publication.

U.S. military authorities, upon occupying New Mexico, which then included all territory to the west to California, generally followed the precedents of earlier Spanish and Mexican authorities, regarding the Pueblo Indians as "civilized" and friendly, and the nomadic tribes as "savage" and untrustworthy. Pueblo leaders visited Gen. Stephen W. Kearny in Santa Fe and, after mutual expressions of good will were exchanged, easily entered into understandings whereby Pueblo life continued much as it had for centuries. Military action was taken against the Navajo and threatened against other nomadic tribes, but not, initially, against any Pueblo village.

Although some Anglo-Americans viewed the Pueblos as weak, docile, even cowardly, this reflected their ignorance of the Pueblo Rebellion of 1680 when all Spaniards in New Mexico were killed or driven out; and of the 1837 uprising against Mexican rule which attempted but failed to achieve the same end.

The Pueblo Indians' strong spirit of independence and bravery was exhibited again in December 1846 and January 1847, in an uprising against the U.S. occupation. It was led mainly by individuals of mixed Spanish and Indian descent. Pueblo Indians and Hispanic New Mexicans attacked troops and defied the U.S.-imposed civil government, killing and scalping Charles Bent, the governor, in his Taos home. The heart of the uprising was crushed when the thick adobe walls of the ancient mission church at Taos were breached by artillery and all defenders within were killed. Peace was restored, but it was clear that Anglo-Americans ruled with a heavy hand.

John Porter Bloom

BIBLIOGRAPHY

Ortiz, Alfonso, and William C. Sturtevant, eds. *Handbook of North American Indians: Southwest.* Vol. 9. 1979.

Dutton, Bertha P. *Indians of the American Southwest.* 1975.

Puros

Puros is the name given to one of two major divisions among liberals in nineteenth-century Mexico; the others are called *moderados* (or moderates). Although both groups believed in principle in constitutionalism and the rights to free speech, juridical equality, and individual liberties, the *puros* (which means literally the "pure ones") were the more radical and anticlerical political faction. *Puros* demanded reduction of the influence and wealth of the Catholic Church, which at the time was the only religion permitted in Mexico. The church controlled all birth, marriage, and death rituals and records. Various clerical organizations, including convents, monasteries, pious funds, brotherhoods, temples, and parishes owned substantial amounts of real estate, particularly in the capital city. To *puros*, political power was a tool they intended to use to transform Mexican society and to increase liberty and equality. Many *puros* had significant ties to militia forces and state governments. Prominent *puros* included Ponciano Arriaga, Blas Balcárcel, Valentín Gómez Farías, Melchor Ocampo, Ignacio Ramírez, Francisco Suárez Iriarte, and Francisco Zarco.

The support of the *puros* for federalism and local control of military forces links them to a series of factions that can be traced back to the early years of the republic, but the term *puro* was apparently first used in late 1846 in reference to supporters of Vice President Valentín Gómez Farías. While encharged with presidential authority during the absence of President Antonio López de Santa Anna, Gómez Farías issued a decree that sought to mortgage property belonging to the Catholic Church to help fund the war effort. In reaction, moderates, conservatives, and the clergy supported an uprising by elite militia that was known as the Polkos Revolt. The decree was withdrawn, and President Santa Anna replaced Gómez Farías in power.

The conflict between the political factions weakened the efforts of the Mexican government to resist the U.S. invasion. The *puros* opposed the Treaty of Guadalupe Hidalgo, which had been negotiated by the moderates, and some *puros* sought to continue armed resistance to U.S. forces. The division between *moderados* and *puros* continued through the era of the Reforma (during the 1850s) and French Intervention, with the *puros* pushing for more rapid reduction of the church's wealth and power and the retention of republican government. In principle, liberals sought to promote individual liberty, but explicit religious toleration was too controversial to be included even in the generally liberal Constitution of 1857. The *puros* formed an important part of the liberal alliance that defeated the conservatives in the Wars of the Reform and the French Intervention. The Constitution of 1857 remained the fundamental law of Mexico until it was replaced by the revolutionary Constitution of 1917.

Donald F. Stevens

BIBLIOGRAPHY

Costeloe, Michael P. "The Mexican Church in the Rebellion of the Polkos." *Hispanic American Historical Review* 46 (May 1966): 170–178.

Hale, Charles A. *Mexican Liberalism in the Age of Mora, 1821–1853.* 1968.

Santoni, Pedro. *Mexicans at Arms: Puro Federalists and the Politics of War, 1845–1848.* 1996.

Scholes, Walter V. *Mexican Politics during the Juárez Regime, 1855–1872.* 1957.

Stevens, Donald F. *Origins of Instability in Early Republican Mexico.* 1991.

Quitman, John A.

U.S. major general John A. Quitman (1799–1858) was born in Rhinebeck, New York. Quitman settled in Natchez, Mississippi, in 1821, where he practiced law and prospered in state politics. Militaristic by nature, Quitman organized the Natchez Fencibles (a volunteer militia company), rose to major general in Mississippi's militia, and led volunteers to revolutionary Texas in 1836.

Appointed volunteer brigadier general by President James K. Polk on 1 July 1846, Quitman has been judged by many historians the ablest of Polk's volunteer generals. He commanded the 2d Volunteer Brigade in Gen. Zachary Taylor's Monterrey campaign and demonstrated conspicuous bravery and leadership in the fighting on 21 and 23 September 1846, for which he was voted a sword by Congress (2 March 1847). After occupying Victoria on 29 December 1846, Quitman's troops were transferred to Gen. Winfield Scott's army. Quitman participated in Scott's capture of Vera Cruz and commanded an independent operation against coastal Alvarado (30 March–2 April 1847) before rejoining Scott.

Brig. Gen. John A. Quitman. Daguerreotype, c. 1846. From the collection of William J. Schultz, M.D.

On 14 April 1847, he was commissioned major general in the regular army by President Polk. Given command of the 4th ("Volunteer") Division, Quitman achieved fame in the storming of Chapultepec and the Garita Belén (Belén Gate) during the U.S. conquest of Mexico City on 13 and 14 September 1847. Scott then appointed Quitman Civil and Military Governor of Mexico City. Quitman returned to the United States that November, and was mustered out of the army on 20 July 1848.

Following the war, Quitman served as governor of Mississippi (1850–1851) and U.S. representative (1855–1858) and gained notoriety for his advocacy of secession and his attempt to organize a private military expedition to liberate Cuba from Spanish rule. Throughout his later years, he maintained ties to the Aztec Club (an organization of U.S. officers who had participated in the U.S.–Mexican War) which he had joined and served as president while in Mexico City.

Robert E. May

BIBLIOGRAPHY

May, Robert E. *John A. Quitman: Old South Crusader.* 1985.

Quitman Family Papers, 1760–1926. Southern Historical Collection, University of North Carolina Library, Chapel Hill, North Carolina.

Racism

Historians disagree as to exactly when racism first manifested itself against Mexicans in the borderlands. Texas was the first setting where Anglo-Americans encountered Mexicans in adversarial roles. One group of historians believes the Texas Revolution of 1836 was precipitated by an antagonism that can be traced to ethnic or racial prejudice, cultural differences, religious beliefs, and economic competition; to late eighteenth or early nineteenth century contact United States citizens had made with Latin American countries; and to the Black Legend, the belief held by Spain's European enemies that Spain was a particularly evil and intolerant nation given its treatment of foreigners, competitors, and colonized people. Others argue that racism was not overt before 1836, that in fact it cannot be documented until years after the U.S.–Mexican War when Anglo-Americans and Mexicans came into greater contact and vied for economic control of the U.S. Southwest. Whatever the source of racism against Mexicans, some Anglo-Americans of the time used the success of the Texas Revolution as an example of their racial superiority and the destiny of their civilization to overcome "less advanced" races. For many, the Texas episode reaffirmed the triumph of good over Mexican backwardness, corruption, political instability, and tyranny.

Racist sentiments were expressed openly in the years just before the U.S.–Mexican War in the idea of "Anglo-Saxonism"—a notion that emphasized the racial superiority of U.S. Anglo-Americans and predicted the destiny of the white race to dominate much of North America. Anglo-Saxonism was applied widely in Mexico's far north during this period, as white Anglo-American settlers needed to justify their taking Mexico's lands.

Views that Anglo-Americans reported about the Mexicans' biological nature also evidenced racism. Travelers encountering Mexicans in California, New Mexico, and Texas remarked with unabashed candor on the mixed-blood nature of the Mexicans, detecting signs of African, Indian, and Spanish amalgamation. Miscegenation, in their eyes, had produced an entire mongrel race, cursing any progeny with the flaws of the parent races. Thus, many Anglo-Americans associated Mexicans with deficiency.

Educated U.S. government officials also believed the natives in Mexico proper were no different from the Mexicans that travelers and settlers met in the far north. To these high-ranking diplomats, the Mexican population consisted of unhygienic, swarthy hybrids with a predilection for deception, indolence, and vice.

People in Mexico had their own negative feelings toward the United States, but their prejudice never assumed a form of rabid hatred or took on the guise of racial arrogance. Mexicans based their attitudes on different premises than did Anglo-Americans. Distrust and dislike of Anglos rested on suspicions that the United States had designs on Mexico's territory; on incidents known in Mexico about Anglo-Americans disparaging Mexicans; on the history of Anglo-Americans' relations with Indians in the U.S. West (Mexicans feared that Anglos also considered them candidates for extermination, as had been the case with the Indian tribes); and on the U.S. institution of African slavery, regarded in Mexico as inhumane. Mexicans also believed that the much-touted reputation of Anglos for inexhaustible energy and ambition and for political stability posed a threat to their nation.

Once the war began, U.S. racist attitudes toward Mexico witnessed fuller elaboration. Some U.S. journalists described the conflict as one of those historic episodes that periodically broke out between advanced and "barbaric" peoples. Others perceived it as a learning experience for Mexico's citizens, whose country was now engulfed in a monumental conflict with a superior civilization.

The common U.S. soldier engaged in the fighting expressed views that mirrored the racism on the home front. Many believed Mexicans undeserving of the beneficence that nature had bestowed on their country, attributing even to the wealthier classes an incapacity for developing the country's rich soil. The soldiers imputed inferior traits to the darker-skinned natives, also believing Mexicans to be prone to chicanery, ignorance, laziness, and treachery. To the U.S. soldiers, Mexico's population had made few strides in the arts, literature, and architecture. Anglos viewed the Mexicans' religion as a backward rendition of U.S. Christianity, a pagan-like Catholicism preached by immoral priests.

Following the Treaty of Guadalupe Hidalgo in 1848 and the U.S. acquisition of territory, racism in the Southwest became more open. The need to convert the borderlands into a productive agricultural region and the desire to subordinate workers for use in ranches, mines, railroads, and light industries all engendered negative responses. The Anglo-Americans thought Mexicans ill-suited for full participation in U.S. public life and despite treaty guarantees turned to violence and segregationist practices as well as political mechanisms to immobilize Mexican-American voters.

As for Mexico, it faced disarray in the wake of the war. The loss of half of its territory seemed the culmination of misfortune that dated to the 1820s when the country had gone through one tumult after another. But it also led to a healthy debate among the intelligentsia about the future of their country, as liberals and conservatives both sought to impose their political philosophy on Mexico in an effort to save the nation. The liberals saw the country's survival in republican institutions; the conservatives argued for a monarchy, noting the ineffectiveness of republicanism between 1824 and 1848. The war also led to bitter feelings toward the United States. "Yankeephobia" colored Mexico's relations toward the victor, and Mexicans came to view the United States as a hotbed of colonialism, imperialism, and racial intolerance.

Arnoldo De León

BIBLIOGRAPHY

Brack, Gene M. *Mexico Views Manifest Destiny, 1821–1846: An Essay on the Origins of the Mexican War.* 1975.

Crisp, James E. "Race, Revolution, and the Texas Republic: Toward a New Interpretation." In *The Texas Military Experience: From the Texas Revolution through World War II*, edited by Joseph G. Dawson. 1995.

De León, Arnoldo. *The Mexican Image in Nineteenth Century Texas.* 1982.

Hale, Charles A. "The War with the United States and the Crisis in Mexican Thought." *The Americas* 14 (1957): 153–173.

Horsman, Reginald. *Race and Manifest Destiny: The Origins of American Racial Anglo-Saxonism.* 1981.

McCaffrey, James M. *Army of Manifest Destiny: The American Soldier in the Mexican War, 1846–1848.* 1992.

Railroads

During the U.S.–Mexican War, there were no railroads in the southwestern United States or in northern Mexico, but railroads did play an important role in the war. In a strategic sense, many in the United States, using Manifest Destiny as their rationale, believed that Mexico blocked the "natural route" of a southern railway to the Pacific Ocean. This desire for a railroad to the Pacific may be cited as one of the causes of the war. Logistically, railroads were important because the network that linked major cities and rural areas in the eastern and southern United States was used to move troops and supplies southward, closer to the Gulf of Mexico, where they could be moved overland or by sea to Mexico. Even at this rather early date, railroad transport was recognized as faster, and more dependable, than movement by river or road. Trains of the period could average about twenty miles per hour, meaning that a trip normally requiring weeks could be made in days.

The South appears to have been especially prone to sending troops by rail. For example, in May 1846, Georgia governor George W. Crawford ordered companies of the 1st Georgia Infantry to travel by rail to the regiment's rendezvous at Columbus. In his order he mentioned the Central of Georgia, the Georgia, and the Western and Atlantic railroads. He later billed the War Department for the cost. The companies of the 1st Mississippi Rifles traveled by rail from central Mississippi to the rendezvous at Vicksburg shortly after the war began in 1846, using the recently completed line that ran from Jackson to Vicksburg. The line was used again in July 1847 to carry the discharged volunteers and their guests to a barbecue held in Jackson to honor the regiment. An estimated three thousand persons attended, many of them carried on special trains that ran from Vicksburg to Jackson for the special occasion.

Another troop transport by rail occurred in August 1848, when members of the recently discharged 1st North Carolina received free passage from Wilmington to destinations within the state on the Raleigh and Gaston Railroad. Some of the inland companies of the 1st South Carolinia Infantry took the train to the regiment's rendezvous at Charleston. Once formed, the entire regiment received orders to move by rail from Charleston to Mobile by way of Montgomery. Because the railroads were in their infancy during this period and had trouble accommodating large numbers of traveling troops, a problem arose at Atlanta when a lack of coaches forced several companies to march one hundred fifty miles overland from Atlanta to Notasulga, Alabama. There, still unable to board the train, the battalion booked passage at

Montgomery on two steamboats bound for Mobile, where they finally rejoined the rest of their regiment. Such rail operations also occurred in the North. In Pennsylvania in July 1848, members of the 1st Pennsylvania Infantry traveled the last leg of their journey home on the Allegheny & Portage Railroad. This use of railroads in the U.S.–Mexican War represented the first military deployment by rail in U.S. history.

Richard Francaviglia

BIBLIOGRAPHY

Kurtz, Wilbur G., Jr. "The First Regiment of Georgia Volunteers in the Mexican War." *Georgia Historical Quarterly* 27 (December 1943): 306, 319.

Lander, Ernest M., Jr. *The Reluctant Imperialists: Calhoun, the South Carolinians, and the Mexican War.* 1980.

Oswandel, J. Jacob. *Notes of the Mexican War, 1846–47–48.* 1885.

Wallace, Lee Alphonso, Jr. "North Carolina in the War with Mexico." Master's thesis, University of North Carolina at Chapel Hill, 1950.

Winders, Richard B. "The Role of the Mississippi Volunteers in Northern Mexico, 1846–1848." Master's thesis, University of Texas at Arlington, 1990.

Ramos Arizpe, Miguel

Mexican politician Miguel Ramos Arizpe (1775–1843) was born 15 February at Valle de Las Labores (present-day Ramos Arizpe), Coahuila. Ordained to the priesthood in 1803, he was nominated to a number of important church positions at Nuevo León and Nuevo Santander and received a doctorate in law in Mexico City.

In 1811 Ramos Arizpe sailed to Cadiz as a delegate to the Cortes (parliament) representing seven Mexican provinces, as well as Venezuela and Puerto Rico. He spoke out in favor of avant-garde federalist ideas, precursors of the concept of the free municipality, and was jailed in 1815 by order of King Fernando VII, charged with instigating and conspiring with Mexican and South American revolutionaries. He was freed by the Revolucion de Riego in 1820 and served as a delegate to the new Cortes, now in Madrid, until 1822.

Ramos Arizpe returned to Mexico and was elected Coahuila's representative to the General Congress of 1823 and 1824. He was then named to the influential position of president of the commission charged with drafting the federalist Constitution of 1824. Historians generally agree that Arizpe used the U.S. constitution as a guide, and that notwithstanding his ecclesiastical status, he was greatly aided in his work by members of the York-rite Masons.

In the administration of President Guadalupe Victoria, Ramos Arizpe served as secretary of justice for ecclesiastical affairs, retaining that post and adding the portfolio of min-

ister of finance under President Gomez Pedraza. Later he served as Mexico's minister plenipotentiary to Colombia.

Miguel Ramos Arizpe is the author of the famous *Memoria de las Provinces Internas Oriente,* describing aptly the resources of Coahuila and Texas, which was read at the Cortes in Cadiz in 1812. He died in Puebla 18 April 1843. At his death he was dean of the city's cathedral, a dignity second only to the archbishop in status.

Carlos González Salas

BIBLIOGRAPHY

Alessio Robles, Vito. *Coahuila y Texas en la epoca Colonial.* 1983.

Alessio Robles, Vito. *Ramos Arizpe.* 1937.

González Salas, Carlos. *Miguel Ramos Arizpe.* 1990.

Toro, Alfonso. *Dos Constituyentes de 1824: Miguel Ramos Arizpe y Lorenzo de Zavala.* 1925.

Rancho Davis

During the U.S.–Mexican War, a small village known as Rancho Davis sprang up on the site of present-day Rio Grande City, a small Texas border town in Starr County, located on the Río Grande, about thirty miles northwest of the city of McAllen. The land on which the town is situated, Porción 80, was given to Henry Clay Davis on the occasion of his wedding to Hilaria de la Garza as a present from her family, one of the founding families of Camargo, which is located just across the Río Grande. Davis, a Kentuckian, came to Texas in 1836 and had participated in the Somervell Expedition in 1842.

The principal occupation of the inhabitants of Rancho Davis was trade with the U.S. forces that garrisoned Camargo. This trade often involved smuggling contraband whiskey and other goods. A wood yard was also located there to supply fuel to the many steamboats that plied the Río Grande bringing supplies to Gen. Zachary Taylor's forces.

Following the cessation of hostilities on 26 October 1848, Fort Ringgold was established near Rancho Davis. By provision of the Treaty of Guadalupe Hidalgo, the United States had pledged to stop the incursion of Indian raiding parties into Mexico from the United States, and the fort was built at this strategic location to accomplish that end. Fort Ringgold continued in active service until 1946, when the site was deeded to the school district.

On 16 September 1851 the Mexican revolutionary José Mariá Jesús Carvajal launched an invasion of northern Mexico from Rancho Davis. The purpose of this illegal filibustering expedition, which came to be known as the Merchant's War, was to separate northern Mexico from the Republic of Mexico, forming the so-called Republic of the Sierra Madre. Carvajal's forces were driven back across the

Río Grande in March 1852, where he and his principal followers were arrested by the U.S. government on charges of violation of the Neutrality Act.

Joseph E. Chance

BIBLIOGRAPHY

Robertson, Brian. *Wild Horse Desert: The Heritage of South Texas.* 1985.

Vielé, Teresa Griffin. *Following the Drum.* 1984.

Webb, Walter P. *The Handbook of Texas.* 3 vols. 1952.

Rangel, Joaquín

Born in Mexico City, Joaquín Rangel (1803–1874) joined the Mexican army as a second lieutenant in 1823. He rose through the ranks during the next twenty years and in 1844 was appointed general and artillery chief of Gen. Antonio López de Santa Anna's army. Rangel played a significant role in Mexican political and military affairs during the war with the United States.

On 7 June 1845 at the behest of the *puros*, a pro-war faction, Rangel led a coup d'état against President José Joaquín de Herrera. The uprising did not succeed partly because Rangel commanded the rebels to call for Santa Anna—whose name was still anathema in Mexico—during the mutiny. Nearly two years later, when the revolt of the *polkos* broke out late in February 1847 against the acting chief executive, *puro* politician Valentín Gómez Farías, Rangel commanded the central military fortress in Mexico City known as the Ciudadela. At first Rangel remained loyal to the government but later withdrew his support, thus contributing to the demise of the *puros* as a viable political bloc.

Over the next few months Rangel made several contributions to the Mexican war effort. He was ordered by Santa Anna to salvage the remains of the Mexican army following the Battle of Cerro Gordo and saw action in the campaign for Mexico City. On the afternoon of 13 September Rangel led his brigade in a vigorous defense of the Garita San Cosme against the attacking U.S. soldiers. By 5 P.M., however, Rangel had been severely wounded, and his principal gun, a 24-pound howitzer, had become unserviceable. The U.S. army entered Mexico City one hour later.

After the war Rangel held a variety of civilian and military posts. He served as a deputy to the national congress (1852–1853), was promoted to brigadier general in 1854 by Santa Anna, and two years later was appointed colonel of the "Libertad" national guard battalion by President Ignacio Comonfort. Rangel died in 1874 of a fever in the Cacahuatal of San Pablo.

Pedro Santoni

BIBLIOGRAPHY

Alcaraz, Ramón, ed. *The Other Side; or, Notes for the History of the War between Mexico and the United States.* Translated by Albert C. Ramsey. 1970. Originally published as *Apuntes para la historia de la Guerra entre México y los Estado Unidos,* 1848.

Costeloe, Michael P. *The Central Republic in Mexico, 1835–1846: Hombres de Bien in the Age of Santa Anna.* 1993.

Roa Bárcena, José María. *Recuerdos de la invasion norteamericana (1846–1848).* 3 vols. 1947.

Rea, Joaquín

Mexican guerrilla commander Joaquín Rea (c. 1790–1850) immigrated as a youth from Spain to Tecpan, Guerrero, then in 1811 joined the insurgency for Mexican independence. He later became a merchant in Acapulco and engaged in a lucrative trade with South America. Rea campaigned at various times with the conservative general Nicolás Bravo against liberal commanders in the southwest, first Vicente Guerrero then Juan Álvarez, but joined forces with the liberals when the United States invaded in 1846. Rea organized irregular forces in the state of Puebla and conducted guerrilla operations against U.S. forces. On 13 September 1847 Rea began a siege of the state capital, the city of Puebla, held by a U.S. garrison under Col. Thomas Childs. Gen. Antonio López de Santa Anna arrived on 22 September, after the fall of Mexico City, to assist the siege and thus cut the invaders' supply lines. A U.S. column under Brig. Gen. Joseph Lane relieved the city on 12 October, after pausing long enough to ransack the town and rape the women of Huamantla, Puebla, in retaliation for the death of a popular officer. The outnumbered Rea retired westward to Atlixco, regrouped, and launched further raids. Following the war he renewed his struggle against Álvarez and was killed shortly thereafter by liberal forces in Tecuanapa, Guerrero.

Jeffrey M. Pilcher

BIBLIOGRAPHY

Bauer, K. Jack. *The Mexican War, 1846–1848.* 1974.

Diccionario Porrúa: De história, biografía, y geografía de México. 6th ed., 1995.

Winders, Richard Bruce. "Puebla's Forgotten Heroes." *Military History of the West* 24 (Spring 1994): 1–23.

Recriminations, Mexican

On 14 September 1847 Gen. Winfield Scott entered Mexico City and took contol of the National Palace. After a few days of mopping-up operations, the U.S. force effectively subdued the capital's guerrilla resistance, and only sporadic sniping disturbed the U.S. Army's control of the city. Within a month most units of the Mexican national army had suspended military activities outside of Mexico City, and the U.S. commander was able to administer the country. Mexican patriots were incredulous as they wondered how this foreign domination could have been accomplished with such little resistance. The main forces of the national army had suffered utter defeat and humiliation, military leaders had refused to support the people's uprising in the capital, and the nation's executive had surrendered without a determined fight. A pall of despondency and cynicism descended over the nation. Several Mexican intellectuals responded to these unhappy events by engaging in bitter self-reproach and self-recrimination. No longer focusing their attacks on the U.S. forces, Mexican editorialists and politicians targeted each other as the primary objects of vilification. Finger pointing and blame for Mexico's defeat became common fare in the press and in published pamphlets.

Such self-effacing responses on the part of Mexican intellectuals were a reflection of commonplace nineteenth-century assumptions regarding the root causes for defeat and victory in warfare. The prevailing military wisdom hearkened back to Napoleonic and Clausewitzian beliefs concerning the triumphal, conquering spirit of the victor. Bravery, zeal, tenacity, discipline, and obedience were all taken to be the decisive, determining factors in war and were generally assumed to be fundamentally innate. That is, it was assumed that a conquering nation, race, or people possessed an abundance of these characteristics, as compared with a relative deficiency of such attributes in the character of the nations or races that suffered defeat. These assumptions allowed the U.S. Army and the U.S. public to engage in jubilant self-congratulation and to announce U.S. preeminence, while those in vanquished Mexico were forced to confront the agonizing opposite about themselves.

This focus on human nature and morale has shaped and characterized both the U.S. and Mexican histories of the conflict. Consequently, other explanations for Mexico's military defeat have received insufficient attention. In both the United States and Mexico, this nineteenth-century fixation on Napoleonic notions of the "martial spirit" obfuscated alternative contemporary interpretations available immediately following the war. Instead of denigrating, racialist rhetoric, these other accounts emphasized the crucial importance of adequate funding, the quality of supply and munitions, the flexibility of command structures, and strategy and tactics.

M. Bruce Colcleugh

BIBLIOGRAPHY

Hale, Charles A. "The War with the United States and the Crisis in Mexican Thought." *The Americas* 14, no. 2 (October 1957): 153–175.

Otero, Mariano. *Consideraciones sobre la situación política y social de la República Mexicana en el año de 1848.* 1848.

Recruitment

This entry consists of two separate articles: **Mexican Recruitment** *and* **U.S. Army Recruitment.** *See also* **Volunteers.**

Mexican Recruitment

Pervasive disdain for military service, a sentiment carried over from the colonial period, compelled the Mexican war ministry to rely almost exclusively on conscription to fill permanent army ranks. Widespread evasion of the levy (*leva*), a coercive means of military conscription, and manpower competition from both the active and civic militias obliged the states to impress vagrants, criminals, and other social misfits to meet annual recruiting quotas. Following induction the low pay, harsh discipline, and wretched living conditions encouraged rampant desertion. Those who remained routinely sold clothing and equipment, raided the commissary, or hunted wild game to make ends meet.

To surmount such resistance and enhance soldier quality, the war ministry replaced the *leva* in 1840 with an annual lottery (*sorteo*). Conducted under the supervision of local judges on the last Sunday of October, *sorteo* eligibility was limited to all bachelors and childless widowers between the ages of 18 and 40 who met established health and height prerequisites. Entering service on 15 December, selectees signed a contract specifying their service obligations and the army's reciprocal responsibilities. The six-year term to which they were obligated could, with certain reservations, be served by a paid substitute. If that substitute deserted, however, the original selectee was liable for the balance of his service term.

Despite greater equitability, the *sorteo* proved unable to accommodate army manpower requirements. Personnel shortfalls on the eve of hostilities with the United States obliged the Mexican government to reinstitute the *leva,* a move that once again filled army ranks with insouciant conscripts prone to mutiny and desertion. The quality of the force was further debased by a presidential decree issued on 23 April 1846, that directed the arrest and trial of all persons lacking visible means of support and their induction into the army if convicted of vagrancy.

William A. DePalo, Jr.

BIBLIOGRAPHY

Balbontín, Manuel. *Estado militar de la República Mexicana en 1846,* pp.12–14. 1890.

Decreto para reemplazar las bajas del ejército mexicano por Sorteo General, 26 January 1839. Archivo General de la Nación (AGN). Guerra y Marina (GM). Vol. 8.

Escalante Gonzalbo, Fernando. *Ciudadanos imaginarios: Memorial de los afanes y desventuras de la virtud y apología del vicio triunfante en la Republica Mexicana,* pp. 164–165, 176. 1992.

Green, Stanley C. *The Mexican Republic: The First Decade, 1823–1832*, pp. 184–185. 1987.

Memoria del Secretarío de Estado y del despacho de Guerra y Marina, pp. 9–16 and estados 2 and 3. 1828.

Memoria del Secretarío de Estado y del despacho de Guerra y Marina, pp. 14–15, 18–20. 1839.

U.S. Army Recruitment

In 1845, U.S. Army regulations specified the enlistment of active and able-bodied free white men between the ages of eighteen and thirty-five. Before the U.S.–Mexican War, the General Recruiting Service operated stations throughout the eastern United States, with the cities of New York, Boston, Philadelphia, and Newport, Kentucky, providing over half of the enlistees for the regular service. Stern discipline, little possibility for advancement, low pay, bad food, and poor living conditions, coupled with the U.S. public's prejudices against a permanent military establishment, prevented large numbers of native-born men from enlisting for a five-year term. Consequently, approximately 60 percent of the army was foreign-born in 1845, with Ireland and Germany providing the greatest numbers of foreign-born enlistees. On 19 May 1846, Congress increased regimental strength, and individual regiments sent company officers on recruiting details throughout the United States. Despite enlistment bonuses, most regular units remained under strength throughout the war.

Potential recruits were inspected by army surgeons, who rejected any man with any physical deformities or ailments that rendered him unfit for military service. In addition to the medical inspection, new soldiers received a close haircut, were well washed from head to foot, and were issued military uniforms following the disposal of their civilian clothing. Although the regulations called for the enlistment of single men, married men were allowed to reenlist. The wives of these veterans frequently served as one of the four washerwomen authorized by regulation for each company.

In February 1847, Congress authorized the creation of ten new regular regiments, essentially volunteers in federal service, for the war's duration. Commanding officers were political patronage appointees named by President James K. Polk. To encourage enlistment, land warrants were offered to all enlistees. This changed the composition of the regulars, as native-born troops viewed finite terms of service, coupled with the land bonus, as a viable military option and enlisted in larger proportions. Regardless of enlistment terms and national origin, over thirty-one thousand men served as U.S. regulars during the course of the U.S.–Mexican War.

Robert P. Wettemann, Jr.

BIBLIOGRAPHY

McCaffrey, James. *Army of Manifest Destiny: The American Soldier in the Mexican War, 1846–1848*. 1992.

Winders, Richard Bruce. "Mr. Polk's Army: Politics, Patronage, and the American Military in the Mexican War." Ph.D. diss., Texas Christian University, 1994.

Rejón, Manuel Crescencio

Born in the Yucatán, Mexican politician and foreign minister Manuel Crescencio Rejón (1799–1849) became a lifelong ardent federalist—or *puro*—and outspoken critic of U.S. expansion. He graduated from the Seminario Conciliar in Mérida with a degree in philosophy in 1818. After independence he was named to congress, coauthored the Constitution of 1824, and became a newspaper editor and commentator. He fought attempts by the United States to abrogate the terms of the Adams-Onís Treaty and became a leading voice in the federalist movement. In 1841, while persecuted by the Anastasio Bustamante regime, he coauthored Yucatán's radical constitution, which clarified many of the basic principles of Mexican liberalism.

As minister of foreign relations in 1844, Rejón took an intransigent stand toward the U.S. annexation of Texas. While in exile in Havana in 1846, Rejón was instrumental in forging the alliance between Antonio López de Santa Anna and Valentín Gómez Farías and in orchestrating Santa Anna's return to Mexico. He became one of the ideological forces behind the regimes of José Mariano Salas, Gómez Farías, and Santa Anna. Rejón served briefly as minister of foreign relations from August to October 1846 until a confrontation with Salas forced him to resign. He occupied the post again in the cabinet of Gómez Farías from February to April 1847, and was a deputy in congress later in the year.

Rejón tirelessly denounced U.S. peace overtures during the war and took an uncompromising position toward the loss of national territory. Beginning in 1847, he vigorously fought against treaty ratification in the belief that the United States would ultimately tire of the war and withdraw. He published an eloquent treatise rejecting the Treaty of Guadalupe Hidalgo in 1848. Rejón died on 7 October 1849 while preparing a plan to expand the Mexican navy.

Aaron P. Mahr Yáñez

BIBLIOGRAPHY

Ramírez, José. *Mexico during the War with the United States*. Edited by Walter Scholes and translated by Eliot Scherr. 1950.

Robinson, Cecil, ed. and trans. *The View from Chapultepec: Mexican Writers on the Mexican-American War*. 1989.

Santoni, Pedro. *Mexicans at Arms: Puro Federalists and the Politics of War, 1845–1848*. 1996.

Religion

On the eve of the U.S.–Mexican War, the contrast between the religious climates in Mexico and in the United States could hardly have been starker or more conspicuous. In Mexico, Catholicism retained a virtual monopoly over the religious life of the country and remained the only faith permitted by law. In the United States, the number and variety of religious denominations continued to expand rapidly. In Mexico, the church still enjoyed special political and economic privileges that were guaranteed by law, including the clergy's customary exemption from taxation and the *fueros* (privileges), which guaranteed churchmen accused of crimes the right to trial in a clerical rather than a civil court of law. In the United States, the churches had long since been disestablished, and religious denominations slowly continued to shed their remaining civil privileges as the separation of church and state continued to grow. In Mexico, a large proportion of the clergy, including the higher clergy, were barely literate enough to read the mass; in the United States, the clergy remained one of the better educated professions within an increasingly literate society. In Mexico, the church enjoyed little religious or spiritual vitality by the middle of the 1840s. In the United States, the contagion of revivals known as the Second Great Awakening had sparked a religious fervor that lasted for decades, and the proportion of the U.S. population that belonged to a church continued to climb throughout the first half of the nineteenth century. In Mexico, the church remained a consistent defender of the social and economic status quo, thereby perpetuating the enormous social and economic gulf between rich and poor. In the United States, evangelical Protestantism had by the 1840s become the primary inspiration for a host of political and social reforms designed to improve the lives of even the lowliest citizens.

On the eve of the U.S.–Mexican War the religious climate in the United States was also marked by a growing hostility toward Roman Catholics, a resentment that had existed since the earliest English settlements in North America and that had increased after 1830, when the number of Catholic immigrants to the United States began to increase. For example, the continuing expansion of the frontier inspired the creation of Protestant missionary societies designed to "Christianize" the West and to prevent its evangelization by Catholic missionaries.

With the beginning of hostilities against Mexico, the United States found itself at war with a nation whose people were predominantly Roman Catholic. Because the religious differences between the United States and Mexico were profound and conspicuous, the war might easily have inspired more intense and more widespread outbursts of anti-Catholicism throughout the United States. At the war's outset, President James K. Polk took steps to avoid a resurgence of hostility toward Catholics within the United States. The president hoped to promote respect for Catholicism both at home and abroad in order to prevent the war from becoming construed as a religious conflict between the largely Protestant United States and predominantly Catholic Mexico. The Polk administration successfully encouraged recruitment of Catholic immigrants into the U.S. military, hoping that these troops would vindicate their patriotism on the battlefield. The president appointed the first Roman Catholic chaplains to the U.S. army. Their presence in the field discouraged anti-Catholic feeling within the U.S. military and also helped to dispel Mexican fears that a U.S. victory would imperil Mexican Catholicism.

President Polk instructed U.S. military officers to treat Mexican Catholicism with consistent respect during the U.S. occupation of Mexican territory. Military orders promulgated by U.S. field commanders helped extend the policy of religious toleration throughout the ranks. Although U.S. troops sometimes committed atrocities against Mexican religious institutions, the official military proclamations helped to keep the number of depredations at a minimum.

Despite the administration's efforts, many U.S. Protestant leaders—including preachers, editors, evangelists, and missionaries on the frontier—attempted to fan the flames of anti-Catholicism throughout the war years. Protestant publications often used the war as a pretext for denouncing Catholicism in the United States and south of the border. Seizing on the notorious wartime desertions of the largely Irish-American San Patricio Battalion, they questioned the patriotism of Catholic immigrant soldiers serving in the U.S. military and portrayed them as especially inclined to desert. They complained that the appointment of Roman Catholic chaplains would provide a forum for the conversion of countless U.S. soldiers to Catholicism. They denounced and ridiculed myriad Catholic aspects of Mexican life and society: the allegedly unintelligible rites, oppressive and concupiscent priests, and complaisant and ignorant laity. They encouraged Protestant missionaries to evangelize the inhabitants of newly conquered territories, hoping that the war would result in a waning of Catholicism throughout Mexico, as well as an eclipse of Catholic influence within the United States.

Roman Catholic newspapers in the United States envisioned the war as a chance to defend their faith and to advertise the patriotism of U.S. Catholics. They praised the valor and patriotism of Irish- and German-Catholic immigrants. They urged and applauded the appointment of Roman Catholic chaplains to minister to U.S. soldiers. They countered Protestant denunciations of Mexican Catholicism and instead depicted it in a largely favorable way. When they did concede certain weaknesses in Mexican Catholicism, they attributed such flaws to alleged deficiencies in Mexican culture rather than to failings inherent in the faith. They denounced Protestant attempts to evangelize Mexican Catholics and complained whenever U.S. troops abused or attacked Mexican Catholicism. In varied ways, the Catholic press sought to portray Roman Catholicism as wholly compatible with the demands of life in the United States.

Despite the preoccupation of Protestant and Catholic newspapers with religious aspects of the war, the country as a whole viewed the conflict from a broader perspective. Most U.S. citizens refused to question the patriotism of their Catholic compatriots, perhaps in part because so many Protestant churches—including such old-line denominations as the Congregationalists and the Unitarians, as well as a substantial number of Presbyterians and Northern Baptists—opposed the war. The emerging theme of Manifest Destiny usually eclipsed earlier public attention to hostility between Protestants and Catholics in the United States. The country envisioned its struggle against Mexico in military, political, and racial rather than religious terms.

Isaac McDaniel, OSB

BIBLIOGRAPHY

Callcott, Wilfrid Hardy. *Church and State in Mexico, 1822–1857.* 1965.

Ellsworth, Clayton S. "The American Churches and the Mexican War." *American Historical Review* 45 (1940): 301–326.

Hinckley, Ted C. "American Anti-Catholicism during the Mexican War." *Pacific Historical Review* 23 (1962): 121–137.

Hueston, Robert F. *The Catholic Press and Nativism, 1840–1860.* 1976.

Johannsen, Robert W. *To the Halls of the Montezumas: The Mexican War in the American Imagination.* 1985.

Knobel, Dale T. *Paddy and the Republic: Ethnicity and Nationality in Antebellum America.* 1986.

Schroeder, John H. *Mr. Polk's War: American Opposition and Dissent.* 1973.

Wynn, Dennis J. "The San Patricios and the United States–Mexican War of 1846–1848." Ph.D. diss., Loyola University of Chicago, 1982.

See also **Catholic Church; Mormonism; Protestantism**

Remustered Volunteers

See **Volunteers, Remustered**

Republicanism, U.S.

The republic, and the ideals for which it stood, took on a mystical meaning for the men and women living in the United States during the first half of the nineteenth century. Much of the reverence accorded the institution could be traced to the war for independence from Great Britain. School children living in the Age of Jackson were taught that their forefathers had broken with the corrupt monarchical system of the old world and instituted a form that represented the will of the people—the republic.

Americans were infatuated with the concept of establishing a republic and relied on Rome as their model. Classical architecture came into vogue as did classical languages and literature. Even George Washington was compared to Cincinnatus, the Roman general who had put aside his sword and returned to his fields once Rome no longer required his military services. The republican spirit, with its emphasis on the rights and privileges of citizenship, permeated U.S. society, helping to pave the way for democratic reforms such as the granting of suffrage to all white males.

The United States expressed delight as one by one Spain's New World colonies declared their independence and established republics of their own. Their enthusiasm cooled, however, as the former Spanish colonies failed to live up to the republican standards expected by the United States. Indeed, punishing a corrupt republic became a common theme in the United States during the mid-nineteenth century, an idea expressed by many of its citizens as a reason for waging war against Mexico from 1846 to 1848.

Public opinion in the United States, however, was divided on the future of the republic as the nation's boundaries expanded. While Democrats claimed the republican form of government could be spread across a wide distance and include countless people, Whigs held another view. To them, the republic was much more fragile and was in danger of collapsing if extended too far and too fast. In the end, the Mexican Cession and the slavery issue placed pressure on the republic that caused it to break apart, only to be reassembled after four years of the Civil War.

Richard Bruce Winders

BIBLIOGRAPHY

Johannsen, Robert W. *To the Halls of the Montezumas: The Mexican War in the American Imagination.* 1985.

Merk, Frederick. *Manifest Destiny and Mission in American History.* 1970.

Wiebe, Robert H. *The Opening of American Society: From the Adoption of the Constitution to the Eve of Disunion.* 1985.

Resaca de la Palma, Battle of

The battle of Resaca de la Palma, or Resaca de Guerrero, was fought on 9 May 1846, about five miles north of the Río Grande in present-day Brownsville, Texas. In the battles at Palo Alto on 8 May and at Resaca de la Palma the following day, Gen. Zachary Taylor's Army of Occupation confronted Gen. Mariano Arista's Division of the North for con-

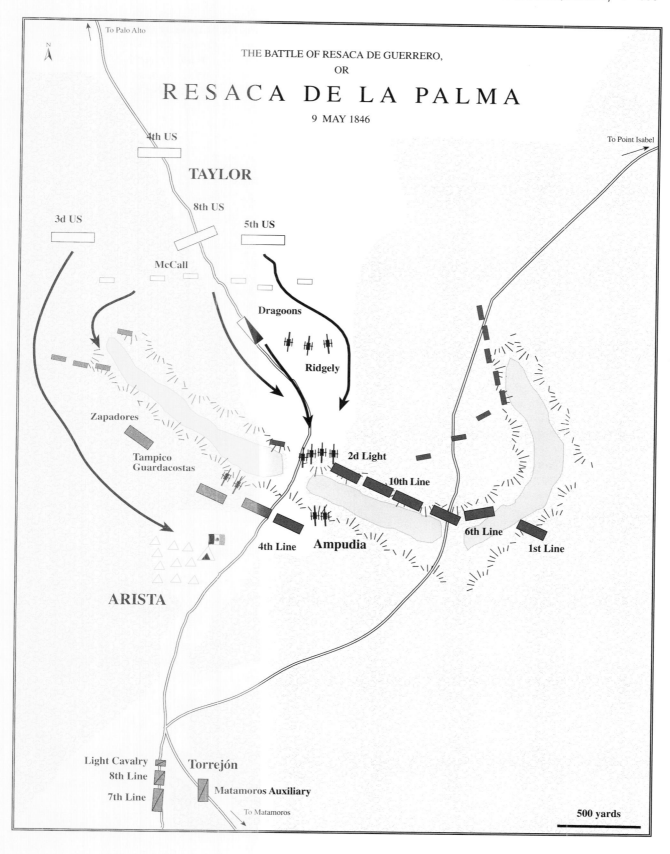

To Palo Alto

N

THE BATTLE OF RESACA DE GUERRERO,
OR
RESACA DE LA PALMA
9 MAY 1846

To Point Isabel

4th US

TAYLOR

8th US

3d US

5th US

McCall

Dragoons

Ridgely

Zapadores

2d Light

10th Line

Tampico
Guardacostas

6th Line

4th Line

Ampudia

1st Line

ARISTA

Light Cavalry
8th Line

Torrejón

7th Line

Matamoros **Auxiliary**

To Matamoros

500 yards

trol of the Río Grande in southern Texas. Taylor's victories there became the catalyst for his campaign into northeastern Mexico.

On 1 May Taylor moved the bulk of his army from Fort Texas, its forward field fortification on the northern bank of the Río Grande opposite Matamoros, to its supply depot thirty miles away at Point Isabel to gather supplies and reinforcements and tend to the depot's fortification. Seizing the opportunity, Arista crossed the river and moved his army between the two U.S. positions, while the Matamoros garrison besieged the fort. Taylor's army set out from Point Isabel toward the Río Grande to relieve the fort on 7 May. On the afternoon of 8 May the two armies met on the plains of Palo Alto, with Arista determined to block the U.S. advance and Taylor equally resolved to cut his way through to the river. The ensuing battle was inconclusive, although the U.S. forces held an advantage in the mobility and proficiency of their field artillery.

The next morning, Arista withdrew his battle-weary troops from Palo Alto and redeployed them five miles south in a more defensible position at Resaca de la Palma. An old abandoned bed of the Río Grande, the *resaca* formed a ravine across the road to Matamoros. Placing his infantry along the ravine walls and his sharpshooters forward in the dense chaparral, Arista hoped to reduce the capability of Taylor's artillery. Arista concentrated his own artillery at points on or near the road crossing and held his sizable cavalry force in reserve some distance to the rear. His force numbered about 3,600 men.

Taylor resumed his march to the river from Palo Alto with just over 1,800 men in the early afternoon of 9 May. Capt. George McCall led an advance unit on foot to the left and right of the road, while Lt. Randolph Ridgely advanced his battery of "flying" artillery—a sobriquet earned the day before at Palo Alto for its rapid deployment during combat—down the narrow road. Three infantry regiments followed closely behind.

Unlike the more conventional battle at Palo Alto the day before, the battle at Resaca de la Palma developed into a hand-to-hand contest in the dense brush. Regimental order was lost as the U.S. troops fought through the chaparral against stubborn resistance from the entrenched Mexican infantry line. As small parties of U.S. infantry broke through the Mexican left flank, Taylor ordered Capt. Charles May's dragoons to charge the Mexican guns at the road crossing. May charged down the road and cleared the guns, but he continued advancing behind the Mexican line before realizing he lacked infantry support. He quickly gathered his forces and charged back, taking Gen. Rómulo Díaz de la Vega, who had refused to leave the guns, prisoner. May's charge silenced the guns long enough for Ridgely to advance his battery and allow the U.S. infantry to push through the road crossing. With the Mexican left flank giving way and

the artillery silenced, the Mexican right began to wither. Arista, who until this time had left command to his second, Gen. Pedro de Ampudia, hastily gathered up his cavalry reserves and attempted two futile charges against the U.S. troops. In his rapid retreat, Arista left behind his division's supplies and records, as well as his personal belongings, which the U.S. forces plundered. In a series of skirmishes, the Mexican troops were forced across the river. The siege of Fort Texas was relieved that afternoon and Taylor occupied Matamoros a week later.

The hand-to-hand fighting at Resaca de la Palma took a heavy toll on both forces. The U.S. troops counted 45 killed

---

Battle of Resaca de la Palma
Order of Battle
9 May 1846

Mexican Forces

Commander
Gen. Mariano Arista

Infantry
2d Light Regiment
1st Line Regiment
2d Line Regiment
4th Line Regiment
6th Line Regiment
10th Line Regiment
Tampico Guardacostas
Zapadores

Cavalry
Light Regiment of Mexico
7th Line Regiment
8th Line Regiment
Presidial Companies
Matamoros Auxiliary

Artillery
approximately 13 pieces

U.S. Forces

Commander
Gen. Zachary Taylor

Infantry
3d Infantry
4th Infantry
5th Infantry
8th Infantry
2d Dragoons (part)

Cavalry
2d Dragoons (part)

Artillery
Company C, 3d Artillery (Ringgold's light battery)

in battle and 98 wounded. Arista reported 160 troops killed and 228 wounded.

The U.S. victory at Resaca de la Palma was definitive and gave the United States firm control of the disputed land between the Nueces River and the Río Grande. Arista's Northern Division was decimated. Shortly afterward, at Linares, Nuevo León, Arista relinquished command and played no significant role thereafter in the war.

Aaron P. Mahr Yáñez

BIBLIOGRAPHY

Alcaraz, Ramón, ed. *The Other Side; or, Notes for the History of the War between Mexico and the United States.* Translated by Albert C. Ramsey. 1970. Originally published as *Apuntes para la historia de la Guerra entre México y los Estado Unidos,* 1848.

Bauer, K. Jack. "The Battles on the Rio Grande: Palo Alto and Resaca de la Palma, 8–9 May 1846." In *America's First Battles, 1776–1965,* edited by Charles Heller and William Stofft. 1986.

Brooks, Nathan Covington. *A Complete History of the Mexican War.* 1965.

Henry, William S. *Campaign Sketches of the War with Mexico.* 1847.

Smith, Justin H. *The War with Mexico.* 2 vols. 1919. Reprint, 1963.

U.S. House Executive Doc. No. 209, 29th Cong., 1st sess., 1–31.

Ridgely, Randolph

Randolph Ridgely (1814–1846), brevet captain, U.S. Artillery, was born on 14 July in Anne Arundel County, Maryland, the son of Elizabeth and Charles Sterett Ridgely. Ridgely graduated from the United States Military Academy in 1837 and was assigned to Company C, 3d Artillery, commanded by Maj. Samuel Ringgold. This elite company, first to be designated as horse artillery, developed tactics for the army's new highly mobile bronze six-pounder, a weapon that would dominate the battlefields of the U.S.–Mexican War.

During the Battle of Palo Alto on 8 May 1846, Ridgely's guns manned the right flank and were responsible for repelling a flanking movement by Mexican cavalry. With the death of Major Ringgold at Palo Alto, Ridgely assumed command of Company C and led it into battle the next day, 9 May 1846, at Resaca de la Palma. For his heroism on this day he was awarded a brevet. Ridgely declined to accept the brevet, feeling that if he deserved a brevet for his actions at the Battle of Resaca de la Palma, he also deserved a second brevet for his actions the day before at the Battle of Palo Alto. However, he accepted a staff appointment as assistant adjutant-general at the rank of brevet captain on 7 July 1846, a position he assumed in addition to his regular duties with Company C.

Ridgely served with distinction in the Battle of Monterrey, 21–27 September 1846, but his light field artillery had little effect on the solid masonry walls that lined the streets of Monterrey. Noted as an expert horseback rider, Ridgely ironically met his end while riding for pleasure in the streets of Monterrey. His horse stumbled on a loose paving stone and lurched forward, throwing him head first onto the street. Ridgely lingered on in a coma for two days, but died on 27 October 1846.

One of the most popular men in the army, Ridgely's death was a shock to all. The Kentucky orator Thomas F. Marshall expressed the feeling of many when he said, "As well might one expect to hear of an eagle dying from the fall of his wings as to hear of Randolph Ridgely's dying from the fall of his horse."

Ridgely's body was interred near the camp of his company at Walnut Springs, on the outskirts of Monterrey, and was later returned to Baltimore, Maryland, where it was reburied in Greenmount Cemetery. The City of Baltimore awarded a sword to his family to commemorate Ridgely's heroism in Mexico.

Joseph E. Chance

BIBLIOGRAPHY

Heitman, Francis B. *Historical Register and Dictionary of the United States Army.* 1903.

Newman, Harry Wright. *Anne Arundel Gentry: A Genealogical History of Some Early Families of Anne Arundel County, Maryland.* 1979.

Riflemen

See **Voltigeurs and Foot Riflemen, U.S.**

Rincón, Manuel

Mexican general Manuel E. Rincón (1784–1849) was born in Perote, Vera Cruz, on 30 July. He began his military career in 1809 as an insurgent, fighting the royalist army for Mexican independence. Embracing independence leader Col. Agustín de Iturbide's Plan of Iguala in 1821, Rincón was elevated to colonel on 9 October 1821 as a reward for his loyalty. Promoted to brigade general two years later, Rincón held various positions of increasing responsibility including governor of Vera Cruz and inspector of active militias. While serving as commandant-general of Mexico, he was elected senator to the National Legislative Assembly of 1843.

As governor and commandant-general of Vera Cruz, Rincón had the dubious distinction of surrendering the port city to French admiral Charles Baudin, an action for which he was relieved of command and court-martialed. Although Rincón was absolved of any culpability for the loss of Vera

Cruz, poor health kept him generally inactive until Gen. Winfield Scott's march on the capital motivated him to offer his service for the impending valley campaign. Posted to the Churubusco convent, Rincón conducted a tenacious defense that held the attacking U.S. forces at bay until depleted ammunition supplies finally forced the garrison's capitulation. The rigors of such intense combat aggravated Rincón's already fragile health, compelling his permanent retirement to Cuernavaca, where he succumbed to his infirmities the following year.

William A. DePalo, Jr.

BIBLIOGRAPHY

Carreño, Alberto, M., ed. *Jefes del Ejército Mexicano en 1847: Biografías de generales de división y de brigada y de coroneles del ejército por fines del año 1847*, pp. 29–32. 1914.

DePalo, William A., Jr. *The Mexican National Army, 1822–1852*, pp. 68–69, 131, 143. 1997.

Diccionario Porrúa: de história, biografía, y geografía de México, p. 2951. 6th ed. 1995.

Noriega Elío, Cecilia. *El constituyente de 1842*, pp. 222–223. 1986.

Roa Bárcena, José María. *Recuerdos de la invasión Norteamericana (1846–1848)*, vol. 2, pp. 257–261, 275–276. 1947.

Ringgold, Samuel

U.S. Army artillery officer Samuel Ringgold (1800–1846) was born in Washington, D.C. He entered West Point in 1814, graduating in 1818. He then was assigned to the Corps of Artillery and sent to Great Britain and France to study European artillery practices. With the reorganization of U.S. Army artillery in 1821, Ringgold was assigned briefly to the 2d Artillery Regiment before being transferred to the 3d Artillery. He spent most of his military career between 1818 and 1823 as an aide to Gen. Winfield Scott. Ringgold was promoted to first lieutenant in 1823 and to captain in 1826. In February 1838 he received a brevet promotion to major for meritorious conduct against the Seminoles in Florida.

Ringgold was one of the U.S. Army's few tactical innovators in an era of doctrinal stagnation. He was an outspoken advocate of light field guns using highly mobile tactics. In September 1838 Ringgold's Company C, 3d Artillery was the first of four U.S. artillery companies to be organized as light artillery units. Tactics for the new units were supposed to be based on Capt. Robert Anderson's 1839 translation of the French *Instructions for Field Artillery, Horse and Foot*. Preferring British methods over the French, Ringgold revised the *Instructions* along British lines, and the manual was reissued by the U.S. Army in 1843.

Ringgold had the opportunity to prove his tactical theories in combat. During the Battle of Palo Alto on 8 May 1846, the light batteries of Ringgold and Lt. James Duncan fired eight rounds for every one fired by the Mexican artillery. While directing his battery's fire, Ringgold was struck by a shell that mangled both his legs. He died of his wounds three days later.

David T. Zabecki

BIBLIOGRAPHY

Birkhimer, William E. *Historical Sketch of the Artillery, United States Army*. 1884.

Dillon, Lester R., Jr. *American Artillery in the Mexican War, 1846–1847*. 1975.

Downey, Fairfax. *The Sound of the Guns: The Story of the American Artillery*. 1955.

Río Grande, Republic of the

An armed federalist movement against the central republic developed between 1838 and 1840 in the frontier states of Tamaulipas, Nuevo León, and Coahuila. Having sided with Texas, these states lent the movement its separatist character. The movement's principal leader was Antonio Canales Rosillo, a highly influential politician in the region, who, along with his political group, had been ousted from the position of power he occupied in the government of the state of Tamaulipas when centralism was introduced there. The Tamaulipas government stirred with ideas against the new centralist system, which had stripped it of its own revenues, wrested decision-making powers from its members, and imposed strict trade limitations. Moreover, since the independence of Texas in 1836, the army maintained a high profile in Tamaulipas, which caused friction with the civilian population. In October 1838 the Matamoros city council members were arrested for conspiracy against the central government, along with Juan Nepomuceno Molano, the prefect of the northern district and Canales's brother-in-law. Canales avoided arrest only because he was at the market in Saltillo. Apprised of the situation, he took up arms near Reynosa on 2 November 1838 and rapidly gathered numerous recruits. His attack on Matamoros was fruitless. The city defended itself under the leadership of Gen. Valentín Canalizo and Gen. Pedro de Ampudia. Canales later united with Pedro Lemus of Tampico, a city also in rebellion and occupied by Gen. José Urrea. They advanced on Monterrey, but Canales ultimately lost faith in Lemus and retreated to the northern townships. The opposition, on the other hand, had much faith in Gen. Juan Pablo Anaya, the former insurgent and renowned military man who had taken refuge in Nuevo León under the protection of the federalist governor, Manuel María del Llano. These states immediately prepared to assist Texas in obtaining weapons and supplies, despite the fact that the Mexican republic maintained a state of war against its former province and did not recognize its independence. Nevertheless, the Mexican opposition was received in Texas under the authorization of President Mirabeau B. Lamar. He saw the split between federalists and centralists as a means of lessening the possibility of a Mexican reconquest of Texas and so decided to maintain diplomatic relations with the Mexican rebels. These relations were very discreet, however, because Lamar did not wish to create problems with Great Britain, which was about to officially recognize the Republic of Texas, and which also had strong influence in Mexico. This situation meant a de facto recognition of Texas independence by the federalists, albeit with the understanding that the Tamaulipas-Texas border was the Nueces River and not the Río Grande. The federalists were harshly criticized in Mexico for their involvement with Texas and accused of treason, while the press in Texas and New Orleans invented the idea that they intended to create a so-called Republic of the Río Grande. At the end of 1839, Canales led an offensive and occupied the northern townships in Tamaulipas. Once again he attacked Matamoros but was unsuccessful. He led another offensive against Monterrey, where he was repulsed by Gen. Mariano Arista, the new centralist chief who had been ordered by President Anastasio Bustamante to bring peace to the border states.

In the political realm, the federalists organized in January 1840 a provisional government of the Eastern Districts, which was based on the Constitution of 1824. It was led by Jesús Cárdenas and had for spokesmen Juan Nepomuceno Molano, Juan N. Margain, Policarpo Martínez, and José María Flores. This government took up residence in Ciudad Guerrero, where it published the periodical *El Correo del Río Bravo del Norte*. Nevertheless, things were not going well militarily. Gen. Isidro Reyes roundly defeated the federalists in Morelos, Coahuila, capturing one of the chief rebel leaders, Antonio Zapata. Under General Arista's orders, Zapata was executed and beheaded, and his head was displayed publicly as a warning.

In September 1840, Juan Nepomuceno Molano led an attack against Ciudad Victoria, accompanied by a group of Texan and U.S. adventurers who demanded rights to whatever booty was taken, but they were detained. Pursued by Arista's forces, Molano advanced across the eastern Sierra Madre to Saltillo. There he met up with another column of the army and was forced to negotiate an armistice, upon which the Anglos departed for Texas. General Arista granted concessions to the rebels because they had demonstrated organization and a capacity for resistance, and because the pacification of the border states was a priority with the Mexican government, which still hoped to regain Texas. The opposition thereby regained their positions of regional power, while at the same time forging an alliance with Arista, a military leader with a political future. Despite being a chimera, the notion of the creation of a new country along the

Río Grande prevailed in Texas. In 1846 Gen. Zachary Taylor used the idea while occupying Matamoros, when he ordered that a newspaper be created and named after the republic to further stimulate the forces of separatism in northeastern Mexico. This newspaper was received so coolly by the Mexican opposition, however, that Taylor had its title changed to *The American Flag*. The notion of this supposed republic led to the creation of another myth, that of the Republic of the Sierra Madre, which was used as a means to accuse as traitors politicians from northeastern Mexico during the 1850s.

Octavio Herrera

BIBLIOGRAPHY

Nance, Joseph M. *After San Jacinto, The Texas-Mexican Frontier, 1836–1841.* 1963.

Vázquez, Josefina Z. Vázquez. "La supuesta República del Río Grande." *Historia Mexicana,* 36, no. 3 (July–September 1986): 49–80.

Vigness, David M. "The Republic of the Rio Grande, an Example of Separatism in North Mexico." Ph.D. diss., University of Texas, Austin. 1951.

Río Grande Campaign

Responding to Mexico's protest against the U.S. annexation of Texas in 1845, troops commanded by Bvt. Brig. Gen. Zachary Taylor encamped on the beach at Corpus Christi, Texas, on 25 July of that year. Diplomatic efforts to avoid confrontation having failed, Taylor marched out on 8 March 1846 to establish control over the area between the Río Grande and the Nueces River. The former was claimed as the boundary by Texas, the latter by Mexico. The United States supported the Texas claim to this area along the lower Río Grande and wanted to force the issue by a show of military strength.

General Taylor's Army of Occupation consisted of about 3,500 officers and men with a train of more than 300 wagons and carts. A supporting force under Maj. John Munroe, consisting chiefly of quartermaster, artillery, and engineer troops, was ordered to proceed by ship to Taylor's destination, the mouth of the Río Grande. Taylor's permanent rank at this time was colonel of the U.S. 6th Infantry Regiment. His advance guard of U.S. 2d Dragoons was commanded by Col. David E. Twiggs; the 1st Brigade (8th Infantry and an artillery battalion) by Taylor's second in command, Col. (brevet brigadier general) William J. Worth; the 2d Brigade (5th and 7th Infantries) by Col. James S. McIntosh; and the 3d Brigade (3d and 4th Infantries) was under Col. William Whistler. At Arroyo Colorado some Mexican cavalry seemed to threaten their advance, but the march was largely uneventful and they arrived opposite Matamoros on 28 March. The Mexicans were in view and spirits were high. The bore-

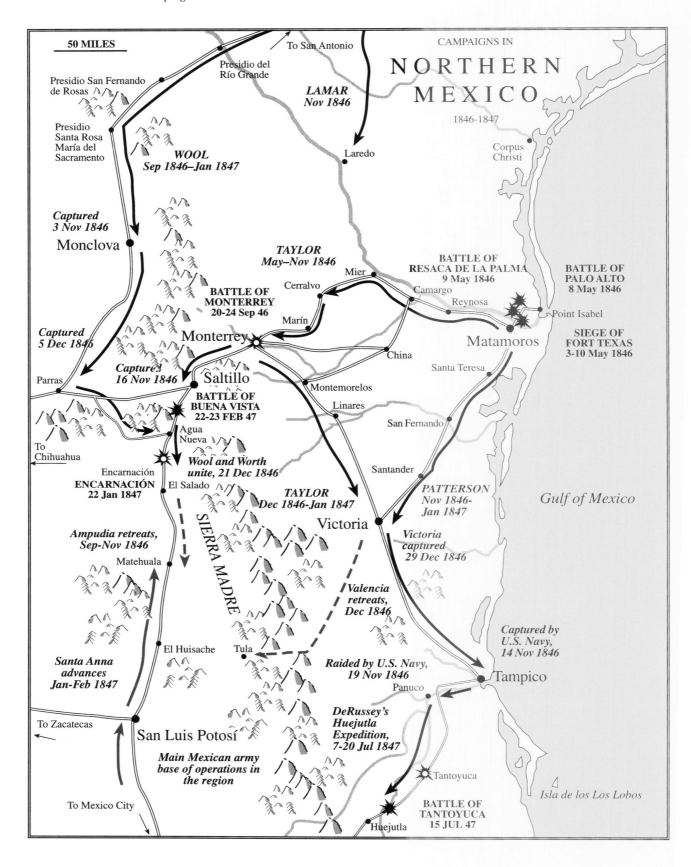

CAMPAIGNS IN NORTHERN MEXICO 1846-1847

dom of confinement to camp and endless drilling at Corpus Christi had ended.

Construction of Fort Texas, an earthwork, commenced almost immediately to face the Mexican batteries in Matamoros, and a standoff developed. Each side observed and felt out the other, waiting for reinforcements and new instructions.

On 23 April a skirmish occurred when Gen. Anastasio Torrejón with 1,600 cavalry crossed the river a few miles upstream. Capt. Seth Thornton and most of his command of some sixty-three U.S. dragoons were captured. President James K. Polk used this incident as the basis for a dramatic phrase in his war message to Congress, already in preparation when the news arrived: "Mexico has . . . shed American blood upon the American soil." War was declared by the United States and calls went out to the states for volunteers to fight in Mexico. Volunteers were to sign up for only six months, given the common assumption that the war would end within that period.

Needing to bring up men and supplies from the Gulf Coast some thirty miles away, Taylor marched for Point Isabel on 1 May, leaving the fort occupied by the 7th Infantry and some artillery under Maj. Jacob Brown. Taylor had just arrived at Point Isabel when sounds of intense artillery bombardment were heard from the direction of Fort Texas. When the Army of Occupation started its return on 7 May the U.S. forces knew they would have to fight. The battles at Palo Alto and Resaca de la Palma ensued on the next two days, significant victories for Taylor and especially the U.S. "flying" artillery. Fort Texas was renamed Fort Brown in honor of its commander, who died after being struck by a shell on 5 May. The city of Brownsville grew up around the fort's site and further commemorates his memory.

In Washington, D.C., on 13 May, President Polk signed the War Bill. Actions unfolded rapidly to enlarge Taylor's force and win the war. With the threat of a Mexican attack across the Río Grande much reduced, and cooperative understanding established with Commo. David E. Connor of the U.S. Home Squadron, needed artillery, many other supplies, and volunteer and regular reinforcements could be brought in by sea. Taylor's immediate military objective was to drive Mexican troops not only from Matamoros but also from the entire south bank of the river. He planned next to capture Monterrey, a major interior city.

Matamoros was taken easily: after waiting for new instructions, Gen. Mariano Arista evacuated the city on the night of 17 May and Taylor took possession peacefully, to the relief of most inhabitants. Along with captured public property, Taylor now had responsibility for some three hundred Mexican military sick and wounded. Reynosa, Camargo, and other Mexican towns were soon occupied without significant fighting. Steamboats could then be used to deliver the dramatically increasing cargoes of men and matériel.

Taylor's forces had established camps by the end of May at points all along both sides of the river up to one hundred or so miles from its mouth. Conditions were far from idyllic for the troops, however, for the heat of summer was oppressive. Their equipment was poor, their supplies uncertain, their standards for sanitation and orderliness were primitive, and their commissioned leaders, including medical officers, were often totally inadequate to cope with such chaotic conditions.

A flood of volunteer troop reinforcements began to arrive by 11 May at Point Isabel. In the war-inspired enthusiasm of the moment in Louisiana, some eight thousand men had signed up to serve for three months. They had been recruited by Gen. Edmund P. Gaines, commanding at New Orleans, without proper authority. Taylor, however, would accept these men only if they agreed to serve for six months. With few exceptions they refused; the brutal heat and other conditions on the Río Grande overwhelmed them, and their hopes for military glory were dashed because the battles of Palo Alto and Resaca de la Palma had ended all organized Mexican opposition in the area. More than 140 of these volunteers died of illness before they could return home.

Taylor meantime had specifically requested Texas volunteers, who began arriving in late May. The Texas infantry regiment served only briefly but the two mounted regiments performed long and significant service. Taylor put these Texas Rangers, as they came to be known, to work fighting guerrillas and scouting routes to Mexico's interior. The Río Grande campaign, referring to the initial occupation of the lowest parts of the valley, transitioned into Taylor's campaign against Monterrey.

John Porter Bloom

BIBLIOGRAPHY

Bauer, K. Jack. *Zachary Taylor: Soldier, Planter, Statesman of the Old Southwest.* 1985.

Kendall, George Wilkins. *The War between the United States and Mexico Illustrated. . . .* 1851.

Roa Bárcena, José María. *Recuerdos de la Invasión Norteamericana, 1846–1848, por un Joven de Entonces.* 1883.

Sides, Joseph C. *Fort Brown Historical.* 1942.

Smith, Justin H. *The War with Mexico.* 2 vols. 1919. Reprint, 1963.

Wilcox, Cadmus Marcellus. *History of the Mexican War.* 1892.

Río Grande City

See **Rancho Davis**

Ritchie, Thomas

Influential editor and political writer Thomas Ritchie (1778–1854) was born in Tappahannock, Essex County, Virginia on 5 November. After receiving a proper education, he moved to Fredericksburg and became a schoolteacher. He left Fredericksburg in 1803 due to ill health and moved to Richmond where on 9 May 1804, he started the *Richmond Enquirer*. The paper ran for forty-one years, three times a week, with Ritchie doing most of the writing and editing himself. Shortly after he started the newspaper, he married Isabella Foushee, the daughter of an active "war hawk," and became involved in politics. The *Richmond Enquirer* became the "Democratic Bible," mainly because Ritchie was an outspoken opponent of Whig politicians Henry Clay and John C. Calhoun.

Ritchie was an avid supporter of President James K. Polk and the annexation of Texas. Between the years 1845 and 1851, Ritchie edited the *Washington Union,* the famous administration-sponsored newspaper that first ran the headline, "American blood has been spilled on American soil." Polk saw to it that Ritchie had advance copies of speeches and first notice of front-line dispatches from the U.S.–Mexican War. Although Thomas Ritchie never held public office, his opinion was well respected among the political leaders of his time, and he did much to shape public opinion concerning U.S. expansion. When the Treaty of Guadalupe Hidalgo was proposed, Ritchie stated the treaty should be accepted since it provided "peace and security for the future," although he was disappointed more territory had not been gained. After he retired from the *Washington Union,* his time was split between Washington, D.C., and his daughter's home. Many famous political figures of the time mourned Ritchie's death on 31 July 1854.

Carlyn E. Davis

BIBLIOGRAPHY

Amber, Charles Henry. *Thomas Ritchie: A Study in Virginia Politics.* 1913.

Eisenhower, John S. D. *So Far from God: The U.S. War with Mexico, 1846–1848.* 1989.

White, Leonard D. *The Jacksonians: A Study in Administrative History, 1829–1861.* 1965.

Robertson, Sterling C.

Soldier and colonizer Sterling Clack Robertson (1785–1842) was born in Nashville, Tennessee, on 2 October to Elijah and Sarah (Maclin) Robertson. He served under Maj. Gen. William Carroll at the Battle of New Orleans. In 1822 he and seventy other stockholders of the Texas Association requested permission from the government of Mexico to settle families in Mexican Texas. Robertson signed a subcontract with the Texas Association in 1830 to introduce two hundred families to Texas although he, along with his partner Alexander Thomson, were prevented from settling them because of Mexico's Law of April 6 (1830), which prohibited further colonization from the United States. In 1831 his colony was transferred to Stephen F. Austin and Samuel May Williams, producing a controversy between the two families and among historians that lingers still. Central to the controversy was the fact that Robertson blamed Austin for invalidation of his contract. He and his heirs believed that Austin unscrupulously used his influence with the Mexican government to have Robertson's contract cancelled so that Austin could take it over. Robertson obtained a colony in his own name in 1834. After becoming a captain in the Texas Rangers in 1836, he was elected a delegate to the independence convention at Washington-on-the-Brazos, where he signed the Texas declaration of independence from the Republic of Mexico as well as the constitution for the new Republic of Texas. Robertson served as a senator in the republic's congress from 1836 to 1838. He died in Robertson County on 4 March 1842. His remains were reinterred in the State Cemetery of Texas in Austin in 1935.

Jodella K. Dyreson

BIBLIOGRAPHY

Biographical Directory of the Texan Conventions and Congresses 1832–1845. 1941.

McLean, Malcolm D., comp. and ed. *Papers Concerning Robertson's Colony in Texas.* 1974–1993.

Rosa, Luis de la

See **de la Rosa**, Luis

Rosillo, Antonio Canales

See **Canales** Rosillo, Antonio

Ruiz, Francisco

Francisco Antonio Ruiz (1804–1876), prominent native-born citizen of San Antonio, Texas, was mayor of San Antonio during the famous Alamo battle in 1836; when the Alamo fell, Mexican general Antonio López de Santa Anna ordered Ruiz to supervise the disposal of corpses. Ruiz served on the San Antonio city council (1837–1841) after Texas won independence from Mexico in 1836.

Like many Texas residents of Mexican or Spanish descent (Tejanos), Ruiz opposed U.S. annexation of Texas. He contended that the issue of annexation should be decided by those who had participated in the Texas Revolution, not by newcomers to Texas. When Texas became a state in 1845, Ruiz chose to live with the Native Americans on the frontier rather than submit to U.S. rule.

Ruiz's absence from his hometown during the U.S.–Mexican War reflects the Tejano viewpoint on that conflict. While at least one hundred forty Tejanos fought for Texas independence from Mexico (1835–1836), only a few soldiers with Spanish surnames enlisted with U.S. forces during the U.S.–Mexican War. Contemporary observers noted that many Tejanos abandoned Texas and stayed in Mexico for the duration of the war.

Ruiz is sometimes confused with his father, José Francisco Ruiz, who was a signer of the Texas declaration of independence (1836) and represented San Antonio as a senator in the first congress of the Republic of Texas (1836–1837). The elder Ruiz died in 1840.

Francisco Antonio returned to San Antonio sometime after the U.S.–Mexican War, but he was not as prominent in public affairs as he had been previously. He died at his hometown in 1876.

Timothy M. Matovina

BIBLIOGRAPHY

Matovina, Timothy M. *Tejano Religion and Ethnicity: San Antonio, 1821–1860.* 1995.

Santos, Richard G. *José Francisco Ruiz.* 1966.

Rusk, Thomas J.

Thomas Jefferson Rusk (1803–1857), commander-in-chief of the Texas army and U.S. senator from Texas, was born 5 December in Clemson, South Carolina. He arrived in Texas in January 1835 in pursuit of a group of swindlers who had cheated him in a fraudulent gold-mining scheme in Georgia. Falling quickly into the political scene in Texas he rose to a position of prominence, being named secretary of war in the provisional government formed during the rebellion against Mexico. Rusk was with Gen. Sam Houston at the battle of San Jacinto in April 1836 and took command of the Texas army in May when Houston was wounded, serving as commander-in-chief until October. He also led forces to Victoria, Texas, after the battle to secure the region following the Mexican retreat.

From 1838 to 1839, Rusk led forces around Nacogdoches against Vicente Córdova, who led a group of discontented Tejanos, Indians, and blacks in an uprising protesting discrimination by Anglo Texans. As Córdova and the area Tejanos had not been supportive of the revolution in 1836 and had been viewed since then as troublemakers, Rusk felt justified in overriding Houston's relatively conciliatory position with more aggressive tactics. Córdova's ill-fated stand ended in his retreat to Mexico and ultimate death in the Woll expedition in 1842.

During the years of the Republic of Texas, Rusk served in a variety of positions in the government, and by the time of annexation in 1846 he was regarded as virtually the equal in reputation of Sam Houston. Rusk chaired the convention that approved Texas's acceptance of the terms of annexation into the United States.

When the Texas legislature needed to elect two senators to serve in Washington, D.C., immediately after annexation, Rusk and Houston were the unanimous choices. They arrived in the national capital in May 1846, and Rusk immediately renewed his acquaintance with South Carolina senator John C. Calhoun, whom he had known in his younger years. Thus, Rusk was not without influential contacts in Washington, although he believed his relationship with Calhoun hindered any close contact with President James K. Polk. Despite chilly relations with the president (or perhaps because of them), both Rusk and Houston were offered positions of major general with the army invading Mexico, but both declined.

Although Texas was key to the motivation for the war against Mexico, Rusk and Houston seem to have remained fairly low-profile during the war. Only as the war was nearing its conclusion, when the opposition Whig party had gained control of Congress, was Rusk directly challenged on Texas's role in the conflict. High-ranking Whigs in Congress such as Daniel Webster and Henry Clay accused Texas of claiming too much territory. They argued that the Nueces River, not the Río Grande, should have been the natural southern border of Texas, as Mexico had claimed before the war started. Rusk addressed this issue in a 17 February 1848 speech to Congress that received national attention.

Rusk was intimately familiar with the details of the Texas Revolution and its result, and he spoke from firsthand experience. He had been at San Jacinto when Mexican president general Antonio López de Santa Anna surrendered and had witnessed Santa Anna signing the document that granted Texas independence. Rusk stated that Santa Anna had agreed to the Río Grande as the southern and western border of Texas, and the first congress of the newly independent state of Texas had so specified that boundary. Thus, when Congress had offered to annex Texas in 1845, there could have been no question as to the boundary. President Polk, therefore, was justified not only in stationing troops, under Gen. Zachary Taylor, in southern Texas in early 1846 but also in pursuing war against Mexico when Mexican forces crossed the Río Grande.

The war was not without justification, Rusk argued. Texans had suffered at the hands of Mexican authorities since 1836; he detailed attacks against innocent women and children and claimed that Texans were held without charge in Mexican prisons. He claimed that the disputed area between the Nueces River and the Río Grande "was occupied chiefly by the widows of those who had fallen in the contest with

Santa Anna . . . Texas could never be induced to withdraw protection from these widows and their orphans." Neither, he argued, could the U.S. government.

Rusk's speech was reprinted and distributed across the country. He believed the war had gone on too long due to the congressional controversy, which he thought encouraged the Mexican government to hold out for better terms. Rusk spent the next few months working for Sam Houston's bid for the Democratic presidential nomination and defending Texan soldiers against Whig political attacks. During the 1848 campaign, Whigs circulated letters supposedly sent by Zachary Taylor describing atrocities committed by Texan troops. Taylor denied writing the letters, but they received wide coverage. Rusk next came to public notice during the debates on the Compromise of 1850, when he encouraged Texas to cede its northwestern lands in return for sufficient money ($10 million in cash and credit) to clear the state of debt.

Rusk remained a senator until 1857 when, despondent for more than a year over the death of his wife, he committed suicide.

Paul K. Davis

BIBLIOGRAPHY

Clarke, Mary Whatley. *Thomas J. Rusk: Soldier, Statesman, Jurist.* 1971.

Congressional Globe. 30th Congress, 17 February 1848.

Huston, Cleburne. *Towering Texan.* 1971.

Lack, Paul. "The Córdova Revolt." In *Tejano Journey, 1770–1850,* edited by Gerald Poyo. 1996.

Papers of Thomas J. Rusk. Barker Center, Austin, Texas.

Sacramento, Battle of

On 28 February 1847 the 1st Missouri Regiment of Mounted Volunteers (about one thousand soldiers) led by Col. Alexander W. Doniphan fought a Mexican army gathered at the Río Sacramento, fifteen miles north of Chihuahua City, Mexico (*see map on following page*). Gen. José A. Heredia commanded three thousand Mexican soldiers, one-third of whom were regulars; the others were national guardsmen or local troops. Heredia's chief subordinate was Gen. Pedro García Conde, former minister of war and one of Mexico's best military engineers, who had designed a series of cannon redoubts above the Arroyo Seco.

Before attacking, Doniphan sent officers to scout the Mexican positions. The Mexican leaders, in planning their emplacements, had erroneously believed that a deep gulch on their left flank was impassable. The invaders rushed forward and built a dirt ramp, allowing them to advance and avoid the strength of the Mexican positions. Heredia promptly attacked with a troop of lancers, but they were turned back by U.S. artillery fire. The invading force deployed in line of battle and, supported by artillery, assaulted the Mexican redoubts. The battle lasted three hours. Only 12 U.S. soldiers were killed or wounded, but 169 Mexicans were killed, 300 wounded, and 79 taken prisoner.

The Battle of Sacramento led to the fall of Chihuahua City on 2 March 1847. The loss deprived the Mexicans of the significant morale boost that would have resulted from a victory over any U.S. force. Doniphan's victory also helped protect the U.S. capture of New Mexico; had the Mexicans won at Sacramento they could have moved northward in an attempt to recapture Santa Fe.

Joseph G. Dawson III

BIBLIOGRAPHY

Bauer, K. Jack. *The Mexican War.* 1974.

Connelley, William E. *Doniphan's Expedition.* 1907.

Salas, José Mariano

José Mariano Salas (1797–1867) began his military career as a member of the Spanish infantry. He accepted the Plan of Iguala and supported Mexico's independence from Spain in 1821. During the Mexican campaign against the Texas revolt for independence, he led a column in the attack against the Alamo. At the time of the U.S. invasion in 1846, Salas controlled the *ciudadela*—the chief barracks of Mexico City. With Mexican politics in disarray, he shared the reins of government together with Valentín Gómez Farías on 5 August, proclaiming the unity of the Mexican federation and opposition to the invading U.S. forces. Salas restored freedom of the press, called for new congressional elections, and declared the Constitution of 1824 in effect. He acted as president until 23 December.

Antonio López de Santa Anna returned to Mexico City 15 September to find Salas in control of the government. In early December the senate held a presidential election, which Santa Anna narrowly won. Gómez Farías was selected as vice president over the *moderado*-supported Melchor Ocampo. Salas refused to relinquish the office until his dismissal by Santa Anna. Once Salas stepped down, he conducted a campaign of guerrilla warfare until captured by Gen. Winfield Scott's advancing troops. After the war, he continued to exercise influence on Mexico's military and politics. In 1863, at the age of seventy-two, Salas served as one of three members of a provisional regency established by the French occupation forces during the attempt by Na-

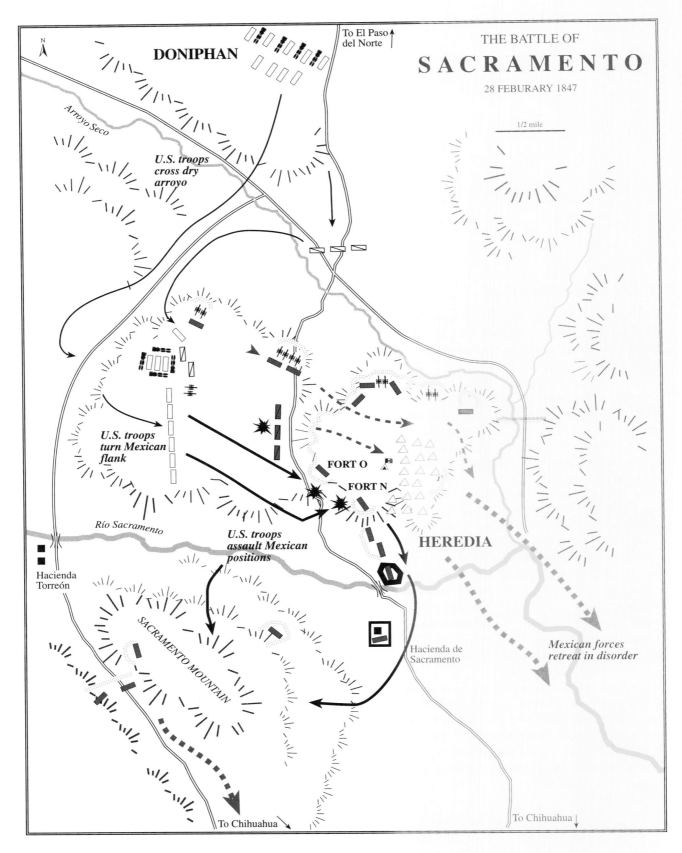

DONIPHAN

To El Paso
del Norte

THE BATTLE OF

SACRAMENTO

28 FEBURARY 1847

1/2 mile

Arroyo Seco

U.S. troops
cross dry
arroyo

U.S. troops
turn Mexican
flank

FORT O

FORT N

Río Sacramento

U.S. troops
assault Mexican
positions

HEREDIA

Hacienda
Torreón

SACRAMENTO MOUNTAIN

Hacienda de
Sacramento

Mexican forces
retreat in disorder

To Chihuahua

To Chihuahua

Saltillo. John Frost, *Pictorial History of Mexico and the Mexican War*, 1862

poléon III (reigned from 1852 to 1871) to install Archduke Maximilian as ruler of Mexico in the 1860s.

Robin Robinson

BIBLIOGRAPHY

Diccionario Porrúa: historia, biografía y geografía de Mexico. 6th ed. 1995.

Echanove Trujillo, Carlos A. *La vida pasional e inquieta de don Crescencio Rejón.* 1941.

Eisenhower, John S. D. *So Far from God: The U.S. War with Mexico, 1846–1848.* 1989.

Ramírez, José Fernando. *Mexico during the War with the United States.* Translated by Elliott B. Scherr. 1950.

Ridley, Jasper. *Maximilian and Juárez.* 1992.

Smith, Justin H. *The War with Mexico.* 2 vols. 1919. Reprint, 1963.

Saltillo

A city of approximately 15,000 inhabitants whose economy was based primarily on commerce, Saltillo was the last urban area occupied by the U.S. Army in northeastern Mexico. After the Mexican army retreated to San Luis Potosí in October 1846, the troops of Gen. Zachary Taylor entered Saltillo on 16 November and remained there until July 1848.

During this period, the governor of Coahuila and the state congress abandoned the city, leaving political chief Eduardo González in nominal charge. Religious holy day celebrations, which were at the center of the city's civic and cultural life, were suspended, for fear of interference from the majority non-Catholic occupying forces.

The U.S. military leaders—Gen. John E. Wool, Maj. John Macrae Washington, Col. Samuel R. Curtis, and Col. John

Francis Hamtrack—issued decrees prohibiting the sale of liquor, regulated the sale and procurement of other products, and punished guerrillas and vagrants. The civilian population that remained in Saltillo, generally speaking, was not hostile toward the U.S. soldiers; many Mexicans did not have a clear sense of patriotism and they understood the threat that foreign occupation of the city signified. There was, however, guerrilla activity in the area surrounding Saltillo, and some residents of the city, such as Braulio Flores, also known as the "Sleeping King," surreptitiously murdered U.S. troops at night. Some residents of Saltillo, such as Catarino Escobedo, were hanged by U.S. authorities because they had joined the guerrillas.

Eduardo González himself was arrested by U.S. authorities as a spy in April 1847 but was released by 28 September. U.S. forces were supplied by the Sánchez Navarro family, the principal landholders in Coahuila at the time. In addition, a number of volunteers, such as William Deam, James Vandergriff, and Howard Vandergriff of Illinois, Jesse Jenkins of Pennsylvania, and George Upperman, married young women from the area. Others, such as the paramedic Josiah Gregg and the self-proclaimed vice consul George M. Collinworth, decided to remain permanently in Saltillo after the war. Marriages between U.S. volunteers and Mexican women attest to the fact that *saltillenses* accepted foreigners as long as they were Catholic, regardless of the fact that they were enemies of the fatherland. This suggests that the sense of patriotism among residents of Saltillo was much less developed than their religious beliefs.

On 22 and 23 February 1847, the Battle of Buena Vista took place south of Saltillo. The wounded were attended to in the present-day Santiago Cathedral, which was converted to a field hospital.

Some of history's first war photographs were taken in Saltillo. About thirty daguerreotypes, probably taken by J. H. William Smith or William P. Schwartz, show U.S. soldiers, streets, buildings, and people of the city. In 1847 two English-language newspapers were being published in Saltillo: *The Picket Guard* and *The Sentinel*.

Carlos Recio Da Villa

BIBLIOGRAPHY

Alessio Robles, Vito. *Saltillo en la historia y en la leyenda*. 1934.

Cuellar Valdés, Pablo M. *Historia de la ciudad de Saltillo*. 1982.

Sandweiss, Martha, et al. *Eyewitness to War*. 1989.

Villareal Lozano, Javier. *Los ojos ajenos, viajeros en Saltillo (1603–1910)*. 1993.

San Antonio

From 1845 to 1846 San Antonio, Texas, was the rendezvous point for U.S. forces under the command of Brig. Gen. John E. Wool. Regular troops led by Col. William Shelby arrived at San Antonio during the fall of 1845. General Wool joined them on 14 August 1846 and spent six weeks drilling both volunteers and regulars before leading them south for an intended invasion of Chihuahua. The main body of troops, some fourteen hundred strong, departed San Antonio on 26 September. Wool's forces included two infantry regiments from Illinois, a cavalry regiment from Arkansas, and a small contingent of regulars.

Most of the U.S. forces stayed at Camp Crockett, about three miles outside San Antonio. Although soldiers' diaries and letters include complaints about bad weather, insufficient provisions, inadequate medical attention, and the incompetence of their commanding officers, in general, the battle preparation the troops received at San Antonio was successful.

Several companies of Texas volunteers were also mustered at San Antonio, beginning with Capt. Richard A. Gillespie's Texas Mounted Rangers in September 1845. Volunteers continued to enlist at San Antonio and other sites in Texas through the spring of 1847, particularly as U.S. forces advanced deeper into Mexico, necessitating more volunteers to defend their lines of communication from guerrilla attack.

According to contemporary observers, San Antonio's predominantly Tejano (Mexican-descent) population had an ambivalent relationship with U.S. troops, who offered the civilians protection from Native American raiders, but also taunted local residents because of their Mexican heritage. Despite such conflicts, the U.S.–Mexican War changed San Antonio significantly as it marked the city's inception as a major center for the U.S. armed forces.

Timothy M. Matovina

BIBLIOGRAPHY

Barton, Henry W. *Texas Volunteers in the Mexican War*. 1970.

Hinton, Harwood P. "The Military Career of John Ellis Wool, 1812–1863." Ph.D. diss., University of Wisconsin, 1960.

San Felipe de Jésus de China

See **China**

San Jacinto, Battle of

On 21 April 1836, the climactic engagement of the Texas Revolution occurred near the confluence of Buffalo Bayou and the San Jacinto River. Gen. Antonio López de Santa Anna hoped to conclude his 1836 campaign by capturing officials of the insurgent government at Harrisburg. Separating from his main force, the Mexican Army of Operations in Texas, he set out on 14 April at the head of seven hundred troops. Near midnight on 15 April, his advance units arrived in Harrisburg only to learn the politicos had fled hours earlier. On 18 April Santa Anna burned Harrisburg and sped toward New Washington on the coast, where he discovered that the rebel government had escaped to Galveston Island.

Meanwhile Gen. Sam Houston, commander of the Texas army, had learned from captured dispatches that Santa Anna commanded the small Mexican unit in New Washington and—more important—that he was isolated from the bulk of his army. Houston rushed to exploit his antagonist's mistake. On 20 April Houston placed his forces in an oak grove near Lynch's Ferry on the Lynchburg-Harrisburg Road, positioned between the Mexican general and his main force. Returning from New Washington later that day, Santa Anna found his line of march blocked by Houston's forces and sent a courier to Gen. Martín Perfecto de Cos. That afternoon, attempts to reconnoiter the Texian position produced minor artillery and cavalry skirmishes.

On Thursday morning, 21 April, Cos arrived on the field with some 660 troops. The reinforcements increased Santa Anna's force to about 1,360, placing Houston, with 910 effectives, at a numerical disadvantage. Around noon Houston held a council of war that voted for an immediate attack, lest more Mexican reinforcements arrive.

The battle opened around 4:30 P.M. Because rising ground and high grass screened the Texian advance, the assault took the Mexicans by surprise. When initial attempts to rally failed, Mexican soldiers degenerated into what one of their officers described as "a bewildered and panic-stricken herd." The battle lasted no more than eighteen minutes; the slaughter continued much longer. Vengeful Texians shouting "Remember the Alamo—Remember Goliad" killed some 630 Mexicans and captured another 730. Of 910 Texians engaged, only 9 lost their lives; 30 sustained wounds, including General Houston. Santa Anna escaped the battlefield, but Texians captured him on 22 April, holding him as a prisoner of war until 20 November. The rebels won a notable victory at San Jacinto, but only with the apprehension of the Mexican commander did the triumph become decisive.

Following the battle the Mexican army withdrew across the Río Grande. Assertions that Texas won its independence at San Jacinto, however, are extravagant. Although the victory provided the Republic of Texas time to develop a government, the constant danger of invasion harried its existence. Mexicans were loath to surrender their claim on Texas and would not completely do so until the Treaty of Guadalupe Hidalgo in 1848.

Stephen L. Hardin

BIBLIOGRAPHY

Delgado, Pedro. *Mexican Account of the Battle of San Jacinto.* 1919.

Hardin, Stephen L. *Texian Iliad: A Military History of the Texas Revolution, 1835–1836.* 1994.

Jenkins, John H., ed. *The Papers of the Texas Revolution.* 10 vols. 1973.

Tolbert, Frank X. *The Day of San Jacinto.* 1959.

San José, Siege of

On 8 November 1847, with the threat looming in Baja California of a revolt against U.S. rule, Commo. W. Branford Shubrick of the U.S. Navy's Pacific Squadron placed a small marine detachment at San José del Cabo. Lt. Charles Heywood commanded the twenty-four-man garrison, which occupied the remains of a Spanish mission and a nearby house. Twenty Mexican civilians supportive of the United States augmented their numbers. In mid-November, with the U.S. Navy's ships operating off Mazatlán, Mexican captain Manuel Pineda assembled a force of more than one hundred men to capture the isolated posts at La Paz and San José. After two unsuccessful assaults on La Paz, Pineda ordered an attack on San José.

Lieutenant Heywood refused a demand to surrender on 19 November. That night Mexican troops attacked the U.S. positions but were beaten off. The following evening they launched another attack, which was also repulsed. During this second assault the defenders' fire killed Lt. José Antonio Mijares of the Mexican navy. On 21 November two U.S. whaling ships arrived off San José. When it appeared that another attack might take place, the civilian crews reinforced the beleaguered garrison. Meanwhile, by 24 November Commodore Shubrick had learned of the attack and sent the *Southampton* with supplies and troops to San José. The ship arrived two days later but by this time the Mexicans had withdrawn.

In late January 1848 Captain Pineda mounted a second siege of the town. U.S. naval support had again been withdrawn from San José, and although Lieutenant Heywood's command had been reinforced, the U.S. forces were extremely short of supplies. On 22 January the Mexicans captured a foraging party and on 4 February they occupied the town. The marines and sailors made several efforts to clear Mexican forces from the town, but they eventually found themselves trapped in the mission, short of water and other provisions. On the evening of 14 February the ship *Cyane* brought Cmdr. Samuel F. Du Pont and one hundred men to break the siege and secure the town.

David J. Coles

BIBLIOGRAPHY

Bauer, K. Jack. *The Mexican War, 1846–1848.* 1974.

Bauer, K. Jack. *Surfboats and Horse Marines: U.S. Naval Operations in the Mexican War, 1846–48.* 1969.

Gerhard, Peter. "Baja California in the Mexican War." *Pacific Historical Review* 14 (November 1945): 418–424.

Harlow, Neal. *California Conquered: War and Peace on the Pacific, 1846–1850.* 1982.

San Juan de Ulúa

Hernán Cortés established a defensive position on the island of San Juan de Ulúa in 1519, just offshore from Vera Cruz on Gallega Reef. In 1588, Italian engineer Bautista Antonelli designed a fortress for the island, but not until 1771 was construction begun on the massive stone walls that formed the "castle" of San Juan de Ulúa. As part of the extensive defensive system of the Caribbean ordered by King Charles III of Spain, the imposing structure could garrison 2,500 men and stood guard over Mexico's principal port. In 1838 the fortress played a part in the heroic actions of Antonio López de Santa Anna as he defied the French attack in the Pastry War.

In 1846, as rumors of an attack by the United States circulated in Vera Cruz, the fort was in disrepair, many of its weapons covered with rust. Gen. Ignacio Mora y Villamil, the most competent engineer in the Mexican army, initiated work to repair the defenses, but his task was far from complete when U.S. forces arrived off the coast. As Gen. Winfield Scott launched his attack against Vera Cruz on 9 March 1847, he showed great respect for the firepower of San Juan, landing his troops well out of range of its guns. Cmdr. Josiah Tattnall, aboard *Spitfire,* bombarded the fortress on two occasions but did little damage. General Scott did not have to test its defenses by assault, however, for San Juan surrendered along with the city of Vera Cruz on 27 March 1847. Today the guns of San Juan de Ulúa are silent, but the mas-sive fortress stands as a monument to Mexico's struggles of the past.

Edward H. Moseley

BIBLIOGRAPHY

Bauer, K. Jack. *Surfboats and Horse Marines: U.S. Naval Operations in the Mexican War, 1846–1848.* 1969.

Benitez, Fernando, and José Emilio Pacheco. *Crónica del puerto de Veracruz.* 1986.

Bobb, Bernard. *The Viceregency of Antonio María Bucareli in New Spain, 1771–1779.* 1962.

San Luis Potosí

This entry consists of two separate articles: State of San Luis Potosí *and* City of San Luis Potosí.

State of San Luis Potosí

Spanish settlers first arrived in the San Luis Potosí region in the late 1500s in search of silver. By the early seventeenth century silver mines operated in Guadalcázar and the capital city of San Luis Potosí, and throughout the colonial era the silver mines of the state of San Luis Potosí produced tremendous amounts of wealth for the Spanish crown. During Mexico's War for Independence (1810–1821) San Luis Potosí remained a royalist stronghold, although some insurgent

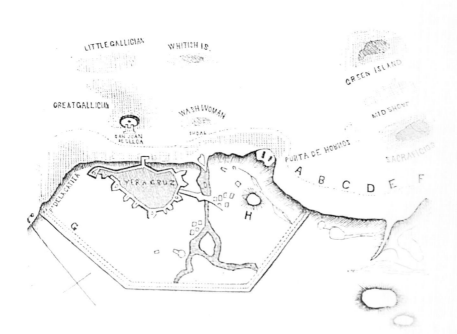

Vera Cruz and San Juan de Ulúa. John Frost, *Pictorial History of Mexico and the Mexican War,* 1862

bands operated in the state under the leadership of Mariano Jiménez. The state of San Luis Potosí contains a number of important cities including the capital (which bears its name), Cerritos, Ciudad del Maíz, Guadalcázar, Matehuala, Río Verde, and Tamazunchale.

During the U.S.–Mexican War, the state of San Luis Potosí served as a major base of unconventional military operations for the Mexican army. Popular guerrilla armies, armed and financed by landowners such as Pablo Verástegui of the Hacienda de San Diego in Río Verde, operated throughout the state and harassed U.S. troops along the Vera Cruz–Mexico City route and around the cities of Monterrey and Saltillo. In the Huasteca, a mountainous region in the eastern portion of the state, popular peasant militias assisted the Mexican army by engaging U.S. forces around the city of Tampico. The participation of San Luis Potosí's citizenry in the national defense contributed greatly to the Mexican army's northeastern theater of operations. By making the occupation of northeastern Mexico costly, these citizen militias prevented the U.S. Army from occupying the state of San Luis Potosí.

Mark Saad Saka

BIBLIOGRAPHY

Bauer, Jack K. *The Mexican War, 1846–1848.* 1974.

Muro, Manuel. *Historia de San Luis Potosí.* 1973.

Saka, Mark Saad. "Peasant Nationalism and Social Unrest in the Mexican Countryside, 1848–1884." Ph.D. diss., University of Houston, 1995.

Valázquez, Primo Feliciano. *Historia de San Luis Potosí.* 1982.

City of San Luis Potosí

San Luis Potosí played an important role in domestic Mexican politics during the course of the U.S.–Mexican War. In December 1845 the city served as a launching point for the successful rebellion led by Maj. Gen. Mariano Paredes y Arrillaga against Mexican president José Joaquín de Herrera. Later, in October 1846, Ramón Adame led a successful pro–Santa Anna revolt in the city. Finally, during the peace negotiations between U.S. representative Nicolas P. Trist and Mexican president Manuel de la Peña y Peña, an anti-peace rebellion originated in San Luis Potosí that threatened to stall the signing of the Treaty of Guadalupe Hidalgo.

San Luis Potosí also played a prominent role in the defense of Mexico during the U.S. invasion. After the city of Monterrey fell to Gen. Zachary Taylor's forces in September 1846—which opened the possibility to the United States of a quick overland invasion of Mexico—Gen. Antonio López de Santa Anna arrived in San Luis Potosí with the intention of rebuilding a new army capable of defeating the U.S. forces. The Mexican army prepared to defend Mexico City by strengthening the defenses of the city of San Luis Potosí. Mexican general Ignacio Mora y Villamil built a lengthy an-

ticavalry trench around the city with assistance from the local citizenry and hacienda workers supplied by nearby estates. Local citizens and the church supplied the army with financial and material assistance, and most haciendas in the San Luis Potosí region supplied the army and subsequent civilian militias with mules and corn to aid in the city's defense. The fortified San Luis Potosí defenses helped convince General Taylor that a direct southward invasion of Mexico City would be difficult, if not impossible. Santa Anna's forces used the city of San Luis Potosí as a base from which to launch military operations against the U.S. Army around Monterrey. The active participation of civilians in the digging of the anticavalry trenches and their inclusion into the national defense earned the city the patriotic distinction of "San Luis de la Patria."

Mark Saad Saka

BIBLIOGRAPHY

Bauer, Jack K. *The Mexican War, 1846–1848.* 1974.

Muro, Manuel. *Historia de San Luis Potosí.* 1973.

Saka, Mark Saad. "Peasant Nationalism and Social Unrest in the Mexican Countryside, 1848–1884." Ph.D. diss., University of Houston, 1995.

Valázquez, Primo Feliciano. *Historia de San Luis Potosí.* 1982.

San Pasqual

Before dawn on the morning of 6 December 1846, U.S. forces under Gen. Stephen W. Kearny rode across the valley of San Pasqual, California, to attack a Mexican (Californio) force led by Maj. Andrés Pico. In the initial charge, Capt. Abraham Johnston and a dragoon were killed by fire from the few firearms carried by the Californios, most of whom were armed with eight-foot lances.

After a short melee, Maj. Pico led his men down the valley in apparent retreat to a huge rock outcropping where his force divided, one group going straight ahead and the other swinging to the right behind the hill. Capt. Benjamin Moore, seeing the Californios getting away, galloped after them urging his men to follow. His troops, mounted on weary horses and mules, charged along in no orderly fashion but strung out at the pace each mount could sustain. When Maj. Pico saw Moore and noted the disorder of his men, he ordered a charge in which his men, mostly *vaqueros* and expert horsemen, inflicted heavy damage on the U.S. troops. Kearny's forces suffered 21 killed and 17 wounded, the Californios probably 6 dead and 12 wounded. The next day, after a short skirmish, the Californios surrounded Kearny's men on a low promontory and held them there for three days until U.S. naval reinforcements arrived.

Both sides claimed victory for the battle on 6 December, but it gave the Californios a tremendous boost in morale.

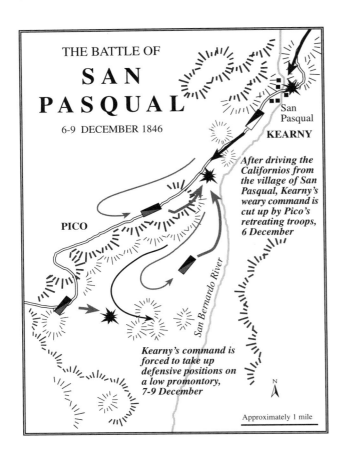

THE BATTLE OF
SAN PASQUAL
6-9 DECEMBER 1846

After driving the Californios from the village of San Pasqual, Kearny's weary command is cut up by Pico's retreating troops, 6 December

San Pasqual

KEARNY

PICO

San Bernardo River

Kearny's command is forced to take up defensive positions on a low promontory, 7-9 December

N

Approximately 1 mile

General Kearny was able to unite his force with Commo. Robert F. Stockton's naval units to continue the conquest of California.

Ron Hinrichs

BIBLIOGRAPHY

Emory, William H. *Notes of a Military Reconnaissance from Fort Leavenworth, in Missouri, to San Diego, in California, in 1846.* 1848.

Gillespie, Archibald H. "Gillespie and the Conquest of California, from Letters Dated February 11, 1846, to July 8, 1848, to the Secretary of the Navy." *California Historical Society Quarterly* 17 (1938): 123–140, 271–284, 325–350.

Griffin, John S. "A Doctor Comes to California, the Diary of John S. Griffin, Assistant Surgeon with Kearny's Dragoons, 1846–1847." *California Historical Society Quarterly,* Special Publication no. 18 (1943).

San Patricio Battalion

During the U.S.–Mexican War, a unique unit of the Mexican army was formed primarily of deserters from U.S. forces. Created by an Irish-American defector named John Riley, the unit was first organized as a company and later increased to two companies, battalion strength. Named for the patron saint of Ireland, the outfit became known as the Batallón de San Patricio, or Saint Patrick's Battalion, and the men were called San Patricios.

The San Patricios fought as artillerymen in the battles of Matamoros, Monterrey, Buena Vista, and Cerro Gordo. Transferred to the infantry, the two companies, of 102 men each, participated in the spirited defense of the Churubusco convent, where they suffered devastating casualties—60 percent of the men were either killed or captured and several were wounded. After military trials, 70 of the captured San Patricios were found guilty of desertion and sentenced to death, but Gen. Winfield Scott pardoned 5 men, reduced the sentences of 15 others to fifty lashes and branding with a two-inch letter *D* on the right cheek, and confirmed capital punishment for the remaining 50.

Reasons for the soldiers' desertion included brutal military discipline, harassment of foreign-born soldiers, drunkenness, lure of women, religious differences, and enticement offered by the Mexican government.

Although most U.S. citizens regarded the San Patricios as traitors, Mexicans still consider them heroes and honor their memory with public ceremonies on St. Patrick's Day and on 12 September each year, the anniversary of the executions.

Robert Ryal Miller

BIBLIOGRAPHY

Callaghan, James. "The San Patricios." *American Heritage* 46 (1995): 68–70, 73–74, 77–81.

Miller, Robert Ryal. *Shamrock and Sword: The Saint Patrick's Battalion in the U.S.–Mexican War.* 1989.

Santa Anna, Antonio López de

Mexican general and politician Antonio López de Santa Anna (1794–1876) was born 21 February to Spanish parents in Jalapa in the province of Vera Cruz, where his father was a minor royal official. Santa Anna chose a career in the royal army, but in April 1821 he abandoned the Spanish cause and fought to establish Mexican independence. From his power base in Vera Cruz and his position among the military he established his credentials as a republican, a federalist, and a contender for power at the center. In 1829 he decisively defeated a Spanish invasion force at Tampico, a victory that gave him national status, and in 1832 he organized a successful rebellion against the government of Anastasio Bustamante. Congress confirmed his power by electing him president in March 1833, with the liberal Valentín Gómez Farías as vice president. Santa Anna did not have a specific policy or belong to a party; he was content to allow the politicians their space, returning to his estate at Manga de Clavo and observing reactions to the anticlerical program of Gómez

Antonio López de Santa Anna. Santa Anna is depicted with Gen. Mariano Arista (left) and an unidentified lancer (Fayette Robinson, *Mexico and Her Military Chieftains*, 1851).

Farías and his threats to other privileged groups. He concluded that liberal reformism was a minority creed and anticlericalism an unpopular cause.

In April 1834 he emerged from Manga de Clavo, entered Mexico City as a savior of the Constitution of 1824, and activated his presidency. His policies reassured the clergy, rewarded the army, and marginalized federalists and liberals. He did not act from religious or political convictions, simply from the calculation that powerful elites would keep him in power if he in turn dispensed patronage and guaranteed order. This meant the restoration of strong central government, and in 1834 he orchestrated a working alliance among centralists, clerics, generals, and property owners. Santa Anna personally led the forces that defeated federalist opposition in a single battle in Zacatecas, and centralism was officially enshrined in the Constitution of 1836, which established a strong eight-year presidential system and a congress elected by voters with high property qualifications. Santa Anna had spent fifteen years making himself a Mexican hero, cultivating his power base, and projecting his image as the Napoléon of the West. With power firmly in his hands, he withdrew once again to his hacienda, pleading reasons of health. He wanted to possess power rather than administer it; so he stayed in Manga de Clavo while his agents occupied the government.

Santa Anna was a man of unimposing stature, melancholic in appearance, with dark hair and eyes and a white complexion. In 1825 he married Inés de la Paz García, who was a supportive wife for nineteen years. He scandalized many Mexicans when, six weeks after her death, he married María Dolores de Tosta, fifteen years old, when he was fifty.

Santa Anna recognized early that he needed a personal base for his political career. He acquired a number of haciendas in Vera Cruz—483,000 acres was the final count—which provided a high income from livestock and rents. These were more than houses and estates. Manga de Clavo in particular was a fortress, headquarters, and political retreat. When disaster threatened, when it was necessary to withdraw from the fray, disconcert his enemies, raise his demands, or simply recuperate, he headed for Manga de Clavo. And when he decided to act, to remove a government, or to seize power, he rode out from Manga de Clavo. Like any *caudillo,* he attracted support from interest groups and in turn sought to increase his following. His regional base comprised the provincial bureaucracy, the popular sectors of rural Vera Cruz, and the peons of his own estates. At the national level his primary support was the military, among whom he had old comrades who looked to him for promotion and rewards. His civilian supporters were led by a group of personal friends and cronies, the *santanistas,* politicians who helped and collaborated, and bureaucrats who aspired to high office. He was also a favorite of the *agiotistas,* the financial speculators of the time, many of whom played important roles in his periodic returns to power. He was known to reward his supporters by granting them import licenses, contracts for war supplies, and franchises for public works; and he expected a commission for himself from financial transactions that he authorized. Outside his main clients Santa Anna also received the occasional support of other elite groups—landowners, clergy, and entrepreneurs—though none of these was directly dependent on his favor. There was no sign of social awareness or populist preference in the policy of Santa Anna. His tariff policy owed little to any concern for the artisan classes and even less to economic ideas. He simply maneuvered among interest groups, sometimes favoring the cotton growers of Vera Cruz, sometimes importers, and sometimes manufacturers.

Santa Anna changed from royalist to republican, from federalist to centralist without betraying policy or principles, for he apparently had none. Inconsistency was one of his strengths: it enabled him to appeal to each of the parties, or to rebuff them all. He offered himself as a leader for Mexico, above institutions and faithful to only one idea: Mexico needed strong government, and the centralist regime of 1834 to 1846 was the appropriate model. In practice this design did not work, however, because the central government was too weak and impoverished to exercise its powers in the departments. The departments were dominated by army generals and civil governors and contained many politicians who were outraged not only by the defeat of liberalism but also by their loss of opportunities. Santa Anna, therefore, faced numerous and costly revolts against the national government. Although these were suppressed, it was not so easy to overcome the revolt of Texas, and the situation in Texas in turn further destabilized relations between the center and the regions.

Santa Anna made Texas his exclusive campaign. He aimed to crush the revolt as he would that of any other Mexican state, yet he was unaware of the real situation. He boasted to the British minister that if he found that the U.S. government was aiding the rebels, he would march his army on to Washington, D.C., and place the Mexican flag on the Capitol. The campaign brought out the flaws in his character and belied the leadership qualities of which he boasted. It was a personal, not a national, war effort. To pay for his army of six thousand, he mortgaged his own properties and raised revenue from forced loans and private advances. He tried to play every part, from general to corporal, unable to organize or delegate. On the expedition itself his military and moral judgments were badly flawed and raised doubts among some of his own officers. His execution of the prisoners at the Alamo and at La Bahía (present-day Goliad) were the actions of a warlord rather than a statesman. After his defeat on the banks of the San Jacinto River, a defeat he blamed on others, Santa Anna tried to escape disguised as a peasant. When taken prisoner on 22 April 1836, he was not only commander-in-chief of the Mexican forces but also

president of Mexico. Even worse, he allowed his army to evacuate Texas without a fight and without negotiating; on 14 May he signed a treaty with the president of the Republic of Texas, designed as a preliminary to Mexican recognition of Texas independence, which he claimed he could deliver. Returning to Vera Cruz in February 1837 after detention and humiliation in the United States, he was received with the honors due his rank but without enthusiasm. He retired to Manga de Clavo, ignoring the presidency and justifying his campaign in a pompous and boastful manifesto, blaming everything on circumstances beyond his control. The conservative regime that he had installed in 1834 continued to rule the country without him, from April 1837 under new president Anastasio Bustamante.

Santa Anna was soon presented with an opportunity to restore his name. The French blockade and invasion of Vera Cruz in 1838, an exercise in gunboat diplomacy on behalf of French claims, enabled him to play a hero's role. He marched to Vera Cruz, where outright victory eluded him, but he managed to obscure the result with a dramatic gesture. Facing the enemy sword in hand as the French artillery fired, he was wounded in the left leg, which had to be amputated, and he retired to his hacienda to recuperate, taking his leg with him. The limb was later transferred to Mexico City where it was placed in a ceremonial resting place. By late February 1839 the victor was fit enough to return to the capital as interim president during Bustamante's absence during a campaign against rebel generals, and he was received with acclaim by politicians and the public alike. Staying long enough to claim a measure of military and political success, he retired again to his hacienda, the defeat at San Jacinto forgotten.

Yet Mexico was still not governed to Santa Anna's liking. In 1841 and 1842, from his rural base and in collaboration with the military, he launched two initiatives: first, to remove the ineffective Bustamante, then to dissolve the liberal congress. A handpicked committee of leading conservative army officers, clerics, landowners, and lawyers produced a new constitution (1843) that was centralist, conservative, pro-executive, and imposed even higher income qualifications for voting than the Constitution of 1836. The privileges of the army and the clergy were specifically guaranteed. Thus, Santa Anna, on the basis of his personal preeminence, at last came to power on his own terms through an understanding among the traditional interest groups, particularly the military, bureaucrats, and wealthy businessmen, who were manipulated by Santa Anna and rewarded by him. His success in the presidential election of late 1843 confirmed the result.

In 1843 and 1844 Santa Anna established in effect a military dictatorship, exercised from Manga de Clavo, fortified by occasional forays into Mexico City, and projected through an elaborate public ritual. His ultimate power base remained the army and the financiers. Army loyalty was bought through inflated budgets, generous promotions, and prompt payment of troops. It was an expensive government. War with Yucatán, conflict over Texas, problems with frontier Indians, peasant uprisings in the south, all served as reasons to justify constant demands for money. Funds were also diverted to enrich Santa Anna and his friends, and it was during this regime that he expanded his properties in the state of Vera Cruz, where he had five thousand men on his personal payroll. The economics of dictatorship relied on short-term, high-interest loans from Santa Anna's favorite group of speculators. The secret of success was to reward each of his support groups in turn—the army, the bureaucracy, the Vera Cruz planters, the import merchants, and the regional interests—but to help his financiers most of all. Santa Anna also had the support of the church, which earned his good will by paying taxes and forced loans, conscious that the alternative to the dictator was anticlericalism. But a regime based exclusively on interest groups, in a country where the elite notoriously refused to pay direct taxes, inevitably found its support base contracting once the money ran out. Even the financiers protested when the government stopped payment on debts owed to many speculators and made repayment depend on further loans. Meanwhile, the military was not providing security: from Oaxaca, Puebla, Sonora, and Yucatán, news of war, rebellion, and independence underlined the basic instability of Santa Anna's Mexico. To defend the dictatorship he asked for more money; when congress, the only institution in Mexico to resist the dictator, refused to collaborate, he raised money by decree and closed congress. His proposals to raise taxes on rural property and on mining and industry were regarded as a betrayal of the very interest groups that had helped him to power; in response, these groups persuaded the military to rebel against the dictator. The garrisons in Guadalajara and Mexico City rose in revolt and congress took steps to depose him; Santa Anna was further demoralized by rioting in the streets of the capital and shouts of "Death to the cripple!" while a mob insulted his disentombed leg. Renouncing his office, he became a common fugitive and was lucky to survive an assassination attempt. In May 1845 he was exiled to Cuba for life.

Santa Anna spent less than two years in exile. In that time Mexico had four different governments and even more finance ministers, none of whom had enough credibility to reassure prospective taxpayers. Life without Santa Anna proved difficult for Mexicans. As federalists and conservatives continued to confront each other, the army was alerted by attempts to reform it, and officers still occasionally "pronounced" for Santa Anna. While generals and politicians destabilized Mexico from within, invaders from the United States attacked from without.

By 1845 Mexico was ready to accept an independent Texas but not a Texas annexed to the United States. U.S.

expansionism, encouraged by Mexican anarchy, brought the two countries to war in April 1846. Mexico did not have a government equipped for war, and much of its fighting spirit was expended in civil conflict rather than action against the United States. In September 1846, with Mexican approval and with the permission of the United States that allowed him to pass the blockade at Vera Cruz, Santa Anna was recalled as president with Valentín Gómez Farías as vice president, to govern on a platform of federalism and to prepare for war with the United States. It was an unlikely alliance—conservative centralist with liberal federalist—but at least it identified the vital roles: Santa Anna to lead the army, Gómez Farías to raise the money. Gómez Farías, liberal that he was, sought to finance the war by confiscating church property, which provoked the rebellion of the *polkos,* a clerical protest supported by army officers. Having used the liberals to threaten the church, Santa Anna then forced the latter to accept a different deal, a forced loan of 1.5 million pesos. It was blackmail, well understood by all parties, including the principal victim, the ousted Gómez Farías.

While Mexicans spent their energies in civil war, the war with the United States drew nearer. Santa Anna's leadership was again puzzling. He drove his ragged army across Mexico's northern deserts to confront, without pause for rest or tactical assessment, a numerically inferior but better prepared U.S. force. On 23 February 1846 at La Angostura, Santa Anna exposed his army to U.S. artillery fire, to which he had no effective reply. He himself fought bravely, and his ill-equipped troops did all that could reasonably be expected of them, but after great carnage he withdrew his battered army and returned southward, leaving the U.S. forces in the field.

Santa Anna renewed the struggle for supplies, troops, a victory, but achieved none. He mortgaged his own property, scraped together his private resources, recruited his own peons, but to no avail. Solidarity with the war effort did not exist: the majority of Mexicans remained indifferent as to who won, indifferent to the fate of Santa Anna. There was no nationalism and little patriotism. The war, and the deals to end the war, were not really between nation and nation. Various political groups, including that of Santa Anna, struggled not to defend the country but to strike a bargain with the United States that would benefit their own party. Under these conditions there was no united front to prevent the U.S. forces from landing near Vera Cruz and making their way inland. Santa Anna attempted to stop them at Cerro Gordo, near Puebla, but he was outmaneuvered, his defenses were bypassed, and his troops exposed to yet more slaughter. The battle for Mexico City was his last chance, but again there were questions about his role. Santa Anna did not lack courage, and after the defeat at Cerro Gordo his negotiating skills managed to slow the U.S. advance; but he was deficient in military tactics, and he failed to make the most of his resources or to capitalize on local hostility toward the invaders. Few nationalist guerrillas challenged the U.S. forces; no mass resistance barred their way. The Mexicans fought fiercely, especially when their own communities were at risk, but they had no feeling for a national cause and they were not reassured by their own side. The defense of Mexico City depended partly on Santa Anna's ability to raise troops and his readiness to lead from the front, but even more on the efforts of Mexican volunteers and citizens in arms. Neither, however, was sufficient to prevent the U.S. forces, superior in equipment and artillery, from occupying the capital on 15 September 1847. Amid final scenes of chaos, heroism, and terror the Mexicans were forced to accept defeat. Santa Anna, convinced that he could not win and unwilling to accept responsibility for an inglorious peace, resigned as president on 16 September and eventually left the country. A new government negotiated the Treaty of Guadalupe Hidalgo in February 1848, in which Mexico traded its only asset, territory, for immunity from further claims and a dollar indemnity.

Some in Mexico denounced Santa Anna as a traitor who had delivered Mexico to the enemy. Others pointed out that the president had not personally avoided action, and although he was not a great general neither was he a traitor. Others described him as a good planner and a disastrous executor. Santa Anna was probably the only Mexican in 1846 who could bring together the people and resources needed to defend the country, and this presumably was why he was recalled by many of those who, in 1845, had been most active in expelling him. He lost an army at La Angostura and another at Cerro Gordo, but he was still capable of raising a third for defense of the capital. He was not a great national leader. He was a *caudillo* who could evoke support in specific interest groups but could not arouse a nation. And despite its *caudillos,* its generals, and its warriors, Mexico could not prevent the loss of California, Texas, and the northern states, or inspire in its inhabitants a lasting loyalty. The Santa Anna years saw only a partial achievement of Mexican nationalism. Independence from Spain had been won and defended. But national unity had been seriously impaired and almost half the national territory lost beyond recall.

After the war Santa Anna had enough money to keep him in voluntary exile in Colombia, confident that his day would come again. Mexico still needed him and soon showed that it preferred a *caudillo* to a congress. The reasons were not obscure. Postwar conditions frightened people of property. The Caste War in Yucatán, peasant demands for land and subsistence, Indian insurrection in the center and the north, and social protest in the towns took Mexico to the verge of anarchy and posed questions that the federal regime of 1848 through 1852 could not answer. Like all previous governments, the federalists experienced taxpayer resistance and

budget deficits, which led to unpaid armies, disaffection, and occasional rebellion. Federalism was viewed as a vested interest, good for its politicians, and bad for the rest of the country. In 1852 a movement for the recall of Santa Anna gathered momentum, as the centralists, financiers, military, and all who desired law and order collaborated for the return to power of Santa Anna, "the man necessary in the present circumstances."

Various interests took credit for the restoration. But the conservatives, with their political machine, and the *agiotistas,* with their money, were the prime movers. Both were willing to support a dictatorship dedicated to strong central government, economic development, and social order. Both needed the military in order to retain power, and thus Santa Anna returned to office, on 20 April 1853, through a triple alliance of the army, the conservatives, and the financiers. He was fifty-nine and this was his eleventh presidency. In fact it became a personal dictatorship: he abolished federalism, imposed a rigidly centralist government, ruled without a constitution, and took no steps to call a constituent congress. Direct taxes on property and incomes were again imposed by decree, supplemented by various consumer taxes; even so, revenue was insufficient to meet inflated army budgets. In December 1853 Santa Anna concluded a deal with the United States, selling the Mesilla Valley in southern Arizona, the so-called Gadsden Purchase, for $15 million, subsequently reduced by the purchasers to $10 million. This enabled him to maintain political stability, leave the church immune, and retain some independence from the financiers. But stability was an illusion. As political dissent grew, Santa Anna resorted to even greater exercise of personal power, surrounded himself with cronies, muzzled the press, and acquired the right to continue in office indefinitely, even to name his successor. He seems not to have understood the character of midcentury liberals, their pressure for political reform and social opportunity, and their search for allies.

A central government in Mexico was vulnerable to two dangers, provincial rebellion and military dissent, which together posed a formidable threat. Santa Anna's dream of permanent dictatorship was frustrated only by the regional power of his rival Juan Álvarez, *caudillo* of the south, leader of an amorphous group of landowners, Indians, mestizos, and blacks, and traditional supporters of federalism. When the dictator began to place his own civil and military officials in the south, Álvarez was provoked into rebellion, charging Santa Anna with selling Mexican territory to the United States and establishing a despotic government. The Plan of Ayutla (11 March 1854) thus united the southern *caudillo* and the military behind a constitutional program that would convoke a congress and seek "liberal institutions."

The Ayutla Revolution in the south had financial implications for Santa Anna. Taxation was high enough to be unpopular yet its yield was too low to cover expenditures.

The dictator financed his regime with money from the Gadsden Purchase (which after the reduction by the purchasers to $10 million was further reduced by selling the land in advance at a heavy discount to speculators), and from deals with the *agiotistas*, who propped up the last two years of the dictatorship in the hope of promoting infrastructure development. But development never came, and during 1855, disillusioned by the corruption, waste, and economic failure of the dictatorship, the *agiotistas* decided that Santa Anna was no longer a good investment and switched their support to the men of Ayutla. At this point the dictatorship simply ran out of money and could not pay its officials, its soldiers, or its debtors. Santa Anna left Mexico City for Vera Cruz and Havana in the early hours of 9 August 1855 and formally abdicated on 12 August, blaming his failure on the malice of his enemies and the ingratitude of Mexicans. After twenty years of exile and two attempts to make a political comeback, he was allowed to return to Mexico in 1874 but not to recover his confiscated estates. He died in modest circumstances in the capital on 21 June 1876 at the age of eighty-two.

Santa Anna has been viewed with mixed feelings by Mexicans and by historians. At the end of his last dictatorship his enemies accused him of two specific offenses: he had sold national territory illegally to the United States and he had established a despotic government. As a hero, a survivor, and a manipulator he has admirers. But his critics have emphasized his opportunism, duplicity, and abuse of power and concluded that Mexico lost more than it gained from his rule. Mexican historian Moisés González Navarro observed that Santa Anna's lack of principles encouraged political parties to think that they could use him to advance their own, with the result that he was always recalled in hope. "In reality he worked only for his personal cause. For a third of a century this was his major strength, but in time it became his greatest weakness."

John Lynch

BIBLIOGRAPHY

Calderón de la Barca, Frances E. *Life in Mexico.* 1931.

Callcott, Wilfrid Hardy. *Santa Anna: The Story of an Enigma Who Once Was Mexico.* 1936.

Costeloe, Michael P. *The Central Republic in Mexico, 1835–1846: Hombres de Bien in the Age of Santa Anna.* 1993.

Díaz Díaz, Fernando. *Caudillos y caciques: Antonio López de Santa Anna y Juan Álvarez.* 1972.

Fowler, Will. "The Repeated Rise of General Antonio López de Santa Anna in the so-called Age of Chaos (Mexico, 1821–1855)." In *Authoritarianism in Latin America since Independence,* edited by Will Fowler. 1996.

Fuentes Mares, José. *Santa Anna, el hombre.* 5th ed. 1984.

González Navarro, Moisés. *Anatomía del poder en México (1848–1853).* 1977.

Jones, Oakah L. *Santa Anna.* 1968.

Olivera, Ruth R., and Liliane Crété. *Life in Mexico under Santa Anna, 1822–1855.* 1991.

Tenenbaum, Barbara A. *The Politics of Penury: Debts and Taxes in Mexico, 1821–1856.* 1986.

Vázquez Mantecón, Carmen. *Santa Anna y la encrucijada del estado: La dictadura (1853–1855).* 1986.

Yáñez, Agustín. *Santa Anna: Espectro de una sociedad.* 1982.

Santa Cruz de Rosales, Battle of

At Santa Fe, New Mexico, on 4 February 1848, Brig. Gen. Sterling Price, commander of the Ninth Military Department, received a report that a large Mexican army under Gen. José Urrea was advancing on El Paso del Norte (present-day Juárez, Mexico) from the south. Price, who had long been eager to conduct a campaign to Chihuahua, ordered several companies under his command, both regular and volunteer, to concentrate at El Paso, where he arrived on 23 February. There Price learned that the report of Urrea's army was false; nevertheless, he decided to continue south and attack the small force under Governor Ángel Trías at Chihuahua City, 280 miles away. Near Sacramento, on 7 March, Price received a message from Trías protesting the U.S. advance, claiming that a treaty of peace had recently been signed. Unconvinced, Price pushed on to Chihuahua, occupying the capital city late that night. Governor Trías had retreated with his army to Santa Cruz de Rosales, a town 60 miles southeast, and Price continued in pursuit with about 250 men, arriving at Santa Cruz de Rosales at dawn on 9 March. Price demanded unconditional surrender; Trías refused, again insisting that a treaty had been signed. Price agreed to forestall his attack for a few days to give the Mexican commander time to obtain confirmation of the new peace, which also gave Price time to bring up his artillery and additional troops that had fallen behind during his forced marches. On the morning of 16 March, with the arrival of his reinforcements and still no confirmation of the treaty, Price commenced the attack with a long artillery bombardment. That afternoon, Price ordered three storming parties to take the town. Near dusk, Price's men had fought their way to the plaza, when Trías surrendered. Trías's force, which had numbered some 804 men, suffered, in Price's estimation, 238 killed (Trías reported the casualties at 32 killed and 25 or 30 wounded, as well as 11 citizens killed). Out of Price's army of 665 men, 4 were killed and 19 wounded. The Battle of Santa Cruz de Rosales was the last engagement of the U.S.–Mexican War; the Treaty of Guadalupe Hidalgo had indeed been signed more than a month before the battle.

Mark L. Gardner

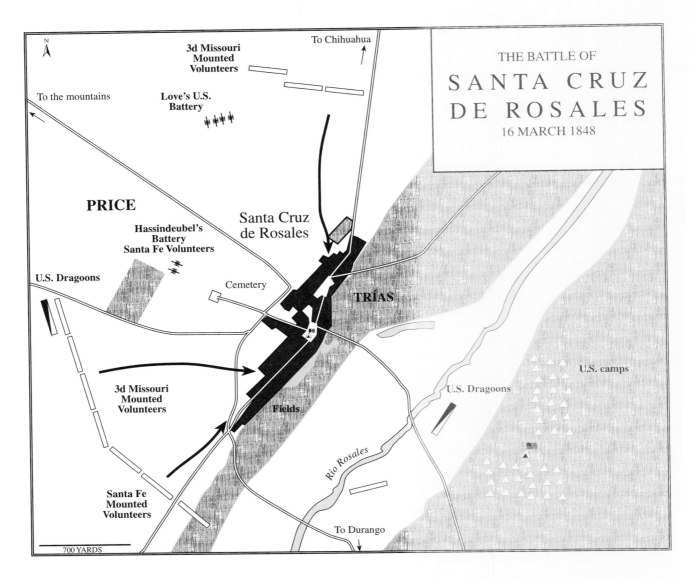

THE BATTLE OF

SANTA CRUZ DE ROSALES

16 MARCH 1848

BIBLIOGRAPHY

Johnston, Abraham Robinson, et al. *Marching with the Army of the West, 1846–1848*. Edited by Ralph Bieber. 1936.

Shalhope, Robert E. *Sterling Price: Portrait of a Southerner.* 1971.

U.S. Congress. House. *Message from the President of the United States . . .* 30th Cong., 2d sess., 1848. H. Ex. Doc. 1. Serial 537.

Santa Fe

This entry consists of two separate articles: **City of Santa Fe** *and* **Santa Fe Expedition.**

City of Santa Fe

Founded by Spaniards in 1610, Santa Fe was the capital of the Mexican Department of New Mexico and the western terminus of the Santa Fe Trail, an important trade route with the United States established in 1821. The exotic Santa Fe trade was a source of fascination in the United States, and many Americans, including U.S. volunteers who would march on New Mexico during the U.S.–Mexican War, envisioned Santa Fe as a place of wonderful edifices and enormous wealth. It was actually a sprawling town of narrow dirt streets and flat-roofed adobe buildings that looked to one soldier in the U.S. Army of the West like "a parcel of brick yards."

Situated on the east side of the Río Grande, Santa Fe fell

within territory claimed by the young Republic of Texas. In 1841 Texas sent an expedition of merchants and soldiers overland to Santa Fe with the combined mission of opening trade with the New Mexico capital and asserting Texas sovereignty. The expedition was a failure; its members were captured by Mexican soldiers under Governor Manuel Armijo before reaching Santa Fe and sent on a harrowing march to Mexico City. With the U.S. annexation of Texas in 1845, however, Texas's boundary claim passed to the United States and was offered as justification for the conquest of New Mexico during the U.S.–Mexican War.

From Santa Fe, in August 1846, Governor Armijo attempted to organize a defense against the rapidly approaching U.S. Army of the West under Col. (later general) Stephen W. Kearny. When Armijo suddenly disbanded his army and fled south, many of Santa Fe's residents temporarily deserted the town in fear but returned after the Army of the West peacefully occupied the capital on 18 August. Construction began immediately on a star fort, named Fort Marcy, on a hill overlooking the town. Missouri and, later, Illinois Volunteers garrisoned Santa Fe throughout the war. The first soldiers brought with them an epidemic of measles, which proved disastrous for Santa Fe's children. The occupation army also was hit hard with sickness and disease during its first fall and winter in the capital; by 1 March 1847 there were approximately 190 soldiers buried in the new burial ground near Fort Marcy.

U.S. occupation resulted in a large influx of cash from the army payroll and various army expenditures, and this translated into big business for Santa Fe's gambling halls and saloons. Reports of dissipation and a lack of discipline among the troops in Santa Fe eventually made their way east. In December 1846 several prominent New Mexicans plotted to overthrow the U.S. forces in Santa Fe; the plot was discovered, however, and several of the conspirators were arrested and tried before military courts-martial. All were acquitted. While there were surely many Santa Fe residents who continued to be unhappy with the occupation army, there were no further resistance efforts in the capital.

After the annexation of New Mexico by the United States in 1848, Santa Fe remained the seat of government in the new territory. Its noted Palace of the Governors, erected at the time of Santa Fe's founding, became the oldest public building in the United States.

Mark L. Gardner

BIBLIOGRAPHY

Allison, W. H. H., ed. "Santa Fe in 1846." *Old Santa Fe* 2 (April 1915): 392–406.

Noble, David Grant, ed. *Santa Fe: History of an Ancient City.* 1989.

Twitchell, Ralph Emerson. *Old Santa Fe: The Story of New Mexico's Ancient Capital.* 1925.

Santa Fe Expedition

Since 1836 the Texas Republic had claimed the Río Grande as its southern and western boundary. To buttress this claim, and in an attempt to divert to Texas the revenues of the lucrative Santa Fe–St. Louis trade, estimated at $5 million annually, President Mirabeau B. Lamar dispatched a force of 320 men to New Mexico in June 1841. Santa Fe, he believed, was eager to gain its independence from Mexico and would welcome his offer of annexation and trade.

Ill-equipped and poorly led, the expedition soon ran into difficulty. After a tortuous march through uncharted territory, harassed by Comanches and weak from thirst and hunger, the exhausted Texians reached their destination only to find that the citizens of Santa Fe were hostile to Lamar's proposal. Mexican troops under the command of Governor Manuel Armijo captured the advance party of the expedition without resistance on 17 September; the remaining members of the expedition surrendered on 5 October.

The Santa Fe prisoners were marched to Mexico City, enduring harsh treatment at the hands of their captors during the journey. News of the failure of the expedition and the prisoners' subsequent ordeal prompted calls in the Texas Republic for reprisals against Mexico. In the United States, prominent political leaders appealed to the Mexican government for clemency. In April 1842, U.S. minister Waddy Thompson secured the release of all the prisoners except for José Antonio Navarro, a signer of the Texas declaration of independence, who was held in Mexico until 1844.

The expedition gained special notoriety as a result of the literary efforts of one of its members, George Wilkins Kendall, cofounder of the New Orleans *Picayune*. In 1844 Kendall published his two-volume *Narrative of the Texan Santa Fe Expedition*, which immediately became a best-selling account of the episode, creating much anti-Mexican feeling in the United States on the eve of the war with Mexico.

Sam W. Haynes

BIBLIOGRAPHY

Kendall, George Wilkins. *Narrative of the Texan Santa Fe Expedition.* 1844.

Loomis, Noel M. *The Texan-Santa Fé Pioneers.* 1958.

Santa Fe–Chihuahua Trail

The Santa Fe–Chihuahua Trail was part of the magnificent *El Camino Real de Tierra Adentro,* Royal Road to the Interior, which stretched in its entirety from the port of Vera Cruz through Mexico City, Durango, and Chihuahua to Santa Fe, as early as the sixteenth century. An extension continued beyond, to Taos. In the Spanish and Mexican periods, monthly and annual mail carriers and supply trains provided service between Santa Fe and Mexico City, maintaining it as a permanent route.

All segments of the Santa Fe–Chihuahua Trail were traversed by U.S. troops during the U.S.-Mexican War. This portion of the Camino Real had come into use by Anglo-Americans after the Santa Fe Trail, the route from Missouri to Santa Fe, was opened to U.S. traders in 1821. The government of newly independent Mexico was eager to levy tariffs on traders from the United States, and the people of New Mexico and northern Mexico were anxious to obtain goods more cheaply than before; thus, trade flourished down the Santa Fe Trail. At first selling their merchandise in New Mexico, U.S. traders soon found their market saturated and sought opportunities for commerce in Chihuahua, Durango, and elsewhere in northern Mexico. By 1840 at least half of the merchandise carried to Santa Fe was destined for sale in present-day northern Mexico.

Thus, in the summer of 1846, the Army of the West under Col. (soon to be general) Stephen W. Kearny, hurrying down the Santa Fe Trail, pursued and was accompanied and followed by both U.S. and Mexican traders. A few traders beat the army to Santa Fe and hastened on to Chihuahua in search of quick profits, but most traders found themselves under military purview. In anticipation of Col. Alexander Doniphan's march to El Paso and Chihuahua, for instance, traders had to wait for the military column at Fray Cristóbal. Only after the troops had begun to cross the *Jornada del Muerto* were the traders permitted to follow.

The traders did not figure importantly in the Battle of Brazito, 25 December 1846, but their service was widely recognized in the Battle of Sacramento on 28 February 1847. Formed into an informal "trader and teamster battalion" under "Major" Samuel C. Owens, who was killed in action, they anchored an important part of the battlefield. They suffered under heavy Mexican fire. Much has been written also of the services and claimed services of other traders, notably James Wiley Magoffin and the Glasgow brothers, Edward and William, in negotiations between the U.S. invaders and Mexican authorities.

The approximately 560-mile route between Santa Fe and Chihuahua is generally followed by present-day highways and railways. In New Mexico, departing Santa Fe, travelers took a fairly direct route to the Río Grande and followed it south, giving them the opportunity to visit all the villages, haciendas, and pueblos near the river, to a point below Socorro. Although it was possible to follow the river's course farther south, canyons and marshes made it so difficult that travelers preferred the hardships of the shorter route—dangerous from lack of water and threat of Indian ambush—the *Jornada del Muerto*.

Passing through the Mesilla Valley and the Pass of the North (El Paso del Norte) to the present-day city of Ciudad Juárez, the difficult desert route on beyond to Chihuahua approximated the route of present-day Mexican National Highway 45.

John Porter Bloom

BIBLIOGRAPHY

Gardner, Mark L., ed. *Brothers on the Santa Fe and Chihuahua Trails: Edward James Glasgow and William Henry Glasgow, 1846–1848.* 1993.

Moorhead, Max L. *New Mexico's Royal Road: Trade and Travel on the Chihuahua Trail.* 1958.

Scott, Winfield

Winfield Scott (1786–1866) was born near Petersburg, Virginia, on 13 June. On 3 May 1808 he was appointed a captain in the regular light artillery and assigned to duty in New Orleans. Promoted to lieutenant colonel of the 2d Artillery with the outbreak of the War of 1812, Scott was assigned to the Niagara frontier where he distinguished himself at the battle of Queenston Heights, 13 October 1812. Promoted to colonel to rank from 12 March 1813 and then to brigadier general on 9 March 1814 for his successful assault on Fort

Winfield Scott. John Frost, *Pictorial History of Mexico and the Mexican War,* 1862

George on 27 May 1813, he was assigned as commander of the camp of instruction at Buffalo. There Scott trained recruits to become the equals of British regulars. In 1814, Scott's brigade played a prominent role in the battles of the Chippewa, 5 July, and Lundy's Lane, 25 July 1814. Severely wounded at Lundy's Lane, Scott was breveted major general to date from the day of the battle and on 3 November was awarded a gold medal by the U.S. Congress.

In 1835 he published his highly influential *Infantry Tactics*, the army's first standard drill manual. In July 1832 he was assigned to command of the U.S. regulars in the Black Hawk War and later that year helped to pacify the Nullification threat in Charleston, South Carolina. In 1836 he took command of the forces engaged first against the Seminoles in Florida and later against the Creeks in Georgia. Although a master of European-style strategy and tactics, Scott was unable to adapt to the guerrilla warfare employed by Native Americans, and after two fruitless campaigns he was relieved of command. In 1838 he was engaged in various diplomatic missions to the British and Canadians and supervised the forced removal of the Cherokees to Oklahoma.

On 25 June 1841, Scott was elevated to command of the U.S. Army with the permanent rank of major general. Politically active and outspoken in his opposition to the Democratic administration of President James K. Polk, at the outbreak of the U.S.–Mexican War Scott was passed over for command of the Army of Observation of Texas. Although Gen. Zachary Taylor won a string of victories in Texas and northern Mexico, a U.S. advance beyond Monterrey was logistically infeasible. It was also, for President Polk, politically dangerous, as Taylor, like Scott, was a Whig and rapidly gaining support as a potential presidential nominee. Much against his will, therefore, in November 1846, Polk approved Scott's bold plan to lead an amphibious assault on Mexico's gulf coast and to follow the route of Cortés to "the halls of the Montezumas."

Although often viewed by his contemporaries as egotistical and even pompous, Scott was also the most humane and scientific soldier that America had yet produced. Widely read in eighteenth-century military history texts that stressed the primacy of limited objectives, maneuver, and occupation of territory above the ruthless destruction of total war, Scott concluded that battle was to be avoided unless imperatively necessary and that the carefully crafted siege was superior to the costly assault on a fortified enemy position. This philosophy was precisely correct for the campaign against Mexico City, 260 miles deep into Mexican territory and defended by vastly superior numbers.

In preparing for the campaign, Scott was meticulous in his logistical planning, and on the battlefield his insistence on superior discipline, training, and tactics avoided needless casualties. Further, his reliance on a cadre of West Point–trained staff officers brought a level of professional expertise

to U.S. arms never before experienced.

Coming ashore below Vera Cruz on 9 March 1847 in a model amphibious landing, Scott laid siege to the vital Mexican port, accepting the city's surrender on 27 March. Fearing the coming of the yellow fever season, Scott led his army inland on 8 April, outflanking and routing the forces of Gen. Antonio López de Santa Anna at Cerro Gordo on 18 April, thus gaining the high ground beyond the coast and placing his army out of range of the dreaded *vomito*. Pressing toward Mexico City, Scott occupied Puebla on 15 May but was forced to wait there until 7 August while volunteer regiments that had served their time were mustered out and fresh volunteers joined the army. Resuming his advance on the Mexican capital, Scott won two major victories on 20 August, the first at Contreras and the second at Churubusco, which drove Santa Anna's army back into the city.

Hoping to end the war without having to take Mexico City by storm, Scott agreed to an armistice on 25 August to negotiate peace terms; he abrogated the truce when Santa Anna violated its provisions by reinforcing and fortifying his position. Fighting resumed with a costly U.S. victory at El Molino del Rey on 8 September and at Chapultepec on 13 September. Mexico City fell to Scott's army the following day.

With an army that never mustered more than ten thousand effectives, Scott had won half a dozen major victories and captured Mexico City, all at the cost of what was probably the lowest casualty rate commensurate with such an ambitious campaign. Moreover, his strict regard for the rights of civilians in occupied territory not only served to suppress potential guerrilla activities on his rear but motivated a delegation of the first citizens of Mexico City to urge him to declare himself dictator for six years. His success, however, made him as great a threat to the Democratic administration as Taylor, so President Polk removed him from command and convened a court of inquiry to investigate Scott's alleged misconduct during the campaign. He was cleared of all charges, and on 9 March 1848, on his return to the United States, Congress rewarded his U.S.–Mexican War services with a second gold medal.

Scott lost the Whig presidential nomination to Zachary Taylor in 1848, and in 1852, as the Whig candidate, his reputation as "Old Fuss and Feathers"—a stickler for "spit and polish" in the age of Jacksonian democracy—contributed greatly to his overwhelming defeat by Franklin Pierce, his former subordinate in the U.S.–Mexican War. Scott was breveted lieutenant general on 22 February 1855, to rank from 29 March 1847, the only U.S. Army officer to hold that grade between George Washington and Ulysses S. Grant.

In September 1859 Scott embarked on a diplomatic mission to Puget Sound in present-day Washington state, where he helped to prevent an armed clash between British and U.S.

interests over the possession of San Juan Island. Returning to the East where threat of secession and civil war was becoming intense, Scott urged President James Buchanan's administration to prepare the nation for war. By the time of Abraham Lincoln's inauguration, however, no such preparations had been made, and Scott despaired of holding any federal property in the South.

His strategic conception for the impending Civil War, known as the Anaconda Plan, called for seizure of the Mississippi River and blockade of southern ports by the Union navy, thus strangling the seceded states into resuming their places in the Union and precluding the need for a war of annihilation and the lasting regional hatred that a protracted civil war would engender. Despite its initial rejection, Scott's plan ultimately found its way into the strategic formula crafted by Lincoln and Grant in 1864.

In 1861, however, Scott was nearly seventy-five years old and suffering from dropsy and vertigo. He bore the brunt of the blame for the Union debacle at First Manassas. When George B. McClellan intrigued his way into command of the Army of the Potomac, Scott resigned from the U.S. Army on 31 October 1862. He died at West Point on 29 May 1866 and is buried there at the Post Cemetery.

Thomas W. Cutrer

BIBLIOGRAPHY

Elliot, Charles Wilson. *Winfield Scott: The Soldier and the Man.* 1937.

Hitchcock, Ethan Allen. *Fifty Years in Camp and Field: Diary of Major-General Ethan Allen Hitchcock, U.S.A.* Edited by W. A. Croffut. 1909.

Keyes, Erasmus D. *Fifty Years of Observation of Men and Events, Civil and Military.* 1884.

Myers, William Starr, ed. *The Mexican War Diary of George B. McClellan.* 1917.

Scott, Winfield. *Memoirs of Lieut.-General Winfield Scott, LL.D.* 1864.

Smith, E. Kirby. *To Mexico with Scott: Letters of Captain E. Kirby Smith to His Wife.* 1917.

Williams, T. Harry, ed. *With Beauregard in Mexico: The Mexican War Reminiscences of P. G. T. Beauregard.* 1956.

Scott's Armistice

Although his army was seriously reduced by the recent fighting and far from its base of supply, Gen. Winfield Scott believed that his victories at Contreras and Churubusco, 20 August 1847, would lead to immediate peace negotiations. By 22 August, Scott's army was in full view of Mexico City, and a squadron of U.S. dragoons had ridden to within twenty yards of the city's gates. Scott refrained from entering the city, however, believing that "a treaty would be more easily negotiated with the Mexican government in posses-

sion of the capital than if it was scattered and the capital in the hands of the invader."

Many Mexicans realized that only an armistice could save their capital from occupation. Early on the morning of 21 August, as Scott and U.S. envoy Nicholas P. Trist rode toward Tacubaya, they met Brig. Gen. Ignacio Mora y Villamil bearing letters and Gen. Antonio López de Santa Anna's verbal request for a twelve-month armistice. Although Scott instantly rejected the notion of a year-long cease-fire, he wrote directly to Santa Anna declaring himself "willing to sign, on reasonable terms, a short armistice."

Santa Anna's minister of war, Brig. Gen. Lino José Alcorta, accepted Scott's proposal on 22 August and, with Mora and Brig. Gen. Benito Quijana, met with U.S. commissioners Generals John A. Quitman, Franklin Pierce, and Persifor F. Smith at Tacubaya at 4:00 P.M. to negotiate terms. The armistice, ratified by Scott 23 August and by Santa Anna the following day, ended hostilities within seventy-eight miles of the capital, halted reinforcements to and fortification by both armies, allowed supplies to enter Mexico City, permitted U.S. quartermasters to purchase provisions in the Mexican capital, and facilitated prisoner exchange.

The truce was beset with misunderstandings and violations from the start. The U.S. military complained that Santa Anna violated the injunctions against reconnaissance, fortification, and reinforcement, and Mexican troops and civilians hampered U.S. efforts to purchase supplies in the city. On 26 August a wagon train, sent to purchase supplies, was attacked by a mob of stone-throwing *léperos* (rabble) and turned back at the city gate. Although Mexican authorities thereafter provided a calvalry escort, only army pack mules, entering the city by night, were allowed to take out supplies.

Nevertheless, Scott and Trist assumed that the armistice was a prelude to serious negotiations. Trist met with the Mexican negotiators—Mora, former president José Joaquín de Herrera, José Bernardo Couto, and Miguel Atristain—from 27 August through 6 September at Atzcapuzalco, a village northwest of Mexico City. Among Trist's demands were Mexican cession of New Mexico and both Upper and Lower California and a U.S. right-of-way across the Isthmus of Tehuantepec. For these concessions, the United States was willing to pay $30 million. Under pressure from the war factions within his government and the army and from the citizens of Mexico City, however, Santa Anna rejected U.S. terms. Mexico instead insisted on the immediate U.S. evacuation of Mexican territory, payment of Mexican debts to U.S. citizens, and a statement that the U.S. war effort had been entirely an attempt to seize Mexican territory.

On 3 September Santa Anna banned further sale of provisions to Scott's army; ordered the concentration at Mexico City of all forces within thirty leagues of the capital; and, on 4 or 5 September began to strengthen Mexico City's fortifications. In response, at 4:00 P.M., on 6 September, Scott abrogated the armistice.

Santa Anna issued a proclamation to the citizens of the capital announcing his determination to "preserve your altars from infamous violation, and your daughters and your wives from the extremity of insult." On 7 September, Capt. Ephraim Kirby Smith wrote to his wife, "Tomorrow will be a day of slaughter." It was, indeed, to be the bloodiest day of the war. With Scott's army now committed to taking the enemy capital by storm, the U.S. forces struck at El Molino del Rey where Smith and 115 of his comrades were killed in action. Further heavy fighting followed on the thirteenth at Chapultepec, the Belén Gate, and the San Cosme Gate. The failure of negotiations at Atzcapuzalco resulted in 1,600 U.S. and 4,000 Mexican soldiers killed and wounded before Mexico City capitulated on 14 September.

Thomas W. Cutrer

BIBLIOGRAPHY

Crawford, Ann Fears, ed. *The Eagle: The Autobiography of Santa Anna.* 1967.

Hitchcock, Ethan Allen. *Fifty Years in Camp and Field: Diary of Major-General Ethan Allen Hitchcock, U. S. A.* Edited by W. A. Croffut. 1909.

Myers, William Starr, ed. *The Mexican War Diary of George B. McClellan.* 1917.

Nortrup, Jack. "Nicholas Trist's Mission to Mexico: A Reinterpretation." *Southwestern Historical Quarterly* 71 (January 1968): 321–346.

Scott, Winfield. *Memoirs of Lieut.-General Winfield Scott, LL.D.* 1864.

Smith, E. Kirby. *To Mexico with Scott: Letters of Captain E. Kirby Smith to His Wife.* 1917.

Williams, T. Harry, ed. *With Beauregard in Mexico: The Mexican War Reminiscences of P. G. T. Beauregard.* 1956.

Seguín, Erasmo

A member of a prominent San Antonio, Texas, family, politician Juan José María Erasmo Seguín (1782–1857) had a career in public service that spanned three sovereignties: Spain, Mexico, and the Republic of Texas. He assumed his first public office, postmaster, in 1807 and retained it with only two interruptions for nearly thirty years. In 1820 he was elected *alcalde ordinario* (combined mayor and justice of the peace) for 1821, the first of a number of municipal offices he held during the Mexican period. In 1823 Seguín was elected as Texas representative to the constituent congress in Mexico City that wrote the federal Constitution of 1824. After he returned from that duty, he received appointment as quartermaster for the Department of Béxar, a post he held until the Texas Revolution.

Seguín was a strong supporter of Mexican federalism and Anglo-American immigration to Texas. He became an ally of Stephen F. Austin from the time the latter first came to Texas in 1821, and he lobbied for the liberal treatment of the slave property and religious conscience of the new settlers. He sided with the Texians in the rebellion against Mexico and, although he did not participate militarily, he did contribute supplies to their cause. During the first years of the Republic of Texas he served as a magistrate in San Antonio but by 1842 had retired to private life. From then until his death he devoted himself to stock and crop farming on his property in what is now Wilson County, Texas.

Jesús F. de la Teja

BIBLIOGRAPHY

de la Teja, Jesús F., ed. *A Revolution Remembered: The Memoirs and Selected Correspondence of Juan N. Seguín.* 1991.

Vernon, Ida. "Activities of the Seguins in Early Texas History." *West Texas Historical Association Year Book* 25 (1949): 11–38.

Seguín, Juan Nepomuceno

Born in Spanish-colonial San Antonio, Texas, Texas politician Juan Nepomuceno Seguín (1806–1890) was a member of one of the town's prominent families. (His father was Juan José María Erasmo Seguín.) Having become politically involved in local and state affairs during the Mexican period, he served on the San Antonio city council and as interim *jefe político* (lieutenant governor) for the Department of Béxar in 1834. A strong supporter of the federalist cause, Seguín took up arms in the Texas Revolution of late 1835 to 1836, organizing a company of Tejano cavalry, which saw action at the Siege of Béxar in December 1835 and fought at the Battle of San Jacinto in April 1836.

Seguín participated in the political and economic life of the Republic of Texas until his self-imposed exile in 1842. Elected to the Texas senate toward the end of the second congress in early 1838, he also served in the third and fourth congresses as chairman of the Committee on Military Affairs. He resigned his senate seat in October 1840 to participate in Gen. Antonio Canales's abortive effort to establish a Republic of the Río Grande. In early 1841 Seguín became mayor of San Antonio. As a competitor in the land speculation business and as mayor, however, he created resentment and distrust among the Anglo-Americans who arrived in San Antonio following Texas independence. This distrust became open hostility when he was accused of conspiring in Gen. Rafael Vázquez's invasion of South Texas in March 1842, and in April 1842 Seguín was forced to flee to Mexico.

Between 1842 and 1848, Seguín saw military service in Mexico. According to his memoirs, when he arrived in Mexico the authorities gave him the option of providing military service or going to jail. Seguín chose to lead a company of irregular cavalry of Tejano ex-patriots, which made up part of the force under Gen. Adrian Woll that briefly captured San Antonio in September 1842. Following the expedition's return to Mexico another Tejano unit was organized under Seguín, the *Escuadrón Auxiliar de Béjar,* which was charged with frontier defense between Laredo and Presidio del Río Grande (present-day Guerrero, Coahuila). In 1845 he wrote to Texas president Anson Jones regarding the Mexican government's willingness to negotiate with Texas if it would forgo annexation by the United States. During the U.S.–Mexican War Seguín's unit saw action at Buena Vista and conducted guerrilla actions. He successfully eluded the efforts of Texas Rangers under Capt. Ben McCulloch to capture him, but nothing else is known of his activities during the war.

In 1848 Seguín returned to the San Antonio area, where he again became involved in politics. In 1852 he won election as a Béxar County justice of the peace and later helped found the Democratic Party in Béxar County. There is no information about his activities during the Civil War, but in 1869 he served for a time as Wilson County judge, his last public service in Texas. In early 1870 he took his family to live in the border town of Nuevo Laredo, where he spent the last twenty years of his life.

Jesús F. de la Teja

BIBLIOGRAPHY

de la Teja, Jesús F., ed. *A Revolution Remembered: The Memoirs and Selected Correspondence of Juan N. Seguín.* 1991.

Robbins, Jerry D. "Juan Seguin." Master's thesis, Southwest Texas State University, 1962.

Vernon, Ida. "Activities of the Seguins in Early Texas History." *West Texas Historical Association Year Book* 25 (1949): 11–38.

Seno Mexicano

See **Trans-Nueces**

Shannon, Wilson

U.S. minister to Mexico Wilson Shannon (1802–1877) was a native of Belmont County, Ohio. Shannon practiced law and was an active partisan in local Democratic politics before winning election as governor of Ohio in 1838. Following an unsuccessful reelection bid in 1840, Shannon won a second gubernatorial term in 1842.

In 1844 Shannon was nominated by President John Tyler to replace Waddy Thompson as U.S. minister to Mexico. When Shannon arrived in the Mexican capital in September, U.S.–Mexican relations were at a low ebb, owing to the Tyler

administration's efforts to revive the Texas annexation issue. The new diplomatic initiative from Washington, D.C., prompted the centralist government of Antonio López de Santa Anna to issue a series of bellicose proclamations threatening to reconquer Texas. Acting on orders from the U.S. State Department, Shannon issued a protest against this prospective Mexican policy. A series of angry diplomatic notes between Shannon and Mexican foreign minister Manuel Crescencio Rejón were exchanged, which led the inexperienced U.S. minister to break off diplomatic relations. For the next six months Shannon remained in the Mexican capital but had no further communication with Mexican leaders as tension between the two countries mounted. With the inauguration of James K. Polk as president in March 1845, Shannon was recalled.

In 1849 Shannon led an expedition to the gold mines of California, but he returned to Ohio in the early 1850s. After serving one term in Congress (1853–1855) Shannon was appointed territorial governor of Kansas (1855–1856), where he attempted vainly to prevent the outbreak of violence between Free-Soiler and proslavery groups. After the Civil War he practiced law in Lawrence, Kansas, where he died in 1877.

Sam W. Haynes

BIBLIOGRAPHY

Pitchford, Louis Cleveland. "The Diplomatic Representatives from the United States to Mexico, 1826–48." Ph.D. diss., University of Colorado, 1965.

Shields, James

James Shields (1806–1879), brigadier general of the U.S. volunteers, was an Irish Catholic who immigrated to the United States at age sixteen. After an injury ended his seafaring career, he served as a volunteer in the Seminole War. Admitted to the Illinois bar in 1832, the popular Democrat was elected state representative in 1835 and served as auditor and supreme court justice before being named general land office commissioner by President James K. Polk in 1845.

In 1846 Shields was appointed brigadier general of volunteers and subsequently served under Generals John Ellis Wool, Zachary Taylor, and Winfield Scott. Believed to be mortally wounded at Cerro Gordo, Shields returned to service after only nine weeks and was brevetted major general for gallantry. Shields magnanimously served under Brig. Gen. Persifor F. Smith during the Battles of Contreras and Churubusco (20 August 1847). Initially criticized for failing to lead his men from exposed positions at Churubusco, Shields's brigade nonetheless captured more than eight hundred Mexican soldiers. At Chapultepec, while leading his men on foot after his horse had been shot out from under him, a Mexican musket ball shattered Shields's arm, thus ending his participation in the war. Shields's military record, coupled with his unassuming attitude, made him one of the more well-received of President James K. Polk's politically appointed generals. Shields remained in Mexico recovering from his injuries until July 1848, when his volunteer brigade was sent home and he was dismissed from service.

After the U.S.–Mexican War, he represented Illinois (1849–1855) and Minnesota (1857–1859) in the U.S. Senate before serving as a general during the Civil War. He later lived in California and Missouri, representing the latter in the U.S. Senate from 1878 until his death. In 1893 the state of Illinois placed Shields's statue in the U.S. Capitol, memorializing him as a warrior, jurist, and statesman.

Robert P. Wettemann, Jr.

BIBLIOGRAPHY

Castle, Henry A. "General James Shields: Soldier, Orator, Statesman." *Minnesota Historical Society Collections* 15 (1915): 711–730.

Condon, William H. *Life of Major General James Shields: Hero of Three Wars and Senator from Three States.* 1900.

Sierra Gorda Revolt

Government confiscation of communal forestlands in the Sierra Gorda (a region of rugged mountains and hot valleys in north-central Mexico) in January 1847 ignited a revolutionary agrarian movement among resident charcoal makers and woodcutters that soon attracted disgruntled hacienda peons, army deserters, and bandits. Led by Eleuterio Quiróz, former muleteer from the Tapanco hacienda in San Luis Potosí, rebel attacks by early 1848 had spread to nearby haciendas. The government responded by extending amnesty even to deserters and attempting to co-opt Quiróz and his leaders with cash stipends. Neither approach had the desired effect, and hostilities continued to escalate.

Believing that U.S. forces were aiding the insurgents, the Mexican government diverted Div. Gen. Anastasio Bustamante and several permanent army infantry regiments into the Sierra Gorda. After some initial progress, Bustamante was compelled to suspend his counterguerrilla campaign on 10 February 1849 to deal with the mutiny of Lt. Col. Leonardo Márquez. This distraction enabled the insurgents to seize several strategically important points. The war ministry countered by sending two more army battalions and two thousand additional national guardsmen from neighboring states. This gave the federal commander sufficient strength to secure the most vulnerable haciendas, forcing the rebels to venture farther from their sanctuary to find undefended targets.

The revolt persisted until October 1849 when government soldiers captured Quiróz during his desperate attempt to seize San Luis Potosí. Found guilty of treason by a military tribunal, the insurgent chieftain was executed two months later. His most zealous supporters were amnestied and resettled in military colonies along the northern frontier, where their aggression and guerrilla warfare talents could be channeled toward fending off relentless Indian attacks.

William A. DePalo, Jr.

BIBLIOGRAPHY

DePalo, William A., Jr. *The Mexican National Army, 1822–1852,* pp. 151–154, 241. 1997.

Memoria del Secretarío de Estado y del despacho de Guerra y Marina, 5–7 and estado 1. 1850.

Reglamento para el establicimiento de las colonias militares en la Sierra Gorda, 26 October 1849. Archivo General de la Nación (AGN), Guerra y Marina (GM), Vol. 15.

Reina, Leticia. *Las rebeliones campesinas en México (1819–1906),* pp. 291–292, 299. 1980.

Zamacois, Niceto de. *Historia de México desde sus tiempos más remotos hasta nuestros días.* Vol. 13, pp. 265, 270–271, 300–301. 1876–1888.

Sierra Madre, Republic of the

Although the Treaty of Guadalupe Hidalgo, which ended the U.S.–Mexican War in 1848, established the Río Grande as the Texas–Mexico boundary, the area along the river remained in frequent turmoil for three decades after the war. In fact, a type of "cold war" existed between Texans and Mexicans along the border that frequently erupted into hostilities. Indian depredations and the flight of fugitive slaves into Mexico were specific issues that troubled Texan–Mexican relations. The most troublesome issue, however, was the continued desire of many Texans to acquire all or part of Mexico. In particular, Texas expansionists hoped to establish a "Republic of the Sierra Madre" that would encompass a large part of what are today Coahuila, Nuevo León, and Tamaulipas. The idea of a Republic of the Sierra Madre, expansionists hoped, would appeal to Mexican federalists, especially in Matamoros, who felt politically isolated from the centralist Mexican government and who had close economic ties to the United States.

The possibility of creating a Republic of the Sierra Madre presented itself in 1851 in the revolution of La Loba led by Mexican general José María Jesus Carvajal. Inspired by the creation of the Republic of the Río Grande, an abortive federalist attempt at independence in South Texas and northern Mexico in 1840, the energetic and ambitious Carvajal bragged of becoming the George Washington of Mexico.

On 3 September 1851 General Carvajal and his sympathizers met at La Loba, near Guerrero, upriver from Camargo and Mier, where the Plan of La Loba was finalized.

The plan called for a federalist government with the main powers reserved to the states. Should these demands be refused, Carvajal resolved to form an independent republic. Carvajal's campaign was heavily financed by Brownsville and Matamoros merchants who had grown tired of the Mexican federal government's imposition of tariffs on goods imported and exported across the river, and who were clamoring for a permanent free trade zone. In Carvajal the merchants saw the possibility of establishing an independent republic that would support free commerce across the border. Carvajal successfully attacked Camargo on 17 September 1851, but in the "Merchants War" on the Río Grande that followed, he lost a series of important battles to Mexican troops.

Carvajal's failure resulted from his inability to enlist Mexican federalists. Many Mexicans resented Carvajal's inclusion of some four hundred Texans in his army, most notable a contingent of discharged Texas Rangers led by the already legendary John S. Ford. Although Brownsville merchants provided badly needed arms for the army, the presence of so many Texans alienated the Mexicans. Ford, a U.S.–Mexican War veteran, was motivated by Carvajal's promise to return to Texas escaped slaves who were living in northern Mexico.

Frederick Law Olmsted, an astute journalist who passed through Texas in 1855, wrote that many Texans continued to hope for the creation of a Republic of the Sierra Madre that would halt the flight of runaway slaves. In the U.S. Senate in 1858, Sam Houston proposed the creation of a protectorate over all of Mexico. Houston predicted that "the wisdom of the project would eventually be recognized and that, like the annexation of Texas, it would be taken up by the masses and carried over the heads of the politicians." The idea was dealt a serious setback, however, when Sen. William H. Seward of New York persuaded the Senate to table Houston's resolution. In his only speech in the 1859 Texas gubernatorial campaign, Houston again raised the idea of a protectorate, which he argued would secure the return of escaped slaves, achieve U.S. expansion, and "build us up in proud defiance of the rest of the world." As governor of Texas during the Cortina War in the Lower Río Grande Valley in 1859 and 1860, Houston attempted to carry out his scheme for a protectorate by encouraging the Knights of the Golden Circle, a filibustering group advocating the creation of a slaveholding empire in Mexico, Central America, and the Caribbean, to invade Mexico. The secessionist movement soon overshadowed Houston's protectorate scheme, however, and by the spring of 1861 his plan was dead.

Yet Texans did not abandon their aspirations of securing additional territory from Mexico. Repeatedly after the Civil War the subject of a Republic of the Sierra Madre or a protectorate in Mexico continued to surface. As late as 1877, the *San Antonio Daily Express* was seriously discussing the need to establish the Texas boundary along the Sierra Madre and, if necessary, impose a protectorate over all of Mexico.

Nasser Momayezi

BIBLIOGRAPHY

Gordon, Webster Michael. "Texan Manifest Destiny and the Mexican Border Conflict." Ph.D. diss., Indiana University, 1972.

Kearney, Milo, and Anthony Knopp. *Boom and Bust: The Historical Cycles of Matamoros and Brownsville.* 1991.

Maril, Robert Lee. *Poorest of Americans: The Mexican Americans of the Lower Rio Grande Valley of Texas.* 1986.

Tyler, Ronnie C. *Santiago Vidaurri and the Southern Confederacy.* 1973.

Slang

Language changes constantly, giving each period in time its own distinct idioms. The conflict between Mexico, Texas, and the United States had a particularly rich lexicon because it mixed English and Spanish as well as regional colloquialisms.

U.S. regulars and volunteers incorporated Spanish words and phrases into their own vocabulary. Soldiers frequently used Spanish words for common items such as milk, bread, beans, and meat. *Vamos* became the byword for leaving or going. Young women, especially attractive ones, were *señoritas*. A *fandango* could mean either a spirited fight or a dance. A *stampede* referred to a false alarm. The term *mustang* could be applied to either a wild horse or an individual with a wild streak.

Mexicans incorporated English words into their language, too. Soldiers from the United States were sometimes referred to as *Los Goddammes* in reference to their habit of constant swearing. The word *devil* was frequently used in combination with *Texan* and *volunteer*, making *Los Diablos Tejanos* and *Los Diablos Voluntarios* common phrases.

Words of racial derision were also common on both sides with *gringo* and *greaser* being among the best known. Some writers have claimed *gringo*, a word used to denote a North American, was a corruption of a popular song title, "Green Grow the Lilacs." Another more likely explanation, however, is that it was an old Spanish word meaning *foreigner*. *Greaser* was an unflattering term used by U.S. soldiers to describe Mexicans. While some U.S. soldiers reserved the term for the lower classes, others used it as a blanket appellation for all inhabitants of Mexico.

Richard Bruce Winders

BIBLIOGRAPHY

Bloom, John Porter. "With the American Army into Mexico, 1846–1848." Ph.D. diss., Emory University, 1956.

Winders, Richard Bruce. *Mr. Polk's Army.* 1997.

Slavery

The issue of slavery was linked to the U.S.–Mexican War from the beginning of the conflict. Many Northerners believed that slavery was the major cause of the war—that President James K. Polk's administration was following a policy designed deliberately to acquire more territory for slave states. During the war, Northerners demanded a policy that would prevent expansion of slavery into the territories acquired from Mexico; Southerners demanded that the territories be open to slavery. After the war the debate over whether to allow slavery in the new territories paralyzed the nation for nearly four years, set the stage for the abortive Nashville secession convention, and exacerbated sectional tensions in the decade before the U.S. Civil War.

The war with Mexico was directly connected to the annexation of Texas, which many Northerners saw as part of a proslavery conspiracy. In fact, the Texas Revolution of 1836 in part resulted from the refusal of emigrants from the southern United States to accept Mexico's ban on slavery. Once independent, Texas became a giant "Empire for Slavery," and annexation brought this empire into the United States, providing seemingly limitless amounts of territory for the expansion of slavery. The aggressive moves by the Polk administration toward Mexico were seen as a part of the proslavery conspiracy by a slaveowning, proslavery Southern president.

The contrast between Polk's policy toward Mexico and his policy toward the Northwest was instructive to many Northerners. Polk campaigned in 1844 on the slogan of "fifty-four forty or fight," and the Democratic platform of that year called for the acquisition of "the whole of the territory of Oregon," which extended well into present-day British Columbia. In the end, however, Polk refused to fight for this territory, and his diplomatic efforts to gain all of the Northwest were weak and conciliatory. This was a reasonable approach because a war with Great Britain would have been costly and perhaps unwinnable. In the Southwest, however, Polk demanded that Mexico recognize the Río Grande as the border for Texas, farther south than anyone in Mexico had ever proposed. When Mexico refused to recognize this border or to make other territorial concessions, Polk prepared for war. Thus, many Northerners believed that Polk was more interested in expansion that would aid slavery than in expansion that would aid the North.

From the moment the war with Mexico began, Northerners argued that it was designed to gain land that could be open to slavery. Under the Missouri Compromise (1820) all western territory south of the southern boundary of Missouri (below 36°30′) would be open to slavery. However, in 1820 most of the western land south of the 36°30′ parallel belonged to Mexico. Thus, slavery could expand westward only through acquisition of northern Mexico. The Massa-chusetts legislature declared the war was unconstitutional because it was being fought for "the triple object of extending slavery, of strengthening the slave power, and of obtaining control of the free states." The charge of a proslavery war had a telling effect in the North, where the Whigs made huge gains in the 1846 congressional elections.

The Whigs might have been even more successful had it not been for the Wilmot Proviso. In August 1846 Democratic representative David Wilmot of Pennsylvania proposed the proviso as an amendment to an appropriations bill of $2 million to fund the war. The proviso declared "that, as an express and fundamental condition to the acquisition of any territory from the Republic of Mexico . . . neither slavery nor involuntary servitude shall ever exist in any part of said territory." Whigs, who were generally hostile to the war, saw the proviso as a way to embarrass President Polk, a Democrat, and to drive a wedge between Southern and Northern Democrats. Northern Democrats endorsed the proviso because it allowed them to avoid the charge that their support for the war would lead to more slave states.

In the House of Representatives all Northern Whigs and all but four Northern Democrats supported the proviso, which passed in the House by a vote of 85 to 79. In the Senate, however, five Northern Democrats joined all Southern senators to defeat the proviso. This defeat left the government paralyzed in the years after the war. After 1846 Southerners demanded the right to take their slaves into the new territories, arguing that the federal lands should be open to all citizens and all constitutionally protected forms of property. In response, Northerners in the House blocked all attempts to organize the new territories while permitting slavery.

Southern opposition to the proviso was as much emotional as practical. Few Southerners believed slavery would thrive in present-day Nevada, Utah, or New Mexico. Many Southerners agreed with U.S. representative Alexander Stephens, a Georgia Whig (and future vice president of the Confederate States of America), that the proviso was a "humbug" with little economic value to slaveowners. But Stephens also argued that the proviso was "an insult to the South" that could not be tolerated. In the Senate, the uncompromising John C. Calhoun responded to the proviso with an assertion that any ban on slavery in the territories was unconstitutional. After ratification of the Treaty of Guadalupe Hidalgo, ending the war with Mexico, Calhoun declared that if the South "yields now" on the question of slavery in the territories, "all will be lost."

The problem of slavery in the new territories split the Democratic Party in 1848, with former president Martin Van Buren running as the candidate of the Free Soil Party. Most of his 291,263 votes came from Northerners who usually voted for the Democratic Party. This set the stage for the electoral victory of Zachary Taylor, the "hero" of the U.S.–

Mexican War, who was running on the Whig ticket. A slaveowning Southerner, Taylor opposed the proviso because, in his estimation, it insulted the South. However, he also opposed allowing slavery in either California or New Mexico because the majority of their populations opposed it. When Texas attempted to annex portions of New Mexico in 1850, Taylor ordered federal troops to defend the integrity of the territory. Taylor also believed the proviso was unnecessary because he doubted slavery could prosper or even survive in the Southwest. The Compromise of 1850 finally ended the debate over slavery in the Mexican Cession. Under the compromise, California entered the Union as a free state and slavery was permitted in the remaining territories.

Paul Finkelman

BIBLIOGRAPHY

Campbell, Randolph B. *An Empire for Slavery: The Peculiar Institution in Texas, 1821–1865.* 1991.

Merk, Frederick. *Slavery and the Annexation of Texas.* 1972.

Morrison, Chaplain W. *Democratic Politics and Sectionalism: The Wilmot Proviso Controversy.* 1967.

Savell, Richard. *Ballots for Freedom: Antislavery Politics in the United States.* 1976.

Wilson, Henry. *Rise and Fall of the Slave Power in America.* 3 vols. 1872–1879. Reprint, 1969.

See also **Abolitionism**

Slidell, John

John Slidell (c. 1793–1871) was a New Orleans politician who served in the U.S. House of Representatives before being nominated by President James K. Polk in 1845 to restore diplomatic relations with Mexico.

Polk appointed Slidell minister to Mexico on 10 November 1845, after being assured by John Black, the U.S. consul in Mexico City, that Slidell would be welcome in Mexico. Polk's instructions emphasized that Slidell was to negotiate all matters at issue between the United States and Mexico—including U.S. claims against Mexico due to past depredations on U.S. citizens and the disputed southern and western boundary for Texas—as well as to try to take advantage of Mexico's weak hold on California, a province desired by U.S. expansionists. Polk also instructed Slidell to give up U.S. claims in exchange for a favorable Texas boundary and in addition pay Mexico $25 million for California. On 17 December Slidell was sent amended instructions that told him not to press the issue of California if that blocked resolution of a boundary for Texas and settlement of the claims issue. Unknown to Polk, Mexico had already reacted negatively to Slidell because of his status as an envoy extraordinary and minister plenipotentiary.

On 12 January 1846 Polk received news of Slidell's impending rejection by the Mexican government. Slidell wrote that Mexico's apparent change of heart demonstrated that the outstanding differences between the United States and Mexico could not be resolved through peaceful negotiation. Mexican officials suggested to Slidell that they might receive him in the status of commissioner and talk with him about Texas only, the implication being that Mexico expected to be compensated for the loss of Texas before renewing full diplomatic relations. Mexican foreign minister Manuel de la Peña y Peña believed that this is what he had stipulated the preceding October in his communications with Consul Black. Slidell, in a letter to U.S. Secretary of State James Buchanan, commented that "This is a contingency which could not have been anticipated, and for which your instructions have consequently not provided."

The following day, Polk ordered Gen. Zachary Taylor's U.S. Army, which had been encamped on the southern bank of the Nueces River in Texas, to move southward to the Río Grande and occupy with force the area about which the Mexican government apparently refused to negotiate. He hoped that this ploy would force an irresolute Mexican government to deal with Slidell on all outstanding issues. The proud U.S. president was unwilling to retreat. So was the proud Mexican government; it viewed Taylor's advance as an invasion of Mexico beyond the Department of Texas, whose southern boundary was the Nueces River. As neither side would change the position that it perceived it had agreed to the preceding October, war became unavoidable. On 23 January, Polk received official notification of Slidell's rejection. Slidell confided to Secretary of State Buchanan that any diminution of his original status would be interpreted in Mexico as timidity. The opportunity for negotiation had passed, although Slidell remained in Mexico until the end of March, vainly seeking acceptance by the Mexican government in his original capacity.

Following his failed mission, Slidell became Louisiana's leading politician in the 1850s and a Confederate agent to France during the Civil War. After that war, Slidell resided in Europe until his death.

Ward M. McAfee

BIBLIOGRAPHY

Bergeron, Paul H. *The Presidency of James K. Polk.* 1987.

McAfee, Ward M. "A Reconsideration of the Origins of the Mexican-American War." *Southern California Quarterly* 62 (1980): 49–65.

McAfee, Ward M., and J. Cordell Robinson, eds. *Origins of the Mexican War.* 2 vols. 1982.

Pletcher, David M. *The Diplomacy of Annexation: Texas, Oregon, and the Mexican War.* 1973.

Slidell Mission

See **Diplomacy**, *article on* **U.S. Diplomacy**

Sloat, John D.

John D. Sloat (1781–1867), U.S. naval officer and first U.S. military governor of California, was born in New York City. A veteran of the War of 1812, he fought pirates in Caribbean waters in the 1820s and in 1840 became commandant of the Portsmouth navy yard. In 1844 he took command of the U.S. Pacific Squadron. In that capacity, his orders instructed him to seize Monterey and secure San Francisco Bay (then called Yerba Buena) as soon as he received news of hostilities between the United States and Mexico. The embarrassing premature seizure of Monterey by Commo. Thomas ap Catesby Jones in 1842 made Sloat cautious about committing a similar faux pas. On 17 May 1846, while at Mazatlán, Sloat heard rumors of fighting along the Río Grande, but he waited for more definite word. Hearing of Sloat's delay, U.S. Secretary of the Navy George Bancroft wrote him a reprimand regarding his "most unfortunate and unwarranted inactivity," but Sloat did not receive this chastisement until after he had finally acted to carry out his orders.

At the end of May, Sloat received definite word of Gen. Zachary Taylor's engagements near the Río Grande and embarked his flotilla for the waters of Alta California. No Mexican flag flew over Monterey at the time of Sloat's arrival. Indeed, Monterey had ceased to serve as the province's capital, which had been moved to Los Angeles.

In early July, when Sloat arrived off the coast of California, he still lacked news of a formal U.S. declaration of war. (That would not arrive in California until 17 August.) For several days, while cruising between Monterey and San Francisco, Sloat continued to fret over whether to carry out his orders. Receiving news of the Bear Flag Revolt and the involvement of both Capt. John C. Frémont and Lt. Archibald Gillespie in this enterprise, Sloat decided to act, fearing that British naval forces in the area might intervene to quell the Bear Flaggers unless he involved his own troops. On 7 July, after five days of waiting, U.S. marines landed at Monterey and raised the U.S. flag. The same was done at San Francisco. In ill health, three days after his sixty-fifth birthday, Sloat turned over command to his successor, Robert Stockton, and on 29 July left for the United States, having served as California's first U.S. military governor for less than one month.

Sloat's subsequent life was marked by command of the Norfolk navy yard from 1847 to 1851 and advancement to rear admiral in 1866, largely for service to the Union navy during the Civil War. He died in New Brighton, New York, in 1867.

Ward M. McAfee

BIBLIOGRAPHY

Bauer, K. Jack. *Surfboats and Horse Marines: U.S. Naval Operations in The Mexican War, 1846–48.* 1969.

Harlow, Neal. *California Conquered: War and Peace on the Pacific, 1846–1850.* 1982.

Smith, Justin

Historian Justin Harvey Smith (1857–1930) was one of the first serious students of the war with Mexico. Born in Boscawen, New Hampshire, on 13 January, he graduated valedictorian from Dartmouth in 1877 before attending the Union Theological Seminary in New York (1879–1881). Abandoning a ministerial career, he joined the publishing firm of Charles Scribners Sons, moving to Ginn and Company in 1890, where he worked as both businessman and editor.

Returning to Dartmouth in 1898 as professor of modern history, Smith published *The Troubadours at Home* (1899), *Arnold's March from Cambridge to Quebec* (1903), and *Our Struggle for the Fourteenth Colony: Canada and the American Revolution* (1907) before resigning in 1908. Devoting full time to research, he penned *The Annexation of Texas* (1911) and his magnum opus, *War with Mexico* (1919), receiving the Pulitzer and Loubat Prizes for the latter work. Chairman of the American Historical Association's Historical Manuscripts Commission (1917–1923), Smith edited "Letters of General Antonio López de Santa Anna Relating to the War between the United States and Mexico, 1846–1848." Weakened by an accident in 1929, Smith died of a heart attack while walking in Brooklyn in 1930. His *War with Mexico* remains one of the seminal works on the war.

Robert P. Wettemann, Jr.

BIBLIOGRAPHY

"Personal." *American Historical Review* 35 (July 1930): 941–942.

Smith, Justin H. *The War with Mexico.* 2 vols. 1919. Reprint, 1963.

Smith, Persifor F.

A colonel of the U.S. Mounted Rifles, Persifor F. Smith (1798–1858) was born in Philadelphia on 16 November to Mary Anne Frazer and Jonathan Smith. He graduated from the College of New Jersey (Princeton) in 1815 and moved to New Orleans with lawyer's credentials in 1819. He became the state adjutant general in 1835 and commanded a regiment of Louisiana, and later Pennsylvania, volunteers during the Second Seminole War (1835–1842).

Smith raised an unauthorized brigade of Louisiana volunteers for the U.S.–Mexican War and arrived at Matamoros on 22 May 1846. He accepted the position of colonel in the regular army on 27 May, commanding the Mounted Rifles. At Monterrey (21–23 September 1846), Smith participated in the assault on Federation and Independence Hills, which earned him a commendation as brevet brigadier general. He transferred to Gen. Winfield Scott's army and commanded a brigade of cavalry. He led U.S. forces at Contreras (19–20 August 1847) for which he received a second commendation as brevet major general. He fought at Churubusco (20 August), Chapultepec (12–13 September), and Garita de Belén (13 September). Smith was a commissioner for the Tacubaya armistice and with Col. William J. Worth successfully negotiated the suspension of hostilities stipulated in the Treaty of Guadalupe Hidalgo. In October Smith assumed the governorship of Mexico City and was commander at Vera Cruz during the U.S. withdrawal during June and July 1848.

Smith commanded several departments in the western United States after the war and accepted the rank of brigadier general on 30 December 1856. He died at Fort Leavenworth on 17 May 1858 and was buried in Philadelphia.

Jimmy L. Bryan, Jr.

BIBLIOGRAPHY

Brown, Canter, Jr. "Persifor F. Smith, the Louisiana Volunteers, and Florida's Second Seminole War." *Louisiana History* 34 (1993): 389–410.

Living Age (Boston), 5 June 1858, 799–800.

Snively Expedition

The Snively Expedition in 1843 was initiated by the Republic of Texas against Mexico in retribution for offenses against Texians by the Mexican government during the Santa Fe Expedition in early 1842, the Mier Expedition in December 1842, and Gen. Adrian Woll's raid and occupation of San Antonio in September 1842. On 28 January 1843 Jacob Snively successfully petitioned the government of Texas to lead an expedition to raid the property of Mexican traders traveling along portions of the Santa Fe Trail that passed through territory claimed by Texas. On 24 April nearly 175 men met at Fort Johnson, Texas. Calling themselves the Battalion of Invincibles, they unanimously elected Snively as leader.

The unit marched westward along the Red River, then north until reaching the Arkansas River in present-day Kansas on 27 May. Snively partisans patrolled south of the Arkansas River in search of a Mexican caravan. On 20 June Col. Charles A. Warfield and a remnant of his command from his expedition joined the Battalion of Invincibles.

Warfield also had received a commission from Texas to wage war on Mexican Santa Fe Trail commerce. In May 1843, after Warfield and his unit had attacked the New Mexican town of Mora, killing five defenders and capturing eighteen, local Mexican militia reinforcements had responded, stampeding Warfield's horses and capturing five of his men. The defeated Texian had retreated and disbanded his force before encountering Snively.

After combining forces the Texians soon encountered one hundred Mexican militiamen from Taos. In the fight that followed seventeen Mexicans were killed, and eighty-two were captured. The Texians suffered no casualties and took the Mexicans' horses, weapons, and other supplies as plunder.

After several days of no further action, the men grew restless, and friction developed in the command as some men expressed a desire to return home. On 28 June the party divided into two groups—the "mountaineers" led by Snively, and the "home boys" commanded by Capt. Eli Chandler.

Both groups headed back toward the Arkansas River. On 30 June the mountaineers encountered two hundred U.S. dragoons under the command of Capt. Philip St. George Cooke escorting a Mexican caravan on the north bank of the river, clearly on U.S. soil. The dragoons crossed the Arkansas and surrounded Snively's Texians, ordering them to surrender most of their weapons. About fifty Texians accepted Cooke's offer of safe escort to Missouri, while the rest, including Snively, rejoined Chandler on 2 July.

Snively urged an attack on the now unguarded caravan but found little enthusiasm from his command; he resigned in anger on 9 July. Eventually, some seventy of the adventurers chose to remain on the plains and elected Warfield as their commander. On 13 July Warfield's Texians overtook the elusive Mexican caravan but by that time it had a sizable escort from New Mexico. Frustrated over what they considered a lost opportunity caused by needless U.S. meddling, the Texians abandoned their mission. The Battalion of Invincibles disbanded for good on 6 August 1843 at Bird's Fort on the Trinity River.

Cory Hendricks

BIBLIOGRAPHY

Carroll, H. Bailey. "Steward A. Miller and the Snively Expedition of 1843." *Southwestern Historical Quarterly* 54 (January 1951): 261–286.

Oates, Stephen B. "The Hard Luck Story of the Snively Expedition." *American West* (August 1967).

Oates, Stephen B., ed. "Hugh F. Young's Account of the Snively Expedition as Told to John S. Ford." *Southwestern Historical Quarterly* 70 (July 1966).

Yoakum, Henderson K. *History of Texas from its First Settlement in 1685 to its Annexation to the United States in 1846.* 1855.

Soldaderas

Accompanying every Mexican army was a shadow army of women known as *soldaderas*. More than just camp followers in the classical sense, these women came to be the supply system of most Mexican armies. Mothers, wives, girlfriends, and sisters of the soldiers in the ranks, *soldaderas* excelled at keeping their loved ones fed, clothed, and healthy while on campaign, often relieving the Mexican government of that burden. On several occasions, the leaders of Mexico's military tried to curtail or abolish the custom of *soldaderas*, but they met with little success and many of these leaders came to rely on the women to help them fight wars.

In Gen. Antonio López de Santa Anna's campaign against Texas, an estimated fifteen hundred *soldaderas* and their children began the march from San Luis Potosí for the Río Grande. The punishing march and weather caused most to fall out or turn back, and fewer than three hundred remained when the army arrived in San Antonio.

In the U.S.–Mexican War, *soldaderas* once again came to the aid of their fighting men, participating by the thousands. Their service often came at a price, however. María Josefa Zozaya, a *soldadera* with Gen. Pedro de Ampudia's army in Nuevo León, was lauded as the "Angel of Monterrey" by U.S. troops who watched her tend wounded Mexican soldiers until felled by a bullet herself.

Donald S. Frazier

BIBLIOGRAPHY

DePalo, William A., Jr. *The Mexican National Army, 1822–1852.* 1997.

Salas, Elizabeth. *Soldaderas in the Mexican Military: Myths and History.* 1990.

Somervell Expedition

In retaliation for Mexican attacks on the Texas frontier in the spring and fall of 1842, Texas president Sam Houston sanctioned in early October an invasion of the lower Río Grande Valley, appointing Gen. Alexander Somervell to lead the campaign. From the outset the expedition was plagued by poor leadership, bad weather, meager supplies, and a lack of discipline among the men under Somervell's command. On 25 November the army left San Antonio, and after a slow and difficult march arrived in Laredo on 8 December. When the Texians learned that the impoverished Mexican citizenry could offer little in the way of supplies or spoils, many soldiers ran amok and sacked the town. Believing that the Mexican army was at that time moving against his intractable and ill-prepared force, Somervell showed little interest in pursuing the objectives of his mission, much to the anger of many of his men. On 19 December, after making a brief, half-hearted foray across the Río Grande to demand supplies from the citizens of Guerrero, he called off the campaign and gave the order to march north. Only 187 Texians obeyed the order; more than 300 separated from Somervell's command and elected William Fisher to lead them into Mexico, an enterprise that would be known as the Mier Expedition.

Sam W. Haynes

BIBLIOGRAPHY

Green, Thomas Jefferson. *Journal of the Expedition Against Mier.* 1845.

Haynes, Sam W. *Soldiers of Misfortune: The Somervell and Mier Expeditions.* 1990.

Sonora Revolt of 1837

Like the Texas Revolution of 1836, the Sonora Revolt of 1837 reflected the clash between centralism and federalism that characterized Mexican politics of the period. The revolt also combined elements of a personal feud and a civil-military conflict, pitting Manuel María Gándara against Gen. José Urrea. Gándara was the first governor of Sonora under the new centralist Constitution of 1836, while Urrea served as commandant-general of Sonora and Sinaloa. Urrea revolted in the name of federalism against the central government on 26 December 1837. Gándara initially supported Urrea's revolt, only to see an emergency session of the state legislature in March 1838 appoint Urrea the new federalist governor. Urrea then attempted to expand the revolt by invading the neighboring state of Sinaloa. Urrea's invasion enjoyed some early success, including the capture of the key port of Mazatlán, but on 6 May forces of the central government recaptured Mazatlán, forcing Urrea's return to Sonora.

Gándara took advantage of Urrea's absence by pronouncing in favor of centralism on 16 May 1838 and declaring himself governor. Urrea returned to Sonora but eventually suffered defeat at the hands of the centralist forces aided by Indian allies. By November 1838 Gándara had regained control of Sonora, effectively bringing an end to the Revolt of 1837. Urrea returned as governor of Sonora in May 1842, touching off a two-year civil war with Gándara and his followers. The Sonora Revolt of 1837 typified the personalism, militarism, and political opportunism that cut across the centralist-federalist conflict and made northern Mexico a tempting target for further U.S. expansion.

Don M. Coerver

BIBLIOGRAPHY

Stagg, Albert. *The Almadas and Alamos, 1783–1867.* 1978.

Voss, Stuart F. *On the Periphery of Nineteenth-Century Mexico: Sonora and Sinaloa, 1810–1877.* 1982.

Sonora y Sinaloa

Well into the nineteenth century, Sonora and Sinaloa operated on the periphery of developments in Mexico. Physically isolated from the Mexican heartland, the area was left to develop on its own for most of the Mexican colonial period. The growing population, which was attracted by mining, as well as the central government's security concerns about the northwestern frontier, led to the creation of the province of Sonora-Sinaloa in 1721. In 1776 Sonora-Sinaloa became part of the *Provincias Internas,* an administrative unit established to defend the entire northern frontier of New Spain. In 1786, in a further attempt to centralize royal control over the frontier, the Spanish crown transformed the province of Sonora-Sinaloa into the Intendancy of Arizpe.

Mexico's War for Independence (1810–1821) largely bypassed the northwestern region; in fact, the Intendancy of Arizpe continued to function as a political unit for two years after independence. One of the most pressing issues was whether Sonora and Sinaloa would remain united in an independent Mexico; urban rivalries and differing security needs led to demands for division. Early indications were that Sonora and Sinaloa would be separate entities, but the federal Constitution of 1824 combined the two into the state of Occidente. The constitution also had a provision preventing any modifications in the state until 1830. As soon as it was legally possible, most of the political elites in both regions petitioned for separation. In October 1830 the national congress declared the division of the state of Occidente into the states of Sonora and Sinaloa, effective March 1831.

With the division completed, attention shifted to urban rivalries and the federalist-centralist conflict. There were struggles over the location of capitals in both states. In Sonora, Hermosillo contested successfully with the longtime administrative center of Arizpe; in Sinaloa, Culiacán emerged as state capital, at the expense of the traditional center of Cosalá. Each state also had a major port: Guaymas in Sonora and Mazatlán in Sinaloa. In the late 1830s both states increasingly were caught up in the national conflict over the movement toward centralization. This clash briefly brought the political fates of the two states together when the federalist Sonora Revolt of 1837 spilled over into Sinaloa in 1838. These unsettled political conditions continued until the outbreak of war between Mexico and the United States in 1846.

As had happened with other national and international developments, the war between the United States and Mexico largely bypassed Sonora and Sinaloa. Mexican officials feared early in the war that the United States might invade Sonora, but the only U.S. military action there was the incursion of Gen. Stephen W. Kearny's Army of the West into the far northern part of Sonora enroute to campaign in California. U.S. forces also occupied the ports of Guaymas and Mazatlán. The war left the Sonorans with a well-grounded fear of further U.S. expansion and created an even more complicated security problem with respect to the Indians, as the United States did little to prevent Apache raids across the new international boundary.

Don M. Coerver

BIBLIOGRAPHY

Bobb, Bernard E. *The Viceregency of Antonio María Bucareli in New Spain, 1771–1779.* 1962.

Stagg, Albert. *The Almadas and Alamos, 1783–1867.* 1978.

Villa, Eduardo W. *Historia del estado de Sonora.* 2d ed. 1951.

Voss, Stuart F. *On the Periphery of Nineteenth-Century Mexico: Sonora and Sinaloa, 1810–1877.* 1982.

Spain

Spain, as the former ruler of most of the nations comprising Latin America, kept a keen interest in the internal and external affairs of its former colonies. Spain became the external ally of Mexican centralists, especially those who favored a return to monarchy and the enthronement of a European prince. Spain also championed the causes of the Roman Catholic church in Mexico. In 1829 Spain intervened militarily against a federalist regime in Mexico City by seizing the port of Tampico before being driven off by disease and Mexican troops. Spain, for economic and political reasons, continued to seek an opportunity to restore stability—and its own influence—to Mexico.

During the course of the conflict between the United States and Mexico, Spain attempted to steer its former colony away from a military collision with its North American neighbor and, by inference, into a closer diplomatic dependence on Spain. Salvador Bermúdez de Castro, Spanish minister to Mexico, urged European arbitration after the failure of John Slidell's mission in 1845 to settle the U.S.–Mexican boundary. When these urgings were ignored and war broke out, Spain kept its diplomatic distance from Mexico. Leopoldo O'Donnell, comandante general of Cuba, forbade Mexican privateers to call on Cuban ports, and Spanish warships captured the Mexican privateer *Unica* in the Mediterranean and drove *La Rosita* away from shipping lanes. At the end of the war, Spain again sought a part in negotiating a treaty between the United States and Mexico, but its overtures were disregarded.

Donald S. Frazier

BIBLIOGRAPHY

Eisenhower, John S. D. *So Far from God: The U.S. War with Mexico.* 1989.

Smith, Justin. *The War with Mexico.* 2 vols. 1919. Reprint, 1963.

Spot Resolutions

Abraham Lincoln entered the U.S. House of Representatives in 1847 at the age of thirty-eight, full of ambition for a distinguished national career. He was the only Whig Party representative from the state of Illinois and intended to demonstrate his abilities by joining the Whig assault on President James K. Polk's U.S.–Mexican War policies.

Shortly after taking his seat in Congress, on 22 December 1847 Lincoln introduced the "Spot Resolutions," a set of eight questions designed to challenge President Polk's version of the war's origins. Lincoln pressed for answers regarding the exact "spot" where the fighting began. After receiving neither a response from the president nor action from Congress, Lincoln offered his maiden speech on 12 January 1848, asserting that the Mexicans had not been the aggressors, as Polk and the Democrats had been claiming, and that the war was unjustified and unnecessary.

Lincoln's position was politically risky and, as it turned out, somewhat ill-advised. Despite his hopes, the Washington, D.C., community and national party leaders barely noticed the effort. Back in Illinois, however, the response was more heated and decidedly negative. Lincoln received scathing criticism not only from local Democrats, who dubbed him "Spotty" Lincoln, but also from some of his Whig allies, who considered the speech political suicide.

The war came to an end only a few months after the introduction of the resolutions. A rather deflated Lincoln left Congress the next year, although mainly for other reasons. However, the notoriety he gained as a war opponent lingered for the next decade and was an element of some importance in Lincoln's prepresidential career.

Matthew Pinsker

BIBLIOGRAPHY

Boritt, Gabor S. "A Question of Political Suicide? Lincoln's Opposition to the Mexican War." *Journal of the Illinois State Historical Society* 67 (1974): 79–100.

Donald, David Herbert. *Lincoln*. 1995.

Riddle, Donald W. *Congressman Abraham Lincoln*. 1957.

Steamships

The U.S.–Mexican War provided a powerful boost for expanding the U.S. steam navy. Opposed by many powerful figures both within and outside the navy, steam power proved useful in many roles during the war, most strikingly in blockade duties and shelling coastal targets where tide and wind proved difficult for sailing craft. Light-draft steamers *Scorpion, Scourge, Spitfire,* and *Vixen,* all purchased in New York and converted into warships, were especially effective in river operations such as the two forays up the Río Tabasco and the army landing at Vera Cruz. Frequently the steamers towed smaller sailing ships into position as during the Río Tabasco expeditions, but there was at least one instance of a steamer towing a sailing frigate into position, off the mouth of the Río Papaloapan.

The powerful *Mississippi* (1,692 tons; armed with two 10-inch and two 8-inch guns) and *Princeton* (672 tons; one 8-inch gun and eight 42-pounder carronades), the largest steamers in the navy, were particularly useful to the Home Squadron during the war. Although too deep in draft to participate in river expeditions because there was usually a bar across the river mouths, they provided fast and reliable service regardless of wind conditions. Proof of this came in November 1846 when the *Mississippi* steamed from Tampico to Matamoros and then on to New Orleans to obtain troops and supplies, returning to its starting point in only thirteen days, a record for that time.

Taking note of the steam vessels' success during the war, in March 1847 Congress passed an appropriations bill for the construction of four steamers—*Susquehanna, Powhatan, Saranac,* and *San Jacinto*—that subsequently saw considerable service.

Spencer C. Tucker

BIBLIOGRAPHY

Bennett, Frank M. *The Steam Navy of the United States*. 1896. Reprint, 1972.

Canney, Donald L. *The Old Steam Navy*. Vol. 1, *Frigates, Sloops, and Gunboats, 1815–1885*. 1990.

Emmons, George F. *The Navy of the United States. From the Commencement, 1753 to 1853; With a Brief History of Each Vessel's Service and Fate as Appears upon Record*. 1853.

Stockton, Robert F.

Robert F. Stockton (1795–1866) had a long military career beginning in 1811 when the New Jersey native joined the navy as a midshipman. He took part in the defense of Fort McHenry in Baltimore, Maryland, and subsequently served in the Mediterranean and off the African coast. Stockton developed a passion for politics first as a Jacksonian, next as a Whig, and finally as a Democrat and maintained close relationships with Presidents Andrew Jackson and John Tyler. In addition, the veteran officer advocated advances in naval technology and armaments. He supported experiments with screw propulsion and developed a 12-inch cannon, the "Peacemaker." Unfortunately the weapon exploded disastrously during an 1844 test firing aboard the warship *Princeton*, killing Secretary of State Abel Upshur and several other dignitaries.

After a tour off the Texas coast during the spring and summer of 1845, Stockton received orders to join the Pacific Squadron. Arriving off Monterey in July 1846, he took over command of the squadron from Commo. John D. Sloat and immediately became embroiled in the confusing political and military situation in California. Stockton issued a controversial proclamation calling for a restoration of order under U.S. rule. He enlisted the support of Col. John C. Frémont's Bear Flag detachment and within one month completed the occupation of California, which he proclaimed a U.S. territory on 17 August 1846.

Mexican loyalists quickly organized a revolt in southern California against the U.S. forces, recapturing Los Angeles in late September. Three months later Stockton's forces, reinforced with troops under Brig. Gen. Stephen W. Kearny, began a reoccupation of the region. After skirmishes at San Gabriel and outside Los Angeles, Stockton captured the town for a second time in early January 1847. Having quelled the uprising, Stockton and Kearny argued over control of the new Californian government, a feud that ended with the former's replacement shortly thereafter.

Stockton left the navy in 1850 and served in the U.S. Senate for two years. He attended the 1861 Washington Peace Conference but took no active role in the Civil War. He died at Princeton, New Jersey, on 7 October 1866.

David J. Coles

BIBLIOGRAPHY

Bauer, K. Jack. *Surfboats and Horse Marines: U.S. Naval Operations in the Mexican War, 1846–48.* 1969.

Bayard, Samuel John. *A Sketch of the Life of Com. Robert F. Stockton.* 1856.

Harlow, Neal. *California Conquered: War and Peace on the Pacific, 1846–1850.* 1982.

Storm, Jane McManus

See **Cazneau, Jane McManus Storm**

Supplies

This entry consists of two separate articles: **Mexican Supplies** *and* **U.S. Supplies.**

Mexican Supplies

Supplying the Mexican army with food, clothing, and ammunition proved to be a constant problem from 1821 to 1854. Officers complained of a shortage of funds and matériel from the central government while their troops shivered in worn-out uniforms, ate whatever they could scrounge, and fought with antique firearms and cannon with unreliable ammunition.

Elaborate regulations called for a well-organized supply structure resembling a regular quartermaster and commissary service. During the Texas campaign of 1835 to 1836, the Mexican army authorized a system of commissioners for every division in the field. These officers, usually colonels, handled government funds and had to post a bond of 10,000 pesos. To aid them, each had an accountant who posted bond at 4,000 pesos, a treasurer who also bonded at 4,000 pesos, and six junior officers and their clerks stationed at a central depot. By 1840 regulations added a provider of food and supplies, a storekeeper, paymaster, and two clerks added to each divisional depot. In addition, the Mexican army organized recruiting and training depots at San Luis Potosí and Mexico City, each housing a replacement battalion composed of four infantry companies and two companies of cavalry.

In reality, though, the Mexican supply system rarely operated as planned. Funds rarely arrived on time or in the amount required, and necessary materials often proved scarce in the vicinity of the army in the field, especially when officers offered to pay with drafts against the national treasury. As a result, each unit faced overwhelming challenges to maintain its readiness and often pressed supplies and recruits from the people along their route of march. *Soldaderas,* women who accompanied the army in a semi-official role, became the backbone of the informal supply system as they foraged for food and prepared it for the troops.

Transportation was lacking as well. Mexican armies hired mule trains and carts on an as-needed basis to haul food and ammunition with the army. This included, in many cases, hauling artillery, meaning that untrained civilians had charge of these valuable weapons.

Arms and ammunition supply also proved a problem. Mexico had an excellent arsenal in Mexico City, and two gunpowder mills, but the weapons and cartridges produced were of inferior quality. Misshapen cannon projectiles did not fly true, and heavy powder charges in musket cartridges caused many of the infantry to anticipate the kick of their weapon and fire high or from the hip in combat. This lack of logistical support undermined the morale of the army and often kept it from being effective while on campaign.

Donald S. Frazier

BIBLIOGRAPHY

DePalo, William A., Jr. *The Mexican National Army, 1822–1852.* 1997.

Hefter, Joseph. *El soldado Mexicano, 1837–1847.* 1958.

Smith, Justin H. *The War with Mexico.* 2 vols. 1919. Reprint, 1963.

See also **Soldaderas**

U.S. Supplies

U.S. supplies were the responsibility of the Quartermaster Department of the U.S. Army, led by Brig. Gen. Thomas S. Jesup. The department was staffed in 1845 by a total of

Mexican *arrieros*. Keeping the army supplied was a problem for the duration of the war, and civilian muleteers were hired to transport both food and ammunition (Brantz Mayer, *Mexico As It Was and As It Is*, 1844).

thirty-seven officers, a number that had been unchanged since 1838. It was only after ten months of war that Congress approved a modest addition of four permanent quartermasters and ten assistant quartermasters. With this small department General Jesup labored to supply the needs of an army of regulars and volunteers that at times exceeded 25,000 men, on duty from California to New Mexico and south of the Río Grande in northeastern and central Mexico.

The Quartermaster Department was charged with the movement and supply of the armies in the field. The needs of the army included such diverse supplies as steam and sailing ships, uniforms and accouterments, wagons, horses and mules, tents, and even pontoon bridges when needed. In short, everything from horseshoes to uniform buckles that an army might need was the responsibility of the quartermaster. By the outbreak of war in 1846, procurement officers were feverishly contracting with private manufacturers to supply goods and were chartering shipping to deliver these goods. When shipping could not be chartered, the department purchased the needed vessels outright.

Rations were the responsibility of the Subsistence Department, separate from the Quartermaster Department and headed by Col. George Gibson. The daily diet of the soldier in the field consisted of twelve ounces of pork or bacon, or twenty ounces of beef; either eighteen ounces of soft bread or flour, twelve ounces of hard bread, or twenty ounces of cornmeal; the third staple was eight quarts of peas or beans per hundred men. The men supplemented this diet by hunting or by bartering with local inhabitants.

Shortages were inevitable at the beginning of the war as a lag time was needed for manufacturers to complete their contracts and for the needed supplies to be shipped.

Gen. Zachary Taylor complained to the government in Washington, D.C., about a shortage of means for transportation: wagons, mules, horses, shallow-draft steamboats, and pontoon bridges. A lack of these items slowed Taylor's advance on Monterrey until August 1846. In a remarkably short time, however, even these needs were alleviated by an enterprising General Jesup.

The supplies that reached Taylor's forces in Saltillo during 1847 were the result of an extensive and expensive chain of transportation. Supplies reaching south Texas at Brazos Santiago had to be off-loaded into shallow-draft lighters for landing. From Brazos Santiago, these supplies were loaded on wagons and hauled to the mouth of the Río Grande. From the wagons, the supplies were loaded onto river steamers to be transported up river to the nominal head of river travel, Camargo, Mexico. From Camargo, the supplies were again loaded onto wagons and burros to be hauled overland some 180 miles to Saltillo.

In central Mexico, Gen. Winfield Scott, occupying Puebla in May 1847, could not keep open lines of communication with Vera Cruz due to shortages in manpower. Supplies landing at Vera Cruz had to be escorted by a large force of soldiers to prevent capture by Mexican guerrillas. U.S. troops suffered from hunger: one soldier even reported that growling stomachs could be heard throughout the ranks. Scott was able to purchase a great deal of food from the Mexican populace, however, which alleviated some of the problem.

Joseph E. Chance

BIBLIOGRAPHY

McCaffrey, James M. *Army of Manifest Destiny: The American Soldier in the Mexican War, 1846–1848.* 1992.

Orr, William J., and Robert Ryal Miller, eds. *An Immigrant Soldier in the Mexican War.* 1995.

Risch, Erna. *Quartermaster Support of the Army: A History of the Corps, 1775–1939.* 1962.

Smith, Justin H. *The War with Mexico.* 2 vols. 1919. Reprint, 1963.

Sutter's Fort

A Swiss adventurer named John Augustus Sutter established Sutter's Fort in 1839 at the site of present-day Sacramento, now California's capital city. Constructed far from the coastal Californio settlements, Sutter envisioned it protecting an interior empire that would attract U.S. pioneers moving overland. While he received his land grant from a Mexican governor, his plans included encouragement of illegal U.S. immigration into the Mexican province, something that Californios generally viewed with dread. In the years just prior to the U.S.–Mexican War, U.S. pioneers were making their way over the Sierra Nevada into the Sacramento Valley in the vicinity of Sutter's Fort.

The fort and its environs played a significant role in the events that brought the war to California. The area served as the hub of Anglo-American population in the region. There, after being expelled from the Monterey Bay area by Gen. José Castro in March 1846, Capt. John C. Frémont stirred up local settlers with his talk of rough handling by the Californios. Frémont returned two months later, after conferring with Lt. Archibald Gillespie in southern Oregon. Meanwhile, Anglo-American farmers had whipped themselves into a frenzy over supposed plans of Castro's Californio forces to drive them from the province. Frémont's return sparked these settlers to move precipitously against Californio settlements north of San Francisco Bay. Thus the Bear Flag Revolt began a month before the arrival of official U.S. forces in California. Sutter's Fort was used to house Californio prisoners of war taken in that first month of conflict.

At the conclusion of the U.S.–Mexican War, Sutter's Fort proved significant again. In late January 1848 gold was discovered on the American River by one of Sutter's workmen at a sawmill (Sutter's Mill), located forty-five miles north of the fort. One week later, unaware of the discovery near Sutter's Fort that would lead to the California gold rush, U.S. and Mexican negotiators signed the Treaty of Guadalupe Hidalgo, bringing an end to the U.S.–Mexican War.

Ward M. McAfee

BIBLIOGRAPHY

Hawgood, John A. "The Pattern of Yankee Infiltration in Mexican Alta California, 1821–1846." *Pacific Historical Review* 27 (1958): 27–38.

Zollinger, James P. *Sutter: The Man and His Empire.* 1939.

Tabasco River Expedition

The U.S. Navy performed its primary task of securing control of the seas in the war zone so effectively that it was also able to undertake the secondary operations of seizing Mexican towns. Home Squadron commander Commo. David Conner accepted Commo. Matthew C. Perry's suggestion to send a naval force up the Río Tabasco (also known as Río Grijalva) in the Yucatán Peninsula to capture or destroy Mexican vessels, ordnance, and munitions. Perry's force consisted of the steam frigate *Mississippi*, small steamers *McLane* and *Vixen*, and schooners *Reefer*, *Bonita*, *Nonata*, and *Forward*. Their crews were augmented by a 253-man landing force of marines and seamen from the *Raritan* and *Cumberland*.

The expedition left its anchorages along the Gulf Coast on 16 October 1846. A storm separated the *Reefer* from the other vessels and it missed the attack on San Juan Bautista, generally referred to as Tabasco in U.S. sources. The remaining vessels reached the mouth of the Río Tabasco on 22 October. The following day the *Mississippi* and *McLane* remained behind while the other vessels crossed the bar and took the town of Frontera (weakly defended by fewer than three hundred men manning a fort with four 24-pounder guns) and three vessels—the steamer *Petrita* and two schooners.

Perry left some men to garrison Frontera, supported by the larger ships across the bar, and then set out with the remaining force seventy-two miles upriver to Tabasco. The *Petrita*, carrying the landing party, led the way, followed by the *Vixen* towing the *Forward* and *Bonita*. Fort Acachapan, well situated at a bend in the river, could have been a serious obstacle to the U.S. forces, but its garrison fled on their arrival.

On the 25th the U.S. ships anchored at Tabasco and seized two schooners, two brigs, and two sloops. In an ensuing skirmish the U.S. forces sustained five casualties (four killed) while the Mexicans lost five soldiers and four civilians killed. On 26 October Perry's small force departed Tabasco, arriving at Frontera the next morning. Two of the prizes were taken into U.S. service; the others were lost in a storm at the end of November.

In June 1847 Commodore Perry, then commanding the Home Squadron, mounted another, larger assault on Tabasco. Deep-draft vessels unable to cross the bar all contributed men and boats. Perry had his flag in the steamer *Scorpion*.

On 14 June the ships crossed the bar at the mouth of the river and occupied Frontera without resistance. The same day, after coaling, they headed up river. The *Scorpion* led, towing the *Vesuvius, Washington,* and boats of the *Mississippi* and *John Adams*. The steamer *Spitfire* towed *Stromboli, Bonita,* and boats of the *Albany*. The *Scourge* towed the merchant schooner *Spitfire*, which carried explosives to blow up reported river obstacles. Bringing up the rear was the *Vixen*, towing *Etna* and boats of *Raritan, Decatur,* and *Germantown*. In all the forty ships' boats carried 1,173 men. Also included in the tows were seven surfboats, each carrying a 6-pounder fieldpiece.

The force covered forty miles the first day. Perry gained the respect of his men by exposing himself to Mexican shore fire as the expedition moved up river. On 16 July Perry ordered the naval brigade ashore just below Seven Palms to provide flank security and force the Mexicans to withdraw from their defensive positions around river obstacles. The 1,173 men and their seven fieldpieces were landed in just ten minutes. After his land artillery had fired on Fort Acachapan, Perry, sword in hand, personally led a charge. In the engagement the naval brigade, although poorly trained for land operations, routed a force of some nine hundred Mexicans behind strong defenses. The Mexicans sustained thirty

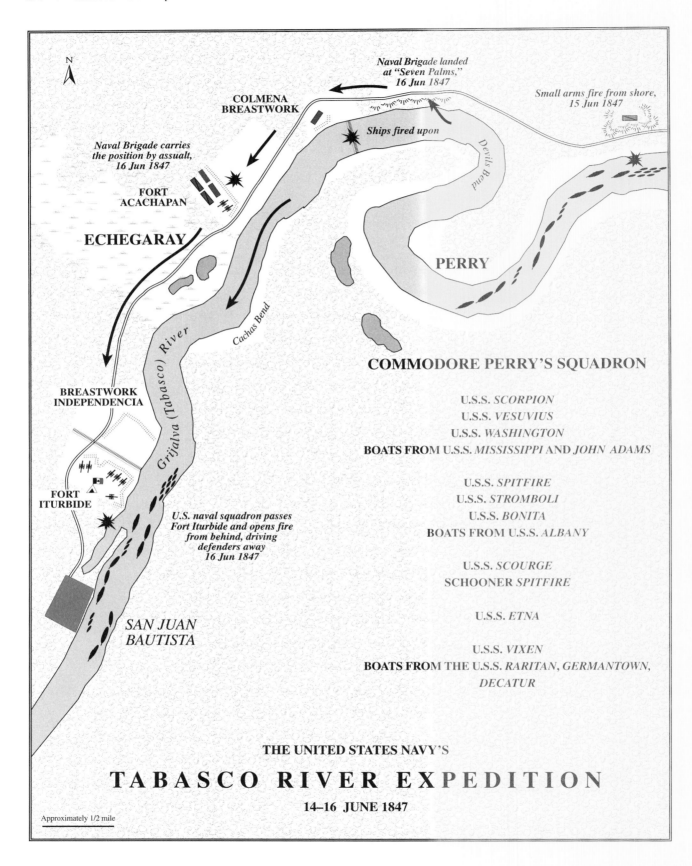

N

Naval Brigade landed
at "Seven Palms,"
16 Jun 1847

COLMENA
BREASTWORK

Small arms fire from shore,
15 Jun 1847

Ships fired upon

Naval Brigade carries
the position by assualt,
16 Jun 1847

FORT
ACACHAPAN

Devils Bend

ECHEGARAY

PERRY

Cachas Bend

COMMODORE PERRY'S SQUADRON

Grijalva (Tabasco) River

U.S.S. SCORPION
U.S.S. VESUVIUS
U.S.S. WASHINGTON
BOATS FROM U.S.S. MISSISSIPPI AND JOHN ADAMS

BREASTWORK
INDEPENDENCIA

U.S.S. SPITFIRE
U.S.S. STROMBOLI
U.S.S. BONITA
BOATS FROM U.S.S. ALBANY

FORT
ITURBIDE

U.S.S. SCOURGE
SCHOONER SPITFIRE

U.S. naval squadron passes
Fort Iturbide and opens fire
from behind, driving
defenders away
16 Jun 1847

U.S.S. ETNA

U.S.S. VIXEN
BOATS FROM THE U.S.S. RARITAN, GERMANTOWN,
DECATUR

SAN JUAN
BAUTISTA

THE UNITED STATES NAVY'S

TABASCO RIVER EXPEDITION

14–16 JUNE 1847

Approximately 1/2 mile

casualties; five U.S. troops were wounded. During the skirmish, crews of the vessels below La Colmena succeeded in removing obstacles after first loosening them with explosives. Both the land and river forces then converged on Tabasco, with the ships arriving first. At that point every Mexican port of consequence on the Gulf Coast was in U.S. hands.

Over the next week Perry supervised the destruction of contraband, fortifications, and the magazine, as well as the transfer of guns from the fort to the flotilla. Pending instructions from the Navy Department, Perry decided to garrison Tabasco with a marine force, supported by the *Spitfire, Scourge,* and *Etna.* On 24 June, the Mexicans mounted a night assault on Tabasco. The U.S. force repelled the attack but lacked sufficient strength to pursue. When Cmdr. Abraham Bigelow arrived in the *Scorpion* to assume command, he requested reinforcements. Perry responded by sending the *Vixen,* one gun, and one hundred sailors and marines. Mexican guerrillas continued to harass the U.S. forces, however; ultimately this and yellow fever forced Perry to order a withdrawal. The garrison evacuated Tabasco on 21 to 22 July, although a U.S. force continued to hold Frontera and was thus able to cut off trade to and from the interior.

Naval historian Kenneth Hagan wrote that the Tabasco raid "involved a demonstration of inspirational naval leadership at the top. . . . " Commodore Conner's creation of a self-contained naval brigade, exploited by Perry, was an important boost to U.S. Navy amphibious operations.

Spencer C. Tucker

BIBLIOGRAPHY

Bauer, K. Jack. *Surfboats and Horse Marines: U.S. Naval Operations in the Mexican War, 1846–48.* 1969.

Hagan, Kenneth J. *This People's Navy: The Making of American Sea Power.* 1991.

Knox, Dudley W. *A History of the United States Navy.* 1936.

Smith, Justin H. *The War with Mexico.* 2 vols. 1919. Reprint, 1963.

Tactics

This entry consists of two separate articles: **Mexican Tactics** *and* **U.S. Tactics.**

Mexican Tactics

The tactics of the Mexican army refer to how Mexican troops were used in battle and the way in which they moved and fought in combat. Like most armies of the nineteenth century, Mexico used a system of linear tactics that relied on volley fire and bayonet shock assault to defeat enemy formations.

In 1821 the new nation of Mexico organized its standing army as two-battalion regiments but soon afterward—because of attrition and political turmoil—converted to single-battalion organizations. In 1839 the Mexican army reorganized again following the British pattern of numbered regiments of two battalions each, one regular (*permanente*) formation mated to an active (*activo*) militia formation. Mexican infantry battalions had eight companies of up to eighty men each including a light company (*cazadores*), often armed with rifles, and a grenadier company (*granadero*) for skirmishing and other specialized duties. They marched to the battlefield in "Indian file," or double column, and fought in double rank lines. To handle their weapons in these formations, the Mexican soldiers followed a manual of arms, or a system of drill, designed for efficient use of their individual weapons. Inherited from the Spanish 1814 drill manual, the regulations called for twenty-two basic positions for carrying the weapons, including orders such as "shoulder arms, present arms, rest arms, review arms, raise arms, cover arms, and arms at ease." In formation, the army observed a front of four feet per man, and three feet between files. In 1843 the infantry drill was simplified by the adoption of a system designed by Capt. Juan Ordoñez.

Mexican infantry firepower came from Brown Bess East India Pattern smoothbore muskets, English Baker rifles, or muskets of other patterns. An eleven-step procedure loaded the weapons, while four commands controlled the volume of fire. Mexican line companies most often fired their volleys from the hip and often shot high, and there was little training in marksmanship or fire discipline. The drill manual made allowances for rapid firing by reducing the number of loading commands to four. Mexican infantry tactics also used large numbers of sharpshooters and skirmishers, skills at which the soldiers excelled. In 1835 this skill was institutionalized by the creation of three light infantry battalions, a fourth being added in 1846.

Bayonets figured large in Mexican drill. In 1844 a new method of bayonet fighting was adopted after Lt. Col. José Lopez Uraga's adaptation of the 1836 French drill. When on the defensive, especially when charged by cavalry, Mexican tactics called for units to create a circular formation, presenting a hedge of bayonets to the oncoming enemy.

The pride of the Mexican army was its cavalry. Armed with pistol, carbine, sword, and lance, extensive drill and training was required to keep that arm efficient. Cavalry also fought in line of battle, but it made use of columns four troopers wide as well. Mexican cavalry regiments contained eight companies, but most were deployed as squadrons of two companies each. This arm contained several specialty organizations including light cavalry and hussars. The tactical doctrine for all mounted troops originated with the pre-1821 Spanish army. Even though Mexico's cavalry was theoretically armed and trained for shock charges, the lack of

Mexican dragoons exercising. John Frost, *Pictorial History of Mexico and the Mexican War,* 1862

quality horses of enough size prevented this technique from being effective in practice.

The artillery of Mexico was organized into three "foot" brigades of eight companies and one mounted brigade of six companies. Each company, numbering approximately sixty to eighty men and corresponding to a battery in the U.S. service, served four guns on average. In 1843 the Mexican government authorized the creation of a school for artillery and engineering instruction, but funding never materialized. In fact, by 1846 civilian contractors handled most transportation for the Mexican artillery, severely hampering its mobility under fire and its effectiveness on the battlefield. Mexico also organized a regiment of sappers (*zapadores*) to serve as engineers in the army. A lack of training and equipment, however, relegated them primarily to the role of infantry.

Donald S. Frazier

BIBLIOGRAPHY

DePalo, William A., Jr. *The Mexican National Army, 1822–1852.* 1997.

Hefter, Joseph. *El soldado Mexicano, 1837–1847.* 1958.

Smith, Justin H. *The War with Mexico.* 2 vols. 1919. Reprint, 1963.

U.S. Tactics

U.S. Army tactics during the U.S.–Mexican War, as in earlier American and European conflicts, assumed that line infantrymen would carry the common shoulder arm of the era, the smoothbore musket. The 1st Mississippi Rifles became famous for their weapons, but this regiment was an exception, not the rule. During the U.S.–Mexican War, the War Department issued roughly thirty-eight thousand smoothbore muskets and only about ten thousand 54-caliber rifles. The musket's poor accuracy and short range limited its effectiveness. With humorous exaggeration, Lt. Ulysses S. Grant claimed that a man using a musket from a distance of a few hundred yards "might fire at you all day without you finding it out."

Because the smoothbores lacked accuracy, infantrymen armed with them had to form in close order and fire in volleys. No one soldier was expected to hit a particular target, but a tight front of men could deliver a deadly mass of lead. The basic drill manual of the U.S.–Mexican War, Maj. Gen. Winfield Scott's three-volume *Infantry Tactics* (1835), which went through nine editions through 1861 dictated that ranks

Drilling the volunteers. John Frost, *Pictorial History of Mexico and the Mexican War,* 1862

would form just thirteen inches apart and that the soldiers would dress their formation by touching elbows.

Effective volleying required discipline and order. Whether commanding a single company or a field army, an officer formed his units carefully. One veteran boasted of Maj. Gen. Zachary Taylor's deployment for the Battle of Palo Alto on 8 May 1846: "our Army was drawn up with as much care and precision as on a drill ground."

Successful offensives depended on careful formations and orderly attacks. It was usually more important to advance deliberately than rapidly. Attackers were to march with a "direct step" of thirty-eight inches, at a steady "common time" rate of ninety steps per minute. During a charge, officers might speed up the advance to a "quick time" of 110 steps per minute.

Commanders sometimes deployed small numbers of skirmishers, soldiers spread out in loose order in front of the main body of troops. Scott's *Tactics* assumed that one or two companies per regiment would serve as skirmishers, but the ratio used on the battlefields of the U.S.–Mexican War was lower than this. Commanders were reluctant to deploy large numbers of soldiers in loose order, because they became difficult to control.

U.S. officers in Mexico used tactics that featured close-ordered formations, deliberate advances, musketry volleys, and bayonet charges. Lt. Isaac I. Stevens recounted that at Churubusco, on 20 August 1847, "The enemy's intrenched [sic] works were carried at the point of the bayonet." A veteran of the Battle of Resaca de la Palma wrote soon afterward, "We rushed ahead to the very mouths of [the Mexican field] pieces, stormed their entrenchments, and with deafening shouts carried all before us. It was a hand to hand conflict, a fight to the death, we bayoneted their men at the pieces."

The short range of the musket added to the importance of the bayonet, and it also made the artillery a viable offensive weapon. A defending line of infantry had a limited zone of fire and so the field guns sometimes advanced with their own foot soldiers, or even ahead of them. Fighting on either the offensive or defensive, the U.S. Army's light batteries (also known as the "Flying Artillery") capitalized on their splendid mobility. "They move over the ground like lightning," claimed a Massachusetts staff officer, "and with great accuracy too. They are the strongest arm of our service."

The limited range of the musket also gave mounted units some opportunities, however rare, to make saber attacks. At Resaca de la Palma, Capt. Charles A. May of the 2d Dragoons led a column of fours that rode over a Mexican battery and captured a general officer. Some accounts exaggerated the significance of this action, which became the most famous saber charge of the war. Rather than making wild dashes like this one, the dragoons far more often served as couriers, provided reconnaissance, fought as skirmishers, covered the flanks of infantry positions, or stood in reserve.

The U.S. experience in Mexico reinforced the assumption that the offensive was superior to the defensive. On many of the war's battlefields, U.S. troops attacked and carried strongly defended positions, at a fairly low cost in casualties. Close-order musket and bayonet tactics succeeded for them in every major engagement of the conflict. Whether the Mexican defenders protected themselves with fieldworks or not seemed to make little difference. Doubtless an overwhelming majority of U.S. veterans agreed with the admittedly prideful remarks of a 1st Artillery lieutenant about the Battle of Monterrey, 21–23 September 1846, and believed his comments applied to most of the war's large battles. "The enemy," this officer contended, "had the advantage of numbers. . . . They chose their positions[,] and strong ones[,] to fight us, but notwithstanding all their advantages, they were beaten as badly as an army ever was."

Perry D. Jamieson

BIBLIOGRAPHY

Bauer, K. Jack. *The Mexican War 1846–1848.* 1974.

Halleck, Henry W. *Elements of Military Art and Science.* 1846. 3d ed., 1862.

Hattaway, Herman, and Archer Jones. *How the North Won: A Military History of the Civil War.* 1983.

McWhiney, Grady, and Perry D. Jamieson. *Attack and Die: Civil War Military Tactics and the Southern Heritage.* 1982.

Scott, Winfield. *Infantry-Tactics; Or, Rules for the Exercise and Manoeuvres of the United States Infantry.* 1835. 10th ed., 1861.

Smith, Justin H. *The War with Mexico.* 2 vols. 1919. Reprint, 1963.

Tamaulipas

The state of Tamaulipas was the first territory of Mexico to be invaded by U.S. forces. In fact, Gen. Zachary Taylor's 1845 occupation of Corpus Christi at the mouth of the Nueces River, which formed the border between Tamaulipas and Texas, was the act that precipitated the war. The skirmish at Carricitos, U.S. victories at the battles of Palo Alto and Resaca de la Palma, and the U.S. occupation of Matamoros took place in Tamaulipas in May 1846. The U.S. Army then advanced on the towns of Reynosa, Camargo, and Mier, while Laredo was occupied by a Texian force. Taking advantage of the Río Grande's navigability, General Taylor set up a supply center in Camargo for his campaign against Monterrey and promoted free trade in order to finance the campaign. He later advanced on Tampico, but after learning that the port was already occupied by Gen. Winfield Scott, he returned to Monterrey after stopping briefly in Ciudad Victoria, the state capital. The occupation of Tampico in November 1846 by the U.S. Army and Navy met with no resistance because Gen. Anastasio Parrodi evacuated the plaza under orders from Gen. Antonio López de Santa Anna, which provoked a conflict with the governor of the state, Francisco Vital Fernández. During the war guerrillas under the generals Antonio Canales, José Urrea, and José María Carvajal operated in Tamaulipas against U.S. forces. They were unable to drive U.S. forces out, however, and the U.S. Army remained in Matamoros and Tampico until June 1848, when the Treaty of Guadalupe Hidalgo went into effect. Under this treaty, one-third of the territory of Tamaulipas, the area between the Río Grande and the Nueces River, was lost to the United States.

Octavio Herrera

BIBLIOGRAPHY

Zorrilla, Juan Fidel, et al., *Tamaulipas. Una historia compartida 1810–1921.* Vol. I, pp. 162–172. 1993.

Tampico

This entry consists of two separate articles: **City of Tampico** *and* **Battle of 1829**.

City of Tampico

Located on the Río Pánuco near its confluence with the Gulf of Mexico, Tampico was Mexico's second most important Gulf port (only to Vera Cruz) at the outbreak of war with the United States. Even before the United States targeted it for occupation, Tampico had attracted foreign aggressors. In July 1829 Spain had mounted a short-lived reconquest that took the town, only to be driven out months later by Mexican troops under Gen. Antonio López de Santa Anna.

In May 1846 the U.S. Navy blockaded the port. The United States viewed Tampico as a potential starting point for the invasion of central Mexico. Based largely on the false assumption that adequate roads led inland, the idea of using Tampico as the landing site was abandoned in favor of Vera Cruz. Tampico did have considerable commercial value as a convenient port, however. It was only some 250 miles from the Río Grande and it was the principal city of the state of Tamaulipas, an area slated by some for U.S. acquisition.

Tampico was lightly fortified and garrisoned by some twelve hundred regular army troops and National Guardsmen under Gen. Anastasio Parrodi. Aware of U.S. plans to take Tampico, General Santa Anna in October 1846 ordered Parrodi to withdraw.

In November the U.S. Navy Home Squadron under Commo. David Conner took Tampico unopposed, beginning the occupation of the port city. Despite its tropical environment, which plagued U.S. soldiers, Tampico played an important role in the U.S. prosecution of the war and served as a staging area for troops from Gen. Zachary Taylor's command that joined Gen. Winfield Scott's invasion of central Mexico.

David Coffey

BIBLIOGRAPHY

Eisenhower, John S. D. *So Far from God: The U.S. War with Mexico, 1846–1848.* 1989.

Meyer, Michael C., and William L. Sherman. *The Course of Mexican History.* 5th ed. 1995.

Smith, Justin H. *The War with Mexico.* 2 vols. 1919. Reprint, 1963.

Battle of 1829

The Battle of 1829 at Tampico was a failed attempt by Spain to reconquer Mexico. Following Mexican government decrees in 1827 and 1828 expelling Spanish citizens, King Ferdinand VII ordered an invasion of the newly independent republic. Brig. Gen. Isidro Barradas sailed from Havana, Cuba, with 3,556 veteran soldiers on 5 July 1829, but with the loss of one ship, only about three thousand men landed on 27 July at Cabo Rojo, forty miles south of Tampico. The inhabitants of Tampico abandoned the town without destroying it as ordered; nevertheless, yellow fever and other tropical diseases fell upon the invaders even before the Mexicans could organize a resistance.

On 21 August, Gen. Antonio López de Santa Anna led some four thousand men in an attack on Tampico, but the Spanish troops had constructed excellent defenses and repulsed the poorly trained and equipped Mexicans. Skirmishes continued for the next few weeks, until a hurricane struck from 9 to 11 September, destroying much of the town. On 12 September, Barradas surrendered. While the Spanish had lost only 85 killed and 130 wounded, yellow fever had incapacitated 863. In addition, R. Adm. Angel Laborde, who had quarreled with General Barradas during the voyage from Cuba to Mexico, failed to resupply the expedition, questioned the surrender agreement, and refused to evacuate the suffering troops until mid-November. King Ferdinand began planning a second invasion attempt in 1830 but could not carry through because of domestic instability. The battle made Santa Anna a national hero, and the Mexican congress acclaimed him *Benemérito de la Patria* (national hero).

Jeffrey M. Pilcher

BIBLIOGRAPHY

Sánchez Lamego, Miguel A. *La invasión española de 1829*. 1971.

Sims, Harold Dana. *The Expulsion of Mexico's Spaniards, 1821–1836*. 1990.

Tampico Expedition

The Tampico Expedition was one of the many military reactions against the centralist regime of Antonio López de Santa Anna. In October 1835 filibuster George Fisher and exiled Mexican general José Antonio Mexía began raising volunteers and money for an expedition to attack the Mexican port city of Tampico in support of the federalist cause. They planned their expedition in New Orleans, and decided that a march into Tampico would rally liberals in the garrison and precipitate in Mexico's eastern states an insurrection similar to those already under way in Coahuila, Texas, and Zacatecas. Fisher and Mexía communicated their intentions to revolutionaries in Texas who expressed great enthusiasm for the project but did not officially sanction the event or move to support it.

Despite this lack of Texian support, Mexía, Fisher, and 150 U.S. and Mexican adventurers left New Orleans on 6 November 1835 aboard the schooner *Mary Jane,* which ran aground off Tampico on 14 November. After gathering his forces, Mexía discovered that the liberals in the garrison had launched their revolt the day before and had been defeated by Tampico's commander, Col. Gregorio Gomez, with the aid of centralist troops rushed north from Tuxpan. Mexía pushed ahead with his plan anyway and attacked Tampico on 15 November, but failed badly. The adventurers fled to the safety of a waiting ship, leaving behind thirty-one prisoners, most of whom fell before firing squads. Mexía and Fisher disembarked with the survivors at Velasco, Texas, on 3 December, their expedition a total disaster.

As with many Texians, Elisha M. Pease, a young soldier in the Texas Revolution, was quick to put distance between the cause in which he fought and the filibustering adventure of Fisher and Mexía. "Say nothing about the expedition to Tampico," he wrote his father in 1837. "Texians disclaim any connection with that affair, it was gotten up by some citizens of New Orleans, for private purposes only."

Josh Lee Winegarner

BIBLIOGRAPHY

Barker, Eugene C. "The Tampico Expedition." *Texas State Historical Association Quarterly* 6, no. 3 (Jan. 1903):169–186.

Turner, F.H. "The Mejia Expedition." *Texas State Historical Association Quarterly,* 7, no. 1 (July 1903):1–28.

Taos Revolt

The Taos Revolt of 19 January 1847 resulted from New Mexican resistance to U.S. occupation of the territory. Although the U.S. Army of the West met no armed opposition when it invaded New Mexico in August 1846, some residents were discontent with the sudden change of power and the ease with which it had been accomplished. In Santa Fe, capital of the territory, several prominent New Mexicans plotted in December to overthrow U.S. forces there. The leaders were Tomás Ortiz, formerly chief *alcalde* (mayor) of Santa Fe, and Diego Archuleta, who had been second-in-command of Mexican forces under New Mexican governor Manuel Armijo. U.S. territorial governor Charles Bent learned of the plot on 17 December and subsequently ordered the arrest of the conspirators. Ortiz and Archuleta fled south, avoiding capture. Although several arrests were made, some of these individuals were later released for lack of evidence, and the remaining suspects were acquitted before a military court-martial in January 1847. It was generally believed that the movement had been suppressed. Seventy miles to the north of Santa Fe, at Taos, however, animosity toward U.S. rule remained high.

In the early hours of 19 January, an armed mob of Pueblo Indians and Mexicans gathered in Taos and demanded the release of some Pueblo Indians being held in the local jail. When the prefect, Cornelio Vigil, attempted to prevent their release, he was killed; the mob then rampaged through the streets, searching out and killing Anglo-Americans and U.S. sympathizers—the Taos Revolt was born. Among the six victims in Taos was Governor Bent, who had recently arrived in town to see his family.

After their initial strike in Taos, the leaders of the insurgents sent "circulars" to various villages and towns, including Santa Fe, encouraging the inhabitants to join the rebel-

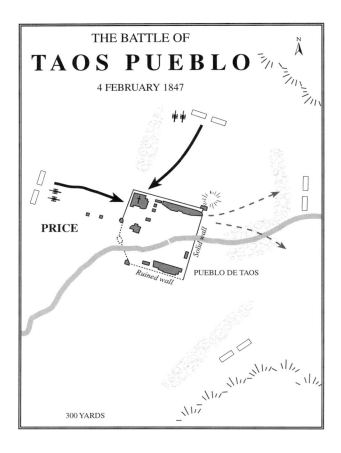

THE BATTLE OF
TAOS PUEBLO
4 FEBRUARY 1847

N

PRICE

Solid wall

Ruined wall

PUEBLO DE TAOS

300 YARDS

had swelled to approximately 1,500, the following day near the village of Santa Cruz de la Cañada. After a brief fight, the insurgents fled their hilltop positions with a loss of 36 killed, including Tafoya. Another fight occurred on 29 January in a narrow canyon on the Taos road near Embudo; again the insurgents were driven in front of Price's army. Four days later Price passed through Taos and found the insurgents fortified within the nearby Taos Indian Pueblo and its church. After an ineffective artillery barrage, Price postponed the attack to the following day. His artillery opened fire at 9 A.M. on 4 February, and two hours later Price ordered his men to storm the church. Under heavy fire, some of his men reached the church's adobe wall, chopped holes in it, and threw several shells in by hand. The six-pounder cannon was then run up and fired several times into the breach in the wall, after which the church was taken. Many of the defenders fled to the interior of the adjacent pueblo while others tried to escape to the mountains; these latter were cut down by St. Vrain's "avengers." The insurgents surrendered the next day, their losses estimated at 150, including Chavez. Price's force suffered 7 killed and 45 wounded. Charged with "rebellious conduct," Montoya was tried by military court-martial, convicted, and hanged on 7 February. Tomasito was murdered by a dragoon while being held for trial. Many more participants in the Taos Revolt were tried in Santa Fe and Taos in March and April on the charges of murder and treason. (The treason charges resulted from Gen. Stephen W. Kearny's premature granting of U.S. citizenship to all New Mexicans.)

On 25 January a detachment of 80 Missouri Volunteers under Capt. Israel R. Hendley had engaged Manuel Cortez and his followers at Mora, but the Volunteers withdrew to Las Vegas after Hendley was killed while storming the fortified village. Capt. Jesse I. Morin led a command of about 200 men and one piece of artillery back to Mora on 1 February. The insurgents abandoned the town in the face of Morin's advance, and Morin's troops burned the village to the ground. Cortez, the only survivor of the leaders of the Taos Revolt, continued to resist U.S. occupation, organizing guerrilla activity in eastern New Mexico and along the Santa Fe Trail until nearly the end of the U.S.–Mexican War.

Mark L. Gardner

lion. On 20 and 21 January, several hundred Mexicans and Indians besieged Simeon Turley's flour mill and distillery at Arroyo Hondo, twelve miles north of Taos, eventually setting fire to the compound and killing seven of its approximately ten defenders. Across the mountains to the east, at the village of Mora, seven Anglo-Americans and one Frenchman were killed on 20 January by a group under Manuel Cortez, a leader in the Taos Revolt who had hurried to Mora with the news of the rebellion.

Led by Pablo Chavez, Pablo Montoya (who called himself the "Santa Anna of the north"), Jesús Tafoya, and Tomasito (a Pueblo Indian), the Taos insurgents headed south to liberate Santa Fe. Col. Sterling Price, commander of U.S. forces in New Mexico, learned of the revolt on 20 January and immediately called in his outlying commands for a campaign against the insurgents. Ceran St. Vrain, a business partner of Governor Bent, quickly raised a volunteer company, nicknamed the "avengers," composed of laborers, merchants, and mountain men then in Santa Fe. Price moved out of the capital on 23 January with 353 men (which included St. Vrain's volunteers) and four mountain howitzers; he added two companies and a six-pounder cannon while on the march. Price first encountered the insurgents, whose ranks

BIBLIOGRAPHY

Cheetham, Francis T. "The First Term of the American Court in Taos, New Mexico." *New Mexico Historical Review* 1 (1926): 23–41.

Cutts, James M. *The Conquest of California and New Mexico.* 1847.

Gardner, Mark L., and Marc Simmons, eds. *The Mexican War Correspondence of Richard Smith Elliott.* 1997.

Goodrich, James W. "Revolt at Mora, 1847." *New Mexico Historical Review* 47 (1972): 49–60.

McNierney, Michael, ed. *Taos 1847: The Revolt in Contemporary Accounts.* 1980.

Sunseri, Alvin R. "Revolt in Taos, 1846–47: Resistance to U.S. Occupation." *El Palacio* (Fall 1990): 40–47.

U.S. Congress. Senate. *Insurrection Against the Military Government in New Mexico and California, 1847 and 1848.* 56th Cong., 1st sess., 1900. S. Doc. 442.

Taylor, Zachary

In early 1845 Gen. Zachary Taylor (1784–1850) was an aging career army officer who simply looked forward to retiring and settling down to become a prosperous southern planter. His actions during the U.S.–Mexican War, however, made him famous beyond expectations. Exercising personal traits of aggressiveness and dogged persistence, along with a remarkable ability to inspire confidence in his soldiers, he forged a series of battlefield victories and emerged from the war a national hero, lauded by the U.S. public as a natural contender for the White House. No other president except for two military heroes—Ulysses S. Grant and Dwight D. Eisenhower—sprang from such obscurity as did Taylor.

Born in Orange County, Virginia, 24 November 1784, the son of Richard and Sarah Dabney (Strother) Taylor, Zachary

Zachary Taylor. This poster-size engraving (1847), depicting Taylor as a hero of the U.S.–Mexican War, was probably designed with the 1848 presidential campaign in mind (Library of Congress).

Taylor had a respectable family background. As an infant he moved with his parents to the western frontier near Louisville, Kentucky. Receiving only a rudimentary education, he secured a first lieutenant's commission in the U.S. Army in 1808 and rose to captain two years later. In 1810 he married Margaret Mackall Smith; they had six children, including an only son, Richard, a future Confederate general. Recognized for effective fighting in Indiana Territory during the War of 1812, Taylor received a major's brevet. After service in the Black Hawk War in 1832 he saw combat command in Florida during the Seminole War (1837–1840) and was brevetted brigadier general. Taylor's frontier-style crustiness and bold leadership prompted his troops to nickname him "Old Rough and Ready."

Taylor was sixty years old in mid-1845 when he reluctantly accepted orders to serve as one of the U.S. commanders who would see action during the U.S.–Mexican War. As evidence of President James K. Polk's determination to defend the disputed southern portion of the recently annexed state of Texas, Taylor's Army of Occupation, comprising only about 3,500 men, encamped at Corpus Christi, Texas. In March 1846 Taylor received orders to move to the banks of the lower Río Grande, where he established Fort Texas (later renamed Fort Brown) opposite Matamoros, Mexico. Mexican officials viewed this as a deliberate invasion of their country's territory. In May a force of Mexicans under Gen. Mariano Arista attacked a small patrol of Taylor's dragoons under Capt. Seth B. Thornton, an incident President James K. Polk used to call for a declaration of war.

With Fort Texas under siege, on 1 May Taylor made a hurried foray to the U.S. arsenal at Point Isabel for cannon and supplies. In Taylor's absence General Arista began a bombardment of the fort and moved his army to intercept the outnumbered U.S. force and cut off their return. The two forces met on 8 May at Palo Alto, in the first major engagement of the U.S.–Mexican War, with Taylor using his artillery effectively against Arista's troops. The next day, at Resaca de la Palma, Taylor's infantry and cavalry forced the Mexicans to retreat across the Río Grande. Lieutenant Meade described Taylor after two days of fighting: "When the victory was ours beyond a doubt [General Taylor] said to me, 'Suppose I had taken the advice of those who did not wish me to advance. . . . Had I been opposed to British or French troops, I should have hesitated, but knowing as I do the Mexican character, I was confident they could not bring an army to defeat the gallant little band I command." Nearly as important as achieving two quick victories, Taylor's personal conduct galvanized his inexperienced soldiers to assert courage of their own. Meade wrote, "During the action of Resaca . . . [Taylor urged,] 'Let us go nearer' and immediately rode to the very front of the battle," Meade recalled. "This was not foolhardiness . . . but a studied act, the object being in his own person to impress on others the necessity on such an occasion of disregarding their personal safety." When news of Taylor's decisive triumphs reached a U.S. public tired of political stalemate and hungry for military success, he became an instant hero.

Receiving promotion to major general, Taylor quickly crossed the Río Grande and pushed his small army, now more than six thousand men, into northern Mexico toward Monterrey. Meade observed, "He was capable of enduring great physical fatigue, and was in the habit on the march of riding a very fast walking brown horse which kept all his staff in a trot, and at night the General would dismount fresh and unfatigued, when all around were broken down."

Although slowed somewhat by logistical problems, Taylor approached Monterrey and laid seige on 21 to 23 September. Although he succeeded in battering Mexican general Pedro de Ampudia's defenders, Taylor faced mounting casualties and dwindling supplies. Believing that President Polk meant to persuade the Mexican government to negotiate terms of surrender at that time, Taylor agreed to a temporary armistice that allowed Ampudia's forces to evacuate the town. Despite Polk's outrage at Taylor's unauthorized leniency, the U.S. public viewed Monterrey as another victory. "General Taylor's motives . . . were most honorable," asserted Lieutenant Meade. "He knew perfectly well, as did the whole army, that the Mexicans were in our power. . . . [General Taylor meant] to open the door to negotiations for peace . . . to stop the effusion of blood not only of soldiers, but of women and children, of the old and infirm." Yet some of Taylor's men doubted such wisdom, one soldier remarking, "The Treaty made at Monterrey is enough to disgust any true American."

Convinced that northern Mexico no longer offered strategic advantages and determined to reduce—for political reasons—the headstrong Taylor's growing popularity among the U.S. public, President Polk authorized Gen. Winfield Scott to take most of Taylor's best forces, including nearly all of his regular army soldiers. These men Scott added to his main expeditionary army, captured Vera Cruz on the Gulf of Mexico, and began marching overland to Mexico City. As a result, Taylor's simmering ire toward Polk and his resentment of Scott intensified. "Taylor had taken a violent dislike to Scott," noted Col. Ethan Allen Hitchcock. "He disliked most of our men in power."

When Gen. Antonio López de Santa Anna, Mexico's supreme commander, learned of Taylor's sudden vulnerability he saw an opportunity to drive the invaders back to the Río Grande, and immediately advanced with an army of about twenty thousand men against Taylor, who now fielded probably no more than five thousand, many of whom were volunteers who had never seen hard fighting. Moving aggressively Taylor had already shifted the bulk of his troops, under Gen. John E. Wool, several miles south of Saltillo to a mountain plain called Buena Vista, though Taylor re-

mained in Saltillo to guard U.S. supplies. In brutal combat on 22 and 23 February 1847 U.S. forces repulsed Mexican assaults. Lieutenant Meade recalled, "On the field of Buena Vista, which General Taylor did not reach on the 23rd until 10 o'clock [in the morning] . . . the day was considered lost by General John Ellis Wool and many more. Yet the moment General Taylor appeared, the cry resounded 'Old Zack has come' and instantly the spirits of all revived, and a reinforcement of 5,000 men could not have had the moral effect produced by the arrival of this single old man." After Buena Vista, the war in northern Mexico was essentially over. Taylor left Mexico in November 1847, hugely popular with the U.S. public, but at odds with Polk and Scott.

Taylor's victories in Mexico set off a popular clamor during 1848 for his nomination to the presidency. A man of simple habits and plain appearance, Taylor reluctantly agreed, declaring a preference for the Whig Party's nomination. Many political leaders expressed doubts about his worthiness for high office, especially when he admitted to never having even voted in a major election. According to Lieutenant Meade, however, "General Taylor was a social man, very fond of conversing. . . . His education was by no means deficient. . . . He was especially well versed in our early political history and was a hard student of the current politics of the day." Taylor had long viewed George Washington as a model of a soldier-statesman with convictions of conservatism and nationalism.

Largely because of Taylor's relatively brief presidency, and especially because of his political stubbornness, historians have minimized the importance of his actions in the White House. Despite his status as a wealthy slaveholder, Taylor shunned the Whig Party's moderate leadership and adhered to its growing antislavery faction. Although he affirmed slavery's inviolability as it existed in the South, he staunchly opposed the expansion of slavery into the vast western territories acquired from Mexico. Thus, he spearheaded the federal government's resistance to Texas's long-standing claims to the eastern half of New Mexico Territory. Rejecting demands in Congress for a compromise that would allow popular sovereignty to dictate slavery's future in the territories (with only California admitted as a free state), Taylor vowed, if necessary, to command an army to crush a threatened armed invasion of New Mexico by empire-seeking Texans.

After four decades of rigorous military service, Taylor tired under the increasing pressures of the presidency. At a 4th of July ceremony celebrating the construction of the Washington Monument, Taylor endured the hot weather by consuming quantities of cold water, followed by cherries and iced milk. Stricken with probable acute gastroenteritis and a high fever and given possibly harmful medical treatment, he died 9 July 1850. (Taylor's body was exhumed in 1991 to answer historians' suspicions he may have suffered arsenic poisoning; no arsenic was found.) Taylor's death removed a major obstacle to Congress's adopting the Compromise of 1850, legislation that defined the borders of Texas and temporarily settled the status of slavery in the West.

Although Zachary Taylor did not have Winfield Scott's mastery of strategy and tactics, as a battlefield commander he radiated a sense of confidence, exerted a defiant determination, and displayed an ability to lead men in combat. Springing from Taylor's character and temperament, his example of aggressive command leadership made deep and lasting impressions on dozens of young officers, especially future Civil War leaders such as Jefferson Davis, Thomas J. Jackson, and Ulysses S. Grant.

T. Michael Parrish

BIBLIOGRAPHY

Bauer, K. Jack. *Zachary Taylor; Soldier, Planter, Statesman of the Old Southwest.* 1985.

Dyer, Brainerd. *Zachary Taylor.* 1946.

Hamilton, Holman. *Zachary Taylor: Soldier of the Republic.* 1941.

Hamilton, Holman. *Zachary Taylor: Soldier in the White House.* 1951.

Lavender, David. *Climax at Buena Vista: The American Campaigns in Northeastern Mexico, 1846–47.* 1966.

Meade, George Gordon. Manuscript on Zachary Taylor during the Mexican War. Historical Society of Pennsylvania, Philadelphia, Pennsylvania.

Stegmaier, Mark J. *Texas, New Mexico, and the Compromise of 1850.* 1996.

Taylor's Armistice

Maj. Gen. Zachary Taylor's armistice, negotiated at Monterrey, Mexico, on 24 September 1846, was one of the most controversial events of the U.S.–Mexican War and a major turning point in Taylor's military career. On 21 September Taylor had laid siege to Monterrey, a strategically important town in northern Mexico. Well fortified and reputedly impregnable, Monterrey was defended by a force commanded by Gen. Pedro de Ampudia. Ineffective artillery barrages, haphazard infantry assaults, and vicious house-to-house street fighting left Taylor's troops badly mauled and nearly stymied, although they had forced the Mexicans to retreat behind barricades at the town's center.

By continuing the siege Taylor might have achieved outright victory, but his small army of 6,220 effectives had suffered 120 men killed, 368 wounded, and 43 missing (about 8.5 percent casualties) and was running low on ammunition with no immediate prospect for being resupplied. Taylor also wanted to avoid inflicting needless harm on Monterrey's civilians. Moreover, he was operating under the conviction that a conciliatory gesture toward the Mexicans would enhance the prospect of a negotiated peace settlement by U.S. officials, who were anxious to suspend hostilities and put an end to the war.

Having suffered enough himself—Ampudia had lost around 400 men, about 5 percent of his 7,303 troops—Taylor's antagonist reassured Taylor that diplomatic peace efforts would benefit from an armistice. Early on 24 September negotiations were initiated between U.S. and Mexican officers. The Mexicans agreed to evacuate the town within one week, and in return were allowed to keep their personal arms and a battery of field artillery. All other weapons and supplies were left behind. Taylor agreed to abide by the armistice for eight weeks or until either the U.S. or Mexican government nullified it. "These terms are liberal," Taylor wrote privately, "but not considered too much so by all reflecting men . . . considering our situation; besides it was thought it would be judicious to act with magnanimity toward a prostrate foe . . . as their [sic] was a genl [sic] wish for peace on the part of the [Mexican] nation."

Because of pervasive delays in communications, however, Taylor had not yet received word of the change in U.S. policy, that U.S. officials had decided to press for military victory rather than continue to seek a diplomatic solution to the war. President James K. Polk was outraged at the news of Taylor's armistice. Polk canceled the armistice but dared not relieve or even censure Taylor publicly. In the eyes of an adoring U.S. public, which considered the fall of Monterrey a wonderful victory, Taylor had become more of a hero, so that the Democrat Polk rightly feared and resented him as a prospective Whig candidate for the 1848 presidential race. In this atmosphere of mutual mistrust and animosity, Taylor's victory at Buena Vista in February 1847—a battle that resulted from his disregard for Polk's orders—redoubled Taylor's stature as a popular hero and a contender for the presidency.

T. Michael Parrish

BIBLIOGRAPHY

Bauer, K. Jack. *The Mexican War, 1846–1848.* 1974.

Bauer, K. Jack. *Zachary Taylor: Soldier, Planter, Statesman of the Old Southwest.* 1985.

Dyer, Brainerd. *Zachary Taylor.* 1946.

Hamilton, Holman. *Zachary Taylor: Soldier of the Republic.* 1941.

Smith, Justin H. *The War with Mexico.* 2 vols. 1919. Reprint, 1963.

Tejada, Miguel Lerdo de

See **Lerdo de Tejada, Miguel**

Tejanos

Tejanos were the native Mexicans of Texas—the residents and government officials—when the first U.S. settlers entered Texas with Stephen F. Austin after 1821. In the twentieth century their descendants would be called Mexican Americans. Tejanos played a supportive role in sponsoring Austin's colonists under the colonization program and many supported and served in the Texas Revolution against Gen. Antonio López de Santa Anna's Mexican army in 1836 as well. After the revolution, however, as newcomers from the United States arrived with strongly anti-Mexican attitudes, most of the Tejanos became disaffected from the Texas government. Tejano communities such as Nacogdoches, La Bahía (present-day Goliad), and Victoria were almost depopulated of Tejanos who fled the disorder and indiscriminate violence against Tejanos and Mexicans in Texas that occurred after the Battle of San Jacinto.

By the time of the U.S.–Mexican War, Tejanos had for their own safety gone into self-imposed exile in Louisiana or Mexico or had retreated into isolated Tejano enclaves, avoiding direct conflict with the immigrants from the United States. One such enclave was San Antonio, which remained the only sizable population of Tejanos by 1845. Tejanos there were isolated economically and politically from the rest of Texas.

Approximately eight thousand Mexicans lived in the region south of the Nueces River and north of the Río Grande, called the Seno Mexicano, but this was the disputed area that the United States claimed and that Mexico had never conceded. The Mexican government maintained its claim to Texas by refusing to recognize Santa Anna's concession after his defeat in the 1836 battle of San Jacinto. The United States held the advantage of possession of Texas. But Mexico adamantly claimed that the region south of the Nueces River had never been a part of Texas, even before the Texas Revolution.

When Gen. Zachary Taylor moved into Corpus Christi to prepare for war, the twenty or so Mexican families of Corpus Christi had little choice but to tolerate the huge military presence. Military journals indicate that the U.S. troops bought food and spirits from these Mexicans. The troops abused their welcome to the point that General Taylor placed restrictions on their visits into the Mexican community. The army quartermaster reportedly purchased cattle, food, and horses from these and other Mexicans on the nearby ranches. The citizens of Laredo and the Mexican towns along the Río Grande also provided beef, chickens, eggs, and horses to the U.S. Army, and reluctantly accepted the occupiers as their government by force.

Apparently no Tejanos or Mexicans joined Taylor's ranks. The rosters of Taylor's army, Capt. Mirabeau B. Lamar's troops, and the Texas Rangers reveal not a single Mexican name. Indeed, it is more likely that the ranchers of Camargo, Laredo, Mier, and Reynosa joined ranks as volunteers with the Mexican army. Gen. Antonio Canales, a civic and military leader of Camargo, for example, regularly recruited his *ranchero* cavalry from the ranches north of the Río Grande. Military journals from the U.S. and Mexican armies reveal that Canales's *rancheros* performed daring feats in the service of the Mexican army. In one case, Canales's *rancheros* lariated a mounted Texas Ranger, choking him to death as they pulled him from his horse. Canales's cavalry squadrons and the volunteer cavalry squadrons of Camargo, Mier, and Reynosa served as independent light cavalry units, harassing Taylor's supply convoys along the Río Grande in guerrilla tactics. These were most likely the residents of the ranching communities north of the Río Grande, who after 1848 would be labeled as Tejanos.

Andrés Tijerina

BIBLIOGRAPHY

Covian Martinez, Vidal Efrén. *Compendio de historia de Tamaulipas.* 4 vols. 1973.

Henry, W. S. *Campaign Sketches of the War with Mexico.* 1847.

Lamar, Mirabeau B. *The Papers of Mirabeau Buonaparte Lamar.* 6 vols. 1921–1927.

McClintock, William A. "Journal of a Trip through Texas and Northern Mexico in 1846–1847." *Southwestern Historical Quarterly* 34 (1930–1931): 20–37, 141–158, 231–256.

Montemayor, Francisco J. *Sabinas Hidalgo en la tradición, leyenda, historia.* 1948.

Roa Barcena, José María. *Recuerdos de la invasion norteamericana (1846–1848).* 2 vols. 1947.

Téllez, Rafael

In the spring of 1846, the Mexican government dispatched Col. Rafael Téllez (1???–1???) to the port of Mazatlán, in the state of Sinaloa, reportedly to lead a military expedition into Alta California to protect the province from U.S. forces. Documents in Téllez's possession, however, indicated that then-president Gen. Mariano Paredes y Arrillaga only wanted to appease Mexican public opinion and did not intend the expedition to sail.

Téllez arrived in Mazatlán in April. One month later, he took over as military commander general and led a rebellion calling for the restoration of federalism and the return of Gen. Antonio López de Santa Anna (then in exile in Cuba). Téllez did not embark for California even after the triumph of the August 1846 rebellion of the Ciudadela (whose goals were similar to the ones of the May rebellion in Mazatlán). The expedition was cancelled in September because the new government did not provide Téllez with the necessary reinforcements.

Téllez, who had been replaced as Sinaloa's military commander general in December, illegally assumed the post following an early January 1847 rebellion that sought to establish a Santa Anna dictatorship. After defeating the forces of the legitimate military commander general on 15 September, Téllez and his followers took over Mazatlán. The disarray in Sinaloa that resulted from these and other developments made it easy for U.S. forces to occupy Mazatlán that November. After being advised by U.S. commodore W. Branford Shubrick to surrender, Téllez evacuated the city and withdrew to Palos Prietos.

The U.S. occupation of Mazatlán, which lasted until the end of the war, also cut off Téllez from his financial resources. He surrendered to Mexican government forces in late January 1848.

Pedro Santoni

BIBLIOGRAPHY

Alcaraz, Ramón, ed. *The Other Side; or, Notes for the History of the War between Mexico and the United States.* Translated by Albert C. Ramsey. 1970. Originally published as *Apuntes para la historia de la Guerra entre México y los Estado Unidos,* 1848.

Smith, Justin H. *The War with Mexico.* 2 vols. 1919. Reprint, 1963.

Temple, Henry John

British foreign secretary Henry John Temple, Lord Palmerston (1784–1865), was born 20 October in London. He was educated at Harrow, Edinburgh, and Cambridge. Palmerston promoted a balance of power in Europe along with advancing Great Britain's interests abroad. His deepest concern was to protect the rights of British citizens everywhere. Palmerston's parliamentary obligations lasted fifty-eight years, including two terms as prime minister.

Palmerston succeeded Lord Aberdeen (George Hamilton-Gordon) in the foreign office immediately after the U.S.–Mexican War began. He advanced Aberdeen's policies, including nonintervention and general accommodation, toward the United States as long as British interests were not threatened.

Palmerston dealt directly with issues initiated by Mexico. When asked by France and Mexico to negotiate an alliance treaty between them, Palmerston responded negatively, noting that with the issue of the Oregon Territory just settled, there was no need to antagonize the United States. He also refused Antonio López de Santa Anna's offer in 1846 to cede California to Great Britain, and instead urged the Mexican government to settle as soon as possible with the United States.

While Palmerston's attitude toward the United States was politically conciliatory, he thought U.S. citizens were socially inept and he disapproved of slavery. He also held President James K. Polk in low regard.

Palmerston's attention during the U.S.–Mexican War was focused primarily on the European continent, especially France. By the end of the war, his concentration was fully on Europe as the Revolution of 1848 loomed. His main efforts toward North America by this time were somewhat limited to protecting the lives and properties of British citizens caught up in the war.

Palmerston continued to have a prominent political career. He served as prime minister from 1855 to 1865 (except during a short time in 1858 and 1859). Palmerston died 18 October 1865, shortly after his reelection as prime minister.

Tracy M. Shilcutt

BIBLIOGRAPHY

Bourne, Kenneth. *Palmerston.* 1982.

Pletcher, David M. *The Diplomacy of Annexation: Texas, Oregon and the Mexican War.* 1973.

Ten Regiment Bill

In December 1846, President James K. Polk's administration recognized the need for additional troops and requested that Congress create ten new regiments of regulars. The bill passed the House on 11 January 1847, but was delayed in the Senate by partisan wrangling for another month. Polk signed the Ten Regiment Bill into law on 11 February 1847.

The bill authorized the creation of the 9th, 10th, 11th, 12th, 13th, 14th, 15th and 16th U.S. Infantry Regiments, the 3d U.S. Dragoons, and the Regiment of Voltigeurs and Foot Riflemen. Because these units were intended only for the U.S.–Mexican War, most regular officers refrained from transferring to them because they feared they would lose their commissions when the regiments were discharged at the war's end. Thus, the officers of the new regiments were mainly Democratic appointees. The War Department levied quotas on states for their share of recruits for the new regiments, and land warrants were offered to induce recruitment. Rushed to the front piecemeal, some of the new regiments saw action in the battles for Mexico City. These troops performed garrison duty in Mexico until disbanded in the summer of 1848.

The creation of these regiments, designated the New Establishment, sparked new legislation regarding their organization. A bill signed into law on 3 March 1847 specified that the regiments be organized into divisions and brigades. The bill also gave Congress the authority to appoint new generals to command the additional troops.

Franklin Pierce, George Cadwalader, Enos D. Hopping, Caleb Cushing, and Sterling Price were brought into the service as brigadier generals, and two current brigadier generals of volunteers, John A. Quitman and Gideon J. Pillow, were promoted to the higher rank of major general.

Richard Bruce Winders

BIBLIOGRAPHY

Callan, John F. *The Military Laws of the United States. Relating to the Army, Volunteers, Militia, and to Bounty Lands and Pensions. From the Foundation of the Government to the Year 1863.* 1863.

Smith, Justin H. *The War with Mexico.* 2 vols. 1919. Reprint, 1963.

Terán, Manuel de Mier y

See **Mier y Terán, Manuel de**

Terrés, Andrés

A native of Barcelona, Spain, Andrés Terrés (1777–1850) was a career army officer who fought in the Iberian Peninsula against Napoléon Bonaparte from 1808 to 1814. He supported the royalist cause during Mexico's War of Independence, and in 1823 turned away from Agustín de Iturbide and adhered to the Plan of Casa Mata. Terrés was promoted to general in 1842 and he commanded the Mexican troops at the Garita Belén (Belén Gate) when the U.S. Army launched its final assault on Mexico City.

After Chapultepec Castle fell to U.S. forces on the morning of 13 September 1847, Gen. Antonio López de Santa Anna prepared to defend the Belén Gate. To support the two hundred men and three four-pounders under Terrés, Santa Anna brought up four artillery pieces and posted additional infantry detachments in support of the guns. Before leaving for the San Cosme Gate, however, Santa Anna failed to place these troops under Terrés's orders, an omission that later proved costly.

As U.S. troops gained ground along the causeway, the defenders of the Belén Gate came under heavy infantry and artillery fire. The garrison was further demoralized when part of the Mexican infantry, which Terrés considered his reserve, withdrew unexpectedly. In addition, Terrés's cannon ammunition had failed, so he decided at about one o'clock to abandon the position. Terrés took the artillery with him and sought refuge inside the Ciudadela.

Santa Anna was irate on learning of the loss of the Belén Gate. He met Terrés at the Ciudadela, struck him across the face with his horsewhip, and placed him under arrest. For the remainder of the afternoon Santa Anna led an assortment of troops in a vain effort to dislodge the U.S. forces from the Belén Gate.

By May 1849 a council of war had absolved Terrés of all guilt. Santa Anna subsequently also made amends during his last presidential term. He issued a decree in May 1853 restoring Terrés's rank and providing a pension for his wife and daughters.

Pedro Santoni

BIBLIOGRAPHY

Rives, George. *The United States and Mexico, 1821–1848.* 2 vols. Reprint, 1969.

Roa Bárcena, José María. *Recuerdos de la invasión norteamericana (1846–1848).* 3 vols. 1947.

Smith, Justin. *The War with Mexico.* 2 vols. 1919. Reprint, 1963.

Territories

This entry consists of two separate articles: **Mexican Territories** *and* **U.S. Territories**.

Mexican Territories

Mexico's inability to establish permanent central control over its territories was a critical factor in the war with the United States. Mexico exercised less supervision over its states and territories than had Spain, which had improved its command over the borderlands during the eighteenth century. After Mexican independence in 1821, federalism appealed to regions along the northern and southern periphery out of a desire for free trade and self-rule. Frontier states and territories had been accustomed to receiving assistance in fighting Indians, which was not forthcoming from the central government after independence. The absence of economic integration and decent roads as well as the neglect of colonization projects led to an eventual lapse of allegiance to the national government. The loss of Texas in 1836 was a resounding blow to Mexico City. The question as to when Texas would be annexed to the United States in part determined the outbreak of hostilities between Mexico and the United States. California enjoyed a tranquil autonomy while New Mexico became sullen and divided. Merchants in northern and coastal regions profited from free trade rather than the protectionism demanded by Mexico City. Smuggling made Monterrey and Pacific ports into lucrative commercial areas. In Yucatán, the elites revolted and sought outright independence from Mexico. Constant revolts in the north and southeast would divert scarce funds, resources, and manpower from the effort to prepare for war against the U.S. invaders. This discord also meant that states and territories along the periphery would not provide resources to the central government for the war effort.

In California, the key event was secularization of the missions in 1834. This created a large class of California rancher-farmers eager to trade hides and tallow and led to a class structure less rigid than that in Mexico. *Rancho* life and strong family values dominated California society. Increasingly close commercial ties to U.S. ports meant that U.S. settlers were not forced to accept the Catholic religion or to pay taxes. California found that its trade depended on the sea rather than on overland trade with New Mexico or through Sonora. The only alternative was trade with U.S. and British merchants.

New Mexicans, on the other hand, were predominantly of Spanish ancestry rather than Mexican and carried on active overland trade with U.S. merchants in St. Louis. The growing Santa Fe trade and presence of U.S. merchants allowed many New Mexico elites to prosper and favor closer U.S. relations. New Mexico governor Albino Pérez attempted to enforce the rigid central control favored by Antonio López de Santa Anna. His moral and financial excesses, combined with his imposition of the tenets of the centralist Constitution of 1836, led to a revolt in August 1837 in which Pérez and sixteen other officials were killed. Most *Nuevo Mexicanos* desired municipal control or village control in the indigenous tradition.

Yucatán resisted centralist control more intensively than other regions in Mexico. Santa Anna's dictatorship angered the white Yucatecan elite because the national government's authoritarianism infringed on their ability to usurp land and water rights to produce sugar and henequen and to prosper from free trade. Higher tariffs, the stationing of federal troops, and local conscription provoked a successful revolt by 1839.

Yucatán soon broke away from Mexico. In 1841, the Yucatecan legislature created an ultra-federalist constitution. When Santa Anna closed Yucatecan trade with Mexican ports, the Yucatecans hired a fleet of warships from the Texas navy. This step later resulted in harmonious ties with the U.S. Navy during the U.S.-Mexican War. Meanwhile, the governor declared the "sovereign nation" of Yucatán. In December 1843 a compromise—the *convenios* agreement—was agreed to in Mexico City whereby Yucatán was allowed some autonomy. The Mexican government violated the deal by decreeing that major Yucatecan products could not be exported duty free, and Yucatán declared its independence two weeks after the national congress formally repudiated the *convenios* in December 1845.

A month later Campeche revolted successfully against the state legislature in Mérida in order to protects its merchant fleets from U.S. naval forces. Backed by Maya supporters, Campeche leaders took over Yucatán in January 1847 and did not resist the U.S. occupation of the ports of Laguna and Carmen. But the outbreak of a Maya revolt resulted in the wholesale slaughter of several hundred thousand inhabitants of Yucatán, which led the governor of Yucatán to offer its sovereignty to the United States. Elsewhere in the southeast, the states of Chiapas and Tabasco considered union with Guatemala.

Douglas W. Richmond

BIBLIOGRAPHY

Richmond, Douglas W. "Yucatán's Struggle for Sovereignty during the Mexican–U.S. Conflict, 1836–1848." *La ciudad y el campo en la historia de México,* edited by Richard Sánchez, Eric Van Young, and Gisela Von Wobeser, pp. 173–183. 1992.

Weber, David. *The Mexican Frontier, 1821–1846: The American Southwest under Mexico.* 1982.

See also **California; New Mexico; Texas;** *and* **Yucatecan Revolt**

U.S. Territories

The United States originally consisted simply of thirteen autonomous states. Trans-Appalachian cessions by various of these produced the first territories, or public domain, which became the U.S. government's greatest financial asset and means to expanding power. Louisiana Territory (1803), the Floridas (1819), and Oregon Territory (1846) followed as major acquisitions through purchase or negotiation. Texas was annexed directly as a state (1845). Now the desire for Mexican lands plunged the United States into war and internal conflict.

The U.S. Constitution provided no mechanism for administering territories, merely empowering Congress "to dispose of and make all needful Rules and Regulations" for them, and to admit new states. However, the Northwest Ordinance of 1787 placed territories into temporary colonial status and required basic features such as religious freedom and common law. Congress appointed territorial governors, secretaries, and judges, all under federal control. Territories reaching five thousand free male inhabitants could form legislatures. Eventually a population of sixty thousand and a republican constitution qualified a territory for statehood equal to all other states. Significantly, the ordinance prohibited slavery north of the Ohio River.

On land policy, the Ordinance of 1785 directed that territories be surveyed, divided into six-mile-square townships, and sold in 640-acre lots. Subsequent reductions in minimum lot size, even to eighty acres, encouraged individual settlers yet failed to stem large-scale speculation. The Preemption Act of 1841 accommodated settlement realities by allowing squatters pre-survey claims and first purchase at the lowest price. Territorial policy thus both followed and fostered rapid expansion.

Manifest Destiny expansionism found force in President James K. Polk, whose rebuffed attempts to purchase New Mexico and his major objective, California, moved him to use war as a means to territorial ends. Frustrated by Mexico's persistent wartime intransigence over cessions. Polk finally achieved his goal in 1848 with the Treaty of Guadalupe Hidalgo, gaining Mexican recognition of the Río Grande border and adding 529,000 square miles and the important California ports to U.S. territory.

The war with Mexico also glaringly reopened the quarrel over slavery in the territories, intensifying sectionalism and threatening party disintegration. The 36°30' line established by the 1820 Missouri Compromise to separate slave from free territory within the Louisiana Purchase was obsolete. With "Mr. Polk's War" underway, the Wilmot Proviso sought to prohibit slavery in any lands won from Mexico while John C. Calhoun's resolutions claimed that Congress had no right to exclude slavery in any U.S. territories. The sharp debate continued with the new territorial acquisition and reached fever pitch in 1849 when gold-rush California applied for free-soil statehood. The resulting Compromise of 1850 included the Texas and New Mexico Act under which the federal government purchased Texas' northwestern claim and organized it with New Mexico Territory, and the Utah Act which organized Utah Territory. In 1853 the Gadsden Purchase, peacefully acquired from Mexico, filled out the Pacific Southwest and the contiguous United States. The matter of territorial slavery, however, remained divisive and volatile in U.S. politics until the explosion of the Civil War.

David Alan Greer

BIBLIOGRAPHY

Dick, Everett. *The Lure of the Land: A Social History of the Public Lands from the Articles of Confederation to the New Deal.* 1970.

Feller, Daniel. *The Public Lands in Jacksonian America.* 1984.

Pletcher, David. M. *The Diplomacy of Annexation: Texas, Oregon, and the Mexican War.* 1973.

Van Deusen, G.G. *The Jacksonian Era, 1828–1848.* 1959.

See also **Expansionism and Imperialism; Manifest Destiny;** *and* **Slavery**

Texas

This entry consists of four separate articles: **Overview; Nationalism in Texas; Conflicts with Mexico, 1836–1845;** *and* **Annexation of Texas.**

See also **Tejanos; Texas Declaration of Independence; Texas Revolts of 1832;** *and* **Texas Revolution.**

Overview

Texas was the geographical, political, and cultural setting from which the U.S.–Mexican War emerged. Anglo-Americans made up the majority of the population in Texas by the 1820s. Disputes between Mexico and Texas, a state in union with Coahuila under the Mexican constitution of 1824, led eventually to the Texas Revolution in 1835 and 1836. During this conflict Texas received aid and soldiers from the United States; Mexican officials believed, with justification, that without this U.S. assistance to Texas, Mexico would have prevailed in the war. The independent Republic of Texas from its inception sought annexation by the United States, posing a serious international relations issue. Whether in the form of full-scale military operations, incursions, skirmishes, retaliatory raids, or rumor of war, belligerence characterized relations in the disputed Texas-Mexico borderlands. Events in Texas initiated many tensions between the United States and Mexico and repeatedly pitted current and former citizens of the two countries against one another.

Following independence in 1821, Mexico adopted liberal land policies designed to populate its sparsely inhabited northeastern frontier. This approach was intended both to stimulate prosperity and to fill a space toward which adventurers from the United States had already begun to gravitate. In a decade and a half the population of Texas increased tenfold, with nearly 75 percent being Anglo-Americans and at least another 10 percent being their black "servants," held in de facto bondage in contravention of at least the spirit of Mexican national law. Mexican leaders, especially the ardent nationalists, began implementing means to restrict Anglo-American immigration in the 1830s and thereby brought on protest and efforts to retain the looser traditions of federalism. Many leaders in Texas also advocated separate statehood in a manner that aroused more suspicions by the Mexican central government. A cycle of conflict and struggle had ensued by 1832, with Mexico seeking or taking action to govern Texas more firmly, which led to protest and some armed resistance; these in turn created alarm at the prospects of rebellion and Mexican determination to prevail by force if necessary.

In 1835 war put an end to this cycle. Although the official Texas purpose in taking up arms was to maintain rights within the republic under the now defunct Constitution of 1824, all pretense ended in March 1836, when a convention of Texians declared independence. On 21 April a victory at the Battle of San Jacinto saved Texas from what appeared to be certain defeat following losses in San Antonio at the Alamo and at several sites near the coast around Goliad. The subsequent retreat of the Mexican army in conformance with instructions by captured President Antonio López de Santa Anna brought a respite from war to the newly declared nation.

Nationhood posed numerous challenges for the meager resources of the Republic of Texas. The government gained recognition by other nations and maintained the support of most of its inhabitants. At the same time, however, it continually struggled with problems of debt and defense, causing a majority to favor annexation by the United States from the outset.

Sam Houston easily won election as the first president and

took over from the interim chief executive, the unpopular David G. Burnet, in October 1836. Houston set out to build a consensus by enrolling many of the leading figures of the republic in his cabinet and by following a moderate course. He reduced the size and influence of the army, keeping expenditures to a minimum. Diplomatic recognition came from the United States on 3 March 1837, the day after the first anniversary of Texas independence, followed by France in September 1839. Great Britain and other European states subsequently established formal commercial relations as well.

Mexico never accepted the independence of Texas, and the threat of military conflict always loomed. Further complicating relations, Texas claimed the Río Grande (which had never been a provincial Texas demarcation) as its boundary, although the Republic of Texas did not govern territory south or west of the Nueces River.

Internal conflict also posed military challenges. Indians in frontier areas—roughly all the land north of the road traditionally known as El Camino Real, which connected Nacogdoches and San Augustine in the northeast with San Antonio in the southwest—challenged those who ventured out from towns and established farmlands. In 1838 and 1839 a collection of Indians and Tejanos, discontented at the Texians' lack of respect for their claims to land and property, rebelled in the Nacogdoches region under Vicente Córdova in desperate hope of support from Mexico, which never came. In 1839, under new president Mirabeau B. Lamar, the government reinitiated battle against the Cherokees and others who had been implicated in the Córdova Rebellion and drove them to areas north of the Red River. Houston's avoidance of war through patient negotiation and trade also ended on the southwestern frontier as the Lamar administration engaged in pursuit and retaliatory expeditions against the Comanches. Significant engagements occurred in 1840 in and around Victoria and San Antonio, and along the Colorado River north of Anglo-Texan and Mexican settlements.

Lamar also took a more aggressive stance toward Mexico, particularly in aiding federalist rebellions against the national government. He loaned portions of the Texas navy to antigovernment forces in Yucatán, allowed guerrillas operating in the Matamoros area to recruit volunteers in Texas, and attempted to claim Santa Fe by force under the pretext of a defensively armed trading venture. These activities resulted in Mexican expeditions into Texas. One, under Rafael Vásquez in March 1842, remained but a short time. A second force, reportedly twelve thousand men led by Gen. Adrian Woll in September 1842, captured San Antonio and fought pitched battles against hastily assembled Texas volunteers.

Lamar took his expansive and expensive course because he felt strongly that bold measures were needed to promote Texas nationalism. He also articulated views common to the growing number of southern nationalists in the United States, asserting that union with a nation increasingly bedeviled by northern abolitionists threatened slavery in Texas. Yet, his policies led mostly to increased debt and exposure of military vulnerability, thus weakening the fortunes of Texas nationhood.

The failure of Lamar's ambitious schemes paved the way for the return of the more prudent Houston. He inherited tense relations with Mexico, embittered demands for retaliatory invasions of Mexico from Texas firebrands, runaway inflation, and mounting debt. Houston saw little choice but to retrench; however, the demands for a military response were too strong to ignore. Houston attempted to defuse these by sending forces toward the Río Grande under Gen. Alexander Somervell, a man of irresolute temperament. The soldiers chafed under their leader's inconclusive direction, and about three hundred of them, when ordered back to San Antonio, refused to give up their goal of punishing and plundering. Some of them sacked the town of Laredo and then found themselves trapped and hopelessly outnumbered at Mier. Those captured were marched toward Mexico City where they were to be imprisoned. After a failed breakout attempt during the march, Mexican authorities executed one-tenth of the prisoners. These incidents fed anti-Mexican sentiment and placed further pressure on Houston to act boldly, but he disavowed responsibility for the actions of those who had continued to fight in violation of Somervell's orders.

Houston once again cut expenditures, relied mostly on volunteer, militia, or ranger forces for defense, sought to defend Texas by diplomatic means, and continued to pursue annexation. If complete security and financial stability never came to the Texas Republic, it nevertheless showed signs of growth. The population increased as the government continued the Mexican policy of granting land to all true settlers in smaller plots or to colonizing agents in larger grants. By 1845 there were 150,000 people in Texas. The percentage of slaves in the population had increased from just over 10 percent to almost 25 percent at the time of annexation.

The growth in population in part reflected a short-lived lessening of military tensions. By 1844 and 1845 a smoldering peace prevailed both with Mexico and with the Comanches. The young nation had developed a resilient military tradition of hard fighting by citizen-soldiers of various descriptions. On the northeastern frontier the tribes of Indians had been largely evicted or reduced to acceptance of Anglo-Texan domination. As it entered its fourth presidential election in 1844, Texas had achieved substantial political stability. Overwhelming sentiment in favor of annexation still prevailed, however, and the measure gained approval in 1845 almost without opposition in Texas.

Controversies over its southern and western boundaries played a significant role in Texas in the first five years of its statehood, following annexation on 29 December 1845. The U.S. government pressed the former Republic of Texas claim of the Río Grande to its source as the boundary with Mexico, and in support of this claim U.S. forces occupied disputed territory south of the Nueces River. Because this stance became the basis for the U.S. war against Mexico, the state government of Texas maintained its claims after the treaty of Guadalupe Hidalgo in 1848 transferred New Mexico and additional southwestern territory to the United States. The issue of the size and scope of the state of Texas involved internal U.S. social and political conflict as well, because the larger Texas was, the more slavery would be expanded. Texas governors George T. Wood and Peter H. Bell sought to defend claims to those portions of New Mexico east of the Río Grande, even attempting to organize county government and threatening armed occupation. President Zachary Taylor firmly sent federal reinforcements to New Mexico in 1850 and made public their orders to turn back any Texas force of occupation. The U.S. Congress resolved this dispute with a bill setting the Texas–New Mexico boundary with demarcations at the intersection of the Red River and 100° east longitude, north to 36° 30′ north latitude, west to 103° east longitude, south to 32° north latitude; and west to the Río Grande. This measure, along with a $10 million financial incentive to the Texas government and its bondholders, gained passage as part of the Compromise of 1850 and received strong support in Texas. Thus, in the end the disputed boundary of Texas took on a scope and shape that had never been part of its heritage.

Paul D. Lack

BIBLIOGRAPHY

Lack, Paul D. *The Texas Revolutionary Experience: A Political and Social History, 1835–1836.* 1992.

Nackman, Mark E. *A Nation within a Nation: The Rise of Texas Nationalism.* 1975.

Nance, Joseph M. *Attack and Counterattack: The Texas-Mexican Frontier, 1842.* 1964.

Siegel, Stanley. *A Political History of the Texas Republic, 1836–1845.* 1956.

Weber, David J. *The Mexican Frontier, 1821–1846: The American Southwest under Mexico.* 1982.

Nationalism in Texas

Texas nationalism was a powerful patriotic sentiment articulated and displayed by settlers from the United States and Europe in the period from 1836 to the U.S.-Mexican War. Texas nationalism was evident in the years immediately following annexation in 1845 to 1854 and for more than a century thereafter. The 1850 dispute over the New Mexico boundary was the first of many quarrels between Texans and the federal government.

The Anglo-Americans who emigrated to Texas in the years between 1821 and 1846 cut themselves off politically and economically from the United States. Left to themselves to make homes and lives in Texas, they developed a sense of commonality and independence. Other racial and ethnic groups in Texas—native Mexicans, blacks, and Indians—were not assimilated into this new society and were left powerless, with the exception of a few notable Tejanos (Texas partisans of Mexican descent).

The common experience of frontier community building in an alien and inhospitable environment, the war for independence, the struggle for nationhood as the Republic of Texas, and unceasing border defense against Mexico and the plains Indians—all yielded an esprit de corps among Texians. They viewed themselves (as did their U.S. and European contemporaries) as a distinct nationality under the Lone Star flag.

The seeds of Texas nationalism were planted during the years of Mexican rule, from 1821 until the 1836 Texas Revolution. Under a centralized Mexican system of government, the expatriate U.S. settlers were given few opportunities for political participation. The contrast between Mexican ways and their own, between Mexican people and themselves, created a heightened self-awareness. Affiliating with neither Mexico nor the United States, they became Texian.

The decade of Texas nationhood, 1836 to 1845, impressed a stamp of identity on all who would call themselves Texians. The Lone Star Republic took its place among the nations of the Western world, vying for credit, settlement, and trade, as well as for prestige and respect. A measure of the new nation's success was its recognition by the United States and the leading powers of Europe. Mexico, however, rejected the Texian presumption of nationality and vowed to reclaim the country.

The Republic of Texas established its boundaries in 1836 by congressional fiat to include the territory of neighboring Mexican states north and east of the Río Grande, extending to portions of the present-day U.S. states of Colorado, Kansas, New Mexico, and Wyoming. Not content with these extravagant claims, the Texas congress in 1842 added more than half of the remaining territory of the Mexican Republic, including the two Californias, Chihuahua, New Mexico, and Sonora, as well as portions of Coahuila, Durango, Sinaloa, and Tamaulipas. Such extreme and unilateral expressions of Texas sovereignty predictably outraged the Mexican government, made diplomatic recognition unthinkable, and set forth an era of hostility that would not terminate officially until the Treaty of Guadalupe Hidalgo in 1848.

The Texians far from reconsidering their self-proclaimed boundaries, took pride in the size of their nation. Mexico, however, was determined to conquer Texas. The two countries frequently threatened each other with invasion and each made two attempts. Rumors of incursions for most of the era of Texas nationhood kept its citizens in perpetual war-readiness. Spokesmen for the infant republic fixed on their border enemy to ensure political stability and solidarity under trying economic circumstances.

Many Texians held Mexico and its population in contempt. With their corps of rangers and irregulars inured to the rigors of plains warfare, Texians relished the prospect of a head-on clash with Mexican regulars. The U.S. annexation of Texas precipitated the war and gave them their chance to advance on Mexico.

Mark E. Nackman

BIBLIOGRAPHY

Haynes, Sam W. *Soldiers of Misfortune: The Somervell and Mier Expeditions.* 1990.

Nackman, Mark E. *A Nation within a Nation: The Rise of Texas Nationalism.* 1975.

Conflicts with Mexico, 1836–1845

Following the Battle of San Jacinto, David G. Burnet, president of Texas's ad interim government, and the captive Gen. Antonio López de Santa Anna, president of Mexico, signed the Treaties of Velasco. Neither side complied with the terms of the document, and Mexico refused to recognize either Texas's independence or its claims that the Río Grande formed its southern and western boundaries. Minor border raids and threatening pronouncements, however, rather than open conflict, characterized relations during the next two years. Internal convulsions prevented Mexico from carrying out its threats to subdue Texas, and election of Sam Houston as Republic of Texas president in September 1836 further cooled war sentiment. Rather than use force to resolve his impoverished government's continuing disputes with Mexico, Houston opposed a projected invasion of Matamoros, disbanded most of the Texas army, and pressed for annexation by the United States.

Mirabeau B. Lamar, elected president of the Republic of Texas in late 1838, took a much more aggressive stance. Lamar feared a Mexican–Indian alliance against Texas; mixed groups of Mexican soldiers, Tejanos, and a few Indians, led by Capt. Vicente Córdova and Mexican trader Manuel Flores, were crushed by Lamar's forces in East Texas. (The Texas government considered the Córdova episode an example of Mexico's intrigue against the Republic of Texas.) Lamar also allowed Mexican rebels to recruit in Texas, dispatched the Texas navy to support an insurrection in Yucatán, and backed attempts by the self-styled Republic of the Río Grande to break away from Mexico City. Most dramatically, in summer 1841 he sent 320 men to establish Texas's claim to Santa Fe. Short on supplies and lacking reliable information, members of the ill-fated expedition surrendered to Mexican authorities upon reaching their destination.

Although the Santa Fe expedition antagonized Mexico, where Santa Anna regained power in 1842, his eagerness to gain revenge against the rebellious Texians, a cause that remained a popular domestic issue, was tempered by his awareness that Mexico could not afford a full-scale war. He did, however, send 700 Mexican troops, commanded by Gen. Rafael Vásquez, across the Río Grande, and they occupied San Antonio for two days in early March. Houston, who had been elected for a second term as president the year before, also sought to avoid a major confrontation. He dispatched Brig. Gen. Alexander Somervell to take charge of the Texian volunteers organizing in the area but vetoed a declaration of war.

Conflicts continued along the South Texas frontiers. In early July, 450 Mexican soldiers defeated a smaller Texian force at the Battle of Lipantitlan, west of present-day Corpus Christi. On 11 September, Brig. Gen. Adrian Woll's Mexican army of 1,400 troops captured San Antonio after a brief defense by some of the town's residents. Woll immediately found himself under pressure from Maj. John C. Hays's Ranger company and masses of Texian volunteers. On 16 July, a detachment of Woll's cavalry routed Capt. Nicholas M. Dawson and 52 Texians, but the same day, another of Woll's detachments was defeated at the Battle of Salado Creek by Capt. Matthew Caldwell's forces. The Mexican army retreated from San Antonio two days later; near the Hondo River, Hays and Captain Caldwell botched a combined attempt to destroy Woll's rear guard.

Once again, Houston assigned Somervell the task of responding to the Mexican threat. His 750-strong Southwestern Army of Operations occupied Laredo on 8 December. After a brief foray into Guerrero, Mexico, Somervell ordered his army to fall back north of the Río Grande. However, three hundred of his men mutinied, elected Capt. William Fisher their commander, and marched on Mier, which they hoped to pillage. Instead, they found nine hundred Mexican troops, led by Gen. Pedro de Ampudia. Following a sharp encounter that left sixteen Texians and at least forty Mexicans dead, the Texians surrendered as prisoners of war. Many of the Texians captured at Mier were later executed, in the infamous Black Bean episode, following several escape attempts.

War fever in Texas cooled dramatically following the defeat, as many residents of the Lone Star Republic began to realize how precarious their independence really was. Texian raiding parties into New Mexico, led by Col. Charles A. Warfield and Col. Jacob Snively, failed to gain control of the lucrative Santa Fe Trail. Houston and his successor, Anson Jones, believed annexation, not continued warfare with Mexico, was the ultimate answer to the Texas Republic's problems. In Mexico, internal threats to his government led Santa Anna to consider an end to hostilities. Both sides declared an armistice in summer 1843, which they generally

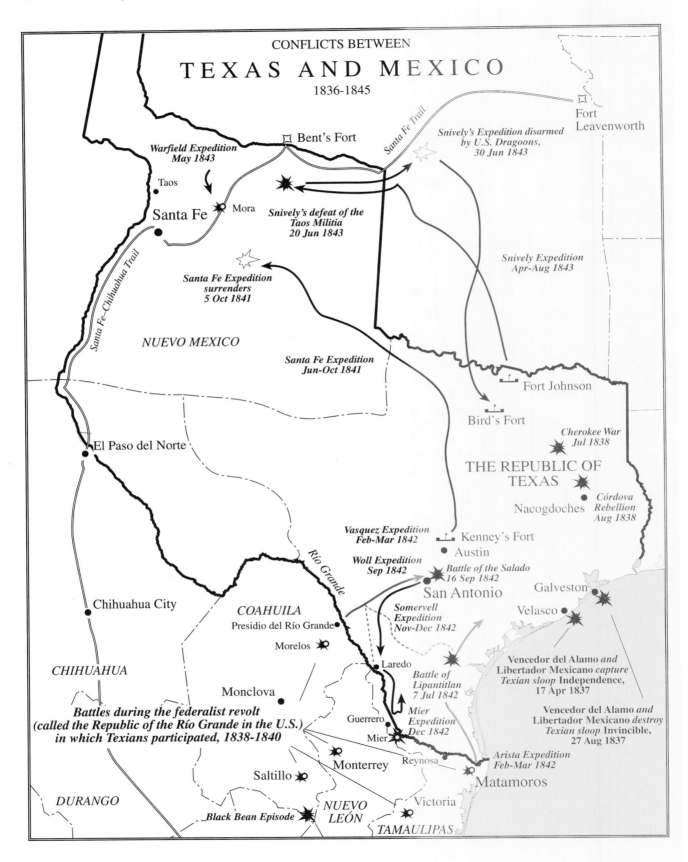

CONFLICTS BETWEEN

TEXAS AND MEXICO

1836-1845

Santa Fe Trail

☐ Fort Leavenworth

☐ Bent's Fort

Warfield Expedition
May 1843

Snively's Expedition disarmed
by U.S. Dragoons,
30 Jun 1843

Taos

Santa Fe ○ Mora

Snively's defeat of the
Taos Militia
20 Jun 1843

Snively Expedition
Apr–Aug 1843

Santa Fe Expedition
surrenders
5 Oct 1841

NUEVO MEXICO

Santa Fe–Chihuahua Trail

Santa Fe Expedition
Jun–Oct 1841

⊥ Fort Johnson

⊥ Bird's Fort

✴ *Cherokee War*
Jul 1838

THE REPUBLIC OF
TEXAS ✴

✕ El Paso del Norte

Nacogdoches

Córdova
Rebellion
Aug 1838

Vasquez Expedition
Feb–Mar 1842

⊥ Kenney's Fort

● Austin

Woll Expedition
Sep 1842

Battle of the Salado
16 Sep 1842

Galveston

Río Grande

Chihuahua City

COAHUILA

Presidio del Río Grande ●

Morelos ✴

San Antonio

Velasco

Somervell
Expedition
Nov–Dec 1842

Vencedor del Alamo and
Libertador Mexicano capture
Texian sloop Independence,
17 Apr 1837

CHIHUAHUA

Monclova ●

Battles during the federalist revolt
(called the Republic of the Río Grande in the U.S.)
in which Texians participated, 1838–1840

Laredo

Battle of
Lipantitlan
7 Jul 1842

Guerrero ●

Mier ✴

Mier
Expedition
Dec 1842

Vencedor del Alamo and
Libertador Mexicano destroy
Texian sloop Invincible,
27 Aug 1837

✴

Reynosa

Arista Expedition
Feb–Mar 1842

Monterrey

Saltillo ✴

DURANGO

Black Bean Episode ✴

NUEVO
LEÓN

Matamoros

Victoria ✴

TAMAULIPAS

observed until Texas was annexed by the United States. The last of the Mier expedition prisoners were released from Mexico's Perote Castle on 15 September 1844.

Robert Wooster

BIBLIOGRAPHY

Binkley, William Campbell. "The Last Stage of Texan Military Operations against Mexico, 1843." *Southwestern Historical Quarterly* 22 (1919): 260–271.

Haynes, Sam W. *Soldiers of Misfortune: The Somervell and Mier Expeditions.* 1990.

Nance, Joseph Milton. *After San Jacinto: The Texas-Mexican Frontier, 1836–1841.* 1963.

Nance, Joseph Milton. *Attack and Counterattack: The Texas-Mexican Frontier, 1842.* 1964.

Wooster, Ralph A. "Texas Military Operations against Mexico, 1842–43." *Southwestern Historical Quarterly* 67 (1964): 465–484.

Annexation of Texas

The annexation of Texas by the United States in 1845 was one of the immediate causes of the U.S.–Mexican War, which began in May 1846. Although contemporaries then and historians since have differed over the extent to which annexation actually contributed to the causes of the war, Mexico and many opponents of slavery in the United States claimed annexation was a direct and primary cause. At the very least, annexation was a serious insult to Mexican national pride. War might subsequently have been averted by a U.S. government intent on keeping the peace by assuaging Mexican pride and compromising on other issues. The incoming administration of President James K. Polk, however, was in no mood to do either. Like many in his country, Polk did not believe the United States had done anything wrong by annexing Texas. Moreover, the new president brought an aggressive territorial agenda to the White House. If Mexico did not bend, Polk was willing to use confrontation and, if necessary, war to acquire California and the Southwest.

After Texas became an independent republic in 1836, the issue of annexation to the United States arose quickly but met resistance from those in the northeastern United States, who feared the expansion of slavery and war with Mexico. An 1843 pro-annexation movement began to gain popular and political strength among southern and western Democrats. Politically beleaguered President John Tyler embraced annexation as a means to get reelected and to forestall British diplomatic objectives in Texas. After initial missteps, the administration signed a treaty with the Republic of Texas in April 1844. This agreement produced a major debate in the Senate, which defeated ratification by a large bipartisan margin in June.

Annexation also played a key role in the presidential election of 1844. The issue was instrumental in depriving Martin Van Buren of the Democratic nomination and in helping nominee James K. Polk upset Whig Henry Clay in a close presidential contest. After the election, outgoing President Tyler reintroduced annexation to Congress in the form of a joint resolution requiring only a majority in each house, not the two-thirds margin required for Senate ratification of a treaty. As it had been in 1844, the debate in early 1845 was heated, but this time the measure passed both the House and Senate. The Republic of Texas subsequently accepted the offer and entered the Union as a state in December 1845.

Annexation involved significant constitutional, diplomatic, and political issues, but the debate was never confined to these issues because abolitionism, slavery, and sectional controversy engulfed the Texas question. As the annexation issue played out between 1843 and 1845, the question of genuine national interest was overshadowed by the rising politics of slavery and sectional self-interest. In the process, national politics were transformed. Once the U.S.–Mexican War began, President Polk desperately attempted to keep his territorial objectives of New Mexico and California separate from the sectional politics of slavery. He failed. Within ninety days of the outbreak of war, the introduction of the Wilmot Proviso in Congress ensured that expansion, sectionalism, slavery, and the war would be inseparably linked.

John H. Schroeder

BIBLIOGRAPHY

Cooper, William J. *The South and the Politics of Slavery, 1828–56.* 1978.

Merk, Frederick. *Slavery and the Annexation of Texas.* 1972.

Pletcher, David M. *The Diplomacy of Annexation: Texas, Oregon, and the Mexican War.* 1973.

Schroeder, John H. "Annexation or Independence: The Texas Issue in American Politics, 1836–1845." *Southwestern Historical Quarterly* 89 (1985): 137–164.

Texas-Comanche Relations

Relations between the Comanche Indians and the Republic of Texas continued in a pattern similar to what had developed under Spanish and Mexican rule, except that warfare was more frequent and more intense. After 1836 settlers moved in greater numbers to the edges of the northern and western plains that the nomadic buffalo hunter-warrior Comanches had dominated for most of the previous century. As a result, the Comanches pursued more opportunities for economic gain by raiding, which generated retaliation after retaliation by both sides. The Texas government, especially when Sam Houston was president (1837–1838, 1842–1844), attempted to achieve peace through trade and negotiation, but citizen-soldiers frequently took matters into their own hands. The Comanches, well equipped for mounted warfare, but united into bands numbering into the hundreds for only short periods, were matched by Texas volunteers armed with increasing firepower and a desire for revenge.

Houston's pursuit of peace was hampered as well by congressional refusal to ratify boundary lines or other treaties. President Mirabeau B. Lamar between 1839 and 1841 favored war as a means to pacify the frontier. In spring 1840 more than thirty Comanches died and an equal number were captured in the Council House fight in San Antonio, which was precipitated by mutual deceptions concerning a prisoner exchange. Panateka Comanche chief Buffalo Hump then led a force of five hundred against the town of Victoria near the Gulf Coast. Mounted Texas volunteers caught these raiders on their trek back to the plains and killed about fifty of them at Plum Creek in August 1840. In October an organized expedition under John H. Moore destroyed a large camp on the Colorado River some two hundred miles beyond the nearest Anglo-Texan settlements. These incidents, added to Houston's renewed quest of trade-for-peace agreements, led to fewer hostilities, but Comanche–Texas tensions were again on the rise by 1845 when annexation brought the U.S. government onto the scene.

Paul D. Lack

BIBLIOGRAPHY
Hoebel, E. Adamson, and Ernest Wallace. *The Comanches.* 1952.
Lipscomb, Carol A. "Comanche Indians." In *The New Handbook of Texas,* 2: 242–245. 1996.

Texas Declaration of Independence

Since October 1835 Texas had been at war, but its leaders had issued only equivocal and perhaps even disingenuous public statements of the purpose of the rebellion. Representatives from the municipalities of Texas debated the issue at the Consultation in November but adopted a position that their cause was to maintain the rights of Texas under the Mexican Constitution of 1824, a structure that had been set aside previously by President Antonio López de Santa Anna. The purpose of this stance was to attract support from Mexican federalists and to maintain a semblance of internal consensus.

Even Stephen F. Austin, whose supporters had constructed this cautious course, understood that independence was mainly a question of timing. Members of the Texas army pushed hard and impatiently for independence. In December 1835 a group of them at Goliad approved a declaration of independence replete with hotly anti-Mexican and antipolitician language. The inept Texas government managed to call for elections in February 1836 to elect delegates to a convention to meet the next month. In most sections of Texas, representatives of the army perspective and other advocates of independence won easily and without public debate on the matter.

The small number of delegates who opposed independence gave in with little resistance amid growing awareness of the arrival of an army of six thousand under Santa Anna to suppress the Secession of Texas. The convention met at Washington-on-the-Brazos and on 2 March 1836 adopted a declaration of independence that asserted the right of revolution and justified the action on the basis that Mexico had succumbed to chronic instability and military despotism. It maintained that the people of Texas had remonstrated against abuses but received only contemptuous repression and a "war of extermination" in return. Thus, Mexico had dissolved the social compact, and Texas had to separate for reasons of "self-preservation."

The delegates approved and signed the document with virtually no debate. Copies of the declaration were then printed and distributed as a means of rallying support for the cause in both Texas and the United States.

Paul D. Lack

BIBLIOGRAPHY
Greer, James K. "The Committee on the Texas Declaration of Independence." *Southwestern Historical Quarterly* 30 (April 1927): 239–251.
Lack, Paul D. *The Texas Revolutionary Experience: A Political and Social History, 1835–1836.* 1992.

Texas Rangers

Texas Rangers had existed as frontier paramilitary units in Texas since 1823 and by 1845 were practically the only armed units in the new state of Texas that—under the complex militia laws of the United States—could be mustered into the regular army.

These mounted men, as volunteers to the U.S. Army, were known variously as Texas Mounted Volunteers, Texas Mounted Rangers, Mounted Riflemen, Texas Mounted Rifles, and even the Texas Militia. They served as scouts, light cavalry, assault infantry, and spies in the Monterrey campaign of Gen. Zachary Taylor; as guerrilla fighters at and after the assault on Mexico City by Gen. Winfield Scott; and as frontier guards, largely against Indian forays along the Río Grande and on the western frontier of Texas.

The Rangers, known before the U.S.–Mexican War as frontier guards, were natural choices to support regular troops. They already had such experience in the Texas Revolution of 1836 and were known for quick action, untiring pursuit, and a legendary ability to fight. Their opponents—Mexican troops, bandits, and the Comanche—applied other names to the service, none polite.

Relations between Mexico and Texas had been strained well before the Texas Revolution, and many a man in Ranger service had a burning desire for revenge. After 1836, Mexican forays into Texas and expeditionary Texan forces en-

Texas Ranger. John Frost, *Pictorial History of Mexico and the Mexican War*, 1862

tering Mexico had worsened feelings. By 1845, the Rangers were willing to enlist in a war that, for them, was a continuation of Texas's armed conflict with Mexico.

U.S. law allowing the mustering of militia forces into the regular army called for short enlistment periods (but allowed subsequent enlistments every three months) from organized state forces. Texas, as a former independent nation with no state militia, had few groups that fit the early law. The Rangers did.

The initial muster essentially served under General Taylor, who had approval to request volunteer troops from Texas. The first group in federal service to officially use the word *ranger* was Capt. Richard A. Gillespie's company, Texas Mounted Rangers of San Antonio. This enlistment, 28 September 1845, was intended, on paper, for frontier defense. As the men accompanied the regular army, the group name was changed to the 1st and 2d Regiments of Texas Mounted Volunteers.

The captaincy of the many units, as they entered the regular war campaign, also changed, producing leaders from skillfully effective to ineptly brutal. The most famous were John C. "Jack" Hays, a respected Texas Ranger captain; Ben McCulloch, who became legendary as a scout; and Samuel H. Walker, connected directly with the use and design of Colt revolvers.

Because of reenlistment procedure and lost records, the number of Rangers in federal service is not known. Some six thousand Texans may have been in federal volunteer service, many as mounted "rangers." A few groups, such as David C. Cady's company of Texas Mounted Rangers, stayed for various lengths of time, generally in federal service, on the frontier to protect against Indian raids.

Probably the most famous military action—other than scouting assignments—was the volunteers' support, as infantry, of the assault on Monterrey in General Taylor's campaign. In one of several engagements, volunteers including Colonel Hays and Lieutenant Colonel Walker joined the pre-dawn infantry scramble up the western face of Loma Independencia during the successful attack in September 1846.

In all campaigns, the Rangers—as they were called, whatever their official title—drew attention. They were outfitted in outlandish dress, bearded, always well-armed, and often dirty and rough. Many were doctors and lawyers, while a notable number had college degrees. Useful as scouts and guerrilla warriors, they also were charged with undeniably brutal killings. Flouting their full rejection of military procedure, discipline, and drill, they earned the name *los diablos Tejanos.*

The volunteers were of critical importance to General Taylor and of some value to Scott's campaign, but opinion is still divided on the influence the Rangers had on the army's dragoons or later light cavalry. Certainly, Rangers had developed methods of their own while learning much from Mexican vaqueros and Comanche warriors. The Rangers' methods of fast field movement, resolute charges, and unearthly yells influenced mounted men of the regular army, but the most obvious bequest was the Rangers' use of the rifle and repeating handguns. Samuel Colt's first five-shooters and the famous six-shot Walker Colt replaced the saber as close weaponry for mounted defense or assault.

John L. Davis

BIBLIOGRAPHY

Barton, Henry W. *Texas Volunteers in the Mexican War.* 1970.

Davis, John L. *The Texas Rangers, Images and Incidents.* 1991.

Oates, Stephen B. "*Los Diablos Tejanos:* The Texas Rangers." In *The Mexican War, Changing Interpretations,* edited by Odie B. Faulk and Joseph A. Stout Jr. 1973.

Reid, Samuel C., Jr. *The Scouting Expeditions of McCulloch's Texas Rangers.* 1847. Reprint, 1970.

Wilkins, Frederick. *The Highly Irregular Irregulars: Texas Rangers in the Mexican War.* 1990.

Texas Revolts of 1832

With passage of the Law of April 6, 1830, Mexico established new garrisons to monitor entrances into eastern Texas at the mouths of the Trinity (Anáhuac, outside of Stephen F.

Austin's colony) and Brazos (Velasco, within Austin's colony) Rivers and where the Old Spanish Trail crossed the Brazos River (Tenoxtitlán, north of Austin's colony, just north of present-day state highway 21). The size of the garrison at Nacogdoches, under the command of Col. José de las Piedras, was increased. Col. Juan Davis Bradburn, a former resident of Tennessee and militia officer at the Battle of New Orleans, now a career officer in the Mexican army and commandant at Anáhuac, became the focus of Anglo-Texan hostility because his strict interpretation of orders to enforce Mexican laws offended his former countrymen.

William B. Travis led citizen complaints against Bradburn, and after a prank termed sedition by the commandant, was jailed along with several others. Friends of the men negotiated unsuccessfully for their release, and on 10 June 1832 attacked the fort. A truce the next day was violated by both sides, and some Brazos residents returned home to get two cannon to bombard the fort. While waiting for the cannon, the Texians camped at nearby Turtle Bayou where, on 13 June, they drafted resolutions explaining their action. It was, they said, part of the two-year civil war between the centralist administration and federalist reformers. The Texans claimed to have attacked Bradburn, the centralist commander, in the name of reformer Gen. Antonio López de Santa Anna. As *santanistas,* the Texans were not rebelling against the nation, only against the despotic centralist administration.

The second incident took place on the Brazos when the locals commandeered a schooner at Brazoria, loaded the cannon on board, and started downriver to pass beneath the guns of the small fort at Velasco. On 26 June about 150 Anglo-Texans led by John Austin and Henry Smith fired on Col. Domingo Ugartechea's small force of less than 100, leading to casualties on both sides. Having exhausted his ammunition, Ugartechea formally surrendered 29 June, although damage to the schooner prevented the Texans from moving the cannon to Anáhuac. On 16 July five warships arrived at Velasco with federalist Col. José Antonio Mexía and Stephen Austin on board. The Texans convinced Mexía that they were loyal federalists.

Colonel Piedras, in response to Bradburn's call for help, approached the village of Liberty thirty miles from Anáhuac. Believing his force was outnumbered, he agreed on 28 June to release Travis and the others to civil authority at Liberty and to remove Bradburn from command. Piedras reached Anáhuac on 1 July. Bradburn agreed to step down; in fear for his life he fled to New Orleans with the aid of local Anglo-Texan tories. Following Piedras's departure on 8 July, the Anáhuac garrison mutinied and joined the *santanista* movement.

When Piedras reached Nacogdoches, he found that Anglo-Texans on Ayish Bayou (present-day San Augustine) were ready to join the *santanistas.* On 2 August they infiltrated

Nacogdoches and demanded that Piedras join Santa Anna's cause. He refused and a battle ensued, resulting in casualties. During the night Piedras withdrew his troops westward, but the Anglo-Texans surrounded them the next day on the Angelina River. Piedras relinquished command to his second officer, who officially surrendered the troops and joined the *santanista* movement; Piedras was allowed to return to Tampico. The other garrisons in Texas also pronounced in favor of Santa Anna, and the civil war ended in December. The Texians capitalized on the federalist victory and sent petitions for various reforms to Mexico City the following spring. Troops and customs collectors did not return to Texas until January 1835, when President Santa Anna renounced federalism and increasingly favored a strong central government.

Margaret Swett Henson

BIBLIOGRAPHY

Henson, Margaret Swett. *Juan Davis Bradburn: A Reappraisal of the Mexican Commander of Anahuac.* 1982.

Henson, Margaret Swett. *The Cartwrights of San Augustine.* 1993.

Texas Revolution

This entry consists of two separate articles: **Causes of the Revolution** *and* **Course of the Revolution**. *See also* **Army, Texas**; **Navy, Texas**; Texas Declaration of Independence.

Causes of the Revolution

Anglo-American immigration into Texas, a Mexican province, began during the 1820s following an immigration policy implemented by Mexico to protect its territory. Plagued by numerous problems associated with its recent independence from Spain and lacking the numbers to populate the area with its own citizens, Mexico turned to westward-moving U.S. settlers in hopes of deterring an unauthorized takeover of its northern lands.

Stephen F. Austin brought several families to the region as early as 1821 under an agreement his father, Moses, had negotiated with Spain, but most of the Anglo-American settlement of Texas thereafter came under the provisions of Mexico's State Colonization Law of 1825. The statute, passed by the Coahuila y Texas legislature, was intended to promote the economic development of the province; its framers believed that Anglo-American settlers would help protect Texas from Indians, encourage commerce, resurrect the ranching industry, and bring about the cultivation of cotton lands.

Soon after implementation of the new policy, however, problems arose between Anglo-American settlers and Mexican authorities. Most of the immigrants lived in the eastern section of the province—far from the Mexican communities of San Antonio, Goliad, and Victoria—and for them Texas provided an abundance of available lands for personal use, opportunities for turning a profit through commerce (smuggling), and the tolerance to continue U.S. political practices. The Mexican authorities, however, soon viewed the immigrants as unwilling to conform to Mexican laws. The immigrants violated the provisions of the Colonization Law of 1825 by squatting on lands, engaging in illegal transfer and sale of goods, carrying on Protestant beliefs, and maintaining slavery.

In response to these situations, as well as to the Fredonia Rebellion of 1826 (a local disturbance in Nacogdoches in which a local land agent, Haden Edwards, sought independence from Mexico, albeit without success), the Mexican national congress in 1830 passed the Law of April 6. This law's objectives were to stop immigration from the United States by nullifying the contracts that allowed Anglo-American land agents to bring settlers into the province and to prohibit further importation of slaves. It also included provisions to control commerce along the Gulf of Mexico, and called for erecting military posts to enforce the new law.

Texans disliked the Law of April 6 because it had the potential to stifle economic growth in the province. The articles regulating commerce (which established tariffs and more clearly designated ports along the Gulf for navigation) produced a confrontation between Mexican officials and the more militant settlers in Anáhuac in June 1832. On the pretext that the local Mexican commander would not release William Barret Travis—who had been jailed for attempting to obtain the release of two slaves through subterfuge—Anglo-Americans from around Anáhuac laid siege to the garrison. Though higher-ranking Mexican officials defused the situation, the settlers complained that the treatment of Travis violated the customary U.S. principle of arrest by warrant and the rights to bail and to trial by jury.

Not all Anglo-American Texans condoned the actions of the militants at Anáhuac; some settlers in the province wanted to find solutions to their problems with the Mexican government through more peaceful means. This faction (which later became known as the "peace party") met with authorities at San Felipe de Austin in October 1832 and urged the national government to allow resumption of immigration into Texas. Other settlers, belonging to what would become the "war party," held their own meeting in 1833, making demands on the national government that included the separation of Texas from Coahuila; they noted that given Texas's status as a territory under the state of Coahuila, it could not press its own agenda in the legislature. Neither of these conventions produced immediate results.

In 1833, a liberal coup led by Antonio López de Santa Anna brought more sympathetic rule to the people in Texas. The new Mexican congress lifted the most restrictive provisions of the Law of April 6, notably the one stopping immigration. But this period of government was short-lived, for in 1834 President Santa Anna ousted the liberals and established a new centralist political structure that severely reduced decision-making power at the state and local levels.

This turn of events produced revolts throughout Mexico. The state of Zacatecas led the groundswell of discontent, but Santa Anna quickly smashed the resistance. The legislature of Coahuila similarly remonstrated, announcing that it would not submit to centralist authority, and set out to raise money through the sale of lands to finance the cause of states' rights. In Texas, Mexican military commanders reported that Anglo-American speculators had bought some of these lands and that rumor held that they would sell their property to finance an army against the national government. In response to such concerns, Mexico in late spring of 1835 prepared to dispatch an army to Texas.

As stories circulated of the imminent arrival of troops, Anglo-American Texans led by William B. Travis attacked and successfully subdued the military garrison at Anáhuac. The assault on the post was based on, as the one of 1832 had been, unpopular customs duties, but its leaders were members of the "war party," who calculated that their actions would rally other Texans behind the banner of independence from Mexico. For Mexico, the attack on the military installation signaled the long-feared secessionist movement, especially since Texans harbored both Travis and the Anglo-American speculators.

Arnoldo De León

BIBLIOGRAPHY

Campbell, Randolph B. *An Empire for Slavery: The Peculiar Institution in Texas, 1821–1865.* 1989.

de la Teja, Jesús F., and John Wheat. "Béxar: Profile of a Tejano Community, 1820–1832." *Southwestern Historical Quarterly* 89 (1985):7–34.

Lack, Paul D. *The Texas Revolutionary Experience: A Social and Political History.* 1992.

McLean, Malcolm D. *Papers Concerning Robertson's Colony in Texas.* 1974–1993.

Reichstein, Andreas. *Rise of the Lone Star: The Making of Texas.* 1989.

Weber, David J. *The Mexican Frontier, 1821–1846: The American Southwest under Mexico.* 1982.

Course of the Revolution

Popular misconception distorts the true nature of the conflict that wrested Texas from Mexico. The prevalent designations—the Texas Revolution or the War for Texas Independence—are misleading. The struggle was not strictly a revolution; hostilities began in October 1835 as a simple revolt. Nor was it initially a bid for complete separation from the Mexican republic. Both newly arrived Texians and native

Tejanos fought for local autonomy under the federalist system created by the Mexican Constitution of 1824, not to completely restructure society. Likewise, the war did not begin as a "culture conflict." Indeed, several Tejanos joined their *norteamericano* neighbors to resist the regime of dictator Antonio López de Santa Anna.

Events unfolded during two distinct operations: the campaigns of 1835 and 1836. The first was an effort by Texians and their Tejano allies to rid the province of centralist battalions commanded by Gen. Martín Perfecto de Cos. The second was Santa Anna's attempt at reconquest, a venture in which he was nearly successful.

CAMPAIGN OF 1835

Military operations began on 2 October 1835 when a squadron of centralist cavalry commanded by Lt. Francisco de Castañeda arrived at Gonzales and demanded the return of a cannon that Mexican authorities had given to the settlers to use for protection against Indian attacks. The residents refused, hoisting over the artillery a banner brandishing the bellicose challenge: "COME AND TAKE IT." The Texians then attacked the centralist camp. Obeying his orders to avoid "compromising the honor of Mexican arms," Castañeda abandoned the field and withdrew to San Antonio de Béxar. The Texians claimed victory.

Texian rebels achieved success again on 10 October when a contingent of Matagorda volunteers captured Presidio La Bahía outside present-day Goliad. General Cos had stripped the garrison during his march to Béxar and a mere skeleton force defended the post. Commanded by Capt. George Collinsworth, the Texian force took the fort in a surprise night attack. With Goliad under their control, the Texians gained centralist military goods and a vital strategic advantage. They could now deny Cos, ensconced in Béxar, the use of the Gulf as an avenue for additional supplies and reinforcements.

Back in Gonzales, militiamen from numerous Texian settlements volunteered for service. Flocking to that settlement on the Guadalupe River, they greeted *empresario* Stephen F. Austin, who was elected commander of the self-styled "Army of the People." By 12 October the rebel force was on the march. "But one spirit and one purpose animates the people of this part of the country," General Austin reported, "and that is to take Béxar, and drive the military out of Texas."

Austin conducted a wide sweep below the town, ostensibly intending to sever communications between the centralist garrison and the Mexican interior. In reality, Cos's cavalry patrols routinely slipped through gaps in the Texian cordon because Austin did not have enough horsemen to cover every approach into the town.

Allies loyal to the Constitution of 1824, however, were on the way. On 15 October, Victoria *alcalde* Plácido Benavides joined the federalist ranks with some thirty mounted *ran-*

cheros. Then on 22 October, Juan N. Seguín entered the rebel camp with thirty-seven federalists. A few days later forty Tejanos under Salvador Flores and Manuel Leal arrived. Austin lauded the value of the Mexican federalists who "acquitted themselves to their credit as patriots and soldiers."

On 28 October a ninety-two-man reconnaissance led by Col. James Bowie and Capt. James W. Fannin clashed with Cos's units near the Mission Purísima Concepción. Taking cover in a horseshoe bend of the San Antonio River, Texian riflemen quickly thinned the centralist ranks. Cos lost about seventy-six killed or wounded and fell back into the fortified Béxar. Bowie suffered the loss of only one soldier.

Phillip Dimmitt, the new rebel commander in Goliad, prepared an expedition against Fort Lipantitlán, on the Nueces River. A Texian force commanded by Adjutant Ira J. Westover captured the fort on 3 November. The next day Westover defeated the centralist garrison—which had been away on a scout when the fort had fallen—at the Battle of Nueces Crossing. Once again the accuracy of Kentucky long rifles in the hands of experienced sharpshooters proved decisive. The centralist post commander, Capt. Nicolás Rodriguez, led the remnants of his unit to Matamoros. With the loss of Fort Lipantitlán, Cos lost his link of communication between Béxar and the Mexican interior.

The siege continued to strangle Cos in Béxar, but its ultimate success remained in question. General Austin faced numerous problems. The volunteers grew bored. Without immediate fighting, many left for home; some abandoned ranks to speculate in land; others found relief from their ennui by drinking corn liquor. Drunks careened through camp firing off rifles and wasting precious powder and ball. Austin implored the politicians: "In the name of Almighty God, send no more ardent spirits into this camp." In addition, Austin grew so weak from illness that a slave had to assist him to mount a horse.

On 18 November, Austin learned that he had won appointment as commissioner to the United States. The news delighted him: "I can be of service to Texas by going to the U.S. and I wish to go there." On 24 November, Austin paraded the Army of the People and asked for a vote concerning the wisdom of continuing the siege. Some 405 pledged to remain, but only if they could elect Austin's replacement. The headstrong volunteers chose Col. Edward Burleson, an experienced ranger captain and Indian fighter, and the siege proceeded.

On 5 December, Burleson commanded a reserve force in the federalist camp while Col. Ben Milam and Col. Francis W. Johnson led some 550 volunteers in an assault of the encircled San Antonio. Inside the beleaguered town, General Cos and about 800 centralist troops fought valiantly. Denied supplies and reinforcements, they fought street-to-street, house-to-house, and on occasion room-to-room. On the

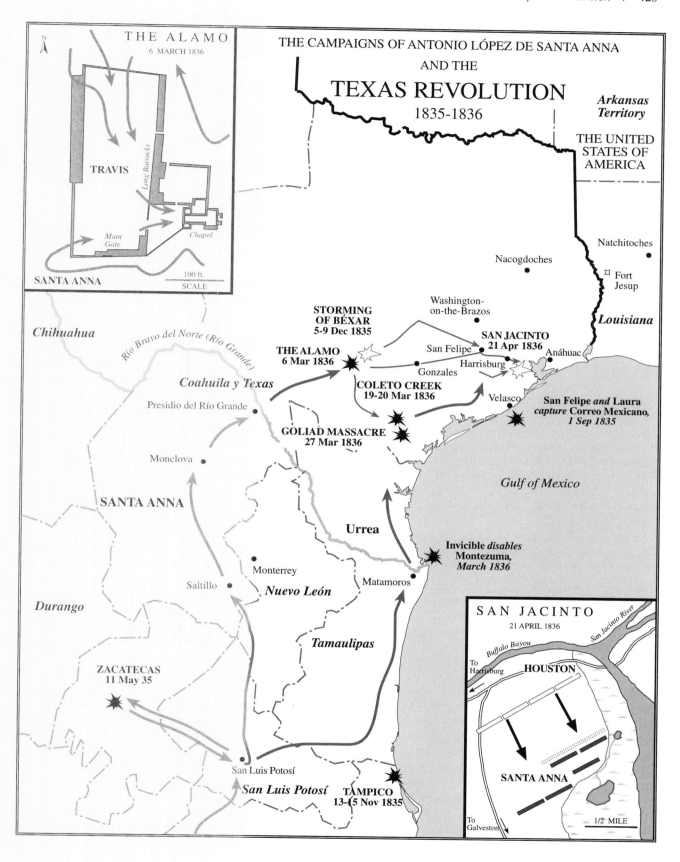

THE ALAMO
6 MARCH 1836

TRAVIS

Long Barracks

Main Gate

Chapel

SANTA ANNA

100 ft.
SCALE

THE CAMPAIGNS OF ANTONIO LÓPEZ DE SANTA ANNA
AND THE
TEXAS REVOLUTION
1835-1836

Arkansas Territory

THE UNITED STATES OF AMERICA

Natchitoches

Nacogdoches

Fort Jesup

Washington-on-the-Brazos

Louisiana

Chihuahua

Río Bravo del Norte (Río Grande)

STORMING OF BÉXAR
5-9 Dec 1835

THE ALAMO
6 Mar 1836

Coahuila y Texas

Presidio del Río Grande

SAN JACINTO
21 Apr 1836

San Felipe

Anáhuac

Gonzales

Harrisburg

COLETO CREEK
19-20 Mar 1836

Velasco

San Felipe *and* Laura *capture* Correo Mexicano, *1 Sep 1835*

GOLIAD MASSACRE
27 Mar 1836

Monclova

SANTA ANNA

Gulf of Mexico

Urrea

Invicible *disables* Montezuma, *March 1836*

Monterrey

Matamoros

Saltillo

Nuevo León

Durango

Tamaulipas

ZACATECAS
11 May 35

SAN JACINTO
21 APRIL 1836

San Jacinto River

Buffalo Bayou

To Harrisburg

HOUSTON

SANTA ANNA

San Luis Potosí

San Luis Potosí

TAMPICO
13-15 Nov 1835

To Galveston

1/2 MILE

The Texas Campaigns
Orders of Battles
1835–1836

Mexican Forces

Commander

Gen. Antonio López de Santa Anna

Cavalry

Permanente Units

Doloros (Zacatecas, 1835; Alamo, 1836)
Vera Cruz (Zacatecas, 1835)
Tampico (Zacatecas, 1835; Coleto Creek, 1836
San Jacinto 1836)
Presidials Río Grande

Activo and other militia units

Cuaulta Dragoons (Coleto Creek, 1836)
Guanajuanto (Coleto Creek, 1836; San Jacinto, 1836)
Guardia Victoria (Coleto Creek, 1836)
Rancheros de Guadalupe de los Santos (Coleto Creek, 1836)

Infantry

Permanente Units

Morelos Battalion
Jimenez Battalion (Alamo, 1836; Coleto Creek, 1836)
Matamoros Battalion (Alamo, 1836; San Jacinto, 1836)
Allende Battalion (Zacatecas 1835; Alamo, 1836)
Aldama Battalion (Alamo, 1836; San Jacinto, 1836)
Guerrero Battalion (San Jacinto, 1836)
Zapadores (Zacatecas, 1835; Alamo, 1836)

Activo Militia Units

San Luis Potosí Battalion (Zacatecas, 1835; Alamo, 1836; Coleto Creek, 1836)
Toluca Battalion (Alamo, 1836; San Jacinto, 1836)
Querétaro Battalion (Zacatecas, 1835)
Guanajuato Battalion (Zacatecas, 1935)
First Mexico Battalion (Zacatecas, 1835)
Guadalajara Battalion (Zacatecas, 1835; San Jacinto, 1836)
Tres Villas Battalion (Coleto Creek, 1836; Goliad Massacre, 1836)

Texas Forces

The Alamo (6 March 1836)
Infantry (3 companies)
Volunteers (3 companies)
Cavalry (1 company)
Artillery (2 companies)

Coleto Creek (19–20 March 1836)
Lafayette Battalion (6 companies)
Georgia Battalion (5 companies)
Artillery (1 company)
Cavalry (1 company)

San Jacinto (21 April 1836)
Regular Artillery Corps (1 company)
Regular Infantry Battalion (2 companies)
1st Texas Volunteers (8 companies)
2nd Texas Volunteers (10 companies)
Cavalry Corps (3 companies)

---

fifty-eight Texian delegates met at San Felipe de Austin. Paricipants of the Constitution of 1835 elected Branch T. Archer president of the Consultation and affirmed their loyalty to federalist principles and the Mexican Constitution of 1824. Some were already advocating complete separation from Mexico, but the majority believed that such a step would alienate potential allies: local Tejanos and Mexican federalists in Coahuila. Delegates also created a provisional government and elected Henry Smith as governor, with James W. Robinson as lieutenant governor, and organized the General Council. That body would contain representatives from the settlements who would function as a parliament. The most pressing obstacle facing the Consultation was the lack of funds to continue the war effort. It therefore named Branch T. Archer, William H. Wharton, and Stephen F. Austin agents to the United States with instructions to solicit loans and promote the Texian cause. About the same time, the Consultation chose Sam Houston commander of the regular army—a hollow appointment as that force existed only on paper.

By December contention threatened the activities of the provisional government. Advocates of independence became more strident, while the ruling elite remained steadfast to the Constitution of 1824. On 20 December, the garrison at the Presidio La Bahía—consisting primarily of newly arrived volunteers from the United States—pressed the issue when they announced the Goliad Declaration of Independence. The General Council in San Felipe de Austin repudiated the document, denouncing it as willful and premature.

Two facts, however, became abundantly clear: the provisional government was ill-equipped to govern events that were spiraling out of control, and the issue of independence was not going away. Therefore, the Consultation called for a meeting for the following March to establish an ad interim

---

third day of fighting, a centralist sniper killed Milam. Cos surrendered on 10 December. Burleson offered to parole the centralists on the condition that they retreat to a point south of the Río Grande and never again take up arms against the federalist Constitution of 1824. Cos accepted the terms and withdrew toward the Mexican interior. The Army of the People had accomplished its twin goals; it had taken Béxar and driven the centralist military out of Texas.

The political events of 1835 were only slightly less chaotic than those of a military nature. Between 3 and 14 November,

Houston, Santa Anna, and Cos. This lithograph (perhaps 1836 or 1837) is an imaginative portrayal of the surrender of Gen. Antonio López de Santa Anna and Gen. Martín Perfecto de Cos to Sam Houston after the Battle of San Jacinto (Library of Congress).

government and draft a constitution. The delegates would table the issue of independence until then. By March 1836, however, centralist forces were in Texas in an effort to regain control.

CAMPAIGN OF 1836

Following the capture of San Antonio in December 1835, many Texians believed the war was won and most of the rebels returned to their homes. In January and February 1836, however, President and commanding general Antonio López de Santa Anna launched his campaign of reconquest against the rebellious province.

From the Mexican interior, two main roads led into Texas. The first was the Atascosito Raoad, which extended from Matamoros northward through San Patricio, Refugio, Goliad, Victoria, and into the heart of Austin's colony. The second was the Old San Antonio Road, which crossed the Río

Grande and wound northeastward through San Antonio de Béxar, Bastrop, Nacogdoches, San Augustine, and across the Sabine River into Louisiana. Two forts blocked these approaches into Texas: the Presidio La Bahía at Goliad and the Alamo at San Antonio. Each installation functioned as a frontier picket guard, ready to alert the Texas settlements of a centralist advance. Col. James C. Neill had command of the Béxar garrison. At Goliad, some ninety miles to the southeast, Col. James W. Fannin commanded a four hundred-man-force inside the Presidio La Bahía, which the rebels renamed Fort Defiance. Both Neill and Fannin determined to stall the centralist force on the frontier, but they were both aware that without speedy reinforcements neither the Alamo nor Fort Defiance could long withstand a siege.

Santa Anna intended to crush the rebels in a strategic pincer movement. On 16 February, he crossed the Río Grande. Correctly surmising that the Texians expected him to advance from the south via the Laredo Road, he marched up the Old San Antonio Road, making an indirect approach from the west. On 17 February Gen. José Urrea forded the Río Grande at Matamoros and moved up the Atascosito Road with a force of some 550 men. His part in the strategic plan involved a sweep of the coastal prairies, which would culminate in the recapture of Goliad.

While Santa Anna was marching north, the Texian representatives were bickering, primarily about a scheme to capture Matamoros. Governor Smith opposed the Matamoros Expedition; Lieutenant Governor Robinson and the General Council supported it. The rift widened into a complete schism. Smith proclaimed the Council dissolved. The General Council responded by impeaching Smith and continued to meet, with Robinson serving as acting governor.

Santa Anna's advance elements arrived in Béxar on 23 February 1836 and lay siege to the Alamo, commanded by Lt. Col. William B. Travis. On 6 March—day thirteen of the siege—Santa Anna launched an assault and wiped out all of the fort's defenders, including frontiersmen James Bowie and David Crockett.

While Santa Anna's guns hammered the walls of the Alamo, fifty-nine Texian delegates convened at Washington-on-the-Brazos. The expected help from Mexican federalists had not been forthcoming and U.S. bankers had no interest in funding domestic Mexican squabbles. Consequently, on 2 March, Texian delegates signed a declaration of independence. Among the signatories were three native Mexicans: Lorenzo de Zavala, José Antonio Navarro, and José Francisco Ruiz.

With the pressing issue of independence settled, the Texian Convention of 1836 drafted a constitution for the newly created nation. Adopted by the delegates on 16 March, the document was a plagiarized collage of the U.S. Constitution and those of several Southern states. The members of the Convention then declared themselves the legitimate government of Texas and appointed Sam Houston "Commander in Chief of all the land forces of the Texan Army, both regulars, volunteers, and militia, while in actual service." For the first time, one individual exercised unity of command. As its final act, the Convention appointed an ad interim body to direct business until the establishment of a regular government. It named David G. Burnet president, Lorenzo de Zavala vice president, Samuel P. Carson secretary of state, Bailey Hardeman secretary of the treasury, Thomas Jefferson Rusk secretary of war, Robert Potter secretary of the navy, and David Thomas attorney general.

As the Texas politicos attempted to form a government, General Urrea conducted a brilliant sweep of the coastal bend. He achieved initial success when his forces surprised and overwhelmed detached Texian contingents at San Patricio and Refugio. Obeying General Houston's orders, Fannin abandoned Goliad with plans to fall back to the Colorado

River. Urrea overtook Fannin's retreating force on the open prairie between Goliad and Victoria and, after strong resistance at the Battle of Coleto Creek on 19 March, Fannin surrendered his command—then the largest Texian unit. On 27 March, during the so-called Goliad Massacre, Mexican soldiers executed Fannin and most of his command.

Earlier that month, on 11 March, General Houston had arrived in Gonzales to take command of 374 volunteers gathered there to relieve the Alamo. The troops at that post had been dead since 6 March, but Houston would not have that intelligence confirmed until 13 March. On that date Alamo widow Susanna Dickinson rode into town with details of the siege and the final assault. She also reported that Santa Anna and a 5,000-man force were on the march toward Gonzales. Because the Alamo had fallen, Santa Anna's army might easily sweep in behind Fort Defiance, so Houston dispatched orders to Goliad for Fannin to abandon the town and retire to Victoria on the Guadalupe River.

Houston's plans hinged on Fannin's prompt withdrawal. With 374 volunteers, Houston dared not engage Santa Anna's main force at Gonzales. The rebel general sought to rendezvous with the Goliad garrison. He was confident that with Fannin's 400 men he could stop the Mexican advance at the Colorado River.

On the night of 13 March, Houston began his retreat. His small contingent crossed the Colorado River on 17 March and took up a position at Burnam's Ferry. Houston realized, however, that it was not a good place to make a stand because even if he did manage to halt Santa Anna's main force there, Urrea could cross the Colorado farther down river and then drive into the heart of the Texian settlements. Houston burned the ferry and marched down the east bank, reaching Beason's Crossing on 19 March.

Conditions improved at Beason's. Understanding the seriousness of the threat facing their country, settlers flocked to Houston's army, increasing it to about 1,400 effectives. Spring rains swelled the Colorado River, temporarily rendering it impassable for the Mexicans. Also, Santa Anna had divided his forces in an attempt to locate the elusive rebel army. If Texians could not hope to fight the entire Mexican army, they might at least defeat a portion of it. Enraged at the reports of the Alamo slaughter, volunteers were spoiling for a fight.

On 21 March they got their chance when a Mexican division numbering between 600 and 800 under Gen. Joaquín Ramírez y Sesma arrived opposite Beason's Crossing and pitched camp. His lieutenants urged General Houston to cross the river and attack Ramírez before he could be reinforced, but Houston authorized only a reconnaissance-in-force. He was waiting for Fannin's division to arrive, which he expected at any time.

On 23 March Houston learned of Fannin's defeat and capture, news that totally upset his strategic planning. On

26 March Houston ordered a retreat to San Felipe on the Brazos River. The rebel army reached San Felipe on 28 March, but after spending only one night there, Houston ordered another retreat to Jared Groce's plantation, twenty miles upriver. The abandonment of San Felipe, the oldest Anglo-American settlement in Texas, caused a storm of protest. Two companies bluntly refused to retreat further. Capt. Moseley Baker's company remained to guard the San Felipe crossing. Capt. Wiley Martin took his company about twenty-five miles downriver to defend the Fort Bend crossing. Disgusted with constant retreat, many volunteers deserted to assist their families who had joined the Runaway Scrape, a wild exodus toward the Louisiana border. On 29 March, the day it began the march to Groce's, the Texian army had dwindled to a mere 500.

Houston used the two weeks on the Brazos River to good advantage. There he drilled the soldiers in the rudiments of linear combat. Austrian-born George Erath admitted that the "delay at Groce's had a good effect in disciplining us and in giving us information on military tactics." Also, through the efforts of the Texian surgeons, most of those stricken with maladies brought on by almost constant exposure to spring rains gradually improved.

Texian soldiers regained their health and self-confidence, but they and the interim government were dissatisfied with Houston's performance. President Burnet addressed a scathing letter to Houston in which he urged him to engage the Mexican forces. "The country expects you to fight," he lectured. "The salvation of the country depends on your doing so."

On 12 April Houston broke camp at Groce's. It required two days to transport all the men and supplies to the east bank of the Brazos. The general then marched his army eastward but gave no hint of its destination. Many believed they were marching toward the Mexicans and battle; others believed they were journeying toward the Sabine River and shameful safety.

On 16 April the rebel army reached a major crossroads, both literally and metaphorically. The north road led to Nacogdoches and safety, the other toward Harrisburg and confrontation. Tension was high as the army approached the crossroads. Many swore they would mutiny if the general ordered the army north. Some called loudly for Houston's removal. As the moment of decision approached, the general lingered toward the rear of the column. As the lead elements approached the fork, a shout sounded through the ranks: "To the right boys, to the right." The willful revolutionaries took the road to Harrisburg; Houston followed the army.

On 18 April Houston received captured dispatches that revealed that Santa Anna was at the head of a small force in New Washington. Santa Anna, believing Houston was still at Groce's plantation, had abandoned his pursuit of the rebel army. Finding San Felipe in ashes he traveled down river to Fort Bend, where he learned that officials of the insurgent government were at Harrisburg, a mere thirty miles away. If he could capture and hang the political ringleaders, he could let his subordinates deal with the rebel army. On 14 April he took personal command of a 500-man force and detached himself from the main army so he could travel faster. But he was not fast enough. When he arrived in Harrisburg he learned that President Burnet and his cabinet had departed only an hour before. Santa Anna dispatched dragoons in rapid pursuit, but the Texian politicos escaped to Galveston Island. On 18 April Santa Anna burned Harrisburg and rushed toward New Washington. That same day, Houston acquired the captured dispatches and realized that his rival had made a fatal blunder.

On 20 April Houston took position in an oak grove near Lynch's Ferry on the Lynchburg-Harrisburg Road; the rebel army placed itself between the Mexican general and his main force. Returning from New Washington later that day, Santa Anna found his line of march blocked by the Texians. He sent a courier to General Cos at Fort Bend. That afternoon Mexican attempts to reconnoiter the Texian position produced minor artillery and cavalry skirmishes.

On Thursday morning, 21 April, Cos arrived on the field with some 540 troops. The reinforcements increased Santa Anna's force to about 1,240. Houston, with 910 effectives, had lost the numerical advantage. Around noon, Houston called a council of war. It voted for an immediate attack, lest additional Mexican reinforcements arrive.

Houston launched his assault around 4:30 P.M. Because rising ground and high grass screened the Texian approach, the attack caught the Mexicans by surprise. After initial attempts to rally failed, Mexican soldiers fled in what one of their officers described as "a bewildered and panic-stricken herd." The fighting lasted no more than eighteen minutes; the slaughter continued much longer. Vengeful rebels shouting "Remember the Alamo" and "Remember Goliad," killed some 630 Mexicans and captured another 730. Of the 910 Texians engaged, only 9 lost their lives; 30 sustained wounds, including General Houston. Santa Anna escaped the battlefield, but Texians captured him on 22 April. Houston won a notable victory at San Jacinto, but only the capture of the Mexican commander made the triumph decisive.

The San Jacinto campaign, however, did not accomplish as much as some writers suggest. Many maintain that the Texians defeated the Mexican army at San Jacinto, but the contingent Santa Anna brought to the shores of Buffalo Bayou was only a small portion of his total force. Generals Filisola and Urrea each commanded divisions that were larger than the entire Texian army. Following the Battle of San Jacinto, the Mexicans retreated south of the Río Grande, but the breakdown of logistics influenced that decision far more than the threat of Texian arms.

Some also claim that Texas won its independence at San

Jacinto, but during the decade that it existed as a sovereign nation, Mexicans never surrendered their claim to the province. Not until the Treaty of Guadalupe Hidalgo in 1848 did they agree to abandon Texas and accept the Río Grande as the international boundary.

Stephen L. Hardin

BIBLIOGRAPHY

Hardin, Stephen L. *Texian Iliad: A Military History of the Texas Revolution.* 1994.

Jenkins, John H., ed. *The Papers of the Texas Revolution, 1835–1836.* 1973.

Lack, Paul D. *The Texas Revolutionary Experience: A Political and Social History, 1835–1836.* 1992.

Poyo, Gerald E., ed. *Tejano Journey, 1770–1859.* 1996.

Siegel, Stanley. *A Political History of the Texas Republic, 1836–1845.* 1956.

Texas Tories

From 1832 to 1836 Anglo-Texans who were satisfied with Mexican control of Texas were known as Texas tories. Also called the "peace party" by contemporaries, Texas tories were prevalent in three Anglo-Texan settlements: Gonzales, the lower Brazos River, and along the lower Trinity River. These conservatives resisted calls from the "war party" to rebel against Mexican authorities or to sever ties with Mexico between the 1832 attacks against Anáhuac, Velasco, and Nacogdoches, the convention at Washington-on-the-Brazos, and the adoption of the Texas declaration of independence on 2 March 1836. In 1832 tory sentiment was strongest east of the Trinity River among former residents of southwestern Louisiana, who had become cattle raisers in Spanish Louisiana in the 1790s after fleeing their Carolina homes following the American Revolution. The Barrows, Whites, and other families, unhappy with the U.S. purchase of the Louisiana Territory, moved to Mexican Texas in the 1820s, although they continued to smuggle their livestock to markets in Louisiana. They had no quarrel with Mexican laws, and on 20 April 1836 several tories rode eastward to the San Jacinto River to serve as guides to the Sabine River area for Gen. Antonio López de Santa Anna's army. The victory of Sam Houston's army over Santa Anna's on 21 April, however, caused a change of mind, and some tories even served in the army of the Republic of Texas during the summer of 1836.

Tory sentiment also was strong among the older colonists in Stephen F. Austin's colony along the Brazos and Green De Witt's colony at Gonzales. Those who had received generous land grants and sworn loyalty to Mexico in the mid-1820s hesitated to sever ties; this was especially true among most of Austin's old friends and relatives. The hot-headed William B. Travis and others who had come to Texas at the end of the colonial period and had not received a headright (a grant of land given to a person who would settle or develop it) lacked this feeling of loyalty or respect for Mexican culture. In general it was the young and brash newcomers who agitated to separate from Mexico. After the Battle of San Jacinto on 21 April 1836, those who had espoused tory sentiment kept low profiles. Only a few tories were punished for their loyalty to Mexico.

Margaret Swett Henson

BIBLIOGRAPHY

Henson, Margaret Swett. "Tory Sentiment in Anglo-Texan Public Opinion, 1832–1836." *Southwestern Historical Quarterly* 90 (1986): 1–34.

Lack, Paul D. *The Texas Revolutionary Experience: A Political and Social History, 1835–1836.* 1992.

See also **Texas** Revolts of 1832

Thompson, Waddy

A prosperous attorney and planter, Waddy Thompson (1798–1868) served two terms in the South Carolina legislature (1826–1830) before being elected to the U.S. Congress as a Whig in 1835. Thompson resigned after serving three terms, and in 1842 was appointed U.S. minister to Mexico by President William Henry Harrison. Although Thompson had championed recognition of the Republic of Texas in 1836, a move he saw as a necessary first step toward annexation, the new minister proved to be a pleasant surprise for the Mexican government. During his stay in Mexico he became fluent in Spanish and developed a cordial working relationship with Mexican leaders that was based on mutual respect, notwithstanding a number of crises that strained U.S.–Mexican relations during his tenure. These included the unauthorized seizure of Monterey, California, by U.S. commodore Thomas ap Catesby Jones and the violation of Mexican territorial sovereignty by Texians in the Santa Fe Expedition in 1841 and the Mier Expedition in 1842. Thompson used his influence with Mexican president Antonio López de Santa Anna to gain the release of many Texians incarcerated in Mexico. Thompson also worked out a new claims agreement with the Mexican government in 1843, although mounting debts forced Mexico to suspend claims payments to the United States one year later.

Thompson resigned his post and returned to the United States in spring 1844. A staunch supporter of Henry Clay, Thompson was anxious to disassociate himself from President John Tyler's unpopular administration, which was then engaged in a campaign to bring about the annexation of Texas, a policy Thompson then opposed. In 1846 Thompson published *Recollections of Mexico*, which was one of the few travel books by a U.S. writer during this period to express a compassionate regard for Mexico's leaders and its people.

He remained a vocal if ineffective critic of the annexation of Texas and of the U.S.–Mexican War in the years that followed. After the Civil War Thompson moved to Florida, where he died in 1868.

Sam W. Haynes

BIBLIOGRAPHY

Haynes, Sam W. *Soldiers of Misfortune: The Somervell and Mier Expeditions.* 1990.

Thompson, Henry T. *Waddy Thompson, Jr.* 1929.

Thoreau, Henry David

Author and political dissident Henry David Thoreau (1817–1862) is best known for his twenty-six-month stay in a self-built cabin on the shores of Walden Pond, the events of which were chronicled in his *Walden* (1854). Associated with the transcendental movement, Thoreau believed that each individual should eschew convention and should instead seek out divine law, which was knowable through contemplation of nature. His unyielding personal code often led him into conflict with civil authority, as was the case with his 1846 arrest because of his refusal to pay a poll tax. His refusal was an act of protest against the U.S.–Mexican War, which Thoreau felt was being fought at the urging of unscrupulous southerners anxious to spread slavery into the West.

After Thoreau's release, the famed transcendental thinker Ralph Waldo Emerson asked Thoreau why he had been jailed. Thoreau's terse reply was "Why did you not?" An apocryphal version of the story has Emerson visit the jailed Thoreau and ask his friend, "Henry, why are you in jail?" In this version, Thoreau's reply is "Waldo, why are you not?" Eyewitness testimony suggests that Emerson did not visit the jail and did not approve of Thoreau's action.

The experience resulted in Thoreau's authorship of the essay *Civil Disobedience* (1849), a document that in later generations formed the philosophical basis for the effective nonviolent protests of Mohandas Gandhi and Martin Luther King Jr. In it, Thoreau wrote that if a law "is of such a nature that it requires you to be the agent of injustice to another, then, I say, break the law."

Chuck Etheridge

BIBLIOGRAPHY

Boller, Paul. *American Transcendentalism: An Intellectual Inquiry.* 1974.

Harding, Walter. *The Days of Henry David Thoreau: A Biography.* 1982.

Harding, Walter, et al., ed. *The Writings of Henry David Thoreau.* 1970–.

Longstreth, T. Morris. *Henry David Thoreau: American Rebel.* 1963.

Matthiessen, F. O. *American Renaissance: Art and Expression in the Age of Emerson and Whitman.* 1941.

Thorns, Horns, and Stingers

Encounters with "thorns, horns, and stingers" (a popular phrase of the day) filled diaries and letters of U.S. soldiers who sojourned in Mexico during the U.S.–Mexican War. Reptiles were some of the first inhabitants to greet U.S. soldiers who entered the Río Grande Valley. Killing rattlesnakes became an everyday occupation for troops camped in the chaparral along the river. Fewer snakes were found in Mexico's mountains and high central plateau but the creatures lived in the tropical forests surrounding Tampico and Vera Cruz. Iguanas also thrived in the tropics and provided a food source for local inhabitants. Another reptile, the horned toad, gave credence to the idea that all the creatures of the region were armed with some means of protection.

Insects were constant tormenters. Mosquitoes blanketed the coastal plains and tropical forests. Camps and barracks were breeding grounds for lice and fleas. Annoying as these pests were, science had not yet realized the connection between insects and disease. Although not technically an insect, tarantulas amazed the soldiers who had never seen spiders so large. In arid regions, scorpions often crawled into shoes during the night, ready to give an unsuspecting soldier who might forget to check for such unwelcome visitors a painful surprise.

The mesquite tree and cactus could form an almost impenetrable wall, capable of ripping the clothes and skin of intruders to shreds. American soldiers tried to avoid these thickets for another reason: they formed a hiding place for bandits and guerrillas who wore chaps to protect themselves from the sharp spikes.

Richard Bruce Winders

BIBLIOGRAPHY

McCaffrey, James M. *The Army of Manifest Destiny: The American Soldier in the Mexican War, 1846–1848.* 1990.

Scott, Henry L. *Military Dictionary: Comprising the Technical Definitions; Information On Raising and Keeping Troops; Actual Service, Including Makeshift and Improved Matériel; And Law, Government, Regulation, and Administration Relating to Land Forces.* 1864.

Winders, Richard Bruce. "Mr. Polk's Army: Politics, Patronage, and the American Military in the Mexican War." Ph.D. diss., Texas Christain University, 1994.

Thornton Affair

On 24 April 1846, suspecting that Mexican troops under Gen. Mariano Arista had secretly crossed the Río Grande to attack his forces, Gen. Zachary Taylor sent a squadron (companies C and F) of the 2d Dragoons, led by Capt. Seth B. Thornton, to patrol the region adjacent to Fort Texas (later Fort Brown). On the afternoon of 25 April Thornton and his men sought shelter from the rain at Rancho de Carricitos, about twenty miles upriver. (The exact location is unknown.) Upon entering a clearing in front of the hacienda the dragoons were fired on by Mexican soldiers hiding in the nearby chaparral. These troops, commanded by Gen. Anastasio Torrejón, consisted of a battalion of sappers, some cavalry, and two companies of the 2d Light Infantry, numbering in all about 1,600 men.

Caught by surprise and greatly outnumbered, Captain Thornton and his men returned fire as they tried desperately to escape. Surrounded by Mexican troops on three sides and cut off on the fourth by the Río Grande, they were finally forced to surrender. Thornton, who was knocked unconscious when he fell off his horse, was at first believed to be dead.

The actual number of U.S. soldiers who participated in this action is uncertain. General Taylor's dispatch to the War Department states that the squadron consisted of sixty-three soldiers, of whom sixteen were killed or wounded, while a contemporary news report in *Niles' National Register* lists the names of no less than sixty-nine officers and men. Of these, said the paper, fourteen were killed outright and fifty-five soldiers (including Thornton) were taken prisoner, two of whom afterward died of their wounds. Captain Hardee, Thornton's second in command, said the party was made up of fifty-two dragoons. In contrast, General Torrejón reported he took seventy men prisoner. Regardless of their number, the captives were held at Matamoros, where Hardee reported they were well-treated. The men were later exchanged for Mexican prisoners. On 26 April, in a note to Torrejón, General Arista congratulated him on his victory, calling it the "preliminary of glorious deeds that [Mexico's] happy sons will in future present to her."

In Washington, D.C., General Taylor's report of the action was received on 9 May. Two days later, President James K. Polk addressed a joint session of Congress, declaring "Mexico has passed the boundary of the United States, has invaded our territory and shed American blood upon the American soil. She has proclaimed that hostilities have commenced, and that the two nations are now at war." On 13 May, as a result of the Thornton affair, both houses voted in favor of declaring war against Mexico.

Steven R. Butler

BIBLIOGRAPHY

Alcaraz, Ramón, ed. *The Other Side; or, Notes for the History of the War between Mexico and the United States.* Translated by Albert C. Ramsey. 1970. Originally published as *Apuntes para la historia de la Guerra entre México y los Estado Unidos,* 1848.

Butler, Steven R. *A Documentary History of the Mexican War.* 1995.

Chatfield, W. H. *The Twin Cities, Brownsville, Texas and Matamoros, Mexico.* 1893.

Niles' National Register, Baltimore, Maryland, May 23, 1846.

Quaife, Milo Milton, ed. *The Diary of James K. Polk.* 1910.

Thorpe, Thomas B. *Our Army on the Rio Grande.* 1846.

Tolsá, Eugenio

Mexican general Eugenio Tolsá (1796–1837) was born in the port of Vera Cruz, the second son of Spanish sculptor Manuel Tolsá. In 1812 he joined the viceroyal army as a veteran cadet in the Lobera Battalion and earned the rank of cavalry captain fighting against Mexican rebels. On 22 April 1821, in command of a force of dragoons in Texcoco, he joined Gen. Agustín de Iturbide's independence movement. A year later, in reward for his services, he received the rank of colonel. Tolsá retired from the army in 1823 and took on police duties, acting as chief of the Public Security Corps in Mexico City. Even so, he participated in the campaign against the Spanish invasion in 1829. He rejoined the army in 1832 and served in centralist President Anastasio Bustamante's unsuccessful campaign against the federalist rebellion of Gen. Antonio López de Santa Anna, earning the rank of brigadier general. During Santa Anna's first presidency, General Tolsá switched sides and served from 1834 to 1835 in the campaign against a federalist congress and vice president Valentín Gómez Farías. Tolsá organized one of the divisions of the army that marched on Zacatecas to crush a rebellion, headed by that city's national guard, in support of Gómez Farías. Tolsá was replaced as commander of the division but led the Reserve Brigade during the siege of Zacatecas.

In the Texas campaign from October 1835 to August 1836 Tolsá commanded a brigade that included the battalions "Guerrero" and "Primero Activo de Mexico," forty horses, and five artillery pieces. He distinguished himself at the head of this unit in the battle on the Río Colorado on 26 March and at the Atascosito on 2 April. After General Santa Anna occupied Béxar, Tolsá and his brigade formed part of the advance guard on the road to San Jacinto. Tolsá died 14 September 1837 while serving as commander general of Querétaro.

Faustino A. Aquino Sánchez

BIBLIOGRAPHY

Escontría, Alfredo. *Obra y personalidad del escultor y arquitecto Don Manuel Tolsá.* 1929.

Topographical Engineers

During the U.S.–Mexican War the U.S. Army Corps of Topographical Engineers carried out reconnaissances and helped prepare defenses and fortifications. The corps' functions included exploration, mapping, and civil works projects. This freed the larger Corps of Engineers to concentrate on its combat role to support the army in the field and to build coastal fortifications.

Topographers had served in the army since the American Revolution. During the period of national expansion the Corps of Topographical Engineers evolved into an agency supporting Manifest Destiny. It functioned as a subordinate bureau of the Corps of Engineers between 1818 and 1831, and a separate bureau between 1831 and 1838, and a separate corps from 1838 to 1863. In 1863 Congress merged it with the Corps of Engineers.

Most of the topographical engineers—twenty-six of its forty-six officers (the corps had no enlisted personnel) between 1846 and 1848—served in or near combat zones. These included the famed explorer Bvt. Capt. John C. Frémont, who played a key role in seizing California. William H. Emory, a first lieutenant, led a topographical party that mapped and described Brig. Gen. Stephen W. Kearny's route across the Southwest to California. A party consisting of 2d Lt. James W. Abert and 2d Lt. William G. Peck mapped the newly conquered territory of New Mexico. Two second lieutenants, George G. Meade and John Pope, carried out topographic duties on Gen. Zachary Taylor's staff, and Capt. George W. Hughes accompanied Brig. Gen. John E. Wool's force into northern Mexico. Capt. Joseph E. Johnston served as a topographer under Gen. Winfield Scott but transferred to the elite Voltigeur (light infantry) Regiment. Later in the war Hughes and Emory served under Scott as leaders of a volunteer infantry regiment.

While carrying out their duties, this small corps of officers continued their geographic and scientific discoveries. Their investigations, accomplished in the midst of the war, broadened geographic knowledge about the little-known regions of the Southwest and Mexico.

Adrian G. Traas

BIBLIOGRAPHY

Goetzman, William H. *Army Explorations in the American West, 1803–1863.* 1959.

Ryan, Gary David. "War Department Topographical Bureau, 1831–1863: An Administrative History." Ph.D. diss., American University, 1968.

Schubert, Frank N., ed. *The Nation Builders: A Sesquicentennial History of the Corps of Topographical Engineers, 1838–1863.* 1988.

Traas, Adrian G. *From the Golden Gate to Mexico City: The U.S. Army Topographical Engineers in the Mexican War, 1846–1848.* 1993.

Tornel, José María

José María Tornel y Mendivil (1789–1853), Mexican general and politician, was born in Orizaba, Vera Cruz. He studied at the seminary in Tehuacán (which provided elementary and high school education) and San Ildefonso College in Mexico City. He then joined the army of Epitacio Sánchez in the fight for independence from Spain.

Tornel joined Agustín de Iturbide's movement in 1821. President Guadalupe Victoria appointed Tornel his private secretary, and President Vicente Guerrero appointed him special envoy and plenipotentiary minister of Mexico to the United States; Tornel carried out these functions from November 1829 to February 1831. He returned to Mexico in 1832, and from then on he had close bonds with Gen. Antonio López de Santa Anna and collaborated with him during his presidential terms, mainly as secretary of war or governor of the Federal District.

He supported the monarchist military rebellion of Gen. Mariano Paredes y Arrillaga against Gen. José Joaquin de Herrera's administration in December 1845. Paredes y Arrillaga appointed Tornel secretary of war, and he remained in charge from February to July 1846. Therefore, General Tornel was in command of military affairs when the war started in May 1846. During the U.S. invasion, Tornel persuaded General Santa Anna not to abandon military and political command after the Battle of Cerro Gordo in April 1847. When General Santa Anna decided to resist the invading U.S. army in the Valley of Mexico, he named Tornel *cuartel general maestre* of the Mexican army and in August 1847 governor of the Federal District. The *cuartel general maestre* transmitted the General Staff's orders to the various army corps. Tornel was very active in his roles and remained with General Santa Anna during the defense of Mexico City.

Besides being a man of action, General Tornel was always keen on science, art, and education. He wrote *Tejas y los Estados Unidos de América, en sus relaciones con la República Mejicana* in 1837 and *Breve reseña histórica* in 1852. He promoted the foundation of the Lancaster Company, an institution devoted to the education of poor children; and he ran the prestigious Colegio de Minería from 1843 until his death in 1853.

Reynaldo Sordo Cedeño

BIBLIOGRAPHY

Bosch García, Carlos. *Material para la historia de las relaciones entre México y los Estados Unidos, 1829–1848.* 1957.

Sordo Cedeño, Reynaldo. "El general Tornel y la guerra de Texas." *Historia Mexicana* 42 (April–June 1993): 919–953.

Tornel Decree

Revolt in the early 1830s against President Antonio López de Santa Anna's centralist regime threatened to tear apart the Mexican republic. Mexican liberals had turned to the United States for help, and money, men, and arms flowed from New Orleans and other U.S. cities in support of the revolutionaries.

Mexican officials, noting the influx of assistance to the rebels, decided to implement a strict policy intended to prevent interference from outsiders. Minister of War José María Tornel drafted a proclamation with the approval of the Mexican congress. Called the Tornel Decree for its author, the document declared, "Foreigners landing on the coast of the republic or invading its territory by land, armed with the intention of attacking our country, will be deemed pirates and dealt with as such. . . . " Dated 30 December 1835, the Tornel Decree provided the rationale for the policy of no quarter adopted by Mexican troops in their effort to bring the rebellion to a close.

Writing in the early 1840s, Waddy Thompson, U.S. minister to Mexico, described a conversation he had with Santa Anna about the Texas Revolution. Santa Anna, once again the president of Mexico, stated to Thompson, "the campaign of Texas had been commenced under a special act of the Mexican congress, providing that no prisoners should be made." While this can be interpreted as an attempt to fix the blame on the Mexican government for atrocities committed by his troops, there is no doubt that the Tornel Decree was directly linked to events at the Alamo and at Goliad.

Richard Bruce Winders

BIBLIOGRAPHY

Thompson, Waddy. *Recollections of Mexico.* 1846.

[Tornel Decree]. *Telegraph and Texas Register.* 12 March 1836.

See also **Appendix** *for a translation of the Tornel Decree*

Torrejón, Anastasio

Born in the Llanos de Apan, Anastasio Torrejón (c. 1802–18??) joined the Royalist army as a cadet lieutenant in 1816 and fought against Mexican insurgents, earning the rank of lieutenant colonel before the end of the War for Independence. In 1823 he declared for Antonio López de Santa Anna's Plan de Casa Mata and helped establish the Mexican Republic. A highly decorated soldier, Torrejón reached the rank of brigadier general by 1840 and supported Anastasio Bustamante's government against a revolt led by Santa Anna. In 1845 Torrejón helped Mariano Paredes y Arrillaga overthrow President José Joaquín de Herrera. The following year, Torrejón arrived in Matamoros in charge of a cavalry brigade. On 25 April 1846 his command attacked and destroyed a dragoon detachment under U.S. captain Seth Thornton, the event that led the United States to declare war on the pretext that "American blood had been shed on American soil."

In the ensuing campaign, Torrejón's troops covered the Río Grande crossing of Gen. Mariano Arista's army and were engaged at Palo Alto and Resaca de la Palma. In the aftermath of these battles, Torrejón received orders to cover the army's withdrawal to Monterrey. His command defended that city and later fought at Buena Vista, where Torrejón was bruised by a shell fragment. His 3d Cavalry Brigade turned the U.S. left and nearly won the battle for the Mexicans.

In the battles for Mexico City, Torrejón led his troops at Contreras, where the brigade suffered heavy losses, after which Torrejón was accused of a lack of diligence to orders. Despite this slur on his reputation, his cavalry covered the Mexican retreat to Mexico City, and his troops fought again in defense of the San Cosme Garita (gate). In 1854 Torrejón was named commandant general of Michoacán.

Donald S. Frazier

BIBLIOGRAPHY

Carreño, Alberto M., ed. *Jefes del ejército Mexicano en 1847: Biografías de generales de división y brigadad y de coroneles del ejército Mexicano por fines del año de 1847.* 1914.

Smith, Justin H. *The War with Mexico.* 2 vols. 1919. Reprint, 1963.

Trade

The history of commerce between early national Mexico and the United States remains largely untold due to the lack of good serial data. Mexican export and import figures are neither consistent nor comprehensive; on the U.S. side, overland exports from the United States to Mexico went unrecorded until 1893. Maritime trade statistics, collected by the U.S. Treasury from 1824 onward, reveal that Mexico traded silver—mostly specie and some bullion—for manufactured cloth, for wheat flour coming through New Orleans, and for raw cotton for the Mexican textile industry, which tariffs enacted by Mexico in 1829, 1837, and 1842–1843 attempted to protect. Still, before 1838, finished cotton accounted for between 30 and 40 percent of domestic U.S. exports to Mexico. Moreover, before 1841, reexports constituted at least half of all U.S. exports to Mexico by value every year. Such quantitative evidence suggests what other qualitative information confirms: before the Texas Revolution (1835–1836), the composition of U.S. exports and reexports to Mexico reflected mostly economic factors and commercial restrictions. After that, political and diplomatic calculations came into play, as the United States and Great Britain competed more directly for influence in Mexico.

Their respective patterns of trade, which had earlier paralleled each other, falling and rising together, began to move in opposite directions, exhibiting reversed peaks and troughs.

English goods reached Mexico through Texas; this is one reason Texas dominated the political economy of trade between 1825 and 1848. At first, Tejanos were supposed to buy and sell from Mexican army quartermasters at set prices. However, to encourage settlement of the northern frontier, Mexico granted Texas settlers a seven-year exemption from tariffs in 1823. Attempts to collect duties in the early 1830s exacerbated political tensions, leading one economic historian to label the U.S.–Mexican War as an "irrepressible" conflict. Texas had no coastal customs house until 1830, but it is clear that Texas cotton was shipped to New Orleans on U.S. vessels. British merchant companies also gave U.S. traders serious competition in California.

In many ways, the most legendary trade between the United States and Mexico involved individual traders along the Santa Fe Trail. The New Mexico–Chihuahua trade remained active until 1846, as incalculable quantities of silver and mules flowed from the northern provinces to Missouri. Mexican and U.S. scholars differ over the degree of commercial and cultural influence exerted by U.S. traders over New Mexico's inhabitants. But the reorientation of the region away from Mexico and toward the United States was evident, leading a present-day authority on the Southwest, David Weber, to conclude: "The Mexican era saw the *pobladores* break loose from the grasp of Spanish mercantilism only to be embraced by American capitalism."

For the United States, overall trade flows to and from Mexico were small, but their effects could be significant. Regional markets, particularly in Texas, were probably much affected by the overland trade in cattle, horses, and mules. Before the Panic of 1837 in the United States, substantial flows of Mexican silver helped drive up U.S. prices. Wealthy Mexicans also purchased bonds of the individual states of the United States and lost money when these states suspended payment during the panic.

After the U.S.–Mexican War, Mexico's trade with the United States grew more rapidly than its trade with Europe, so that over the rest of the century the United States accounted for an increasing share of Mexico's foreign commerce. The willingness of a nascent generation of Mexican liberals to back away from protectionism and to countenance freer trade also accounted for this shift. These Mexicans, ever wary of U.S. commercial and military power, believed that opening markets to the United States would prevent further loss of territory. The rapid growth of the U.S. economy after 1840 both enlarged the U.S. market for Mexican goods and made the United States an even larger supplier of finished goods to Mexico. But it was not until the 1880s that the integration of the two economies really accelerated. The completion of rail links between the two countries was critical in this regard, as was the now openly favorable policy of the regime of Mexican dictator Porfirio Díaz toward foreign investment.

It is customary to state that trade follows the flag, that diplomacy opens the way for more intensive commercial relations. Before the war with the United States, Mexicans generally believed that the principle was reversed, and that Yankee traders were generally followed by U.S. armies. It was not until the later part of the nineteenth century that the more usual pattern held, for only then was a strengthened Mexican state really in a position to control access to its territory and, hence, to its markets.

Linda K. Salvucci

BIBLIOGRAPHY

Almonte, Juan. *Noticia estadística sobre Tejas.* 1835. Translated by Carlos E. Castañeda as "Statistical Report on Texas." *Southwestern Historical Quarterly* 28 (1925): 177–222.

Boyle, Susan Calafate. *Los Capitalistas: Hispano Merchants on the Santa Fe Trail.* 1997.

Gregg, Josiah. *Commerce of the Prairies.* 1844.

Herrera Canales, Inés. *El comercio exterior de Mexico. 1821–1875.* 1977.

Moyano Pahissa, Angela. *El comercio de Santa Fe y la guerra del 47.* 1976.

Salvucci, Richard J. "The Origins and Progress of U.S.–Mexican Trade, 1825–1884: 'Hoc opus, hic labor est.' " *Hispanic American Historical Review* 71, no. 4 (1991): 697–735.

Weber, David J. *The Mexican Frontier, 1821–1846: The American Southwest under Mexico.* 1982.

Traders Battalion

The Traders Battalion was a volunteer infantry unit of approximately 150 overland merchants and teamsters who had accompanied Col. Alexander W. Doniphan's expedition to Chihuahua. Doniphan had been ordered to report with his regiment of Missouri Volunteers to Gen. John E. Wool at Chihuahua City. He learned upon his arrival at El Paso del Norte on 29 December 1846, however, that Wool had not marched on Chihuahua. (Wool's Chihuahua campaign had in fact been abandoned.) Doniphan decided to proceed to Chihuahua anyway, but, confident that he would encounter a large Mexican force, he ordered the formation of the Traders Battalion on 9 February 1847 to augment his small army. This battalion was organized from members of the merchant caravan of some three hundred wagons traveling south with Doniphan for protection. Two companies were formed: merchant Edward James Glasgow was elected captain of Company A; wagonmaster Henry Skillman, captain of Company B; and merchant Samuel C. Owens, their major.

U.S. traders at Doniphan's camp. John Frost, *Pictorial History of Mexico and the Mexican War*, 1862

At the Battle of Sacramento on 28 February 1847, eighteen miles outside of Chihuahua, Doniphan used the merchant and army wagons to conceal the strength of his army as he maneuvered it into position. The wagons then remained in the rear of Doniphan's attacking force to serve as fortifications if the Missouri Volunteers were repulsed. The Traders Battalion was charged with protecting these wagons, but because Doniphan's Missourians drove the Mexican army under Gen. José Heredia from the field, the battalion did not enter the fight. Major Owens, however, joined in the first charge on the Mexican positions and was killed while rashly firing into an enemy redoubt (many suspected that Owens sought death). Although battalion members returned to their former civilian pursuits immediately after the battle, they were not mustered out of service until 5 April 1847. Because Doniphan had not been authorized to form such a unit (and the muster rolls had been subsequently lost in Washington), several Traders Battalion veterans were denied pensions late in life.

Mark L. Gardner

BIBLIOGRAPHY

Connelley, William E. [ed.]. *War with Mexico, 1846–1847; Doniphan's Expedition and the Conquest of New Mexico and California.* 1907.

Gardner, Mark L., ed. *Brothers on the Santa Fe and Chihuahua Trails: Edward James Glasgow and William Henry Glasgow, 1846–1848.* 1993.

U.S. Congress. Senate. *Memorial and Resolutions of the Mexican War Veteran Volunteer Association . . . 55th Cong., 2d sess., 1898. S. Doc. 146. Serial 3600.

Trans-Nueces

Referred to as the Seno Mexicano by Mexicans, the Trans-Nueces was the region between the Nueces River and the Río Grande. In Spanish, the term Seno Mexicano means the Gulf of Mexico, but it was used more generally to refer to the coastal plains from the Nueces River south to the southern border of the Mexican state of Tamaulipas. The boundary of this region within present-day Texas extended from Corpus Christi on the Gulf Coast westward along the Nueces River, southward to Laredo, and eastward along the Río Grande to Matamoros and the Gulf Coast. Mexico's longstanding claim to this region as part of its northern state of Tamaulipas was based on the fact that the state and municipal governments there had been established and functioning since the mid-eighteenth century. Residents of the region considered themselves Mexicans rather than Tejanos, as the native Mexicans in Texas were called. Following its 1836 declaration of independence, the Republic of Texas also claimed the region, although Texas neither occupied it nor controlled it militarily. The United States supported the Texas claim, but had begun to develop its own claim to Texas before annexing it as a state in 1845.

Approximately 8,000 Mexicans lived in the disputed region, most either in a few small villages or on large ranches. The largest town was Laredo, which had a population of 1,891 according to a census carried out by Capt. Mirabeau B. Lamar when he and U.S. forces occupied the town in 1846.

Lamar occupied Laredo and held it in the initial phase of the U.S.–Mexican War. One of his lieutenants occupied Presidio (near present-day Eagle Pass, Texas), which toward the end of the war had fewer than 300 Mexican and Texian residents. Other villages included Corpus Christi with about 20 Mexican families and a few Anglo-Americans and San Patricio with 20 Irish families and 8 Mexican families. Scores of Mexican ranching communities also dotted the region between the Nueces River and the Río Grande, each containing from 20 to 150 ranch family members and workers. Many of these villagers and ranchers sold beef, eggs, spirits, and supplies to Gen. Zachary Taylor's army as it made its way toward the Río Grande. Some also served as guides and muleteers for the U.S. Army.

Along the south bank of the Río Grande, several thousand Mexican residents lived in the towns of Camargo, Matamoros, Mier, and Reynosa. In fact, the Mexican residents of these settlements were close relatives of the families living north of the Río Grande, who were also under the municipal jurisdiction of the towns on the south bank of the Río Grande.

In general, the Mexicans of the Seno Mexicano resisted the U.S. encroachment on and claim to their land. On separate occasions, the Mexican villagers petitioned Captain Lamar and General Taylor in 1846 to allow their region to remain a part of the Republic of Mexico. The petitions were denied. The residents of one Mexican village near present-day Harlingen burned their homes and fields rather than let them fall into Taylor's hands on his approach to Matamoros. Mexican residents of the river towns contributed beans, corn, and other supplies to the Mexican army and volunteered as auxiliary forces. Indeed, a cavalry force of approximately five hundred *ranchero* riders was recruited from these towns by Gen. Antonio Canales, a lawyer and political leader of Camargo. Canales intially offered to support General Taylor in exchange for Taylor's support for an independent Republic of the Río Grande that would consist of these towns and the surrounding ranching frontier. Taylor refused, however, and Canales led his *ranchero* cavalry on guerrilla-style raids of Taylor's supply convoys throughout the region.

After the Treaty of Guadalupe Hidalgo in 1848, the Trans-Nueces region was occupied by the U.S. Army and formally incorporated into Texas and the United States, at which time the region's residents became U.S. citizens.

Andrés Tijerina

BIBLIOGRAPHY

Castañeda, Carlos E. *Our Catholic Heritage in Texas, 1519–1936.* Vol. 2. 1936.

Covian Martinez, Vidal Efrén. *Compendio de historia de Tamaulipas.* 4 vols. 1973.

Roa Barcena, José María. *Recuerdos de la invasion norteamericana (1846–1848).* 2 vols. 1947.

United States. *The Seventh Census of the United States, 1850. Texas* MSS (microfilm).

Travis, William B.

Commander of Texas revolutionary forces during the Battle of the Alamo, William Barret Travis (1809–1836) was born in Edgefield District, now Saluda County, South Carolina, on 9 August. His family moved to Conecuh County, Alabama, in 1818. Travis read for the law in Monroeville, practiced law, joined the Masonic lodge and the Alabama militia, and published a newspaper, the *Claiborne Herald.* Then he moved to Texas without explanation; by 1835 his wife had begun divorce proceedings on the grounds of desertion.

Travis opened a law office in Anáhuac in 1831 and quickly became involved in a dispute with Mexican colonel Juan Davis Bradburn over customs collections and other problems produced by the Law of April 6, 1830. Bradburn arrested Travis, but he was released by Col. José de las Piedras to defuse tension.

Travis moved his law practice to San Felipe and became secretary of the *ayuntamiento,* or local governing body. In 1835 he returned to Anáhuac with volunteers to capture the command of Capt. Antonio Tenorio, who had been sent to resume customs collections.

Travis participated in the march from Gonzales to San Antonio in October 1835 and served as a scout for Stephen F. Austin's Army of the People until just before the Battle of San Antonio (5–10 December 1835). He returned to San Felipe before the battle to recruit men and while there received a commission as lieutenant colonel of cavalry from the Consultation. He returned to San Antonio in January 1836 by order of Interim Governor Henry Smith and succeeded Col. James C. Neill as commander of the forces in the Alamo. Travis was forced to share command with Col. James Bowie, whose volunteers would obey only the famous knife fighter. Travis and all of the Alamo's defenders perished when their fortress fell to Gen. Antonio López de Santa Anna on 6 March 1836.

One of the strongest myths of the Alamo concerns Travis's "line in the dirt." When it was clear that no Texian reinforcements would arrive in time to aid the defenders, Travis allegedly drew a line in the dirt and asked those who were willing to join him in a fight to the death to step across it. All but one did, a man named Moses Lewis Rose. None of the Alamo survivors recounted this incident at the time; the story was first told by a third-hand source more than twenty years later, in 1857. "Remember the Alamo" became the battle cry of vengeance at the Battle of San Jacinto (21 April 1836); subsequent claims to Texas eventually led to the U.S.–Mexican War.

Archie P. McDonald

BIBLIOGRAPHY

McDonald, Archie P. *Travis*. 1976. Rev. ed., 1995.

McDonald, Archie P. *Travis: One Chief Rol'd among the Rest.* The Kathryn Stoner O'Connor Lectures on Texas History, no. 1. 1986.

Treaties

In addition to the following articles, see also **Adams-Onís Treaty;** **Clayton-Bulwer Treaty; McLane-Ocampo Treaty**

Treaties of Velasco

Gen. Antonio López de Santa Anna, disguised as a common soldier, was captured by Texian forces the day after the Battle of San Jacinto (21 April 1836). Although it was the desire of the Texas army to hang him for his crimes at the Alamo and La Bahía (present-day Goliad), Sam Houston understood his value as a diplomatic pawn, and Texas president David G. Burnet concurred in this view. Santa Anna met with Vice President Lorenzo de Zavala, and understanding that his life was at stake, agreed to sign two treaties at Velasco, on the Texas coast, where he had been taken to ensure his safety.

By the terms of the treaties, parts of which were kept secret, Santa Anna promised to immediately cease hostilities against Texas and to work for a durable and lasting peace. As Mexican troops evacuated Texas beyond the Río Grande, they would have to restore captured property. Most important, Mexico agreed to recognize Texas independence with the boundary placed at the Río Grande. In return for those concessions, the Lone Star Republic pledged to return Santa Anna alive to Mexico. Made possible by the stunning victory at San Jacinto, the treaties of Velasco ensured the independence of Texas. The government of Mexico asserted that these treaties were invalid because Santa Anna was a captive when they were signed and that, therefore, no formal agreements on recognition and boundaries were ever made between Texas and Mexico.

Stanley E. Siegel

BIBLIOGRAPHY

Schmitz, Joseph W. *Texan Statecraft, 1836–1845*. 1941.

Siegel, Stanley. *A Political History of the Texas Republic, 1836–1845*. 1956.

Treaty of 1832

Following the War of 1812, the character of Native American–U.S. relations changed. As the threat of British intervention ceased, and as the number of land-hungry settlers increased, the U.S. government no longer felt the need to accommodate its indigenous allies. Between 1816 and 1850 scores of treaties were negotiated in which Indian tribes ceded their lands east of the Mississippi River to the United States and agreed to move to territory west of the Mississippi River (present-day Oklahoma).

Federal policy, established in the Indian Removal Act of 1830, resulted in removal of the Sac, Fox, and Kickapoo peoples of the Ohio country, as well as the southern Chickasaws, Choctaws, Creeks, Cherokees, and Seminoles. Typical of removal policy was the treaty between the United States and the Seminoles signed in 1832 at Payne's Landing, Florida, by U.S. negotiator James Gadsden and fifteen Seminole representatives.

Affixing their Xs to the treaty, the chiefs agreed to relinquish to the United States by 1835 all lands they occupied in Florida and emigrate to Creek country west of the Mississippi River. The Seminoles were to receive $15,400 and additional compensation for cattle and property. Claims against them for stolen slaves were liquidated.

As 1835 drew nearer, however, many Seminoles (and their African slaves) began to oppose the treaty, and they resisted removal for seven years. After arriving in Oklahoma in 1842, immigrant Seminoles faced the hostility of Osages, Comanches, and Texans. Eventually, more than three hundred Seminoles joined the Mexicans and their Kickapoo allies in their struggle against Texas. At times the Texans made use of other displaced tribes, such as the Choctaws, to serve as auxiliaries against the Seminoles. The Anglo communities of West Texas were not free of the threat of Comanche attack until 1875, at which time the Seminoles and Kickapoos settled into a more peaceful life on the plains of Coahuila.

W. Dirk Raat

BIBLIOGRAPHY

Hagan, William T. *American Indians*. 1979.

Moseley, Edward H. "Indians from the Eastern United States and the Defense of Northeastern Mexico, 1855–1864." *Southwestern Social Science Quarterly* 46 (1965): 273–280.

"Treaty between the United States and the Seminole (North American Indians), signed at Payne's Landing, 9 May 1832." In *The Consolidated Treaty Series*, edited and annotated by Clive Parry. Vol. 82, pp. 397–399. 1969.

Treaty of Cahuenga

The Treaty of Cahuenga, signed 12 January 1847 by Lt. Col. John C. Frémont for the United States and Gen. Andrés Pico for the Californios, ended the resistance of the Mexican citizens of upper California to the U.S. occupation of California during the U.S.–Mexican War.

The United States had officially claimed California on 7 July 1846 and immediately occupied the province. The northern Californios generally offered only minor resistance, but those in the south expelled the U.S. forces from Los Angeles in September 1846 and defeated Gen. Stephen W. Kearny's recently arrived army in December. After rescuing General Kearny's army, the American commander, Commo. Robert F. Stockton, moved his and Kearny's army north to retake Los Angeles and simultaneously asked Lieutenant Colonel Frémont to bring his army south from the San Francisco area to assist. While Frémont was still north of town, camped at the foot of Cahuenga Pass, near the San Fernando mission, Stockton and Kearny defeated the Californios and reentered Los Angeles on 10 January 1847.

Knowing Frémont was in the area, the defeated Californios sought him out to begin the process of surrender. They turned to Frémont because of their resentment of Stockton for his harsh actions during his occupation of Los Angeles. Under Frémont's overview, both sides appointed commissioners, who drafted a surrender document. The document required the Californios to surrender their public arms, to return home, to obey the laws of the United States, and to not resume hostilities. Life, property, and citizenship were to be protected, and Californios were not required to take an oath of allegiance until a final treaty was signed. Those who wished could leave the country. The capitulation, ending all resistance to the U.S. conquest of California, was signed by the commissioners, Frémont as the self-styled military commandant of the U.S. forces, and Pico as "Chief of the National Forces" of the Californios. An additional article, signed 16 January, canceled paroles of prisoners on both sides. Six other provisions—calling for elections, protection of priests, retention of incumbents in office, recognition of public debts, and destroyed property—were apparently approved on the 18th, but their exact status is unclear.

Frémont's signing of the treaty was controversial. There was the question of whether or not Frémont had the authority to sign such a treaty, as he was not the commander of the U.S. troops in California; both Stockton and Kearny outranked him and were close by. Frémont's action exasperated both of his superiors, who saw it as insubordinate, and who worried that Frémont may not have known of the U.S. victory and might have given away more than necessary in the armistice. As it turned out, he had not given too much, and Stockton forgave Frémont's rashness enough to appoint him governor of California. Most historians believe that, beyond Frémont's usual desire for the spotlight, his actions were based on his hope to establish a conciliatory atmosphere in California during his governorship.

Raymond Starr

BIBLIOGRAPHY

Bancroft, Hubert Howe. *History of California.* Vol. 5. *1846–1848.* 1886.

Harlow, Neal. *California Conquered: War and Peace on the Pacific, 1846–1850.* 1982.

Rolle, Andrew. *John Charles Fremont: Character as Destiny.* 1991.

Tays, George, ed. "Pío Pico's Correspondence with the Mexican Government, 1846–1848." *California Historical Society Quarterly* 13 (1934): 134–136.

Treaty of Guadalupe Hidalgo

The Treaty of Guadalupe Hidalgo ended the U.S.–Mexican War. Signed on 2 February 1848, it is the oldest treaty still in force between the United States and Mexico. As a result of the treaty, the United States acquired more than 500,000 square miles of valuable territory and emerged as a world power in the late nineteenth century.

Beyond territorial gains and losses, the treaty has been important in shaping the international and domestic histories of both Mexico and the United States. During the U.S.–Mexican War, U.S. leaders assumed an attitude of moral superiority in their negotiations of the treaty. They viewed the forcible incorporation of almost one-half of Mexico's national territory as an event foreordained by providence, fulfilling Manifest Destiny to spread the benefits of U.S. democracy to the lesser peoples of the continent. Because of its military victory the United States virtually dictated the terms of settlement. The treaty established a pattern of political and military inequality between the two countries, and this lopsided relationship has stalked Mexican-U.S. relations ever since.

The treaty in draft form was brought to Mexico by Nicholas P. Trist, the U.S. peace commissioner, in the summer of 1847. In its basic form it called for the cession of Alta and Baja California and New Mexico, the right of transit across the Tehuantepec isthmus, and the Río Grande as the southern border of Texas. In exchange the United States would pay up to $20 million to Mexico and assume up to $3 million in U.S. citizens' claims against Mexico. In subsequent negotiations the demand for Baja California and the right of transit were dropped.

After the military campaign, which had resulted in U.S. occupation of most of Mexico's major cities, the Mexican government agreed to meet with Trist to discuss peace terms. Just before negotiations were to begin, however, Trist received instructions from President James K. Polk ordering him to return to Washington, D.C. Trist, however, decided to stay on and meet with the Mexican representatives, even though he lacked official status.

Negotiations began in earnest in January 1848. The Mexican government, headed by the ad interim Mexican president Manuel de la Peña y Peña, quickly agreed to the boundary issues: Texas's southern boundary would be the Río Grande, the cession of Alta California would include the port of San Diego, and Mexico would give up its territory between Texas and California, with a boundary to be surveyed. Mexican peace commissioners Luis G. Cuevas, Bernardo Couto, and Miguel Atristain spent a good deal of time on various drafts of Articles VIII and IX, which dealt with the issues of property rights and U.S. citizenship for Mexican citizens in the newly ceded regions. The Mexican commissioners succeeded in amplifying the texts of the two articles. They also introduced Article XI, which gave the United States responsibility for controlling hostile Indian incursions originating on the U.S. side of the border. (Article XI proved to be a source of irritation between the two nations and was subsequently negated by the Gadsden Treaty of 1854.)

On his own initiative, Trist offered an indemnity of $15 million, judging that this would gain acceptance for the treaty among those who felt that the United States had already paid enough in "blood and treasure."

After reaching agreement on all these issues, Trist drew up an English-language draft of the treaty and Cuevas translated it into Spanish, preserving the idiom and thought rather than the literal meaning. Finally, on 2 February 1848, the Mexican representatives met Trist in the Villa of Guadalupe Hidalgo, across from the shrine of the patron saint of Mexico. They signed the treaty and then celebrated a mass together at the basilica.

Signing the treaty was only the beginning of the process; it still had to be ratified by the congresses of both the United States and Mexico. No one could foresee how the Polk administration would receive a treaty negotiated by an unofficial agent; nor could they know the twists and turns of the Mexican political scene for the next few months. In both the U.S. and Mexican governments there was opposition to the treaty. In the United States, the northern abolitionists opposed the annexation of Mexican territory. In the Mexican congress, a sizable minority was in favor of continuing the fight. Nevertheless both countries ratified the document. The signing of the Treaty of Guadalupe Hidalgo marked the end of a war and the beginning of a lengthy U.S. political debate over slavery in the acquired territories, as well as continued conflict with Mexico over boundaries.

The Treaty of Guadalupe Hidalgo looms larger in the history of Mexico than in that of the United States. Partly because of the loss of valuable territory, the treaty ensured that Mexico would remain an underdeveloped country well into the twentieth century. Mexican historians and politicians view this treaty as a bitter lesson in U.S. aggression. As a result of the humiliation of the war and the loss of more than half of the national territory, young Mexicans embraced a reform movement, headed by Benito Juárez, governor of Oaxaca, who had opposed the treaty. In the 1850s the reformers came to power in Mexico vowing to strengthen the country's political system so that never again would they be victims of U.S. aggression. Benito Juárez's La Reforma was the start of a political and economic modernization process that continues to this day in Mexico.

The Treaty of Guadalupe Hidalgo has had implications not only for relations between the two countries but also for international law. Interpretations of the provisions of the treaty have been important in disputes over international boundaries, water and mineral rights, and the civil and property rights of the descendants of the Mexicans in the ceded territories. Since 1848 there have been hundreds of court cases citing the Treaty of Guadalupe Hidalgo as a basis for land claims, but few Mexican claimants were successful in retaining their land.

Since 1848 Native Americans and Mexican Americans have struggled to achieve political and social equality within the United States, often citing the Treaty of Guadalupe Hidalgo as a document that promised civil and property rights. Although the treaty promised U.S. citizenship to former Mexican citizens, the Native Americans in the ceded territories, who in fact were Mexican citizens, were not given full U.S. citizenship until the 1930s. Former Mexican citizens were almost universally considered foreigners by the U.S. settlers who moved into the new territories. In the first half century after ratification of the Treaty of Guadalupe Hidalgo, hundreds of state, territorial, and federal legal bodies produced a complex tapestry of conflicting opinions and decisions bearing on the meaning of the treaty. The property rights seemingly guaranteed in Articles VIII and IX of the treaty (and in the Protocol of Querétaro) were not all they seemed. In U.S. courts, the property rights of former Mexican citizens in California, New Mexico, and Texas proved to be fragile. Within a generation the Mexican-Americans became a disenfranchised, poverty-stricken minority.

Richard Griswold del Castillo

BIBLIOGRAPHY

Chacon Gómez, Fernando. "The Intended and Actual Effects of Article VIII of the Treaty of Guadalupe Hidalgo: Mexican Treaty Rights under International and Domestic Law." Ph.D. diss., University of Michigan, 1977.

Griswold del Castillo, Richard. *The Treaty of Guadalupe Hidalgo: A Legacy of Conflict.* 1990.

Pletcher, David M. *The Diplomacy of Annexation: Texas, Oregon, and the Mexican War.* 1973.

See also **Appendix** *for full text of the treaty*

Trías Álvarez, Ángel

Ángel Trías Álvarez (1807–1867), governor of Chihuahua, was born in Chihuahua City and educated in Europe. A nephew of liberal general Juan Álvarez, Trías campaigned against Apaches in the 1830s and became governor of Chihuahua in 1845. When the United States invaded in 1846, Trías prepared to defend the northern state, organizing militia troops and overseeing the casting of artillery at his personal expense. In February 1847, after the surrender of New Mexico, a column under Col. Alexander W. Doniphan advanced from El Paso toward Chihuahua City. Governor Trías assigned defensive fortifications to one of Mexico's foremost engineers, Gen. Pedro García Conde, who established a strong position on the Sacramento River; command of the troops was entrusted to Brig. Gen. José A. Heredia. On 28 February, U.S. forces attacked and overcame the Mexican defenses. Trías withdrew his capital to Parral until the army of occupation withdrew in April.

In March 1848, after the Treaty of Guadalupe Hidalgo had ended the war, the governor of New Mexico, Sterling Price, on his own initiative, launched a second invasion of Chihuahua. Once again Trías rode out to meet the aggressors. On 16 March he fell captive at the Battle of Santa Cruz de Rosales but was released when Governor Price obeyed federal orders and withdrew from Mexico.

During the postwar border survey commission's dispute over the Mesilla Valley, Trías mobilized state forces against the threat of yet another invasion from New Mexico. He continued as a leader in state politics for two decades and assisted Benito Juárez while in Chihuahua during the French intervention. He died in Chihuahua, in a town later named Labor de Trías in his honor.

Jeffrey M. Pilcher

BIBLIOGRAPHY

Bauer, K. Jack. *The Mexican War, 1846–1848.* 1974.
Diccionario Porrúa: De história, biografía, y geografía de México. 6th ed. 1995.
Roeder, Ralph. *Juarez and His Mexico.* 1947.

Trist, Nicholas P.

U.S. diplomat Nicholas Philip Trist (1800–1874) was the remarkable executive agent who defied a president and sacrificed his career to negotiate the treaty that ended the U.S.–Mexican War. Born in Charlottesville, Virginia, and raised in Louisiana, he attended the College of Orleans and West Point but resigned from the latter in 1821 without graduating. He then read law in New Orleans with Edward Livingston before moving to the Charlottesville office of Thomas Jefferson, a family friend whose granddaughter Trist married in 1824. Resident briefly at Monticello, he witnessed the great Virginian's death in 1826 and afterward administered Jefferson's estate.

Aristocratic in temperament, Trist could be pompous, headstrong, and self-righteous, but he was also idealistic, principled, and driven by a strong sense of duty. He lacked ambition and was repeatedly rescued from financial diffi-

Nicholas P. Trist. John Frost, *Pictorial History of Mexico and the Mexican War,* 1862

culty by influential acquaintances who admired his character, suffered his ponderous correspondence, and invariably promoted his interests. Jefferson secured Trist's West Point appointment, Henry Clay found him a clerkship in the U.S. State Department in 1828, and President Andrew Jackson employed him as a private secretary before appointing him consul in Havana in 1833, a post Trist held until 1841.

President James K. Polk presented Trist with his historic opportunity by returning him to the State Department in 1845 as its chief clerk. In April 1847, on the recommendation of Secretary of State James Buchanan, Polk commissioned Trist executive agent to arrange a peace with Mexico. A quarrel with Gen. Winfield Scott marred Trist's arrival at Vera Cruz in May, Polk having predisposed his envoy against the general and Scott suspecting the president of trying to undermine his authority. Although mutual good sense fostered a reconciliation and a close friendship between Scott and Trist, their initial feud and Trist's conciliatory posture during early negotiations dismayed Polk. On 6 October the president, dissatisfied with Trist's handling of the negotiations, ordered his agent recalled. Crestfallen, Trist prepared to leave, but in early December he changed his mind, ignored the recall, and reopened negotiations. On 2 February 1848, in line with his original instructions, he successfully completed the Treaty of Guadalupe Hidalgo. Polk, furious with his disobedient emissary but mindful of the treaty's merits, accepted the settlement. The president afterward punished

Trist by refusing to pay him beyond the date the diplomat received his recall in Mexico City.

Trist's unauthorized but courageous actions deflated a growing sentiment in the United States to acquire all of Mexico and extricated Polk from the quagmire of an increasingly unpopular war. Acceptable because it met the president's essential territorial objectives, his achievement nevertheless weighed heavily on Trist's conscience. Biographer Robert Drexler, indeed, offers evidence that this unlikely agent of Manifest Destiny was embarrassed by the terms the imperative of peace required him to force on the beleaguered Mexicans.

Trist returned home to eke out a meager living as a paymaster for the Philadelphia, Wilmington, and Baltimore Railroad. In 1870 President Ulysses S. Grant appointed him postmaster in Alexandria, Virginia, and the following year Congress finally awarded him the monetary compensation denied by Polk. Trist died in Alexandria, largely unnoticed, on 11 February 1874.

L. Marshall Hall

BIBLIOGRAPHY

Drexler, Robert W. *Guilty of Making Peace: A Biography of Nicholas P. Trist.* 1991.

Graebner, Norman A. *Empire on the Pacific: A Study in American Continental Expansion.* 1955. 2d ed., 1983.

Pletcher, David M. *The Diplomacy of Annexation: Texas, Oregon, and the Mexican War.* 1973.

Sears, Louis M. "Nicholas P. Trist, a Diplomat with Ideals." *Mississippi Valley Historical Review* 11 (1924): 85–98.

Tucson

Founded by Spanish-speaking pioneers in 1775, Tucson remained a Sonora frontier garrison *presidio* until the Gadsden Purchase transferred it to the United States in 1853. Although Tucson was unimportant to U.S. strategists during the U.S.–Mexican War, sharp encounters took place there.

Encouraged by at least eight Spanish land grants, Tucson was becoming a prosperous extension of northern New Spain by 1800. It was a self-sufficient agrarian community supporting *presidio* troops. Although its residents had little contact with other Spanish communities, Tucson maintained extensive relations with indigenous tribes. A wall enclosed and protected the community until 1856.

The political and financial turmoil that followed Mexican independence weakened Tucson because the missions were abandoned, the *presidios* were neglected, and rations used to pacify the indigenous peoples were no longer available. Although not eager to break with Mexico, *Tucsonenses* were dissatisfied with their hardship living conditions. They backed Mariano Paredes y Arrillaga when he overthrew José

Joaquín de Herrera with northern assistance in 1846. Tucson adhered formally to the 1843 *Bases Orgánicas* but demanded a federalist general, José Urrea, as leader of the Department of the North.

During the U.S.–Mexican War, Tucson had mixed relations with U.S. forces. On at least two occasions, U.S. troops entered Tucson. The Mormon Battalion passed through Tucson in December 1846. When the Mexican commander, Gen. Antonio Comadrán, learned that U.S. forces were on the outskirts, he urged them to bypass Tucson. Desperate for supplies, however, Lt. Col. Philip St. George Cooke insisted that his Mormon Battalion be permitted to enter. Comadrán then withdrew his one-hundred-man force, which was greatly outnumbered, and the citizens of Tucson evacuated to the nearby mission San Xavier. Thus, Cooke encountered no resistance when he entered Tucson on 17 December 1846. Realizing that the Mormons were well-intentioned, Tucson's civilians then began to trade eagerly with U.S. forces.

Such courtesy and respect was absent during the next encounter. In November 1847 a detachment of sixty U.S. troops rode near Tucson on their way to California in order to consolidate the still shaky U.S. occupation there. These forces were aggressive. They attempted unsuccessfully to assault the walls for four days. Because taking Tucson was not important to U.S. strategy in the region, a detail of five soldiers from Fort Bliss, Texas, rode in to recall this force. This event was the last conflict in Tucson during the U.S.–Mexican War.

Douglas W. Richmond

BIBLIOGRAPHY

Getty, Harry. *Interethnic Relationships in the Community of Tucson.* 1976.

Sheridan, Thomas E. *Los Tucsonenses: The Mexican Community in Tucson, 1854–1941.* 1986.

Tuxpan, Battle of

The Battle of Tuxpan between the U.S. Navy and Mexican forces occurred 18 April 1847. Located midway between Tampico and Vera Cruz, Tuxpan was similar to Mexico's other Gulf ports, except for Vera Cruz, in that it lay upstream—about eight miles up the Río Tuxpan—and was protected by shoal water at the river's mouth. By early April 1847 Tuxpan was the only important Gulf Coast port not in U.S. hands.

In March 1847 Commo. Matthew C. Perry organized and drilled an infantry brigade. Drawn from the squadron, it was the first in the history of the U.S. Navy. Numbering at one point more than two thousand men, it also had ten brass guns.

Perry considered the capture of Tuxpan a matter of honor for the navy because Tuxpan was in part defended by guns taken from the USS *Truxtun,* which had run aground. The town was well situated for defense with batteries on high ground, including one atop a forty-foot cliff. Gen. Don Martín Perfecto de Cos, a brother-in-law of Antonio López de Santa Anna, commanded the Mexican garrison.

Perry's landing force consisted of 1,489 officers and men and four guns. The naval portion of the attacking force consisted of the steamers *Spitfire, Vixen,* and *Scourge,* three schooners, and three bomb brigs. The expedition rendezvoused at Lobos Island and arrived off the Río Tuxpan 17 April. Because the water was only eight feet deep at the bar, Perry had his men lighten the larger *Spitfire* and *Vixen* by removing their masts. The flagship *Mississippi* anchored offshore and Perry shifted his flag to the *Spitfire.*

Early on the morning of 18 April the three steamers crossed the bar and steamed upriver, each towing a sail gunboat and ten barges carrying the landing parties. About 2:30 P.M. the expedition came under fire from the principal Mexican shore battery defending Tuxpan. The *Spitfire* pushed ahead with the other vessels following under oar and sail. The Mexicans then fired grape and canister, and future Confederate officer Raphael Semmes remembered that "the affair began to be a little serious."

Cmdr. Franklin Buchanan and his landing party got ashore first and quickly overran the principal shore battery. By 4:00 P.M. the U.S. force had secured all the forts at a cost of only two U.S. sailors killed and twelve wounded. The next day Perry disarmed Tuxpan, destroying the forts and removing anything of use to the Mexican forces, including the guns from the *Truxtun* and military stores.

On 22 April Perry's shore parties withdrew, leaving the *Albany* and *Reefer* to guard the river mouth. Perry then ordered his squadron against Tabasco, the last significant port still in Mexican hands.

Spencer C. Tucker

BIBLIOGRAPHY

Bauer, K. Jack. *Surfboats and Horse Marines. U.S. Naval Operations in the Mexican War. 1846–48.* 1969.

Morison, Samuel Eliot. *"Old Bruin." Commodore Matthew Calbraith Perry.* 1967.

Semmes, Raphael. *Service Afloat and Ashore during the Mexican War.* 1851.

Smith, Justin H. *The War with Mexico.* 2 vols. 1919. Reprint, 1963.

Twiggs, David E.

U.S. general David Emanuel Twiggs (1790–1862), son of Revolutionary War hero John Twiggs, was born near Augusta, Georgia, on 14 February. During the Creek War (1813–1814), David Twiggs commanded small groups of regulars in the Mississippi Territory. He became a major after the War of 1812 and participated in Andrew Jackson's invasion of Florida (later known as the First Seminole War) and in virtually every phase of the Second Seminole War. Promoted to colonel, he was commanding the 2d Regiment of Dragoons at the beginning of the U.S.–Mexican War.

Twiggs first served under Gen. Zachary Taylor in northern Mexico. While encamped with Taylor's army between the Nueces River and the Río Grande in early 1846, Twiggs's argument with Brig. Gen. William J. Worth led to Worth temporarily quitting the service. As Taylor's second-in-command during Worth's absence, Twiggs played a conspicuous role at the Battles of Palo Alto and Resaca de la Palma. After the U.S. Army crossed the Río Grande, Twiggs became military governor of Matamoros. Worth returned as the army moved toward Monterrey, however, and Twiggs's unit played only a small role in the Battle of Monterrey. Following the capture of Monterrey, Twiggs and Worth were ordered to join Gen. Winfield Scott's upcoming Mexico City campaign.

Twiggs's division was the last to disembark at Vera Cruz on 9 March. After the surrender of Vera Cruz, Twiggs's division led the march toward Mexico City on 8 April 1846. Within a few days, he approached the heavily fortified pass of Cerro Gordo. After nearly walking into a trap laid by Gen. Antonio López de Santa Anna, Twiggs awaited the arrival of General Scott. Planning to flank the Mexican position on 17 April, Scott gave Twiggs the honor of leading the attack. Twiggs's men overran the Mexican positions but failed to cut off the Mexicans' retreat.

After waiting in Puebla several months for reinforcements, the U.S. Army resumed its march on Mexico City. The campaign's final phase began on 7 August 1846, but Twiggs's division played only a small role. His men distracted part of the Mexican army while U.S. forces traversed El Pedregal south of Mexico City. Several weeks later, they again carried out a diversionary attack, this time against the South Gate of Mexico City, while the bulk of the army stormed Chapultepec.

After enjoying a couple of months of rest in Mexico City, Twiggs was ordered back to Vera Cruz, where, as military governor, he organized the transportation of supplies to the interior. He remained at that post until the Treaty of Guadalupe Hidalgo was ratified and then returned to the United States.

His service in the U.S.–Mexican War earned Twiggs a brevet promotion to major general and a ceremonial sword from Congress. He then served in Texas and along the Gulf Coast. During the 1861 secession crisis, Twiggs as commander of the Department of Texas vainly sought instructions from the War Department before surrendering to Confederate sympathizers. When the U.S. government discharged him from the service, he briefly served as a Confederate general in New Orleans. He then retired to his ancestral home outside of Augusta, where he died on 15 July 1862.

Jeanne T. Heidler
David S. Heidler

BIBLIOGRAPHY

Heidler, Jeanne T. "The Military Career of David Emanuel Twiggs." Ph.D. diss., Auburn University, 1988.

Tyler, John

U.S. statesman and president John Tyler (1790–1862) was raised in Charles City County, Virginia. He attended William and Mary College and thereafter was admitted to the bar of his native county. Tyler was elected governor of Virginia after stints in the Virginia legislature and the U.S. House. In 1827 Tyler entered the U.S. Senate and soon became associated with anti-Jackson forces coalescing to create the Whig Party. In 1840, although he had little sympathy with the economic principles espoused by Sen. Henry Clay and other party leaders, Tyler was elected vice president on the Whig ticket as William Henry Harrison's running mate.

In 1841 Tyler became the first vice president to succeed to the presidency when Harrison, after only one month in office, died of pneumonia. "His Accidency" immediately broke

John Tyler. Library of Congress

with Clay and other Whig leaders over domestic policy, but his administration scored a number of foreign policy successes, including a trade pact with China. Tyler's administration experienced growing friction with Great Britain over (1) the Oregon Territory issue, (2) the Canada–Maine boundary disputes, (3) the *Caroline* and *Creole* cases, involving an ongoing dispute over a U.S. steamer the British had destroyed on the Niagara River on the suspicion it was assisting Canadian insurgents, and the British refusal to return mutinous slaves who had escaped to the Bahamas, and (4) Great Britain's sponsorship of the worldwide abolition movement. Secretary of State Daniel Webster successfully negotiated the Webster–Ashburton Treaty (1842), which resolved many of these difficulties, but he resigned when it became clear that the annexation of Texas, which Webster opposed, would be next on Tyler's agenda.

Since the establishment of the Republic of Texas in 1836 after its successful war of independence against Mexico, proslavery forces throughout the United States and the citizens of Texas favored annexation. Abolitionists, particularly Northern Whigs, opposed it, branding the annexationists conspirators bent on spreading slavery. The issue was further complicated by Mexico's continuing belligerent stand against both Texas independence and the possibility of U.S. annexation. Through numerous reliable "unofficial" sources, the Tyler administration learned that Great Britain had offered to guarantee Texas independence and protection against attacks from Mexico if Texas abolished slavery. By 1842, with the rising tide of Manifest Destiny sweeping the nation, Tyler directed his new secretary of state, Abel Upshur, a strong proponent of annexation, to initiate talks between the United States and Texas. By February, when Upshur was killed in an accidental explosion on board the USS *Princeton,* Tyler was nearly ready to present an annexation treaty to the Senate. Tyler thereupon appointed John C. Calhoun, who resumed Upshur's work with vigor.

Tyler presented the annexation treaty to the Senate on 22 April, stressing the will of the Texas people, the commercial and strategic value of Texas, and the dangers of allowing Texas to fall under British dominion. While the Senate debated the issue the Democratic Party nominated James K. Polk for president on an expansionist platform. Nevertheless, the treaty failed by a vote of 35 to 16. Undaunted after the June rejection of the treaty, Tyler continued to move toward annexation by a joint resolution of Congress. Polk's election over Whig nominee Clay in a campaign marked by considerable discussion of the issue gave annexation renewed momentum. Tyler interpreted Polk's election as a mandate to annex Texas. In the four months between the election and the inauguration of his successor, Tyler moved decisively toward the acquisition of Texas. He dispatched to Mexico City Ohioan Wilson Shannon, who clashed with Mexican foreign minister Manual Crescencio Rejón, exacerbating already bitter exchanges between Rejón and Secretary of State Calhoun. Meanwhile, Tyler sent Andrew Jackson Donelson to Texas to assess the political climate regarding annexation. Donelson found the issue far from certain. Some Texians were disappointed with the Senate's earlier rejection of the annexation treaty, while Sam Houston and President Anson Jones were lukewarm on the subject. The British chargé d'affaires was also on the scene urging that Texas reject the U.S. initiative. At Tyler's urging, both the House and Senate sponsored bills to annex Texas. A compromise bill passed the Senate on 27 February, with four days remaining before Polk's inauguration. Tyler signed the joint resolution on 1 March and on 3 March sent a dispatch to Donelson with instructions to offer Texas annexation to the United States as a single state. Immediately following Tyler's dispatch to Donelson, the Mexican minister to the United States, Juan N. Almonte, demanded his passports, diplomatic relations were broken between the United States and Mexico, and the issue was taken up by the new president. After Tyler left office in 1845 he remained active in politics and played the role of elder statesman.

In February 1861 after the election of Abraham Lincoln, Tyler chaired the Peace Convention which met in Washington, D.C., to conciliate between President Lincoln and Southern secessionists. The Convention submitted a series of compromise initiatives to Congress, including an amendment in essence restoring the Missouri Compromise line west to the Pacific, guaranteeing slavery in perpetuity where it already existed. The proposals were rejected by both sides, and secession was not averted. In April Tyler attended Virginia's secession convention and voted in favor of the state's secession from the Union. Though elected to the Confederate House of Representatives, Tyler did not live long enough to serve. He died in Richmond on 18 January 1862 at the age of 72.

James M. Denham

BIBLIOGRAPHY

Eisenhower, John S. D. *So Far from God: The U.S. War with Mexico, 1846–1848.* 1989.

Peterson, Norma Lois. *The Presidencies of William Henry Harrison and John Tyler.* 1989.

Seager, Robert. *And Tyler Too: A Biography of John and Julia Gardiner Tyler.* 1963.

Wiltse, Charles M. *John C. Calhoun: Sectionalist, 1840–1850.* 1951.

Ugartechea, Domingo de

Domingo de Ugartechea (1???–1839) first came to Texas as a junior cadet with the Spanish army in 1813 and fought against the insurgents at the Battle of the Medina. He returned to Texas in 1832 as a colonel in charge of the 125-man Mexican garrison at Velasco. Here, he fought and lost a bloody battle on 26 June against Texians, who allowed him to evacuate the fort with honors of war. In 1835 he received the post of commandant general of Coahuila y Texas as well as commander of the forces at the San Antonio de Béxar presidio. Under orders, troops from Colonel Ugartechea's command initiated the Battle of Gonzales on 2 October 1835 that sparked the Texas Revolution. Ugartechea, along with the recently arrived Gen. Martín Perfecto de Cos, defended San Antonio against a Texian force before surrendering on 9 December. He retreated with his troops to Laredo but joined the invasion force of Gen. Antonio López de Santa Anna in 1836. He commanded garrisons on the coast until he was forced to leave Texas following the Mexican loss at the Battle of San Jacinto. Afterward Ugartechea served in Matamoros, where he attempted to instigate Indian wars against Texians. He died while fighting federalist insurgents at Saltillo on 24 May 1839.

Jennifer A. Shimp

BIBLIOGRAPHY

Alessio Robles, Vito. *Coahuila y Texas*. 1946.

Hardin, Steve. *Texian Iliad*. 1994.

Lack, Paul. *The Texas Revolutionary Experience*. 1992.

Uniforms

This entry consists of two separate articles: **Mexican Uniforms** *and* U.S. Uniforms.

Mexican Uniforms

With Mexican independence in 1821, the former Spanish colonial military was slowly reorganized through a series of reforms in 1823 and 1827. The Mexican military adopted a style of uniform based on European influences, which was changed at least six times between 1821 and 1848, yet retained a strong French flavor. This consisted of a high-collared wool tunic, cut at the waist with tails, pants of wool cloth, and a leather or felt shako for headgear. For fatigue and off duty, a white canvas roundabout jacket without tails and white canvas pants were worn with a small wool peaked garrison cap for headgear. A leather bootee was also prescribed, but in many cases sandals were worn instead, while many *soldados* preferred to go barefoot, despite standing orders against it.

In 1832, a new series of regulations were undertaken that called for the infantry to wear a dark blue tailcoat of Querétaro cloth, with a scarlet collar, lapels, and cuffs, and yellow (brass) buttons with light blue wool pants. Cavalry was to be issued a scarlet Querétaro cloth tailcoat with green collar, lapels and cuffs, white (pewter or lead) buttons, and mounted pants with an antelope skin seat, flared at the ankle with cloth stripe on the seams. Headgear consisted of a tanned cowhide helmet. Both cavalry and infantry wore the canvas or sailcloth pants and coat for fatigue or off duty. Less than a year later, a new regulation of 1833 changed the uniforms again. The lapelled coat was replaced by a single breasted coatee of the same color. Despite the regulation changes, for the next six years both styles of uniforms were worn. The shakos, which were bell-crowned, were trimmed in brass furniture. The plumes or pom-poms were green for *cazadores*, red for *granadoros*, and the national colors of green, white, and red for the *fusileros*.

In 1839, new regulations were adopted that gave each of the recently reorganized infantry battalions their own distinctive lapels and turnback colors. Owing to the constantly changing political situation, these regulations were revoked in 1840 only to be reinstated in 1841. The style of the dark blue coatee and trousers remained somewhat the same, while the shako became shorter and more stove-piped. There was a variety of styles in both the shako and the garrison cap, which was still worn for fatigue or off duty. First sergeants were distinguished by two silk epaulettes. Second sergeants wore one epaulette on the right shoulder. Cavalry noncommissioned officers wore green epaulettes, while infantry wore red.

Some units had distinctive uniforms of their own, such as the Grenadier Guards of the Supreme, raised in 1841, the 11th Lina Regiment (whose coats were white, trimmed in sky blue), and the Ligero Regiments, who in the field wore grey tailless jackets with grey U.S.-style forage caps trimmed in red.

Mexican cavalry fell into the same regulation changes and also had some distinctive uniforms for special units. The Tulancingo Cuirassiers wore traditional French-style helmets and brass cuirass with the national coat of arms on the front. The Hussars of the Guard of the Supreme Power, the Mounted Rifle Regiment, and the Jalisco Lancers were among these specially uniformed regiments.

The only units not affected by the changes during this period appear to be the standing frontier *presidial* companies. These units wore the same uniform that had been adopted at the time of independence, consisting of a medium blue wool coat, red collar and cuffs, with blue trousers and the traditional wide-brimmed wool hat. Only the California companies deviated from the traditional uniform, with grey side-buttoned chaparral pants and on-garrison-duty shakos.

Mexican officers, enjoying the privilege of rank, wore uniforms also based on European styles. After 1839, the traditional Peninsular-style tailcoats gave way to the frock coat, while bicorne hats were replaced by French-style kepis. Buttons were imported, gold- or silver-plated with the national crest, and consisted of several different styles and sizes. Rank was distinguished by the epaulettes. Cavalry officers wore silver, and the infantry wore gold. The elaborate nature of the epaulettes decreased for the lower-grade officers, with lieutenants wearing one epaulette on the right shoulder and sub-lieutenants wearing one on the left.

While the regulations were quickly adopted, Mexico experienced a critical shortage of materials during most of this period. In many cases, the dress uniform was often worn in combination with the fatigue uniform. The most popular combination appears to have been the blue wool tailcoats with the white canvas pants. Some Mexican units at La Angostura were reported to have been dressed in "rags" with hurriedly made shakos constructed from palmetto leaves. During this period the regulations called for every *soldado* to be issued a barracks cap; three shirts; a cloth tailcoat; two canvas jackets; one pair each of gala pants, wool pants, and canvas pants; a neck stock; a shako with cords; an overcoat; and shoes. However, very rarely did supply ever cover demand.

One difficulty in the documentation of Mexican uniforms of this period is that while the regulations have survived, actual examples of original uniforms, particularly those of the *soldados,* have not. Some headgear and bits of insignia can be found in public and private collections, but the detailed documentation of Mexican uniforms remains a work in progress.

Kevin R. Young

BIBLIOGRAPHY

Brown, A. S., and J. and Neito A. Hefter. *El Soldado Mexicano, 1837–1847.* 1958

Hooker, T. D. "Uniforms of the Mexican Army, 1837–1847." *Tradition Magazine,* nos. 65 and 66.

U.S. Uniforms

The uniforms worn by U.S. Army regulars in the U.S.–Mexican War were remarkably different from the full-dress uniforms depicted in most contemporary art. Regular soldiers of the infantry and artillery were issued trousers and short jackets constructed from a stout and heavy sky-blue woolen kersey, a well napped wool woven in a twill pattern. Corps designations were indicated by the color of collar braid and buttons. Infantry jackets were trimmed in white with pewter buttons. Artillerymen wore jackets with brass buttons and yellow lace. The uniforms were tight fitting and quite uncomfortable in both the arid and tropical areas of the country. Dragoons, the mounted branch of the service, were also issued sky-blue trousers. Their jackets were ornately trimmed in yellow lace and of more expensive dark blue fabric.

All corps were issued the 1839 model pattern forage cap. Its brass letter denoted company while side buttons indicated corps. Though rakish in design it offered little protection from the harsh rays of the sun. Many officers and even some enlisted men discarded this item for the more practical wide-brimmed straw hat.

Officers were specified a dark-blue woolen frock coat, the button denoting corps: silver for infantry, gold for artillery and dragoons. Rank was indicated by shoulder boards, the embroidery corresponding with the button. Shoulder boards were generally one inch in width and three inches in length, worn on top of the coat at a point crossing the shoulder and butting against the sleeve cap. The rank system is still in use in the U.S. Army of the present day. A stripe in the corps' color ran down the outseam of the trousers. As officers provided their own garments, deviations occurred in the regulations with some individuals sporting civilian attire. Com-

Lt. E. Armstrong. Daguerreotype, c. 1846. In this typical photographic portrait of the period, most likely taken before his departure for Mexico, the lieutenant wears the ornate, impractical uniform of a dragoon officer. From the collection of William J. Schultz, M.D.

pany officers wore white leather shoulder belts to support their swords. Mounted officers and dragoons were given waist belts. All officers were required to wear a sash tied about the waist.

Sergeants of artillery and infantry were allowed the privilege of carrying swords and wearing the stripe on the trousers. In addition, the first sergeant of each company was issued a red sash. Until the regulation change in 1847 and its introduction of upward-pointing chevrons, no designation was made for corporals when out of dress uniform.

Each soldier was issued a cotton haversack to contain the daily ration, a canteen, and white leather belts to support his cartridge box and bayonet scabbard. The cloth knapsack, painted to render it waterproof, contained the soldier's other possessions, including his blanket. Rolled and strapped to the top was his greatcoat, which could serve as an extra blanket or raincoat.

Unlike the regulars, volunteers were required to supply their own clothing. Many companies wore garments made by hometown women. Some had no uniform at all, merely wearing what was on hand when they were mustered into service. Late in the war, volunteers were able to draw a fresh issue from the government stores. Being clothed as regulars

did not sit well with many volunteers and was the cause of no little grumbling in the ranks.

Steve Abolt

BIBLIOGRAPHY

Ferrell, Robert H., ed. *Monterrey is Ours! The Mexican War Letters of Lieutenant Dana 1845–1847.* 1990.

Gideon, J., and G. S. Gideon. *General Regulations for the Army, 1847,* pp. 186–215. By authority of the War Department. 1847.

Katcher, Philip R. N. *The Mexican-American War 1846–1848.* Osprey Men-At-Arms Series. Color plates by G. A. Embleton. 1976. Reprint, 1989.

Kimmel, Ross M. "American Forces in the War with Mexico, 1846–48." *Military Illustrated Past and Present 40* (September 1991): pp. 27–36; 42 (November 1991): 33–41; 45 (February 1992): 11–15; 47 (April 1992): 8–14; 48 (May 1992): 28–31.

United States, 1821–1854

This entry consists of two articles, each of which considers a significant trend of the era: **A Romantic Nationalism** *discusses the spirit of "Young America";* **Sectionalism** *examines the forces countering national unity.*

A Romantic Nationalism

On 4 March, 1845, a cold rainy day in Washington, D.C., James Knox Polk stood on the east portico of the Capitol, sheltered by an umbrella, and read his inaugural address. At age forty-nine, the youngest president in the nation's history, he was still awed by the unexpected turn of fortune that had brought him his party's nomination and his victory over Henry Clay, one of the country's most respected and experienced leaders, in the 1844 presidential election. In his remarks he moved beyond the usual recital of the principles that would guide his administration to address what America meant to him. "This heaven-favored land," he declared, enjoyed the "most admirable and wisest system of well-regulated self-government . . . ever devised by human minds" wherein the fire of libery warmed "the hearts of happy millions" and invited "all the nations of the earth to imitate our example." "Who shall assign limits," Polk asked, "to the achievements of free minds and free hands under the protection of this glorious Union?" (Polk, 1897, vol. 4, pp. 373–376).

It was a ringing statement of faith by the youngest president of a youthful nation. Many of the elements of what the country's romantics called the spirit of the age were echoed in Polk's remarks: the providential dispensation, the appeal to the hearts of the people, the freedom of the individual within a system of popular self-government, the absence of limits on individuals' opportunities to improve themselves. The sentiments were not new, but it was only as the country approached the midpoint of the nineteenth century that they became an article of national faith.

YOUNG AMERICA

It was "an astonishing age," wrote Richard S. Fisher in 1850 in *The Book of the World* (I, p. 109) and it belonged to the United States. Technological discoveries, mind-boggling in their impact, had issued, one after another, from the nation's inventive genius. The railroad and the magnetic telegraph annihilated both distance and time. It was an Age of Movement, declared the influential newspaper editor Horace Greeley, when to stand still was to fall behind. The locomotive became a metaphor for the nation. The United States was a "go a-head" country, and Americans were a "go a-head" people. "Go a-head" became a national motto, both intriguing and puzzling to Charles Dickens, who sought to fathom its meaning during his visit to the United States in 1842. Any person who travels on anything slower than a locomotive, one political leader solemnly announced, cannot keep pace with the spirit of the age (Greeley, 1848, p. 54).

Foreign travelers to the United States during the 1830s and 1840s were particularly annoyed by the bluster and brag they encountered in their journeys. By the mid-1840s, annoyance had turned into ridicule, especially among English writers, who scoffed at what they called the "ubiquitous qualities of the Universal Yankee nation." They took exception to claims by U.S. politicians and the public that Zachary Taylor was a more brilliant military commander than Napoléon Bonaparte or the Duke of Wellington. And they reacted with amazement to the claim that the march of Col. Alexander W. Doniphan's Missouri Volunteers across the deserts of northern Mexico surpassed the retreat of the ancient Greek army under Xenophon from Persia. When Alexander Mackay toured the United States during the U.S.–Mexican War, he observed the debates in the House of Representatives, where he listened in amazement to a congressman quoting from the Book of Genesis to prove the U.S. claim to the whole of Oregon.

Attacks by English authors were answered in kind by U.S. writers, whose new heights of verbosity were often mixed with a caustic Anglophobia. Walt Whitman, editor of a Brooklyn newspaper, shrugged off the slurs that were directed against "Yankeedoodle-dom" as but another demonstration of Great Britain's "spiteful meanness." "Let the Old World wag on under its cumbrous load of form and conservatism," Whitman wrote, "we are of a newer, fresher race and land" (Whitman, 1920, vol. 1, pp. 46–47 and 32–33).

"Young America" became a popular slogan of the period, and tributes to the Young American became subject matter for poets and essayists. In December 1845, Edwin DeLeon, southern editor and self-styled "scion of this Young America," published an address entitled "The Position and Duties of 'Young America'" that provided the concept with a phil-osophical basis. "Nations," wrote DeLeon, "like men, have their seasons of infancy, manly vigor, and decreptitude." The United States, the "young Giant of the West," stood "in the full flush of exulting manhood, and the worn-out Powers of the Old World may not hope either to restrain or impede his onward progress." DeLeon spoke at a time of increasing tension and fears of war, both with Great Britain over the Oregon boundary question, a matter of considerable concern, and with Mexico over Texas annexation, a matter of less concern. Whether it be in Texas or in Oregon, wherever the extension of the area of freedom might take the United States, DeLeon added, let us be prepared to guard it against the "profaning foot of any foreign foe" (DeLeon, p. 25).

To DeLeon, the United States was coming of age, moving into manhood, at a time when the lives of its people were changing dramatically in a host of different ways, spurred on by the rise of an industrial establishment, technological improvements in transportation and communication, the growth of cities, and an increasing flow of immigrants from Europe. At the same time, Americans were reaching beyond their borders. An expanding commerce, an increase in travel made possible by steam power on land and sea, and a heightened interest in exploration were carrying Americans to the far corners of the globe. Clipper ships regularly carried goods back and forth between the country's eastern port cities and China, while large bulky wagons lumbered to northern Mexico, turning the Sante Fe Trail into a busy highway. Fur traders roamed the northern and central Rocky Mountains, penetrating the Pacific Northwest and California, and a flourishing coastal trade brought New England merchant ships to California's shores. Whaling vessels from northeastern ports were carrying the U.S. flag into the Pacific and Indian Oceans. Thousands of Americans were making the long trek overland to new homes in the lush western valleys of Oregon, where they immediately called for the extension of U.S. laws and institutions. Hundreds more were on their way to California. By 1846, the U.S. population in Oregon exceeded nine thousand; as many as five hundred U.S. farmers called California home. The numbers would continue to increase.

YOUNG AMERICA AT WAR

The war with Mexico was the first major national crisis faced by the United States during this period of unprecedented social and economic change, and it immediately became a significant element in the effort to define a role for the young republic. Whether we call it romantic nationalism or the spirit of the age, Young America or Manifest Destiny and mission, the popular feeling was critical to the country's growth and development. Beneath all the exaggerated rhetoric that it generated were ideas of substance that exerted a profound and powerful influence on the shaping of the na-

OREGON TERRITORY
(Boundary settled 1846)

UNORGANIZED TERRITORY

THE REPUBLIC OF MEXICO

DISPUTED TERRITORY

FORT SNELLING

Iowa

Illinois Indiana Ohio

Missouri St. Louis

FORT LEAVENWORTH

Michigan

New York

Pennsylvania

Washington, D. C.

Virginia

Kentucky

Arkansas Tennessee North Carolina

Mississippi South Carolina

Louisiana Alabama Georgia

Texas

FORT JESUP New Orleans Pensacola

San Antonio

Florida

Corpus Christi

Maine
Vermont New Hampshire
Massachusetts
Rhode Island
Connecticut
New Jersey
Delaware
Maryland

The Bahamas (British)

Cuba (Spanish)

Haiti

Jamaica (British)

THE UNITED STATES OF AMERICA
1846

tion. They provided the backdrop before which the drama of the U.S.–Mexican War was played out.

The spirit of the age was evident at the war's beginning in the response of young Americans to the call for volunteers. Many of those who responded were motivated by a thirst for adventure mixed with a sense of patriotic duty. They perceived themselves as travelers, as explorers, and as pioneers (they were called the "go a-head" volunteers), opening one more window through which Americans back home could view a remote and exotic clime, sharing their romantic fascination with alien manners and customs and with an antiquity they could not find in their own country.

To Walt Whitman, U.S. fighting men reflected the patriotism of the country's common people. The mass demonstrations that celebrated the victories in Mexico in city after city moved Whitman to declare that there was no more "admirable impulse in the human soul than *patriotism*." The large gatherings convinced him that the U.S.–Mexican War was a great democratic mission. Although he argued that military superiority was not by itself a sign of national greatness, he believed that the triumphs on the battlefield would "elevate the *true* self-respect of the American people" to a point commensurate with "such a great nation as ours really is." Like many others, he found the roots of patriotism in the nation's revolutionary origins. Analogies were constantly drawn between the "spirit of '76" and the "spirit of '46," and the volunteers were as often admonished to show the world that the patriotism of the fathers could still be found in the hearts of the sons (pp. 82–85).

The war touched the lives of the U.S. public more intimately and with greater immediacy than any event to that time. Coinciding with the "print explosion" of the mid-nineteenth century, of which the penny press was but one manifestation, the war was reported in more detail than "any previous war in any part of the world." Fast steam presses, innovative techniques in news gathering, the employment of war correspondents for the first time (including many volunteers who reported the war for their hometown newspapers), the use of the new magnetic telegraph, and the rapid proliferation of books and periodicals, all combined to carry the war into people's lives on an unprecedented scale. The episodes of the war, the experiences of its combatants in camp and field, even the intentions and feelings of the Mexican foe were "more thoroughly known by mankind, than those of any war that has ever taken place" (Mott, 1941, pp. 248–249; *Niles' National Register* [September 25, 1847], p. 53).

THE AFTERMATH

What did the end of the U.S.–Mexican War mean to the people of the United States? For one thing, as the May 1848 *Democratic Review* suggested, it meant the "reduction of our enormous expenses by the withdrawal of the army, and the cessation with it of the excessive jobbing which has been so long going on" (p. 472). The war had cost the nation about $100 million; its demands had resulted in a drain of specie to Mexico that had been only partially offset by unprecedented exports of U.S. grain to Europe. The news of Mexico's ratification of the peace treaty coincided with the opening of bids in Washington, D.C., for a new government loan, and the effect of the announcement that the war had ended was immediately apparent. The entire new loan was taken by U.S. and British banking houses on terms that were highly advantageous to the government. "Shrewd capitalists as the large European bankers are," crowed the *New-York Tribune*, "they must be convinced that this Government is no longer an experiment, and that its bonds are as good security as those of any debt-ridden State of Europe" (March 7, 1848).

Vast new territories had become part of the United States, although some commentators felt that these areas—the "impenetrable moutains and dry narrow valleys" of California and the "trackless, treeless . . . and utterly uninhabitable" New Mexico—would prove useless. Most of the new land, it was thought, would become the haunt of savages and outlawed desperadoes, a drain on the national treasury, and a constant threat to the nation's frontier settlements. Mexico, some believed, had forced a shrewd bargain, ridding itself of worthless territory and receiving $15 million from the United States for the sacrifice.

Americans quickly assigned a significance to the U.S. triumph in Mexico that reflected national pride. The U.S.–Mexican War was the country's first foreign war, fought on foreign soil far from the U.S. population centers. The vast area covered by the military campaigns and the difficult terrain over which much of the fighting took place had raised serious problems for supply, communications, and transportation. For the first time, the nation was forced to raise, train, and equip large numbers of volunteer troops, and to move the troops quickly to the areas of military operation. The efficiency with which the young republic met these problems seemed to demonstrate its energy and strength.

Some critics of the war conceded, after the peace treaty had been signed, that the war had shown "that a people . . . devoted to the arts of peace, possessing free political institutions, can vanquish a military people, governed by military despots (*Merchant's Magazine* [April 1848], p. 463). The war, many agreed, had won new respect for the "model republic" and had convincingly refuted the arguments of those who claimed that republics, lacking a powerful centralized government, could not successfully wage a foreign war.

On 4 July 1848, the long-awaited ratification of the treaty by the Mexican congress arrived at the White House, the same day that the cornerstone of the Washington Monument was dedicated—an auspicious coincidence. The dedication address was delivered by Robert C. Winthrop, leader of the Whig Party, Massachusetts representative, and Speaker of the House of Representatives. The day, he noted, not only commemorated the achievement of U.S. independence but also marked "the precise epoch at which we have arrived in the world's history." A war against a foreign foe had just been won, and he paid tribute to the "veterans of the line and the volunteers" who stood before him. Winthrop pointed out that the revolutions at that moment convulsing Europe were popular uprisings in which the "influence of our own insitutions" and the "results of our own example" could be seen. "The great doctrines of our own Revolution," he said, "are proclaimed as emphatically this day in Paris, as they were seventy-two years this day in Philadelphia" (Winthrop, 1876, pp. 9–28).

Finally, Winthrop invoked the language of Young America. The "great American-built locomotive, 'Liberty,' " he declared, still held its course "on the track of human freedom, unimpeded and unimpaired; gathering strength as it goes; developing new energies to meet new exigencies," with a speed that "knows no parallel."

Robert W. Johannsen

BIBLIOGRAPHY

Blau, Joseph L., ed. *Social Theories of Jacksonian Democracy.* 1954.

Brooks, Nathan Covington. *Complete History of the Mexican War.* 1849.

DeLeon, Edwin. *The Position and Duties of "Young America": An*

Address Delivered Before the Two Literary Societies of the South Carolina College, December 1845. 1845.

Greeley, Horace. "The Age We Live In." *Nineteenth Century* 1 (1848): 54.

Johannsen, Robert W., ed. *Democracy on Trial.* 2d ed. 1988.

Johannsen, Robert W. *The Frontier, the Union, and Stephen A. Douglas.* 1989.

Johannsen, Robert W. *To the Halls of the Montezumas: The Mexican War in the American Imagination.* 1985.

Livermore, Abiel Abbot. *The War with Mexico Reviewed.* 1850.

Mott, Frank Luther. *American Journalism: A History of Newspapers in the United States through 250 Years, 1690 to 1940.* 1941.

Polk, James K. "Inaugural Address, March 4, 1845." In *Messages and Papers of the Presidents, 1789–1897,* compiled by James D. Richardson. 1897.

Somkin, Fred. *Unquiet Eagle: Memory and Desire in the Idea of American Freedom: 1815–1860.* 1967.

Stanton, William. *The Great United States Exploring Expedition of 1838–1842.* 1975.

Whitman, Walt. *The Gathering of the Forces.* Edited by Cleveland Rodgers and John Black. 1920.

Winthrop, Robert C. "National Monument to Washington: An Oration Delivered at the Seat of Government, on the Occasion of Laying the Corner-Stone of the National Monument to Washington, July 4, 1848." In *Washington, Bowdoin, and Franklin as Portrayed in Occasional Addresses.* 1876.

See also **Expansionism and Imperialism; Literature; Manifest Destiny; Newspapers,** *article on* **U.S. Press; Railroads;** *and* **Young America Movement**

Sectionalism

Powerful forces were at work in the United States from 1821 to 1854. The nation suffered from growing pains that would ultimately shape and color this period just as much as the boundless enthusiasm expressed in the newspapers and literature of the time.

The concept of Manifest Destiny with its quasi-religious tenets influenced this period profoundly, both motivating the U.S. appetite for territory and in turn being used by the U.S. government and public to justify its expansion. Born from a Puritan sense of "calling" and "election," the spirit that moved the citizens of the young republic drew strength from their nation's history. As the story was remembered, idealistic New Englanders, motivated by a love of God, conquered the wilderness and brought salvation and civilization to its indigenous inhabitants. These "Indians" were natural pagans and savages, and either converted to English views of correct behavior or faced extinction. According to this perception of events, God had smiled on these activities and blessed the Christian nation by removing the obstacles from its path. Territorial expansion up to 1821 had seemingly been authored by the divine being, and U.S. citizens saw themselves as humble tools of the cosmic plan.

Although the Consitution promised to keep state and church separate, Protestantism rose to the level of a national religion. Catholicism, with its tie to a foreign leader in Rome, was viewed as a threat by this Protestant republic. Recent Irish immigrants became targets—as foreigners as well as Catholics—as the residents of northeastern cities rioted and burned churches and convents. Anti-Catholic sentiment affected the U.S. attitude toward Mexico because much of the U.S. public believed that Catholicism, with its autocratic hierarchy, was an inappropriate religion for a republic. Other Christian sects bore the burden of persecution as well. Protestant vigilantes drove Joseph Smith and his followers from New York, Ohio, Missouri, and Illinois before the Mormons ultimately fled to a potential desert utopia in present-day Utah.

From 1821 to 1854, Republicanism also made an indelible mark on the United States. Believing that the republican form of government was superior to all others, citizens of the United States justified their hostility toward Mexico as retribution for that nation's transgressions against republican ideals. Instead of a sister republic, Mexico was viewed as a haven for dictators and in need of redemption. Europeans, too, were targets of this republican scorn. The Monroe Doctrine reserved Latin America as a zone of influence for the United States. During this period, U.S. foreign policy and public opinion were decidedly anti-British, as Great Britain was considered to be the leading booster of monarchies, aristocrats, and autocrats worldwide.

Racism also was a critical component of U.S. national philosophy after 1821. Since their arrival on the East Coast, Anglo-Saxons had advanced steadily across the continent, seemingly proving the superiority of whites of west European stock over all others. Indians fell before Anglo-Saxon progress while Africans occupied their "natural" position as servants and slaves. Mexicans, described by some U.S. writers and thinkers of the age as a mongrel race, were a mix of many inferior elements according to this view—Indian backwardness coupled with Spanish sloth and African inferiority created a mixed race in desperate need of U.S. intervention. This belief in white Anglo-Saxon superiority made it easy to justify President Andrew Jackson's policy of Indian removal: the land belonged to those who would make it produce. Many Protestant Americans believed the same policy applied to Mexicans.

A spirit of militarism existed in the United States that provided a means to accomplish continental conquest. While militarism is usually thought of as a late-nineteenth-century occurrence, the Jacksonian period was a militant era. From 1821 to 1854, heroic deeds were not only a way to prove one's devotion to the "American Ideal" but also often served as a springboard to political office. Beginning with George Washington, the United States venerated war heroes and often trusted them with high office. Andrew Jackson rose from regional fame to national prominence, as did William Henry Harrison, Richard M. Johnson, and even Sam Houston. The U.S.–Mexican War created three presidents—Zachary Taylor, Franklin Pierce, and Jefferson Davis. The nation's willingness to use military force became almost evangelistic in nature as U.S. military leaders stood ready to fight to make their vision of the world come true.

The United States, however, was far from achieving national consensus over the future of the republic. Nowhere was this more evident than in the realm of politics. In 1821 the nation enjoyed the "Era of Good Feelings" as Democrats wielded one-party rule. By 1824, however, cracks had appeared in this unified façade, and by 1828, it had begun to crumble. By 1836, the Whig Party led a ferocious opposition to Andrew Jackson's type of democracy, and by 1840 this political countermovement elected William Henry Harrison to the presidency. The wrangling of these two parties dramatically shaped national affairs and the character of the age, but they destroyed themselves in the process. The emergence of the Republican Party in 1854 initiated a new direction in U.S. politics and marked the end of the Jacksonian era and its struggles.

In fact, the new age was the bitter result of strong undercurrents long tugging at the nation. By 1854, even casual observers noted that the United States was really two nations—North and South—marked by strong cultural differences. Northerners, where the Puritan imprint remained strong, claimed industry and righteousness as the national character and saw government as the ally of reform. Southerners, infused with ideas of individual liberty, descended from an oppressed people, and the products of a rural and agricultural lifestyle, viewed meddlesome outsiders with suspicion, whether they were reformers, Puritans, or politicians.

Economics also was markedly different between the two sections. In the South, a newly wealthy elite vied with old-money aristocrats to control the region and to sway the nation. Their wealth, prestige, and power rested on personal empires built with slave labor. This landed gentry, despite their limited numbers, gained increasing influence over the affairs of the United States and were viewed by many as having a retarding effect on the nation's future. Slavery, then, became linked intellectually and politically to any opposition or support held toward this group and would serve as the axis on which the nation's destiny increasingly turned. In 1846, many Southerners had become strong expansionists while Northerners saw the addition of territory as benefiting mainly the slave-owning elite.

In contrast, the wealth of the North came from immigrant labor and industry. Free labor built fortunes in the North, and this wealth in turn sponsored a newly potent political element that vied with traditional elites for power. In the national arena, these industrialists found themselves at cross-purposes with many other political factions and built coalitions to overcome this opposition. Before long, traditional economic issues faded from view, but not from importance, as the national dialogue turned away from outward expansion and toward national reform targeted mainly at the U.S. South. Whether righteous indignation or economic motives drove this reform impulse is still hotly debated.

Industrialism, while arguably as inhumane as slavery, did bring prosperity to a wider cross-section of people while bringing upon society a variety of ills. Working and living conditions were primitive as skilled and unskilled workers flocked to northern cities to support the mushrooming factory economy. Not all found success or even comfort, and many immigrants were marginalized by competing U.S.–born laborers cloaked in the rhetoric of nativism. As a result, many of these new citizens suffered a second-class citizen status. By 1846, many had joined the U.S. Army to advance their chances in what came to be seen as a mildly hostile and coldly indifferent society.

Even native-born citizens of the United States held economic fears. The nation's fiscal health was far from steadily robust, and "panics" occurred with every generation. For the average inhabitant of the United States, life was a quest for stability. For most people in this agrarian nation, stability meant land, giving the desire for Manifest Destiny an extremely practical edge. Each panic led to westward immigration, and every period of prosperity led to population booms. This cycle, as much as any rhetoric or national philosophy, explained why the United States was the "go-ahead" nation. Its people, far from unified in purpose, believed that prosperity lay with a change of status within a highly fluid society.

The United States of 1821 to 1854 was a frustrating and complicated place. Its currents and passions, fears and motivations profoundly influenced relations with Mexico and sculpted an important era in the history the world. After the resolution of border issues between the two nations in 1854, however, the enthusiastic but unbalanced spirit of the United States would seek new outlets, with violent results.

Donald S. Frazier
Richard Bruce Winders

BIBLIOGRAPHY

Benson, Lee. *The Concept of Jacksonian Democracy.* 1961.

Binkley, Wilfred E. *American Political Parties: Their National History.* 1971.

Hietala, Thomas. *Manifest Destiny: Anxious Aggrandizement in Late Jacksonian America.* 1985.

Horsman, Reginald. *Race and Manifest Destiny: The Origins of American Radical Anglo-Saxonism.* 1981.

Merk, Frederick. *Manifest Destiny and Mission in American History.* 1995.

Potter, David M. *The Impending Crises: 1848–1861.* 1973.

Schlesinger, Arthur, Jr. *The Age of Jackson.* 1945.

See also Abolitionism; Democratic Party; Free-Soil Party; Republicanism, U.S.; Slavery; Whig Party

United States Military Academy

See Military Academy, United States

Urrea, José

Mexican general José Urrea (1797–1849) was born to a military family at the frontier *presidio* of Horcasitas. Urrea began his army career at age eleven as a cadet in the *presidio* of San Rafael de Buenavista. Like most of his contemporaries, he participated in the royalist counterinsurgency campaigns before embracing the Plan of Iguala in 1821. Removed from military service for being on the losing side of the 1828 Tulancingo *cuartelazo* (military garrison uprising), Urrea was reinstated the following year as recompense for his performance against the Spanish expeditionary army.

Promoted to brigade general in 1835, Urrea held the post of commandant-general of Durango when summoned to join the Army of Operations being assembled to suppress the Texian rebels. The army's most proficient commander, he captured the entire Goliad garrison at Coleto Creek. His appeal to spare the prisoners' lives was overruled by Gen. Antonio López de Santa Anna, who cited the Mexican congress's decree of 30 December 1835 mandating the execution of all foreigners taken in battle or bearing arms against the nation.

Urrea's distinguished service in the Texas campaign led to his appointment in 1837 as commandant-general of Sonora. Rather than assume his new post immediately, the truculent general led a military column into neighboring Sinaloa to coerce that district into the federalist fold. Brought to battle and defeated by the division general (equivalent to a U.S. Army major general) Mariano Paredes y Arrillaga near Mazatlán in May 1838, Urrea sought temporary refuge in Durango. Making his way to Tampico, he and fellow federalist conspirator José Antonio Mexía fomented a rebellion in October that coincided with the French blockade of Mexico's Gulf Coast. This uprising lasted until 3 May 1839, when Div. Gen. Gabriel Valencia decisively defeated the rebels in a fierce engagement near Pueblo de Acajete. Mexía was captured and summarily executed; but the resilient Urrea withdrew to Tampico where he lingered until Brig. Gen. Mariano

Arista forced the city's surrender on 5 June. Escaping once more, Urrea remained at large until October 1839, when he was apprehended in Tuxpan.

Urrea was incarcerated in Mexico City's dungeon of the Inquisition for the next nine months, when his federalist supporters engineered his escape on 15 July 1840. Once liberated, he seized the national palace, arrested centralist president Anastasio Bustamante, and invited Valentín Gómez Farías to assume political leadership of the insurrection. When the rebellion collapsed after twelve days of unprecedented destruction, the customarily lenient terms of capitulation enabled Urrea to return to Durango, where he bided his time until Bustamante's ouster the following year. Appointed commandant-general and governor of Sonora in 1842, Urrea remained at that post fending off centralist challenges and Apache depredations until his election to the national congress in April 1845.

At the outbreak of war with the United States he commanded a brigade of cavalry and mounted irregulars, which he used skillfully to interdict U.S. supply lines between Monterrey and Matamoros and to raid supply depots. Withdrawing across the mountains when Gen. Zachary Taylor's northern campaign ground to a halt, Urrea continued guerrilla operations in Tamaulipas until the war ended. Thereafter, he sponsored yet another disturbance in Tamaulipas in 1848 that, while unsuccessful, managed to disrupt the postwar government's Sierra Gorda pacification campaign.

William A. DePalo, Jr.

BIBLIOGRAPHY

Almada, Francisco R. *Diccionario de historia, geografía y biografía sonorenses,* pp. 806–810. 1990.

Costeloe, Michael P. "A Pronunciamiento in Nineteenth Century Mexico: 15 de julio de 1840." *Mexican Studies/Estudios Mexicanos* 4 (Summer 1988): 249.

"Diario de las operaciones militares de Gral. José Urrea sobre la campaña de Téjas, Victoria de Durango, 1838." *Documentos para la historia de la guerra de Téjas,* pp. 20–23. 1952.

Diccionario Porrúa: de História, Biografía, y Geografía de México. 6th ed., pp. 3644–3645. 1995.

Hu-DeHart, Evelyn. *Yaqui Resistance and Survival: The Struggle for Land and Autonomy, 1821–1910,* pp. 59–68. 1984.

Roa Bárcena, José María. *Recuerdos de la invasión norteamericana, 1846–1848.* 3 vols. Vol. 1, pp. 199–201. 1947.

Vigness, David M. "La expedición Urrea-Mejía." *Historia Mexicana* 2 (July 1955–June 1956): 212–216.

Voss, Stuart F. *On the Periphery of Nineteenth Century Mexico: Sonora and Sinaloa, 1810–1877,* pp. 96–104. 1982.

U.S. Mounted Rifles

See Mounted Rifles, U.S.

U.S. Volunteers

See **Volunteers, U.S.**

Utah

For centuries the Great Basin, today known as the state of Utah, was the home of the Shoshoni and Ute Indians. The first recorded intrusion of Europeans was in 1776, with the arrival of Spanish Franciscan priests Francisco Dominguez and Silvestre Velez de Escalante, whose travels gave Mexico claim to the Great Basin region. In the nineteenth century U.S. explorers, fur trappers, and mountain men mapped the area, giving credence to U.S. claims to the same territory.

In 1833 Oregon-bound pioneers visited the Great Basin, hoping to find it habitable, but concluded, "Hell is not one mile from this place," and rode away. It was not until the arrival of the Mormon pioneers that the Great Basin had a permanent colony of non-native settlers. Brigham Young, Mormon leader, ignored the admonitions of mountain man Jim Bridger against large-scale colonization in the area and announced on 24 July 1847, "This is the right place."

The Mormon choice of settling in the Great Basin caused some confusion: to which government did they owe their allegiance? Mexico, the United States, and to some extent Great Britain claimed sovereignty. It was not until seven months after the arrival of the Mormons that the Treaty of Guadalupe Hidalgo, ending the U.S.–Mexican War, settled the sovereignty issue. The compromise of September 1850 gave further clarity by dividing the newly conquered southwest into the territories of Utah and New Mexico. Utah remained a territory for forty-six years before being admitted as a state on 4 January 1896.

Susan Easton Black

BIBLIOGRAPHY

Larson, Gustive O. *Outline History of Utah and the Mormons.* 1958.

Powell, Allan Ken, ed. *Utah History Encyclopedia.* 1994.

See also **Mormonism**

V

Valencia, Gabriel

A career soldier, Gabriel Valencia (1799–1848) was born in Mexico City in 1799. After serving in the Spanish army, he joined the Mexican revolutionaries in 1821 and quickly became a power behind the *caudillo* politics of Mexico. In 1831, Valencia received the rank of brigade general and associated himself with the centralist leadership. Valencia accompanied Gen. Antonio López de Santa Anna's invasion of Texas in 1836 although he was not actively engaged, but he did aid in the defeat of the French in the 1838 Pastry War. Valencia's forces captured and executed federalist Gen. José Antonio Mexía in 1838, and he scattered federalist insurgents at the battle of Acajete in 1839. With his popularity on the rise, Valencia developed aspirations to dictatorship, although some described him as a "vulgar, ambitious upstart."

Valencia emerged as a key player in Mexican politics in the 1840s. As commander of the garrison of Mexico City, he defended the centralist regime of Anastasio Bustamante against rebels led by José Urrea and Valentín Gomez Farias in the 15 July 1840 revolt. The following year, however, he aided Santa Anna in a successful general uprising against President Bustamante. Shortly afterward, Santa Anna rewarded Valencia, whom he considered to be a potentially dangerous rival, by advancing him to the rank of division general. He also aided Valencia in amassing a sizable personal fortune in an effort to buy his loyalty.

Valencia, however, maintained his own agenda. In the 1844 revolution, Valencia led pro-congress forces against Santa Anna and the following year helped overthrow President José Joaquín de Herrera, hoping to gain that office himself. Instead, a military junta chose Mariano Paredes y Arillaga. During the war with the United States, Valencia served in the northeast at Tula and San Luis Potosí in the summer of 1847 and urged a counter-offensive against Gen. Zachary Taylor's army. His recommendations often bordered on insubordination, and he apparently coveted overall command of the army.

When U.S. troops threatened Mexico City, Valencia led reinforcements to the capital but failed to actively oppose the U.S. advance east of the city. In an effort to retard Valencia's ambitions, Santa Anna ordered him to the difficult southern approaches of Mexico City, hoping to remove him from a position of potential glory in light of initial U.S. troop movements. Instead, General Scott's troops surprised Santa Anna—and Valencia—by overrunning the Mexican forces at Contreras. After the capital fell, the militarily disgraced Valencia withdrew to Querétero. He surrendered to U.S. forces on 2 January 1848, after it became apparent that further resistance was futile. He died later that year in Mexico City.

Donald S. Frazier

BIBLIOGRAPHY

Costeloe, Michael. *The Central Republic in Mexico, 1835–1846: Hombres de Bien in the Age of Santa Anna.* 1993.

DePalo, William A., Jr. *The Mexican National Army.* 1997.

Smith, Justin H. *The War with Mexico.* 2 vols. 1919. Reprint, 1963.

Vallejo, Mariano Guadalupe

Mariano Guadalupe Vallejo (1807–1890) was a Californio political leader, *ranchero,* and entrepreneur. The highest rank Vallejo achieved in the Mexican army was colonel, but after he served as California's military governor (commandant-general, 1836–1842) he became known as "General Vallejo." To avoid becoming involved in a civil war, he dismissed his Sonoma troops in November 1844, and from then until the end of the U.S.–Mexican War he remained, militarily speaking, a neutral. His main impact during the U.S.–Mexican War was as a United States apologist. Widely respected for his political acumen, he had argued persuasively for a U.S. protectorate before the U.S.–Mexican conflict. Nevertheless, fearing the potential problems created by U.S. immigration, Vallejo in 1845 urged Mexico to buy Sutter's Fort and thus deprive U.S. malcontents of a rallying point. His letters of warning to Mexico regarding U.S. immigration and California's defenselessness were accurate and sometimes prescient.

Vallejo was the first Californio *ranchero* to suffer from the U.S. conflict with Mexico. On 14 June 1846 his undefended headquarters at Sonoma was raided by members of the revolutionary Bear Flag Party—made up primarily of U.S. immigrants. Vallejo surrendered 250 stands of arms and other supplies belonging to the Mexican government. He was then taken to Sutter's Fort on the Sacramento River, where from 16 June until 2 August 1846 he was imprisoned by order of Capt. John C. Frémont. His unjustified imprisonment played a role in stiffening the Californios' resistance to U.S. occupation. Vallejo's cattle, horses, and agricultural products were requisitioned by U.S. forces, but Vallejo took no direct part in aiding the United States against Mexican troops. The U.S. government later awarded him $48,700 of the $117,875 damages he requested, which was the largest single payment for damages made by the U.S. government to a Mexican citizen living in California.

Alan Rosenus

BIBLIOGRAPHY

Emparan, Madie Brown. *The Vallejos of California.* 1967.

Rosenus, Alan. *General M. G. Vallejo and the Advent of the Americans.* 1995.

Van Buren, Martin

Martin Van Buren (1782–1862) eagerly became involved in New York state politics in the early 1800s and took charge of the Republican machine that controlled state politics. He assumed the presidency of the United States three days after U.S. recognition of Texas independence on 1 March 1837. Texas immediately pressured Van Buren to approve actions for U.S. annexation of Texas, but he opposed it because he believed the United States should stay out of the conflict between Mexico and Texas, and he did not want to exacerbate the sectional conflict between the Northern and Southern regions of the United States. Van Buren thus pushed the debate into the legislature to delay the matter.

Annexation remained an issue throughout the early 1840s. In 1844 Van Buren sought the Democratic nomination. The Democrats were divided over the annexation issue. Many Northern party members were against annexation because they wanted to curtail the expansion of slavery, while Southern Democrats favored annexation. The sectional di-

vision, continued hostilities between Mexico and Texas, and the view that the annexation was a hostile act toward Mexico encouraged Van Buren to continue his opposition to annexation. This led the Southern branch of the Democratic Party to reject Van Buren's nomination and nominate instead James K. Polk, who supported annexation of Texas as well as general expansion for the United States. On 4 March 1845, the United States annexed Texas and that same year elected Polk to the presidency. Van Buren strongly denounced annexation and the U.S.–Mexican War, which Polk declared in May 1846.

After the U.S.–Mexican War commenced, the party became divided even more over the issue of slavery in the territories. Van Buren did not wish to divide the party yet felt committed to his ideals and the prevention of the spread of slavery and thus supported the antislavery faction. He never faltered, remaining a staunch opponent of both annexation and the war.

Van Buren remained active in politics during and after the U.S.–Mexican War, but he soon thereafter retired from politics and died peacefully in his hometown of Kinderhook, New York, in 1862.

Angela D. Moore

BIBLIOGRAPHY

Cole, Donald B. *Martin Van Buren and the American Political System.* 1984.

Niven, John. *Martin Van Buren: The Romantic Age of American Politics.* 1983.

Vander Linden, Pedro

Belgian military physician Pedro Vander Linden (1804–1860) was born in Brussels. He graduated as a military physician and distinguished himself in the Dutch–Belgian War of 1830 to 1832. He joined the Mexican army in 1837 as a surgeon in the Allende Battalion where he befriended Gen. Antonio López de Santa Anna, who in 1842 promoted him to colonel. In 1845 he was awarded the directorship of the Military Health Corps for supporting the Herrera government during the June uprising led by Gen. Joaquín Rangel. In 1846 he was director of the Military Hospital of Instruction and inspector general of the Military Medical Corps. In 1847 Vander Linden participated in the campaigns against the United States and was present at major battles including La Angostura (where he served as negotiator between General Santa Anna and Gen. Zachary Taylor), Cerro Gordo (where he was captured), Contreras, Churubusco, El Molino del Rey, Chapultepec, Garita Belén (Belén Gate), and San Cosme. At all of these battles he was noted for the outstanding and painstaking care he took in treating the wounded. During the U.S. occupation, he served on the city council of Mexico City, for which he was later accused of treason and forced to leave the country. He rejoined the army in 1853, and in 1855, under the Santa Anna government, founded the Military Hospital of Mexico City. He died in Guadalajara, a victim of a typhus epidemic.

Faustino A. Aquino Sánchez

BIBLIOGRAPHY

Cárdenas de la Peña, Enrique. *Mil personajes en el México del siglo XIX.* 1979.

Diccionario Porrúa: De história, biografía, y geografía de México. 6th ed. 1995.

Roa Bárcena, José María. *Recuerdos de la invasión Norteamericana, 1846–1848.* 1947.

Vasquez Expedition

In the spring of 1842 a Mexican army of approximately seven hundred men marched into Texas under the command of Gen. Rafael Vasquez. In the years following Texas's declaration of independence in 1836, Mexican leaders had periodically threatened to renew hostilities against Texas. Lacking the resources to attempt reconquest, the Mexican government under President Antonio López de Santa Anna in the early 1840s ordered its army to harass the Texas frontier, hoping to discourage settlement and capital investment in the young Republic of Texas. Accordingly, in spring 1842 General Vasquez's forces marched into Texas, seizing San Antonio on 5 March. Forewarned of the Mexican advance, most Anglo-American residents had already hastened toward the interior, leaving the town open to Vasquez and his men.

Early reports of the invasion threw Anglo Texians into a panic, as hundreds of settlers fled to the safety of settlements in East Texas. The attack sparked calls for reprisals against Mexico, which President Sam Houston, an advocate of defensive measures, opposed. By the summer of 1842 the war fever had passed, only to revive when Santa Anna ordered a second invasion, the Woll Expedition, in the fall of 1842.

Sam W. Haynes

BIBLIOGRAPHY

Haynes, Sam W. *Soldiers of Misfortune: The Somervell and Mier Expeditions.* 1990.

Sánchez Lamego, Miguel A. *The Second Mexican–Texan War, 1841–1843.* 1972.

Vázquez, Ciriaco

A native of Vera Cruz, Mexican general Ciriaco Vázquez (1794–1847) entered military service on 29 December 1809 as a cadet in the Vera Cruz Infantry Regiment of the Line. He served the royalist cause until 30 March 1821, when he joined a cohort of his regiment that rallied to the independence army. For his distinguished performance in the campaign that ousted the Spanish expeditionary army from Tampico in September 1829, Vázquez was elevated to the rank of brigade general and named to the Mexican commission sent to Havana to monitor the terms of capitulation. Thereafter, he held various positions of increased responsibility including military commander of Vera Cruz, Jalapa, and Isla del Carmen.

When the war with the United States began, Vázquez was commanding an infantry brigade in the Army of the North. Assigned to observe the terrain between Tamaulipas and Matehualpa, his brigade did not participate in any major actions. Reassigned in March 1847 to the newly activated Army of the East, Vázquez commanded the Mexican position on el Telégrafo during the defense of Cerro Gordo. On the morning of 18 April, he fell mortally wounded while attempting to rally his troops, who had been unnerved by the unexpected appearance of Col. William S. Harney's brigade. In recognition of his heroic leadership and valor at Cerro Gordo, the government promoted Vázquez posthumously to division general.

William A. DePalo, Jr.

BIBLIOGRAPHY

Carreño, Alberto M., ed. *Jefes del Ejército Mexicano en 1847: Biografías de generales de división y de brigada y de coroneles del Ejército por fines del año 1847,* pp. 90–95. 1914.

DePalo, William A., Jr. *The Mexican National Army, 1822–1852,* pp. 121, 123. 1997.

Martínez Caraza, Leopoldo. *La intervención Norteamericana en México, 1846–1848,* pp. 156–158. 1981.

Roa Bárcena, José María. *Recuerdos de la invasión Norteamericana, 1846–1848.* 3 vols. Vol. 2, pp. 42–48. 1947.

Vega, Rómulo Díaz de la

See **Díaz de la Vega, Rómulo**

Vera Cruz Campaign

Vera Cruz, Mexico's most important port and the principal gateway into the nation, was considered to be a formidable position. Gen. Winfield Scott remarked that the guardian fortress of San Juan de Ulúa possessed sufficient firepower to sink the entire U.S. fleet. With the outbreak of hostilities in the U.S.–Mexican War the United States made no attempt to assail the walled city, but Secretary of the Navy George Bancroft ordered it blockaded, along with all other Gulf ports. Commo. David E. Conner, commander of the navy's Home Squadron, established a base at Antón Lizardo, only twelve miles south of the city.

By late 1846 President James K. Polk was aware that there

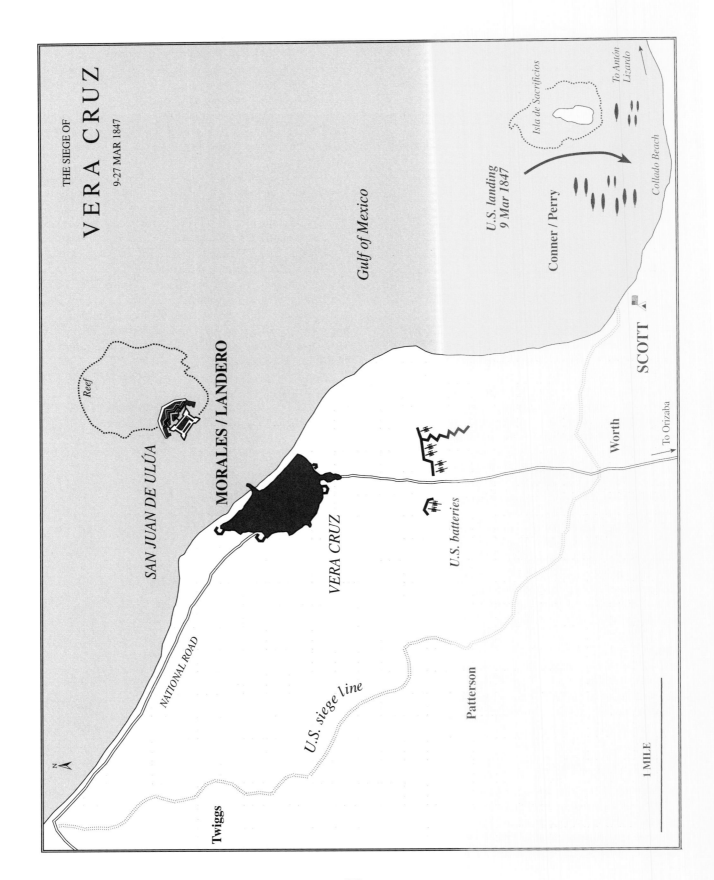

THE SIEGE OF

VERA CRUZ

9-27 MAR 1847

Reef

SAN JUAN DE ULÚA

MORALES / LANDERO

Gulf of Mexico

Isla de Sacrificios

To Antón
Lizardo

U.S. landing
9 Mar 1847

Conner / Perry

Collado Beach

VERA CRUZ

U.S. batteries

SCOTT

Worth

To Orizaba

U.S. siege line

Patterson

NATIONAL ROAD

Twiggs

N

1 MILE

458

Siege of Vera Cruz
Order of Battle
9–28 March 1847

Mexican Forces

Commander
Gen. Juan Morales

Garrison at Vera Cruz

Infantry
2d Line Regiment
8th Line Regiment
11th Line Regiment (1 company)
3d Light
Sappers
Enlisted Marines
The Libres of Puebla, National Guard
National Guard of Orizava
National Guard of Vera Cruz
National Guard of Coatepec
Activo Battalion of Oaxaca
Activo Battalion of Tehuantepec

Artillery
150-man detachment, regulars
80-man detachment, National Guard

Garrison at San Juan de Ulúa

Infantry
Activo Battalion of Puebla
Activo Battalion of Jamiltepec
Companies from the Activo Battalions of Tuxpan, Tampico,
   and Alvarado

Artillery
450 men

Note: General Scott reported capturing 400 pieces of artillery at Vera Cruz and San Juan de Ulúa.

U.S. Forces

Commander
Gen. Winfield Scott

Infantry
2d Infantry
3d Infantry
4th Infantry
5th Infantry
6th Infantry
7th Infantry
8th Infantry
1st Artillery (serving as infantry)
2d Artillery (serving as infantry)
3d Artillery (serving as infantry)
4th Artillery (serving as infantry)
1st Regiment Mounted Rifles (dismounted)
Company A, Engineers
U.S. Marine Battalion
1st Alabama Volunteers
1st Georgia Volunteers
3d Illinois Volunteers
4th Illinois Volunteers
1st Kentucky Volunteers
2d New York Volunteers
1st Pennsylvania Volunteers
2d Pennsylvania Volunteers
1st South Carolina Volunteers
1st Tennessee Volunteers
2d Tennessee Volunteers

Cavalry
1st Dragoons
2d Dragoons
1st Tennessee Volunteer Cavalry

Artillery
Company K, 1st Artillery (Taylor's light battery)
Company A, 2d Artillery (Duncan's light battery)
Steptoe's Field Battery, 3d Artillery
Howitzer and rocket company
Ordnance Department siege train

was a growing impatience in the United States to end the war with Mexico. Wishing to conclude the conflict as quickly as possible, he gave orders to allow exiled Gen. Antonio López de Santa Anna to slip through the blockade at Vera Cruz, with the expectation that the Mexican leader would negotiate a treaty that would satisfy U.S. territorial ambitions. Santa Anna not only failed to bring an end to the war but also fanned the flames of Mexican nationalism.

It is against this background that President Polk began to plan a new military campaign centered on Vera Cruz. He hoped at first that merely the occupation of the port would be sufficient to force a Mexican surrender; he soon realized, however, that a landing on the coast would have to be followed by a march to Mexico City.

Commodore Conner suggested a landing south of Vera Cruz, out of range of the guns of San Juan de Ulúa, and emphasized that naval support of an invasion could be given from his Antón Lizardo base. By November 1846 Gen. Winfield Scott presented a blueprint for such an operation. He insisted that a landing be made no later than 1 February

1847 followed by a rapid march into the interior to avoid the dreaded *vómito negro* (yellow fever) that plagued the coastal region. While the plan was being refined, the president had to select a commander. Scott, the most experienced general in the army and principal designer of the operation, would have seemed the logical choice, but this was by no means assured; Polk, painfully aware of Scott's ties to the Whig Party, attempted to persuade Congress to allow him to award the command to Democratic senator Thomas Hart Benton. When the Senate rejected the plan, Polk reluctantly named Scott to the position.

Grateful for his selection, and believing that he had the full confidence of the president, Scott worked tirelessly to implement the expedition. The largest amphibious operation in U.S. history before World War II, the invasion involved moving some fifteen thousand men and their weapons and equipment from Tampico, the mouth of the Río Grande, and other more distant locations to the beachhead at Vera Cruz. Quartermaster General Thomas S. Jesup demonstrated great skill in organizing the shipment of men, weapons, and thousands of items essential for the project. Raising an army was more difficult than gathering supplies; when Congress failed to supply new regiments in time to initiate the operation Scott insisted that a large portion of Gen. Zachary Taylor's seasoned army be shifted to the new front. Taylor, already bitter over what he considered to be a lack of support from President Polk, resented being forced to contribute the very heart of his army to the new campaign.

General Scott left New York at the end of November 1846 and stopped briefly in New Orleans, where he picked up information relating to the small coral island of Lobos, midway between Tampico and Vera Cruz, which would be used as a rendezvous point for his invasion. Arriving at the mouth of the Río Grande in late December, Scott found that key supplies, including the landing craft, had not arrived. The commander agonized that the healthy season for the campaign was swiftly running out; the target date of 1 February 1847 simply could not be met. By mid-February, however, the general set sail aboard the *Massachusetts*. Stopping briefly at Tampico, where Gen. Robert Patterson had massed some six thousand men, the commander and his growing force moved on 21 February to the main rendezvous point, Lobos Island. On 3 March 1847 the combined force set sail to the south, arriving at Antón Lizardo two days later.

Scott planned to move his three divisions to the protected area of the Isla de Sacrificios on army transports. Commodore Conner offered to provide navy ships for that transfer, pointing out that the larger vessels would cause less congestion in the narrow passage between Sacrificios and Collado Beach, the selected landing point south of Vera Cruz. The general-in-chief wisely accepted the offer and announced that the landing would take place on 8 March. Unfavorable weather forced a delay, but on the following morning, 9 March 1847, conditions were perfect and the long-delayed Vera Cruz attack was launched. The movement was one of precision and coordination between navy and army elements. Mexican lancers rode along the sand dunes behind Collado Beach but quickly scattered when the U.S. ships' guns opened fire. As Gen. William J. Worth led the first wave ashore, there was no opposition. The Mexican commander, Gen. Juan Morales, remained behind the stone walls of Vera Cruz. By midnight some ten thousand men had been placed ashore without a single loss of life.

On the following morning the operation continued. Additional supplies were brought ashore, and General Scott established his command post near the beach at "Fort Washington." General Morales, with some three thousand men, remained in the city, and another thousand Mexican soldiers occupied San Juan, protected by its massive walls and about one hundred heavy guns. Some U.S. officers called for an immediate assault against the walled city, but Scott, wishing to avoid high casualties, decided that he would attempt to take the prize by siege. During the following days the three U.S. divisions were positioned in a half moon around the city. Artillery and mortars were pulled through the heavy sand under the supervision of the corps of engineers. Commodore Conner suggested that the navy could play an even more effective role by bringing some of its heavy guns ashore. Scott hesitated at first but eventually accepted the offer, not only to bring the guns ashore, but also to have them operated by navy crews.

On 21 March, just as the bombardment was about to begin, Commo. Matthew C. Perry replaced Conner as commander of the Home Squadron. Although the change came at an awkward time, it did not adversely affect the operation; naval support of the attack went on as planned. Before opening the barrage, General Scott offered to allow noncombatants to leave the city, but Morales declined. The army batteries opened fire on 22 March, assisted by the naval ships. To further tighten his grip on the defenses, Scott ordered his forces to cut off all supplies into the city, including water. On 24 March the navy guns were in place on shore and joined in the shelling; the battery included three 32-pounders and two French 8-inch *Paixhans* that fired 68-pound exploding shells and were more effective than the army artillery. Although San Juan was barely damaged, broad holes were opened in the walls of Vera Cruz, and many buildings were damaged. Mexican counterfire was only slightly effective, in part due to inferior ammunition. The people in the city faced great hardship and suffering, but the U.S. commander refused to grant a truce. General Morales resigned, turning over his position to Gen. Juan Landero, who sought terms on 25 March. Scott rejected efforts to negotiate, insisting that he would only entertain terms of a surrender.

On 28 March the Mexican defenders marched out of Vera Cruz, stacked their arms, and surrendered to the invading

Parade of U.S.–Mexican War veterans. From the collection of William J. Schultz, M.D.

army. At the same time, the garrison of San Juan de Ulúa struck its colors and joined in the capitulation. The way lay open for Scott's march inland; he selected the National Road, which passed from the coastal plain to the healthy elevation of the provincial city of Jalapa. His path was contested by General Santa Anna, but after the U.S. victory at the Battle of Cerro Gordo, the way was open to Jalapa, Puebla, and eventually to the Valley of Mexico. Vera Cruz remained under U.S. control throughout the war and served as a point of supply and reenforcement for the invading army. Thus, the capture of Vera Cruz was the first step in the decisive campaign of the war.

Edward H. Moseley

BIBLIOGRAPHY

Bauer, K. Jack. *Surfboats and Horse Marines: U.S. Naval Operations in the Mexican War, 1846–48.* 1969.

Clark, Paul C., Jr., and Edward H. Moseley. "D-Day Veracruz, 1847—A Grand Design." *Joint Force Quarterly* (Winter 1995–1996, no. 10): 102–115.

Elliott, Charles Winslow. *Winfield Scott: The Soldier and the Man.* 1937.

Lott, W. S. "The Landing of the Expedition against Vera Cruz in 1847." *Military Service Institution of the United States* 24 (May 1899): 422–428.

Morison, Samuel Eliot. *"Old Bruin" Commodore Matthew C. Perry, 1794–1858.* 1967.

Quaife, Milo Milton, ed. *The Diary of James K. Polk during His Presidency, 1845 to 1849.* 4 vols. 1910.

Scott, Winfield. *Memoirs of Lieut. General Scott, LL.D., Written by Himself.* 2 vols. 1864.

Semmes, Raphael. *Service Afloat and Ashore during the Mexican War.* 1851.

Veterans Organizations

The earliest U.S.–Mexican War veterans organization was the Aztec Club, formed in occupied Mexico City in 1847 by 149 U.S. Army officers. Membership was later extended to any officer with U.S.–Mexican War service. Their descendants carry on the club's traditions to the present day.

Following the Civil War, several U.S.–Mexican War veterans groups were organized at the state and regional levels. Almost all were subordinate to the National Association of Veterans of the Mexican War, founded in Washington, D.C., in January 1874 by Alexander Kenaday, a former dragoon sergeant who had previously formed a veterans association in San Francisco, California. As secretary of the N.A.V.M.W., a post he held for twenty-three years, Kenaday almost single-handedly conducted the organization's business, handled its correspondence, and published a monthly newspaper called *The Vedette*.

From 1874 to 1910, the N.A.V.M.W. held an annual reunion of U.S.–Mexican War veterans at various cities throughout the United States. In 1876 it issued a bronze service medal to its members. Its primary goal, achieved in January 1887, was federal legislation granting an eight-dollar per month service pension. Another goal, a national U.S.–Mexican War veterans monument, never materialized. After Kenaday's death in 1897, a new secretary, Mrs. Moore Murdock, successfully pressed Congress to increase pensions to twelve dollars per month. In 1901 Mrs. Murdock founded a womens auxiliary, the Dames of 1846.

In 1989 a national lineage society, the Descendants of Mexican War Veterans, was formed to honor all U.S. veterans of the war with Mexico.

Steven R. Butler

BIBLIOGRAPHY

Butler, Steven R. "Alexander Kenaday and the National Association of Veterans of the Mexican War." *Mexican War Quarterly* 1 (1992): 10–21.

Butler, Steven R. "M. Moore Murdock: Angel of the Veterans." *Mexican War Journal* 3 (1994): 18–33.

Butler, Steven R., ed. *The Descendants of Mexican War Veterans 1994 Roster and Bylaws of the Organization.* 1994.

Eisenhower, John S. D. *So Far from God: The U.S. War with Mexico, 1846–1848.* 1989.

National Association of Veterans of the Mexican War. *Proceedings of the Second Annual Reunion.* 1875.

National Association of Veterans of the Mexican War. *Origins and Progress of the National Association of Veterans of the Mexican War.* 1887.

Wilcox, Cadmus Mercellus. *History of the Mexican War.* 1892.

See also **Pensions**

Victoria, Guadalupe

Guadalupe Victoria (1785–1843), the first president of Mexico, was born Miguel Fernández y Félix in obscurity in Durango. He studied to become a lawyer at the Colegio de San Ildefonso in Mexico City before he joined the 1810 insurgency against Spain. Fernández y Félix joined the forces of José María Morelos y Pavón, who had his officers pledge eternal loyalty to the Virgin of Guadalupe. At this point, Fernández y Félix changed his name to the pseudonym by which he is known.

Magnificently successful during the heyday of the insurrection, Guadalupe Victoria became the principal insurgent leader in Vera Cruz before suffering a series of defeats. Refusing to accept a royal pardon, he wandered for years in mountain forests between Puebla and Vera Cruz, holding out until the collapse of Spanish power. Guadalupe Victoria served in the junta that ruled Mexico before the establishment of a republic. Soldiers acting as statesmen became an unfortunate precedent in Mexican governance.

Elected Mexico's first president in June 1824, Guadalupe Victoria became the only leader of the early republic to serve out his full term. Tall, homely, and modest, Guadalupe Victoria attempted to work with his opponents. Although a federalist, he invited conservatives to join his cabinet; but his regime suffered from a worsening financial situation and increasingly bitter political strife. Despite attempting a policy of goodwill, Victoria was not decisive and simply lacked the talent to govern. His health failed considerably after his election, and he suffered chronic debilitating illness, probably a brain tumor. Vice President Gen. Nicolás Bravo joined a revolt by other conservative generals in 1827 that attempted to dismiss federalists within the regime, until the conservatives were in turn put down by another revolt. Clearly the political chaos that disrupted Mexican politics in the first half of the nineteenth century originated during Victoria's regime.

From 1831 to 1843 Guadalupe Victoria served as a governor and senator. He was one of two Mexican generals who concluded a treaty with France on 9 March 1838 that ended the Pastry War. Guadalupe Victoria died in 1843.

Douglas W. Richmond

BIBLIOGRAPHY

Calderón de la Barca, Frances. *Life in Mexico.* 1973.

Flaccus, Elmer. "Guadalupe Victoria: His Personality as a Cause of his Failure." *The Americas* 23 (1967): 297–311.

Victoria and Tampico, Occupation of

By late November 1846, as the focus of the U.S.–Mexican War began to shift from northern to central Mexico, Gen. Winfield Scott was engaged in planning an invasion of central Mexico. Initially the Mexican port city of Tampico was considered the best entry point for a campaign that would lead to Mexico City. Commo. David Conner, commanding the U.S. Home Squadron's blockade of the Mexican coast, had earlier determined that the city was poorly defended. When Gen. Antonio López de Santa Anna discovered from a captured dispatch that the city was to be taken, he ordered

Mexican forces to abandon it. Tampico was occupied by the U.S. Navy on 14 November 1846.

General Santa Anna had hoped that any planned U.S. invasion of central Mexico would be launched from Tampico because there were no good roads from there to either San Luis Potosí or Mexico City. The U.S. war department, encouraged by the easy capture of Tampico, felt that the precarious hold on Tampico needed to be secured and issued orders for reinforcements.

Maj. Gen. Robert Patterson, then at Camargo commanding a large contingent of volunteer soldiers, received orders transmitted directly from Secretary of War William L. Marcy to proceed to Tampico. Gen. Zachary Taylor indignantly protested this unusual order in a letter of 15 October 1846 to Marcy: "... The Department of War should refrain from corresponding directly with my subordinates ... Confusion and disaster alone can result. ... " But regardless of the blunder in military protocol by Marcy, the plans were set to proceed. Patterson's forces were to secure the defenses of Tampico and prepare for the campaign against central Mexico. Patterson's column of volunteers departed Camargo by early December 1846, proceeding down the Río Grande by steamboats. When concentrated at Matamoros, Patterson's forces were ordered to march overland to Tampico.

Meanwhile, General Taylor's force of regulars and volunteers at Monterrey and Saltillo were ordered to stand on the defensive and secure the Mexican territory captured during the earlier part of the year. The defense of this vast region by a small occupying force was dependent largely on the terrain. Northeastern Mexico was effectively isolated from the remainder of the country by the rugged Sierra Madre Oriental, which extended northwestward from Victoria to Monterrey. The only known passage through this range was the pass from Saltillo to Monterrey, which was controlled by U.S. forces. To make sure that his flanks were protected, Taylor decided in early December 1846 to command an expedition from Monterrey to Victoria, along the edge of the mountains, to determine if there were alternate passes. Unsure if Victoria, the capital city of Tamaulipas, was heavily defended, Taylor planned to coordinate his advance on Victoria with the march of Patterson's forces from the north, in case of Mexican resistance. As the two U.S. columns converged on Victoria, Gen. Gabriel Valencia, commanding the Victoria district, begged General Santa Anna for orders to attack the straggling columns of U.S. troops. But Santa Anna refused, knowing that if a battle was initiated, no reinforcements could be brought to Valencia's aid across the mountains that separated Victoria from the major Mexican base at San Luis Potosí. The Mexican military abandoned the city, which was occupied by U.S. forces on 29 December 1846.

Ultimately, the starting point for General Scott's attack on central Mexico was moved from Tampico to Vera Cruz after it was discovered that there were no major roads from Tampico inland to Mexico City. Patterson's forces were subsequently transported from Tampico to join Scott's forces in the invasion of Vera Cruz. Taylor's forces in northern Mexico were stripped of almost all regular troops and many volunteer regiments, which became part of Scott's Vera Cruz invasion army. General Santa Anna saw that the time had arrived for him to engage U.S. forces, and he issued orders to march north from San Luis Potosí and attack the weakened U.S. garrison at Saltillo.

Joseph E. Chance

BIBLIOGRAPHY

Bauer, K. Jack. *The Mexican War, 1846–1848.* 1974.

Claiborne, J. F. H. *Life and Correspondence of John A. Quitman.* 1860.

French, Samuel G. *Two Wars: An Autobiography of Gen. Samuel G. French.* 1901.

Henry, W. S. *Campaign Sketches of the War with Mexico.* 1847.

U.S. Congress. *Mexican War Correspondence.* 30th Cong., 1st sess., 1848, Exec. Doc. 60.

See also **Rio Grande Campaign** *for map*

Vidaurri, Santiago

Mexican official and strongman Santiago Vidaurri (1809–1867) was born in Lampazos, Nuevo León, on 25 July and grew up in the area of Monterrey. As a young man he was arrested for cutting off the hand of a soldier in a fight. When the municipal authorities discovered that the prisoner was well educated they hired him as a scribe; in 1837 he was promoted to chief assistant to the governor of Nuevo León, a post he held for several years. In 1841 Gen. Mariano Arista sent Vidaurri as a spy to report on the Santa Fe Expedition of Texas president Mirabeau B. Lamar. Having accomplished his mission, the young official returned to Monterrey to continue his administrative duties. After 1845, Vidaurri disappears from the official accounts, and there is no record of his activities during the occupation of Monterrey by the army of Gen. Zachary Taylor.

After the Treaty of Guadalupe Hidalgo, Vidaurri returned to the Mexican political stage, embracing the concepts of liberalism. On 23 May 1855, his small army, led by Juan Zuazua, seized the city of Monterrey. Forming an alliance with liberal forces in central Mexico but never sharing control in the northeast, Vidaurri became one of the most powerful regional *caudillos* in the nation. During the early phases of the War of Reform he supported Benito Juárez but broke with the liberal president rather than share lucrative customs revenues along the U.S.–Mexico border. When the Hapsburg prince Maximilian was placed upon a puppet Mexican throne by French forces in 1864, Vidaurri deserted the liberal cause and joined the Empire. When Porfirio Díaz captured Mexico City in 1867, he arrested the former northern strongman and had him executed as a traitor to Mexico.

Edward H. Moseley

BIBLIOGRAPHY

Roel, Santiago, ed. *Correspondencia particular de D. Santiago Vidaurri, gobernador de Nuevo León, 1855–1864.* 1946.

Tyler, Ronnie C. *Santiago Vidaurri and the Southern Confederacy.* 1973.

Villamil, Ignacio Mora y

See Mora y Villamil, Ignacio

Voltigeurs and Foot Riflemen, U.S.

The Ten Regiment Bill, signed into law in February 1847, authorized a specialized regiment called Voltigeurs and Foot Riflemen, an idea adapted from the French. In theory, all the men were armed with rifles, and half were mounted and half were on foot. The idea was for the dismounted men to climb up behind their mounted counterparts and ride to battle together, making the regiment highly mobile. The U.S. version, however, never received mounts; thus, it was a regiment of foot riflemen. A battery of four rockets and six 12-pounder Mountain Howitzers was authorized to serve with the regiment. The regiment's uniform was distinctive—dark gray jackets, trousers with white trim, and buttons marked with a *V*—but it is not known if the regiment actually received these garments or wore the sky blue uniforms of regular infantry.

The Voltigeurs landed at Vera Cruz in late spring 1847 and served in central Mexico. At least two companies arrived behind schedule and were used as escorts on the National Road. Eight companies, however, saw action in the battles for Mexico City. The regiment was badly bloodied at the Battle of Molino del Rey where five officers and ninety-five men were casualties. The regiment remained in Mexico City after its fall until 1 March 1848, when it was ordered to occupy Toluca. Withdrawn from Mexico in July, the regiment was mustered out of service at Fort McHenry, Maryland. While the regiment had performed well, the concept of voltigeurs never developed into a part of the U.S. military establishment. Several voltigeur officers later served in the Civil War, including confederate general Joseph E. Johnston, who was lieutenant colonel of the regiment.

Richard Bruce Winders

BIBLIOGRAPHY

Robarts, William H. *Mexican War Veterans: A Complete Roster of the Regular and Volunteer Troops in the War between the United States and Mexico. From 1846 to 1848.* 1887.

Smith, Justin H. *The War with Mexico.* 2 vols. 1919. Reprint, 1963.

Zeh, Frederick. *An Immigrant Soldier in the Mexican War.* 1995.

Volunteers

This entry consists of two separate articles: **U.S. Volunteers** *and* **Remustered Volunteers**.

U.S. Volunteers

Two components comprised the U.S. Army during the U.S.–Mexican War: regulars and volunteers. Unlike regulars, volunteer units were raised by the individual states of the Union. Regular units of the Old Establishment were created by Congress, and their officers received commissions from Congress. The rank and file enlisted for a specific time—usually five years.

The importance of the volunteer in the U.S. military establishment had its origin in legislation laying the founda-

Col. Jonathan Stevenson of the New York Volunteers. Daguerreotype, c. 1846. From the collection of William J. Schultz, M.D.

tion for the regular army and state militias. The nation's founders, determined to keep only a small force of regulars to avoid the dangers associated with a large standing army, depended on each state to supply additional troops in case of regional or national emergency. Specifically, the militia could be called out to quell insurrection, repel invasion, and enforce the nation's laws. The War of 1812, however, pointed out serious flaws in this early system of national defense. First, militiamen were bound by law to only a three-month enlistment, and second, state officials were reluctant to allow their troops to serve outside their state borders. These features made the militia an ineffective offensive force.

Congress increasingly relied on volunteers as a means to overcome the problems associated with true militia. The Militia Law of 1792 had authorized volunteer units as adjuncts to militia divisions. The use of volunteers—militiamen who were willing to perform active service—was expanded when Congress created a corps of volunteers to augment the regular army during the War of 1812. The concept was again used in the 1830s to raise troops for the conflict between U.S. forces and the Seminole Indians in Florida.

During the U.S.–Mexican War, the War Department raised 73,532 volunteers, but this includes several thousand men who never set foot on Mexican soil. Also included in this number are volunteers called illegally by Gen. Edmund P. Gaines in May 1846 shortly after the battles of Palo Alto and Resaca de la Palma. The 12,601 men who responded to his call arrived on the Río Grande only to learn that the War Department had no place for them. Dejected and irate, most returned home.

Congress, meeting in session 13 May 1846, authorized President James K. Polk to call 50,000 volunteers as part of the effort to mobilize for war. The War Department issued the initial call to the states of the Old Northwest (Ohio, Illinois, and Indiana) and Old Southwest (Alabama, Mississippi, Tennessee, and Kentucky). Only 18,210 of the authorized number were actually mustered into service at that time, as Polk waited to see if the full corps would be needed. Optimism that the war would be short led to wording in the legislation that allowed volunteers to leave the service at the end of twelve months. When it became apparent in late 1846 that the war was far from over and that most of the twelve-month volunteers wanted to leave the service in spring of 1847, the U.S. government had to scramble to find replacements. The twelve-month volunteers had fought at Monterrey and Buena Vista and had garrisoned towns in northern Mexico. A few were selected to accompany Gen. Winfield Scott to central Mexico and were present at the Siege of Vera Cruz and the Battle of Cerro Gordo. Of the 18,000 twelve-month volunteers, 631 reenlisted in reconstituted units designated "remustered" volunteers.

The War Department closed the twelve-month loophole when it issued a second call for volunteers. Troops raised in

Unidentified volunteer private. Daguerreotype, c. 1846, taken in New Orleans. From the collection of William J. Schultz, M.D.

the autumn and winter of 1846 were told their enlistment was "for the war." While some of these 33,596 troops were "lucky enough" to be assigned to Scott's column, many were sent to northern Mexico and New Mexico where the fighting had ceased except for antiguerrilla operations. Most volunteers who answered this second call spent fifteen months in Mexico, trapped in garrison duty with little hope for action.

The Quartermaster Department was unprepared to uniform the volunteer corps when the war began, having enough supplies only for the small regular army. To meet the emergency Congress authorized for volunteers a clothing allowance of $3.50 per month. This practice led to volunteer uniforms in a variety of colors and styles. Some units wore uniforms patterned after their state's militia. Some colonels contracted with local tailors to produce their regiments' uniforms. There was variation even within regiments, however, as individual companies sometimes had their own distinct uniform. Replacing worn-out clothing was a serious problem for volunteer troops in Mexico. Some commanders raided Quartermaster stocks and took uniforms intended for regulars. The Quartermaster Department issued captured Mexican uniforms to volunteers in central Mexico in an effort to alleviate the situation. By the time Congress voted to provide volunteers with uniforms, the Treaty of Guadalupe Hidalgo had been signed and the troops were on their way home.

Although considered U.S. troops by the War Department, volunteers did not view themselves as such and retained strong ties to their home states; after all, volunteers were raised using a state apparatus—the militia system. Military duty was seen as a way to bring honor to one's state and local community. Volunteers maintained close contact with their families and friends, expecting to reenter society at the expiration of their enlistment. As citizen soldiers, volunteers were "citizens" first in all matters.

Volunteers earned a reputation as rowdy and undisciplined. The tradition that allowed them to choose their own officers was partly to blame. Many volunteer officers, elected to their positions by friends and neighbors, refrained from disciplining their troops rather than risk their disapproval. Moreover, volunteers often viewed their officers in the same light as other elected officials and expected favors in return for their support. Additionally, freed from the constraints of their own society, volunteers often behaved in ways they would never have considered at home. Their willingness to rob and ransack prompted some regulars to observe that the volunteers made war not only on the government of Mexico, but also on its people. Nevertheless, with leadership, training, and time, some volunteers became useful troops, as evidenced by Col. Jefferson Davis and the 1st Mississippi Rifles.

Richard Bruce Winders

BIBLIOGRAPHY

Callan, John F. *Military Laws of the United States.* 1863.

Scott, Henry L. *Military Dictionary.* 1864. Reprint, 1984.

Smith, Justin. *War with Mexico.* 2 vols. 1919. Reprint, 1963.

Winders, Richard Bruce. *Mr. Polk's Army.* 1997.

Remustered Volunteers

The U.S. government had hoped that the military campaigns begun in the fall of 1846 would cause Mexico to sue for peace, but the U.S. occupation of New Mexico, the capture of Monterrey, and the presence of U.S. forces in California failed to end Mexican resistance. Faced with a longer war than President James K. Polk and his supporters had expected, Congress recognized the need to raise more troops. Two actions were taken in response to this development: the War Department called up the remainder of the volunteers authorized under the Act of 13 May 1846, and Congress passed the Ten Regiment Bill on 11 February 1847.

Knowing it would take months to raise new regiments, officials turned to twelve-month volunteers who were already in the field but soon to be discharged as a potential source of manpower. U.S. commanders in Mexico pleaded with volunteers to remain at their posts and to see the war through to its end, but the majority of these citizen-soldiers believed that they had already done their duty and returned home almost en masse at the expiration of their one-year terms. Several hundred chose to stay with the army; they were remustered into the service and formed into four separate units of mounted volunteers: Capt. Gaston Meares's company near Saltillo; Capt. James Boyd's company in central Mexico; Maj. Robert Walker's battalion in New Mexico; and Capt. Chatham Roberdeau Wheat's company in central Mexico. Although other discharged volunteers re-enlisted in new volunteer regiments when they returned home, they were not designated remustered volunteers.

Richard Bruce Winders

BIBLIOGRAPHY

U.S. Congress. House. *Military Forces Employed in the Mexican War: Letter from the Secretary of War Transmitting Information in answer to a resolution of the House, of July 31, 1848, relative to the military forces employed in the late war with Mexico.* 31st Cong., 1st sess., Executive Document No. 24.

Winders, Richard Bruce. *Mr. Polk's Army: The American Military Experience in the Mexican War.* 1997.

Winders, Richard Bruce. "Mr. Polk's Army: Politics, Patronage, and the American Military in the Mexican War." Ph.D. diss., Texas Christian University, 1994.

See also **Ten Regiment Bill**

Walker, Robert J.

Robert J. Walker (1801–1869) was secretary of the treasury under President James K. Polk and the most influential member of his cabinet. Born in Pennsylvania, Walker gained prominence as a young man when he advanced Andrew Jackson's bid for the presidency. Despite his growing influence in Pennsylvania politics, Walker moved to Natchez, Mississippi, in 1826 where he practiced law and speculated in land and slaves. The Mississippi legislature elected him twice to the U.S. Senate, where he served from 1836 to early 1845. In Polk's administration Walker supported policies to expand the nation's trade and territory. He proposed and won lower tariffs in 1846, urged rigorous prosecution of the war against Mexico, and favored a large territorial indemnity and transit rights across the Isthmus of Tehuantepec to promote commerce.

Early in the war Walker supported acquiring Mexican territory north of 26° north latitude. By late 1847 he suggested taking all of Mexico if necessary to end the war. To help finance the conquest of Mexico and ease the burden on the U.S. treasury, Walker and Polk lifted the blockade on Mexican trade and levied import duties and export fees on precious metals. The treasury primarily relied on loans, not taxes, to fund the war, a policy that sharply increased the national debt. Financing the prolonged war placed a heavy burden on Walker and impaired his health—one wag observed in 1847 that Walker seemed as exhausted as the treasury over which he presided.

Not satisfied with the acquisition of California and New Mexico, Walker joined Polk in 1848 in advocating the annexation of Yucatán and Cuba. A vital force in the annexation of Texas, a defender of slavery, and a states-rights champion in the 1830s and 1840s, Walker in the early 1850s returned to private life and personal business. President James Buchanan, however, appointed him governor of Kansas Territory in early 1857. Walker believed that most Kansas voters opposed the expansion of slavery into the territory, so he supported the free-soil side in the dispute. At odds with the administration, Walker resigned his post late that year. A Unionist Democrat during the Civil War, he aided the North's cause by selling bonds in Great Britain. Walker died in Washington, D.C., in 1869.

Thomas Hietala

BIBLIOGRAPHY

Hietala, Thomas R. *Manifest Design*, pp. 26–32, 41–42, 49–53, 183–184, 199–201, 245. 1985.

"Robert J. Walker." *United States Magazine and Democratic Review* (February 1845): 157–164.

Robert J. Walker Papers. Library of Congress, National Archives, Washington, D.C.

Shenton, James P. *Robert John Walker, A Politician from Jackson to Lincoln.* 1961.

Walker, Samuel

Samuel Hamilton Walker (1817–1847), lieutenant colonel, 1st Texas Mounted Riflemen, was born 24 February in Prince George's County, Maryland, a son of Elizabeth and Nathan Walker. He participated in the Second Seminole War before moving to Texas in January 1842. Walker served in the Somervell and Mier Expeditions to the Río Grande during which he fell prisoner on 24 December 1842 near Mier, Mexico. He escaped from Mexico in July 1843 and joined John C. Hays's Texas Rangers in 1844, participating in several battles with Indians.

On 21 April 1846 Walker organized a company of rangers and scouted for Gen. Zachary Taylor on the Río Grande,

Samuel Walker leading a company of Texas Rangers. John Frost, *Pictorial History of Mexico and the Mexican War*, 1862

fighting at Palo Alto and Resaca de la Palma. He received a captain's commission in the U.S. Mounted Rifles but served first with Hays's Texas regiment as lieutenant colonel and fought at Monterrey, 19–24 September 1846. After Hays's men disbanded on 30 September, Walker traveled to Maryland and New York to recruit his company. He met Samuel Colt, inventor of the Colt Revolver, and offered improvements that resulted in the production of the Walker Colt.

Walker reached Gen. Winfield Scott's army in May 1847 and served under Gen. Joseph Lane fighting guerrillas on the Vera Cruz road. On 20 June he won a victory at Las Vegas and led a charge into Huamantla on 9 October where he was killed. The national press had followed Walker's career since his service on the Río Grande and reported his death as that of a fallen hero. Although he was killed while an officer in the regular army, the nation celebrated Walker as a Texas Ranger. He was buried in San Antonio.

Jimmy L. Bryan, Jr.

BIBLIOGRAPHY

Sibley, Marilyn McAdams, ed. *Samuel H. Walker's Account of the Mier Expedition*. 1978.

Spurlin, Charles. "Ranger Walker in the Mexican War." *Military History of Texas and the Southwest* 9 (1971): 259–279.

Walker, William

Physician, lawyer, and filibuster William Walker (1824–1860) was born in Nashville, Tennessee, in May 1824. He graduated in 1843 from the University of Pennsylvania Medical School, studied medicine in Europe, and returned to Nashville in 1845 to practice as a physician. He quickly tired of medicine and went to New Orleans, where he studied law and practiced it for a short time. In 1848 he became assistant editor of the *New Orleans Crescent*.

In 1850 Walker journeyed to California where he became

assistant editor of the *San Francisco Daily Herald*. Like many adventurers of the era, he believed Mexico was vulnerable to losing more of its territory after the U.S.–Mexican War. In 1853 he led a filibustering expedition into Baja California to separate this region and ultimately Sonora from Mexico. With approximately fifty supporters he traveled by ship to La Paz, Baja California, where he proclaimed himself "President of the Republic of Lower California." A short time later he claimed he "annexed" Sonora to his new republic. The Mexican government sent a naval force to end this filibustering threat. Walker and his party narrowly escaped by traveling overland to the U.S. border. Although U.S. authorities brought Walker to trial for violation of neutrality laws, no court of Californians would convict him.

In 1855, still determined to be president of a Latin American country, Walker organized men to filibuster to Nicaragua. At Granada, Nicaragua, in 1855, he proclaimed himself president. Although forced to leave in 1856, Walker returned in August 1860 but established his camp on the coast of Honduras, hoping to go from there to Nicaragua. Honduran authorities, with the assistance of a British warship, captured and executed him in September.

Joseph A. Stout, Jr.

BIBLIOGRAPHY

Allen, Merritt Parmalee. *William Walker, Filibuster*. 1932.

Greene, Laurence. *The Filibuster: The Career of William Walker*. 1937.

Scroggs, William O. *Filibusters and Financiers: The Story of William Walker and His Associates*. 1916.

Stout, Joseph A., Jr. *The Liberators: Filibustering Expeditions into Mexico 1848–1862, and the Last Thrust of Manifest Destiny*. 1973.

Walnut Springs

Located on the northeast outskirts of Monterrey, Mexico, Walnut Springs was the campground for the 6,640 officers and men of the U. S. forces that captured Monterrey during 21 to 27 September 1846. The site was selected personally by Gen. Zachary Taylor on 19 September 1846, as his forces arrived within the range of Mexican cannons located on the defensive perimeter of Monterrey. This site, wooded with stately oak and pecan trees and watered by several springs, continued to be used as the principal camp for U.S. soldiers at Monterrey for the remainder of the war (*see illustration on following page*). General Taylor also lived on the site throughout his stay in northern Mexico, and it was here that William Carl Brown Jr. created his well-known painting of Taylor and his staff.

The cemetery of the 3d Infantry was located at Walnut Springs. Surrounded by a wall of neatly dressed limestone blocks four feet high and adorned by a rectangular pillar surmounted by a cross, the cemetery became the final resting site of many of the officers slain in the attack on Monterrey. The remains of Maj. William W. Lear, Bvt. Maj. Lewis Nelson Morris, Capt. George P. Field, Capt. Philip Nordbourne Barbour, 1st Lieut. Douglass Simms Irwin, 2d Lieut. Robert Hazlitt of the 3d Infantry, and 2d Lieut. Rankin Dilworth of the 1st Infantry were interred within these walls. The mortal remains of Brig. Gen. Thomas L. Hamer were temporarily buried at the site and later moved to Ohio for reburial. The practice of reburial in the United States of U.S. soldiers slain in Mexico was largely a private matter, and no records exist as to their number.

A correspondent to the New Orleans *Picayune* reported by 1851 that the walls of the cemetery had been entirely destroyed, but the graves remained unmolested. Searches were made in 1965 by Carter L. Hilsabeck and in 1996 by Joseph E. Chance for remains of the camp at Walnut Springs and the cemetery, but the urban sprawl of modern industrial Monterrey has covered the site. A small cemetery that met the historical descriptions was located near Ojo Nogal, a Monterrey suburb, but the headstones were those of Mexicans. It was a common practice, however, to bury over the sites of old graves.

Joseph E. Chance

BIBLIOGRAPHY

Henry, W. S. *Campaign Sketches of the War with Mexico*. 1847.

New Orleans *Picayune*, March 13, 1851.

Wislizenus, Adolphus. *Memoirs of a Tour of Northern Mexico*. 1969.

War Aims

This entry consists of two separate articles: **Mexican War Aims** *and* **U.S. War Aims**.

Mexican War Aims

On 6 March 1845, the Mexican minister in Washington, D.C., broke diplomatic relations with the United States, shortly after the U.S. Congress approved the annexation of Texas. In Mexico, the extremist press demanded a declaration of war and a military campaign to recover Texas, believing that these actions were the only way to defend the integrity of Mexico's national territory and to stop U.S. expansionism. President José Joaquín de Herrera, considering Mexico's internal weakness and the lack of both funds and an adequate army, decided to avoid conflict, even if it meant losing Texas. He was even willing to meet with a U.S. representative to discuss the issue. Herrera was supported by the moderate liberals; however, the radical liberals (*puros*) and the conservatives demanded a firmer attitude against the United States, which led Herrera to refuse to meet U.S. emissary John Slidell. Meanwhile, Gen. Mariano Paredes y Ar-

View of Monterrey from Walnut Springs. John Frost, *Pictorial History of Mexico and the Mexican War*, 1862

rillaga rebelled against Herrera, accused him of treason, and promised to declare war immediately. After assuming the presidency, he too realized Mexico's situation and, like his predecessor, adopted a conciliatory policy; yet he too refused to meet with Slidell and hostilities began soon thereafter. The U.S. Army crossed the Nueces River and reached Matamoros on 28 March. On 23 April Paredes y Arrillaga began to organize the defense of the country, although the formal declaration of war did not occur until 2 July, almost two months after the U.S. declaration.

The complex and divisive political situation in Mexico complicated the military defense. The *puros* allied with Gen. Antonio López de Santa Anna, believing that he was the only leader who could successfully organize the defense of independence and territorial integrity. Even the moderate liberals, worried by consecutive military defeats by the U.S.

Army, were willing to achieve unity and continue war; some, though, opposed a traditional military offensive and advocated instead the use of guerrilla tactics.

On 4 August, the liberals formed a temporary government that ruled until the end of the year and supported war. Santa Anna and Valentín Gómez Farías were elected president and vice president, respectively, on 6 December, amid calls to save the nation's honor. But the military situation was desperate: the U.S. forces controlled northern Mexico, and another army, which disembarked at Vera Cruz on 29 March 1847, was marching toward Mexico City. The press and the various groups gradually changed their attitudes, influenced by the military superiority and irrepressible advance of the U.S. forces, the deteriorating condition of the Mexican army, and the country's economic crisis. The moderate liberals were willing to buy peace with land, and many conservatives wanted to reach an agreement with the United States. They were willing to support the moderates because they feared that continuing the war would mean their property would be confiscated. Some of the *puros*, frustrated because they had lost power when Gómez Farías was ousted, agreed to negotiate. They wanted the United States to forgo territorial gains in exchange for a temporary protectorate and to help Mexico establish an authentic democratic republic. Santa Anna's supporters wanted to continue fighting, whether for patriotism or for reasons of personal benefit.

U.S. forces cleared all approaches to Mexico City on 20 August, and an armistice was called to permit negotiations. The war party prevailed in the Mexican congress, however, and those who would meet with the U.S. commissioner Nicholas P. Trist were instructed to act as if Mexico had not been defeated and to relinquish only Texas, and only as far as the Nueces River. Thus no agreement was reached and hostilities started again on 6 September.

Mexico City surrendered 14 September, Santa Anna resigned the presidency two days later, and a moderate liberal government succeeded him, establishing itself in the city of Querétaro. During the next nine months, opinions against and in favor of war were heard. Conservative and moderate liberals desired peace. However, moderate liberals were divided into two groups, the first led by Luis de la Rosa and Luis Gonzaga Cuevas, who would accept sacrifice of an important part of the territory in order to achieve peace with the United States. Mariano Otero led the second group, which desired a more honorable, although less realistic agreement: to cede only Texas and, if necessary, to define the boundary at the Río Bravo. The *puros*, on the other hand, believed Mexico should continue the war until all U.S. troops left the country. Some of them, like Manuel Crescencio Rejón, still believed that Mexico could win a prolonged guerrilla war. The different proposals were heard in December at the congress. Considering the desperate situation, Otero's group and the *puros* were defeated. Mexico was ready to negotiate.

Peace talks began on 2 January 1848, and the Treaty of Guadalupe Hidalgo was signed on 2 February. It was returned to Mexico in May, approved by the U.S. Senate and signed by President James K. Polk, but several of its amendments led to arguments between the Mexican war and peace parties. President Manuel de la Peña y Peña submitted the treaty to congress, claiming that Mexico had achieved the best possible terms in the worst of situations and that the only way out was to accept the modified treaty. He also said that if the conflict continued, so would Mexico's internal problems and that more territory would be lost. So, despite disagreements, Congress approved the treaty. The president's ratification and the exchange of ratifications by the end of the month confirmed the success of the peace party.

Ana Rosa Suárez Argüello

BIBLIOGRAPHY

Alcaraz, Ramón ed. *The Other Side; or Notes for the History of the War between Mexico and the United States.* Translated by Albert C. Ramsey. 1970. Originally published as *Apuntes para la historia de la Guerra entre México y los Estados Unidos,* 1848.

Briseño Senosiáin, Lillian, et al. *Valentín Gómez Farías y su lucha por el federalismo 1822–1858.* 1991.

Bosch García, Carlos. *Documentos de la relación de México con los Estados Unidos.* 4 vols. 1983–1985.

Griswold del Castillo, Richard. *The Treaty of Guadalupe Hidalgo: A Legacy of Conflict.* 1990.

Peña y Reyes, Antonio de la, ed. *Algunos documentos sobre el Tratado de Guadalupe y la situación de México durante la invasión americana.* 1971.

Pletcher, David M. *The Diplomacy of Annexation: Texas, Oregon, and the Mexican War.* 1973.

Riva Palacio, Vicente, coord. *México a través de los siglos.* 5 vols. 1887.

Roa Bárcena, José María. *Recuerdos de la invasión norteamericana (1846–1848).* 3 vols. 1947.

Vázquez, Josefina Z., and Lorenzo Meyer. *México frente a Estados Unidos: Un ensayo histórico, 1776–1980.* 1982.

Velasco Márquez, Jesús. *La opinión pública y la guerra del 47.* 1975.

Zamacois, Niceto de. *Historia de México desde sus tiempos más remotos hasta nuestros días, escrita en vista de todo lo que de irrecusable han dado a luz los más caracterizados historiadores, y en virtud de documentos auténticos no publicados todavía, tomados del Archivo Nacional de Méjico, de las bibliotecas públicas, y de los preciosos manuscritos que, hasta hace poco, existían en las de los conventos de aquel país.* 20 vols. 1876–1882.

U.S. War Aims

On 11 May 1846, two days after learning that U.S. dragoons had been fired on by Mexican troops near the banks of the Río Grande, President James K. Polk asked Congress to declare war against Mexico on the grounds that "American blood" had been shed on "American soil." While some members of Congress maintained that the Trans-Nueces region, where the attack had occurred, was not U.S. territory, Polk insisted that the area been acquired by the United States when it annexed Texas in 1845. By declaring war against Mexico, the administration sought to force its southern neighbor to accept U.S. sovereignty over this disputed territory. In addition, Polk cited other "insults" and "injuries" that necessitated a declaration of war against Mexico: the Mexican government's failure to pay $3.5 million in outstanding claims owed to U.S. citizens and its recent refusal to normalize diplomatic relations by rejecting John Slidell as U.S. minister to Mexico.

The redress of U.S. grievances against Mexico represented only a part of the president's war aims, however. Although Polk declined to say so publicly, he was eager to obtain New Mexico and California, and critics of the war suspected that Polk had manufactured the conflict in order to seize these territories from Mexico. Polk insisted that he had not gone to war to obtain the southwest for the United States, but he was well aware that a Mexican defeat would enable the U.S. government to demand territorial concessions in the peace negotiations that followed. Indeed, as early as June 1845, Polk had ordered the Pacific fleet to remain on alert and to seize California in the event of war between the two countries.

That territorial objectives were of paramount importance for Polk became evident when, two days after the war message was read to Congress, Secretary of State James Buchanan showed the president a diplomatic document he had drafted on the war's causes. Anxious to allay the fears of foreign governments, which might provide support to Mexico if they believed the war was being waged for territorial aggrandizement, Buchanan stated that the United States did not go to war to obtain California, New Mexico, or any other portion of Mexican territory. Polk's reaction was to insist that Buchanan delete any reference to the "no territory" pledge, remarking that he considered such assurances "unnecessary and improper." Although the United States had not gone to war for conquest, Polk intended to claim some territorial indemnity from Mexico to defray the costs of waging war.

Despite an uninterrupted string of U.S. victories in 1846 and 1847, Polk's efforts to obtain New Mexico and California were stymied by Mexico's refusal to negotiate a peace treaty. The president's determination to expand the nation's boundaries also ran into stiff opposition at home from Whigs and antislavery Democrats, who suspected that the administration's expansionist policies stemmed from a desire to extend slavery. To ensure that the South did not benefit from the war, David Wilmot, a Pennsylvania Democrat, proposed a proviso to an appropriations bill in August 1846 prohibiting slavery in any territory acquired from Mexico. Although the Wilmot Proviso failed to pass the Senate, it introduced a new dimension to the growing controversy over the war's aims, polarizing the Northern and Southern wings of the Democratic Party over the slavery issue.

As the war dragged on, the debate over the status of slavery in the southwest threatened to become so divisive that opponents of the administration called on the president to formally disavow any territorial ambitions whatsoever in the war with Mexico. In his third annual message in December 1847, Polk rejected out of hand his critics' call for a peace without territorial compensation. To accept the "no territory" doctrine, he argued, "would be a public acknowledge-

ment that our country was wrong . . . an admission unfounded in fact, and degrading to the national character."

Meanwhile, support for seizing even more territory from Mexico than Polk or his advisers had envisioned at the outset of the war was rapidly gaining ground. By 1847 many expansionist politicians and pundits began to call not merely for the acquisition of Mexico's northernmost provinces, but also for further territorial cessions below the Río Grande, while some demanded nothing less than that country's complete absorption by the United States. A number of prominent party leaders, among them Secretary of State Buchanan—whose about-face on the territorial issue may have been calculated to enhance his prospects as a contender for the Democratic presidential nomination—and Secretary of the Treasury Robert J. Walker called for the annexation of Mexico. Although Polk never endorsed the "All of Mexico" movement, by the fall of 1847 he favored increasing the size of the territorial indemnity, one that would include Tampico, Mexico's second largest port. Only the threat of further cessions, he believed, would induce Mexican leaders to negotiate a peace treaty.

The debate over how much territory to take from Mexico came to an abrupt end in February 1848, however, with the news that Nicholas P. Trist, acting on earlier instructions from the U.S. government, had signed the Treaty of Guadalupe Hidalgo with Mexican peace commissioners on 2 February. According to the terms of the treaty, Mexico ceded New Mexico and California, for which it received $15 million and the assumption by the United States of claims against the Mexican government. Despite opposition from Democrats, who argued that the agreement did not take enough territory from Mexico, and Whigs, who maintained that it took too much, the Senate ratified the treaty on 10 March by a vote of 38 to 14. The question of whether these territories would become free or slave states in the Union would continue to divide both parties along sectional lines until the Compromise of 1850.

Sam W. Haynes

BIBLIOGRAPHY

Haynes, Sam W. *James K. Polk and the Expansionist Impulse.* 1996.

Quaife, Milo M., ed. *The Diary of Jame K. Polk during his Presidency, 1845 to 1849.* 1910.

Richardson, James D. *A Compilation of the Messages and Papers of the Presidents*, vol. 4. 1898.

War Correspondents

The modern war correspondent was first introduced during the U.S.–Mexican War. Several types of war correspondents reported the war. In addition to the full-time reporters, of whom there were probably fewer than ten, most representing

New Orleans newspapers, numerous free-lance writers were found anywhere there was a military presence. Many enlistees had made arrangements with their hometown papers to send home dispatches. Editors as well as their underlings served in the army, with sixteen from Massachusetts alone. During this era most newspapermen were referred to as "printers," and virtually every company of volunteers employed at least one.

Newspapermen were abundant during the conflict because so many had volunteered to fight the Mexican army. In one company of volunteers, there were at least twenty New Orleans printers. Among them were three correspondents for the New Orleans *Delta*: James L. Freaner, J. G. H. Tobin, known for his sketches "From Captain Tobin's Knapsack," and John H. Peoples, better known by his pseudonym "Chaparral."

The most celebrated correspondent of the war was George Wilkins Kendall, who cofounded the New Orleans *Picayune* with Francis Lumsden in 1837. Kendall was so anxious to witness warfare himself that he left Gen. Zachary Taylor's command temporarily to join the Texas Rangers under Capt. Ben McCulloch. Kendall covered most of the battles of General Taylor and Gen. Winfield Scott, including those at Chapultepec, Monterrey, Cerro Gordo, and Churubusco.

Lumsden attempted to raise his own New Orleans regiment, but he ended his recruiting drive when a better-equipped mounted company from Georgia passed through the Crescent City on its way to the border and elected Lumsden as its leader.

Also representing the *Picayune* was Christopher Mason Haile, a Kendall protégé and graduate of West Point. He joined Scott's staff during the siege of Vera Cruz and became widely known for his humorous letters in the paper signed "Pardon Jones."

One of Kendall's chief rivals was James L. Freaner, correspondent for the New Orleans *Delta*, who published his dispatches under the pseudonym "Mustang." He acquired his sobriquet at the battle of Monterrey, where he killed an officer of the lancers and seized his charger. In February 1848, Nicholas P. Trist entrusted Freaner to carry the Treaty of Guadalupe Hidalgo to Washington, D.C.

Although few newspapers outside the deep South sent correspondents, others were present. For example, in 1846 the *New York Herald* claimed that its five correspondents in Mexico "had more talent than those of any other paper," and Lucian J. Eastin published firsthand accounts under the initial "E" in the *Jefferson Inquirer* of Jefferson City, Missouri. Also, numerous correspondents and printers founded newspapers, which were collectively referred to as the "Anglo-Saxon Press," in Mexico's occupied cities.

The only known woman correspondent to cover the front lines was Jane McManus Storm, whose dispatches appeared under the pseudonyms "Montgomery" and "Cora Mont-gomery" in the New York *Sun*. She was the only member of the press to report from behind Mexican lines and was one of the few to criticize both U.S. military efforts and her fellow war reporters.

Mitchel Roth

BIBLIOGRAPHY

Copeland, Fayette. *Kendall of the Picayune.* 1943. Reprint, 1970.

Johanssen, Robert W. *To the Halls of the Montezumas: The Mexican War in the American Imagination.* 1985.

Reilly, Tom. "Jane McManus Storms: Letters from the Mexican War, 1846–1848." *Southwestern Historical Quarterly* 85 (July 1981): 21–44.

Sandweiss, Martha A., Rick Stewart, and Ben W. Huseman. *Eyewitness to War: Prints and Daguerrotypes of the Mexican War, 1846–1848.* 1979.

War Crimes

See **Atrocities**

War Message, Polk's

On 11 May 1846, two days after receiving the news that U.S. troops on the Río Grande had been attacked by Mexican forces, President James K. Polk asked Congress to declare war against Mexico. Ignoring Mexican claims to the Trans-Nueces, where the skirmish had occurred, Polk declared that "American blood" had been shed on "American soil." To further support his call for a declaration of war, Polk listed the "insults" and "injuries" that the United States had suffered at the hands of Mexico: the Mexican government's refusal to pay outstanding claims owed to U.S. citizens; its refusal to recognize the U.S. annexation of Texas or the Río Grande as the legitimate boundary of Texas; and its rejection of John Slidell as U.S. minister plenipotentiary to Mexico.

The Polk administration and its supporters in Congress moved quickly to capitalize on public anger at the Mexican attack on U.S. forces, ramming the war bill through Congress with limited debate. Administration loyalists skillfully added to the bill a preamble restating Polk's position that war existed "by act of the Republic of Mexico," thereby coupling the declaration of war with the measure to vote men and supplies for Gen. Zachary Taylor's army. Even Whigs who believed the war unjustified felt compelled to vote in favor of the measure for fear of seeming unpatriotic in a time of national emergency. The bill passed handily in the House by a vote of 173 to 14 and in the Senate by a vote of 40 to 2, with three senators abstaining. Despite the lopsided margins in favor of the bill, many leaders of both parties questioned Polk's motives for waging war against Mexico. As a result, the broad, bipartisan support for the president's decision disintegrated in the months ahead.

Sam W. Haynes

BIBLIOGRAPHY
Bergeron, Paul H. *The Presidency of James K. Polk.* 1987.
Haynes, Sam W. *James K. Polk and the Expansionist Impulse.* 1996.

Weapons

This entry consists of four separate articles: **Weapons Technology;** **Coastal and Naval Weapons;** **Field Artillery;** *and* **Small Arms.** *See also* **Colt Revolver** *and* **Mississippi Rifle.**

Weapons Technology

The years from 1821 to 1854 witnessed many advances in weapons technology. Smoothbore muskets gave way to rifles, percussion replaced flintlock ignition, rifles became militarily reliable, and sabers and lances fell before revolving cylinder pistols. Only artillery escaped this technology revolution without major changes.

For mounted troops, sabers prevailed during the beginning of the period but were increasingly supplemented by pistols. The most common edged weapon among U.S. troops by the time of the U.S.–Mexican War was the model 1833, also known as "Old Wrist Breaker" due to its heavy two-pound blade. Among Mexican horsemen, the preferred weapon was the lance, backed by a lighter saber.

Firearms also were carried by mounted troops. The revolver took the place of edged weapons for mounted service after the 1835 introduction of Samuel Colt's revolver. Improvements to this weapon eventually led to a heavy pistol capable of firing six full-power loads, giving it remarkable destructive power for its day. In addition, most U.S. carbines and Mexican *escopetas* (carbines) appeared clumsy in comparison to the sturdy revolvers. In 1846 Maj. Gen. Zachary Taylor was so impressed with the Colt revolvers his officers were carrying that he had 1,000 ordered for his troops followed by 1,000 more after his troops tested them in the field.

Long arms—muskets and rifles—changed the most during this period. In 1821 the flintlock musket of .69 or .75 caliber was the typical weapon used by most armies. Typically a muzzle loader, its rate of fire was three to four shots per minute with frequent misfires due to its primitive flint and steel ignition system. As the flintlock era waned, the percussion system came into its own, using a system in which the hammer delivered a sharp blow to an explosive cap, instead of the open pan ignition method it replaced. Many of the previous flintlock muskets were converted into percussion cap muskets, primarily because of the lower rate of misfire. Mexican troops had little access to the new system, however, and U.S. troops mistrusted what they considered an untested invention.

Percussion firearms helped advance the usefulness of military rifles. Among Mexican troops, the reliable Baker rifle, a flintlock, continued to give good service. In the United States, however, the Model 1841, which was .54 caliber and had a thirty-three-inch barrel, became the first useful rifle in U.S. service. It was reliable, accurate, and easy to use and immediately became popular with civilians and soldiers alike, acquiring the name Mississippi Rifle due to its use by the Mississippi Volunteers in the U.S.–Mexican War. In addition to its superior percussion system, the Model 1841 also had significantly more power than previous rifles, including Bakers, firing a bullet eight inches into a tree from one hundred yards. Later in 1848, Christian Sharps introduced a successful breech-loading rifle, replacing the unreliable flintlock Hall rifle in U.S. units. The various Sharps rifles and carbines were some of the most widely used guns in the United States until the late 1850s.

The final obstacle to efficient military rifles was overcome in 1849 with the invention of the minié ball. This bullet had a conical head instead of being round like the bullets it replaced, providing it with better ballistic profiles. In addition, its base was hollow, which expanded to fit rifling grooves and gave it a better seal as it traveled down the barrel. This innovation also allowed bullets to be cast in a smaller caliber than the rifle bore, which made it easier to load. As a result, accuracy and range improved without decreasing the rate of fire. By 1854 the era of smoothbore muskets was past as most armies had reequipped with rifles.

Among artillery, most of the innovations came from improved tactics and lighter-weight guns and carriages. The workhorse of all armies of the period remained the direct-fire, muzzle-loading smoothbore field gun of from 6- to 12-pound caliber. Experiments had been made with breech-loading and rifled weapons, but both of these innovations remained imperfect. For the most part, inventors and designers focused their attention on the size and shape of the cannon barrels so they could increase the power of the charge used to propel munitions down range. Most true innovations to artillery occurred later in the nineteenth century.

Craft Hughes

BIBLIOGRAPHY
Dupuy, R. E., and Trevor N. Dupuy. *Encyclopedia of Military History.* 1977.
Peterson, Harold L. *Pageant of the Gun.* 1967.
Tunis, Edwin. *Weapons.* 1954.

Coastal and Naval Weapons

Naval guns of the U.S.–Mexican War were muzzle-loading smoothbores. Virtually all were made of iron, which—although heavier—was far cheaper than bronze. Naval ordnance of the 1840s was in a state of transition. Ship batteries were changing from many small broadside guns to a few larger guns in pivot mounts, and batteries entirely of guns designed to fire only solid shot were giving way to mixed batteries of shot and shell guns. Although the use of shells was opposed by many old hands in the navy, who considered them highly dangerous, they had been proven very effective against wooden ships. Projected at relatively low velocity, a shell could lodge in the side of an opposing vessel; the shell's subsequent explosion not only tore irregular holes in the hull, which were difficult to patch, but also caused considerable splintering, which produced the majority of personnel casualties in the age of sail. In addition, shell guns could be lighter than solid shot guns because they fired smaller powder charges.

In March 1845 Secretary of the Navy George Bancroft convened a board of captains to suggest changes in ship armament for the navy. Its recommendations, which were approved, doubled the number of shell guns on all classes of ships. The new regulations also established the 32-pounder (in six weight classes) as the standard gun of the U.S. Navy and provided for a new, lighter 55 hundred weight [cwt] class of 8-inch shell gun (1 cwt = 112 pounds). The new system had two classes of guns designed for shell: 10-inch (89 cwt, 10-inch bore) and 8-inch (90, 63, and 55 cwt; all 8-inch bore). Other, smaller, guns fired shot: 64-pounder (106 cwt, 8-inch bore) and 32-pounders (61, 57, 51, 46, 42, 33, and 27 cwt; all 6.4-inch bore). The 32-pounders of 42 and 33 cwt had powder chambers at the bottom of their bores.

The navy phased the new system in gradually. U.S. Navy vessels during the U.S.–Mexican War thus carried many older 42- and 32-pounder carronades as well as the older, smaller long guns: 24-pounders (5.82-inch bore), 18-pounders (5.3-inch bore), 12-pounders (4.62-inch bore) and 9-pounders (4.2-inch bore). At the other extreme the navy used at least four 10-inch army columbiads, large-bore guns developed to project explosive shell in flat trajectory. Mounted one gun each on four bomb brigs (two-masted, shallow-draft sailing ships), they were used for shore bombardment.

Guns aboard Mexican warships were for the most part small. After the British repossessed the *Guadalupe* and more powerful *Montezuma* (both of which had at least one 68-pounder in addition to other guns), the largest guns on Mexican warships were 32-pounders; most carried only a single 24- or 12-pounder.

For the U.S. Navy the war demonstrated the need for a boat gun designed specifically for the small coastal craft that were vital in blockading the Mexican coasts. Although the navy had a few small carronades in storage, these were seldom on ships or put to use. The navy met the shortage during the war by using army 6- and 12-pounder field pieces and mountain howitzers, small carronades, and some old light 4.4-inch howitzers from storehouses in the various navy yards.

The U.S.–Mexican War heightened navy interest in developing a system of scientifically based ordnance. At the end of the war Lt. John Dahlgren was assigned to the Washington Navy Yard with the task of testing the suitability of the army's mountain howitzer as a boat gun and establishing range tables for the various classes of 32-pounder guns. His work led ultimately to development of the Dahlgren boat howitzer and the class of heavy guns named for him.

Spencer C. Tucker

BIBLIOGRAPHY

Tucker, Spencer C. *Arming the Fleet: U.S. Navy Ordnance in the Muzzle-loading Era.* 1989.

Field Artillery

Black powder, smoothbore, muzzle-loading artillery approached the apex of its development in the late 1840s. The guns of the U.S.–Mexican War, however, were only marginally improved versions of the cannon that had been in general use for three hundred years. Starting after the war and continuing through the Civil War, developments in rifled bores, smokeless powder, and ultimately breech-loading and recoil systems drastically altered artillery and changed its role on the battlefield.

The cannon of the U.S.–Mexican War fell into three primary categories, based on their construction and ballistic characteristics. The most widely used artillery piece was the gun, which was long in relation to the size of its bore and fired projectiles at a high velocity and flat trajectory. The mortar was a short, stubby weapon that fired only at high angles. While mortars had relatively short ranges, they could fire over intermediate obstructions to engage targets in defilade. The howitzer fired at a trajectory between that of the gun and the mortar, and its range was greater than that of the mortar, but less than that of the gun. The howitzer was more mobile in the field than the mortar, and it could fire a larger projectile than could a gun of similar weight. Generically, all artillery pieces were—and still are—called guns. Modern artillery is still organized into these three categories.

According to an old gunner's axiom, the real weapon of the artillery is the projectile, the gun is merely the means to point it at the target. Gunners on both sides of the U.S.–Mexican War carried an impressive family of exploding and nonexploding projectiles in the ammunition chests on their caissons and limbers.

Solid shot, essentially a cast iron sphere, was the basic

round of the gun. At ranges out to 1,500 yards, solid shot had a devastating effect on the closely packed infantry formations of the day. As the enemy's attacking infantry closed to approximately 300 yards, gunners switched to grape shot, clusters of iron balls one to two inches in diameter. Grape also was effective against cavalry charges. At ranges from 100 yards to point-blank, the gunners switched to canister, musket balls packed into a tin cylinder, which in effect turned the cannon into a huge shotgun.

Shell was a hollow iron projectile filled with a time-fuzed exploding charge. If the shell also was packed with musket balls inside the explosive, it was called spherical case shot. This type of round was developed in the early 1800s by Lt. Henry Shrapnel of the Royal Artillery. Normally, mortars fired only shell. Howitzers could fire any ammunition but were most effective when firing spherical case and shell. Spherical case was most effective when set for an air burst just above the heads of enemy troops. Because the black powder time fuzes of the era burned erratically, the proper adjustment of these rounds was an art most artillery officers found difficult to master. Despite its difficulty of use, however, spherical case extended the range of antipersonnel scatterable ammunition far beyond that of grape. From the 1840s on, spherical case replaced grape in the basic ammunition loads of U.S. field guns.

Both the Mexican army and the U.S. Army entered the war with a wide array of cannon sizes and types, but the U.S. Army had more modern systems. Between 1841 and 1844, the U.S. Army completely revamped its artillery inventory, eliminating iron guns and relying almost entirely on cannon made of bronze. Iron guns were heavier than bronze guns of a comparable size, and bronze tubes were far more reliable and less prone to bursting. Mexican field artillery was generally slower and less responsive in combat. The Mexican army also did not have horse or mounted artillery units, which placed them at a tactical disadvantage in battles such as those at Palo Alto and Buena Vista.

David T. Zabecki

BIBLIOGRAPHY

Dillon, Lester R., Jr. *American Artillery in the Mexican War. 1846–1847.* 1975.

Mauncy, Albert. *Artillery through the Ages: A Short Illustrated History of Cannon Emphasizing Types Used in America.* 1949.

Peterson, Harold L. *Round Shot and Rammers.* 1969.

Small Arms

Dramatic advances in small arms design in the United States afforded U.S. troops significant advantages over their relatively poorly armed Mexican opponents. U.S. soldiers entered the field with some of the most modern weapons of the day, while Mexican troops typically carried obsolete relics of the late eighteenth and early nineteenth centuries. Some

Mexican irregulars were armed with even earlier miquelet-lock muskets which had been introduced in the seventeenth century by Spanish colonialists.

Most Mexican infantrymen were issued outdated .75-caliber India-pattern Brown Bess smoothbore muskets. A few fielded more accurate and longer ranged .625-caliber Baker rifles. These arms were surplus British flintlocks that Great Britain sold to Mexico as the United Kingdom converted to percussion arms. By the time the muskets entered Mexican service they were well-worn and prone to malfunction. Although armed with various combinations of sabers, single-shot flintlock pistols, and carbines known as *escopetas,* cavalrymen found the lance their most reliable weapon.

Small arms development in the United States was in a transitional phase at the outbreak of hostilities. Most infantrymen were armed with .69-caliber smoothbore, flintlock muskets manufactured by the Harpers Ferry and Springfield federal arsenals as well as by various civilian contractors. The most common types were the Model 1816 and the Model 1835. As the war progressed, armorers converted a number of the flintlocks into more reliable percussion arms, although it is unclear how many actually reached the troops in the field.

At the onset of hostilities, the U.S. Army had three primary-issue percussion long arms in limited service. Except for its percussion ignition system, the mass-produced Model 1842 differed little from earlier flintlocks. The Model 1841 percussion rifle and the Hall carbine were more radical in design and performance. Manufactured by Harpers Ferry and by civilian contractors, the Model 1841 featured a rifled barrel and a smaller .54-caliber projectile, which afforded it significant advantages in range and accuracy. The Model 1841 could achieve deadly fire at several hundred yards compared to the dubious accuracy of the standard musket at fifty yards. Dubbed the Mississippi Rifle due to its impressive performance in the hands of Col. Jefferson Davis's Mississippi Volunteers, the 1841 was a favorite among the troops.

The Hall carbine was a more controversial weapon. Although it had a smooth bore, the Hall's advanced breech-loading mechanism was a distinct advantage for mounted troops. Less mechanically adept soldiers, however, found the Hall difficult to operate and maintain. As a consequence, during the war the army also issued more conventional muzzleloading carbines such as the Model 1847 cavalry musketoon. Others, however, appreciated that the Hall's breech-block could be removed and used as a high-powered pocket pistol—a handy weapon in rough-and-tumble cantinas.

Cavalry troops also typically carried .54-caliber, single-shot, muzzleloading pistols. The most common were the Models 1819 and 1836, manufactured by civilian contractors such as North, Waters, and Johnson. Originally produced as flintlocks, a limited number were converted to percussion as the war progressed. The Model 1842 was originally designed as a percussion weapon, as were a limited number of Deringer-produced Model 1842 Navy pistols, which also had rifled barrels.

In 1847 the army distributed one thousand .44-caliber Colt Walker Model revolvers to five companies of United States Dragoons. An improvement over the Texas Rangers' .36-caliber Colt Paterson revolvers, the Walker Model's increased firepower proved decisive in a number of cavalry engagements.

Jeff Kinard

BIBLIOGRAPHY

Blackmore, Howard L. *British Military Firearms.* 1961.

Flayderman, Norm. *Flayderman's Guide to Antique American Firearms.* 1987.

Katcher, Philip R. N. *The Mexican-American War, 1846–1848.* 1989.

Steffen, Randy. *The Horse Soldier, 1776–1943.* Vol. 1. 1977.

Wilkins, Frederick. *The Highly Irregular Irregulars: Texas Rangers in the Mexican War.* 1990.

Webster, Daniel

Born in Salisbury, New Hampshire, U.S. statesman and orator Daniel Webster (1782–1852) was a graduate of Dartmouth College. He served as New Hampshire representative to the U.S. Congress during the War of 1812. Webster was U.S. secretary of state from 1841 to 1843, where he opposed President John Tyler's actions to annex Texas for its proslavery stance. Instead, he pressed for Mexican recognition of Texas statehood.

During the term of President James Polk in 1845, as U.S. senator from Massachusetts Webster abstained from voting on the declaration of war against Mexico. The Whig Party of Massachusetts, of which Webster was a member, was against any U.S. expansion and opposed the spread of slavery into any territory. After the declaration of war, the party adopted a strict antislavery position, which isolated Massachusetts Whigs from the rest of the nation. Webster adamantly opposed this attempt to turn the Whig Party into an instrument for abolishing slavery, and emphasized the Whig Party's need to remain flexible. Webster's antislavery and antiexpansion stance, however, did not waver as peace terms and a settlement were discussed toward the end of the U.S.–Mexican War. President Polk pursued a policy that encouraged the expansion of slavery into the areas acquired from Mexico. David Wilmot, U.S. representative from Pennsylvania, introduced the Wilmot Proviso, which called for the prohibition of slavery in any territory acquired from Mexico as a result of the war. In response, Webster voiced his antiexpansion position, stating that war should not be fought to acquire new territory and that the United States should not take territory from the Republic of Mexico. Webster argued

Daniel Webster. Engraving by J. A. J. Wilcox (Library of Congress)

that to prohibit the expansion of slavery the United States should pursue a policy of nonexpansion. His solution was ignored, however, as the United States acquired new territory in the name of national security.

Webster's antislavery stance, especially his attitude toward U.S. expansion, changed little during the rest of his career. Again in 1850, he returned to the position of U.S. secretary of state under President Millard Fillmore and served until 1852, when he retired suffering from intestinal disorders. Webster died at his home in Marshfield, Massachusetts, on 24 October 1852.

Both he and Fillmore had hoped for a presidential nomination; Webster repudiated the candidacy of Gen. Winfield Scott and prophesied the downfall of the Whig Party.

Cassandra Britt

BIBLIOGRAPHY

Bartlett, Irving H. *Daniel Webster.* 1978.

Dalzell, Robert F. *Daniel Webster and the Trial of American Nationalism, 1843–1852.* 1973.

Whig Party

The Whig Party was the opposition party in the United States during the U.S.–Mexican War. The Whig Party was less expansionist and less enthusiastic about waging the war than the Democratic Party. In the presidential election of 1844, when the Democratic candidate, James K. Polk, endorsed the annexation of Texas, the Whig candidate, Henry Clay, opposed annexation unless it could be accomplished without war or domestic controversy. Polk's narrow victory in the election was used to justify the annexation of Texas by joint resolution of the two houses of Congress, against Whig objections that this was unconstitutional. In 1845, Polk ordered the U.S. Army into the disputed area between the Nueces River and the Río Grande, and hostilities ensued the following year.

Besides moral disapproval of what they considered aggressive war, the Whigs' opposition had practical sources. Party leaders feared that taking land from Mexico would provoke sectional dispute over whether or not slavery should expand into the newly acquired territory. Such divisiveness would harm the Whig Party more than the Democratic Party because northern Democrats were generally more willing to defer to the Southern wing of their party. However, Whig opposition to the war was often muted by prudence. The Federalist Party had been ruined by its opposition to the War of 1812, and the example was not lost on the Whigs.

President Polk's call for war in May 1846 was pushed through Congress without time for debate or investigation of its claims. The few Whig members of Congress who voted against it were antislavery stalwarts such as John Quincy Adams of Massachusetts and Joshua Giddings of Ohio. Many moderate and conservative Whigs, however, were suspicious of Polk's justifications for war and denounced his war message afterward as misleading. One of these was Abraham Lincoln, representative from Illinois, who on 22 December 1847 demanded to know whether the "spot" where, according to Polk, the Mexicans had "shed the blood of our fellow *citizens* on *our own soil*" was not in fact a disputed area populated chiefly by Mexicans (*Collected Works of Abraham Lincoln*, 1, 421–422).

During the war, most Whigs in Congress voted in favor of military appropriations because they did not wish to seem unpatriotic or unsupportive of the men in uniform; however, they demonstrated their opposition to the war in other ways. Whig senator John J. Crittenden of Kentucky was seeking a negotiated peace within a month of the outbreak of hostilities. Most forceful of all the Whigs was Sen. Thomas Corwin of Ohio. "If I were a Mexican," he declared on 11 February 1847, "I would tell you, 'Have you not room in your own country to bury your dead men? If you come into mine we will greet you with bloody hands and welcome you to hospitable graves' " (*Life and Speeches of Thomas Corwin*, p. 305).

President Polk sought whenever possible to appoint Democrats to military commands; ironically, however, the two principal U.S. generals turned out to be Whigs: Zachary Taylor and Winfield Scott. Party differences thus contributed to the tense relationships between the president and his commanders in the field.

Whig magazines such as the *American Review* and newspapers such as the *New York Tribune* denounced Polk's conduct of the war, including his plan to make the war pay for itself by levying taxes on the civilian population of occupied Mexico. Henry Clay, seeking another Whig presidential nomination in the coming 1848 election, delivered a major address on the war at Lexington, Kentucky, on 13 November 1847. "This is no war of defence," he declared, "but one unnecessary and of offensive aggression" (*The Papers of Henry Clay,* 10, 364). Clay blamed the conflict on President Polk and called for peace to be negotiated on the basis of no territorial acquisitions beyond Texas.

Despite the dramatic military successes of the U.S. forces, the war against Mexico was not popular with large sections of the electorate, and the midterm congressional elections of 1846 went against the Democrats. Under the Constitution as it then stood, however, the new Congress did not meet until December 1847, by which time the major campaigns of the war had been fought. The Whigs used their new majority in the House of Representatives to pass a resolution in January 1848 declaring that the war had been "unnecessarily and unconstitutionally begun by the President of the United States." A month later Polk felt it politically necessary to accept a peace treaty negotiated by Nicholas P. Trist in defiance of the president's instructions.

The issues debated between the Whig and Democratic parties over the war, its causes, conduct, and consequences, have continued to be debated by historians ever since.

Daniel Walker Howe

BIBLIOGRAPHY

Howe, Daniel Walker. *The Political Culture of the American Whigs.* 1979.

Merk, Frederick. "Dissent in the Mexican War." In *Dissent in Three American Wars,* by Samuel Eliot Morison, Frederick Merk, and Frank Freidel. 1970.

Schroeder, John H. *Mr. Polk's War: American Opposition and Dissent, 1846–1848.* 1973.

Wells, Ronald A. "The War with Mexico." In *The Wars of America: Christian Views,* edited by Ronald A. Wells. 1991.

Wickliffe, Charles A.

U.S. politician and diplomat Charles A. Wickliffe (1788–1869) was born 8 June in Washington County, Kentucky. After studying law, Wickliffe was admitted to the bar in Bardstown, Kentucky, where he became a leading politician. Beginning in the 1820s, Wickliffe served ten years in the U.S. House of Representatives. In 1836, he was elected lieutenant governor of Kentucky, serving the last few months of the term as governor after James Clark died in office. President John Tyler appointed him postmaster general in 1841.

In 1845, President James K. Polk ordered Wickliffe to Galveston, Texas, on a secret diplomatic mission. Originally ordered to thwart European efforts to forestall the U.S. annexation of Texas, Wickliffe and Commo. Robert F. Stockton pressured the Republic of Texas government to move troops across the Río Grande. Wickliffe hoped that by encouraging hostilities between Texas and Mexico, it would be easier for the United States to annex Texas under the guise of protection. Although unable to persuade the Texas government to invade Mexico, he did much to increase popular support in Texas for annexation and to dispel European plans to stop annexation. Due to the secrecy of Wickliffe's mission, little is known of President Polk's involvement in the scheme.

Wickliffe ran as a Peace Democrat in the 1863 Kentucky gubernatorial race, losing to Thomas E. Bramlette. Wickliffe died 31 October 1869.

Jason Bullock

BIBLIOGRAPHY

Kerr, Judge Charles, ed. *History of Kentucky.* 1922.

Price, Glenn W. *Origins of the War with Mexico: The Polk-Stockton Intrigue.* 1967.

Wilmot, David

David Wilmot (1814–1868) was born in Bethany, Pennsylvania, on 20 January, the son of a prosperous merchant. He studied law and practiced for ten years but was always more interested in politics. Elected as Democratic representative from Pennsylvania, Wilmot introduced the Wilmot Proviso as an amendment to a House appropriations bill in August 1846. The proviso would have prohibited slavery in all of the territories acquired from Mexico. Although repeatedly passed by the House of Representatives, with its huge Northern majority, the Senate, where the South had a temporary majority, always defeated it.

Representative Wilmot symbolized the dilemma of northern Democrats who were unhappy with the administration of President James K. Polk and the internal tensions caused by Southern domination of the Democratic Party. Wilmot represented a traditionally Democratic district and initially supported most of the Polk administration's policies. However, Polk had alienated a number of northern Democrats by his veto of a bill to improve rivers and harbors in the Midwest, his veto of the Walker Tariff, which hurt manufacturing regions in the North, and his failure to appoint any Democrats who supported Martin Van Buren to patronage positions. Wilmot, like many other northern members of his party, had supported the nomination of Van Buren in 1844. Northern Democrats also were enraged by Polk's concessions to Great Britain on land claims in the Northwest,

where slavery was prohibited. In the presidential campaign of 1844, Polk had called for the United States to establish control over the entire Oregon Territory, up to the 54th parallel. Some Americans adopted the slogan, "54°40′ or fight" in an effort to support this claim. But, once in office, Polk reached a compromise with Great Britain to place the boundary at 49° north latitude. On the other hand, Polk aggressively went after more land in the southwest, leading to the war with Mexico.

Wilmot was reelected in 1846 and in 1848 but was forced out of the 1850 election by Pennsylvania Democrats loyal to James Buchanan and sympathetic to Southern demands to allow slavery in the territories. Wilmot helped create the Republican Party in Pennsylvania and served briefly in the Senate from 1861 to 1863. After leaving the Senate Wilmot was appointed by President Abraham Lincoln to the federal court of claims, where he served until his death in 1868.

Paul Finkelman

BIBLIOGRAPHY

Foner, Eric. "The Wilmot Proviso Revisited." *Journal of American History* 61 (September 1969): 270.

Going, Charles Buxton. *David Wilmot, Free Soiler: A Biography of the Great Advocate of the Wilmot Proviso.* 1924.

Morrison, Chaplain W. *Democratic Politics and Sectionalism: The Wilmot Proviso Controversy.* 1967.

Wilmot Proviso

In August 1846 David Wilmot, a Democratic representative from Pennsylvania, proposed his proviso as an amendment to an appropriations bill of $2 million to fund the war with Mexico. The proviso declared "that, as an express and fundamental condition to the acquisition of any territory from the Republic of Mexico . . . neither slavery nor involuntary servitude shall ever exist in any part of said territory." The proviso solved a major dilemma for northern Democrats. Northern Democrats favored Manifest Destiny and territorial expansion and consequently supported the war, but their support for the war would damage their political position at home if the war were perceived as part of a larger plan to expand slavery into the new territories.

When first introduced the proviso easily passed the House of Representatives, with every Northern Whig and all but four Northern Democrats voting for the amendment. With the exception of two Whig representatives, every Southerner opposed the proviso. The Senate adjourned before it could take up consideration of the bill. In February 1847 the House appended the proviso to a $3-million appropriations bill. Again, the vote was overwhelmingly sectional. The Senate passed the bill but deleted the proviso. The House accepted the bill without the proviso when twenty-three

Northern Democrats changed their votes under strong pressure from President James K. Polk.

Northerners continued to add the proviso to a number of other bills, but always the Senate rejected the amendment, and in the end Congress never adopted the proviso. Nevertheless Wilmot's amendment came to symbolize the entire debate over the extension of slavery into the territories. Every northern state legislature but one endorsed the proviso. The debate galvanized northern Democrats, many of whom supported the Free-Soil Party candidacy of Martin Van Buren in 1848, and some, like Wilmot, later joined the Republican Party. Furthermore, the proviso debate illustrated how the problem of slavery in the territories threatened harmony within the Democratic Party and the nation itself.

Paul Finkelman

BIBLIOGRAPHY

Foner, Eric. "The Wilmot Proviso Revisited." *Journal of American History* 61 (September 1969): 270.

Morrison, Chaplain W. *Democratic Politics and Sectionalism: The Wilmot Proviso Controversy.* 1967

Silbey, Joel. *The Shrine of Party: Congressional Voting Behavior, 1841–1852.* 1967.

Woll's Expedition

On 11 September 1842, a Mexican army under Gen. Adrian Woll captured San Antonio in the second major invasion of the Texas frontier that year. After a brief but spirited defense of the town, the Anglo Texan residents surrendered. District court had been in session that week in San Antonio, and the captives included the judge and two members of the Republic of Texas congress, as well as several attorneys and clerks.

For a week Woll held the town, while a force of Texans was hastily organized under the command of Maj. John C. Hays and Mathew Caldwell. On 17 September the Texas force engaged Woll's forces on the outskirts of San Antonio, repulsing several assaults by Mexican infantry. During the course of the fighting, a company of fifty-three Fayette County, Texas, militiamen under the command of Capt. Nicholas Mosby Dawson arrived, but they were intercepted by Mexican cavalry before they could join the Texians. Two managed to escape; the others were killed or taken prisoner.

Two days after the fighting, the Mexican troops left San Antonio and marched south, taking with them their Texas prisoners and as many as two hundred Tejanos, who feared reprisals from Anglo Texans if they remained in the area. Hays and Caldwell pursued the retreating Mexican army and near the Hondo River attacked Woll's rearguard before breaking off the pursuit.

The Woll invasion led to renewed calls in Texas for reprisals against Mexico, prompting President Sam Houston to

sanction an invasion of the lower Río Grande valley, which ended with the defeat of Texas forces at Ciudad Mier on 26 December 1842.

Sam W. Haynes

BIBLIOGRAPHY

Haynes, Sam W. *Soldiers of Misfortune: The Somervell and Mier Expeditions.* 1990.

Sánchez Lamego, Miguel A. *The Second Mexican-Texan War, 1841–1843.* 1972.

Women

This entry consists of two separate articles: **Women in Mexico** *and* **Women in the United States.**

Women in Mexico

The life of Mexican women during the war with the United States depended on many factors, including wealth and ethnicity. One factor that affected the experience of women was their social status. Spanish ancestry usually provided an elevated status. In general, the wealthy were descended from Spanish families who had received early land grants from the Spanish crown (although *mestizos*, especially military men who had defended the Spanish *presidios*, later received land grants as well). Wealthy women were perceived as being more Hispanic or European than Mexican. These women held significant economic power both as large property owners and as consumers; among them were Ana Maria de la Guerra, of the elite de la Guerra y Noriega family of Santa Barbara in California, who was married to Alfred Robinson, author of *Life in California* (1848), and Juana Machado Alipaz de Ridington, born into a military family, who left written record of her life in Alta California. Some wealthy *ranchero* widows prospered by selling horses and mules to the U.S. military. Women such as Fermina Espinosa allegedly broke horses, tended cattle, and cut lumber. Historian Carolina Castillo Crimm noted that these rich widows often had to defend their landholdings in court. In communities such as San Antonio, Texas, and Abiquiu, New Mexico, widows outnumbered widowers because of frontier conditions, the U.S.–Mexican War, and Indian wars. There were women such as Apolinaria Lorenzana who never married but still acquired ranches of their own and businesswomen such as Gertrudis Barcelo who ran a gambling hall and invested her profits in trade and land.

On the other hand, if a woman came from a peasant background she often became the target of discrimination and prejudice not only from the Anglo-American community but also from the wealthy Hispanics, who perceived Indian or *mestizo* ancestry as inferior. This differentiation continued after the war. Mexican women on the frontier, like their

Mexican peasant women working in a washhouse. Robert A. Wilson, *Mexico: Its Peasants and Priests*, 1856

Anglo-American counterparts, maintained the household and helped to work the family farm, or *rancho*. *Mestizo* women also worked as *peones* for *patrons* on the large ranches. Mexican women who lived near towns sold vegetables, tortillas, and other items at the *mercado* (market). Peasant women traveled with the military acting as cooks and performing other services, such as providing information and supplies, acting as nurses, and even overseeing burial arrangements. Often known as "corn grinders," these women spent many hours working over the *metates* grinding the corn for tortillas. Elizabeth Salas in *Soldaderas in the Mexican Military* found that these women joined the military primarily to earn a living, rather than for protection or companionship. In fact, women supported the war effort in many ways. Francisca Reyes aided in resisting the Anglo-American presence by burying in her yard an old cannon nicknamed *el pedrero de la vieja* (the old woman's rock gun), which was later dug up and used in the Battle of Dominguez Ranch near Los Angeles.

Yolanda Garcia Romero

BIBLIOGRAPHY

Alcaraz, Ramón, ed. *The Other Side; or Notes for the History of the War between Mexico and the United States.* Translated by Albert C. Ramsey. 1970. Originally published as *Apuntes para la historia de la Guerra entre México y los Estados Unidos,* 1848.

Dysart, Jane. "Mexican Women of Texas, 1830–1860: The Assimilation Process." *Western Historical Quarterly* 7 (1976): 365–375.

Lecompte, Janet. *Rebellion in Rio Arriba.* 1985.

Ruiz, Ramon Eduardo, ed. *The Mexican War.* 1963.

Women in the United States

Women in the United States during the 1840s lived in a society with well-ordered Victorian ideals in which both status and place were rigidly defined, and movements and social intercourse between the sexes minutely circumscribed. Because biology was thought to determine one's role in life, women received little formal education. Women in the 1840s were taught to be and act feminine and demure; to suffer in silence; to never forget duty to home and family; and to be submissive, deferring to men in all matters civic, financial, and political. Domestic economy, that is, the housekeeping skills—cleaning, cooking, sewing—and the rearing of children was deemed a female's only proper interest. Because women were considered the purer sex and more pious than men, they were expected to be the spiritual guardians of their families and communities.

While the U.S. war with Mexico had little long-lasting impact on U.S. women in general, it did affect temporarily the lives of thousands of individual women. First, it enabled them to express their patriotism in various ways. They gave banquets, dances, parties, and picnics when the men left for, or returned from, the war. They used their sewing skills to make uniforms, flags, banners, quilts, and blankets. They mailed packages of books, gifts, magazines, and newspapers to the troops, and, most important, they wrote thousands of letters to the lonely, homesick men in Mexico who craved news from the States.

Another way the war affected U.S. women was that, with their men away, thousands of women had to face unfamiliar domestic situations. They were forced to manage farms and businesses, to attend to livestock and crops, to cope with machinery and the maintenance of houses and equipment, to make financial decisions, and to deal with myriad other new and perplexing problems. Although women dealt admirably with these challenges, because of the tenacity of Victorian society they quickly reverted to their subservient role when the men returned.

The most lasting impact of the war on many women was that their men did not return. The loss of a father, husband, or son changed lives forever. Hundreds of women were widowed, and many were left not only bereft but also destitute, their sole financial support gone. Too, many were left with children to raise alone.

While many women opposed the war on humanitarian grounds there was no organized, nationwide feminine anti-war movement, although a handful of pioneer suffragists who belonged to New England abolition societies spoke out against the war. In the main, if a woman opposed the war she did so quietly and primarily because of personal fears for her man who was in harm's way. One woman who spoke out publicly against the war was Margaret Fuller, a pacifist and *New York Tribune* journalist, who carried on her opposition from Europe, where she spent the duration of the war. Fuller's antiwar stance was counteracted by women closer to the conflict: Jane Cazneau, a journalist for the New York *Sun* and tireless promoter of the doctrine of Manifest Destiny, who lived in Eagle Pass, Texas, spoke Spanish, relished diplomatic intrigue and war politics, and favored the annexation of Mexico; Ann Chase, wife of the U.S. consul in Tampico, who expressed her sentiments by passing critical secrets and information about Mexican troop movements to the U.S. Army; and Sarah Borginnis, who was a battlefield nurse and entrepreneur who supported U.S. forces in Texas and Mexico.

Linda D. Vance

BIBLIOGRAPHY

Balducci, Carolyn F. *Margaret Fuller: A Life of Passion and Defiance.* 1991.

Cashion, Peggy. "Women and the Mexican War, 1846–1848." Master's thesis, The University of Texas at Arlington, 1990.

Cazneau, Jane. *Eagle Pass or Life on the Border.* 1966.

Clinton, Catherine. *The Other Civil War: American Women in the Nineteenth Century.* 1984.

Welter, Barbara. *Dimity Convictions: The American Woman in the Nineteenth Century.* 1976.

Wool, John E.

U.S. general and occupation commander in northeastern Mexico, John Ellis Wool (1784–1869) was born 29 February in Newburgh, New York. He operated a store in Troy (near Albany), and excelled as a militia officer. In the War of 1812 as a regular army officer, he won distinction in the battles of Queenston and Plattsburgh, rising from captain to brevet lieutenant colonel. In the peacetime army, Wool served as an inspector general of the army from 1816 to 1841. He studied artillery weaponry in Europe (1832); supervised preparations for the removal of the Cherokees from the South (1836–1837); and during the Canadian Patriot War, suppressed gunrunning on the New York–Canadian border (1838). In 1841, Brig. Gen. John E. Wool became commander of the Eastern Department of the Army.

In June and July 1846 Wool supervised the muster and shipment of ten volunteer regiments from the Ohio and lower Mississippi valleys to Gen. Zachary Taylor's army on the Mexican border. In August, at San Antonio, Texas, he organized the Center Division to invade Chihuahua and on 8 October crossed the Río Grande at Presidio del Río Grande (near Eagle Pass) into Coahuila with 3,400 men. When

John E. Wool. John Frost, *Pictorial History of Mexico and the Mexican War*, 1862

scouts reported it would be impossible to take wheeled vehicles from Monclova west into Chihuahua, Wool requested (and received) permission from Taylor to join his forces and took station at Parras. On 17 December Wool, responding to an urgent request from Gen. William J. Worth, at Saltillo, for help in meeting a Mexican army of 15,000 under Gen. Antonio López de Santa Anna that was advancing north into that sector from San Luis Potosí, marched in haste from Parras and swung south of Saltillo to Rancho Agua Nueva. By mid-February, Taylor had concentrated 4,000 men there to face Mexican forces.

On 21 February 1847, at Wool's insistence, Taylor retreated north to a defensive position near Rancho Buena Vista, six miles south of Saltillo. Wool made the initial troop deployment, but the next day Taylor pulled units from the line and left to check Saltillo defenses. On the morning of 23 February Wool's weakened left flank was crumbling when Taylor returned with help. Wool personally, and with couriers, maneuvered artillery and infantry to meet the Mexican assault. In the afternoon, he was fired on while responding to a Mexican truce flag but raced to safety. Taylor's forces repelled Mexican attacks until dark, when Santa Anna withdrew his forces. In the late spring of 1848 Wool received a major general's brevet and later was presented with ornate swords by the U.S. Congress, New York State, and the town of Troy for his action there.

From March to December 1847, Wool commanded the Saltillo district. Fresh troops replaced battle veterans in June. Wool encouraged Mexicans to return to their homes and battled guerrilla bands in the vicinity. In December at Monterrey, Wool took command (Taylor was on leave) of the occupation forces in Coahuila, Nuevo León, and Tamaulipas. Lacking instructions for military government, he improvised to govern. He paid liberally for supplies, expanded commerce, and in February 1848 issued an amnesty to Mexicans within his jurisdiction. His district commanders reopened schools, restored local police, and started tax collection. In the spring Wool sent an expedition to Zacatecas to map the territory and escort silver shipments to the border. In July, with peace, he evacuated his forces from Mexico.

After the war Wool again commanded the army's Eastern Department and briefly headed the Division of the Pacific (1854–1857). In 1861 he shipped volunteer regiments to Washington, D.C. In the spring of 1862 his forces at Fortress Monroe, Virginia, captured Confederate Norfolk; that fall, at Baltimore (Middle Department), he guarded the Baltimore and Ohio Railroad. In July 1863, while commanding the Department of New York and New England, he tried to stop the New York City draft riots.

Retired on 1 August 1863 at age seventy-nine, Wool died on 11 November 1869 in Troy.

Harwood P. Hinton

BIBLIOGRAPHY

Carleton, James H. *The Battle of Buena Vista.* 1848.

Eisenhower, John S. D. *So Far from God: The U.S. War with Mexico, 1846–1848.* 1989.

Hinton, Harwood P. "The Military Career of John Ellis Wool, 1812–1863." Ph.D. diss., University of Wisconsin, 1960.

Wool's March

The epic march of U.S. troops under the command of Brig. Gen. John E. Wool, made from September 1846 through January 1847, proved to be one of the most famous of the U.S.–Mexican War and contributed greatly to the subsequent U.S. victory at Buena Vista. On 11 June 1846 General Wool, then in Cincinnati, Ohio, directing the enlistment of volunteers, received orders to proceed to San Antonio, Texas, to organize a force to occupy the Mexican state of Chihuahua. Accompanied by a regiment of Illinois volunteers, Wool traveled first to New Orleans, where he requisitioned equipment and arms. By the end of July he left New Orleans, sailing to Port Lavaca, Texas, and then marching overland to San Antonio, arriving on 14 August. The following day he took command of the Army of Chihuahua.

Over the next several weeks, additional forces reached San Antonio, while supplies and transportation were stockpiled. Wool, a regular officer whose career dated back to the War of 1812, implemented a rigid system of camp rules and regulations, which enraged the volunteer soldiers of his command but that proved invaluable during the coming campaign. By late September he had gathered some 3,400 troops, including two Illinois volunteer infantry regiments, volunteer cavalry regiments from Arkansas and Texas, two companies of regulars from the 6th Infantry, two regular dragoon companies, a regular artillery battery, and a scattering of support personnel. Capt. Robert E. Lee accompanied the expedition as engineer.

The advance party departed San Antonio on 23 September, with Col. William S. Harney and the main body leaving three days later. Wool followed with a small escort, while two Illinois regiments waited for sufficient transportation. By 8 October the vanguard had reached the Río Grande opposite Presidio. Four days later the main force crossed the river on pontoon barges and encamped nearby. While there, relations between Wool and his volunteers continued to deteriorate, with the citizen-soldiers bitterly critical of the general's overbearing attitude and his insistence on strict discipline. To Wool's credit he did issue strong orders against the harassment of Mexican civilians and the destruction of private property.

After waiting for the arrival of the 1st and 2d Illinois Regiments, the column marched west from Presidio del Río Grande and then south through the Mexican state of Coahuila, occupying Monclova on 3 November. Wool stopped there to await expiration of the armistice implemented following the Battle of Monterrey. Wool planned to continue on to Parras, some two hundred miles to the south, before turning his command northwest toward Chihuahua, but by this time he, Maj. Gen. Zachary Taylor, and President James K. Polk had all determined that the movement into Chihuahua was unnecessary and that Wool's force could be put to best use supporting Taylor's main army. Taylor, though, was slow to provide specific instructions, and Wool's grumbling troops remained at Monclova for nearly a month.

Finally, in late November, Taylor ordered Wool to Parras to collect grain and other supplies. In the event of a Mexican thrust to the north, Wool could also support U.S. forces at Saltillo. After an exhausting march, the command arrived in Parras on 5 December. Less than two weeks later the general received news that Mexican forces threatened Saltillo, and he once more assembled his weary troops for another forced march. The attack did not materialize, but Wool's arrival at Agua Nueva, south of Saltillo, had reinforced the small U.S. force in the critical period before the Battle of Buena Vista.

David J. Coles

BIBLIOGRAPHY

Baylies, Francis. *A Narrative of Major General Wool's Campaign in Mexico, in the Years 1846, 1847 & 1848.* 1851. Reprint, 1975.

Freeman, Douglas Southall. *R. E. Lee.* 1934.

Hinton, Harwood Perry. "The Military Career of John Ellis Wool, 1812–1863." Ph.D. diss., University of Wisconsin, 1960.

William J. Worth. John Frost, *Pictorial History of Mexico and the Mexican War*, 1862

Worth, William J.

U.S. general William Jenkins Worth (1794–1849) was born in Hudson, New York, 1 March. Worth began his military career in 1813 as a first lieutenant in the 23d Infantry. During the War of 1812, he served as Brig. Gen. Winfield Scott's aide-de-camp, winning a brevet to captain, then major.

Following the War of 1812, Worth served at a variety of posts, including an eight-year stint as commandant of cadets at the U.S. Military Academy. During the Second Seminole War he became colonel of the 8th Infantry. By 1841 he had assumed command of the entire conflict; he is generally credited with bringing the war to a close, and he was brevetted a brigadier general.

During the U.S.–Mexican War, Worth served under Gen. Zachary Taylor for much of the campaign in northern Mexico and under Gen. Winfield Scott in the Mexico City campaign. Before hostilities and as a member of Taylor's Army of Occupation, Worth became embroiled in a controversy over rank, claiming the post of Taylor's second-in-command based on his brevet as brigadier general. President James K. Polk ultimately ruled in favor of Col. David E. Twiggs, who claimed the post based on linear rank. At this, Worth resigned from the army and stormed off to Washington, D.C., to plead his case. In his absence, fighting began when Mexicans attacked Capt. Seth Thornton's dragoons near Fort Texas. When Worth learned of the fighting he withdrew his resignation and returned to Mexico, although too late to participate in the first two battles of the war, at Palo Alto and Resaca de la Palma.

After moving up the Río Grande to Camargo and establishing a supply base at Cerralvo, Worth's division joined the general advance toward Monterrey. Taylor sent Worth and approximately two thousand men around to the north and then southwest of the city to cut the road to Saltillo. Not only did Worth and his men cut the road, they stormed the fortified Bishop's Palace and drove into the city. Three days of hand-to-hand fighting ended with an armistice and the evacuation of the Mexican army on 24 September 1846. Worth was named military governor of Monterrey following the Mexicans' departure.

When Taylor received orders from Washington, D.C., on 2 November, to cancel the armistice, he selected Saltillo as his next objective. Worth's division led the advance and took the town without a fight on 17 November 1846. On 9 January 1847, rumors that the bulk of Taylor's regular forces would be sent to the Gulf Coast for another campaign proved true, and Worth received orders to move his division to the mouth of the Río Grande to prepare for General Scott's campaign against Mexico City. After his arrival on 22 January, he spent the next month helping Scott plan the operation. In February, Worth imagined that a large Mexican force was about to attack him, and his alarm compelled both Taylor and Twiggs to race to his relief. Not until Christmas did events reveal that Worth's fears were unfounded.

On 9 March 1847 Worth's division led the army ashore at Vera Cruz and took up positions on the extreme right of Scott's siege line. After almost three weeks of bombardment the Mexicans sued for terms, and Worth served as one of the negotiators. When the Mexican army left the city, Worth became its military governor.

Scott, eager to gain the interior before the fever season, set 8 April for the army to begin its advance on Mexico City. Worth was furious when Scott placed Worth's rival, General Twiggs, in the vanguard. Some historians mark this as the beginning of the Scott-Worth rift.

The campaign's first major engagement was at Cerro Gordo. Worth's division helped pursue the fleeing Mexican army and, after the battle, moved with the rest of the army to Jalapa. From there, Scott sent Worth's division ahead through Perote to Puebla. Worth entered Puebla on 15 May and opened negotiations with its civilian government, agreeing to terms that would soon prove controversial, including a provision that gave Mexican courts jurisdiction over crimes against U.S. personnel. When Scott entered Puebla, he nullified the agreement by declaring martial law.

Scott's declaration revived the feud with Worth that had started in Vera Cruz. Scott also ordered Worth to rescind a handbill that warned U.S. soldiers about Puebla markets selling them poisoned food. Worth demanded a court of inquiry, but it not only found against him, it recommended that Scott reprimand him. Scott, however, circulated the reprimand only among brigade and division commanders.

Because volunteers whose terms of service had expired had to be replaced before advancing on Mexico City, Scott's army did not leave Puebla until 7 August. Worth's division departed on 9 August, the third of four divisions to take up the march. He supported Scott's decision to approach Mexico City from the south, although during the first major engagement of this final phase Worth's division remained idle outside of Contreras. The same day (20 August), however, his division bore the brunt of fighting at Churubusco. Following these frays the Mexicans asked for a truce, which Scott granted.

After hearing rumors that Mexicans were melting down church bells and casting them into cannon at El Molino del Rey, which violated the truce, Scott canceled it on 7 September and ordered Worth's division to attack El Molino del Rey. On 8 September, Worth's men suffered heavy casualties in an ultimately successful attack that revealed the rumors regarding the cannon were false.

U.S. forces nevertheless began preparations for the final assault on Mexico City. General Scott decided to attack the city by way of the fortified hill of Chapultepec and thus gave rise to yet another controversy involving his subordinates. Following the 12 September bombardment of the Mexican positions, Worth and his division trailed Gen. Gideon Pillow's division up the western slope of the hill the next day. After helping to secure the military academy and its fortifications, Worth led his men down the hill along one of the causeways toward the city. Taking heavy fire, Worth pushed into the heart of the city. Other divisions were simultaneously entering at other points, forcing a Mexican military evacuation to Guadalupe Hidalgo.

This devastating victory at Mexico City served as a prelude to months of sputtering negotiations with the Mexican government and tremendous dissension in the upper echelons of the U.S. Army. Most of the trouble started with General Pillow's report following Chapultepec, which exaggerated his activities and discounted the role played by General Scott. An anonymous letter then appeared in a U.S. newspaper being published in Mexico. The letter gave Worth credit for the army's southern approach to Mexico City. Scott, mistakenly believing that Worth was responsible for the letter, chastised him for violating regulations. Worth's angry response included an appeal to President Polk for vindication. Scott relieved Worth of his command and ordered his arrest.

After deliberating with his cabinet, Polk ordered a court of inquiry to be conducted in Mexico and removed Scott from command. Between the time these instructions arrived in Mexico (February) and the court's convening (March), intermediaries had arranged an uneasy truce between Worth and Scott. When the court met, it had to deal only with the Pillow controversy. In fact, Worth subsequently was restored to his command and was the last general to lead his men out of Mexico City, on 12 June 1848.

After leaving Mexico, Worth immediately went to Washington, D.C., and after a short leave reported to his new post in Texas as commander of the Departments of Texas and New Mexico. Shortly after arriving, in December 1848, he contracted cholera. He died in Texas on 7 May 1849.

Jeanne T. Heidler
David S. Heidler

BIBLIOGRAPHY

Hitchcock, Ethan Allen. *Fifty Years in Camp and Field: Diary of Major-General Ethan Allen Hitchcock, U.S.A.* Edited by W. A. Croffut. 1909.

Wallace, Edward S. *General William Jenkins Worth: Monterrey's Forgotten Hero.* 1953.

Y-Z

Yell, Archibald

U.S. politician Archibald Yell (1797–1847) served as colonel of the Arkansas Mounted Volunteers. Born in Jefferson County, Tennessee, in August 1797, Yell enlisted in the Tennessee militia under Andrew Jackson at age seventeen. He fought at Pensacola (1814) during the Creek War, at New Orleans (1815) in the War of 1812, and in the First Seminole War (1818). After he passed the bar, Yell established a law practice at Shelbyville, Tennessee, entering politics as a Jacksonian Democrat. After a term in the Tennessee legislature in 1827, he moved to Arkansas. Yell was the state's first representative to Congress in 1836 and was elected governor in 1840. He began another term in Congress in 1845.

A close friend of James K. Polk, Yell was an ardent expansionist. Before he took office as U.S. president, Polk selected Yell as an unofficial agent to Texas to arouse sentiment for annexation. In 1846, with Polk's blessing, Yell vacated his seat in Congress to enter the U.S.–Mexican War. He obtained the command of the Arkansas Mounted Volunteers as colonel and joined Gen. Zachary Taylor's army in October 1846. Yell was often criticized as a military officer, especially for inability or unwillingness, as Gen. John E. Wool charged, to discipline his troops, who were responsible for offenses against Mexican civilians. His conduct at Buena Vista (22–23 February 1847), which included bickering with Col. Humphrey Marshall of Kentucky over seniority, did little to redeem his reputation until he led a charge and was killed by a Mexican lancer. Celebrated in the United States as a war hero, he was buried in Fayetteville, Arkansas.

Jimmy L. Bryan, Jr.

BIBLIOGRAPHY

Bauer, K. Jack. *The Mexican War, 1846–1848.* 1974.

Hughes, William W. *Archibald Yell.* 1988.

Young America Movement

More a slogan than an organized cause, the phrase *Young America* came into use in the United States during the mid-1840s. It derived from the Young Italy and Young Europe movements that followed France's July Revolution of 1830 as well as from Ralph Waldo Emerson's 1844 lecture "The Young American" in Boston to the Mercantile Library Association and Edwin de Leon's 1845 commencement address in Charleston at South Carolina College. Young America rhetoric celebrated the robust youth of the United States as compared to the supposedly declining, feeble countries of Europe. Young Americans emphasized their nation's freedom from stifling traditions, its economic progress and republican political traditions, its rapid growth, and its anticipated greatness.

The Young America movement both reflected and helped to foster the climate of U.S. nationalism and territorial expansionism that played such an important role in producing and sustaining the U.S.–Mexican War. The period's most stridently expansionist politicians and ideologues tended to be Democrats in their twenties or thirties—such as Stephen A. Douglas, John L. O'Sullivan, Andrew Kennedy, and Walt Whitman—who espoused Young America tenets.

Following the outbreak of revolution throughout much of Europe in 1848, Young Americans increasingly took up the cause of European republicanism while continuing to advocate their nation's territorial expansion, particularly by means of the annexation of Spain's colony of Cuba. The Young America movement climaxed in 1852 with Stephen Douglas's unsuccessful candidacy for the Democratic presidential nomination. The slogan, however, continued to be applied to political topics, as well as many other matters, long after that date.

Robert E. May

BIBLIOGRAPHY

Curti, Merle E. "Young America." *American Historical Review* 32 (1926): 34–55.

Danborn, David B. "The Young America Movement." *Journal of the Illinois State Historical Society* 67 (1974): 294–306.

See also **United States, 1821–1854**, *article on* **Romantic Nationalism**

Yucatecan Revolt

The Yucatecan revolt of 1847, commonly known as the Caste War of Yucatán, represents one of the episodes in the region's modern history when North American influences conditioned rural mobilizations. Geographically isolated from and politically marginalized by the Mexican state throughout the nineteenth century, the Yucatán peninsula was oriented more toward the United States, Central America, and the Caribbean islands. The United States, at war with Mexico in the late 1840s but involved in an expanding commercial relationship with Yucatán, played a part in both the outbreak and the outcome of the bloody Caste War.

The weakness of the Mexican state and the increasing power of Yucatán's white elites provided the political preconditions for two attempts at secession during the decade beginning in 1836 that led to the 1847 Maya peasant revolt. These prominent local landowners and merchants, based in Mérida, the state capital located in the northwestern quadrant of the peninsula, or in neighboring Campeche, its political and economic rival, competed fiercely among themselves but remained united in their desire for regional autonomy. During the protracted conflict from 1839 to 1843 between regionalist Yucatán and the centralist Mexican republic, Yucatecan elites recruited Maya peasants to fight, promising them, among other things, to return lands that had been lost to expanding sugar production. The *yucatecos* successfully drove the Mexican forces from the peninsula, but the white elites reneged on their promise to distribute land to Maya recruits—a decision they would later regret.

Yucatecan disenchantment flared again when the war with the United States broke out in May 1846. Tensions between *meridano* and *campechano* elites worsened as the United States played on Yucatecan separatism and the factionalism of the regional elite to secure its strategic war objectives. In December 1846, Campeche revolted against both Mexico and Mérida, declaring for an independent Yucatán that would remain unconditionally neutral in the war against the United States. *Campechano* leaders mobilized the Maya on the state's southeastern frontier to join the fight against Mérida, providing them with guns and ammunition and allowing them to form their own battalions under their own lead-

ers. In the course of the fighting, the Maya came to identify their real enemies: the dominant white society whose sugar plantations were destroying their subsistence-based communities. The elite *campechano* revolt triumphed quickly—by January 1847—but in the process detonated what would become Latin America's most successful indigenous peasant rebellion.

Although triggered by a series of elite disputes, the 1847 revolt was neither simply a race war nor a residuum of elite factional conflict fanned by U.S. diplomats and soldiers. Rather, the Maya peasantry, armed by the Yucatecan elites, seized the opportunity that elite factionalism provided to pursue a social revolution aimed at halting the encroachment of commercial agriculture and erasing caste distinctions. Because of their fear of the Maya peasantry and their subsequent lynching of several Maya leaders, the white elites bear the major responsibility for redefining a social conflict into a race war.

By the spring of 1848, the *yucatecos* were besieged in Mérida and Campeche, the last white redoubts in a peninsula otherwise under free Maya control. That the whites managed to recover was due in part to the support of many Maya peons, who worked on the northwestern haciendas, and to the receipt of foreign assistance, principally from the United States. In mid-1848, the United States delivered guns and powder taken from captured Mexican troops via Commo. Matthew Perry's Home Squadron. Yucatecan governor Santiago Méndez had previously sent special envoy Justo Sierra O'Reilly to Washington in 1847, hoping to secure recognition of Yucatán as a neutral in the war between the United States and Mexico. Despite the defeat of President James K. Polk's Bill for the Relief of the Yucatán, Sierra's lobby did prompt almost a thousand U.S. volunteers (including those U.S.–Mexican War veterans called "the first of the American filibusters") and soldiers of fortune to offer their services against the Maya.

Ultimately, however, it was the government of Mexico that bailed out the Yucatecans. Yucatán agreed to reunite with Mexico if the central government would help turn the tide against the Maya rebels. On 17 August 1848, with all U.S. warships removed from Yucatecan waters and the Maya threat to Mérida and Campeche lifted, Yucatán rejoined the Mexican republic.

Although complete pacification of the Maya would take decades, the white elites gradually regained their hegemony. The rebellion reduced the peninsula's population by almost half, and elite fears of "another Caste War" plagued regional and national politics into the twentieth century. The 1847 Yucatecan revolt destroyed the profitable sugar industry on the southeastern frontier—thus accomplishing one of the Maya's fundamental objectives—yet in so doing it shaped possibilities for another kind of monoculture: large-scale henequen (Yucatecan sisal) production in the northwest of the peninsula.

Gilbert M. Joseph

BIBLIOGRAPHY

Joseph, Gilbert M. "The United States, Feuding Elites, and Rural Revolt in Yucatán, 1836–1915." In *Rural Revolt in Mexico and U.S. Intervention,* edited by Daniel Nugent, pp. 167–197. 1988.

Reed, Nelson. *The Caste War of Yucatán.* 1964.

Rugeley, Terry. *Yucatán's Maya Peasantry and the Origins of the Caste War.* 1996.

Zacatecas

Zacatecas, capital of the state of Zacatecas, was founded in the seventeenth century as a Franciscan convent. The center of much of colonial Mexico's mineral wealth, it enjoyed a privileged place under Spanish rule and developed a strong sense of local identity, or *patria chica.* After Mexican independence, the people of Zacatecas backed primarily federalist causes. When Antonio López de Santa Anna proclaimed himself president of Mexico in 1834, Zacatecas refused to acknowledge him and his central government; legislators of the district held that the Constitution of 1824 was the legitimate framework of government. To consolidate his power, Santa Anna passed a decree on 31 March 1835 reducing the size and strength of the nation's militia. When the powerful militia of Zacatecas refused to cooperate, Santa Anna declared a state of rebellion. "The devil, who in this country never takes a holiday," wrote German mining engineer Eduard Harkort, "ignited the flames of revolution in the formerly peaceful Zacatecas."

Santa Anna marched in April to discipline the rebels with an army of 3,400 men aided by Generals Martín Perfecto de Cos and Juan José Andrade. Don Francisco Garcia, the governor of Zacatecas, assembled an army of 5,000 poorly armed militia. General Andrade, in a ruse designed by Santa Anna, left the centralist army and rode into the city with his command claiming that he, too, would fight for the federalist cause. Governor Garcia believed him.

On 10 May Santa Anna and his troops arrived on the Plains of Guadalupe outside the city and demanded that Garcia surrender. He refused. At five o'clock the following morning, Santa Anna attacked Garcia's army from all sides and, aided by Andrade's perfidy, routed the rebels in a two-hour battle. "Our loss was due in no small part to the cowardice of Garcia, who ran away at the first shot," Harkort added, "and to the cowardice of the troops, who by entire battalions threw away their weapons in the darkness before ever seeing an enemy soldier." Santa Anna's centralist troops killed 2,000 rebels and captured another 2,700 while losing

Centralist Units in the Zacatecas Revolt
1835

Cavalry Permanente Units
Vera Cruz Regiment
Dolores Regiment
Tampico Regiment

Infantry Permanente Units
Allende Battalion
Zapadores Battalion

Activo Militia Units
Querétaro Battalion
First Mexico Battalion
Guanajuato Battalion
Guadalajara Battalion
San Luis Potosí Battalion

only 100 men. For two days after the battle, Santa Anna and his men pillaged and plundered the rich mining city.

Federalists everywhere took note of Santa Anna's brutality. In Texas, settlers branded the president a tyrant, and the cruel reputation of his centralist regime grew to mythical proportions. Texians subsequently used Santa Anna's conduct in Zacatecas as a justification for revolution against his government.

Lee Ann Woodall

BIBLIOGRAPHY

Bancroft, Hubert Howe. *History of the North Mexican States and Texas.* 1889.

Brister, Luis E., ed. and trans. *In Mexican Prisons: The Journal of Eduard Harkort, 1832–1834.* 1986.

Robinson, Fayette. *Mexico and Her Military Chieftains.* 1847.

Zavala, Lorenzo de

Mexican politician and signer of the Texas declaration of independence Lorenzo de Zavala (1788–1836) was born near Mérida, Yucatán, and received a classical education. Between 1810 and 1813 he and fellow liberals discussed the ideas of the Enlightenment and established the first newspaper in Mérida. His increasing anticlericalism led to his arrest in 1814 when Ferdinand VII returned to the Spanish throne. He spent three years in prison in the harbor of Vera Cruz where he taught himself English, read medical books, and became a Freemason. Elected a Yucatán deputy to the Cortes in Madrid in 1820, he returned home in 1822 and served in the constituent congress in Mexico City. An admirer of the U.S. constitution, Zavala became a leader in the federalist faction and helped shape the 1824 Mexican constitution. He served as senator from Yucatán from 1824 to 1827, when he became governor of the State of Mexico where he instituted reforms in education and distributed absentee-owned land to Indian villagers. A close friend of Joel Poinsett, the first U.S. minister to Mexico, Zavala was active in the York-rite lodges established with Poinsett's help, where the members were reform-minded federalists opposing the centralist-dominated conservative Scottish-rite Masons. Zavala supported fellow *yorkino* Vicente Guerrero for president in 1828 and became secretary of the treasury, implementing wise but unpopular reforms to stabilize Mexico's economy. When a centralist coup overthrew Guerrero, Zavala fled to the United States in 1830 with fellow refugees.

Between 1830 and 1832 he traveled around the United States and Europe, the latter in connection with the sale of his Texas *empresario* contract to the New York investors in the Galveston Bay and Texas Land Company. He wrote a travel journal favorable to the United States and worked on his multivolume *Ensayo histórico de las revoluciones de Mégico;* he also married a New York widow (his Yucatán wife died leaving two adult children), who bore him three children. He returned to his governorship in Mexico in 1832 when federalist victories in the civil war assured the election of Antonio López de Santa Anna as federalist president. In 1833 Santa Anna named Zavala Mexico's first minister to France. His stay in Paris was marred by Santa Anna's growing centralism, and when the president began destroying the Constitution of 1824, Zavala denounced him. Recalled by the angry president, Zavala ignored the summons in 1835 and went instead to New York and then Texas.

Federalist refugees in New Orleans in 1835 planned to overthrow Santa Anna: Zavala would foster revolt in Texas to create a diversion for his friend, José Antonio Mexía, who would sail to Tampico (a doomed undertaking) where he expected to recruit federalists. Federalist vice president Valentín Gómez Farías, a New Orleans refugee, would then return home and restore the Constitution of 1824. Zavala reached Texas in July 1835, shortly after a few Texans had captured the recently reestablished Mexican garrison at Anáhuac. Zavala's advice was appreciated by some Texans, but others regarded him with suspicion: his previous experience among cosmopolitan intellectuals in Europe and the United States did not prepare him for the anti-Mexican prejudice he saw in Texas. His neighbors at Harrisburg (near present-day Houston) elected him a delegate to the November Consultation that organized a separate state of Texas (joined to neighboring Coahuila since 1824) but rejected a call for independence. Elected to attend the 1 March 1836 convention, Zavala, accepting the inevitable, signed the declaration of independence on 2 March and was unanimously chosen interim vice president of the new Republic of Texas. The only

delegate who had previously helped create a national constitution, Zavala served on several key committees.

On 24 April, three days after the Battle of San Jacinto, Zavala arrived at the battleground from Galveston Island (where the government was temporarily encamped) and met the captive Santa Anna. Vice President Zavala helped negotiate the two Treaties of Velasco (one public, the other secret) signed 14 May 1836, with Santa Anna promising to not take up arms against the Texans in the future and establishing the Río Grande—not the Nueces River, the traditional southwestern boundary of Texas—as the Texas-Mexico boundary. The secret treaty allowed Santa Anna to return to Mexico where he agreed to work to recognize Texan independence. A mob prevented Santa Anna's departure in June, and he remained a prisoner until fall, while Mexico refused to recognize Santa Anna's endorsement while a prisoner. Zavala and Texas president David G. Burnet resigned in October so that newly elected president Sam Houston could assume the office. Zavala had suffered with malaria since arriving in Texas, and a boating accident in the chilly waters in front of his home on the San Jacinto River led to his death on 15 November 1836, eleven days before Santa Anna returned to Mexico.

Margaret Swett Henson

BIBLIOGRAPHY

Estep, Raymond. "The Life of Lorenzo de Zavala." Ph.D. diss., University of Texas, 1942. Published in Spanish as *Lorenzo de Zavala: Profeta de liberalismo mexicano.* 1952.

Henson, Margaret Swett. *Lorenzo de Zavala: The Pragmatic Idealist.* 1996.

Zerecero, Anastasio

Mexican politician Anastasio Zerecero (1799–1875) was born in Mexico City. Zerecero studied law and belonged to a society that favored the insurgents during the Wars of Independence. He joined the York-rite Masons in the 1820s and participated in the campaign to expel the Spaniards from Mexico. Zerecero also helped instigate the 1828 Parián riot. Exiled in 1830 by the conservative Anastasio Bustamante government, Zerecero remained a leading *puro* supporter over the next fifteen years.

As war with the United States became imminent, Zerecero again championed the *puros'* banner. He wrote for the bellicose newspaper *La Voz del Pueblo* in 1845 and subsequently worked to undermine the monarchist conspiracy headed by Gen. Mariano Paredes y Arrillaga. Zerecero's activities also highlight the reasons why many politically conscious Mexicans feared the *puros.* Zerecero wrote an inflammatory article in October 1846 for the official government newspaper; to carry on with the war effort, the piece suggested, the urban poor should seize the fortunes of the wealthy and hand them to Mexican soldiers. The ensuing outcry led to Zerecero's removal from the newspaper. Also at that time Zerecero led an unsuccessful effort to prevent Mexico City's well-to-do from arming their own civic militia units.

One year later, as U.S. troops neared Mexico City, Zerecero joined the civic militia and fought in the battles for the Mexican capital. During the postwar era he backed the 1854 Ayutla rebellion and resisted the French intervention. Zerecero then held several legal posts and, six years before his death in 1875, wrote *Memorias para la historia de las revoluciones en México* [. . .].

Pedro Santoni

BIBLIOGRAPHY

Diccionario Porrúa: De historia, biografía, y geografía de México. 4 vols. 6th ed. 1995.

Di Tella, Torcuato S. *National Politics in Early Independent Mexico, 1820–1847.* 1996.

Santoni, Pedro. *Mexicans at Arms: Puro Federalists and the Politics of War.* 1996.

Zozaya, María Josefa

Stories surrounding María Josefa Zozaya seem to be a composite of the experiences and contributions, both real and legendary, of two women. In one version, Zozaya, known as the "Angel of Monterrey," was an older woman who rallied the troops and became a casualty in the Battle of Monterrey in September 1846. Another interpretation, found in *Apuntes para la historia de la guerra entre Mexico y Los Estados Unidos* (1848), described Zozaya as a young, beautiful woman. During the Monterrey battle, Zozaya was said to have been on the rooftops with the Mexican army handing out food and supplies.

The legend of Zozaya may be compared to that of Adelita of the Mexican Revolution (1910–1921). Adelita, a nurse, became legendary for her contributions to the Revolution and was named in countless ballads, or *corridos*. She became so popular that *Adelita* became the general term for nurses in the revolutionary armies, which led to much confusion regarding the real identity of the original Adelita.

In similar fashion, the popularity of the stories about María Josefa Zozaya has contributed to the uncertainty about her identity. What does remain undisputed is that she supported the Mexican troops against the U.S. presence.

Yolanda Garcia Romero

BIBLIOGRAPHY

Dysart, Jane. "Mexican Women of Texas, 1830–1860: The Assimilation Process." *Western Historical Quarterly* 7 (1976): 365–375.

Weems, John Edward. *To Conquer a Peace: The War between the United States and Mexico.* 1974.

APPENDIX 1

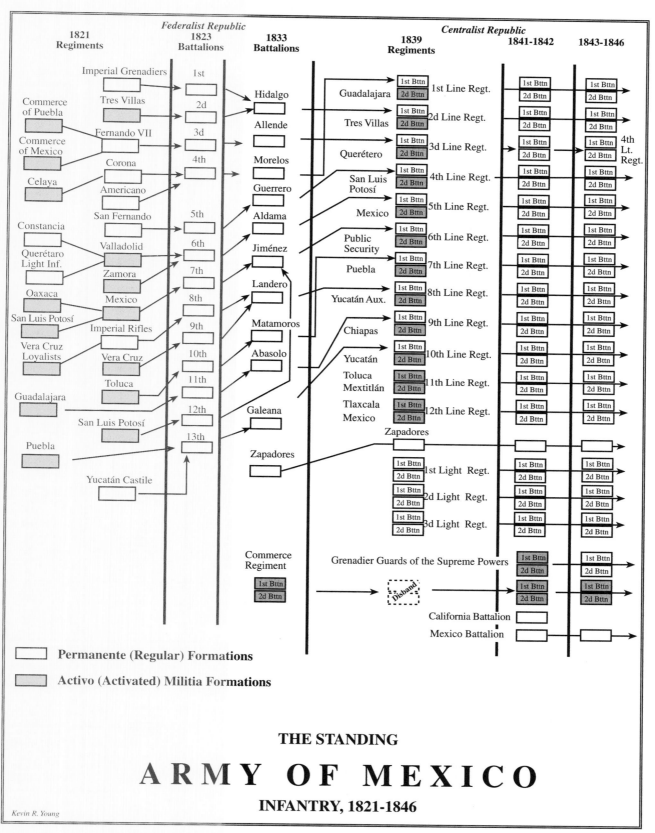

Permanente (Regular) Formations

Activo (Activated) Militia Formations

THE STANDING

ARMY OF MEXICO

INFANTRY, 1821-1846

Kevin R. Young

APPENDIX 2

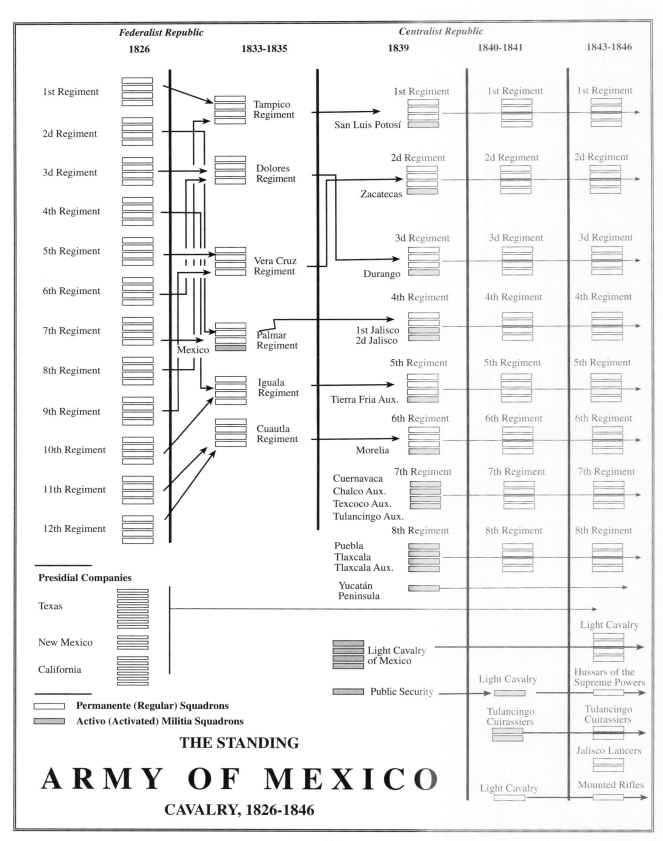

Federalist Republic

1826   1833-1835

Centralist Republic

1839   1840-1841   1843-1846

1st Regiment

2d Regiment

3d Regiment

4th Regiment

5th Regiment

6th Regiment

7th Regiment

8th Regiment

9th Regiment

10th Regiment

11th Regiment

12th Regiment

Tampico Regiment

Dolores Regiment

Vera Cruz Regiment

Mexico

Palmar Regiment

Iguala Regiment

Cuautla Regiment

1st Regiment   1st Regiment   1st Regiment
San Luis Potosí

2d Regiment   2d Regiment   2d Regiment
Zacatecas

3d Regiment   3d Regiment   3d Regiment
Durango

4th Regiment   4th Regiment   4th Regiment
1st Jalisco
2d Jalisco

5th Regiment   5th Regiment   5th Regiment
Tierra Fria Aux.

6th Regiment   6th Regiment   6th Regiment
Morelia

7th Regiment   7th Regiment   7th Regiment
Cuernavaca
Chalco Aux.
Texcoco Aux.
Tulancingo Aux.

8th Regiment   8th Regiment   8th Regiment
Puebla
Tlaxcala
Tlaxcala Aux.

Yucatán
Peninsula

Presidial Companies

Texas

New Mexico

California

Light Cavalry
of Mexico

Public Security

Light Cavalry

Hussars of the
Supreme Powers

Light Cavalry

Tulancingo
Cuirassiers

Tulancingo
Cuirassiers

Jalisco Lancers

Light Cavalry   Mounted Rifles

☐ **Permanente (Regular) Squadrons**
▦ **Activo (Activated) Militia Squadrons**

THE STANDING

ARMY OF MEXICO

CAVALRY, 1826-1846

Appendix 3

U.S. Forces Employed in the War with Mexico

REGULARS

Old Establishment

Force	Duration of Service
General Staff	permanent
U.S. Engineers	permanent
U.S. Topographical Engineers	permanent
Ordnance Department	permanent
1st Dragoons	permanent
2d Dragoons	permanent
Regiment of Mounted Rifles	permanent
1st Artillery	permanent
2d Artillery	permanent
3d Artillery	permanent
4th Artillery	permanent
1st Infantry	permanent
2d Infantry	permanent
3d Infantry	permanent
4th Infantry	permanent
5th Infantry	permanent
6th Infantry	permanent
7th Infantry	permanent
8th Infantry	permanent

New Establishment

Force	Duration of Service
3d Dragoons	war
9th Infantry	war
10th Infantry	war
11th Infantry	war
12th Infantry	war
13th Infantry	war
14th Infantry	war
15th Infantry	war
16th Infantry	war
Regiment of Voltigeurs	war
Battalion of U.S. Marines	attached to Scott's column

VOLUNTEERS

Force	Duration of Service
1st Alabama Infantry	6 months
Raiford's Battalion of Alabama Infantry	6 months
Platt's Battalion of Alabama Infantry	6 months
1st Alabama Infantry	war
Seibal's Battalion of Alabama Infantry	war
MaGee's Company of Alabama Cavalry	war
1st Arkansas Cavalry	12 months
Gray's Battalion of Arkansas Volunteers	12 months
Engart's Company of Arkansas Cavalry	war
Meares' Company of Remustered [Arkansas] Mounted Volunteers	war
Fremont's Battalion of California Volunteers	war in California
Maddox's Company of California Volunteers	war in California
Burton's Detachment of California Volunteers	12 months
Johnson's Company of Florida Infantry	12 months
Kelley's Company of Florida Infantry	12 months
Livingston's Company of Florida Volunteers	war
Fisher's Company of Florida Volunteers	war
1st Georgia Infantry	12 months
Seymour's Battalion of Georgia Infantry	war
Calhoun's Battalion of Georgia Cavalry	war
1st Illinois Infantry	12 months
2d Illinois Infantry	12 months
3d Illinois Infantry	12 months
4th Illinois Infantry	12 months
5th Illinois Infantry	war
6th Illinois Infantry	war
Dunlap's Battalion of Illinois Cavalry	war
Parker's Company of Iowa Cavalry	12 months
Morgan's Company of Iowa Infantry	12 months
Morgan's Company of Iowa Cavalry	war
1st Indiana Infantry	12 months
2d Indiana Infantry	12 months
3d Indiana Infantry	12 months
4th Indiana Infantry	war
5th Indiana Infantry	war
1st Kentucky Cavalry	12 months
1st Kentucky Infantry	12 months
2d Kentucky Infantry	12 months
3d Kentucky Infantry	war

U.S. Forces Employed in the War with Mexico (*continued*)

VOLUNTEERS (*continued*)

Force	Duration of Service
4th Kentucky Infantry	war
Gally's Louisiana Artillery Battalion	3 months
Gally's Louisiana Artillery Battalion	6 months
1st Louisiana Infantry	6 months
2d Louisiana Infantry	6 months
3d Louisiana Infantry	6 months
4th Louisiana Infantry	6 months
5th Louisiana Infantry	6 months
6th Louisiana Infantry	6 months
Biscoe's Battalion of Louisiana Cavalry	12 months
Blanchard's Company of Louisiana Infantry	12 months
1st Louisiana Infantry	12 months
Fiesca's Battalion of Louisiana Infantry	war
1st Maryland and District of Columbia Battalion	12 months
2d Maryland and District of Columbia Battalion	war
Boyd's Company of Remustered [Maryland] Mounted Volunteers	war
1st Massachusetts Infantry	war
Gage's Company of Michigan Infantry	war
1st Michigan Infantry	war
1st Mississippi Rifles	12 months
2d Mississippi Rifles	war
Anderson's Battalion of Mississippi Rifles	war
Woodruff's New Jersey Battalion of Infantry	war
1st Missouri Infantry	6 months
Holt's Battalion of Missouri Infantry	12 months
Willock's Battalion of Missouri Cavalry	12 months
Doniphan's Regiment of Missouri Cavalry	12 months
Price's Regiment of Missouri Cavalry	12 months
Clarke's Battalion of Missouri Volunteers	12 months
Easton's Battalion of Missouri Infantry	war
Rall's Regiment of Missouri Cavalry	war
Powell's Battalion of Missouri Cavalry	war
Gilpin's Battalion of Missouri Cavalry	war
Walker's Battalion of Remustered [Missouri] Mounted Volunteers	war
Mormon Battalion	12 months
Davis' Company of Mormon Volunteers	12 months
1st New York Infantry	12 months
2d New York Infantry	war
1st North Carolina Infantry	war
1st Ohio Infantry	12 months
2d Ohio Infantry	12 months
3d Ohio Infantry	12 months
Camp Washington [Ohio] Volunteers	12 months
4th Ohio Infantry	war
5th Ohio Infantry	war
Kenneally's and Riddle's Companies of Ohio Infantry	war
Duncan's Company of Ohio Cavalry	war
1st Pennsylvania Infantry	war
2d Pennsylvania Infantry	war
Companies of Pennsylvania Infantry	war
1st South Carolina Infantry	war
1st Tennessee Cavalry	12 months
1st Tennessee Infantry	12 months
2d Tennessee Infantry	12 months
3d Tennessee Infantry	war
4th Tennessee Infantry	war
5th Tennessee Infantry	war
Wheat's Battalion of Remustered [Tennessee] Mounted Volunteers	war
Henderson's Texas Volunteers	3 months
Hay's Regiment of Texas Mounted Volunteers	6 months
Wood's Regiment of Texas Mounted Volunteers	6 months
Johnston's Regiment of Texas Infantry	6 months
Cooper's Regiment of Texas Mounted Volunteers	6 months
Smith's Battalion of Texas Mounted Volunteers	6 months
Hay's Regiment of Texas Mounted Volunteers	6 months
Blackbeaver's Company of Texas Mounted Volunteers	6 months
Hay's Battalion of Texas Mounted Volunteers	12 months
Bell's Regiment of Texas Mounted Volunteers	12 months
McCulloch's and Gray's Companies of Mounted Volunteers	12 months
Battalion of Texas Infantry	12 months
Chevallie's Battalion of Texas Mounted Volunteers	war
Battalion of Texas Mounted Volunteers	war
1st Virginia Infantry	war
Knowlton's Company of Wisconsin Infantry	12 months

U.S. Forces Employed in the War with **Mexico** (continued)	
VOLUNTEERS (*continued*)	
Force	*Duration of Service*
Knowlton's Company of Wisconsin Infantry	war

Unofficial Volunteer Units

Force	*Duration of Service*
Battalion of Santa Fe Traders	Chihuahua Expedition
St. Vrain's Battalion of Santa Fe Traders	Taos Revolt
McKinstry's Quartermaster Company	Mexico City Campaign

Appendix 4

Mexican Navy, 1846

Type	Name	Battery	Tonnage	Size	Crew	Disposition (if known)
Steam Frigate (Iron Hull)	*Guadalupe*	2 × British 68 pdrs (8-inch) shell guns 2 × 68 pdrs (8-inch) shell guns 4 × long 12 pdrs	775	200′ × 34′ × 10′	200	Transferred to British owners
Steam Frigate	*Montezuma*	1 × 68 pdr (8-inch) shell guns 2 × long 32 pdrs 4 × 32 pdr carronades 1 × long 9 pdr	1,111	204′ × 34′ × 11′	230	Transferred to British owners
Brig	*Mexicano* (ex *Yucateco*)	14 × 18 pdr carronades 2 × 8 pdr howitzers	208	108′ × 27′ × 11.5′	100	Scuttled at Alvarado, April 1847
Brig	*Veracruzano Libre* (ex *Santa Anna*)	1 × long 32 pdr 6 × 18 pdr carronades 2 × 12 pdr howitzers	174	103′ × 24′ × 10.5′	70	Scuttled at Alvarado, April 1847
Brig	*Zempoalteca*	6 × long 12 pdr carronades	200		100	Scuttled at Alvarado, April 1847
Schooner	*Aguila*	1 × long 32 pdr 6 × 18 pdr carronades	130	99′ × 23′ × 10′	40	Scuttled at Alvarado, April 1847
Schooner	*Anáhuac*	1 × long 9 pdr 2 × 6 pdrs	105		70	Burned at Guaymas, 7 Oct. 1846
Schooner	*Guerrero*	1 × 24 pdr	48.5	64′ × 19′ × 6′	25	Scuttled at Alvarado, April 1847
Schooner	*Isabel* (later U.S.S. *Falcon*)	1 × 24 pdr	74	68.5′ × 19′ × 6′	25	Captured at Tampico, 14 Nov. 1846
Schooner	*Libertad* (ex *Campecheno*)	1 × long 12 pdr	89	78′ × 20′ × 7.5′	70	Scuttled at Alvarado, April 1847
Schooner	*Morelos*	1 × 12 pdr	59	74′ × 18′ × 7′	30	Scuttled at Alvarado, April 1847
Schooner	*Pueblana* (later U.S.S. *Tampico*)	1 × 24 pdr	74	68.5′ × 19′ × 6′	25	Captured at Tampico, 14 Nov. 1846

Mexican Navy, 1846 (*continued*)

Type	Name	Battery	Tonnage	Size	Crew	Disposition (if known)
Schooner	*Queretana*	1 × 24 pdr	75		32	Scuttled at Alvarado, April 1847
Schooner	*Sonorense*	1 × 12 pdr	27		20	Burned at Guaymas, 7 Oct. 1846
Schooner	*Unión* (later U.S.S. *Union*)	1 × 24 pdr	74	68.5′ × 19′ × 6′	25	Captured at Tampico, 14 Nov. 1846
Schooner	*Victoria*	1 × 24 pdr	48.5	64′ × 19′ × 6′	25	Scuttled at Alvarado, April 1847

Appendix 5

		United States Navy				
		Home Squadron				
Type	*Name*	*Battery*	*Tonnage*	*Size*	*Crew*	*Disposition (if known)*
Ship-of-the-Line	*Ohio*[1]	12 × 8-inch guns 28 × 42 pdrs 44 × 32 pdrs	2,757	197′ × 53.75′ × 26.5′	820	
1st Class Frigate	*Cumberland*	8 × 8-inch guns 42 × 32 pdrs	1,708	175′ × 45′ × 22.3′	480	
1st Class Frigate	*Potomac*	8 × 8-inch guns 42 × 32 pdrs	1,708	175′ × 45′ × 22.3′	480	
1st Class Frigate	*Raritan*	8 × 8-inch guns 42 × 32 pdrs	1,708	175′ × 45′ × 22.3′	480	
1st Class Sloop of War	*Albany*	4 × 8-inch guns 18 × 32 pdrs	1,042	148′ × 38.5′ × 17.5′	210	
1st Class Sloop of War	*Germantown*	4 × 8-inch guns 18 × 32 pdrs	942	150′ × 36′ × 17.25′	210	
1st Class Sloop of War	*Saratoga*	4 × 8-inch guns 18 × 32 pdrs	882	146.3′ × 38′ × 16.75′	275	
1st Class Sloop of War	*St. Mary's*	4 × 8-inch guns 18 × 32 pdrs	958	150′ × 37.3′ × 17.25′	210	
1st Class Steamer	*Mississippi*	2 × 10-inch guns 8 × 8-inch guns	1,732	220′ × 66.5′ × 21.75′	257	
1st Class Steamer	*Princeton*	1 × 8-inch gun 12 × 42 pdr carronades	672	156.5′ × 30.5′ × 20′	166	
2nd Class Sloop of War	*Boston*	4 × 8-inch guns 16 × 32 pdrs	700	127′ × 35′ × 16.5′	190	Wrecked 15 Nov. 1846 Bahama Islands
2nd Class Sloop of War	*Falmouth*	22 × 24 pdrs	703	127.5′ × 36′ × 17′	190	
2nd Class Sloop of War	*John Adams*	22 × 24 pdrs	700	127′ × 35′ × 16.5′	190	
3rd Class Sloop of War	*Decatur*	16 × 32 pdrs	566	117′ × 32′ × 15.6′	150	
3rd Class Steamer	*Iris* (ex merchant *Iris*)	1 × 32 pdr carronade	388	153′ × 26.3′ × 11′	48	
3rd Class Steamer	*Scorpion* (ex *Aurora*)	2 × 8-inch guns 2 × 18 pdr carronades	339	160.75′ × 24.5′ × 9.75′	61	

[1]*Ohio* also served in the Pacific Squadron

United States Navy
Home Squadron (*continued*)

Type	Name	Battery	Tonnage	Size	Crew	Disposition (if known)
3rd Class Steamer (Iron Hull)	Scourge (ex Bangor)	1 × 32 pdr 2 × 24 pdr carronades	230	120' × 23' × 9'	61	
3rd Class Steamer	Spitfire	1 × 8-inch gun 2 × 32 pdr carronades	241	118' × 22.5' × 8.25'	50	
3rd Class Steamer	Vixen	2 × 32 pdr carronades	241	118' × 22.5' × 8.25'	50	
3rd Class Steamer	Water Witch	1 × 8-inch gun 2 × 32 pdrs	255	131' × 21.75' × 7.25'	54	
Bomb Brig	Etna (ex Walcott)	1 × 10-inch columbiad	182	84' × 25.5' × 10.25'	47	
Bomb Brig	Hecla (ex I.L. Richardson)	1 × 10-inch columbiad	195		47	
Bomb Brig	Stromboli (ex Howard)	1 × 10-inch columbiad	182		47	
Bomb Brig	Vesuvius (ex St. Marys)	1 × 10-inch columbiad	240		47	
Brig	Lawrence	2 × 32 pdrs 8 × 32 pdr carronades	364	109.75' × 26.25' × 13'	80	
Brig	Perry	2 × 32 pdrs 6 × 32 pdr carronades	280	105' × 25.5' × 13.25'	80	
Brig	Porpoise	2 × 9 pdrs 9 × 24 pdr carronades	224	88' × 25' × 13'		
Brig	Somers	10 × 32 pdr carronades	259	100' × 25' × 13'	80	Capsized off Isla Verde, near Vera Cruz, 8 Dec. 1846
Brig	Truxtun	10 × 32 pdr carronades	331	100' × 27.3' × 13'	80	Wrecked near Tuxpan 14 Aug. 1846
Coast Survey Brig	Washington	1 × 42 pdr		91.25' × 22'		
Revenue Cutter	Ewing	6 × 12 pdrs			170	
Revenue Cutter	Forward	6 × 12 pdrs			150	
Revenue Cutter	Santa Anna					
Revenue Cutter	Van Buren	4 × 12 pdrs	112	73.3' × 20.5' × 7.3'		
Revenue Cutter	Woodbury	4 × 12 pdrs 1 × 6 pdrs	112	73.3' × 20.5' × 7.3'		
Revenue Steamer	Legare	1 × 18 pdr 1 × 12 pdr 1 × 9 pdr 2 × 4 pdrs	364	140' × 24' × 6.5'		
Revenue Steamer	McLane	6 × 12 pdrs	369	161' × 17' × 10'		Converted to Lightship

United States Navy
Home Squadron (*continued*)

Type	Name	Battery	Tonnage	Size	Crew	Disposition (if known)
Revenue Steamer	*Spencer*	4 × 12 pdrs 1 × 18 pdr carronade	398	160' × 24' × 9.25'		
Schooner	*Bonita*	1 × 32 pd carronade	74	59' × 19' × 7'	40	
Schooner	*Falcon* (ex *Isabel*)	1 × 24 pdr	74	68.5' × 19' × 6'	25	Taken at Tampico 14 Nov. 1846
Schooner	*Flirt*	2 × 18 pdr carronades	150		33	
Schooner	*Mahonese* (ex merchant *Mahonese*)	1 × 24 pdr	100			Taken at Tampico 14 Nov. 1846
Schooner	*Morris* (ex *Laura Virginia*)					Taken at Frontera 23 Oct. 1846
Schooner	*Nonata* (ex *Belle*) (ex Mexican *Nonata*)	4 × 42 pdr carronades	122			Taken in Gulf of Mexico 21 Aug. 1846
Schooner	*On-ka-hy-e*	2 guns	200	96' × 22' × 12.75'		
Schooner	*Petrel*	1 × 32 pdr carronade	74	59' × 19' × 7'	40	
Schooner	*Reefer*	1 × 32 pdr carronade	74	59' × 19' × 7'	40	
Schooner	*Tampico* (ex *Pueblana*)	1 × 24 pdr	74	68.5' × 19' × 6'	25	Taken at Tampico 14 Nov. 1846
Schooner	*Union* (ex *Unión*)	1 × 24 pdr	74	68.5' × 19' × 6'	25	Taken at Tampico 14 Nov. 1846; wrecked off Vera Cruz 16 Dec. 1846
Steamer (Iron Hull)	*Hunter*		96	100' × 18'	50	Wrecked on Isla Verde, near Vera Cruz, 21 March 1847
Steamer	*Petrita* (ex *Champion*) (ex *Secretary*) (ex Mexican *Petrita*)	1 × 24 pdr carronade	200			Taken at Frontera 23 Oct. 1846; foundered in Alvarado River 15 April 1848
Storeship	*Electra* (ex *Rolla*)	2 × 18 pd carronades	248.5		21	
Storeship	*Fredonia* (ex merchant *Fredonia*)	4 × 24 pdr carronades	800	160' × 33' × 20.5'	37	
Storeship	*Relief*	4 × 18 pdr gunnades 2 × 12 pdr gunnades	467	109' × 30.75' × 16.5'	44	
Storeship	*Supply* (ex merchant *Supply*)	4 × 24 pdr carronades	547		37	

Pacific Squadron

Type	Name	Battery	Tonnage	Size	Crew	Disposition (if known)
Ship-of-the-Line	*Columbus*	8 × 8-inch guns 56 × 32 pdrs 22 × 32 pdr carronades	2,480	193′ × 53.5′ × 26′	780	
Razee	*Independence*	8 × 8-inch guns 48 × 32 pdrs	1,891	188′ × 51.5′ × 24.3′	750	
1st Class Frigate	*Congress*	8 × 8-inch guns 46 × 32 pdrs	1,867	179′ × 48′ × 22.5′	480	
1st Class Frigate	*Savannah*	4 × 8-inch guns 28 × 32 pdrs 22 × 42 pdr carronades	1,708	175′ × 45′ × 22.3′	480	
1st Class Sloop of War	*Portsmouth*	4 × 8-inch guns 18 × 32 pdrs	1,022	153′ × 38′ × 17.5′	210	
2nd Class Sloop of War	*Cyane*	20 × 32 pdrs	792	132.3′ × 36′ × 16.5′	200	
2nd Class Sloop of War	*Levant*	4 × 8-inch guns 18 × 32 pdrs	792	132.3′ × 36′ × 16.5′	200	
2nd Class Sloop of War	*Warren*	24 × 32 pdrs	691	127′ × 34.5′ × 16.5′	190	
3rd Class Sloop of War	*Dale*	16 × 32 pdrs	566	117′ × 32′ × 15.6′	150	
3rd Class Sloop of War	*Preble*	16 × 32 pdrs	566	117′ × 32′ × 15.6′	150	
Bark	*Whinton*					Impressed in Gulf of California 1847
Brig	*Malek Adhel* (ex merchant *Malek Adhel*)	2 × 9 pdrs 10 × 6 pdrs	114	80′ × 20.5′ × 7.75′		Taken at Mazatlan 7 Sept. 1846
Schooner	*Julia*					Taken at La Paz, Baja California 14 Sept. 1846
Schooner	*Libertad*	1 × 9 pdr				
Schooner	*Shark*	2 × 9 pdrs 10 × 24 pdr carronades	198	86′ × 24.5′ × 12.3′	100	Wrecked at mouth of Columbia River 10 Sept. 1846
Storeship	*Erie*	4 × 9 pdrs	611	118′ × 32.3′ × 18′	43	
Storeship	*Lexington*	4 × 9 pdrs 2 × 32 pdr carronades	691	127′ × 34.5′ × 16.5′	43	
Storeship	*Southampton*	2 × 42 pdr carronades 4 × 18 pdr carronades 2 × 12 pdr gunnades	567	152.5′ × 27.75′ × 16′	43	

APPENDIX 6

Texan Navy
Texan Navy, 1836–1837

Type	Name	Battery	Tonnage	Size	Crew	Disposition (if known)
Schooner	San Felipe	7 × 12 pdrs			70	Destroyed 6 Nov 1836
Schooner	Independence (ex Ingham)	1 × long 9 pdr 13 × 6 pdrs	App. 125		40	Captured off Velasco, 1837; Later Mexican Independencia
Schooner	Brutus	1 × long 18 pdr 9 × 6 pdrs	160		40	Wrecked, Galveston Island, 1837
Schooner	Invincible		125			Wrecked, Galveston Island, 1837
Schooner	Liberty (ex William Robbins)		60			Sold, 1836

Texan Navy, 1839–1846

Type	Name	Battery	Tonnage	Size	Crew	Disposition (if known)
Sloop of War	Austin	16 × 24 pdrs 2 × 18 pdrs 2 × long 18 pdrs	600	125′ × 31′ × 12.5′	175	Taken into U.S. Navy, 1846; scrapped 1848
Brig	Wharton (ex Colorado)	15 × 18 pdrs 1 × long 9 pdr	405	110′ × 28′ × 11′	140	Taken into U.S. Navy, 1846; sold
Brig	Archer	14 × 18 pdrs	405	110′ × 28′ × 11′	140	Taken into U.S. Navy, 1846; sold
Schooner	San Bernard (ex Scorpion)	4 × 12 pdrs 1 × long 12 pdr	170	66′ × 21.5′ × 8′	82	Taken into U.S. Navy, 1846; sold
Schooner	San Antonio (ex Asp)	4 × 12 pdrs	170	66′ × 21.5′ × 8′	82	Failed mutiny 11 Feb. 1842, New Orleans; lost at sea, Oct 1842
Schooner	San Jacinto (ex Viper)	4 × 12 pdrs 1 × long 9 pdr	170	66′ × 21.5′ × 8′	82	Wrecked Aug. 1840, Arcas Island
Sidewheel Steamer	Zavala (ex Charleston)			210′ × 24′ × 12′	126	Beached May 1842, Galveston Island; broken up 1844

APPENDIX 7

THE TORNEL DECREE

As it appeared, in English translation, in the *Telegraph and Texas Register*

Mexico, War and Navy Department

Circular. The government has received information that, in the United States of North America, meetings are being called for the avowed purpose of getting up and fitting out expeditions against the Republic of Mexico, in order to send assistance to the rebels, foster the civil war, and inflict upon our country all the calamities, by which it is followed. In the United States, our ancient ally, expeditions are now organized similar to that headed by the traitor Jose Antonio Mexia and some have even set out for Texas. They have been furnished with every kind of ammunition, by means of which the revolted colonies are enabled to resist and fight the nation from which they received but immense benefits. The government is also positively informed that these acts, condemned by the wisdom of the laws of the United States, are also reported by the general government, with which the best intelligence and greatest [tear in paper]ony still prevail. However, as these adventurers and speculators have succeeded in escaping the penalties inflicted by the laws of their own country, it becomes necessary to adopt measures for their punishment. His excellency the president ad interim, anxious to repress these aggressions which constitute not only an offense to the sovereignty of the Mexican nation, but also to evident violation of international laws as they are generally adopted, has ordered the following decrees to be enforced.

1. Foreigners landing on the coast of the republic or invading its territory by land, armed with the intention of attacking our country, will be deemed pirates and dealt with as such, being citizens of no nation presently at war with the republic, and fighting under no recognized flag.
2. All foreigners who will import either by sea or land, in the places occupied by the rebels, either arms or ammunition of any kind for the use of them, will be deemed pirates and punished as such.

I send to you these decrees, that you may cause them to be fully executed.

Tornel

Mexico 30ᵗʰ Dec. 1835

Telegraph and Texas Register, 12 March 1836. Courtesy of the Daughters of the Republic of Texas Library.

APPENDIX 8

DECLARATION OF THE PEOPLE OF TEXAS IN GENERAL CONVENTION ASSEMBLED

Whereas, General Antonio Lopez de Santa Anna, and other military chieftains, have, by force of arms, overthrown the federal institutions of Mexico, and dissolved the social compact which existed between Texas and the other members of the Mexican confederacy; now the good people of Texas, availing themselves of their natural rights,

SOLEMNLY DECLARE,

1st. That they have taken up arms in defence of their rights and liberties, which were threatened by the encroachments of military despots, and in defence of the republican principles of the federal constitution of Mexico, of eighteen and twenty-four.

2d. That Texas is no longer morally or civilly bound by the compact of union; yet, stimulated by the generosity and sympathy common to a free people, they offer their support and assistance to such of the members of the Mexican confederacy as will take up arms against military despotism.

3d. That they do not acknowledge that the present authorities of the nominal Mexican republic have the right to govern within the limits of Texas.

4th. That they will not cease to carry on war against the said authorities whilst their troops are within the limits of Texas.

5th. That they hold it to be their right during the disorganization of the federal system, and the reign of despotism, to withdraw from the union, to establish an independent government, or to adopt such measures as they may deem best calculated to protect their rights and liberties, but that they will continue faithful to the Mexican government so long as that nation is governed by the constitution and laws that were formed for the government of the political association.

6th. That Texas is responsible for the expense of her armies now in the field.

7th. That the public faith of Texas is pledged for the payment of any debts contracted by her agents.

8th. That she will reward, by donations in lands, all who volunteer their services in her present struggle, and receive them as citizens.

These declarations we solemnly avow to the world; and call God to witness their truth and sincerity, and invoke defeat and disgrace upon our heads, should we prove guilty of duplicity.

Mr. Mitchell, from the committee appointed in pursuance of a resolution offered by him yesterday, reported progress, and asked and obtained leave to sit again.

Mr. Royal moved that five hundred copies of the report from the committee of twelve be printed.

Mr. Everitt proposed, as an amendment, one thousand be substituted for five hundred, which being accepted by the mover, Mr. Royal, was adopted by the house.

Mr. S. Houston moved that each member of this consultation sign the declaration made by the committee of twelve, (which, on the suggestion of the President, was laid over till the report be enrolled) as soon as enrolled.

Mr. Clements called up his resolution, offered yesterday, which being read, Mr. Perry proposed an amendment, which was accepted. Mr. Wharton moved its reference to a special committee.

Mr. Perry suggested, that as the permanent council had already acted on this subject, it might not, perhaps, be necessary.

On the suggestion of Mr. Royal, both the original resolution, as offered by Mr. Clements, and the amendment proposed by Mr. Perry, were withdrawn, and the following, embracing both, was offered by Mr. Clements:

Resolved, That a committee of five be appointed to report amendments to the acts of the council on the subject of rangers on the frontiers, and to extend the line from the Colorado to the Cibollo river.

Whereupon the following members were appointed that committee: Messrs. D. Parker, Clements, Lester, Perry and Martin.

The rule of the house being suspended in this case, Mr. Millard submitted the following:

Resolved, That a committee of twelve, one from each municipality represented in this consultation, be appointed by the president to draw up and submit a plan or system of a provisional government for all Texas which was adopted.

In pursuance of the above, the president named the following members to compose that committee: Messrs. Millard, Jones, Wilson, Dyer, Hoxie, Lester, H. Smith, Arrington, Thompson, Robinson, Everitt and A. Houston.

Mr. Millard asked and obtained leave to retire with the committee of which he was chairman.

On motion of Mr. W. Smith, the house adjourned to two o'clock P.M.

Two o'clock p. m.

The house met pursuant to adjournment.

On motion of Mr. S. Houston, in order to afford to the several committees time to prepare their reports,

The house adjourned until to-morrow morning 9 o'clock.

San Felipe de Austin, Nov. 8, 1835.
Nine o'clock A.M.

APPENDIX 9

THE TEXAS DECLARATION OF INDEPENDENCE
2 March 1836

A quarrel between Governor Henry Smith and the Council in January, 1836, paralyzed the Provisional Government of Texas. Fortunately, the Council had called for an election on February 1 to select delegates to a convention at Washington on March 1 to form a new government. Public sentiment, reflected by the attitude of the forty-one delegates on hand for the opening session, favored a declaration of independence. After the Convention had been organized, the first act of President Richard Ellis was to appoint a committee consisting of George C. Childress, chairman, James Gaines, Bailey Hardeman, Edward Conrad, and Collin McKinney to draft a declaration of independence. The following report of the committee, supposedly written by Childress and closely paralleling the United States Declaration of 1776, was unanimously adopted the next day.

THE DECLARATION OF INDEPENDENCE Made by the Delegates of The People of Texas in General Convention, at Washington, ON MARCH 2nd, 1836.

When a government has ceased to protect the lives, liberty and property of the people, from whom its legitimate powers are derived, and for the advancement of whose happiness it was instituted; and so far from being a guarantee for their inestimable and inalienable rights, becomes an instrument in the hands of evil rulers for their suppression. When the federal republican constitution of their country, which they have sworn to support, no longer has a substantial existence, and the whole nature of their government has been forcibly changed, without their consent, from a restricted federative republic, composed of sovereign states, to a consolidated central military despotism, in which every interest is disregarded but that of the army and the priesthood, both the eternal enemies of civil liberty, the ever ready minions of power, and the usual instruments of tyrants. When, long after the spirit of the constitution has departed, moderation is at length so far lost by those in power, that even the semblance of freedom is removed, and the forms themselves of the constitution discontinued, and so far from their petitions and remonstrances being regarded, the agents who bear them are thrown into dungeons, and mercenary armies sent forth to enforce a new government upon them at the point of the bayonet.

When, in consequence of such acts of malfeasance and abduction on the part of the government, anarchy prevails, and civil society is dissolved into its original elements, in such a crisis, the first law of nature, the right of self-preservation, the inherent and inalienable right of the people to appeal to first principles, and take their political affairs into their own hands in extreme cases, enjoins it as a right towards themselves, and a sacred obligation to their posterity, to abolish such government, and create another in its stead, calculated to rescue them from impending dangers, and to secure their welfare and happiness.

Nations, as well as individuals, are amenable for their acts to the public opinion of mankind. A statement of a part of our grievances is therefore submitted to an impartial world, in justification of the hazardous but unavoidable step now taken, of severing our political connection with the Mexican people, and assuming an independent attitude among the nations of the earth.

The Mexican government, by its colonization laws, invited and induced the Anglo American population of Texas to colonize its wilderness under the pledged faith of a written constitution, that they should continue to enjoy that constitutional liberty and republican government to which they had been habituated in the land of their birth, the United States of America.

In this expectation they have been cruelly disappointed, inasmuch as the Mexican nation has acquiesced to the late changes made in the government by General Antonio Lopez de Santa Anna, who, having overturned the constitution of his country, now offers, as the cruel alternative, either to abandon our homes, acquired by so many privations, or submit to the most intolerable of all tyranny, the combined despotism of the sword and the priesthood.

It hath sacrificed our welfare to the state of Coahuila by which our interests have been continually depressed through a jealous and partial course of legislation, carried on at a far distant seat of government, by a hostile majority, in an unknown tongue, and this too, notwithstanding we have petitioned in the humblest terms for the establishment of a separate state government, and have, in accordance with the provisions of the national constitution, presented to the general congress a republican constitution, which was, without a just cause, contemptuously rejected.

It incarcerated in a dungeon, for a long time, one of our citizens, for no other cause but a zealous endeavor to procure the acceptance of our constitution, and the establishment of a state government.

It has failed and refused to secure, on a firm basis, the right of trial by jury, that palladium of civil liberty, and only safe guarantee for the life, liberty, and property of the citizen.

It has failed to establish any public system of education,

although possessed of almost boundless resources, (the pubic domain,) and although it is an axiom in political science, that unless a people are educated and enlightened, it is idle to expect the continuance of civil liberty, or the capacity for self government.

It has suffered the military commandants, stationed among us, to exercise arbitrary acts of oppression and tyranny, thus trampling upon the most sacred rights of the citizens, and rendering the military superior to the civil power.

It has dissolved, by force of arms, the state congress of Coahuila and Texas, and obliged our representatives to fly for their lives from the seat of government, thus depriving us of the fundamental political right of representation.

It has demanded the surrender of a number of our citizens, and ordered military detachments to seize and carry them into the interior for trial, in contempt of the civil authorities, and in defiance of the laws and the constitution.

It has made piratical attacks upon our commerce, by commissioning foreign desperadoes, and authorizing them to seize our vessels, and convey the property of our citizens to far distant parts for confiscation.

It denies us the right of worshiping the Almighty according to the dictates of our own conscience, by the support of a national religion, calculated to promote the temporal interest of its human functionaries, rather than the glory of the true and living God.

It has demanded us to deliver up our arms, which are essential to our defence—the rightful property of freemen—and formidable only to tyrannical governments.

It has invaded our country both by sea and by land, with the intent to lay waste our territory, and drive us from our homes; and has now a large mercenary army advancing, to carry on against us a war of extermination.

It has, through its emissaries, incited the merciless savage, with the tomahawk and scalping knife, to massacre the inhabitants of our defenceless frontiers.

It has been, during the whole time of our connection with it, the contemptible sport and victim of successive military revolutions, and hath continually exhibited every characteristic of a weak, corrupt, and tyrannical government.

These, and other grievances, were patiently borne by the people of Texas, until they reached that point at which forbearance ceases to be a virtue. We then took up arms in defence of the national constitution. We appealed to our Mexican brethren for assistance: our appeal has been made in vain; though months have elapsed, no sympathetic response has yet been heard from the interior. We are, therefore, forced to the melancholy conclusion, that the Mexican people have acquiesced in the destruction of their liberty, and the substitution therefor of a military government; that they are unfit to be free, and incapable of self government.

The necessity of self-preservation, therefore, now decrees our eternal political separation.

WE, *therefore, the delegates, with plenary powers, of the people of Texas, in solemn convention assembled, appealing to a candid world for the necessities of our condition, do hereby resolve and declare, that our political connection wish the Mexican nation has forever ended, and that the people of Texas do now constitute a* FREE, SOVEREIGN, *and* INDEPENDENT REPUBLIC, *and are fully invested with all the rights and attributes which properly belong to independent nations; and, conscious of the rectitude of our intentions, we fearlessly and confidently commit the issue to the supreme Arbiter of the destinies of nations.*

In witness whereof we have hereunto subscribed our names.

RICHARD ELLIS,
President and Delegate from Red River,

ALBERT H. S. KIMBLE, *Secretary,*

C. B. Stewart,	William B. Leates,
James Collingsworth,	M. B. Menard,
Edwin Waller,	A. B. Hardin,
A. Brigham,	John W. Bunton,
John S. D. Byrom,	Thomas J. Gazley,
Francis Ruis,	R. M. Coleman,
J. Antonio Navarro,	Sterling C. Robertson,
William D. Lacy,	George C. Childress,
William Menifee,	Baily Hardiman,
John Fisher,	Robert Potter,
Matthew Caldwell,	Charles Taylor,
John S. Roberts,	Samuel P. Carson,
Robert Hamilton,	Thomas J. Rusk,
Collin McKinney,	William C. Crawford,
A. H. Latimore,	John Turner,
James Power,	Benjamin Briggs Goodrich,
Sam. Houston,	James G. Swisher,
Edward Conrad,	George W. Barnet,
Martin Palmer,	Jesse Grimes,
James Gaines,	E. O. Legrand,
William Clark, jun.,	David Thomas,
Sydney O. Pennington,	S. Rhoads Fisher,
William Motley,	John W. Bower,
Lorenzo de Zavala,	J. B. Woods,
George W. Smyth,	Andrew Briscoe,
Stephen H. Everett,	Thomas Barnett,
Elijah Stepp,	Jesse B. Badgett,
Claiborne West,	Stephen W. Blount.

From *Laws of the Republic of Texas* (Printed by Order of the Secretary of State, 2 vols.; Houston, 1838), I, 3–7.

APPENDIX 10

GOVERNMENTS OF MEXICO
1843-1851

GENERAL D. ANTONIO LÓPEZ DE SANTA ANNA

On 4 March 1843 Don Antonio de Santa Anna took charge as the provisional president of the Republic. He left the presidency that same year on 4 October, naming Don Valentín Canalizo as the interim president.

Government Ministry Officials during this Period

State and Foreign Relations
4 March 1843–4 October 1843 — Don José Ma. De Bocanegra

Justice
4 March 1843–16 July 1843 — Don Pedro Velez
17 July 1843–4 October 1843 — Don Manuel Baranda

Military
4 March 1843–19 September 1843 — Don José María Tornel
20 September 1843–4 October 1843 — Don José Ma. Díaz Noriega, O.M.E.

Treasury
4 March 1843–4 October 1843 — Don Ignacio Trigueros

GENERAL D. VALENTÍN CANALIZO

Don Valentín Canalizo was named interim president by decree on 2 October 1843, having been sworn in and taking office on 4 October. He governed with this title until 1 February 1844, until which time he was sworn in as interim constitutional president, named by the Senate on the 27th of the previous January. He exercised power until 4 June 1844.

Government Ministry Officials during this Period

State and Foreign Relations
4 October 1843–4 June 1844 — Don José Ma. De Bocanegra

Justice
4 October 1843–4 June 1844 — Don Manuel Barranda

Military
4 October 1843–25 October 1843 — Don José Ma. Díaz Noriega, O.M.E.
26 October 1843–26 March 1844 — Don José Ma. Tornel
27 March 1844–10 April 1844 — Don José Ma. Díaz Noriega, O.M.E.
11 April 1844–June 1844 — Don José Ma. Tornel

Treasury
4 October 1843–4 June 1844 — Don Ignacio Trigueros

GENERAL D. ANTONIO LÓPEZ DE SANTA ANNA

On 4 June 1844 Don Antonio López de Santa Anna was sworn in as constitutional president of the Republic, voted by the departmental assemblies on 1 November 1843 and declared by the House of Representatives on 2 January 1844. He left the presidency on 12 September 1844, using the license that was conceded to him on 7 September 1844.

Government Ministry Officials during this Period

State and Foreign Relations
4 June 1844–24 July 1844 — Don José María de Bocanegra
25 July 1844–4 August 1844 — Don José Ma. Ortiz Monasterio, O.M.E.
5 August 1844–18 August 1844 — Don José María de Bocanegra
19 August 1844–12 September 1844 — Don Manuel Crescencio Rejón

Justice
4 June 1844–12 September 1844 — Don Manuel Baranda

Military
4 June 1844–10 June 1844 — Don José María Tornel
11 June 1844–12 September 1844 — Don Isidro Reyes

Treasury
4 June 1844–12 September 1844 — Don Ignacio Trigueros

GENERAL D. JOSÉ JOAQUÍN DE HERRERA

Don Valentín Canalizo, named interim president by the Senate on 7 September 1844, was found absent. Don José Joaquín de Herrera, being president of the council, took office in his place on 12 September 1844. He left office on 21 September 1844 upon the appearance of Mr. Valentín Canalizo to take charge of the government.

GENERAL D. VALENTÍN CANALIZO

The Senate named Mr. Canalizo the interim president of the Republic on 7 September 1844. He was sworn in and took office on 21 September of that same year. He governed until 6 December 1844, at which time a revolution broke out in the capital.

GENERAL D. JOSÉ JOAQUÍN DE HERRERA

As a consequence of the revolutionary movement, Don José Joaquín de Herrera took charge of the government as president of the council on 6 December 1844. On 7 December 1844 he was named interim president by the Senate. The departmental assemblies voted him as constitutional president on 1 August 1845. He was sworn into office on 16 September of that same year. His presidency lasted until 30 December 1845, at which time the revolution of the Citadel triumphed.

GENERAL D. MARIANO PAREDES Y ARRILLAGA
On 4 January 1846 Don Mariano Paredes y Arrillaga was sworn into office, having been appointed the day before by the Ruling Committee. On 12 June 1846 he was reelected by the Special Congress and was sworn in on the thirteenth. Don Nicolás Bravo was named vice president. The administration of General Paredes relinquished control on 28 July by being awarded control of the Army by decree passed on 20 June of that same year.

GENERAL D. NICOLÁS BRAVO
By virtue of the decree that gave General Paredes the power to take control of the Army on 20 June 1846, Don Nicolás Bravo took the office of president on 28 July 1846. The revolution proclaimed in the Citadel in the early hours of the morning of 4 August 1846 put an end to his short administration.

GENERAL D. MARIANO SALAS
As leader of the revolution proclaimed in the Citadel in the early hours of the morning of 4 August 1846, General D. Mariano Salas took possession of the government on 5 August. He gave over the control of the administration to Don Valentín Gómez Farías on 23 December 1846.

GENERAL D. PEDRO MARÍA ANAYA
On 2 April 1847 Congress named General Don Pedro María Anaya as substitute president as a consequence of the permission granted to Congress by General Santa Anna and because he was relieved of the office of vice president the day before. He ceased to function as president on 20 May.

GENERAL D. ANTONIO LÓPEZ DE SANTA ANNA
On 20 May 1847 General D. Antonio López de Santa Anna again was charged with the office of the presidency, the same office he renounced in the village of Guadalupe Hidalgo on 16 September of that same year. (Following is a quote about the general from the impressions published by a contemporary of the war of 1847: "Having made so many efforts can suggest the most unblemished patriotism in order to fight the American Army; he had counted on the cooperation of the governors of the states and the majority of them remained cold spectators of the struggle, as if they had not been Mexicans; he had confided in the honor, skill and discipline of several leaders, and he had the feeling that some were showing signs of insubordination, in his judgment, and he felt that there were others possessing the most miserable cowardice,

though these were few in number. One of the scenes that was recorded into memory with indelible characters occurred in San Juan Teotihuacan. General Santa Anna referred to the heroic deeds of Generals Leon y Balderas, of Xicotencatl, of Cano, of Martinez de Castro, and of the many who sacrificed themselves for the sake of the motherland by defending its independence, with tears he paid the tribute due to their memory; but upon lamenting the death of the many students of the Military Institute, that even though they were children, they showed the foreign enemy that they knew to die and not to surrender, he exclaimed, 'If I had given charge of the cavalry to two of these students, there would have not been a single American soldier in the Valley of Mexico.' This quote was recorded because it is the most expressive eulogy that the general of an army could have made regarding the bravery of the corps to which he referred".)

DON VALENTÍN GÓMEZ FARÍAS
On 23 December 1846 Congress named Don Antonio López de Santa Anna as interim president and Don Valentín Gómez Farías as vice president. Valentin Gomez Farias took possession of the office of president as Santa Anna was not to be found. He governed until 21 March 1847.

GENERAL D. ANTONIO LÓPEZ DE SANTA ANNA
On the night of 21 March 1847, D. Antonio López de Santa Anna was sworn into office and took possession of the government of the Republic in the village of Guadalupe Hidalgo, before a commission of Congress. He left the presidency on 2 April 1847, making use of the permission granted to him.

LICENCIADO DON MANUEL DE LA PEÑA Y PEÑA
As a consequence of the renunciation of the presidency by General Santa Anna on 16 September 1847, Don Manuel de la Peña y Peña, president of the Supreme Court of Justice, was to establish the government in the city of Toluca on 26 September, the nation having been leaderless from the 17 to 25 September. He left the presidency on 13 November.

GENERAL D. PEDRO MARÍA ANAYA
Interim president elect, General D. Pedro María Anaya exercised power in Querétaro from 13 November 1847 until 8 January 1848.

LICENCIADO DE MANUEL DE LA PEÑA Y PEÑA
As president of the Supreme Court of Justice, Don Manuel de la Peña y Peña was given charge as president of the Republic on 8 January 1848. He governed until 3 June, the day that he took over as constitutional president. On 2 February 1848 he negotiated the treaty of peace and friendship among the commissioners of Mexico and of the United States. The treaty was ratified in Querétaro on 30 May 1848.

GENERAL D. JOSÉ JOAQUÍN DE HERRERA

Constitutional president elect Don José Joaquín de Herrera took charge of the government on 3 June 1848. His office ended on 18 January 1851, on which day Don Mariano Arista was sworn into office.

SOURCE: *Gobiernos de México, Diccionario Porrúa*, 5th edition

APPENDIX 11

POLK'S WAR MESSAGE
11 May 1846

To the Senate and House of Representatives:

The existing state of the relations between the United States and Mexico renders it proper that I should bring the subject to the consideration of Congress. . . .

In my message at the commencement of the present session I informed you that upon the earnest appeal both of the Congress and convention of Texas I had ordered an efficient military force to take a position "between the Nueces and the Del Norte." This had become necessary to meet a threatened invasion of Texas by the Mexican forces, for which extensive military preparations had been made. The invasion was threatened solely because Texas had determined, in accordance with a solemn resolution of the Congress of the United States, to annex herself to our Union, and under these circumstances it was plainly our duty to extend our protection over her citizens and soil.

This force was concentrated at Corpus Christi, and remained there until after I had received such information from Mexico as rendered it probable, if not certain, that the Mexican Government would refuse to receive our envoy.

Meantime Texas, by the final action of our Congress, had become an integral part of our Union. The Congress of Texas, by its act of December 19, 1836, had declared the Rio del Norte to be the boundary of that Republic. Its jurisdiction had been extended and exercised beyond the Nueces. The country between that river and the Del Norte had been represented in the Congress and in the convention of Texas, had thus taken part in the act of annexation itself, and is now included within one of our Congressional districts. Our own Congress had, moreover, with great unanimity, by the act approved December 31, 1845, recognized the country beyond the Nueces as a part of our territory by including it within our own revenue system, and a revenue officer to reside within that district has been appointed by and with the advice and consent of the Senate. It became, therefore, of urgent necessity to provide for the defense of that portion of our country. Accordingly, on the 13th of January last instructions were issued to the general in command of these troops to occupy the left bank of the Del Norte. This river, which is the southwestern boundary of the State of Texas, is an exposed frontier.

The movement of the troops to the Del Norte was made by the commanding general under positive instructions to abstain from all aggressive acts toward Mexico or Mexican citizens and to regard the relations between that Republic and the United States as peaceful unless she should declare war or commit acts of hostility indicative of a state of war. . . .

The Mexican forces at Matamoras assumed a belligerent attitude, and on the 12th of April General Ampudia, then in command, notified General Taylor to break up his camp within twenty-four hours and to retire beyond the Nueces River, and in the event of his failure to comply with these demands announced that arms, and arms alone, must decide the question. But no open act of hostility was committed until the 24th of April. On that day General Arista, who had succeeded to the command of the Mexican forces, communicated to General Taylor that "he considered hostilities commenced and should prosecute them." A party of dragoons of 63 men and officers were on the same day dispatched from the American camp up the Rio del Norte, on its left bank, to ascertain whether the Mexican troops had crossed or were preparing to cross the river, "became engaged with a large body of these troops, and after a short affair, in which some 16 were killed and wounded, appear to have been surrounded and compelled to surrender." . . .

The cup of forbearance had been exhausted even before the recent information from the frontier of the Del Norte. But now, after reiterated menaces, Mexico has passed the boundary of the United States, has invaded our territory and shed American blood upon the American soil. She has proclaimed that hostilities have commenced, and that the two nations are now at war.

As war exists, and notwithstanding all our efforts to avoid it, exists by the act of Mexico herself, we are called upon by every consideration of duty and patriotism to vindicate with decision the honor, the rights, and the interests of our country. . . .

In further vindication of our rights and defense of our territory, I invoke the prompt action of Congress to recognize the existence of the war, and to place at the disposition of the Executive the means of prosecuting the war with vigor, and thus hastening the restoration of peace. . . .

SOURCE: James D. Richardson, ed., *A Compilation of the Messages and Papers of the Presidents,* vol. 4, pp. 437ff. 1897–1916.

APPENDIX 12

THE COMPLETE TEXT OF THE TREATY OF GUADALUPE HIDALGO AND THE PROTOCOL OF QUERÉTARO

In the name of Almighty God:

The United States of America, and the United Mexican States, animated by a sincere desire to put an end to the calamities of the war which unhappily exists between the two Republics, and to establish upon a solid basis relations of peace and friendship, which shall confer reciprocal benefits upon the citizens of both, and assure the concord, harmony and mutual confidence, wherein the two peoples should live, as good neighbours, have for that purpose appointed their respective Plenipotentiaries: that is to say, the President of the United States has appointed Nicholas P. Trist, a citizen of the United States, and the President of the Mexican Republic has appointed Don Luis Gonzaga Cuevas, Don Bernardo Couto, and Don Miguel Atristain, citizens of the said Republic; who, after a reciprocal communication of their respective full powers, have, under the protection of Almighty God, the author of Peace, arranged, agreed upon, and signed the following

Treaty of Peace, Friendship, Limits and Settlement between the United States of America and the Mexican Republic.

ARTICLE I.

There shall be firm and universal peace between the United States of America and the Mexican Republic, and between their respective countries, territories, cities, towns and people, without exception of places or persons.

ARTICLE II.

Immediately upon the signature of this Treaty, a convention shall be entered into between a Commissioner or Commissioners appointed by the General in Chief of the forces of the United States, and such as may be appointed by the Mexican Government, to the end that a provisional suspension of hostilities shall take place, and that, in the places occupied by the said forces, constitutional order may be re-established, as regards the political, administrative, and judicial branches, so far as this shall be permitted by the circumstances of military occupation.

ARTICLE III.

Immediately upon the ratification of the present treaty by the Government of the United States, orders shall be transmitted to the Commanders of their land and naval forces, requiring the latter, (provided this treaty shall then have been ratified by the Government of the Mexican Republic and the ratifications exchanged) immediately to desist from blockading any Mexican ports; and requiring the former (under the same condition) to commence, at the earliest moment practicable, withdrawing all troops of the United States then in the interior of the Mexican Republic, to points, that shall be selected by common agreement, at a distance from the sea-ports, not exceeding thirty leagues; and such evacuation of the interior of the Republic shall be completed with the least possible delay; the Mexican Government hereby binding itself to afford every facility in it's power for rendering the same convenient to the troops, on their march and in their new positions, and for promoting a good understanding between them and the inhabitants. In like manner, orders shall be despatched to the persons in charge of the Custom Houses at all ports occupied by the forces of the United States, requiring them (under the same condition) immediately to deliver possession of the same to the persons authorized by the Mexican Government to receive it, together with all bonds and evidences of debt for duties on importations and on exportations, not yet fallen due. Moreover, a faithful and exact account shall be made out, showing the entire amount of all duties on imports and on exports, collected at such Custom Houses, or elsewhere in Mexico, by authority of the United States, from and after the day of ratification of this treaty by the Government of the Mexican Republic; and also an account of the cost of collection; and such entire amount, deducting only the cost of collection, shall be delivered to the Mexican Government, at the City of Mexico, within three months after the exchange of ratifications.

The evacuation of the Capital of the Mexican Republic by the troops of the United States, in virtue of the above stipulation, shall be completed in one month after the orders there stipulated for shall have been received by the commander of said troops, or sooner if possible.

ARTICLE IV.

Immediately after the exchange of ratifications of the present treaty, all castles, forts, territories, places and possessions, which have been taken or occupied by the forces of the United States during the present war, within the limits of the Mexican Republic, as about to be established by the following Article, shall be definitively restored to the said Republic, together with all the artillery, arms, apparatus of war, munitions and other public property, which were in the said castles and forts when captured, and which shall remain there at the time when this treaty shall be duly ratified by the Government of the Mexican Republic. To this end, immediately upon the signature of this treaty, orders shall be despatched to the American officers commanding such castles and forts, securing against the removal or destruction of any such artillery, arms, apparatus of war, munitions or other public property. The City of Mexico, within the inner line of intrenchments surrounding the said City, is comprehended in the above stipulations, as regards the restoration of artillery, apparatus of war, &c.

The final evacuation of the territory of the Mexican Republic, by the forces of the United States, shall be completed in three months from the said exchange of ratifications, or sooner, if possible: the Mexican Government hereby engaging, as in the foregoing Article, to use all means in it's power for facilitating such evacuation, and rendering it convenient to the troops, and for promoting a good understanding between them and the inhabitants.

If, however, the ratification of this treaty by both parties should not take place in time to allow the embarcation of the troops of the United States to be completed before the commencement of the sickly season, at the Mexican Ports on the Gulf of Mexico; in such case a friendly arrangement shall be entered into between the General in Chief of the said troops and the Mexican Government, whereby healthy and otherwise suitable places at a distance from the ports not exceeding thirty leagues shall be designated for the residence of such troops as may not yet have embarked, until the return of the healthy season. And the space of time here referred to, as comprehending the sickly season, shall be understood to extend from the first day of May to the first day of November.

All prisoners of war taken on either side, on land or on sea, shall be restored as soon as practicable after the exchange of ratifications of this treaty. It is also agreed that if any Mexicans should now be held as captives by any savage tribe within the limits of the United States, as about to be established by the following Article, the Government of the said United States will exact the release of such captives, and cause them to be restored to their country.

Article V.

The Boundary line between the two Republics shall commence in the Gulf of Mexico, three leagues from land, opposite the mouth of the Rio Grande, otherwise called Rio Bravo del Norte, or opposite the mouth of it's deepest branch, if it should have more than one branch emptying directly into the sea; from thence, up the middle of that river, following the deepest channel, where it has more than one, to the point where it strikes the southern boundary of New Mexico; thence, westwardly, along the whole southern boundary of New Mexico (which runs north of the town called *Paso*) to it's western termination; thence, northward, along the western line of New Mexico, until it intersects the first branch of the river Gila; (or if it should not intersect any branch of that river, then, to the point on the said line nearest to such branch, and thence in a direct line to the same;) thence down the middle of the said branch and of the said river, until it empties into the Rio Colorado; thence, across the Rio Colorado, following the division line between Upper and Lower California, to the Pacific Ocean.

The southern and western limits of New Mexico, mentioned in this Article, are those laid down in the Map, entitled "*Map of the United Mexican States, as organized and defined by various acts of the Congress of said Republic, and constructed according to the best Authorities. Revised Edition. Published at New York in 1847 by J. Disturnell:*" of which Map a Copy is added to this treaty, bearing the signatures and seals of the Undersigned Plenipotentiaries. And, in order to preclude all difficulty in tracing upon the ground the limit separating Upper from Lower California, it is agreed that the said limit shall consist of a straight line, drawn from the middle of the Rio Gila, where it unites with the Colorado, to a point on the coast of the Pacific Ocean, distant one marine league due south of the southernmost point of the Port of San Diego, according to the plan of said port, made in the year 1782 by Don Juan Pantoja, second sailing master of the Spanish fleet, and published at Madrid in the year 1802, in the Atlas to the voyage of the schooners *Sutil* and *Mexicana:* of which plan a copy is hereunto added, signed and sealed by the respective plenipotentiaries.

In order to designate the Boundary line with due precision, upon authoritative maps, and to establish upon the ground landmarks which shall show the limits of both Republics, as described in the present Article, the two Governments shall each appoint a Commissioner and a Surveyor, who, before the expiration of one year from the date of the exchange of ratifications of this treaty, shall meet at the Port of San Diego, and proceed to run and mark the said boundary in it's whole course, to the Mouth of the Rio Bravo del Norte. They shall keep journals and make out plans of their operations; and the result, agreed upon by them, shall be deemed a part of this Treaty, and shall have the same force as if it were inserted therein. The two Governments will amicably agree regarding what may be necessary to these persons, and also as to their respective escorts, should such be necessary.

The Boundary line established by this Article shall be religiously respected by each of the two Republics, and no change shall ever be made therein, except by the express and free consent of both nations, lawfully given by the General Government of each, in conformity with it's own constitution.

ARTICLE VI.

The Vessels and citizens of the United States shall, in all time, have a free and uninterrupted passage by the Gulf of California, and by the River Colorado below it's confluence with the Gila, to and from their possessions situated north of the Boundary line defined in the preceding Article: it being understood, that this passage is to be by navigating the Gulf of California and the River Colorado, and not by land, without the express consent of the Mexican Government.

If, by the examinations which may be made, it should be ascertained to be practicable and advantageous to construct a road, canal or railway, which should, in whole or in part, run upon the river Gila, or upon it's right or it's left bank, within the space of one marine league from either margin of the river, the Governments of both Republics will form an agreement regarding it's construction, in order that it may serve equally for the use and advantage of both countries.

ARTICLE VII.

The river Gila, and the part of the Rio Bravo del Norte lying below the southern boundary of New Mexico, being, agreeably to the fifth Article, divided in the middle between the two Republics, the navigation of the Gila and of the Bravo below said boundary shall be free and common to the vessels and citizens of both countries; and neither shall, without the consent of the other, construct any work that may impede or interrupt, in whole or in part, the exercise of this right: not even for the purpose of favouring new methods of navigation. Nor shall any tax or contribution, under any denomination or title, be levied upon vessels or persons navigating the same, or upon merchandise or effects transported thereon, except in the case of landing upon one of their shores. If, for the purpose of making the said rivers navigable, or for maintaining them in such state, it should be necessary or advantageous to establish any tax or contribution, this shall not be done without the consent of both Governments.

The stipulations contained in the present Article shall not impair the territorial rights of either Republic, within it's established limits.

ARTICLE VIII.

Mexicans now established in territories previously belonging to Mexico, and which remain for the future within the limits of the United States, as defined by the present treaty, shall be free to continue where they now reside, or to remove at any time to the Mexican Republic, retaining the property which they possess in the said territories, or disposing thereof, and removing the proceeds wherever they please; without their being subjected, on this account, to any contribution, tax or charge whatever.

Those who shall prefer to remain in the said territories, may either retain the title and rights of Mexican citizens, or acquire those of citizens of the United States. But they shall be under the obligation to make their election within one year from the date of the exchange of ratifications of this treaty: and those who shall remain in the said territories, after the expiration of that year, without having declared their intention to retain the character of Mexicans, shall be considered to have elected to become citizens of the United States.

In the said territories, property of every kind, now belonging to Mexicans, not established there, shall be inviolably respected. The present owners, the heirs of these, and all Mexicans who may hereafter acquire said property by contract, shall enjoy with respect to it, guaranties equally ample as if the same belonged to citizens of the United States.

ARTICLE IX.

The Mexicans who, in the territories aforesaid, shall not preserve the character of citizens of the Mexican Republic, conformably with what is stipulated in the preceding article, shall be incorporated into the Union of the United States and be admitted, at the proper time (to be judged of by the Congress of the United States) to the enjoyment of all the rights of citizens of the United States according to the principles of the Constitution; and in the mean time shall be maintained and protected in the free enjoyment of their liberty and property, and secured in the free exercise of their religion without restriction.

[One of the amendments of the U.S. Senate struck out Article X.]

ARTICLE XI.

Considering that a great part of the territories which, by the present Treaty, are to be comprehended for the future within the limits of the United States, is now occupied by savage tribes, who will hereafter be under the exclusive controul [sic] of the Government of the United States, and whose incursions within the territory of Mexico would be prejudicial in the extreme; it is solemnly agreed that all such incursions shall be forcibly restrained by the Government of the United States, whensoever this may be necessary; and that when they cannot be prevented, they shall be punished by the said Government, and satisfaction for the same shall be exacted: all in the same way, and with equal diligence and energy, as if the same incursions were meditated or committed within it's own territory against it's own citizens.

It shall not be lawful, under any pretext whatever, for any inhabitant of the United States, to purchase or acquire any Mexican or any foreigner residing in Mexico, who may have been captured by Indians inhabiting the territory of either of the two Republics, nor to purchase or acquire horses, mules, cattle or property of any kind, stolen within Mexican territory by such Indians.

And, in the event of any person or persons, captured within Mexican Territory by Indians, being carried into the territory of the United States, the Government of the latter engages and binds itself in the most solemn manner, so soon as it shall know of such captives being within it's territory, and shall be able so to do, through the faithful exercise of it's influence and power, to rescue them and return them to their country, or deliver them to the agent or representative of the Mexican Government. The Mexican Authorities will, as far as practicable, give to the Government of the United States notice of such captures; and it's agent shall pay the expenses incurred in the maintenance and transmission of the rescued captives; who, in the mean time, shall be treated with the utmost hospitality by the American authorities at the place where they may be. But if the Government of the United States, before receiving such notice from Mexico, should obtain intelligence through any other channel, of the existence of Mexican captives within it's territory, it will proceed forthwith to effect their release and delivery to the Mexican agent, as above stipulated.

For the purpose of giving to these stipulations the fullest possible efficacy, thereby affording the security and redress demanded by their true spirit and intent, the Government of the United States will now and hereafter pass, without unnecessary delay, and always vigilantly enforce, such laws as the nature of the subject may require. And finally, the sacredness of this obligation shall never be lost sight of by the said Government, when providing for the removal of the Indians from any portion of the said territories, or for it's being settled by citizens of the United States; but on the contrary special care shall then be taken not to place it's Indian occupants under the necessity of seeking new homes, by committing those invasions which the United States have solemnly obliged themselves to restrain.

ARTICLE XII.

In consideration of the extension acquired by the boundaries of the United States, as defined in the fifth Article of the present Treaty, the Government of the United States engages to pay to that of the Mexican Republic the sum of fifteen Millions of Dollars.

Immediately after this treaty shall have been duly ratified by the Government of the Mexican Republic, the sum of three millions of dollars shall be paid to the said Government by that of the United States at the city of Mexico, in the gold or silver coin of Mexico. The remaining twelve millions of dollars shall be paid at the same place and in the same coin, in annual instalments of three millions of dollars each, together with interest on the same at the rate of six per centum per annum. This interest shall begin to run upon the whole sum of twelve millions, from the day of the ratification of the present treaty by the Mexican Government, and the first of the instalments shall be paid at the expiration of one year from the same day. Together with each annual instalment, as it falls due, the whole interest accruing on such instalment from the beginning shall also be paid.

ARTICLE XIII.

The United States engage moreover, to assume and pay to the claimants all the amounts now due them, and those hereafter to become due, by reason of the claims already liquidated and decided against the Mexican Republic, under the conventions between the two Republics severally concluded on the eleventh day of April eighteen hundred and thirty-nine, and on the thirtieth day of January eighteen hundred and forty three: so that the Mexican Republic shall be absolutely exempt for the future, from all expense whatever on account of the said claims.

ARTICLE XIV.

The United States do furthermore discharge the Mexican Republic from all claims of citizens of the United States, not heretofore decided against the Mexican Government, which may have arisen previously to the date of the signature of this treaty: which discharge shall be final and perpetual, whether the said claims be rejected or be allowed by the Board of Commissioners provided for in the following Article, and whatever shall be the total amount of those allowed.

ARTICLE XV.

The United States, exonerating Mexico from all demands on account of the claims of their citizens mentioned in the preceding Article, and considering them entirely and forever cancelled, whatever their amount may be, undertake to make satisfaction for the same, to an amount not exceeding three and one quarter millions of Dollars. To ascertain the validity and amount of those claims, a Board of Commissioners shall be established by the Government of the United States, whose awards shall be final and conclusive: provided that in deciding upon the validity of each claim, the board shall be guided and governed by the principles and rules of decision prescribed by the first and fifth Articles of the unratified convention, concluded at the City of Mexico on the twentieth day of November, one thousand eight hundred and forty-three; and in no case shall an award be made in favour of any claim not embraced by these principles and rules.

If, in the opinion of the said Board of Commissioners, or of the claimants, any books, records or documents in the possession or power of the Government of the Mexican Republic, shall be deemed necessary to the just decision of any claim, the Commissioners or the claimants, through them, shall, within such period as Congress may designate, make an application in writing for the same, addressed to the Mexican Minister for Foreign Affairs, to be transmitted by the Secretary of State of the United States; and the Mexican Government engages, at the earliest possible moment after the receipt of such demand, to cause any of the books, records or documents, so specified, which shall be in their possession or power, (or authenticated Copies or extracts of the same) to be transmitted to the said Secretary of State, who shall immediately deliver them over to the said Board of Commissioners: provided that no such application shall be made, by, or at the instance of, any claimant, until the facts which it is expected to prove by such books, records or documents, shall have been stated under oath or affirmation.

ARTICLE XVI.

Each of the contracting parties reserves to itself the entire right to fortify whatever point within it's territory, it may judge proper so to fortify, for it's security.

ARTICLE XVII.

The Treaty of Amity, Commerce and Navigation, concluded at the city of Mexico on the fifth day of April A.D. 1831, between the United States of America and the United Mexican States, except the additional Article, and except so far as the stipulations of the said treaty may be incompatible with any stipulation contained in the present treaty, is hereby revived for the period of eight years from the day of the exchange of ratifications of this treaty, with the same force and virtue as if incorporated therein; it being understood that each of the contracting parties reserves to itself the right, at any time after the said period of eight years shall have expired, to terminate the same by giving one year's notice of such intention to the other party.

ARTICLE XVIII.

All supplies whatever for troops of the United States in Mexico, arriving at ports in the occupation of such troops, previous to the final evacuation thereof, although subsequently to the restoration of the Custom Houses at such ports, shall be entirely exempt from duties and charges of any kind: the Government of the United States hereby engaging and pledging it's faith to establish, and vigilantly to enforce, all possible guards for securing the revenue of Mexico, by preventing the importation, under cover of this stipulation, of any articles, other than such, both in kind and in quantity, as shall really be wanted for the use and consumption of the forces of the United States during the time they may remain in Mexico. To this end, it shall be the duty of all officers and agents of the United States to denounce to the Mexican Authorities at the respective ports, any attempts at a fraudulent abuse of this stipulation, which they may know of or may have reason to suspect, and to give to such authorities all the aid in their power with regard thereto: and every such attempt, when duly proved and established by sentence of a competent tribunal, shall be punished by the confiscation of the property so attempted to be fraudulently introduced.

ARTICLE XIX.

With respect to all merchandise, effects and property whatsoever, imported into ports of Mexico whilst in the occupation of the forces of the United States, whether by citizens of either republic, or by citizens or subjects of any neutral nation, the following rules shall be observed:

I. All such merchandise, effects and property, if imported previously to the restoration of the Custom Houses to the Mexican Authorities, as stipulated for in the third Article of this treaty, shall be exempt from confiscation, although the importation of the same be prohibited by the Mexican tariff.

II. The same perfect exemption shall be enjoyed by all such merchandise, effects and property, imported subsequently to the restoration of the Custom Houses, and previously to the sixty days fixed in the following Article for the coming into force of the Mexican tariff at such ports respectively: the said merchandise, effects and property being, however, at the time of their importation, subject to the payment of duties, as provided for in the said following Article.

III. All merchandise, effects and property described in the two rules foregoing, shall, during their continuance at the place of importation, or upon their leaving such place for the interior, be exempt from all duty, tax or impost of every kind, under whatsoever title or denomination. Nor shall they be there subjected to any charge whatsoever upon the sale thereof.

IV. All merchandise, effects and property, described in the first and second rules, which shall have been removed to any place in the interior, whilst such place was in the occupation of the forces of the United States, shall, during their continuance therein, be exempt from all tax upon the sale or consumption thereof, and from every kind of impost or contribution, under whatsoever title or denomination.

V. But if any merchandise, effects or property, described in the first and second rules, shall be removed to any place not occupied at the time by the forces of the United States, they shall, upon their introduction into such place, or upon their sale or consumption there, be subject to the same duties, which, under the Mexican laws, they would be required to pay in such cases, if they had been imported in time of peace through the Maritime Custom Houses, and had there paid the duties conformably with the Mexican tariff.

VI. The owners of all merchandise, effects or property, described in the first and second rules, and existing in any port of Mexico, shall have the right to reship the same, exempt from all tax, impost or contribution whatever.

With respect to the metals, or other property exported from any Mexican port, whilst in the occupation of the forces of the United States, and previously to the restoration of the Custom House at such port, no person shall be required by the Mexican Authorities, whether General or State, to pay any tax, duty or contribution upon any such exportation, or in any manner to account for the same to the said Authorities.

Article XX.

Through consideration for the interests of commerce generally, it is agreed, that if less than sixty days should elapse between the date of the signature of this treaty and the restoration of the Custom Houses, conformably with the stipulation in the third Article, in such case, all merchandise, effects and property whatsoever, arriving at the Mexican ports after the restoration of the said Custom Houses, and previously to the expiration of sixty days after the day of the signature of this treaty, shall be admitted to entry; and no other duties shall be levied thereon than the duties established by the tariff found in force at such Custom Houses, at the time of the restoration of the same. And to all such merchandise, effects and property, the rules established by the preceding Article shall apply.

Article XXI.

If unhappily any disagreement should hereafter arise between the Governments of the two Republics, whether with respect to the interpretation of any stipulation in this treaty, or with respect to any other particular concerning the political or commercial relations of the two Nations, the said Governments, in the name of those Nations, do promise to each other, that they will endeavour in the most sincere and earnest manner, to settle the differences so arising, and to preserve the state of peace and friendship, in which the two countries are now placing themselves: using, for this end, mutual representations and pacific negotiations. And, if by these means, they should not be enabled to come to an agreement, a resort shall not, on this account, be had to reprisals, aggression or hostility of any kind, by the one Republic against the other, until the Government of that which deems itself aggrieved, shall have maturely considered, in the spirit

of peace and good neighbourship, whether it would not be better that such difference should be settled by the arbitration of Commissioners appointed on each side, or by that of a friendly nation. And should such course be proposed by either party, it shall be acceded to by the other, unless deemed by it altogether incompatible with the nature of the difference, or the circumstances of the case.

Article XXII.

If (which is not to be expected, and which God forbid!) war should unhappily break out between the two Republics, they do now, with a view to such calamity, solemnly pledge themselves to each other and to the world, to observe the following rules: absolutely, where the nature of the subject permits, and as closely as possible in all cases where such absolute observance shall be impossible.

I. The merchants of either Republic, then residing in the other, shall be allowed to remain twelve months (for those dwelling in the interior) and six months (for those dwelling at the sea-ports) to collect their debts and settle their affairs; during which periods, they shall enjoy the same protection, and be on the same footing, in all respects, as the citizens or subjects of the most friendly nations; and, at the expiration thereof, or at any time before, they shall have full liberty to depart, carrying off all their effects, without molestation or hindrance: conforming therein to the same laws, which the citizens or subjects of the most friendly nations are required to conform to. Upon the entrance of the armies of either nation into the territories of the other, women and children, ecclesiastics, scholars of every faculty, cultivators of the earth, merchants, artizans, manufacturers and fishermen, unarmed and inhabiting unfortified towns, villages or places, and in general all persons whose occupations are for the common subsistence and benefit of mankind, shall be allowed to continue their respective employments, unmolested in their persons. Nor shall their houses or goods be burnt or otherwise destroyed: nor their cattle taken, nor, their fields wasted, by the armed force, into whose power, by the events of war, they may happen to fall; but if the necessity arise to take any thing from them for the use of such armed force, the same shall be paid for at an equitable price. All churches, hospitals, schools, colleges, libraries and other establishments for charitable and beneficent purposes, shall be respected, and all persons connected with the same protected in the discharge of their duties and the pursuit of their vocations.

II. In order that the fate of prisoners of war may be alleviated, all such practices as those of sending them into distant, inclement or unwholesome districts, or crowding them into close and noxious places, shall be studiously avoided. They shall not be confined in dungeons, prison-ships or prisons; nor be put in irons, or bound, or otherwise restrained in the use of their limbs. The officers shall enjoy liberty on their paroles, within convenient districts, and have comfortable quarters; and the common soldiers shall be disposed in cantonments, open and extensive enough for air and exercise, and lodged in barracks as roomy and good as are provided by the party in whose power they are for it's own troops. But if any officer shall break his parole by leaving the district so assigned him, or any other prisoner shall escape from the limits of his cantonment, after they shall have been designated to him, such individual, officer, or other prisoner shall forfeit so much of the benefit of this Article as provides for his liberty on parole or in cantonment. And if an officer so breaking his parole, or any common soldier so escaping from the limits assigned him, shall afterwards be found in arms, previously to his being regularly exchanged, the person so offending shall be dealt with according to the established laws of war. The officers shall be daily furnished by the party in whose power they are, with as many rations, and of the same articles as are allowed either in kind or by commutation, to officers of equal rank in it's own army; and all others shall be daily furnished with such ration as is allowed to a common soldier in it's own service: the value of all which supplies shall, at the close of the war, or at periods to be agreed upon between the respective commanders, be paid by the other party, on a mutual adjustment of accounts for the subsistence of prisoners; and such accounts shall not be mingled with or set off against any others, nor the balance due on them be withheld, as a compensation or reprisal for any cause whatever, real or pretended. Each party shall be allowed to keep a Commissary of prisoners, appointed by itself, with every cantonment of prisoners, in possession of the other; which Commissary shall see the prisoners as often as he pleases; shall be allowed to receive, exempt from all duties or taxes, and to distribute whatever comforts may be sent to them by their friends; and shall be free to transmit his reports in open letters to the party by whom he is employed.

And it is declared that neither the pretence that war dissolves all treaties, nor any other whatever, shall be considered as annulling or suspending the solemn covenant contained in this Article. On the contrary the state of war is precisely that for which it is provided; and during which it's stipulations are to be as sacredly observed as the most acknowledged obligations under the law of nature or nations.

ARTICLE XXIII.

This Treaty shall be ratified by the President of the United States of America, by and with the advice and consent of the Senate thereof; and by the President of the Mexican Republic, with the previous approbation of it's General Congress: and the ratifications shall be exchanged in the city of Washington or at the seat of government of Mexico, in four months from the date of the signature hereof, or sooner if practicable.

In faith whereof, we, the respective Plenipotentiaries, have signed this Treaty of Peace, Friendship, Limits and Settlement, and have hereunto affixed our seals respectively. Done in Quintuplicate at the city of Guadalupe Hidalgo on the second day of February in the Year of Our Lord one thousand eight hundred and forty eight.

N. P. TRIST. [Seal]
LUIS G. CUEVAS [Seal]
BERNARDO COUTO [Seal]
MIGˡ ATRISTAIN [Seal]

U.S. Senate Amendments

The U.S. Senate amended Articles III, IX, XI, XII, and XXIII and ratified the treaty on 10 March 1848. The treaty as amended was ratified by the Mexican government on 30 May 1848.

The opening sentences of Article III were amended to make the exchange of ratifications and not simply the ratifications themselves a precondition for ordering the removal of U.S. blockades of Mexican ports and the withdrawal of U.S. troops. In fact, the Mexican ratification and the formal exchange occurred on the same day.

The original Article IX was replaced with a longer text adapted, as the first paragraph of the original had been, from Article III of the Treaty for the Cession of Louisiana. The final text read

ARTICLE IX.

The Mexicans who, in the territories aforesaid, shall not preserve the character of citizens of the Mexican Republic, conformably with what is stipulated in the preceding Article, shall be incorporated into the Union of the United States, and admitted as soon as possible, according to the principles of the Federal Constitution, to the enjoyment of all the rights of citizens of the United States. In the mean time, they shall be maintained and protected in the enjoyment of their liberty, their property, and the civil rights now vested in them according to the Mexican laws. With respect to political rights, their condition shall be on an equality with that of the inhabitants of the other territories of the United States; and at least equally good as that of the inhabitants of Louisiana and the Floridas, when these provinces, by transfer from the French Republic and the Crown of Spain, became territories of the United States.

The same most ample guaranty shall be enjoyed by all ecclesiastics and religious corporations or communities, as well in the discharge of the offices of their ministry, as in the enjoyment of their property of every kind, whether individual or corporate. This guaranty shall embrace all temples, houses and edifices dedicated to the Roman Catholic worship; as well as all property destined to it's support, or to that of schools, hospitals and other foundations for charitable or beneficent purposes. No property of this nature shall be considered as having become the property of the American Government, or as subject to be, by it, disposed of or diverted to other uses.

Finally, the relations and communication between the Catholics living in the territories aforesaid, and their respective ecclesiastical authorities, shall be open, free and exempt from all hindrance whatever, even although such authorities should reside within the limits of the Mexican Republic, as defined by this treaty; and this freedom shall continue, so long as a new demarcation of ecclesiastical districts shall not have been made, conformably with the laws of the Roman Catholic Church.

The U.S. Senate struck Article X completely from the treaty. It read

ARTICLE X.

All grants of land made by the Mexican Government or by the competent authorities, in territories previously appertaining to Mexico, and remaining for the future within the limits of the United States, shall be respected as valid, to the same extent that the same grants would be valid, if the said territories had remained within the limits of Mexico. But the grantees of lands in Texas, put in possession thereof, who, by reason of the circumstances of the country since the beginning of the troubles between Texas and the Mexican Government, may have been prevented from fulfilling all the conditions of their grants, shall be under the obligation to fulfill the said conditions within the periods limited in the same respectively; such periods to be now counted from the date of the exchange of ratifications of this treaty: in default of which the said grants shall not be obligatory upon the State of Texas, in virtue of the stipulations contained in this Article.

The foregoing stipulation in regard to grantees of land in Texas, is extended to all grantees of land in the territories aforesaid, elsewhere than in Texas, put in possession under such grants; and, in default of the fulfilment of the conditions of any such grant, within the new period, which, as is above stipulated, begins with the day of the exchange of ratifications of this treaty, the same shall be null and void.

The Mexican Government declares that no grant whatever of lands in Texas has been made since the second day of March one thousand eight hundred and thirty six; and that no grant whatever of lands in any of the territories aforesaid has been made since the thirteenth day of May one thousand eight hundred and forty-six.

The U.S. Senate removed from the end of the second paragraph of Article XI the following phrase, "nor to provide

such Indians with fire-arms or ammunition by sale or otherwise" thus retaining the right of the United States to arm nomadic tribes living within its borders, even if such arms were used on raids into Mexico.

Article XII was cut substantially; the excised text appears below in italics.

ARTICLE XII.

In consideration of the extension acquired by the boundaries of the United States, as defined in the fifth Article of the present Treaty, the Government of the United States engages to pay to that of the Mexican Republic the sum of fifteen Millions of Dollars, *in the one or the other of the two modes below specified. The Mexican Government shall, at the time of ratifying this treaty, declare which of these two modes of payment it prefers; and the mode so elected by it shall be conformed to by that of the United States.*

First mode of payment: Immediately after this treaty shall have been duly ratified by the Government of the Mexican Republic, the sum of three Millions of Dollars shall be paid to the said Government by that of the United States at the city of Mexico, in the gold or silver coin of Mexico. For the remaining twelve millions of dollars, the United States shall create a stock, bearing an interest of six per centum per annum, commencing on the day of the ratification of this Treaty by the Government of the Mexican Republic, and payable annually at the city of Washington: the principal of said stock to be redeemable there, at the pleasure of the Government of the United States, at any time after two years from the exchange of ratifications of this treaty; six months public notice of the intention to redeem the same being previously given. Certificates of such stock, in proper form, for such sums as shall be specified by the Mexican Government, and transferable by the said Government, shall be delivered to the same by that of the United States.

Second mode of payment: Immediately after this treaty shall have been duly ratified by the Government of the Mexican Republic, the sum of three millions of dollars shall be paid to the said Government by that of the United States at the city of Mexico, in the gold or silver coin of Mexico. The remaining twelve millions of dollars shall be paid at the same place and in the same coin, in annual instalments of three millions of dollars each, together with interest on the same at the rate of six per centum per annum. This interest shall begin to run upon the whole sum of twelve millions, from the day of the ratification of the present treaty by the Mexican Government, and the first of the instalments shall be paid at the expiration of one year from the same day. Together with each annual instalment, as it falls due, the whole interest accruing on such instalment from the beginning shall also be paid. *Certificates in proper form, for the said instalments respectively, in such sums as shall be desired by the*

Mexican Government, and transferable by it, shall be delivered to the said Government by that of the United States.

The U.S. Senate amended Article XXIII to allow the exchange of ratifications to take place not only at Washington, D.C., but also "at the seat of Government of Mexico," which is where the exchange took place.

The original treaty also included an additional and secret article which was not ratified by the U.S. Senate or by the government of Mexico, extending the deadline for the exchange of ratifications from four months to eight months after the original signing. The article was rendered unnecessary by the U.S. Senate's amendment of Article XXIII permitting the exchange to take place in Mexico.

Additional and Secret Article

Of the Treaty of Peace, Friendship, Limits and Settlement between the United States of America and the Mexican Republic, signed this day by their respective Plenipotentiaries.

In view of the possibility that the exchange of the ratifications of this treaty may, by the circumstances in which the Mexican Republic is placed, be delayed longer than the term of four months fixed by it's twenty-third Article for the exchange of ratifications of the same; it is hereby agreed that such delay shall not, in any manner, affect the force and validity of this Treaty, unless it should exceed the term of eight months, counted from the date of the signature thereof.

This Article is to have the same force and virtue as if inserted in the treaty to which it is an Addition.

In faith whereof, we, the respective Plenipotentiaries have signed this Additional and Secret Article, and have hereunto affixed our seals respectively. Done in Quintuplicate at the City of Guadalupe Hidalgo on the second day of February, in the year of Our Lord one thousand eight hundred and forty-eight.

> N. P. Trist. [Seal]
> Luis G. Cuevas [Seal]
> Bernardo Couto [Seal]
> Mig.ᴵ Atristain [Seal]

On 26 May 1848, the day following the ratification of the amended treaty by the Mexican senate, U.S. commissioners Nathan Clifford and Ambrose Sevier explained to the Mexican government the intent of the U.S. Senate's amendments. Mexican minister of foreign relations Luis Rosa suggested the commissioners form these explanations into a document, which was later called the Protocol of Querétaro.

PROTOCOL OF QUERÉTARO

In the city of Queretaro on the twenty sixth of the month of May eighteen hundred and forty-eight at a conference between Their Excellencies Nathan Clifford and Ambrose H. Sevier Commissioners of the United States of America, with full powers from their Government to make to the Mexican Republic suitable explanations in regard to the amendments which the Senate and Government of the said United States have made in the treaty of peace, friendship, limits and definitive settlement between the two Republics, signed in Guadalupe Hidalgo, on the second day of February of the present year, and His Excellency Don Luis de la Rosa, Minister of Foreign Affairs of the Republic of Mexico, it was agreed, after adequate conversation respecting the changes alluded to, to record in the present protocol the following explanations which Their aforesaid Excellencies the Commissioners gave in the name of their Government and in fulfillment of the Commission conferred upon them near the Mexican Republic.

First.

The american [sic] Government by suppressing the IXᵗʰ article of the Treaty of Guadalupe and substituting the III. article of the Treaty of Louisiana did not intend to diminish in any way what was agreed upon by the aforesaid article IXᵗʰ in favor of the inhabitants of the territories ceded by Mexico. Its understanding that all of that agreement is contained in the IIIᵈ article of the Treaty of Louisiana. In consequence, all the privileges and guarantees, civil, political and religious, which would have been possessed by the inhabitants of the ceded territories, if the IXᵗʰ article of the Treaty had been retained, will be enjoyed by them without any difference under the article which has been substituted.

Second.

The American Government by suppressing the Xᵗʰ article of the Treaty of Guadalupe did not in any way intend to annul the grants of lands made by Mexico in the ceded territories. These grants, notwithstanding the suppression of the article of the Treaty, preserve the legal value which they may possess; and the grantees may cause their legitimate titles to be acknowledged before the american tribunals.

Conformably to the law of the United-States, legitimate titles to every description of property personal and real, existing in the ceded territories, are those which were legitimate titles under the Mexican law in California and New-Mexico up to the 13ᵗʰ of May 1.846, and in Texas up to the 2ᵈ March 1.836.

Third.

The Government of the United States by suppressing the concluding paragraph of article XIIᵗʰ of the Treaty, did not intend to deprive the Mexican Republic of the free and unrestrained faculty of ceding, conveying or transferring at any time (as it may judge best) the sum of the twelfe [sic] millions of dollars which the same Government of the United-States is to deliver in the places designated by the amended article.

And these explanations having been accepted by the Minister of Foreign Affairs of the Mexican Republic, he declared in name of his Government that with the understanding conveyed by them, the same Government would proceed to ratify the Treaty of Guadalupe as modified by the Senate and Government of the United States. In testimony of which their Excellencies the aforesaid Commissioners and the Minister

have signed and sealed in quintuplicate the present protocol.

[Seal] A. H. SEVIER.
[Seal] NATHAN CLIFFORD
[Seal] LUIS DE LA ROSA

SOURCE: Hunter Miller, ed., *Treaties and Other International Acts of the United States of America,* vol. 5 (Washington, D.C.: U.S. Government Printing Office, 1937).

Outline of Contents

This outline provides a general overview of the conceptual scheme of this work. The outline is divided into six major parts, as follows:

I. Peoples of the Region

African Americans
Apaches
    Chiricahua Apaches
    Gileño and Mimbreño Apaches
    Lipan Apaches
    Mescalero Apaches
Border Cultures
Caddo Indians
Californios
Castes
Cherokees
Class Structure in Mexico
Comanches
Immigration
    Immigration to California
    Immigration to Texas

Immigration to New Mexico
Indian Policy
    Mexican Policy
    Texan Policy
    U.S. Policy
Indians
    Overview
    Indian Raids
Léperos
Nuevo Mexicanos
Peonage
Pueblo Indians
Racism
Tejanos
Texas–Comanche Relations
Women
    Women in Mexico
    Women in the United States

II. The Land

Overview Articles
Agriculture
Borderlands
Boundary Commissions
Boundary Disputes
Cartography
Empresarios
Geography and Climate
Land Grants
Land Speculation
Thorns, Horns, and Stingers

Regions and Countries
France
Great Britain
Mexico, 1821–1854
Spain
Texas
    Overview
    Nationalism in Texas
Trans-Nueces

United States, 1821–1854
    A Romantic Nationalism
    Sectionalism

States, Provinces, and Territories
Arizona
Baja California
California
    Overview
Chihuahua, State of
Coahuila y Texas
Cuba
Durango, State of
Gadsden Purchase
Louisiana Purchase
Mexican Cession
New Mexico
    Overview
Nuevo León
Oregon Territory
Puebla
    State of Puebla
San Luis Potosí
    State of San Luis Potosí
Sonora y Sinaloa
Tamaulipas
Territories
    Mexican Territories
    U.S. Territories
Texas
    Annexation of Texas
Utah

Cities and Other Places
Brazos Santiago
Camargo
Cerralvo
China
Corpus Christi
Fort Texas
Jalapa
Laredo and Nuevo Laredo

IV. Military History

Overview Articles

Army Life
   Life in the Mexican Army
   Life in the U.S. Army
Atrocities
Bomb Brigs
Camp Followers
   Mexican Camp Followers
   U.S. Camp Followers
Civil War Generals
Colt Revolver
Deserters
Foraging
Forts
Guerrillas
Military Colonies, Mexican
Mississippi Rifle
Naval Blockade
Numbers and Losses
Occupation of Mexico
Patronage in the U.S. Military
Presidios
Prisoners of War
   Mexican Prisoners
   Texan Prisoners
   U.S. Prisoners
Privateers
Soldaderas
Supplies
   Mexican Supplies
   U.S. Supplies
Tactics
   Mexican Tactics
   U.S. Tactics
Texas
   Conflicts with Mexico, 1836–1845
Uniforms
   Mexican Uniforms
   U.S. Uniforms
Weapons
   Weapons Technology
   Coastal and Naval Weapons
   Field Artillery
   Small Arms

Mexican, Texan, and U.S. Military Organization

Army, Mexican
   Overview
   Organization of the Mexican Army
   Postwar Reforms
Army, Texas

Army, U.S.
   Organization
   Army of Observation and
      Occupation
   Army of the West
Marines, U.S.
Military Academy, Mexican
Military Academy, United States
Military Contractors, U.S.
Militia, Mexican Civic
Militia, U.S.
Navy, Mexican
Navy, Texan
Navy, U.S.
Recruitment
   Mexican Recruitment
   U.S. Army Recruitment
Volunteers
   U.S. Volunteers

Military Units

Flying Artillery
Lancers
Mexican Spy Company
Mormon Battalion
Mounted Rifles, U.S.
San Patricio Battalion
Texas Rangers
Topographical Engineers
Traders Battalion
Voltigeurs and Foot Riflemen, U.S.
Volunteers
   Remustered Volunteers

Campaigns and Expeditions

Alvarado Expedition
Ayutla Revolution
Bear Flag Revolt
California
   U.S. Occupation
Córdova Rebellion
Doniphan's March
Fredonia Rebellion
Huasteca Revolts
Huejutla Expedition
Lower California Campaign
Mexico City Campaign
   The March to Mexico City
   Assault on Mexico City
   Defending the Road to Mexico
Mier Expedition
Monterey, California
   Monterey Incident of 1842

New Mexico
   Revolt of 1837
   U.S. Occupation
Pastry War of 1838
Polkos Revolt
Río Grande, Republic of the
Río Grande Campaign
Santa Fe
   Santa Fe Expedition
Sierra Gorda Revolt
Sierra Madre, Republic of the
Snively Expedition
Somervell Expedition
Sonora Revolt of 1837
Tabasco River Expedition
Tampico Expedition
Taos Revolt
Texas Revolts of 1832
Texas Revolution
   Causes of the Revolution
   Course of the Revolution
Vasquez Expedition
Vera Cruz Campaign
Woll's Expedition
Wool's March
Yucatecan Revolt
Zacatecas

Battles

Alamo
Béxar, Siege of
Brazito, Battle of
Buena Vista, Battle of
Cañoncito, Battle of
Cerro Gordo, Battle of
Chapultepec, Battle of
Coleto Creek, Battle of
Contreras and Churubusco
Encarnación, Hacienda de
Fort Texas, Siege of
Huamantla, Battle of
La Mesa, Battle of
Molino del Rey, Battle of
Monterrey, Mexico, Battle of
Mulegé, Battle of
Palo Alto, Battle of
Puebla
   Siege of Puebla
Resaca de la Palma, Battle of
Sacramento, Battle of
San Jacinto, Battle of
San José, Siege of
San Pasqual
Santa Cruz de Rosales, Battle of

INDEX

Note: Page numbers in **boldface** indicate main article on subject. Page numbers in *italics* indicate illustrations or maps.

Hidalgo Battalion, National Guard, 91, 111

Hill, D. H., 321

Hill, Stephen G., 30

Hilsabeck, Carter L., 469

Historia de las relaciones entre México y los Estados Unidos, 1819–1848 (Bosch García), 196

Historia de las relaciones entre México y los Estados Unidos de América (Zorrilla), 196

Historia de Méjico (Alamán y Escalada), 6

Historia general de México (anthology), 196

Historiography, **193–197**
  American, 31, 38, 194–195, 212, 215, 332, 389
  assessment of Santa Anna, 377
  focus on human nature and morale, 351
  Magoffin (Susan) eyewitness accounts, 234
  Mexican, 6, 47, 64, 153, 195–196, 276, 431

History of the Conquest of Mexico (Prescott), 228, 332

History of the United States from the Discovery of the American Continent (Bancroft), 38

Hitchcock, Ethan Allen, 147, 245, 406

Hoffman, Charles Fenno, 229

Hoffman, Willam, 57

Hois Comanches. *See* Penateka Comanches

Holley, Myron, 227

Home Squadron, U.S.
  bomb brigs, 47
  Brazos Santiagos, 57
  Conner command, 107, 361
  Gulf Coast blockade, 236–237, 283–285
  Marine Corps companion operations, 236
  Perry (Matthew C.) command, 318, 397, 460
  steamships, 393
  Tabasco River Expedition, 397
  Tampico occupation, 402

Homestead Act, Texas (1838), 218

Hondo River, 241, 415

Honduras, 99, 152, 469

Hooker, Joseph, 35

Hopi Indians, 344

Hopping, Enos D., 25, 409

Horned toads, 429

Horse artillery. *See* Flying artillery

Hospitals, 191

Hot region, Mexico, 283

House of Representatives, U.S.
  abolitionists, 177
  Adams, John Quincy, 2–3
  Ashmun Amendment passage, 31
  Calhoun, John C., 69
  Clay as Speaker, 98
  contested 1824 presidential election decision, 137

Crockett, David, 119

Free-Soil Party memebers, 166

Giddings, Joshua, 177

Immortal Fourteen, 203

Lincoln's "Spot Resolutions," 106, 341, 393

members from Texas, 41, 105

Polk as Speaker, 327

Texas annexation opposition, 178

Texas annexation resolution, 43, 443

Whig-backed resolution against U.S.-Mexican War, 478

Whig majority coalition with dissident Democrats, 106

Wilmot Proviso passage, 106, 387, 479

Houston, Sam, **197–198**, 210
  Alamo plan, 7
  British relations, 143
  Cherokee ties, 114, 197, 204
  Córdova Rebellion policy, 114, 363
  Democratic presidential nomination bid, 364
  Flacco relations, 156
  Indian accomodation and treaties, 204, 205, 413, 417, 418
  Johnston animosity, 212
  Jordan attack on, 213
  Knights of the Golden Circle relationship, 216
  Lamar policy disagreements, 218, 413
  Mexican accomodation by, 415
  Mexican protectorate proposal, 386
  Mexican surrender to, *422*
  as military hero, 452
  prosecution of Moore (Edwin Ward), 276, 287
  San Jacinto victory, 61, 197, 363, 369, 422, 427–428
  Santa Anna clemency rationale, 130, 436
  Somervell expedition authorization, 156, 192, 260, 391, 415
  Texas annexation advocacy, 197, 324, 413, 415
  Texas annexation negotiations, 197, 209, 443
  as Texas congressman, 105
  Texas flag design, 158
  and Texas independence, 53, 324
  as Texas military commander-in-chief, 23, 100, 286, 287, 425, 426–428
  Texas presidency, 62, 192, 212, 324, 325, 412–413, 490
  Texas presidential reelection, 218
  Texas Rangers, 189
  unionism, 198
  U.S.-Mexican War, 363
  Woll's Expedition reprisal, 480

Houston, Texas, 325

Howell, Varina, 123

Howitzer, 475

Huamantla, Battle of (1847), **198**
  Santa Anna defeat, 324

triggering U.S. retaliatory atrocities, 33, 198, 259, 350

Walker (Samuel W.) death at, 33, 102, 198, 259, 279, 468

Huasteca peasant militias, 371

Huasteca revolts (1846–1848), 193, **198–200**, *250*
  Mexican elites' interpretations of, 203–204

Hudson, Frederic, 183

Huejutla Expedition (1847), 173, **200**, 335

Hughes, George W., 259, 431

Hull, Joseph B., 231

Hunkers, 326

Hunter, Charles G., 11, 234, 286

Hunter, Maria, 234

Huntington Library (San Marino, California), 280

Hurly, A., 319

Hussars of the Guard of the Supreme Powers, 61
  Cerro Gordo battle, 89
  Churubusco battle, 111
  Mexico City defense, 258
  uniform, 446

Huston, Felix, **200**, 212

I

Ide, William B., 40, **201**

Iguanas, 429

Illinois
  Douglas, Stephen A., 135
  Lincoln as Whig U.S. representative, 393
  Shields, James, 384, 385
  volunteers, 89, 91, 292, 367, 379, 459, 465, 483

Illiteracy, 28, 109

Immigrant Soldier in the Mexican War, An (Miller), 195

Immigration to Arizona, 19, 48–49

Immigration to California, **201–202**
  Bear Flag Revolt, 167
  Frémont support, 166–167
  Larkin encouragement of, 223
  racism of U.S. settlers, 178
  Vallejo's warnings to Mexico on, 456

Immigration to Mexico, **202**

Immigration to New Mexico, **202**

Immigration to Texas
  Anglo-American conventions of 1832–1833, 113–114
  Anglo-Americans, 4–5, 50, 129, 144, 197, 261, 412, 414, 420–421, 885
  Fredonia Rebellion, 165–166
  Indians from United States, 204
  land headrights, 221
  Mexía policies, 244
  Mexican Law of April 6, 1830, curbing, 85, 125, 129, 421
  Mexican settlement program, 304, 420–421

Lamar, Mirabeau B. (*continued*)
  disbandment of regular army, 23
  Fisher appointment by, 156
  Laredo occupation, 223, 435
  military appointees, 242
  New Mexican foray, 32–33, 50, 242,
    325, 379, 413, 415, 463
  Texan army, 408
  Texan navy, 287
  Texas congressional opponents, 105
  Texas flag design, 158
  Texas presidency, 62, 106, 197, 324,
    415
  Texas Rangers, 189
  Yucatán rebellion aid, 131
Lamar, Rebecca Johnston, 242
La Mesa, Battle of (1847), 72, **218–219**,
  236
La Messila, 290
Lamy, Jean Baptiste, 238
Lancaster Company, 431
Lancers, 72, **219–220**, 309, 320, 371, 373,
  399, 474, 476
Land, William, 52
Land contractors. *See Empresarios*
Lander, Ernest McPherson, 195
Landero, Juan José, **220**, 276–277, 460
Land grants, **220–221**
  borderlands, 49
  California, 376
  empresarios, 50, 144, 221, 428
  Mexican military colonies, 263
  for Texan military service, 287
  Texas Constitution on, 110
  by Texas Republic, 105–106, 413
  Texas tories and, 428
  for U.S. army enlistment, 352
Lands, Indian
  Texas treaties, 204–205
  Treaty of 1832, 436
  U.S. means of acquisition, 147, 149,
    205–206
Land speculation, 54, 220–221, **221–222**
  Burnet holdings, 62
  Butler (Anthony W.) holdings, 64
  Maverick (Samuel) holdings, 240
  Seguín (Juan Nepomuceno) holdings,
    383
  in Texas, 54, 62, 220–221, 221–222,
    240, 421
Lane, Joseph, 189, **222**
  Huamantla battle, 198, 259
  National Road guerrilla resistance, 259
  Puebla occupation, 259, 350
  Puebla siege relief, 343
  rank and dates of appointment and
    commission, 25
  Texas Rangers command, 161, 259
  Walker (Samuel) service with, 468
Language. *See Slang*
"La Pasadita" (song), 281
La Patria (New Orleans Spanish-language
  newspaper), 294

La Paz, Baja California, 37, 176, 279, 369,
  469
La Razón (Mexican newspaper), 77
Laredo and Nuevo Laredo, **222–223**, 402
  sacking by Somervell forces, 391, 413,
    415
  Tejanos, 384, 408
  in Trans-Nueces, 434, 435
Laredo Guards, 218
Laredo Road, 426
Larkin, Thomas O., **223**
  Bear Flag Revolt policy, 41
  secret mission to promote Texas
    annexation, 146
  as U.S. consul in California, 168
  warnings about British interests in
    California, 86–87
La Rosita (Mexican privateer), 336, 392
Las Animas, Battle of (1847), 259
Las Cruces, New Mexico, 243
Las Vegas, Battle of (1847), 468
Las Vegas, New Mexico, 291
La Tenería, 272
Latin America
  as Knights of the Golden Circle target,
    215–216
  leaders' view of Cuba, 120
  Monroe Doctrine on, 451
  U.S. filibustering expeditions, 152
  See also specific countries
Latter-day Saints. *See* Mormon Battalion;
  Mormonism
Laudanum, 191
Laura (Texian ship), 286
Lava field. *See* Pedregal lava field
La Vallette, Elie, 231
La Verdad (Spanish-English newspaper),
  88
La Voz del Pueblo (Mexican newspaper),
  293, 491
Law of April 6, 1830. *See* Decree of 1830
Law of January 1847, 214
Lawrenceburg, Tennese, 274
Laws of the Indies, 203
Lawson, Thomas, 16, 24, 191
Lays of the Palmetto (Simms), 229
Lea, Luke, 206
Leal, Manuel, 424
Lear, William W., 469
Lee, Elliott, 238
Lee, Robert E., 147, 216, 483
  Aztec Club membership, 34
  Cerro Gordo reconnaissance, 89
  Confederate Army commission, 95
  Contreras and Churubusco battles, 113
  engineering skills, 113, 256, 263
  march to Mexico City, 113, 256
Leftwich, Robert, 221
Legacy of the war in Mexico, **223–225**
Legacy of the war in the United States,
  225–226
Legends of Mexico: The Battle of Taylor
  (Lippard), 228

Le Moyne, Jean Baptiste, 292
Lemus, Pedro, 358
Léon, Alonso de, 99
León, Antonio, 56, 133, **226**, 268
Léperos, 82, 98, **226–227**
Lerdo de Tejada, Miguel, 227
Lerdo de Tejada, Sebastian, 116
Lerdo Law of 1856, 34, 227
Leroux, Antoine, 19
Letcher, Robert P., 181
"Letters of General Antonio López de
  Santa Anna Relating to the War
  between the United States and
  Mexico, 1846–1848 (Smith ed.), 389
Leutze, Emanuel, 31
Levy (*leva*). *See* Conscription
Lewis and Clark Expedition, 53
Lexington (U.S. ship), 231
Liberals, Mexican
  Álvarez, Juan, 12, 376
  Ayutla Revolution installing, 108
  Baz, Juan José, 39–40
  civic militia as bulwark, 265
  class system, 97
  congressional elections (1846), 104
  conservative view as foreign-influenced,
    107
  Constitution of 1824, 108–109
  Constitution of 1842, 109
  defeat of conservative-backed French
    Intervention, 224
  factional division over U.S. war, 324
  free trade policy, 433
  Indian policy, 203–204
  Juárez leadership, 214
  on lack of national unity, 85
  Lafragua policies, 217
  Lerdo de Tejada (Miguel) economic
    theory, 227
  moderados vs. *puros,* 104, 267, 324,
    344–345
  Mora, José María Luis, 276
  National Rite Masonic Order, 165
  peonage reform recommendations, 316
  postwar prescription for survival, 348,
    376
  press, 293–294
  radicals. *See Puros*
  reaction to proposed Sierra Madre
    republic, 386
  Rejón, Manuel Crescencio, 352
  response to U.S. expansionism, 86, 224,
    469
  Santa Anna defeats of, 373
  U.S.-Mexican War aims, 470–471
  view of United States, 337
  War of the Reform, 13
  York rite association, 166, 248
Libertad (Mexican national guard
  battalion), 350
Libertador Mexicano (Mexican ship), 285,
  286
Liberty (Texas ship), 287

Mounted Rifles, U.S., 198, **278–279**
Carson commission, 77
Cerro Gordo battle, 89
Chapultepec battle, 91
Colt revolver, 102
Contreras and Churubusco battles, 111
creation of, 24, 235, 278
Mexico City Campaign, 255, 258, 259
Mississippi rifle use, 266
Smith (Persifor F.) service, 389–390
Texas Rangers, 419
uniform, 278, 446
Vera Cruz campaign, 459
Walker (Samuel) service, 259, 279, 468
See also Voltigeurs and Foot Riflemen, U.S.
Mounted volunteer units, 466
Movement for the Acquisition of All of Mexico, The (Fuller), 194
Movimiento de la Acordada, 248
Moyano Pahissa, Angela, 196
Mr. Polk's Army: The American Military Experience in the Mexican War, The (Winders), 195
Mulegé, Battle of (1847), 37, **279**, *284*
Mules, 328, 394, 396, 432
Mumps, 190
Munford, Carlton R., 95
Munitions. *See* Artillery; Weapons; *specific kinds*
Munroe, John, 359
Murdock, Mrs. Moore, 461
Museums and archives, **279–280**
Music, Mexican, **280–281**
army band book, 28
Music, U.S., **281–282**
army musicians, 26
sheet music collection, 280, *282*
Musket balls, 476
Muskets, 399, 474, 476
drawbacks of, 400, 401
Músquiz, Ramón, 100
"Mustang" (pseud. of James L. Freaner), 165, 296, 473
Mustang (slang meaning), 386
Mutiny, 244

N

Nachitoches, Louisiana, 50
Nacogdoches
Córdova Rebellion, 114–115
creation as Mexican department, 99
Fredonia Rebellion, 165–166, 421
Spanish founding, 48
Tejano and Indian uprisings (1838–1839), 23, 204, 363, 413
Tejano disaffection, 408
Texas Revolts of 1832, 54, 125, 420, 428
Texas tories' loyalty to Mexico, 428
U.S. settlers, 62, 119, 165, 202

NAFTA. *See* North American Free Trade Agreement of 1993
Napoléon I, emperor of France, 164, 230, 410
Napoléon III, emperor of France, 164, 165, 252, 365, 367
Narbona, Miguel, 16
Narrative of the Texan Santa Fe Expedition (Kendall), 31, 215, 379
Nash, John H., 201
Nashville secession convention, 387
Natchez (ship), 179
Natchez Fencibles, 345
National anthem, Mexican, 281
National Archives and Records Administration, U.S., 279, 280
National Association of Veterans of the Mexican War, 315, 461
National Bridge, Battle of (1847), 259, *260*
National guard, Mexican, 22, 23, 104
Chapultepec battle, 91
Churubusco battle, 111
Vera Cruz defense, 459
National Highway 45, 380
Nationalism
American, 447–450, 487
Mexican, 224
Mexican *patria chica* hampering, 312–313
See also Patriotism
National Republican Party, 137–138
National Rite Masons, 166
National Road, Mexico, **283**, 342
guerrilla bands, 239, 258–259, 283, 371
intelligence-gathering for Scott, 244–245
map of topography, 255
march to Mexico City, 253–256, 258–259, 283, 324
Scott's march from Vera Cruz, 89
Scott's march into Vera Cruz, 461
terrain, 283
U.S. defense of, **258–259**, 278
Voltigeurs companies as escorts, 464
National Society of the Colonial Dames in the State of Texas, 275
Native Americans. *See* Indian policy *headings*; Indians; *specific groups*
Nativism, 140, 452
Naturalist records, 144, 191
Naturopathy, 191
Navajo Indians, 206, 289, 291, 292, 299
Naval Academy, U.S. (Annapolis), 38
Naval blockade, **283–285**
artist renderings, 31
Baja California, 37, 231
Guaymas, 19, *284*
Gulf Coast, 11, 47, 107, 236–237, 285, 288, 318, 402
of Matamoros, 287
Mexican public opinion, 338–339
of Tampico (1846), 402
Texas Revolution, 287

U.S. escort of Santa Anna through, 32, 459
U.S. Marine ships, 236
of Vera Cruz (1838–1839). *See* Pastry War of 1838
of Vera Cruz (1846), 10, 31, 285, 288, 457, *458*, 459
See also Privateers
Naval weapons, 47, 393, 397, 475
Navarro, José Antonio, 285, 335, 379, 426
N.A.V.M.W. *See* National Association of the Veterans of the Mexican War
Navy, Mexican, 189, 283, 285–286, 287
Navy, Texan, 189, 275–276, 286–287
Navy, U.S., **287–289**
African American service quota, 3
Alvarado expedition, 11
amphibious operation, 107, 236–237, 288–289, 381, 460
bomb brigs, 47
California presence, 168, 177; *See also* Pacific Squadron
Chase (Ann) espionage for, 93
Conner, David, 107
historiography, 194
infantry brigade, 440
Jones, Thomas ap Catesby, 212–213
Lower California campaign, 231
Mackenzie, Alexander Slidell, 233
map of land and sea battles (1846–1848), 284
Marines, 236–237
Moore, Edwin Ward, 275
Naval Academy founding, 38
"Peacemaker" cannon explosion disaster, 178, 393, 442
Perry, Matthew C., 317–318, 440–441
San José siege, 369
Sloat, John D., 389
steamships, 103, 361, 393
Stockton, Robert F., 393–394
Tabasco River Expedition, 288, 397–399
Tampico occupation, 91, 402
Texan naval commissions, 287
Tuxpan battle, 440–441
Vera Cruz landing, 459–460
weapons, 47, 393, 397, 475
Yucatecan ties, 411
See also Home Squadron, U.S.; Naval blockade
Nebel, Carl, 31, 210
Nednhis (Chiricahua Apache band), 15
Neill, James C., 7, 425, 435
Nepomuceno Seguín, Juan. *See* Seguín, Juan Nepomuceno
Netherlands, 131
Nettie Lee Benson Latin American Collection, 280
Neutrality
British, 183
Central American canal treaty, 99
U.S. violations, 129
Neutrality Act, U.S., 287, 350, 469

Prisoners of war, Texan, 125–126, **335**, 417
  Black Bean Episode, 33, 45, 261, 325, 413, 415
  Goliad massacre of, 100, 179
  Perote Castle as prison, 317
  Santa Anna's execution policy, 85
  Thompson (Waddy) diplomatic release efforts, 428
Prisoners of war, U.S., **335**
  Huejutla Expedition, 173, 200
  Perote Castle as prison, 317
Privateers, 285, 286, **335–336**, 392
Privileges. See Fueros
Procurement. See Supplies
Projectiles. See Artillery; Weapons
Pronunciamientos (barracks revolts), 21, 244
Propaganda, 13, 294; See also Public opinion
Property qualifications, Mexican political, 109, 250, 373
Property rights, 126, 438
  Catholic Church, 82, 84, 104
  See also Fueros
Prostitutio. See Camp followers
Protectionism. See Tariffs
Protestantism, **336–337**
  of Anglo-American settlers in Texas, 421
  fervor of U.S. evangelicalism, 83, 336, 353
  Manifest Destiny link, 234, 451
  Mexican public opinion, 339
  Puritanism, 234, 451, 452
  as U.S. national religion, 83, 451
  See also Mormonism; *other specific sects*
Protocol of Querétaro, 126, 438
Provincias Internas, 289, 392; See also Sonora y Sinaloa
Provisions. See Supplies
Prussia, 132, 188
Public debt. See Debt
Public opinion, **337–342**
  antiwar propaganda and, 13
  British on U.S. motives for war with Mexico, 183
  Mexican prewar sentiment, 85–86, **337–338**
  Mexican wartime perceptions, **338–339**
  mixed feelings on banditry, 39
  press effect on, 45, 293, 450
  U.S. political sentiment, 87, **341–342**
  U.S. popular sentiment, 45, 87, **337–341**, 353–354, 449–450, 451
Puebla, city of, **342**
  endemic diseases, 190, 191, 343
  National Road, 293, 342
  Scott encampment, 68, 258, 317, 342–343, 381, 396
  Scott intelligence network, 101
  Worth's martial law decree, 485
  Worth's troop installation, 31, 254, 342–343

See also Puebla, Siege of *listing below*
Puebla, Siege of (1847), **342–344**
  Huamantla battle, 198
  Lane regiment performance, 222, 259, 343
  map, 343
  Rea leadership, 259, 350
Puebla, State of, **342**
  dissatisfaction with Santa Anna, 375
  Gaona as commandant-general, 172
  Jarero as commandant-general, 211
  mestizos rebellions, 98, 199
  Mexican Spy Company, **244–245**, 343
  National Road, 283, 342
  Pérez as governor, 316
  textile mills, 4
  See also Tuxpan
Puebla Battalion, Activo Militia, 61
Puebla Light Squadron, Activo Militia, 61
Puebla Regiment, Activo Militia, 89
Pueblo
  Activo Battalion, 459
  Mormon Battalion, 277
Pueblo Indians, 206, 238, 289, 290, 292, **344**, 404; See also Taos Revolt
Pueblo Rebellion (1680), 289, 298, 344
Puget Sound, 381–382
Punitive expedition (1916), 224
Puntiagucla, 95
Purísma Bridge, 272, 424
Puritanism, 234, 451, 452
Puros, **344–345**
  Ayutla Revolution, 34
  Carbajal's writings, 77
  congressional deputies (1846), 104
  coup against Herrera, 350
  exiles in New Orleans, 244
  Gómez Farías leadership, 104, 180, 324
  as Gómez Pedraza opponents, 180–181
  González Cosío support, 181
  Juárez prominence, 104
  militia revival by, 264, 265, 329
  moderado campaign against, 116
  moderados beliefs vs., 104, 267, 344, 345
  Paredes y Arrillaga ouster by, 104, 126, 180, 323
  political response to U.S.-Mexcan War, 104, 470–471
  polkos revolt against, 104, 116, 180, 181, 267, 345, 350
  press alliance, 293–294
  prominent personalities, 345
  Rangel association, 350
  Rejón leadership, 104, 352
  response to U.S. annexation of Texas, 180, 469
  Tampico Expedition, 403
  Treaty of Guadalupe Hidalgo opposition, 104–105, 118, 181, 267, 345
  U.S.-Mexican War aims, 180, 471
  Zerecero support, 491

Q

Quakers, 1
Quartermaster's Department, U.S., 24, 211, 328, 394–395, 460, 465
Querétaro
  federal government evacuation to, 104, 120, 252, 324
  Filisola as division commander, 153
  Jarauta-led rebellion, 210
  Jarero as commandant-general, 211
  Juvera posts, 214
  as liberal Mexican government site, 471
  rebellion, 98
  Valencia surrender, 455
  See also Protocol of Querétaro
Querétaro Battalion, 91, 490
Querétaro Cavalry regiment, 169
Querétaro Lancers, 214
Querétaro Regiment, Activo Militia, 61
Quijana, Benito, 382
Quinine sulfate, 191
Quiróz, Eleuterio, 39, 385
Quitman, John A., 302, 303, **345–346**
  annexation of Cuba movement, 304
  assault on Mexico City, 256
  Aztec Club membership, 34, 346
  Chapultepec attack, 93
  march to Mexico City, 113, 255
  Marine battalion, 237
  Mexico City armistice negotiations, 321, 382
  promotion as major general, 345, 410
  rank and dates of appointment and commission, 25
  U.S. militia, 265

R

Racism, **347–348**
  borderlands, 49, 347, 348
  California, 73, 178
  derisive terms, 386
  seen as factor in U.S. war against Mexico, 86
  as Manifest Destiny argument, 234–235
  Mexican caste system, 81–82, 97, 98, 480
  Scottish Rite vs. York Rite Masonry, 165
  Texas, 45, 347, 363, 368
  United States, 3–4, 9, 107, 234–235, 451
Radziminski, Charles, 51, 52
Railroads, **348–349**
  as communications link, 103
  diminishing debt peonage, 316
  Gadsden Purchase lands, 51, 54
  Isthmus of Tehuantepec rights, 171
  as metaphor for U.S. spirit, 448, 450
  as U.S. economic factor, 433
  as U.S.-Mexican War factor, 174, 176
Ramírez, Antonio, 179

W